Books by Amy Lowell included in this volume

A DOME OF MANY-COLOURED GLASS

SWORD BLADES AND POPPY SEED

MEN, WOMEN AND GHOSTS

CAN GRANDE'S CASTLE

PICTURES OF THE FLOATING WORLD

LEGENDS

FIR-FLOWER TABLETS

A CRITICAL FABLE

WHAT'S O'CLOCK

EAST WIND

BALLADS FOR SALE

and six previously uncollected poems

THE COMPLETE POETICAL WORKS

OF

Amy Lowell

THE COMPLETE
POETICAL WORKS

OF

Amy Lowell

With an introduction by
LOUIS UNTERMEYER

HOUGHTON MIFFLIN COMPANY BOSTON

The Riverside Press Cambridge

The Riverside Press

CAMBRIDGE · MASSACHUSETTS
PRINTED IN THE U.S.A.

CONTENTS

A Memoir by Louis Untermeyer xxi

A DOME OF MANY-COLOURED GLASS

Lyrical Poems

Before the Altar 1
Suggested by the Cover of a Volume of Keats's Poems 1
Apples of Hesperides 2
Azure and Gold 2
Petals 2
Venetian Glass 3
Fatigue 3
A Japanese Wood-Carving 3
A Little Song 4
Behind a Wall 4
A Winter Ride 4
A Coloured Print by Shokei 5
Song 5
The Fool Errant 5
The Green Bowl 7
Hora Stellatrix 7
Fragment 7
Loon Point 7
Summer 8
"To-morrow to Fresh Woods and Pastures New" 9
The Way 9
ΔΙΨΑ 9
Roads 10
Teatro Bambino. Dublin, N.H. 10
The Road to Avignon 11
New York at Night 12
A Fairy Tale 12
Crowned 13
To Elizabeth Ward Perkins 13
The Promise of the Morning Star 13
J — K. Huysmans 14
March Evening 14

Sonnets

Leisure 15
On Carpaccio's Picture: The Dream of St. Ursula 15
The Matrix 15
Monadnock in Early Spring 15
The Little Garden 15
To an Early Daffodil 16
Listening 16
The Lamp of Life 16
Hero-Worship 16
In Darkness 17

v

CONTENTS

Before Dawn 17
The Poet 17
At Night 17
The Fruit Garden Path 18
Mirage 18
To a Friend 18
A Fixed Idea 18
Dreams 18
Frankincense and Myrrh 19
From One Who Stays 19
Crépuscule du Matin 19
Aftermath 19
The End 20
The Starling 20
Market Day 20
Epitaph in a Church-Yard in Charleston, South Carolina 20
Francis II, King of Naples 21
To John Keats 21

The Boston Athenæum

The Boston Athenæum 21

Verses for Children

Sea Shell 23
Fringed Gentians 23
The Painted Ceiling 24
The Crescent Moon 24
Climbing 24
The Trout 25
Wind 25
The Pleiades 25

SWORD BLADES AND POPPY SEED

Sword Blades and Poppy Seed

Sword Blades and Poppy Seed 27

Sword Blades

The Captured Goddess 31
The Precinct. Rochester 32
The Cyclists 33
Sunshine through a Cobwebbed Window 33
A London Thoroughfare 33
Astigmatism 34
The Coal Picker 35
Storm-Racked 35
Convalescence 35
Patience 35
Apology 36
A Petition 36
A Blockhead 36
Stupidity 37

Irony 37
Happiness 37
The Last Quarter of the Moon 37
A Tale of Starvation 38
The Foreigner 40
Absence 41
A Gift 41
The Bungler 41
Fool's Money Bags 41
Miscast I 42
Miscast II 42
Anticipation 42
Vintage 42
The Tree of Scarlet Berries 42
Obligation 42
The Taxi 43
The Giver of Stars 43
The Temple 43
Epitaph of a Young Poet 43
In Answer to a Request 43

Poppy Seed

The Great Adventure of Max Breuck 44
Sancta Maria, Succurre Miseris 55
After Hearing a Waltz by Bartók 56
Clear, with Light Variable Winds 57
The Basket 58
In a Castle 60
The Book of Hours of Sister Clotilde 61
The Exeter Road 65
The Shadow 66
The Forsaken 71
Late September 72
The Pike 72
The Blue Scarf 72
White and Green 73
Aubade 73
Music 73
A Lady 73
In a Garden 73
A Tulip Garden 74

MEN, WOMEN AND GHOSTS

Figurines in Old Saxe

❈ Patterns 75
Pickthorn Manor 76
The Cremona Violin 88
The Cross-Roads 103
A Roxbury Garden 104
1777 109

Bronze Tablets

The Fruit Shop 111
Malmaison 113
The Hammers 116
Two Travellers in the Place Vendôme 124

War Pictures

The Allies 125
The Bombardment 125
Lead Soldiers 126
The Painter on Silk 128
A Ballad of Footmen 129

The Overgrown Pasture

Reaping 130
Off the Turnpike 131
The Grocery 134
Number 3 on the Docket 136

Clocks Tick a Century

Nightmare: A Tale for an Autumn Evening 139
The Paper Windmill 141
The Red Lacquer Music-Stand 142
Spring Day 145
The Dinner-Party 147
Stravinsky's Three Pieces "Grotesques," for String Quartet 148
Towns in Colour
   Red Slippers 149
   Thompson's Lunch Room — Grand Central Station 149
   An Opera House 150
   Afternoon Rain in State Street 150
   An Aquarium 151

CAN GRANDE'S CASTLE

Sea-Blue and Blood-Red 153
Guns as Keys: and the Great Gate Swings 162
Hedge Island 173
The Bronze Horses 177

PICTURES OF THE FLOATING WORLD

Lacquer Prints

Streets 203
By Messenger 203
Circumstance 203
Angles 203
Vicarious 203
Near Kioto 203
Desolation 203
Yoshiwara Lament 203

CONTENTS

Sunshine 203
Illusion 204
A Year Passes 204
A Lover 204
To a Husband 204
The Fisherman's Wife 204
From China 204
The Pond 204
Autumn 204
Ephemera 204
Document 204
The Emperor's Garden 204
One of the "Hundred Views of Fuji" by Hokusai 204
Disillusion 205
Paper Fishes 205
Meditation 205
The Camellia Tree of Matsue 205
Superstition 205
The Return 205
A Lady to Her Lover 205
Nuance 205
Autumn Haze 205
Peace 205
In Time of War 206
Nuit Blanche 206
Spring Dawn 206
Poetry 206
From a Window 206
Again the New Year Festival 206
Time 206
Legend 206
Pilgrims Ascending Fuji-yama 206
The Kagoes of a Returning Traveller 206
A Street 206
Outside a Gate 206
Road to the Yoshiwara 206
Ox Street, Takanawa 206
A Daimio's Oiran 206
Passing the Bamboo Fence 207
Frosty Evening 207
An Artist 207
A Burnt Offering 207
Daybreak. Yoshiwara 207
Temple Ceremony 207
Two Porters Returning along a Country Road 207
Storm by the Seashore 207
The Exiled Emperor 207
Letter Written from Prison by Two Political Offenders 207
Moon Haze 207
Proportion 207
Constancy 207

Chinoiseries

Reflections 208
Falling Snow 208
Hoar-Frost 208
Gold-Leaf Screen 208
A Poet's Wife 208
Spring Longing 208
Li T'ai Po 209

Planes of Personality
TWO SPEAK TOGETHER

Vernal Equinox 209
The Letter 209
Mise en Scène 210
Venus Transiens 210
Madonna of the Evening Flowers 210
Bright Sunlight 210
Ombre Chinoise 211
July Midnight 211
Wheat-in-the-Ear 211
The Weather-Cock Points South 211
The Artist 211
The Garden by Moonlight 212
Interlude 212
Bullion 212
The Wheel of the Sun 212
A Shower 212
Summer Rain 213
April 213
Coq d'Or 213
The Charm 213
After a Storm 213
Opal 214
Wakefulness 214
Orange of Midsummer 214
Shore Grass 214
Autumnal Equinox 214
The Country House 215
Nerves 215
Left Behind 215
Autumn 215
The Sixteenth Floor 215
Strain 215
Haunted 216
Grotesque 216
Snow in April 216
A Sprig of Rosemary 216
Maladie de l'Après-Midi 216
November 217
Nostalgia 217
Preparation 217
A Decade 217

CONTENTS

Penumbra 217
Frimaire 218

EYES, AND EARS, AND WALKING

Solitaire 218
The Back Bay Fens 219
Free Fantasia on Japanese Themes 219
At the Bookseller's 219
Violin Sonata by Vincent d'Indy 220
Winter's Turning 220
Eucharis Amazonica 220
The Two Rains 221
Good Gracious! 221
Trees 221
Dawn Adventure 221
The Corner of Night and Morning 221
Beech, Pine, and Sunlight 221
Planning the Garden 222
Impressionist Picture of a Garden 222
A Bather 223
Dog-Days 223
August (Late Afternoon) 223
Hilly Country 224
Trees in Winter 224
Sea Coal 224
Dolphins in Blue Water 224
Motor Lights on a Hill Road 224

AS TOWARD ONE'S SELF

In a Time of Dearth 225
Aliens 226
Middle Age 226
La Vie de Bohême 226
Flame Apples 226
The Travelling Bear 227
Merchandise 227
The Poem 227
The Peddler of Flowers 227
Balls 228
The Fanatic 228
Fireworks 228
Trades 228
Generations 229
Entente Cordiale 229
Castles in Spain 229

PLUMMETS TO CIRCUMSTANCE

Ely Cathedral 230
William Blake 230
An Incident 230
Peach-Colour to a Soap-Bubble 230
Pyrotechnics 230
The Bookshop 231
Gargoyles 231
To Winky 232

Chopin 233
Appuldurcombe Park 233
The Broken Fountain 234
The Dusty Hour-Glass 235
The Flute 235
Flotsam 235
Little Ivory Figures Pulled with String 236
On the Mantelpiece 236
AS TOWARD WAR
Misericordia 237
Dreams in War Time 237
Spectacles 238
In the Stadium 238
After Writing "The Bronze Horses" 239
The Fort 239
Camouflaged Troop-ship 240
September, 1918 241
The Night before the Parade 241
AS TOWARD IMMORTALITY
On a Certain Critic 242

LEGENDS

Memorandum Confided by a Yucca to a Passion-Vine. *Peru* . . . 245
A Legend of Porcelain. *China* 251
Many Swans. *North America* 261
Funeral Song for the Indian Chief Blackbird. *North America* . . . 273
Witch-Woman. *Yucatan* 276
The Ring and the Castle. *Europe* 278
Gavotte in D Minor. *Europe* 280
The Statue in the Garden. *Europe* 280
Dried Marjoram. *England* 291
Before the Storm. *New England* 295
Four Sides to a House. *New England* 298

FIR-FLOWER TABLETS
Preface 301
Introduction 303

Li T'Ai-po (A.D. *701–762*)

Songs of the Marches 328
The Battle to the South of the City 329
The Perils of the Shu Road 330
Looking at the Moon After Rain 330
The Lonely Wife 331
The Pleasures within the Palace 331
The Young Girls of Yüeh 331
Written in the Character of a Beautiful Woman 332
Songs to the Peonies 332
Spring Grief and Resentment 332
The Palace Woman and the Dragon Robes 333
The Nanking Wine-Shop 333
Fêng Huang T'ai 333
The Northern Flight 333
Fighting to the South of the City 334

Mêng Chiao (Circa A.D. 790)
Sung to the Air: "The Wanderer" 356

Wei Ying-Wu (Circa A.D. 850)
Farewell Words to the Daughter of Yang 356

Wên T'Ing-Yün (Circa A.D. 850)
Sung to the Air: "Looking South" 357

Descendant of Founder Southern T'Ang Dynasty (Circa A.D. 960)
Together We Know Happiness 357

T'Ai Yüan-Ming (A.D. 365–427)
Once More Fields and Gardens 357

Anonymous. Liang Dynasty (A.D. 502–557)
Song of the Snapped Willow 358

Authorship Uncertain. Chou Dynasty. Reign of King Hsüan (826–781 B.C.)
The Cloudy River 358

Emperor Wu of Han (156–87 B.C.)
To the Air: "The Fallen Leaves" 359

Emperor Chao of Han (94–73 B.C.)
Early Autumn at the Pool of Sprinkling Water 359

Emperor Ling of Later Han (A.D. 156–189)
Proclaiming the Joy of Certain Hours 359

Pan Chieh-Yü (Circa 32 B.C.)
A Song of Grief 360

Chiang Ts'Ai-P'In (Circa A.D. 750)
A Letter of Thanks for Precious Pearls 360

Kang Kuei-Fei (Circa A.D. 750)
Dancing 360

Liang Dynasty (A.D. 502–557)
Songs of the Courtesans 360

Mother of the Lord of Sung (Circa 600 B.C.)
The Great Ho River 361

Written Pictures
An Evening Meeting 361
The Emperor's Return 361
Portrait of Beautiful Concubine 361
Calligraphy 362
The Palace Blossoms 362
One Goes a Journey 362
From the Straw Hut among the Seven Peaks 362

On the Classic of the Hills and Sea 362
The Hermit 363
After How Many Years 363
The Inn at the Mountain Pass 364
Li T'ai-po Meditates 364
Pair of Scrolls 364
Two Panels 364
The Return 364
Evening Calm 364
Fishing Picture 364
Spring. Summer. Autumn. 364

A CRITICAL FABLE 389

WHAT'S O'CLOCK 435
East, West, North, and South of a Man 435
Evelyn Ray 437
The Swans 439
Once Jericho 440
Merely Statement 440
Footing up a Total 441
Twenty-Four Hokku on a Modern Theme 441
The Anniversary 443
Song for a Viola d'Amore 443
Prime 444
Vespers 444
In Excelsis 444
White Currants 445
Exercise in Logic 445
Overcast Sunrise 445
Afterglow 445
A Dimension 445
Mackerel Sky 446
The On-Looker 446
Lilacs 446
Purple Grackles 447
Meeting-House Hill 449
Texas 449
Charleston, South Carolina 450
The Middleton Place 450
The Vow 451
The Congressional Library 452
Which, Being Interpreted, Is as May Be, or Otherwise 453
The Sisters 459
View of Teignmouth in Devonshire 461
Fool o' the Moon 465
Tomb Valley 466
The Green Parrakeet 467
Time's Acre 468
Sultry 469
The Enchanted Castle 470

CONTENTS

Autumn and Death 470
Folie de Minuit 471
The Slippers of the Goddess of Beauty 471
The Watershed 472
La Ronde du Diable 473
Morning Song, with Drums 473
A Grave Song 473
A Rhyme out of Motley 474
The Red Knight 474
Nuit Blanche 474
Orientation 474
Pantomime in One Act 474
In a Powder Closet 475
Attitude under an Elm Tree 475
On Reading a Line Underscored by Keats in a Copy of "Palmerin of England" . 476
The Humming-Birds 476
Summer Night Piece 477
Wind and Silver 477
Night Clouds 477
Fugitive 477
The Sand Altar 477
Time-Web 477
Preface to an Occasion 477
Primavera 478
Katydids 478
To Carl Sandburg 478
If I Were Francesco Guardi 479
Eleonora Duse 479

EAST WIND

The Doll 481
The House in Main Street 484
One Winter Night 488
The Day That Was That Day 491
A Dracula of the Hills 493
The Note-Book in the Gate-Legged Table 499
The Rosebud Wall-Paper 503
The Conversion of a Saint 512
The Gravestone 516
The Real Estate Agent's Tale 520
The Landlady of the Whinton Inn Tells a Story 525
"And Pity 'Tis, 'Tis True" 530
The House with the Marble Steps 532

BALLADS FOR SALE

Ballads for Sale 535
  To a Gentleman Who Wanted to See the First Drafts of My Poems in the
  Interests of Psychological Research into the Workings of the Creative Mind . 535
  On Looking at a Copy of Alice Meynell's Poems, Given Me, Years Ago, by a
  Friend 536
  Who Has Not, Cannot Have 537

Mid-Adventure 537
Correspondence 538
To a Lady of Undeniable Beauty and Practised Charm 538
And So, I Think, Diogenes 538
Mesdames Atropos and Clio Engage in a Game of Slap-Stick 539
A Communication 540
The Immortals 541
Apotheosis 542
Behind Time 543

Gouache Pictures of Italy

Palazzo Contarini 546
The Lime Avenue 546
The Water Stair 546
The Stable 547
Fête at Caserta. The Queen of Naples Receives 547
Santa Settimana 547
The Ambassador 548
From Nice to Oneglia 548
Villa Capouana 548
The Church of Santa Chiara, Naples 549
In the Campagna 549

Portraits, Places, and People

To Eleonora Duse. In Answer to a Letter 550
To Eleonora Duse. 1923 550
The Madonna of Carthagena 551
Tune 554
Grievance 555
Paradox 555
Hippocrene 556
Thorn Piece 556
On Christmas Eve 557
A New Year's Card 557
Fact 558
Heraldic 558
Quincunx 558
Carrefour 558
Granadilla 558
Caustic 559
One! Two! Three! 559
Alternatives 559
Threnody 560
Tanka 560
Reflection 560
Pastime 560
After an Illness 560
"Rode the Six Hundred" 561
The Silent Husband 561
The "Plum-Blossom" Concubine Writes to the Emperor Ming Huang . . 561
Old Examination Hall — China 562
Pillar Prints 562

To Two Unknown Ladies 562
Written on the Reverse 565
Silhouette with Sepia Background 566
Aquatint Framed in Gold 567
Miniature 567
Easel Picture 568
The Irony of Death 568
The Grave 568
The Mirror 569
Portrait of an Orchestra Leader 569
Portrait 569
Magnolia Gardens 569
A South Carolina Forest 570
Circus Tents by Lake Michigan 570
St. Louis. June 571
The Revenge 571
Chill 572
Snow 573
Old Snow 573
New Heavens for Old 574
The Sibyl 574
The Madman 574
Dirge 575
Anecdote 576
Epithalamium in the Modern Manner 577
Points of View 577
Shooting the Sun 578
The Customer 578
The Sewing-Book 579
Still Life 580
Ballad of Grinning Death 580
Poetic Justice 581
To Francesca Braggiotti 581
Dance Figure 582
Jazz Dance 582
Proper Invective 584
Dissonance 586
The Book of Stones and Lilies 586
Stalactite 586
The Splendour Falls from Castle Walls 586

Songs of the Pueblo Indians

Women's Harvest Song 588
Basket Dance 588
Women's Song of the Corn 588
Prayer for a Profusion of Sunflowers 589
Prayer for Lightning 589
Flute-Priest Song for Rain 589

UNCOLLECTED POEMS

On "The Cutting of an Agate" (By W. B. Yeats) 591
POETRY AND DRAMA II. SEPTEMBER, 1914.

A Rainy Night 591
    EGOIST II. JULY, 1915.
A Comparison 591
    OTHERS I. AUGUST, 1915.
May Evening in Central Park 591
    POETRY VI. SEPTEMBER, 1915.
The Road to the Mountain 592
    NEW YORK TRIBUNE. MARCH 30, 1919.
Eleonora Duse 592
    POETRY XXII. AUGUST 23, 1923.

A MEMOIR

IT IS almost impossible to separate the legendary and the real Amy Lowell. She was to a great extent the victim of her fabulous quest for novelty, and the legend of her inexhaustibility — a myth which she herself accepted — was probably responsible for her death. No one knows just how many poems she actually wrote, but some six hundred and fifty were preserved in the eleven published volumes brought together in this comprehensive collection, to say nothing of uncompleted and unprinted verses. More impressive, and more significant of the varied interests which compelled her and the drives which undid her, was her bewildering range of ideas and idioms, a constantly shifting kaleidoscope of style and subject matter.

There was little evidence of that range when her first volume was launched on the perilous seas of criticism. I remember that my own review was not only generally patronizing but cruel in its particulars. Unaware of the devotion which was to become a lifetime preoccupation, I implied that the author had not freed herself from a fatuous, fancied kinship to Keats, that her tone was belatedly Tennysonian, and that her indebtedness to Shelley was implicit in more than the title of her book, A Dome of Many-Coloured Glass. That was in 1912.

Two years later, when her next volume was published, it seemed that a wholly new poet and, what was more, a new epoch had appeared. Sword Blades and Poppy Seed sounded some of the first notes in the controversy which raged about the New Poetry. The book heralded the era's growing dissatisfaction with traditional measures and the determination to try new verse forms, strange cadences, and unfamiliar responses to standard sentiments. It startled readers with the first English examples of "polyphonic prose," which John Gould Fletcher claimed he invented, and a series of glittering and often bizarre images, which her detractors charged had been borrowed from the then-emerging Imagists.

The Amy Lowell legend was already in the making; fact and fantasy began to interweave. To the proper Bostonians she was the oddity, locally famous, born February 9, 1874, of an illustrious family descended from Percival Lowell who came to Newburyport in 1637. James Russell Lowell, critic, first editor of the Atlantic Monthly, and wittiest of the New England poets, was her grandfather's cousin. Percival Lowell, the astronomer who in 1905 mathematically proved the existence of a new planet Pluto, and maintained that evidence of "canals" indicated living intelligences on Mars, was a brother. Another brother, Abbott Lawrence Lowell, who confessed he understood little of her poetry, was president of Harvard College.

Amy was educated privately at home and abroad. A precocious small girl, she made her literary debut at the age of eleven. A book entitled *Dream Drops, or Stories from Fairy Land* was a composite effort, chiefly written by her mother and her much older sister, Elizabeth, but it contained contributions by the child. It was published by the Boston firm of Cupples and Hurd and the edition was sold out.

In her teens she exchanged her visions of fairyland for dreams of the theater. She had fallen in love with Sarah Bernhardt and Eleonora Duse; she abandoned hopes of becoming an actress only when a glandular disbalance turned the unusually pretty girl into an abnormally fat woman, "a walking side-show," she said with a mixture of self-pity and self-contempt.

She was forty when I first met her. I was prepared for the monstrous distribution of flesh — although a short woman, she weighed well over two hundred pounds — for the cigars with which she affronted genteel society, and the armada of immense English sheepdogs which intimidated strangers but which were less watchdogs than substitutes for the children she never had. What I was not prepared for was the extraordinary delicacy as well as the dignity of the woman. Instead of seeming a rakish masculine affectation, the cigar merely accentuated her essential femininity. ("My doctor tells me that the paper is what makes cigarettes injurious," she explained.) The disproportionate bulk was forgotten the moment she spoke, for the voice, half prim, half peremptory, drew attention to the tiny mouth, to the fastidiously fine features, the almost transparent porcelain skin, the quizzical but not unkind eyes. I noticed also the incongruously small hands and little ankles. I had heard that her bed was made of two dozen pillows, mattresses being too hard for her, and that the tires of her Pierce Arrow were inflated to only half the normal pressure so that the car would ride without jouncing. With a close friend, Ada Dwyer Russell, a former actress, she lived in a house called Sevenels, not, as has been supposed, because of the seven ells in the structure, but because of seven Lowells. All the doorknobs were sterling silver. The appointments were luxurious, but her working life was strict and severe. Everything possible was done to separate the private poet and the public person.

To safeguard her flights of imagination, as well as her privacy, she kept peculiar hours. She freed herself from most people's usual duties, the daily demands, unsolicited visits by friends, the importunities of the telephone, by sleeping during the day and working at night. It was her custom to wake at about three in the afternoon, consult her housekeeper across a four o'clock breakfast tray, go over the previous night's notes with her two secretaries — one for her creative writing, one for her business affairs — and come down to dinner about eight. Frequently there were guests, important notables as well as little-known poets she was cultivating; but they were aware of her schedule, and their cars were always ordered for eleven-thirty. At midnight she went to her room and began to write, transcribe, and revise. Somewhere between five and six, just before the rest of the household came to life, she would go to bed. It was a way of life any artist might like to enjoy — if he could afford it.

By the time we became friends, Amy Lowell was well on the way to being a celebrity. After she gave up the last hope of appearing on the stage she planned to write for it. When this, too, failed she decided — determined, she said — to be a poet. Waiting until she was thirty-eight before publishing her first mature book, she studied the techniques of verse making, analyzed the way in which the masters had achieved their effects, and paid particular attention to the methods of the innovators. Even before *A Dome of Many-Coloured Glass* was off the press she heard of a few experimenters who had their headquarters in London and who, under the aegis of Ezra Pound, called themselves Imagists. Amy Lowell "invaded" England, met Pound head on, convinced his confreres that she was an even more pugnacious dictator than Pound, and "captured" the group — with the obvious exception of Pound. Returning triumphantly to America, she presented her fellow insurgents to the public in three annual volumes (1915, 1916, 1917) entitled *Some Imagist Poets*. The collections included John Gould Fletcher, "H. D.," D. H. Lawrence, among others, as well as Amy Lowell herself, all of whom rebelled against the "morbid romantic attitude and outworn false generalities" in favor of "the hard, definite word and the clear, uncluttered image." Pound fumed and threatened suit. Amy was delighted. She knew that neither a title nor a school of poets could be copyrighted and, with a flair for publicity which would have made her another fortune as a promoter, wrote him that his suit would be "a good advertisement" and would increase sales of the venture. Pound, occupied with paraphrases from the Chinese, replied (in a letter to me) that he had "no objection to the pleasure others have had in exploiting the label and offering cheap imitations, but I regret the loss of critical distinction between poetry which uses no word which does not contribute to the presentation — and verbosity." He disassociated himself from the American publications of the Imagists and always referred to the group as the "Amygist" movement.

Amy Lowell resented the charge of high-handedness. Pound, she wrote in one of the first letters I received from her, "would have ruined the movement, important though it was, as he has ruined everything he has touched . . . The only thing I object to in your article is your saying that it was under his leadership that 'the Imagists became not only a group but a fighting protest.' It was nothing of the sort. The Imagists during the year and a half in which he headed the movement were unknown and jeered at, when they were not absolutely ignored. It was not until I entered the arena and Ezra dropped out that Imagism had to be considered seriously . . . The name is his; the idea was widespread. But changing the whole public attitude from derision to consideration came from my work."

She began waging a battle on two fronts. She fought with equal ardor as propagandist and poet; she stalked the ramparts of her own beleaguered citadel, went forth to shout down her critics, and stormed enemy battlements clear across the country. She reminded one of Theodore Roosevelt who had the gift of sensing the turn a tendency was about to take and, recognizing the strength of a movement, would place himself at the head of it. Also, in common with Roosevelt the First, she knew when to take up a cause and when to abandon it. When the cult of Imagism broadened into a struggle for free verse she championed *vers libre* in dozens of prefaces, reviews, articles, and on countless public platforms. When the vers libretines gave up their freedom for more orthodox forms, she returned to orderly couplets, strict tercets, rhymed narratives, even to old-fashioned ballads. When Japanese and Chinese poetry became a vogue, she turned a fashion into a lasting achievement with her "adapted" *Fir-Flower Tablets*.

Meanwhile, she was busy with her own poems. Their development as well as their changing centers of interest may be traced in the books which she wrote while beating the drums for her colleagues and haranguing apathetic reviewers. The stories in *Men, Women and Ghosts*, published when she was forty-two, range from experiments in free verse, which project "unrelated" patterns reminiscent of abstract paintings, to tales in "polyphonic prose," which is prose only in its typographical arrangement. The gamut widened from the opening "Patterns," which caused a sensation upon its appearance and became the most anthologized of her poems, to the grim New England narratives, a counterpoint to Frost's *North of Boston*, in "The Overgrown Pasture." Two years later *Can Grande's Castle* extended the limitations of polyphonic prose to sound the widest possible variations in metre, altering the beat to permit long flowing cadences, and mixing rhymes irregularly to achieve a contrapuntal form with orchestral sonority. In "Sea-Blue and Blood-Red" she was able to pack the entire drama of Nelson and Lady Hamilton in a fluctuating progression, half narrative and half oratorio; "Guns as Keys: And the Great Gate Swings" employed the form to contrast "the delicacy and clarity of Japan and the artistic ignorance and gallant self-confidence of America."

She was also hard at work getting a hearing for the poems. A new book was not merely a publishing venture but a campaign. She saw to it that no editorial office, no inner sanctum, was barred to her. Her social standing, her affluence, her militant reputation, her unquestionable charm — she used them all. Her trips to New York, which she considered enemy territory, were planned with expert generalship. Her headquarters were a suite in the Hotel St. Regis. There she held court. Clocks were stopped so that the ticking would not remind her of the passing of time. Windows were draped, and all the mirrors were hidden behind heavy dark hangings. Every poet feels himself to be a disembodied if not a blithe spirit, especially when the fit of inspiration is on him, and Amy Lowell would not risk confronting the sensitive afflatus with the gross reality of all that too, too solid flesh.

From the St. Regis she plotted her plan of war and drew up the battle lines. She maneuvered to get what she considered the best men to write the best reviews for the best mediums. She summoned editors — and they came. She cajoled, browbeat, and generally captivated her critics — and, though they were not certain that she was a great poet, they were convinced that she was a great personality. Sometimes there was a note of belligerence underneath the blandishments. "You advertise so much in the Times," she complained to her publisher, "that you ought to force them into a somewhat less hostile attitude." "I have to be my own impresario," she told me. "There's no point in having a trumpet — or any brass — if you don't blow it."

Trumpets were sounded whenever she argued about poetry; they rang out with special vigor when she spoke of those who opposed the New Dispensation. It took years to transform her ivory tower into a steel-ribbed fortress and to maintain herself on that eminence. Once there, she provoked the attackers to do their worst. "Let them come and push me off," she challenged. "I dare them!" It was a dare that none would accept; it was not merely the picture of her physical bulk which intimidated any possible combatants but the knowledge of her doughty and indomitable spirit.

As a conversationalist she was both pugnacious and persuasive. Heywood Broun recalled a gaily inconsistent talk in which she used every feminine wile to attack feminism. Broun's wife, Ruth Hale, was a belligerent feminist, a charter member of the Lucy Stone League, and Broun attempted to defend the movement. "Amy Lowell leaned back," said Broun, "in a big, easy chair, puffing one of her Manila cigars. 'I have (puff, puff) no patience,' said Miss Lowell, 'with the new-fashioned woman (puff, puff) and her so-called rights. I believe (and here she drew deep of the cigar) in the old-fashioned, conservative woman and all her limitations.'"

She was equally certain about the need for maintaining social and economic conventions, but she was troubled about them. "It is hard to be a true poet," wrote Malcolm Cowley in an otherwise unmalicious review, "when one is rich, blanketed with four per cent debentures and rocked to sleep in a cradle of sound common stocks." With a gentler irony Vachel Lindsay said she was equipped to be not only the state laureate but the Senator from Massachusetts. She was not unaware of a certain ambivalence, a split which separated the poet from the politician, but she showed her consciousness of it on only a few occasions. I remember one of the occasions when the implications of her wealth worried her. We were attending a performance of Gerhart Hauptmann's *The Weavers*, a drama of class conflict which pictured an uprising in the 1840's. Anticipating Ernst Toller's violent *The Machine-Wreckers*, Hauptmann's play reached its climax as the Silesian workers, starving and desperate, destroy not only the machines, which they hold responsible for their distress, but proceed to smash the home of their employer. Amy Lowell could not help thinking of the industrialized town of Lowell which had been named for her forebears and she, who sometimes referred to herself as "the last of the barons," flinched. "This is the future," she whispered as the curtain came down on a scene of pillage. "That is what is going to happen to me!"

That it was unlikely to happen in her time — and in Brookline — scarcely comforted her. The top floor of Sevenels became more and more of a tower soaring over if not altogether safe from the threatening future. There her dreams, translated into poems, became increasingly dramatic and varied, alternately realistic and escapist. Her early love of the theatre led her to find dramas not only in the events of the day but in forgotten fables, stray items tucked away in old newspapers. *Pictures of the Floating World* begins with a set of Japanese lacquer prints, expands into odd "chinoiseries," and develops into startling "planes of personality," tender in "Madonna of the Evening Flowers" and "A Decade," bizarre in "Gargoyles," archaic in "Appuldurcombe Park," revealingly grotesque in

"Dreams in War Time." *Legends*, the most wide-ranging of her volumes, includes an amalgam of Peruvian myths, "Memorandum confided by a Yucca to a Passion-Vine," which sprang from a sentence embedded in Garcilasso de la Vega's saga of the Incas; an Indian song-story, "Many Swans," based "on a Kathlemet text translated by Dr. Franz Boas;" "The Statue in the Garden," a Roman tale found in Burton's *Anatomy of Melancholy*; to say nothing of enlargements of folkstuff from Yucatan, Europe, and New England. The lush variety of material, style, and subject matter flashes through the posthumously published *What's O'Clock*, which was awarded the Pulitzer Prize in 1926. It culminated in her much-quoted apostrophe, "Lilacs," the poem of hers she liked best, with its climatic — and climactic — evocation:

> *Heart-leaves of lilac all over New England,*
> *Roots of lilac under the soil of New England,*
> *Lilac in me because I am New England,*
> *Because my roots are in it,*
> *Because my leaves are of it,*
> *Because my flowers are for it,*
> *Because it is my country*
> *And I speak to it of itself.*

A *Critical Fable* is a further proof of her versatility. Frankly modeled on James Russell Lowell's *A Fable for Critics*, even to the rhymed title page, it was published anonymously. When suspected of its authorship Amy Lowell vehemently denied it. ("From the moment I opened the book I said to myself: Louis is the only person who would have been likely to write this book . . . and now you hastily forestall me by suggesting that *I* have done it — which is one of the neatest little side-steppings I have ever seen!") Although purists complained of the rough rhythms and rougher rhyming, the hit-or-miss lines accomplished many palpable hits. There was penetration and no little humor in her half cutting, half kindly disposals of the leading (and several minor) American poets of her day.

She was a very sick woman when she began her two-volume biography of Keats. "Keats is nearly killing me," she informed me when she was in the midst of it. I did not take the sentence seriously, for I had no idea how grievously the work was affecting her already overburdened body. Long before she undertook to track down all Keats's associations, annotations, and the smallest of minutiae, she had written me, "Do try and get here as early as possible before they have quite minced me to pieces and swept me up in the dustpan." I never knew how terribly handicapped she was by a double hernia that was continually "patched up" but which would never completely heal. Besides, she seemed to delight in multiple commitments; she was not herself unless she was continually attacked, belabored, and occupied to the point of exhaustion. She had written critical books on *Six French Poets* as well as *Tendencies in Modern American Poetry*, and she had amplified the concepts in these books into reviews, lengthy articles, and countless lectures. She had helped start a series of biennial anthologies which we had entitled A *Miscellany of American Poetry* (Frost, Lindsay, Robinson, Sandburg, Aiken, and Teasdale were among the first to be included), and her correspondence about other candidates was constant and often incontinently sharp.

She almost literally gave her lifeblood for Keats. The youthful infatuation for the greatest of lyric poets led to a lifelong passion which was part identification, part obsession. She was certainly thinking not solely of Keats when she wrote, "The stigma of oddness is the price a myopic world always exacts of genius." "How hard, how desperately hard, is the way of the experimenter in art!" And there is not so much analysis of her subject as self-revelation when she wrote: "I do not suppose that anyone not a poet can realize the agony of creating a poem. Every nerve, even every muscle, seems strained to the breaking point. The poem will not be denied; to refuse to write it would be a greater torture. It tears its way out of the brain, splintering and breaking its passage, and leaves that organ in the state of a jelly-fish when the task is done."

It was sometimes said that Amy Lowell had everything a poet should have except passion, that she had perception but lacked feeling, that (in the words of one of her critics) she substituted motion for emotion. A few days after her death on May 12, 1925, Heywood Broun penned an obituary tribute in the New York *World* which took up the animadversions. "She was upon the surface of things a Lowell," wrote Broun, "a New Englander and a spinster. But inside everything was molten like the core of the earth. . . . Given one more gram of emotion, Amy Lowell would have burst into flame and been consumed to cinders."

Her final place in the history of American literature has not yet been determined. Controversy regarding the impact and quality of her poetry still goes on — it has become the fashion to say that she is the poet of the external rather than the internal world. But succeeding generations have a habit of reversing contemporary estimates, and it is more than likely that she will be enthusiastically rediscovered. In any case, the importance of her influence remains unquestioned. Underneath her preoccupation with the need for novelty, the disruption of traditional patterns, and other theoretical departures, she was a dynamic force. She was not only a disturber but an awakener. Her exhilarating differences invigorated the old forms while affecting the new techniques. Her pioneering energy cleared the field of flabby accumulations and helped establish the fresh and free-searching poetry of our day.

LOUIS UNTERMEYER

THE COMPLETE
POETICAL WORKS
OF
Amy Lowell

A DOME OF MANY-COLOURED GLASS

LYRICAL POEMS

BEFORE THE ALTAR

Before the Altar, bowed, he stands
With empty hands;
Upon it perfumed offerings burn
Wreathing with smoke the sacrificial urn.
Not one of all these has he given,
No flame of his has leapt to Heaven
Firesouled, vermilion-hearted,
Forked, and darted,
Consuming what a few spare pence
Have cheaply bought, to fling from hence
In idly-asked petition.

His sole condition
Love and poverty.
And while the moon
Swings slow across the sky,
Athwart a waving pine tree,
And so on
Tips all the needles there
With silver sparkles, bitterly
He gazes, while his soul
Grows hard with thinking of the poor-
ness of his dole.

"Shining and distant Goddess, hear my
prayer
Where you swim in the high air!
With charity look down on me,
Under this tree,
Tending the gifts I have not brought,
The rare and goodly things
I have not sought.
Instead, take from me all my life!

"Upon the wings
Of shimmering moonbeams
I pack my poet's dreams
For you.
My wearing strife,
My courage, my loss,
Into the night I toss

For you.
Golden Divinity,
Deign to look down on me
Who so unworthily
Offers to you:
All life has known.
Seeds withered unsown,
Hopes turning quick to fears,
Laughter which dies in tears.
The shredded remnant of a man
Is all the span
And compass of my offering to you.

"Empty and silent, I
Kneel before your pure, calm majesty.
On this stone, in this urn
I pour my heart and watch it burn,
Myself the sacrifice; but be
Still unmoved: Divinity."

From the altar, bathed in moonlight,
The smoke rose straight in the quiet
night.

SUGGESTED BY THE COVER OF A VOLUME OF KEATS'S POEMS

Wild little bird, who chose thee for a
sign
To put upon the cover of this book?
Who heard thee singing in the distance
dim,
The vague, far greenness of the enshrouding wood,
When the damp freshness of the morning earth
Was full of pungent sweetness and thy
song?

Who followed over moss and twisted
roots,
And pushed through the wet leaves of
trailing vines

Where slanting sunbeams gleamed un-
certainly,
While ever clearer came the dropping
notes,
Until, at last, two widening trunks dis-
closed
Thee singing on a spray of branching
beech,
Hidden, then seen; and always that same
song
Of joyful sweetness, rapture incarnate,
Filled the hushed, rustling stillness of the
wood?

We do not know what bird thou art.
Perhaps
That fairy bird, fabled in island tale,
Who never sings but once, and then his
song
Is of such fearful beauty that he dies
From sheer exuberance of melody.

For this they took thee, little bird, for
this
They captured thee, tilting among the
leaves,
And stamped thee for a symbol on this
book.
For it contains a song surpassing thine,
Richer, more sweet, more poignant. And
the poet
Who felt this burning beauty, and whose
heart
Was full of loveliest things, sang all he
knew
A little while, and then he died; too frail
To hear this untamed, passionate burst
of song.

APPLES OF HESPERIDES

Glinting golden through the trees,
    Apples of Hesperides!
Through the moon-pierced warp of night
Shoot pale shafts of yellow light,
Swaying to the kissing breeze
Swings the treasure, golden-gleaming,
    Apples of Hesperides!

Far and lofty yet they glimmer,
    Apples of Hesperides!
Blinded by their radiant shimmer,
Pushing forward just for these;
Dew-besprinkled, bramble-marred,
Poor duped mortal, travel-scarred,

Always thinking soon to seize
And possess the golden-glistening
    Apples of Hesperides!

Orbed, and glittering, and pendent,
    Apples of Hesperides!
Not one missing, still transcendent,
Clustering like a swarm of bees.
Yielding to no man's desire,
Glowing with a saffron fire,
Splendid, unassailed, the golden
    Apples of Hesperides!

AZURE AND GOLD

April had covered the hills
    With flickering yellows and reds,
The sparkle and coolness of snow
    Was blown from the mountain beds.

Across a deep-sunken stream
    The pink of blossoming trees,
And from windless appleblooms
    The humming of many bees.

The air was of rose and gold
    Arabesqued with the song of birds
Who, swinging unseen under leaves,
    Made music more eager than words.

Of a sudden, aslant the road,
    A brightness to dazzle and stun,
A glint of the bluest blue,
    A flash from a sapphire sun.

Blue-birds so blue, 'twas a dream,
    An impossible, unconceived hue,
The high sky of summer dropped down
    Some rapturous ocean to woo.

Such a colour, such infinite light!
    The heart of a fabulous gem,
Many-faceted, brilliant and rare.
    Centre Stone of the earth's diadem!

.   .   .   .   .

Centre Stone of the Crown of the World,
    "Sincerity" graved on your youth!
And your eyes hold the blue-bird flash,
    The sapphire shaft, which is truth.

PETALS

Life is a stream
On which we strew

Petal by petal the flower of our heart;
The end lost in dream,
They float past our view,
We only watch their glad, early start.

Freighted with hope,
Crimsoned with joy,
We scatter the leaves of our opening rose;
Their widening scope,
Their distant employ,
We shall never know. And the stream
as it flows
Sweeps them away,
Each one is gone
Ever beyond into infinite ways.
We alone stay
While years hurry on,
The flower fared forth, though its frag-
rance still stays.

VENETIAN GLASS

As one who sails upon wide, blue sea
Far out of sight of land, his mind intent
Upon the sailing of his little boat,
On tightening ropes and shaping fair his
course,
Hears suddenly, across the restless sea,
The rhythmic striking of some towered
clock,
And wakes from thoughtless idleness to
time:
Time, the slow pulse which beats eternity!
So through the vacancy of busy life
At intervals you cross my path and bring
The deep solemnity of passing years.
For you I have shed bitter tears, for you
I have relinquished that for which my
heart
Cried out in selfish longing. And to-night
Having just left you, I can say: " 'Tis
well.
Thank God that I have known a soul
so true,
So nobly just, so worthy to be loved!"

FATIGUE

Stupefy my heart to every day's monotony,
Seal up my eyes, I would not look
so far,
Chasten my steps to peaceful regularity,
Bow down my head lest I behold a
star.

Fill my days with work, a thousand calm
necessities
Leaving no moment to consecrate to
hope,
Girdle my thoughts within the dull circumferences
Of facts which form the actual in one
short hour's scope.

Give me dreamless sleep, and loose night's
power over me,
Shut my ears to sounds only tumultuous then,
Bid Fancy slumber, and steal away its
potency,
Or Nature wakes and strives to live
again.

Let each day pass, well ordered in its
usefulness,
Unlit by sunshine, unscarred by storm;
Dower me with strength and curb all
foolish eagerness —
The law exacts obedience. Instruct, I
will conform.

A JAPANESE WOOD-CARVING

High up above the open, welcoming door
It hangs, a piece of wood with colours
dim.
Once, long ago, it was a waving tree
And knew the sun and shadow through
the leaves
Of forest trees, in a thick eastern wood.
The winter snows had bent its branches
down,
The spring had swelled its buds with
coming flowers,
Summer had run like fire through its
veins,
While autumn pelted it with chestnut
burrs,
And strewed the leafy ground with acorn
cups.
Dark midnight storms had roared and
crashed among
Its branches, breaking here and there a
limb;
But every now and then broad sunlit
days
Lovingly lingered, caught among the
leaves.
Yes, it had known all this, and yet to us
It does not speak of mossy forest ways,

Of whispering pine trees or the shim-
mering birch;
But of quick winds, and the salt, sting-
ing sea!
An artist once, with patient, careful knife,
Had fashioned it like to the untamed sea.
Here waves uprear themselves, their tops
blown back
By the gay, sunny wind, which whips
the blue
And breaks it into gleams and sparks of
light.
Among the flashing waves are two white
birds
Which swoop, and soar, and scream for
very joy
At the wild sport. Now diving quickly in,
Questing some glistening fish. Now fly-
ing up,
Their dripping feathers shining in the
sun,
While the wet drops like little glints of
light,
Fall pattering backward to the parent sea.
Gliding along the green and foam-flecked
hollows,
Or skimming some white crest about to
break,
The spirits of the sky deigning to stoop
And play with ocean in a summer mood.
Hanging above the high, wide open door,
It brings to us in quiet, firelit room,
The freedom of the earth's vast solitudes,
Where heaping, sunny waves tumble and
roll,
And seabirds scream in wanton happiness.

A LITTLE SONG

When you, my Dear, are away, away,
How wearily goes the creeping day.
A year drags after morning, and night
Starts another year of candle light.
O Pausing Sun and Lingering Moon!
Grant me, I beg of you, this boon.

Whirl round the earth as never sun
Has his diurnal journey run.
And, Moon, slip past the ladders of air
In a single flash, while your streaming
hair
Catches the stars and pulls them down
To shine on some slumbering Chinese
town.

O Kindly Sun! Understanding Moon!
Bring evening to crowd the footsteps of
noon.

But when that long awaited day
Hangs ripe in the heavens, your voyaging
stay.
Be morning, O Sun! with the lark in song,
Be afternoon for ages long.
And, Moon, let you and your lesser lights
Watch over a century of nights.

BEHIND A WALL

I own a solace shut within my heart,
A garden full of many a quaint delight
And warm with drowsy, poppied sun-
shine; bright,
Flaming with lilies out of whose cups dart
Shining things
With powdered wings.

Here terrace sings to terrace, arbors close
The ends of dreaming paths; a wanton
wind
Jostles the half-ripe pears, and then,
unkind,
Tumbles a-slumber in a pillar rose,
With content
Grown indolent.

By night my garden is o'erhung with
gems
Fixed in an onyx setting. Fireflies
Flicker their lanterns in my dazzled
eyes.
In serried rows I guess the straight, stiff
stems
Of hollyhocks
Against the rocks.

So far and still it is that, listening,
I hear the flowers talking in the dawn;
And where a sunken basin cuts the
lawn,
Cinctured with iris, pale and glistening,
The sudden swish
Of a waking fish.

A WINTER RIDE

Who shall declare the joy of running!
Who shall tell of the pleasures of
flight!

Springing and spurning the tufts of wild
  heather,
Sweeping, wide-winged, through the
  blue dome of light.
Everything mortal has moments immortal,
Swift and God-gifted, immeasurably
  bright.

So with the stretch of the white road
  before me,
Shining snowcrystals rainbowed by the
  sun,
Fields that are white, stained with long,
  cool, blue shadows,
Strong with the strength of my horse
  as we run.
Joy in the touch of the wind and the
  sunlight!
Joy! With the vigorous earth I am one.

A COLOURED PRINT BY SHOKEI

It winds along the face of a cliff
This path which I long to explore,
And over it dashes a waterfall,
  And the air is full of the roar
And the thunderous voice of waters
  which sweep
In a silver torrent over some steep.

It clears the path with a mighty bound
And tumbles below and away,
And the trees and the bushes which grow
  in the rocks
Are wet with its jewelled spray;
The air is misty and heavy with sound,
And small, wet wildflowers star the
  ground.

Oh! The dampness is very good to smell,
  And the path is soft to tread,
And beyond the fall it winds up and on,
  While little streamlets thread
Their own meandering way down the hill
Each singing its own little song, until

I forget that 'tis only a pictured path,
  And I hear the water and wind,
And look through the mist, and strain
  my eyes
  To see what there is behind;
For it must lead to a happy land,
This little path by a waterfall spanned.

SONG

Oh! To be a flower
  Nodding in the sun,
Bending, then upspringing
  As the breezes run;
Holding up
A scent-brimmed cup,
  Full of summer's fragrance to the sum-
  mer sun.

Oh! To be a butterfly
  Still, upon a flower,
Winking with its painted wings,
  Happy in the hour.
Blossoms hold
Mines of gold
  Deep within the farthest heart of each
  chaliced flower.

Oh! To be a cloud
  Blowing through the blue,
Shadowing the mountains,
  Rushing loudly through
Valleys deep
Where torments keep
  Always their plunging thunder and
  their misty arch of blue.

Oh! To be a wave
  Splintering on the sand,
Drawing back, but leaving
  Lingeringly the land.
Rainbow light
Flashes bright
  Telling tales of coral caves half hid
  in yellow sand.

Soon they die, the flowers;
  Insects live a day;
Clouds dissolve in showers;
  Only waves at play
Last forever.
Shall endeavor
  Make a sea of purpose mightier than
  we dream to-day?

THE FOOL ERRANT

The Fool Errant sat by the highway of
  life
  And his gaze wandered up and his
  gaze wandered down,
A vigorous youth, but with no wish to
  walk,
  Yet his longing was great for the distant town.

He whistled a little frivolous tune
Which he felt to be pulsing with
ecstasy,
For he thought that success always fol-
lowed desire,
Such a very superlative fool was he.

A maiden came by on an ambling mule,
Her gown was rose-red and her ker-
chief blue,
On her lap she carried a basket of eggs.
Thought the fool, "There is certainly
room for two."

So he jauntily swaggered towards the
maid
And put out his hand to the bridle-
rein.
"My pretty girl," quoth the fool, "take
me up,
For to ride with you to the town I am
fain."

But the maiden struck at his upraised arm
And pelted him hotly with eggs, a
score.
The mule, lashed into a fury, ran;
The fool went back to his stone and
swore.

Then out of the cloud of settling dust
The burly form of an abbot appeared,
Reading his office he rode to the town.
And the fool got up, for his heart was
cheered.

He stood in the midst of the long, white
road
And swept off his cap till it touched
the ground.
"Ah, Reverent Sir, well met," said the
fool,
"A worthier transport never was found.

"I pray you allow me to mount with you,
Your palfrey seems both sturdy and
young."
The abbot looked up from the holy book
And cried out in anger, "Hold your
tongue!

"How dare you obstruct the King's highroad,
You saucy varlet, get out of my way."

Then he gave the fool a cut with his
whip
And leaving him smarting, he rode
away.

The fool was angry, the fool was sore,
And he cursed the folly of monks and
maids.
"If I could but meet with a man," sighed
the fool,
"For a woman fears, and a friar up-
braids."

Then he saw a flashing of distant steel
And the clanking of harness greeted
his ears,
And up the road journeyed knights-at-
arms,
With waving plumes and glittering
spears.

The fool took notice and slowly arose,
Not quite so sure was his foolish heart.
If priests and women would none of him
Was it likely a knight would take his
part?

They sang as they rode, these lusty boys,
When one chanced to turn toward the
highway's side,
"There's a sorry figure of fun," jested he,
"Well, Sirrah! move back, there is
scarce room to ride."

"Good Sirs, Kind Sirs," begged the crest-
fallen fool,
"I pray of your courtesy speech with
you,
I'm for yonder town, and have no horse
to ride,
Have you never a charger will carry
two?"

Then the company halted and laughed
out loud.
"Was such a request ever made to a
knight?"
"And where are your legs," asked one,
"if you start,
You may be inside the town gates to-
night."

" 'Tis a lazy fellow, let him alone,
They've no room in the town for such
idlers as he."

But one bent from his saddle and said,
"My man,
Art thou not ashamed to beg charity!

"Thou are well set up, and thy legs are
strong,
But it much misgives me lest thou'rt
a fool;
For beggars get only a beggar's crust,
Wise men are reared in a different
school."

Then they clattered away in the dust and
the wind,
And the fool slunk back to his lonely
stone;
He began to see that the man who asks
Must likewise give and not ask alone.

Purple tree-shadows crept over the road,
The level sun flung an orange light,
And the fool laid his head on the hard,
gray stone
And wept as he realized advancing
night.

A great, round moon rose over a hill
And the steady wind blew yet more
cool;
And crouched on a stone a wayfarer
sobbed,
For at last he knew he was only a
fool.

THE GREEN BOWL

This little bowl is like a mossy pool
In a Spring wood, where dogtooth vio-
lets grow
Nodding in chequered sunshine of the
trees;
A quiet place, still, with the sound of
birds,
Where, though unseen, is heard the end-
less song
And murmur of the never resting sea.
'Twas winter, Roger, when you made this
cup,
But coming Spring guided your eager
hand
And round the edge you fashioned young
green leaves,
A proper chalice made to hold the shy
And little flowers of the woods. And
here

They will forget their sad uprooting, lost
In pleasure that this circle of bright
leaves
Should be their setting; once more they
will dream
They hear winds wandering through lofty
trees
And see the sun smiling between the
leaves.

HORA STELLATRIX

The stars hang thick in the apple tree,
The south wind smells of the pungent
sea,
Gold tulip cups are heavy with dew.
The night's for you, Sweetheart, for you!
Starfire rains from the vaulted blue.

Listen! The dancing of unseen leaves.
A drowsy swallow stirs in the eaves.
Only a maiden is sorrowing.
'Tis night and spring, Sweetheart, and
spring!
Starfire lights your heart's blossoming.

In the intimate dark there's never an
ear,
Though the tulips stand on tiptoe to
hear.
So give; ripe fruit must shrivel or fall.
As you are mine, Sweetheart, give all!
Starfire sparkles, your coronal.

FRAGMENT

What is poetry? Is it a mosaic
Of coloured stones which curiously
are wrought
Into a pattern? Rather glass that's
taught
By patient labour any hue to take
And glowing with a sumptuous splendor,
make
Beauty a thing of awe; where sun-
beams caught,
Transmuted fall in sheaves of rainbows
fraught
With storied meaning for religion's sake.

LOON POINT

Softly the water ripples
Against the canoe's curving side,

Softly the birch trees rustle
Flinging over us branches wide.

Softly the moon glints and glistens
As the water takes and leaves,
Like golden ears of corn
Which fall from loose-bound sheaves,

Or like the snow-white petals
Which drop from an overblown rose,
When Summer ripens to Autumn
And the freighted year must close.

From the shore come the scents of a
garden,
And between a gap in the trees
A proud, white statue glimmers
In cold, disdainful ease.

The child of a southern people,
The thought of an alien race,
What does she in this pale, northern
garden,
How reconcile it with her grace?

But the moon in her wayward beauty
Is ever and always the same,
As lovely as when upon Latmos
She watched till Endymion came.

Through the water the moon writes her
legends
In light, on the smooth, wet sand;
They endure for a moment, and vanish,
And no one may understand.

All round us the secret of Nature
Is telling itself to our sight,
We may guess at her meaning but never
Can know the full mystery of night.

But her power of enchantment is on us,
We bow to the spell which she weaves,
Made up of the murmur of waves
And the manifold whisper of leaves.

SUMMER

Some men there are who find in nature
all
Their inspiration, hers the sympathy
Which spurs them on to any great endeavor,
To them the fields and woods are closest
friends,

And they hold dear communion with
the hills;
The voice of waters soothes them with
its fall,
And the great winds bring healing in their
sound.
To them a city is a prison house
Where pent up human forces labour
and strive,
Where beauty dwells not, driven forth
by man;
But where in winter they must live until
Summer gives back the spaces of the
hills.
To me it is not so. I love the earth
And all the gifts of her so lavish hand:
Sunshine and flowers, rivers and rushing
winds,
Thick branches swaying in a winter
storm,
And moonlight playing in a boat's wide
wake;
But more than these, and much, ah,
how much more,
I love the very human heart of man.
Above me spreads the hot, blue mid-
day sky,
Far down the hillside lies the sleeping
lake
Lazily reflecting back the sun,
And scarcely ruffled by the little breeze
Which wanders idly through the nod-
ding ferns.
The blue crest of the distant mountain,
tops
The green crest of the hill on which I
sit;
And it is summer, glorious, deep-toned
summer,
The very crown of nature's changing year
When all her surging life is at its full.
To me alone it is a time of pause,
A void and silent space between two
worlds,
When inspiration lags, and feeling sleeps,
Gathering strength for efforts yet to
come.
For life alone is creator of life,
And closest contact with the human
world
Is like a lantern shining in the night
To light me to a knowledge of myself.
I love the vivid life of winter months
In constant intercourse with human
minds,

When every new experience is gain
And on all sides we feel the great world's
heart;
The pulse and throb of life which makes
us men!

"TO-MORROW TO FRESH WOODS AND PASTURES NEW"

As for a moment he stands, in hardy
masculine beauty,
Poised on the fircrested rock, over the
pool which below him
Gleams in the wavering sunlight, waiting
the shock of his plunging.
So for a moment I stand, my feet planted
firm in the present,
Eagerly scanning the future which is so
soon to possess me.

THE WAY

At first a mere thread of a footpath half
blotted out by the grasses
Sweeping triumphant across it, it wound
between hedges of roses
Whose blossoms were poised above leaves
as pond lilies float on the water,
While hidden by bloom in a hawthorn a
bird filled the morning with singing.

It widened a highway, majestic, stretching ever to distant horizons,
Where shadows of tree-branches wavered,
vague outlines invaded by sunshine;
No sound but the wind as it whispered
the secrets of earth to the flowers,
And the hum of the yellow bees, honey-
laden and dusty with pollen.
And Summer said, "Come, follow onward, with no thought save the longing to wander,
The wind, and the bees, and the flowers,
all singing the great song of Nature,
Are minstrels of change and of promise,
they herald the joy of the Future."

Later the solitude vanished, confused and
distracted the road
Where many were seeking and jostling.
Left behind were the trees and the
flowers.
The half-realized beauty of quiet, the
sacred unconscious communing.

And now he is come to a river, a line of
gray, sullen water,
Not blue and splashing, but dark, rolling
somberly on to the ocean.

But on the far side is a city whose windows flame gold in the sunset.
It lies fair and shining before him, a gem
set betwixt sky and water.
And spanning the river a bridge, frail
promise to longing desire,
Flung by man in his infinite courage,
across the stern force of the water;
And he looks at the river and fears, the
bridge is so slight, yet he ventures
His life to its fragile keeping, if it fails
the waves will engulf him.
O Arches! be strong to uphold him, and
bear him across to the city,
The beautiful city whose spires still glow
with the fires of sunset!

ΔΙΨΑ

Look, Dear, how bright the moonlight is
to-night!
See where it casts the shadow of that tree
Far out upon the grass. And every gust
Of light night wind comes laden with the
scent
Of opening flowers which never bloom
by day:
Night-scented stocks, and four o'clocks,
and that
Pale yellow disk, upreared on its tall
stalk,
The evening primrose, comrade of the
stars.
It seems as though the garden which
you love
Were like a swinging censer, its incense
Floating before us as a reverent act
To sanctify and bless our night of love.
Tell me once more you love me, that 'tis
you
Yes, really you, I touch, so, with my hand;
And tell me it is by your own free will
That you are here, and that you like to be
Just here, with me, under this sailing
pine.
I need to hear it often for my heart
Doubts naturally, and finds it hard to
trust.
Ah, Dearest, you are good to love me so,

And yet I would not have it goodness,
rather
Excess of selfishness in you to need
Me through and through, as flowers need
the sun.
I wonder can it really be that you
And I are here alone, and that the night
Is full of hours, and all the world asleep,
And none can call to you to come away;
For you have given all yourself to me
Making me gentle by your willingness.
Has your life too been waiting for this
time,
Not only mine the sharpness of this joy?
Dear Heart, I love you, worship you as
though
I were a priest before a holy shrine.
I'm glad that you are beautiful, although
Were you not lovely still I needs must
love;
But you are all things, it must have been
so
For otherwise it were not you. Come,
close;
When you are in the circle of my arm
Faith grows a mountain and I take my
stand
Upon its utmost top. Yes, yes, once more
Kiss me, and let me feel you very near
Wanting me wholly, even as I want you.
Have years behind been dark? Will those
to come
Bring unguessed sorrows into our two
lives?
What does it matter, we have had to-
night!
To-night will make us strong, for we
believe
Each in the other, this is a sacrament.
Beloved, is it true?

ROADS

I know a country laced with roads,
They join the hills and they span the
brooks,
They weave like a shuttle between broad
fields,
And slide discreetly through hidden
nooks.
They are canopied like a Persian dome
And carpeted with orient dyes.
They are myriad-voiced, and musical,
And scented with happiest memories.
O Winding roads that I know so well,

Every twist and turn, every hollow and
hill!
They are set in my heart to a pulsing tune
Gay as a honey-bee humming in June.
'Tis the rhythmic beat of a horse's feet
And the pattering paws of a sheep-dog
bitch;
'Tis the creaking trees, and the singing
breeze,
And the rustle of leaves in the road-side
ditch.

A cow in a meadow shakes her bell
And the notes cut sharp through the
autumn air,
Each chattering brook bears a fleet of
leaves
Their cargo the rainbow, and just now
where
The sun splashed bright on the road
ahead
A startled rabbit quivered and fled.
O Uphill roads and roads that dip
down!
You curl your sun-spattered length along,
And your march is beaten into a song
By the softly ringing hoofs of a horse
And the panting breath of the dogs I
love.
The pageant of Autumn follows its course
And the blue sky of Autumn laughs
above.

And the song and the country become as
one,
I see it as music, I hear it as light;
Prismatic and shimmering, trembling to
tone,
The land of desire, my soul's delight.
And always it beats in my listening ears
With the gentle thud of a horse's
stride,
With the swift-falling steps of many dogs,
Following, following at my side.
O Roads that journey to fairyland!
Radiant highways whose vistas gleam,
Leading me on, under crimson leaves,
To the opaline gates of the Castles of
Dream.

TEATRO BAMBINO
DUBLIN, N.H.

How still it is! Sunshine itself here falls
In quiet shafts of light through the
high trees

Which, arching, make a roof above the
walls
Changing from sun to shadow as each
breeze
Lingers a moment, charmed by the
strange sight
Of an Italian theatre, storied, seer
Of vague romance, and time's long history;
Where tiers of grass-grown seats sprinkled
with white,
Sweet-scented clover, form a broken
sphere
Grouped round the stage in hushed
expectancy.

What sound is that which echoes through
the wood?
Is it the reedy note of an oaten pipe?
Perchance a minute more will see the
brood
Of the shaggy forest god, and on his
lip
Will rest the rushes he is wont to play.
His train in woven baskets bear ripe
fruit
And weave a dance with ropes of gray
acorns,
So light their touch the grasses scarcely
sway
As they the measure tread to the lilting
flute.
Alas! 'tis only Fancy thus adorns.

A cloud drifts idly over the shining sun.
How damp it seems, how silent, still,
and strange!
Surely 'twas here some tragedy was done,
And here the chorus sang each coming
change?
Sure this is deep in some sweet, southern
wood,
These are not pines, but cypress tall
and dark;
That is no thrush which sings so
rapturously,
But the nightingale in his most passionate
mood
Bursting his little heart with anguish.
Hark!
The tread of sandalled feet comes
noiselessly.

The silence almost is a sound, and dreams
Take on the semblances of finite
things;

So potent is the spell that what but seems
Elsewhere, is lifted here on Fancy's
wings.
The little woodland theatre seems to
wait,
All tremulous with hope and wistful
joy,
For something that is sure to come at
last,
Some deep emotion, satisfying, great.
It grows a living presence, bold and
shy,
Cradling the future in a glorious past.

THE ROAD TO AVIGNON

A minstrel stands on a marble stair,
Blown by the bright wind, debonair;
Below lies the sea, a sapphire floor,
Above on the terrace a turret door
Frames a lady, listless and wan,
But fair for the eye to rest upon.
The minstrel plucks at his silver strings,
And looking up to the lady, sings: —
    Down the road to Avignon,
    The long, long road to Avignon,
    Across the birdge to Avignon,
    One morning in the spring.

The octagon tower casts a shade
Cool and gray like a cutlass blade;
In sun-baked vines the cicalas spin,
The little green lizards run out and in.
A sail dips over the ocean's rim,
And bubbles rise to the fountain's brim.
The minstrel touches his silver strings,
And gazing up to the lady, sings: —
    Down the road to Avignon,
    The long, long road to Avignon,
    Across the bridge to Avignon,
    One morning in the spring.

Slowly she walks to the balustrade,
Idly notes how the blossoms fade
In the sun's caress; then crosses where
The shadow shelters a carven chair.
Within its curve, supine she lies,
And wearily closes her tired eyes.
The minstrel beseeches his silver strings,
And holding the lady spellbound,
    sings: —
    Down the road to Avignon,
    The long, long road to Avignon,
    Across the bridge to Avignon,
    One morning in the spring.

Clouds sail over the distant trees,
Petals are shaken down by the breeze,
They fall on the terrace tiles like snow;
The sighing of waves sounds, far below.
A humming-bird kisses the lips of a rose
Then laden with honey and love he goes.
The minstrel woos with his silver strings,
And climbing up to the lady, sings: —
    Down the road to Avignon,
    The long, long road to Avignon,
    Across the bridge to Avignon,
    One morning in the spring.

Step by step, and he comes to her,
Fearful lest she suddenly stir.
Sunshine and silence, and each to each,
The lute and his singing their only speech;
He leans above her, her eyes unclose,
The humming-bird enters another rose.
The minstrel hushes his silver strings.
Hark! The beating of humming-birds'
    wings!
    Down the road to Avignon,
    The long, long road to Avignon,
    Across the bridge to Avignon,
    One morning in the spring.

NEW YORK AT NIGHT

A near horizon whose sharp jags
    Cut brutally into a sky
Of leaden heaviness, and crags
Of houses lift their masonry
    Ugly and foul, and chimneys lie
And snort, outlined against the gray
Of lowhung cloud. I hear the sigh
The goaded city gives, not day
Nor night can ease her heart, her an-
    guished labours stay.

Below, straight streets, monotonous,
    From north and south, from east and
    west,
Stretch glittering; and luminous
    Above, one tower tops the rest
    And holds aloft man's constant quest:
Time! Joyless emblem of the greed
    Of millions, robber of the best
Which earth can give, the vulgar creed
Has seared upon the night its flaming
    ruthless screed.

O Night! Whose soothing presence
    brings
    The quiet shining of the stars.
O Night! Whose cloak of darkness clings

So intimately close that scars
    Are hid from our own eyes. Beggars
By day, our wealth is having night
    To burn our souls before altars
Dim and tree-shadowed, where the light
Is shed from a young moon, mysteriously
    bright.

Where art thou hiding, where thy peace?
    This is the hour, but thou are not.
Will waking tumult never cease?
    Hast thou thy votary forgot?
    Nature forsakes this man-begot
And festering wilderness, and now
    The long still hours are here, no jot
Of dear communing do I know;
Instead the glaring, man-filled city groans
    below!

A FAIRY TALE

On winter nights beside the nursery fire
We read the fairy tale, while glowing
    coals
Builded its pictures. There before our
    eyes
We saw the vaulted hall of traceried stone
Uprear itself, the distant ceiling hung
With pendent stalactites like frozen
    vines;
And all along the walls at intervals,
Curled upwards into pillars, roses climbed,
And ramped and were confined, and
    clustered leaves
Divided where there peered a laughing
    face.
The foliage seemed to rustle in the wind,
A silent murmur, carved in still, gray
    stone.
High pointed windows pierced the south-
    ern wall
Whence proud escutcheons flung pris-
    matic fires
To stain the tessellated marble floor
With pools of red, and quivering green,
    and blue;
And in the shade beyond the further door,
Its sober squares of black and white were
    hid
Beneath a restless, shuffling, wide-eyed
    mob
Of lackeys and retainers come to view
The Christening.
A sudden blare of trumpets, and the
    throng
About the entrance parted as the guests

Filed singly in with rare and precious
gifts.
Our eager fancies noted all they brought,
The glorious unattainable delights!
But always there was one unbidden guest
Who cursed the child and left it bitter-
ness.

The fire falls asunder, all is changed,
I am no more a child, and what I see
Is not a fairy tale, but life, my life.
The gifts are there, the many pleasant
things:
Health, wealth, long-settled friendships,
with a name
Which honors all who bear it, and the
power
Of making words obedient. This is much;
But overshadowing all is still the curse,
That never shall I be fulfilled by love!
Along the parching highroad of the world
No other soul shall bear mine company.
Always shall I be teased with semblances,
With cruel impostures, which I trust
awhile
Then dash to pieces, as a careless boy
Flings a kaleidoscope, which shattering
Strews all the ground about with coloured
sherds.
So I behold my visions on the ground
No longer radiant, an ignoble heap
Of broken, dusty glass. And so, unlit,
Even by hope or faith, my dragging steps
Force me forever through the passing
days.

CROWNED

You came to me bearing bright roses,
    Red like the wine of your heart;
You twisted them into a garland
    To set me aside from the mart.
Red roses to crown me your lover,
    And I walked aureoled and apart.

Enslaved and encircled, I bore it,
    Proud token of my gift to you.
The petals waned paler, and shriveled,
    And dropped; and the thorns started
    through.
Bitter thorns to proclaim me your lover,
    A diadem woven with rue.

TO
ELIZABETH WARD PERKINS

Dear Bessie, would my tired rhyme
Had force to rise from apathy,
And shaking off its lethargy
Ring word-tones like a Christmas chime.

But in my soul's high belfry, chill
    The bitter wind of doubt has blown,
    The summer swallows all have flown,
The bells are frost-bound, mute and still.

Upon the crumbling boards the snow
    Has drifted deep, the clappers hang
    Prismed with icicles, their clang
Unheard since ages long ago.

The rope I pull is stiff and cold,
    My straining ears detect no sound
    Except a sigh, as round and round
The wind rocks through the timbers old.

Below, I know the church is bright
    With haloed tapers, warm with prayer;
    But here I only feel the air
Of icy centuries of night.

Beneath my feet the snow is lit
    And gemmed with colours, red, and
    blue,
    Topaz, and green, where light falls
    through
The saints that in the windows sit.

Here darkness seems a spectred thing,
    Voiceless and haunting, while the stars
    Mock with a light of long dead years
The ache of present suffering.

Silent and winter-killed I stand,
    No carol hymns my debt to you;
    But take this frozen thought in lieu,
And thaw its music in your hand.

THE PROMISE OF THE MORNING
STAR

Thou father of the children of my brain
    By thee engendered in my willing heart,
    How can I thank thee for this gift of
    art
Poured out so lavishly, and not in vain.

What thou created never more can die,
    Thy fructifying power lives in me
    And I conceive, knowing it is by thee,
Dear other parent of my poetry!

For I was but a shadow with a name,
    Perhaps by now the very name's forgot;

So strange is Fate that it has been my
   lot
To learn through thee the presence of
   that aim

Which evermore must guide me. All
   unknown,
By me unguessed, by thee not even
   dreamed,
A tree has blossomed in a night that
   seemed
Of stubborn, barren wood. For thou hast
   sown

This seed of beauty in a ground of truth.
   Humbly I dedicate myself, and yet
   I tremble with a sudden fear to set
New music ringing through my fading
   youth.

J—K. HUYSMANS

A flickering glimmer through a window-
   pane,
A dim red glare through mud bespattered
   glass,
Cleaving a path between blown walls of
   sleet
Across uneven pavements sunk in slime
To scatter and then quench itself in mist.
And struggling, slipping, often rudely
   hurled
Against the jutting angle of a wall,
And cursed, and reeled against, and flung
   aside
By drunken brawlers as they shuffled past,
A man was groping to what seemed a
   light.
His eyelids burnt and quivered with the
   strain
Of looking, and against his temples beat
The all enshrouding, suffocating dark.
He stumbled, lurched, and struck against
   a door
That opened, and a howl of obscene mirth
Grated his senses, wallowing on the floor
Lay men, and dogs and women in the dirt.
He sickened, loathing it, and as he gazed
The candle guttered, flared, and then
   went out.

Through travail of ignoble midnight
   streets
He came at last to shelter in a porch
Where gothic saints and warriors made a
   shield

To cover him, and tortured gargoyles spat
One long continuous stream of silver rain
That clattered down from myriad roofs
   and spires
Into a darkness, loud with rushing sound
Of water falling, gurgling as it fell,
But always thickly dark. Then as he
   leaned
Unconscious where, the great oak door
   blew back
And cast him, bruised and dripping, in
   the church.
His eyes from long sojourning in the night
Were blinded now as by some glorious
   sun;
He slowly crawled toward the altar steps.
He could not think, for heavy in his ears
An organ boomed majestic harmonies;
He only knew that what he saw was light!
He bowed himself before a cross of flame
And shut his eyes in fear lest it should
   fade.

MARCH EVENING

Blue through the window burns the twilight;
Heavy, through trees, blows the warm
   south wind.
Glistening, against the chill, gray sky light,
Wet, black branches are barred and
   entwined.

Sodden and spongy, the scarce-green grass
   plot
Dents into pools where a foot has been.
Puddles lie spilt in the road a mass, not
Of water, but steel, with its cold, hard
   sheen.

Faint fades the fire on the hearth, its
   embers
Scattering wide at a stronger gust.
Above, the old weathercock groans, but
   remembers
Creaking, to turn, in its centuried rust.

Dying, forlorn, in dreary sorrow,
Wrapping the mists round her withering form,
Day sinks down; and in darkness to--
   morrow
Travails to birth in the womb of the
   storm.

SONNETS

LEISURE

Leisure, thou goddess of a bygone age,
  When hours were long and days sufficed
    to hold
  Wide-eyed delights and pleasures un-
    controlled
By shortening moments, when no gaunt
    presage
Of undone duties, modern heritage,
  Haunted our happy minds; must thou
    withhold
Thy presence from this over-busy world,
And bearing silence with thee disengage
  Our twined fortunes? Deeps of unhewn
    woods
Alone can cherish thee, alone possess
Thy quiet, teeming vigor. This our crime:
  Not to have worshipped, marred by
    alien moods
That sole condition of all loveliness,
The dreaming lapse of slow, unmeasured
    time.

ON CARPACCIO'S PICTURE THE DREAM OF ST. URSULA

Swept, clean, and still, across the polished
    floor
  From some unshuttered casement, hid
    from sight,
  The level sunshine slants, its greater
    light
Quenching the little lamp which pallid,
    poor,
Flickering, unreplenished, at the door
  Has striven against darkness the long
    night.
  Dawn fills the room, and penetrating,
    bright,
The silent sunbeams through the window
    pour.
And she lies sleeping, ignorant of Fate,
  Enmeshed in listless dreams, her soul
    not yet
Ripened to bear the purport of this day.
  The morning breeze scarce stirs the
    coverlet,
  A shadow falls across the sunlight;
    wait!
A lark is singing as he flies away.

THE MATRIX

Goaded and harassed in the factory
  That tears our life up into bits of days
  Ticked off upon a clock which never
    stays,
Shredding our portion of Eternity,
We break away at last, and steal the key
  Which hides a world empty of hours;
    ways
  Of space unroll, and Heaven overlays
The leafy, sun-lit earth of Fantasy.
  Beyond the ilex shadow glares the sun,
  Scorching against the blue flame of the
    sky.
Brown lily-pads lie heavy and supine
  Within a granite basin, under one
  The bronze-gold glimmer of a carp;
    and I
Reach out my hand and pluck a nec-
    tarine.

MONADNOCK IN EARLY SPRING

Cloud-topped and splendid, dominating
    all
  The little lesser hills which compass
    thee,
  Thou standest, bright with April's
    buoyancy,
Yet holding Winter in some shaded wall
Of stern, steep rock; and startled by the
    call
  Of Spring, thy trees flush with expec-
    tancy
  And cast a cloud of crimson, silently,
Above thy snowy crevices where fall
  Pale shrivelled oak leaves, while the
    snow beneath
Melts at their phantom touch. Another
    year
Is quick with import. Such each year has
    been.
  Unmoved thou watchest all, and all
    bequeath
Some jewel to thy diadem of power,
Thou pledge of greater majesty unseen.

THE LITTLE GARDEN

A little garden on a bleak hillside
  Where deep the heavy, dazzling moun-
    tain snow

Lies far into the spring. The sun's pale glow
Is scarcely able to melt patches wide
About the single rose bush. All denied
Of nature's tender ministries. But no,—
For wonder-working faith has made it blow
With flowers many hued and starry-eyed.
Here sleeps the sun long, idle summer hours;
Here butterflies and bees fare far to rove
Amid the crumpled leaves of poppy flowers;
Here four o'clocks, to the passionate night above
Fling whiffs of perfume, like pale incense showers.
A little garden, loved with a great love!

TO AN EARLY DAFFODIL

Thou yellow trumpeter of laggard Spring!
Thou herald of rich Summer's myriad flowers!
The climbing sun with new recovered powers
Does warm thee into being, through the ring
Of rich, brown earth he woos thee, makes thee fling
Thy green shoots up, inheriting the dowers
Of bending sky and sudden, sweeping showers,
Till ripe and blossoming thou art a thing
To make all nature glad, thou art so gay;
To fill the lonely with a joy untold;
Nodding at every gust of wind to-day,
To-morrow jewelled with raindrops. Always bold
To stand erect, full in the dazzling play
Of April's sun, for thou hast caught his gold.

LISTENING

'Tis you that are the music, not your song.
The song is but a door which, opening wide,
Lets forth the pent-up melody inside,
Your spirit's harmony, which clear and strong

Sings but of you. Throughout your whole life long
Your songs, your thoughts, your doings, each divide
This perfect beauty; waves within a tide
Or single notes amid a glorious throng.
The song of earth has many different chords;
Ocean has many moods and many tones
Yet always ocean. In the damp Spring woods
The painted trillium smiles, while crisp pine cones
Autumn alone can ripen. So is this
One music with a thousand cadences.

THE LAMP OF LIFE

Always we are following a light,
Always the light recedes; with groping hands
We stretch toward this glory, while the lands
We journey through are hidden from our sight
Dim and mysterious, folded deep in night,
We care not, all our utmost need demands
Is but the light, the light! So still it stands
Surely our own if we exert our might.
Fool! Never can'st thou grasp this fleeting gleam,
Its glowing flame would die if it were caught,
Its value is that it doth always seem
But just a little farther on. Distraught,
But lighted ever onward, we are brought
Upon our way unknowing, in a dream.

HERO—WORSHIP

A face seen passing in a crowded street,
A voice heard singing music, large and free;
And from that moment life is changed, and we
Become of more heroic temper, meet
To freely ask and give, a man complete
Radiant because of faith, we dare to be
What Nature meant us. Brave idolatry
Which can conceive a hero! No deceit,
No knowledge taught by unrelenting years,

Can quench this fierce, untamable de-
  sire.
We know that what we long for once
  achieved
Will cease to satisfy. Be still our fears;
If what we worship fail us, still the fire
Burns on, and it is much to have believed.

IN DARKNESS

Must all of worth be travailled for, and
  those
Life's brightest stars rise from a trou-
  bled sea?
Must years go by in sad uncertainty
Leaving us doubting whose the conquer-
  ing blows,
Are we or Fate the victors? Time which
  shows
All inner meanings will reveal, but we
Shall never know the upshot. Ours to
  be
Wasted with longing, shattered in the
  throes,
The agonies of splendid dreams, which
  day
Dims from our vision, but each night
  brings back;
We strive to hold their grandeur, and
  essay
To be the thing we dream. Sudden we
  lack
The flash of insight, life grows drear and
  gray,
And hour follows hour, nerveless, slack.

BEFORE DAWN

Life! Austere arbiter of each man's fate,
  By whom he learns that Nature's stead-
  fast laws
Are as decrees immutable; O pause
Your even forward march! Not yet too
  late
Teach me the needed lesson, when to wait
Inactive as a ship when no wind draws
To stretch the loosened cordage. One
  implores
Thy clemency, whose willfulness innate
Has gone uncurbed and roughshod
  while the years
Have lengthened into decades; now dis-
  tressed

He knows no rule by which to move or
  stay,
And teased with restlessness and desperate fears
He dares not watch in silence thy wise way
Bringing about results none could have
  guessed.

THE POET

What instinct forces man to journey on,
  Urged by a longing blind but domi-
  nant!
Nothing he sees can hold him, nothing
  daunt
His never failing eagerness. The sun
Setting in splendour every night has won
His vassalage; those towers flamboyant
Of airy cloudland palaces now haunt
His daylight wanderings. Forever done
With simple joys and quiet happiness
  He guards the vision of the sunset sky;
Though faint with weariness he must pos-
  sess
Some fragment of the sunset's majesty;
He spurns life's human friendships to
  profess
Life's loneliness of dreaming ecstasy.

AT NIGHT

The wind is singing through the trees to-
  night,
A deep-voiced song of rushing cadences
And crashing intervals. No summer
  breeze
Is this, though hot July is at its height,
Gone is her gentler music; with delight
  She listens to this booming like the
  seas,
These elemental, loud necessities
Which call to her to answer their swift
  might.
Above the tossing trees shines down a
  star,
Quietly bright; this wild, tumultuous
  joy
Quickens nor dims its splendour. And
  my mind,
O Star! is filled with your white light,
  from far,
So suffer me this one night to enjoy
The freedom of the onward sweeping
  wind.

THE FRUIT GARDEN PATH

The path runs straight between the flow-
ering rows,
A moonlit path, hemmed in by beds of
bloom,
Where phlox and marigolds dispute for
room
With tall, red dahlias and the briar rose.
'Tis reckless prodigality which throws
Into the night these wafts of rich per-
fume
Which sweep across the garden like a
plume.
Over the trees a single bright star glows.
Dear garden of my childhood, here my
years
Have run away like little grains of sand;
The moments of my life, its hopes and
fears
Have all found utterance here, where now
I stand;
My eyes ache with the weight of un-
shed tears,
You are my home, do you not understand?

MIRAGE

How is it that, being gone, you fill my
days,
And all the long nights are made glad
by thee?
No loneliness is this, nor misery,
But great content that these should be
the ways
Whereby the Fancy, dreaming as she
strays,
Makes bright and present what she
would be.
And who shall say if the reality
Is not with dreams so pregnant. For de-
lays
And hindrances may bar the wished-for
end;
A thousand misconceptions may prevent
Our souls from coming near enough to
blend;
Let me but think we have the same intent,
That each one needs to call the other,
"friend!"
It may be vain illusion. I'm content.

TO A FRIEND

I ask but one thing of you, only one,
That always you will be my dream of
you;

That never shall I wake to find untrue
All this I have believed and rested on,
Forever vanished, like a vision gone
Out into the night. Alas, how few
There are who strike in us a chord we
knew
Existed, but so seldom heard its tone
We tremble at the half-forgotten
sound.
The world is full of rude awakenings
And heaven-born castles shattered to
the ground,
Yet still our human longing vainly clings
To a belief in beauty through all
wrongs.
O stay your hand, and leave my heart
its songs!

A FIXED IDEA

What torture lurks within a single
thought
When grown too constant, and however
kind,
However welcome still, the weary mind
Aches with its presence. Dull remem-
brance taught
Remembers on unceasingly; unsought
The old delight is with us but to find
That all recurring joy is pain refined,
Become a habit, and we struggle, caught.
You lie upon my heart as on a nest,
Folded in peace, for you can never know
How crushed I am with having you at rest
Heavy upon my life. I love you so
You bind my freedom from its rightful
quest.
In mercy lift your drooping wings and go.

DREAMS

I do not care to talk to you although
Your speech evokes a thousand sym-
pathies,
And all my being's silent harmonies
Wake trembling into music. When you
go
It is as if some sudden, dreadful blow
Had severed all the strings with savage
ease.
No, do not talk; but let us rather seize
This intimate gift of silence which we
know.
Others may guess your thoughts from
what you say,

As storms are guessed from clouds where
    darkness broods.
To me the very essence of the day
Reveals its inner purpose and its moods;
As poplars feel the rain and then
    straightway
Reverse their leaves and shimmer through
    the woods.

FRANKINCENSE AND MYRRH

My heart is tuned to sorrow, and the
    strings
Vibrate most readily to minor chords,
Searching and sad; my mind is stuffed
    with words
Which voice the passion and the ache of
    things:
Illusions beating with their baffled wings
Against the walls of circumstance, and
    hoards
Of torn desires, broken joys; records
Of all a bruised life's maimed imaginings.
Now you are come! You tremble like
    a star
Poised where, behind earth's rim, the sun
    has set,
Your voice has sung across my heart, but
    numb
And mute, I have no tones to answer. Far
Within I kneel before you, speechless yet,
And life ablaze with beauty, I am dumb.

FROM ONE WHO STAYS

How empty seems the town now you are
    gone!
A wilderness of sad streets, where gaunt
    walls
Hide nothing to desire; sunshine falls
Eery, distorted, as it long had shone
On white, dead faces tombed in halls of
    stone.
The whir of motors, stricken through
    with calls
Of playing boys, floats up at intervals;
But all these noises blur to one long moan.
What quest is worth pursuing? And
    how strange
That other men still go accustomed ways!
I hate their interest in the things they do.
A spectre-horde repeating without
    change

An old routine. Alone I know the days
Are still-born, and the world stopped,
    lacking you.

CREPUSCULE DU MATIN

All night I wrestled with a memory
Which knocked insurgent at the gates
    of thought.
The crumbled wreck of years behind
    has wrought
Its disillusion; now I only cry
For peace, for power to forget the lie
Which hope too long has whispered.
    So I sought
The sleep which would not come, and
    night was fraught
With old emotions weeping silently.
I heard your voice again, and knew the
    things
Which you had promised proved an
    empty vaunt.
I felt your clinging hands while night's
    broad wings
Cherished our love in darkness. From
    the lawn
A sudden, quivering birdnote, like a
    taunt.
My arms held nothing but the empty
    dawn.

AFTERMATH

I learnt to write to you in happier
    days,
    And every letter was a piece I chipped
From off my heart, a fragment newly
    clipped
From the mosaic of life; its blues and
    grays,
Its throbbing reds, I gave to earn your
    praise.
To make a pavement for your feet I
    stripped
My soul for you to walk upon, and
    slipped
Beneath your steps to soften all your
    ways.
But now my letters are like blossoms
    pale
We strew upon a grave with hopeless
    tears.
    I ask no recompense, I shall not fail

Although you do not heed; the long, sad
    years
Still pass, and still I scatter flowers frail,
And whisper words of love which no one
    hears.

THE END

Throughout the echoing chambers of my
    brain
I hear your words in mournful cadence
    toll
Like some slow passing-bell which
    warns the soul
Of sundering darkness. Unrelenting, fain
To batter down resistance, fall again
Stroke after stroke, insistent diastole,
The bitter blows of truth, until the
    whole
Is hammered into fact made strangely
    plain.
Where shall I look for comfort? Not
    to you.
Our worlds are drawn apart, our spirit's
    suns
Divided, and the light of mine burnt dim.
Now in the haunted twilight I must do
Your will. I grasp the cup which over-
    runs,
And with my trembling lips I touch the
    rim.

THE STARLING

" 'I can't get out,' said the starling."
    STERNE's *Sentimental Journey*

Forever the impenetrable wall
    Of self confines my poor rebellious soul,
    I never see the towering white clouds
        roll
Before a sturdy wind, save through the
    small
Barred window of my jail. I live a thrall
With all my outer life a clipped, square
    hole,
    Rectangular; a fraction of a scroll
Unwound and winding like a worsted
    ball.
    My thoughts are grown uneager and
        depressed
Through being always mine, my fancy's
    wings
Are moulted and the feathers blown away.
    I weary for desires never guessed,

For alien passions, strange imaginings,
To be some other person for a day.

MARKET DAY

White, glittering sunlight fills the market
    square,
    Spotted and sprigged with shadows.
        Double rows
    Of bartering booths spread out their
        tempting shows
Of globed and golden fruit, the morning
    air
Smells sweet with ripeness, on the pave-
    ment there
    A wicker basket gapes and overflows
    Spilling out cool, blue plums. The
        market glows,
And flaunts, and clatters in its busy care.
    A stately minster at the northern side
Lifts its twin spires to the distant sky,
    Pinnacled, carved and buttressed;
        through the wide
Arched doorway peals an organ, sud-
    denly —
    Crashing, triumphant in its pregnant
        tide,
Quenching the square in vibrant har-
    mony.

EPITAPH IN A CHURCH–YARD IN CHARLESTON, SOUTH CAROLINA

GEORGE AUGUSTUS CLOUGH
A NATIVE OF LIVERPOOL,
DIED SUDDENLY OF "STRANGER'S FEVER"
NOV'R 5TH 1843
AGED 22

He died of "Stranger's Fever" when his
    youth
    Had scarcely melted into manhood, so
    The chiselled legend runs; a brother's
        woe
Laid bare for epitaph. The savage ruth
Of a sunny, bright, but alien land, un-
    couth
    With cruel caressing dealt a mortal
        blow,
    And by this summer sea where flowers
        grow
In tropic splendour, witness to the truth
Of ineradicable race he lies.
    The law of duty urged that he should
        roam,

Should sail from fog and chilly airs to
skies
Clear with deceitful welcome. He had
come
With proud resolve, but still his lonely
eyes
Ached with fatigue at never seeing
home.

FRANCIS II, KING OF NAPLES

WRITTEN AFTER READING TREVELYAN'S
"GARIBALDI AND THE MAKING OF ITALY"

Poor foolish monarch, vacillating, vain,
Decaying victim of a race of kings,
Swift Destiny shook out her purple
wings
And caught him in their shadow; not
again
Could furtive plotting smear another
stain
Across his tarnished honour. Smoulder-
ings
Of sacrificial fires burst their rings
And blotted out in smoke his lost domain.
Bereft of courtiers, only with his queen,
From empty palace down to empty
quay.
No challenge screamed from hostile cara-
bine.

A single vessel waited, shadowy;
All night she ploughed her solitary way
Beneath the stars, and through a tranquil
sea.

TO JOHN KEATS

Great master! Boyish, sympathetic man!
Whose orbed and ripened genius
lightly hung
From life's slim, twisted tendril and
there swung
In crimson-sphered completeness; guard-
ian
Of crystal portals through whose open-
ings fan
The spicéd winds which blew when
earth was young,
Scattering wreaths of stars, as Jove
once flung
A golden shower from heights cerulean.
Crumbled before thy majesty we bow.
Forget thy empurpled state, thy
panoply
Of greatness, and be merciful and near;
A youth who trudged the highroad we
tread now
Singing the miles behind him; so may
we
Faint throbbings of thy music overhear.

THE BOSTON ATHENAEUM

THE BOSTON ATHENAEUM

Thou dear and well-loved haunt of happy
hours,
How often in some distant gallery,
Gained by a little painful spiral stair,
Far from the halls and corridors where
throng
The crowd of casual readers, have I
passed
Long, peaceful hours seated on the floor
Of some retired nook, all lined with
books,
Where reverie and quiet reign supreme!
Above, below, on every side, high shelved
From careless grasp of transient interest,
Stand books we can but dimly see, their
charm
Much greater that their titles are unread;

While on a level with the dusty floor
Others are ranged in orderly confusion,
And we must stoop in painful posture
while
We read their names and learn their his-
tories.
The little gallery winds round about
The middle of a most secluded room,
Midway between the ceiling and the
floor.
A type of those high thoughts, which
while we read
Hover between the earth and furthest
heaven
As fancy wills, leaving the printed page;
For books but give the theme, our hearts
the rest,
Enriching simple words with unguessed
harmony

And overtones of thought we only know.
And as we sit long hours quietly,
Reading at times, and at times simply
    dreaming,
The very room itself becomes a friend,
The confidant of intimate hopes and
    fears;
A place where are engendered pleasant
    thoughts,
And possibilities before unguessed
Come to fruition born of sympathy.
And as in some gay garden stretched upon
A genial southern slope, warmed by the
    sun,
The flowers give their fragrance joyously
To the caressing touch of the hot noon;
So books give up the all of what they
    mean
Only in a congenial atmosphere,
Only when touched by reverent hands,
    and read
By those who love and feel as well as
    think.
For books are more than books, they are
    the life,
The very heart and core of ages past.
The reason why men lived, and worked,
    and died,
The essence and quintessence of their
    lives.
And we may know them better, and
    divine
The inner motives whence their actions
    sprang,
Far better than the men who only knew
Their bodily presence, the soul forever
    hid
From those with no ability to see.
They wait here quietly for us to come
And find them out, and know them for
    our friends;
These men who toiled and wrote only for
    this,
To leave behind such modicum of truth
As each perceived and each alone could
    tell.
Silently waiting that from time to time
It may be given them to illuminate
Dull daily facts with pristine radiance
For some long-waited-for affinity
Who lingers yet in the deep womb of
    time.
The shifting sun pierces the young green
    leaves
Of elm trees, newly coming into bud,

And splashes on the floor and on the
    books
Through old, high, rounded windows,
    dim with age.
The noisy city-sounds of modern life
Float softened to us across the old grave-
    yard.
The room is filled with a warm, mellow
    light,
No garish colours jar on our content,
The books upon the shelves are old and
    worn.
'Twas no belated effort nor attempt
To keep abreast with old as well as new
That placed them here, tricked in a
    modern guise,
Easily got, and held in light esteem.
Our fathers' fathers, slowly and carefully
Gathered them, one by one, when they
    were new
And a delighted world received their
    thoughts
Hungrily; while we but love the more,
Because they are so old and grown so
    dear!
The backs of tarnished gold, the faded
    boards,
The slightly yellowing page, the strange
    old type,
All speak the fashion of another age;
The thoughts peculiar to the man who
    wrote
Arrayed in garb peculiar to the time;
As though the idiom of a man were
    caught
Imprisoned in the idiom of a race.
A nothing truly, yet a link that binds
All ages to their own inheritance,
And stretching backward, dim and dim-
    mer still,
Is lost in a remote antiquity.
Grapes do not come of thorns nor figs of
    thistles,
And even a great poet's divinest thought
Is coloured by the world he knows and
    sees.
The little intimate things of every day,
The trivial nothings that we think not of,
These go to make a part of each man's
    life;
As much a part as do the larger thoughts
He takes account of. Nay, the little things
Of daily life it is which mold, and shape,
And make him apt for noble deeds and
    true.

And as we read some much-loved master-
piece,
Read it as long ago the author read,
With eyes that brimmed with tears as he
saw
The message he believed stamped in type
Inviolable for the slow-coming years;
We know a certain subtle sympathy,
We seem to clasp his hand across the
past,
His words become related to the time,
He is at one with his own glorious creed
And all that in his world was dared and
done.
The long, still, fruitful hours slip away
Shedding their influences as they pass;
We know ourselves the richer to have sat
Upon this dusty floor and dreamed our
dreams.
No other place to us were quite the same,
No other dreams so potent in their charm,
For this is ours! Every twist and turn
Of every narrow stair is known and loved;
Each nook and cranny is our very own;
The dear, old, sleepy place is full of
spells
For us, by right of long inheritance.
The building simply bodies forth a
thought
Peculiarly inherent to the race.
And we, descendants of that elder time,
Have learnt to love the very form in
which
The thought has been embodied to our
years.

And here we feel that we are not alone,
We too are one with our own richest past;
And here that veiled, but ever smoulder-
ing fire
Of race, which rarely seen yet never dies,
Springs up afresh and warms us with its
heat.
And must they take away this treasure
house,
To us so full of thoughts and memories;
To all the world beside a dismal place
Lacking in all this modern age requires
To tempt along the unfamiliar paths
And leafy lanes of old time literatures?
It takes some time for moss and vines to
grow
And warmly cover gaunt and chill stone
walls
Of stately buildings from the cold North
Wind.
The lichen of affection takes as long,
Or longer, ere it lovingly enfolds
A place which since without it were be-
reft,
All stript and bare, shorn of its chiefest
grace.
For what to us were halls and corridors
However large and fitting, if we part
With this which is our birthright; if we
lose
A sentiment profound, unsoundable,
Which Time's slow ripening alone can
make,
And man's blind foolishness so quickly
mar.

VERSES FOR CHILDREN

SEA SHELL

Sea Shell, Sea Shell,
  Sing me a song, O Please!
A song of ships, and sailor men,
  And parrots, and tropical trees,

Of islands lost in the Spanish Main
Which no man ever may find again,
Of fishes and corals under the waves,
And seahorses stabled in great green caves.

Sea Shell, Sea Shell,
Sing of the things you know so well.

FRINGED GENTIANS

Near where I live there is a lake
As blue as blue can be, winds make
It dance as they go blowing by.
I think it curtseys to the sky.

It's just a lake of lovely flowers
And my Mamma says they are ours;
But they are not like those we grow
To be our very own, you know.

We have a splendid garden, there
Are lots of flowers everywhere;

Roses, and pinks, and four o'clocks
And hollyhocks, and evening stocks.

Mamma lets us pick them, but never
Must we pick any gentians — ever!
For if we carried them away.
They'd die of homesickness that day.

THE PAINTED CEILING

My Grandpapa lives in a wonderful house
  With a great many windows and doors,
There are stairs that go up, and stairs
    that go down,
  And such beautiful, slippery floors.

But of all of the rooms, even mother's
    and mine,
  And the bookroom, and parlour and all,
I like the green dining-room so much the
    best
  Because of its ceiling and wall.

Right over your head is a funny round
    hole
  With apples and pears falling through;
There's a big bunch of grapes all purply
    and sweet,
  And melons and pineapples too.

They tumble and tumble, but never come
    down
  Though I've stood underneath a long
    while
With my mouth open wide, for I always
    have hoped
  Just a cherry would drop from the pile.

No matter how early I run there to look
  It has always begun to fall through;
And one night when at bedtime I crept
    in to see,
  It was falling by candle-light too.

I am sure they are magical fruits, and each
    one
  Makes you hear things, or see things,
    or go
Forever invisible; but it's no use,
  And of course I shall just never know.

For the ladder's too heavy to lift, and
    the chairs
  Are not nearly so tall as I need.
I've given up hope, and I feel I shall die
  Without having accomplished the deed.

It's a little bit sad, when you seem very
    near
  To adventures and things of that sort,
Which nearly begin, and then don't; and
    you know
  It is only because you are short.

THE CRESCENT MOON

Slipping softly through the sky
  Little horned, happy moon,
Can you hear me up so high?
  Will you come down soon?

On my nursery window-sill
  Will you stay your steady flight?
And then float away with me
  Through the summer night?

Brushing over tops of trees,
  Playing hide and seek with stars,
Peeping up through shiny clouds
  At Jupiter or Mars.

I shall fill my lap with roses
  Gathered in the Milky Way,
All to carry home to mother.
  Oh! what will she say!

Little rocking, sailing moon,
  Do you hear me shout — Ahoy!
Just a little nearer, moon,
  To please a little boy.

CLIMBING

High up in the apple tree climbing I go,
With the sky above me, the earth below.
Each branch is the step of a wonderful
    stair
Which leads to the town I see shining up
    there.

Climbing, climbing, higher and higher,
The branches blow and I see a spire,
The gleam of a turret, the glint of a dome,
All sparkling and bright, like white sea
    foam.

On and on, from bough to bough,
The leaves are thick, but I push my way
    through;
Before, I have always had to stop,
But to-day I am sure I shall reach the top.

To-day to the end of the marvelous stair,
Where those glittering pinnacles flash in
    the air!
Climbing, climbing, higher I go,
With the sky close above me, the earth
    far below.

THE TROUT

Naughty little speckled trout,
Can't I coax you to come out?
Is it such great fun to play
In the water every day?

Do you pull the Naiads' hair
Hiding in the lilies there?
Do you hunt for fishes' eggs,
Or watch tadpoles grow their legs?

Do you little trouts have school
In some deep sun-glinted pool,
And in recess play at tag
Round that bed of purple flag?

I have tried so hard to catch you,
Hours and hours I've sat to watch you;
But you never will come out,
Naughty little speckled trout!

WIND

He shouts in the sails of the ships at sea,
He steals the down from the honeybee,
He makes the forest trees rustle and sing,
He twirls my kite till it breaks its string.
    Laughing, dancing, sunny wind,
    Whistling, howling, rainy wind,
    North, South, East and West,
    Each is the wind I like the best.

He calls up the fog and hides the hills,
He whirls the wings of the great wind-
    mills,
The weathercocks love him and turn to
    discover
His whereabouts — but he's gone, the
    rover!

Laughing, dancing, sunny wind,
Whistling, howling, rainy wind,
North, South, East and West,
Each is the wind I like the best.

The pine trees toss him their cones with
    glee,
The flowers bend low in courtesy,
Each wave flings up a shower of pearls,
The flag in front of the school unfurls.
    Laughing, dancing, sunny wind,
    Whistling, howling, rainy wind,
    North, South, East and West,
    Each is the wind I like the best.

THE PLEIADES

By day you cannot see the sky
For it is up so very high.
You look and look, but it's so blue
That you can never see right through.

But when night comes it is quite plain,
And all the stars are there again.
They seem just like old friends to me,
I've known them all my life you see.

There is the dipper first, and there
Is Cassiopeia in her chair,
Orion's belt, the Milky Way,
And lots I know but cannot say.

One group looks like a swarm of bees,
Papa says they're the Pleiades;
But I think they must be the toy
Of some nice little angel boy.

Perhaps his jackstones which to-day
He has forgot to put away,
And left them lying on the sky
Where he will find them bye and bye

I wish he'd come and play with me.
We'd have such fun, for it would be
A most unusual thing for boys
To feel that they had stars for toys!

SWORD BLADES
AND POPPY SEED

SWORD BLADES AND POPPY SEED

A drifting, April, twilight sky,
A wind which blew the puddles dry,
And slapped the river into waves
That ran and hid among the staves
Of an old wharf. A watery light
Touched bleak the granite bridge, and
white
Without the slightest tinge of gold,
The city shivered in the cold.
All day my thoughts had lain as dead,
Unborn and bursting in my head.
From time to time I wrote a word
Which lines and circles overscored.
My table seemed a graveyard, full
Of coffins waiting burial.
I seized these vile abortions, tore
Them into jagged bits, and swore
To be the dupe of hope no more.
Into the evening straight I went,
Starved of a day's accomplishment.
Unnoticing, I wandered where
The city gave a space for air,
And on the bridge's parapet
I leant, while pallidly there set
A dim, discouraged, worn-out sun.
Behind me, where the tramways run,
Blossomed bright lights, I turned to leave,
When someone plucked me by the sleeve.
"Your pardon, Sir, but I should be
Most grateful could you lend to me
A carfare, I have lost my purse."
The voice was clear, concise, and terse.
I turned and met the quiet gaze
Of strange eyes flashing through the haze.
The man was old and slightly bent,
Under his cloak some instrument
Disarranged its stately line,
He rested on his cane a fine
And nervous hand, an almandine
Smouldered with dull-red flames, sanguine
It burned in twisted gold, upon
His finger. Like some Spanish don,
Conferring favours even when
Asking an alms, he bowed again

And waited. But my pockets proved
Empty, in vain I poked and shoved,
No hidden penny lurking there
Greeted my search. "Sir, I declare
I have no money, pray forgive,
But let me take you where you live."
And so we plodded through the mire
Where street lamps cast a wavering fire.
I took no note of where we went,
His talk became the element
Wherein my being swam, content.
It flashed like rapiers in the night
Lit by uncertain candle-light,
When on some moon-forsaken sward
A quarrel dies upon a sword.
It hacked and carved like a cutlass blade,
And the noise in the air the broad words
made
Was the cry of the wind at a window-pane
On an Autumn night of sobbing rain.
Then it would run like a steady stream
Under pinnacled bridges where minarets
gleam,
Or lap the air like the lapping tide
Where a marble staircase lifts its wide
Green-spotted steps to a garden gate,
And a waning moon is sinking straight
Down to a black and ominous sea,
While a nightingale sings in a lemon tree.
I walked as though some opiate
Had stung and dulled my brain, a state
Acute and slumbrous. It grew late.
We stopped, a house stood silent, dark.
The old man scratched a match, the spark
Lit up the keyhole of a door,
We entered straight upon a floor
White with finest powdered sand
Carefully sifted, one might stand
Muddy and dripping, and yet no trace
Would stain the boards of this kitchen-
place.
From the chimney, red eyes sparked the
gloom,
And a cricket's chirp filled all the room.
My host threw pine-cones on the fire
And crimson and scarlet glowed the pyre

Wrapped in the golden flame's desire.
The chamber opened like an eye,
As a half-melted cloud in a Summer sky
The soul of the house stood guessed, and
    shy
It peered at the stranger warily.
A little shop with its various ware
Spread on shelves with nicest care.
Pitchers, and jars, and jugs, and pots,
Pipkins, and mugs, and many lots
Of lacquered canisters, black and gold,
Like those in which Chinese tea is sold.
Chests, and puncheons, kegs, and flasks,
Goblets, chalices, firkins, and casks.
In a corner three ancient amphorae leaned
Against the wall, like ships careened.
There was dusky blue of Wedgwood ware,
The carved, white figures fluttering there
Like leaves adrift upon the air.
Classic in touch, but emasculate,
The Greek soul grown effeminate.
The factory of Sèvres had lent
Elegant boxes with ornament
Culled from gardens where fountains
    splashed
And golden carp in the shadows flashed,
Nuzzling for crumbs under lily-pads,
Which ladies threw as the last of fads.
Eggshell trays where gay beaux knelt,
Hand on heart, and daintily spelt
Their love in flowers, brittle and bright,
Artificial and fragile, which told aright
The vows of an eighteenth-century knight.
The cruder tones of old Dutch jugs
Glared from one shelf, where Toby mugs
Endlessly drank the foaming ale,
Its froth grown dusty, awaiting sale.
The glancing light of the burning wood
Played over a group of jars which stood
On a distant shelf, it seemed the sky
Had lent the half-tones of his blazonry
To paint these porcelains with unknown
    hues
Of reds dyed purple and greens turned
    blues,
Of lustres with so evanescent a sheen
Their colours are felt, but never seen.
Strange wingéd dragons writhe about
These vases, poisoned venoms spout,
Impregnate with old Chinese charms;
Sealed urns containing mortal harms,
They fill the mind with thoughts impure,
Pestilent drippings from the ure
Of vicious things. "Ah, I see,"
Said I, "you deal in pottery."

The old man turned and looked at me.
Shook his head gently. "No," said he.

Then from under his cloak he took the
    thing
Which I had wondered to see him bring
Guarded so carefully from sight.
As he laid it down it flashed in the light,
A Toledo blade, with basket hilt,
Damascened with arabesques of gilt,
Or rather gold, and tempered so
It could cut a floating thread at a blow.
The old man smiled, "It has no sheath,
'Twas a little careless to have it beneath
My cloak, for a jostle to my arm
Would have resulted in serious harm.
But it was so fine, I could not wait,
So I brought it with me despite its state."
"An amateur of arms," I thought,
"Bringing home a prize which he has
    bought."
"You care for this sort of thing, Dear Sir?"
"Not in the way which you infer.
I need them in business, that is all."
And he pointed his finger at the wall.
Then I saw what I had not noticed before.
The walls were hung with at least five
    score
Of swords and daggers of every size
Which nations of militant men could de-
    vise.
Poisoned spears from tropic seas,
That natives, under banana trees,
Smear with the juice of some deadly
    snake.
Blood-dipped arrows, which savages make
And tip with feathers, orange and green,
A quivering death, in harlequin sheen.
High up, a fan of glancing steel
Was formed of claymores in a wheel.
Jewelled swords worn at kings' levees
Were suspended next midshipmen's dirks,
    and these
Elbowed stilettos come from Spain,
Chased with some splendid Hidalgo's
    name.
There were Samurai swords from old
    Japan,
And scimitars from Hindoostan,
While the blade of a Turkish yataghan
Made a waving streak of vitreous white
Upon the wall, in the firelight.
Foils with buttons broken or lost
Lay heaped on a chair, among them tossed
The boarding-pike of a privateer.

Against the chimney leaned a queer
Two-handed weapon, with edges dull
As though from hacking on a skull.
The rusted blood corroded it still.
My host took up a paper spill
From a heap which lay in an earthen
   bowl,
And lighted it at a burning coal.
At either end of the table, tall
Wax candles were placed, each in a small,
And slim, and burnished candlestick
Of pewter. The old man lit each wick,
And the room leapt more obviously
Upon my mind, and I could see
What the flickering fire had hid from me.
Above the chimney's yawning throat,
Shoulder high, like the dark wainscote,
Was a mantelshelf of polished oak
Blackened with the pungent smoke
Of firelit nights; a Cromwell clock
Of tarnished brass stood like a rock
In the midst of a heaving, turbulent sea
Of every sort of cutlery.
There lay knives sharpened to any use,
The keenest lancet, and the obtuse
And blunted pruning bill-hook; blades
Of razors, scalpels, shears; cascades
Of penknives, with handles of mother-of-
   pearl,
And scythes, and sickles, and scissors; a
   whirl
Of points and edges, and underneath
Shot the gleam of a saw with bristling
   teeth.
My head grew dizzy, I seemed to hear
A battle-cry from somewhere near,
The clash of arms, and the squeal of
   balls,
And the echoless thud when a dead man
   falls.
A smoky cloud had veiled the room,
Shot through with lurid glares; the gloom
Pounded with shouts and dying groans,
With the drip of blood on cold, hard
   stones.
Sabres and lances in streaks of light
Gleamed through the smoke, and at my
   right
A creese, like a licking serpent's tongue,
Glittered an instant, while it stung.
Streams, and points, and lines of fire!
The livid steel, which man's desire
Had forged and welded, burned white and
   cold.
Every blade which man could mould,

Which could cut, or slash, or cleave, or
   rip,
Or pierce, or thrust, or carve, or strip,
Or gash, or chop, or puncture, or tear,
Or slice, or hack, they all were there.
Nerveless and shaking, round and round,
I stared at the walls and at the ground,
Till the room spun like a whipping top,
And a stern voice in my ear said, "Stop!
I sell no tools for murderers here.
Of what are you thinking! Please clear
Your mind of such imaginings.
Sit down. I will tell you of these things."

He pushed me into a great chair
Of russet leather, poked a flare
Of tumbling flame, with the old long
   sword,
Up the chimney; but said no word.
Slowly he walked to a distant shelf,
And brought back a crock of finest delf.
He rested a moment a blue-veined hand
Upon the cover, then cut a band
Of paper, pasted neatly round,
Opened and poured. A sliding sound
Came from beneath his old white hands,
And I saw a little heap of sands,
Black and smooth. What could they be:
"Pepper," I thought. He looked at me.
"What you see is poppy seed.
Lethean dreams for those in need."
He took up the grains with a gentle hand
And sifted them slowly like hour-glass
   sand.
On his old white finger the almandine
Shot out its rays, incarnadine.
"Visions for those too tired to sleep.
These seeds cast a film over eyes which
   weep.
No single soul in the world could dwell,
Without these poppy-seeds I sell."
For a moment he played with the shining
   stuff,
Passing it through his fingers. Enough
At last, he poured it back into
The china jar of Holland blue,
Which he carefully carried to its place.
Then, with a smile on his aged face,
He drew up a chair to the open space
'Twixt table and chimney. "Without
   preface,
Young man, I will say that what you see
Is not the puzzle you take it to be."
"But surely, Sir, there is something
   strange

In a shop with goods at so wide a range
Each from the other, as swords and seeds.
Your neighbours must have greatly differ-
ing needs."
"My neighbours," he said, and he stroked
his chin,
"Live everywhere from here to Pekin.
But you are wrong, my sort of goods
Is but one thing in all its moods."
He took a shagreen letter case
From his pocket, and with charming grace
Offered me a printed card,
I read the legend, "Ephraim Bard.
Dealer in Words." And that was all.
I stared at the letters, whimsical
Indeed, or was it merely a jest.
He answered my unasked request:
"All books are either dreams or swords,
You can cut, or you can drug, with words.
My firm is a very ancient house,
The entries on my books would rouse
Your wonder, perhaps incredulity.
I inherited from an ancestry
Stretching remotely back and far,
This business, and my clients are
As were those of my grandfather's days,
Writers of books, and poems, and plays.
My swords are tempered for every speech,
For fencing wit, or to carve a breach
Through old abuses the world condones.
In another room are my grindstones and
hones,
For whetting razors and putting a point
On daggers, sometimes I even anoint
The blades with a subtle poison, so
A twofold result may follow the blow.
These are purchased by men who feel
The need of stabbing society's heel,
Which egotism has brought them to think
Is set on their necks. I have foils to pink
An adversary to quaint reply,
And I have customers who buy
Scalpels with which to dissect the brains
And hearts of men. Ultramundanes
Even demand some finer kinds
To open their own souls and minds.
But the other half of my business deals
With visions and fancies. Under seals,
Sorted, and placed in vessels here,
I keep the seeds of an atmosphere.
Each jar contains a different kind
Of poppy seed. From farthest Ind
Come the purple flowers, opium filled,
From which the weirdest myths are dis-
tilled;

My orient porcelains contain them all.
Those Lowestoft pitchers against the wall
Hold a lighter kind of bright conceit;
And those old Saxe vases, out of the heat
On that lowest shelf beside the door,
Have a sort of Ideal, 'couleur d'or.'
Every castle of the air
Sleeps in the fine black grains, and there
Are seeds for every romance, or light
Whiff of a dream for a summer night.
I supply to every want and taste."
'Twas slowly said, in no great haste
He seemed to push his wares, but I
Dumfounded listened. By and by
A log on the fire broke in two.
He looked up quickly, "Sir, and you?"
I groped for something I should say;
Amazement held me numb. "To-day
You sweated at a fruitless task."
He spoke for me, "What do you ask?
How can I serve you?" "My kind host,
My penniless state was not a boast;
I have no money with me." He smiled.
"Not for that money I beguiled
You here; you paid me in advance."
Again I felt as though a trance
Had dimmed my faculties. Again
He spoke, and this time to explain.
"The money I demand is Life,
Your nervous force, your joy, your strife!"
What infamous proposal now
Was made me with so calm a brow?
Bursting through my lethargy,
Indignantly I hurled the cry:
"Is this a nightmare, or am I
Drunk with some infernal wine?
I am no Faust, and what is mine
Is what I call my soul! Old Man!
Devil or Ghost! Your hellish plan
Revolts me. Let me go." "My child,"
And the old tones were very mild,
"I have no wish to barter souls;
My traffic does not ask such tolls.
I am no devil; is there one?
Surely the age of fear is gone.
We live within a daylight world
Lit by the sun, where winds unfurled
Sweep clouds to scatter pattering rain,
And then blow back the sun again.
I sell my fancies, or my swords,
To those who care far more for words,
Ideas, of which they are the sign,
Than any other life-design.
Who buy of me must simply pay
Their whole existence quite away:

Their strength, their manhood, and their
  prime,
Their hours from morning till the time
When evening comes on tiptoe feet,
And losing life, think it complete;
Must miss what other men count being,
To gain the gift of deeper seeing;
Must spurn all ease, all hindering love,
All which could hold or bind; must prove
The farthest boundaries of thought,
And shun no end which these have
  brought;
Then die in satisfaction, knowing
That what was sown was worth the
  sowing.
I claim for all the goods I sell
That they will serve their purpose well,
And though you perish, they will live.
Full measure for your pay I give.
To-day you worked, you thought, in vain.
What since has happened is the train
Your toiling brought. I spoke to you
For my share of the bargain, due."
"My life! And is that all you crave
In pay? What even childhood gave!
I have been dedicate from youth.
Before my God I speak the truth!"
Fatigue, excitement of the past
Few hours broke me down at last.
All day I had forgot to eat,
My nerves betrayed me, lacking meat.
I bowed my head and felt the storm
Plough shattering through my prostrate
  form.
The tearless sobs tore at my heart.
My host withdrew himself apart;
Busied among his crockery,

He paid no farther heed to me.
Exhausted, spent, I huddled there,
Within the arms of the old carved chair.

A long half-hour dragged away,
And then I heard a kind voice say,
"The day will soon be dawning, when
You must begin to work again.
Here are the things which you require."
By the fading light of the dying fire,
And by the guttering candle's flare,
I saw the old man standing there.
He handed me a packet, tied
With crimson tape, and sealed. "Inside
Are seeds of many differing flowers,
To occupy your utmost powers
Of storied vision, and these swords
Are the finest which my shop affords.
Go home and use them; do not spare
Yourself; let that be all your care.
Whatever you have means to buy
Be very sure I can supply."
He slowly walked to the window, flung
It open, and in the grey air rung
The sound of distant matin bells.
I took my parcels. Then, as tells
An ancient mumbling monk his beads,
I tried to thank for his courteous deeds
My strange old friend. "Nay, do not
  talk,"
He urged me, "you have a long walk
Before you. Good-by and Good-day!"
And gently sped upon my way
I stumbled out in the morning hush,
As down the empty street a flush
Ran level from the rising sun.
Another day was just begun.

SWORD BLADES

THE CAPTURED GODDESS

Over the housetops,
Above the rotating chimney-pots,
I have seen a shiver of amethyst,
And blue and cinnamon have flickered
A moment,
At the far end of a dusty street.

Through sheeted rain
Has come a lustre of crimson,
And I have watched moonbeams
Hushed by a film of palest green.

It was her wings,
Goddess!
Who stepped over the clouds,
And laid her rainbow feathers
Aslant on the currents of the air.

I followed her for long,
With gazing eyes and stumbling feet.
I cared not where she led me,
My eyes were full of colours:
Saffrons, rubies, the yellows of beryls,
And the indigo-blue of quartz;
Flights of rose, layers of chrysoprase,

Points of orange, spirals of vermilion,
The spotted gold of tiger-lily petals,
The loud pink of bursting hydrangeas.
I followed,
And watched for the flashing of her wings.

In the city I found her,
The narrow-streeted city.
In the market-place I came upon her,
Bound and trembling.
Her fluted wings were fastened to her
  sides with cords,
She was naked and cold,
For that day the wind blew
Without sunshine.

Men chaffered for her,
They bargained in silver and gold,
In copper, in wheat,
And called their bids across the market-
  place.

The Goddess wept.

Hiding my face I fled,
And the grey wind hissed behind me,
Along the narrow streets.

THE PRECINCT. ROCHESTER

The tall yellow hollyhocks stand,
Still and straight,
With their round blossoms spread open,
In the quiet sunshine.
And still is the old Roman wall,
Rough with jagged bits of flint,
And jutting stones,
Old and cragged,
Quite still in its antiquity.
The pear-trees press their branches against
  it,
And feeling it warm and kindly,
The little pears ripen to yellow and red.
They hang heavy, bursting with juice,
Against the wall.
So old, so still!
The sky is still.
The clouds make no sound
As they slide away
Beyond the Cathedral Tower,
To the river,
And the sea.
It is very quiet,
Very sunny.

The myrtle flowers stretch themselves in
  the sunshine,
But make no sound.
The roses push their little tendrils up,
And climb higher and higher.
In spots they have climbed over the wall.
But they are very still,
They do not seem to move.
And the old wall carries them
Without effort, and quietly
Ripens and shields the vines and blossoms.

A bird in a plane-tree
Sings a few notes,
Cadenced and perfect
They weave into the silence.
The Cathedral bell knocks,
One, two, three, and again.
And then again.
It is a quiet sound.
Calling to prayer,
Hardly scattering the stillness,
Only making it close in more densely.
The gardener picks ripe gooseberries
For the Dean's supper to-night.
It is very quiet,
Very regulated and mellow.
But the wall is old,
It has known many days.
It is a Roman wall,
Left-over and forgotten.

Beyond the Cathedral Close
Yelp and mutter the discontents of peo-
  ple not mellow,
Not well-regulated.
People who care more for bread than for
  beauty,
Who would break the tombs of saints,
And give the painted windows of churches
To their children for toys.
People who say:
"They are dead, we live!
The world is for the living."

Fools! It is always the dead who breed.
Crush the ripe fruit, and cast it aside,
Yet its seeds shall fructify,
And trees rise where your huts were stand-
  ing.
But the little people are ignorant,
They chaffer, and swarm.
They gnaw like rats,
And the foundations of the Cathedral are
  honey-combed.

The Dean is in the Chapter House;
He is reading the architect's bill
For the completed restoration of the
    Cathedral.
He will have ripe gooseberries for supper,
And then he will walk up and down the
    path
By the wall,
And admire the snapdragons and dahlias,
Thinking how quiet and peaceful
The garden is.
The old wall will watch him,
Very quietly and patiently it will watch.
For the wall is old,
It is a Roman wall.

THE CYCLISTS

Spread on the roadway,
With open-blown jackets,
Like black, soaring pinions,
They swoop down the hillside,
    The Cyclists.

Seeming dark-plumaged
Birds, after carrion,
Careening and circling,
Over the dying
Of England.

She lies with her bosom
Beneath them, no longer
The Dominant Mother,
The Virile — but rotting
Before time.

The smell of her, tainted,
Has bitten their nostrils.
Exultant they hover,
And shadow the sun with
Foreboding.

SUNSHINE THROUGH A
COBWEBBED WINDOW

What charm is yours, you faded old-world
    tapestries,
Of outworn, childish mysteries,
    Vague pageants woven on a web of
        dream!
    And we, pushing and fighting in the
        turbid stream
Of modern life, find solace in your tar-
    nished broideries.

Old lichened halls, sun-shaded by huge
    cedar-trees,
The layered branches horizontal stretched,
    like Japanese
Dark-banded prints. Carven cathedrals,
    on a sky
Of faintest colour, where the gothic
    spires fly
And sway like masts, against a shifting
    breeze.

Worm-eaten pages, clasped in old brown
    vellum, shrunk
From over-handling, by some anxious
    monk.
    Or Virgin's Hours, bright with gold
        and graven
    With flowers, and rare birds, and all
        the Saints of Heaven,
And Noah's ark stuck on Ararat, when
    all the world had sunk.

They soothe us like a song, heard in a
    garden, sung
By youthful minstrels, on the moonlight
    flung
    In cadences and falls, to ease a queen,
    Widowed and childless, cowering in a
        screen
Of myrtles, whose life hangs with all its
    threads unstrung.

A LONDON THOROUGHFARE.
2 A.M.

They have watered the street,
It shines in the glare of lamps,
Cold, white lamps,
And lies
Like a slow-moving river,
Barred with silver and black.
Cabs go down it,
One,
And then another,
Between them I hear the shuffling of feet.
Tramps doze on the window-ledges,
Night-walkers pass along the sidewalks.
The city is squalid and sinister,
With the silver-barred street in the midst,
Slow-moving,
A river leading nowhere.

Opposite my window,
The moon cuts,
Clear and round,

Through the plum-coloured night.
She cannot light the city:
It is too bright.
It has white lamps,
And glitters coldly.

I stand in the window and watch the
    moon.
She is thin and lustreless,
But I love her.
I know the moon,
And this is an alien city.

ASTIGMATISM

To Ezra Pound
with Much Friendship and
Admiration and Some Differences
of Opinion

The Poet took his walking-stick
Of fine and polished ebony.
Set in the close-grained wood
Were quaint devices;
Patterns in ambers,
And in the clouded green of jades.
The top was of smooth, yellow ivory,
And a tassel of tarnished gold
Hung by a faded cord from a hole
Pierced in the hard wood,
Circled with silver.
For years the Poet had wrought upon this
    cane.
His wealth had gone to enrich it,
His experiences to pattern it,
His labour to fashion and burnish it.
To him it was perfect,
A work of art and a weapon,
A delight and a defence.
The Poet took his walking-stick
And walked abroad.

Peace be with you, Brother.

The Poet came to a meadow.
Sifted through the grass were daisies,
Open-mouthed, wondering, they gazed at
    the sun.
The Poet struck them with his cane.
The little heads flew off, and they lay
Dying, open-mouthed and wondering,
On the hard ground.
"They are useless. They are not roses,"
    said the Poet.

Peace be with you, Brother. Go your
    ways.

The Poet came to a stream.
Purple and blue flags waded in the water;
In among them hopped the speckled
    frogs;
The wind slid through them, rustling.
The Poet lifted his cane,
And the iris heads fell into the water.
They floated away, torn and drowning.
"Wretched flowers," said the Poet,
"They are not roses."

Peace be with you, Brother. It is your
    affair.

The Poet came to a garden.
Dahlias ripened against a wall,
Gillyflowers stood up bravely for all their
    short stature,
And a trumpet-vine covered an arbour
With the red and gold of its blossoms.
Red and gold like the brass notes of
    trumpets.
The Poet knocked off the stiff heads of
    the dahlias,
And his cane lopped the gillyflowers at
    the ground.
Then he severed the trumpet-blossoms
    from their stems.
Red and gold they lay scattered,
Red and gold, as on a battle field;
Red and gold, prone and dying.
"They were not roses," said the Poet.

Peace be with you, Brother.
But behind you is destruction, and waste
    places.

The Poet came home at evening,
And in the candle-light
He wiped and polished his cane.
The orange candle flame leaped in the
    yellow ambers,
And made the jades undulate like green
    pools.
It played along the bright ebony,
And glowed in the top of cream-coloured
    ivory.
But these things were dead,
Only the candle-light made them seem
    to move.
"It is a pity there were no roses," said
    the Poet.

Peace be with you, Brother. You have
    chosen your part.

THE COAL PICKER

He perches in the slime, inert,
Bedaubed with iridescent dirt.
The oil upon the puddles dries
To colours like a peacock's eyes,
And half-submerged tomato-cans
Shine scaly, as leviathans
Oozily crawling through the mud.
The ground is here and there bestud
With lumps of only part-burned coal.
His duty is to glean the whole,
To pick them from the filth, each one,
To hoard them for the hidden sun
Which glows within each fiery core
And waits to be made free once more.
Their sharp and glistening edges cut
His stiffened fingers. Through the smut
Gleam red the wounds which will not shut.
Wet through and shivering he kneels
And digs the slippery coals: like eels
They slide about. His force all spent,
He counts his small accomplishment.
A half-a-dozen clinker-coals
Which still have fire in their souls.
Fire! And in his thought there burns
The topaz fire of votive urns.
He sees it fling from hill to hill,
And still consumed, is burning still.
Higher and higher leaps the flame,
The smoke an ever-shifting frame.
He sees a Spanish Castle old,
With silver steps and paths of gold.
From myrtle bowers comes the plash
Of fountains, and the emerald flash
Of parrots in the orange trees,
Whose blossoms pasture humming bees.
He knows he feeds the urns whose smoke
Bears visions, that his master-stroke
Is out of dirt and misery
To light the fire of poesy.
He sees the glory, yet he knows
That others cannot see his shows.
To them his smoke is sightless, black,
His votive vessels but a pack
Of old discarded shards, his fire
A peddler's; still to him the pyre
Is incensed, an enduring goal!
He sighs and grubs another coal.

STORM–RACKED

How should I sing when buffeting salt
    waves
And stung with bitter surges, in whose
    might

I toss, a cockleshell? The dreadful
    night
Marshals its undefeated dark and raves
In brutal madness, reeling over graves
Of vanquished men, long-sunken out
    of sight,
Sent wailing down to glut the ghoulish
    sprite
Who haunts foul seaweed forests and
    their caves.
No parting cloud reveals a watery star,
My cries are washed away upon the wind,
My cramped and blistering hands can
    find no spar,
My eyes with hope o'erstrained, are grow-
    ing blind.
But painted on the sky great visions
    burn,
My voice, oblation from a shattered
    urn!

CONVALESCENCE

From out the dragging vastness of the
    sea,
Wave-fettered, bound in sinuous, sea-
    weed strands
He toils toward the rounding beach,
    and stands
One moment, white and dripping, silently,
Cut like a cameo in lazuli,
Then falls, betrayed by shifting shells,
    and lands
Prone in the jeering water, and his
    hands
Clutch for support where no support can
    be.
So up, and down, and forward, inch
    by inch,
He gains upon the shore, where poppies
    glow
And sandflies dance their little lives away.
The sucking waves retard, and tighter
    clinch
The weeds about him, but the land-winds
    blow,
And in the sky there blooms the sun of
    May.

PATIENCE

Be patient with you?
    When the stooping sky
Leans down upon the hills
And tenderly, as one who soothing stills

An anguish, gathers earth to lie
Embraced and girdled. Do the sun-filled
  men
Feel patience then?

Be patient with you?
  When the snow-girt earth
Cracks to let through a spurt
Of sudden green, and from the muddy
  dirt
  A snowdrop leaps, how mark its worth
To eyes frost-hardened, and do weary men
Feel patience then?

Be patient with you?
  When pain's iron bars
Their rivets tighten, stern
To bend and break their victims; as they
  turn,
  Hopeless, there stand the purple jars
Of night to spill oblivion. Do these men
Feel patience then?

Be patient with you?
  You! My sun and moon!
My basketful of flowers!
My money-bag of shining dreams! My
  hours,
  Windless and still, of afternoon!
You are my world and I your citizen.
  What meaning can have patience
  then?

APOLOGY

Be not angry with me that I bear
  Your colours everywhere,
All through each crowded street,
  And meet
The wonder-light in every eye,
  As I go by.

Each plodding wayfarer looks up to gaze,
  Blinded by rainbow haze,
The stuff of happiness,
  No less,
Which wraps me in its glad-hued folds
  Of peacock golds.

Before my feet the dusty, rough-paved
  way
Flushes beneath its gray.
My steps fall ringed with light,
  So bright,
It seems a myriad suns are strown
About the town.

Around me is the sound of steepled bells,
  And rich perfuméd smells
Hang like a wind-forgotten cloud,
  And shroud
Me from close contact with the world.
  I dwell impearled.

You blazon me with jewelled insignia.
  A flaming nebula
Rims in my life. And yet
  You set
The word upon me, unconfessed
  To go unguessed.

A PETITION

I pray to be the tool which to your hand
  Long use has shaped and moulded till
  it be
Apt for your need, and, unconsider-
  ingly,
You take it for its service. I demand
To be forgotten in the woven strand
  Which   grows   the   multi-coloured
  tapestry
  Of your bright life, and through its
  tissues lie
A hidden, strong, sustaining, grey-toned
  band.
  I wish to dwell around your daylight
  dreams,
The railing to the stairway of the clouds,
  To guard your steps securely up, where
  streams
A faery moonshine washing pale the
  crowds
  Of pointed stars. Remember not
  whereby
You mount, protected, to the far-flung
  sky.

A BLOCKHEAD

Before me lies a mass of shapeless days,
  Unseparated atoms, and I must
Sort them apart and live them. Sifted
  dust
Covers   the   formless   heap.   Reprieves,
  delays,
There are none, ever. As a monk who
  prays
  The sliding beads asunder, so I thrust
Each tasteless particle aside, and just
Begin again the task which never stays.
  And I have known a glory of great
  suns,

When days flashed by, pulsing with joy
and fire!
Drunk bubbled wine in goblets of desire,
And felt the whipped blood laughing
as it runs!
Spilt is that liquor, my too hasty hand
Threw down the cup, and did not under-
stand.

STUPIDITY

Dearest, forgive that with my clumsy
touch
I broke and bruised your rose.
I hardly could suppose
It were a thing so fragile that my clutch
Could kill it, thus.

It stood so proudly up upon its stem,
I knew no thought of fear,
And coming very near
Fell, overbalanced, to your garment's hem,
Tearing it down.

Now, stooping, I gather, one by one,
The crimson petals, all
Outspread about my fall.
They hold their fragrance still, a blood-
red cone
Of memory.

And with my words I carve a little jar
To keep their scented dust,
Which, opening, you must
Breathe to your soul, and, breathing,
know me far
More grieved than you.

IRONY

An arid daylight shines along the beach
Dried to a grey monotony of tone,
And stranded jelly-fish melt soft upon
The sun-baked pebbles, far beyond their
reach
Sparkles a wet, reviving sea. Here bleach
The skeletons of fishes, every bone
Polished and stark, like traceries of
stone,
The joints and knuckles hardened each
to each.
And they are dead while waiting for
the sea,
The moon-pursuing sea, to come again.
Their hearts are blown away on the hot
breeze.

Only the shells and stones can wait
to be
Washed bright. For living things, who
suffer pain,
May not endure till time can bring them
ease.

HAPPINESS

Happiness, to some, elation;
Is, to others, mere stagnation.
Days of passive somnolence,
At its wildest, indolence.
Hours of empty quietness,
No delight, and no distress.

Happiness to me is wine,
Effervescent, superfine.
Full of tang and fiery pleasure,
Far too hot to leave me leisure
For a single thought beyond it.
Drunk! Forgetful! This the bond: it
Means to give one's soul to gain
Life's quintessence. Even pain
Pricks to livelier living, then
Wakes the nerves to laugh again,
Rapture's self is three parts sorrow.
Although we must die to-morrow,
Losing every thought but this;
Torn, triumphant, drowned in bliss.

Happiness: We rarely feel it.
I would buy it, beg it, steal it,
Pay in coins of dripping blood
For this one transcendent good.

THE LAST QUARTER OF
THE MOON

How long shall I tarnish the mirror of
life,
A spatter of rust on its polished steel!
The seasons reel
Like a goaded wheel.
Half-numb, half-maddened, my days are
strife.

The night is sliding towards the dawn,
And upturned hills crouch at autumn's
knees.
A torn moon flees
Through the hemlock trees,
The hours have gnawed it to feed their
spawn.

Pursuing and jeering the misshapen thing
A rabble of clouds flares out of the east.
　Like dogs unleashed
　After a beast,
They stream on the sky, an outflung
　string.

A desolate wind, through the unpeopled
　dark,
Shakes the bushes and whistles through
　empty nests,
　And the fierce unrests
　I keep as guests
Crowd my brain with corpses, pallid and
　stark.

Leave me in peace, O Spectres, who
　haunt
My labouring mind, I have fought and
　failed.
　I have not quailed,
　I was all unmailed
And naked I strove, 'tis my only vaunt.

The moon drops into the silver day
As waking out of her swoon she comes.
　I hear the drums
　Of millenniums
Beating the mornings I still must stay.

The years I must watch go in and out,
While I build with water, and dig in air,
　And the trumpets blare
　Hollow despair,
The shuddering trumpets of utter rout.

An atom tossed in a chaos made
Of yeasting worlds, which bubble and
　foam.
　Whence have I come?
　What would be home?
I hear no answer. I am afraid!

I crave to be lost like a wind-blown flame.
Pushed into nothingness by a breath,
　And quench in a wreath
　Of engulfing death
This fight for a God, or this devil's game.

A TALE OF STARVATION

There once was a man whom the gods
　didn't love,
　And a disagreeable man was he.

He loathed his neighbours, and his
　neighbours hated him,
　And he cursed eternally.

He damned the sun, and he damned the
　stars,
　And he blasted the winds in the sky.
He sent to Hell every green, growing
　thing,
　And he raved at the birds as they fly.

His oaths were many, and his range was
　wide,
　He swore in fancy ways;
But his meaning was plain: that no
　created thing
Was other than a hurt to his gaze.

He dwelt all alone, underneath a leaning
　hill,
　And windows toward the hill there
　were none,
And on the other side they were white-
　washed thick,
　To keep out every spark of the sun.

When he went to market he walked all
　the way
　Blaspheming at the path he trod.
He cursed at those he bought of, and
　swore at those he sold to,
　By all the names he knew of God.

For his heart was soured in his weary old
　hide,
　And his hopes had curdled in his
　breast.
His friend had been untrue, and his love
　had thrown him over
For the chinking money-bags she liked
　best.

The rats had devoured the contents of
　his grain-bin,
　The deer had trampled on his corn,
His brook had shrivelled in a summer
　drought,
　And his sheep had died unshorn.

His hens wouldn't lay, and his cow broke
　loose,
　And his old horse perished of a colic.
In the loft his wheat-bags were nibbled
　into holes
　By little, glutton mice on a frolic.

So he slowly lost all he ever had,
And the blood in his body dried.
Shrunken and mean he still lived on,
And cursed that future which had
lied.

One day he was digging, a spade or two,
As his aching back could lift,
When he saw something glisten at the
bottom of the trench,
And to get it out he made great shift.

So he dug, and he delved, with care and
pain,
And the veins in his forehead stood
taut.
At the end of an hour, when every bone
cracked,
He gathered up what he had sought.

A dim old vase of crusted glass,
Prismed while it lay buried deep.
Shifting reds and greens, like a pigeon's
neck.
At the touch of the sun began to leap.

It was dull in the tree-shade, but glowing
in the light;
Flashing like an opal-stone,
Carved into a flagon; and the colours
glanced and ran,
Where at first there had seemed to be
none.

It had handles on each side to bear it
up,
And a belly for the gurgling wine.
Its neck was slender, and its mouth was
wide,
And its lip was curled and fine.

The old man saw it in the sun's bright
stare
And the colours started up through the
crust,
And he who had cursed at the yellow sun
Held the flask to it and wiped away
the dust.

And he bore the flask to the brightest
spot,
Where the shadow of the hill fell clear;
And he turned the flask, and he looked
at the flask,
And the sun shone without his sneer.

Then he carried it home, and put it on
a shelf,
But it was only grey in the gloom.
So he fetched a pail, and a bit of
cloth,
And he went outside with a broom.

And he washed his windows just to let
the sun
Lie upon his new-found vase;
And when evening came, he moved it
down
And put it on a table near the place

Where a candle fluttered in a draught
from the door.
The old man forgot to swear,
Watching its shadow grown a mammoth
size,
Dancing in the kitchen there.

He forgot to revile the sun next morning
When he found his vase afire in its
light.
And he carried it out of the house that
day,
And kept it close beside him until
night.

And so it happened from day to day.
The old man fed his life
On the beauty of his vase, on its perfect
shape.
And his soul forgot its former strife.

And the village-folk came and begged to
see
The flagon which was dug from the
ground.
And the old man never thought of an
oath, in his joy
At showing what he had found.

One day the master of the village school
Passed him as he stooped at toil,
Hoeing for a bean-row, and at his side
Was the vase, on the turned-up soil.

"My friend," said the schoolmaster,
pompous and kind,
"That's a valuable thing you have
there,
But it might get broken out of doors,
It should meet with the utmost care

What are you doing with it out here?"
"Why, Sir," said the poor old man,
"I like to have it about, do you see?
To be with it all I can."

"You will smash it," said the school-
master, sternly right,
"Mark my words and see!"
And he walked away, while the old man
looked
At his treasure despondingly.

Then he smiled to himself, for it was
his!
He had toiled for it, and now he
cared.
Yes! loved its shape, and its subtle, swift
hues,
Which his own hard work had bared.

He would carry it round with him every-
where,
As it gave him joy to do.
A fragile vase should not stand in a
bean-row!
Who would dare to say so? Who?

Then his heart was rested, and his fears
gave way,
And he bent to his hoe again. . . .
A clod rolled down, and his foot slipped
back.
And he lurched with a cry of pain.

For the blade of the hoe crashed into
glass,
And the vase fell to iridescent sherds.
The old man's body heaved with slow,
dry sobs.
He did not curse, he had no words.

He gathered the fragments, one by one,
And his fingers were cut and torn.
Then he made a hole in the very place
Whence the beautiful vase had been
borne.

He covered the hole, and he patted it
down,
Then he hobbled to his house and shut
the door.
He tore up his coat and nailed it at the
windows
That no beam of light should cross the
floor.

He sat down in front of the empty
hearth,
And he neither eat nor drank.
In three days they found him, dead and
cold,
And they said: "What a queer old
crank!"

THE FOREIGNER

Have at you, you Devils!
My back's to this tree,
For you're nothing so nice
That the hind-side of me
Would escape your assault.
Come on now, all three!

Here's a dandified gentleman,
Rapier at point,
And a wrist which whirls round
Like a circular joint.
A spatter of blood, man!
That's just to anoint

And make supple your limbs.
'Tis a pity the silk
Of your waistcoat is stained.
Why! Your heart's full of milk,
And so full, it spills over!
I'm not of your ilk.

You said so, and laughed
At my old-fashioned hose,
At the cut of my hair,
At the length of my nose.
To carve it to pattern
I think you propose.

Your pardon, young Sir,
But my nose and my sword
Are proving themselves
In quite perfect accord.
I grieve to have spotted
Your shirt. On my word!

And hullo! You Bully!
That blade's not a stick
To slash right and left,
And my skull is too thick
To be cleft with such cuffs
Of a sword. Now a lick

Down the side of your face.
What a pretty, red line!

Tell the taverns that scar
   Was an honour. Don't whine
That a stranger has marked you.

   .   .   .   .

   The tree's there, You Swine!

Did you think to get in
   At the back, while your friends
Made a little diversion
   In front? So it ends,
With your sword clattering down
   On the ground. 'Tis amends

I make for your courteous
   Reception of me,
A foreigner, landed
   From over the sea.
Your welcome was fervent
   I think you'll agree.

My shoes are not buckled
   With gold, nor my hair
Oiled and scented, my jacket's
   Not satin, I wear
Corded breeches, wide hats,
   And I make people stare!

So I do, but my heart
   Is the heart of a man,
And my thoughts cannot twirl
   In the limited span
'Twixt my head and my heels
   As some other men's can.

I have business more strange
   Than the shape of my boots,
And my interests range
   From the sky, to the roots
Of this dung-hill you live in,
   You half-rotted shoots

Of a mouldering tree!
   Here's at you, once more.
You Apes! You Jack-fools!
   You can show me the door,
And jeer at my ways,
   But you're pinked to the core.

And before I have done,
   I will prick my name in
With the front of my steel,
   And your lily-white skin
Shall be printed with me.
   For I've come here to win!

ABSENCE

My cup is empty to-night,
Cold and dry are its sides,
Chilled by the wind from the open
   window.
Empty and void, it sparkles white in the
   moonlight.
The room is filled with the strange scent
Of wistaria blossoms.
They sway in the moon's radiance
And tap against the wall.
But the cup of my heart is still,
And cold, and empty.

When you come, it brims
Red and trembling with blood,
Heart's blood for your drinking;
To fill your mouth with love
And the bitter-sweet taste of a soul.

A GIFT

See! I give myself to you, Beloved!
My words are little jars
For you to take and put upon a shelf.
Their shapes are quaint and beautiful,
And they have many pleasant colours and
   lustres
To recommend them.
Also the scent from them fills the room
With sweetness of flowers and crushed
   grasses.

When I shall have given you the last one,
You will have the whole of me,
But I shall be dead.

THE BUNGLER

You glow in my heart
Like the flames of uncounted candles.
But when I go to warm my hands,
My clumsiness overturns the light,
And then I stumble
Against the tables and chairs.

FOOL'S MONEY BAGS

Outside the long window,
With his head on the stone sill,
The dog is lying,
Gazing at his Beloved.
His eyes are wet and urgent,
And his body is taut and shaking.

It is cold on the terrace;
A pale wind licks along the stone slabs,
But the dog gazes through the glass
And is content.

The Beloved is writing a letter.
Occasionally she speaks to the dog,
But she is thinking of her writing.
Does she, too, give her devotion to one
Not worthy?

MISCAST

I

I have whetted my brain until it is like
    a Damascus blade,
So keen that it nicks off the floating
    fringes of passers-by,
So sharp that the air would turn its edge
Were it to be twisted in flight.
Licking   passions   have   bitten   their
    arabesques into it,
And the mark of them lies, in and out,
Worm-like,
With the beauty of corroded copper pat-
    terning white steel.
My brain is curved like a scimitar,
And sighs at its cutting
Like a sickle mowing grass.
    But of what use is all this to me!
    I, who am set to crack stones
    In a country lane!

MISCAST

II

My heart is like a cleft pomegranate
Bleeding crimson seeds
And dripping them on the ground.
My heart gapes because it is ripe and
    over-full,
And its seeds are bursting from it.

But how is this other than a torment
    to me!
I, who am shut up, with broken crockery,
In a dark closet!

ANTICIPATION

I have been temperate always,
But I am like to be very drunk
With your coming.
There have been times
I feared to walk down the street

Lest I should reel with the wine of you,
And jerk against my neighbours
As they go by.
I am parched now, and my tongue is
    horrible in my mouth,
But my brain is noisy
With the clash and gurgle of filling
    wine-cups.

VINTAGE

I will mix me a drink of stars, —
Large stars with polychrome needles,
Small stars jetting maroon and crimson,
Cool, quiet, green stars.
I will tear them out of the sky,
And squeeze them over an old silver cup,
And I will pour the cold scorn of my
    Beloved into it,
So that my drink shall be bubbled with
    ice.

It will lap and scratch
As I swallow it down;
And I shall feel it as a serpent of fire,
Coiling and twisting in my belly.
His snortings will rise to my head,
And I shall be hot, and laugh,
Forgetting that I have ever known a
    woman.

THE TREE OF SCARLET BERRIES

The rain gullies the garden paths
And tinkles on the broad sides of grass
    blades.
A tree, at the end of my arm, is hazy
    with mist.
Even so, I can see that it has red berries,
A scarlet fruit,
Filmed over with moisture.
It seems as though the rain,
Dripping from it,
Should be tinged with colour.
I desire the berries,
But, in the mist, I only scratch my hand
    on the thorns.
Probably, too, they are bitter.

OBLIGATION

Hold your apron wide
That I may pour my gifts into it,
So that scarcely shall your two arms
    hinder them
From falling to the ground.

I would pour them upon you
And cover you,
For greatly do I feel this need
Of giving you something,
Even these poor things.

Dearest of my Heart!

THE TAXI

When I go away from you
The world beats dead
Like a slackened drum.
I call out for you against the jutted stars
And shout into the ridges of the wind.
Streets coming fast,
One after the other,
Wedge you away from me,
And the lamps of the city prick my eyes
So that I can no longer see your face.
Why should I leave you,
To wound myself upon the sharp edges
of the night?

THE GIVER OF STARS

Hold your soul open for my welcoming.
Let the quiet of your spirit bathe me
With its clear and rippled coolness,
That, loose-limbed and weary, I find rest,
Outstretched upon your peace, as on a
bed of ivory.

Let the flickering flame of your soul play
all about me,
That into my limbs may come the keen-
ness of fire,
The life and joy of tongues of flame,
And, going out from you, tightly strung
and in tune,
I may rouse the blear-eyed world,
And pour into it the beauty which you
have begotten.

THE TEMPLE

Between us leapt a gold and scarlet flame.
Into the hollow of the cupped, arched
blue
Of Heaven it rose. Its flickering
tongues up-drew
And vanished in the sunshine. How it
came
We guessed not, nor what thing could be
its name.

From each to each had sprung those
sparks which flew
Together into fire. But we knew
The winds would slap and quench it in
their game.
And so we graved and fashioned
marble blocks
To treasure it, and placed them round
about.
With pillared porticos we wreathed the
whole,
And roofed it with bright bronze. Be-
hind carved locks
Flowered the tall and sheltered flame.
Without,
The baffled winds thrust at a column's
bole.

EPITAPH OF A YOUNG POET WHO DIED BEFORE HAVING ACHIEVED SUCCESS

Beneath this sod lie the remains
Of one who died of growing pains.

IN ANSWER TO A REQUEST

You ask me for a sonnet. Ah, my Dear,
Can clocks tick back to yesterday at
noon?
Can cracked and fallen leaves recall
last June
And leap up on the boughs, now stiff
and sere?
For your sake, I would go and seek the
year,
Faded beyond the purple ranks of
dune,
Blown sands of drifted hours, which
the moon
Streaks with a ghostly finger, and her
sneer
Pulls at my lengthening shadow. Yes,
'tis that!
My shadow stretches forward, and the
ground
Is dark in front because the light's
behind.
It is grotesque, with such a funny hat,
In watching it and walking I have
found
More than enough to occupy my mind.

I cannot turn, the light would make me
blind.

POPPY SEED

THE GREAT ADVENTURE OF MAX BREUCK

I

A yellow band of light upon the street
Pours from an open door, and makes a wide
Pathway of bright gold across a sheet
Of calm and liquid moonshine. From inside
Come shouts and streams of laughter, and a snatch
Of song, soon drowned and lost again in mirth,
The clip of tankards on a table top,
And stir of booted heels. Against the patch
Of candle-light a shadow falls, its girth
Proclaims the host himself, and master of his shop.

II

This is the tavern of one Hilverdink,
Jan Hilverdink, whose wines are much esteemed.
Within his cellar men can have to drink
The rarest cordials old monks ever schemed
To coax from pulpy grapes, and with nice art
Improve and spice their virgin juiciness.
Here froths the amber beer of many a brew,
Crowning each pewter tankard with as smart
A cap as ever in his wantonness
Winter set glittering on top of an old yew.

III

Tall candles stand upon the table, where
Are twisted glasses, ruby-sparked with wine,
Clarets and ports. Those topaz bumpers were
Drained from slim, long-necked bottles of the Rhine.
The centre of the board is piled with pipes,

Slender and clean, the still unbaptized clay
Awaits its burning fate. Behind, the vault
Stretches from dim to dark, a groping way
Bordered by casks and puncheons, whose brass stripes
And bands gleam dully still, beyond the gay tumult.

IV

"For good old Master Hilverdink, a toast!"
Clamoured a youth with tassels on his boots.
"Bring out your oldest brandy for a boast,
From that small barrel in the very roots
Of your deep cellar, man. Why here is Max!
Ho! Welcome, Max, you're scarcely here in time.
We want to drink to old Jan's luck, and smoke
His best tobacco for a grand climax.
Here, Jan, a paper, fragrant as crushed thyme,
We'll have the best to wish you luck, or may we choke!"

V

Max Breuck unclasped his broadcloth cloak, and sat.
"Well thought of, Franz; here's luck to Mynheer Jan."
The host set down a jar; then to a vat
Lost in the distance of his cellar, ran.
Max took a pipe as graceful as the stem
Of some long tulip, crammed it full, and drew
The pungent smoke deep to his grateful lung.
It curled all blue throughout the cave and flew
Into the silver night. At once there flung
Into the crowded shop a boy, who cried to them:

VI

"Oh, sirs, is there some learned lawyer
here,
Some advocate, or all-wise counsellor?
My master sent me to inquire where
Such men do mostly be, but every door
Was shut and barred, for late has grown
the hour.
I pray you tell me where I may now find
One versed in law, the matter will not
wait."
"I am a lawyer, boy," said Max, "my
mind
Is not locked to my business, though 'tis
late.
I shall be glad to serve what way is in
my power."

VII

Then once more, cloaked and ready, he
set out,
Tripping the footsteps of the eager boy
Along the dappled cobbles, while the rout
Within the tavern jeered at his employ.
Through new-burst elm leaves filtered the
white moon,
Who peered and splashed between the
twinkling boughs,
Flooded the open spaces, and took flight
Before tall, serried houses in platoon,
Guarded by shadows. Past the Custom
House
They took their hurried way in the
Spring-scented night.

VIII

Before a door which fronted a canal
The boy halted. A dim tree-shaded spot.
The water lapped the stones in musical
And rhythmic tappings, and a galliot
Slumbered at anchor with no light
aboard.
The boy knocked twice, and steps ap-
proached. A flame
Winked through the keyhole, then a key
was turned,
And through the open door Max went
toward
Another door, whence sound of voices
came.
He entered a large room where candelabra
burned.

IX

An aged man in quilted dressing gown
Rose up to greet him. "Sir," said Max,
"you sent
Your messenger to seek throughout the
town
A lawyer. I have small accomplishment,
But I am at your service, and my name
Is Max Breuck, Counsellor, at your com-
mand."
"Mynheer," replied the aged man,
"obliged
Am I, and count myself much privileged.
I am Cornelius Kurler, and my fame
Is better known on distant oceans than
on land.

X

My ship has tasted water in strange seas,
And bartered goods at still uncharted
isles.
She's oft coquetted with a tropic breeze,
And sheered off hurricanes with jaunty
smiles."
"Tush, Kurler," here broke in the other
man,
"Enough of poetry, draw the deed and
sign."
The old man seemed to wizen at the
voice,
"My good friend, Grootver, — " he at
once began.
"No introductions, let us have some wine,
And business, now that you at last have
made your choice."

XI

A harsh and disagreeable man he proved
to be,
This Grootver, with no single kindly
thought.
Kurler explained, his old hands nervously
Twisting his beard. His vessel he had
bought
From Grootver. He had thought to soon
repay
The ducats borrowed, but an adverse
wind
Had so delayed him that his cargo
brought
But half its proper price, the very day

He came to port he stepped ashore to find
The market glutted and his counted
profits naught.

Little by little Max made out the way
That Grootver pressed that poor harassed
old man.
His money he must have, too long delay
Had turned the usurer to a ruffian.
"But let me take my ship, with many
bales
Of cotton stuffs dyed crimson, green, and
blue,
Cunningly patterned, made to suit the
taste
Of mandarin's ladies; when my battered
sails
Open for home, such stores will I bring
you
That all your former ventures will be
counted waste.

XIII

Such light and foamy silks, like crinkled
cream,
And indigo more blue than sun-whipped
seas,
Spices and fragrant trees, a massive beam
Of sandalwood, and pungent China teas,
Tobacco, coffee!" Grootver only laughed.
Max heard it all, and worse than all he
heard
The deed to which the sailor gave his
word.
He shivered, 'twas as if the villain gaffed
The old man with a boat-hook; bleeding,
spent,
He begged for life nor knew at all the
road he went.

XIV

For Kurler had a daughter, young and
gay,
Carefully reared and shielded, rarely seen.
But on one black and most unfriendly day
Grootver had caught her as she passed
between
The kitchen and the garden. She had run
In fear of him, his evil leering eye,
And when he came she, bolted in her
room,

Refused to show, though gave no reason
why.
The spinning of her future had begun,
On quiet nights she heard the whirring
of her doom.

XV

Max mended an old goosequill by the fire,
Loathing his work, but seeing no thing
to do.
He felt his hands were building up the
pyre
To burn two souls, and seized with
vertigo
He staggered to his chair. Before him lay
White paper still unspotted by a crime.
"Now, young man, write," said Grootver
in his ear.
" 'If in two years my vessel should yet
stay
From Amsterdam, I give Grootver, some-
time
A friend, my daughter for his lawful wife.'
Now swear."

XVI

And Kurler swore, a palsied, tottering
sound,
And traced his name, a shaking, wandering line.
Then dazed he sat there, speechless from
his wound.
Grootver got up: "Fair voyage, the brigantine!"
He shuffled from the room, and left the
house.
His footsteps wore to silence down the
street.
At last the aged man began to rouse.
With help he once more gained his
trembling feet.
"My daughter, Mynheer Breuck, is
friendless now.
Will you watch over her? I ask a solemn
vow."

XVII

Max laid his hand upon the old man's
arm,
"Before God, sir, I vow, when you are
gone,
So to protect your daughter from all harm

As one man may." Thus sorrowful,
forlorn,
The situation to Max Breuck appeared,
He gave his promise almost without
thought,
Nor looked to see a difficulty. "Bred
Gently to watch a mother left alone;
Bound by a dying father's wish, who
feared
The world's accustomed harshness when
he should be dead;

XVIII

Such was my case from youth, Mynheer
Kurler.
Last Winter she died also, and my days
Are passed in work, lest I should grieve
for her,
And undo habits used to earn her praise.
My leisure I will gladly give to see
Your household and your daughter pros-
perous."
The sailor said his thanks, but turned
away.
He could not brook that his humility,
So little wonted, and so tremulous,
Should first before a stranger make such
great display.

XIX

"Come here to-morrow as the bells ring
noon,
I sail at the full sea, my daughter then
I will make known to you. 'Twill be a
boon
If after I have bid good-by, and when
Her eyeballs scorch with watching me
depart,
You bring her home again. She lives
with one
Old serving-woman, who has brought her
up,
But that is no friend for so free a heart.
No head to match her questions. It is
done.
And I must sail away to come and brim
her cup.

XX

My ship's the fastest that owns Amsterdam
As home, so not a letter can you send.

I shall be back, before to where I am
Another ship could reach. Now your
stipend — "
Quickly Breuck interposed. "When you
once more
Tread on the stones which pave our
streets. — Good night!
To-morrow I will be, at stroke of noon,
At the great wharf." Then hurrying, in
spite
Of cake and wine the old man pressed
upon
Him ere he went, he took his leave and
shut the door.

XXI

'Twas noon in Amsterdam, the day was
clear,
And sunshine tipped the pointed roofs
with gold.
The brown canals ran liquid bronze, for
here
The sun sank deep into the waters cold.
And every clock and belfry in the town
Hammered, and struck, and rang. Such
peals of bells,
To shake the sunny morning into life,
And to proclaim the middle, and the
crown,
Of this most sparkling daytime! The
crowd swells,
Laughing and pushing toward the quays
in friendly strife.

XXII

The "Horn of Fortune" sails away to-day.
At highest tide she lets her anchor go,
And starts for China. Saucy popinjay!
Giddy in freshest paint she curtseys low,
And beckons to her boats to let her start.
Blue is the ocean, with a flashing breeze.
The shining waves are quick to take her
part.
They push and spatter her. Her sails are
loose,
Her tackles hanging, waiting men to seize
And haul them taut, with chanty-singing,
as they choose.

XXIII

At the great wharf's edge Mynheer Kurler
stands,
And by his side, his daughter, young
Christine.

Max Breuck is there, his hat held in his
hands,
Bowing before them both. The brigantine
Bounces impatient at the long delay,
Curvets and jumps, a cable's length from
shore.
A heavy galliot unloads on the walls
Round, yellow cheeses, like gold cannon
balls
Stacked on the stones in pyramids. Once
more
Kurler has kissed Christine, and now he
is away.

XXIV

Christine stood rigid like a frozen stone,
Her hands wrung pale in effort at control.
Max moved aside and let her be alone,
For grief exacts each penny of its toll.
The dancing boat tossed on the glinting
sea.
A sun-path swallowed it in flaming light,
Then, shrunk a cockleshell, it came again
Upon the other side. Now on the lee
It took the "Horn of Fortune." Strain-
ing sight
Could see it hauled aboard, men pulling
on the crane.

XXV

Then up above the eager brigantine,
Along her slender masts, the sails took
flight,
Were sheeted home, and ropes were
coiled. The shine
Of the wet anchor, when its heavy weight
Rose splashing to the deck. These things
they saw,
Christine and Max, upon the crowded
quay.
They saw the sails grow white, then blue
in shade,
The ship had turned, caught in a windy
flaw
She glided imperceptibly away,
Drew farther off and in the bright sky
seemed to fade.

XXVI

Home, through the emptying streets, Max
took Christine,
Who would have hid her sorrow from his
gaze.

Before the iron gateway, clasped be-
tween
Each garden wall, he stopped. She, in
amaze,
Asked, "Do you enter not then, Mynheer
Breuck?
My father told me of your courtesy.
Since I am now your charge, 'tis meet
for me
To show such hospitality as maiden
may,
Without disdaining rules must not be
broke.
Katrina will have coffee, and she bakes
to-day."

XXVII

She straight unhasped the tall, beflowered
gate.
Curled into tendrils, twisted into cones
Of leaves and roses, iron infoliate,
It guards the pleasance, and its stiffened
bones
Are budded with much peering at the
rows,
And beds, and arbours, which it keeps
inside.
Max started at the beauty, at the glare
Of tints. At either end was set a wide
Path strewn with fine, red gravel, and
such shows
Of tulips in their splendour flaunted
everywhere!

XXVIII

From side to side, midway each path,
there ran
A longer one which cut the space in two.
And, like a tunnel some magician
Has wrought in twinkling green, an alley
grew,
Pleached thick and walled with apple
trees; their flowers
Incensed the garden, and when Autumn
came
The plump and heavy apples crowding
stood
And tapped against the arbour. Then the
dame
Katrina shook them down, in pelting
showers
They plunged to earth, and died trans-
formed to sugared food.

XXIX

Against the high, encircling walls were
  grapes,
Nailed close to feel the baking of the sun
From glowing bricks. Their microscopic
  shapes
Half hidden by serrated leaves. And one
Old cherry tossed its branches near the
  door.
Bordered along the wall, in beds between,
Flickering, streaming, nodding in the air,
The pride of all the garden, there were
  more
Tulips than Max had ever dreamed or
  seen.
They jostled, mobbed, and danced. Max
  stood at helpless stare.

XXX

"Within the arbour, Mynheer Breuck, I'll
  bring
Coffee and cakes, a pipe, and Father's
  best
Tobacco, brought from countries har-
  bouring
Dawn's earliest footstep. Wait." With
  girlish zest
To please her guest she flew. A moment
  more
She came again, with her old nurse be-
  hind.
Then, sitting on the bench and knitting
  fast,
She talked as someone with a noble store
Of hidden fancies, blown upon the wind,
Eager to flutter forth and leave their
  silent past.

XXXI

The little apple leaves above their heads
Let fall a quivering sunshine. Quiet, cool,
In blossomed boughs they sat. Beyond,
  the beds
Of tulips blazed, a proper vestibule
And antechamber to the rainbow. Dyes
Of prismed richness: Carmine. Madder.
  Blues
Tinging dark browns to purple. Silvers
  flushed
To amethyst and tinct with gold. Round
  eyes

Of scarlet, spotting tender saffron hues.
Violets sunk to blacks, and reds in orange
  crushed.

XXXII

Of every pattern and in every shade.
Nacreous, iridescent, mottled, checked.
Some purest sulphur-yellow, others made
An ivory-white with disks of copper
  flecked.
Sprinkled and striped, tasselled, or keenest
  edged.
Striated, powdered, freckled, long or short.
They bloomed, and seemed strange won-
  der-moths new-fledged,
Born of the spectrum wedded to a flame.
The shade within the arbour made a port
To o'ertaxed eyes, its still, green twilight
  rest became.

XXXIII

Her knitting-needles clicked and Christine
  talked,
This child matured to woman unaware,
The first time left alone. Now dreams
  once balked
Found utterance. Max thought her very
  fair.
Beneath her cap her ornaments shone
  gold,
And purest gold they were. Kurler was
  rich
And heedful. Her old maiden aunt had
  died
Whose darling care she was. Now, growing bold,
She asked, had Max a sister? Dropped a
  stitch
At her own candour. Then she paused
  and softly sighed.

XXXIV

Two years was long! She loved her father
  well,
But fears she had not. He had always
  been
Just sailed or sailing. And she must not
  dwell
On sad thoughts, he had told her so, and
  seen
Her smile at parting. But she sighed once
  more.

Two years was long; 'twas not one hour
  yet!
Mynheer Grootver she would not see at
  all.
Yes, yes, she knew, but ere the date so set,
The "Horn of Fortune" would be at the
  wall.
When Max had bid farewell, she watched
  him from the door.

XXXV

The next day, and the next, Max went to
  ask
The health of Jufvrouw Kurler, and the
  news:
Another tulip blown, or the great task
Of gathering petals which the high wind
  strews;
The polishing of floors, the pictured tiles
Well scrubbed, and oaken chairs most
  deftly oiled.
Such things were Christine's world, and
  his was she.
Winter drew near, his sun was in her
  smiles.
Another Spring, and at his law he toiled,
Unspoken hope counselled a wise effi-
  ciency.

XXXVI

Max Breuck was honour's soul, he knew
  himself
The guardian of this girl; no more, no
  less.
As one in charge of guineas on a shelf
Loose in a china teapot, may confess
His need, but may not borrow till his
  friend
Comes back to give. So Max, in honour,
  said
No word of love or marriage; but the days
He clipped off on his almanac. The end
Must come! The second year, with feet
  of lead,
Lagged slowly by till Spring had plumped
  the willow sprays.

XXXVII

Two years had made Christine a woman
  grown,
With dignity and gently certain pride.
But all her childhood fancies had not
  flown,

Her thoughts in lovely dreamings seemed
  to glide.
Max was her trusted friend, did she con-
  fess
A closer happiness? Max could not tell.
Two years were over and his life he found
Sphered and complete. In restless eager-
  ness
He waited for the "Horn of Fortune."
  Well
Had he his promise kept, abating not one
  pound.

XXXVIII

Spring slipped away to Summer. Still no
  glass
Sighted the brigantine. Then Grootver
  came
Demanding Jufvrouw Kurler. His tres-
  pass
Was justified, for he had won the game.
Christine begged time, more time! Mid-
  summer went,
And Grootver waxed impatient. Still the
  ship
Tarried. Christine, betrayed and weary,
  sank
To dreadful terrors. One day, crazed, she
  sent
For Max. "Come quickly," said her note,
"I skip
The worst distress until we meet. The
  world is blank."

XXXIX

Through the long sunshine of late after-
  noon
Max went to her. In the pleached alley,
  lost
In bitter reverie, he found her soon.
And sitting down beside her, at the cost
Of all his secret, "Dear," said he, "what
  thing
So suddenly has happened?" Then, in
  tears,
She told that Grootver, on the following
  morn,
Would come to marry her, and shud-
  dering:
"I will die rather, death has lesser fears."
Max felt the shackles drop from the oath
  which he had sworn.

XL

"My Dearest One, the hid joy of my
  heart!
I love you, oh! you must indeed have
  known.
In strictest honour I have played my part;
But all this misery has overthrown
My scruples. If you love me, marry me
Before the sun has dipped behind those
  trees.
You cannot be wed twice, and Grootver,
  foiled,
Can eat his anger. My care it shall be
To pay your father's debt, by such degrees
As I can compass, and for years I've
  greatly toiled.

XLI

This is not haste, Christine, for long
  I've known
My love, and silence forced upon my lips.
I worship you with all the strength I've
  shown
In keeping faith." With pleading finger
  tips
He touched her arm. "Christine! Be-
  loved! Think.
Let us not tempt the future. Dearest,
  speak,
I love you. Do my words fall too swift
  now?
They've been in leash so long upon the
  brink."
She sat quite still, her body loose and
  weak.
Then into him she melted, all her soul at
  flow.

XLII

And they were married ere the westering
  sun
Had disappeared behind the garden trees.
The evening poured on them its benison,
And flower-scents, that only night-time
  frees,
Rose up around them from the beamy
  ground,
Silvered and shadowed by a tranquil
  moon.
Within the arbour, long they lay em-
  braced,

In such enraptured sweetness as they
  found
Close-partnered each to each, and thinking soon
To be enwoven, long ere night to morning faced.

XLIII

At last Max spoke, "Dear Heart, this
  night is ours,
To watch it pale, together, into dawn,
Pressing our souls apart like opening
  flowers
Until our lives, through quivering bodies
  drawn,
Are mingled and confounded. Then, far
  spent,
Our eyes will close to undisturbéd rest.
For that desired thing I leave you now.
To pinnacle this day's accomplishment,
By telling Grootver that a bootless quest
Is his, and that his schemes have met a
  knock-down blow."

XLIV

But Christine clung to him with sobbing
  cries,
Pleading for love's sake that he leave her
  not.
And wound her arms about his knees and
  thighs
As he stood over her. With dread, begot
Of Grootver's name, and silence, and the
  night,
She shook and trembled. Words in moaning plaint
Wooed him to stay. She feared, she
  knew not why,
Yet greatly feared. She seemed some anguished saint
Martyred by visions. Max Breuck soothed
  her fright
With wisdom, then stepped out under the
  cooling sky.

XLV

But at the gate once more she held him
  close
And quenched her heart again upon his
  lips.
"My Sweetheart, why this terror? I propose

But to be gone one hour! Evening slips
Away, this errand must be done." "Max!
Max!
First goes my father, if I lose you now!"
She grasped him as in panic lest she
drown.
Softly he laughed, "One hour through
the town
By moonlight! That's no place for foul
attacks.
Dearest, be comforted, and clear that
troubled brow.

XLVI

One hour, Dear, and then, no more alone.
We front another day as man and wife.
I shall be back almost before I'm gone,
And midnight shall anoint and crown our
life."
Then through the gate he passed. Along
the street
She watched his buttons gleaming in the
moon.
He stopped to wave and turned the gar-
den wall.
Straight she sank down upon a mossy seat.
Her senses, mist-encircled by a swoon,
Swayed to unconsciousness beneath its
wreathing pall.

XLVII

Briskly Max walked beside the still canal.
His step was firm with purpose. Not a jot
He feared this meeting, nor the rancorous
gall
Grootver would spit on him who marred
his plot.
He dreaded no man, since he could pro-
tect
Christine. His wife! He stopped and
laughed aloud.
His starved life had not fitted him for joy.
It strained him to the utmost to reject
Even this hour with her. His heart beat
loud.
"Damn Grootver, who can force my time
to this employ!"

XLVIII

He laughed again. What boyish uncon-
trol
To be so racked. Then felt his ticking
watch.

In half an hour Grootver would know the
whole.
And he would be returned, lifting the
latch
Of his own gate, eager to take Christine
And crush her to his lips. How bear delay?
He broke into a run. In front, a line
Of candle-light banded the cobbled street.
Hilverdink's tavern! Not for many a day
Had he been there to take his old, accus-
tomed seat.

XLIV

"Why, Max! Stop, Max!" And out they
came pell-mell,
His old companions. "Max, where have
you been?
Not drink with us? Indeed you serve us
well!
How many months is it since we have
seen
You here? Jan, Jan, you slow, old dod-
dering goat!
Here's Mynheer Breuck come back again
at last,
Stir your old bones to welcome him. Fie,
Max,
Business! And after hours! Fill your
throat;
Here's beer or brandy. Now, boys, hold
him fast.
Put down your cane, dear man. What
really vicious whacks!"

L

They forced him to a seat, and held him
there,
Despite his anger, while the hideous joke
Was tossed from hand to hand. Franz
poured with care
A brimming glass of whiskey. "Here,
we've broke
Into a virgin barrel for you, drink!
Tut! Tut! Just hear him! Married! Who,
and when?
Married, and out on business. Clever
Spark!
Which lie's the likeliest? Come, Max, do
think."
Swollen with fury, struggling with these
men,
Max cursed hilarity which must needs
have a mark.

LI

Forcing himself to steadiness, he tried
To quell the uproar, told them what he
  dared
Of his own life and circumstance. Implied
Most urgent matters, time could ill be
  spared.
In jesting mood his comrades heard his
  tale,
And scoffed at it. He felt his anger more
Goaded and bursting; — "Cowards! Is
  no one loth
To mock at duty — " Here they called
  for ale,
And forced a pipe upon him. With an
  oath
He shivered it to fragments on the earthen
floor.

LII

Sobered a little by his violence,
And by the host who begged them to be
  still,
Nor injure his good name, "Max, no
  offence,"
They blurted, "you may leave now if you
  will."
"One moment, Max," said Franz. "We've
  gone too far.
I ask your pardon for our foolish joke.
It started in a wager ere you came.
The talk somehow had fall'n on drugs,
  a jar
I brought from China, herbs the natives
  smoke,
Was with me, and I thought merely to
  play a game.

LIII

Its properties are to induce a sleep
Fraught with adventure, and the flight of
  time
Is inconceivable in swiftness. Deep
Sunken in slumber, imageries sublime
Flatter the senses, or some fearful dream
Holds them enmeshed. Years pass which
  on the clock
Are but so many seconds. We agreed
That the next man who came should
  prove the scheme;

And you were he. Jan handed you the
  crock.
Two whiffs! And then the pipe was broke,
  and you were freed."

LIV

"It is a lie, a damned, infernal lie!"
Max Breuck was maddened now. "An-
  other jest
Of your befuddled wits. I know not why
I am to be your butt. At my request
You'll choose among you one who'll an-
  swer for
Your most unseasonable mirth. Good-
  night
And good-by, — gentlemen. You'll hear
  from me."
But Franz had caught him at the very
  door,
"It is no lie, Max Breuck, and for your
  plight
I am to blame. Come back, and we'll talk
  quietly.

LV

You have no business, that is why we
  laughed,
Since you had none a few minutes ago.
As to your wedding, naturally we chaffed,
Knowing the length of time it takes to do
A simple thing like that in this slow world.
Indeed, Max, 'twas a dream. Forgive me
  then.
I'll burn the drug if you prefer." But
  Breuck
Muttered and stared, — "A lie." And
  then he hurled,
Distraught, this word at Franz: "Prove it.
  And when
It's proven, I'll believe. That thing shall
  be your work.

LVI

I'll give you just one week to make your
  case.
On August thirty-first, eighteen-fourteen,
I shall require your proof." With won-
  dering face
Franz cried, "A week to August, and
  fourteen
The year! You're mad, 'tis April now.

April, and eighteen-twelve." Max stag-
gered, caught
A chair, — "April two years ago! Indeed,
Or you, or I, are mad. I know not how
Either could blunder so." Hilverdink
brought
"The Amsterdam Gazette," and Max was
forced to read.

LVII

"Eighteen hundred and twelve," in larg-
est print;
And next to it, "April the twenty-first."
The letters smeared and jumbled, but by
dint
Of straining every nerve to meet the worst,
He read it, and into his pounding brain
Tumbled a horror. Like a roaring sea
Foreboding shipwreck, came the message
plain:
"This is two years ago! What of Chris-
tine?"
He fled the cellar, in his agony
Running to outstrip Fate, and save his
holy shrine.

LVIII

The darkened buildings echoed to his feet
Clap-clapping on the pavement as he ran.
Across moon-misted squares clamoured
his fleet
And terror-wingéd steps. His heart began
To labour at the speed. And still no sign,
No flutter of a leaf against the sky.
And this should be the garden wall, and
round
The corner, the old gate. No even line
Was this! No wall! And then a fearful
cry
Shattered the stillness. Two stiff houses
filled the ground.

LIX

Shoulder to shoulder, like dragoons in
line,
They stood, and Max knew them to be
the ones
To right and left of Kurler's garden. Spine
Rigid next frozen spine. No mellow tones
Of ancient gilded iron, undulate,
Expanding in wide circles and broad
curves,

The twisted iron of the garden gate,
Was there. The houses touched and left
no space
Between. With glassy eyes and shaking
nerves
Max fled. Then mad with fear, fled still,
and left that place.

LX

Stumbling and panting, on he ran, and on.
His slobbering lips could only cry, "Chris-
tine!
My Dearest Love! My Wife! Where are
you gone?
What future is our past? What satur-
nine,
Sardonic devil's jest has bid us live
Two years together in a puff of smoke?
It was no dream, I swear it! In some star,
Or still imprisoned in Time's egg, you give
Me love. I feel it. Dearest Dear, this
stroke
Shall never part us, I will reach to where
you are."

LXI

His burning eyeballs stared into the dark.
The moon had long been set. And still
he cried:
"Christine! My Love! Christine!" A
sudden spark
Pricked through the gloom, and shortly
Max espied
With his uncertain vision, so within
Distracted he could scarcely trust its truth,
A latticed window where a crimson gleam
Spangled the blackness, and hung from
a pin,
An iron crane, were three gilt balls. His
youth
Had taught their meaning, now they
closed upon his dream.

LXII

Softly he knocked against the casement,
wide
It flew, and a cracked voice his business
there
Demanded. The door opened, and inside
Max stepped. He saw a candle held in air
Above the head of a gray-bearded Jew.
"Simeon Isaacs, Mynheer, can I serve

You?" "Yes, I think you can. Do you keep arms?
I want a pistol." Quick the old man grew
Livid. "Mynheer, a pistol! Let me swerve
You from your purpose. Life brings often false alarms — "

LXIII

"Peace, good old Isaacs, why should you suppose
My purpose deadly. In good truth I've been
Blest above others. You have many rows
Of pistols it would seem. Here, this shagreen
Case holds one that I fancy. Silvered mounts
Are to my taste. These letters 'C.D.L.'
Its former owner? Dead, you say. Poor Ghost!
'Twill serve my turn though — " Hastily he counts
The florins down upon the table. "Well,
Good-night, and wish me luck for your to-morrow's toast."

LXIV

Into the night again he hurried, now
Pale and in haste; and far beyond the town
He set his goal. And then he wondered how
Poor C.D.L. had come to die. "It's grown
Handy in killing, maybe, this I've bought,
And will work punctually." His sorrow fell
Upon his senses, shutting out all else.
Again he wept, and called, and blindly fought
The heavy miles away. "Christine. I'm well.
I'm coming. My Own Wife!" He lurched with failing pulse.

LXV

Along the dyke the keen air blew in gusts,
And grasses bent and wailed before the wind.
The Zuider Zee, which croons all night and thrusts

Long stealthy fingers up some way to find
And crumble down the stones, moaned baffled. Here
The wide-armed windmills looked like gallows-trees.
No lights were burning in the distant thorps.
Max laid aside his coat. His mind, half-clear,
Babbled "Christine!" A shot split through the breeze.
The cold stars winked and glittered at his chilling corpse.

SANCTA MARIA, SUCCURRE MISERIS

Dear Virgin Mary, far away,
Look down from Heaven while I pray.
Open your golden casement high,
And lean way out beyond the sky.
I am so little, it may be
A task for you to harken me.

O Lady Mary, I have bought
A candle, as the good priest taught.
I only had one penny, so
Old Goody Jenkins let it go.
It is a little bent, you see.
But Oh, be merciful to me!

I have not anything to give,
Yet I so long for him to live.
A year ago he sailed away
And not a word unto to-day.
I've strained my eyes from the sea-wall
But never does he come at all.

Other ships have entered port
Their voyages finished, long or short,
And other sailors have received
Their welcomes, while I sat and grieved.
My heart is bursting for his hail,
O Virgin, let me spy his sail.

Hull down on the edge of a sun-soaked sea
Sparkle the bellying sails for me.
Taut to the push of a rousing wind
Shaking the sea till it foams behind,
The tightened rigging is shrill with the song:
"We are back again who were gone so long."

One afternoon I bumped my head.
I sat on a post and wished I were dead
Like father and mother, for no one cared
Whither I went or how I fared.
A man's voice said, "My little lad,
Here's a bit of a toy to make you glad."

Then I opened my eyes and saw him
  plain,
With his sleeves rolled up, and the dark
  blue stain
Of tattooed skin, where a flock of quail
Flew up to his shoulder and met the tail
Of a dragon curled, all pink and green,
Which sprawled on his back, when it was
  seen.

He held out his hand and gave to me
The most marvellous top which could
  ever be.
It had ivory eyes, and jet-black rings,
And a red stone carved into little wings,
All joined by a twisted golden line,
And set in the brown wood, even and
  fine.

Forgive me, Lady, I have not brought
My treasure to you as I ought,
But he said to keep it for his sake
And comfort myself with it, and take
Joy in its spinning, and so I do.
It couldn't mean quite the same to you.

Every day I met him there,
Where the fisher-nets dry in the sunny air.
He told me stories of courts and kings,
Of storms at sea, of lots of things.
The top he said was a sort of sign
That something in the big world was
  mine.

> Blue and white on a sun-shot
>   ocean.
> Against the horizon a glint in
>   motion.
> Full in the grasp of a shoving
>   wind,
> Trailing her bubbles of foam be-
>   hind,
> Singing and shouting to port she
>   races,
> A flying harp, with her sheets and
>   braces.

O Queen of Heaven, give me heed,
I am in very utmost need.

He loved me, he was all I had,
And when he came it made the sad
Thoughts disappear. This very day
Send his ship home to me I pray.

I'll be a priest, if you want it so,
I'll work till I have enough to go
And study Latin to say the prayers
On the rosary our old priest wears.
I wished to be a sailor too,
But I will give myself to you.

I'll never even spin my top,
But put it away in a box. I'll stop
Whistling the sailor-songs he taught.
I'll save my pennies till I have bought
A silver heart in the market square,
I've seen some beautiful, white ones there.

I'll give up all I want to do
And do whatever you tell me to.
Heavenly Lady, take away
All the games I like to play,
Take my life to fill the score,
Only bring him back once more!

> The poplars shiver and turn their
>   leaves,
> And the wind through the belfry
>   moans and grieves.
> The gray dust whirls in the market
>   square,
> And the silver hearts are covered
>   with care
> By thick tarpaulins. Once again
> The bay is black under heavy rain.

The Queen of Heaven has shut her door.
A little boy weeps and prays no more.

AFTER HEARING A WALTZ BY BARTOK

But why did I kill him? Why? Why?
  In the small, gilded room, near the
    stair?
My ears rack and throb with his cry,
  And his eyes goggle under his hair,
  As my fingers sink into the fair
White skin of his throat. It was I!

I killed him! My God! Don't you hear?
  I shook him until his red tongue
Hung flapping out through the black,
  queer,

Swollen lines of his lips. And I clung
With my nails drawing blood, while I
flung
The loose, heavy body in fear.

Fear lest he should still not be dead.
I was drunk with the lust of his life.
The blood-drops oozed slow from his
head
And dabbled a chair. And our strife
Lasted one reeling second, his knife
Lay and winked in the lights overhead.

And the waltz from the ballroom I heard,
When I called him a low, sneaking cur.
And the wail of the violins stirred
My brute anger with visions of her.
As I throttled his windpipe, the purr
Of his breath with the waltz became
blurred.

I have ridden ten miles through the dark,
With that music, an infernal din,
Pounding rhythmic inside me. Just Hark!
One! Two! Three! And my fingers sink
in
To his flesh when the violins, thin
And straining with passion, grow stark.

One! Two! Three! Oh, the horror of
sound!
While she danced I was crushing his
throat.
He had tasted the joy of her, wound
Round her body, and I heard him gloat
On the favour. That instant I smote.
One! Two! Three! How the dancers swirl
round!

He is here in the room, in my arm,
His limp body hangs on the spin
Of the waltz we are dancing, a swarm
Of blood-drops is hemming us in!
Round and round! One! Two! Three!
And his sin
Is red like his tongue lolling warm.

One! Two! Three! And the drums are his
knell.
He is heavy, his feet beat the floor
As I drag him about in the swell
Of the waltz. With a menacing roar,
The trumpets crash in through the
door.
One! Two! Three! clangs his funeral bell.

One! Two! Three! In the chaos of space
Rolls the earth to the hideous glee
Of death! And so cramped is this place,
I stifle and pant. One! Two! Three!
Round and round! God! 'Tis he throttles
me!
He has covered my mouth with his face!

And his blood has dripped into my heart!
And my heart beats and labours. One!
Two!
Three! His dead limbs have coiled every
part
Of my body in tentacles. Through
My ears the waltz jangles. Like glue
His dead body holds me athwart.

One! Two! Three! Give me air! Oh! My
God!
One! Two! Three! I am drowning in
slime!
One! Two! Three! And his corpse, like a
clod,
Beats me into a jelly! The chime,
One! Two! Three! And his dead legs
keep time.
Air! Give me air! Air! My God!

CLEAR, WITH LIGHT VARIABLE WINDS

The fountain bent and straightened itself
In the night wind,
Blowing like a flower.
It gleamed and glittered,
A tall white lily,
Under the eye of the golden moon.
From a stone seat,
Beneath a blossoming lime,
The man watched it.
And the spray pattered
On the dim grass at his feet.

The fountain tossed its water,
Up and up, like silver marbles.
Is that an arm he sees?
And for one moment
Does he catch the moving curve
Of a thigh?
The fountain gurgled and splashed,
And the man's face was wet.

Is it singing that he hears?
A song of playing at ball?
The moonlight shines on the straight
column of water,

And through it he sees a woman,
Tossing the water-balls.
Her breasts point outwards,
And the nipples are like buds of peonies.
Her flanks ripple as she plays,
And the water is not more undulating
Than the lines of her body.

"Come," she sings, "Poet!
Am I not more worth than your day
    ladies,
Covered with awkward stuffs,
Unreal, unbeautiful?
What do you fear in taking me?
Is not the night for poets?
I am your dream,
Recurrent as water,
Gemmed with the moon!"

She steps to the edge of the pool
And the water runs, rustling, down her
    sides.
She stretches out her arms,
And the fountain streams behind her
Like an opened veil.

.   .   .   .   .

In the morning the gardeners came to
    their work.
"There is something in the fountain,"
    said one.
They shuddered as they laid their dead
    master
On the grass.
"I will close his eyes," said the head
    gardener,
"It is uncanny to see a dead man staring
    at the sun."

THE BASKET

I

The inkstand is full of ink, and the
paper lies white and unspotted, in the
round light thrown by a candle. Puffs of
darkness sweep into the corners, and keep
rolling through the room behind his
chair. The air is silver and pearl, for the
night is liquid with moonlight.
    See how the roof glitters, like ice!
    Over there, a slice of yellow cuts into
the silver-blue, and beside it stand two
geraniums, purple because the light is
silver-blue, to-night.

See! She is coming, the young woman
with the bright hair. She swings a basket
as she walks, which she places on the sill,
between the geranium stalks. He laughs,
and crumples his paper as he leans forward to look. "The Basket Filled with
Moonlight," what a title for a book!
    The bellying clouds swing over the
housetops.

He has forgotten the woman in the
room with the geraniums. He is beating
his brain, and in his ear-drums hammers
his heavy pulse. She sits on the window-
sill, with the basket in her lap. And tap!
She cracks a nut. And tap! Another.
Tap! Tap! Tap! The shells ricochet upon
the roof, and get into the gutters, and
bounce over the edge and disappear.
    "It is very queer," thinks Peter, "the
basket was empty, I'm sure. How could
nuts appear from the atmosphere?"
    The silver-blue moonlight makes the
geraniums purple, and the roof glitters
like ice.

II

Five o'clock. The geraniums are very
gay in their crimson array. The bellying
clouds swing over the housetops, and
over the roofs goes Peter to pay his morning's work with a holiday.
    "Annette, it is I. Have you finished?
Can I come?"
    Peter jumps through the window.
    "Dear, are you alone?"
    "Look, Peter, the dome of the taber-
nacle is done. This gold thread is so very
high, I am glad it is morning, a starry
sky would have seen me bankrupt. Sit
down, now tell me, is your story going
well?"
    The golden dome glittered in the
orange of the setting sun. On the walls,
at intervals, hung altar-cloths and chas-
ubles, and copes, and stoles, and coffin
palls. All stiff with rich embroidery, and
stitched with so much artistry, they seemed
like spun and woven gems, or flower-buds
new-opened on their stems.
    Annette looked at the geraniums, very
red against the blue sky.
    "No matter how I try, I cannot find
any thread of such a red. My bleeding

hearts drip stuff muddy in comparison.
Heigh-ho! See my little pecking dove?
I'm in love with my own temple. Only
that halo's wrong. The colour's too
strong, or not strong enough. I don't
know. My eyes are tired. Oh, Peter,
don't be so rough; it is valuable. I won't
do any more. I promise. You tyrannise,
Dear, that's enough. Now sit down and
amuse me while I rest."

The shadows of the geraniums creep
over the floor, and begin to climb the
opposite wall.

Peter watches her, fluid with fatigue,
floating, and drifting, and undulant in
the orange glow. His senses flow towards
her, where she lies supine and dreaming.
Seeming drowned in a golden halo.
The pungent smell of the geraniums is
hard to bear.

He pushes against her knees, and
brushes his lips across her languid hands.
His lips are hot and speechless. He woos
her, quivering, and the room is filled with
shadows, for the sun has set. But she only
understands the ways of a needle through
delicate stuffs, and the shock of one colour on another. She does not see that
this is the same, and querulously murmurs
his name.
"Peter, I don't want it. I am tired."
And he, the undesired, burns and is
consumed.
There is a crescent moon on the rim
of the sky.

III

"Go home, now, Peter. To-night is
full moon. I must be alone."
"How soon the moon is full again!
Annette, let me stay. Indeed, Dear Love,
I shall not go away. My God, but you
keep me starved! You write 'No Entrance
Here,' over all the doors. Is it not strange,
my Dear, that loving, yet you deny me
entrance everywhere. Would marriage
strike you blind, or, hating bonds as you
do, why should I be denied the rights of
loving if I leave you free? You want the
whole of me, you pick my brains to rest
you, but you give me not one heart-beat.
Oh, forgive me, Sweet! I suffer in my

loving, and you know it. I cannot feed
my life on being a poet. Let me stay."
"As you please, poor Peter, but it will
hurt me if you do. It will crush your
heart and squeeze the love out."
He answered gruffly, "I know what I'm
about."
"Only remember one thing from to-
night. My work is taxing and I must have
sight! I MUST!"

The clear moon looks in between the
geraniums. On the wall, the shadow of
the man is divided from the shadow of
the woman by a silver thread.

They are eyes, hundreds of eyes, round
like marbles! Unwinking, for there are no
lids. Blue, black, gray, and hazel, and the
irises are cased in the whites, and they
glitter and spark under the moon. The
basket is heaped with human eyes. She
cracks off the whites and throws them
away. They ricochet upon the roof, and
get into the gutters, and bounce over the
edge and disappear. But she is here,
quietly sitting on the window-sill, eating
human eyes.

The silver-blue moonlight makes the
geraniums purple, and the roof shines like
ice.

IV

How hot the sheets are! His skin is
tormented with pricks, and over him
sticks, and never moves, an eye. It lights
the sky with blood, and drips blood. And
the drops sizzle on his bare skin, and he
smells them burning in, and branding
his body with the name "Annette."
The blood-red sky is outside his window now. Is it blood or fire? Merciful
God! Fire! And his heart wrenches and
pounds "Annette!"
The lead of the roof is scorching, he
ricochets, gets to the edge, bounces over
and disappears.
The bellying clouds are red as they
swing over the housetops.

V

The air is of silver and pearl, for the
night is liquid with moonlight. How the
ruin glistens, like a palace of ice! Only
two black holes swallow the brilliance of

the moon. Deflowered windows, sockets without sight.

A man stands before the house. He sees the silver-blue moonlight, and set in it, over his head, staring and flickering, eyes of geranium red.

Annette!

IN A CASTLE

I

Over the yawning chimney hangs the fog.   Drip — hiss — drip — hiss — fall the raindrops on the oaken log which burns, and steams, and smokes the ceiling beams.   Drip — hiss — the rain never stops.

The wide, state bed shivers beneath its velvet coverlet. Above, dim, in the smoke, a tarnished coronet gleams dully. Overhead hammers and chinks the rain. Fearfully wails the wind down distant corridors, and there comes the swish and sigh of rushes lifted off the floors. The arras blows sidewise out from the wall, and then falls back again.

It is my lady's key, confided with much nice cunning, whisperingly. He enters on a sob of wind, which gutters the candles almost to swaling. The fire flutters and drops.   Drip — hiss — the rain never stops. He shuts the door. The rushes fall again to stillness along the floor. Outside, the wind goes wailing.

The velvet coverlet of the wide bed is smooth and cold. Above, in the firelight, winks the coronet of tarnished gold. The knight shivers in his coat of fur, and holds out his hands to the withering flame. She is always the same, a sweet coquette. He will wait for her.

How the log hisses and drips! How warm and satisfying will be her lips!

It is wide and cold, the state bed; but when her head lies under the coronet, and her eyes are full and wet with love, and when she holds out her arms, and the velvet counterpane half slips from her, and alarms her trembling modesty, how

eagerly he will leap to cover her, and blot himself beneath the quilt, making her laugh and tremble.

Is it guilt to free a lady from her palsied lord, absent and fighting, terribly abhorred?

He stirs a booted heel and kicks a rolling coal. His spur clinks on the hearth. Overhead, the rain hammers and chinks. She is so pure and whole. Only because he has her soul will she resign herself to him, for where the soul has gone, the body must be given as a sign. He takes her by the divine right of the only lover. He has sworn to fight her lord, and wed her after. Should he be overborne, she will die adoring him, forlorn, shriven by her great love.

Above, the coronet winks in the darkness.   Drip — hiss — fall the raindrops. The arras blows out from the wall, and a door bangs in a far-off hall.

The candles swale. In the gale the moat below plunges and spatters. Will the lady lose courage and not come? The rain claps on a loosened rafter. Is that laughter?

The room is filled with lisps and whispers. Something mutters. One candle drowns and the other gutters. Is that the rain which pads and patters, is it the wind through the winding entries which chatters? The state bed is very cold and he is alone. How far from the wall the arras is blown!

Christ's Death! It is no storm which makes these little chuckling sounds. By the Great Wounds of Holy Jesus, it is his dear lady, kissing and clasping someone! Through the sobbing storm he hears her love take form and flutter out in words. They prick into his ears and stun his desire, which lies within him, hard and dead, like frozen fire. And the little noise never stops.

Drip — hiss — the rain drops.

He tears down the arras from before an inner chamber's bolted door.

II

The state bed shivers in the watery dawn. Drip — hiss — fall the raindrops. For the storm never stops.

On the velvet coverlet lie two bodies, stripped and fair in the cold, grey air. Drip — hiss — fall the blood-drops, for the bleeding never stops. The bodies lie quietly. At each side of the bed, on the floor, is a head. A man's on this side, a woman's on that, and the red blood oozes along the rush mat.

A wisp of paper is twisted carefully into the strands of the dead man's hair. It says, "My Lord: Your wife's paramour has paid with his life for the high favour."

Through the lady's silver fillet is wound another paper. It reads, "Most noble Lord: Your wife's misdeeds are as a double-stranded necklace of beads. But I have engaged that, on your return, she shall welcome you here. She will not spurn your love as before, you have still the best part of her. Her blood was red, her body white, they will both be here for your delight. The soul inside was a lump of dirt, I have rid you of that with a spurt of my sword point. Good luck to your pleasure. She will be quite complaisant, my friend, I wager." The end was a splashed flourish of ink.

Hark! In the passage is heard the clink of armour, the tread of a heavy man. The door bursts open and standing there, his thin hair wavering in the glare of steely daylight, is my Lord of Clair.

Over the yawning chimney hangs the fog. Drip — hiss — drip — hiss — fall the raindrops. Overhead hammers and chinks the rain which never stops.

The velvet coverlet is sodden and wet, yet the roof beams are tight. Overhead, the coronet gleams with its blackened gold, winking and blinking. Among the rushes three corpses are growing cold.

III

In the castle church you may see them stand,
Two sumptuous tombs on either hand
Of the choir, my Lord's and my Lady's,
grand
In sculptured filigrees. And where the
transepts of the church expand,
A crusader, come from the Holy Land,
Lies with crossed legs and embroidered
band.
The page's name became a brand
For shame. He was buried in crawling
sand,
After having been burnt by royal com-
mand.

THE BOOK OF HOURS OF SISTER CLOTILDE

The Bell in the convent tower swung,
High overhead the great sun hung,
A navel for the curving sky.
The air was a blue clarity.
    Swallows flew,
    And a cock crew.

The iron clanging sank through the light
    air,
Rustled over with blowing branches. A
    flare
Of spotted green, and a snake had gone
Into the bed where the snowdrops shone
    In green new-started,
    Their white bells parted.

Two by two, in a long brown line,
The nuns were walking to breathe the fine
Bright April air. They must go in soon
And work at their tasks all the afternoon.
    But this time is theirs!
    They walk in pairs.

First comes the Abbess, preoccupied
And slow, as a woman often tried,
With her temper in bond. Then the
    oldest nun.
Then younger and younger, until the last
    one
    Has a laugh on her lips,
    And fairly skips.

They wind about the gravel walks
And all the long line buzzes and talks.
They step in time to the ringing bell,
With scarcely a shadow. The sun is well
    In the core of a sky
    Domed silverly.

Sister Marguérite said: "The pears will
    soon bud."

Sister Angélique said she must get her
    spud
And free the earth round the jasmine
    roots.
Sister Véronique said: "Oh, look at those
    shoots!
There's a crocus up,
With a purple cup."

But Sister Clotilde said nothing at all,
She looked up and down the old grey wall
To see if a lizard were basking there.
She looked across the garden to where
    A sycamore
    Flanked the garden door.

She was restless, although her little feet
    danced,
And quite unsatisfied, for it chanced
Her morning's work had hung in her mind
And would not take form. She could not
    find
    The beautifulness
    For the Virgin's dress.

Should it be of pink, or damasked blue?
Or perhaps lilac with gold shotted
    through?
Should it be banded with yellow and
    white
Roses, or sparked like a frosty night?
    Or a crimson sheen
    Over some sort of green?

But Clotilde's eyes saw nothing new
In all the garden, no single hue
So lovely or so marvellous
That its use would not seem impious.
    So on she walked,
    And the others talked.

Sister Elisabeth edged away
From what her companion had to say,
For Sister Marthe saw the world in little,
She weighed every grain and recorded each
    tittle.
    She did plain stitching
    And worked in the kitchen.

"Sister Radegonde knows the apples won't
    last,
I told her so this Friday past.
I must speak to her before Compline."
Her words were like dust motes in slant-
    ing sunshine.

The other nun sighed,
With her pleasure quite dried.

Suddenly Sister Berthe cried out:
"The snowdrops are blooming!" They
    turned about.
The little white cups bent over the
    ground,
And in among the light stems wound
    A crested snake,
    With his eyes awake.

His body was green with a metal bright-
    ness
Like an emerald set in a kind of whiteness,
And all down his curling length were disks,
Evil vermilion asterisks,
    They paled and flooded
    As wounds fresh-blooded.

His crest was amber glittered with blue,
And opaque so the sun came shining
    through.
It seemed a crown with fiery points.
When he quivered all down his scaly
    joints,
    From every slot
    The sparkles shot.

The nuns huddled tightly together, fear
Catching their senses. But Clotilde must
    peer
More closely at the beautiful snake,
She seemed entranced and eased. Could
    she make
    Colours so rare,
    The dress were there.

The Abbess shook off her lethargy.
"Sisters, we will walk on," said she.
Sidling away from the snowdrop bed,
The line curved forwards, the Abbess
    ahead.
    Only Clotilde
    Was the last to yield.

When the recreation hour was done
Each went in to her task. Alone
In the library, with its great north light,
Clotilde wrought at an exquisite
    Wreath of flowers
    For her Book of Hours.

She twined the little crocus blooms
With snowdrops and daffodils, the glooms

Of laurel leaves were interwoven
With Stars-of-Bethlehem, and cloven
    Fritillaries,
    Whose colour varies.

They framed the picture she had made,
Half-delighted and half-afraid.
In a courtyard with a lozenged floor
The Virgin watched, and through the
    arched door
    The angel came
    Like a springing flame.

His wings were dipped in violet fire,
His limbs were strung to holy desire.
He lowered his head and passed under
    the arch,
And the air seemed beating a solemn
    march.
    The Virgin waited
    With eyes dilated.

Her face was quiet and innocent,
And beautiful with her strange assent.
A silver thread about her head
Her halo was poised. But in the stead
    Of her gown, there remained
    The vellum, unstained.

Clotilde painted the flowers patiently,
Lingering over each tint and dye.
She could spend great pains, now she had
    seen
That curious, unimagined green.
    A colour so strange
    It had seemed to change.

She thought it had altered while she
    gazed.
At first it had been simple green; then
    glazed
All over with twisting flames, each spot
A molten colour, trembling and hot,
    And every eye
    Seemed to liquefy.

She had made a plan, and her spirits
    danced.
After all, she had only glanced
At that wonderful snake, and she must
    know
Just what hues made the creature throw
    Those splashes and sprays
    Of prismed rays.

When evening prayers were sung and
    said,
The nuns lit their tapers and went to bed.
And soon in the convent there was no
    light,
For the moon did not rise until late that
    night,
    Only the shine
    Of the lamp at the shrine.

Clotilde lay still in her trembling sheets.
Her heart shook her body with its beats.
She could not see till the moon should
    rise,
So she whispered prayers and kept her
    eyes
    On the window-square
    Till light should be there.

The faintest shadow of a branch
Fell on the floor. Clotilde, grown staunch
With solemn purpose, softly rose
And fluttered down between the rows
    Of sleeping nuns.
    She almost runs.

She must go out through the little side
    door
Lest the nuns who were always praying
    before
The Virgin's altar should hear her pass.
She pushed the bolts, and over the grass
    The red moon's brim
    Mounted its rim.

Her shadow crept up the convent wall
As she swiftly left it, over all
The garden lay the level glow
Of a moon coming up, very big and slow.
    The gravel glistened.
    She stopped and listened.

It was still, and the moonlight was getting
    clearer.
She laughed a little, but she felt queerer
Than ever before. The snowdrop bed
Was reached and she bent down her
    head.
    On the striped ground
    The snake was wound.

For a moment Clotilde paused in alarm,
Then she rolled up her sleeve and
    stretched out her arm.

She thought she heard steps, she must be
    quick.
She darted her hand out, and seized the
    thick
        Wriggling slime,
        Only just in time.

The old gardener came muttering down
    the path,
And his shadow fell like a broad, black
    swath.
And covered Clotilde and the angry
    snake.
He bit her, but what difference did that
    make!
        The Virgin should dress
        In his loveliness.

The gardener was covering his new-set
    plants
For the night was chilly, and nothing
    daunts
Your lover of growing things. He spied
Something to do and turned aside,
        And the moonlight streamed
        On Clotilde, and gleamed.

His business finished the gardener rose.
He shook and swore, for the moonlight
    shows
A girl with a fire-tongued serpent, she
Grasping him, laughing, while quietly
        Her eyes are weeping.
        Is he sleeping?

He thinks it is some holy vision,
Brushes that aside and with decision
Jumps — and hits the snake with his
    stick,
Crushes his spine, and then with quick,
        Urgent command
        Takes her hand.

The gardener sucks the poison and spits,
Cursing and praying as befits
A poor old man half out of his wits.
"Whatever possessed you, Sister, it's
        Hatched of a devil
        And very evil.

It's one of them horrid basilisks
You read about. They say a man risks
His life to touch it, but I guess I've
    sucked it
Out by now. Lucky I chucked it

Away from you.
I guess you'll do."

"Oh, no, François, this beautiful beast
Was sent to me, to me the least
Worthy in all our convent, so I
Could finish my picture of the Most High
        And Holy Queen,
        In her dress of green.

He is dead now, but his colours won't
    fade
At once, and by noon I shall have made
The Virgin's robe. Oh, François, see
How kindly the moon shines down on
    me!
        I can't die yet,
        For the task was set."

"You won't die now, for I've sucked it
    away,"
Grumbled old François, "so have your
    play.
If the Virgin is set on snake's colours so
    strong, — "
"François, don't say things like that, it
    is wrong."
So Clotilde vented
Her creed. He repented.

"He can't do no more harm, Sister," said
    he.
"Paint as much as you like." And gingerly
He picked up the snake with his stick.
    Clotilde
Thanked him, and begged that he would
    shield
        Her secret, though itching
        To talk in the kitchen.

The gardener promised, not very pleased,
And Clotilde, with the strain of adventure
    eased,
Walked quickly home, while the half-high
    moon
Made her beautiful snake-skin sparkle,
    and soon
        In her bed she lay
        And waited for day.

At dawn's first saffron-spired warning
Clotilde was up. And all that morning,
Except when she went to the chapel to
    pray,
She painted, and when the April day

Was hot with sun,
Clotilde had done.

Done! She drooped, though her heart
beat loud
At the beauty before her, and her spirit
bowed
To the Virgin her finely-touched thought
had made.
A lady, in excellence arrayed,
And wonder-souled,
Christ's Blessed Mould!

From long fasting Clotilde felt weary and
faint,
But her eyes were starred like those of a
saint
Enmeshed in Heaven's beatitude.
A sudden clamour hurled its rude
Force to break
Her vision awake.

The door nearly leapt from its hinges,
pushed
By the multitude of nuns. They hushed
When they saw Clotilde, in perfect quiet,
Smiling, a little perplexed at the riot.
And all the hive
Buzzed "She's alive!"

Old François had told. He had found the
strain
Of silence too great, and preferred the
pain
Of a conscience outraged. The news had
spread,
And all were convinced Clotilde must be
dead.
For François, to spite them,
Had not seen fit to right them.

The Abbess, unwontedly trembling and
mild,
Put her arms round Clotilde and wept,
"My child,
Has the Holy Mother showed you this
grace,
To spare you while you imaged her face?
How could we have guessed
Our convent so blessed!

A miracle! But Oh! My Lamb!
To have you die! And I, who am
A hollow, living shell, the grave
Is empty of me. Holy Mary, I crave

To be taken, Dear Mother,
Instead of this other."

She dropped on her knees and silently
prayed,
With anguished hands and tears delayed
To a painful slowness. The minutes drew
To fractions. Then the west wind blew
The sound of a bell,
On a gusty swell.

It came skipping over the slates of the
roof,
And the bright bell-notes seemed a re-
proof
To grief, in the eye of so fair a day.
The Abbess, comforted, ceased to pray.
And the sun lit the flowers
In Clotilde's Book of Hours.

It glistened the green of the Virgin's dress
And made the red spots, in a flushed
excess,
Pulse and start; and the violet wings
Of the angel were colour which shines
and sings.
The book seemed a choir
Of rainbow fire.

The Abbess crossed herself, and each nun
Did the same, then one by one,
They filed to the chapel, that incensed
prayers
Might plead for the life of this sister of
theirs.
Clotilde, the Inspired!

She only felt tired.

. . . . .

The old chronicles say she did not die
Until heavy with years. And that is why
There hangs in the convent church a
basket
Of osiered silver, a holy casket,
And treasured therein
A dried snake-skin.

THE EXETER ROAD

Panels of claret and blue which shine
Under the moon like lees of wine.
A coronet done in a golden scroll,
And wheels which blunder and creak as
they roll

Through the muddy ruts of a moorland
track.
They daren't look back!

They are whipping and cursing the horses.
Lord!
What brutes men are when they think
they're scored.
Behind, my bay gelding gallops with me,
In a steaming sweat, it is fine to see
That coach, all claret, and gold, and blue,
Hop about and slue.

They are scared half out of their wits,
poor souls.
For my lord has a casket full of rolls
Of minted sovereigns, and silver bars.
I laugh to think how he'll show his scars
In London to-morrow. He whines with
rage
In his varnished cage.

My lady has shoved her rings over her
toes.
'Tis an ancient trick every night-rider
knows.
But I shall relieve her of them yet,
When I see she limps in the minuet
I must beg to celebrate this night,
And the green moonlight.

There's nothing to hurry about, the plain
Is hours long, and the mud's a strain.
My gelding's uncommonly strong in the
loins,
In half an hour I'll bag the coins.
'Tis a clear, sweet night on the turn of
Spring.
The chase is the thing!

How the coach flashes and wobbles, the
moon
Dripping down so quietly on it. A tune
Is beating out of the curses and screams,
And the cracking all through the painted
seams.
Steady, old horse, we'll keep it in sight.
'Tis a rare fine night!

There's a clump of trees on the dip of the
down,
And the sky shimmers where it hangs
over the town.
It seems a shame to break the air
In two with this pistol, but I've my share

Of drudgery like other men.
His hat? Amen!

Hold up, you beast, now what the devil!
Confound this moor for a pockholed, evil,
Rotten marsh. My right leg's snapped.
'Tis a mercy he's rolled, but I'm nicely
capped.
A broken-legged man and a broken-legged
horse!
They'll get me, of course.

The cursed coach will reach the town
And they'll all come out, every loafer
grown
A lion to handcuff a man that's down.
What's that? Oh, the coachman's bul-
leted hat!
I'll give it a head to fit it pat.
Thank you! No cravat.

They handcuffed the body just for style,
And they hung him in chains for the
volatile
Wind to scour him flesh from bones.
Way out on the moor you can hear the
the groans
His gibbet makes when it blows a gale.
'Tis a common tale.

THE SHADOW

Paul Jannes was working very late,
For this watch must be done by eight
To-morrow or the Cardinal
Would certainly be vexed. Of all
His customers the old prelate
Was the most important, for his state
Descended to his watches and rings,
And he gave his mistresses many things
To make them forget his age and smile
When he paid his visits, and they could
while
The time away with a diamond locket
Exceedingly well. So they picked his
pocket,
And he paid in jewels for his slobbering
kisses.
This watch was made to buy him blisses
From an Austrian countess on her way
Home, and she meant to start next day.
Paul worked by the pointed, tulip flame
Of a tallow candle, and became
So absorbed, that his old clock made him
wince

Striking the hour a moment since.
Its echo, only half apprehended,
Lingered about the room. He ended
Screwing the little rubies in,
Setting the wheels to lock and spin,
Curling the infinitesimal springs,
Fixing the filigree hands. Chippings
Of precious stones lay strewn about.
The table before him was a rout
Of splashes and sparks of coloured light.
There was yellow gold in sheets, and quite
A heap of emeralds, and steel.
Here was a gem, there was a wheel.
And glasses lay like limpid lakes
Shining and still, and there were flakes
Of silver, and shavings of pearl,
And little wires all awhirl
With the light of the candle. He took the watch
And wound its hands about to match
The time, then glanced up to take the hour
From the hanging clock.
                Good, Merciful Power!
How came that shadow on the wall,
No woman was in the room! His tall
Chiffonier stood gaunt behind
His chair. His old cloak, rabbit-lined,
Hung from a peg. The door was closed.
Just for a moment he must have dozed.
He looked again, and saw it plain.
The silhouette made a blue-black stain
On the opposite wall, and it never wavered
Even when the candle quavered
Under his panting breath. What made
That beautiful, dreadful thing, that shade
Of something so lovely, so exquisite,
Cast from a substance which the sight
Had not been tutored to perceive?
Paul brushed his eyes across his sleeve.

Clear-cut, the Shadow on the wall
Gleamed black, and never moved at all.

Paul's watches were like amulets,
Wrought into patterns and rosettes;
The cases were all set with stones,
And wreathing lines, and shining zones.
He knew the beauty in a curve,
And the Shadow tortured every nerve
With its perfect rhythm of outline
Cutting the whitewashed wall. So fine
Was the neck he knew he could have spanned

It about with the fingers of one hand.
The chin rose to a mouth he guessed,
But could not see, the lips were pressed
Loosely together, the edges close,
And the proud and delicate line of the nose
Melted into a brow, and there
Broke into undulant waves of hair.
The lady was edged with the stamp of race.
A singular vision in such a place.

He moved the candle to the tall
Chiffonier; the Shadow stayed on the wall.
He threw his cloak upon a chair,
And still the lady's face was there.
From every corner of the room
He saw, in the patch of light, the gloom
That was the lady. Her violet bloom
Was almost brighter than that which came
From his candle's tulip-flame.
He set the filigree hands; he laid
The watch in the case which he had made;
He put on his rabbit cloak, and snuffed
His candle out. The room seemed stuffed
With darkness. Softly he crossed the floor,
And let himself out through the door.

The sun was flashing from every pin
And wheel, when Paul let himself in.
The whitewashed walls were hot with light.
The room was the core of chrysolite,
Burning and simmering with fiery might.
The sun was so bright that no shadow could fall
From the furniture upon the wall.
Paul sighed as he looked at the empty space
Where a glare usurped the lady's place.
He settled himself to his work, but his mind
Wandered, and he would wake to find
His hand suspended, his eyes grown dim,
And nothing advanced beyond the rim
Of his dreaming. The Cardinal sent to pay
For his watch, which had purchased so fine a day.
But Paul could hardly touch the gold,
It seemed the price of his Shadow, sold.

With the first twilight he struck a match
And watched the little blue stars hatch
Into an egg of perfect flame.
He lit his candle, and almost in shame
At his eagerness, lifted his eyes.
The Shadow was there, and its precise
Outline etched the cold, white wall.
The young man swore, "By God! You, Paul,
There's something the matter with your brain.
Go home now and sleep off the strain."

The next day was a storm, the rain
Whispered and scratched at the window-pane.
A grey and shadowless morning filled
The little shop. The watches, chilled,
Were dead and sparkless as burnt-out coals.
The gems lay on the table like shoals
Of stranded shells, their colours faded,
Mere heaps of stone, dull and degraded.
Paul's head was heavy, his hands obeyed
No orders, for his fancy strayed.
His work became a simple round
Of watches repaired and watches wound.
The slanting ribbons of the rain
Broke themselves on the window-pane,
But Paul saw the silver lines in vain.
Only when the candle was lit
And on the wall just opposite
He watched again the coming of IT,
Could he trace a line for the joy of his soul
And over his hands regain control.

Paul lingered late in his shop that night
And the designs which his delight
Sketched on paper seemed to be
A tribute offered wistfully
To the beautiful shadow of her who came
And hovered over his candle flame.
In the morning he selected all
His perfect jacinths. One large opal
Hung like a milky, rainbow moon
In the centre, and blown in loose festoon
The red stones quivered on silver threads
To the outer edge, where a single, fine
Band of mother-of-pearl the line
Completed. On the other side,
The creamy porcelain of the face
Bore diamond hours, and no lace
Of cotton or silk could ever be
Tossed into being more airily

Than the filmy golden hands; the time
Seemed to tick away in rhyme.
When, at dusk, the Shadow grew
Upon the wall, Paul's work was through.
Holding the watch, he spoke to her:
"Lady, Beautiful Shadow, stir
Into one brief sign of being.
Turn your eyes this way, and seeing
This watch, made from those sweet curves
Where your hair from your forehead swerves,
Accept the gift which I have wrought
With your fairness in my thought.
Grant me this, and I shall be
Honoured overwhelmingly."

The Shadow rested black and still,
And the wind sighed over the window-sill.
Paul put the despised watch away
And laid out before him his array
Of stones and metals, and when the morning
Struck the stones to their best adorning,
He chose the brightest, and this new watch
Was so light and thin it seemed to catch
The sunlight's nothingness, and its gleam.
Topazes ran in a foamy stream
Over the cover, the hands were studded
With garnets, and seemed red roses, budded.
The face was of crystal, and engraved
Upon it the figures flashed and waved
With zircons, and beryls, and amethysts.
It took a week to make, and his trysts
At night with the Shadow were his alone.
Paul swore not to speak till his task was done.
The night that the jewel was worthy to give,
Paul watched the long hours of daylight live
To the faintest streak; then lit his light,
And sharp against the wall's pure white
The outline of the Shadow started
Into form. His burning-hearted
Words so long imprisoned swelled
To tumbling speech. Like one compelled,
He told the lady all his love,
And holding out the watch above
His head, he knelt, imploring some
Littlest sign.
                    The Shadow was dumb.

Weeks passed, Paul worked in fevered
haste,
And everything he made he placed
Before his lady. The Shadow kept
Its perfect passiveness. Paul wept.
He wooed her with the work of his hands,
He waited for those dear commands
She never gave. No word, no motion,
Eased the ache of his devotion.
His days passed in a strain of toil,
His nights burnt up in a seething coil.
Seasons shot by, uncognisant
He worked. The Shadow came to haunt
Even his days. Sometimes quite plain
He saw on the wall the blackberry stain
Of his lady's picture. No sun was bright
Enough to dazzle that from his sight.

There were moments when he groaned to
see
His life spilled out so uselessly,
Begging for boons the Shade refused,
His finest workmanship abused,
The iridescent bubbles he blew
Into lovely existence, poor and few
In the shadowed eyes. Then he would
curse
Himself and her! The Universe!
And more, the beauty he could not make,
And give her, for her comfort's sake!
He would beat his weary, empty hands
Upon the table, would hold up strands
Of silver and gold, and ask her why
She scorned the best which he could buy.
He would pray as to some high-niched
saint,
That she would cure him of the taint
Of failure. He would clutch the wall
With his bleeding fingers, if she should fall
He could catch, and hold her, and make
her live!
With sobs he would ask her to forgive
All he had done. And broken, spent,
He would call himself impertinent;
Presumptuous; a tradesman; a nothing;
driven
To madness by the sight of Heaven.
At other times he would take the things
He had made, and winding them on
strings,
Hang garlands before her, and burn per-
fumes,
Chanting strangely, while the fumes
Wreathed and blotted the shadow face,
As with a cloudy, nacreous lace.

There were days when he wooed as a
lover, sighed
In tenderness, spoke to his bride,
Urged her to patience, said his skill
Should break the spell. A man's sworn
will
Could compass life, even that, he knew.
By Christ's Blood! He would prove it
true!
The edge of the Shadow never blurred.
The lips of the Shadow never stirred.

He would climb on chairs to reach her
lips,
And pat her hair with his finger-tips.
But instead of young, warm flesh return-
ing
His warmth, the wall was cold and burn-
ing
Like stinging ice, and his passion, chilled,
Lay in his heart like some dead thing
killed
At the moment of birth. Then, deadly
sick,
He would lie in a swoon for hours, while
thick
Phantasmagoria crowded his brain,
And his body shrieked in the clutch of
pain.
The crisis passed, he would wake and
smile
With a vacant joy, half-imbecile
And quite confused, not being certain
Why he was suffering; a curtain
Fallen over the tortured mind beguiled
His sorrow. Like a little child
He would play with his watches and
gems, with glee
Calling the Shadow to look and see
How the spots on the ceiling danced
prettily
When he flashed his stones. "Mother,
the green
Has slid so cunningly in between
The blue and the yellow. Oh, please look
down!"
Then, with a pitiful, puzzled frown,
He would get up slowly from his play
And walk round the room, feeling his way
From table to chair, from chair to door,
Stepping over the cracks in the floor,
Till reaching the table again, her face
Would bring recollection, and no solace
Could balm his hurt till unconsciousness.
Stifled him and his great distress.

One morning he threw the street door
wide
On coming in, and his vigorous stride
Made the tools on his table rattle and
jump.
In his hands he carried a new-burst clump
Of laurel blossoms, whose smooth-barked
stalks
Were pliant with sap. As a husband talks
To the wife he left an hour ago,
Paul spoke to the Shadow. "Dear, you
know
To-day the calendar calls it Spring,
And I woke this morning gathering
Asphodels, in my dreams, for you.
So I rushed out to see what flowers blew
Their pink-and-purple-scented souls
Across the town-wind's dusty scrolls,
And made the approach to the Market
Square
A garden with smells and sunny air.
I feel so well and happy to-day,
I think I shall take a Holiday.
And to-night we will have a little treat.
I am going to bring you something to
eat!"
He looked at the Shadow anxiously.
It was quite grave and silent. He
Shut the outer door and came
And leant against the window-frame.
"Dearest," he said, "we live apart
Although I bear you in my heart.
We look out each from a different world.
At any moment we may be hurled
Asunder. They follow their orbits, we
Obey their laws entirely.
Now you must come, or I go there,
Unless we are willing to live the flare
Of a lighted instant and have it gone."

A bee in the laurels began to drone.
A loosened petal fluttered prone.

"Man grows by eating, if you eat
You will be filled with our life, sweet
Will be our planet in your mouth.
If not, I must parch in death's wide
drouth
Until I gain to where you are,
And give you myself in whatever star
May happen. O You Beloved of Me!
Is it not ordered cleverly?"
The Shadow, bloomed like a plum, and
clear,
Hung in the sunlight. It did not hear.

Paul slipped away as the dusk began
To dim the little shop. He ran
To the nearest inn, and chose with care
As much as his thin purse could bear.
As rapt-souled monks watch over the
baking
Of the sacred wafer, and through the
making
Of the holy wine whisper secret prayers
That God will bless this labour of theirs;
So Paul, in a sober ecstasy,
Purchased the best which he could buy.
Returning, he brushed his tools aside,
And laid across the table a wide
Napkin. He put a glass and plate
On either side, in duplicate.
Over the lady's, excellent
With loveliness, the laurels bent.
In the centre the white-flaked pastry
stood,
And beside it the wine flask. Red as
blood
Was the wine which should bring the
lustihood
Of human life to his lady's veins.
When all was ready, all which pertains
To a simple meal was there, with eyes
Lit by the joy of his great emprise,
He reverently bade her come,
And forsake for him her distant home.
He put meat on her plate and filled her
glass,
And waited what should come to pass.

The Shadow lay quietly on the wall.
From the street outside came a watch-
man's call:
"A cloudy night. Rain beginning to fall."

And still he waited. The clock's slow tick
Knocked on the silence. Paul turned sick.
He filled his own glass full of wine;
From his pocket he took a paper. The
twine
Was knotted, and he searched a knife
From his jumbled tools. The cord of life
Snapped as he cut the little string.
He knew that he must do the thing
He feared. He shook powder into the
wine,
And holding it up so the candle's shine
Sparked a ruby through its heart,
He drank it. "Dear, never apart
Again! You have said it was mine to do.
It is done, and I am come to you!"

Paul Jannes let the empty wine-glass fall,
And held out his arms. The insentient
wall
Stared down at him with its cold, white
glare
Unstained! The Shadow was not there!
Paul clutched and tore at his tightening
throat.
He felt the veins in his body bloat,
And the hot blood run like fire and
stones
Along the sides of his cracking bones.
But he laughed as he staggered towards
the door,
And he laughed aloud as he sank on the
floor.

The Coroner took the body away,
And the watches were sold that Saturday.
The Auctioneer said one could seldom
buy
Such watches, and the prices were high.

THE FORSAKEN

Holy Mother of God, Merciful Mary.
Hear me! I am very weary. I have come
from a village miles away, all day I have
been coming, and I ache for such far
roaming. I cannot walk as light as I
used, and my thoughts grow confused. I
am heavier than I was. Mary Mother,
you know the cause!

Beautiful Holy Lady, take my shame
away from me! Let this fear be only
seeming, let it be that I am dreaming.
For months I have hoped it was so, now
I am afraid I know. Lady, why should
this be shame, just because I haven't got
his name. He loved me, yes, Lady, he
did, and he couldn't keep it hid. We
meant to marry. Why did he die?

That day when they told me he had
gone down in the avalanche, and could
not be found until the snow melted in
Spring, I did nothing. I could not cry.
Why should he die? Why should he die
and his child live? His little child alive
in me, for my comfort. No, Good God,
for my misery! I cannot face the shame,
to be a mother, and not married, and the
poor child to be reviled for having no
father. Merciful Mother, Holy Virgin,

take away this sin I did. Let the baby
not be. Only take the stigma off of me!

I have told no one but you, Holy Mary.
My mother would call me "whore," and
spit upon me; the priest would have me
repent, and have the rest of my life spent
in a convent. I am no whore, no bad
woman, he loved me, and we were to be
married. I carried him always in my
heart, what did it matter if I gave him
the least part of me too? You were a
virgin, Holy Mother, but you had a son,
you know there are times when a woman
must give all. There is some call to give
and hold back nothing. I swear I obeyed
God then, and this child who lives in me
is the sign. What am I saying? He is
dead, my beautiful, strong man! I shall
never feel him caress me again. This is
the only baby I shall have. Oh, Holy
Virgin, protect my baby! My little, helpless baby!

He will look like his father, and he
will be as fast a runner and as good a
shot. Not that he shall be no scholar
neither. He shall go to school in winter,
and learn to read and write, and my
father will teach him to carve, so that he
can make the little horses, and cows, and
chamois, out of white wood. Oh, No!
No! No! How can I think such things,
I am not good. My father will have
nothing to do with my boy, I shall be
an outcast thing. Oh, Mother of our
Lord God, be merciful, take away my
shame! Let my body be as it was before
he came. No little baby for me to keep
underneath my heart for those long
months. To live for and to get comfort
from. I cannot go home and tell my
mother. She is so hard and righteous. She
never loved my father, and we were born
for duty, not for love. I cannot face it.
Holy Mother, take my baby away! Take
away my little baby! I don't want it, I
can't bear it!

And I shall have nothing, nothing! Just
be known as a good girl. Have other men
want to marry me, whom I could not
touch, after having known my man.
Known the length and breadth of his
beautiful white body, and the depth of

his love, on the high Summer Alp, with
the moon above, and the pine-needles all
shiny in the light of it. He is gone, my
man, I shall never hear him or feel him
again, but I could not touch another. I
would rather lie under the snow with my
own man in my arms!

So I shall live on and on. Just a good
woman. With nothing to warm my heart
where he lay, and where he left his baby
for me to care for. I shall not be quite
human, I think. Merely a stone-dead
creature. They will respect me. What
do I care for respect! You didn't care for
people's tongues when you were carrying
our Lord Jesus. God had my man give
me my baby, when He knew that He was
going to take him away. His lips will
comfort me, his hands will soothe me.
All day I will work at my lace-making and
all night I will keep him warm by my side
and pray the blessed Angels to cover him
with their wings. Dear Mother, what is
it that sings? I hear voices singing, and
lovely silver trumpets through it all. They
seem just on the other side of the wall.
Let me keep my baby, Holy Mother. He
is only a poor lace-maker's baby, with a
stain upon him, but give me strength to
bring him up to be a man.

LATE SEPTEMBER

Tang of fruitage in the air;
Red boughs bursting everywhere;
Shimmering of seeded grass;
Hooded gentians all a'mass.

Warmth of earth, and cloudless wind
Tearing off the husky rind,
Blowing feathered seeds to fall
By the sun-baked, sheltering wall.

Beech trees in a golden haze;
Hardy sumachs all ablaze,
Glowing through the silver birches.
How that pine tree shouts and lurches!

From the sunny door-jamb high,
Swings the shell of a butterfly.
Scrape of insect violins
Through the stubble shrilly dins.

Every blade's a minaret
Where a small muezzin's set,

Loudly calling us to pray
At the miracle of day.

Then the purple-lidded night
Westering comes, her footsteps light
Guided by the radiant boon
Of a sickle-shaped new moon.

THE PIKE

In the brown water,
Thick and silver-sheened in the sunshine,
Liquid and cool in the shade of the reeds,
A pike dozed.
Lost among the shadows of stems
He lay unnoticed.
Suddenly he flicked his tail,
And a green-and-copper brightness
Ran under the water.

Out from under the reeds
Came the olive-green light,
And orange flashed up
Through the sun-thickened water.
So the fish passed across the pool,
Green and copper,
A darkness and a gleam,
And the blurred reflections of the willows
    on the opposite bank
Received it.

THE BLUE SCARF

Pale, with the blue of high zeniths, shim-
    mered over the silver, brocaded
In smooth, running patterns, a soft stuff,
    with dark knotted fringes, it lies there,
Warm from a woman's soft shoulders,
    and my fingers close on it, caressing.
Where is she, the woman who wore it?
    The scent of her lingers and drugs me!
A languor, fire-shotted, runs through me,
    and I crush the scarf down on my face,
And gulp in the warmth and the blue-
    ness, and my eyes swim in cool-tinted
    heavens.
Around me are columns of marble, and
    a diapered, sun-flickered pavement.
Rose-leaves blow and patter against it.
Below the stone steps a lute tinkles.

A jar of green jade throws its shadow
    half over the floor. A big-bellied
Frog hops through the sunlight and plops
    in the gold-bubbled water of a basin,

Sunk in the black and white marble. The
west wind has lifted a scarf
On the seat close beside me, the blue of
it is a violent outrage of colour.
She draws it more closely about her, and
it ripples beneath her slight stirring.
Her kisses are sharp buds of fire; and I
burn back against her, a jewel
Hard and white; a stalked, flaming flower;
till I break to a handful of cinders,
And open my eyes to the scarf, shining
blue in the afternoon sunshine.

How loud clocks can tick when a room
is empty, and one is alone!

WHITE AND GREEN

Hey! My daffodil-crowned,
Slim and without sandals!
As the sudden spurt of flame upon darkness
So my eyeballs are startled with you,
Supple-limbed youth among the fruit-
trees,
Light runner through tasselled orchards.
You are an almond flower unsheathed
Leaping and flickering between the
budded branches.

AUBADE

As I would free the white almond from
the green husk
So would I strip your trappings off,
Beloved.
And fingering the smooth and polished
kernel
I should see that in my hands glittered a
gem beyond counting.

MUSIC

The neighbour sits in his window and
plays the flute.
From my bed I can hear him,
And the round notes flutter and tap about
the room,
And hit against each other,
Blurring to unexpected chords.
It is very beautiful,
With the little flute-notes all about me,
In the darkness.

In the daytime,
The neighbour eats bread and onions with
one hand
And copies music with the other.

He is fat and has a bald head,
So I do not look at him,
But run quickly past his window.
There is always the sky to look at,
Or the water in the well!

But when night comes and he plays his
flute,
I think of him as a young man,
With gold seals hanging from his watch,
And a blue coat with silver buttons.
As I lie in my bed
The flute-notes push against my ears and
lips,
And I go to sleep, dreaming.

A LADY

You are beautiful and faded
Like an old opera tune
Played upon a harpsichord;
Or like the sun-flooded silks
Of an eighteenth-century boudoir.
In your eyes
Smoulder the fallen roses of out-lived
minutes,
And the perfume of your soul
Is vague and suffusing,
With the pungence of sealed spice-jars.
Your half-tones delight me,
And I grow mad with gazing
At your blent colours.

My vigour is a new-minted penny,
Which I cast at your feet.
Gather it up from the dust,
That its sparkle may amuse you.

IN A GARDEN

Gushing from the mouths of stone men
To spread at ease under the sky
In granite-lipped basins,
Where iris dabble their feet
And rustle to a passing wind,
The water fills the garden with its rush-
ing,
In the midst of the quiet of close-clipped
lawns.

Damp smell the ferns in tunnels of stone,
Where trickle and plash the fountains,
Marble fountains, yellowed with much
water.

Splashing down moss-tarnished steps
It falls, the water;

And the air is throbbing with it.
With its gurgling and running.
With its leaping, and deep, cool murmur.

And I wished for night and you.
I wanted to see you in the swimming-
pool,
White and shining in the silver-flecked
water.
While the moon rode over the garden,
High in the arch of night,
And the scent of the lilacs was heavy with
stillness.

Night, and the water, and you in your
whiteness, bathing!

A TULIP GARDEN

Guarded within the old red wall's em-
brace,
Marshalled like soldiers in gay company,
The tulips stand arrayed. Here in-
fantry
Wheels out into the sunlight. What bold
grace
Sets off their tunics, white with crimson
lace!
Here are platoons of gold-frocked
cavalry,
With scarlet sabres tossing in the eye
Of purple batteries, every gun in place.
Forward they come, with flaunting
colours spread,
With torches burning, stepping out in
time
To some quick, unheard march. Our
ears are dead,
We cannot catch the tune. In panto-
mime
Parades that army. With our utmost
powers
We hear the wind stream through a
bed of flowers.

MEN, WOMEN AND GHOSTS

FIGURINES IN OLD SAXE

PATTERNS

I walk down the garden paths,
And all the daffodils
Are blowing, and the bright blue squills.
I walk down the patterned garden-paths
In my stiff, brocaded gown.
With my powdered hair and jewelled fan,
I too am a rare
Pattern. As I wander down
The garden paths.

My dress is richly figured,
And the train
Makes a pink and silver stain
On the gravel, and the thrift
Of the borders.
Just a plate of current fashion
Tripping by in high-heeled, ribboned
shoes.
Not a softness anywhere about me,
Only whalebone and brocade.
And I sink on a seat in the shade
Of a lime tree. For my passion
Wars against the stiff brocade.
The daffodils and squills
Flutter in the breeze
As they please.
And I weep;
For the lime-tree is in blossom
And one small flower has dropped upon
my bosom.

And the plashing of waterdrops
In the marble fountain
Comes down the garden-paths.
The dripping never stops.
Underneath my stiffened gown
Is the softness of a woman bathing in a
marble basin,
A basin in the midst of hedges grown
So thick, she cannot see her lover hiding,
But she guesses he is near,
And the sliding of the water
Seems the stroking of a dear
Hand upon her.
What is Summer in a fine brocaded gown!

I should like to see it lying in a heap
upon the ground.
All the pink and silver crumpled up on
the ground.

I would be the pink and silver as I ran
along the paths,
And he would stumble after,
Bewildered by my laughter.
I should see the sun flashing from his
sword-hilt and buckles on his shoes.
I would choose
To lead him in a maze along the pat-
terned paths,
A bright and laughing maze for my heavy-
booted lover.
Till he caught me in the shade,
And the buttons of his waistcoat bruised
my body as he clasped me,
Aching, melting, unafraid.
With the shadows of the leaves and the
sundrops,
And the plopping of the waterdrops,
All about us in the open afternoon —
I am very like to swoon
With the weight of this brocade,
For the sun sifts through the shade.

Underneath the fallen blossom
In my bosom,
Is a letter I have hid.
It was brought to me this morning by a
rider from the Duke.
"Madam, we regret to inform you that
Lord Hartwell
Died in action Thursday se'nnight."
As I read it in the white, morning sun-
light,
The letters squirmed like snakes.
"Any answer, Madam," said my footman.
"No," I told him.
"See that the messenger takes some re-
freshment.
No, no answer."
And I walked into the garden,
Up and down the patterned paths,
In my stiff, correct brocade.

The blue and yellow flowers stood up
proudly in the sun,
Each one.
I stood upright too,
Held rigid to the pattern
By the stiffness of my gown.
Up and down I walked.
Up and down.

In a month he would have been my
husband.
In a month, here, underneath this lime,
We would have broken the pattern;
He for me, and I for him,
He as Colonel, I as Lady,
On this shady seat.
He had a whim
That sunlight carried blessing.
And I answered, "It shall be as you have
said."
Now he is dead.

In Summer and in Winter I shall walk
Up and down
The patterned garden-paths
In my stiff, brocaded gown.
The squills and daffodils
Will give place to pillared roses, and to
asters, and to snow.
I shall go
Up and down,
In my gown.
Gorgeously arrayed,
Boned and stayed.
And the softness of my body will be
guarded from embrace
By each button, hook, and lace.
For the man who should loose me is
dead,
Fighting with the Duke in Flanders,
In a pattern called a war.
Christ! What are patterns for?

PICKTHORN MANOR

I

How fresh the Dartle's little waves that
day!
A steely silver, underlined with blue,
And flashing where the round clouds,
blown away,
Let drop the yellow sunshine to gleam
through
And tip the edges of the waves with
shifts

And spots of whitest fire, hard like
gems
Cut from the midnight moons they
were, and sharp
As wind through leafless stems.
The Lady Eunice walked between the
drifts
Of blooming cherry-trees, and watched
the rifts
Of clouds drawn through the
river's azure warp.

II

Her little feet tapped softly down the
path.
Her soul was listless; even the morning
breeze
Fluttering the trees and strewing a light
swath
Of fallen petals on the grass, could
please
Her not at all. She brushed a hair aside
With a swift move, and a half-angry
frown.
She stopped to pull a daffodil or
two,
And held them to her gown
To test the colours; put them at her
side,
Then at her breast, and loosened them
and tried
Some new arrangement, but it
would not do.

III

A lady in a Manor-house, alone,
Whose husband is in Flanders with
the Duke
Of Marlborough and Prince Eugene, she's
grown
Too apathetic even to rebuke
Her idleness. What is she on this Earth?
No woman surely, since she neither
can
Be wed nor single, must not let her
mind
Build thoughts upon a man
Except for hers. Indeed that were no
dearth
Were her Lord here, for well she knew
his worth,
And when she thought of him
her eyes were kind.

IV

Too lately wed to have forgot the wooing.
Too unaccustomed as a bride to feel
Other than strange delight at her wife's
  doing.
Even at the thought a gentle blush
  would steal
Over her face, and then her lips would
  frame
Some little word of loving, and her
  eyes
  Would brim and spill their tears,
    when all they saw
Was the bright sun, slantwise
Through burgeoning trees, and all the
  morning's flame
Burning and quivering round her. With
  quick shame
She shut her heart and bent be-
  fore the law.

V

He was a soldier, she was proud of that.
This was his house and she would keep
  it well.
His honour was in fighting, hers in what
He'd left her here in charge of. Then
  a spell
Of conscience sent her through the or-
  chard spying
Upon the gardeners. Were their tools
  about?
  Were any branches broken? Had
    the weeds
Been duly taken out
Under the 'spaliered pears, and were
  these lying
Nailed snug against the sunny bricks and
  drying
  Their leaves and satisfying all their
    needs?

VI

She picked a stone up with a little pout,
Stones looked so ill in well-kept flower-
  borders.
Where should she put it? All the paths
  about
Were strewn with fair, red gravel by
  her orders.
No stone could mar their sifted smoothness. So

She hurried to the river. At the
  edge
  She stood a moment charmed by the
    swift blue
Beyond the river sedge.
She watched it curdling, crinkling, and
  the snow
Purfled upon its wave-tops. Then, "Hullo,
  My beauty, gently, or you'll wrig-
    gle through."

VII

The Lady Eunice caught a willow spray
To save herself from tumbling in the
  shallows
Which rippled to her feet. Then straight
  away
She peered down stream among the
  budding sallows.
A youth in leather breeches and a shirt
Of finest broidered lawn lay out upon
  An overhanging bole and deftly
    swayed
  A well-hooked fish which shone
In the pale lemon sunshine like a spurt
Of silver, bowed and damascened, and
  girt
  With crimson spots and moons
    which waned and played.

VIII

The fish hung circled for a moment,
  ringed
And bright; then flung itself out, a
  thin blade
Of spotted lightning, and its tail was
  winged
With chipped and sparkled sunshine.
  And the shade
Broke up and splintered into shafts of
  light
Wheeling about the fish, who churned
  the air
  And made the fish-line hum, and
    bent the rod
Almost to snapping. Care
The young man took against the twigs,
  with slight,
Deft movements he kept fish and line
  in tight
  Obedience to his will with every
    prod.

IX

He lay there, and the fish hung just
    beyond.
He seemed uncertain what more he
    should do.
He drew back, pulled the rod to corre-
    spond,
Tossed it and caught it; every time he
    threw,
He caught it nearer to the point. At last
The fish was near enough to touch. He
    paused.
Eunice knew well the craft —
    "What's got the thing!"
She cried. "What can have caused —
Where is his net? The moment will be
    past.
The fish will wriggle free." She stopped
    aghast.
    He turned and bowed. One arm
        was in a sling.

X

The broad, black ribbon she had thought
    his basket
Must hang from, held instead a useless
    arm.
"I do not wonder, Madam, that you ask
    it."
He smiled, for she had spoke aloud.
    "The charm
Of trout fishing is in my eyes enhanced
When you must play your fish on land
    as well."
    "How will you take him?" Eunice
    asked. "In truth
I really cannot tell.
'Twas stupid of me, but it simply chanced
I never thought of that until he glanced
    Into the branches. 'Tis a bit un-
        couth."

XI

He watched the fish against the blowing
    sky,
Writhing and glittering, pulling at the
    line.
"The hook is fast, I might just let him
    die,"
He mused. "But that would jar against
    your fine
Sense of true sportsmanship, I know it
    would,"

Cried Eunice. "Let me do it." Swift
    and light
She ran towards him. "It is so long
    now
Since I have felt a bite,
I lost all heart for everything." She
    stood,
Supple and strong, beside him, and her
    blood
    Tingled her lissom body to a glow.

XII

She quickly seized the fish and with a
    stone
Ended its flurry, then removed the
    hook,
Untied the fly with well-poised fingers.
    Done,
She asked him where he kept his fish-
    ing-book.
He pointed to a coat flung on the
    ground.
She searched the pockets, found a sha-
    green case,
    Replaced the fly, noticed a golden
    stamp
Filling the middle space.
Two letters half rubbed out were there,
    and round
About them gay rococo flowers wound
    And tossed a spray of roses to
    the clamp.

XIII

The Lady Eunice puzzled over these.
    "G.D." the young man gravely said.
    "My name
Is Gervase Deane. Your servant, if you
    please."
"Oh, Sir, indeed I know you, for your
    fame
For exploits in the field has reached my
    ears.
I did not know you wounded and
    returned."
    "But just come back, Madam. A
    silly prick
To gain me such unearned
Holiday making. And you, it appears,
Must be Sir Everard's lady. And my
    fears
    At being caught a-trespassing were
    quick."

XIV

He looked so rueful that she laughed out
    loud.
"You are forgiven, Mr. Deane. Even
    more,
I offer you the fishing, and am proud
That you should find it pleasant from
    this shore.
Nobody fishes now, my husband used
    To angle daily, and I too with him.
    He loved the spotted trout, and pike,
      and dace,
    He even had a whim
That flies my fingers tied swiftly confused
The greater fish. And he must be ex-
    cused,
    Love weaves odd fancies in a
      lonely place."

XV

She sighed because it seemed so long ago,
    Those days with Everard; unthinking
      took
The path back to the orchard. Strolling
    so
She walked, and he beside her. In a
    nook
Where a stone seat withdrew beneath low
    boughs,
Full-blossomed, hummed with bees,
    they sat them down.
    She questioned him about the war,
    the share
Her husband had, and grown
Eager by his clear answers, straight allows
Her hidden hopes and fears to speak,
    and rouse
    Her numbed love, which had
    slumbered unaware.

XVI

Under the orchard trees daffodils danced
    And jostled, turning sideways to the
    wind.
A dropping cherry petal softly glanced
    Over her hair, and slid away behind.
At the far end through twisted cherry-
    trees
    The old house glowed, geranium-hued,
      with bricks
      Bloomed in the sun like roses, low
      and long,
Gabled, and with quaint tricks

Of chimneys carved and fretted. Out of
    these
Grey smoke was shaken, which the faint
    Spring breeze
    Tossed into nothing. Then a
    thrush's song

XVII

Needled its way through sound of bees
    and river.
    The notes fell, round and starred,
      between young leaves,
Trilled to a spiral lilt, stopped on a
    quiver.
The Lady Eunice listens and believes.
Gervase has many tales of her dear Lord,
    His bravery, his knowledge, his charmed
    life.
    She quite forgets who's speaking in
    the gladness
Of being this man's wife.
Gervase is wounded, grave indeed, the
    word
Is kindly said, but to a softer chord
    She strings her voice to ask with
    wistful sadness,

XVIII

"And is Sir Everard still unscathed? I
    fain
    Would know the truth." "Quite well,
    dear Lady, quite."
She smiled in her content. "So many
    slain,
    You must forgive me for a little
    fright."
And he forgave her, not alone for that,
But because she was fingering his heart,
    Pressing and squeezing it, and think-
    ing so
Only to ease her smart
Of painful, apprehensive longing. At
Their feet the river swirled and chucked.
    They sat
    An hour there. The thrush flew
    to and fro.

XIX

The Lady Eunice supped alone that day,
    As always since Sir Everard had gone,
In the oak-panelled parlour, whose array
    Of faded portraits in carved mouldings
    shone.

Warriors and ladies, armoured, ruffed,
     peruked.
Van Dykes with long, slim fingers; Hol-
     beins, stout
And heavy-featured; and one Rubens
     dame,
A peony just burst out,
With flaunting, crimson flesh. Eunice
     rebuked
Her thoughts of gentler blood, when
     these had duked
It with the best, and scorned to
     change their name.

XX

A sturdy family, and old besides,
     Much older than her own, the Earls
     of Crowe.
Since Saxon days, these men had sought
     their brides
Among the highest born, but always so,
Taking them to themselves, their wealth,
     their lands,
But never their titles. Stern perhaps,
     but strong,
The Framptons fed their blood from
     richest streams,
Scorning the common throng.
Gazing upon these men, she understands
The toughness of the web wrought from
     such strands,
     And pride of Everard colours all
     her dreams.

XXI

Eunice forgets to eat, watching their
     faces
     Flickering in the wind-blown candle's
     shine.
Blue-coated lackeys tiptoe to their places,
     And set out plates of fruit and jugs of
     wine.
The table glitters black like Winter ice.
     The Dartle's rushing, and the gentle
     clash
     Of blossomed branches, drifts into
     her ears.
And through the casement sash
She sees each cherry stem a pointed slice
Of splintered moonlight, topped with all
     the spice
     And shimmer of the blossoms it
     uprears.

XXII

"In such a night — " she laid the book
     aside,
     She could outnight the poet by think-
     ing back.
In such a night she came here as a bride.
     The date was graven in the almanack
Of her clasped memory. In this very
     room
     Had Everard uncloaked her. On this
     seat
     Had drawn her to him, bade her
     note the trees,
How white they were and sweet
And later, coming to her, her dear groom,
Her Lord, had lain beside her in the
     gloom
     Of moon and shade, and whis-
     pered her to ease.

XXIII

Her little taper made the room seem vast,
     Caverned and empty. And her beating
     heart
Rapped through the silence all about her
     cast
Like some loud, dreadful death-watch
     taking part
In this sad vigil. Slowly she undrest,
     Put out the light and crept into her
     bed.
     The linen sheets were fragrant, but
     so cold.
And brimming tears she shed,
Sobbing and quivering in her barren nest,
Her weeping lips into the pillow prest,
     Her eyes sealed fast within its
     smothering fold.

XXIV

The morning brought her a more stoic
     mind,
     And sunshine struck across the polished
     floor.
She wondered whether this day she should
     find
     Gervase a-fishing, and so listen more,
Much more again, to all he had to tell.
     And he was there, but waiting to begin
     Until she came. They fished awhile,
     then went
To the old seat within

The cherry's shade. He pleased her very
    well
By his discourse. But ever he must dwell
    Upon Sir Everard. Each incident

XXV

Must be related and each term explained.
    How troops were set in battle, how a
    siege
Was ordered and conducted. She com-
    plained
Because he bungled at the fall of Liége.
The curious names of parts of forts she
    knew,
    And aired with conscious pride her
    ravelins,
    And counterscarps, and lunes. The
    day drew on,
And his dead fish's fins
In the hot sunshine turned a mauve-green
    hue.
At last Gervase, guessing the hour, with-
    drew.
    But she sat long in still oblivion.

XXVI

Then he would bring her books, and read
    to her
    The poems of Dr. Donne, and the
    blue river
Would murmur through the reading, and
    a stir
Of birds and bees make the white
    petals shiver,
And one or two would flutter prone and
    lie
Spotting the smooth-clipped grass. The
    days went by
Threaded with talk and verses. Green
    leaves pushed
Through blossoms stubbornly.
Gervase, unconscious of dishonesty,
Fell into strong and watchful loving, free
    He thought, since always would
    his lips be hushed.

XXVII

But lips do not stay silent at command,
    And Gervase strove in vain to order his.
Luckily Eunice did not understand
    That he but read himself aloud, for
    this

Their friendship would have snapped.
    She treated him
And spoilt him like a brother. It was
    now
    "Gervase" and "Eunice" with them,
    and he dined
Whenever she'd allow,
In the oak parlour, underneath the dim
Old pictured Framptons, opposite her
    slim
    Figure, so bright against the chair
    behind.

XXVIII

Eunice was happier than she had been
    For many days, and yet the hours were
    long.
All Gervase told to her but made her
    lean
More heavily upon the past. Among
Her hopes she lived, even when she was
    giving
    Her morning orders, even when she
    twined
    Nosegays to deck her parlours. With
    the thought
Of Everard, her mind
Solaced its solitude, and in her striving
To do as he would wish was all her living.
    She welcomed Gervase for the
    news he brought.

XXIX

Black-hearts and white-hearts, bubbled
    with the sun,
    Hid in their leaves and knocked against
    each other.
Eunice was standing, panting with her
    run
Up to the tool-house just to get another
Basket. All those which she had brought
    were filled,
    And still Gervase pelted her from
    above.
    The buckles of his shoes flashed
    higher and higher
Until his shoulders strove
Quite through the top. "Eunice, your
    spirit's filled
This tree. White-hearts!" He shook, and
    cherries spilled
    And spat out from the leaves like
    falling fire.

XXX

The wide, sun-winged June morning
    spread itself
Over the quiet garden. And they
    packed
Full twenty baskets with the fruit. "My
    shelf
Of cordials will be stored with what it
    lacked.
In future, none of us will drink strong ale,
    But cherry-brandy." "Vastly good, I
    vow,"
    And Gervase gave the tree another
    shake.
The cherries seemed to flow
Out of the sky in cloudfuls, like blown
    hail.
Swift Lady Eunice ran, her farthingale,
    Unnoticed, tangling in a fallen
    rake.

XXXI

She gave a little cry and fell quite prone
In the long grass, and lay there very
    still.
Gervase leapt from the tree at her soft
    moan,
And kneeling over her, with clumsy
    skill
Unloosed her bodice, fanned her with his
    hat,
And his unguarded lips pronounced his
    heart.
    "Eunice, my Dearest Girl, where are
    you hurt?"
His trembling fingers dart
Over her limbs seeking some wound. She
    strove
To answer, opened wide her eyes, above
    Her knelt Sir Everard, with face
    alert.

XXXII

Her eyelids fell again at that sweet sight,
"My Love!" she murmured, "Dearest!
    Oh, my Dear!"
He took her in his arms and bore her
    right
And tenderly to the old seat, and
    "Here
I have you mine at last," she said, and
    swooned

Under his kisses. When she came once
    more
To sight of him, she smiled in com-
    fort knowing
Herself laid as before
Close covered on his breast. And all her
    glowing
Youth answered him, and ever nearer
    growing
She twined him in her arms and
    soft festooned

XXXIII

Herself about him like a flowering vine,
    Drawing his lips to cling upon her own.
A ray of sunlight pierced the leaves to
    shine
Where her half-opened bodice let be
    shown
Her white throat fluttering to his soft
    caress,
    Half-gasping with her gladness. And
    her pledge
She whispers, melting with delight.
    A twig
Snaps in the hornbeam hedge.
A cackling laugh tears through the quiet-
    ness.
Eunice starts up in terrible distress.
    "My God! What's that?" Her
    staring eyes are big.

XXXIV

Revulsed emotion set her body shaking
    As though she had an ague. Gervase
    swore,
Jumped to his feet in such a dreadful
    taking
His face was ghastly with the look it
    wore.
Crouching and slipping through the trees,
    a man
    In worn, blue livery, a humpbacked
    thing,
    Made off. But turned every few
    steps to gaze
At Eunice, and to fling
Vile looks and gestures back. "The ruf-
    fian!
By Christ's Death! I will split him to
    a span
    Of hog's thongs." She grasped at
    his sleeve, "Gervase!

XXXV

What are you doing here? Put down
    that sword,
That's only poor old Tony, crazed and
    lame.
We never notice him. With my dear
    Lord
I ought not to have minded that he
    came.
But, Gervase, it surprises me that you
    Should so lack grace to stay here."
    With one hand
She held her gaping bodice to conceal
Her breast. "I must demand
Your instant absence. Everard, but new
Returned, will hardly care for guests.
    Adieu."
    "Eunice, you're mad." His brain
    began to reel.

XXXVI

He tried again to take her, tried to twist
Her arms about him. Truly, she had
    said
Nothing should ever part them. In a mist
She pushed him from her, clasping her
    aching head
In both her hands, and rocked and
    sobbed aloud.
    "Oh! Where is Everard? What does
    this mean?
    So lately come to leave me thus
    alone!"
But Gervase had not seen
Sir Everard. Then, gently, to her bowed
And sickening spirit, he told of her proud
Surrender to him. He could hear
    her moan.

XXXVII

Then shame swept over her and held her
    numb,
    Hiding her anguished face against the
    seat.
At last she rose, a woman stricken —
    dumb —
And trailed away with slowly-dragging
    feet.
Gervase looked after her, but feared to
    pass
The barrier set between them. All his
    rare

Joy broke to fragments — worse than
    that, unreal.
And standing lonely there,
His swollen heart burst out, and on the
    grass
He flung himself and wept. He knew,
    alas!
The loss so great his life could
    never heal.

XXXVIII

For days thereafter Eunice lived retired,
    Waited upon by one old serving-maid.
She would not leave her chamber, and
    desired
Only to hide herself. She was afraid
Of what her eyes might trick her into
    seeing,
Of what her longing urge her then to do.
    What was this dreadful illness soli-
    tude
    Had tortured her into?
Her hours went by in a long constant
    fleeing
The thought of that one morning. And
    her being
    Bruised itself on a happening so
    rude.

XXXIX

It grew ripe Summer, when one morning
    came
    Her tirewoman with a letter, printed
Upon the seal were the Deane crest and
    name.
With utmost gentleness, the letter
    hinted
His understanding and his deep regret.
    But would she not permit him once
    again
    To pay her his profound respects?
    No word
Of what had passed should pain
Her resolution. Only let them get
Back the old comradeship. Her eyes
    were wet
    With starting tears, now truly she
    deplored

XL

His misery. Yes, she was wrong to keep
    Away from him. He hardly was to
    blame.

'Twas she — she shuddered and began to weep.
'Twas her fault! Hers! Her everlasting shame
Was that she suffered him, whom not at all
She loved. Poor Boy! Yes, they must still be friends.
She owed him that to keep the balance straight.
It was such poor amends
Which she could make for rousing hopes to gall
Him with their unfulfilment. Tragical
It was, and she must leave him desolate.

XLI

Hard silence he had forced upon his lips
For long and long, and would have done so still
Had not she — here she pressed her finger tips
Against her heavy eyes. Then with forced will
She wrote that he might come, sealed with the arms
Of Crowe and Frampton twined. Her heart felt lighter
When this was done. It seemed her constant care
Might some day cease to fright her.
Illness could be no crime, and dreadful harms
Did come from too much sunshine. Her alarms
Would lessen when she saw him standing there,

XLII

Simple and kind, a brother just returned
From journeying, and he would treat her so.
She knew his honest heart, and if there burned
A spark in it he would not let it show.
But when he really came, and stood beside
Her underneath the fruitless cherry boughs,
He seemed a tired man, gaunt, leaden-eyed.
He made her no more vows,

Nor did he mention one thing he had tried
To put into his letter. War supplied
Him topics. And his mind seemed occupied.

XLIII

Daily they met. And gravely walked and talked.
He read her no more verses, and he stayed
Only until their conversation, balked
Of every natural channel, fled dismayed.
Again the next day she would meet him, trying
To give her tone some healthy sprightliness,
But his uneager dignity soon chilled
Her well-prepared address.
Thus Summer waned, and in the mornings, crying
Of wild geese startled Eunice, and their flying
Whirred overhead for days and never stilled.

XLIV

One afternoon of grey clouds and white wind,
Eunice awaited Gervase by the river.
The Dartle splashed among the reeds and whined
Over the willow-roots, and a long sliver
Of caked and slobbered foam crept up the bank.
All through the garden, drifts of skirling leaves
Blew up, and settled down, and blew again.
The cherry-trees were weaves
Of empty, knotted branches, and a dank
Mist hid the house, mouldy it smelt and rank
With sodden wood, and still unfalling rain.

XLV

Eunice paced up and down. No joy she took
At meeting Gervase, but the custom grown

Still held her. He was late. She sudden
    shook,
And caught at her stopped heart. Her
    eyes had shown
Sir Everard emerging from the mist.
His uniform was travel-stained and torn,
    His jackboots muddy, and his eager
        stride
Jangled his spurs. A thorn
Entangled, trailed behind him. To the
    tryst
He hastened. Eunice shuddered, ran — a
    twist
    Round a sharp turning and she
        fled to hide.

XLVI

But he had seen her as she swiftly ran,
    A flash of white against the river's grey.
"Eunice," he called. "My darling. Eu-
    nice. Can
You hear me? It is Everard. All day
I have been riding like the very devil
    To reach you sooner. Are you startled,
        Dear?"
    He broke into a run and followed
        her,
And caught her, faint with fear,
Cowering and trembling as though she
    some evil
Spirit were seeing. "What means this
    uncivil
    Greeting, Dear Heart?" He saw
        her senses blur.

XLVII

Swaying and catching at the seat, she
    tried
    To speak, but only gurgled in her
        throat.
At last, straining to hold herself, she
    cried
    To him for pity, and her strange words
        smote
A coldness through him, for she begged
    Gervase
To leave her, 'twas too much a second
    time.
    Gervase must go, always Gervase, her
        mind
Repeated like a rhyme
This name he did not know. In sad
    amaze

He watched her, and that hunted, fearful
    gaze,
    So unremembering and so unkind.

XLVIII

Softly he spoke to her, patiently dealt
    With what he feared her madness. By
        and by
He pierced her understanding. Then he
    knelt
Upon the seat, and took her hands:
    "Now try
To think a minute I am come, my Dear,
    Unharmed and back on furlough. Are
        you glad
    To have your lover home again? To
        me,
Pickthorn has never had
A greater pleasantness. Could you not
    bear
To come and sit awhile beside me here?
    A stone between us surely should
        not be."

XLIX

She smiled a little wan and ravelled smile,
    Then came to him and on his shoulder
        laid
Her head, and they two rested there
    awhile,
    Each taking comfort. Not a word was
        said.
But when he put his hand upon her
    breast
    And felt her beating heart, and with
        his lips
    Sought solace for her and himself,
        She started
As one sharp lashed with whips,
And pushed him from her, moaning, his
    dumb quest
Denied and shuddered from. And he,
    distrest,
    Loosened his wife, and long they
        sat there, parted.

L

Eunice was very quiet all that day,
    A little dazed, and yet she seemed con-
        tent.
At candle-time, he asked if she would play
    Upon her harpsichord, at once she went

And tinkled airs from Lully's *Carnival*
   And *Bacchus*, newly brought away
     from France.
    Then jaunted through a lively riga-
     doon
    To please him with a dance
By Purcell, for he said that surely all
Good Englishmen had pride in national
   Accomplishment. But tiring of it
    soon

LI

He whispered her that if she had for-
   given
   His startling her that afternoon, the
    clock
Marked early bed-time. Surely it was
   Heaven
   He entered when she opened to his
    knock.
The hours rustled in the trailing wind
   Over the chimney. Close they lay and
    knew
    Only that they were wedded. At
     his touch
    Anxiety she threw
Away like a shed garment, and inclined
Herself to cherish him, her happy mind
    Quivering, unthinking, loving over-
     much.

LII

Eunice lay long awake in the cool
   night
   After her husband slept. She gazed with
    joy
Into the shadows, painting them with
   bright
   Pictures of all her future life's em-
    ploy.
Twin gems they were, set to a single
   jewel,
   Each shining with the other. Soft she
    turned
   And felt his breath upon her hair,
    and prayed
   Her happiness was earned.
Past Earls of Crowe should give their
   blood for fuel
To light this Frampton's hearth-fire. By
   no cruel
    Affrightings would she ever be
    dismayed.

LIII

When Everard, next day, asked her in
   joke
   What name it was that she had called
    him by,
She told him of Gervase, and as she
   spoke
   She hardly realized it was a lie.
Her vision she related, but she hid
   The fondness into which she had been
    led.
    Sir Everard just laughed and pinched
     her ear,
   And quite out of her head
The matter drifted. Then Sir Everard
   chid
Himself for laziness, and off he rid
    To see his men and count his
    farming-gear.

LIV

At supper he seemed overspread with
   gloom,
   But gave no reason why, he only asked
More questions of Gervase, and round the
   room
   He walked with restless strides. At last
    he tasked
Her with a greater feeling for this man
   Than she had given. Eunice quick
    denied
    The slightest interest other than a
    friend
   Might claim. But he replied
He thought she underrated. Then a ban
He put on talk and music. He'd a plan
    To work at, draining swamps at
    Pickthorn End.

LV

Next morning Eunice found her Lord
   still changed,
   Hard and unkind, with bursts of anger.
    Pride
Kept him from speaking out. His prob-
    ings ranged
   All round his torment. Lady Eunice
    tried
To sooth him. So a week went by, and
   then
   His anguish flooded over; with clenched
    hands

Striving to stem his words, he told
   her plain
Tony had seen them, "brands
Burning in Hell," the man had said.
   Again
Eunice described her vision, and how
   when
Awoke at last she had known
   dreadful pain.

LVI

He could not credit it, and misery fed
Upon his spirit, day by day it grew.
To Gervase he forbade the house, and led
The Lady Eunice such a life she flew
At his approaching footsteps. Winter
   came
Snowing and blustering through the
   Manor trees.
All the roof-edges spiked with icicles
In fluted companies.
The Lady Eunice with her tambour-frame
Kept herself sighing company. The flame
Of the birch fire glittered on the
   walls.

LVII

A letter was brought to her as she sat,
Unsealed, unsigned. It told her that
   his wound,
The writer's, had so well recovered that
To join his regiment he felt him bound.
But would she not wish him one short
   "Godspeed,"
He asked no more. Her greeting would
   suffice.
He had resolved he never should re-
   turn.
Would she this sacrifice
Make for a dying man? How could she
   read the rest! But forcing her
   eyes to the deed,
She read. Then dropped it in the
   fire to burn.

LVIII

Gervase had set the river for their meet-
   ing
As farthest from the farms where
   Everard
Spent all his days. How should he
   know such cheating
Was quite expected, at least no dullard

Was Everard Frampton. Hours by hours
   he hid
Among the willows watching. Dusk
   had come,
And from the Manor he had long
   been gone.
Eunice her burdensome
Task set about. Hooded and cloaked, she
   slid
Over the slippery paths, and soon amid
The sallows saw a boat tied to a
   stone.

LIX

Gervase arose, and kissed her hand, then
   pointed
Into the boat. She shook her head,
   but he
Begged her to realize why, and with dis-
   jointed
Words told her of what peril there
   might be
From listeners along the river bank.
A push would take them out of ear-
   shot. Ten
Minutes was all he asked, then she
   should land,
He go away again,
Forever this time. Yet how could he
   thank
Her for so much compassion. Here she
   sank
Upon a thwart, and bid him quick
   unstrand

LX

His boat. He cast the rope, and shoved
   the keel
Free of the gravel; jumped, and dropped
   beside
Her; took the oars, and they began to
   steal
Under the overhanging trees. A wide
Gash of red lantern-light cleft like a
   blade
Into the gloom, and struck on Eunice
   sitting
Rigid and stark upon the after
   thwart.
It blazed upon their flitting
In merciless light. A moment so it
   stayed,

Then was extinguished, and Sir Everard
made
One leap, and landed just a frac-
tion short.

LXI

His weight upon the gunwale tipped the
boat
To straining balance. Everard lurched
and seized
His wife and held her smothered to his
coat.
"Everard, loose me, we shall drown — "
and squeezed
Against him, she beat with her hands. He
gasped
"Never, by God!" The slidden boat
gave way
And the black foamy water split —
and met.
Bubbled up through the spray.
A wailing rose and in the branches rasped,
And creaked, and stilled. Over the tree-
tops, clasped
In the blue evening, a clear moon
was set.

LXII

They lie entangled in the twisting roots,
Embraced forever. Their cold marriage
bed
Close-canopied and curtained by the
shoots
Of willows and pale birches. At the
head,
White lilies, like still swans, placidly float
And sway above the pebbles. Here are
waves
Sun-smitten for a threaded counter-
pane
Gold-woven on their graves.
In perfect quietness they sleep, remote
In the green, rippled twilight. Death has
smote
Them to perpetual oneness who
were twain.

THE CREMONA VIOLIN

PART FIRST

Frau Concert-Meister Altgelt shut the
door.
A storm was rising, heavy gusts of wind

Swirled through the trees, and scattered
leaves before
Her on the clean, flagged path. The sky
behind
The distant town was black, and sharp
defined
Against it shone the lines of roofs and
towers,
Superimposed and flat like cardboard
flowers.

A pasted city on a purple ground,
Picked out with luminous paint, it
seemed. The cloud
Split on an edge of lightning, and a sound
Of rivers full and rushing boomed through
bowed,
Tossed, hissing branches. Thunder
rumbled loud
Beyond the town fast swallowing into
gloom.
Frau Altgelt closed the windows of each
room.

She bustled round to shake by constant
moving
The strange, weird atmosphere. She
stirred the fire,
She twitched the supper-cloth as though
improving
Its careful setting, then her own attire
Came in for notice, tiptoeing higher and
higher
She peered into the wall-glass, now ad-
justing
A straying lock, or else a ribbon thrusting

This way or that to suit her. At last
sitting,
Or rather plumping down upon a chair,
She took her work, the stocking she was
knitting,
And watched the rain upon the window
glare
In white, bright drops. Through the black
glass a flare
Of lightning squirmed about her needles.
"Oh!"
She cried. "What can be keeping Theo-
dore so!"

A roll of thunder set the casements clapping.
Frau Altgelt flung her work aside and
ran,

Pulled open the house door, with kerchief
    flapping
She stood and gazed along the street. A
    man
Flung back the garden-gate and nearly
    ran
Her down as she stood in the door. "Why,
    Dear,
What in the name of patience brings you
    here?

Quick, Lotta, shut the door, my violin
I fear is wetted. Now, Dear, bring a light.
This clasp is very much too worn and
    thin.
I'll take the other fiddle out to-night
If it still rains. Tut! Tut! my child, you're
    quite
Clumsy. Here, help me, hold the case
    while I —
Give me the candle. No, the inside's dry.

Thank God for that! Well, Lotta, how
    are you?
A bad storm, but the house still stands,
    I see.
Is my pipe filled, my Dear? I'll have a
    few
Puffs and a snooze before I eat my tea.
What do you say? That you were feared
    for me?
Nonsense, my child. Yes, kiss me, now
    don't talk.
I need a rest, the theatre's a long walk."

Her needles still, her hands upon her lap
Patiently laid, Charlotta Altgelt sat
And watched the rain-run window. In
    his nap
Her husband stirred and muttered. Seeing
    that,
Charlotta rose and softly, pit-a-pat,
Climbed up the stairs, and in her little
    room
Found sighing comfort with a moon in
    bloom.

But even rainy windows, silver-lit
By a new-burst, storm-whetted moon,
    may give
But poor content to loneliness, and it
Was hard for young Charlotta so to strive
And down her eagerness and learn to live
In placid quiet. While her husband slept,
Charlotta in her upper chamber wept.

Herr Concert-Meister Altgelt was a man
Gentle and unambitious, that alone
Had kept him back. He played as few
    men can,
Drawing out of his instrument a tone
So shimmering-sweet and palpitant, it
    shone
Like a bright thread of sound hung in
    the air,
Afloat and swinging upward, slim and fair.

Above all things, above Charlotta his wife,
Herr Altgelt loved his violin, a fine
Cremona pattern, Stradivari's life
Was flowering out of early discipline
When this was fashioned. Of soft-cutting
    pine
The belly was. The back of broadly
    curled
Maple, the head made thick and sharply
    whirled.

The slanting, youthful sound-holes
        through
    The belly of fine, vigorous pine
    Mellowed each note and blew
    It out again with a woody flavour
    Tanged and fragrant as fir-trees are
    When breezes in their needles jar.

    The varnish was an orange-brown
    Lustered like glass that's long laid
        down
    Under a crumbling villa stone.
    Purfled stoutly, with mitres which
        point
    Straight up the corners. Each curve
        and joint
    Clear, and bold, and thin.
    Such was Herr Theodore's violin.

Seven o'clock, the Concert-Meister gone
With his best violin, the rain being
    stopped,
Frau Lotta in the kitchen sat alone
Watching the embers which the fire
    dropped.
The china shone upon the dresser, topped
By polished copper vessels which her skill
Kept brightly burnished. It was very still.

An air from *Orféo* hummed in her head.
Herr Altgelt had been practising before
The night's performance. Charlotta had
    plead

With him to stay with her. Even at the
door
She'd begged him not to go. "I do implore
You for this evening, Theodore," she had
said.
"Leave them to-night, and stay with me,
instead."

"A silly poppet!" Theodore pinched her
ear.
"You'd like to have our good Elector turn
Me out I think." "But, Theodore, some-
thing queer
Ails me. Oh, do but notice how they
burn,
My cheeks! The thunder worried me.
You're stern,
And cold, and only love your work, I
know.
But Theodore, for this evening, do not
go."

But he had gone, hurriedly at the end,
For she had kept him talking. Now she
sat
Alone again, always alone, the trend
Of all her thinking brought her back to
that
She wished to banish. What would life
be? What?
For she was young, and loved, while he
was moved
Only by music. Each day that was
proved.

Each day he rose and practised. While
he played,
She stopped her work and listened, and
her heart
Swelled painfully beneath her bodice.
Swayed
And longing, she would hide from him
her smart.
"Well, Lottchen, will that do?" Then
what a start
She gave, and she would run to him and
cry,
And he would gently chide her, "Fie,
Dear, fie.

I'm glad I played it well. But such a
taking!
You'll hear the thing enough before I've
done."

And she would draw away from him, still
shaking.
Had he but guessed she was another one,
Another violin. Her strings were aching,
Stretched to the touch of his bow hand,
again
He played and she almost broke at the
strain.

Where was the use of thinking of it now,
Sitting alone and listening to the clock!
She'd best make haste and knit another
row.
Three hours at least must pass before his
knock
Would startle her. It always was a shock.
She   listened — listened — for   so   long
before,
That when it came her hearing almost
tore.

She caught herself just starting in to
listen.
What nerves she had: rattling like brittle
sticks!
She wandered to the window, for the
glisten
Of a bright moon was tempting. Snuffed
the wicks
Of her two candles. Still she could not fix
To anything. The moon in a broad
swath
Beckoned her out and down the garden-
path.

Against the house, her hollyhocks stood
high
And black, their shadows doubling them.
The night
Was white and still with moonlight, and
a sigh
Of blowing leaves was there, and the dim
flight
Of insects, and the smell of aconite,
And stocks, and Marvel of Peru. She
flitted
Along the path, where blocks of shadow
pitted

The even flags. She let herself go dreaming
Of Theodore her husband, and the tune
From *Orféo* swam through her mind, but
seeming

Changed — shriller. Of a sudden, a clear moon
Showed her a passer-by, inopportune
Indeed, but here he was, whistling and striding.
Lotta squeezed in between the currants, hiding.

"The best laid plans of mice and men," alas!
The stranger came indeed, but did not pass.
Instead, he leant upon the garden-gate,
Folding his arms and whistling. Lotta's state,
Crouched in the prickly currants, on wet grass,
Was far from pleasant. Still the stranger stayed,
And Lotta in her currants watched, dismayed.

He seemed a proper fellow standing there
In the bright moonshine. His cocked hat was laced
With silver, and he wore his own brown hair
Tied, but unpowdered. His whole bearing graced
A fine cloth coat, and ruffled shirt, and chased
Sword-hilt. Charlotta looked, but her position
Was hardly easy. When would his volition

Suggest his walking on? And then that tune!
A half-a-dozen bars from *Orféo*
Gone over and over, and murdered. What Fortune
Had brought him there to stare about him so?
"Ach, Gott im Himmel! Why will he not go!"
Thought Lotta, but the young man whistled on,
And seemed in no great hurry to be gone.

Charlotta, crouched among the currant bushes,
Watched the moon slowly dip from twig to twig.
If Theodore should chance to come, and blushes

Streamed over her. He would not care a fig,
He'd only laugh. She pushed aside a sprig
Of sharp-edged leaves and peered, then she uprose
Amid her bushes. "Sir," said she, "pray whose

Garden do you suppose you're watching? Why
Do you stand there? I really must insist
Upon your leaving. 'Tis unmannerly
To stay so long." The young man gave a twist
And turned about, and in the amethyst
Moonlight he saw her like a nymph half-risen
From the green bushes which had been her prison.

He swept his hat off in a hurried bow.
"Your pardon, Madam, I had no idea
I was not quite alone, and that is how
I came to stay. My trespass was not sheer
Impertinence. I thought no one was here,
And really gardens cry to be admired.
To-night especially it seemed required.

And may I beg to introduce myself?
Heinrich Marohl of Munich. And your name?"
Charlotta told him. And the artful elf
Promptly exclaimed about her husband's fame.
So Lotta, half-unwilling, slowly came
To conversation with him. When she went
Into the house, she found the evening spent.

Theodore arrived quite wearied out and teased,
With all excitement in him burned away.
It had gone well, he said, the audience pleased,
And he had played his very best to-day,
But afterwards he had been forced to stay
And practise with the stupid ones. His head
Ached furiously, and he must get to bed.

PART SECOND

Herr Concert-Meister Altgelt played,
And the four strings of his violin
Were spinning like bees on a day in
    Spring.
The notes rose into the wide sun-mote
Which slanted through the window,
They lay like coloured beads a-row,
They knocked together and parted,
And started to dance,
Skipping, tripping, each one slipping
Under and over the others so
That the polychrome fire streamed
    like a lance
Or a comet's tail,
Behind them.
Then a wail arose — crescendo —
And dropped from off the end of
    the bow,
And the dancing stopped.
A scent of lilies filled the room,
Long and slow. Each large white
    bloom
Breathed a sound which was holy
    perfume from a blessed censer,
And the hum of an organ tone,
And they waved like fans in a hall
    of stone
Over a bier standing there in the
    center, alone.
Each lily bent slowly as it was blown.
Like smoke they rose from the
    violin —
Then faded as a swifter bowing
Jumbled the notes like wavelets
    flowing
In a splashing, pashing, rippling
    motion
Between broad meadows to an ocean
Wide as a day and blue as a flower,
Where every hour
Gulls dipped, and scattered, and
    squawked, and squealed.
And over the marshes the Angelus
    pealed,
And the prows of the fishing-boats
    were spattered
With spray.
And away a couple of frigates were
    starting
To race to Java with all sails set,
Topgallants, and royals, and stun-
    sails, and jibs,

And wide moonsails; and the shin-
    ing rails
Were polished so bright they sparked
    in the sun.
All the sails went up with a run:
"They call me Hanging Johnny,
    Away-i-oh;
They call me Hanging Johnny,
    So hang, boys, hang."
And the sun had set and the high
    moon whitened,
And the ship heeled over to the
    breeze.
He drew her into the shade of the
    sails,
And whispered tales
Of voyages in the China seas,
And his arm around her
Held and bound her.
She almost swooned,
With the breeze and the moon
And the slipping sea,
And he beside her,
Touching her, leaning —
The ship careening,
With the white moon steadily shin-
    ing over
Her and her lover,
Theodore, still her lover!

Then a quiver fell on the crowded
    notes,
And slowly floated
A single note which spread and
    spread
Till it filled the room with a shim-
    mer like gold,
And noises shivered throughout its
    length,
And tried its strength.
They pulled it, and tore it,
And the stuff waned thinner, but
    still it bore it.
Then a wide rent
Split the arching tent,
And balls of fire spurted through,
Spitting yellow, and mauve, and
    blue.
One by one they were quenched as
    they fell,
Only the blue burned steadily.
Paler and paler it grew, and — faded
    — away.
    Herr Altgelt stopped.

"Well, Lottachen, my Dear, what do
    you say?
I think I'm in good trim. Now let's have
    dinner.
What's this, my Love, you're very sweet
    to-day.
I wonder how it happens I'm the winner
Of so much sweetness. But I think you're
    thinner;
You're like a bag of feathers on my knee.
Why, Lotta child, you're almost stran-
    gling me.

I'm glad you're going out this afternoon.
The days are getting short, and I'm so
    tied
At the Court Theatre my poor little bride
Has not much junketing I fear, but soon
I'll ask our manager to grant a boon.
To-night, perhaps, I'll get a pass for you,
And when I go, why Lotta can come too.

Now dinner, Love. I want some onion
    soup
To whip me up till that rehearsal's over.
You know it's odd how some women can
    stoop!
Fräulein Gebnitz has taken on a lover,
A Jew named Goldstein. No one can dis-
    cover
If it's his money. But she lives alone
Practically. Gebnitz is a stone,

Pores over books all day, and has no ear
For his wife's singing. Artists must have
    men;
They need appreciation. But it's queer
What messes people make of their lives,
    when
They should know more. If Gebnitz finds
    out, then
His wife will pack. Yes, shut the door
    at once.
I did not feel it cold, I am a dunce."

Frau Altgelt tied her bonnet on and went
Into the streets. A bright, crisp Autumn
    wind
Flirted her skirts and hair. A turbulent,
Audacious wind it was, now close behind,
Pushing her bonnet forward till it twined
The strings across her face, then from in
    front
Slantingly swinging at her with a shunt,

Until she lay against it, struggling, push-
    ing,
Dismayed to find her clothing tightly
    bound
Around her, every fold and wrinkle crush-
    ing
Itself upon her, so that she was wound
In draperies as clinging as those found
Sucking about a sea nymph on the frieze
Of some old Grecian temple. In the
    breeze

The shops and houses had a quality
Of hard and dazzling colour; something
    sharp
And buoyant, like white, puffing sails at
    sea.
The city streets were twanging like a
    harp.
Charlotta caught the movement, skip-
    pingly
She blew along the pavement, hardly
    knowing
Toward what destination she was going.

She fetched up opposite a jeweller's shop,
Where filigreed tiaras shone like crowns,
And necklaces of emeralds seemed to drop
And then float up again with lightness.
    Browns
Of stripéd agates struck her like cold
    frowns
Amid the gaiety of topaz seals,
Carved though they were with heads, and
    arms, and wheels.

A row of pencils knobbed with quartz or
    sard
Delighted her. And rings of every size
Turned smartly round like hoops before
    her eyes,
Amethyst-flamed or ruby-girdled, jarred
To spokes and flashing triangles, and
    starred
Like rockets bursting on a festal day.
Charlotta could not tear herself away.

With eyes glued tightly on a golden
    box,
Whose rare enamel piqued her with its
    hue,
Changeable, iridescent, shuttlecocks
Of shades and lustres always darting
    through
Its level, superimposing sheet of blue,

Charlotta did not hear footsteps approaching.
She started at the words: "Am I en-
croaching?"

"Oh, Heinrich, how you frightened me! I
thought
We were to meet at three, is it quite
that?"
"No, it is not," he answered, "but I've
caught
The trick of missing you. One thing is
flat,
I cannot go on this way. Life is what
Might best be conjured up by the word:
'Hell.'
Dearest, when will you come?" Lotta, to
quell

His effervescence, pointed to the gems
Within the window, asked him to admire
A bracelet or a buckle. But one stems
Uneasily the burning of a fire.
Heinrich was chafing, pricked by his
desire.
Little by little she wooed him to her
mood
Until at last he promised to be good.

But here he started on another tack;
To buy a jewel, which one would Lotta
choose.
She vainly urged against him all her lack
Of other trinkets. Should she dare to use
A ring or brooch her husband might ac-
cuse
Her of extravagance, and ask to see
A strict accounting, or still worse might
be.

But Heinrich would not be persuaded.
Why
Should he not give her what he liked?
And in
He went, determined certainly to buy
A thing so beautiful that it would win
Her wavering fancy. Altgelt's violin
He would outscore by such a handsome
jewel
That Lotta could no longer be so cruel!

Pity Charlotta, torn in diverse ways.
If she went in with him, the shopman
might
Recognize her, give her her name; in days

To come he could denounce her. In her
fright
She almost fled. But Heinrich would be
quite
Capable of pursuing. By and by
She pushed the door and entered hurriedly.

It took some pains to keep him from
bestowing
A pair of ruby earrings, carved like roses,
The setting twined to represent the growing
Tendrils and leaves, upon her. "Who
supposes
I could obtain such things! It simply
closes
All comfort for me." So he changed his
mind
And bought as slight a gift as he could
find.

A locket, frosted over with seed pearls,
Oblong and slim, for wearing at the neck,
Or hidden in the bosom; their joined curls
Should lie in it. And further to bedeck
His love, Heinrich had picked a whiff, a
fleck
The merest puff of a thin, linked chain
To hang it from. Lotta could not refrain

From weeping as they sauntered down
the street.
She did not want the locket, yet she did.
To have him love her she found very
sweet,
But it is hard to keep love always hid.
Then there was something in her heart
which chid
Her, told her she loved Theodore in him,
That all these meetings were a foolish
whim.

She thought of Theodore and the life
they led,
So near together, but so little mingled.
The great clouds bulged and bellied over-
head,
And the fresh wind about her body
tingled;
The crane of a large warehouse creaked
and jingled;
Charlotta held her breath for very fear,
About her in the street she seemed to
hear:

"They call me Hanging Johnny
    Away-i-oh;
They call me Hanging Johnny
    So hang, boys, hang."

And it was Theodore, under the racing
    skies,
Who held her and who whispered in her
    ear.
She knew her heart was telling her no
    lies,
Beating and hammering. He was so dear,
The touch of him would send her in a
    queer
Swoon that was half an ecstasy. And
    yearning
For Theodore, she wandered, slowly turn-
    ing

Street after street as Heinrich wished it so.
He had some aim, she had forgotten
    what.
Their progress was confused and very
    slow,
But at the last they reached a lonely spot,
A garden far above the highest shot
Of soaring steeple. At their feet, the
    town
Spread open like a chequer-board laid
    down.

Lotta was dimly conscious of the rest,
Vaguely remembered how he clasped the
    chain
About her neck. She treated it in jest,
And saw his face cloud over with sharp
    pain.
Then suddenly she felt as though a strain
Were put upon her, collared like a slave,
Leashed in the meshes of this thing he
    gave.

She seized the flimsy rings with both her
    hands
To snap it, but they held with odd per-
    sistence.
Her eyes were blinded by two wind-blown
    strands
Of hair which had been loosened. Her
    resistance
Melted within her, from remotest dis-
    tance,
Misty, unreal, his face grew warm and
    near,
And giving way she knew him very dear.

For long he held her, and they both
    gazed down
At the wide city, and its blue, bridged
    river.
From wooing he jested with her, snipped
    the blown
Strands of her hair, and tied them with
    a sliver
Cut from his own head. But she gave a
    shiver
When, opening the locket, they were
    placed
Under the glass, commingled and en-
    laced.

"When will you have it so with us?" He
    sighed.
She shook her head. He pressed her
    further. "No,
No, Heinrich, Theodore loves me," and
    she tried
To free herself and rise. He held her so,
Clipped by his arms, she could not move
    nor go.
"But you love me," he whispered, with
    his face
Burning against her through her kerchief's
    lace.

Frau Altgelt knew she toyed with fire,
    knew
That what her husband lit this other man
Fanned to hot flame. She told herself
    that few
Women were so discreet as she, who ran
No danger since she knew what things
    to ban.
She opened her house door at five o'clock,
A short half-hour before her husband's
    knock.

PART THIRD

The *Residenz-Theater* sparked and
    hummed
With lights and people. Gebnitz was to
    sing,
That rare soprano. All the fiddles
    strummed
With tuning up; the wood-winds made
    a ring
Of reedy bubbling noises, and the sting
Of sharp, red brass pierced every ear-
    drum; patting
From muffled tympani made a dark slat-
    ting

Across the silver shimmering of flutes;
A bassoon grunted, and an oboe wailed;
The 'celli pizzicato-ed like great lutes,
And mutterings of double basses trailed
Away to silence, while loud harp-strings
    hailed
Their thin, bright colours down in such
    a scatter
They lost themselves amid the general
    clatter.

Frau Altgelt in the gallery, alone,
Felt lifted up into another world.
Before her eyes a thousand candles shone
In the great chandeliers. A maze of
    curled
And powdered periwigs past her eyes
    swirled.
She smelt the smoke of candles guttering,
And caught the glint of jewelled fans
    fluttering

All round her in the boxes. Red and gold,
The house, like rubies set in filigree,
Filliped the candlelight about, and bold
Young sparks with eye-glasses, unblush-
    ingly
Ogled fair beauties in the balcony.
An officer went by, his steel spurs jan-
    gling.
Behind Charlotta an old man was
    wrangling

About a play-bill he had bought and lost.
Three drunken soldiers had to be ejected.
Frau Altgelt's eyes stared at the vacant
    post
Of Concert-Meister, she at once detected
The stir which brought him. But she felt
    neglected
When with no glance about him or her
    way,
He lifted up his violin to play.

The curtain went up? Perhaps. If so,
Charlotta never saw it go.
The famous Fräulein Gebnitz' sing-
    ing
Only came to her like the ringing
Of bells at a festa
Which swing in the air
And nobody realizes they are there.
They jingle and jangle,
And clang, and bang.
And never a soul could tell whether
    they rang,

For the plopping of guns and rockets
And the chinking of silver to spend,
    in one's pockets,
And the shuffling and clapping of
    feet,
And the loud flapping
Of flags, with the drums,
As the military comes.
It's a famous tune to walk to,
And I wonder where they're off to.
Step-step-stepping to the beating of
    the drums.
But the rhythm changes as though
    a mist
Were curling and twisting
Over the landscape.
For a moment a rhythmless, tuneless
    fog
Encompasses her. Then her senses
    jog
To the breath of a stately minuet.
Herr Altgelt's violin is set
In tune to the slow, sweeping bows,
    and retreats and advances,
To curtsies brushing the waxen floor
    as the Court dances.
Long and peaceful like warm Sum-
    mer nights
When stars shine in the quiet river.
    And against the lights
Blundering insects knock,
And the *Rathaus* clock
Booms twice, through the shrill
    sounds
Of flutes and horns in the lamplit
    grounds.
Pressed against him in the mazy
    wavering
Of a country dance, with her short
    breath quavering
She leans upon the beating, throb-
    bing
Music. Laughing, sobbing,
Feet gliding after sliding feet;
His — hers —
The ballroom blurs —
She feels the air
Lifting her hair,
And the lapping of water on the
    stone stair.
He is there! He is there!
Twang harps, and squeal, you thin
    violins,
That the dancers may dance, and
    never discover

The old stone stair leading down to
the river
With the chestnut-tree branches
hanging over
Her and her lover.
Theodore, still her lover!

The evening passed like this, in a half
faint,
Delirium with waking intervals
Which were the entr'acts. Under the
restraint
Of a large company, the constant calls
For oranges or syrops from the stalls
Outside, the talk, the passing to and fro,
Lotta sat ill at ease, incognito.

She heard the Gebnitz praised, the tenor
lauded,
The music vaunted as most excellent.
The scenery and the costumes were ap-
plauded,
The latter it was whispered had been sent
From Italy. The Herr Direktor spent
A fortune on them, so the gossips said.
Charlotta felt a lightness in her head.

When the next act began, her eyes were
swimming,
Her prodded ears were aching and con-
fused.
The first notes from the orchestra sent
skimming
Her outward consciousness. Her brain
was fused
Into the music, Theodore's music! Used
To hear him play, she caught his single
tone.
For all she noticed they two were alone.

PART FOURTH

Frau Altgelt waited in the chilly street,
Hustled by lackeys who ran up and down
Shouting their coachmen's names; forced
to retreat
A pace or two by lurching chairmen;
thrown
Rudely aside by linkboys; boldly shown
The ogling rapture in two bleary eyes
Thrust close to hers in most unpleasant
wise.

Escaping these, she hit a liveried arm,
Was sworn at by this glittering gentleman
And ordered off. However, no great harm

Came to her. But she looked a trifle wan
When Theodore, her belated guardian,
Emerged. She snuggled up against him,
trembling,
Half out of fear, half out of the assem-
bling

Of all the thoughts and needs his play-
ing had given.
Had she enjoyed herself, he wished to
know.
"Oh! Theodore, can't you feel that it
was Heaven!"
"Heaven! My Lottachen, and was it so?
Gebnitz was in good voice, but all the
flow
Of her last aria was spoiled by Klops,
A wretched flutist, she was mad as hops."

He was so simple, so matter-of-fact,
Charlotta Altgelt knew not what to say
To bring him to her dream. His lack of
tact
Kept him explaining all the homeward way
How this thing had gone well, that badly.
"Stay,
Theodore!" she cried at last. "You know
to me
Nothing was real, it was an ecstasy."

And he was heartily glad she had enjoyed
Herself so much, and said so. "But it's
good
To be got home again." He was em-
ployed
In looking at his violin, the wood
Was old, and evening air did it no good.
But when he drew up to the table for tea
Something about his wife's vivacity

Struck him as hectic, worried him in
short.
He talked of this and that but watched
her close.
Tea over, he endeavoured to extort
The cause of her excitement. She arose
And stood beside him, trying to compose
Herself, all whipt to quivering, curdled life,
And he, poor fool, misunderstood his
wife.

Suddenly, broken through her anxious
grasp,
Her music-kindled love crashed on him
there.

Amazed, he felt her fling against him,
    clasp
Her arms about him, weighing down his
    chair,
Sobbing out all her hours of despair.
"Theodore, a woman needs to hear things
    proved.
Unless you tell me, I feel I'm not loved."

Theodore went under in this tearing
    wave,
He yielded to it, and its headlong flow
Filled him with all the energy she gave.
He was a youth again, and this bright
    glow,
This living, vivid joy he had to show
Her what she was to him. Laughing and
    crying
She asked assurances there's no denying.

Over and over again her questions, till
He quite convinced her, every now and
    then
She kissed him, shivering as though
    doubting still.
But later when they were composed and
    when
She dared relax her probings, "Lotta-
    chen,"
He asked, "how is it your love has with-
    stood
My inadvertence? I was made of wood."

She told him, and no doubt she meant it
    truly,
That he was sun, and grass, and wind,
    and sky
To her. And even if conscience were un-
    ruly
She salved it by neat sophistries, but why
Suppose her insincere, it was no lie
She said, for Heinrich was as much forgot
As though he'd never been within ear-
    shot.

But Theodore's hands in straying and
    caressing
Fumbled against the locket where it lay
Upon her neck. "What is this thing I'm
    pressing?"
He asked. "Let's bring it to the light of
    day."
He lifted up the locket. "It should stay
Outside, my Dear. Your mother has good
    taste.
To keep it hidden surely is a waste."

Pity again Charlotta, straight aroused
Out of her happiness. The locket brought
A chilly jet of truth upon her, soused
Under its icy spurting she was caught,
And choked, and frozen. Suddenly she
    sought
The clasp, but with such art was this con-
    trived
Her fumbling fingers never once arrived

Upon it. Feeling, twisting, round and
    round,
She pulled the chain quite through the
    locket's ring
And still it held. Her neck, encompassed,
    bound,
Chafed at the sliding meshes. Such a
    thing
To hurl her out of joy! A gilded string
Binding her folly to her, and those curls
Which lay entwined beneath the clus-
    tered pearls!

Again she tried to break the cord. It
    stood.
"Unclasp it, Theodore," she begged. But
    he
Refused, and being in a happy mood,
Twitted her with her inefficiency,
Then looking at her very seriously:
"I think, Charlotta, it is well to have
Always about one what a mother gave.

As she has taken the great pains to send
This jewel to you from Dresden, it will
    be
Ingratitude if you do not intend
To carry it about you constantly.
With her fine taste you cannot disagree,
The locket is most beautifully designed."
He opened it and there the curls were,
    twined.

Charlotta's heart dropped beats like knit-
    ting-stitches.
She burned a moment, flaming; then she
    froze.
Her face was jerked by little, nervous
    twitches,
She heard her husband asking: "What
    are those?"
Put out her hand quickly to interpose,
But stopped, the gesture half-complete,
    astounded
At the calm way the question was pro-
    pounded.

"A pretty fancy, Dear, I do declare.
Indeed I will not let you put it off.
A lovely thought; yours and your mother's
hair!"
Charlotta hid a gasp under a cough.
"Never with my connivance shall you
doff
This charming gift." He kissed her on
the cheek,
And Lotta suffered him, quite crushed
and meek.

When later in their room she lay awake,
Watching the moonlight slip along the
floor,
She felt the chain and wept for
Theodore's sake.
She had loved Heinrich also, and the core
Of truth, unlovely, startled her. Where-
fore
She vowed from now to break this double
life
And see herself only as Theodore's wife.

PART FIFTH

It was no easy matter to convince
Heinrich that it was finished. Hard to
say
That though they could not meet (he
saw her wince)
She still must keep the locket to allay
Suspicion in her husband. She would pay
Him from her savings bit by bit — the
oath
He swore at that was startling to them
both.

Her resolution taken, Frau Altgelt
Adhered to it, and suffered no regret.
She found her husband all that she had
felt
His music to contain. Her days were set
In his as though she were an amulet
Cased in bright gold. She joyed in her
confining;
Her eyes put out her looking-glass with
shining.

Charlotta was so gay that old, dull tasks
Were furbished up to seem like rituals.
She baked and brewed as one who only
asks
The right to serve. Her daily manuals
Of prayer were duties, and her festivals

When Theodore praised some dish, or
frankly said
She had a knack in making up a bed.

So Autumn went, and all the mountains
round
The city glittered white with fallen snow,
For it was Winter. Over the hard ground
Herr Altgelt's footsteps came, each one
a blow.
On the swept flags behind the currant
row
Charlotta stood to greet him. But his lip
Only flicked hers. His Concert-Meister-
ship

Was first again. This evening he had got
Important news. The opera ordered from
Young Mozart was arrived. That old
despot,
The Bishop of Salzburg, had let him
come
Himself to lead it, and the parts, still hot
From copying, had been tried over. Never
Had any music started such a fever.

The orchestra had cheered till they were
hoarse,
The singers clapped and clapped. The
town was made,
With such a great attraction through the
course
Of Carnival time. In what utter shade
All other cities would be left! The trade
In music would all drift here naturally.
In his excitement he forgot his tea.

Lotta was forced to take his cup and
put
It in his hand. But still he rattled on,
Sipping at intervals. The new catgut
Strings he was using gave out such a tone
The "Maestro" had remarked it, and had
gone
Out of his way to praise him. Lotta
smiled,
He was as happy as a little child.

From that day on, Herr Altgelt, more and
more
Absorbed himself in work. Lotta at first
Was patient and well-wishing. But it
wore
Upon her when two weeks had brought
no burst

Of loving from him. Then she feared
the worst;
That his short interest in her was a light
Flared up an instant only in the night.

Idomeneo was the opera's name,
A name that poor Charlotta learnt to
hate.
Herr Altgelt worked so hard he seldom
came
Home for his tea, and it was very late,
Past midnight sometimes, when he
knocked. His state
Was like a flabby orange whose crushed
skin
Is thin with pulling, and all dented in.

He practised every morning and her
heart
Followed his bow. But often she would
sit,
While he was playing, quite withdrawn
apart,
Absently fingering and touching it,
The locket, which now seemed to her a
bit
Of some gone youth. His music drew her
tears,
And through the notes he played, her
dreading ears

Heard Heinrich's voice, saying he had
not changed;
Beer merchants had no ecstasies to take
Their minds off love. So far her thoughts
had ranged
Away from her stern vow, she chanced to
take
Her way, one morning, quite by a mistake,
Along the street where Heinrich had his
shop.
What harm to pass it since she should
not stop!

It matters nothing how one day she
met
Him on a bridge, and blushed, and hurried by.
Nor how the following week he stood
to let
Her pass, the pavement narrowing suddenly.
How once he took her basket, and once
he

Pulled back a rearing horse who might
have struck
Her with his hoofs. It seemed the oddest
luck

How many times their business took them
each
Right to the other. Then at last he spoke,
But she would only nod, he got no
speech
From her. Next time he treated it in
joke,
And that so lightly that her vow she
broke
And answered. So they drifted into seeing
Each other as before. There was no
fleeing.

Christmas was over and the Carnival
Was very near, and tripping from each
tongue
Was talk of the new opera. Each book-
stall
Flaunted it out in bills, what airs were
sung,
What singers hired. Pictures of the
young
"Maestro" were for sale. The town was
mad.
Only Charlotta felt depressed and sad.

Each day now brought a struggle 'twixt
her will
And Heinrich's. 'Twixt her love for
Theodore
And him. Sometimes she wished to kill
Herself to solve her problem. For a score
Of reasons Heinrich tempted her. He
bore
Her moods with patience, and so surely
urged
Himself upon her, she was slowly merged

Into his way of thinking, and to fly
With him seemed easy. But next morn-
ing would
The Stradivarius undo her mood.
Then she would realize that she must
cleave
Always to Theodore. And she would try
To convince Heinrich she should never
leave,
And afterwards she would go home and
grieve.

All thought in Munich centered on the
    part
Of January when there would be given
Idomeneo by Wolfgang Mozart.
The twenty-ninth was fixed. And all
    seats, even
Those almost at the ceiling, which were
    driven
Behind the highest gallery, were sold.
The inches of the theatre went for
    gold.

Herr Altgelt was a shadow worn so thin
With work, he hardly printed black be-
    hind
The candle. He and his old violin
Made up one person. He was not unkind,
But dazed outside his playing, and the
    rind,
The pine and the maple of his fiddle,
    guarded
A part of him which he had quite dis-
    carded.

    It woke in the silence of frost-bright
        nights,
    In little lights,
    Like will-o'-the-wisps flickering, flut-
        tering,
    Here — there —
    Spurting, sputtering,
    Fading and lighting,
    Together, asunder —
    Till Lotta sat up in bed with won-
        der,
    And the faint grey patch of the
        window shone
    Upon her sitting there, alone.
    For Theodore slept.

The twenty-eighth was last rehearsal day,
'Twas called for noon, so early morning
    meant
Herr Altgelt's only time in which to play
His part alone. Drawn like a monk who's
    spent
Himself in prayer and fasting, Theodore
    went
Into the kitchen, with a weary word
Of cheer to Lotta, careless if she heard.

    Lotta heard more than his spoken
        word.
    She heard the vibrating of strings
        and wood.

She was washing the dishes, her
    hands all suds,
When the sound began,
Long as the span
Of a white road snaking about a hill.
The orchards are filled
With cherry blossoms at butterfly
    poise.
Hawthorn buds are cracking,
And in the distance a shepherd is
    clacking
His shears, snip-snipping the wool
    from his sheep.
The notes are asleep,
Lying adrift on the air
In level lines
Like sunlight hanging in pines and
    pines,
Strung and threaded,
All imbedded
In the blue-green of the hazy pines.
Lines — long, straight lines!
And stems,
Long, straight stems
Pushing up
To the cup of blue, blue sky.
Stems growing misty
With the many of them,
Red-green mist
Of the trees,
And these
Wood-flavoured notes.
The back is maple and the belly is
    pine.
The rich notes twine
As though weaving in and out of
    leaves,
Broad leaves
Flapping slowly like elephants' ears,
Waving and falling.
Another sound peers
Through little pine fingers,
And lingers, peeping.
Ping! Ping! pizzicato, something is
    cheeping.
There is a twittering up in the
    branches,
A chirp and a lilt,
And crimson atilt on a swaying twig.
Wings! Wings!
And a little ruffled-out throat which
    sings.
The forest bends, tumultuous
With song.
The woodpecker knocks,

And the song-sparrow trills,
Every fir, and cedar, and yew
Has a nest or a bird,
It is quite absurd
To hear them cutting across each
    other:
Peewits, and thrushes, and larks, all
    at once,
And a loud cuckoo is trying to
    smother
A wood-pigeon perched on a birch,
"Roo —coo — oo — oo — "
"Cuckoo! Cuckoo! That's one for
    you!"
A blackbird whistles, how sharp, how
    shrill!
And the great trees toss
And leaves blow down,
You can almost hear them splash on
    the ground.
The whistle again:
It is double and loud!
The leaves are splashing,
And water is dashing
Over those creepers, for they are
    shrouds;
And men are running up them to
    furl the sails,
For there is a capful of wind to-day,
And we are already well under way.
The deck is aslant in the bubbling
    breeze.
"Theodore, please.
Oh, Dear, how you tease!"
And the boatswain's whistle sounds
    again,
And the men pull on the sheets:
"My name is Hanging Johnny,
        Away-i-oh;
They call me Hanging Johnny,
        So hang, boys, hang."
The trees of the forest are masts,
    tall masts;
They are swinging over
Her and her lover.
Almost swooning
Under the ballooning canvas,
She lies
Looking up in his eyes
As he bends farther over.
Theodore, still her lover!

The suds were dried upon Charlotta's
    hands,
She leant against the table for support,

Wholly forgotten. Theodore's eyes were
    brands
Burning upon his music. He stopped
    short.
Charlotta almost heard the sound of
    bands
Snapping. She put one hand up to her
    heart,
Her fingers touched the locket with a
    start.

Herr Altgelt put his violin away
Listlessly. "Lotta, I must have some rest.
The strain will be a hideous one to-day.
Don't speak to me at all. It will be best
If I am quiet till I go." And lest
She disobey, he left her. On the stairs
She heard his mounting steps. What use
    were prayers!

He could not hear, he was not there, for
    she
Was married to a mummy, a machine.
Her hand closed on the locket bitterly.
Before her, on a chair, lay the shagreen
Case of his violin. She saw the clean
Sun flash the open clasp. The locket's
    edge
Cut at her fingers like a pushing wedge.

A heavy cart went by, a distant bell
Chimed ten, the fire flickered in the grate.
She was alone. Her throat began to swell
With sobs. What kept her here, why
    should she wait?
The violin she had begun to hate
Lay in its case before her. Here she flung
The cover open. With the fiddle swung

Over her head, the hanging clock's loud
    ticking
Caught on her ear. 'Twas slow, and as
    she paused
The little door in it came open, flicking
A wooden cuckoo out: "Cuckoo!" It
    caused
The forest dream to come again.
    "Cuckoo!"
Smashed on the grate, the violin broke
    in two.

"Cuckoo! Cuckoo!" the clock kept
    striking on;
But no one listened. Frau Altgelt had
    gone.

THE CROSS–ROADS

A bullet through his heart at dawn. On the table a letter signed with a woman's name. A wind that goes howling round the house, and weeping as in shame. Cold November dawn peeping through the windows, cold dawn creeping over the floor, creeping up his cold legs, creeping over his cold body, creeping across his cold face. A glaze of thin yellow sunlight on the staring eyes. Wind howling through bent branches. A wind which never dies down. Howling, wailing. The gazing eyes glitter in the sunlight. The lids are frozen open and the eyes glitter.

The thudding of a pick on hard earth. A space grinding and crunching. Overhead, branches writhing, winding, interlacing, unwinding, scattering; tortured twinings, tossings, creakings. Wind flinging branches apart, drawing them together, whispering and whining among them. A waning, lobsided moon cutting through black clouds. A stream of pebbles and earth and the empty spade gleams clear in the moonlight, then is rammed again into the black earth. Tramping of feet. Men and horses. Squeaking of wheels.
"Whoa! Ready, Jim?"
"All ready."
Something falls, settles, is still. Suicides have no coffin.
"Give us the stake, Jim. Now."
Pound! Pound!
"He'll never walk. Nailed to the ground."
An ash stick pierces his heart, if it buds the roots will hold him. He is a part of the earth now, clay to clay. Overhead the branches sway, and writhe, and twist in the wind. He'll never walk with a bullet in his heart, and an ash stick nailing him to the cold, black ground.

Six months he lay still. Six months. And the water welled up in his body, and soft blue spots chequered it. He lay still, for the ash stick held him in place. Six months! Then her face came out of a mist of green. Pink and white and frail like Dresden china, lilies-of-the-valley at her breast, puce-coloured silk sheening about her. Under the young green leaves, the horse at a foot-pace, the high yellow wheels of the chaise scarcely turning, her face, rippling like grain a-blowing, under her puce-coloured bonnet; and burning beside her, flaming within his correct blue coat and brass buttons, is someone. What has dimmed the sun? The horse steps on a rolling stone; a wind in the branches makes a moan. The little leaves tremble and shake, turn and quake, over and over, tearing their stems. There is a shower of young leaves, and a sudden-sprung gale wails in the trees.

The yellow-wheeled chaise is rocking — rocking, and all the branches are knocking — knocking. The sun in the sky is a flat, red plate, the branches creak and grate. She screams and cowers, for the green foliage is a lowering wave surging to smother her. But she sees nothing. The stake holds firm. The body writhes, the body squirms. The blue spots widen, the flesh tears, but the stake wears well in the deep, black ground. It holds the body in the still, black ground.

Two years! The body has been in the ground two years. It is worn away; it is clay to clay. Where the heart moulders, a greenish dust, the stake is thrust. Late August it is, and night; a night flauntingly jewelled with stars, a night of shooting stars and loud insect noises. Down the road to Tilbury, silence — and the slow flapping of large leaves. Down the road to Sutton, silence — and the darkness of heavy-foliaged trees. Down the road to Wayfleet, silence — and the whirring scrape of insects in the branches. Down the road to Edgarstown, silence — and stars like stepping-stones in a pathway overhead. It is very quiet at the cross-roads, and the sign-board points the way down the four roads, endlessly points the way where nobody wishes to go.

A horse is galloping, galloping up from Sutton. Shaking the wide, still leaves as he goes under them. Striking sparks with his iron shoes; silencing the katydids. Dr. Morgan riding to a child-birth over Tilbury way; riding to deliver a woman of her first-born son. One o'clock from Wayfleet bell tower, what a shower of shoot ing stars! And a breeze all of a sudden, jarring the big leaves and making them jerk up and down. Dr. Morgan's hat is blown from his head, the horse swerves, and curves away from the sign-post. An oath — spurs — a blurring of grey mist. A quick left twist, and the gelding is snorting and racing down the Tilbury road with the wind dropping away behind him.

The stake has wrenched, the stake has started, the body, flesh from flesh, has parted. But the bones hold tight, socket and ball, and clamping them down in the hard, black ground is the stake, wedged through ribs and spine. The bones may twist, and heave, and twine, but the stake holds them still in line. The breeze goes down, and the round stars shine, for the stake holds the fleshless bones in line.

Twenty years now! Twenty long years! The body has powdered itself away; it is clay to clay. It is brown earth mingled with brown earth. Only flaky bones remain, lain together so long they fit, although not one bone is knit to another. The stake is there too, rotted through, but upright still, and still piercing down between ribs and spine in a straight line.

Yellow stillness is on the cross-roads, yellow stillness is on the trees. The leaves hang drooping, wan. The four roads point four yellow ways, saffron and gamboge ribbons to the gaze. A little swirl of dust blows up Tilbury road, the wind which fans it has not strength to do more; it ceases, and the dust settles down. A little whirl of wind comes up Tilbury road. It brings a sound of wheels and feet. The wind reels a moment and faints to nothing under the sign-post. Wind again, wheels and feet louder. Wind again — again — again. A drop of rain, flat into the dust. Drop! — Drop! Thick heavy raindrops, and a shrieking wind bending the great trees and wrenching off their leaves.

Under the black sky, bowed and dripping with rain, up Tilbury road, comes the procession. A funeral procession, bound for the graveyard at Wayfleet. Feet and wheels — feet and wheels. And among them one who is carried.

The bones in the deep, still earth shiver and pull. There is a quiver through the rotted stake. Then stake and bones fall together in a little puffing of dust.

Like meshes of linked steel the rain shuts down behind the procession, now well along the Wayfleet road.

He wavers like smoke in the buffeting wind. His fingers blow out like smoke, his head ripples in the gale. Under the sign-post, in the pouring rain, he stands, and watches another quavering figure drifting down the Wayfleet road. Then swiftly he streams after it. It flickers among the trees. He licks out and winds about them. Over, under, blown, contorted. Spindrift after spindrift; smoke following smoke. There is a wailing through the trees, a wailing of fear, and after it laughter — laughter — laughter, skirling up to the black sky. Lightning jags over the funeral procession. A heavy clap of thunder. Then darkness and rain, and the sound of feet and wheels.

A ROXBURY GARDEN

I

HOOPS

Blue and pink sashes,
Criss-cross shoes,
Minna and Stella run out into the garden
To play at hoop.

Up and down the garden-paths they race,
In the yellow sunshine,
Each with a big round hoop
White as a stripped willow-wand.

Round and round turn the hoops,
Their diamond whiteness cleaving the
    yellow sunshine.
The gravel crunches and squeaks beneath
    them,
And a large pebble springs them into the
    air
To go whirling for a foot or two
Before they touch the earth again
In a series of little jumps.

Spring, Hoops!
Spit out a shower of blue and white
    brightness.
The little criss-cross shoes twinkle behind
    you,

The pink and blue sashes flutter like flags,
The hoop-sticks are ready to beat you.
Turn, turn, Hoops! In the yellow sun-
    shine.
Turn your stripped willow whiteness
Along the smooth paths.

Stella sings:
"Round and round, rolls my hoop,
Scarcely touching the ground,
With a swoop,
And a bound,
Round and round.
With a bumpety, crunching, scatter-
    ing sound,
Down the garden it flies;
In our eyes
The sun lies.
See it spin
Out and in;
Through the paths it goes whirling,
About the beds curling.
Sway now to the loop,
Faster, faster, my hoop.
Round you come,
Up you come,
Quick and straight as before.
Run, run, my hoop, run,
Away from the sun."

And the great hoop bounds along the
    path,
Leaping into the wind-bright air.
Minna sings:
"Turn, hoop,
Burn hoop,
Twist and twine
Hoop of mine.
Flash along,
Leap along,
Right at the sun.
Run, hoop, run.
Faster and faster,
Whirl, twirl.
Wheel like fire,
And spin like glass;
Fire's no whiter
Glass is no brighter.
Dance,
Prance,
Over and over,
About and about,
With the top of you under,
And the bottom at top,
But never a stop."

Turn about, hoop, to the tap of my
    stick,
I follow behind you
To touch and remind you
Burn and glitter, so white and quick,
Round and round, to the tap of a
    stick."

The hoop flies along between the flower-
    beds,
Swaying the flowers with the wind of its
    passing.

Besides the foxglove-border roll the hoops,
And the little pink and white bells shake
    and jingle
Up and down their tall spires;
They roll under the snow-ball bush,
And the ground behind them is strewn
    with white petals;
They swirl round a corner,
And jar a bee out of a Canterbury bell;
They cast their shadows for an instant
Over a bed of pansies,
Catch against the spurs of a columbine,
Jostle the quietness from a cluster of
    monk's-hood.
Pat! Pat! behind them come the little
    criss-cross shoes,
And the blue and pink sashes stream out
    in flappings of colour.

Stella sings:
"Hoop, hoop,
Roll along,
Faster bowl along,
Hoop.
Slow, to the turning,
Now go! — Go!
Quick!
Here's the stick.
Rat-a-tap-tap it,
Pat it, flap it.
Fly like a bird or a yellow-backed bee,
See how soon you can reach that tree.
Here is a path that is perfectly straight.
Roll along, hoop, or we shall be late."

Minna sings:
"Trip about, slip about, whip about
Hoop.
Wheel like a top at its quickest spin,
Then, dear hoop, we shall surely win.
First to the greenhouse and then to
    the wall

Circle and circle,
And let the wind push you,
Poke you,
Brush you,
And not let you fall.
Whirring you round like a wreath of
    mist.
Hoopety hoop,
Twist,
Twist."

Tap! Tap! go the hoop-sticks,
And the hoops bowl along under a grape
    arbour.
For an instant their willow whiteness is
    green,
Pale white-green.
Then they are out in the sunshine,
Leaving the half-formed grape clusters
A-tremble under their big leaves.

"I will beat you, Minna," cries Stella,
Hitting her hoop smartly with her stick.
"Stella, Stella, we are winning," calls
    Minna,
As her hoop curves round a bed of clove-
    pinks.
A humming-bird whizzes past Stella's ear,
And two or three yellow-and-black butter-
    flies
Flutter, startled, out of a pillar rose.

Round and round race the litle girls
After their great white hoops.

Suddenly Minna stops.
Her hoop wavers an instant,
But she catches it up on her stick.
"Listen, Stella!"
Both the little girls are listening;
And the scents of the garden rise up
    quietly about them.
"It's the chaise! It's Father!
Perhaps he's brought us a book from Bos-
    ton."
Twinkle, twinkle, the little criss-cross
    shoes
Up the garden path.
Blue — pink — an instant, against the
    syringa hedge.
But the hoops, white as stripped willow-
    wands,
Lie in the grass,
And the grasshoppers jump back and
    forth
Over them.

II

BATTLEDORE AND SHUTTLECOCK .

The shuttlecock soars upward
In a parabola of whiteness,
Turns,
And sinks to a perfect arc.
Plat! the battledore strikes it,
And it rises again,
Without haste,
Winged and curving,
Tracing its white flight
Against the clipped hemlock-trees.
Plat!
Up again,
Orange and sparkling with sun,
Rounding under the blue sky,
Dropping,
Fading to grey-green
In the shadow of the coned hemlocks.

"Ninety-one." "Ninety-two." "Ninety-
    three."
The arms of the little girls
Come up — and up —
Precisely,
Like mechanical toys.
The battledores beat at nothing,
And toss the dazzle of snow
Off their parchment drums.
"Ninety-four." Plat!
"Ninety-five." Plat!
Back and forth
Goes the shuttlecock,
Icicle-white,
Leaping at the sharp-edged clouds,
Overturning,
Falling,
Down,
And down,
Tinctured with pink
From the upthrusting shine
Of Oriental poppies.

The little girls sway to the counting
    rhythm;
Left foot,
Right foot.
Plat! Plat!
Yellow heat twines round the handles of
    the battledores,
The parchment cracks with dryness;
But the shuttlecock
Swings slowly into the ice-blue sky,
Heaving up on the warm air

Like a foam-bubble on a wave,
With feathers slanted and sustaining.
Higher,
Until the earth turns beneath it;
Poised and swinging,
With all the garden flowing beneath it,
Scarlet, and blue, and purple, and
white —
Blurred colour reflections in rippled
water —
Changing — streaming —
For the moment that Stella takes to lift
her arm.
Then the shuttlecock relinquishes,
Bows,
Descends;
And the sharp blue spears of the air
Thrust it to earth.

Again it mounts,
Stepping up on the rising scents of
flowers,
Buoyed up and under by the shining heat.
Above the foxgloves,
Above the guelder-roses,
Above the greenhouse glitter,
Till the shafts of cooler air
Meet it,
Deflect it,
Reject it,
Then down,
Down,
Past the greenhouse,
Past the guelder-rose bush,
Past the foxgloves.

"Ninety-nine," Stella's battledore springs
to the impact.
Plunk! Like the snap of a taut string.
"Oh! Minna!"
The shuttlecock drops zigzagedly,
Out of orbit,
Hits the path,
And rolls over quite still.
Dead white feathers,
With a weight at the end.

III

GARDEN GAMES

The tall clock is striking twelve;
And the little girls stop in the hall to
watch it,
And the big ships rocking in a half-circle

Above the dial.
Twelve o'clock!
Down the side steps
Go the little girls,
Under their big round straw hats.
Minna's has a pink ribbon,
Stella's a blue,
That is the way they know which is
which.
Twelve o'clock!
An hour yet before dinner.
Mother is busy in the still-room,
And Hannah is making gingerbread.
Slowly, with lagging steps,
They follow the garden-path,
Crushing a leaf of box for its acrid smell,
Discussing what they shall do,
And doing nothing.

"Stella, see that grasshopper
Climbing up the bank!
What a jump!
Almost as long as my arm."
Run, children, run.
For the grasshopper is leaping away,
In half-circle curves,
Shuttlecock curves,
Over the grasses.
Hand in hand, the little girls call to him:
"Grandfather, grandfather gray,
Give me molasses, or I'll throw you
away."
The grasshopper leaps into the sunlight,
Golden-green,
And is gone.

"Let's catch a bee."
Round whirl the little girls,
And up the garden.
Two heads are thrust among the Canter-
bury bells,
Listening,
And fingers clasp and unclasp behind
backs
In a strain of silence.

White bells,
Blue bells,
Hollow and reflexed.
Deep tunnels of blue and white dimness,
Cool wine-tunnels for bees.
There is a floundering and buzzing over
Minna's head.
"Bend it down, Stella. Quick! Quick!"
The wide mouth of a blossom

Is pressed together in Minna's fingers.
The stem flies up, jiggling its flower-bells,
And Minna holds the dark blue cup in
    her hand,
With the bee
Imprisoned in it.
Whirr! Buzz! Bump!
Bump! Whiz! Bang!
BANG!!
The blue flower tears across like paper,
And a gold-black bee darts away in the
    sunshine.

"If we could fly, we could catch him."
The sunshine is hot on Stella's upturned
    face,
As she stares after the bee.
"We'll follow him in a dove chariot.
Come on, Stella."
Run, children,
Along the red gravel paths,
For a bee is hard to catch,
Even with a chariot of doves.

Tall, still, and cowled,
Stand the monk's-hoods;
Taller than the heads of the little girls.
A blossom for Minna.
A blossom for Stella.
Off comes the cowl,
And there is a purple-painted chariot;
Off comes the forward petal,
And there are two little green doves,
With green traces tying them to the
    chariot.
"Now we will get in, and fly right up to
    the clouds.
Fly, Doves, up in the sky,
With Minna and me,
After the bee."

Up one path,
Down another,
Run the little girls,
Holding their dove chariots in front of
    them;
But the bee is hidden in the trumpet of
    a honeysuckle,
With his wings folded along his back.

The dove chariots are thrown away,
And the little girls wander slowly through
    the garden,
Sucking the salvia tips,
And squeezing the snapdragons

To make them gape.
"I'm so hot,
Let's pick a pansy
And see the little man in his bath,
And play we're he."
A royal bath-tub,
Hung with purple stuffs and yellow.
The great purple-yellow wings
Rise up behind the little red and green
    man;
The purple-yellow wings fan him,
He dabbles his feet in cool green.
Off with the green sheath,
And there are two spindly legs.
"Heigho!" sighs Minna.
"Heigho!" sighs Stella.
There is not a flutter of wind,
And the sun is directly overhead.

Along the edge of the garden
Walk the little girls.
Their hats, round and yellow like cheeses,
Are dangling by the ribbons.
The grass is a tumult of buttercups and
    daisies;
Buttercups and daisies streaming away
Up the hill.
The garden is purple, and pink, and
    orange, and scarlet;
The garden is hot with colours.
But the meadow is only yellow, and
    white, and green,
Cool, and long, and quiet.
The little girls pick buttercups
And hold them under each other's chins.
"You're as gold as Grandfather's snuff-
    box.
You're going to be very rich, Minna."
"Oh-o-o! Then I'll ask my husband to
    give me a pair of garnet earrings
Just like Aunt Nancy's.
I wonder if he will.
I know. We'll tell fortunes.
That's what we'll do."
Plump down in the meadow grass,
Stella and Minna,
With their round yellow hats,
Like cheeses,
Beside them.
Drop,
Drop,
Daisy petals.
"One I love,
Two I love,
Three I love I say . . ."

The ground is peppered with daisy petals,
And the little girls nibble the golden
    centres,
And play it is cake.

A bell rings.
Dinner-time;
And after dinner there are lessons.

1777

I

THE TRUMPET-VINE ARBOUR

The throats of the little red trumpet-
    flowers are wide open,
And the clangour of brass beats against
    the hot sunlight.
They bray and blare at the burning sky.
Red! Red! Coarse notes of red,
Trumpeted at the blue sky.
In long streaks of sound, molten metal,
The vine declares itself.
Clang! — from its red and yellow trum-
    pets.
Clang! — from its long, nasal trumpets,
Splitting the sunlight into ribbons, tat-
    tered and shot with noise.

I sit in the cool arbour, in a green-and-
    gold twilight.
It is very still, for I cannot hear the
    trumpets,
I only know that they are red and open,
And that the sun above the arbour shakes
    with heat.
My quill is newly mended,
And makes fine-drawn lines with its point.
Down the long, white paper it makes
    little lines,
Just lines — up — down — criss-cross.
My heart is strained out at the pin-point
    of my quill;
It is thin and writhing like the marks of
    the pen.
My hand marches to a squeaky tune,
It marches down the paper to a squealing
    of fifes.
My pen and the trumpet-flowers,
And Washington's armies away over the
    smoke-tree to the Southwest.
"Yankee Doodle," my Darling! It is you
    against the British,
Marching in your ragged shoes to batter
    down King George.

What have you got in your hat? Not a
    feather, I wager.
Just a hay-straw, for it is the harvest you
    are fighting for.
Hay in your hat, and the whites of their
    eyes for a target!
Like Bunker Hill, two years ago, when I
    watched all day from the house-top
Through Father's spy-glass.
The red city, and the blue, bright water,
And puffs of smoke which you made.
Twenty miles away,
Round by Cambridge, or over the Neck,
But the smoke was white — white!
To-day the trumpet-flowers are red —
    red —
And I cannot see you fighting,
But old Mr. Dimond has fled to Canada,
And Myra sings "Yankee Doodle" at her
    milking.
The red throats of the trumpets bray and
    clang in the sunshine,
And the smoke-tree puffs dun blossoms
    into the blue air.

II

THE CITY OF FALLING LEAVES

Leaves fall,
Brown leaves,
Yellow leaves streaked with brown.
They fall,
Flutter,
Fall again.
The brown leaves,
And the streaked yellow leaves,
Loosen on their branches
And drift slowly downwards.
One,
One, two, three,
One, two, five.
All Venice is a falling of Autumn
    leaves —
Brown,
And yellow streaked with brown.

"That sonnet, *Abate*,
Beautiful,
I am exhausted by it.
Your phrases turn about my heart
And stifle me to swooning.
Open the window, I beg.
Lord! What a strumming of fiddles and
    mandolins!
'Tis really a shame to stop indoors.

Call my maid, or I will make you lace me
   yourself.
Fie, how hot it is, not a breath of air!
See how straight the leaves are falling.
Marianna, I will have the yellow satin
   caught up with silver fringe,
It peeps out delightfully from under a
   mantle.
Am I well painted to-day, *caro Abate
mio?*
You will be proud of me at the *Ridotto,*
   hey?
Proud of being *Cavalier' Servente* to such
   a lady?"
"Can you doubt it, *Bellissima Contessa?*
A pinch more rouge on the right cheek,
And Venus herself shines less . . ."
"You bore me, *Abate,*
I vow I must change you!
A letter, Achmet?
Run and look out of the window, *Abate.*
I will read my letter in peace."
The little black slave with the yellow
   satin turban
Gazes at his mistress with strained eyes.
His yellow turban and black skin
Are gorgeous — barbaric.
The yellow satin dress with its silver
   flashings
Lies on a chair
Beside a black mantle and a black mask.
Yellow and black,
Gorgeous — barbaric.
The lady reads her letter,
And the leaves drift slowly
Past the long windows.
"How silly you look, my dear *Abate,*
With that great brown leaf in your wig.
Pluck it off, I beg you,
Or I shall die of laughing."

A yellow wall
Aflare in the sunlight,
Chequered with shadows,
Shadows of vine leaves,
Shadows of masks,
Masks coming, printing themselves for an
   instant,
Then passing on,
More masks always replacing them.
Masks with tricorns and rapiers sticking
   out behind
Pursuing masks with plumes and high
   heels,
The sunlight shining under their insteps.

One,
One, two,
One, two, three,
There is a thronging of shadows on the
   hot wall,
Filigreed at the top with moving leaves.
Yellow sunlight and black shadows,
Yellow and black,
Gorgeous — barbaric.
Two masks stand together,
And the shadow of a leaf falls through
   them,
Marking the wall where they are not.
From hat-tip to shoulder-tip,
From elbow to sword-hilt,
The leaf falls.
The shadows mingle,
Blur together,
Slide along the wall and disappear.

Gold of mosaics and candles,
And night blackness lurking in the ceiling
   beams.
Saint Mark's glitters with flames and re-
   flections.
A cloak brushes aside,
And the yellow of satin
Licks out over the coloured inlays of the
   pavement.
Under the gold crucifixes
There is a meeting of hands
Reaching from black mantles.
Sighing embraces, bold investigations,
Hide in confessionals,
Sheltered by the shuffling of feet.
Gorgeous — barbaric
In its mail of jewels and gold,
Saint Mark's looks down at the swarm
   of black masks;
And outside in the palace gardens brown
   leaves fall,
Flutter,
Fall.
Brown,
And yellow streaked with brown.

Blue-black, the sky over Venice,
With a pricking of yellow stars.
There is no moon,
And the waves push darkly against the
   prow
Of the gondola,
Coming from Malamocco
And streaming toward Venice.
It is black under the gondola hood,

But the yellow of a satin dress
Glares out like the eye of a watching
  tiger.
Yellow compassed about with darkness,
Yellow and black,
Gorgeous — barbaric.
The boatman sings,
It is Tasso that he sings;
The lovers seek each other beneath their
  mantles,

And the gondola drifts over the lagoon,
  aslant to the coming dawn.
But at Malamocco in front,
In Venice behind,
Fall the leaves,
Brown,
And yellow streaked with brown.
They fall,
Flutter,
Fall.

BRONZE TABLETS

THE FRUIT SHOP

Cross-ribboned shoes; a muslin gown,
High-waisted, girdled with bright blue;
A straw poke bonnet which hid the frown
She pluckered her little brows into
As she picked her dainty passage through
The dusty street. "Ah, Mademoiselle,
A dirty pathway, we need rain,
My poor fruits suffer, and the shell
Of this nut's too big for its kernel, lain
Here in the sun it has shrunk again.
The baker down at the corner says
We need a battle to shake the clouds;
But I am a man of peace, my ways
Don't look to the killing of men in crowds.
Poor fellows with guns and bayonets for
  shrouds!
Pray, Mademoiselle, come out of the sun.
Let me dust off that wicker chair. It's
  cool
In here, for the green leaves I have run
In a curtain over the door, make a pool
Of shade. You see the pears on that
  stool —
The shadow keeps them plump and fair."
Over the fruiterer's door, the leaves
Held back the sun, a greenish flare
Quivered and sparked the shop, the
  sheaves
Of sunbeams, glanced from the sign on
  the eaves,
Shot from the golden letters, broke
And splintered to little scattered lights.
Jeanne Tourmont entered the shop, her
  poke
Bonnet tilted itself to rights,
And her face looked out like the moon on
  nights
Of flickering clouds. "Monsieur Popain, I

Want gooseberries, an apple or two,
Or excellent plums, but not if they're
  high;
Haven't you some which a strong wind
  blew?
I've only a couple of francs for you."
Monsieur Popain shrugged and rubbed his
  hands.
What could he do, the times were sad.
A couple of francs and such demands!
And asking for fruits a little bad.
Wind-blown indeed! He never had
Anything else than the very best.
He pointed to baskets of blunted pears
With the thin skin tight like a bursting
  vest,
All yellow, and red, and brown, in smears.
Monsieur Popain's voice denoted tears.
He picked up a pear with tender care,
And pressed it with his hardened thumb.
"Smell it, Mademoiselle, the perfume
  there
Is like lavender, and sweet thoughts come
Only from having a dish at home.
And those grapes! They melt in the
  mouth like wine,
Just a click of the tongue, and they burst
  to honey.
They're only this morning off the vine,
And I paid for them down in silver money.
The Corporal's widow is witness, her pony
Brought them in at sunrise to-day.
Those oranges — Gold! They're almost
  red.
They seem little chips just broken away
From the sun itself. Or perhaps instead
You'd like a pomegranate, they're rarely
  gay,
When you split them the seeds are like
  crimson spray.

Yes, they're high, they're high, and those
Turkey figs,
They all come from the South, and Nel-
son's ships
Make it a little hard for our rigs.
They must be forever giving the slips
To the cursed English, and when men
clips
Through powder to bring them, why
dainties mounts
A bit in price. Those almonds now,
I'll strip off that husk, when one dis-
counts
A life or two in a nigger row
With the man who grew them, it does
seem how
They would come dear; and then the
fight
At sea perhaps, our boats have heels
And mostly they sail along at night,
But once in a way they're caught; one
feels
Ivory's not better nor finer — why peels
From an almond kernel are worth two
sous.
It's hard to sell them now," he sighed.
"Purses are tight, but I shall not lose.
There's plenty of cheaper things to
choose."
He picked some currants out of a wide
Earthen bowl. "They make the tongue
Almost fly out to suck them, bride
Currants they are, they were planted
long
Ago for some new Marquise, among
Other great beauties, before the Château
Was left to rot. Now the Gardener's
wife,
He that marched off to his death at Ma-
rengo,
Sells them to me; she keeps her life
From snuffing out, with her pruning
knife.
She's a poor old thing, but she learnt the
trade
When her man was young, and the young
Marquis
Couldn't have enough garden. The flow-
ers he made
All new! And the fruits! But 'twas said
that he
Was no friend to the people, and so they
laid
Some charge against him, a cavalcade
Of citizens took him away; they meant

Well, but I think there was some mis-
take.
He just pottered round in his garden, bent
On growing things; we were so awake
In those days for the New Republic's
sake.
He's gone, and the garden is all that's
left
Not in ruin, but the currants and apri-
cots,
And peaches, furred and sweet, with a
cleft
Full of morning dew, in those green-
glazed pots,
Why, Mademoiselle, there is never an eft
Or worm among them, and as for theft,
How the old woman keeps them I cannot
say,
But they're finer than any grown this
way."
Jeanne Tourmont drew back the filigree
ring
Of her striped silk purse, tipped it upside
down
And shook it, two coins fell with a ding
Of striking silver, beneath her gown
One rolled, the other lay, a thing
Sparked white and sharply glistening,
In a drop of sunlight between two
shades.
She jerked the purse, took its empty
ends
And crumpled them toward the centre
braids.
The whole collapsed to a mass of blends
Of colours and stripes. "Monsieur Po-
pain, friends
We have always been. In the days be-
fore
The Great Revolution my aunt was kind
When you needed help. You need no
more;
'Tis we now who must beg at your door,
And will you refuse?" The little man
Bustled, denied, his heart was good,
But times were hard. He went to a
pan
And poured upon the counter a flood
Of pungent raspberries, tanged like wood.
He took a melon with rough green rind
And rubbed it well with his apron tip.
Then he hunted over the shop to find
Some walnuts cracking at the lip,
And added to these a barberry slip
Whose acrid, oval berries hung

Like fringe and trembled. He reached
a round
Basket, with handles, from where it
swung
Against the wall, laid it on the ground
And filled it, then he searched and found
The francs Jeanne Tourmont had let fall.
"You'll return the basket, Mademoi-
selle?"
She smiled, "The next time that I call,
Monsieur. You know that very well."
'Twas lightly said, but meant to tell.
Monsieur Popain bowed, somewhat
abashed.
She took her basket and stepped out.
The sunlight was so bright it flashed
Her eyes to blindness, and the rout
Of the little street was all about.
Through glare and noise she stumbled,
dazed.
The heavy basket was a care.
She heard a shout and almost grazed
The panels of a chaise and pair.
The postboy yelled, and an amazed
Face from the carriage window gazed.
She jumped back just in time, her heart
Beating with fear. Through whirling
light
The chaise departed, but her smart
Was keen and bitter. In the white
Dust of the street she saw a bright
Streak of colours, wet and gay,
Red like blood. Crushed but fair,
Her fruit stained the cobbles of the way.
Monsieur Popain joined her there.
"Tiens, Mademoiselle,
        c'est le Général Bonaparte, partant
            pour la Guerre!"

MALMAISON

I

How the slates of the roof sparkle in
the sun, over there, over there, beyond
the high wall! How quietly the Seine
runs in loops and windings, over there,
over there, sliding through the green
countryside! Like ships of the line, stately
with canvas, the tall clouds pass along
the sky, over the glittering roof, over the
trees, over the looped and curving river.
A breeze quivers through the linden-
trees. Roses bloom at Malmaison. Roses!
Roses! But the road is dusty. Already
the Citoyenne Beauharnais wearies of

her walk. Her skin is chalked and powdered with dust, she smells dust, and
behind the wall are roses! Roses with
smooth open petals, poised above rippling leaves . . . Roses . . . They have
told her so. The Citoyenne Beauharnais
shrugs her shoulders and makes a little
face. She must mend her pace if she
would be back in time for dinner. Roses
indeed! The guillotine more likely.

The tiered clouds float over Malmaison, and the slate roof sparkles in the
sun.

II

Gallop! Gallop! The General brooks
no delay. Make way, good people, and
scatter out of his path, you, and your
hens, and your dogs, and your children.
The General is returned from Egypt, and
is come in a *calèche* and four to visit
his new property. Throw open the gates,
you, Porter of Malmaison. Pull off your
cap, my man, this is your master, the
husband of Madame. Faster! Faster!
A jerk and a jingle and they are arrived,
he and she. Madame has red eyes. Fie!
It is for joy at her husband's return.
Learn your place, Porter. A gentleman
here for two months? Fie! Fie, then!
Since when have you taken to gossiping.
Madame may have a brother, I suppose.
That — all green, and red, and glitter,
with flesh as dark as ebony — that is a
slave; a blood-thirsty, stabbing, slashing
heathen, come from the hot countries
to cure your tongue of idle whispering.

A fine afternoon it is, with tall bright
clouds sailing over the trees.

"Bonaparte, *mon ami*, the trees are
golden like my star, the star I pinned
to your destiny when I married you. The
gypsy, you remember her prophecy! My
dear friend, not here, the servants are
watching; send them away, and that
flashing splendour, Roustan. Superb —
Imperial, but . . . My dear, your arm
is trembling; I faint to feel it touching
me! No, no, Bonaparte, not that —
spare me that — did we not bury that
last night! You hurt me, my friend, you

are so hot and strong. Not long, Dear,
no, thank God, not long."
The looped river runs saffron, for the
sun is setting. It is getting dark. Dark.
Darker. In the moonlight, the slate roof
shines palely milkily white.
The roses have faded at Malmaison,
nipped by the frost. What need for
roses? Smooth, open petals — her arms.
Fragrant, outcurved petals — her breasts.
He rises like a sun above her, stooping
to touch the petals, press them wider.
Eagles. Bees. What are they to open
roses! A little shivering breeze runs
through the linden-trees, and the tiered
clouds blow across the sky like ships of
the line, stately with canvas.

III

The gates stand wide at Malmaison,
stand wide all day. The gravel of the
avenue glints under the continual rolling
of wheels. An officer gallops up with his
sabre clicking; a mameluke gallops down
with his charger kicking. *Valets de pied*
run about in ones, and twos, and groups,
like swirled blown leaves. Tramp! Tramp!
The guard is changing, and the grenadiers
off duty lounge out of sight, ranging
along the roads toward Paris.
The slate roof sparkles in the sun, but
it sparkles milkily, vaguely, the great
glass-houses put out its shining. Glass,
stone, and onyx now for the sun's mirror. Much has come to pass at Malmaison. New rocks and fountains, blocks of
carven marble, fluted pillars uprearing
antique temples, vases and urns in unexpected places, bridges of stone, bridges
of wood, arbours and statues, and a flood
of flowers everywhere, new flowers, rare
flowers, parterre after parterre of flowers.
Indeed, the roses bloom at Malmaison.
It is youth, youth untrammeled and advancing, trundling a country ahead of
it as though it were a hoop. Laughter,
and spur janglings in tessellated vestibules. Tripping of clocked and embroidered stockings in little low-heeled shoes
over smooth grass-plots. India muslins
spangled with silver patterns slide through
trees — mingle — separate — white day
fireflies flashing moon-brilliance in the
shade of foliage.

"The kangaroos! I vow, Captain, I
must see the kangaroos."
"As you please, dear Lady, but I recommend the shady linden alley and feeding the cockatoos."
"They say that Madame Bonaparte's
breed of sheep is the best in all France."
"And, oh, have you seen the enchanting little cedar she planted when the
First Consul sent home the news of the
victory of Marengo?"
Picking, choosing, the chattering company flits to and fro. Over the trees the
great clouds go, tiered, stately, like ships
of the line bright with canvas.
Prisoners'-base, and its swooping, veering, racing, giggling, bumping. The First
Consul runs plump into M. de Beauharnais and falls. But he picks himself
up smartly, and starts after M. Isabey.
Too late, M. Le Premier Consul, Mademoiselle Hortense is out after you.
Quickly, my dear Sir! Stir your short
legs, she is swift and eager, and as graceful as her mother. She is there, that
other, playing too, but lightly, warily,
bearing herself with care, rather floating
out upon the air than running, never
far from goal. She is there, borne up
above her guests as something indefin-
ably fair, a rose above periwinkles. A
blown rose, smooth as satin, reflexed,
one loosened petal hanging back and
down. A rose that undulates languorously
as the breeze takes it, resting upon its
leaves in a faintness of perfume.

There are rumours about the First Consul. Malmaison is full of women, and
Paris is only two leagues distant. Madame Bonaparte stands on the wooden
bridge at sunset, and watches a black
swan pushing the pink and silver water
in front of him as he swims, crinkling
its smoothness into pleats of changing colour with his breast. Madame Bonaparte
presses against the parapet of the bridge,
and the crushed roses at her belt melt,
petal by petal, into the pink water.

IV

A vile day, Porter. But keep your wits
about you. The Empress will soon be
here. Queer, without the Emperor! It

is indeed, but best not consider that. Scratch your head and prick up your ears. Divorce is not for you to debate about. She is late? Ah, well, the roads are muddy. The rain spears are as sharp as whetted knives. They dart down and down, edged and shining. Clop-trop! Clop-trop! A carriage grows out of the mist. Hist, Porter. You can keep on your hat. It is only Her Majesty's dogs and her parrot. Clop-trop! The Ladies in Waiting, Porter. Clop-trop! It is Her Majesty. At least, I suppose it is, but the blinds are drawn.

"In all the years I have served Her Majesty she never before passed the gate without giving me a smile!"

You're a droll fellow, to expect the Empress to put out her head in the pouring rain and salute you. She has affairs of her own to think about.

Clang the gate, no need for further waiting, nobody else will be coming to Malmaison to-night.

White under her veil, drained and shaking, the woman crosses the antechamber. Empress! Empress! Foolish splendour, perished to dust. Ashes of roses, ashes of youth. Empress forsooth!

Over the glass domes of the hot-houses drenches the rain. Behind her a clock ticks — ticks again. The sound knocks upon her thought with the echoing shudder of hollow vases. She places her hands on her ears, but the minutes pass, knocking. Tears in Malmaison. And years to come each knocking by, minute after minute. Years, many years, and tears, and cold pouring rain.

"I feel as though I had died, and the only sensation I have is that I am no more."

Rain! Heavy, thudding rain!

V

The roses bloom at Malmaison. And not only roses. Tulips, myrtles, geraniums, camelias, rhododendrons, dahlias, double hyacinths. All the year through, under glass, under the sky, flowers bud, expand, die, and give way to others, always others. From distant countries they have been brought, and taught to live in the cool temperateness of France. There is the *Bonapartea* from Peru; the *Napoleone Impériale*; the *Josephinia Imperatrix*, a pearl-white flower, purple-shadowed, the calix pricked out with crimson points. Malmaison wears its flowers as a lady wears her gems, flauntingly, assertively. Malmaison decks herself to hide the hollow within.

The glass-houses grow and grow, and every year fling up hotter reflections to the sailing sun.

The cost runs into millions, but a woman must have something to console herself for a broken heart. One can play backgammon and patience, and then patience and backgammon, and stake gold napoleons on each game won. Sport truly! It is an unruly spirit which could ask better. With her jewels, her laces, her shawls; her two hundred and twenty dresses, her fichus, her veils; her pictures, her busts, her birds. It is absurd that she cannot be happy. The Emperor smarts under the thought of her ingratitude. What could he do more? And yet she spends, spends as never before. It is ridiculous. Can she not enjoy life at a smaller figure? Was ever monarch plagued with so extravagant an ex-wife. She owes her chocolate-merchant, her candle-merchant, her sweetmeat purveyor; her grocer, her butcher, her poulterer; her architect, and the shopkeeper who sells her rouge; her perfumer, her dressmaker, her merchant of shoes. She owes for fans, plants, engravings, and chairs. She owes masons and carpenters, vintners, *lingères*. The lady's affairs are in sad confusion. And why? Why?

Can a river flow when the spring is dry?

Night. The Empress sits alone, and the clock ticks, one after one. The clock nicks off the edges of her life. She is chipped like an old bit of china; she is frayed like a garment of last year's wearing. She is soft, crinkled, like a fading rose. And each minute flows by brushing against her, shearing off another and another petal. The Empress crushes her breasts with her hands and weeps. And the tall clouds sail over Malmaison like a procession of stately ships bound for the moon.

Scarlet, clear-blue, purple epauletted with gold. It is a parade of soldiers sweeping up the avenue. Eight horses, eight Imperial harnesses, four caparisoned postilions, a carriage with the Emperor's arms on the panels. Ho, Porter, pop out your eyes, and no wonder. Where else under the Heavens could you see such splendour!

They sit on a stone seat. The little man in the green coat of a Colonel of Chasseurs, and the lady, beautiful as a satin seed-pod, and as pale. The house has memories. The satin seed-pod holds his germs of Empire. We will stay here, under the blue sky and the turreted white clouds. She draws him; he feels her faded loveliness urge him to replenish it. Her soft transparent texture woos his nervous fingering. He speaks to her of debts, of resignation; of her children, and his; he promises that she shall see the King of Rome; he says some harsh things and some pleasant. But she is there, close to him, rose toned to amber, white shot with violet, pungent to his nostrils as embalmed rose-leaves in a twilit room.

Suddenly the Emperor calls his carriage and rolls away across the looping Seine.

VI

Crystal-blue brightness over the glass-houses. Crystal-blue streaks and ripples over the lake. A macaw on a gilded perch screams; they have forgotten to take out his dinner. The windows shake. Boom! Boom! It is the rumbling of Prussian cannon beyond Pecq. Roses bloom at Malmaison. Roses! Roses! Swimming above their leaves, rotting beneath them. Fallen flowers strew the unraked walks. Fallen flowers for a fallen Emperor! The General in charge of him draws back and watches. Snatches of music — snarling, sneering music of bagpipes. They say a Scotch regiment is besieging Saint-Denis. The Emperor wipes his face, or is it his eyes. His tired eyes which see nowhere the grace they long for. Josephine! Somebody asks him a question, he does not answer, somebody else does that. There are voices, but one voice he does not hear, and yet he hears

it all the time. Josephine! The Emperor puts up his hand to screen his face. The white light of a bright cloud spears sharply through the linden-trees. Vive l'Empereur! There are troops passing beyond the wall, troops which sing and call. Boom! A pink rose is jarred off its stem and falls at the Emperor's feet.

"Very well. I go." Where! Does it matter? There is no sword to clatter. Nothing but soft brushing gravel and a gate which shuts with a click.

"Quick, fellow, don't spare your horses."

A whip cracks, wheels turn, why burn one's eyes following a fleck of dust.

VII

Over the slate roof tall clouds, like ships of the line, pass along the sky. The glass-houses glitter splotchily, for many of their lights are broken. Roses bloom, fiery cinders quenching under damp weeds. Wreckage and misery, and a trailing of petty deeds smearing over old recollections.

The musty rooms are empty and their shutters are closed, only in the gallery there is a stuffed black swan, covered with dust. When you touch it, the feathers come off and float softly to the ground. Through a chink in the shutters, one can see the stately clouds crossing the sky toward the Roman arches of the Marly Aqueduct.

THE HAMMERS

I

FRINDSBURY, KENT, 1786

Bang!
Bang!
Tap!
Tap-a-tap! Rap!
All through the lead and silver Winter days,
All through the copper of Autumn hazes.
Tap to the red rising sun,
Tap to the purple setting sun.
Four years pass before the job is done.
Two thousand oak trees grown and felled,
Two thousand oaks from the hedgerows
of the Weald,

Sussex has yielded two thousand oaks
With huge boles
Round which the tape rolls
Thirty mortal feet, say the village folks.
Two hundred loads of elm and Scottish
    fir;
Planking from Dantzig.
My! What timber goes into a ship!
Tap! Tap!
Two years they have seasoned her ribs on
    the ways,
Tapping, tapping.
You can hear, though there's nothing
    where you gaze.
Through the fog down the reaches of the
    river,
The tapping goes on like heart-beats in
    a fever.
The church-bells chime
Hours and hours,
Dropping days in showers.
Bang! Rap! Tap!
Go the hammers all the time.
They have planked up her timbers
And the nails are driven to the head;
They have decked her over,
And again, and again.
The shoring-up beams shudder at the
    strain.
Black and blue breeches,
Pigtails bound and shining:
Like ants crawling about,
The hull swarms with carpenters, running
    in and out.
Joiners, calkers,
And they are all terrible talkers.
Jem Wilson has been to sea and he tells
    some wonderful tales
Of whales, and spice islands,
And pirates off the Barbary coast.
He boasts magnificently, with his mouth
    full of nails.
Stephen Pibold has a tenor voice,
He shifts his quid of tobacco and sings:
    "The second in command was blear-
        eyed Ned:
        While the surgeon his limb was a-
            lopping,
    A nine-pounder came and smack went
        his head,
        Pull away, pull away, pull away! I
            say;
    Rare news for my Meg of Wapping!"
Every Sunday
People come in crowds

(After church-time, of course)
In curricles, and gigs, and wagons,
And some have brought cold chicken and
    flagons
Of wine,
And beer in stoppered jugs.
"Dear! Dear! But I tell 'ee 'twill be a
    fine ship.
There's none finer in any of the slips at
    Chatham."

The third Summer's roses have started in
    to blow,
When the fine stern carving is begun.
Flutings, and twinings, and long slow
    swirls,
Bits of deal shaved away to thin spiral
    curls.
Tap! Tap! A cornucopia is nailed into
    place.
Rap-a-tap! They are putting up a railing
    filigreed like Irish lace.
The Three Towns' people never saw such
    grace.
And the paint on it! The richest gold
    leaf!
Why, the glitter when the sun is shining
    passes belief.
And that row of glass windows tipped to-
    ward the sky
Are rubies and carbuncles when the day
    is dry.
Oh, my! Oh, my!
They have coppered up the bottom,
And the copper nails
Stand about and sparkle in big wooden
    pails.
Bang! Clash! Bang!
    "And he swigg'd, and Nick swigg'd,
        And Ben swigg'd, and Dick swigg'd,
    And I swigg'd, and all of us swigg'd it,
        And swore there was nothing like
            grog."
It seems they sing,
Even though coppering is not an easy
    thing.
What a splendid specimen of humanity
    is a true British workman,
Say the people of the Three Towns,
As they walk about the dockyard
To the sound of the evening church-bells.
And so artistic, too, each one tells his
    neighbour.
What immense taste and labour!
Miss Jessie Prime, in a pink silk bonnet,

Titters with delight as her eyes fall upon
it,
When she steps lightly down from
Lawyer Green's whisky;
Such amazing beauty makes one feel
frisky,
She explains.
Mr. Nichols says he is delighted
(He is the firm);
His work is all requited
If Miss Jessie can approve.
Miss Jessie answers that the ship is "a
love."
The sides are yellow as marigold,
The port-lids are red when the ports are
up;
Blood-red squares like an even chequer
Of yellow asters and portulaca.
There is a wide "black strake" at the
waterline
And above is a blue like the sky when
the weather is fine.
The inner bulwarks are painted red.
"Why?" asks Miss Jessie. " 'Tis a horrid
note."
Mr. Nichols clears his throat,
And tells her the launching date is set.
He says, "Be careful, the paint is wet."
But Miss Jessie has touched it, her
sprigged muslin gown
Has a blood-red streak from the shoulder
down.
"It looks like blood," says Miss Jessie
with a frown.

Tap! Tap! Rap!
An October day, with waves running in
blue-white lines and a capful of
wind.
Three broad flags ripple out behind
Where the masts will be:
Royal Standard at the main,
Admiralty flag at the fore,
Union Jack at the mizzen.
The hammers tap harder, faster,
They must finish by noon.
The last nail is driven.
But the wind has increased to half a
gale,
And the ship shakes and quivers upon
the ways.
The Commissioner of Chatham Dock-
yard is coming
In his ten-oared barge from the King's
Stairs;

The Marine's band will play "God Save
Great George Our King;"
And there is to be a dinner afterwards at
the Crown, with speeches.
The wind screeches, and flaps the flags
till they pound like hammers.
The wind hums over the ship,
And slips round the dog-shores,
Jostling them almost to falling.
There is no time now to wait for Com-
missioners and marine bands.
Mr. Nichols has a bottle of port in his
hands.
He leans over, holding his hat, and shouts
to the men below:
"Let her go!"
Bang! Bang! Pound!
The dog-shores fall to the ground,
And the ship slides down the greased
planking.
A splintering of glass,
And port wine running all over the white
and copper stem timbers.
"Success to his Majesty's ship, the Bel-
lerophon!"
And the red wine washes away in the
waters of the Medway.

II

Paris, March, 1814

Fine yellow sunlight down the rue du
Mont Thabor.
Ten o'clock striking from all the clock-
towers of Paris.
Over the door of a shop, in gilt letters:
"Martin — Parfumeur," and something
more.
A large gilded wooden something.
Listen! What a ringing of hammers!
Tap!
Tap!
Squeak!
Tap! Squeak! Tap-a-tap!
"Blaise."
"Oui, M'sieu."
"Don't touch the letters. My name
stays."
"Bien, M'sieu."
"Just take down the eagle, and the shield
with the bees."
"As M'sieu pleases."
Tap! Squeak! Tap!
The man on the ladder hammers steadily
for a minute or two,

Then stops.
"Hé! Patron!
They are fastened well, Nom d'un Chien!
What if I break them?"
"Break away,
You and Paul must have them down
   to-day."
"Bien."
And the hammers start again,
Drum-beating at the something of gilded
   wood.
Sunshine in a golden flood
Lighting up the yellow fronts of houses,
Glittering each window to a flash.
Squeak! Squeak! Tap!
The hammers beat and rap.
A Prussian hussar on a grey horse goes
   by at a dash.
From other shops, the noise of striking
   blows:
Pounds, thumps, and whacks;
Wooden sounds: splinters — cracks.
Paris is full of the galloping of horses and
   the knocking of hammers.
"Hullo! Friend Martin, is business slack
That you are in the street this morning?
   Don't turn your back
And scuttle into your shop like a rabbit
   to its hole.
I've just been taking a stroll.
The stinking Cossacks are bivouacked all
   up and down the Champs Elysées.
I can't get the smell of them out of my
   nostrils.
Dirty fellows, who don't believe in frills
Like washing. Ah, mon vieux, you'd have
   to go
Out of business if you lived in Russia. So!
We've given up being perfumers to the
   Emperor, have we?
Blaise,
Be careful of the hen,
Maybe I can find a use for her one of
   these days.
That eagle's rather well cut, Martin.
But I'm sick of smelling Cossack,
Take me inside and let me put my head
   into a stack
Of orris-root and musk."
Within the shop, the light is dimmed to
   a pearl-and-green dusk
Out of which dreamily sparkle counters
   and shelves of glass,
Containing phials, and bowls, and jars,
   and dishes; a mass

Of aqueous transparence made solid by
   threads of gold.
Gold and glass,
And scents which whiff across the green
   twilight and pass.
The perfumer sits down and shakes his
   head:
"Always the same, Monsieur Antoine,
You artists are wonderful folk indeed."
But Antoine Vernet does not heed.
He is reading the names on the bottles
   and bowls,
Done in fine gilt letters with wonderful
   scrolls.
"What have we here? 'Eau Impérial
   Odontalgique.'
I must say, mon cher, your names are
   chic.
But it won't do, positively it will not
   do.
Elba doesn't count. Ah, here is another:
'Baume du Commandeur.' That's better.
   He needs something to smother
Regrets. A little lubricant, too,
Might be useful. I have it,
'Sage Oil,' perhaps he'll be good now;
   with it we'll submit
This fine German rouge. I fear he is
   pale."
"Monsieur Antoine, don't rail
At misfortune. He treated me well and
   fairly."
"And you prefer him to Bourbons, admit
   it squarely."
"Heaven forbid!" Bang! Whack!
Squeak! Squeak! Crack!
CRASH!
"Oh, Lord, Martin! That shield is hash.
The whole street is covered with golden
   bees.
They look like so many yellow peas,
Lying there in the mud. I'd like to paint
   it.
'Plum pudding of Empire.' That's rather
   quaint, it
Might take with the Kings. Shall I try?"
"Oh, Sir,
You distress me, you do." "Poor old
   Martin's purr!
But he hasn't a scratch in him, I know.
Now let us get back to the powders and
   patches.
Foolish man,
The Kings are here now. We must hit
   on a plan

To change all these titles as fast as we
can.
'Bouquet Impératrice.' Tut! Tut! Give
me some ink —
'Bouquet de la Reine,' what do you think?
Not the same receipt?
Now, Martin, put away your conceit.
Who will ever know?
'Extract of Nobility' — excellent, since
most of them are killed."
"But, Monsieur Antoine — "
"You are self-willed,
Martin. You need a salve
For your conscience, do you?
Very well, we'll halve
The compliments, also the pastes and
dentifrices;
Send some to the Kings, and some to
the Empresses.
'Oil of Bitter Almonds' — the Empress
Josephine can have that.
'Oil of Parma Violets' fits the other one
pat."
Rap! Rap! Bang!
"What a hideous clatter!
Blaise seems determined to batter
That poor old turkey into bits,
And pound to jelly my excellent wits.
Come, come, Martin, you mustn't shirk.
'The night cometh soon' — etc. Don't
jerk
Me up like that. 'Essence de la Val-
lière —
That has a charmingly Bourbon air.
And, oh! Magnificent! Listen to this! —
'Vinaigre des Quatre Voleurs.' Nothing
amiss
With that — England, Austria, Russia,
and Prussia!
Martin, you're a wonder,
Upheavals of continents can't keep you
under."
"Monsieur Antoine, I am grieved indeed
At such levity. What France has gone
through — "
"Very true, Martin, very true,
But never forget that a man must feed."
Pound! Pound! Thump!
Pound!
"Look here, in another minute Blaise will
drop that bird on the ground."
Martin shrugs his shoulders. "Ah, well,
what then? — "
Antoine, with a laugh: "I'll give you two
sous for that antiquated hen."

The Imperial Eagle sells for two sous,
And the lilies go up.
A man must choose!

III

PARIS, APRIL, 1814

Cold, impassive, the marble arch of the
Place du Carrousel.
Haughty, contemptuous, the marble arch
of the Place du Carrousel.
Like a woman raped by force, rising above
her fate,
Borne up by the cold rigidity of hate,
Stands the marble arch of the Place du
Carrousel.
Tap! Clink-a-tink!
Tap! Rap! Chink!
What falls to the ground like a streak of
flame?
Hush! It is only a bit of bronze flashing
in the sun.
What are all those soldiers? Those are
not the uniforms of France.
Alas! No! The uniforms of France,
Great Imperial France, are done.
They will rot away in chests and hang to
dusty tatters in barn lofts.
These are other armies. And their name?
Hush, be still for shame;
Be still and imperturable like the marble
arch.
Another bright spark falls through the
blue air.
Over the Place du Carrousel a wailing of
despair.
Crowd your horses back upon the people,
Uhlans and Hungarian Lancers,
They see too much.
Unfortunately, Gentlemen of the In-
vading Armies, what they do not see,
they hear.
Tap! Clink-a-tink!
Tap!
Another sharp spear
Of brightness,
And a ringing of quick metal lightness
On hard stones.
Workmen are chipping off the names of
Napoleon's victories
From the triumphal arch of the Place du
Carrousel.
Do they need so much force to quell the
crowd?

An old Grenadier of the line groans
aloud,
And each hammer tap points the sob of a
woman.
Russia, Prussia, Austria, and the faded-
white-lily Bourbon king
Think it well
To guard against tumult,
A mob is an undependable thing.
Ding! Ding!
Vienna is scattered all over the Place du
Carrousel
In glittering, bent, and twisted letters.
Your betters have clattered over Vienna
before,
Officer of his Imperial Majesty our
Father-in-Law!
Tink! Tink!
A workman's chisel can strew you to the
winds,
Munich.
Do they think
To pleasure Paris, used to the fall of
cities,
By giving her a fall of letters!
It is a month too late.
One month, and our lily-white Bourbon
king
Has done a colossal thing;
He has curdled love,
And soured the desires of a people.
Still the letters fall,
The workmen creep up and down their
ladders like lizards on a wall.
Tap! Tap! Tink!
Clink! Clink!
"Oh, merciful God, they will not touch
Austerlitz!
Strike me blind, my God, my eyes can
never look on that.
I would give the other leg to save it, it
took one.
Curse them! Curse them! Aim at his
hat.
Give me the stone. Why didn't you give
it to me?
I would not have missed. Curse him!
Curse all of them! They have got the
'A'!"
Ding! Ding!
"I saw the Terror, but I never saw so
horrible a thing as this.
Vive l'Empereur! Vive l'Empereur!"
"Don't strike him, Fritz.
The mob will rise if you do.

Just run him out to the quai,
That will get him out of the way.
They are almost through."
Clink! Tink! Ding!
Clear as the sudden ring
Of a bell
"Z" strikes the pavement.
Farewell, Austerlitz, Tilsit, Presbourg;
Farewell, greatness departed.
Farewell, Imperial honours, knocked
broadcast by the beating hammers of
ignorant workmen.
Straight, in the Spring moonlight,
Rises the deflowered arch.
In the silence, shining bright,
She stands naked and unsubdued.
Her marble coldness will endure the
march
Of decades.
Rend her bronzes, hammers;
Cast down her inscriptions.
She is unconquerable, austere,
Cold as the moon that swims above her
When the nights are clear.

IV

CROISSY, ILE-DE-FRANCE, JUNE, 1815

"Whoa! Victorine.
Devil take the mare! I've never seen so
vicious a beast.
She kicked Jules the last time she was
here,
He's been lame ever since, poor chap."
Rap! Tap!
Tap-a-tap-a-tap! Tap! Tap!
"I'd rather be lame than dead at Water-
loo, M'sieu Charles."
"Sacré Bleu! Don't mention Waterloo,
and the damned grinning British.
We didn't run in the old days.
There wasn't any running at Jena.
Those were decent days,
And decent men, who stood up and
fought.
We never got beaten, because we
wouldn't be.
See!"
"You would have taught them, wouldn't
you, Sergeant Boignet?
But to-day it's everyone for himself,
And the Emperor isn't what he was."
"How the Devil do you know that?
If he was beaten, the cause

Is the green geese in his army, led by
traitors.
Oh, I say no names, Monsieur Charles,
You needn't hammer so loud.
If there are any spies lurking behind the
bellows,
I beg they come out. Dirty fellows!"
The old Sergeant seizes a red-hot poker
And advances, brandishing it, into the
shadows.
The rows of horses flick
Placid tails.
Victorine gives a savage kick
As the nails
Go in. Tap! Tap!
Jules draws a horseshoe from the fire
And beats it from red to peacock-blue
and black,
Purpling darker at each whack.
Ding! Dang! Dong!
Ding-a-ding-dong!
It is a long time since any one spoke.
Then the blacksmith brushes his hand
over his eyes,
"Well," he sighs,
"He's broke."
The Sergeant charges out from behind
the bellows.
"It's the green geese, I tell you,
Their hearts are all whites and yellows,
There's no red in them. Red!
That's what we want. Fouché should be fed
To the guillotine, and all Paris dance the
carmagnole.
That would breed jolly fine lick-bloods
To lead his armies to victory."
"Ancient history, Sergeant.
He's done."
"Say that again, Monsieur Charles, and
I'll stun
You where you stand for a dung-eating
Royalist."
The Sergeant gives the poker a savage
twist;
He is as purple as the cooling horseshoes.
The air from the bellows creaks through
the flues.
Tap! Tap! The blacksmith shoes Vic-
torine,
And through the doorway a fine sheen
Of leaves flutters, with the sun between.
By a spurt of fire from the forge
You can see the Sergeant, with swollen
gorge,
Puffing, and gurgling, and choking;

The bellows keep on croaking.
They wheeze,
And sneeze,
Creak! Bang! Squeeze!
And the hammer strokes fall like buzzing
bees
Or pattering rain,
Or faster than these,
Like the hum of a waterfall struck by a
breeze.
Clank! from the bellow's chain pulled up
and down.
Clank!
And sunshine twinkles on Victorine's
flank,
Starting it to blue,
Dropping it to black.
Clack! Clack!
Tap-a-tap! Tap!
Lord! What galloping! Some mishap
Is making that man ride so furiously.
"François, you!
Victorine won't be through
For another quarter of an hour." "As
you hope to die,
Work faster, man, the order has come."
"What order? Speak out. Are you
dumb?"
"A chaise, without arms on the panels,
at the gate
In the far side-wall, and just to wait.
We must be there in half an hour with
swift cattle.
You're a stupid fool if you don't hear that
rattle.
Those are German guns. Can't you guess
the rest?
Nantes, Rochefort, possibly Brest."
Tap! Tap! as though the hammers were
mad.
Dang! Ding! Creak! The farrier's lad
Jerks the bellows till he cracks their bones,
And the stifled air hiccoughs and groans.
The Sergeant is lying on the floor
Stone dead, and his hat with the *tricolore*
Cockade has rolled off into the cinders.
Victorine snorts and lays back her ears.
What glistens on the anvil? Sweat or
tears?

V

ST. HELENA, MAY, 1821

Tap! Tap! Tap!
Through the white tropic night.

Tap! Tap!
Beat the hammers,
Unwearied, indefatigable.
They are hanging dull black cloth about
the dead.
Lustreless black cloth
Which chokes the radiance of the moon-
light
And puts out the little moving shadows
of leaves.
Tap! Tap!
The knocking makes the candles quaver,
And the long black hangings waver
Tap! Tap! Tap!
Tap! Tap!
In the ears which do not heed.
Tap! Tap!
Above the eyelids which do not flicker.
Tap! Tap!
Over the hands which do not stir.
Chiselled like a cameo of white agate
against the hangings,
Struck to brilliance by the falling moon-
light,
A face!
Sharp as a frozen flame,
Beautiful as an altar lamp of silver,
And still. Perfectly still.
In the next room, the men chatter
As they eat their midnight lunches.
A knife hits against a platter.
But the figure on the bed
Between the stifling black hangings
Is cold and motionless,
Played over by the moonlight from the
windows
And the indistinct shadows of leaves.

Tap! Tap!
Upholsterer Darling has a fine shop in
Jamestown.
Tap! Tap!
Andrew Darling has ridden hard from
Longwood to see to the work in his
shop in Jamestown.
He has a corps of men in it, toiling and
swearing,
Knocking, and measuring, and planing,
and squaring,
Working from a chart with figures,
Comparing with their rules,
Setting this and that part together with
their tools.
Tap! Tap! Tap!
Haste indeed!

So great is the need
That carpenters have been taken from
the new church,
Joiners have been called from shaping
pews and lecterns
To work of greater urgency.
Coffins!
Coffins is what they are making this
bright Summer morning.
Coffins — and all to measurement.
There is a tin coffin,
A deal coffin,
A lead coffin,
And Captain Bennett's best mahogany
dining-table
Has been sawed up for the grand outer
coffin.
Tap! Tap! Tap!
Sunshine outside in the square,
But inside, only hollow coffins and the
tapping upon them.
The men whistle,
And the coffins grow under their hammers
In the darkness of the shop.
Tap! Tap! Tap!

Tramp of men.
Steady tramp of men.
Slit-eyed Chinese with long pigtails
Bearing oblong things upon their
shoulders
March slowly along the road to Long-
wood.
Their feet fall softly in the dust of the
road;
Sometimes they call gutturally to each
other and stop to shift shoulders.
Four coffins for the little dead man,
Four fine coffins,
And one of them Captain Bennett's din-
ing-table!
And sixteen splendid Chinamen, all
strong and able
And of assured neutrality.
Ah! George of England, Lord Bathurst
& Co.
Your princely munificence makes one's
heart glow.
Huzza! Huzza! For the Lion of England!

Tap! Tap! Tap!
Marble likeness of an Emperor,
Dead man, who burst your heart against
a world too narrow,

The hammers drum you to your last
throne
Which always you shall hold alone.
Tap! Tap!
The glory of your past is faded as a sunset
fire,
Your day lingers only like the tones of a
wind-lyre
In a twilit room.
Here is the emptiness of your dream
Scattered about you.
Coins of yesterday,
Double napoleons stamped with Consul
or Emperor,
Strange as those of Herculaneum —
And you just dead!
Not one spool of thread
Will these buy in any market-place.
Lay them over him,
They are the baubles of a crown of
mist
Worn in a vision and melted away at
waking.
Tap! Tap!
His heart strained at kingdoms
And now it is content with a silver dish.
Strange World! Strange Wayfarer!
Strange Destiny!
Lower it gently beside him and let it
lie.
Tap! Tap! Tap!

TWO TRAVELLERS IN THE PLACE VENDOME

Reign of Louis Philippe

A great tall column spearing at the sky
With a little man on top. Goodness!
Tell me why?
He looks a silly thing enough to stand
up there so high.

What a strange fellow, like a soldier in
a play,
Tight-fitting coat with the tails cut away,
High-crowned hat which the brims over-
lay.

Two-horned hat makes an outline like a
bow.
Must have a sword, I can see the light
glow
Between a dark line and his leg. Vertigo

I get gazing up at him, a pygmy flashed
with sun.
A weathercock or scarecrow or both
things in one?
As bright as a jewelled crown hung above
a throne.

Say, what is the use of him if he doesn't
turn?
Just put up to glitter there, like a torch
to burn,
A sort of sacrificial show in a lofty urn?

But why a little soldier in an obsolete
dress?
I'd rather see a Goddess with a spear, I
confess.
Something allegorical and fine. Why,
yes —

I cannot take my eyes from him. I don't
know why at all.
I've looked so long the whole thing
swims. I feel he ought to fall.
Foreshortened there among the clouds
he's pitifully small.

What do you say? There used to be an
Emperor standing there,
With flowing robes and laurel crown.
Really? Yet I declare
Those spiral battles round the shaft don't
seem just his affair.

A togaed, laurelled man's I mean. Now
this chap seems to feel
As though he owned those soldiers.
Whew! How he makes one reel,
Swinging round above his circling armies
in a wheel.

Sweeping round the sky in an orbit like
the sun's,
Flashing sparks like cannon-balls from his
own long guns.
Perhaps my sight is tired, but that figure
simply stuns.

How low the houses seem, and all the
people are mere flies.
That fellow pokes his hat up till it
scratches on the skies.
Impudent! Audacious! But, by Jove, he
blinds the eyes!

WAR PICTURES

THE ALLIES

August 14th, 1914

Into the brazen, burnished sky, the cry hurls itself. The zigzagging cry of hoarse throats, it floats against the hard winds, and binds the head of the serpent to its tail, the long snail-slow serpent of marching men. Men weighed down with rifles and knapsacks, and parching with war. The cry jars and splits against the brazen, burnished sky.

This is the war of wars, and the cause? Has this writhing worm of men a cause?

Crackling against the polished sky is an eagle with a sword. The eagle is red and its head is flame.

In the shoulder of the worm is a teacher.

His tongue laps the war-sucked air in drought, but he yells defiance at the red-eyed eagle, and in his ears are the bells of new philosophies, and their tinkling drowns the sputter of the burning sword. He shrieks, "God damn you! When you are broken, the word will strike out new shoots."

His boots are tight, the sun is hot, and he may be shot, but he is in the shoulder of the worm.

A dust speck in the worm's belly is a poet.

He laughs at the flaring eagle and makes a long nose with his fingers. He will fight for smooth, white sheets of paper, and uncurdled ink. The sputtering sword cannot make him blink, and his thoughts are wet and rippling. They cool his heart.

He will tear the eagle out of the sky and give the earth tranquillity, and loveliness printed on white paper.

The eye of the serpent is an owner of mills.

He looks at the glaring sword which has snapped his machinery and struck away his men.

But it will all come again, when the sword is broken to a million dying stars, and there are no more wars.

Bankers, butchers, shop-keepers, painters, farmers — men, sway and sweat. They will fight for the earth, for the increase of the slow, sure roots of peace, for the release of hidden forces. They jibe at the eagle and his scorching sword.

One! Two! — One! Two! — clump the heavy boots. The cry hurtles against the sky.

Each man pulls his belt a little tighter, and shifts his gun to make it lighter. Each man thinks of a woman, and slaps out a curse at the eagle. The sword jumps in the hot sky, and the worm crawls on to the battle, stubbornly.

This is the war of wars, from eye to tail the serpent has one cause:

PEACE!

THE BOMBARDMENT

Slowly, without force, the rain drops into the city. It stops a moment on the carved head of Saint John, then slides on again, slipping and trickling over his stone cloak. It splashes from the lead conduit of a gargoyle, and falls from it in turmoil on the stones in the Cathedral square. Where are the people, and why does the fretted steeple sweep about in the sky? Boom! The sound swings against the rain. Boom, again! After it, only water rushing in the gutters, and the turmoil from the spout of the gargoyle. Silence. Ripples and mutters. Boom!

The room is damp, but warm. Little flashes swarm about from the firelight. The lustres of the chandelier are bright, and clusters of rubies leap in the bohemian glasses on the *étagère*. Her hands are restless, but the white masses of her hair are quite still. Boom! Will it never cease to torture, this iteration! Boom! The vibration shatters a glass on the *étagère*. It lies there, formless and glowing, with all its crimson gleams shot out of pattern, spilled, flowing red, blood-red. A thin bell-note pricks through the silence. A door creaks. The old lady speaks: "Victor, clear away that broken glass." "Alas! Madame, the bohemian glass!" "Yes, Victor, one hundred years ago my father brought it — " Boom! The room shakes, the servitor quakes. Another goblet shivers and breaks. Boom!

It rustles at the window-pane, the smooth, streaming rain, and he is shut within its clash and murmur. Inside is his candle, his table, his ink, his pen, and his dreams. He is thinking, and the walls are pierced with beams of sunshine, slipping through young green. A fountain tosses itself up at the blue sky, and through the spattered water in the basin he can see copper carp, lazily floating among cold leaves. A wind-harp in a cedar-tree grieves and whispers, and words blow into his brain, bubbled, iridescent, shooting up like flowers of fire, higher and higher. Boom! The flame-flowers snap on their slender stems. The fountain rears up in long broken spears of dishevelled water and flattens into the earth. Boom! And there is only the room, the table, the candle, and the sliding rain. Again, Boom! — Boom! — Boom! He stuffs his fingers into his ears. He sees corpses, and cries out in fright. Boom! It is night, and they are shelling the city! Boom! Boom!

A child wakes and is afraid, and weeps in the darkness. What has made the bed shake? "Mother, where are you? I am awake." "Hush, my Darling, I am here." "But, Mother, something so queer happened, the room shook." Boom! "Oh! What is it? What is the matter?" Boom! "Where is Father? I am so afraid." Boom! The child sobs and shrieks. The house trembles and creaks. Boom!

Retorts, globes, tubes, and phials lie shattered. All his trials oozing across the floor. The life that was his choosing, lonely, urgent, goaded by a hope, all gone. A weary man in a ruined laboratory, that is his story. Boom! Gloom and ignorance, and the jig of drunken brutes. Diseases like snakes crawling over the earth, leaving trails of slime. Wails from people

burying their dead. Through the window, he can see the rocking steeple. A ball of fire falls on the lead of the roof, and the sky tears apart on a spike of flame. Up the spire, behind the lacings of stone, zigzagging in and out of the carved tracings, squirms the fire. It spouts like yellow wheat from the gargoyles, coils round the head of Saint John, and aureoles him in light. It leaps into the night and hisses against the rain. The Cathedral is a burning stain on the white, wet night.

Boom! The Cathedral is a torch, and the houses next to it begin to scorch. Boom! The bohemian glass on the *étagère* is no longer there. Boom! A stalk of flame sways against the red damask curtains. The old lady cannot walk. She watches the creeping stalk and counts. Boom! — Boom! — Boom!

The poet rushes into the street, and the rain wraps him in a sheet of silver. But it is threaded with gold and powdered with scarlet beads. The city burns. Quivering, spearing, thrusting, lapping, streaming, run the flames. Over roofs, and walls, and shops, and stalls. Smearing its gold on the sky, the fire dances, lances itself through the doors, and lisps and chuckles along the floors.

The child wakes again and screams at the yellow petalled flower flickering at the window. The little red lips of flame creep along the ceiling beams.

The old man sits among his broken experiments and looks at the burning Cathedral. Now the streets are swarming with people. They seek shelter and crowd into the cellars. They shout and call, and over all, slowly and without force, the rain drops into the city. Boom! And the steeple crashes down among the people. Boom! Boom, again! The water rushes along the gutters. The fire roars and mutters. Boom!

LEAD SOLDIERS

The nursery fire burns brightly, crackling in cheerful little explosions and trails

of sparks up the back of the chimney.
Miniature rockets peppering the black
bricks with golden stars, as though a gala
flamed a night of victorious wars.

The nodding mandarin on the bookcase moves his head forward and back,
slowly, and looks into the air with his
blue-green eyes. He stares into the air
and nods — forward and back. The red
rose in his hand is a crimson splash on
his yellow coat. Forward and back, and
his blue-green eyes stare into the air,
and he nods — nods.

Tommy's soldiers march to battle,
Trumpets flare and snare-drums
    rattle.
Bayonets flash, and sabres glance —
How the horses snort and prance!
Cannon drawn up in a line
Glitter in the dizzy shine
Of the morning sunlight. Flags
Ripple colours in great jags.
Red blows out, then blue, then green,
Then all three — a weaving sheen
Of prismed patriotism. March
Tommy's soldiers, stiff and starch,
Boldly stepping to the rattle
Of the drums, they go to battle.

Tommy lies on his stomach on the
floor and directs his columns. He puts
his infantry in front, and before them
ambles a mounted band. Their instruments make a strand of gold before the
scarlet-tunicked soldiers, and they take
very long steps on their little green platforms, and from the ranks bursts the song
of Tommy's soldiers marching to battle.
The song jolts a little as the green platforms stick on the thick carpet. Tommy
wheels his guns round the edge of a box
of blocks, and places a squad of cavalry
on the commanding eminence of a footstool.

The fire snaps pleasantly, and the old
Chinaman nods — nods. The fire makes
the red rose in his hand glow and twist.
Hist! That is a bold song Tommy's
soldiers sing as they march along to
battle.
Crack! Rattle! The sparks fly up the
chimney.

Tommy's army's off to war —
Not a soldier knows what for.
But he knows about his rifle,
How to shoot it, and a trifle
Of the proper thing to do
When it's he who is shot through.
Like a cleverly trained flea,
He can follow instantly
Orders, and some quick commands
Really make severe demands
On a mind that's none too rapid,
Leaden brains tend to the vapid.
But how beautifully dressed
Is this army! How impressed
Tommy is when at his heel
All his baggage wagons wheel
About the patterned carpet, and
Moving up his heavy guns
He sees them glow with diamond
    suns
Flashing all along each barrel.
And the gold and blue apparel
Of his gunners is a joy.
Tommy is a lucky boy.
    Boom! Boom! Ta-ra!

The old mandarin nods under his
purple umbrella. The rose in his hand
shoots its petals up in thin quills of
crimson. Then they collapse and shrivel
like red embers. The fire sizzles.

Tommy is galloping his cavalry, two
by two, over the floor. They must pass
the open terror of the door and gain the
enemy encamped under the wash-stand.
The mounted band is very grand, playing
allegro and leading the infantry on at the
double quick. The tassel of the hearth-
rug has flung down the bass-drum, and he
and his dapple-grey horse lie overtripped,
slipped out of line, with the little lead
drumsticks glistening to the fire's shine.
The fire burns and crackles, and tickles
the tripped bass-drum with its sparkles.
The marching army hitches its little
green platforms valiantly, and steadily
approaches the door. The overturned
bass-drummer, lying on the hearth-rug,
melting in the heat, softens and sheds
tears. The song jeers at his impotence,
and flaunts the glory of the martial and
still upstanding, vaunting the deeds it
will do. For are not Tommy's soldiers
all bright and new?

Tommy's leaden soldiers we,
Glittering with efficiency.
Not a button's out of place,
Tons and tons of golden lace
Wind about our officers.
Every manly bosom stirs
At the thought of killing — killing!
Tommy's dearest wish fulfilling.
We are gaudy, savage, strong,
And our loins so ripe we long
First to kill, then procreate,
Doubling so the laws of Fate.
On their women we have sworn
To graft our sons. And overborne
They'll rear us younger soldiers, so
Shall our race endure and grow,
Waxing greater in the wombs
Borrowed of them, while damp
    tombs
Rot their men. O Glorious War!
Goad us with your points, Great
    Star!

The china mandarin on the bookcase
nods slowly, forward and back — forward
and back — and the red rose writhes and
wriggles, thrusting its flaming petals under and over one another like tortured
snakes.
The fire strokes them with its dartles,
and purrs at them, and the old man nods.

Tommy does not hear the song. He
only sees the beautiful, new, gaily-col-
oured lead soldiers. They belong to him,
and he is very proud and happy. He
shouts his orders aloud, and gallops his
cavalry past the door to the wash-stand.
He creeps over the floor on his hands and
knees to one battalion and another, but
he sees only the bright colours of his
soldiers and the beautiful precision of
their gestures. He is a lucky boy to
have such fine lead soldiers to enjoy.

Tommy catches his toe in the leg of
the wash-stand, and jars the pitcher. He
snatches at it with his hands, but it is
too late. The pitcher falls, and as it
goes, he sees the white water flow over
its lip. It slips between his fingers and
crashes to the floor. But it is not water
which oozes to the door. The stain is
glutinous and dark, a spark from the firelight heads it to red. In and out, be-

tween the fine, new soldiers, licking over
the carpet, squirms the stream of blood,
lapping at the little green platforms, and
flapping itself against the painted uniforms.

The nodding mandarin moves his head
slowly, forward and back. The rose is
broken, and where it fell is black blood.
The old mandarin leers under his purple
umbrella, and nods — forward and back,
staring into the air with blue-green eyes.
Every time his head comes forward a
rosebud pushes between his lips, rushes
into full bloom, and drips to the ground
with a splashing sound. The pool of
black blood grows and grows, with each
dropped rose, and spreads out to join the
stream from the wash-stand. The beautiful army of lead soldiers steps boldly forward, but the little green platforms are
covered in the rising streams of blood.

The nursery fire burns brightly and
flings fan-bursts of stars up the chimney,
as though a gala flamed a night of victorious wars.

THE PAINTER ON SILK

There was a man
Who made his living
By painting roses
Upon silk.

He sat in an upper chamber
And painted,
And the noises of the street
Meant nothing to him.

When he heard bugles, and fifes, and
    drums,
He thought of red, and yellow, and white
    roses
Bursting in the sunshine,
And smiled as he worked.

He thought only of roses,
And silk.
When he could get no more silk
He stopped painting
And only thought
Of roses.

The day the conquerors
Entered the city,

The old man
Lay dying.
He heard the bugles and drums,
And wished he could paint the roses
Bursting into sound.

A BALLAD OF FOOTMEN

Now what in the name of the sun and
    the stars
Is the meaning of this most unholy of
    wars?

Do men find life so full of humour and
    joy
That for want of excitement they smash
    up the toy?

Fifteen millions of soldiers with popguns
    and horses
All bent upon killing, because their "of
    courses"

Are not quite the same. All these men
    by the ears,
And nine nations of women choking with
    tears,

It is folly to think that the will of a king
Can force men to make ducks and drakes
    of a thing

They value, and life is, at least one sup-
    poses,
Of some little interest, even if roses

Have not grown up between one foot
    and the other.
What a marvel bureaucracy is, which can
    smother

Such quite elementary feelings, and tag
A man with a number, and set him to wag

His legs and his arms at the word of com-
    mand
Or the blow of a whistle! He's certainly
    damned,

Fit only for mince-meat, if a little gold
    lace
And an upturned moustache can set him
    to face

Bullets, and bayonets, and death, and
    diseases,
Because some one he calls his Emperor,
    pleases.

If each man were to lay down his weapon,
    and say,
With a click of his heels, "I wish you
    Good-day,"

Now what, may I ask, could the Emperor
    do?
A king and his minions are really so few.

Angry? Oh, of course, a most furious
    Emperor!
But the men are so many they need not
    mind his temper, or

The dire results which could not be in-
    flicted.
With no one to execute sentence, convicted

Is just the weak wind from an old, broken
    bellows.
What lackeys men are, who might be
    such fine fellows!

To be killing each other, unmercifully,
At an order, as though one said, "Bring
    up the tea."

Or is it that tasting the blood on their jaws
They lap at it, drunk with its ferment,
    and laws

So patiently builded, are nothing to
    drinking
More blood, any blood. They don't no-
    tice its stinking.

I don't suppose tigers do, fighting cocks,
    sparrows,
And, as to men — what are men, when
    their marrows

Are running with blood they have gulped;
    it is plain
Such excellent sport does not recollect
    pain.

Toll the bells in the steeples left stand-
    ing. Half-mast
The flags which meant order, for order
    is past.

Take the dust of the streets and sprinkle
    your head,
The civilization we've worked for is dead.

Squeeze into this archway, the head of
    the line
Has just swung round the corner to *Die
    Wacht am Rhein.*

THE OVERGROWN PASTURE

REAPING

You want to know what's the matter
  with me, do yer?
My! Ain't men blinder'n moles?
It ain't nothin' new, be sure o' that.
Why, ef you'd had eyes you'd ha' seed
Me changin' under your very nose,
Each day a little diff'rent.
But you never see nothin', you don't.
Don't touch me, Jake,
Don't you dars't to touch me,
I ain't in no humour.
That's what's come over me;
Jest a change clear through.
You lay still, an' I'll tell yer,
I've had it on my mind to tell yer
Fer some time.
It's a strain livin' a lie from mornin' till
  night,
An' I'm goin' to put an end to it right
  now.
An' don't make any mistake about one
  thing,
When I married yer I loved yer.
Why, your voice 'ud make
Me go hot and cold all over,
An' your kisses most stopped my heart
  from beatin'.
Lord! I was a silly fool.
But that's the way 'twas.
Well, I married yer
An' thought Heav'n was comin'
To set on the door-step.
Heav'n didn't do no settin',
Though the first year warn't so bad.
The baby's fever threw you off some, I
  guess,
An' then I took her death real hard,
An' a mopey wife kind o' disgusts a man.
I ain't blamin' yer exactly.
But that's how 'twas.
Do lay quiet,
I know I'm slow, but it's harder to say'n
  I thought.
There come a time when I got to be
More wife agin than mother.
The mother part was sort of a waste
When we didn't have no other child.
But you'd got used ter lots o' things,
An' you was all took up with the farm.

Many's the time I've laid awake
Watchin' the moon go clear through the
  elm-tree,
Out o' sight.
I'd foller yer around like a dog,
An' set in the chair you'd be'n settin' in,
Jest to feel its arms around me,
So long's I didn't have yours.
It preyed on me, I guess,
Longin' and longin'
While you was busy all day, and snorin'
  all night.
Yes, I know you're wide awake now,
But now ain't then,
An' I guess you'll think diff'rent
When I'm done.
Do you mind the day you went to Had-
  rock?
I didn't want to stay home for reasons,
But you said someone'd have to be here
'Cause Elmer was comin' to see t' th'
  telephone.
An' you never see why I was so set on
  goin' with yer,
Our married life hadn't be'n any great
  shakes,
Still marriage is marriage, an' I was raised
  God-fearin'.
But, Lord, you didn't notice nothin',
An' Elmer hangin' around all Winter!
'Twas a lovely mornin'.
The apple-trees was just elegant
With their blossoms all flared out,
An' there warn't a cloud in the sky.
You went, but you wouldn't pay no 'tention
  to what I said,
An' I heard the Ford chuggin' for most
  a mile,
The air was so still.
Then Elmer come.
It's no use your frettin', Jake,
I'll tell you all about it.
I know what I'm doin',
An' what's worse, I know what I done.
Elmer fixed th' telephone in about two
  minits,
An' he didn't seem in no hurry to go,
An' I don't know as I wanted him to go
  either,
I was awful mad at your not takin' me
  with yer,

An' I was tired o' wishin' and wishin'
An' gittin' no comfort.
I guess it ain't necessary to tell yer all
the things.
He stayed to dinner,
An' he helped me do the dishes,
An' he said a home was a fine thing,
An' I said dishes warn't a home
Nor yet the room they're in.
He said a lot o' things,
An' I fended him off at first,
But he got talkin' all around me,
Clost up to the things I'd be'n thinkin',
What's the use o' me goin' on, Jake,
You know.
He got all he wanted,
An' I give it to him,
An' what's more, I'm glad!
I ain't dead, anyway,
An' somebody thinks I'm somethin'.
Keep away, Jake,
You can kill me to-morrer if you want to,
But I'm goin' to have my say.
Funny thing! Guess I ain't made to hold
a man.
Elmer ain't be'n here for more'n two
months.
I don't want to pretend nothin',
Mebbe if he'd be'n lately
I shouldn't have told yer.
I'll go away in the mornin', o' course.
What you want the light fer?
I don't look no diff'rent.
Ain't the moon bright enough
To look at a woman that's deceived yer
by?
Don't, Jake, don't, you can't love me now!
It ain't a question of forgiveness.
Why! I'd be thinkin' o' Elmer ev'ry
minute;
It ain't decent.
Oh, my God! It ain't decent any more
either way!

OFF THE TURNPIKE

Good ev'nin', Mis' Priest.
I jest stepped in to tell you Good-bye.
Yes, it's all over.
All my things is packed
An' every last one o' them boxes
Is on Bradley's team
Bein' hauled over to th' depot.
No, I ain't goin' back agin.
I'm stoppin' over to French's fer to-night,

And goin' down first train in th' mornin'.
Yes, it do seem kinder queer
Not to be goin' to see Cherry's Orchard
no more,
But Land Sakes! When a change's
comin',
Why, I al'ays say it can't come too quick.
Now, that's real kind o' you,
Your doughnuts is always so tasty.
Yes, I'm goin' to Chicago,
To my niece,
She's married to a fine man, hardware
business,
An' doin' real well, she tells me.
Lizzie's be'n at me to go out ther for the
longest while.
She ain't got no kith nor kin to Chicago,
you know
She's rented me a real nice little flat,
Same house as hers,
An' I'm goin' to try that city livin' folks
say's so pleasant.
Oh, yes, he was real generous,
Paid me a sight o' money fer the Orchard;
I told him 'twouldn't yield nothin' but
stones,
But he ain't farmin' it.
Lor', no, Mis' Priest,
He's jest took it to set and look at the
view.
Mebbe he wouldn't be so stuck on the
view
Ef he'd seed it every mornin' and night
for forty year
Same's as I have.
I dessay it's pretty enough,
But it's so pressed into me
I c'n see't with my eyes shut.
No. I ain't cold, Mis' Priest,
Don't shut th' door.
I'll be all right in a minit.
But I ain't a mite sorry to leave that view.
Well, mebbe 'tis queer to feel so,
An' mebbe 'taint.
My! But that tea's revivin'.
Old things ain't always pleasant things,
Mis' Priest.
No, no, I don't cal'late on comin' back,
That's why I'd ruther be to Chicago,
Boston's too near.
It ain't cold, Mis' Priest,
It's jest my thoughts.
I ain't sick, only —
Mis' Priest, ef you've nothin' ter take yer
time,

An' have a mind to listen,
There's somethin' I'd like ter speak about.
I ain't never mentioned it,
But I'd like to tell yer 'fore I go.
Would you mind lowerin' them shades,
Fall twilight's awful grey,
An' that fire's real cosy with the shades
drawed.
Well, I guess folks about here think I've
be'n dret'ful onsociable.
You needn't say 'taint so, 'cause I know
diff'rent.
An' what's more, it's true.
Well, the reason is I've be'n scared out
o' my life.
Scared ev'ry minit o' th' time, fer eight
year.
Eight mortal year 'tis, come next June.
'Twas on the eighteenth o' June,
Six months after I'd buried my hus-
band,
That somethin' happened ter me.
Mebbe you'll mind that afore that
I was a cheery body.
Hiram was too,
Al'ays liked to ask a neighbor in,
An' ev'n when he died,
Barrin' low sperrits, I warn't averse to
seein' nobody.
But that eighteenth o' June changed
ev'rythin'.
I was doin' most o' th' farmwork myself,
With jest a hired boy, Clarence King,
'twas,
Comin' in fer an hour or two.
Well, that eighteenth o' June
I was goin' round,
Lockin' up and seein' to things 'fore I
went to bed.
I was jest steppin' out t' th' barn,
Goin' round outside 'stead o' through
the shed,
'Cause there was such a sight o' moon-
light
Somehow or another I thought 'twould
be pretty outdoors.
I got settled for pretty things that night,
I guess.
I ain't stuck on 'em no more.
Well, them laylock bushes side o' th'
house
Was real lovely.
Glitt'rin' and shakin' in the moonlight,
An' the smell o' them rose right up
An' most took my breath away.

The colour o' the spikes was all faded
out,
They never keep their colour when the
moon's on 'em,
But the smell fair 'toxicated me.
I was al'ays partial to a sweet scent,
An' I went close up t' th' bushes
So's to put my face right into a flower.
Mis' Priest, jest's I got breathin' in that
laylock bloom
I saw, layin' right at my feet,
A man's hand!
It was as white's the side o' th' house,
And sparklin' like that lum'nous paint
they put on gate-posts.
I screamed right out,
I couldn't help it,
An' I could hear my scream
Goin' over an' over
In that echo be'ind th' barn.
Hearin' it agin an' agin like that
Scared me so, I dar'sn't scream any
more.
I jest stood ther,
And looked at that hand.
I thought the echo'd begin to hammer
like my heart,
But it didn't.
There was only th' wind,
Sighin' through the laylock leaves,
An' slappin' 'em up agin the house.
Well, I guess I looked at that hand
Most ten minits,
An' it never moved,
Jest lay there white as white.
After a while I got to thinkin' that o'
course
'Twas some drunken tramp over from
Redfield.
That calmed me some,
An' I commenced to think I'd better git
him out
From under them laylocks.
I planned to drag him in t' th' barn
An' lock him in ther till Clarence come
in th' mornin'.
I got so mad thinkin' o' that all-fired
brazen tramp
Asleep in my laylocks,
I jest stooped down and grabbed th'
hand and give it an awful pull.
Then I bumped right down settin' on
the ground.
Mis' Priest, ther warn't no body come
with the hand.

No, it ain't cold, it's jest I can't abear
    thinkin' of it,
Ev'n now.
I'll take a sip o' tea.
Thank you, Mis' Priest, that's better.
I'd rather finish now I've begun.
Thank you, jest the same.
I dropped the hand's ef it'd be'n red hot
'Stead o' ice cold.
Fer a minit or two I jest laid on that
    grass
Pantin'.
Then I up and run to them laylocks
An' pulled 'em every which way.
True es I'm settin' here, Mis' Priest,
Ther warn't nothin' ther.
I peeked an' pryed all about 'em,
But ther warn't no man ther
Neither livin' nor dead.
But the hand was ther all right,
Upside down, the way I'd dropped it,
And glist'nin' fit to dazzle yer.
I don't know how I done it,
An' I don't know why I done it,
But I wanted to git that dret'ful hand
    out o' sight
I got in t' th' barn, somehow,
An' felt roun' till I got a spade.
I couldn't stop fer a lantern,
Besides, the moonlight was bright enough
    in all conscience.
Then I scooped that awful thing up in
    th' spade.
I had a sight o' trouble doin' it.
It slid off, and tipped over, and I
    couldn't bear
Ev'n to touch it with my foot to prop it,
But I done it somehow.
Then I carried it off be'ind the barn,
Clost to an old apple-tree
Where you couldn't see from the house,
An' I buried it,
Good an' deep.

I don't rec'lect nothin' more o' that
    night.
Clarence woke me up in th' mornin',
Hollerin' fer me to come down and set
    th' milk.
When he'd gone,
I stole roun' to the apple-tree
And seed the earth all new turned
Where I left it in my hurry.
I did a heap o' gardenin'
That mornin'.

I couldn't cut no big sods
Fear Clarence would notice and ask me
    what I wanted 'em fer,
So I got teeny bits o' turf here and ther,
And no one couldn't tell ther'd be'n any
    diggin'
When I got through.
They was awful days after that, Mis'
    Priest,
I used ter go every mornin' and poke
    about them bushes,
An' up and down the fence,
Ter find the body that hand come off of.
But I couldn't never find nothin'.
I'd lay awake nights
Hearin' them laylocks blowin' and
    whiskin'.
At last I had Clarence cut 'em down
An' make a big bonfire of 'em.
I told him the smell made me sick,
An' that warn't no lie,
I can't abear the smell on 'em now.
An' no wonder, es you say.
I fretted somethin' awful 'bout that hand
I wondered, could it be Hiram's,
But folks don't rob graveyards hereabouts.
Besides, Hiram's hands warn't that awful,
    starin' white.
I give up seein' people,
I was afeared I'd say somethin'.
You know what folks thought o' me
Better'n I do, I dessay,
But mebbe now you'll see I couldn't do
    nothin' diff'rent.
But I stuck it out,
I warn't goin' to be downed
By no loose hand, no matter how it come
    ther
But that ain't the worst, Mis' Priest,
Not by a long ways.
Two year ago, Mr. Densmore made me
    an offer for Cherry's Orchard.
Well, I'd got used to th' thought o'
    bein' sort o' blighted,
An' I warn't scared no more.
Lived down my fear, I guess.
I'd kinder got used to the' thought o'
    that awful night,
And I didn't mope much about it.
Only I never went out o' doors by moon-
    light;
That stuck.
Well, when Mr. Densmore's offer come,
I started thinkin' 'bout the place
An' all the things that had gone on ther.

Thinks I, I guess I'll go and see where
I put the hand.
I was foolhardy with the long time that
had gone by.
I know'd the place real well,
Fer I'd put it right in between two o'
the apple roots.
I don't know what possessed me, Mis'
Priest,
But I kinder wanted to know
That the hand had been flesh and bone,
anyway.
It had sorter bothered me, thinkin' I
might ha' imagined it.
I took a mornin' when the sun was real
pleasant and warm;
I guessed I wouldn't jump for a few old
bones.
But I did jump, somethin' wicked.
Ther warn't no bones!
Ther warn't nothin'!
Not ev'n the gold ring I'd minded bein'
on the little finger.
I don't know ef ther ever was anythin'.
I've worried myself sick over it.
I be'n diggin' and diggin' day in and
day out
Till Clarence ketched me at it.
Oh, I know'd real well what you all
thought,
An' I ain't sayin' you're not right,
But I ain't goin' to end in no county
'sylum
If I c'n help it.
The shiv'rin' fits come on me sudden
like.
I know 'em, don't you trouble.
I've fretted considerable about the 'sylum,
I guess I be'n frettin' all the time I ain't
be'n diggin'.
But anyhow I can't dig to Chicago, can I?
Thank you, Mis' Priest,
I'm better now. I only dropped in in
passin'.
I'll jest be steppin' along down to
French's.
No, I won't be seein' nobody in the
mornin',
It's a pretty early start.
Don't you stand ther, Mis' Priest,
The wind'll blow yer lamp out,
An' I c'n see easy, I got aholt o' the
gate now.
I ain't a mite tired, thank you.
Good-night.

THE GROCERY

"Hullo, Alice!"
"Hullo, Leon!"
"Say, Alice, gi' me a couple
O' them two for five cigars,
Will yer?"
"Where's your nickel?"
"My! Ain't you close!
Can't trust a feller, can yer."
"Trust you. Why
What you owe this store
Would set you up in business.
I can't think why Father 'lows it."
"Yer Father's a sight more neighbourly
Than you be. That's a fact.
Besides, he knows I got a vote."
"A vote! Oh, yes, you got a vote!
A lot o' good the Senate'll be to Father
When all his bank account
Has run away in credits.
There's your cigars,
If you can relish smokin'
With all you owe us standin'."
"I dunno as that make 'em taste any
diff'rent.
You ain't fair to me, Alice, 'deed you
ain't.
I work when anythin's doin'.
I'll get a carpenterin' job next Summer
sure.
Cleve was tellin' me to-day he'd take me
on come Spring."
"Come Spring, and this December!
I've no patience with you, Leon,
Shilly-shallyin' the way you do.
Here, lift over them crates o' oranges
I wanter fix 'em in the winder."
"It riles yer, don't it, me not havin'
work.
You pepper up about it somethin' good.
You pick an' pick, and that don't help
a mite.
Say, Alice, do come in out o' that winder.
Th' oranges c'n wait,
An' I don't like talkin' to yer back."
"Don't you! Well, you'd better make
the best o' what you can git.
Maybe you won't have my back to talk
to soon.
They look good in pyramids with the
'lectric light on 'em,
Don't they?
Now hand me the bananas
An' I'll string 'em right acrost."

"What do yer mean
'Bout me not havin' you to talk to?
Are yer springin' somethin' on me?"
"I don't know 'bout springin'
When I'm tellin' you right out.
I'm goin' away, that's all."
"Where? Why?
What yer mean — goin' away?"
"I've took a place
Down to Boston, in a candy store
For the holidays."
"Good Land, Alice,
What in the Heavens fer!"
"To earn some money,
And to git away from here, I guess."
"Ain't yer Father got enough?
Don't he give yer proper pocket-money?"
"He'd have a plenty, if you folks paid
him."
"He's rich I tell yer.
I never figured he'd be close with you."
"Oh, he ain't. Not close.
That ain't why.
But I must git away from here.
I must! I must!"
"You got a lot o' reason in yer
To-night.
How long d' you cal'late
You'll be gone?"
"Maybe for always."
"What ails yer, Alice?
Talkin' wild like that.
Ain't you an' me goin' to be married
Some day."
"Some day! Some day!
I guess the sun'll never rise on some day."
"So that's the trouble.
Same old story.
'Cause I ain't got the cash to settle right
now.
You know I love yer,
An' I'll marry yer as soon
As I c'n raise the money."
"You've said that any time these five
year,
But you don't do nothin'.'"
"Wot could I do?
Ther ain't no work here Winters.
Not fer a carpenter, ther ain't."
"I guess you warn't born a carpenter.
Ther's ice-cuttin' a plenty."
"I got a dret'ful tender throat;
Dr. Smiles he told me
I mustn't resk ice-cuttin'."
"Why haven't you gone to Boston,

And hunted up a job?"
"Have yer forgot the time I went ex-
pressin'
In the American office, down ther?"
"And come back two weeks later!
No, I ain't."
"You didn't want I should git hurted,
Did yer?
I'm a sight too light fer all that liftin'
work.
My back was commencin' to strain, as
'twas.
Ef I was like yer brother now,
I'd ha' be'n down to the city long ago.
But I'm too clumsy fer a dancer.
I ain't got Arthur's luck."
"Do you call it luck to be a disgrace to
your folks,
And git locked up in jail!"
"Oh, come now, Alice,
'Disgrace' is a mite strong.
Why, the jail was a joke.
Art's all right."
"All right!
All right to dance, and smirk, and lie
For a livin',
And then in the end
Lead a silly girl to give you
What warn't hers to give
By pretendin' you'd marry her —
And she a pupil."
"He'd ha' married her right enough,
Her folks was millionaires."
"Yes, he'd ha' married her!
Thank God, they saved her that."
"Art's a fine feller.
I wish I had his luck.
Swellin' round in Hart, Schaffner & Marx
fancy suits,
And eatin' in rest'rants.
But somebody's got to stick to the old
place,
Else Foxfield'd have to shut up shop,
Hey, Alice?"
"You admire him!
You admire Arthur!
You'd be like him only you can't dance.
Oh, Shame! Shame!
And I've been like that silly girl.
Fooled with your promises,
And I give you all I had.
I knew it, oh, I knew it,
But I wanted to git away 'fore I proved
it.
You've shamed me through and through.

Why couldn't you hold your tongue,
And spared me seein' you
As you really are."
"What the Devil's the row?
I only said Art was lucky.
What are you spitfirin' at me fer?
Ferget it, Alice.
We've had good times, ain't we?
I'll see Cleve 'bout that job agin to-
morrer,
And we'll be married 'fore hayin' time."
"It's like you to remind me o' hayin'
time.
I've good cause to love it, ain't I?
Many's the night I've hid my face in the
dark
To shut out thinkin'!"
"Why, that ain't nothin'.
You ain't be'n half so kind to me
As lots o' fellers' girls.
Gi' me a kiss, Dear,
And let's make up."
"Make up!
You poor fool.
Do you suppose I care a ten cent piece
For you now.
You've killed yourself for me.
Done it out o' your own mouth.
You've took away my home,
I hate the sight o' the place.
You're all over it,
Every stick an' stone means you,
An' I hate 'em all."
"Alice, I say,
Don't go on like that.
I can't marry yer
Boardin' in one room,
But I'll see Cleve to-morrer,
I'll make him — "
"Oh, you fool!
You terrible fool!"
"Alice, don't go yit,
Wait a minit,
I'll see Cleve — "
"You terrible fool!"
"Alice, don't go.
Alice — " (Door slams)

NUMBER 3 ON THE DOCKET

The lawyer, are you?
Well! I ain't got nothin' to say.
Nothin'!
I told the perlice I hadn't nothin'.
They know'd real well 'twas me.

Ther warn't no supposin',
Ketchin' me in the woods as they did,
An' me in my house dress.
Folks don't walk miles an' miles
In the drifted snow,
With no hat nor wrap on 'em
Ef everythin's all right, I guess.
All right? Ha! Ha! Ha!
Nothin' warn't right with me.
Never was.
Oh, Lord! Why did I do it?
Why ain't it yesterday, and Ed here
agin?
Many's the time I've set up with him
nights
When he had cramps, or rheumatizm, or
somethin'.
I used ter nurse him same's ef he was a
baby.
I wouldn't hurt him, I love him!
Don't you dare to say I killed him.
'Twarn't me!
Somethin' got aholt o' me. I couldn't
help it.
Oh, what shall I do! What shall I do!
Yes, Sir.
No, Sir.
I beg your pardon, I — I —
Oh, I'm a wicked woman!
An' I'm desolate, desolate!
Why warn't I struck dead or paralyzed
Afore my hands done it.
Oh, my God, what shall I do!
No, Sir, ther ain't no extenuatin' cir-
cumstances,
An' I don't want none.
I want a bolt o' lightnin'
To strike me dead right now!
Oh, I'll tell yer.
But it won't make no diff'rence.
Nothin' will.
Yes, I killed him.
Why do yer make me say it?
It's cruel! Cruel!
I killed him because o' th' silence.
The long, long silence,
That watched all around me,
And he wouldn't break it.
I tried to make him,
Time an' agin,
But he was terrible taciturn, Ed was.
He never spoke 'cept when he had to,
An then he'd only say "yes" and "no."
You can't even guess what that silence
was.

I'd hear it whisperin' in my ears,
An' I got frightened, 'twas so thick,
An' al'ays comin' back.
Ef Ed would ha' talked sometimes
It would ha' driven it away;
But he never would.
He didn't hear it same as I did.
You see, Sir,
Our farm was off'n the main road,
And set away back under the mountain;
And the village was seven mile off,
Measurin' after you'd got out o' our lane.
We didn't have no hired man,
'Cept in hayin' time;
An' Dane's place,
That was the nearest,
Was clear way 'tother side the mountain.
They used Marley post-office
An' ours was Benton.
Ther was a cart-track took yer to Dane's
     in Summer,
An' it warn't above two miles that way,
But it warn't never broke out Winters.
I used to dread the Winters.
Seem's ef I couldn't abear to see the
     golden-rod bloomin';
Winter'd come so quick after that.
You don't know what snow's like when
     yer with it
Day in an' day out.
Ed would be out all day loggin',
An' I set at home and look at the snow
Layin' over everythin';
It 'ud dazzle me blind,
Till it warn't white any more, but black
     as ink.
Then the quiet 'ud commence rushin' past
     my ears
Till I most went mad listenin' to it.
Many's the time I've dropped a pan on
     the floor
Jest to hear it clatter.
I was most frantic when dinner-time come
An' Ed was back from the woods.
I'd ha' give my soul to hear him speak.
But he'd never say a word till I asked him
Did he like the raised biscuits or what-
     ever,
An' then sometimes he'd jest nod his
     answer.
Then he'd go out agin,
An' I'd watch him from the kitchen
     winder.
It seemed the woods come marchin' out
     to meet him

An' the trees 'ud press round him an'
     hustle him.
I got so I was scared o' th' trees.
I thought they come nearer,
Every day a little nearer,
Closin' up round the house.
I never went in t' th' woods Winters,
Though in Summer I liked 'em well
     enough.
It warn't so bad when my little boy was
     with us.
He used to go sleddin' and skatin',
An' every day his father fetched him to
     school in the pung
An' brought him back agin.
We scraped an' scraped fer Neddy,
We wanted him to have a education.
We sent him to High School,
An' then he went up to Boston to Tech-
     nology.
He was a minin' engineer,
An' doin' real well,
A credit to his bringin' up.
But his very first position ther was an
     explosion in the mine.
And I'm glad! I'm glad!
He ain't here to see me now.
Neddy! Neddy!
I'm your mother still, Neddy.
Don't turn from me like that.
I can't abear it. I can't! I can't!
What did you say?
Oh, yes, Sir.
I'm here.
I'm very sorry,
I don't know what I'm sayin'.
No, Sir,
Not till after Neddy died.
'Twas the next Winter the silence come,
I don't remember noticin' it afore.
That was five year ago,
An' it's been gittin' worse an' worse.
I asked Ed to put in a telephone.
I though ef I felt the whisperin' comin'
     on
I could ring up some o' th' folks.
But Ed wouldn't hear of it.
He said we'd paid so much for Neddy
We couldn't hardly git along as 'twas.
An' he never understood me wantin' to
     talk.
Well, this year was worse'n all the others;
We had a terrible spell o' stormy weather,
An' the snow lay so thick
You couldn't see the fences even.

Out o' doors was as flat as the palm o'
 my hand,
Ther warn't a hump or a holler
Fer as you could see.
It was so quiet.
The snappin' o' the branches back in the
 wood-lot
Sounded like pistol shots.
Ed was out all day
Same as usual.
An' it seemed he talked less'n ever.
He didn't even say 'Good-mornin',' once
 or twice,
An' jest nodded or shook his head when
 I asked him things.
On Monday he said he'd got to go over
 to Benton
Fer some oats.
I'd oughter ha' gone with him,
But 'twas washin' day
An' I was afeared the fine weather'd
 break,
An' I couldn't do my dryin'.
All my life I'd done my work punctual,
An' I couldn't fix my conscience
To go junketin' on a washin'-day.
I can't tell you what that day was to me.
It dragged an' dragged,
Fer ther warn't no Ed ter break it in the
 middle
Fer dinner.
Every time I stopped stirrin' the water
I heerd the whisperin' all about me.
I stopped oftener'n I should
To see ef 'twas still ther,
An' it al'ays was.
An' gittin' louder
It seemed ter me.
Once I threw up the winder to feel the
 wind.
That seemed most alive somehow.
But the woods looked so kind of men-
 acin'
I closed it quick
An' started to mangle's hard's I could,
The squeakin' was comfortin'.
Well, Ed come home 'bout four.
I seen him down the road,

An' I run out through the shed inter
 th' barn
To meet him quicker.
I hollered out, 'Hullo!'
But he didn't say nothin',
He jest drove right in
An' climbed out o' th' sleigh
An' commenced unharnessin'.
I asked him a heap o' questions;
Who he'd seed
An' what he'd done.
Once in a while he'd nod or shake,
But most o' th' time he didn't do nothin'.
'Twas gittin' dark then,
An' I was in a state,
With the loneliness
An' Ed payin' no attention
Like somethin' warn't livin'.
All of a sudden it come,
I don't know what,
But I jest couldn't stand no more.
It didn't seem's though that was Ed,
An' it didn't seem as though I was me.
I had to break a way out somehow,
Somethin' was closin' in
An' I was stiflin'.
Ed's loggin' axe was ther,
An' I took it.
Oh, my God!
I can't see nothin' else afore me all the
 time.
I run out inter th' woods,
Seemed as ef they was pullin' me;
An' all the time I was wadin' through the
 snow
I seed Ed in front of me
Where I'd laid him.
An' I see him now.
There! There!
What you holdin' me fer?
I want ter go to Ed,
He's bleedin'.
Stop holdin' me.
I got to go.
I'm comin', Ed.
I'll be ther in a minit.
Oh, I'm so tired!
    (Faints)

CLOCKS TICK A CENTURY

NIGHTMARE: A TALE FOR AN AUTUMN EVENING

AFTER A PRINT BY GEORGE CRUIKSHANK

It was a gusty night,
With the wind booming, and swooping,
Looping round corners,
Sliding over the cobble-stones,
Whipping and veering,
And careering over the roofs
Like a thousand clattering horses.
Mr. Spruggins had been dining in the city,
Mr. Spruggins was none too steady in his gait,
And the wind played ball with Mr. Spruggins
And laughed as it whistled past him.
It rolled him along the street,
With his little feet pit-a-patting on the flags of the sidewalk,
And his muffler and his coat-tails blown straight out behind him.
It pumped him against area railings,
And chuckled in his ear when he said "Ouch!"
Sometimes it lifted him clear off his little patting feet
And bore him in triumph over three grey flagstones and a quarter.
The moon dodged in and out of clouds, winking.
It was all very unpleasant for Mr. Spruggins,
And when the wind flung him hard against his own front door
It was a relief,
Although the breath was quite knocked out of him.
The gas-lamp in front of the house flared up,
And the keyhole was as big as a barn door;
The gas-lamp flickered away to a sputtering blue star,
And the keyhole went out with it.
Such a stabbing, and jabbing,
And sticking, and picking,
And poking, and pushing, and prying
With that key;
And there is no denying that Mr. Spruggins rapped out an oath or two,

Rub-a-dub-dubbing them out to a real snare-drum roll.
But the door opened at last,
And Mr. Spruggins blew through it into his own hall
And slammed the door to so hard
That the knocker banged five times before it stopped.
Mr. Spruggins struck a light and lit a candle,
And all the time the moon winked at him through the window.
"Why couldn't you find the keyhole, Spruggins?"
Taunted the wind.
"I can find the keyhole."
And the wind, thin as a wire,
Darted in and seized the candle flame
And knocked it over to one side
And pummelled it down — down — down — !
But Mr. Spruggins held the candle so close that it singed his chin,
And ran and stumbled up the stairs in a surprisingly agile manner,
For the wind through the keyhole kept saying, "Spruggins! Spruggins!" behind him.
The fire in his bedroom burned brightly.
The room with its crimson bed and window curtains
Was as red and glowing as a carbuncle.
It was still and warm.
There was no wind here, for the windows were fastened;
And no moon,
For the curtains were drawn.
The candle flame stood up like a pointed pear
In a wide brass dish.
Mr. Spruggins sighed with content;
He was safe at home.
The fire glowed — red and yellow roses
In the black basket of the grate —
And the bed with its crimson hangings
Seemed a great peony,
Wide open and placid.
Mr. Spruggins slipped off his top-coat and his muffler.
He slipped off his bottle-green coat
And his flowered waistcoat.
He put on a flannel dressing-gown,

And tied a peaked night-cap under his
chin.
He wound his large gold watch
And placed it under his pillow.
Then he tiptoed over to the window and
pulled back the curtain.
There was the moon dodging in and out
of the clouds;
But behind him was his quiet candle.
There was the wind whisking along the
street.
The window rattled, but it was fastened.
Did the wind say, "Spruggins"?
All Mr. Spruggins heard was "S-s-s-s-s — "
Dying away down the street.
He dropped the curtain and got into bed.
Martha had been in the last thing with
the warming-pan;
The bed was warm,
And Mr. Spruggins sank into feathers,
With the familiar ticking of his watch
just under his head.
Mr. Spruggins dozed.
He had forgotten to put out the candle,
But it did not make much difference as
the fire was so bright . . .
Too bright!
The red and yellow roses pricked his eye-
lids,
They scorched him back to consciousness.
He tried to shift his position;
He could not move.
Something weighed him down,
He could not breathe.
He was gasping,
Pinned down and suffocating.
He opened his eyes.
The curtains of the window were flung
back,
The fire and the candle were out,
And the room was filled with green moon-
light.
And pressed against the window-pane
Was a wide, round face,
Winking — winking —
Solemnly dropping one eyelid after the
other.
Tick — tock — went the watch under
his pillow,
Wink — wink — went the face at the
window.
It was not the fire roses which had
pricked him,
It was the winking eyes.
Mr. Spruggins tried to bounce up;

He could not, because —
His heart flapped up into his mouth
And fell back dead.
On his chest was a fat pink pig,
On the pig a blackamoor
With a ten pound weight for a cap.
His mustachios kept curling up and down
like angry snakes,
And his eyes rolled round and round,
With the pupils coming into sight, and
disappearing,
And appearing again on the other side.
The holsters at his saddle-bow were two
port bottles,
And a curved table-knife hung at his belt
for a scimitar,
While a fork and a keg of spirits were
strapped to the saddle behind.
He dug his spurs into the pig,
Which trampled and snorted,
And stamped its cloven feet deeper into
Mr. Spruggins.
Then the green light on the floor began
to undulate.
It heaved and hollowed,
It rose like a tide,
Sea-green,
Full of claws and scales
And wriggles.
The air above his bed began to move;
It weighed over him
In a mass of draggled feathers.
Not one lifted to stir the air.
They drooped and dripped
With a smell of port wine and brandy,
Closing down, slowly,
Trickling drops on the bed-quilt.
Suddenly the window fell in with a great
scatter of glass,
And the moon burst into the room,
Sizzling — "S s-s-s-s — Spruggins! Sprug-
gins!"
It rolled toward him,
A green ball of flame,
With two eyes in the center,
A red eye and a yellow eye,
Dropping their lids slowly,
One after the other.
Mr. Spruggins tried to scream,
But the blackamoor
Leapt off his pig
With a cry,
Drew his scimitar,
And plunged it into Mr. Spruggins's
mouth.

Mr. Spruggins got up in the cold dawn
And remade the fire.
Then he crept back to bed
By the light which seeped in under the
    window curtains,
And lay there, shivering,
While the bells of St. George the Martyr
    chimed the quarter after seven.

THE PAPER WINDMILL

The little boy pressed his face against
the window-pane and looked out at the
bright sunshiny morning. The cobblestones of the square glistened like mica.
In the trees, a breeze danced and pranced,
and shook drops of sunlight like falling
golden coins into the brown water of
the canal. Down stream slowly drifted
a long string of galliots piled with crimson cheeses. The little boy thought they
looked as if they were roc's eggs, blocks
of big ruby eggs. He said, "Oh!" with
delight, and pressed against the window
with all his might.

The golden cock on the top of the
Stadhuis gleamed. His beak was open
like a pair of scissors and a narrow piece
of blue sky was wedged in it. "Cock-a-
doodle-do," cried the little boy. "Can't
you hear me through the window, Gold
Cocky? Cock-a-doodle-do! You should
crow when you see the eggs of your
cousin, the great roc." But the golden
cock stood stock still, with his fine tail
blowing in the wind. He could not
understand the little boy, for he said
"*Cocorico*" when he said anything. But
he was hung in the air to swing, not to
sing. His eyes glittered to the bright
West wind, and the crimson cheeses
drifted away down the canal.

It was very dull there in the big room.
Outside in the square, the wind was playing tag with some fallen leaves. A man
passed, with a dogcart beside him full
of smart, new milkcans. They rattled out
a gay tune: "Tiddity-tum-ti-ti. Have
some milk for your tea. Cream for your
coffee to drink to-night, thick, and
smooth, and sweet, and white," and the
man's sabots beat an accompaniment:
"Plop! trop! milk for your tea. Plop!

trop! drink it to-night." It was very
pleasant out there, but it was lonely here
in the big room. The little boy gulped at
a tear.

It was queer how dull all his toys were.
They were so still. Nothing was still in
the square. If he took his eyes away a
moment it had changed. The milkman
had disappeared round the corner, there
was only an old woman with a basket of
green stuff on her head, picking her way
over the shiny stones. But the wind
pulled the leaves in the basket this way
and that, and displayed them to beautiful
advantage. The sun patted them con-
descendingly on their flat surfaces, and
they seemed sprinkled with silver. The
little boy sighed as he looked at his disordered toys on the floor. They were motionless, and their colours were dull. The
dark wainscoting absorbed the sun. There
was none left for toys.

The square was quite empty now. Only
the wind ran round and round it, spinning. Away over in the corner where a
street opened into the square, the wind
had stopped. Stopped running, that is,
for it never stopped spinning. It whirred,
and whirled, and gyrated, and turned. It
burned like a great coloured sun. It
hummed, and buzzed, and sparked, and
darted. There were flashes of blue, and
long smearing lines of saffron, and quick
jabs of green. And over it all was a sheen
like a myriad cut diamonds. Round and
round it went, the huge wind-wheel, and
the little boy's head reeled with watching
it. The whole square was filled with its
rays, blazing and leaping round after one
another, faster and faster. The little boy
could not speak, he could only gaze, staring in amaze.

The wind-wheel was coming down the
square. Nearer and nearer it came, a great
disk of spinning flame. It was opposite
the window now, and the little boy could
see it plainly, but it was something more
than the wind which he saw. A man was
carrying a huge fan-shaped frame on his
shoulder, and stuck in it were many little
painted paper windmills, each one scur-
rying round in the breeze. They were

bright and beautiful, and the sight was one to please anybody, and how much more a little boy who had only stupid, motionless toys to enjoy.

The little boy clapped his hands, and his eyes danced and whizzed, for the cireling windmills made him dizzy. Closer and closer came the windmill man, and held up his big fan to the little boy in the window of the Ambassador's house. Only a pane of glass between the boy and the windmills. They slid round before his eyes in rapidly revolving splendour. There were wheels and wheels of colours — big, little, thick, thin — all one clear, perfect spin. The windmill vendor dipped and raised them again, and the little boy's face was glued to the window-pane. Oh! What a glorious, wonderful plaything! Rings and rings of windy colour always moving! How had any one ever preferred those other toys which never stirred. "Nursie, come quickly. Look! I want a windmill. See! It is never still. You will buy me one, won't you? I want that silver one, with the big ring of blue."

So a servant was sent to buy that one: silver, ringed with blue, and smartly it twirled about in the servant's hands as he stood a moment to pay the vendor. Then he entered the house, and in another minute he was standing in the nursery door, with some crumpled paper on the end of a stick which he held out to the little boy. "But I wanted a windmill which went round," cried the little boy. "That is the one you asked for, Master Charles," Nursie was a bit impatient, she had mending to do. "See it is silver, and here is the blue." "But it is only a blue streak," sobbed the little boy. "I wanted a blue ring, and this silver doesn't sparkle." "Well, Master Charles, that is what you wanted, now run away and play with it, for I am very busy."

The little boy hid his tears against the friendly window-pane. On the floor lay the motionless, crumpled bit of paper on the end of its stick. But far away across

the square was the windmill vendor, with his big wheel of whirring splendour. It spun round in a blaze like a whirling rainbow, and the sun gleamed upon it, and the wind whipped it, until it seemed a maze of spattering diamonds. *"Cocorico!"* crowed the golden cock on the top of the *Stadhuis*. "That is something worth crowing for." But the little boy did not hear him, he was sobbing over the crumpled bit of paper on the floor.

THE RED LACQUER MUSIC–STAND

A music-stand of crimson lacquer, long since brought
In some fast clipper-ship from China, quaintly wrought
With bossed and carven flowers and fruits in blackening gold,
The slender shaft all twined about and thickly scrolled
With vine leaves and young twisted tendrils, whirling, curling,
Flinging their new shoots over the four wings, and swirling
Out on the three wide feet in golden lumps and streams;
Petals and apples in high relief, and where the seams
Are worn with handling, through the polished crimson sheen,
Long streaks of black, the under lacquer, shine out clean.
Four desks, adjustable, to suit the heights of players
Sitting to viols or standing up to sing, four layers
Of music to serve every instrument, are there,
And on the apex a large flat-topped golden pear.
It burns in red and yellow, dusty, smouldering lights,
When the sun flares the old barn-chamber with its flights
And skips upon the crystal knobs of dim sideboards,
Legless and mouldy, and hops, glint to glint, on hoards
Of scythes, and spades, and dinner-horns, so the old tools

Are little candles throwing brightness
round in pools.
With Oriental splendour, red and gold,
the dust
Covering its flames like smoke and thin-
ning as a gust
Of brighter sunshine makes the colours
leap and range,
The strange old music-stand seems to
strike out and change;
To stroke and tear the darkness with
sharp golden claws;
To dart a forked, vermilion tongue from
open jaws;
To puff out bitter smoke which chokes
the sun; and fade
Back to a still, faint outline obliterate in
shade.
Creeping up the ladder into the loft, the
Boy
Stands watching, very still, prickly and
hot with joy.
He sees the dusty sun-mote slit by streaks
of red,
He sees it split and stream, and all about
his head
Spikes and spears of gold are licking,
pricking, flicking,
Scratching against the walls and furniture,
and nicking
The darkness into sparks, chipping away
the gloom.
The Boy's nose smarts with the pungence
in the room.
The wind pushes an elm branch from
before the door
And the sun widens out all along the floor,
Filling the barn-chamber with white,
straightforward light,
So not one blurred outline can tease the
mind to fright.

"O All ye Works of the Lord, Bless ye
the Lord;
Praise Him, and Magnify Him for ever.
O let the Earth Bless the Lord; Yea,
let it Praise
Him, and Magnify Him for ever.
O ye Mountains and Hills, Bless ye the
Lord; Praise
Him, and Magnify Him for ever.
O All ye Green Things upon the Earth,
Bless ye the Lord; Praise Him, and
Magnify Him for ever."

The Boy will praise his God on an altar
builded fair,
Will heap it with the Works of the Lord.
In the morning air,
Spices shall burn on it, and by their pale
smoke curled,
Like shoots of all the Green Things, the
God of this bright World
Shall see the Boy's desire to pay his debt
of praise.
The Boy turns round about, seeking with
careful gaze
An altar meet and worthy, but each table
and chair
Has some defect, each piece is needing
some repair
To perfect it; the chairs have broken legs
and backs,
The tables are uneven, and every highboy
lacks
A handle or a drawer, the desks are
bruised and worn,
And even a wide sofa has its cane seat
torn.
Only in the gloom far in the corner there
The lacquer music-stand is elegant and
rare,
Clear and slim of line, with its four wings
outspread,
The sound of old quartets, a tenuous,
faint thread,
Hanging and floating over it, it stands
supreme —
Black, and gold, and crimson, in one
twisted scheme!

A candle on the bookcase feels a draught
and wavers,
Stippling the white-washed walls with
dancing shades and quavers.
A bed-post, grown colossal, jigs about
the ceiling,
And shadows, strangely altered, stain the
walls, revealing
Eagles, and rabbits, and weird faces
pulled awry,
And hands which fetch and carry things
incessantly.
Under the Eastern window, where the
morning sun
Must touch it, stands the music-stand,
and on each one
Of its broad platforms is a pyramid of
stones,

And metals, and dried flowers, and pine
and hemlock cones,
An oriole's nest with the four eggs neatly
blown,
The rattle of a rattlesnake, and three
large brown
Butternuts uncracked, six butterflies im-
paled
With a green luna moth, a snake-skin
freshly scaled,
Some sunflower seeds, wampum, and a
bloody-tooth shell,
A blue jay feather, all together piled pell-
mell
The stand will hold no more. The Boy
with humming head
Looks once again, blows out the light,
and creeps to bed.

The Boy keeps solemn vigil, while out-
side the wind
Blows gustily and clear, and slaps against
the blind.
He hardly tries to sleep, so sharp his
ecstasy
It burns his soul to emptiness, and sets
it free
For adoration only, for worship. Dedi-
cate,
His unsheathed soul is naked in its
novitiate.
The hours strike below from the clock
on the stair.
The Boy is a white flame suspiring in
prayer.
Morning will bring the sun, the Golden
Eye of Him
Whose splendour must be veiled by
starry cherubim,
Whose Feet shimmer like crystal in the
streets of Heaven.
Like an open rose the sun will stand up
even,
Fronting the window-sill, and when the
casement glows
Rose-red with the new-blown morning,
then the fire which flows
From the sun will fall upon the altar and
ignite
The spices, and his sacrifice will burn in
perfumed light.
Over the music-stand the ghosts of
sounds will swim,
Viols d'amore and *hautbois* accorded to
a hymn.

The Boy will see the faintest breath of
angels' wings
Fanning the smoke, and voices will flower
through the strings.
He dares no farther vision, and with
scalding eyes
Waits upon the daylight and his great
emprise.

The cold, grey light of dawn was whiten-
ing the wall
When the Boy, fine-drawn by sleepless-
ness, started his ritual.
He washed, all shivering and pointed like
a flame.
He threw the shutters open, and in the
window-frame
The morning glimmered like a tarnished
Venice glass.
He took his Chinese pastilles and put
them in a mass
Upon the mantelpiece till he could seek
a plate
Worthy to hold them burning. Alas! He
had been late
In thinking of this need, and now he
could not find
Platter or saucer rare enough to ease his
mind.
The house was not astir, and he dared
not go down
Into the barn-chamber, lest some door
should be blown
And slam before the draught he made as
he went out.
The light was growing yellower, and still
he looked about.
A flash of almost crimson from the gilded
pear
Upon the music-stand, startled him waiting there.
The sun would rise and he would meet
it unprepared,
Labelled a fool in having missed what
he had dared.
He ran across the room, took his pastilles
and laid
Them on the flat-topped pear, most carefully displayed
To light with ease, then stood a little
to one side,
Focussed a burning-glass and painstak-
ingly tried
To hold it angled so the bunched and
prismed rays

Should leap upon each other and spring
into a blaze.
Sharp as a wheeling edge of disked, carnation flame,
Gem-hard and cutting upward, slowly the
round sun came.
The arrowed fire caught the burning-
glass and glanced,
Split to a multitude of pointed spears,
and lanced,
A deeper, hotter flame, it took the incense
pile
Which welcomed it and broke into a
little smile
Of yellow flamelets, creeping, crackling,
thrusting up,
A golden, red-slashed lily in a lacquer cup.

"O ye Fire and Heat, Bless ye the
Lord; Praise
Him, and Magnify Him for ever.
O ye Winter and Summer, Bless ye the
Lord; Praise
Him, and Magnify Him for ever.
O ye Nights and Days, Bless ye the
Lord; Praise
Him, and Magnify Him for ever.
O ye Lightnings and Clouds, Bless ye
the Lord;
Praise Him, and Magnify Him for ever."

A moment so it hung, wide-curved,
bright-petalled, seeming
A chalice foamed with sunrise. The Boy
woke from his dreaming.
A spike of flame had caught the card of
butterflies,
The oriole's nest took fire, soon all four
galleries
Where he had spread his treasures were
become one tongue
Of gleaming, brutal fire. The Boy instantly swung
His pitcher off the wash-stand and turned
it upside down.
The flames drooped back and sizzled, and
all his senses grown
Acute by fear, the Boy grabbed the quilt
from his bed
And flung it over all, and then with aching head
He watched the early sunshine glint on
the remains
Of his holy offering. The lacquer stand
had stains

Ugly and charred all over, and where the
golden pear
Had been, a deep, black hole gaped
miserably. His dear
Treasures were puffs of ashes; only the
stones were there,
Winking in the brightness.
                    The clock upon the stair
Struck five, and in the kitchen someone
shook a grate.
The Boy began to dress, for it was getting late.

SPRING DAY

BATH

The day is fresh-washed and fair, and
there is a smell of tulips and narcissus in
the air.
The sunshine pours in at the bath-
room window and bores through the
water in the bath-tub in lathes and
planes of greenish-white. It cleaves the
water into flaws like a jewel, and cracks
it to bright light.
Little spots of sunshine lie on the surface of the water and dance, dance, and
their reflections wobble deliciously over
the ceiling; a stir of my finger sets them
whirring, reeling. I move a foot, and
the planes of light in the water jar. I lie
back and laugh, and let the green-white
water, the sun-flawed beryl water, flow
over me. The day is almost too bright
to bear, the green water covers me from
the too bright day. I will lie here awhile
and play with the water and the sun
spots.
The sky is blue and high. A crow flaps
by the window, and there is a whiff of
tulips and narcissus in the air.

BREAKFAST TABLE

In the fresh-washed sunlight, the breakfast table is decked and white. It offers
itself in flat surrender, tendering tastes,
and smells, and colours, and metals, and
grains, and the white cloth falls over its
side, draped and wide. Wheels of white
glitter in the silver coffee-pot, hot and
spinning like catherine-wheels, they
whirl, and twirl — and my eyes begin to
smart, the little white, dazzling wheels
prick them like darts. Placid and peace-

ful, the rolls of bread spread themselves in the sun to bask. A stack of butter-pats, pyramidal, shout orange through the white, scream, flutter, call: "Yellow! Yellow! Yellow!" Coffee steam rises in a stream, clouds the silver tea-service with mist, and twists up into the sunlight, revolved, involuted, suspiring higher and higher, fluting in a thin spiral up the high blue sky. A crow flies by and croaks at the coffee steam. The day is new and fair with good smells in the air.

WALK

Over the street the white clouds meet, and sheer away without touching.

On the sidewalks, boys are playing marbles. Glass marbles, with amber and blue hearts, roll together and part with a sweet clashing noise. The boys strike them with black and red striped agates. The glass marbles spit crimson when they are hit, and slip into the gutters under rushing brown water. I smell tulips and narcissus in the air, but there are no flowers anywhere, only white dust whipping up the street, and a girl with a gay Spring hat and blowing skirts. The dust and the wind flirt at her ankles and her neat, high-heeled patent leather shoes. Tap, tap, the little heels pat the pavement, and the wind rustles among the flowers on her hat.

A water-cart crawls slowly on the other side of the way. It is green and gay with new paint, and rumbles contentedly, sprinkling clear water over the white dust. Clear zigzagging water, which smells of tulips and narcissus.

The thickening branches make a pink *grisaille* against the blue sky.

Whoop! The clouds go dashing at each other and sheer away just in time. Whoop! And a man's hat careers down the street in front of the white dust, leaps into the branches of a tree, veers away and trundles ahead of the wind, jarring the sunlight into spokes of rose-colour and green.

A motor-car cuts a swathe through the bright air, sharp-beaked, irresistible, shouting to the wind to make way. A glare of dust and sunshine tosses together behind it, and settles down. The

sky is quiet and high, and the morning is fair with fresh-washed air.

MIDDAY AND AFTERNOON

Swirl of crowded streets. Shock and recoil of traffic. The stock-still brick façade of an old church, against which the waves of people lurch and withdraw. Flare of sunshine down side-streets. Eddies of light in the windows of chemists' shops, with their blue, gold, purple jars, darting colours far into the crowd. Loud bangs and tremors, murmurings out of high windows, whirring of machine belts, blurring of horses and motors. A quick spin and shudder of brakes on an electric car, and the jar of a church-bell knocking against the metal blue of the sky. I am a piece of the town, a bit of blown dust, thrust along with the crowd. Proud to feel the pavement under me, reeling with feet. Feet tripping, skipping, lagging, dragging, plodding doggedly, or springing up and advancing on firm elastic insteps. A boy is selling papers, I smell them clean and new from the press. They are fresh like the air, and pungent as tulips and narcissus.

The blue sky pales to lemon, and great tongues of gold blind the shop-windows, putting out their contents in a flood of flame.

NIGHT AND SLEEP

The day takes her ease in slippered yellow. Electric signs gleam out along the shop fronts, following each other. They grow, and grow, and blow into patterns of fire-flowers as the sky fades. Trades scream in spots of light at the unruffled night. Twinkle, jab, snap, that means a new play; and over the way: plop, drop, quiver, is the sidelong sliver of a watchmaker's sign with its length on another street. A gigantic mug of beer effervesces to the atmosphere over a tall building, but the sky is high and has her own stars, why should she heed ours?

I leave the city with speed. Wheels whirl to take me back to my trees and my quietness. The breeze which blows with me is fresh-washed and clean, it has come but recently from the high sky.

There are no flowers in bloom yet, but the earth of my garden smells of tulips and narcissus.

My room is tranquil and friendly. Out of the window I can see the distant city, a band of twinkling gems, little flower-heads with no stems. I cannot see the beer-glass, nor the letters of the restaurants and shops I passed, now the signs blur and all together make the city, glowing on a night of fine weather, like a garden stirring and blowing for the Spring.

The night is fresh-washed and fair and there is a whiff of flowers in the air.

Wrap me close, sheets of lavender. Pour your blue and purple dreams into my ears. The breeze whispers at the shutters and mutters queer tales of old days, and cobbled streets, and youths leaping their horses down marble stairways. Pale blue lavender, you are the colour of the sky when it is fresh-washed and fair . . . I smell the stars . . . they are like tulips and narcissus . . . I smell them in the air.

THE DINNER–PARTY

FISH

"So . . . " they said,
With their wine-glasses delicately poised,
Mocking at the thing they cannot understand.
"So . . . " they said again,
Amused and insolent.
The silver on the table glittered,
And the red wine in the glasses
Seemed the blood I had wasted
In a foolish cause.

GAME

The gentleman with the grey-and-black whiskers
Sneered languidly over his quail.
Then my heart flew up and laboured,
And I burst from my own holding
And hurled myself forward.
With straight blows I beat upon him,
Furiously, with red-hot anger, I thrust against him.
But my weapon slithered over his polished surface,

And I recoiled upon myself,
Panting.

DRAWING-ROOM

In a dress all softness and half-tones,
Indolent and half-reclined,
She lay upon a couch,
With the firelight reflected in her jewels.
But her eyes had no reflection,
Thy swam in a grey smoke,
The smoke of smouldering ashes,
The smoke of her cindered heart.

COFFEE

They sat in a circle with their coffee-cups.
One dropped in a lump of sugar,
One stirred with a spoon.
I saw them as a circle of ghosts
Sipping blackness out of beautiful china,
And mildly protesting against my coarseness
In being alive.

TALK

They took dead men's souls
And pinned them on their breasts for ornament;
Their cuff-links and tiaras
Were gems dug from a grave;
They were ghouls battening on exhumed thoughts;
And I took a green liqueur from a servant
So that he might come near me
And give me the comfort of a living thing.

ELEVEN O'CLOCK

The front door was hard and heavy,
It shut behind me on the house of ghosts.
I flattened my feet on the pavement
To feel it solid under me;
I ran my hand along the railings
And shook them,
And pressed their pointed bars
Into my palms.
The hurt of it reassured me,
And I did it again and again
Until they were bruised.
When I woke in the night
I laughed to find them aching,
For only living flesh can suffer.

STRAVINSKY'S THREE PIECES "GROTESQUES," FOR STRING QUARTET

First Movement

Thin-voiced, nasal pipes
Drawing sound out and out
Until it is a screeching thread,
Sharp and cutting, sharp and cutting,
It hurts.
Whee-e-e!
Bump! Bump! Tong-ti-bump!
There are drums here,
Banging,
And wooden shoes beating the round, grey stones
Of the market-place.
Whee-e-e!
Sabots slapping the worn, old stones,
And a shaking and cracking of dancing bones;
Clumsy and hard they are,
And uneven,
Losing half a beat
Because the stones are slippery.
Bump-e-ty-tong! Whee-e-! Tong!
The thin Spring leaves
Shake to the banging of shoes.
Shoes beat, slap,
Shuffle, rap,
And the nasal pipes squeal with their pigs' voices,
Little pigs' voices
Weaving among the dancers,
A fine white thread
Linking up the dancers,
Bang! Bump! Tong!
Petticoats,
Stockings,
Sabots,
Delirium flapping its thigh-bones;
Red, blue, yellow,
Drunkenness steaming in colours;
Red, yellow, blue,
Colours and flesh weaving together,
In and out, with the dance,
Coarse stuffs and hot flesh weaving together.
Pigs' cries white and tenuous,
White and painful,
White and —
Bump!
Tong!

Second Movement

Pale violin music whiffs across the moon,
A pale smoke of violin music blows over the moon,
Cherry petals fall and flutter,
And the white Pierrot,
Wreathed in the smoke of the violins,
Splashed with cherry petals falling, falling,
Claws a grave for himself in the fresh earth
With his finger-nails.

Third Movement

An organ growls in the heavy roof-groins of a church,
It wheezes and coughs.
The nave is blue with incense,
Writhing, twisting,
Snaking over the heads of the chanting priests.
Requiem aeternam dona ei, Domine;
The priests whine their bastard Latin
And the censers swing and click.
The priests walk endlessly
Round and round,
Droning their Latin
Off the key.
The organ crashes out in a flaring chord,
And the priests hitch their chant up half a tone.
Dies illa, dies irae,
Calamitatis et miseriae,
Dies magna et amara valde.
A wind rattles the leaded windows.
The little pear-shaped candle flames leap and flutter,
Dies illa, dies irae;
The swaying smoke drifts over the altar,
Calamitatis et miseriae;
The shuffling priests sprinkle holy water,
Dies magna et amara valde;
And there is a stark stillness in the midst of them
Stretched upon a bier.
His ears are stone to the organ,
His eyes are flint to the candles,
His body is ice to the water.
Chant, priests,
Whine, shuffle, genuflect,
He will always be as rigid as he is now
Until he crumbles away in a dust heap.

Lacrymosa dies illa,
Qua resurget ex favilla
Judicandus homo reus.
Above the grey pillars the roof is in darkness.

TOWNS IN COLOUR

I

RED SLIPPERS

Red slippers in a shop-window, and outside in the street, flaws of grey, windy sleet!

Behind the polished glass, the slippers hang in long threads of red, festooning from the ceiling like stalactites of blood, flooding the eyes of passers-by with dripping colour, jamming their crimson reflections against the windows of cabs and tramcars, screaming their claret and salmon into the teeth of the sleet, plopping their little round maroon lights upon the tops of umbrellas.

The row of white, sparkling shop fronts is gashed and bleeding, it bleeds red slippers. They spout under the electric light, fluid and fluctuating, a hot rain — and freeze again to red slippers, myriadly multiplied in the mirror side of the window.

They balance upon arched insteps like springing bridges of crimson lacquer; they swing up over curved heels like whirling tanagers sucked in a windpocket; they flatten out, heelless, like July ponds, flared and burnished by red rockets.

Snap, snap, they are cracker-sparks of scarlet in the white, monotonous block of shops.

They plunge the clangour of billions of vermilion trumpets into the crowd outside, and echo in faint rose over the pavement.

People hurry by, for these are only shoes, and in a window, farther down, is a big lotus bud of cardboard whose petals open every few minutes and reveal a wax doll, with staring bead eyes and flaxen hair, lolling awkwardly in its flower chair.

One has often seen shoes, but whoever saw a cardboard lotus bud before?

The flaws of grey, windy sleet beat on the shop-window where there are only red slippers.

II

THOMPSON'S LUNCH ROOM — GRAND CENTRAL STATION

Study in Whites

Wax-white —
Floor, ceiling, walls.
Ivory shadows
Over the pavement
Polished to cream surfaces
By constant sweeping.
The big room is coloured like the petals
Of a great magnolia,
And has a patina
Of flower bloom
Which makes it shine dimly
Under the electric lamps.
Chairs are ranged in rows
Like sepia seeds
Waiting fulfilment.
The chalk-white spot of a cook's cap
Moves unglossily against the vaguely
    bright wall —
Dull chalk-white striking the retina like
    a blow
Through the wavering uncertainty of
    steam.
Vitreous-white of glasses with green re-
    flections,
Ice-green carboys, shifting — greener,
    bluer — with the jar of moving water.
Jagged green-white bowls of pressed glass
Rearing snow-peaks of chipped sugar
Above the lighthouse-shaped castors
Of grey pepper and grey-white salt.
Grey-white placards: "Oyster Stew, Corn-
    beef Hash, Frankfurters":
Marble slabs veined with words in mean-
    dering lines.
Dropping on the white counter like horn
    notes
Through a web of violins,
The flat yellow lights of oranges,
The cube-red splashes of apples,
In high plated *épergnes.*
The electric clock jerks every half-minute:
"Coming! — Past!"

"Three beef-steaks and a chicken-pie,"
Bawled through a slide while the clock
    jerks heavily.
A man carries a china mug of coffee to
    a distant chair.
Two rice puddings and a salmon salad
Are pushed over the counter;
The unfulfilled chairs open to receive
    them.
A spoon falls upon the floor with the
    impact of metal striking stone,
And the sound throws across the room
Sharp, invisible zigzags
Of silver.

III

An Opera House

Within the gold square of the proscenium
    arch,
A curtain of orange velvet hangs in stiff
    folds,
Its tassels jarring slightly when someone
    crosses the stage behind.
Gold carving edges the balconies,
Rims the boxes,
Runs up and down fluted pillars.
Little knife-stabs of gold
Shine out whenever a box door is opened.
Gold clusters
Flash in soft explosions
On the blue darkness,
Suck back to a point,
And disappear.
Hoops of gold
Circle necks, wrists, fingers,
Pierce ears,
Poise on heads
And fly up above them in coloured
    sparkles.
Gold!
Gold!
The opera house is a treasure-box of gold.
Gold in a broad smear across the orches-
    tra pit:
Gold of horns, trumpets, tubas;
Gold — spun-gold, twittering-gold, snap-
    ping-gold
Of harps.
The conductor raises his baton,
The brass blares out
Crass, crude,
Parvenu, fat, powerful,
Golden.

Rich as the fat, clapping hands in the
    boxes.
Cymbals, gigantic, coin-shaped,
Crash.
The orange curtain parts
And the prima-donna steps forward.
One note,
A drop: transparent, iridescent,
A gold bubble,
It floats . . . floats . . .
And bursts against the lips of a bank
    president
In the grand tier.

IV

Afternoon Rain in State Street

Cross-hatchings of rain against grey walls,
Slant lines of black rain
In front of the up and down, wet stone
    sides of buildings.
Below,
Greasy, shiny, black, horizontal,
The street.
And over it, umbrellas,
Black polished dots
Struck to white
An instant,
Stream in two flat lines
Slipping past each other with the smooth-
    ness of oil.
Like a four-sided wedge
The Custom House Tower
Pokes at the low, flat sky,
Pushing it farther and farther up,
Lifting it away from the house-tops,
Lifting it in one piece as though it were
    a sheet of tin,
With the lever of its apex.
The cross-hatchings of rain cut the Tower
    obliquely,
Scratching lines of black wire across it,
Mutilating its perpendicular grey surface
With the sharp precision of tools.
The city is rigid with straight lines and
    angles,
A chequered table of blacks and greys.
Oblong blocks of flatness
Crawl by with low-geared engines,
And pass to short upright squares
Shrinking with distance.
A steamer in the basin blows its whistle,
And the sound shoots across the rain
    hatchings,

A narrow, level bar of steel.
Hard cubes of lemon
Superimpose themselves upon the fronts
  of buildings
As the windows light up.
But the lemon cubes are edged with
  angles
Upon which they cannot impinge.
Up, straight, down, straight — square.
Crumpled grey-white papers
Blow along the side-walks,
Contorted, horrible,
Without curves.
A horse steps in a puddle,
And white, glaring water spurts up
In stiff, outflaring lines,
Like the rattling stems of reeds.
The city is heraldic with angles,
A sombre escutcheon of argent and sable
And countercoloured bends of rain
Hung over a four-square civilization.
When a street lamp comes out,
I gaze at it for full thirty seconds
To rest my brain with the suffering, round
  brilliance of its globe.

V

An Aquarium

Streaks of green and yellow iridescence,
Silver shiftings,
Rings veering out of rings,
Silver — gold —
Grey-green opaqueness sliding down,
With sharp white bubbles
Shooting and dancing,
Flinging quickly outward.
Nosing the bubbles,
Swallowing them,
Fish.
Blue shadows against silver-saffron water,
The light rippling over them
In steel-bright tremors.
Outspread translucent fins
Flute, fold, and relapse;
The threaded light prints through them
  on the pebbles
In scarcely tarnished twinklings.

Curving of spotted spines,
Slow up-shifts,
Lazy convolutions:
Then a sudden swift straightening
And darting below:
Oblique grey shadows
Athwart a pale casement.
Roped and curled,
Green man-eating eels
Slumber in undulate rhythms,
With crests laid horizontal on their
  backs.
Barred fish,
Striped fish,
Uneven disks of fish,
Slip, slide, whirl, turn,
And never touch.
Metallic blue fish,
With fins wide and yellow and swaying
Like Oriental fans,
Hold the sun in their bellies
And glow with light:
Blue brilliance cut by black bars.
An oblong pane of straw-coloured shim-
  mer,
Across it, in a tangent,
A smear of rose, black, silver,
Short twists and upstartings,
Rose-black, in a setting of bubbles:
Sunshine playing between red and black
  flowers
On a blue and gold lawn.
Shadows and polished surfaces,
Facets of mauve and purple,
A constant modulation of values.
Shaft-shaped,
With green bead eyes;
Thick-nosed,
Heliotrope-coloured;
Swift spots of chrysolite and coral;
In the midst of green, pearl, amethyst
  irradiations.

Outside,
A willow-tree flickers
With little white jerks,
And long blue waves
Rise steadily beyond the outer islands.

CAN GRANDE'S CASTLE

SEA–BLUE AND BLOOD–RED

I

THE MEDITERRANEAN

Blue as the tip of a salvia blossom, the inverted cup of the sky arches over the sea. Up to meet it, in a flat band of glaring colour, rises the water. The sky is unspecked by clouds, but the sea is flecked with pink and white light shadows, and silver scintillations snip-snap over the tops of the waves.

Something moves along the horizon. A puff of wind blowing up the edges of the silver-blue sky? Clouds! Clouds! Great thunderheads marching along the skyline! No, by Jove! The sun shining on sails! Vessels, hull down, with only their tiers of canvas showing. Beautiful ballooning thunderheads dipping one after another below the blue band of the sea.

II

NAPLES

Red tiles, yellow stucco, layer on layer of windows, roofs, and balconies, Naples pushes up the hill away from the curving bay. A red, half-closed eye, Vesuvius watches and waits. All Naples prates of this and that, and runs about its little business, shouting, bawling, incessantly calling its wares. Fish frying, macaroni drying, seven feet piles of red and white broccoli, grapes heaped high with rosemary, sliced pomegranates dripping seeds, plucked and bleeding chickens, figs on spits, lemons in baskets, melons cut and quartered nicely, "*Ah, che bella cosa!*" They even sell water, clear crystal water for a *paul* or two. And everything done to a hullabaloo. They jabber over cheese, they chatter over wine, they gabble at the corners in the bright sunshine. And piercing through the noise is the beggar-whine, always, like an undertone, the beggar-whine; and always the crimson, watching eye of Vesuvius.

Have you seen her — the Ambassadress? Ah, *Bellissima Creatura! Una Donna Rara!* She is fairer than the Blessed Virgin; and good! Never was such a soul in such a body! The rôle of her benefactions would stretch from here to Posilipo. And she loves the people, loves to go among them and speak to this one and that, and her apple-blossom face under the big blue hat works miracles like the Holy Images in the Churches.

In her great house with the red marble stairway, Lady Hamilton holds brilliant sway. From her boudoir windows she can see the bay, and on the left, hanging there, a flame in a cresset, the blood-red glare of Vesuvius staring at the clear blue air.

Blood-red on a night of stars, red like a wound, with lava scars. In the round wall-mirrors of her boudoir, is the blackness of the bay, the whiteness of a star, and the bleeding redness of the mountain's core. Nothing more. All night long, in the mirrors, nothing more. Black water, red stain, and above, a star with its silver rain.

Over the people, over the king, trip the little Ambassadorial feet; fleet and light as a pigeon's wing, they brush over the artists, the friars, the *abbés*, the Court. They bear her higher and higher at each step. Up and over the hearts of Naples goes the beautiful Lady Hamilton till she reaches even to the Queen; then rests in a sheening, shimmering altitude, between earth and sky, high and floating as the red crater of Vesuvius. Buoyed up and sustained in a blood-red destiny, all on fire for the world to see.

Proud Lady Hamilton! Superb Lady Hamilton! Quivering, blood-swept, vivid Lady Hamilton! Your vigour is enough to awake the dead, as you tread the newly uncovered courtyards of Pompeii. There is a murmur all over the opera house when you enter your box. And your frocks! Jesu! What frocks! "India painting on wyte sattin!" And a new camlet shawl, all sea-blue and blood-red, in an intricate pattern, given by Sir William to help you do your marvelous "Attitudes." Incomparable actress! No theatre built is big enough to compass you. It takes a world; and centuries shall elbow each other aside to watch you act your part. Art, Emma, or heart? The blood-red cone of Vesuvius glows in the night.

She sings "Luce Bella," and Naples cries "Brava! Ancora!" and claps its hands. She dances the tarantella, and poses before a screen with the red-blue shawl. It is the frescoes of Pompeii unfrozen; it is the fine-cut profiles of Sicilian coins; it is Apollo Belvedere himself — Goethe has said it. She wears a Turkish dress, and her face is sweet and lively as rippled water.

The lava-streams of Vesuvius descend as far as Portici. She climbs the peak of fire at midnight — five miles of flame. A blood-red mountain, seeping tears of blood. She skips over glowing ashes and laughs at the pale, faded moon, wan in the light of the red-hot lava. What a night! Spires and sparks of livid flame shooting into the black sky. Blood-red smears of fire; blood-red gashes, flashing her out against the smouldering mountain. A tossing fountain of blood-red jets, it sets her hair flicking into the air like licking flamelets of a burning aureole. Blood-red is everywhere. She wears it as a halo and diadem. Emma, Emma Hamilton, Ambassadress of Great Britain to the Kingdom of the Two Sicilies.

III

ABOUKIR BAY, EGYPT

North-north-west, and a whole-sail breeze, ruffling up the larkspur-blue sea, breaking the tops of the waves into egg-white foam, shoving ripple after ripple of pale jade-green over the shoals of Aboukir Bay. Away to the East rolls in the sluggish water of old Nile. West

and South — hot, yellow land. Ships at anchor. Thirteen ships flying the tricolore, and riding at ease in a patch of blue water inside a jade-green hem. What of them? Ah, fine ships! The Orient, one hundred and twenty guns, Franklin, Tonnant, each with eighty. Weighty metal to float on a patch of blue with a green hem. They ride stem to stern, in a long line, pointing the way to Aboukir Bay.

To the North are thunderheads, ballooning silver-white thunderheads rising up out of the horizon. The thunderheads draw steadily up into the blue-blossomed sky. A topgallant breeze pushes them rapidly over the white-specked water. One, two, six, ten, thirteen separate tiered clouds, and the wind sings loud in their shrouds and spars. The royals are furled, but the topgallantsails and topsails are full and straining. Thirteen white thunderheads bearing down on Aboukir Bay.

The Admiral is working the stump of his right arm; do not cross his hawse, I advise you. "Youngster to the mast-head. What! Going without your glass, and be damned to you! Let me know what you see, immediately."

"The enemy fleet, Sir, at anchor in the bay."

"Bend on the signal to form in line of battle, Sir Ed'ard."

The bright wind straightens the signal pennants until they stand out rigid like boards.

"Captain Hood reports eleven fathoms, Sir, and shall he bear up and sound?"

"Signal Captain Hood to lead, sounding."

"By the mark ten! A quarter less nine! By the deep eight!"

Round to starboard swing the white thunderheads, the water of their bows washing over the green jade hem. An orange sunset steams in the shrouds, and glints upon the muzzles of the cannon in the open ports. The hammocks are down; the guns run out and primed; beside each is a pile of canister and grape; gunners are blowing on their matches;

snatches of fife music drift down to the lower decks. In the cockpits, the surgeons are feeling the edges of knives and saws; men think of their wives and swear softly, spitting on their hands.

"Let go that anchor! By God, she hangs!"

Past the *Guerrier* slides the *Goliath*, but the anchor drops and stops her on the inner quarter of the *Conquérant*. The *Zealous* brings up on the bow of the *Guerrier*, the *Orion*, *Theseus*, *Audacious*, are all come to, inside the French ships.

The *Vanguard*, Admiral's pennant flying, is lying outside the *Spartiate*, distant only a pistol shot.

In a pattern like a country dance, each balanced justly by its neighbour, lightly, with no apparent labour, the ships slip into place, and lace a design of white sails and yellow yards on the purple, flowing water. Almighty Providence, what a day! Twenty-three ships in one small bay, and away to the Eastward, the water of old Nile rolling sluggishly between its sand-bars.

Seven hundred and forty guns open fire on the French fleet. The sun sinks into the purple-red water, its low, straight light playing gold on the slaughter. Yellow fire, shot with red, in wheat sheafs from the guns; and a racket and ripping which jerks the nerves, then stuns, until another broadside crashes the ears alive again. The men shine with soot and sweat, and slip in the blood which wets the deck.

The surgeons cut and cut, but men die steadily. It is heady work, this firing into ships not fifty feet distant. Lilac and grey, the heaving bay, slapped and torn by thousands of splashings of shot and spars. Great red stars peer through the smoke, a mast is broke short off at the lashings and falls overboard, with the rising moon flashing in its top-hamper.

There is a rattle of musketry; pipe-clayed, red-coated marines swab, and fire, and swab. A round shot finishes the job, and tears its way out through splintering bulwarks. The roar of broadside after broadside echoes from the shore in a long, hoarse humming. Drums beat in little fire-cracker snappings, and a boat-swain's whistle wires, thin and sharp, through the din, and breaks short off against the scream of a gun crew, cut to bits by a bursting cannon.

Three times they clear the *Vanguard's* guns of a muck of corpses, but each new crew comes on with a cheer and each discharge is a jeer of derision.

The Admiral is hit. A flying sliver of iron has shivered his head and opened it, the skin lies quivering over his one good eye. He sees red, blood-red, and the roar of the guns sounds like water running over stones. He has to be led below.

Eight bells, and the poop of the *Orient* is on fire. "Higher, men, train your guns a little higher. Don't give them a loop-hole to scotch the flame. 'Tis their new fine paint they'll have to blame." Yellow and red, waving tiger-lilies, the flames shoot up — round, serrated petals, flung out of the black-and-silver cup of the bay. Each stay is wound with a flickering fringe. The ropes curl up and shrivel as though a twinge of pain withered them. Spasm after spasm convulses the ship. A Clap! — A Crash! — A Boom! — and silence. The ships have ceased firing.

Ten, twenty, forty seconds . . .

Then a dash of water as masts and spars fall from an immense height, and in the room of the floating, licking tiger-lily is a chasm of yellow and red whirling eddies. The guns start firing again.

Foot after foot across the sky goes the moon, with her train of swirling silver-blue stars.

The day is fair. In the clear Egyptian air, the water of Aboukir Bay is as blue as the bottom flowers of a larkspur spray. The shoals are green with a white metal sheen, and between its sand-bars the Nile can be seen, slowly rolling out to sea.

The Admiral's head is bound up, and his eye is bloodshot and very red, but he is sitting at his desk writing, for all that. Through the stern windows is the blue of the sea, and reflections dance waveringly on his paper. This is what he has written:

"VANGUARD. MOUTH OF THE NILE.
August 8th, 1798.

MY DEAR SIR: —
Almighty God has made me the happy
instrument in destroying the enemy's
fleet; which, I hope, will be a blessing
to Europe . . . I hope there will be no
difficulty in our getting refitted at Naples
. . .

Your most obliged and affectionate
HORATIO NELSON."

Dance, little reflections of blue water,
dance, while there is yet time.

IV

NAPLES

"Get out of the way, with your skew-
bald ass. Heu! Heu!" There is scant
room for the quality to pass up and down
the whole Strada di Toledo. Such a
running to and fro! Such a clacking, and
clapping, and fleering, and cheering. Holy
Mother of God, the town has gone mad.
Listen to the bells. They will crack the
very doors of Heaven with their jangling.
The sky seems the hot half-hollow of
a clanging bell. I verily believe they
will rock the steeples off their foundations. Ding! *Dang!* Dong! Jingle-
Jingle! Clank! Clink! Twitter! Tingle!
Half Naples is hanging on the ropes, I
vow it is louder than when they crown
the Pope. The lapis-lazuli pillars in
Jesus Church positively lurch with the
noise; the carvings of Santa Chiara are
at swinging poise. In San Domenico Maggiore, the altar quivers; Santa Maria del
Carmine's chimes run like rivers tinkling
over stones; the big bell of the Cathedral
hammers and drones. It is gay to-day,
with all the bells of Naples at play.
That's a fine equipage; those bays shine
like satin. Why, it is the British Ambassadress, and two British officers with
her in the carriage! Where is her hat?
Tut, you fool, she doesn't need one, she
is wearing a ribbon like a Roman senator.
Blue it is, and there are gold letters:
"Nelson and Victory." The woman is
undoubtedly mad, but it is a madness
which kindles. "*Viva Nelson! Viva
Miladi!*" Half a hundred hats are flying
in the air like kites, and all the white

handkerchiefs in Naples wave from the
balconies.

Brava, Emma Hamilton, a fig for the
laws of good taste, your heart beats blood,
not water. Let pale-livered ladies wave
decorously; do you drive the streets and
tell the *lazzaroni* the good news. Proud
Lady Hamilton! Mad, whole-hearted
Lady Hamilton! *Viva! Viva ancora!* Wear
your Nelson-anchor earrings for the sun
to flash in; cut a dash in your new blue
shawl, spotted with these same anchors.
What if lily-tongued dandies dip their
pens in gall to jeer at you, your blood is
alive. The red of it stains a bright band
across the pages of history. The others
are ghosts, rotting in aged tombs. Light
your three thousand lamps, that your
windows spark and twinkle "Nelson"
for all the world to see, and even the
little wavelets of the bay have a largess of
gold petals dropped from his name.
Rule, Britannia, though she doesn't deserve it; it is all Nelson and the Ambassadress, in the streets of Naples.

He has rooms at the Palazzo Sesso,
the British Admiral, and all day long
he watches the red, half-closed eye of
Vesuvius gazing down at his riding ships.
At night, there is a red plume over the
mountain, and the light of it fills the
room with a crimson glow, it might be
a gala lit for him. His eyes swim. In
the open sky hangs a steel-white star, and
a bar of silver cuts through the red reflections of the mirrors. Red and silver,
for the bay is not blue at night.

"Oh brave Nelson, oh God bless and
protect our brave deliverer, oh, Nelson,
Nelson, what do we not owe to you."
Sea-blue, the warp; but the thread of
the woof is bolted red. Fiddlers and dinners — Well, or Hell! as the case may
be. Queens, populace — these are things,
like guns, to face. Rostral Columns and
birthday fêtes jar the nerves of a wounded
head; it is better in bed, in the rosy gloom
of a plume-lit room.
So the Admiral rests in the Palazzo
Sesso, the guest of his Ambassador, and
his ships ride at anchor under the flaming
mountain.
The shuttle shoots, the shuttle weaves.

The red thread to the blue thread cleaves. The web is plaiting which nothing unreaves.

The Admiral buys the Ambassadress a table, a pleasant tribute to hospitality. It is of satin-wood, sprinkled over with little flying loves arrayed in pink and blue sashes. They sit at this table for hours, he and she, discussing the destiny of the Kingdom of the Two Sicilies, and her voice is like water tinkling over stones, and her face is like the same water twinkling in shallows.

She counts his money for him, and laughs at his inability to reduce *carolins* to English sixpences. She drives him out to Caserta to see the Queen, and parades him on the Chiaia to delight the common people. She is always before him, a mist of rose and silver, a damask irradiation, shading and lighting like a palpitant gem.

In the evenings, by the light of two wax candles, the Admiral writes kind acknowledgements to the tributes of half a world. Moslem and Christian sweetly united to stamp out liberty. It is an inspiring sight to see. Rule Britannia indeed, with Slavs and Turks boosting up her footstool. The Sultan has sent a Special Envoy bearing gifts: the *Chelenck* — "Plume of Triumph," all in diamonds, and a pelisse of sables, just as bonds of his eternal gratitude. "*Viva il Turco!*" says Lady Hamilton. The Mother of His Sultanic Majesty begs that the Admiral's pocket may be the repository of a diamond-studded box to hold his snuff. The Russian Tzar, a bit self-centered as most monarchs are, sends him his portrait, diamond-framed of course. The King of Sardinia glosses over his fewer gems by the richness of his compliments. The East India Company, secure of its trade, has paid him ten thousand pounds. The Turkish Company has given him plate. A grateful country augments his state by creating him the smallest kind of peer, with a couple of tuppences a year, and veneering it over by a grant of arms. Arms for an arm, but what for an eye! Does the Admiral smile as he writes his reply? Writes with his left hand that he is aware of the

high honour it will be to bear this shield: "A chief undulated argent, from which a palm-tree issuant, between a disabled ship on the dexter, and a ruinous battery on the sinister, all proper." "Very proper, indeed," nods Sir William, but Lady Hamilton prods the coloured paper shield a trifle scornfully. "If I was King of England, I would make you Duke Nelson, Marquis Nile, Earl Aboukir, Viscount Pyramid, Baron Crocodile and Prince Victory." "My dear Emma, what a child you are," says Sir William, but the Admiral looks out of the window at the blood-red mountain and says nothing at all.

Something shakes Naples. Shakes so violently that it makes the candles on the Admiral's writing-table flicker. Earthquakes, perhaps. Aye, earthquakes, but not from the red, plumed mountain. The dreadful tread of marching men is rocking the Bourbon Kingdom of the Two Sicilies, and the *fanfare* of Republican trumpets blows over the city like a great wind. It swirls the dust of Monarchy in front of it, across Naples and out over the Chiaia to the sea.

The Admiral walks his quarter-deck with the blue bay beneath him, but his eyes are red with the glare of Vesuvius, and the blood beats in and out of his heart so rapidly that he is almost stifled. All Naples is red to the Admiral, but the core of crimson is the Palazzo Sesso, in whose windows, at night, the silver stars flash so brightly. "Crimson and silver," thinks the Admiral, "O Emma, Emma Hamilton!"

It is December now, and Naples is heaving and shuddering with the force of the Earth shock. There is no firm ground on which to stand. Beneath the Queen's footsteps is a rocking jelly. Even the water of the bay boils and churns and knocks loudly against the wooden sides of the British ships.

Over the satin-wood table, the Admiral and the Ambassadress sit in consultation, and red fire flares between them across its polished surface. "My adorable, unfortunate Queen! Dear,

dear Queen!" Lady Hamilton's eyes are carbuncles burning into the Admiral's soul. He is dazzled, confused, used to the glare on blue water he thinks he sees it now. It is Duty and Kings. Caste versus riff-raff. The roast beef of old England against fried frogs' legs.

Red, blood-red, figures the weaving pattern, red blushing over blue, flushing the fabric purple, like lees of wine.

A blustering night to go to a party. But the coach is ready, and Lord Nelson is arrived from his ship. Official persons cannot give the slip to other official persons, and it is Kelim Effendi who gives the reception, the Sultan's Special Envoy. "Wait," to the coachman; then lights, jewels, sword-clickings, compliments, a promenade round the rooms, bowing, and a quick, unwatched exit from a side door. Someone will wake the snoring coachman hours hence and send him away. But it will not be his Master or Mistress. These hurry through dark, windy streets to the Molesiglio. How the waves flow by in the darkness! "A heavy ground-swell," says the Admiral, but there is a lull in the wind. A pass-word in English — we are all very English tonight. "Can you find your way, Emma?" Sir William is perturbed. But the Ambassadress is gone, gone lightly, swiftly, up the dark mole and disappeared through a postern in the wall. She is aflame, scorching with red and gold fires, a torch of scarlet and ochre, a meteor of sulphur and chrome dashed with vermilion.

There are massacres in the streets of Naples; in the Palace, a cowering Queen. This is melodrama, and Emma is the Princess of Opera Bouffe. Opera Bouffe, with Death as Pulchinello. Ho! Ho! You laugh. A merry fellow, and how if Death had you by the gizzard? Comedy and Tragedy shift masks, but Emma is intent on her task and sees neither. Frightened, vacillating monarchs to guide down a twisting stair; but there is Nelson climbing up. And there are lanterns, cutlasses, pistols, and, at last, the night air, black slapping water, and boats.

They are afloat, off the trembling, quivering soil of Naples, and their way is lit by a blood-red glimmer from the tossing fires of Vesuvius.

V

PALERMO, ET AL.

Storm-tossed water, and an island set in a sea as blue as the bottom flowers of a spike of larkspur, come upon out of a hurly-burly of wind, and rain, and jagged waves. Through it all has walked the Ambassadress like some starry saint, pouring mercy out of full hands. The Admiral sees her misted with rose and purple, radiating comfort in a phosphoric glow. Is it wise to light one's life with an iridescence? Perhaps not, but the bolt is shot.

The stuff is weaving. Now one thread is uppermost, now another, making striae of reds and blues, or clouding colour over colour.

There are lemon groves, and cool stars, and love flooding beneath them. There are slanting decks, and full sails, and telescopes, wearying to a one-eyed man. Then a span of sunlight under pink oleanders; and evenings beneath painted ceilings, surrounded by the hum of a court.

Naples again, with cannon blazing. A haze of orders, documents, pardons, and a hanging. Palermo, and Dukedoms and "Nostro Liberatore." One cannot see everything with one eye. Flight is impossible, but misted vision shows strange shapes. It is Opera Bouffe, with Tragedy in the front row. Downing Street hints reproof, mentions stories of gaming-tables and high piles of gold. What nonsense to talk of a duel! Sir William and the Admiral live like brothers. But they will not be silent, those others. "Poor Lady Nelson, what will she do?" Still it is true that the lady in question is a bit of a shrew.

Blood beats back and forth under the lemon groves, proving itself a right of way. "I worship, nay, adore you, and if you was single, and I found you under a hedge, I would instantly marry you. Santa Emma! As truly as I believe in God, do I believe you are a saint." If the lady is a saint and he her acolyte, it is by a Divine right. These are the ways of Heaven; the Admiral prays and knows himself forgiven and absolved.

Revolve slowly, shuttle of the blue thread, red is a strong colour under Sicilian skies.

VI

LEGHORN TO LONDON

A Court, an Ambassador, and a great Admiral, in travelling carriages rolling over the map of Europe. Straining up hills, bowling along levels, rolling down slopes, and all to the tune of "Hip! Hip! Hurrah!" From Leghorn to Florence, to Ancona, to Trieste, is one long *Festa*. Every steeple sways with clashing bells, and people line the roads, yelling "*Viva Nelson! Hola! Hola! Viva Inghilterra!*" Wherever they go, it is a triumphal progress and a pinny-pinny-poppy-show. Whips crack, sparks fly, sails fill — another section of the map is left behind. Carriages again, up hill and down, from the seaboard straight into Austria.

Hip! Hip! Hip! The wheels roll into Vienna. Then what a to-do! Concerts, Operas, Fireworks too. Dinners where one hundred six-foot grenadiers do the waiting at table. Such grandiloquence! Such splendid, regal magnificence! Trumpets and cannons, and Nelson's health; the Jew wealth of Baron Arnstein, and the excellent wine of his cellars. Haydn conducts an oratorio while the guests are playing faro. Delightful city! What a pity one must leave! These are rewards worthy of the Battle of the Nile. You smile. Tut! Tut! Remember they are only foreigners; the true British breed writes home scurvy letters for all London to read. Hip! Hip! God save the King!

For two months, the travelling carriages stand in the stables; but horses are put to them at last, and they are off again. No Court this time; but what is a fleeing Queen to a victorious Admiral! Up hill, down dale, round and round roll the sparkling wheels, kicking up all the big and little stones of Austria. "Huzza for the Victor of Aboukir!"

shouts the populace. The traces tighten, and the carriages are gone. In and out of Prague roll the wheels, and across the border into Germany.

Dresden at last, but an Electress turning her back on Lady Hamilton. A stuffy state, with a fussy etiquette! Why distress oneself for such a rebuff? Emma will get even with them yet. It is enough for her to do her "Attitudes," and to perfection. And still — and still — But Lady Hamilton has an iron will.

Proud Lady Hamilton! Blood-betrayed, hot-hearted Lady Hamilton! The wheels roll out of Dresden, and Lady Hamilton looks at the Admiral. "Oh, Nelson, Nelson." But the whips are cracking and one cannot hear.

Roll over Germany, wheels. Roll through Magdeburg, Lodwostz, Anhalt. Roll up to the banks of the Elbe, and deposit your travellers in a boat once more. Along the green shores of the green-and-brown river to Hamburg, where merchants and bankers are waiting to honour the man who has saved their gold. Huzza for Nelson, Saviour of Banks! Where is the frigate a thankful country might have sent him? Not there. Why did he come overland, forsooth? The Lion and the Unicorn are uncouth beasts, but we do not mind in the least. No, indeed! We take a packet and land at Yarmouth.

"Hip! Hip! Hip! God save the King! Long live Nelson, Britain's Pride!" The common people are beside themselves with joy, there is no alloy to their welcome. Before *The Wrestler's* inn, troops are paraded. And every road is arcaded with flags and flowers. "He is ours! Hip! Hip! Nelson!" Cavalcades of volunteer cavalry march before him. Two days to London, and every road bordered with smiling faces. They cannot go faster than a footpace because the carriage is drawn by men. Muskets pop, and every shop in every town is a flutter of bunting.

Red, Lady Hamilton, red welcome for your Admiral. Red over foggy London. Bow bells peeling, and the crowded streets reeling through fast tears. Years,

Emma, and Naples covered by their ashes.

Blood-red, his heart flashes to hers, but the great city of London is blurred to both of them.

VII

MERTON

Early Autumn, and a light breeze rustling through the trees of Paradise Merton, and pashing the ripples of the Little Nile against the sides of the arched stone bridge. It is ten o'clock, and through the blowing leaves, the lighted windows of the house twinkle like red, pulsing stars. Far down the road is a jingle of harness, and a crunching of wheels. Out of the darkness flare the lamps of a post-chaise, blazing basilisk eyes, making the smooth sides of leaves shine, as they approach, the darkness swallowing in behind them. A rattle, a stamping of hoofs, and the chaise comes to a stand opposite a wooden gate. It is not late, maybe a bit ahead of time. The post-boy eases himself in the saddle, and loosens his reins. The light from the red windows glitters in the varnished panels of the chaise.

How tear himself away from so dear a home! Can he wrench himself apart, can he pull his heart out of his body? Her face is pitiful with tears. Two years gone, and only a fortnight returned. His head hums with the rushing of his blood. "Wife in the sight of Heaven" — surely one life between them now, and yet the summons has come. Blue water is calling, the peaked seas beckon.

The Admiral kneels beside his child's bed, and prays. These are the ways of the Almighty. "His will be done." Pathetic trust, thrusting aside desire. The fire on the hearth is faint and glowing, and throws long shadows across the room. How quiet it is, how far from battles and crowning seas.

She strains him in her arms, she whispers, sobbing, "Dearest husband of my heart, you are all the world to Emma." She delays his going by minute and minute. "My Dearest and most Beloved, God protect you and my dear Horatia

and grant us a happy meeting. Amen! Amen!"

Tear, blue shuttle, through the impeding red, but have a care lest the thread snap in following.

"God bless you, George. Take care of Lady Hamilton." He shakes his brother-in-law by the hand. The chaise door bangs. The post-boy flicks his whip, the horses start forward. Red windows through flecking trees. Blood-red windows growing dimmer behind him, until they are only a shimmer in the distance. His eyes smart, searching for their faint glimmer through blowing trees. His eyes smart with tears, and fears which seem to haunt him. All night he drives, through Guildford, over Hindhead, on his way to Portsmouth.

VIII

AT SEA, OFF CAPE TRAFALGAR

Blue as the tip of a deep blue salvia blossom, the inverted cup of the sky arches over the sea. Up to meet it, in a concave curve of bright colour, rises the water, flat, unrippled, for the wind scarcely stirs. How comes the sky so full of clouds on the horizon, with none over head? Clouds! Great clouds of canvas! Mighty ballooning clouds, bearing thunder and crinkled lightning in their folds. They roll up out of the horizon, tiered, stately. Sixty-four great thunder-clouds, more perhaps, throwing their shadows over ten miles of sea.

Boats dash back and forth. Their ordered oars sparkling like silver as they lift and fall. Frigate captains receiving instructions, coming aboard the flagship, departing from it. Blue and white, with a silver flashing of boats.

Thirty-three clouds headed South, twenty-three others converging upon them! They move over the water as silently as the drifting air. Lines to lines, drawing nearer on the faint impulse of the breeze.

Blue coated, flashing with stars, the Admiral walks up and down the poop.

Stars on his breast, in his eyes the white glare of the sea. The enemy wears, looping end to end, and waits, poised in a half-circle like a pale new moon upon the water. The British ships point straight to the hollow between the horns, and even their stu'nsails are set. Arrows flung at a crescent over smooth blue water.

"Now, Blackwood, I am going to amuse the fleet with a signal. Mr. Pasco, I wish to say to the fleet, 'England confides that every man will do his duty.' You must be quick, for I have one more to make, which is for close action."

"If your Lordship will permit me to substitute 'expects' for 'confides,' it will take less time, because 'expects' is in the vocabulary and 'confides' must be spelt."

Flutter flags, fling out your message to the advancing arrows. Ripple and fly over the Admiral's head. Signal flags are of all colours, but the Admiral sees only the red. It beats above him, outlined against the salvia-blue sky. A crimson blossom sprung from his heart, the banner royal of his Destiny struck out sharply against the blue of Heaven.

Frigate Captain Blackwood bids goodbye to the Admiral. "I trust, my Lord, that on my return to the *Victory*, I shall find your Lordship well and in possession of twenty prizes." A gash of blood-colour cuts across the blue sky, or is it that the Admiral's eyes are tired with the flashing of the sea? "God bless you, Blackwood, I shall never speak to you again." What is it that haunts his mind? He is blinded by red, blood-red fading to rose, smeared purple, blotted out by blue. Larkspur sea and blue sky above it, with the flickering flags of his signal standing out in cameo.

Boom! A shot passes through the main topgallantsail of the *Victory*. The ship is under fire. Her guns cannot bear while she is head on. Straight at the floating half-moon of ships goes the *Victory*, leading her line, muffled in the choking smoke of the *Bucentaure's* guns. The sun is dimmed, but through the smoke-cloud prick diamond sparkles from the Admiral's stars as he walks up and down the quarter-deck.

Red glare of guns in the Admiral's eyes. Red stripe of marines drawn up on the poop. Eight are carried off by a single shot, and the red stripe liquefies, and seeps, lapping, down the gangway. Every stu'nsail boom is shot away. The blue of the sea has vanished; there is only the red of cannon, and the white twinkling sparks of the Admiral's stars.

The bows of the *Victory* cross the wake of the *Bucentaure*, and one after another, as they bear, the double-shotted guns tear through the woodwork of the French ship. The *Victory* slips past like a shooting shuttle, and runs on board the *Redoubtable*, seventy-four, and their spars lock, with a shock which almost stops their headway.

It is a glorious Autumn day outside the puff-ball of smoke. A still, blue sea, unruffled, banded to silver by a clear sun.

Guns of the *Victory*, guns of the *Redoubtable*, exploding incessantly, making one long draw of sound. Rattling upon it, rain on a tin roof, the pop-pop of muskets from the mizzen-top of the *Redoubtable*. There are sharpshooters in the mizzen-top, aiming at the fog below. Suddenly, through it, spears the gleam of diamonds; it is the Admiral's stars, reflecting the flashes of the guns.

Red blood in a flood before his eyes. Red from horizon to zenith, crushing down like beaten metal. The Admiral falls to his knees, to his side, and lies there, and the crimson glare closes over him, a cupped inexorable end. "They have done for me at last, Hardy. My back-bone is shot through."

The blue thread is snapped and the bolt falls from the loom. Weave, shuttle of the red thread. Weave over and under yourself in a scarlet ecstasy. It is all red now he comes to die. Red, with the white sparkles of those cursed stars.

Carry him gently down, and let no man know that it is the Admiral who has fallen. He covers his face and his stars with his handkerchief. The white glitter is quenched; the white glitter of his life will shine no more. "Doctor, I am gone.

I leave Lady Hamilton and my daughter Horatia as a legacy to my Country." Pathetic trust, thrusting aside knowledge. Flint, the men who sit in Parliament, flint which no knocking can spark to fire. But you still believe in men's goodness, knowing only your own heart. "Let my dear Lady Hamilton have my hair, and all other things belonging to me."

The red darkens, and is filled with tossing fires. He sees Vesuvius, and over it the single brilliance of a star.

"One would like to live a little longer, but thank God, I have done my duty."

Slower, slower, passes the red thread and stops. The weaving is done.

In the log-book of the *Victory*, it is written: "Partial firing continued until 4:30, when a victory having been re- ported to the Right Honourable Lord Viscount Nelson, K.B., he died of his wound."

IX
CALAIS

It is a timber-yard, pungent with the smell of wood: Oak, Pine, and Cedar. But under the piles of white boards, they say there are bones rotting. An old guide to Calais speaks of a wooden marker shaped like a battledore, handle downwards, on the broad part of which was scratched: "Emma Hamilton, England's Friend." It was a poor thing and now even that has gone. Let us buy an oak chip for remembrance. It will only cost a sou.

GUNS AS KEYS: AND THE GREAT GATE SWINGS

PART I

Due East, far West. Distant as the nests of the opposite winds. Removed as fire and water are, as the clouds and the roots of the hills, as the wills of youth and age. Let the key-guns be mounted, make a brave show of waging war, and pry off the lid of Pandora's box once more. Get in at any cost, and let out at little, so it seems, but wait — wait — there is much to follow through the Great Gate!

They do not see things in quite that way, on this bright November day, with sun flashing, and waves splashing, up and down Chesapeake Bay. On shore, all the papers are running to press with huge headlines: "Commodore Perry Sails." Dining-tables buzz with travellers' tales of old Japan culled from Dutch writers. But we are not like the Dutch. No shutting the stars and stripes up on an island. Pooh! We must trade wherever we have a mind. Naturally!

The wharves of Norfolk are falling behind, becoming smaller, confused with the warehouses and the trees. On the impetus of the strong South breeze, the paddle-wheel steam frigate, *Mississippi*, of the United States Navy, sails down the flashing bay. Sails away, and steams away, for her furnaces are burning, and her paddle-wheels turning, and all her sails are set and full. Pull, men, to the old chorus:

"A Yankee ship sails down the river,
Blow, boys, blow;
Her masts and spars they shine like silver,
Blow, my bully boys, blow."

But what is the use? That plaguy brass band blares out with "The Star Spangled Banner," and you cannot hear the men because of it. Which is a pity, thinks the Commodore, in his cabin, studying the map, and marking stepping-stones: Madeira, Cape Town, Mauritius, Singapore, nice firm stepping-places for seven-league boots. Flag-stones up and down a hemisphere.

My! How she throws the water off from her bows, and how those paddle-wheels churn her along at the rate of seven good knots! You are a proud lady, Mrs. *Mississippi*, curtseying down Chesapeake Bay, all a-flutter with red white and blue ribbons.

At Mishima in the Province of Kai,
Three men are trying to measure a
   pine tree
By the length of their outstretched
   arms.
Trying to span the bole of a huge
   pine tree
By the spread of their lifted arms.
Attempting to compress its girth
Within the limit of their extended
   arms.
Beyond, Fuji,
Majestic, inevitable,
Wreathed over by wisps of cloud.
The clouds draw about the moun-
   tain,
But there are gaps.
The men reach about the pine tree,
But their hands break apart;
The rough bark escape their hand-
   clasps;
The tree is unencircled.
Three men are trying to measure
   the stem of a gigantic pine tree,
With their arms,
At Mishima in the Province of Kai.

Furnaces are burning good Cumber-
land coal at the rate of twenty-six tons
per diem, and the paddle-wheels turn
round and round in an iris of spray. She
noses her way through a wallowing sea;
foots it, bit by bit, over the slanting
wave slopes; pants along, thrust forward
by her breathing furnaces, urged ahead
by the wind draft flattening against her
taut sails.
The Commodore, leaning over the
taffrail, sees the peak of Madeira sweep
up out of the haze. The *Mississippi*
glides into smooth water, and anchors
under the lee of the "Desertas."

Ah! the purple bougainvillia! And
the sweet smells of the heliotrope and
geranium hedges! Ox-drawn sledges clattering over cobbles — what a fine pause
in an endless voyaging. Stars and stripes
demanding five hundred tons of coal, ten
thousand gallons of water, resting for a
moment on a round stepping-stone, with

the drying sails slatting about in the
warm wind.
"Get out your accordion, Jim, and give
us the 'Suwannee River' to show those
Dagoes what a tune is. Pipe up with the
chorus, boys. Let her go."
The green water flows past Madeira.
Flows under the paddle-boards, making
them clip and clap. The green water
washes along the sides of the Commodore's steam flagship and passes away
to leeward.
"Hitch up your trousers, Black Face,
and do a horn-pipe. It's a fine quiet
night for a double shuffle. Keep her
going, Jim. Louder. That's the ticket.
Gosh, but you can spin, Blackey!"

The road is hilly
Outside the Tiger Gate,
And striped with shadows from a
   bow moon
Slowly sinking to the horizon.
The roadway twinkles with the bob-
   bing of paper lanterns,
Melon-shaped, round, oblong,
Lighting the steps of those who pass
   along it;
And there is a sweet singing of many
   semi,
From the cages which an insect-seller
Carries on his back.

Westward of the Canaries, in a wind-
blazing sea. Engineers, there, extinguish
the furnaces; carpenters, quick, your
screwdrivers and mallets, and unship the
paddle-boards. Break out her sails, quar-
termasters, the wind will carry her faster
than she can steam, for the trades have
her now, and are whipping her along in
fine clipper style. Key-guns, your muzzles
shine like basalt above the tumbling
waves. Polished basalt cameoed upon
malachite. Yankee-doodle-dandy! A fine
upstanding ship, clouded with canvas,
slipping along like a trotting filly out of
the Commodore's own stables. White
sails and sailors, blue-coated officers, and
red in a star sparked through the claret
decanter on the Commodore's luncheon
table.
The Commodore is writing to his wife,
to be posted at the next stopping place.

Two years is a long time to be upon the sea.

Nigi-oi of Matsuba-ya
Celebrated oiran,
Courtesan of unrivalled beauty,
The great silk mercer, Mitsui,
Counts himself a fortunate man
As he watches her parade in front of him
In her robes of glazed blue silk
Embroidered with singing nightin-
gales.
He puffs his little silver pipe
And arranges a fold of her dress.
He parts it at the neck
And laughs when the falling plum-
blossoms
Tickle her naked breasts.
The next morning he makes out a bill
To the Director of the Dutch Fac-
tory at Nagasaki
For three times the amount of the goods
Forwarded that day in two small junks
In the care of a trusted clerk.

The North-east trades have smoothed away into hot, blue doldrums. Paddle-wheels to the rescue. Thank God, we live in an age of invention. What air there is, is dead ahead. The deck is a bed of cinders, we wear a smoke cloud like a funeral plume. Funeral — of whom? Of the little heathens inside the Gate? Wait! Wait! These monkey-men have got to trade, Uncle Sam has laid his plans with care, see those black guns sizzling there. "It's deuced hot," says a lieutenant, "I wish I could look in at a hop in Newport this evening."

The one hundred and sixty streets
in the Sanno quarter
Are honey-gold,
Honey-gold from the gold-foil screens in the houses,
Honey-gold from the fresh yellow mats;
The lintels are draped with bright colours,
And from eaves and poles

Red and white paper lanterns
Glitter and swing.
Through the one hundred and sixty decorated streets of the Sanno quarter,
Trails the procession,
With a bright slowness,
To the music of flutes and drums.
Great white sails of cotton
Belly out along the honey-gold streets.
Sword bearers,
Spear bearers,
Mask bearers,
Grinning masks of mountain genii,
And a white cock on a drum
Above a purple sheet.
Over the flower hats of the peo-
ple,
Shines the sacred palanquin,
"Car of gentle motion,"
Upheld by fifty men,
Stalwart servants of the god,
Bending under the weight of mirror-
black lacquer,
Of pillars and roof-tree
Wrapped in chased and gilded copper.
Portly silk tassels sway to the march-
ing of feet,
Wreaths of gold and silver flowers
Shoot sudden scintillations at the gold-foil screens.
The golden phoenix on the roof of the palanquin
Spreads its wings,
And seems about to take flight
Over the one hundred and sixty streets
Straight into the white heart
Of the curved blue sky.
Six black oxen,
With white and red trappings,
Draw platforms on which are musicians, dancers, actors,
Who posture and sing,
Dance and parade,
Up and down the honey-gold streets,
To the sweet playing of flutes,
And the ever-repeating beat of heavy drums,
To the constant banging of heavily beaten drums,
To the insistent repeating rhythm of beautiful great drums.

Across the equator and panting down to Saint Helena, trailing smoke like a mourning veil. Jamestown jetty, and all the officers in the ship making at once for Longwood. Napoleon! Ah, tales — tales — with nobody to tell them. A bronze eagle caged by floating woodwork. A heart burst with beating on a flat drop-curtain of sea and sky. Nothing now but pigs in a sty. Pigs rooting in the Emperor's bedroom. God be praised, we have a plumed smoking ship to take us away from this desolation.

> "Boney was a warrior
> Away-i-oh;
> Boney was a warrior,
> John François."

"Oh, shut up, Jack, you make me sick. Those pigs are like worms eating a corpse. Bah!"

The ladies,
Wistaria Blossom, Cloth-of-Silk, and
    Deep Snow,
With their ten attendants,
Are come to Asakusa
To gaze at peonies.
To admire crimson-carmine peonies,
To stare in admiration at bomb-
    shaped, white and sulphur
    peonies,
To caress with a soft finger
Single, rose-flat peonies,
Tight, incurved, red-edged peonies,
Spin-wheel circle, amaranth peonies.
To smell the acrid pungence of
    peony blooms,
And dream for months afterwards
Of the temple garden at Asakusa,
Where they walked together
Looking at peonies.

The Gate! The Gate! The far-shining Gate! Pat your guns and thank your stars you have not come too late. The Orient's a sleepy place, as all globe-trotters say. We'll get there soon enough, my lads, and carry it away. That's a good enough song to round the Cape with, and there's the Table Cloth on Table Mountain and we've drawn a bead over half the curving world. Three cheers for Old Glory, fellows.

A Daimio's procession
Winds between two green hills,
A line of thin, sharp, shining,
    pointed spears
Above red coats
And yellow mushroom hats.
A man leading an ox
Has cast himself upon the ground,
He rubs his forehead in the dust,
While his ox gazes with wide, moon
    eyes
At the glittering spears
Majestically parading
Between two green hills.

Down, down, down, to the bottom of the map; but we must up again, high on the other side. America, sailing the seas of a planet to stock the shop counters at home. Commerce-raiding a nation; pulling apart the curtains of a temple and calling it trade. Magnificent mission! Every shop-till in every bye-street will bless you. Force the shut gate with the muzzles of your black cannon. Then wait — wait for fifty years — and see who has conquered.

But now the *Mississippi* must brave the Cape, in a crashing of bitter seas. The wind blows East, the wind blows West, there is no rest under these clashing clouds. Petrel whirl by like torn newspapers along a street. Albatrosses fly close to the mastheads. Dread purrs over this stormy ocean, and the smell of the water is the dead, oozing dampness of tombs.

Tiger rain on the temple bridge of
    carved greenstone,
Slanting tiger lines of rain on the
    lichened lanterns of the gateway,
On the stone statues of mythical
    warriors.
Striped rain making the bells of the
    pagoda roofs flutter,
Tiger-footing on the bluish stones
    of the court-yard,
Beating, snapping, on the cheese-
    rounds of open umbrellas,
Licking, tiger-tongued, over the
    straw mat which a pilgrim wears
    upon his shoulders,
Gnawing, tiger-toothed, into the
    paper mask

Which he carries on his back.
Tiger-clawed rain scattering the
peach-blossoms,
Tiger tails of rain lashing furiously
among the cryptomerias.

"Land — O." Mauritius. Stepping-
stone four. The coaling ships have arrived, and the shore is a hive of Negroes,
and Malays, and Lascars, and Chinese.
The clip and clatter of tongues is un-
ceasing. "What awful brutes!" "Obviously, but the fruits they sell are good."
"Food, fellows, bully good food." Yankee
money for pine-apples, shaddocks,
mangoes. "Who were Paul and Virginia?" "Oh, a couple of spooneys who
died here, in a shipwreck, because the
lady wouldn't take off her smock." "I
say, Fred, that's a shabby way to put it.
You've no sentiment." "Maybe. I don't
read much myself, and when I do, I
prefer United States, something like old
Artemus Ward, for instance." "Oh, dry
up, and let's get some donkeys and go
for a gallop. We've got to begin coaling
to-morrow, remember."

The beautiful dresses,
Blue, Green, Mauve, Yellow;
And the beautiful green pointed hats
Like Chinese porcelains!
See, a band of geisha
Is imitating the state procession of
a Corean Ambassador,
Under painted streamers,
On an early afternoon.

The hot sun burns the tar up out of
the deck. The paddle-wheels turn, flinging the cupped water over their shoulders.
Heat smoulders along the horizon. The
shadow of the ship floats off the starboard quarter, floats like a dark cloth
upon the sea. The watch is pulling on
the topsail halliards:

"O Sally Brown of New York City,
Ay, ay, roll and go."

Like a tired beetle, the *Mississippi* creeps
over the flat, glass water, creeps on,
breathing heavily. Creeps — creeps —
and sighs and settles at Pointe de Galle,
Ceylon.

Spice islands speckling the Spanish
Main. Fairy tales and stolen readings.
Saint John's Eve! Midsummer Madness!
Here it is all true. But the smell of the
spice-trees is not so nice as the smell of
new-mown hay on the Commodore's field
at Tarrytown. But what can one say to
forests of rose-wood, satin-wood, ebony!
To the talipot tree, one leaf of which
can cover several people with its single
shade. Trade! Trade! Trade in spices
for an earlier generation. We dream of
lacquers and precious stones. Of spinning telegraph wires across painted fans.
Ceylon is an old story, ours will be the
glory of more important conquests.
But wait — wait. No one is likely to
force the Gate. The smoke of golden
Virginia tobacco floats through the blue
palms. "You say you killed forty elephants with this rifle!" "Indeed, yes, and
a trifling bag, too."

Down the ninety-mile rapids
Of the Heaven Dragon River,
He came,
With his bowmen,
And his spearmen,
Borne in a gilded palanquin,
To pass the Winter in Yedo
By the Shōgun's decree.
To pass the Winter idling in the
Yoshiwara,
While his bowmen and spearmen
Gamble away their rusted weapons
Every evening
At the Hour of the Cock.

Her Britannic Majesty's frigate *Cleopatra* salutes the *Mississippi* as she sails
into the harbour of Singapore. Vessels
galore choke the wharves. From China,
Siam, Malaya; Sumatra, Europe, America. This is the bargain counter of the
East. Goods — Goods, dumped ashore
to change boats and sail on again. Oaths
and cupidity; greasy clothes and greasy
dollars wound into turbans. Opium and
birds'-nests exchanged for tea, cassia,
nankeens; gold thread bartered for Brummagem buttons. Pockets knives told off
against teapots. Lots and lots of cheap
damaged porcelains, and trains of silken
bales awaiting advantageous sales to
Yankee merchantmen. The figure-head

of the *Mississippi* should be a beneficent angel. With her guns to persuade, she should lay the foundation of such a market on the shores of Japan. "We will do what we can," writes the Commodore, in his cabin.

Outside the drapery shop of
    Taketani Sabai,
Strips of dyed cloth are hanging out
    to dry.
Fine Arimitsu cloth,
Fine blue and white cloth,
Falling from a high staging,
Falling like falling water,
Like blue and white unbroken water
Sliding over a high cliff,
Like the Ono Fall on the Kisokaido
    Road.
Outside the shop of Taketani Sabai,
They have hung the fine dyed cloth
In strips out to dry.

Romance and heroism; and all to make one dollar two. Through grey fog and fresh blue breezes, through heat, and sleet, and sheeted rain. For centuries men have pursued the will-o'-the-wisp — trade. And they have got — what? All civilization weighed in twopenny scales and fastened with string. A sailing planet packed in a dry-goods box. Knocks, and shocks, and blocks of extended knowledge, contended for and won. Cloves and nutmegs, and science stowed among the grains. Your gains are not in silver, mariners, but in the songs of violins, and the thin voices whispering through printed books.

"It looks like a dinner-plate," thinks the officer of the watch, as the *Mississippi* sails up the muddy river to Canton, with the Dragon's Cave Fort on one side, and the Girl's Shoe Fort on the other.

The Great Gate looms in the distant mist, and the anchored squadron waits and rests, but its coming is as certain as the equinoxes, and the lightning bolts of its guns are ready to tear off centuries like husks of corn.

The Commodore sips bottled water from Saratoga, and makes out a report for the State Department. The men play pitch-and-toss, and the officers poker, and the betting gives heavy odds against the little monkey-men.

On the floor of the reception room
    of the Palace
They have laid a white quilt,
And on the quilt, two red rugs;
And they have set up two screens
    of white paper
To hide that which should not be
    seen.
At the four corners, they have placed
    lanterns,
And now they come.
Six attendants,
Three to sit on either side of the
    condemned man,
Walking slowly.
Three to the right,
Three to the left,
And he between them
In his dress of ceremony
With the great wings.
Shadow wings, thrown by the
    lantern light,
Trail over the red rugs to the
    polished floor,
Trail away unnoticed,
For there is a sharp glitter from a
    dagger
Borne past the lanterns on a silver
    tray.
"O my Master,
I would borrow your sword,
For it may be a consolation to you
To perish by a sword to which you
    are accustomed."
Stone, the face of the condemned
    man,
Stone, the face of the executioner,
And yet before this moment
These were master and pupil,
Honoured and according homage,
And this is an act of honourable
    devotion.
Each face is passive,
Hewed as out of strong stone,
Cold as a statue above a temple
    porch.
Down slips the dress of ceremony to
    the girdle.
Plunge the dagger to its hilt.
A trickle of blood runs along the
    white flesh
And soaks into the girdle silk.

Slowly across from left to right,
Slowly, upcutting at the end,
But the executioner leaps to his feet,
Poises the sword —
Did it flash, hover, descend?
There is a thud, a horrible rolling,
And the heavy sound of a loosened,
    falling body,
Then only the throbbing of blood
Spurting into the red rugs.
For he who was a man is that thing
Crumpled up on the floor,
Broken, and crushed into the red
    rugs.
The friend wipes the sword,
And his face is calm and frozen
As a stone statue on a Winter night
Above a temple gateway.

PART II

Four vessels giving easily to the low-
running waves and cat's-paw breezes of
a Summer sea. July, 1853, Mid-Century,
but just on the turn. Mid-Century, with
the vanishing half fluttering behind on a
foam-bubbled wake. Four war ships
steering for the "Land of Great Peace,"
caparisoned in state, cleaving a jewelled
ocean to a Dragon Gate. Behind it, the
quiet of afternoon. Golden light reflecting from the inner sides of shut portals.
War is an old wives' tale, a frail beautiful embroidery of other ages. The panoply of battle fades. Arrows rust in
arsenals, spears stand useless on their
butts in vestibules. Cannon lie un-
mounted in castle yards, and rats and
snakes make nests in them and rear
their young in unmolested satisfaction.
    The sun of Mid-Summer lies over the
"Land of Great Peace," and behind the
shut gate they do not hear the paddle-
wheels of distant vessels unceasingly turning and advancing, through the jewelled
scintillations of the encircling sea.

Susquehanna and *Mississippi*, steamers,
towing *Saratoga* and *Plymouth*, sloops of
war. Moving on in the very eye of the
wind, with not a snip of canvas upon
their slim yards. Fuji! — a point above
nothing, for there is a haze. Stop gazing,
that is the bugle to clear decks and shot
guns. We must be prepared, as we run

up the coast straight to the Bay of Yedo.
"I say, fellows, those boats think they
can catch us, they don't know that this
is Yankee steam." Bang! The shore guns
are at work. And that smoke-ball would
be a rocket at night, but we cannot see
the gleam in this sunshine.
    Black with people are the bluffs of
Uraga, watching the "fire-ships," lipping
windless up the bay. Say all the prayers
you know, priests of Shinto and Buddha.
Ah! The great splashing of the wheels
stops, a chain rattles. The anchor drops
at the Hour of the Ape.
    A clock on the Commodore's chest of
drawers strikes five with a silvery tinkle.

Boats are coming from all directions.
Beautiful boats of unpainted wood,
broad of beam, with tapering sterns, and
clean runs. Swiftly they come, with shouting rowers standing to their oars. The
shore glitters with spears and lacquered
hats. Compactly the boats advance, and
each carries a flag — white-black-white
— and the stripes break and blow. But
the towlines are cast loose when the
rowers would make them fast to the
"black ships," and those who would
climb the chains slip back dismayed,
checked by a show of cutlasses, pistols,
pikes. "*Naru Hodo!*" This is amazing,
unprecedented! Even the Vice-Governor,
though he boards the *Susquehanna*, cannot see the Commodore. "His High
Mighty Mysteriousness, Lord of the Forbidden Interior," remains in his cabin.
Extraordinary! Horrible!
    Rockets rise from the forts, and their
trails of sparks glitter faintly now, and
their bombs break in faded colours as
the sun goes down.
    Bolt the gate, monkey-men, but it is
late to begin turning locks so rusty and
worn.

Darkness over rice-fields and hills. The
Gold Gate hides in shadow. Upon the
indigo-dark water, millions of white jelly-
fish drift, like lotus-petals over an inland
lake. The land buzzes with prayer, low,
dim smoke hanging in air; and every hill
gashes and glares with shooting fires. The
fire-bells are ringing in double time, and

a heavy swinging boom clashes from the great bells of temples. Couriers lash their horses, riding furiously to Yedo; junks and scull-boats arrive hourly at Shinagawa with news; runners, bearing dispatches, pant in government offices. The hollow doors of the Great Gate beat with alarms. The charmed Dragon Country shakes and trembles. Iyéyoshi, twelfth Shōgun of the Tokugawa line, sits in his city. Sits in the midst of one million, two hundred thousand trembling souls, and his mind rolls forward and back like a ball on a circular runway, and finds no goal. Roll, poor distracted mind of a sick man. What can you do but wait, trusting in your Dragon Gate, for how should you know that it is rusted.

But there is a sign over the "black ships." A wedge-shaped tail of blue sparklets, edged with red, trails above them as though a Dragon were pouring violet sulphurous spume from steaming nostrils, and the hulls and rigging are pale, quivering, bright as Taira ghosts on the sea of Nagatō.

Up and down walk sentinels, fore and aft, and at the side gangways. There is a pile of round shot and four stands of grape beside each gun; and carbines, and pistols, and cutlasses, are laid in the boats. Floating arsenals — floating sample-rooms for the wares of a continent; shop-counters, flanked with weapons, adrift among the jelly-fishes.

Eight bells, and the meteor washes away before the wet, white wisps of dawn.

Through the countrysides of the "Land of Great Peace," flowers are blooming. The greenish-white, sterile blossoms of hydrangeas boom faintly, like distant inaudible bombs of colour exploding in the woods. Weigelas prick the pink of their slender trumpets against green backgrounds. The fan-shaped leaves of ladies' slippers rustle under cryptomerias.

Midsummer heat curls about the cinnamon-red tree-boles along the Tokaido. The road ripples and glints with the passing to and fro, and beyond, in the roadstead, the "black ships" swing at their anchors and wait.

All up and down the Eastern shore of the bay is a feverish digging, patting, plastering. Forts to be built in an hour to resist the barbarians, if, peradventure, they can. Japan turned to, what will it not do! Fishermen and palanquin-bearers, packhorse-leaders and farm-labourers, even women and children, pat and plaster. Disaster batters at the Dragon Gate. Batters at the door of Yedo, where Samurai unpack their armour, and whet and feather their arrows.

Daimios smoke innumerable pipes, and drink unnumbered cups of tea, discussing — discussing — "What is to be done?" The Shōgun is no Emperor. What shall they do if the "hairy devils" take a notion to go to Kiōto! Then indeed would the Tokugawa fall. The prisons are crammed with those who advise opening the Gate. Open the Gate, and let the State scatter like dust to the winds! Absurd! Unthinkable! Suppress the "brocade pictures" of the floating monsters with which book-sellers and picture-shop keepers are delighting and affrighting the populace. Place a ban on speech. Preach, inert Daimios — the Commodore will *not* go to Nagasaki, and the roar of his guns will drown the clattering fall of your Dragon Doors if you do not open them in time. East and West, and trade shaded by heroism. Hokusai is dead, but his pupils are lampooning your carpet soldiers. Spare the dynasty — parley, procrastinate. Appoint two Princes to receive the Commodore, at once, since he will not wait over long. At Kurihama, for he must not come to Yedo.

Flip — flap — flutter — flags in front of the Conference House. Built over night, it seems, with unpainted peaked summits of roofs gleaming like ricks of grain. Flip — flutter — flap — variously-tinted flags, in a crescent under nine tall standards whose long scarlet pennons brush the ground. Beat — tap — fill and relapse — the wind pushing against taut white cloth screens, bellying out the Shōgun's crest of heart-shaped Asarum leaves in the panels, crumpling them to indefinite figures of scarlet spotting white. Flip — ripple — brighten — over serried ranks of soldiers on the beach. Sword-bearers, spear-bearers, archers, lancers, and those who carry heavy, antiquated matchlocks. The block of them five thousand armed men, drawn up in front of a cracking golden door. But behind their bristling spears, the cracks are hidden.

Braying, blasting blares from two brass bands, approaching in glittering boats over glittering water. One is playing the "Overture" from "William Tell," the other, "The Last Rose of Summer," and the way the notes clash, and shock, and shatter, and dissolve, is wonderful to hear. Queer barbarian music, and the monkey-soldiers stand stock still, listening to its reverberation humming in the folded doors of the Great Gate.

Stuff your ears, monkey-soldiers, screw your faces, shudder up and down your spines. Cannon! Cannon! from one of the "black ships." Thirteen thudding explosions, thirteen red dragon tongues, thirteen clouds of smoke like the breath of the mountain gods. Thirteen hammer strokes shaking the Great Gate, and the seams in the metal widen. Open Sesame, shotless guns; and "The Only, High, Grand and Mighty, Invisible Mysteriousness, Chief Barbarian" reveals himself, and steps into his barge.

Up, oars, down; drip — sun-spray — rowlock-rattle. To shore! To shore! Set foot upon the sacred soil of the "Land of Great Peace," with its five thousand armed men doing nothing with their spears and matchlocks, because of the genii in the black guns aboard the "black ships."

One hundred marines in a line up the wharf. One hundred sailors, man to man, opposite them. Officers, two deep; and, up the centre — the Procession. Bands together now: "Hail Columbia." Marines in file, sailors after, a staff with the American flag borne by seamen, another with the Commodore's broad pennant. Two boys, dressed for ceremony, carrying the President's letter and credentials in golden boxes. Tall, blue-black negroes on either side of — THE COMMODORE! Walking slowly, gold, blue, steel-glitter, up to the Conference House, walking in state up to an ancient tottering Gate, lately closed securely, but now gaping. Bands, rain your music against this golden barrier, harry the ears of the monkey-

men. The doors are ajar, and the Commodore has entered.

Prince of Idzu — Prince of Iwami — in winged dresses of gold brocade, at the end of a red carpet, under violet, silken hangings, under crests of scarlet heart-shaped Asarum leaves, guardians of a scarlet lacquered box, guardians of golden doors, worn thin and bending.

In silence the blue-black negroes advance and take the golden boxes from the page boys; in silence they open them and unwrap blue velvet coverings. Silently they display the documents to the Prince of Idzu — the Prince of Iwami — motionless, inscrutable — beyond the red carpet.

The vellum crackles as it is unfolded, and the long silk-gold cords of the seals drop their gold tassels to straight glistening inches and swing slowly — gold tassels clock-ticking before a doomed, burnished gate.

The negroes lay the vellum documents upon the scarlet lacquered box; bow, and retire.

"I am desirous that our two countries should trade with each other." Careful letters, carefully traced on rich parchment, and the low sun casts the shadow of the Gate far inland over high hills.

"The letter of the President of the United States will be delivered to the Emperor. Therefore you can now go."

The Commodore, rising: "I will return for the answer during the coming Spring."

But ships are frail, and seas are fickle, one can nail fresh plating over the thin gate before Spring. Prince of Idzu — Prince of Iwami — inscrutable statesmen, insensate idiots, trusting blithely to a lock when the key-guns are trained even now upon it.

Withdraw, Procession. Dip oars back to the "black ships." Slip cables and depart, for day after day will lapse and nothing can retard a coming Spring.

Panic Winter throughout the "Land of Great Peace." Panic, and haste, wasting energies and accomplishing nothing. Kiōto has heard, and prays, trembling.

Priests at the shrine of Isé whine long, slow supplications from dawn to dawn, and through days dropping down again from morning. Iyéyoshi is dead, and Iyésada rules in Yedo; thirteenth Shōgun of the Tokugawa. Rules and struggles, rescinds laws, urges reforms; breathless, agitated endeavours to patch and polish where is only corroding and puffed particles of dust.

It is Winter still in the Bay of Yedo, though the plum-trees of Kamata and Kinagawa are white and fluttering.

Winter, with green, high, angular seas. But over the water, far toward China, are burning the furnaces of three great steamers, and four sailing vessels heel over, with decks slanted and sails full and pulling.

"There's a bit of a lop, this morning. Mr. Jones, you'd better take in those royals."

"Ay, ay, Sir. Tumble up here, men! Tumble up! Lay aloft and stow royals. Haul out to leeward."

"To my,
    Ay,
And we'll *furl*
    Ay,
And pay Paddy Doyle for his Boots."

"Taut band — knot away."

Chug! Chug! go the wheels of the consorts, salting smoke-stacks with whirled spray.

The Commodore lights a cigar, and paces up and down the quarter-deck of the *Powhatan*. "I wonder what the old yellow devils will do," he muses.

Forty feet high, the camellia trees, with hard, green buds unburst. It is early yet for camellias, and the green buds and the glazed green leaves toss frantically in a blustering March wind. Sheltered behind the forty feet high camellia trees, on the hills of Idzu, stand watchmen straining their eyes over a broken dazzle of sea. Just at the edge of moonlight and sunlight — moon setting; sun rising — they come. Seven war ships heeled over and flashing, dashing through heaped waves, sleeping a moment in hollows, leaping

over ridges, sweeping forward in a strain of canvas and a train of red-black smoke.

"The fire-ships! The fire-ships!"

Slip the bridles of your horses, messengers, and clatter down the Tokaido; scatter pedestrians, palanquins, slow moving cattle, right and left into the cryptomerias; rattle over bridges, spatter dust into shop-windows. To Yedo! To Yedo! For Spring is here, and the fire-ships have come!

Seven vessels, flying the stars and stripes, three more shortly to join them, with ripe, fruit-bearing guns pointed inland.

Princes evince doubt, distrust. Learning must beat learning. Appoint a Professor of the University. Delay, prevaricate. How long can the play continue? Hayashi, learned scholar of Confucius and Mencius — he shall confer with the barbarians at Uraga. Shall he! Word comes that the Mighty Chief of Ships will not go to Uraga. Steam is up, and — Horror! Consternation! The squadron moves toward Yedo! Sailors, midshipmen, lieutenants, pack yards and crosstrees, seeing temple gates, castle towers, flowered pagodas, and look-outs looming distantly clear, and the Commodore on deck can hear the slow booming of the bells from the temples of Shiba and Asakusa.

You must capitulate, great Princes of a quivering gate. Say Yokohama, and the Commodore will agree, for they must not come to Yedo.

Rows of japonicas in full bloom outside the Conference House. Flags, and streamers, and musicians, and pikemen. Five hundred officers, seamen, marines, and the Commodore following in his white-painted gig. A jig of fortune indeed, with a sailor and a professor manoeuvring for terms, chess-playing each other in a game of future centuries.

The Americans bring presents. Presents now, to be bought hereafter. Good will, to head long bills of imports. Occidental mechanisms to push the Orient into limbo. Fox-moves of interpreters, and Pandora's box with a contents rated far too low.

Round and round goes the little train on its circular railroad, at twenty miles an hour, with grave dignitaries seated on its roof. Smiles, gestures, at messages running over wire, a mile away. Touch the harrows, the ploughs, the flails, and shudder at the "spirit pictures" of the daguerreotype machine. These Barbarians have harnessed gods and dragons. They build boats which will not sink, and tinker little gold wheels till they follow the swinging of the sun.

Run to the Conference House. See, feel, listen. And shrug deprecating shoulders at the glisten of silk and lacquer given in return. What are cups cut out of conch-shells, and red-dyed figured crêpe, to railroads, and burning engines!

Go on board the "black ships" and drink mint juleps and brandy smashes, and click your tongues over sweet puddings. Offer the strangers pickled plums, sugared fruits, candied walnuts. Bruit the news far inland through the mouths of countrymen. Who thinks of the Great Gate! Its portals are pushed so far back that the shining edges of them can scarcely be observed. The Commodore has never swerved a moment from his purpose, and the dragon mouths of his guns have conquered without the need of a single powder-horn.

The Commodore writes in his cabin. Writes an account of what he has done.

The sands of centuries run fast, one slides, and another, each falling into a smother of dust.

A locomotive in pay for a Whistler; telegraph wires buying a revolution; weights and measures and Audubon's birds in exchange for fear. Yellow monkey-men leaping out of Pandora's box, shaking the rocks of the Western coast-line. Golden California bartering panic for prints. The dressing-gowns of a continent won at the cost of security. Artists and philosophers lost in the hour-glass sand pouring through an open Gate.

Ten ships sailing for China on a fair May wind. Ten ships sailing from one world into another, but never again into the one they left. Two years and a tip-turn is accomplished. Over the globe and back, Rip Van Winkle ships. Slip into your docks in Newport, in Norfolk, in Charlestown. You have blown off the locks of the East, and what is coming will come.

POSTLUDE

In the Castle moat, lotus flowers are
  blooming,
They shine with the light of an
  early moon
Brightening above the Castle towers.
They shine in the dark circles of
  their unreflecting leaves.
Pale blossoms,
Pale towers,
Pale moon,
Deserted ancient moat
About an ancient stronghold,
Your bowmen are departed,
Your strong walls are silent,
Their only echo
A croaking of frogs.
Frogs croaking at the moon
In the ancient moat
Of an ancient, crumbling Castle.

1903. JAPAN

The high cliffs of the Kegon waterfall, and a young man carving words on the trunk of a tree. He finishes, pauses an instant, and then leaps into the foam-cloud rising from below. But, on the tree-trunk, the newly-cut words blaze white and hard as though set with diamonds:

"How mightily and steadily go Heaven and Earth! How infinite the duration of Past and Present! Try to measure this vastness with five feet. A word explains the Truth of the whole Universe — *unknowable.* To cure my agony I have decided to die. Now, as I stand on the crest of this rock, no uneasiness is left in me. For the first time I know that extreme pessimism and extreme optimism are one."

1903. AMERICA

"Nocturne — Blue   and   Silver —
  Battersea Bridge.

Nocturne — Grey and Silver — Chelsea Embankment. Variations in Violet and Green." Pictures in a glass-roofed gallery, and all day long the throng of people is so

great that one can scarcely see them. Debits — credits? Flux and flow through a wide gateway. Occident — Orient — after fifty years.

HEDGE ISLAND

A Retrospect and a Prophecy

Hedges of England, peppered with sloes; hedges of England, rows and rows of thorn and brier raying out from the fire where London burns with its steaming lights, throwing a glare on the sky o' nights. Hedges of England, road after road, lane after lane, and on again to the sea at the North, to the sea at the East, blackberry hedges, and man and beast plod and trot and gallop between hedges of England, clipped and clean; beech, and laurel, and hornbeam, and yew, wheels whirl under, and circle through, tunnels of green to the sea at the South; wind-blown hedges to mark the mouth of Thames or Humber, the Western rim. Star-point hedges, smooth and trim.

Star-point indeed, with all His Majesty's mails agog every night for the provinces. Twenty-seven fine crimson coaches drawn up in double file in Lombard Street. Great gold-starred coaches, blazing with royal insignia, waiting in line at the Post-Office. Eight of a Summer's evening, and the sun only just gone down. "Lincoln," "Winchester," "Portsmouth," shouted from the Post-Office steps; and the Portsmouth chestnuts come up to the collar with a jolt, and stop again, dancing, as the bags are hoisted up. "Gloucester," "Oxford," "Bristol," "York," "Norwich." Rein in those bays of the Norwich team, they shy badly at the fan-gleam of the lamp over the Post-Office door. "All in. No more." The stones of St. Martin's-le-Grand sparkle under the slap of iron shoes. Off you go, bays, and the greys of the Dover mail start forward, twitching, hitching, champing, stamping, their little feet pat the ground in patterns and their bits

fleck foam. "Whoa! Steady!" With a rush they are gone. But Glasgow is ready with a team of piebalds and sorrels, driven chess-board fashion. Bang down, lids of mail-boxes — thunder-lids, making the horses start. They part and pull, push each other sideways, sprawl on the slippery pavement, and gather wave-like and crashing to a leap. Spicey tits those! Tootle-too! A nice calculation for the gate, not a minute to spare, with the wheelers well up in the bit and the leaders carrying bar. Forty-two hours to Scotland, and we have a coachman who keeps his horses like clock-work. Whips flick, buckles click, and wheels turn faster and faster till the spokes blur. "Sound your horn, Walter." Make it echo back and forth from the fronts of houses. Good-night, London, we are carrying the mails to the North. Big, burning light which is London, we dip over Highgate hill and leave you. The air is steady, the night is bright, the roads are firm. The wheels hum like a gigantic spinning-jenny. Up North, where the hedges bloom with roses. Through Whetstone Gate to Alconbury Hill. Stop at the *Wheatsheaf* one minute for the change. They always have an eye open here, it takes thirty seconds to drink a pot of beer, even the post-boys sleep in their spurs. The wheels purr over the gravel. "Give the off-hand leader a cut on the cheek!" Whip! Whew! This is the first night of three. Three nights to Glasgow; hedges — hedges — shoot and flow. Eleven miles an hour, and the hedges are showered with glow-worms. The hedges and the glow-worms are very still, but we make a prodigious clatter. What does it matter? It is good for these yokels to be waked up. Tootle-toot! The diamond-paned lattice of a cottage flies open. Post-office here. Throw them on their haunches. Bag up — bag down — and the village has grown indistinct behind. The old moon is racing us, she slices through trees like a knife through cheese. Distant clocks strike midnight. The coach rocks — this is a galloping stage. We have a roan near-wheel and a grey off-wheel and our leaders are chestnuts, "quick as light, clever as cats."

The sickle-flame of our lamps cuts past sequences of trees and well-plashed quickset hedges — hedges of England, long shafts of the nimbus of London. Hurdles here and there. Park palings. Reflections in windows. On — on — through the night to the North. Over stretched roads, with a soft, continuous motion like slipping water. Nights and days unwinding down long roads.

In the green dawn, spires and bell-towers start up and stare at us. Hoary old woods nod and beckon. A castle turret glitters through trees. There is a perfume of wild-rose and honey-bine, twining in the hedges — Northerly hedges, sliding away behind us. The pole-chains tinkle tunes and play a saraband with sheep-bells beyond the hedges. Wedges of fields — square, flat, slatted green with corn, purple with cabbages. The stable clocks of Gayhurst and Tyringham chime from either side of the road. The Ouse twinkles blue among smooth meadows. Go! Go! News of the World! Perhaps a victory! the "Nile" or "Salamanca"! Perhaps a proclamation, or a fall in the rate of consols. Whatever it is, the hedges of England hear it first. Hear it, and flick and flutter their leaves, and catch the dust of it on their shining backs. Bear it over the dumpling hills and the humpbacked bridges. Start it down the rivers: Eden, Eshe, Sark, Milk, Driff, and Clyde. Shout it to the sculptured corbels of old churches. Lurch round corners with it, and stop with a snap before the claret-coloured brick front of the Bell at Derby, and call it to the ostler as he runs out with fresh horses. The twenty Corinthian columns of pale primrose alabaster at Keddleston Hall tremble with its importance. Even the runaway couples bound for Gretna Green cheer and wave. Laurels, and ribbons, and

a red flag on our roof. "Wellesley forever!"

Dust dims the hedges. A light travelling chariot running sixteen miles an hour with four blood mares doing their bravest. Whip, bound, and cut again. Loose rein, quick spur. He stands up in the chariot and shakes a bag full of broad guineas, you can hear them — clinking, chinking — even above the roar of wheels. "Go it! Go it! We are getting away from them. Fifty guineas to each of you if we get there in time." Quietly wait, grey hedges, it will all happen again: quick whip, spur, strain. Two purple-faced gentlemen in another chariot, black geldings smoking hot, blood and froth flipped over the hedges. They hail the coach: "How far ahead? Can we catch them?" "Ten minutes gone by. Not more." The post-boys wale their lunging horses. Rattle, reel, and plunge.

But the runaways have Jack Ainslee from the Bush, Carlisle. He rides in a yellow jacket, and he knows every by-lane and wood between here and the border. In an hour he will have them at Gretna, and to-night the lady will write to her family at Doncaster, and the down mail will carry the letter, with tenpence halfpenny to pay for news that nobody wishes to hear.

"Buy a pottle of plums, Good Sir." "Cherries, fine, ripe cherries O." Get your plums and cherries, and hurry into the White Horse Celler for a last rum and milk. You are a poet, bound to Dover over Westminster Bridge. Ah, well, all the same. You are an Essex farmer, grown fat by selling your peas at Covent Garden Market at four guineas a pint. Certainly; as you please. You are a prebend of Exeter or Wells, timing your journey to the Cathedral Close. If you choose. You are a Corinthian Buck going to Brighton by the Age which runs "with a fury." Mercury on a box seat.

Get up, bearers and top-boots. Shoot the last parcel in. Now — "Let 'em go. I have 'em." That was a jerk, but the coachman lets fly his whip and quirks his off-wheeler on the thigh. Out and under the archway of the coach-yard, with the guard playing "Sally in our Alley" on his key-bugle. White with sun, the streets of London. Cloud-shadows run ahead of us along the streets. Morning. Summer. England. "Have a light, Sir? Tobacco tastes well in this fresh air."

Hedges of England, how many wheels spatter you in a day? How many coaches roll between you on their star-point way? What rainbow colours slide past you with the fluency of water? Crimson mails rumble and glide the night through, but the Cambridge *Telegraph* is a brilliant blue. The *Bull and Mouth* coaches are buttercup yellow, those of the *Bull* are painted red, while the *Bell and Crown* sports a dark maroon with light red wheels. They whirl in a flurry of dust and colours. Soon all this will drop asunder like the broken glass of a kaleidoscope. Hedges, you will see other pictures. New colours will flow beside you. New shapes will intersect you. Tut! Tut! Have you not hawthorn blossoms and the hips and haws of roses?

Trundle between your sharp-shorn hedges, old *Tally-hoes*, and *Comets*, and *Regents*. Stop at the *George*, and turn with a flourish into the yard, where a strapper is washing a mud-splashed chaise, and the horsekeeper is putting a "point" on that best whip of yours. "Coach stops here half an hour, Gentlemen: dinner quite ready." A long oak corridor. Then a burst of sunshine through leaded windows, spangling a floor, iris-tinting rounds of beef, and flaked veal pies, and rose-marbled hams, and great succulent cheeses. Wine-glasses take it and break it, and it quivers away over the table-cloth in faint rainbows; or, straight and sudden, stamps a startling silver whorl on the polished side of a teapot of hot bohea. A tortoise-shell cat naps between red geraniums, and myrtle sprigs tap the stuccoed wall, gently blowing to and fro. Ah, hedges of England, have you led to this? Do you always conduct to galleried inns, snug bars, beds hung with flowered chintz, sheets smelling of lavender?

What of the target practice off Spithead? What of the rocking seventy-fours, flocking like gulls about the harbour entrances? Hedges of England, can they root you in the sea?

Your leaves rustle to the quick breeze of wheels incessantly turning. This island might be a treadmill kept floating right side up by galloping hoofs.

Gabled roofs of *Green Dragons*, and *Catherine Wheels*, and *Crowns*, ivy-covered walls, cool cellars holding bins and bins of old port, and claret, and burgundy. You cannot hear the din of passing chaises, underground, there is only the sound of beer running into a jug as the landlord turns the spiggot of a barrel. Green sponge of England, your heart is red with wine. "Fine spirits and brandies." Ha! Ha! Good old England, drinking, blinking, dreading new ideas. Queer, bluff, burly England. You have Nelsons, and Wellesleys, and Tom Cribbs, but you have also Wordsworths and Romneys, and (a whisper in your ear) Arkwrights and Stevensons.

"Time's up, Gentlemen; take your places, please!" The horn rings out, the bars rattle, the horses sidle and paw and swing; swish — clip — with the long whip, and away to the hedges again. The high, bordering hedges, leading to Salisbury, and Bath, and Exeter.

Christmas weather with a hard frost. Hips and haws sparkle in the hedges, garnets and carnelians scattered on green baize. The edges of the coachman's hat are notched with icicles. The horses slip on the frozen roads. Loads are heavy at this time of year, with rabbits and pheasants tied under the coach, but it is all hearty Christmas cheer, rushing between the hedges to get there in time for the plum-pudding. Old England forever! And coach-horns, and waits, and Cathedral organs hail the Star of Bethlehem.

But our star, our London, gutters with fog. The Thames rolls like smoke under charcoal. The dome of St. Paul's is gone, so is the spire of St. Martin's-in-the-Fields, only the fires of torches are brisk and tossing. Tossing torches; tossing heads of horses. Eight mails following each other out of London by torchlight. Scarcely can we see the red flare of the horn lantern in the hand of the ostler at the *Peacock*, but his voice blocks squarely into the fog: "*York Highflyer*," "*Leeds Union*," "*Stamford Regent*." Coach lamps stream and stare, and key-bugles play fugues with each other; "Oh, Dear, What Can the Matter Be?" and "The Flaxen Headed Plough-boy" canon and catch as the mails take the road. There will be no "springing" the horses over the "hospital ground" on a day like this; we cannot make more than three miles an hour in such a fog. Hedges of England, you are only ledges from which water drips back to the sea. The rain is so heavy the coach sways. There will be floods farther on. Floods over the river Mole, with apples, and trees, and hurdles floating. Have a care with your leaders there, they have lost the road, and the wheelers have toppled into a ditch of swirling, curling water. The wheelers flounder and squeal and drown, but the coach is hung up on the stump of a willow-tree, and the passengers have only a broken leg or two among them.

Double thong your team, Coachman, that creaking gibbet on the top of Hindhead is an awesome sight at the fall of night, with the wind roaring and squeaking over the heather. The murder, they say, was done at this spot. Give it to them on the flank, good and hot. "Lord, I wish I had a nip of cherry-brandy." "What was that; down in the bowl!" "Drop my arm, Damn you! or you will roll the coach over!" Teeth chatter, bony castanets — click — click — to a ghastly tune, click — click — on the gallows-tree, where it blows so windily. Blows the caged bones all about, one or two of them have dropped out. The up coach will see them lying on the ground like snow-flakes tomorrow. But we shall be floundering in a drift, and shifting the mailbags to one of the horses so that the guard can carry them on. Hedges of England, smothered in snow. Hedges of England, row after row, flat and obliterate down to the sea; but the chains are choked on the gallows-tree. Round about England the toothed waves snarl, gnarling her cliffs of chalk and marl. Crabbed England, consuming beef and pudding, and pouring down magnums of port, to cheat the elements. Go it, England, you will beat Bonaparte yet. What have you to do with ideas! You have Bishops, and Squires, and Manor-houses, and — rum.

London shakes with bells. Loud, bright bells lashing over roofs and steeples, exploding in the sunlight with the brilliance of rockets. Every clock-tower drips a tune. The people are merry-making, for this is the King's Birthday and the mails parade this afternoon.

"Messrs. Vidler and Parrat request the pleasure of Mr. Chaplin's company on Thursday the twenty-eighth of May, to a cold collation at three o'clock and to see the Procession of the Mails."

What a magnificent spectacle! A coil of coaches progressing round and round Lincoln's Inn Fields. Sun-mottled harness, gold and scarlet guards, horns throwing off sprays of light and music. Liverpool, Manchester — blacks and greys; Bristol, Devonport — satin bays; Holyhead — chestnuts; Halifax — roans, blue-specked, rose-specked . . . On their box-seat thrones sit the mighty coachmen, twisting their horses this way and that with a turn of the wrist. These are the spokes of a wheeling sun, these are the rays of London's aureole. This is her star-fire, reduced by a prism to separate sparks. Cheer, good people! Chuck up your hats, and buy violets to pin in your coats. You shall see it all tonight, when the King's arms shine in lamps from every housefront, and the mails, done parading, crack their whips and depart. England forever! Hurrah!

England forever — going to the Prize Fight on Copthorne Common. England forever, with a blue coat and scarlet lining hanging over the back of the tilbury. England driving a gig and one horse; England set up with a curricle and two. England in donkey-carts and coaches.

England swearing, pushing, drinking, happy, off to see the "Game Chicken" punch the "Nonpareil's" face to a black-and-blue jelly. Good old England, drunk as a lord, cursing the turn-pike men. Your hedges will be a nest of broken bottles before night, and clouds of dust will quench the perfume of your flowers: I bet you three bulls to a tanner you can't smell a rose for a week.

They've got the soldiers out farther along. "Damn the soldiers! Drive through them, Watson." A fine, manly business; are we slaves? "Britons never — never —" Waves lap the shores of England, waves like watchdogs growling; and long hedges bind her like a bundle. Sit safe, England, trussed and knotted; while your strings hold, all will be well.

But in the distance there is a puff of steam. Just a puff, but it will do. Post-boys, coachmen, guards, chaises, melt like meadow rime before the sun.

You spun your webs over England, hedge to hedge. You kept England bound together by your spinning wheels. But it is gone. They have driven a wedge of iron into your heart. They have dried up the sea, and made pathways in the swimming air. They have tapped the barrels in your cellars and your throats are parched and bleeding. But still the hedges blow for the Spring, and dusty soldiers smell your roses as they tramp to Aldershot or Dorchester.

England forever! Star-pointed and shining. Flinging her hedges out and asunder to embrace the world.

THE BRONZE HORSES

Elements

Earth, Air, Water, and Fire! Earth beneath, Air encompassing, Water within its boundaries. But Fire is nothing, comes from nothing, goes nowhither. Fire leaps forth and dies, yet is everything sprung out of Fire.

The flame grows and drops away, and where it stood is vapour, and where was the vapour is swift revolution, and where was the revolution is spinning resistance, and where the resistance endured is crystallization. Fire melts, and the absence of Fire cools and freezes. So are metals fused in twisted flames and take on a form other than that they have known, and this new form shall be to them rebirth and making. For in it they will stand upon the Earth, and in it they will defy the Air, and in it they will suffer the Water.

But Fire, coming again, the substance changes and is transformed. Therefore are things known only between burning and burning. The quickly consumed more swiftly vanish, yet all must feel the heat of the flame which waits in obscurity, knowing its own time and what work it has to do.

Rome

The blue sky of Italy; the blue sky of Rome. Sunlight pouring white and clear from the wide-stretched sky. Sunlight sliding softly over white marble, lying in jasmine circles before cool porticoes, striking sharply upon roofs and domes, recoiling before straight façades of grey granite, foiled and beaten by the deep halls of temples.

Sunlight on tiles and tufa, sunlight on basalt and porphyry. The sky stripes Rome with sun and shadow; strips of yellow, strips of blue, pepper-dots of purple and orange. It whip-lashes the four great horses of gilded bronze, harnessed to the bronze *quadriga* on the Arch of Nero, and they trot slowly forward without moving. The horses tread the marbles of Rome beneath their feet. Their golden flanks quiver in the sunlight. One foot paws in the air. A step, and they will lance into the air, Pegasus-like, stepping the wind. But they do not take the step. They wait — poised, treading Rome as they trod Alexandria, as they trod the narrow Island of Cos. The spokes of the *quadriga* wheels flash, but they do not turn. They burn like day-stars above the

Arch of Nero. The horses poise over Rome, a constellation of morning, triumphant above Emperors, proud, indifferent, enduring, relentlessly spurning the hot dust of Rome. Hot dust clouds up about them, but not one particle sticks to their gilded manes. Dust is nothing, a mere smoke of disappearing hours. Slowly they trot forward without moving, and time passes and passes them, brushing along their sides like wind.

People go and come in the streets of Rome, shuffling over the basalt paving-stones in their high latcheted sandals. White and purple, like the white sun and the purple shadows, the senators pass, followed by a crowd of slaves. Waves of brown-coated populace efface themselves before a litter, carried by eight Cappadocians in light-red tunics; as it moves along, there is the flicker of a violet *stola* and the blowing edge of a *palla* of sky-white blue. A lady, going to the bath to lie for an hour in the crimson and wine-red reflections of a marble chamber, to glide over a floor of green and white stones into a Carraran basin, where the green and blue water will cover her rose and blue-veined flesh with a slipping veil. Aqua Claudia, Aqua Virgo, Aqua Marcia, drawn from the hills to lie against a woman's body. Her breasts round hollows for themselves in the sky-green water, her fingers sift the pale water and drop it from her as a lark drops notes backwards into the sky. The lady lies against the lipping water, supine and indolent, a pomegranate, a passion-flower, a silver-flamed lily, lapped, slapped, lulled, by the ripples which stir under her faintly moving hands.

Later, beneath a painting of twelve dancing girls upon a gold ground, the slaves will anoint her with cassia, or nakte, or spikenard, or balsam, and she will go home in the swaying litter to eat the tongues of red flamingoes, and drink honey-wine flavoured with far-smelling mint.

Legionaries ravish Egypt for her entertainment; they bring her roses from Alexandria at a cost of thirty thousand pounds. Yet she would rather be at Baiae, one is so restricted in one's pleasures in Rome! The games are not until next week, and her favourite gladiator, Naxos, is in training just now, therefore time drags. The lady lags over her quail and peacocks' eggs. How dull it is. White, and blue, and stupid. Rome!

Smoke flutters and veers from the top of the Temple of Vesta. Altar smoke winding up to the gilded horses as they tread above Rome. Below — laughing, jangling, pushing and rushing. Two carts are jammed at a street corner, and the oaths of the drivers mingle, and snap, and corrode, like hot fused metal, one against another. They hiss and sputter, making a confused chord through which the squeal of a derrick winding up a granite slab pierces, shrill and nervous, a sharp boring sound, shoring through the wide, white light of the Roman sky. People are selling things: matches, broken glass, peas, sausages, cakes. A string of donkeys, with panniers loaded with red asparagus and pale-green rue, minces past the derrick, the donkeys squeeze one by one, with little patting feet, between the derrick and the choked crossing. "Hey! Gallus, have you heard that Caesar has paid a million *sestertii* for a Murrhine vase. It is green and white, flaked like a Spring onion, and has the head of Minerva cut in it, sharp as a signet." "And who has a better right indeed, now that Titus has conquered Judea. He will be here next week, they say, and then we shall have a triumph worth looking at." "Famous indeed! We need something. It's been abominably monotonous lately. Why, there was not enough blood spilled in the games last week to give one the least appetite. I'm damned stale, for one."

Still, over Rome, the white sun sails the blue, stretching sky, casting orange and purple striae down upon the marble city, cool and majestic, between cool hills, white and omnipotent, dying of languor, amusing herself for a moment with the little boats floating up the Tiber bringing the good grain of Carthage, then relaxed and falling as water falls, dropping into the bath. Weak as water; without contour as water; colourless as water; Rome bathes, and relaxes, and melts. Fluid and fluctuating, a liquid city pouring itself back into the streams of the earth. And above, on the Arch of Nero, hard, metallic, firm, cold, and permanent, the bronze horses trot slowly, not moving, and the moon casts the fine-edged shadow of them down upon the paving-stones.

Hills of the city: Pincian, Esquiline, Caelian, Aventine, the crimson tip of the sun burns against you, and you start into sudden clearness and glow red, red-gold, saffron, gradually diminishing to an outline of blue. The sun mounts over Rome, and the Arch of Augustus glitters like a cleft pomegranate; the Temples of Julius Caesar, Castor, and Saturn, turn carbuncle, and rose, and diamond. Columns divide into double edges of flash and shadow; domes glare, inverted beryls hanging over arrested scintillations. The fountains flake and fringe with the scatter of the sun. The mosaic floors of *atriums* are no longer stone, but variegated fire; higher, on the walls, the pictures painted in the white earth of Melos, the red earth of Sinope, the yellow ochre of Attica, erupt into flame. The legs of satyrs jerk with desire, the dancers whirl in torch-bright involutions. Grapes split and burst, spurting spots and sparks of sun.

It is morning in Rome, and the bronze horses on the Arch of Nero trot quietly forward without moving, but no one can see them, they are only a dazzle, a shock of stronger light against the white-blue sky.

Morning in Rome; and the whole city foams out to meet it, seething, simmering, surging, seeping. All between the Janiculum and the Palatine is undulating with people. Scarlet, violet, and purple togas pattern the mass of black and brown. Murex-dyed silk dresses flow beside raw woolen fabrics. The altars smoke incense, the bridges shake under the caking mass of sight-seers. "Titus! Titus! *Io triumphe!*" Even now the troops are collected near the Temple of Apollo, outside the gates, waiting for the signal to march. In the parching Roman morning, the hot dust rises and clouds over the city — an aureole of triumph. The horses on the Arch of Nero paw the golden dust, but it passes, passes, brushing along their burnished sides like wind.

What is that sound? The marble city shivers to the treading of feet. Caesar's legions marching, foot — foot — hundreds, thousands of feet. They beat the ground, rounding each step double. Coming — coming — cohort after cohort, with brazen trumpets marking the time. One — two — one — two — laurel-crowned each one of you, cactus-fibred, harsh as sand grinding the rocks of a treeless land, rough and salt as a Dead Sea wind, only the fallen are left behind. Blood-red plumes, jarring to the footfalls; they have passed through the gate, they are in the walls of the mother city, of marble Rome. Their tunics are purple embroidered with gold, their armour clanks as they walk, the cold steel of their swords is chill in the sun, each is a hero, one by one, endless companies, the soldiers come. Back to Rome with a victor's spoils, with a victor's wreath on every head, and Judah broken is dead, dead! "*Io triumphe!*" The shout knocks and breaks upon the spears of the legionaries.

The God of the Jews is overborne, he has failed his people. See the stuffs from the Syrian looms, and the vestments of many-colours, they were taken from the great Temple at Jerusalem. And the watching crowds split their voices acclaiming the divine triumph. Mars, and Juno, and Minerva, and the rest, those gods are the best who bring victory! And the beasts they have over there! Is that a crocodile? And that bird with a tail as long as a banner, what do you call that? Look at the elephants, and the dromedaries! They are harnessed in jewels. Oh! Oh! The beautiful sight! Here come the prisoners, dirty creatures. "That's a good-looking girl there. I have rather a fancy for a Jewess. I'll get her, by Bacchus, if I have to mortgage my farm. A man too, of course, to keep the breed going; it will be a good investment, although, to be sure, I want the girl myself. Castor and Pollux, did you see that picture! Ten men disembowelled on the steps of the altar. That is better than a gladiator show any day. I wish I had been there.

Simon, oh, Simon! Spit at him, Lucullus. Thumbs down for Simon! Fancy getting him alive, I wonder he didn't kill himself first like Cleopatra. This is a glorious day, I haven't had such fun in years."

The bronze horses tread quietly above the triumphing multitudes. They too have been spoils of war, yet they stand here on the Arch of Nero dominating Rome. Time passes — passes — but the horses, calm and contained, move forward, dividing one minute from another and leaving each behind.

You should be still now, Roman populace. These are the decorations of the Penetralia, the holy Sanctuary which your soldiers have profaned. But the people jeer and scoff, and comment on the queer articles carried on the heads of the soldiers. Tragedy indeed! They see no tragedy, only an immense spectacle, unique and satisfying. The crowd clears its throat and spits and shouts "Io triumphe! Io triumphe!" against the cracking blare of brazen trumpets.

Slowly they come, the symbols of a beaten religion: the Golden Table for the Shew-Bread, the Silver Trumpets that sounded the Jubilee, the Seven-Branched Candlestick, the very Tables of the Law which Moses brought down from Mount Sinai. Can Jupiter conquer these? Slowly they pass, glinting in the sunlight, staring in the light of day, mocked and exhibited. Lord God of Hosts, fall upon these people, send your thunders upon them, hurl the lightnings of your wrath against this multitude, raze their marble city so that not one stone remain standing. But the sun shines unclouded, and the holy vessels pass onward through the Campus Martius, through the Circus Flaminius, up the Via Sacra to the Capitol, and then . . . The bronze horses look into the brilliant sky, they trot slowly without moving, they advance slowly, one foot raised. There is always another step — one, and another. How many does not matter, so that each is taken.

The *spolia opima* have passed. The crowd holds its breath and quivers. Every-

one is tiptoed up to see above his neighbour; they sway and brace themselves in their serried ranks. Away, over the heads, silver eagles glitter, each one marking the passage of a legion. The "Victorious Legion" goes by, the "Indomitable Legion," the "Spanish Legion," and those with a crested lark on their helmets, and that other whose centurions are almost smothered under the shining reflections of the medallions fastened to their armour. Cohort after cohort, legion on the heels of legion, the glistening greaves rise and flash and drop and pale, scaling from sparkle to dullness in a series of rhythmic angles, constantly repeated. They swing to the tones of straight brass trumpets, they jut out and fall at the call of spiral bugles. Above them, the pointed shields move evenly, right to left — right to left. The horses curvet and prance, and shiver back, checked, on their haunches; the javelins of the horsemen are so many broad-ended sticks of flame.

Those are the eagles of the Imperial Guard, and behind are two golden chariots. "Io triumphe!" The roar drowns the trumpets and bugles, the clatter of the horses' hoofs is a mere rattle of sand ricocheting against the voice of welcoming Rome. The Emperor Vespasian rides in one chariot, in the other stands Titus. Titus, who has subdued Judea, who has humbled Jehovah, and brought the sacred vessels of the Lord God of Hosts back with him as a worthy offering to the people of Rome. Cheer, therefore, good people, you have the Throne of Heaven to recline upon; you are possessed of the awful majesty of the God of the Jews; beneath your feet are spread the emblems of the Most High; and your hands are made free of the sacred instruments of Salvation.

What god is that who falls before pikes and spears! Here is another god, his face and hands stained with vermilion, after the manner of the Capitoline Jupiter. His car is of ivory and gold, green plumes nod over the heads of his horses, the military bracelets on his arms seem like circling serpents of bitter flame. The milk-white horses draw him slowly to the Capitol, step by step, along the Via Triumphalis, and step by step the old golden horses on the Arch of Nero tread down the hours of the lapsing day.

That night, forty elephants bearing candelabra light up the ranges of pillars supporting the triple portico of the Capitol. Forty illuminated elephants — and the light of their candles is reflected in the polished sides of the great horses, above, on the Arch of Nero, slowly trotting forward, stationary yet moving, in the soft night which hangs over Rome.

PAVANE TO A BRASS ORCHESTRA

Water falls from the sky, and green-fanged lightning mouths the heavens. The Earth rolls upon itself, incessantly creating morning and evening. The moon calls to the waters, swinging them forward and back, and the sun draws closer and as rhythmically recedes, advancing in the pattern of an ancient dance, making a figure of leaves and aridness. Harmony of chords and pauses, fugue of returning balances, canon and canon repeating the theme of Earth, Air, and Water.

A single cymbal-crash of Fire, and for an instant the concerted music ceases. But it resumes — Earth, Air, and Water, and out of it rise the metals, unconsumed. Brazen cymbals, trumpets of silver, bells of bronze. They mock at fire. They burn upon themselves and retain their entities. Not yet the flame which shall destroy them. They shall know all flames but one. They shall be polished and corroded, yet shall they persist and play the music which accompanies the strange ceremonious dance of the sun.

CONSTANTINOPLE

Empire of the East! Byzantium! Constantinople! The Golden City of the World. A crystal fixed in aquamarines; a jewel-box set down in a seaside garden. All the seas are as blue as Spring lupins, and there are so many seas. Look where you please, forward, back, or down, there is water. The deep blue water of crisp ripples, the long light shimmer of flat undulations, the white glare, smoothing into purple, of a sun-struck ebb. The Bosphorus winds North to the Black Sea.

The Golden Horn curves into the Sweet Waters. The edge of the city swerves away from the Sea of Marmora. Aquamarines, did I say? Sapphires, beryls, lapis-lazuli, amethysts, and felspar. Whatever stones there are, bluer than gentians, bluer than cornflowers, bluer than asters, bluer than periwinkles. So blue that the city must be golden to complement the water. A gold city, shimmering and simmering, starting up like mica from the green of lemon trees, and olives, and cypresses.

Gold! Gold! Walls and columns covered with gold. Domes of churches resplendent with gold. Innumerable statues of "bronze fairer than pure gold," and courts paved with golden tiles. Beyond the white and rose-coloured walls of Saint Sophia, the city rounds for fourteen great miles; fourteen miles of onychite, and porphyry, and marble; fourteen miles of colonnades, and baths, and porticoes; fourteen miles of gay, garish, gaudy, glaring gold. Why, even the Imperial *triremes* in the harbour have gold embroidered gonfalons, and the dolphins, ruffling out of the water between them, catch the colour and dive, each a sharp cutting disk-edge of yellow flame.

It is the same up above, where statues spark like stars jutted from a mid-day sky. There are golden Emperors at every crossing, and golden Virgins crowding every church-front. And, in the centre of the great Hippodrome, facing the *triremes* and the leaping dolphins, is a fine chariot of Corinthian brass. Four horses harnessed to a gilded *quadriga*. The horses pace evenly forward, in a moment they will be trampling upon space, facing out to sea on the currents of the morning breeze. But their heads are arched and checked, gracefully they pause, one leg uplifted, seized and baffled by the arrested movement. They are the horses of Constantine, brought from Rome, so people say, buzzing in the Augustaion. "Fine horses, hey?" "A good breed, Persia from the look of them, though they're a bit thick in the barrel for the horses they bring us from there." "They bring us their worst, most likely." "Oh, I don't know, we buy pretty well. Why, only the other day I gave a mint of money for a cargo of Egyptian maize." "Lucky dog, you'll make on that, with all the harvest here ruined by the locusts."

It is a pretty little wind which plays along the sides of the gilded horses, a coquettish little sea wind, blowing and listing and finally dropping away altogether and going to sleep in a plane-tree behind the Hippodrome.

Constantinople is a yellow honey-comb, with fat bees buzzing in all its many-sided cells. Bees come over the flower-blue seas; bees humming from the Steppes of Tartary, from the long line of Nile-fed Egypt. Tush! What would you! Where there is gold there are always men about it; to steal it, to guard it, to sit and rot under its lotus-shining brilliance. The very army is woven of threads drawn from the edges of the world. Byzantines are merchantmen, they roll and flounder in the midst of gold coins, they tumble and wallow in money-baths, they sit and chuckle under a continuous money-spray. And ringed about them is the army, paid to shovel back the scattering gold pieces: Dalmatians with swords and arrows; Macedonians with silver belts and gilt shields; Scholarii, clad in rose-coloured tunics; Varangians, shouldering double battle-axes. When they walk, the rattle of them can be heard pattering back from every wall and doorway. It clacks and cracks even in the Copper Market, above the clang of cooking pots and the wrangling whine of Jewish traders. Constantinople chatters, buzzes, screams, growls, howls, squeals, snorts, brays, croaks, screeches, crows, neighs, gabbles, purrs, hisses, brawls, roars, shouts, mutters, calls, in every sort of crotchet and demi-semi-quaver, wavering up in a great contrapuntal murmur — adagio, maestoso, capriccioso, scherzo, staccato, crescendo, vivace, veloce, brio — brio — brio!! A racket of dissonance, a hubbub of harmony. Chords? Discords? Answer: Byzantium!

People pluck the strings of rebecks and psalteries; they shock the cords of lyres; they batter tin drums, and shatter the guts of kettle-drums when the Emperor goes to Saint Sophia to worship at an altar of precious stones fused into a bed of gold and silver, and, as he walks up the nave between the columns of green granite, and the columns of porphyry, under the golden lily on the Octagonal Tower, the bells pour their notes over the roofs, spilling them in single jets down on each side of the wide roofs. Drip — drip — drip — out of their hearts of beaten bronze, slipping and drowning in the noise of the crowds clustered below.

On the top of the Hippodrome, the bronze horses trot toward the lupin-coloured Sea of Marmora, slowly, without moving; and, behind them, the spokes of the *quadriga* wheels remain separate and single, with the blue sky showing between each one.

What a city is this, builded of gold and alabaster, with myrtle and roses strewn over its floors, and doors of embossed silver opening upon golden trees where jewelled birds sing clock-work notes, and fountains flow from the beaks of silver eagles. All this splendour cooped within the fourteen miles of a single city, forsooth! In Britain, they sit under oaken beams; in France, they eat with hunting-knives; in Germany, men wear coats of their wives' weaving. In Italy — but there is a Pope in Italy! The bronze horses pause on the marble Hippodrome, and days blow over them, brushing their sides like wind.

It is May eleventh in Constantinople, and the Spring-blue sea shivers like a field of lupins run over by a breeze. Every tree and shrub spouted over every garden-wall flouts a chromatic sequence of greens. A long string of camels on the Bridge of Justinian moves, black and ostrich-like, against the sheen of water. A swallow sheers past the bronze horses and drops among the pillars on top of the curve of the Hippodrome; the great cistern on the Spina reflects a speckless sky. It is race-day in Constantinople, and the town is turned out upon the benches of the Hippodrome, waiting for the procession to begin. "Hola! You fellows on the top tier, do you see anything?"

"Nothing yet, but I hear music." "Music! Oh, Lord! I should think you did. Clear the flagged course there, the procession is coming." "Down in front. Sit down, you." "Listen. Oh, dear, I'm so fidgety. If the Green doesn't win, I'm out a fortune." "Keep still, will you, we can't hear the music, you talk so loud." "Here they come! Green! Green! Green! Drown those Blues over there. Oh, Green, I say!"

Away beyond, through the gates, flageolets are squealing, and trumpets are splitting their brass throats and choking over the sound. Patter — patter — patter — horses' hoofs on flagstones. They are coming under the paved arch. There is the President of the Games in a tunic embroidered with golden palm-branches; there is the Emperor in his pearl-lappeted cap, and his vermilion buskins; and here are the racers — Green — Blue — driving their chariots, easily standing in their high-wheeled chariots. The sun whitens the knives in their girdles, the reins flash in the sun like ribbons of spun glass. Three-year-olds in the Green chariot, so black they are blue. Four blue-black horses, with the sheen of their flanks glistening like the grain of polished wood. The little ears point forward, their teeth tease the bits. They snort and jerk, and the chariot wheels quirk over an outstanding stone and jolt down, flat and rumbling. The Blue chariot-driver handles a team of greys, white as the storks who nest in the cemetery beyond the Moslem quarter. He gathers up his reins, and the horses fall back against the pole, clattering, then fling forward, meet the bit, rear up, and swing inward, settling gradually into a nervous jigging as they follow round the course. "Blue! Blue! Go for him, Blue!" from the North Corner. "Hurrah for the Blue! Blue to Eternity!" Slowly the procession winds round the Spina, and the crowd stands up on the seats and yells and cheers and waves handkerchiefs, sixty thousand voices making such a noise that only the high screaming of the flageolets can be heard above it. The horses toss and twitch, the harness jingles, and the gilded eggs and dolphins on the Spina coruscate in versicoloured stars.

Above the Emperor's balcony, the bronze horses move quietly forward, and the sun outlines the great muscles of their lifted legs.

They have reached the Grand Stand again, and the chariots are shut and barred in their stalls. The multitude, rustling as though they were paper being folded, settles down into their seats. The President drops a napkin, the bars are unlocked, and the chariots in a double rush take the straight at top speed, Blue leading, Green saving up for the turn at the curve. Round the three cones at the end, Blue on one wheel, Green undercutting him. Blue turns wide to right himself, takes the outside course and flashes up the long edge so that you cannot count two till he curves again. Down to the Green Corner, Blue's off horses slipping just before the cones, one hits the pole, loses balance and falls, drags a moment, catches his feet as the chariot slows for the circle, gathers, plunges, and lunges up and on, while the Greens on the benches groan and curse. But the black team is worse off, the inside near colt has got his leg over a trace. Green checks his animals, the horse kicks free, but Blue licks past him on the up way, and is ahead at the North turn by a wheel length. Green goes round, flogging to make up time. Two eggs and dolphins gone, three more to go. The pace has been slow so far, now they must brace up. Bets run high, screamed out above the rumble of the chariots. "Ten on the Green." "Odds fifty for the Blue." "Double mine; those greys have him." "The blacks, the blacks, lay you a hundred to one the blacks beat." Down, round, up, round, down, so fast they are only dust puffs, one can scarcely see which is which. The horses are badly blown now, and the drivers yell to them, and thrash their churning flanks. The course is wet with sweat and blood, the wheels slide over the wet course. Green negotiates the South curve with his chariot sideways; Blue skids over to the flagged way and lames a horse on the stones. The Emperor is on his feet, staring through his emerald spy-glass. Once more round for the last egg and dolphin.

Down for the last time, Blue's lame horse delays him, but he flays him with the whip and the Green Corner finds them abreast. The Greens on the seats burst up standing. "Too far out! Well turned!" "The Green's got it!" "Well done, Hirpinus!" The Green driver disappears up the long side to the goal, waving his right hand, but Blue's lame horse staggers, stumbles, and goes down, settling into the dust with a moan. Vortex of dust, struggling horses, golden glitter of the broken chariot. "Overthrown, by the Holy Moses! And hurt too! Well, well, he did his best, that beast always looked skittish to me." "Is he dead, do you think? They've got the litter." "Most likely. Green! Green! See, they're crowning him. Green and the people! Oh-hé! Green!"

Cool and imperturbable, the four great gilt horses slowly pace above the marble columns of the Grand Stand. They gaze out upon the lupin-blue water beyond the Southern curve. Can they see the Island of Corfu from up there, do you think? There are vessels at the Island of Corfu waiting to continue a journey. The great horses trot forward without moving, and the dust of the race-track sifts over them and blows away.

Constantinople from the Abbey of San Stefano: bubbles of opal and amber thrust up in a distant sky, pigeon-coloured nebulae closing the end of a long horizon. Tilting to the little waves of a harbour, the good ships, *Aquila, Paradiso, Pellegrina*, leaders of a fleet of galleys: *dromi, hippogogi*, vessels carrying timber for turrets, strong vessels holding mangonels. Proud vessels under an ancient Doge, keeping Saint John's Day at the Abbey of San Stefano, within sight of Constantinople.

Knights in blue and crimson inlaid armour clank up and down the gangplanks of the vessels. Flags and banners flap loosely at the mast-heads. There is the banner of Baldwin of Flanders, the standard of Louis of Blois, the oriflamme of Boniface of Montferrat, the pennon of Hugh, Count of Saint Paul, and last, greatest, the gonfalon of Saint Mark,

dripped so low it almost touches the deck, with the lion of Venice crumpled in its windless folds.

Saint John's Day, and High Mass in the Abbey of San Stefano. They need God's help who would pass over the double walls and the four hundred towers of Constantinople. *Te Deum Laudamus!* The armoured knights make the sign of the cross, lightly touching the crimson and azure devices on their breasts with mailed forefingers.

South wind to the rescue; that was a good mass. "Boatswain, what's the direction of that cat's-paw, veering round a bit? Good."

Fifty vessels making silver paths in the Summer-blue Sea of Marmora. Fifty vessels passing the Sweet Waters, blowing up the Bosphorus.

Strike your raucous gongs, City of Byzantium. Run about like ants between your golden palaces. These vessels are the chalices of God's wrath. The spirit of Christ walking upon the waters. Or is it anti-Christ? This is the true Church. Have we not the stone on which Jacob slept, the rod which Moses turned into a serpent, a portion of the bread of the Last Supper? We are the Virgin's chosen abiding place; why, the picture which Saint Luke painted of her is in our keeping. We have pulled the sun's rays from the statue of Constantine and put up the Cross instead. Will that bring us nothing? Cluster round the pink and white striped churches, throng the alabaster churches, fill the naves with a sound of chanting. Strike the terrorgongs and call out the soldiers, for even now the plumed knights are disembarking, and the snarling of their trumpets mingles with the beating of the gongs.

The bronze horses on the Hippodrome, harnessed to the gilded *quadriga*, step forward slowly. They proceed in a measured cadence. They advance without moving. There are lights and agitation in the city, but the air about the horses has the violet touch of night.

Now, now, you crossbowmen and

archers, you go first. Stand along the gunwales and be ready to jump. Keep those horses still there, don't let them get out of order. Lucky we thought of the hides. Their damnable Greek fire can't hurt us now. Up to the bridge, knights. Three of you abreast, on a level with the towers. What's a shower of arrows against armour! An honourable dint blotting out the head of a heron, half a plume sheared off a helmet so that it leers cock-eyed through the press. Tut! Tut! Little things, the way of war. Jar, jolt, mud — the knights clash together like jumbled chess-men, then leap over the bridges. Confusion — contusion — raps — bangs — lurches — blows — battle-axes thumping on tin shields; bolts bumping against leathern bucklers. "A Boniface to the Rescue!" "Baldwin forever!" "Viva San Marco!" Such a pounding, pummelling, pitching, pointing, piercing, pushing, pelting, poking, panting, punching, parrying, pulling, prodding, puking, piling, passing, you never did see. Stones pour out of the mangonels; arrows fly thick as mist. Swords twist against swords, bill-hooks batter bill-hooks, staves rattle upon staves. One, two, five men up a scaling ladder. Chop down on the first, and he rolls off the ladder with his skull in two halves; rip up the bowels of the second, he drips off the ladder like an overturned pail. But the third catches his adversary between the legs with a pike and pitches him over as one would toss a truss of hay. Way for the three ladder men! Their feet are on the tower, their plumes flower, argent and gold, above the muck of slaughter. From the main truck of the ships there is a constant seeping of Venetians over the walls of Constantinople. They flow into the city, they throw themselves upon the beleaguered city. They smash her defenders, and crash her soldiers to mere bits of broken metal.

Byzantines, Copts, Russians, Persians, Armenians, Moslems, the great army of the Franks is knocking at the gates of your towers. Open the gates. Open, open, or we will tear down your doors, and breach the triple thickness of your walls. Seventeen burning boats indeed, and have the Venetians no boat-hooks?

They make pretty fireworks to pleasure our knights of an evening when they come to sup with Doge Dandolo. At night we will sleep, but in the morning we will kill again. Under your tents, helmeted knights; into your cabin, old Doge. The stars glitter in the Sea of Marmora, and above the city, black in the brilliance of the stars, the great horses of Constantinople advance, pausing, blotting their shadows against the sprinkled sky.

From June until September, the fracas goes on. The chanting of masses, the shouting of battle songs, sweep antiphonally over Constantinople. They blend and blur, but what is that light tinkling? Tambourines? What is that snapping? Castanets? What is that yellow light in the direction of the Saracen mosque? My God! Fire! Gold of metals, you have met your king. Ringed and crowned, he takes his place in the jewelled city. Gold of fire mounted upon all the lesser golds. The twin tongues of flame flaunt above the housetops. Banners of scarlet, spears of saffron, spikes of rose and melted orange. What are the little flags of the Crusaders to these! They clamoured for pay and won the elements. Over the Peninsula of Marmora it comes. The whips of its fire-thongs lash the golden city. A conflagration half a league wide. Magnificent churches, splendid palaces, great commercial streets, are burning. Golden domes melt and liquefy, and people flee from the dripping of them. Lakes of gold lie upon the pavements; pillars crack and tumble, making dams and bridges over the hot gold. Two days, two nights, the fire rages, and through the roar of it the little cries of frightened birds come thin and pitiful. Earth pleading with fire. Earth begging quarter of the awful majesty of fire. The birds wheel over Constantinople; they perch upon the cool bronze horses standing above the Hippodrome. The quiet horses who wait and advance. This is not their fire, they trample on the luminousness of flames, their strong hind legs plant them firmly on the marble coping. They watch the falling of the fire, they gaze upon the ruins spread about them, and the pungence of charred wood brushes along their tarnished sides like wind.

The Franks have made an Emperor and now the Greeks have murdered him. The Doge asks for fifty *centenaria* in gold to pay his sailors. Who will pay, now that the Emperor is dead? Declare a siege and pay yourselves, Count, and Marquis, and Doge. Set your ships bow to stern, a half a league of them. Sail up the Golden Horn, and attack the walls in a hundred places. You fail to-day, but you will win to-morrow. Bring up your battering-rams and ballistae; hurl stones from your mangonels; run up your scaling ladders and across your skin bridges. Winter is over and Spring is in your veins. Your blood mounts like sap, mount up the ladder after it. Two ships to a tower, and four towers taken. Three gates battered in. The city falls. Cruel saints, you have betrayed your votaries. Even the relic of the Virgin's dress in the Panhagia of Blachernae has been useless. The knights enter Byzantium, and their flickering pennants are the flamelets of a new conflagration. Fire of flesh burning in the blood of the populace. They would make the sign of the cross, would they, so that the Franks may spare them? But the sap is up in the Frankish veins, the fire calls for fuel. Blood burns to who will ignite it. The swords itch for the taste of entrails, the lances twitch at sight of a Byzantine. Feed, Fire! Here are men, and women, and children, full of blood for the relish of your weapons. Spring sap, how many women! Good Frankish seed for the women of Byzantium. Blood and lust, you shall empty yourselves upon the city. Your swords shall exhaust themselves upon these Greeks. Your hands shall satisfy themselves with gold. Spit at the priests. This is the Greek church, not ours. Grab the sacred furniture of the churches, fornicate upon the high altar of Saint Sophia, and load the jewels upon the donkeys you have driven into the church to receive them. Old pagan Crusaders, this is the Orgy of Spring! Lust and blood, the birthright of the world.

The bright, shining horses tread upon the clean coping of the Hippodrome, and the Sea of Marmora lies before them like a lupin field run over by a breeze.

What are you now, Constantinople? A sacked city; and the tale of your plundering shall outdo the tale of your splendours for wonder. Three days they pillage you. Burmese rubies rattle in the pockets of common soldiers. The golden tree is hacked to bits and carried off by crossbowmen. An infantry sergeant hiccoughs over the wine he drinks from an altar cup. The knights live in palaces and dip their plumes under the arch of the Emperor's bed-chamber.

In the Sea of Marmora, the good ships *Aquila*, *Paradiso*, *Pellegrina* swing at anchor. The *dromi* and *hippogogi* ride free and empty. They bob to the horses high above them on the Hippodrome. They dance to the rhythmic beat of hammers floating out to them from the city of Constantinople.

Throb — throb — a dying pulse counts its vibrations. Throb — throb — and each stroke means a gobbet of gold. They tear it down from the walls and doors, they rip it from ceilings and pry it up from floors. They chip it off altars, they rip it out of panels, they hew it from obelisks, they gouge it from enamels. This is a death dance, a whirligig, a skeleton city footing a jig, a tarantella quirked to hammer-stroke time; a corpse in motley ogling a crime. Tap — tap — tap — goes the pantomime.

Grinning devils watch church cutting the throat of church. Chuckling gargoyles in France, in Britain, rub their stomachs and squeeze themselves together in an ecstasy of delight. Ho! Ho! Marquis Boniface, Count Hugh, Sieur Louis. What plunder do you carry home? What relics do you bring to your Gothic cathedrals? The head of Saint Clement? The arm of John the Baptist? A bit of the wood of the True Cross? Statues are only so much metal, but these are treasures worth fighting for. Fighting, quotha! Murdering, stealing. The Pope will absolve you, only bring him home a tear of Christ, and you will see. A tear of Christ! *Eli, Eli, lama sabachthani!*

Oh, pitiful world! Pitiful knights in your inlaid armour! Pitiful Doge, preening himself in the Palace of Blachernae!

Above the despoiled city, the Corinthian horses trot calmly forward, without moving, and the *quadriga* behind them glitters in the sun.

People have blood, but statues have gold, and silver, and bronze. Melt them! Melt them! "Gee! Haw!" Guide the oxen carefully. Four oxen to drag the head of Juno to the furnace. White oxen to transport Minerva; fawn-coloured oxen for the colossal Hercules of Lysippus. Pour them into the furnaces so that they run out mere soft metal ripe for coining. Two foot-sergeants as much as a knight. Flatten out Constantinople. Raze her many standing statues, shave the Augustaion to a stark stretch of paving-stones. Melt the bones of beauty, indomitable Crusaders, and pay the Venetians fifty thousand silver marks as befits an honest company of dedicated gentlemen.

"The Doge wants those horses, does he? Just as they are, unmelted? Holy Saint Christopher, what for? Pity he didn't speak sooner, I sent Walter the Smith to cut the gold off them this morning, but it sticks like the very devil and he hasn't done much. Well, well, the Doge can have them. A man with a whim must be given way to, particularly when he owns all the ships. How about that gilded chariot?" "Oh, he can't manage that. Just the horses. You were in a mighty hurry with that cutting, it seems to me. You've made them look like zebras, and he'll not like that. He's a bit of a connoisseur in horse-flesh, even if he does live in the water. Wants to mate them to the dolphins probably, and go a-campaigning astride of fishes. Ha! Ha! Ha!"

"Steady there, lower the horses carefully, they are for the Doge." One — one — one — one — down from the top of the Hippodrome. One — one — one — one — on ox-carts rumbling toward the water's edge, in boats rowing over the lupin-coloured sea. Great horses, trot calmly on your sides, roll quietly to the heaving of the bright sea. Above you, sails go up, anchors are weighed. The gonfalon of Saint Mark flings its extended lion to the freshening wind. To Venice, *Aquila*, *Paradiso*, *Pellegrina*, with your attendant *dromi!* To Venice! Over the running waves of the Spring-blue sea.

BENEATH A CROOKED RAINBOW

As the seasons of Earth are Fire, so are the seasons of men. The departure of Fire is a change, and the coming of Fire is a greater change. Demand not that which is over, but acclaim what is still to come. So the Earth builds up her cities, and falls upon them with weeds and nettles; and Water flows over the orchards of past centuries. On the sand-hills shall apple trees flourish, and in the water-courses shall be gathered a harvest of plums. Earth, Air, and Water abide in fluctuation. But man, in the days between his birth and dying, fashions metals to himself, and they are without heat or cold. In the Winter solstice, they are not altered like the Air, nor hardened like the Water, nor shrivelled like the Earth, and the heats of Summer bring them no burgeoning. Therefore are metals outside the elements. Between melting and melting they are beyond the Water, and apart from the Earth, and severed from the Air. Fire alone is of them, and master. Withdrawn from Fire, they dwell in isolation.

VENICE

Venice anadyomene! City of reflections! A cloud of rose and violet poised upon a changing sea. City of soft waters washing marble stairways, of feet moving over stones with the continuous sound of slipping water. Floating, wavering city, shot through with the silver threads of water, woven with the green-gold of flowing water, your marble Rivas block the tides as they sweep in over the Lagoons, your towers fling golden figures of Fortune into the carnation sky at sunset, the polished marble of the walls of old palaces burns red to the flaring torches set in cressets before your doors.

Strange city, belonging neither to earth nor water, where the slender spandrels of vines melt into the carvings of arched windows, and crabs ferry themselves through the moon-green water rippling over the steps of a decaying church.

Beautiful, faded city. The sea wind has dimmed your Oriental extravagance to an iris of rose, and amber, and lilac. You are dim and reminiscent like the frayed hangings of your State Chambers, and the stucco of your house-fronts crumbles into the canals with a gentle dripping which no one notices.

A tabernacle set in glass, an ivory ornament resting upon a table of polished steel. It is the surface of the sea, spangled, crinkled, engine-turned to whorls of blue and silver, ridged in waves of flower-green and gold. Sequins of gold skip upon the water, crocus-yellow flames dart against white smoothness and disappear, wafers of many colours float and intermingle. The Lagoons are a white fire burning to the blue band of the Lido, restlessly shifting under the cool, still, faint peaks of the Euganean Hills.

Where is there such another city? She has taken all the Orient to herself. She has treated with Barbarossa, with Palaeologus, with the Pope, the Tzar, the Caliph, the Sultan, and the Grand Khan. Her returning vessels have discharged upon the mole metals and jewels, pearls from the Gulf of Oman, silks from Damascus, camel's-hair fabrics from Erzeroum. The columns of Saint John of Acre have been landed on her jetties, and the great lions from the Piraeus. Now she rests and glitters, holding her treasures lightly, taking them for granted, chatting among the fringes, and tinkling sherbet spoons of an evening in the dark shadow of the Campanile.

Up from the flickering water, beyond the laced colonnades of the Ducal Palace — golden bubbles, flung out upon a sky of ripe blue. Arches of white and scarlet flowers, pillars of porphyry, columns of jasper, open loggias of deep-green serpentine flaked with snow. In the architraves, stones chipped and patterned, the blues studded with greens, the greens circling round yellows, reds of every depth, clear purples, heliotropes clouded into a vague white. Above them, all about them, the restless movement of carven stone; it is involuted and grotesque, it is acanthus leaves and roses, it is palm branches and vine tendrils, it is feathers and the tails of birds, all blowing on a day of *scirocco*. Angels rise among the swirling acanthus leaves, angels and leaves weaving an upstarting line, ending in the great star of Christ struck upon the edge of a golden dome. Saint Mark's Church, gazing down the length of the chequered Piazza, thrusting itself upon the black and white pavement, rising out of the flat tiles in a rattle of colours, soaring toward the full sky like a broken prism whirling at last into the gold bubbles of its five wide domes. The Campanile mounts above it, but the Campanile is only brick, even if it has a pointed top which you cannot see without lying on your back. The pigeons can fly up to it, but the pigeons prefer the angles and hollows of the sculptured church.

Saint Mark's Church — and over the chief arch, among the capitals of foaming leaves and bent grasses, trample four great horses. They are of gold, of gilding so fine that it has not faded. They are tarnished here and there, but their fair colour overcomes the green corroding and is a blinding to the eyes in sunshine. Four magnificent, muscular horses, lightly stepping upon traceried columns, one forefoot raised to launch them forward. They stand over the high door, caught back a moment before springing, held an instant to the perfection of a movement about to begin, and the pigeons circle round them brushing against their sides like wind.

But, dear me, Saint Mark's is the only thing in the Piazza that is not talking, and walking to and fro, and cheapening shoe buckles at a stall, and playing *panfil* and *bassetta* at little round tables by the wall, and singing to guitars, and whistling to poodles, and shouting to acquaintances, and giving orders to servants, and whispering a scandal behind fans, and carrying tomatoes in copper pans, and flying on messages, and lying to creditors, and spying on suspects, and colliding with masked loungers, and crying out the merits of fried fish, caught when the tide comes leaping through the Tre Porti. A dish of tea at a coffee-house, and then cross one leg over the other and wait. She will be here by seven o'clock, and a faithful *cicisbeo* has her charms to muse upon until then. Ah, Venice, chattering, flattering, occupied Venice, what are the sculptured angels and golden horses to you. You are far too busy to glance at them. They are chiefly remarkable as curiosities, for whoever saw a real angel, and as to a real horse — "I saw a stuffed one for a *soldo*, the other day, in the Campo San Polo. *Un elephanto*, Gastone, taller than my shoulder and the eyes were made of glass, they would pass for perfect any day."

Ah, the beautiful palaces, with their gateways of gilded iron frilled into arms and coronets, quilled into shooting leaves and tendrils, filled with rosettes, fretted by heraldic emblems! Ah, the beautiful taste, which wastes no time on heavy stone, but cuts flowers, and foliage, and flourishes, and ribbons out of — stucco! Bows of stucco glued about a ceiling by Tiepolo, and ranged underneath, frail white-and-gold, rose-and-gold, green-and-gold chairs, fair consoles of polished lacquer supporting great mirrors of Murano. Hangings of blue silk with silver fringes, behind your folds, la Signora Benzona accords a favour to the Cavalier Giuseppe Trevis. Upon a salmon-coloured sofa striped with pistachio-green, the Cavaliera Contarini flirts with both her *cicisbei* at once, in a charming impartiality. Kisses? Ah, indeed, certainly kisses. Hands tickling against hands? But assuredly, one for each of you. The heel of a left slipper caught against a buckled shoe, the toe of a right foot pressed beneath a broader sole; but the toll is finished. "Tut! Tut! Gentlemen! With the other present! Have you no delicacy? To-night perhaps, after the Ridotto, we will take a *giro* in my gondola as far as Malamocco, Signor Bianchi. And to-morrow, Carlo Pin, will you go to church with me? There is something in the tones of an organ, I know not what exactly, but it has its effect."

"You rang, *Illustrissima?*" "Of course I rang, Stupid, did you think it was the cat?" "Your nobility desires?" "The time, Blockhead, what is the time?" "Past seven, *Illustrissima.*" "Ye Gods, how time passes when one sleeps! Bring my chocolate at once, and call Giannina." With a yawn, the lady rises, just as the sun fades away from the flying figure of Fortune on the top of the Dogana. "Candles, Moracchio." And the misty mirrors prick and pulsate with reflections of blurred flame. Flame-points, and behind them the puce-coloured curtains of a bed; an escritoire with feathered pens and Spanish wax; a table with rouge-pots and powder-boxes; a lady, naked as a Venus, slipping into a silk shift. In the misty mirrors, she is all curves and colour, all slenderness and tapering, all languor and vivacity. Even Giannina murmurs, "*Che bella Madonna mia!*" as she pulls the shift into place. But the door is ajar, a mere harmless crack to make a fuss about. "Only one eye, *Cara Mia*, I assure you the other saw nothing but the panel. I ask for so much, and I have only taken the pleasure of one little eye. I must kiss them, *Signora Bellissima*, two little red berries, like the fruit of the *potentillas* in the grass at Sant 'Elena. *Musica! Musica!* The barque of music is coming down the canal. Sit on my knee a moment, the Casino can wait; and after you have won a thousand *zecchini*, will you be a second Danae and go with me to the early morning market? Then you shall come home and sleep all day in the great bed among the roses I shall buy for you. With your gold? Perhaps, my dearest tease, the luck has deserted me lately. But there are ways of paying, are there not, and I am an honourable man."

The great horses of Saint Mark's trot softly forward on their sculptured pedestals, without moving. Behind them, the glass of the arched window is dark, but the Piazza is a bowl of light, a tambourine of little bell-stroke laughter. The golden horses step forward, dimly shimmering in the light of the lamps below, and the pigeons sleep quietly on the stands at their feet.

Green Lion of Saint Mark upon your high pedestal! Winged Lion of Saint Mark, your head turned over the blinding Lagoons to the blue Lido, your tail pointing down the sweeping flow of the Grand Canal! What do you see, Green Lion of the Patron Saint? Boats? Masts? Quaint paintings on the broad bows of *bragozzi*, orange sails contra-crossing one another over tossing ripples. Gondolas tipping to the oars of the *barcajuoli*, slipping under the Ponte della Paglia, dipping between sardine *topi*, skipping past the Piazzetta, curving away to the Giudecca, where it lies beyond the crystal pinnacles of Santa Maria della Salute and San Giorgio Maggiore which has the lustre of roses.

What do you smell, Lion? Boiling hot chestnuts, fried cuttles, fried puffs of pastry; the pungent odour of salt water and of dead fish; the nostalgic aroma of sandal-wood and myrrh, of musk, of leopard skins and the twin tusks of elephants.

And you, great Lion of the Ducal Palace, what goes on at your feet? People knotted together or scattering, pattering over the old stones in impertinent satin slippers, flippantly tapping the pavement with red heels. Whirls of people circle like the pigeons, knots of people spot the greyness of the stones, ribbons of people file along the colonnades, rayed lines of people between the Procuratie stripe the pavement sideways, criss-cross, at oblique angles. Spangles snap and fade; gems glitter. A gentleman in a buttercup-coloured coat goes by with a bouquet. A sea-green gown brocaded with cherry and violet stays an instant before a stall to buy a packet of ambergris. Pilgrims with staffs and cockles knock the stones as they shuffle along, a water-carrier shouts out a song. A scarlet sacristan jingles his keys; purple robes of justices saunter at ease. Messer Goldoni hustles by to a rehearsal, and three famous *castrati*, i Signori Pacchierotti, Aprili, Rubenelli, rustle their mantles and adjust their masks, ogling the ladies with gold lorgnons. Blind men sniffle into flageolets, marionette men hurry on to a distant Campo in a flurry of cotton streamers. If Venice is a flowing of water, it is also a flowing of

people. All Europe runs into this wide square. There is Monsieur Montesquieu, just from France, taking notes on the sly; there is Mrs. Piozzi, from England, with an eye to everything, even chicken-coops; Herr Goethe, from the Court at Weimar, trying to overcome a fit of mental indigestion; Madame Vigée le Brun, questioning the merit of her work and that of Rosalba Carriera. You have much to watch, Lion, the whole earth cannot match the pageant of this great square, in the limpid sun-shot air, between the towering Campanile and the blaze of Saint Mark's angels. Star-fish patterns, jelly-fish rounds of colour, if the sea quivers with variety so does the Piazza. But above, on the façade of the jewelled church, the horses do not change. They stand vigorous and immovable, stepping lightly as though poised upon glass. Metal horses set upon shifting shards of glass, and the soft dipthongs of the Venetian dialect float over them like wind.

There are two Venices, the one we walk upon, and the one which wavers up to us inverted from the water of the canals. The silver prow of a gondola winds round a wall, and in the moss-brown water another gondola joins it, bottom to bottom, with the teeth of the prow infinitely repeated. A cypress closes the end of a *rio*, and driven into the thick water another cypress spindles beneath us, and the wake of our boat leaves its foliage cut to tatters as it passes on. We plough through the veined pinks and subdued scarlets of the façades of palaces; we sheer a path through a spotted sky and blunt the tip of a soaring campanile. Are we swimming in the heavens, turned legend and constellation? Truly it seems so. "How you go on, Cavalier, certainly you are a foreigner to notice such things. The Lido, Giuseppe. I have a nostalgia for flowers to-day, and besides, abroad so early in the afternoon — what shocking style! The custom of the country, my dear Sir, here we go to bed by sunlight as you will see."

Sweep out of the broad canal, turn to the hanging snow summits. Oh, the beautiful silver light, the blue light shimmering with silver. The clear sunlight on rose brick and amber marble. The sky so pale it is white, so bright it is yellow, so cloudless it is blue. Oh, the shafts of sapphire striping the wide water, the specks of gold dancing along it, the diamond roses opening and shutting upon its surface! Some one is singing in a distant boat:

"*Amanti, ci vuole costanza in amor'*
    Amando,
        Penando,
    Si speri, si, si."

The lady shrugs her shoulders. "These fishermen are very droll. What do the *canaglia* know about love. Breeding, yes, that is certainly their affair, but love! *Più presto*, Giuseppe. How the sun burns!" Rock over the streaked Lagoon, gondola, pock the blue strips with white, shock purple shadows through the silver strata, set blocks of iris cannoning against gold. This is the rainbow over which we are floating, and the heart-shaped city behind us is a reliquary of old ivory laid upon azure silk. Your hand, Signor the Foreigner, be careful lest she wet those fine French stockings, they cost I do not know how much a pair. Now run away across the Lido, gathering violets and periwinkles. The lady has a whim for a *villeggiatura*, and why not? Those scarlet pomegranate blossoms will look well in her hair to-night at the opera. But one cannot linger long, already the Dolomites are turning pink, and there is a whole night ahead of us to be cajoled somehow. A mile away from Venice and it is too far. "*Felicissima notte!*" Wax candles shine in the windows. The little stars of the gondola lanterns glide between dark walls. Broken moonlight shivers in the canals. And the masks come out, thronging the streets and squares with a chequerwork of black cloaks and white faces. Little white faces floating like pond-lilies above the water. Floating faces adrift over unfathomable depths. Have you ever heard the words, *Libertà, Independenza, e Eguaglianza?* "What stuff and nonsense! Of course I have read your great writer, Rousseau; I cried my heart out over 'La Nouvelle Héloïse,' but in practice! Wake my servants, the lazy fellows are always asleep, you will find them curled up on the stairs most likely. It is

time we went to the *Mendicanti* to hear the oratorio. Ah, but those poor orphans sing with a charm! It makes one weep to hear them, only the old *Maestro di Capella* will beat time with his music on the grill. It is quite ridiculous, they could go through it perfectly without him. *Misericordia!* The red light! That is the gondola of the Supreme Tribunal taking some poor soul to the Piombi; God protect him! But it does not concern us, my friend. *Ridiamo a duetto!*" Little tinkling drops from the oars of the boatmen, little tinkling laughter wafted across the moonlight.

Four horses parading in front of a splendid church. Four ancient horses with ears pointed forward, listening. One foot is raised, they advance without moving. To what do they listen? To the serenades they have heard so often? *Cavatine, canzonette*, dance songs, hymns, for six hundred years the songs of Venice have drifted past them, lightly, as the wings of pigeons. And month by month the old moon has sailed over them, as she did in Constantinople, as she did in Rome.

Saint Stephen's Day, and the Carnival! For weeks now Venice will be amused. Folly to think of anything but fun. Toot the fifes! Bang the drums! Did you ever see anything so jolly in all your life before? Keep your elbows to your sides, there isn't room to square them. "My! What a flare! Rockets in broad daylight! I declare they make the old horses of Saint Mark's blush pink when they burst. Thirsty? So am I, what will you have? Wine or oranges? Don't jostle so, old fellow, we can look in the window as well as you. See that apothecary's stall, isn't that a gay festoon? Curse me, if it isn't made of leeches; what will these shopkeepers do next! That mask has a well-turned ankle. Good evening, my charmer. You are as beautiful as a parrot, as white as linen, as light as a rabbit. Ay! O-o-h! The she-camel! She aimed her *confetti* right at my eye. Come on, Tito, let's go and see them behead the bull. Hold on a minute though, somebody's pulling my cloak. Just one little squeeze, Beauty, you shouldn't tweak a man's cloak if you don't want to be squeezed. You plump little pudding, you little pecking pigeon, I'll get more next time. Wow! Here comes Arlecchino. Push back, push back, the comedians are coming. Stow in your fat belly, *'lustrissimo*, you take up room enough for two."

Somebody beats a gong, and three drummers cleave a path through the crowd. Bang! *Bang!* BANG! So loud it splits the hearing. Mattachino leaps down the path. He is in white, with red lacings and red shoes. On his arm is a basket of eggs. Right, left, into the crowd, skim the eggs. Duck — jump — it is no use. Plump, on some one's front; pat, against some one's hat. The eggs crack, and scented waters run out of them, filling the air with the sweet smells of musk and bergamot. But here is a wheel of colours rolling down the path. Clown! Clown! It is Arlecchino, in his patched coat. It was green and he has botched it with red, or is it yellow, or possibly blue. It is hard to tell, he turns so fast. Three somersaults, and he comes up standing, and makes a long nose, and sweeps off his hat with the hare's fud, and glares solemnly into the eyes of a gentleman in spectacles. "Sir," says Arlecchino, "have you by chance a toothache? I can tell you how to cure it. Take an apple, cut it into four equal parts, put one of these into your mouth, and thrust your head into an oven until the apple is baked. I swear on my honour you will never have the toothache again." Zip! Sizz! No use in the cane. A pirouette and he is away again. A handspring, a double cut-under, and the parti-coloured rags are only a tag bouncing up out of surging black mantles. But there is something more wonderful yet. Set your faces to the Piazzetta, people; push, slam, jam, to keep your places. "A balloon is going up from the Dogana del Mare, a balloon like a moon or something else starry. A meteor, a comet, I don't really know what; it looks, so they say, like a huge apricot, or a pear — yes, that's surely the thing — blushing red, mellow yellow, a fruit on the wing, garlanded with streamers and tails, all a-whirl and a-flutter. Cut the string and she sails, till she lands in the gutter." "How do you know she lands in the gutter, Booby?" "Where else should she land, unless in the sea?" "You're a fool, I suppose you sat up all night writing that dog-gerel." "Not at all, it is an improvisation." "Here, keep back, you can't push past me with your talk. Oh! Look! Look!"

That is a balloon. It rises slowly — slowly — above the Dogana. It wavers, dips, and poises; it mounts in the silver air, it floats without direction; suspended in movement, it hangs, a clear pear of red and yellow, opposite the melting, opal-tinted city. And the reflection of it also floats, perfect in colour but cooler, perfect in outline but more vague, in the glassy water of the Grand Canal. The blue sky sustains it; the blue water encloses it. Then balloon and reflection swing gently seaward. One ascends, the other descends. Each dwindles to a speck. Ah, the semblance is gone, the water has nothing; but the sky focusses about a point of fire, a formless iridescence sailing higher, become a mere burning, until that too is absorbed in the brilliance of the clouds.

You cheer, people, but you do not know for what. A beautiful toy? Undoubtedly you think so. Shout yourselves hoarse, you who have conquered the sea, do you underestimate the air? Joke, laugh, purblind populace. You have been vouchsafed an awful vision, and you do nothing but clap your hands.

That is over, and here is Pantalone calling to you. "Going — going — I am selling my furniture. Two dozen chairs of fine holland; fourteen tables of almond paste; six majolica mattresses full of scrapings of haycocks; a semolina bedcover; six truffled cushions; two pavilions of spider-web trimmed with tassels made from the moustaches of Swiss door-keepers. Oh! The Moon! The Moon! The good little yellow moon, no bigger than an omelet of eight eggs. Come, I will throw in the moon. A quarter-ducat for the moon, good people. Take your opportunity."

Great gold horses, quietly stepping above the little mandarin figures, strong horses above the whirling porcelain figures, are the pigeons the only birds in Venice? Have the swallows told you nothing, flying from the West? The bells of Saint Mark's Church ring midnight. The carnival is over.

In the deserted square, the pavement is littered with feathers, *confetti*, orange-peel, and pumpkin-seeds. But the golden horses on the balcony over the high door trot forward, without moving, and the shadow of the arch above them is thrown farther and farther forward as the moon drops toward the Lagoon.

Bronze armies marching on a sea-shell city. Slanted muskets filing over the passes of tall Alps. Who is this man who leads you, carven in new bronze, supple as metal still cooling, firm as metal from a fresh-broken mold? A bright bronze general heading armies. The tread of his grenadiers is awful, continuous. How will it be in the streets of the glass city? These men are the flying letters of a new gospel. They are the tablets of another law. Twenty-eight, this general! Ah, but the metal is well compounded. He has been victorious in fourteen pitched battles and seventy fights; he has taken five hundred field pieces, and two thousand of heavy calibre; he has sent thirty millions back to the treasury of France. The Kings of Naples and Sardinia write him friendly letters; the Pope and the Duke of Parma weary themselves with compliments. The English have retired from Genoa, Leghorn, and Corsica.

Little glass masks, have you heard nothing of this man? What of the new French ambassador, Citizen Lallemont? You have seen his gondoliers and the *tricolore* cockade in their caps? It is a puzzling business, but you can hardly expect us to be alarmed, we have been a republic for centuries. Still, these new ideas are intriguing, they say several gentlemen have adopted them. "Alvise Pisani, my Dear, and Abbate Colalto, also Bragadin, and Soranza, and Labbia. Oh, there was much talk about it last night. Such strange notions! But the cockade is very pretty. I have the ribbon, and I am going to make a few. Signora Fontana gave me the pattern."

Columbus discovered America. Ah, it was then you should have made your cockades. Is it Bonaparte or the Cape of Good Hope which has compassed your destiny? Little porcelain figures, can you stand the shock of bronze?

No, evidently. The quills of the Senate secretaries are worn blunt, writing note after note to the General of the Armies. But still he marches forward, and his soldiers, dressed as peasants, have invaded Breschia and Bergamo. And what a man! Never satisfied. He must have this — that — and other things as well. He must have guns, cannon, horses, mules, food, forage. What is all this talk of a Cisalpine Republic? The Senate wavers like so many sea anemones in an advancing tide. Ascension Day is approaching. Shall the Doge go in the *Bucentoro* to wed the sea "in token of real and perpetual dominion"? The Senate dictates, the secretaries write, and the *Arsenalotti* polish the brasses of the *Bucentoro* and wait. Brightly shine the overpolished brasses of the *Bucentoro*, but the ships in the Arsenal are in bad repair and the crews wanting.

It is Holy Saturday in Venice, and solemn processions march to the churches. The slow chanting of choirs rises above the floating city, but in the Citizen Lallemont's apartments is a jangling of spurred heels, a clanking of cavalry sabres. General Junot arrived in the small hours of the night. Holy Saturday is nothing to a reformed Frenchman; the General's business will not wait, he must see the Signory at once. Desert your churches, convene the College in haste. A bronze man cannot be opposed by a Senate of glass. Is it for fantasy that so many people are wearing the *tricolore*, or is it politeness to the visiting general? But what does he say? French soldiers murdered! Nonsense, a mere street row between Bergamese. But Junot thunders and clanks his sabre. A sword is a terrible thing in a cabinet of biscuit figurines. Let that pass. He has gone. But Venice is shaken. The stately palaces totter on their rotting piles, the *campi* buzz with voices, the Piazza undulates to a gesticulating multitude. Only the pigeons wheel unconcernedly about the Campanile, and the great horses stand, poised and majestic, beneath the mounting angels of Saint Mark's Church.

Ascension Day draws nearer. The brasses of the *Bucentoro* shine like gold. Surely the Doge will not desert his bride; or has the jilt tired of her long subjection? False water, upon your breast rock many navies, how should you remain true to a ship which fears to wet its keel. The *Bucentoro* glitters in the Arsenal, she blazes with glass and gilding drawn up safely on a runway of dry planks, while over the sea, beyond the Lido, rises the spark of sails. The vessel is hull down, but the tiers of canvas lift up, one after the other: skysails, royals, topgallantsails, topsails, mainsails, and at last, the woodwork. Then gleaming ports, then streaming water flashed from a curved bow. A good ship, but she flys the *tricolore*. This is no wedding barge, there is no winged lion on that flag. There is no music, no choir singing hymns. Men run to and fro in San Nicolo Fort, peering through spyglasses. Ah, she will observe the rules, the skysails come down, then the royals — but why in thunder do not the topgallantsails follow? The fellow is coming right under the fort. Guns. He salutes. Answer from the fort. Citizen Lallemont has agreed that no French vessel shall enter the port, even the English do not attempt it. But the son of a dog comes on. Send out boats, Comandatore Pizzamano. *Per Dio*, he is passing them! Touch off the cannon as a warning. One shot. Two. Some one is on the poop with a speaking-trumpet. "What ship is that?" "*Le Libérateur d'Italie. Le Capitaine Laugier. Marine de la République Française.*" "It is forbidden to enter the port, *Signor Capitano Laugier*." "We intend to anchor outside." Do you! Then why not clew up those damned topgallantsails. My God! She is past the fort. She has slipped through the entrance; she is in the Lagoon. Her forefoot cuts the diamond water, she sheers her way through the calm colour reflections, her bow points straight at the rose and violet city swimming under the light clouds of early afternoon. Shock! Shiver! Foul of a Venetian galley, by all that's holy. What beastly seamanship! The Venetians

will not stand it, I tell you. Pop! Pop! Those are muskets, drop on them with cutlasses, *mes enfants*. Chop into the cursed foreigners. "*Non vogliamo forestieri qui.*" Boom! The cannon of Fort Sant' Andrea. Good guns, well pointed, the smoke from them draws a shade over the water. Down come the topgallantsails. You have paid a price for your entrance, Captain Laugier, but it is not enough. "*Viva San Marco!*" Detestable voices, these Venetians. That cry is confusing. Puff! The smoke goes by. Three marines have fallen. The cannon fire at intervals of two minutes. Hot work under a burning sky. Hot work on a burning deck. The smoothness of the water is flecked with bits of wood. A dead body rolls overboard, and bobs up and down beside the ships. A sailor slips from a yard, and is spiked on an upturned bayonet. Over the water comes the pealing of many bells. Captain Laugier is dead, and the city tolls his requiem. Strike your colours, beaten Frenchmen. Bronze cannot walk upon the sea. You have failed and succeeded, for upon your Captain's fallen body the bronze feet have found their bridge. Do you rejoice, old Arsenal? A captive boat towed up to you again! Ah, the cannon firing has brought the rain. Yes, and thunder too, and in the thunder a voice of bronze. The *Bucentoro* will not take the water this year. Cover up the brasses, *Arsenalotti*. Ascension Day is nothing to Venice now.

Yesterday this was matter for rejoicing, but to-day . . . Get the best rowers, order relays of horses on the mainland, post hot foot to the Commissioners at Grätz. One ship is nothing, but if they send twenty! What has the bronze General already said to the Commissioners? The Senate wonders, and wears itself out in speculation. They will give money, they will plunder the pockets of the populace to save Venice. Can a child save his toys when manhood is upon him? The century is old, already another lies in its arms. Month by month a new moon rises over Venice, but century by century! They cannot see, these Senators. They cannot hear the General cutting the Commissioners short in a sort of fury. "I wish no more Inquisition, no more Senate. I will be an Attila for Venice. This government is old; it must fall!" Pretty words from bronze to porcelain. A stain on a brave, new gospel. "Save Venice," the letter urges, and the Commissioners depart for Trieste. But the doors are locked. The General blocks his entrances. "I cannot receive you, Gentlemen, you and your Senate are disgusting to the French blood." A pantomime before a temple, with a priest acting the part of chief comedian. Strange burlesque, arabesquing the characters of a creed. You think this man is a greedy conqueror. Go home, thinking. Your moment flutters off the calendar, your world dissolves and another takes its place. This is the cock-crow of ghosts. Slowly pass up the canal, slowly enter the Ducal Palace. Debate, everlastingly debate. And while you quibble the communication with the continent is cut.

He has declared war, the bronze General. What can be done? The little glass figures crack under the strain. Condulmer will not fight. Pesaro flees to Austria. So the measure awaits a vote. A grave Senate consulting a ballot-box as to whether it shall cut its throat. This is not suicide, but murder; this is not murder, but the turned leaf of an almanac. "Divide! Divide!" What is the writing on the other side? *"Viva la Libertà,"* shouts General Salimbeni from a window. Stupid crowd, it will not give a cheer. It is queer what an unconscionable objection people have to dying. *"Viva San Marco!"* shouts General Salimbeni. Ah, now you hear! Such a racket, and the old lion flag hoisted everywhere. But that was a rash thing to do. It brings the crash. They fight, fight for old Saint Mark, they smash, burn, demolish. Who wore the *tricolore?* Plunder their houses. No you don't, no selling us to foreigners. They cannot read, the people, they do not see that the print has changed. By dint of cannon you can stop them. Stop them suddenly like a clock dropped from a wall.

Venice! Venice! The star-wakes gleam and shatter in your still canals, and the great horses pace forward, vigorous, unconcerned, beautiful, treading your grief as they tread the passing winds.

The riot is over, but another may break out. A dead republic cannot control its citizens. General Baraguey d'Hilliers is at Mestre. His dragoons will keep order. Shame, nobles and abdicated Senate! But can one blame the inactivity of the dead? French dragoons in little boats. The 5th and 63rd of the line proceeding to Venice in forty little boats. Grenadiers embarked for a funeral. Soldiers cracking jokes, and steady oar-strokes, warping them over the water toward Venice. A dark city, scarcely a lamp is lit. A match-spark slits the darkness, a drummer is lighting his pipe. Ah, there are walls ahead. The dull bones of the dead. Water swashes against marble. They are in the canal, their voices echo from doors and porches. Forty boats, and the bobble of them washes the water step and step above its usual height on the stairways. "C'est une église ça!" "Mais, oui, Bêta, tu pensais pourtant pas que tu entrais en France. Nous sommes dans une sale ville aristocratique, et je m'en fiche, moi!" Brave brigadier, spit into the canal, what else can a man of the new order do to show his enlightenment. Two regiments of seasoned soldiers, two regiments of free citizens, forty boat-loads of thinking men to goad a moribund nation into the millennium. The new century arriving with a flower in its button-hole, the *carmagnole* ousting the *furlana*. Perhaps — perhaps — but years pile up and then collapse. Will gaps start between one and another? Settle your gunstraps, 63rd of the line, we land here by the dim shine of a lantern held by a bombardier. Tier and tier the soldiers march through Venice. Their steps racket like the mallets of marble-cutters in the narrow *calli*, and the sound of them over bridges is the drum-beating of hard rain.

There are soldiers everywhere, Venice is stuffed with soldiers. They are at the Arsenal, on the Rialto, at San Stefano, and four hundred stack muskets, and hang their bearskins on the top of them, in the middle of the Piazza.

Golden horses, the sound of violins is

hushed, the pigeons who brush past you in the red and rising sunlight have just been perching on crossed bayonets. Set your faces to this army, advance toward them, paw the air over their heads. They do not observe you — yet. You are confounded with jewels, and leaves, and statues. You are a part of the great church, even though you stand poised to leave it, and already a sergeant has seen you. "Tiens," says he, "voilà les quatre chevaux d'or. Ah, mais ils sont magnifiques! Et quelle drôle d'idée de les avoir montés sur la Cathédrale."

The century wanes, the moon-century is gnawed and eaten, but the feet of the great horses stand upon its fragments, full-tilted to an arrested advance, and the green corroding on their sides is hidden in the glare of gold.

"For the honour and independence of the infant Cisalpine Republic, the affectionate and loving Republic of France orders and commands — "

What does she command? Precisely, that the new Government shall walk in solemn procession round the Piazza, and that a mass of thanksgiving shall be celebrated in Saint Mark's Church and the image of the Virgin exposed to the rejoicing congregation. Who would have supposed that Venetians could be so dumb. The acclamations seem mostly in the French tongue. Never mind, it takes more than a day to translate a creed into a new language. Liberty is a great prize, good Venetians, although it must be admitted that she appears in disguise for the moment. She wears a mask, that is all, and you should be accustomed to masks. The soldiers bask in the warm sunshine, and doubtless the inhabitants bask in the sight of the soldiers, but they conceal their satisfaction very adroitly. Still, General Baraguey d'Hilliers has no doubt that it is there. This liberation of a free people is a famous exploit. He is a bit nettled at their apathy, for he has always heard that they were of a gay temperament. "Sacré Bleu! And we are giving them so much!"

Indeed, this giving is done with a magnificent generosity. It is exactly on Ascension Day that Bonaparte writes from Montebello: "Conformably to your desire, Citizens, I have ordered the municipalities of Padua and Treviso to allow the passage of the foodstuffs necessary to the provisionment of the town of Venice."

"Real and perpetual dominion," and now a boatload of food is a condescension! Pink and purple water, your little ripples jest at these emblazoned palaces, your waves chuckle down the long Rivas, you reflect the new flag of Venice which even the Dey of Algiers refuses to respect, and patter your light heels upon it as on a dancing-floor. There will be no more use for the Bucentoro, of course. So rip off the gilding, pack up the mirrors, chop the timbers into firewood. This is good work for soldiers with nothing to do. There are other ships to be dismantled too, and some few seaworthy enough to send to the army at Corfu. But if they have taken away Ascension Day, the French will give Venice a new fête. Ah! and one so beautiful! Beat the drums, ring the church-bells, set up a Tree of Liberty in the Great Square, this fête is past telling. So writes the Citizen Arnault, from his room in the Queen of England inn. He bites his pen, he looks out on the little canal with its narrow bridge, he fusses with his watch-chain. It is not easy to write to the bronze General. He dips in the ink and starts again. "The people take no active part in what goes on here. They have seen the lions fall without making any sign of joy." That certainly is queer. Perhaps Citizen Arnault did not hear that gondolier, who, when they chiselled out "Pax tibi, Marce, evangelista meus" on the lion's book, and chiselled in "Diritti dell' uomo e del cittadino," exclaimed: "The lion has turned over a new leaf." Does that sound like grief? Certainly not, think the French soldiers, and yet the Doge's robes, the Golden Book, burn in silence, until a corporal strikes up the "Marseillaise." They make a grand blaze too; why, the boatmen far off in the hazy Lagoon can hear the crackle of it snapping over the water. Then the columns! The columns produce a lovely effect, one all wound with tricolore flags and with this inscription: "To the French, regenerators of

Italy, Venice grateful," on its front, and on the back, "Bonaparte." The other is not so gay, but most proper and desirable. It is hung with crêpe, and the letters read: "To the shade of the victim of oligarchy, "Venice sorrowful," and, "Laugier." To be sure there has been considerable excitement, and the great green lion has been thrown down and shattered in at least eighty fragments, but the soldiers did it. The populace were simply stolid and staring. Citizen Arnault fidgets in his chair. But other affairs march better. He has found the only copy of Anacharsis which is known to be in Venice; he is going to hunt for Homer, for he wants to put it with the Ossian of Cesarotti which he has already taken from the Library. Here his pen runs rapidly, he has an inspiration. "There are four superb horses which the Venetians took when, in company with the French, they sacked Constantinople. These horses are placed over the portal of the Ducal Church. Have not the French some right to claim them, or at least to accept them of Venetian gratitude?" The bronze General has an eye to a man, witness this really excellent plan. Fold your letter, Citizen. Press your fob down upon the seal. You may feel proud as you ring for candles, no one will have hurt Venice more than you.

The blue night softens the broken top of the column in the Piazzetta where it juts against the sky. The violet night sifts shadows over the white, mounting angels of Saint Mark's Church; it throws an aureole of lilac over the star of Christ and melts it into the glimmering dome behind. But upon the horses it clashes with the glitter of steel. Blue striking gold, and together producing a white-heart fire. Cold, as in great fire, hard as in new-kindled fire, outlined as behind a flame which folds back upon itself in lack of fuel, the great horses stand. They strain forward, they recoil even when starting, they raise one foot and hold it lifted, and all about them the stones of the jewelled church writhe, and convolute, and glisten, and dash the foam of their tendrils against the clear curve of the moulded flanks.

The Treaty of Campo Formio! A mask stripped off a Carnival figure, and behold, the sneering face of death! What of the creed the French were bringing the Venetians! Was it greed after all, or has a seed been sown? If so, the flowering will be long delayed. The French are leaving us, and almost we wish they would remain. For Austria! What does it matter that the *Bucentoro* is broken up; the lions from the Piraeus loaded into a vessel; books, parchments, pictures, packed in travelling cases! What does anything matter! A gondolier snaps his fingers: "*Francese non tutti ladri, ma Buona-parte!*" Hush, my friend, that is a dangerous remark, for Madame Bonaparte has descended upon Venice in a whirlwind of laughter, might have made friends had she not been received in an overturned storehouse. But she stays only three days, and the song of the gondoliers who row her away can scarcely be heard for the hammering they make, putting up an immense scaffolding in front of Saint Mark's Church. They have erected poles too, and tackle. It is an awful nuisance, for soldiers are not skilled in carpenter work, and no Venetian will lend a hand. A grand ship sails for Toulon as soon as the horses are on board.

Golden horses, at last you leave your pedestals, you swing in the blue-and-silver air, you paw the reflections flung by rippled water, and the starved pigeons whirl about you chattering. One — one — one — one! The tackle creaks, the little squeaks of the pigeons are sharp and pitiful. A gash in the front of the great Church. A blank window framing nothing. The leaves of the sculptures curl, the swirling angels mount steadily, the star of Christ is the pointed jet of a flame, but the horses drop — drop — They descend slowly, they jerk, and stop, and start again, and one — one — one — one — they touch the pavement. Women throw shawls over their heads and weep; men pull off their caps and mutter prayers and imprecations. Then silently they form into a procession and march after the hand-carts, down to the quay, down to the waiting vessel. Slow feet following to a grave. Here is a sign, but hardly of joy. This is a march of mourning. Depart, vessel, draw out over the bright Lagoon, grow faint, vague, blur and disappear. The murder is accomplished. To-morrow come the Austrians.

BONFIRES BURN PURPLE

Then the energy which peoples the Earth crystallized into a single man. And this man was Water, and Fire, and Flesh. His core had the strength of metal, and the hardness of metal was in his actions, and upon him the sun struck as upon polished metal. So he went to and fro among the nations, gleaming as with jewels. Of himself were the monuments he erected, and his laws were engraved tablets of fairest bronze. But there grew a great terror among the lesser peoples of the Earth, and they ran hither and yon like the ants, they swarmed like beetles, and they saw themselves impotent, merely making tracks in sand. Now as speed is heat, so did this man soften with the haste of his going. For Fire is supreme even over metal, and the Fire in him overcame the strong metal, so that his limbs failed, and his brain was hot and molten. Then was he consumed, but those of his monuments which harboured not Fire, and were without spirit, and cold, these endured. In the midst of leaping flame, they kept their semblances, and turning many colours in heat, still they cooled as the Fire cooled. For metal is unassailable from without, only a spark in the mid-most circle can force a double action which pours it into Water, and volatilizes it into Air, and sifts it to ashes which are Earth. For man can fashion effigies, but the spark of Life he can neither infuse nor control.

As a sharp sun this man passed across his century, and of the cenotaphs of his burning, some remain as a shadow of splendour in the streets of his city, but others have returned whence he gathered them, for the years of these are many and the touch of kings upon them is as the dropping of particles of dust.

VENICE AGAIN

Sunday evening, May 23, 1915. A beautiful Sunday evening with the Lagoon just going purple, and the angel on the tip of the new Campanile dissolved to a spurt of crocus-coloured flame. Up into the plum-green sky mount the angels of the Basilica of Saint Mark, their wings, curved up and feathered to the fragility of a blowing leaf, making incisive stabs of whiteness against the sky.

An organ moans in the great nave, and the high voices of choristers float out through the open door and surge down the long Piazza. The chugging of a motor-boat breaks into the chant, swirls it, churns upon it, and fades to a distant pulsing down the Grand Canal. The Campanile angel goes suddenly crimson, pales to rose, dies out in lilac, and remains dark, almost invisible, until the starting of stars behind it gives it a new solidity in hiding them.

In the warm twilight, the little white tables of the Café Florian are like petals dropped from the rose of the moon. For a moment they are weird and magical, but the abrupt glare of electric lights touches them back into mere tables: mere tables, flecked with coffee-cups and liqueur-glasses; mere tables, crumpling the lower halves of newspapers with their hard edges; mere tables, where gesticulating arms rest their elbows, and ice-cream plates nearly meet disaster in the excitement of a heated discussion. Venice discusses. What will the Government do? Austria has asked that her troops might cross over Italian territory, South of Switzerland, in order to attack the French frontier. Austria! "I tell you, Luigi, that alliance the Government made with the Central Powers was a ghastly blunder. You could never have got Italians to fight on the side of Austrians. Blood is thicker than ink, fortunately. But we are ready, thanks to Commandante Cadorna. It was a foregone conclusion, ever since we refused passage to their troops." "I saw Signor Colsanto, yesterday. He told me that the order had come from the General Board of Antiquities and Fine Arts to remove everything possible to Rome, and protect what can't be moved. He begins the work to-morrow." "He does! Well, that tells us. Here, Boy, Boy, give me a paper. Listen to that roar! There you are, *cinque centesimi*.

Well, we're off, Luigi. It's declared. Italy at war with Austria again. Thank God, we've wiped off the stain of that abominable treaty." With heads bared, the crowd stands, and shouts, and cheers, and the pigeons fleer away in frightened circles to the sculptured porticoes of the Basilica. The crowd bursts into a sweeping song. A great patriotic chorus. It echoes from side to side of the Piazza, it runs down the colonnades of the Procuratie like a splashing tide, it dashes upon the arched portals of Saint Mark's and flicks upward in jets of broken music. Wild, shooting, rolling music; vibrant, solemn, dedicated music; throbbing music flung out of loud-pounding hearts. The Piazza holds the sound of it and lifts it up as one raises an offering before an altar. Higher — higher — the song is lifted, it engulfs the four golden horses over the centre door of the church. The horses are as brazen cymbals crashing back the great song in a cadence of struck metal, the carven capitals are fluted reeds to this mighty anthem, the architraves bandy it to and fro in revolving canons of harmony. Up, up, spires the song, and the mounting angels call it to one another in an ascending scale even to the star of fire on the topmost pinnacle which is the Christ, even into the distant sky where it curves up and over falling down to the four horizons, to the highest point of the aconite-blue sky, the sky of the Kingdom of Italy.

Garibaldi's Hymn! For war is declared and Italy has joined the Allies!

Soft night falling upon Venice. Summer night over the moon-city, the flower-city. *Fiore di Mare!* Garden of lights in the midst of dark waters, your star-blossoms will be quenched, the strings of your guitars will snap and slacken. Nights, you will gird on strange armour, and grow loud and strident. But now — The gilded horses shimmer above the portico of Saint Mark's! How still they are, and powerful. Pride, motion, activity set in a frozen patience.

Suddenly — Boom! A signal gun. Then immediately the shrill shriek of a steam whistle, and another, and whistles

and whistles, from factories and boats, yawling, snarling, mewling, screeching, a cracked cacophony of horror.

Minutes — one — two — three — and the batteries of the Aerial-Guard Station begin to fire. Shells — red and black, white and grey — bellow, snap, and crash into the blue-black sky. A whirr — the Italian planes are rising. Their white centre lights throw a halo about them, and, tip and tip, a red light and a green, spark out to a great spread, closing together as the planes gain in altitude. Up they go, the red, white, and green circles underneath their wings and on either side of the fan-tails bright in the glow of the white centre light. Up, up, slanting in mounting circles. "Holy Mother of God! What is it?" Taubes over the city, flying at a great height, flying in a wedge like a flight of wild geese. Boom! The anti-aircraft guns are flinging up strings of luminous balls. Range 10,000 feet, try 10,500. Loud detonations, echoing far over the Lagoon. The navigation lights of the Italian planes are a faint triangle of bright dots. They climb in deliberate spirals, up and up, up and up. They seem to hang. They hover without direction. Ah, there are the Taubes, specks dotting the beam of a search-light. One of them is banking. Two Italian machines dart up over him. He spins, round — round — top-whirling, sleeping in speed, to us below he seems stationary. Pup-pup-pup-pup-pup — machine-guns, clicking like distant typewriters, firing with indescribable rapidity. The Italian planes drop signal balloons, they hang in the air like suspended sky-rockets, they float down, amber balls, steadily burning. The ground guns answer, and white buds of smoke appear in the sky. They seem to blossom out of darkness, silver roses beyond the silver shaft of the search-light. The air is broken with noise: thunder-drumming of cannon, sharp pocking of machine-guns, snap and crack of rifles. Above, the specks loop, and glide, and zigzag. The spinning Taube nose-dives, recovers, and zums upward, topping its adversary. Another Taube swoops in over a Nieuport and wags its tail, spraying lead bullets into the Italian in a wide, wing-and-wing arc. The sky is bitten

red with stinging shrapnel. Two machines charge head on, the Taube swerves
and rams the right wing of the Nieuport.
Flame! Flame leaping and dropping. A
smear from zenith to — following it, the
eye hits the shadow of a roof. Blackness.
One poor devil gone, and the attacking
plane is still airworthy though damaged.
It wobbles out of the search-light and
disappears, rocking. Two Taubes shake
themselves free of the tangle, they glide
down — down — all round them are ribbons of "flaming onions," they avoid
them and pass on down, close over the
city, unscathed, so close you can see the
black crosses on their wings with a glass.
Rifles crack at them from roofs. Pooh!
You might as well try to stop them with
pea-shooters. They curve, turn, and hang
up-wind. Small shells beat about them
with a report like twanged harp-strings.
"*Klar zum Werfen?*" "*Jahwol.*" "*Gut
doch, werfen.*" Words cannot carry
down thousands of feet, but the ominous
hovering is a sort of speech. People
wring their hands and clutch their
throats, some cover their ears. Z-z-z-z-z!
That whine would pierce any covering.
The bomb has passed below the roofs.
Nothing. A pause. Then a report, breaking the hearing, leaving only the appre-
hension of a great light and no sound.
They have hit us! *Misericordia!* They
have hit Venice One — two — four —
ten bombs. People sob and pray, the
water lashes the Rivas as though there
were a storm. Another machine falls,
shooting down in silence. It is not on
fire, it merely falls. Then slowly the
Taubes draw off. The search-light shifts,
seeking them. The gun-fire is spaced
more widely. Field-glasses fail to show
even a speck. There is silence. The silence of a pulse which has stopped. But
the people walk in the brightness of fire.
Fire from the Rio della Tanna, from the
Rio del Carmine, from the quarter of
Santa Lucia. Bells peal in a fury, fire-
boats hurry with forced engines along the
canals. Water streams jet upon the fire;
and, in the golden light, the glittering
horses of Saint Mark's pace forward, silent, calm, determined in their advance,
above the portal of the untouched
church.

The night turns grey, and silver, and
opens into a blue morning. Diamond
roses sparkle on the Lagoon, but the
people passing quickly through the Piazza
are grim, and workmen sniff the smoky
air as they fix ladders and arrange tools.
Venice has tasted war. "*Evviva Italia!*"

City of soft colours, of amber and violet, you are turning grey-green, and grey-
green are the uniforms of the troops who
defend you. The Bersaglièri still wear
their cocks' feathers, but they are green
too, and black. Black as the guns mounted
on pontoons among the Lagoons before
Venice, green as the bundles of reeds
camouflaging them from Austrian observation balloons. Drag up metre after
metre of grey-green cloth, stretch it over
the five golden domes of Saint Mark's
Basilica. Hood their splendour in umbrella bags of cloth, so that not one
glint shall answer the mocking shimmer
of the moon. Barrows and barrows of
nails for the wooden bastion of the Basilica, hods and hods of mortar and narrow bricks to cover the old mosaics of
the lunettes. Cart-loads of tar and planking, and heaps, heaps, hills and mountains of sand — the Lido protecting Venice, as it has done for hundreds of years.
They shovel sand, scoop sand, pour sand,
into bags and bags and bags. Thousands
of bags piled against the bases of columns, rising in front of carved corners,
blotting out altars, throttling the open
points of arches. Porphyries, malachites,
and jades are squarely boarded, pulpits
and fonts disappear in swaddling bands.
Why? The battle front is forty miles
away in Friuli, and Venice is not a
fortified town. Why? Answer, Reims!
Bear witness, Ypres! Do they cover Venice without reason? Nietzsche was a
German, still I believe they read him in
Vienna. Blood and Iron! And is there
not also Blood and Stone, Blood and
Bronze, Blood and Canvas? "Kultur,"
Venetians, in the Rio del Carmine; there
is no time to lose. Take down the great
ceiling pictures in the Ducal Palace and
wrap them on cylinders. Build a high
trestle, and fashion little go-carts which
draw with string.
Hush! They are coming — the four

beautiful horses. They rise in a whirl of disturbed pigeons. They float and descend. The people watch in silence as, one after another, they reach the ground. Across the tiles they step at last, each pulled in a go-cart; merry-go-round horses, detached and solitary, one foot raised, tramp over chequered stones, over chequered centuries. The merry-go-round of years has brought them full circle, for are they not returning to Rome?

For how long? Ask the guns embedded in the snow of glaciers; ask the rivers pierced from their beds, overflowing marshes and meadows, forming a new sea. Seek the answer in the faces of the Grenatieri Brigade, dying to a man, but halting the invaders. Demand it of the women and children fleeing the approach of a bitter army. Provoke the reply in the dryness of those eyes which gaze upon the wreck of Tiepolo's ceiling in the Church of the Scalzi. Yet not in Italy alone shall you find it. The ring of searching must be widened, and France, England, Japan, and America, caught within its edge. Moons and moons, and seas seamed with vessels. Needles stitching the cloth of peace to choke the cannon of war.

The boat draws away from the Riva. The great bronze horses mingle their outlines with the distant mountains. Dim gold, subdued green-gold, flashing faintly to the faint, bright peaks above them. Granite and metal, earth over water. Down the canal, old, beautiful horses, pride of Venice, of Constantinople, of Rome. Wars bite you with their little flames and pass away, but roses and oleanders strew their petals before your going, and you move like a constellation in a space of crimson stars.

So the horses float along the canal, between barred and shuttered palaces, splendid against marble walls in the fire of the sun.

PICTURES OF
THE FLOATING WORLD

LACQUER PRINTS

STREETS

(Adapted from the poet
Yakura Sanjin, 1769)

As I wandered through the eight hun-
dred and eight streets of the city,
I saw nothing so beautiful
As the Women of the Green Houses,
With their girdles of spun gold,
And their long-sleeved dresses,
Coloured like the graining of wood.
As they walk,
The hems of their outer garments flutter
open,
And the blood-red linings glow like sharp-
toothed maple leaves
In Autumn.

BY MESSENGER

One night
When there was a clear moon,
I sat down
To write a poem
About maple-trees.
But the dazzle of moonlight
In the ink
Blinded me,
And I could only write
What I remembered.
Therefore, on the wrapping of my poem
I have inscribed your name.

CIRCUMSTANCE

Upon the maple leaves
The dew shines red,
But on the lotus blossom
It has the pale transparence of tears.

ANGLES

The rain is dark against the white sky,
Or white against the foliage of eucalyp-
tus-trees.

But, in the cistern, it is a sheet of mauve
and amber,
Because of the chrysanthemums
Heaped about its edge.

VICARIOUS

When I stand under the willow-tree
Above the river,
In my straw-coloured silken garment
Embroidered with purple chrysanthemums,
It is not at the bright water
That I am gazing,
But at your portrait,
Which I have caused to be painted
On my fan.

NEAR KIOTO

As I crossed over the bridge of Ari-
warano Narikira,
I saw that the waters were purple
With the floating leaves of maples.

DESOLATION

Under the plum-blossoms are nightingales;
But the sea is hidden in an egg-white
mist,
And they are silent.

YOSHIWARA LAMENT

Golden peacocks
Under blossoming cherry-trees,
But on all the wide sea
There is no boat.

SUNSHINE

The pool is edged with the blade-like
leaves of irises.
If I throw a stone into the placid water,

It suddenly stiffens
Into rings and rings
Of sharp gold wire.

ILLUSION

Walking beside the tree-peonies,
I saw a beetle
Whose wings were of black lacquer
spotted with milk.
I would have caught it,
But it ran from me swiftly
And hid under the stone lotus
Which supports the statue of Buddha.

A YEAR PASSES

Beyond the porcelain fence of the pleasure garden,
I hear the frogs in the blue-green ricefields;
But the sword-shaped moon
Has cut my heart in two.

A LOVER

If I could catch the green lantern of the firefly
I could see to write you a letter.

TO A HUSBAND

Brighter than fireflies upon the Uji River
Are your words in the dark, Beloved.

THE FISHERMAN'S WIFE

When I am alone,
The wind in the pine-trees
Is like the shuffling of waves
Upon the wooden sides of a boat.

FROM CHINA

I thought: —
The moon,
Shining upon the many steps of the palace before me,
Shines also upon the chequered ricefields
Of my native land.
And my tears fell
Like white rice grains
At my feet.

THE POND

Cold, wet leaves
Floating on moss-coloured water,

And the croaking of frogs —
Cracked bell-notes in the twilight.

AUTUMN

All day I have watched the purple vine
leaves
Fall into the water.
And now in the moonlight they still fall,
But each leaf is fringed with silver.

EPHEMERA

Silver-green lanterns tossing among windy
branches:
So an old man thinks
Of the loves of his youth.

DOCUMENT

The great painter, Hokusai,
In his old age,
Wrote these words:
"Profiting by a beautiful Spring day,
In this year of tranquillity,
To warm myself in the sun,
I received a visit from my publisher
Who asked me to do something for
him.
Then I reflected that one should not
forget the glory of arms,
Above all when one was living in
peace;
And in spite of my age,
Which is more than seventy years,
I have found courage to draw those
ancient heroes
Who have been the models of glory."

THE EMPEROR'S GARDEN

Once, in the sultry heats of Midsummer,
An Emperor caused the miniature mountains in his garden
To be covered with white silk,
That so crowned
They might cool his eyes
With the sparkle of snow.

ONE OF THE "HUNDRED VIEWS OF FUJI" BY HOKUSAI

Being thirsty,
I filled a cup with water,
And, behold! Fuji-yama lay upon the
water
Like a dropped leaf!

DISILLUSION

A scholar,
Weary of erecting the fragile towers of
  words,
Went on a pilgrimage to Asama-yama.
And seeing the force of the fire
Spouting from this mighty mountain,
Hurled himself into its crater
And perished.

PAPER FISHES

The paper carp,
At the end of its long bamboo pole,
Takes the wind into its mouth
And emits it at its tail.
So is man,
Forever swallowing the wind.

MEDITATION

A wise man,
Watching the stars pass across the sky,
Remarked:
In the upper air the fireflies move more
  slowly.

THE CAMELLIA TREE
OF MATSUE

At Matsue,
There was a Camellia Tree of great
  beauty
Whose blossoms were white as honey wax
Splashed and streaked with the pink of
  fair coral.
At night,
When the moon rose in the sky,
The Camellia Tree would leave its place
By the gateway,
And wander up and down the garden,
Trailing its roots behind it
Like a train of rustling silk.
The people in the house,
Hearing the scrape of them upon the
  gravel,
Looked out into the garden
And saw the tree,
With its flowers erect and peering,
Pressed against the shōji.
Many nights the tree walked about the
  garden,
Until the women and children
Became frightened,
And the Master of the house

Ordered that it be cut down.
But when the gardener brought his axe
And struck at the trunk of the tree,
There spouted forth a stream of dark
  blood;
And when the stump was torn up,
The hole quivered like an open wound.

SUPERSTITION

I have painted a picture of a ghost
Upon my kite,
And hung it on a tree.
Later, when I loose the string
And let it fly,
The people will cower
And hide their heads,
For fear of the God
Swimming in the clouds.

THE RETURN

Coming up from my boat
In haste to lighten your anxiety,
I saw, reflected in the circular metal
  mirror,
The face and hands of a woman
Arranging her hair.

A LADY TO HER LOVER

The white snows of Winter
Follow the falling of leaves;
Therefore
I have had your portrait cut
In snow-white jade.

NUANCE

Even the iris bends
When a butterfly lights upon it.

AUTUMN HAZE

Is it a dragonfly or a maple leaf
That settles softly down upon the water?

PEACE

Perched upon the muzzle of a cannon
A yellow butterfly is slowly opening and
  shutting its wings.

IN TIME OF WAR

Across the newly-plastered wall,
The darting of red dragonflies
Is like the shooting
Of blood-tipped arrows.

NUIT BLANCHE

The chirping of crickets in the night
Is intermittent,
Like the twinkling of stars.

SPRING DAWN

He wore a coat
With gold and red maple leaves,
He was girt with the two swords,
He carried a peony lantern.
When I awoke,
There was only the blue shadow of the
plum-tree
Upon the shōji.

POETRY

Over the shop where silk is sold
Still the dragon kites are flying.

FROM A WINDOW

Your footfalls on the drum bridge beside
my house
Are like the pattering drops of a passing
shower,
So soon are they gone.

AGAIN THE NEW YEAR FESTIVAL

I have drunk your health
In the red-lacquer wine cups,
But the wind-bells on the bronze lan-
terns
In my garden
Are corroded and fallen.

TIME

Looking at myself in my metal mirror,
I saw, faintly outlined,
The figure of a crane
Engraved upon its back.

LEGEND

When the leaves of the cassia-tree
Turn red in Autumn,

Then the moon,
In which it grows,
Shines for many nights
More brightly.

PILGRIMS ASCENDING
FUJI–YAMA

I should tremble at the falling showers
of ashes
Dislodged by my feet,
Did I not know
That at night they fly upward
And spread themselves once more
Upon the slopes of the Honourable
Mountain.

THE KAGOES OF A RETURNING
TRAVELLER

Diagonally between the cryptomerias,
What I took for the flapping of wings
Was the beating feet of your runners,
O my Lord!

A STREET

Under red umbrellas with cream-white
centres,
A procession of Geisha passes
In front of the silk-shop of Matsuzaka-ya.

OUTSIDE A GATE

On the floor of the empty palanquin
The plum-petals constantly increase.

ROAD TO THE YOSHIWARA

Coming to you along the Nihon Em-
bankment,
Suddenly the road was darkened
By a flock of wild geese
Crossing the moon.

OX STREET, TAKANAWA

What is a rainbow?
Have I not seen its colours and its shape
Duplicated in the melon slices
Lying beside an empty cart?

A DAIMIO'S OIRAN

When I hear your runners shouting:
"Get down! Get down!"
Then I dress my hair
With the little chrysanthemums.

PASSING THE BAMBOO FENCE

What fell upon my open umbrella —
A plum-blossom?

FROSTY EVENING

It is not the bright light in your window
Which dazzles my eyes;
It is the dim outline of your shadow
Moving upon the shōji.

AN ARTIST

The anchorite, Kisen,
Composed a thousand poems
And threw nine hundred and ninety-
nine into the river
Finding one alone worthy of preserva-
tion.

A BURNT OFFERING

Because there was no wind,
The smoke of your letters hung in the
air
For a long time;
And its shape
Was the shape of your face,
My Beloved.

DAYBREAK. YOSHIWARA

Draw your hoods tightly,
You who must depart,
The morning mist
Is grey and miasmic.

TEMPLE CEREMONY

(FROM THE JAPANESE OF SŌJŌ HENJŌ)

Blow softly,
O Wind!
And let no clouds cover the moon
Which lights the posturing steps
Of the most beautiful of dancers.

TWO PORTERS RETURNING ALONG A COUNTRY ROAD

Since an empty kago can be carried upon
the back of one man,
Therefore the other has nothing to do

But gaze at the white circle
Drawn about the flying moon.

STORM BY THE SEASHORE

There is no moon in the sky,
But with each step
I see one grow in the sand
Under my feet.
This interests me so much
That I forget the rain
Beating against the lantern
Which my cloak only partially covers.

THE EXILED EMPEROR

The birds sing to-day,
For to-morrow they will be flown
Many miles across the tossing sea.

LETTER WRITTEN FROM PRISON BY TWO POLITICAL OFFENDERS

When a hero fails of his purpose,
His acts are regarded as those of a vil-
lain and a robber.
Pursuing liberty, suddenly our plans are
defeated.
In public we have been seized and pin-
ioned and caged for many days.
How can we find exit from this place?
Weeping, we seem as fools; laughing, as
rogues.
Alas! for us; we can only be silent.

MOON HAZE

Because the moonlight deceives
Therefore I love it.

PROPORTION

In the sky there is a moon and stars,
And in my garden there are yellow moths
Fluttering about a white azalea bush.

CONSTANCY

Although so many years,
Still the vows we made each other
Remain tied to the great trunk
Of the seven separate trees
In the courtyard of the Crimson Temple
At Nara.

CHINOISERIES

REFLECTIONS

When I looked into your eyes,
I saw a garden
With peonies, and tinkling pagodas,
And round-arched bridges
Over still lakes.
A woman sat beside the water
In a rain-blue, silken garment.
She reached through the water
To pluck the crimson peonies
Beneath the surface,
But as she grasped the stems,
They jarred and broke into white-green
  ripples;
And as she drew out her hand,
The water-drops dripping from it
Stained her rain-blue dress like tears.

FALLING SNOW

The snow whispers about me,
And my wooden clogs
Leave holes behind me in the snow.
But no one will pass this way
Seeking my footsteps,
And when the temple bell rings again
They will be covered and gone.

HOAR–FROST

In the cloud-grey mornings
I heard the herons flying;
And when I came into my garden,
My silken outer-garment
Trailed over withered leaves.
A dried leaf crumbles at a touch,
But I have seen many Autumns
With herons blowing like smoke
Across the sky.

GOLD–LEAF SCREEN

Under the broken clouds of dawn,
The white leopards eat the grapes
In my vineyard.
And in the sunken splendour of twilight,
The ring pheasants perch among the red
  fruit
Of my pomegranate trees.
The bright coloured varnish

Scales off the wheels of my chariots,
For the horses which should draw them
Have gone Northward in a gloom of
  spears.
My stablemen march,
Each with a two-edged spear upon his
  shoulder,
And my orchard tenders have put on the
  green feathered helmets
And girt themselves with blacks bows.
I stand above the terrace of three hun-
  dred rose-trees
And gaze at my despoiled vineyards.
Drums beat among the Northern hills,
But I hear only the rattle of the wind
  on the chipped tiles
Of my roof.

A thousand little stitches in the soul of
  a dead man —
Still one can enjoy these things
Sitting over a fire of camphor wood
In a quilted gown of purple-red silk.

A POET'S WIFE

CHO WĔN-CHŪN TO HER HUSBAND
SSŬ-MA HSIANG-JU

You have taken our love and turned it
  into coins of silver.
You sell the love poems you wrote for
  me,
And with the price of them you buy
  many cups of wine,
I beg that you remain dumb,
That you write no more poems.
For the wine does us both an injury,
And the words of your heart
Have become the common speech of the
  Emperor's concubines.

SPRING LONGING

The South wind blows open the folds
  of my dress,
My feet leave wet tracks in the earth
  of my garden,
The willows along the canal sing
      with new leaves turned upon the
  wind.

I walk along the tow-path
Gazing at the level water.
Should I see a ribbed edge
Running upon its clearness,
I should know that this was caused
By the prow of the boat
In which you are to return.

LI T'AI PO

So, Master, the wine gave you something,
I suppose.

I think I see you,
Your silks all disarranged,
Lolling in a green-marble pavilion,
Ogling the concubines of the Emperor's
Court
Who pass the door
In yellow coats, and white jade ear-drops,
Their hair pleated in folds like the hun-
dred clouds.
I watch you,
Hiccoughing poetry between drinks,
Sinking as the sun sinks,
Sleeping for twenty-four hours,
While they peek at you,
Giggling,
Through the open door.

You found something in the wine,
I imagine,
Since you could not leave it,
Even when, after years of wandering,
You sat in the boat with one sail,
Travelling down the zigzag rivers
On your way back to Court.

You had a dream,
I conjecture.
You saw something under the willow-
lights of the water
Which swept you to dizziness,
So that you toppled over the edge of the
boat,
And gasped, and became your dream.

Twelve hundred years
Or thereabouts,
Did the wine do it?
I would sit in the purple moonlight
And drink three hundred cups,
If I believed it.
Three hundred full cups,
After your excellent fashion,
While in front of me
The river dazzle ran before the moon,
And the light flaws of the evening wind
Scattered the notes of nightingales
Loosely among the kuai trees.

They erected a temple to you:
"Great Doctor,
Prince of Poetry,
Immortal man who loved drink."
I detest wine,
And I have no desire for the temple,
Which under the circumstances
Is fortunate.
But I would sacrifice even sobriety
If, when I was thoroughly drunk,
I could see what you saw
Under the willow-clouded water,
The day you died.

PLANES OF PERSONALITY
Two Speak Together

VERNAL EQUINOX

The scent of hyacinths, like a pale mist,
lies between me and my book;
And the South Wind, washing through
the room,
Makes the candles quiver.
My nerves sting at a spatter of rain on
the shutter,
And I am uneasy with the thrusting of
green shoots
Outside, in the night.

Why are you not here to overpower me
with your tense and urgent love?

THE LETTER

Little cramped words scrawling all over
the paper
Like draggled fly's legs,
What can you tell of the flaring moon
Through the oak leaves?
Or of my uncurtained window and the
bare floor

Spattered with moonlight?
Your silly quirks and twists have nothing
   in them
Of blossoming hawthorns,
And this paper is dull, crisp, smooth,
   virgin of loveliness
Beneath my hand.

I am tired, Beloved, of chafing my heart
   against
The want of you;
Of squeezing it into little inkdrops,
And posting it.
And I scald alone, here, under the fire
Of the great moon.

MISE EN SCENE

When I think of you, Beloved,
I see a smooth and stately garden
With parterres of gold and crimson tulips
And bursting lilac leaves.
There is a low-lipped basin in the midst,
Where a statue of veined cream marble
Perpetually pours water over her shoulder
From a rounded urn.
When the wind blows,
The water-stream blows before it
And spatters into the basin with a light
   tinkling,
And your shawl — the colour of red vio-
   lets —
Flares out behind you in great curves
Like the swirling draperies of a painted
   Madonna.

VENUS TRANSIENS

Tell me,
Was Venus more beautiful
Than you are,
When she topped
The crinkled waves,
Drifting shoreward
On her plaited shell?
Was Botticelli's vision
Fairer than mine;
And were the painted rosebuds
He tossed his lady,
Of better worth
Than the words I blow about you
To cover your too great loveliness
As with a gauze
Of misted silver?
For me,

You stand poised
In the blue and buoyant air,
Cinctured by bright winds,
Treading the sunlight.
And the waves which precede you
Ripple and stir
The sands at my feet.

MADONNA OF THE EVENING
FLOWERS

All day long I have been working,
Now I am tired.
I call: "Where are you?"
But there is only the oak-tree rustling in
   the wind.
The house is very quiet,
The sun shines in on your books,
On your scissors and thimble just put
   down,
But you are not there.
Suddenly I am lonely:
Where are you?
I go about searching.

Then I see you,
Standing under a spire of pale blue lark-
   spur,
With a basket of roses on your arm.
You are cool, like silver,
And you smile.
I think the Canterbury bells are playing
   little tunes.

You tell me that the peonies need spray-
   ing,
That the columbines have overrun all
   bounds,
That the pyrus japonica should be cut
   back and rounded.
You tell me these things.
But I look at you, heart of silver,
White heart-flame of polished silver,
Burning beneath the blue steeples of the
   larkspur,
And I long to kneel instantly at your
   feet,
While all about us peal the loud, sweet
   Te Deums of the Canterbury bells.

BRIGHT SUNLIGHT

The wind has blown a corner of your
   shawl
Into the fountain,

Where it floats and drifts
Among the lily-pads
Like a tissue of sapphires.
But you do not heed it,
Your fingers pick at the lichens
On the stone edge of the basin,
And your eyes follow the tall clouds
As they sail over the ilex-trees.

OMBRE CHINOISE

Red foxgloves against a yellow wall
    streaked with plum-coloured shadows;
A lady with a blue and red sunshade;
The slow dash of waves upon a parapet.
That is all.
Non-existent — immortal —
As solid as the centre of a ring of fine
    gold.

JULY MIDNIGHT

Fireflies flicker in the tops of trees,
Flicker in the lower branches,
Skim along the ground.
Over the moon-white lilies
Is a flashing and ceasing of small, lemon-
    green stars.
As you lean against me,
Moon-white,
The air all about you
Is slit, and pricked, and pointed with
    sparkles of lemon-green flame
Starting out of a background of vague,
    blue trees.

WHEAT–IN–THE–EAR

You stand between the cedars and the
    green spruces,
Brilliantly naked
And I think:
    What are you,
    A gem under sunlight?
    A poised spear?
    A jade cup?
You flash in front of the cedars and the
    tall spruces,
And I see that you are fire —
Sacrificial fire on a jade altar,
Spear-tongue of white, ceremonial fire.
My eyes burn,
My hands are flames seeking you,
But you are as remote from me as a
    bright pointed planet
Set in the distance of an evening sky.

THE WEATHER–COCK
POINTS SOUTH

I put your leaves aside,
One by one:
The stiff, broad outer leaves;
The smaller ones,
Pleasant to touch, veined with purple;
The glazed inner leaves.
One by one
I parted you from your leaves,
Until you stood up like a white flower
Swaying slightly in the evening wind.

White flower,
Flower of wax, of jade, of unstreaked
    agate;
Flower with surfaces of ice,
With shadows faintly crimson.
Where in all the garden is there such a
    flower?
The stars crowd through the lilac leaves
To look at you.
The low moon brightens you with silver.

The bud is more than the calyx.
There is nothing to equal a white bud,
Of no colour, and of all,
Burnished by moonlight,
Thrust upon by a softly-swinging wind.

THE ARTIST

Why do you subdue yourself in golds and
    purples?
Why do you dim yourself with folded
    silks?
Do you not see that I can buy brocades
    in any draper's shop,
And that I am choked in the twilight
    of all these colours?
How pale you would be, and startling,
How quiet;
But your curves would spring upward
Like a clear jet of flung water,
You would quiver like a shot-up spray
    of water,
You would waver, and relapse, and
    tremble.
And I too should tremble,
Watching.

Murex-dyes and tinsel —
And yet I think I could bear your beauty
    unshaded.

THE GARDEN BY MOONLIGHT

A black cat among roses,
Phlox, lilac-misted under a first-quarter
moon,
The sweet smells of heliotrope and night-
scented stock.
The garden is very still,
It is dazed with moonlight,
Contented with perfume,
Dreaming the opium dreams of its folded
poppies.
Firefly lights open and vanish
High as the tip buds of the golden glow
Low as the sweet alyssum flowers at my
feet.
Moon-shimmer on leaves and trellises,
Moon-spikes shafting through the snow-
ball bush.
Only the little faces of the ladies' delight
are alert and staring,
Only the cat, padding between the roses,
Shakes a branch and breaks the chequered
pattern
As water is broken by the falling of a
leaf.
Then you come,
And you are quiet like the garden,
And white like the alyssum flowers,
And beautiful as the silent sparks of the
fireflies.
Ah, Beloved, do you see those orange
lilies?
They knew my mother,
But who belonging to me will they know
When I am gone.

INTERLUDE

When I have baked white cakes
And grated green almonds to spread
upon them;
When I have picked the green crowns
from the strawberries
And piled them, cone-pointed, in a blue
and yellow platter;
When I have smoothed the seam of the
linen I have been working;
What then?
To-morrow it will be the same:
Cakes and strawberries,
And needles in and out of cloth.
If the sun is beautiful on bricks and
pewter,
How much more beautiful is the moon,

Slanting down the gauffered branches of
a plum-tree;
The moon,
Wavering across a bed of tulips;
The moon,
Still,
Upon your face.
You shine, Beloved,
You and the moon.
But which is the reflection?
The clock is striking eleven.
I think, when we have shut and barred
the door,
The night will be dark
Outside.   ·

BULLION

My thoughts
Chink against my ribs
And roll about like silver hail-stones.
I should like to spill them out,
And pour them, all shining,
Over you.
But my heart is shut upon them
And holds them straitly.

Come, You! and open my heart;
That my thoughts torment me no longer,
But glitter in your hair.

THE WHEEL OF THE SUN

I beg you
Hide your face from me.
Draw the tissue of your head-gear
Over your eyes.
For I am blinded by your beauty,
And my heart is strained,
And aches,
Before you.

In the street,
You spread a brightness where you walk,
And I see your lifting silks
And rejoice;
But I cannot look up to your face.
You melt my strength,
And set my knees to trembling.
Shadow yourself that I may love you,
For now it is too great a pain.

A SHOWER

That sputter of rain, flipping the hedge-
rows
And making the highways hiss,

How I love it!
And the touch of you upon my arm
As you press against me that my umbrella
May cover you.

Tinkle of drops on stretched silk.
Wet murmur through green branches.

SUMMER RAIN

All night our room was outer-walled with
   rain.
Drops fell and flattened on the tin roof,
And rang like little disks of metal.
Ping! — Ping! — and there was not a pin-
   point of silence between them.
The rain rattled and clashed,
And the slats of the shutters danced and
   glittered.
But to me the darkness was red-gold and
   crocus-coloured
With your brightness,
And the words you whispered to me
Sprang up and flamed — orange torches
   against the rain.
Torches against the wall of cool, silver
   rain!

APRIL

A bird chirped at my window this morn-
   ing,
And over the sky is drawn a light net-
   work of clouds.
Come,
Let us go out into the open,
For my heart leaps like a fish that is
   ready to spawn.

I will lie under the beech-trees,
Under the grey branches of the beech-
   trees,
In a blueness of little squills and crocuses.
I will lie among the little squills
And be delivered of this overcharge of
   beauty,
And that which is born shall be a joy to
   you
Who love me.

COQ D'OR

I walked along a street at dawn in cold,
   grey light,
Above me lines of windows watched,
   gaunt, dull, drear.

The lamps were fading, and the sky was
   streaked rose-red,
Silhouetting chimneys with their queer,
   round pots.
My feet upon the pavement made a
   knock — knock — knock.
Above the roofs of Westminster, Big Ben
   struck.
The cocks on all the steeples crew in
   clear, flat tones,
And churchyard daisies sprang away from
   thin, bleak bones.
The golden trees were calling me:
   "Come! Come! Come!"
The trees were fresh with daylight, and I
   heard bees hum.
A cart trailed slowly down the street, its
   load young greens,
They sparkled like blown emeralds, and
   then I laughed.
A morning in the city with its upthrust
   spires
All tipped with gold and shining in the
   brisk, blue air,
But the gold is round my forehead and
   the knot still holds
Where you tied it in the shadows, your
   rose-gold hair.

THE CHARM

I lay them before you,
One, two, three silver pieces,
And a copper piece
Dulled with handling.
The first will buy you a cake,
The second a flower,
The third a coloured bead.
The fourth will buy you nothing at all,
Since it has a hole in it.
I beg you, therefore,
String it about your neck,
At least it will remind you of my poverty.

AFTER A STORM

You walk under the ice trees.
They sway, and crackle,
And arch themselves splendidly
To deck your going.
The white sun flips them into colour
Before you.
They are blue,
And mauve,
And emerald.

They are amber,
And jade,
And sardonyx.
They are silver fretted to flame
And startled to stillness,
Bunched, splintered, iridescent.
You walk under the ice trees
And the bright snow creaks as you step
  upon it.
My dogs leap about you,
And their barking strikes upon the air
Like sharp hammer-strokes on metal.
You walk under the ice trees
But you are more dazzling than the ice
  flowers,
And the dogs' barking
Is not so loud to me as your quietness.

You walk under the ice trees
At ten o'clock in the morning.

OPAL

You are ice and fire,
The touch of you burns my hands like
  snow.
You are cold and flame.
You are the crimson of amaryllis,
The silver of moon-touched magnolias.
When I am with you,
My heart is a frozen pond
Gleaming with agitated torches.

WAKEFULNESS

Jolt of market-carts;
Steady drip of horses' hoofs on hard pave-
  ment;
A black sky lacquered over with blueness,
And the lights of Battersea Bridge
Pricking pale in the dawn.
The beautiful hours are passing
And still you sleep!
Tired heart of my joy,
Incurved upon your dreams,
Will the day come before you have
  opened to me?

ORANGE OF MIDSUMMER

You came to me in the pale starting of
  Spring,
And I could not see the world
For the blue mist of wonder before my
  eyes.

You beckoned me over a rainbow bridge,
And I set foot upon it, trembling.
Through pearl and saffron I followed you,
Through heliotrope and rose,
Iridescence after iridescence,
And to me it was all one
Because of the blue mist that held my
  eyes.

You came again, and it was red-hearted
  Summer.
You called to me across a field of poppies
  and wheat,
With a narrow path slicing through it
Straight to an outer boundary of trees.
And I ran along the path,
Brushing over the yellow wheat beside it,
And came upon you under a maple-tree,
  plaiting poppies for a girdle.
"Are you thirsty?" said you,
And held out a cup.
But the water in the cup was scarlet and
  crimson
Like the poppies in your hands.
"It looks like blood," I said.
"Like blood," you said,
"Does it?
But drink it, my Beloved."

SHORE GRASS

The moon is cold over the sand-dunes,
And the clumps of sea-grasses flow and
  glitter;
The thin chime of my watch tells the
  quarter after midnight;
And still I hear nothing
But the windy beating of the sea.

AUTUMNAL EQUINOX

Why do you not sleep, Beloved?

It is so cold that the stars stand out of
  the sky
Like golden nails not driven home.
The fire crackles pleasantly,
And I sit here listening
For your regular breathing from the room
  above.

What keeps you awake, Beloved?
Is it the same nightmare that keeps me
  strained with listening
So that I cannot read?

THE COUNTRY HOUSE

Did the door move, or was it always ajar?
The gladioli on the table are pale mauve.
I smell pale mauve and blue,
Blue soft like bruises — putrid — ooz-
ing —
The air oozes blue — mauve —
And the door with the black line where
it does not shut!

I must pass that door to go to bed,
Or I must stay here
And watch the crack
Oozing air.

Is it — air?

NERVES

The lake is steel-coloured and umber,
And a clutter of gaunt clouds blows
rapidly across the sky.

I wonder why you chose to be buried
In this little grave-yard by the lake-side.
It is all very well on blue mornings,
Summer mornings,
Autumn mornings polished with sunlight.
But in Winter, in the cold storms,
When there is no wind,
And the snow murmurs as it falls!
The grave-stones glimmer in the twilight
As though they were rubbed with phos-
phorous.
The direct road is up a hill,
Through woods —
I will take the lake road,
I can drive faster there.
You used to like to drive with me —
Why does death make you this fearful
thing?
Flick! — flack! — my horse's feet strike
the stones.
There is a house just round the bend.

LEFT BEHIND

White phlox and white hydrangeas,
High, thin clouds,
A low, warm sun.
So it is this afternoon.
But the phlox will be a drift of petals,
And the hydrangeas stained and fallen
Before you come again.

I cannot look at the flowers,
Nor the lifting leaves of the trees.
Without you, there is no garden,
No bright colours,
No shining leaves.
There is only space,
Stretching endlessly forward —
And I walk, bent, unseeing,
Waiting to catch the first faint scuffle
Of withered leaves.

AUTUMN

They brought me a quilled, yellow dahlia,
Opulent, flaunting.
Round gold
Flung out of a pale green stalk.
Round, ripe gold
Of maturity,
Meticulously frilled and flaming,
A fire-ball of proclamation:
Fecundity decked in staring yellow
For all the world to see.
They brought a quilled, yellow dahlia,
To me who am barren.
Shall I send it to you,
You who have taken with you
All I once possessed?

THE SIXTEENTH FLOOR

The noise of the city sounds below me.
It clashes against the houses
And rises like smoke through the narrow
streets.
It polishes the marble fronts of houses,
Grating itself against them,
And they shine in the lamplight
And cast their echoes back upon the
asphalt of the streets.

But I hear no sound of your voice,
The city is incoherent — trivial,
And my brain aches with emptiness.

STRAIN

It is late
And the clock is striking thin hours,
But sleep has become a terror to me,
Lest I wake in the night
Bewildered,
And stretching out my arms to comfort
myself with you,

Clasp instead the cold body of the dark-
ness.
All night it will hunger over me,
And push and undulate against me,
Breathing into my mouth
And passing long fingers through my
    drifting hair.
Only the dawn can loose me from it,
And the grey streaks of morning melt it
    from my side.

Bring many candles,
Though they stab my tired brain
And hurt it.
For I am afraid of the twining of the
    darkness
And dare not sleep.

HAUNTED

See! He trails his toes
Through the long streaks of moonlight,
And the nails of his fingers glitter:
They claw and flash among the tree-tops.
His lips suck at my open window,
And his breath creeps about my body
And lies in pools under my knees.
I can see his mouth sway and wobble,
Sticking itself against the window-jambs,
But the moonlight is bright on the floor,
Without a shadow.
Hark! A hare is strangling in the forest,
And the wind tears a shutter from the
    wall.

GROTESQUE

Why do the lilies goggle their tongues at
    me
When I pluck them;
And writhe, and twist,
And strangle themselves against my
    fingers,
So that I can hardly weave the garland
For your hair?
Why do they shriek your name
And spit at me
When I would cluster them?
Must I kill them
To make them lie still,
And send you a wreath of lolling corpses
To turn putrid and soft
On your forehead
While you dance?

SNOW IN APRIL

Sunshine!
Sunshine!
Smooth blue skies,
Fresh winds through early tree-tops,
Pointed shoots,
White bells,
White and purple cups.
I am a plum-tree
Checked at its flowering.
My blossoms wither,
My branches grow brittle again.
I stretch them out and up,
But the snowflakes fall —
Whirl — and fall.
April and snow,
And my heart stuffed and suffocating
Dead,
With my blossoms brown and dropping
Upon my cold roots.

A SPRIG OF ROSEMARY

I cannot see your face.
When I think of you,
It is your hands which I see.
Your hands
Sewing,
Holding a book,
Resting for a moment on the sill of a
    window.
My eyes keep always the sight of your
    hands,
But my heart holds the sound of your
    voice,
And the soft brightness which is your
    soul.

MALADIE DE L'APRES-MIDI

Why does the clanking of a tip-cart
In the road
Make me so sad?
The sound beats the air
With flat blows,
Dull and continued.

Not even the clear sunshine
Through bronze and green oak leaves,
Nor the crimson spindle of a cedar-tree
Hooded with Virginia creeper,
Nor the humming brightness of the air,
Can comfort my melancholy.

The cart goes slowly,
It creeps at a foot-pace,
And the flat blows of sound
Hurt me,
And bring me nearly to weeping.

NOVEMBER

The vine leaves against the brick walls of
    my house
Are rusty and broken.
Dead leaves gather under the pine-trees,
The brittle boughs of lilac-bushes
Sweep against the stars.
And I sit under a lamp
Trying to write down the emptiness of
    my heart.
Even the cat will not stay with me,
But prefers the rain
Under the meagre shelter of a cellar win-
    dow.

NOSTALGIA

"Through pleasures and palaces" —
Through hotels, and Pullman cars, and
    steamships . . .

Pink and white camellias
        floating in a crystal bowl,
The sharp smell of firewood,
The scrape and rustle of a dog stretching
    himself
        on a hardwood floor,
And your voice, reading — reading —
        to the slow ticking of an old brass
        clock . . .

"Tickets, please!"
And I watch the man in front of me
Fumbling in fourteen pockets,
While the conductor balances his ticket-
    punch
Between his fingers.

PREPARATION

To-day I went into a shop where they sell
    spectacles.

"Sir," said the shopman, "what can I do
    for you?
Are you far-sighted or near-sighted?"

"Neither the one nor the other," said I.
"I can read the messages passing along
    the telegraph wires,
And I can see the antennae of a fly
Perched upon the bridge of my nose."

"Rose-coloured spectacles, perhaps?" sug-
    gested the shopman.

"Indeed, no," said I.
"Were I to add them to my natural
    vision
I should see everything ruined with
    blood."

"Green spectacles," opined the shopman.

"By no means," said I.
"I am far too prone to that colour at mo-
    ments.
No. You can give me some smoked
    glasses
For I have to meet a train this after-
    noon."

"What a world yours must be, Sir."
Observed the shopman as he wrapped up
    the spectacles,
"When it requires to be dimmed by
    smoked glasses."

"Not a world," said I, and laid the money
    down on the counter,
"Certainly not a world.
Good-day."

A DECADE

When you came, you were like red wine
    and honey,
And the taste of you burnt my mouth
    with its sweetness.
Now you are like morning bread,
Smooth and pleasant.
I hardly taste you at all for I know your
    savour,
But I am completely nourished.

PENUMBRA

As I sit here in the quiet Summer night,
Suddenly, from the distant road, there
    comes
The grind and rush of an electric car.
And, from still farther off,

An engine puffs sharply,
Followed by the drawn-out shunting
  scrape of a freight train.
These are the sounds that men make
In the long business of living.
They will always make such sounds,
Years after I am dead and cannot hear
  them.

Sitting here in the Summer night,
I think of my death.
What will it be like for you then?
You will see my chair
With its bright chintz covering
Standing in the afternoon sunshine,
As now.
You will see my narrow table
At which I have written so many hours.
My dogs will push their noses into your
  hand,
And ask — ask —
Clinging to you with puzzled eyes.

The old house will still be here,
The old house which has known me since
  the beginning.
The walls which have watched me while
  I played:
Soldiers, marbles, paper-dolls,
Which have protected me and my books.

The front-door will gaze down among the
  old trees
Where, as a child, I hunted ghosts and
  Indians;
It will look out on the wide gravel sweep
Where I rolled my hoop,
And at the rhododendron bushes
Where I caught black-spotted butterflies.

The old house will guard you,
As I have done.
Its walls and rooms will hold you,
And I shall whisper my thoughts and
  fancies
As always,
From the pages of my books.

You will sit here, some quiet Summer
  night,
Listening to the puffing trains,
But you will not be lonely,
For these things are a part of me.
And my love will go on speaking to you
Through the chairs, and the tables, and
  the pictures,
As it does now through my voice,
And the quick, necessary touch of my
  hand.

FRIMAIRE

Dearest, we are like two flowers
Blooming last in a yellowing garden,
A purple aster flower and a red one
Standing alone in a withered desolation.

The garden plants are shattered and
  seeded,
One brittle leaf scrapes against another,
Fiddling echoes of a rush of petals.
Now only you and I nodding together.

Many were with us; they have all faded.
Only we are purple and crimson,
Only we in the dew-clear mornings,
Smarten into colour as the sun rises.

When I scarcely see you in the flat moon-
  light,
And later when my cold roots tighten,
I am anxious for the morning,
I cannot rest in fear of what may happen.

You or I — and I am a coward.
Surely frost should take the crimson.
Purple is a finer colour,
Very splendid in isolation.

So we nod above the broken
Stems of flowers almost rotted.
Many mornings there cannot be now
For us both. Ah, Dear, I love you!

Eyes, and Ears, and Walking

SOLITAIRE

When night drifts along the streets of the
  city,
And sifts down between the uneven roofs,

My mind begins to peek and peer.
It plays at ball in old, blue Chinese
  gardens,
And shakes wrought dice-cups in Pagan
  temples

Amid the broken flutings of white pillars.
It dances with purple and yellow crocuses
    in its hair,
And its feet shine as they flutter over
    drenched grasses.
How light and laughing my mind is,
When all the good folk have put out
    their bedroom candles,
And the city is still!

THE BACK BAY FENS

Study in Orange and Silver

Through the Spring-thickened branches
I see it floating,
An ivory dome
Headed to gold by the dim sun.

It hangs against a white-misted sky,
And the swollen branches
Open or cover it,
As they blow in the wet wind.

FREE FANTASIA ON JAPANESE THEMES

All the afternoon there has been a chirp-
    ing of birds,
And the sun lies, warm and still, on the
    Western sides of puffed branches.
There is no wind,
Even the little twigs at the ends of the
    branches do not move,
And the needles of the pines are solid,
Bands of inarticulate blackness,
Against the blue-white sky.
Still — but alert —
And my heart is still and alert,
Passive with sunshine
Avid of adventure.

I would experience new emotions —
Submit to strange enchantments —
Bend to influences,
Bizarre, exotic,
Fresh with burgeoning.

I would climb a Sacred Mountain,
Struggle with other pilgrims up a steep
    path through pine-trees
Above to the smooth, treeless slopes,
And prostrate myself before a painted
    shrine,
Beating my hands upon the hot earth,
Quieting my eyes with the distant sparkle
Of the faint Spring sea.

I would recline upon a balcony
In purple curving folds of silk,
And my dress should be silvered with a
    pattern
Of butterflies and swallows,
And the black band of my *obi*
Should flash with gold, circular threads,
And glitter when I moved.
I would lean against the railing
While you sang to me of wars —
Past, and to come —
Sang and played the *samisen*.
Perhaps I would beat a little hand drum
In time to your singing;
Perhaps I would only watch the play of
    light
On the hilts of your two swords.

I would sit in a covered boat,
Rocking slowly to the narrow waves of a
    river,
While above us, an arc of moving lan-
    terns,
Curved a bridge.
And beyond the bridge,
A hiss of gold
Blooming out of blackness,
Rockets exploded,
And died in a soft dripping of coloured
    stars.
We would float between the high trestles,
And drift away from the other boats,
Until the rockets flared without sound
And their falling stars hung silent in the
    sky
Like wistaria clusters above the ancient
    entrance of a temple.

I would anything
Rather than this cold paper,
With, outside, the quiet sun on the sides
    of burgeoning branches,
And inside, only my books.

AT THE BOOKSELLER'S

Hanging from the ceiling by threads
Are prints,
Hundreds of prints
Of actors and courtesans,
Cheap, everyday prints
To delight the common people.
Those which please the most are women
With long, slim fingers,
In dresses of snow-blue,

Of green the colour of the heart of a
young onion,
Of rose, of black, of dead-leaf brown.
Over the dresses runs a light tracing
Of superimposed tissues:
Orange undulations, zigzag cinnabar trel-
lises,
Patterns of purplish paulownias.
In the corner of one of the prints is
written:
"Utamaro has here painted his elegant
visage."
They cost nothing, these pictures,
They are only one of the cheap amuse-
ments of the populace,
Yet they say that the publisher: Tsoutaya,
Has made a fortune.

VIOLIN SONATA BY
VINCENT D'INDY

To Charles Martin Loeffler

A little brown room in a sea of fields,
Fields pink as rose-mallows
Under a fading rose-mallow sky.

Four candles on a tall iron candlestick,
Clustered like altar lights.
Above, the models of four brown Chinese
junks
Sailing round the brown walls,
Silent and motionless.

The quick cut of a vibrating string,
Another, and another,
Biting into the silence.
Notes pierce, sharper and sharper;
They draw up in a freshness of sound,
Higher — higher, to the whiteness of in-
tolerable beauty.
They are jagged and clear,
Like snow peaks against the sky;
They hurt like air too pure to breathe.
Is it catgut and horsehair,
Or flesh sawing against the cold blue
gates of the sky?

The brown Chinese junks sail silently
round the brown walls.

A cricket hurries across the bare floor.

The windows are black, for the sun has
set.

Only the candles,
Clustered like altar lamps upon their tall
candlestick,
Light the violinist as he plays.

WINTER'S TURNING

Snow is still on the ground,
But there is a golden brightness in the air.
Across the river,
Blue,
Blue,
Sweeping widely under the arches
Of many bridges,
Is a spire and a dome,
Clear as though ringed with ice-flakes,
Golden, and pink, and jocund.
On a near-by steeple,
A golden weather-cock flashes smartly,
His open beak "Cock-a-doodle-dooing"
Straight at the ear of Heaven.
A tall apartment house,
Crocus-coloured,
Thrusts up from the street
Like a new-sprung flower.
Another street is edged and patterned
With the bloom of bricks,
Houses and houses of rose-red bricks,
Every window a-glitter.
The city is a parterre,
Blowing and glowing,
Alight with the wind,
Washed over with gold and mercury.
Let us throw up our hats,
For we are past the age of balls
And have none handy.
Let us take hold of hands,
And race along the sidewalks,
And dodge the traffic in crowded streets.
Let us whir with the golden spoke-wheels
Of the sun.
For to-morrow Winter drops into the
waste-basket,
And the calendar calls it March.

EUCHARIS AMAZONICA

Wax-white lilies
        shaped like narcissus,
Frozen snow-rockets
        burst from a thin green stem,
Your trumpets spray antennae
        like cold, sweet notes stabbing air.
In your cups
        is the sharpness of winds,

The white husks of your blooms
    crack as ice cracks.
You strike against the darkness
    as hoar-frost patterning a window.

Wax-white lilies,
Eucharis lilies,
Mary kissed your petals,
And the chill of pure snow
Burned her lips with its six-pointed seal.

THE TWO RAINS

SPRING RAIN

Tinkling of ankle bracelets.
Dull striking
Of jade and sardonyx
From whirling ends of jointed circlets.

SUMMER RAIN

Clashing of bronze bucklers,
Screaming of horses.
Red plumes of head-trappings
Flashing above spears.

GOOD GRACIOUS!

They say there is a fairy in every streak'd
    tulip.
I have rows and rows of them beside my
    door.
Hoop-la! Come out, Brownie,
And I will give you an emerald ear-ring!
You had better come out,
For to-morrow may be stormy,
And I could never bring myself to part
    with my emerald ear-rings
Unless there was a moon.

TREES

The branches of the trees lie in layers
Above and behind each other,
And the sun strikes on the outstanding
    leaves
And turns them white,
And they dance like a spatter of pebbles
Against a green wall.

The trees make a solid path leading up
    in the air.
It looks as though I could walk upon it
If I only had courage to step out of the
    window.

DAWN ADVENTURE

I stood in my window
    looking at the double cherry:
A great height of white stillness,
Underneath a sky
    the colour of milky grey jade.
Suddenly a crow flew between me and the
    tree —
Swooping, falling, in a shadow-black
    curve —
And blotted himself out in the blurred
    branches
    of a leafless ash.
There he stayed for some time,
    and I could only distinguish him
        by his slight moving.
Then a wind caught the upper branches
    of the cherry,
And the long, white stems nodded up and
    down,
    casually, to me in the window,
Nodded — but overhead the grey jade
    clouds
        passed slowly, indifferently, to-
        ward the sea.

THE CORNER OF NIGHT
AND MORNING

Crows are cawing over pine-trees,
They are teaching their young to fly
Above the tall pyramids of double cher-
    ries.
Rose lustre over black lacquer —
The feathers of the young birds reflect
    the rose-rising sun.
Caw! Caw!
I want to go to sleep,
But perhaps it is better to stand in the
    window
And watch the crows teaching their
    young to fly
Over the pines and the pyramidal cherries,
In the rose-gold light
Of five o'clock on a May morning.

BEECH, PINE, AND SUNLIGHT

The sudden April heat
Stretches itself
Under the smooth, leafless branches
Of the beech-tree,
And lies lightly
Upon the great patches

Of purple and white crocus
With their panting, wide-open cups.

A clear wind
Slips through the naked beech boughs,
And their shadows scarcely stir.
But the pine-trees beyond sigh
When it passes over them
And presses back their needles,
And slides gently down their stems.

It is a languor of pale, south-starting sun-
light
Come upon a morning unawaked,
And holding her drowsing.

PLANNING THE GARDEN

Bring pencils, fine pointed,
For our writing must be infinitesimal;
And bring sheets of paper
To spread before us.
Now draw the plan of our garden beds,
And outline the borders and the paths
Correctly.
We will scatter little words
Upon the paper,
Like seeds about to be planted;
We will fill all the whiteness
With little words,
So that the brown earth
Shall never show between our flowers;
Instead, there will be petals and greenness
From April till November.
These narrow lines
Are rose-drifted thrift,
Edging the paths.
And here I plant nodding columbines,
With tree-tall wistarias behind them,
Each stem umbrella'd in its purple fringe.
Winged sweet-peas shall flutter next to
pansies
All down the sunny centre.
Foxglove spears,
Thrust back against the swaying lilac
leaves,
Will bloom and fade before the China
asters
Smear their crude colours over Autumn
hazes.
These double paths dividing make an
angle
For bushes,
Bleeding hearts, I think,
Their flowers jigging

Like little ladies,
Satined, hoop-skirted,
Ready for a ball.
The round black circles
Mean striped and flaunting tulips,
The clustered trumpets of yellow jon-
quils,
And the sharp blue of hyacinths and
squills.
These specks like dotted grain
Are coreopsis, bright as bandanas,
And ice-blue heliotrope with its sticky
leaves,
And mignonette
Whose sober-coloured cones of bloom
Scent quiet mornings.
And poppies! Poppies! Poppies!
The hatchings shall all mean a tide of
poppies,
Crinkled and frail and flowing in the
breeze

Wait just a moment,
Here's an empty space.
Now plant me lilies-of-the-valley —
This pear-tree over them will keep them
cool —
We'll have a lot of them
With white bells jingling.
The steps
Shall be all soft with stone-crop;
And at the top
I'll make an arch of roses,
Crimson,
Bee-enticing.

There, it is done;
Seal up the paper.
Let us go to bed and dream of flowers.

IMPRESSIONIST PICTURE
OF A GARDEN

Give me sunlight, cupped in a paint
brush,
And smear the red of peonies
Over my garden.
Splash blue upon it,
The hard blue of Canterbury bells,
Paling through larkspur
Into heliotrope,
To wash away among forget-me-nots
Dip red again to mix a purple,
And lay on pointed flares of lilacs against
bright green.

Streak yellow for nasturtiums and marsh
    marigolds
And flame it up to orange for my lilies.
Now dot it so — and so — along an edge
Of Iceland poppies.
Swirl it a bit, and faintly,
That is honeysuckle.
Now put a band of brutal, bleeding crim-
    son
And tail it off to pink, to give the roses.
And while you're loaded up with pink,
Just blotch about that bed of phlox.
Fill up with cobalt and dash in a sky
As hot and heavy as you can make it;
Then tree-green pulled up into that
Gives a fine jolt of colour.
Strain it out,
And melt your twigs into the cobalt sky.
Toss on some Chinese white to flash the
    clouds,
And trust the sunlight you've got in your
    paint.
There is the picture.

A BATHER

After a Picture by Andreas Zorn

Thick dappled by circles of sunshine and
    fluttering shade,
Your bright, naked body advances, blown
    over by leaves,
Half-quenched in their various green, just
    a point of you showing,
A knee or a thigh, sudden glimpsed, then
    at once blotted into
The filmy and flickering forest, to start
    out again
Triumphant in smooth, supple roundness,
    edged sharp as white ivory,
Cool, perfect, with rose rarely tinting
    your lips and your breasts,
Swelling out from the green in the opu-
    lent curves of ripe fruit,
And hidden, like fruit, by the swift inter-
    mittence of leaves.
So, clinging to branches and moss, you
    advance on the ledges
Of rock which hang over the stream, with
    the wood-smells about you,
The pungence of strawberry plants, and
    of gum-oozing spruces,
While below runs the water, impatient,
    impatient — to take you,
To splash you, to run down your sides, to
    sing you of deepness,

Of pools brown and golden, with brown
    and-gold flags on their borders,
Of blue, lingering skies floating solemnly
    over your beauty,
Of undulant waters a-sway in the effort
    to hold you,
To keep you submerged and quiescent
    while over you glories
The Summer.
        Oread, Dryad, or Naiad, or just
Woman, clad only in youth and in gal-
    lant perfection,
Standing up in a great burst of sunshine,
    you dazzle my eyes
Like a snow-star, a moon, your effulgence
    burns up in a halo,
For you are the chalice which holds all
    the races of men.

You slip into the pool and the water folds
    over your shoulder,
And over the tree-tops the clouds slowly
    follow your swimming,
And the scent of the woods is sweet on
    this hot Summer morning.

DOG–DAYS

A ladder sticking up at the open window,
The top of an old ladder;
And all of Summer is there.

Great waves and tufts of wistaria surge
    across the window,
And a thin, belated blossom
Jerks up and down in the sunlight;
Purple translucence against the blue sky.
"Tie back this branch," I say,
But my hands are sticky with leaves,
And my nostrils widen to the smell of
    crushed green.
The ladder moves uneasily at the open
    window,
And I call to the man beneath,
"Tie back that branch."

There is a ladder leaning against the win-
    dow-sill,
And a mutter of thunder in the air.

AUGUST

Late Afternoon

Smoke-colour, rose, saffron,
With a hard edge chipping the blue sky

A great cloud hung over the village,
And the white-painted meeting-house,
And the steeple with the gilded weather-
cock
Heading and flashing to the wind.

HILLY COUNTRY

Jangle of cow-bells through pine-trees.
Grasshoppers leaping up out of the grass.
The mountain is bloomed like a grape
(Silver, hazing over purple),
It blocks into the sky like a shadow.
The South wind blows intermittently,
And the clanking of the cow-bells comes
up the hill in gusts.

TREES IN WINTER

PINE-TREES:
      Black clouds slowly swaying
      Over a white earth.

HEMLOCKS:
      Coned green shadows
      Through a falling veil.

ELM-TREES:
      Stiff black threads
      Lacing over silver.

CEDARS:
      Layered undulations
      Roofing naked ground.

ALMONDS:
      Flaring needles
      Stabbing at a grey sky.

WEEPING CHERRIES:
      Tossing smoke
      Swept down by wind.

OAKS:
      Twisted beams
      Cased in alabaster.

SEA COAL

Swift like the tongues of lilies,
Striped Amaryllis
Thrusting out of cloven basalt.
Amber and chalcedony,
And the snapping of sand

On rocks
Glazed by the wind.

DOLPHINS IN BLUE WATER

Hey! Crackerjack — jump!
Blue water,
Pink water,
Swirl, flick, flitter;
Snout into a wave-trough,
Plunge, curl.
Bow over,
Under,
Razor-cut and tumble.
Roll, turn —
Straight — and shoot at the sky,
All rose-flame drippings.
Down ring,
Drop,
Nose under,
Hoop,
Tail,
Dive,
And gone;
With smooth over-swirlings of blue water,
Oil-smooth cobalt,
Slipping, liquid lapis lazuli,
Emerald shadings,
Tintings of pink and ochre.
Prismatic slidings
Underneath a windy sky.

MOTOR LIGHTS ON A HILL ROAD

Yellow-green, yellow-green, yellow-green
      and silver,
Rimple of leaves,
Blowing,
Passing,
Flowing overhead
Arched leaves,
Silver of twisted leaves;
Fan-like yellow glare
On tree-trunks.
Fluted side wake
Breaking from one polished stem to an-
      other.
Swift drop on a disappearing road,
Jolt — a wooden bridge,
And a flat sky opens in front.
Above —
The wide sky careers furiously past a still
      moon.
Suddenly — Slap! — green, yellow,

Leaves and no moon.
Ribbed leaves,
Chamfered light patterns
Playing on a pleaching of leaves.
Wind,
Strong, rushing,
Continuous, like the leaves.
Wind sliding beside us,
Meeting us,
Pointing against us through a yellow-
green tunnel.
Dot . . . Dot . . . Dot . . .
Little square lights of windows,
Black walls stamping into silver mist,
Shingle roofs aflame like mica.
Elliptical cutting curve
Round a piazza where rocking-chairs
creak emptily.
Square white fences
Chequer-boarding backwards.
Plunge at a black hill,
Flash into water-waving fluctuations.
Leaves gush out of the darkness

And boil past in yellow-green curds:
We slip between them with the smooth-
ness of oil.
Hooped yellow light spars
Banding green
Glide toward us,
Impinge upon our progress,
Open and let us through.
Liquid leaves lap the wheels,
Toss,
Splash,
Disappear.
Green and yellow water-slopes hang over
us,
Close behind us,
Push us forward.
We are the centre of a green and yellow
bubble,
Changing,
Expanding,
Skimming over the face of the world —
Green and yellow, occasionally tinged
with silver.

As Toward One's Self

IN A TIME OF DEARTH

Before me,
On either side of me,
I see sand.
If I turn the corner of my house
I see sand.
Long — brown —
Lines and levels of flat
Sand.

If I could see a caravan
Heave over the edge of it:
The camels wobbling and swaying,
Stepping like ostriches,
With rocking palanquins
Whose curtains conceal
Languors and faintnesses,
Muslins tossed aside,
And a disorder of cushions.
The swinging curtains would pique and
solace me.
But I see only sand,
Long, brown sand,
Sand.

If I could see a herd of Arab horses
Galloping,

Their manes and tails pulled straight
By the speed of their going;
Their bodies sleek and round
Like bellying sails.
They would beat the sand with their fore-
feet,
And scatter it with their hind-feet,
So that it whirled in a cloud of orange,
And the sun through it
Was clip-edged, without rays — and dun.
But I only see sand,
Long, brown, hot sand,
Sand.

If I could see a mirage
Blue-white at the horizon,
With palm-trees about it;
Tall, windless palm-trees, grouped about
a glitter.
If I could strain towards it,
And think of the water creeping round
my ankles,
Tickling under my knees,
Leeching up my sides,
Spreading over my back!
But I only feel the grinding beneath my
feet.
And I only see sand,

Long, dry sand,
Scorching sand,
Sand.

If a sand-storm would come
And spit against my windows,
Snapping upon them, and ringing their
    vibrations;
Swirling over the roof,
Seeping under the door-jamb,
Suffocating me and making me struggle
    for air.
But I only see sand,
Sand lying dead in the sun,
Lines and lines of sand,
Sand.

I will paste newspapers over the windows
    to shut out the sand,
I will fit them into one another, and
    fasten the corners.
Then I will strike matches
And read of politics, and murders, and
    festivals,
Three years old.
But I shall not see the sand any more
And I can read
While my matches last.

ALIENS

The chatter of little people
Breaks on my purpose
Like the water-drops which slowly wear
    the rocks to powder.
And while I laugh
My spirit crumbles at their teasing touch.

MIDDLE AGE

Like black ice
Scrolled over with unintelligible patterns
                    by an ignorant skater
Is the dulled surface of my heart.

LA VIE DE BOHEME

Alone, I whet my soul against the keen
Unwrinkled sky, with its long stretching
    blue.
I polish it with sunlight and pale dew,
And damascene it with young blowing
    leaves.
Into the handle of my life I set
Sprays of mignonette

And periwinkle,
Twisted into sheaves.
The colours laugh and twinkle.
Twined bands of roadways, liquid in the
    sheen
Of street lamps and the ruby shine of
    cabs,
Glisten for my delight all down its length;
And there are sudden sparks
Of morning ripplings over tree-fluttered
    pools.
My soul is fretted full of gleams and
    darks,
Pulsing and still.
Smooth-edged, untarnished, girded in my
    soul
I walk the world.

But in its narrow alleys,
The low-hung, dust-thick valleys
Where the mob shuffles its empty tread,
My soul is blunted against dullard wits,
Smeared with sick juices,
Nicked impotent for other than low uses.
Its arabesques and sparkling subtleties
Crusted to grey, and all its changing sur-
    faces
Spread with unpalpitant monotonies.

I re-create myself upon the polished sky:
A honing-strop above converging roofs.
The patterns show again, like buried
    proofs
Of old, lost empires bursting on the eye
In hieroglyphed and graven splendour.
The whirling winds brush past my head,
And prodigal once more, a reckless
    spender
Of disregarded beauty, a defender
Of undesired faiths,
I walk the world.

FLAME APPLES

Little hot apples of fire,
Burst out of the flaming stem
Of my heart,
I do not understand how you quickened
    and grew,
And you amaze me
While I gather you.

I lay you, one by one,
Upon a table.

And now you seem beautiful and strange
to me,
And I stand before you,
Wondering.

THE TRAVELLING BEAR

Grass-blades push up between the cob-
blestones
And catch the sun on their flat sides
Shooting it back,
Gold and emerald,
Into the eyes of passers-by.

And over the cobblestones,
Square-footed and heavy,
Dances the trained bear.
The cobbles cut his feet,
And he has a ring in his nose
Which hurts him;
But still he dances,
For the keeper pricks him with a sharp
stick,
Under his fur.

Now the crowd gapes and chuckles,
And boys and young women shuffle their
feet in time to the dancing bear.
They see him wobbling
Against a dust of emerald and gold,
And they are greatly delighted.

The legs of the bear shake with fatigue,
And his back aches,
And the shining grass-blades dazzle and
confuse him.
But still he dances,
Because of the little, pointed stick.

MERCHANDISE

I made a song one morning,
Sitting in the shade under the hornbeam
hedge.
I played it on my pipe,
And the clear notes delighted me,
And the little hedge-sparrows and the
chipmunks
Also seemed pleased.
So I was very proud
That I had made so good a song.

Would you like to hear my song?
I will play it to you
As I did that evening to my Beloved,

Standing on the moon-bright cobbles
Underneath her window.
But you are not my Beloved,
You must give me a silver shilling,
Round and glittering like the moon.
Copper I will not take,
How should copper pay for a song
All made out of nothing,
And so beautiful!

THE POEM

It is only a little twig
With a green bud at the end;
But if you plant it,
And water it,
And set it where the sun will be above it,
It will grow into a tall bush
With many flowers,
And leaves which thrust hither and
thither
Sparkling.
From its roots will come freshness,
And beneath it the grass-blades
Will bend and recover themselves,
And clash one upon another
In the blowing wind.

But if you take my twig
And throw it into a closet
With mousetraps and blunted tools,
It will shrivel and waste.
And, some day,
When you open the door,
You will think it an old twisted nail,
And sweep it into the dust bin
With other rubbish.

THE PEDDLER OF FLOWERS

I came from the country
With flowers,
Larkspur and roses,
Fretted lilies
In their leaves,
And long, cool lavender.

I carried them
From house to house,
And cried them
Down hot streets.
The sun fell
Upon my flowers,
And the dust of the streets
Blew over my basket.

That night
I slept upon the open seats
Of a circus,
Where all day long
People had watched
The antics
Of a painted clown.

BALLS

Throw the blue ball above the little twigs
of the tree-tops,
And cast the yellow ball straight at the
buzzing stars.

All our life is a flinging of coloured balls
to impossible distances.
And in the end what have we?
A tired arm — a tip-tilted nose.

Ah! Well! Give me the purple one.
Wouldn't it be a fine thing if I could
make it stick
On top of the Methodist steeple?

THE FANATIC

Like Don Quixote, I tilted at a windmill.
On my good, grey horse I spurred at it,
Galloping heavily over the plain.
My lance pierced the framework of a sail
and stuck there,
And the impact sent me sprawling on the
ground.

My horse wandered away, cropping,
But I started up and fell upon the wind-
mill,
With my dagger unsheathed.
Valiantly I stabbed a dipping sail,
But it rose before I could withdraw the
weapon,
And the blade went up with it, gleaming
— flickering.

Then I drew a pistol,
For I am an up-to-date knight
And my armory unrivalled.
I aimed above me,
At the sky between two sails.
Ping! went the bullet,
And a round, blue eye peeked at me
through the wheeling sail.
I fired again —
Two eyes winked at me, jeering.

Then I ran at the windmill with my fists,
But it struck me down and left me.
All night I lay there,
And the great sails turned about and
about,
And brushed me with their shadows,
For there was a moon.

FIREWORKS

You hate me and I hate you,
And we are so polite, we two!

But whenever I see you, I burst apart
And scatter the sky with my blazing
heart.
It spits and sparkles in stars and balls,
Buds into roses — and flares, and falls.

Scarlet buttons, and pale green disks,
Silver spirals and asterisks,
Shoot and tremble in a mist
Peppered with mauve and amethyst.

I shine in the windows and light up the
trees,
And all because I hate you, if you please.

And when you meet me, you rend
asunder
And go up in a flaming wonder
Of saffron cubes, and crimson moons,
And wheels all amaranths and maroons.

Golden lozenges and spades,
Arrows of malachites and jades,
Patens of copper, azure sheaves.
As you mount, you flash in the glossy
leaves.

Such fireworks as we make, we two!
Because you hate me and I hate you.

TRADES

I want to be a carpenter,
To work all day long in clean wood,
Shaving it into little thin slivers
Which screw up into curls behind my
plane;
Pounding square, black nails into white
boards,
With the claws of my hammer glistening
Like the tongue of a snake.
I want to shingle a house,

Sitting on the ridge-pole in a bright
 breeze.
I want to put the shingles on neatly,
Taking great care that each is directly be-
 tween two others.
I want my hands to have the tang of
 wood:
Spruce, Cedar, Cypress.
I want to draw a line on a board with a
 flat pencil,
And then saw along that line,
With the sweet-smelling sawdust piling
 up in a yellow heap at my feet.

That is the life!
Heigh-ho!
It is much easier than to write this poem.

GENERATIONS

You are like the stem
Of a young beech-tree,
Straight and swaying,
Breaking out in golden leaves.
Your walk is like the blowing of a beech-
 tree
On a hill.
Your voice is like leaves
Softly struck upon by a South wind.
Your shadow is no shadow, but a scat-
 tered sunshine;
And at night you pull the sky down to
 you
And hood yourself in stars.

But I am like a great oak under a cloudy
 sky,
Watching a stripling beech grow up at
 my feet.

ENTENTE CORDIALE

The young gentleman from the foreign
 nation
Sat on the sofa and smiled.
He stayed for two hours and I talked to
 him.
He answered agreeably,
He was very precise, very graceful, very
 enthusiastic.

I thought:
Is it possible that there are no nations,
 only individuals?
That it is the few who give gold and
 flowers,
While the many have only copper
So worn that even the stamp is obliter-
 ated?
I talked to the young gentleman from the
 foreign nation,
And the faint smell of copper assailed my
 nostrils:
Copper,
Twisted copper coins dropped by old
 women
Into the alms-boxes of venerable churches.

CASTLES IN SPAIN

I build my poems with little strokes of ink
Drawn shining down white paper, line
 and line,
And there is nothing here which men
 call fine,
Nothing but hieroglyphs to make them
 think.
I have no broad and blowing plain to link
And loop with aqueducts, no golden
 mine
To crest my pillars, no bright twisted
 vine
Which I can train about a fountain's
 brink.
Those others laced their poems from sea
 to sea
And floated navies over fields of grain,
 They fretted their full fancies in
 strong stone
And struck them on the sky. And yet
 I gain;
For bombs and bullets cannot menace
 me,
 Who have no substance to be over-
 thrown.
Cathedrals crash to rubbish, but my
 towers,
 Carved in the whirling and enduring
 brain,
Fade, and persist, and rise again, like
 flowers.

Plummets to Circumstance

ELY CATHEDRAL

Anaemic women, stupidly dressed and
    shod
In squeaky shoes, thump down the nave
    to laud an expurgated God.
Bunches of lights reflect upon the pave-
    ment where
The twenty benches stop, and through
    the close, smelled-over air
Gaunt arches push up their whited
    stones,
And cover the sparse worshippers with
    dead men's bones.
Behind his shambling choristers, with
    flattened feet
And red-flapped hood, the Bishop walks,
    complete
In old, frayed ceremonial. The organ
    wheezes
A mouldy psalm-tune, and a verger
    sneezes.
But the great Cathedral spears into the
    sky
Shouting for joy.

What is the red-flapped Bishop
    praying for, by the by?

WILLIAM BLAKE

He said he saw the spangled wings of
    angels
In a tree at Peckham Rye,
And Elija walking in the haying-fields;
So they beat him for his lies,
And 'prenticed him to an engraver.
Now his books sell for broad, round,
    golden guineas.
That's a bouncing turn of Fortune!
But we have the guineas,
Since our fathers were thrifty men
And knew the value of gold.

AN INCIDENT

William Blake and Catherine Bourchier
were married in the newly rebuilt
Church of Battersea where the windows were beautifully painted to imitate real stained glass.

Pigments or crystal, what did it matter —
    when Jehovah sat on a cloud of curled
    fire over the door-way,
And angels with silver trumpets played
    Hosannas under the wooden groins of
    the peaked roof!
William and Catherine Blake left the
    painted windows behind in the newly
    rebuilt Church of Battersea,
But God and the angels went out with
    them;
And the angels played on their trumpets
    under the plaster ceiling of their
    lodging,
Morning, and evening, and morning,
    forty-five round years.

Has the paint faded in the windows of
    Battersea Church, I wonder?

PEACH–COLOUR TO A
SOAP–BUBBLE

A man made a symphony
Out of the chords of his soul.
The notes ran upon the air like flights of
    chickadees,
They gathered together and hung
As bees above a syringa bush,
They crowded and clicked upon one an-
    other
In a flurry of progression,
And crashed in the simultaneous magnifi-
    cence
Of a grand finale.
All this he heard,
But the neighbors heard only the croak
Of a wheezy, second-hand flageolet.

Forced to seek another lodging
He took refuge under the arch of a
    bridge,
For the river below him might be con-
    venient
Some day.

PYROTECHNICS

I

Our meeting was like the upward swish of
    a rocket
In the blue night.

I do not know when it burst;
But now I stand gaping,
In a glory of falling stars.

II

Hola! Hola! shouts the crowd, as the
catherine-wheels sputter and turn.
Hola! They cheer the flower-pots and set
pieces.
And nobody heeds the cries of a young
man in shirt-sleeves,
Who has burnt his fingers setting them
off.

III

A King and Queen, and a couple of Gen-
erals,
Flame in coloured lights,
Putting out the stars,
And making a great glare over the people
wandering among the booths.
They are very beautiful and impressive,
And all the people say "Ah!"
By and by they begin to go out,
Little by little.
The King's crown goes first,
Then his eyes,
Then his nose and chin.
The Queen goes out from the bottom up,
Until only the topmost jewel of her
tiara is left.
Then that too goes;
And there is nothing but a frame of
twisted wires,
With the stars twinkling through it.

THE BOOKSHOP

Pierrot has grown old.
He wore spectacles
And kept a shop.
Opium and hellebore
He sold
Between the covers of books,
And perfumes distilled from the veins of
old ivory,
And poisons drawn from lotus seeds one
hundred years withered
And thinned to the translucence of
alabaster.
He sang a pale song of repeated cadenzas
In a voice cold as flutes
And shrill as desiccated violins.

I stood before the shop,
Fingering the comfortable vellum of an
ancient volume,
Turning over its leaves,
And the dead moon looked over my
shoulder
And fell with a green smoothness upon
the page.
I read:
"I am the Lord thy God, thou shalt have
none other gods but me."

Through the door came a chuckle of
laughter
Like the tapping of unstrung kettledrums,
For Pierrot had ceased singing for a mo-
ment
To watch me reading.

GARGOYLES

A COMEDY OF OPPOSITIONS

Thimble-rig on a village green,
Snake-charmers under a blue tent
Winding drugged sausage-bellies through
thin arms.
Hiss
Of a yellow and magenta shawl
On a platform
Above trombones.

Tree lights
Drip cockatoos of colour
On broadest shoulders,
Dead eyes swim to a silver fish.
Gluttonous hands tear at apron strings,
Reach at the red side of an apple,
Slide under ice-floes,
And waltz clear through to the tropics
To sit among cocoanuts
And caress bulbous negresses with loquats
in their hair.

A violin scorching on an F-sharp exit.
Stamp.
Stop.
Hayricks, and panting,
Noon roses guessed under calico —
A budded thorn-bush swinging
Against a smoke-dawn.
Hot pressing on sweet straw,
Laughs like whales floundering across air
circles,
Wallows of smoothness,

Loose muscles dissolved upon lip-brush-
ings,
Languid fluctuations,
Sleep oozing over wet flesh,
Cooling under the broad end of an angled
shadow.
Absurd side-wiggle of geese before ele-
phants;
A gold leopard snarls at a white-nosed
donkey;
Panther-purrs rouse childhood to an edge
of contortion;
Trumpets brawl beneath an oscillation of
green balloons.

Why blow apple-blossoms into wind-
dust?
Why drop a butterfly down the throat of
a pig?
Timid shrinkings of a scarlet-runner bean
From pumpkin roughnesses.
Preposterous clamour of a cock for a
tulip.
If your flesh is cold
Warm it on tea-pots
And let them be of Dresden china
With a coreopsis snarled in the handle.
Horse-bargainings do not become temples,
And sarabands are not danced on tea-
trays of German silver.
Thin drums flatten the uprightness of
distance,
A fading of drums shows lilac on the
fallen beech leaves.
Emptiness of drums.
Nothing.

Burr of a rising moon.

TO WINKY

Cat,
Cat,
What are you?
Son, through a thousand generations, of
the black leopards
Padding among the sprigs of young
bamboo;
Descendant of many removals from the
white panthers
Who crouch by night under the loquat-
trees?
You crouch under the orange begonias,
And your eyes are green
With the violence of murder,

Or half-closed and stealthy
Like your sheathed claws.
Slowly, slowly,
You rise and stretch
In a glossiness of beautiful curves,
Of muscles fluctuating under black,
glazed hair.

Cat,
You are a strange creature.
You sit on your haunches
And yawn,
But when you leap
I can almost hear the whine
Of a released string,
And I look to see its flaccid shaking
In the place whence you sprang.

You carry your tail as a banner,
Slowly it passes my chair,
But when I look for you, you are on the
table
Moving easily among the most delicate
porcelains.
Your food is a matter of importance
And you are insistent on having
Your wants attended to,
And yet you will eat a bird and its
feathers
Apparently without injury.

In the night, I hear you crying,
But if I try to find you
There are only the shadows of rhododen-
dron leaves
Brushing the ground.
When you come in out of the rain,
All wet and with your tail full of burrs,
You fawn upon me in coils and subtleties;
But once you are dry
You leave me with a gesture of incon-
ceivable impudence,
Conveyed by the vanishing quirk of your
tail
As you slide through the open door.

You walk as a king scorning his subjects;
You flirt with me as a concubine in robes
of silk.
Cat,
I am afraid of your poisonous beauty,
I have seen you torturing a mouse.
Yet when you lie purring in my lap
I forget everything but how soft you are,

And it is only when I feel your claws
  open upon my hand
That I remember —
Remember a puma lying out on a branch
  above my head
Years ago.

Shall I choke you, Cat,
Or kiss you?
Really I do not know.

CHOPIN

The cat and I
Together in the sultry night
Waited.
He greatly desired a mouse;
I, an idea.
Neither ambition was gratified.
So we watched
In a stiff and painful expectation.
Little breezes pattered among the trees,
And thin stars ticked at us
Faintly,
Exhausted pulses
Squeezing through mist.

Those others, I said!
And my mind rang hollow as I tapped it.
Winky, I said,
Do all other cats catch their mice?

  .   .   .   .

It was low and long,
Ivory white, with doors and windows blotting blue upon it.
Wind choked in pomegranate-trees,
Rain rattled on lead roofs,
And stuttered along twisted conduit-pipes.
An eagle screamed out of the heavy sky,
And some one in the house screamed
"Ah, I knew that you were dead!"

So that was it:
Funeral chants,
And the icy cowls of buried monks;
Organs on iron midnights,
And long wax winding-sheets
Guttered from altar candles.
First this,
Then spitting blood.
Music quenched in blood,
Flights of arpeggios confused by blood,
Flute-showers of notes stung and arrested on a sharp chord,

Tangled in a web of blood.
"I cannot send you the manuscripts, as
  they are not yet finished.
I have been ill as a dog.
My illness has had a pernicious effect on
  the Preludes
Which you will receive God knows
  when."

  .   .   .   .   .

He bore it.
Therefore, Winky, drink some milk
And leave the mouse until to-morrow.
There are no blood-coloured pomegranate
  flowers
Hurling their petals in at the open window,
But you can sit in my lap
And blink at a bunch of cinnamon-eyed
  coreopsis
While I pull your ears
In the manner which you find so infinitely
  agreeable.

APPULDURCOMBE PARK

I am a woman, sick for passion,
Sitting under the golden beech-trees.
I am a woman, sick for passion,
Crumbling the beech leaves to powder in
  my fingers.
The servants say: "Yes, my Lady," and
  "No, my Lady."
And all day long my husband calls me
From his invalid chair:
"Mary, Mary, where are you, Mary? I
  want you."
Why does he want me?
When I come, he only pats my hand
And asks me to settle his cushions.
Poor little beech leaves,
Slowly falling,
Crumbling,
In the great park.
But there are many golden beech leaves
And I am alone.

I am a woman, sick for passion,
Walking between rows of painted tulips.
Parrot flowers, toucan-feathered flowers,
How bright you are!
You hurt me with your colours,
Your reds and yellows lance at me like
  flames.
Oh, I am sick — sick —

And your darting loveliness hurts my
heart.
You burn me with your parrot-tongues.
Flame!
Flame!
My husband taps on the window with his
stick:
"Mary, come in. I want you. You will
take cold."

I am a woman, sick for passion,
Gazing at a white moon hanging over tall
lilies.
The lilies sway and darken,
And a wind ruffles my hair.
There is a scrape of gravel behind me,
A red coat crashes scarlet against the
lilies.
"Cousin-Captain!
I thought you were playing piquet with
Sir Kenelm."
"Piquet, Dear Heart! And such a moon!"
Your red coat chokes me, Cousin-Cap-
tain.
Blood-colour, your coat:
I am sick — sick — for your heart.
Keep away from me, Cousin-Captain.
Your scarlet coat dazzles and confuses
me.
O heart of red blood, what shall I do!
Even the lilies blow for the bee.
Does your heart beat so loud, Beloved?
No, it is the tower-clock chiming eleven.
I must go in and give my husband his
posset.
I hear him calling:
"Mary, where are you? I want you."

I am a woman, sick for passion,
Waiting in the long, black room for the
funeral procession to pass.
I sent a messenger to town last night.
When will you come?
Under my black dress a rose is blooming.
A rose? — a heart? — it rustles for you
with open petals.
Come quickly, Dear,
For the corridors are full of noises.
In this fading light I hear whispers,
And the steady, stealthy purr of the wind.
What keeps you, Cousin-Captain? . . .
What was that?
"Mary, I want you."
Nonsense, he is dead,
Buried by now.

Oh, I am sick of these long, cold cor-
ridors!
Sick — for what?
Why do you not come?

I am a woman, sick — sick —
Sick of the touch of cold paper,
Poisoned with the bitterness of ink.
Snowflakes hiss, and scratch the windows.
"Mary, where are you?"
That voice is like water in my ears;
I cannot empty them.
He wanted me, my husband,
But these stone parlours do not want me.
You do not want me either, Cousin-Cap-
tain.
Your coat lied,
Only your white sword spoke the truth.
"Mary! Mary!"
Will nothing stop the white snow
Sifting,
Sifting?
Will nothing stop that voice,
Drifting through the wide, dark halls?
The tower-clock strikes eleven dully,
stifled with snow.
Softly over the still snow,
Softly over the lonely park,
Softly . . .
Yes, I have only my slippers, but I shall
not take cold.
A little dish of posset.
Do the dead eat?
I have done it so long,
So strangely long.

THE BROKEN FOUNTAIN

Oblong, its jutted ends rounding into
circles,
The old sunken basin lies with its flat,
marble lip
An inch below the terrace tiles.
Over the stagnant water
Slide reflections:
The blue-green of coned yews;
The purple and red of trailing fuchsias
Dripping out of marble urns;
Bright squares of sky
Ribbed by the wake of a swimming
beetle.
Through the blue-bronze water
Wavers the pale uncertainty of a shadow.
An arm flashes through the reflections,
A breast is outlined with leaves.

Outstretched in the quiet water
The statue of a Goddess slumbers.
But when Autumn comes
The beech leaves cover her with a
golden counter-pane.

THE DUSTY HOUR-GLASS

It had been a trim garden,
With parterres of fringed pinks and
gillyflowers,
    and smooth-raked walks.
Silks and satins had brushed the box
edges
    of its alleys.
The curved stone lips of its fishponds
    had held the rippled reflections of
    tricorns and powdered periwigs.
The branches of its trees had glittered
with lanterns,
    and swayed to the music of flutes
    and violins.

Now, the fishponds are green with scum;
The paths and flower-beds
    are run together and overgrown.
Only at one end is an octagonal Summer-
house
    not yet in ruins.
Through the lozenged panes of its win-
dows,
    you can see the interior:
A dusty bench; a fireplace
    with a lacing of letters carved in
    the stone above it;
A broken ball of worsted
    rolled away into a corner.

Dolci, dolci, i giorni passati!

THE FLUTE

"Stop! What are you doing?"
"Playing on an old flute."
"That's Heine's flute — you mustn't
touch it."
"Why not, if I can make it sound."
"I don't know why not, but you
mustn't."
"I don't believe I can — much. It's
full of dust. Still, listen":

The rose moon whitens the lifting
leaves.
Heigh-o! The nightingale sings!

Through boughs and branches the
moon-thread weaves.
Ancient as time are these midnight
things.

The nightingale's notes over-bubble the
night.
Heigh-o! Yet the night is so big!
He stands on his nest in a wafer of
light,
And the nest was once a philosopher's
wig.

Moon-sharp needles, and dew on the
grass.
Heigh-o! It flickers, the breeze!
Kings, philosophers, periwigs pass;
Nightingale eggs hatch under the trees.

Wigs, and pigs, and kings, and courts.
Heigh-o! Rain on the flower!
The old moon thinks her white, bright
thoughts,
And trundles away before the shower.

"Well, you got it to play."
"Yes, a little. And it has lovely silver
mountings."

FLOTSAM

She sat in a Chinese wicker chair
Wide at the top like a spread peacock's
tail,
And toyed with a young man's heart
which she held lightly in her fingers.
She tapped it gently,
Held it up to the sun and looked through
it,
Strung it on a chain of seed-pearls and
fastened it about her neck,
Tossed it into the air and caught it,
Deftly, as though it were a ball.
Before her on the grass sat the young
man.
Sometimes he felt an ache where his
heart had been.
But he brushed it aside.
He was intent on gazing, and had no
time for anything else.
Presently she grew tired and handed him
back his heart,
But he only laid it on the ground beside
him
And went on gazing.

When the maidservant came to tidy up,
She found the heart on the grass.
"What a pretty thing," said the maid-
servant,
"It is red as a ruby!"
So she picked it up,
And carried it into the house,
And ran a ribbon through it,
And hung it on the looking-glass in her
bedroom.
There it hung for many days,
Banging back and forth as the wind blew
it.

LITTLE IVORY FIGURES PULLED WITH STRING

Is it the tinkling of mandolins which disturbs you?
Or the dropping of bitter-orange petals
among the coffee-cups?
Or the slow creeping of the moonlight
between the olive-trees?

> Drop! drop! the rain
> Upon the thin plates of my
> heart.

String your blood to chord with this
music,
Stir your heels upon the cobbles to the
rhythm of a dance-tune.
They have slim thighs and arms of silver;
The moon washes away their garments;
They make a pattern of fleeing feet in the
branch shadows,
And the green grapes knotted about them
Burst as they press against one another.

> The rain knocks upon the
> plates of my heart,
> They are crumpled with its
> beating.

Would you drink only from your brains,
Old Man?
See, the moonlight has reached your
knees,
It falls upon your head in an accolade of
silver.
Rise up on the music,
Fling against the moon-drifts in a whorl
of young light bodies:
Leaping grape-clusters,
Vine leaves tearing from a grey wall.

You shall run, laughing, in a braid of
women,
And weave flowers with the frosty spines
of thorns.
Why do you gaze into your glass,
And jar the spoons with your finger-
tapping?

> The rain is rigid on the plates
> of my heart.
> The murmur of it is loud —
> loud.

ON THE MANTELPIECE

A thousand years went to her making,
A thousand years of experiments in
pastes and glazes.
But now she stands
In all the glory of the finest porcelain
and the most delicate paint,
A Dresden china shepherdess,
Flaunted before a tall mirror
On a high mantelpiece.

"Beautiful shepherdess,
I love the little pink rosettes on your
shoes,
The angle of your hat sets my heart a-
singing.
Drop me the purple rose you carry in your
hand
That I may cherish it,
And that, at my death,
Which I feel is not far off,
It may lie upon my bier."
So the shepherdess threw the purple rose
over the mantelpiece,
But it splintered in fragments on the
hearth.

Then from below there came a sound of
weeping,
And the shepherdess beat her hands
And cried:
"My purple rose is broken,
It was the flower of my heart."
And she jumped off the mantelpiece
And was instantly shattered into seven
hundred and twenty pieces.
But the little brown cricket who sang so
sweetly
Scuttled away into a crevice of the mar-
ble
And went on warming his toes and chirp-
ing.

As Toward War

MISERICORDIA

He earned his bread by making wooden
    soldiers,
With beautiful golden instruments,
Riding dapple-grey horses.
But when he heard the fanfare of trum-
    pets
And the long rattle of drums
As the army marched out of the city,
He took all his soldiers
And burned them in the grate;
And that night he fashioned a ballet-
    dancer
Out of tinted tissue paper,
And the next day he started to carve a
    Pietà
On the steel hilt
Of a cavalry sword.

DREAMS IN WAR TIME

I

I wandered through a house of many
    rooms.
It grew darker and darker,
Until, at last, I could only find my
    way
By passing my fingers along the wall.
Suddenly my hand shot through an open
    window,
And the thorn of a rose I could not see
Pricked it so sharply
That I cried aloud.

II

I dug a grave under an oak-tree.
With infinite care, I stamped my spade
Into the heavy grass.
The sod sucked it,
And I drew it out with effort,
Watching the steel run liquid in the
    moonlight
As it came clear.
I stooped, and dug, and never turned,
For behind me,
On the dried leaves,
My own face lay like a white pebble,
Waiting.

III

I gambled with a silver money.
The dried seed-vessels of "honesty"
Were stacked in front of me.
Dry, white years slipping through my
    fingers
One by one.
One by one, gathered by the Croupier.
"Faites vos jeux, Messieurs."
I staked on the red,
And the black won.
Dry years,
Dead years;
But I had a system,
I always staked on the red.

IV

I painted the leaves of bushes red
And shouted: "Fire! Fire!"
But the neighbors only laughed.
"We cannot warm our hands at them,"
    they said.
Then they cut down my bushes,
And made a bonfire,
And danced about it.
But I covered my face and wept,
For ashes are not beautiful
Even in the dawn.

V

I followed a procession of singing girls
Who danced to the glitter of tambourines
Where the street turned at a lighted
    corner,
I caught the purple dress of one of the
    dancers,
But, as I grasped, it tore,
And the purple dye ran from it
Like blood
Upon the ground.

VI

I wished to post a letter,
But although I paid much,
Still the letter was overweight.
"What is in this package?" said the
    clerk,
"It is very heavy."

"Yes," I said,
"And yet it is only dried fruit."

VII

I had made a kite,
On it I had pasted golden stars
And white torches,
And the tail was spotted scarlet like a
tiger-lily,
And very long.
I flew my kite,
And my soul was contented
Watching it flash against the concave of
the sky.
My friends pointed at the clouds;
They begged me to take in my kite.
But I was happy
Seeing the mirror shock of it
Against the black clouds.
Then the lightening came
And struck the kite.
It puffed — blazed — fell.
But still I walked on,
In the drowning rain,
Slowly winding up the string.

SPECTACLES

He was a landscape architect.

All day he planned Dutch gardens: rec-
tangular, squared with tulips; Italian
gardens: dark with myrtle, thick with
running water; English gardens: prim,
box-edged, espaliered fruit trees flickering on walls, borders of snap-dragons,
pansies, marjoram, rue.

On Saturday afternoons, he did not walk
into the country. He paid a quarter
and went to a cinema show, and gazed
— gazed — at marching soldiers, at guns
firing and recoiling, at waste grounds
strewn with mutilated dead. When he
took off his glasses, there was moisture
upon them, and his eyes hurt. He
could not see to use a periscope, they
said, yet he could draw gardens.

His firm dismissed him for designing a
military garden: forts, and redoubts,
and salients, in hemlock and yew, and
a puzzle of ditches, damp, deep, floored
with forget-me-nots. It was a wonderful thing, but quite mad, of course.

When they took his body from the river,
the eyes were wide open, and the lids
were so stiffened that they buried him
without closing them.

IN THE STADIUM

MARSHAL JOFFRE REVIEWING THE
HARVARD REGIMENT, MAY 12, 1917

A little old man
Huddled up in a corner of a carriage,
Rapidly driven in front of throngs of
people
With his hand held to a perpetual salute.
The people cheer,
But he has heard so much cheering.
On his breast is a row of decorations.
He feels his body recoil before attacks of
pain.

They are all like this:
Napoleon,
Hannibal,
Great Caesar even,
But that he died out of time.
Sick old men,
Driving rapidly before a concourse of
people,
Gay with decorations,
Crumpled with pain.

The drum-major lifts his silver-headed
stick,
And the silver trumpets and tubas,
The great round drums,
Each with an H on them,
Crash out martial music.
Heavily rhythmed march music
For the stepping of a regiment.

Slant lines of rifles,
A twinkle of stepping,
The regiment comes.
The young regiment,
Boys in khaki
With slanted rifles.
The young bodies of boys
Bulwarked in front of us.
The white bodies of young men
Heaped like sandbags
Against the German guns.

This is war:
Boy flung into a breach
Like shovelled earth;

And old men,
Broken,
Driving rapidly before crowds of people
In a glitter of silly decorations.

Behind the boys
And the old men,
Life weeps,
And shreds her garments
To the blowing winds.

AFTER WRITING
"THE BRONZE HORSES"

I am so tired.
I have run across the ages with spiritless
   feet,
I have tracked man where he falls splint-
   ered in defeat,
I have watched him shoot up like green
   sprouts at dawning,
I have seen him blossom, and fruit, and
   offer himself, fawning,
On golden platters to kings.
I have seen him reel with drunk blood,
I have followed him in flood
Sweep over his other selves.
I have written things
Which sucked the breath
Out of my lungs, and hung
My heart up in a frozen death.
I have picked desires
Out of purple fires
And set them on the shelves
Of my mind,
Nonchalantly,
As though my kind
Were unlike these.
But while I did this, by bowels contracted
   in twists of fear.
I felt myself squeeze
Myself dry,
And wished that I could shrivel before
   Destiny
Could snatch me back into the vortex of
   Yesterday.
Wheels and wheels —
And only your hand is firm.
The very paths of my garden squirm
Like snakes between the brittle flowers,
And the sunrise gun cuts off the hours
Of this day and the next.
The long, dusty volumes are the first of
   a text.
Oh, Beloved, must we read?

Must you and I, alone in the midst of
   trees,
See their green alleys printing with the
   screed
Which counts these new men, these
Terrible resurrections of old wars.
I wish I had not seen so much:
The roses that you wear are bloody scars,
And you the moon above a battle-field;
So all my thoughts are grown to such.
A body peeled
Down to a skeleton,
A grinning jaw-bone in a bed of mignon-
   ette.
What good is it to say "Not yet."
I tell you I am tired
And afraid.

THE FORT

The disappearing guns
Are hidden in their concrete emplace-
   ments,
But, above them,
Meadow grasses fall and recover,
Bend and stiffen,
Go dark, burn light,
In the play of gusty wind.
A black-and-orange butterfly
Flits about the butter-and-egg flowers,
And the sea stands up,
Tall in perspective,
With full-spread schooners
Sprinkled upon it
As roses are powdered
Over a ribbon of moiré blue.
The disappearing guns are black
In grey concrete emplacements
With here and there a touch of red rust.

Wind cuts through the grasses,
Rasps upon them,
Draws a bow note out along them.
Swish! — Oh-h-h!
And the low waves
Crash soft constant cymbals
On the shingle beach
At the foot of the cliff.
Good gracious!
A seal!
After how many years?
He turns his head to look at us,
He lolls on his rock contented and hot
   with sun.

The disappearing guns would shoot over
    him
If they were to fire.
Is he held in the harbour
By the submarine nets, I wonder?

"You turn the crank so.
Do you see her move?
If you stand here, you can see the springs
    for the recoil."
Perhaps I can,
But I cannot see the orange butterfly,
Nor the seal,
Nor the little ships
Drawn across the tall, streaked sea.
And all I can hear
Is the jingle of a piano
In the men's quarters
Playing a comic opera tune.

Is it possible that, at night,
The little flitter-bats
Hang under the lever-wheels of the dis-
    appearing guns
In their low emplacements
To escape from the glare
Of the search-lights,
Shooting over the grasses
To the sea?

CAMOUFLAGED TROOP–SHIP

Boston Harbour

Uprightness,
Masts, one behind another,
Syncopated beyond and between one an-
    other,
Clouding together,
Becoming confused.
A mist of grey, blurring stems
Platformed upon horizontal thicknesses.
Decks,
Bows and sterns escaping fore and aft,
A long line of flatness
Darker than the fog of masts,
More solid,
Monotonous grey.
Dull smokestacks
Plotting lustreless clouds.
An ebb-tide
Slowly sucking the refuse of a harbour
Seaward.

The ferry turns;
And there,

On the starboard quarter,
Thrust out from the vapour-wall of ships:
Colour.
Against the perpendicular:
Obliqueness.
In front of the horizontal:
A crenelated edge.
A vessel, grooved and conical,
Shell-shaped, flower-flowing,
Gothic, bizarre, and unrelated.
Black spirals over cream-colour
Broken at a half-way point.
A slab of black amidships.
At the stern,
Lines:
Rising from the water,
Curled round and over,
Whorled, scattered,
Drawn upon one another.
Snakes starting from a still ocean,
Writhing over cream-colour,
Crashed upon and cut down
By a flat, impinging horizon.

The sea is grey and low,
But the vessel is high with upthrusting
    lines:
Hair lines incessantly moving,
Broad bands of black turning evenly over
    emptiness,
Intorting upon their circuits,
Teasing the eye with indefinite motion,
Coming from nothing,
Ending without cessation.
Drowned hair drifting against mother-of
    pearl;
Kelp-aprons
Shredded upon a yellow beach;
Black spray
Salted over cream-grey wave-tops.

You hollow into rising water,
You double-turn under the dripped edges
    of clouds,
You move in a hundred directions,
And keep to a course the eye cannot see.
Your terrible lines
Are swift as the plunge of a kingfisher;
They vanish as one traces them,
They are constantly vanishing,
And yet you swing at anchor in the grey
    harbour
Waiting for your quota of troops.
Men will sail in you,
Netted in whirling paint,

Held like brittle eggs
In an osier basket.
They will sail,
Over black-skinned water,
Into a distance of cream-colour and
vague shadow-shotted blue.

The ferry whistle blows for the landing.
Start the engine
That we may not block
The string of waiting carts.

SEPTEMBER, 1918

This afternoon was the colour of water
falling through sunlight;
The trees glittered with the tumbling of
leaves;
The sidewalks shone like alleys of dropped
maple leaves,
And the houses ran along them laughing
out of square, open windows.
Under a tree in the park,
Two little boys, lying flat on their faces,
Were carefully gathering red berries
To put in a pasteboard box.

Some day there will be no war,
Then I shall take out this afternoon
And turn it in my fingers,
And remark the sweet taste of it upon my
palate,
And note the crisp variety of its flights of
leaves.
To-day I can only gather it
And put it into my lunch-box,
For I have time for nothing
But the endeavour to balance myself
Upon a broken world.

THE NIGHT BEFORE THE PARADE

April 25, 1919

Birds are calling through the rain,
Glass bells dropping across the patter of
falling rain.
The garden soaks, and breathes, and lifts
up the spear-green leaves of tulips
And the long, golden mouths of daffodils
To the downpour,
And the high blossoms of forsythia
Tremble vaguely, and bend to let the
rain run off them
And spill over the little red peony fronds
Uncurling at their feet.

It is wet, and cool, and pleasant.
Why should words rattle upon this quiet-
ness?
"Adders writhe from the sunken
eyes
Of statues, in Persepolis."

Clashes of bells bursting in a grey sky,
And a clock striking jubilees of brass
hours, one after another.
Gas-jets flicker, and spin sudden lights
across the battle-flags draped to
the pillars.
The church sighs in the evening rain,
Kneeling beneath the dim clouds in a
stillness of adoration.
Beauty of stone, of glass, of memories,
Worshipful beauty spotted by the snarl
of words —
"Adders writhe from the sunken
eyes
Of statues, in Persepolis."

They have put up stands,
Flimsy wooden stands to crush out the
little green life of the grass.
To-morrow the crowds will cheer,
And the streets will shine with flags and
gilding.
The people will shout themselves hoarse
When the green helmets and the white
bayonets
Sweep along the streets.
Only the little grass-blades will cry and
languish,
Weeping: "We are the cousins of the
grasses of France,
The kind grasses who cover the graves of
those you have forgotten."
Then they will hiss under the cruel stands,
And the words will run, and glare, and
brighten:
"Adders writhe from the sunken
eyes
Of statues, in Persepolis."

Rain on a roofless city,
Rain over broken walls and towers scattered to a ring of ruins,
Pale splendours of hard stone melted to
the purple bloom of orchises,
And poppies thrust between the basalt
paving-blocks of roads leading to
a waste of blue-tongued thistles.

Where did I see this?
Not in the leafless branches of the ash-
    tree,
Not in the glitter of my wet window-sill,
Not in the smooth garden filling itself
    with good rain.
There are fireworks to-night,
The first for two years.
And listen to the rain!

Listen — listen —
Prayers, and flowers, and a booming of
    guns.
It blurs —
Do I hear anything?
What are you reading?
    "Adders writhe from the sunken
    eyes
    Of statues, in Persepolis."

As Toward Immortality

ON A CERTAIN CRITIC

Well, John Keats,
I know how you felt when you swung out
    of the inn
And started up Box Hill after the moon.
Lord! How she twinkled in and out of
    the box bushes
Where they arched over the path.
How she peeked at you and tempted you,
And how you longed for the "naked
    waist" of her
You had put into your second canto.
You felt her silver running all over you,
And the shine of her flashed in your eyes
So that you stumbled over roots and
    things.
Ah! How beautiful! How beautiful!
Lying out on the open hill
With her white radiance touching you
Lightly,
Flecking over you.
"My Lady of the Moon,
I flow out to your whiteness,
Brightness.
My hands cup themselves
About your disk of pearl and fire;
Lie upon my face,
Burn me with the cold of your hot white
    flame.
Diana,
High, distant Goddess,
I kiss the needles of this furze bush
Because your feet have trodden it.
Moon!
Moon!
I am prone before you.
Pity me,
And drench me in loveliness.
I have written you a poem
I have made a girdle for you of words;

Like a shawl my words will cover you,
So that men may read of you and not be
    burnt as I have been.
Sere my heart until it is a crinkled leaf,
I have held you in it for a moment,
And exchanged my love with yours,
On a high hill at midnight.
Was that your tear or mine, Bright
    Moon?
It was round and full of moonlight.
Don't go!
My God! Don't go!
You escape from me,
You slide through my hands.
Great Immortal Goddess,
Dearly Beloved,
Don't leave me.
My hands clutch at moonbeams,
And catch each other.
My Dear! My Dear!
My beautiful far-shining lady!
Oh! God!
I am tortured with this anguish of un-
    bearable beauty."

Then you stumbled down the hill, John
    Keats,
Perhaps you fell once or twice;
It is a rough path,
And you weren't thinking of that.
Then you wrote,
By a wavering candle,
And the moon frosted your window till it
    looked like a sheet of blue ice.
And as you tumbled into bed, you said:
"It's a piece of luck I thought of coming
    out to Box Hill."

Now comes a sprig little gentleman,
And turns over your manuscript with his
    mincing fingers,

And tabulates places and dates.
He says your moon was a copy-book
    maxim,
And talks about the spirit of solitude,
And the salvation of genius through the
    social order.
I wish you were here to damn him

With a good, round, agreeable oath,
    John Keats,
But just snap your fingers,
You and the moon will still love,
When he and his papers have slithered
    away
In the bodies of innumerable worms.

LEGENDS

MEMORANDUM CONFIDED BY A YUCCA
TO A PASSION-VINE

The Turkey-buzzard was chatting with
the Condor
High up in the White Cordillera.
"Surely our friend the fox is mad," said
he.
"He chases birds no more and his tail
trails languidly
Behind him in the dust.
Why, he got it full of cactus-spines one
day,
Pawing over a plant that stood in his
way.
All the bees are buzzing about it.
Consider a fox who passes by the great
hives of sharp, black honey
And looks at them no more than a heron
would."
"Odd," said the Condor. "Remarkably
peculiar."
And he flapped his wings and flew away
to the porcelain peaks of the distant
Sierra.
So the Turkey-buzzard thought no more
of the matter,
But busied himself with the carcass of
a dead llama.

And the sun boomed onward over the
ice-peaks;
Hot — Hot — Hotter!
And the sun dropped behind the snow-
peaks,
And the cool of shadow was so delicious
that all the squirrels and rabbits and
peccaries and lizards
Flirted their tails;
And the flamingoes in Lake Titicaca
puffed out their gizzards,
And waded into the pink water reflected
from the carmine-tinted mountain
summits;
And the parrots chattered and flashed in
the mimosas;
And the eagles dove like plummets
Upon the unfortunate alpacas.

The animals were enjoying themselves in
the rose-red light that lingers
Flung from the blood-orchid tips of the
mountains
Before the night mists slide over the
foothills.
Ah! But you could see them in the valleys,
Floating and circling like dead men's
fingers
Combing living hair.

In a place of bright quartz rocks,
Sits a small red fox.
He is half in the shade of a cactus-bush.
The birds still fly, but there is a hush
And a sifting of purple through the air:
Blue dims rose,
The evening is fair.
Why is the red fox waiting there,
With his sniffing nose,
And his stiffened pose,
And his narrow eyelids which never close?
"Fox — fox —
Against the rocks.
Are you rooted there till the equinox?"
So the alcamarines flocking home in the
afterglow
Mock the poor fox, but he doesn't seem
to know.
He sits on his haunches, staring high
Into the soft, fruit-green evening sky.

A yellow rose blooms in the glow,
Thin fox frosted by silver snow,
Mica-crystals flecking over indigo.
And a cactus-tree
Grating its thorn-leaves huskily.
Moan of wind and the crackles of an
empty place
At the coming of night.
The fox is alone.
Then in the far green heavens the lady
rises, tall and white.
August and dazzling
In the drooping light,

She shimmers, jubilantly bright.
Breasts and thighs tuned to liquid air,
Loveliness set naked in a firmament.
He sees the slim, smooth arms,
And the virgin waist bending with deli-
cate movement.
Her body sways as a flower stem
Caught in a gust;
And her hair is thrust
Towards him, he can see the gem
Which binds it loosely. His eyes are
greedy
Of the curving undulations and straight
fall
Following down from head to foot, and
all
Cool and unclouded, touching him al-
most.
With hot tongue he pants upon the
splendour
Of this marble beauty, imperious and
unashamed
In her extreme of excellence.
Then he weeps,
Weeps in little yelping barks for the
cold beautiful body
Of the inaccessible moon.
The villagers wake in a startled fright
And tell each other: "A fox bays the
moon to-night."

The moon lives in Cuzco —
It was the Partridge who told him so —
In a temple builded of jointured stone
On an emerald-studded, silver throne.
So the fox set out for Cuzco with his tail
held high to keep it out of the dust.

Tramp! Tramp! Tramp!
What is that noise approaching him?
Quick, behind a stone,
And he watches them come,
The soldiers of the great Inca.
Copper spear-heads running like a river
of gold along the road.
Helmets of tiger-skins, coats of glittering
feathers,
A ripple of colours from one edge of the
way to the other.
Feet of men cadenced to the swing of
weapons.
So many bows, and arrows, and slings,
and darts, and lances,
A twinkling rhythm of reflections to
which the army advances,

And a rainbow banner flickering colours
to the slipping of the wind.
They pass as water passes and the fox is
left behind.
"Those men come from Cuzco," thought
the fox,
And his heart was like lead in his stomach
for wondering if they knew the moon.
Then he trotted on again with his tail
held high to keep it out of the dust.

Pat! Pat! Pat!
What is that sound behind him?
He leaps into a bush of tufted acacia just
in time.
It is a post-runner, doing his stint of five
miles,
Carrying merchandise from the coast.
And the fox's mouth waters as he smells
fish:
Bobos, shads, sardines,
All fading in a little osier basket,
Faint colours whispering the hues of the
rainbow flag.
But the runner must not lag,
These fish are for the Inca's table.
A flash of feet against the heart-shaped
flowers of the yolosuchil
And the jarred leaves settle and are still.
The fox creeps out and resumes his jour-
ney, with his tail held high to keep it
out of the dust.

Over bush and bramble and prick and
thorn
Goes the fox, till his feet are torn,
And his eyes are weary with keeping the
trail
Through ashen wind and clattering hail,
With the hot, round sun lying flat on his
head,
And morning crushing its weight of lead
On scores of trumpet-vines tangled and
dead.
Across swung bridges of plaited reeds
In a whorl of foaming, bursting beads
Of river mist, where a cañon makes a
fall
Of thousands of feet in a sheer rock wall.
Pomegranates toss him scarlet petals,
The little covetous claws of nettles
Catch at his fur, and a sudden gloom
Blocks his path on a drip of bloom.
Over prick and thorn and bush and bram-
ble;

Up pointed boulders with a slip and
scramble,
Past geese with flattened, blue-green
wings
Pulling the ichu grass which springs
In narrow fissures where nothing else
clings;
Through terraced fields of bright-tongued
maize
Licking the hills to a golden blaze;
Under clustered bananas and scented
oaks;
Across dry, high plains where the yucca
chokes.
Dawns explode in bleeding lights
On the snow-still uplands of ghastly
heights
Where long-dead bodies stare through
their hair
Crooking their brittle legs and bare
Ice-tortured arms, and the sun at noon
Is a glassy shell of dull maroon.
Only at night he watches the moon
Stepping along the smooth, pale sky
In a silver florescence. By and by
The red fox reaches the gates of Cuzco,
But his tail is very much bedraggled for he
can no longer hold it up out of the
dust.

Morning playing dimly in the passion-
vines
Hanging over the gates of Cuzco.
Morning picking out a purple flower —
Another — another —
Cascading down the walls of Cuzco.
Scarlet-flashing, uprose the sun
With one deep bell-note of a copper-
crashed gong.
Glory of rose-mist over the Sierra,
Glory of crimson on the tinted turrets
Of the wide old fort under the high cliff.
Glory of vermilion dripping from the
windows,
Glory of saffron streaking all the shadows,
House fronts glaring in fresh young light,
Gold over Cuzco!
Gold!
Gold!
In an orchid flow,
Where the Temple of Pachacamac rose
like a bell
Shining on the city,
With the clear sweet swell of an open
sunrise gong.

White and carnation,
White and carnation,
The sun's great gnomon,
Measuring its shadow on the long sharp
gold polished grass.
Who pass here
In an early year?
Lightning and Thunder,
Servants of the Sun.
Lord of the rainbow's white and purple,
Blue and carnation,
All awhirl to a curl of gold.
He who comes from the land of monkeys,
He who comes from the flying-fishes
playing games with rainbow dolphins,
Pause —
Here before the gates of gold,
Chamfered crown about the Temple,
Sparkling points and twisted spirals,
All of Gold.
Lemon-tinted Gold,
Red-washed fire Gold,
Gold, the planking,
Gold, the roof-tree,
Gold the burnished doors and porches,
And the chairs of the dead Incas:
One long row of stately bodies
Sitting dead in all the dazzle
Glittering with bright green emeralds.
White-haired Incas,
Hoary Incas,
Black and shiny-haired young Incas,
All dead Incas;
With their hands crossed on their breasts
And their eyes cast down, they wait
there.
Terrible and full-fleshed Incas.
Blaze of fire, burning, glaring,
Bright, too bright!
Ah-h-h!
The Sun!
Up through the wide-open Eastern portal.
Broken, sharpened on a thousand plates
of gold,
It falls,
Splintered into prisms on the rainbow
walls.
The Sun steps into his house.
Hush! It is the PRESENCE!

Face of Pachacamac,
Wreathed in burnished flames of swift
fire.
Then on the wind of a thousand voices
rises the hymn:

"Pachacamac
World's Creator,
Mountain-mover,
Heaven-dwelling.
We beseech thee
Send thy showers,
Warm our meadows,
Bless the seed-ears.
Man and woman,
Beast and lizard,
Feathered people,
Whales and fishes,
All implore thee,
Clement God-head,
To make fruitful
These thy creatures.
String their sinews
Ripe for power,
Quicken wombs and
Eggs and rootlets.
Be the Father,
The Begetter.
Pour upon us,
Lord of all things,
Of thy bounty,
Of thy fulness.
So we praise thee,
Swelling Apple,
Gourd of Promise,
Mighty Melon,
Seed-encaser,
Sun and Spirit,
Lord of Morning,
Blood of Mercy,
Pachacamac!"

And the great tide of men's voices echoed
    and curved upon the plates of gold
Lining the Temple
So that it became a wide horn of melody,
And out of it burst the hymn like a red-
    streaked lily thundering to the morning.
Men's voices singing the hymn of ripen-
    ing seed,
Men's voices raised in a phallic chorus to
    the rising sun . . .
Virgin of the sun,
Pale Virgin,
Through the twisting vine-leaves it comes
    to you broken and shivering.
What are you, Virgin?
And who is this all-wise God
That shuts you in a hall of stone?
Cleft asunder,
A white pomegranate with no seeds,

A peascod dropped on a foot-path before
    its peas are blown.
Pale Virgin, go about your baking,
For the shadows shorten and at noon the
    oven will be heated.

Tired little fox outside the fence,
Lie down in the shade of the wall,
For indeed the sun has done you an
    injury.

Now the East wind, called Brisa, blew
    against the clouds;
And the sun rushed up the sky;
And at noon the shadow of the great
    gnomon was not,
No single dark patch lay anywhere about
    its foot,
For the God sat with all his light upon
    the column.
The fox awoke, and sought shelter from
    the heat.
Creeping, he came to a garden of five
    fountains,
Set in green plots, and plots of silver.
For there he saw, mixed, the fruits of
    the sun:
Apples, quinces, loquats, and chirimoyas,
All just after flowering with their fruit-
    balls perfectly formed but each smaller
    than a pepper-grain,
And the fruits of man:
Oranges, melons, cocoanuts and bread-
    fruit,
Fashioned of gold and silver,
Amazing with brightness.
Indian corn sprouted from the earth on
    thin stalks of gold
Which rattled against one another with
    a sweet clashing,
The golden ears escaping smartly out of
    broad recurved leaves of silver,
And silver tassels floated in a twinkle of
    whiteness from their glittering tops.
Golden snails clung to silver palm-
    branches,
Turquoise butterflies flew hither and
    thither
And one alone remained poised; it was
    of polished stone.
The fox gaped for wonder and his tail
    lay prone on a silver lizard,
But this he never noticed.
Then across the sounds of leaves blowing
And metals tapping,

Came music;
A voice singing in a minor key,
Throaty and uncertain as a new-cut
reed.
"Mama Quilla," it sang.
"Mother Moon,
Through the shell of heaven gliding.
Moon of many stars and brothers,
Mistress of the bright-haired rainbow,
Wife and sister of the Sun-god,
Virgin moon who bore him children,
If you die then do we perish.
Mama Quilla,
I, a Virgin,
Crave a blessing,
Ask a guerdon.
O glorious, chaste, and immaculate moon,
Preserve me to my vows.
But, I implore thee,
Take from me, therefore, this my long-
ing,
Let the Spring deal with me gently,
Still my spirit.
Or, devout and pitying mother,
Give me thunder,
Give me lightning,
Break me on a green-stone anvil,
So the flower of my body
Blow to loveliness a moment.
I am past my holding, Mama Quilla,
In the night I smell the strong-scented
blossoms of the daturas,
And my heart snares me in its loneli-
ness."

So the fox crept up to the door where
the Virgin of the Sun sat spinning.
"Can you tell me, Lady," said he, making
a fine bow,
"If the moon lives here in Cuzco?"
Then the Virgin was afraid,
For she did not know that foxes spoke.
"Who are you," she demanded,
"And whence do you come?"
"I am a fox of the Western Country,
And I come from the water-passage of
Lake Titicaca.
I love the moon,
I desire her more than the monkeys of
the Eastern forests
Desire dates,
More than your kinsmen, the Incas,
Desire the land of the Machigangas.
She is more beautiful to me than red
pepper-pods

To the shepherds who walk the moun-
tains with their llamas.
I prize her more greatly than do the
Aquarimas the shrunken skulls of their
enemies.
She is a poison-tree of many branches:
With one, she brushes the waves of the
ocean
So that all the shores are overflown with
the sea at Spring tides;
And, with another, she tickles the nose
of a tapir
Asleep in a grove of vanilla-trees
On the banks of the Amazon;
And I have been blinded by the sweeping
of a third
Above the snow-cornice on Mount Vil-
canota.
Oh, she has many branches
All dripping with silver-white poison,
And I have come here to drink this
poison and die."
"But you cannot possess the moon;
It is sacrilege," cried the Virgin,
And her hands trembled so that the dis-
taff fell to the ground.
"And it is sacrilege for a Virgin of the
Sun to sing of the labours of women,"
said the fox.
Then the fox told of his watching, night
and night, under the cactus-bush,
Of his great pains and hungering,
And the Virgin listened in a tiptoe of
attention,
While the ruby humming-birds splashed
fire across the silver ripple of the gar-
den,
And the fountains sprang and recoiled,
And the Sun sank behind the mountains
of the sea.

Hush!
Hush!
In the House of Acllahua.
The Mamacunas sleep,
The Virgins lie enmeshed in sleep.
Sleep folded on the House of Acllahua,
While the Sun, their master,
Dries the ocean with his swimming.
West to East, all night he swims,
And they in the House of Acllahua sleep.
Only she is waiting, fearing;
Now more gently, gently, gliding,
Through the fluttering silver flowers.
And the fox is waiting,

Sitting under a tamarisk-tree
With his hot tongue hanging out of his
mouth.
Through the thin cloud of tamarisk-
leaves
Falls a tempered moonlight,
A feathered, partial moonlight,
A moonlight growing every moment
stronger,
A shadow growing every minute blacker.
The Virgin and the fox under the black
feathers of the tamarisk-tree,
While the moon walks with a stately
slowness
Down the long, quiet terraces of the sky.

Hush!
Hush!
The garden burns with cold, green fire,
A bat spots black on a gold sweet-briar,
A polished rose on a stem of wire
Sweeps and bends, a blue flung ball
Palpitating,
Undulating,
All the trees and plants girating,
All the metals quivering to song
And the great palmettos beating gongs.
The low, slow notes of the water-reeds
Underscore the glass-sweet beads
Of the little clapping melon seeds.
Gold and silver strings of a lyre
Plucked by the wind, high pitched and
higher,
And the silver moans with a tone of its
own
Fragile as an ixia newly blown.
All the garden sways to a noise
Of humming metal in equipoise.
Stately dates sweep a merry-go-round,
The fountains spring in a sparkle of
sound.
The moonlight falls in a heap on the
ground.
And there is Light!
Light is a crowned effulgence
Thrown up from the flowers and trees,
Delicate, pearled light, barred by beauti-
ful shadows,
Bloomed light, plunging upon the silver-
roofed Temple.
Open, Open,
Door of the Temple of the Moon.
Come forth, dead mothers of dead Incas.
Slow procession of the dead
Filing out of the Temple.

Mama Vello, mother of Huayna Capac,
Mama Runtu,
Mama Ocllo.
Feathered mantles brush the golden
gravel,
Theirs hands are crossed on their breasts,
They are powdered with turquoises and
raw-cut emeralds.
Slowly the Inca mothers form a ring,
They hold a golden chain
Long and broad as the great street of
Cuzco.
Slowly they move in a circle,
Chanting.
Their steps are soft as weeping water.
Their voices are faint as snow dropping
through Autumn dusk.
Suddenly, in the midst of the ring, a great
fall of Light.
It is she — the MOON!
White mist circumvolves about her,
On her head is a diadem of opal-changing
ice,
And hoar-frost follows the stepping of her
feet.
A single emerald, half white, half foaming
green,
Clasps a girdle about her waist.
Terribly she dances in the ring of Inca
mothers.
The garden turns with them as they
move,
Winding and closing about them,
Impelling them toward the Temple,
Up to the Altar.
Trumpets, brazen and vainglorious,
Silver-striking, shouting cymbals,
Open horns, round gourd-drums beaten
to a rattle of flame.
Movement, ghostly, perpetual,
And sound, loud, sweet, sucking from the
four edges of the sky.
Everything swings, and sings, and oscil-
lates, and curves.
Only the moon upon the High Altar is
still.
She stands, struck to immobility,
Then, without haste, unclasps the foam-
ing emerald
And the mists part and fall . . .
Silence —
Silence spread beneath her as a footstool.
The flowers close;
The Inca mothers are dead corpses on
their silver thrones.

But She!
Naked, white, and beautiful,
Poised and infinite;
Flesh,
Spirit,
Woman and Unparalleled Enchantment.
Moon of waters,
Womb of peoples,
Majesty and highest Queen.
So the Goddess burns in a halo of white-
rose fire
For an instant . . .
Yelp! Yelp! Yelp!
The fox has burst from the Virgin's
grasp.
Over the garden,
Up the aisle of the Temple,
With staring eyes
And ghoulish, licking tongue.
Satyr fox assaulting the moon!
THUNDER!!!
Lightning serpents
Wound in great circles above the Tem-
ple.

Sheets of lightning snarling from racing,
purple clouds
And rain roaring down the hot walls of
a copper sky.

The clouds splinter, and a ruined moon
wavers up into the heavens, about her
are three great rings, one of blood, one
of black, and the utmost all of stinging, glutinous, intorting coils of smoke.
Upon the disk of the moon are spots,
black obscene spots, the print of a
fox's paws.

. . . . . .

Bake your cakes of the sacred maize,
Virgin,
Tend the flame the priest has gathered
with his metal sun-glass,
Weave feathered mantles for the Coya,
Burn holy gums to deaden the scent of
the daturas.
If you and the moon have a secret,
Let it rest there.

A LEGEND OF PORCELAIN

Old China sits and broods behind her
ten-thousand-miles-great wall,
And the rivers of old China crawl —
crawl — forever
Toward the distant, ceaselessly waiting
seas.

At King-te-chin in China,
At King-te-chin in the far East of the
Eighteen Provinces of China,
Where all day long the porcelain fac-
tories belch corded smoke,
And all night long the watch-men, strik-
ing the hours on their lizard-skin
drums,
Follow the shadows thrown before
them
From a sky glazed scarlet as it floats over
the fires of burning kilns —
At King-te-chin, in the heart of brooding
China,
Lives Chou-Kiou,
White as milk in a tazza cup,
Red as a pear-tree just dropping its
petals,
Happy as the Spring-faced wind.
Chou-Kiou,

For whom the wild geese break their
flight,
And the fishes seek the darkness of the
lower waters.
Chou-Kiou,
Apt as a son,
Loved as a son,
More precious to her father than blue
earth with stars of silver.
It is Chou-Kiou who paints the fighting
crickets
On the egg-shell cups;
Who covers the Wa-wa cups
With little bully boys;
Who sketches Manchu ladies, Tartar
ladies,
Chasing crimson butterflies with faint
silk fans,
On the slim teapots of young bamboo.
Chou-Kiou,
Bustling all day between the kilns and
the warehouses.
A breath of peach-bloom silk
Turning a pathway —
Puff! She is gone,
As a peach-blossom painted on paper
Caught in a corner of the wind.

King-te-chin in the Province of Kiangsi,
Noblest of the manufactories of porcelain,
Where, from sunrise to sundown,
In the narrow streets,
The porters cry "Way! Way!" for the beautiful dishes
They carry to the barges,
The flat barges which nuzzle and nudge the banks of the river Jao T'cheou;
And the strong stevedore coolies grunt
As they lift the clay bricks quarried in the P'ing-li mountains
Out of the sharp-prowed boats moored along the river Ki-muen.
Mêng Tsung, master of a thousand workmen,
Walks under the red eaves of his buildings
In the tea-green shadow of the willow-trees,
Contemplating his bakers, his mixers, his painters,
The men who carry tcha wood,
And those, nicer-fingered, who turn the shaping wheels.
He walks among the beehive furnaces,
And his nostrils smart with the sharp scent of ashes,
And his ears rattle with the crackle of a hundred flames.
Mêng Tsung, finest of the porcelain-makers of King-te-chin.

In China,
Old China,
What other artists do is his work also;
Does Lu Tzŭ Kang work in jade; the porcelains of Mêng Tsung are ice and rainbows.
What Chu Pi-shan can do in silver,
What Hsiao-hsi in carnelian,
Pao T'ien-chêng in rhinoceros horn,
P'u Chung-ch'ien in carved bamboo,
Chang Ch'ien-li in mother-of-pearl,
All this is nothing.
The bowls of Mêng Tsung are like Spring sun on a rippled river,
Like willow-leaves seen over late ice,
Like bronze bells one hour before sunset.
They are light as the eggs of the yellow-eyebrowed thrush,
And wonderful in colour as the green grapes of Turkestan.

Mêng Tsung walks under the red eaves of his buildings,
Musing on the beauty of old, old China,
Listening to the dull beating of the fish-drums in the monastery on the hill
calling the attention of God to the prayers of his monks.

Beautiful the sun of China,
Beautiful the squares of flooded rice-fields,
The long slopes of tea plants on the hills of Ning-po,
The grey mulberry-trees of Chuki.
Beautiful the cities between the rivers,
But three, and three, and three times more beautiful
The porcelains fashioned by Chou-Kiou.
See them in the sun,
Swept over by the blowing shade of willows,
Moulded like lotus-leaves,
Yellow as the skins of eels,
Black glaze overlaid with gold.
Tell the story of this porcelain
With veins like arbor-vitae leaves and bullock's hair,
Mottled as hare's fur,
Bright and various as the wooded walls of mountains.
Here are the dawn-red wine-cups,
And the cups of snow-blue with no glisten;
Little vases, barely taller than a toad,
And great, three-part vases shining slowly like tarnished silver.
They stand in rows along the flat board
And she checks them, one by one, on a tablet of fir-flower paper,
And her eyes are little copper bells fallen in the midst of tall grass.
Tell the tale of these great jars,
Cloudy coloured as the crystal grape
With white bloom of rice-dust upon them,
Fallen over at the top by pointed bunches
Of the myriad-year wistaria.
Those smaller jars of moonlight enamel, dark and pale,
With undulating lines which seem to change.
Pots green as growing plants are green,
Marked with the hundred-fold crackle of broken ice.
Pallets painted blue with dragons,

And ample dishes, redder than fresh
  blood,
Spotted with crabs' claws,
Splashed with bluish flames of fire.
Here are bowls faintly tinted as tea-dust
Or the fading leaf of the camphor-tree in
  Autumn;
Others as bamboo paper for thickness,
Lightly spattered with vermilion fishes;
And white bowls
Surpassing hoar-frost and the pointed tips
  of icicles.
There are birds painted thinly in dull
  reds,
Fighting-cocks with rose-pink legs and
  crests of silver,
Teapots rough as the skin of the Kio
  orange, or blistered with the little
  flower-buds of the Tsong-tree.
How tell the carminates,
The greens of pale copper,
The leopard-spotted yellows,
The blues, powdered and indefinite as a
  Mei plum!
Globular bodies with bulbous mouths;
Slim, long porcelains confused like a
  weedy sea;
Porcelains, pale as the morning sky
Fluttered with purple wings of finches;
High-footed cups for green wine,
And incense-burners yellow as old Llama
  books
With cranes upon them.
Blue porcelain for the Altar of Heaven,
Yellow for the Altar of Earth,
Red for the Altar of the Sun,
White for the Altar of the Year-star.
All these Chou-Kiou sets down on her fir-
  flower tablet,
Then carefully, carefully, selects a cup
Of so keen a transparence that the sun,
  passing it, can scarcely mark a shadow,
And fills it with water.
Oh! The purple fishes!
The dark-coloured fishes with scales of
  silver!
The blue-black fishes swerving in a trail
  of gold!
They move and flicker,
They swing in procession,
They dart, and hesitate, and float
With flower-waving tails —
The vase is empty again,
Smooth and open and colourless.
The tally is finished,

The sun is sinking in a rose-green sky,
And in the guard-house down the road
The red tallow candles are lighted.

It is the fifth day of the fifth month,
And all the demons of old China
Are chattering down from the mountains
  of the North.
Little Chou-Kiou,
Where are the spears of the sweet-flag
You should have gathered yesterday
And nailed to the door-lintel at the first
  flow of morning?
Little Chou-Kiou,
It is too late,
The guards have clanged the Dragon
  Gate.
Flags do not grow in this trodden city,
Demons laugh at the studded walls of
  men.
You dream of your betrothed
As you roll your tablet,
Your lover sailing the sharp seas,
Your lover of the tall junks
Trading up and down the coast
Glad when the two eyes of his ship
Are turned again to China.
Silly Chou-Kiou,
Absorbed by love and dishes,
Forgetting the evil spirits
Descending from the curled blue moun-
  tains.

.　　.　　.　　.　　.

Open the Gate,
Open the Gate,
His Lordship T'ang Ling,
High official to the Emperor,
Waits without the walls.
Hurry, Guards,
The sun is red,
The gate already casts a shadow.
T'ang Ling is come
To visit the porcelain factories
Of King-te-chin.
Click! Click! — loud and imperious!
It is the mandarin's outrunners,
And the rods they are carrying and strik-
  ing on the ground.
Clash,
Clash,
Gongs.
Feet of men in the clouded dust,
Whipping banners scarlet and gold,
Tablet-bearers carrying his scrolls:

All of his titles,
All of his greatness,
All of his honours,
Who were his fathers,
Grim, dim, warriors,
Poems and speeches.
Pass,
Pass,
Golden the heels of the men of T'ang
    Ling.
Here is one staggering,
Mightily flaunting,
The heavy, flat, superb umbrella!
Spreading crimson as a lotus,
Frozen sun-disk,
Carried high before him.
Clatter! Trip! Clatter! Clatter!
See the caparisoned horses
Glittering and kicking —
How lightly ride the men of T'ang Ling!
They bear the moon fans before his face,
Honourable gentleman.
They raise the golden melon mace.
They have bamboos for the contuma-
    cious,
And chains for persons who resist the
    God-like will.
A space,
Rifting the procession —
Then a bright and massive thing:
His Chair!
Gold thunder carvings,
Mighty lines and fallen spirals,
Dazzling as the sun on cannon,
And he, the Proud One, T'ang Ling,
With his sapphire button,
And the plaques of his coat embroidered
    with one-eyed peacocks' feathers.
Play Ch'ang flutes before him,
Make a loud music of cymbals,
Pluck sharply on the three-stringed
    guitars,
Prostrate yourselves,
And beat the snake-skin drums.
K'otow, Mèng Tsung,
Walk backwards past the beehive fur-
    naces,
T'ang Ling, servant of the Yellow Em-
    peror,
Has come to inspect the porcelain.

You must stay in the Eastern Pavilion,
Chou-Kiou,
Hiding and peeking behind the amethyst
    flowers of the peonies.

But do not forget the sweet-flag
Which you did not hang upon the door.

Tea appears red in white Hsing-chou
    porcelain,
How strange then to offer such to an
    official.
When T'ang Ling came to visit Mèng
    Tsung
They sat under a cinnamon-tree
Examining the "Pieces of a Thousand
    Flowers."
Coiling-dragon tea is best in black cups,
And silver vessels hold the gosling-down
    wine.
Lychees and finger citrons
Delight the palate of the great man,
And flat-land ginger, soft and tender to
    the taste;
But candied melon-rind calls for more
    wine.
One hundred cups is nothing to so high
    an officer.
Already his fingers stray in vague tappings
Among the samples of porcelain.
A dragon bowl, seven days fired, for the
    Palace.
What is T'ang Ling doing with the
    sword —
Does he dream of the campaigns of his
    youth,
Whirling it voraciously before him?
His sword is tempered to an edge of
    flame,
It cleaves the dragon bowl without a
    splinter.
Chou-Kiou,
Chou-Kiou,
Was the river so far that you could not
    reach it yesterday before the twilight
    fell?
The flags which you did not pick must
    spear your heart.

A diamond-marked python scuttles away
    under the potting-shed,
But every one knows that evil spirits take
    many forms.

.   .   .   .   .

Drive,
Frosty sea,
Against the high beak of this junk,
Cover the painted eyes with foam.
Kuan-Yin, Goddess of sailors,

Care for this man;
Even in remembering, his betrothed has
    forgotten him.
It will be long — long —
Before they sit together gazing at the
    flowery candles.
Pirate junks make bitter waiting.
The moon above the potting-sheds is
    cold.

．　　．　　．　　．

Disaster,
A great plague of disaster,
Fallen upon the factory of Mêng Tsung.
Evil spirits in clay, in water, in fire.
The clay weakens in the potter's grasp
And falls to powder on the wheel.
When the furnaces are opened,
The lovely-shaped vessels
Are run into flakes of cream
At the bottom of the seggars.
The tcha wood,
The strong, horned tcha wood,
Crisp, brittle, dried to the very bite of
    fire,
Hewn perfectly,
Split to an even thickness,
Piled with meticulous care by the circular
    pilers —
The tcha wood dies under the touch of
    the lighters,
It crackles as though each pore seeped
    water;
And the men who carry it to the ovens
Swear at the splinters buried in their
    flesh.
Cinnabar vases bake an acrid chrome,
Blue glaze gutters into thorns of yellow,
Fox fingers smear the delicately etched
    designs.
Have the P'ei-se-kong, the colour-mixers,
    gone mad?
The pound — pound — of their pestles
    seems louder than usual.
No — pestles do not strike with such a
    clang:
Devil gongs beat on the roof-tiles,
Devil bells tinkle at the windows,
A bloody moon casts an ape's shadow
On the open space before the warehouse
    door.
There is a wailing of gibbons in the wil-
    low-trees,
But gibbons do not live in the populous
    city of King-te-chin.

In twos, in threes, in companies,
The servants of the factory slink away.
Chou-Kiou weeps at her painting,
For the junk with the watching eyes is
    desperately overdue.

Foxes dance by night in dim, old China,
And the agent of the Emperor demands
    the delivery of the Palace bowls.

Mêng Tsung is a crazy man,
He nods his head and claps his hands,
He sits and plays a game of chess
In a staring, stuttering idleness.
Swallows build in the eye-holes of his
    kilns.

See her pick her way up the stony path,
Her little feet, small as the quarters of a
    sweet orange,
Bear her sadly over the roughness.
The stars hang out of the sky like lotus-
    seeds,
It is the third watch, and the city gates
    are shut.
Taoist priests know many things,
And folk bewitched say nothing of diffi-
    culties.

The whine of an owl trembles along the
    darkness.
She runs,
Flinging her heart forward,
Reaching to it,
Floundering.

"We need light," says the Taoist priest,
And he cuts a bit of paper round like the
    moon
And hangs it on the wall.
And it is the moon,
Smoothly shining,
Silver and lesser silver,
Hanging from a pin.
He steps into the moon to think,
And she sees him drinking rice-wine
And slowly writing on a tablet.
The room is filled with the larkspur scent
    of ink.

The priest steps down from the paper
    moon.
He reads from a scroll,
Droning the words,
Teetering back and forth on wide, horny
    feet:

"The protection of the sweet-flag has been dishonourably neglected.
Chou-Kiou, accursed woman, following the toys of this present life, has hardened her mind to the teaching of the ages,
She, daughter of Mêng Tsung greatest of those who work in porcelain,
Has strayed from the path of her most respected ancestors.
Thinking of love, she forgot filial piety;
Snared by beauty, she permitted her august father's house to go unguarded.
Now a fox has entered the body of her most directly-to-be-commiserated father,
While he by whom she was truly begot lies bound in the cave of the Tiger-peaked mountain.
Weary, weary, the way of an arrogant heart,
Sad, and beyond sadness, the lot of Chou-Kiou.
With her white hands she must labour,
With her 'golden lily' feet she must stumble under terrific burdens.
The breath of her mouth must coax the flame to enter wet wood,
She must sear and burn before the hot furnaces,
And, waking many nights and days, produce in agony a bowl
'Bright as a mirror, blue as the sky, thin as paper, sweet-sounding to the touch as camphor-jade.' "

China!
China!
The voice of Chou-Kiou is very small,
Her eyes are pale,
Her limbs stiff as frozen thorns:
"And if I do this thing,
What of him, Wu, my betrothed?"
"The scroll is written," said the Taoist priest.
The Gods are many and confused in old, dim China.

.   .   .   .   .

Morning leaping from the rims of the mountains;
Darkness leaning farther and farther over a descending sun.
Clouds bring rain,
And winds dry the pools of it.

The North-west wind whirls dust over the willow-trees;
Wild duck and teal cross and re-cross King-te-chin
In search of water,
And the hurry of their wings
Is the rush of the Northern monsoon
Sweeping the gulf of Tonkin.
Chou-Kiou pounds the blue clay,
Kneading it with effort to its finest granules.

Days and Days —
The smartweed reddens on the river shoals;
Eye-fruit and pears are dropping in the gardens;
Floating elm-leaves gild running water;
The pinnacles of the Dragon Mountains are clear above red mist.
Chou-Kiou paints a crane and two mandarin ducks
Under a persimmon-tree.
She dips the jar, and poises it,
But her ears are numb with the heavy sound of the sea.

Cold winds.
Long Autumn.
"Leaves touched by frost are redder than flowers of the second moon."
How drag the great wood,
How build it into a circle of fire,
Waveringly uncertain on the "golden lily" feet?
Shêng! Shêng! The water-clock marks an hour which has gone.

The wind is sad, blowing ceaselessly from the clear stars,
The lamp-flower flickers and dies down.
Is her shadow some one?
Is she, perhaps, not alone?

She raises the bamboo blind,
Snow is falling,
The branches of the Winter plum-tree
Glitter like jade hairpins against a white sky.
Brooms brush little snow,
Her fox father laughs and rattles his chess-men.
Chou-Kiou,
Bones under frosty water

Bleach as white as the jade-coloured
branches of the plum-tree:
You remember now,
Sweeping from dawn till evening
A pathway to the kilns.

She has blown upon the fire and kindled
it,
She has set her fragile bowl in the midst
of the flame.
She lifts her eyes from the red fire
For green Spring is like smoke in the
willow-trees.
The rivers run flooding over the wharves
of King-te-chin.
She hears the porters shouting: "Way!
Way!"
In the streets, going up and down from
the boats.
But about her is only the harsh sound of
fire,
And a crow calling: "Ka! Ka! Ka!"
In a mulberry-tree.

Ashes of fire,
Ashes of the days of the World!
If failure, then another long beginning.
Why hope,
Why think that Spring must bring relent-
ing.
O man of this woman,
Where on all the Spring-flown oceans
Is your junk?
Where your heart that you cannot hear
the cuckoos calling from the fir woods
of the Golden Yoke Cliff?
China blossoms above her sea-beaches,
Her trees break budding to an early sun,
Foot-boats fly along the blue rivers,
But Chou-Kiou sobs as brick by brick she
opens the cooled kiln.

Oh, marvel of lightness!
Oh, colour hidden and all at once em-
phatically clear!
Like a bright moon carved in ice,
Green as the thousand peaks,
Blue as the sky after rain,
Violet as the skin of an egg-plant fruit,
Then once again white,
White as the "secretly-smiling" magnolia,
And singing a note when struck
Sharp and full as all the hundred and
fifty bells
On the Porcelain Tower of Nankin.

This bowl is worth one hundred taels of
silver.
Pour in the black dragon tea,
Plucked in April before the Spring rains,
This shall be a libation to Kuan-Yin,
Goddess of Mercy.
Chou-Kiou has no wine.
Fragrant Goddess, despise not the yellow
tea.
But the tea bubbles,
It moves like waves in a short bay,
It tumbles with a glitter of rainbows.
Wing-flare widening out of the cup —
The great crane sweeps into the air.
He circles round Chou-Kiou,
Circles, circles —
With him are the mandarin ducks.
The air is dark with wings,
It is bright with the clipping and cut-
ting
Of quickly-flickered wings.
In a whirl of wind,
Something comes twirling and dazzling
out of the house,
Flapping in plum-coloured silks,
Confusing with motion,
Blurred,
Without contour.
It is a man —
It is a bit of paper —
It is a bamboo-silk cocoon —
It blows, turning — turning — toward the
bowl,
It is blown into the bowl —
The tea is red,
It leaps, water-spouting, into the air.
It soars over the red roof-tiles,
It glitters like a pagoda hot with
lamps,
And then descends,
Sucking, into the bowl,
Sucking, out of the bowl,
Disappearing where there is no hole.

It is a beautiful piece,
With white and grey peonies and yellow
persimmons.
There are no birds, only flowers,
Starting in a chord of colours out of
violet haze.
Chou-Kiou has fainted,
She does not hear Mêng Tsung
Calling to her from the Terrace of the
Peach-Trees.
        .   .   .   .   .

I read this tale in the "Azure Sky Book-shop," in the ninth month of the sixth year of Tô Kwong.

When I had reached this point, the shadows of a thirty-two-paper kite fell upon my page, and raising my eyes to the sky, the whiteness of the sun dazzled me, and I inadvertently turned over the leaves of the book.

How many I turned, I do not know, but when I could see again after the blindness of the sky I read at once, not daring to go back for the leap of the story upon which I had fallen —

"Pity, pity me,
For my flesh cries night and morning;
The darkness hears me,
And the tongues of the darkness babble back his name.
I am eager and thwarted.
Daughter I am,
And as a daughter I have given my brain and my body
To restore my father's house.
Alone, with bleeding feet and frozen hands,
I have lifted the curse fallen upon my people;
I have toiled without sleep
Until the sight of my eyes was broken.
Hungering for days, chattering with cold and sorrow,
I have not suffered my heart to weaken.
My prayers have risen incessantly to the thirty-three Heavens.
All powerful Goddess, you have regarded me,
And taken me under your protection.
I am a worm,
Spurning the mulberry-leaf to cry upon the moon.
Holy Kuan-Yin, of the thousand eyes, and the thousand arms, and the merciful heart,
I beseech a farther clemency.
You, who answer the longings of the sterile,
Do not mock me with a half-completed pardon.
Daughter I am, Kuan-Yin,
But I am also a woman.
I love as women here in China must not,
But as you know very well they must and do.

Glory has once more entered into my father's heart,
All day he watches his men.
He weighs the precious blue earth and numbers it.
He oversees the lame men who knead the clay,
He praises and chides the painters,
And rises in the night to superintend the firers.
King-te-chin hums like a hive at swarming time
Between its rivers,
And this is the loudest of all the factories of King-te-chin.
Only I am desolate.
I am as the shadow of a bamboo upon bleached sand,
My eyes are black and colourless seeking the boats on the long canals,
My ears rattle waiting for the sharp sound of a voice at the gate.
Once more I will work, Kuan-Yin,
I will use all my skill to honour you.
I will fashion you in such a manner that your eyes will laugh to see it.
I will make a figure of you in fine silk porcelain
And set it in the temple where all can see,
And, looking, their hearts will be to you as coral beads on a string of white gold
For your hand's stretching,
And for an ornament upon your breast forever."

Then Chou-Kiou tightened her willow-coloured girdle
And sat down to the modelling board.
And on the fifteenth day the figure was completed,
Not entirely to Chou-Kiou's dissatisfaction.
Underneath it she wrote: "Made at the Brilliant Colours Hall."
And again: "Reverentially made by Chou-Kiou, daughter of Mêng Tsung Captain of the Banner promoted four honorary grades, also Director of a Porcelain Manufactory at King-te-chin in the Province of Kiangsi: and presented by her to the Temple of the Holy God of Heaven to remain through everlasting time as an offering of a grateful heart and as a glory in the eyes of men: on a fortunate day

in the Spring of the 6th year of the reign of the Emperor Ch'ien-lung."

For days she paints it,
Rubbing the gold with garlic-bulbs
To fix its lustre.
Laying copper-foil about it to heighten the colour,
Setting it with careful blue:
The blue of little stones,
The blue of the precious stone Meï-Koueï-tse-yeou,
The blue of the head of Buddha.
She dreams of beauty,
And the face of the figure is lovely as her dreams;
But has it not been written: "It is useless to cast a net to catch the image of the moon."

Night over China,
Night over old, distant China,
Dark night over the city of King-te-chin.
Chou-Kiou,
Chou-Kiou,
Your eyes are red watching the flames of a furnace,
And the great shield of wood you hold
Scarcely protects you from the bursting heat of the kiln.
For three days and three nights
You have tended a flowing fire;
For two days and two nights
You have watched before a fierce fire;
Now the seggar is red and passing into a white heat,
It is bright in front and behind.
At cock-crow you will stop the fire,
But to-night you watch,
And your eyes are salt
As though you stood before the sea.
A wind teases the willow-trees,
They rustle,
And fling the moonlight from them like spray.

And then snow fell from the midst of the moon.
The flakes were like willow-flowers,
They drifted down slowly,
And the brilliance of the moon struck upon them as they fell
So that all the air was flowing with silver,
And walking in the arc of it was a woman

Who cast a whip-like shadow before her
From the brightness of the snow and the white, round moon.

All the flowers bend toward her,
The grass by the ring-fence lies horizontally to reach her,
She moves with the movement of wind over water,
And it is no longer the moon which casts her shadow
But she who sets shadows curving outward
From the pebbles at her feet.
Her dress is Ch'ing-green playing into scarlet,
Embroidered with the hundred shous;
The hem is a slow delight of gold, the faded, beautiful gold of temple carvings;
In her hair is a lotus,
Red as the sun after rain.
She comes softly — softly —
And the tinkle of her ornaments
Jars the smooth falling of the snow
So that it breaks into jagged lightnings
Which form about her the characters of her holy name:
Kuan-Yin, Goddess of Mercy, of Sailors, of all who know sorrow and grieve in bitterness.

Ochre-red sails are dark in moonlight,
But the red heart of man is like a water-clock dripping the hours;
Lost days weigh many ounces of silver,
But green Spring is worth blood and gold.

Snow ceases falling,
Moonlight is no longer broken, but a single piece.
Her eyebrows are fine as the edge of distant mountains,
Her eyes are clear as the T'ung-T'ing lake in Autumn,
Her face is sweet as almond-flowers in a wind.
The breath of her passing is cool;
Her gesture is a plum-blossom waving.
She mounts the step
And looks into the eye-hole of the kiln.
One — two — three, the pulse of Chou-Kiou,
Beating to a given time, like music.
The coals of the fire are not fierce now

But gentle,
They lie in the form of roses
And the scent of them is the urgent scent
    of musk.

A watchman calls the hour
And strikes on his bamboo drum.
The moon fades down a long green sky.
There is no one on the step,
No flight of silks down the pathway,
Chou-Kiou sickens to a weariness which
    eats her bones.
She rakes the scattered embers.
The firing is done.

Spring day.
How sharp the pheasants' cry,
Like metal!
This year the bamboo flowers,
This year the many-petalled peonies
Are large as rising moons.
The men of the "Brilliant Coloured Fac-
    tory" stand
In their blue jackets,
In their dark-purple silk jackets,
In a curve like the bow moon,
Watching Chou-Kiou advancing to the
    furnace.
And Mêng Tsung stands,
Fearfully watching.
No one must touch,
No one must caution,
No one must pray.
It is between Chou-Kiou and the Gods.
How do her ancestors in the thirty-three
    Heavens?
Do they watch?
Do they listen?
Do they desire and remain silent?
Ten times round her hands
The cloth is wrapped.
Yet will they be blistered —
But it is cool!
Cold!
And the seggar falls apart without a
    touch.

Fragrant Goddess,
Whose heart is of snow and rubies,
Is this the figure made by Chou-Kiou?
Not so, certainly.
Slimmer,
Lovelier,
More quaintly golden.
This face is clouds and flowers,

These eyes are wind and flame,
This body is jade and silver.
Her dress is the smoky green of Autumn
    lakes
Flashed and tinted to immediate scarlet,
It is embroidered with the hundred shous.
Poised is this figure,
Balanced like a music
Of flageolets and harps under the Dawn.
Men cover their faces,
Here is a beauty to turn the dart of
    arrows.
But Chou-Kiou's figure was single,
This is triplicate.
Attendants guard the dazzling Goddess.
One (who dares to see it!) Chou-Kiou,
In her peach-bloom dress with the wil-
    low-coloured girdle,
And clasped and cherished in her hands
The sacred peach.
The other is a man,
Blue-dressed as in running waves,
Bronze and crimson with the rake of the
    sea.
The gate-keepers shout his name,
Swift are his steps,
Like songs for gladness
His footsteps,
He is a straight shaft of sapphire,
He is a peacock feather borne upon a
    spear.
He and she before the Goddess,
Heads in the dust.
Not alone do the bamboos flower;
Here are blossoms and fruit.
Kuan-Yin, Goddess of Mercy, of Sailors,
    of Sterile Women,
For what they pray let them have full
    answer:
Guide them as with a torch,
Scatter snow and heat like the cool of the
    moon,
Defend them against enemies as a moat
    or a city,
Save them in danger as a father or
    mother,
Quicken them as rain and sun,
Bless the seed of this man as corn under
    a rich sun,
Bless the womb of this woman as fishes
    are blessed by the sea.

Then the multitude rose up
And proclaimed them mighty.
They placed her in the scarlet palanquin

And brought her before him.
They lit the flower candles;
With painted lanterns in broad daylight
they lined the roads.
Drums and musicians played forever,
And fireworks blazed in the heart of the
sky.
So the day fell
And the night came,
And the lizard-skin drums struck mid-
night,
And the marriage was accomplished.

Sweetly the moon slept in the willow-
trees,
And the man and the woman slept under
the green eyelids of the Dawn.

.   .   .   .   .

When I finished the book, night had
come.
I could not part with it, so I bought it
for two ounces of silver.
Did I overprize it, do you think?
It is only a tale of old, dead China.

MANY SWANS

Sun Myth of the North
American Indians

When the Goose Moon rose and
walked upon a pale sky, and water made
a noise once more beneath the ice on the
river, his heart was sick with longing for
the great good of the sun. One Winter
again had passed, one Winter like the
last. A long sea with waves biting each
other under grey clouds, a shroud of
snow from ocean to forest, snow mumbling stories of bones and driftwood beyond his red fire. He desired space, light;
he cried to himself about himself, he
made songs of sorrow and wept in the
corner of his house. He gave his children
toys to keep them away from him. His
eyes were dim following the thin sun. He
said to his wife: "I want that sun. Some
day I shall go to see it." And she said:
"Peace, be still. You will wake the children."

So he waited, and the Whirlwind
Moon came, a crescent — mounted, and
marched down beyond the morning, and
was gone. Then the Extreme Cold Moon
came and shone, it mounted, moved
night by night into morning and faded
through day to darkness. He watched
the Old Moon pass, he saw the Eagle
Moon come and go. Slowly the moons
wound across the snow, and many nights
he could not see them, he could only hear
the waves raving foam and fury until
dawn.

Now the Goose Moon told him things,
but his blood lay sluggish within him

until the moon stood full and apart in
the sky. His wife asked why he was silent.
"I have wept my eyes dry," he answered.
"Give me my cedar bow and my two-
winged arrows with the copper points. I
will go into the forest and kill a moose,
and bring fresh meat for the children."

All day he stalked the forest. He saw
the marks of bears' claws on the trees.
He saw the wide tracks of a lynx, and the
little slot-slot of a jumping rabbit, but
nothing came along. Then he made a
melancholy song for himself: "My name
is Many Swans, but I have seen neither
sparrow nor rabbit, neither duck nor
crane. I will go home and sit by the fire
like a woman and spin cedar bark for fish-
lines."

Then silver rain ran upon him through
the branches from the moon, and he
stepped upon open grass and laughed at
the touch of it under his foot. "I will
shoot the moon," he thought, "and cut
it into cakes for the children."

He laid an arrow on his bow and shot,
and the copper tip made it shine like a
star flying. He watched to see it fall, but
it did not. He shot again, and his arrow
was a bright star until he lost it in the
brilliance of the moon. Soon he had shot
all his arrows, and he stood gaping up at
the moonshine wishing he had not lost
them.

Then Many Swans laughed again because his feet touched grass, not snow.
And he gathered twigs and stuck them
in his hair, and saw his shadow like a

tree walking there. But something tapped
the twigs, he stood tangled in something.
With his hand he felt it, it was the
feather head of an arrow. It dangled
from the sky, and the copper tip jangled
upon wood and twinkled brightly. This
— that — and other twinkles, pricking
against the soft flow of the moon, and
the wind crooned in the arrow-feathers
and tinkled the bushes in his hair.

Many Swans laid his hand on the arrow and began to climb — up — up — a
long time. The earth lay beneath him
wide and blue, he climbed through white
moonlight and purple air until he fell
asleep from weariness.

Sunlight struck sidewise on a chain of
arrows; below were cold clouds; above, a
sky blooming like an open flower and he
aiming to the heart of it. Many Swans
saw that up was far, and down was also
far, but he cried to himself that he had
begun his journey to the sun. Then he
pulled a bush from his hair, and the
twigs had leaved and fruited, and there
were salmon-berries dancing beneath the
leaves. "My father, the sun, is good,"
said Many Swans, and he eat the berries
and went on climbing the arrows into the
heart of the sky.

He climbed till the sun set and the
moon rose, and at midmost moon he fell
asleep to the sweeping of the arrow-
ladder like a cradle in the wind.

When dawn struck gold across the
ladder, he awoke. "It is Summer," said
Many Swans, "I cannot go back, it must
be more days down than I have travelled.
I should be ashamed to see my children,
for I have no meat for them." Then he
remembered the bushes, and pulled another from his hair, and there were blue
huckleberries shining like polished wood
in the midst of leaves. "The sun weaves
the seasons," thought Many Swans, "I
have been under and over the warp of
the world, now I am above the world,"
and he went on climbing into the white
heart of the sky.

Another night and day he climbed, and
he eat red huckleberries from his last
bush, and went on — up and up — his
feet scratching on the ladder with a great
noise because of the hush all round him.

When he reached an edge, he stepped
over it carefully, for edges are thin and
he did not wish to fall. He found a tall
pine-tree by a pond. "Beyond can wait,"
reasoned Many Swans, "this is surely a
far country." And he lay down to sleep
under the pine-tree, and it was the fourth
sleep he had had since he went hunting
moose to bring meat to his family.

The shadow crept away from him, and
the sun came and sat upon his eyelids, so
that by and by he opened them and
rubbed his eyes because a woman stared
at him, and she was beautiful as a salmon
leaping in Spring. Her skirt was woven
of red and white cedar bark, she had
carved silver bracelets and copper bracelets set with haliotis shell, and ear-rings
of sharks' teeth. She sparkled like a river
salmon, and her smile was water tipping
to a light South breeze. She pleased the
heart of Many Swans so that fear was not
in him, only longing to take her for himself as a man does a woman, and he asked
her name. "Grass-Bush-and-Blossom is
my name," she answered. "I am come
after you. My grandmother has sent me
to bring you to her house." "And who is
your grandmother?" asked Many Swans.
But the girl shook her head, and took
a pinch of earth from the ground and
threw it toward the sun. "She has many
names. The grass knows her, and the
trees, and the fishes in the sea. I call
her 'grandmother,' but they speak of
her as 'The-One-Who-Walks-All-Over-
the-Sky.'" Many Swans marvelled and
said nothing, for things are different in
a far country.

They walked together, and the man
hungered for the woman and could not
wait. But she said no word, and he eat
up her beauty as though it were a ripe
foam-berry and still went fasting until
his knees trembled, and his heart was like
hot dust, and his hands ached to thrust
upon her and turn her toward him. So
they went, and Many Swans forgot his
wife and children and the earth hanging
below the sharp edge of the sky.

.   .   .   .   .

The South wind sat on a rock and
never ceased to blow, locking the

branches of the trees together; a flock of swans rose out of the South-East, one and seven, making strange, changing lines across a smooth sky. Wild flax-blossoms ran blue over the bases of black and red totem poles. The colours were strong as blood and death, they rattled like painted drums against the eyesight. "Many Swans!" said the girl and smiled. "Blood and death," drummed the totem poles. "Alas!" nodded the flax. The man heeded nothing but the woman and the soles of his feet beating on new ground.

The houses were carved with the figures of the Spring Salmon. They were carved in the form of a rainbow. Hooked noses stood out above doorways, crooked wooden men crouched, frog-shaped, gazing under low eaves. It was a beautiful town, ringing with colours, singing brightly, terribly, in the smooth light. All the way was sombre and gay, and the man walked and said nothing.

They came to a house painted black and carved with stars. In the centre was a round moon with a door in it. So they entered and sat beside the fire, and the woman gave the man fish-roes and gooseberries, but his desire burnt him and he could not eat.

Grass-Bush-and-Blossom saw his trouble, and she led him to a corner, and showed him many things. There were willow arrows and quivers for them. There were mountain-goat blankets and painted blankets of two elk-skins, there were buffalo-skins, and dressed buckskins, and deerskins with young, soft hair. But Many Swans cared for nothing but the swing of the woman's bark skirt, and the sting of her loveliness which gave him no peace.

Grass-Bush-and-Blossom led him to another corner, and showed him crest helmets, and wooden armour; she showed him coppers like red rhododendron blooms, and plumes of eagles' wings. She gave him clubs of whalebone to handle, and cedar trumpets which blow a sound cool and sweet as the noise of bees. But Many Swans found no ease in looking save at her arms between the bracelets, and his trouble grew and pressed upon him until he felt strangled.

She led him farther and showed him a canoe painted silver and vermilion with white figures of fish upon it, and the gunwales fore and aft were set with the teeth of the sea-otter. She lifted out the paddles, the blades were shaped like hearts and striped with fire hues. She said, "Choose. These are mine and my grandmother's. Take what you will." But Many Swans was filled with the glory of her standing as a young tree about to blossom, and he took her and felt her sway and fold about him with the tightness of new leaves. "This" — said Many Swans, "this — for am I not a man!" So they abode and the day ran gently past them, slipping as river water, and evening came, and someone entered, darkening the door.

Then Grass-Bush-and-Blossom wrapped her cedar-bark skirt about her and sprang up, and her silver and copper ornaments rang sweetly with her moving. The-One-Who-Walks-All-Over-the-Sky looked at Many Swans. "You have not waited," she said. "Alas! It is an evil beginning. My son, my son, I wished to love you." But he was glad and thought: "It is a querulous old woman, I shall heed her no more than the crackling of a fire of frost-bitten twigs."

The old woman went behind the door and hung up something. It pleased him. It was shining, When he woke in the night, he saw it in the glow of the fire. He liked it, and he liked the skins he lay on and fold about him with the woman who lay with him. He thought only of these things.

In the morning, the old woman unhooked the shining object and went out, and he turned about to his wife and said sharp, glad words to her and she to him, and the sun shone into the house until evening, and in the night again he was happy, because of the thing that glittered and flashed and moved to and fro, clashing softly on the wall.

The days were many. He did not count them. Every morning the old woman took out the shining thing, and every evening she brought it home, and all night it shone and cried "Ching-a-ling" as it dangled against the wall.

Moons and moons went by, no doubt. Many Swans did not reckon them out.

Was there an earth? Was there a sky?
He remembered nothing. He did not
try. And then one day, wandering along
the street of carved houses, he heard a
song. He heard the beat of rattles and
drums, and the shrill humming of
trumpets blown to a broken rhythm:

"Haiōō'a! Haiōō!
Many salmon are coming ashore,
They are coming ashore to you, the
    post of our heaven,
They are dancing from the salmon's
    country to the shore.
I come to dance before you at the
    right-hand side of the world, over-
    towering, outshining, surpassing
    all: I, the Salmon!
Haiōō'a! Haiōō!"

And the drums rumbled like the first
thunder of a year, and the rattles pattered like rain on flower petals, and the
trumpets hummed as wind hums in
round-leafed trees; and people ran, jumping, out of the Spring Salmon house and
leapt to the edge of the sky and disappeared, falling quickly, calling the song
to one another as they fell so that the
sound of it continued rising up for a long
time.
Many Swans listened, and he recollected that when the Spring salmon jump,
the children say: "Ayuu! Do it again!"
He thought of his children and his wife
whom he had left on the earth, and wondered who had brought them meat, who
had caught fish for them, and he was sad
at his thoughts and wept, saying: "I want
to shoot birds for my children. I want
to spear trout for my children." So he
went back to his house, and his feet
dragged behind him like nets drawn
across sand.
He lay down upon his bed and grieved,
because he had no children in the sky,
and because the wife of his youth was
lost to him. He would not eat, but lay
with his head covered and made no
sound.
Then Grass-Bush-and-Blossom asked
him: "Why do you grieve?" But he was
silent. And again she said: "Why do you
grieve?" But he answered nothing. And
she asked him many times, until at last

he told her of his children, of his other
wife whom he had left, and she was pitiful because she loved him.
When the old woman came, she also
said: "What ails your husband that he
lies there saying nothing?" And Grass-
Bush-and-Blossom answered: "He is
homesick. We must let him depart."
Many Swans heard what she said, and
he got up and made himself ready. Now
the old woman looked sadly at him. "My
son," she said, "I told you it was a bad
beginning. But I wish to love you. Choose
among these things what you will have,
and return to your people."
Many Swans pointed to the shining
thing behind the door and said: "I will
have that." But the old woman would
not give it to him. She offered him
spears of bone, and yew bows, and arrows winged with ducks' feathers. But
he would not have them. She offered
him strings of blue and white shells, and
a copper canoe with a sternboard of
copper and a copper bailer. He would
not take them. He wanted the thing that
glittered and cried "Ching-a-ling" as it
dangled against the wall. She offered him
all that was in the house. But he liked
that great thing that was shining there.
When that thing turned round it was
shining so that one had to close one's
eyes. He said: "That only will I have."
Then she gave it to him, saying: "You
wanted it. I wished to love you, and I do
love you." She hung it on him. "Now
go home."
Many Swans ran swiftly, he ran to the
edge of the sky, there he found the ladder
of the rainbow. He put his foot on it
and went down, and he felt strong and
able to do anything. He forgot the sky
and thought only of the earth.

Many Swans made a song as he went
down the rainbow ladder. He sang with
a loud voice:

"I will go and tear to pieces Mount
    Stevens, I will use it for stones for
    my fire.
I will go and break Mount Qa'tsta'is,
    I will use it for stones for my fire."

All day and all night he went down,
and he was so strong he did not need to

sleep. The next day he made a new song. He shouted it with a great noise:

"I am going all round the world,
I am at the centre of the world,
I am the post of the world,
On account of what I am carrying in my hand."

This pleased him, and he sang it all day and was not tired at all.

Four nights and days he was going down the ladder, and every day he made a song, and the last was the best. This was it:

"Oh wonder! He is making a turmoil on the earth.
Oh wonder! He makes the noise of falling objects on the earth.
Oh wonder! He makes the noise of breaking objects on the earth."

He did not really mean this, but it was a good song. That is the way with people who think themselves clever. Many Swans sang this song a great many times and on the fourth day, when the dawn was red, he touched the earth and walked off upon it.

. . . . .

When Many Swans arrived on the earth, he was not very near his village. He stood beneath a sea-cliff, and the rocks of the cliff were sprinkled with scarlet moss as it might have been a fall of red snow, and lilac moss smouldered between boulders of pink granite. Far out, the sea sparkled all colours like an abalone shell, and red fish sprang from it — one and another, over its surface. As he gazed, a shadow slipped upon the water, and, looking up, he saw a raven flying and overturning as it flew. Red fish, black raven — blood and death — but Many Swans called "Haiohō-hō!" and danced a long time on the sea-sand because he felt happy in his heart.

He heard a robin singing, and as it sang he walked along the shore and counted his fingers for the headlands he must pass to reach home. He saw the canoes come out to fish, he said the names of his friends who should be in them. He thought of his house and the hearth strewn with white shells and sand. When the canoes of twelve rowers passed, he tried to signal them, but they went by too far from land. The way seemed short, for all day he told himself stories of what people would say to him. "I shall be famous, my fame will reach to the ends of the world. People will try to imitate me. Every one will desire to possess my power." So Many Swans said foolish things to himself, and the day seemed short until the evening when he came in sight of his village.

At the dusky time of night, he came to it, and he heard singing, so he knew his people were having a festival. He could hear the dance-sticks clattering on the cedar boards and the moon-rattles whirling, and he could see the smoke curling out of the smoke-holes. Then he shouted very much and ran fast; but, as he ran, the thing which he carried in his hands shook and cried: "We shall strike your town." Then Many Swans went mad; he turned, swirling like a great cloud, he rose as a pillar of smoke and bent in the wind as smoke bends, he streamed as bands of black smoke, and out of him darted flames, red-mouthed flames, so that they scorched his hair. His hands were full of blood, and he yelled "Break! Break! Break! Break!" and did not know whose voice it was shouting.

There was a tree, and a branch standing out from it, and fire came down and hung on the end of the branch. He thought it was copper which swung on the tree, because it twirled and had a hard edge. Then it split as though a wedge had riven it, and burst into purple flame. The tree was consumed, and the fire leapt laughing upon the houses and poured down through the roofs upon the people. The flame-mouths stuck themselves to the houses and sucked the life from all the people, the flames swallowed themselves and brought forth little flames which ran a thousand ways like young serpents just out of their eggs, till the fire girdled the village and the water in front curdled and burned like oil.

Then Many Swans knew what he had done, and he tried to throw away his power which was killing everybody. But he could not do it. The people lay there dead, and his wife and children among the dead people. His heart was sick, and he cried: "The weapon flew into my hands with which I am murdering," and he tried to throw it away, but it stuck to his flesh. He tried to cut it apart with his knife, but the blade turned and blunted. He cried bitterly: "Ka! Ka! Ka! Ka!" and tried to break what he wore on a stone, but it did not break. Then he cut off his hair and blackened his face, and turned inland to the spaces of the forest, for his heart was dead with his people. And the moon followed him over the tops of the trees, but he hated the moon because it reminded him of the sky.

. . . . .

A long time Many Swans wandered in the forest. White-headed eagles flew over the trees and called down to him: "There is the man who killed everybody." By night the owls hooted to each other: "The man who sleeps has blood on him, his mouth is full of blood, he let loose his power on his own people." Many Swans beat upon his breast and pleaded with the owls: "You with ears far apart who hear everything, you the owls, it was not I who killed, but this evil thing I carry and which I cannot put down." But the owls laughed, shrill, mournful, broken laughs, repeating the words they had said, so that Many Swans could not sleep and in the morning he was so weak he shook when he walked.

He walked among pines which flowed before him in straight, opening lines like water, and the wind in the pine-branches wearied his soul as he heard it all day long. At first he eat nothing, but when he stumbled and fell for faintness he gathered currants and partridge-berries and so made his feet carry him on.

He came to a wood of red firs where fire had been before him. The heartwood of the firs was all burnt out, but the trees stood on stilts of sapwood and mocked the man who slew with fire.

He passed through woods of spear-leaf trees, with sharp vines head-high all about them. He thrust the thing he carried into the vines and tried to let go of it, but it would not stay tangled and came away in his hand.

He heard the slap of beavers' tails on water, and saw muskrats building cabins with the stalks of wild rice in shoal water, but they scattered as he came near. The little animals fled before him in fear, chattering to each other. Even the bears deserted the huckleberry bushes when they heard the fall of his foot, so that he walked alone. Above him, the waxwings were catching flies in the spruce-tops, they were happy because it was Summer and warm, they were the only creatures too busy to look down at the man who moved on as one who never stops, making his feet go always because there was nothing else to do.

By and by the trees thinned, and Many Swans saw beyond them to a country of tall grass. He rested here some time eating fox-grapes and blackberries, for indeed he was almost famished, and weary with the sickness of solitude. He thought of the ways of men, and hungered after speech and comforting. But he saw no man, and the prairie frightened him, rolling endlessly to the sky.

At last his blood quickened again, and the longing for people beat a hard pulse in his throat so that he rose and went on, seeking where he might find men. For days he sought, following the trails of wild horses and buffalo, tripping among the crawling pea-vines, bruised and baffled, blind with the sharp shimmer of the grass.

Then suddenly they came, riding out of the distance on both sides of him. These men wore eagle-plume bonnets, and their horses went so fast he could not see their legs. They ran glittering toward one another, whooping and screaming, and the horses' tails streamed out behind them stiffly like bunches of bones. Each man lay prone on his horse and shot arrows, hawk-feathered arrows, owl-feathered arrows, and they were terrible in swiftness because the feathers had not been cut or burned to make them low.

The arrows flew across one another like a swarm of grasshoppers leaping, and the men foamed forward as waves foam at a double tide.

They came near, bright men, fine as whips, striding lithe cat horses. One rode a spotted horse, and on his head was an upright plume of the tail-feathers of the black eagle. One rode a buckskin horse, long-winded and chary as a panther. One rode a sorrel horse painted with zigzag lightnings. One rode a clay-coloured horse, and the figure of a kingfisher was stamped in blue on its shoulder. Wildcat running horses, and their hoofs rang like thunder-drums on the ground, and the men yelled with brass voices:

"We who live are coming.
Ai-ya-ya-yai!
We are coming to kill.
Ai-ya-ya-yai!
We are coming with the snake arrows,
We are coming with the tomahawks
Which swallow their faces.
Ai-ya-ya-yai!
We will hack our enemies.
Ai-ya-ya-yai!
We will take many scalps.
Ai-ya-ya-yai!
We will kill — kill — till every one is dead.
Ai-ya-ya-ya-yai!"

Many Swans lay in a buffalo wallow and hid, and a white fog slid down from the North and covered the prairie. For a little time he heard the war-whoops and the pit-pit of hitting arrows, and then he heard nothing, and he lay beneath the cold fog hurting his ears with listening. When the sky was red in the evening and the fog was lifted, he shifted himself and looked above the grass. "Alas! Alas!" wept Many Swans, "the teeth of their arrows were like dogs' teeth. They have devoured their enemies." For nobody was there, but the arrows were sticking up straight in the ground. Then Many Swans went a long way round that place for he thought that the stomachs of the arrows must be full of blood. And so he went on alone over the prairie, and his heart was black with what he had seen.

· · · · · ·

A stream flowed in a sunwise turn across the prairie, and the name of the stream was "Burnt Water," because it tasted dark like smoke. The prairie ran out tongues of raw colours — blue of camass, red of geranium, yellow of parsley — at the young green grass. The prairie flung up its larks on a string of sunshine, it lay like a catching-sheet beneath the black breasts balancing down on a wind, calling "See it! See it! See it!" in little round voices.

Antelope and buffalo,
Threading the tall green grass they go,
To and fro, to and fro.
And painted Indians ride in a row,
With arrow and bow, arrow and bow,
Hunting the antelope, the buffalo.
Truly they made a gallant show
Across the prairie's bright green flow,
Warriors painted indigo,
Brown antelope, black buffalo,
Long ago.

· · · · · ·

Now when he heard the barking of dogs, and saw the bundles of the dead lashed to the cottonwood-trees, Many Swans knew that he was near a village. He stood still, for he dared not go on because of the thing which he had with him. He said to himself, "My mind is not strong enough to manage it. My mind is afraid of it." But he longed to speak with men, and so he crept a little nearer until he could see the painted tepees standing in the edge of the sunshine, and smell the smoke of dried sweet grass. Many Swans heard the tinkling of small bells from the buffalo tails hung on the tepees, he saw the lodge ears move gently in the breeze. He heard talk, the voices of men, and he cried aloud and wept, holding his hands out toward the village.

Then the thing which he was carrying shook, and said: "We shall strike that town." Many Swans heard it, and he tried to keep quiet. He tried to throw the thing down, but his hands closed. He could not keep his mind, and his senses flew away so that he was crazy. He heard a great voice shouting: "Break! Break! Break! Break!" but he did not know that it was his own voice.

Back over the prairie sprang up a round cloud, and fire rose out of the heart of the grass. The reds and yellows of the flowers exploded into flame, showers of sparks rattled on the metal sky, which turned purple and hurtled itself down upon the earth. Winds charged the fire, lashing it with long thongs of green lightning, herding the flames over the high grass; and the fire screamed and danced and blew blood whistles, and the scarlet feet of the fire clinked a tune of ghost-bells on the shells of the dry cane brakes. Animals ran — ran — ran — and were overtaken, shaken grass glittered up with a roar and spilled its birds like burnt paper into the red air. The eagle's wing melted where it flew, the hills of the prairie grew mountain-high, amazed with light, and were obscured. The people in the village ran — ran — and the fire shot them down with its red and gold arrows and whirled on, crumpling the tepees so that the skins of them popped like corn. Then the bodies of the dead in the trees took fire with a hard smoke, and the burning of the cottonwoods choked Many Swans as he fled. His nostrils smelt the dead, and he was very sick and could not move. Then the fire made a ring round him, and he stood in the midst by the Burnt River and wrung his hands until the skin tore. He took the thing he wore and tried to strip it off in the fork of a tree, but it did not come off at all. He cried: "Ka! Ka! Ka! Ka!" and leapt into the river and tried to drown the thing, but when he rose it rose with him and came out of the water gleaming so that its wake rippled red and silver a long way down the stream.

Then Many Swans lamented bitterly and cried: "The thing I wanted is bad," but he had the thing and he could not part from it. He rolled in the stones and the bushes to scrape it off, but it clung to him and grew in his flesh like hair. Therefore Many Swans dragged himself up to go on, although the heat of the burnt grass scorched his feet and everything was dead about him. He heard nothing, for there was nobody to mock any more.

.   .   .   .   .

Mist rises along the river bottoms, and ghost-voices hiss an old death-song to a false, faint tune. The branches of willows beat on the moon, pound, pound, with a thin, far sound, shaking and shrilling the wonder tale, the thunder tale, of a nation's killing:

The Nation's drum has fallen down.
Beat — beat — and a double beat!
Ashes are the grass of a lodge-pole town.
Rattle — rattle — on a moon that is sinking.
Out of the North come drift winds wailing.
Beat — beat — and a double beat!
In the frost-blue West, a crow is ailing.
The streams, the water streams, are shrinking!

He gave an acre and we gave him brass.
Beat — beat — and a double beat!
Beautiful and bitter are the roses in the grass.
Rattle — rattle — on a moon that is sinking.
A knife painted red and a knife painted black.
Beat — beat — and a double beat!
Green mounds under a hackmatack.
The streams, the water streams, are shrinking!

Is there Summer in the Spring?
Who will bring the South?
Beat — beat — and a double beat!
Shall honey drop from the green snake's mouth?
Rattle — rattle — on a moon that is sinking.
A red-necked buzzard in an incense tree.
Beat — beat — and a double beat!
And a poison leaf from Gethsemane.
The streams, the water streams, are shrinking.

.   .   .   .   .

Now Many Swans walked over cinders, and there was no sprig or root that the fire had left. Therefore he grew weaker day by day, and at night he lay awake tortured for food, and he prayed to the Earth, saying: "Mother Earth have pity on me and give me to eat," but the ears of the Earth were stopped with cinders. Then, after five sleeps, suddenly before him grew a bush of service-berries which the fire had not taken. Many Swans gathered the berries and appeased his hunger. He said: "The berries that grow are blessed, for now I shall live." Yet he knew that he did not want to live, only his hunger raged fiercely within him and he could not stand against it. He took cinders and powdered them, and mixed them with river water, and made his body black, and so he set his back to the river and his face to the mountains and journeyed on.

Up and over the Backbone-of-the-World went Many Swans. Above the peaks of solitude hang the winds of all directions, and because there are a multitude of winds they can hold fire and turn it. Therefore Many Swans felt leaves once more about his face, and the place was kind to his eyes with laurels, and quaking aspens, and honeysuckle-trees. All the bushes and flowers were talking, but it was not about Many Swans. The oaks boasted of their iron sinews: "Fire is a plaything, a ball to be tossed and flung away," and they rustled their leaves and struck their roots farther into the moist soil. The red firs stirred at the challenge: "In Winter your leaves are dry," they called to the oaks, "then the fire-bear can eat you. But our leaves are never dry. They are whips to sting the lips of all fires." But the cedars and the pines said nothing, for they knew that nobody would believe them if they spoke.

Now when the hemlocks ran away from him, and the cold rocks glittered with snow, Many Swans knew that he stood at the peak of the world, and again the longing for men came upon him. "I will descend into a new country," he said. "I will be very careful not to swing the sacred implement, truly it kills people so that they have no time to escape." He thought he could do it, he believed himself, and he knew no rest because of his quest for men.

There was no way to find, but Many Swans went down through the firs, and the yellow pines, and the maples, to a white plain which ran right, and left, and forward, with only a steep sky stopping it very far off; and the sun on the plain was like molten lead pressing him down and his tongue rattled with thirst. So he lifted himself against the weight of the sun and wished a great wish for men and went on, with his desire sobbing in his heart.

To the North was sand, to the East was sand, to the West was sand, to the South was sand, and standing up out of the sand the great flutes of the cactus-trees beckoned him, and flung their flowers out to tempt him — their wax-white flowers, their magenta flowers, their golden-yellow flowers perking through a glass-glitter of spines; all along the ridges of the desert they called to him and he knew not which way to turn. He asked a humming-bird in a scarlet trumpet-flower, and the humming-bird answered: "Across the sunset to the Red Hills." The sun rose and set three times, and again he knew not where to go, so he asked a gilded flicker who was clicking in a giant cactus. And the flicker told him: "Across the sunset to the Red Hills." But when, after many days, he saw no hills, he thought "The birds deceived me," and he asked a desert lily: "Where shall I find men?" And the lily opened her green-and-blue-veined blossom, and discovered the pure whiteness of her heart. "Across the desert to the Red Hills," she told him, and he believed her, and, on the ninth morning after, he saw the hills, and they were heliotrope and salmon, and as the sun lifted, they were red, and when the sun was in the top of the sky, they were blood scarlet. Then Many Swans lay and slept, for he did not wish to reach the hills at nightfall lest the people should take him for an enemy and kill him.

·   ·   ·   ·   ·

In the morning, Many Swans got up and made haste forward to the hills, and soon he was among cornfields, and the rows of the cornfields were newly plowed and from them there came a sound of singing. Then Many Swans felt the fear

come upon him because of the thing he
loathed and yet carried, and he thought:
"If it should kill these people!" The
music of the song was so beautiful that
he shed tears, but his fears overcame his
longing, for already he loved these people
who sang in cornfields at dawn. Many
Swans hid in a tuft of mesquite-bushes
and listened, and the words the people
were singing were these, but the tune was
like a sun wind in the tree-of-green-sticks:

The white corn I am planting,
The white seed of the white corn.
The roots I am planting,
The leaves I am planting,
The ear of many seeds I am planting,
All in one white seed.
Be kind! Be kind!

The blue corn I am planting,
The blue ear of the good blue corn.
I am planting tall rows of corn.
The bluebirds will fly among my
rows,
The blackbirds will fly up and down
my rows,
The humming-birds will be there be-
tween my rows,
Between the rows of blue corn I am
planting.

Beans I am planting.
The pod of the bean is in the seed.
I tie my beans with white lightning
to bring the thunder,
The long thunder which herds the
rain.
I plant the beans.
Be kind! Be kind!

Squash-seeds I am planting
So that the ground may be striped
with yellow,
Horizontal yellow of squash-flowers,
Horizontal white of squash-flowers,
Great squashes of all colours.
I tie the squash plants with the rain-
bow
Which carries the sun on its back.
I am planting squash-seeds.
Be kind! Be kind!

Out of the South, rain will come
whirling;
And from the North I shall see it
standing and approaching.
I shall hear it dropping on my seeds,
Lapping along the stems of my
plants,
Splashing from the high leaves,
Tumbling from the little leaves.

I hear it like a river, running — running —
Among my rows of white corn, running — running —
I hear it like a leaping spring among
my blue corn rows,
I hear it foaming past the bean
sprouts,
I hear water gurgling among my
squashes.

Descend, great cloud-water,
Spout from the mouth of the light-
ning,
Fall down with overturning thunder.
For the rainbow is the morning
When the sun shall raise us corn,
When the bees shall hum to the
corn-blossom,
To the bean-blossom,
To the straight, low blossoms of the
squashes.

Hear me sing to the rain,
To the sun,
To the corn when I am planting it,
To the corn when I am gathering it,
To the squashes when I load them
on my back.
I sing and the god-people hear,
They are kind.

When the song was finished, Many
Swans knew that he must not hurt this
people. He swore, and even upon the
sacred and terrible thing itself, to make
them his safe keeping. Therefore when
they returned up the trail to the Mesa,
he wandered in the desert below among
yellow rabbit-grass and grey iceplants, and
visited the springs, and the shrines full
of prayer-sticks, and his heart distracted
him with love so that he could not stay
still.
That night he heard an elf owl calling

from a pinyon-tree, and he went to the owl and sought to know the name of this people who sang in the fields at dawn. The owl answered: "Do not disturb me, I am singing a love-song. Who are you that you do not know that this is the land of Tusayan." And Many Swans considered in himself: "Truly I have come a long way."

Four moons Many Swans abode on the plain, eating mesquite-pods and old dried nopals, but he kept away from the Mesa lest the thing he had with him should be beyond his strength to hold.

. . . . .

Twixt this side, twixt that side,
Twixt rock-stones and sage-brush,
Twixt bushes and sand,
Go the snakes a smooth way,
Belly-creeping,
Sliding faster than the flash of water
    on a bluebird's wing.

Twixt corn and twixt cactus,
Twixt springside and barren,
Along a cold trail
Slip the snake-people.
Black-tip-tongued Garter Snakes,
Olive-blue Racer Snakes,
Whip Snakes and Rat Snakes,
Great orange Bull Snakes,
And the King of the Snakes,
With his high rings of scarlet,
His high rings of yellow,
His double high black rings,
Detesting his fellows,
The Killer of Rattlers.
Rattle — rattle — rattle —
Rattle — rattle — rattle —
The Rattlers,
The Rattlesnakes.
Hiss-s-s-s!
Ah-h-h-!
White Rattlesnakes,
Green Rattlesnakes,
Black-and-yellow Rattlesnakes,
Barred like tigers
Soft as panthers.
Diamond Rattlesnakes
All spotted,
Six feet long
With tails of snow-shine.
And most awful,

Heaving wrongwise,
The fiend-whisking
Swift Sidewinders.
Rattlesnakes upon the desert
Coiling in a clump of greasewood,
Winding up the Mesa footpath.
Who dares meet them?
Who dares stroke them?
Who dares seize them?
Rattle — rattle — rattle —
Rattle — rattle — hiss-s-s!

They dare, the men of Tusayan. With their eagle-whips, they stroke them. With their sharp bronze hands, they seize them. Run — run — up the Mesa path, dive into the kiva. The jars are ready, drop in the rattlers — Tigers, Diamonds, Sidewinders, drop in Bull Snakes, Whip Snakes, Garters, but hang the King Snake in a basket on the wall, he must not see all these Rattlesnakes, he would die of an apoplexy.

They have hunted them toward the four directions. Toward the yellow North, the blue West, the red South, the white East. Now they sit by the sand altar and smoke, chanting of the clouds and the four-coloured lightning-snakes who bring rain. They have made green prayer-sticks with black points and left them at the shrines to tell the snake-people that their festival is here. Bang! Bang! Drums! And whirl the thunder-whizzers!

"Ho! Ho! Ho! Hear us!
Carry our words to your Mother.
We wash you clean, Snake Brothers.
We sing to you.
We shall dance for you.
Plead with your Mother
That she send the white and green
    rain,
That she look at us with the black
    eyes of the lightning,
So our corn-ears may be double and
    long,
So our melons may swell as thunder-
    clouds
In a ripe wind.
Bring wind!
Bring lightning!
Bring thunder!
Strip our trees with blue-rain arrows.
Ho-Ho-hai! Wa-ha-ně."

Bang! Bang!

Over the floor of the kiva squirm the snakes, fresh from washing. Twixt this side, twixt that side, twixt toes and twixt ankles, go the snakes a smooth way, and the priests coax them with their eagle-feather whips and turn them always backward. Rattle — rattle — rattle — snake-tails threshing a hot air. Whizz! Clatter! Clap! Clap! Corn-gourds shaking in hard hands. A band of light down the ladder, cutting upon a mad darkness.

Cottonwood kisi flickering in a breeze, little sprigs of cotton-leaves clapping hands at Hopi people, crowds of Hopi people waiting in the Plaza to see a monstrous thing. Houses make a shadow, desert is in sunshine, priests step out of kiva.

Antelope priests in front of the kisi, making slow leg-motions to a slow time. Turtle-shell knee-rattles spill a double rhythm, arms shake gourd-rattles, goat-toes; necklaces — turquoise and sea-shell — swing a round of clashing. Striped lightning Antelopes waiting for the Snake Priests. Red-kilted Snake Priests facing them, going forward and back, coming back and over, waving the snake-whips, chanting a hundred ask-songs. Go on, go back — white — black — red blood-feather, white breath-feather, little cottonleaf hands clap — clap — He is at the flap of the kisi, they have given him a spotted rattlesnake. Put him in the mouth, kiss the Snake Brother, fondle him with the tongue.

Tripping on a quick tune, they trot round the square. Rattle — rattle — goat-toes, turtle-shells, snake-tails. Hiss, oily snake-mouths; drip, wide priest-mouths over the snake-skins, wet slimy snake-skins. "Aye-ya-ha! Ay-ye-he! Ha-ha-wa-ha! Oway-ha!" The red snake-whips tremble and purr. Blur, Plaza, with running priests, with streaks of snake-bodies. The Rain-Mother's children are being honoured. They must travel before the setting of the sun.

.   .   .   .   .

When the town was on a roar with dancing, Many Swans heard it far down in the plain, and he could not contain his hunger for his own kind. He felt very strong because the cool of sundown was spreading over the desert. He said, "I need fear nothing. My arms are grown tough in this place, my hands are hard as a sheep's skull. I can surely control this thing," and he set off up the path to ease his sight only, for he had sworn not to discover himself to the people. But when he turned the last point in the road, the thing in his hands shook, and said: "We shall strike that town."

Many Swans was strong, he turned and ran down the Mesa, but, as he was running, a priest passed him carrying a handful of snakes home. As the priest went by him, the thing in Many Swans' hand leapt up, and it was the King Snake. It was all ringed with red and yellow and black flames. It hissed, and looped, and darted its head at the priest and killed him. Now when the priest was dead, all the snakes he was holding burst up with a great noise and went every which way, twixt this side, twixt that side, twixt upwards, twixt downwards, twixt rock-stone and bunch-grass. And they were little slipping flames of hot fire. They went up the hill in fourteen red and black strings, and they were the strings of blood and death. The snakes went up a swift, smooth way, and Many Swans went up with them for he was mad. He beat his hands together to make a drum, and shouted "Break! Break! Break! Break!" And he thought it was the priests above singing a new song.

Many Swans reached the town, but the fire-snakes were running down all the streets. They struck the people so that they died, and the bodies took fire and were consumed. The house windows were hung with snakes who were caught by their tails and swung down, vomiting golden stars into the rain-gutters. In one of the gutters was a blue salvia plant, and as Many Swans passed, it nodded and said "Alas! Alas!" It reminded Many Swans of the flax-flowers in the sky, and his senses came back to him and he tore his clothes and his hair and cried "Ka! Ka! Ka! Ka!" a great many times. Then he beat himself on the sharp rocks and tried to crush the thing he had, but he could not; he tried to split it, but it did not split.

Many Swans saw that he was alone in the world. He lifted his eyes to the thing and cursed it, then he ran to hurl himself over the cliff. Now a boulder curled into the path and, as he turned its edge, The-One-Who-Walks-All-Over-the-Sky stood before him. Her eyes were moons for sadness, and her voice was like the coiling of the sea. She said to him: "I tried to love you; I tried to be kind to your people; why do you cry? You wished for it." She took it off him and left him.

Many Swans looked at the desert. He looked at the dead town. He wept.

FUNERAL SONG
FOR THE INDIAN CHIEF BLACKBIRD

Buried Sitting Upright on a Live Horse on a Bluff Overlooking the Missouri River

He is dead,
Our Chief.
Aï! Aï! Aï! Aï!
Our Chief
On whom has fallen a sickness,
He, our Leader,
Who has grievously died.

At his feet we are gathered,
Warriors, his children,
We have cut our flesh
Before his body.
Our blood drips on the willow-leaves,
The willows with which we have pierced our arms.
We beat the willow-sticks,
We mourn our Brother, our Father,
We chant slow songs
To the listening spirit of the Great Chief Blackbird.

Yesterday,
When the sky was red
And the sun falling through it,
They called to you,
Your ancestors,
From the middle of the sky;
From a cloud, circling above you,
They pronounced your name.

He is dead,
Our Leader.
Aï! Aï! Aï! Aï!
Our Chief, Blackbird.
Beat the willow-sticks,
Let our blood drop before him.

You have sung your death-song,
To your friends you have sung it,
To the grasses of the prairie,
To the river,
Cutting the prairie
As the moon cuts the sky.

See, we lift you,
The blood of our willow-wounds drops upon you.
We dress you in your shirt of white buckskin,
We fasten your leggings of mountain-goat skin,
We lay upon your shoulders
Your robe of the skin of a young buffalo bull.
We clasp your necklace of grizzly bears' claws
About your neck.

We place upon your head
Your war-bonnet of eagle plumes.
All this you have commanded.
Aï! Aï! Aï! Aï!
Strike the willow-sticks.
You shall depart
From among us.
It is time for you to depart,
You are going on a long journey.

Up to the tall cliff
We carry you.
Our blood drips upon the ground.
And your horse,
Your white horse,
Goes with you.
He follows you.
Softly we lead him

After your body,
After your not heavy body
Shrunken in death.

The hawk is flying
Halfway up the sky.
So will you be halfway above the earth.
On the high bluff
You are standing.
The ground trembles
As we place you upon it.

You are dead,
But you hear our songs.
You are dead,
But we lift you on your White Weasel
Horse.
He trembles as the earth trembles.
His skin quivers
At the loose touch of your knees.
Aï! Aï! Aï! Aï!
Leader of the Warriors
To the spirit land you are going.
Our blood cries to you,
Dropping upon the willow-leaves.

Who is this that rides the Wolf Trail at
evening?
Blackbird,
Chief of his people.
His bow is in his hand,
Scarlet the heads of his arrows,
The feathers of his shield sweep the
ground.
Lift him,
Lift him,
Lift the War Chief
To his light-legged horse.
We will stand,
We will see him,
We shall behold his body
Set high on a high horse,
On his own horse,
His white horse of many battles.
We shall see him
As we desire.

You are bright as the sun among trees,
You are dazzling as the long sun running
among the prairie grasses,
You pierce our eyes as a thunder-cloud
rising against the wind.
Who shall be to us as he,
Our Chief?
Your white horse shivers and is still,

He will carry you safely over the Wolf
Trail
To those who are talking about you,
Calling to you to come.

Lay little sods of earth
About the feet of the white horse.
Gather those which contain the seeds
Of camass, and puccoon, and lupin.
Watch that the seeds of the looks-like-a-
plume flower
Spread the earth we are laying against his
sides,
So that, in the time when the ducks and
geese shed their feathers,
The black breasts may drop from the sky
upon them, singing,
As our blood drops on these sods.

Aï! Aï! Aï! Aï!
Proudly he sits his white horse,
His head-feathers make a noise in the
wind.
Great Chief,
Father of people,
Facing the cleft hill,
Facing the long, moving river,
Waiting briefly for the edge of night,
Abiding the coming of the stars,
Poised to leap,
To strike the star-way with the mighty
energy
Of your powerful horse,
To take the Wolf Trail with the shout
of cunning,
To ride streaming over the great sky.
We watch you,
We exalt you,
We cheer you with our hunting-cries,
Our battle-songs,
To the beating of our willow-sticks you
shall ride,
And he, your White Weasel Horse,
Shall bear you above the clouds
To the tepees beyond the star-which-
never-moves.

When the waters are calm
And the fog rises,
Will you appear?
Then will come up out of the waters
Your brothers,
The Otters.
From beneath the high hill
Your voice will echo forth.

Your voice shall be as metal
In the spaces of the sky,
Your war club shall resound through the
sky.
Like your brothers,
The Eagles,
Your voice shall descend to us
Down the slopes of the wind.
You will go round the world,
You will go over and under the world,
You will come to the Place of Spirits.
Aï! Aï! Aï! Aï!
We are pitying ourselves
That he, our Father, is dead.
He is carried like thunder
Across the sky.
The trees are afraid of the wind,
So are we afraid of the whirlwind of our
enemies
Without our Chief to lead us.
When the rain comes
On the wings of crows
In the Spring,
We shall fear even the voice of the owl,
Sitting alone in our lodges
Now that you are gone.

How many the count of your battles!
At night,
When the dogs were still,
Going softly
You would seek the villages of your ene-
mies to destroy them.
You who, all night long,
Were standing up until daylight.
You fought as one who dances singing:
"Heh-yeh! Heh-yeh! Heh-yeh!
Death I bring!
I dance upon those I kill,
I scalp those I kill,
I laugh above those I kill.
Heh-yeh! Heh-yeh! Heh-yeh! Heh-yeh!"
Your enemies were not able to shoot,
Their bow-strings were wet
And the sinews stretched
And slipped off the ends of the bows.
Your arrows were red
As grasshoppers' wings
When they fly high in the sun.
Your enemies were ashamed before you
Since you cut off their heads
And tied their scalps to your bridle-rein.

Now you journey alone,
Journey along the Wolf Trail
Wearily among the little stars.

Aï! Aï! Aï! Aï!
It is time for you to depart,
You are going on a long journey.
You are going in your shoes.
You cannot travel,
Your feet are weary with many steps,
But your round-hoofed horse shall step
for you,
He shall bear you over the trail of stars.
The deer walks alone,
Singing of his shining horns,
So shall you walk
Singing of the great deeds
You have done in this world.

Leader of the Warriors,
Where are you?
We, your children,
Sing a song of five sounds
To your departing spirit.
We sing a song of vermilion,
We stain our hands
And mark the palms of them in red
On the flanks of your horse.
We heap the sods about him,
We hold his head
And stuff his nostrils and ears with earth.
We cover your arms, your shoulders,
Your glittering face,
The feathers flying above your head.
The water-birds will alight upon your
body,
We shall see your grave from below,
From the place where the snipe stand
above their shadows in the water.

Aï! Aï! Aï! Aï!
The Morning Star and the Young Morn-
ing Star
Are together in the sky above the prairie.
How far have you already gone from us?
Our blood drips slowly,
The wounds are closing,
It is time we pulled out the willow-
sprays
And left this place
Before the rising of the sun.

WITCH–WOMAN

"Witch!
Witch!
Cursed black heart,
Cursed gold heart striped with black;
Thighs and breasts I have loved;
Lips virgin to my thought,
Sweeter to me than red figs;
Lying tongue that I have cherished.
Is my heart wicked?
Are my eyes turned against too bright a
    sun?
Do I dazzle, and fear what I cannot see?
It is grievous to lose the heart from the
    body,
Death which tears flesh from flesh is a
    grievous thing;
But death is cool and kind compared to
    this,
This horror which bleeds and kindles,
These kisses shot with poison,
These thoughts cutting me like red knives.
Lord,
Thunderer,
Swift rider on the clashing clouds,
Ruler over brass heavens,
Mighty ruler of the souls of men,
Be merciless to me if I mistake this
    woman,
As I will be merciless if I learn a bitter
    truth.
I burn green oil to you,
Fresh oil from fair young olives,
I pour it upon the ground;
As it drips I invoke your clemency
To send a sign.
Witches are moon-birds,
Witches are the women of the false,
    beautiful moon.
To-night the sign,
Maker of men and gods.
To-night when the full-bellied moon
    swallows the stars.
Grant that I know.
Then will I offer you a beastly thing and
    a broken;
Or else the seed of both
To be your messengers and slaves forever,
My sons, and my sons' sons, and their
    sons after;
And my daughters and theirs throughout
    the ages

For your handmaidens and bedfellows as
    you command.
How the white sword flickers!
How my body twists in the circle of my
    anguish!
Behold, I have loved this woman,
Even now I cry for her,
My arms weaken,
My legs shake and crumble.
Strengthen my thews,
Cord my sinews to withstand a testing.
Let me be as iron before this thing,
As flashing brass to see,
As lightning to fall;
As rain melting before sunshine if I have
    wronged the woman.
The red flame takes the oil,
The blood of my trees is sucked into fire
As my blood is sucked into the fire of
    your wrath and mercy,
O just and vengeful God."

Body touches body. How sweet the
    spread of loosened bodies in the coil
    of sleep, but a gold-black thread is
    between them. An owl calls deep
    in the wood.
Can you see through the night, woman,
    that you stare so upon it? Man,
    what spark do your eyes follow in
    the smouldering darkness?
She stirs. Again the owl calling. She
    rises. Foot after foot as a panther
    treads, through the door — a minute
    more and the fringes of her goat-
    skin are brushing the bushes. She
    pushes past brambles, the briars
    catch little claws in her goat-skin.
    And he who watches? As the tent-
    lap flaps back, he leaps. The bearer
    of the white sword leaps, and follows
    her. Blur of moonshine before —
    behind. He walks by the light of a
    green-oil oath, and the full moon
    floats above them both.
Seeded grass is a pool of grey. Ice-white,
    cloud-white, frosted with the spray
    of the sharp-edged moon. Croon —
    croon — the wind in the feathered
    tops of the grass. They pass — the
    witch-white woman with the gold-

black heart, the flower-white woman
— and his eyes startle, and answer
the bow curve of her going up the
hill.
The night is still, with the wind, and the
moon, and an owl calling.

On the sea side of a hill where the grass
lies tilted to a sheer drop down,
with the sea splash under as the
waves are thrown upon a tooth of
rock. Shock and shatter of a golden
track, and the black sucking back.
The draw of his breath is hard and
cold, the draw of the sea is a rustle
of gold.
Behind a curl of granite stone the man
lies prone. The woman stands like
an obelisk, and her blue-black hair
has a serpent whisk as the wind lifts
it up and scatters it apart. Witch-
heart, are you gold or black? The
woman stands like a marble tower,
and her loosened hair is a thunder-
shower twisted across with lightnings
of burnt gold.

Naked and white, the matron moon urges
the woman. The undulating sea
fingers the rocks and winds stealthily
over them. She opens the goat-skin
wide — it falls.
The walls of the world are crashing down,
she is naked before the naked moon,
the Mother Moon, who sits in a
courtyard of emerald with six black
slaves before her feet. Six — and a
white seventh who dances, turning
in the moonlight, flinging her arms
about the soft air, despairingly lifting herself to her full height, straining tiptoe away from the slope of
the hill.
Witch-breasts turn and turn, witch-
thighs burn, and the feet strike always faster upon the grass. Her
blue-black hair in the moon-haze
blazes like a fire of salt and myrrh.
Sweet as branches of cedar, her
arms; fairer than heaped grain, her
legs; as grape clusters, her knees and
ankles; her back as white grapes with
smooth skins.

She runs through him with the whipping

of young fire. The desire of her is
thongs and weeping. She is the green
oil to his red flame. He peers from
the curl of granite stone. He hears
the moan of the crawling sea, and
sees — as the goat-skin falls so the
flesh falls. . . .
And the triple Heaven-wall falls down,
and the Mother Moon on a ruby
throne is near as a bow-shot above
the hill.
Goat-skin, here, flesh-skin there, a skeleton dancing in the moon-green air,
with a white, white skull and no
hair. Lovely as ribs on a smooth sand
shore, bright as quartz-stones speckling a moor, long and narrow as
Winter reeds, the bones of the skeleton. The wind in the rusty grass
hums a funeral-chant set to a jig.
Dance, silver bones, dance a whirligig in a crepitation of lust. The
waves are drums beating with
slacked guts. Inside the skeleton is
a gold heart striped with black, it
glitters through the clacking bones,
throwing an inverted halo round the
stamping feet.

Scarlet is the ladder dropping from the
moon. Liquid is the ladder — like
water moving yet keeping its shape.
The skeleton mounts like a great grey ape,
and its bones rattle; the rattle of the
bones is the crack of dead trees
bitten by frost. The wind is desolate,
and the sea moans.
But the ruby chair of Mother Moon
shudders, and quickens with a hard
fire. The skeleton has reached the
last rung. It melts and is absorbed
in the burning moon. The moon?
No moon, but a crimson rose afloat
in the sky. A rose? No rose, but a
black-tongued lily. A lily? No lily,
but a purple orchid with dark, writhing bars.

Trumpets mingle with the sea-drums,
scalding trumpets of brass, the wind-
hum changes to a wail of many
voices, the owl has ceased calling.

"White sword are you thirsty?
I give you the green blood of my heart.

I give you her white flesh cast from her
    black soul.
Thunderer,
Vengeful and cruel Father,
God of Hate,
The skins of my eyes have dropped,

With fire you have consumed the oil of
    my heart.
Take my drunken sword,
Some other man may need it.
She was sweeter than red figs.
O cursed God!"

THE RING AND THE CASTLE

A Ballad

"Benjamin Bailey, Benjamin Bailey, why
    do you wake at the stroke of three?"
"I heard the hoot of an owl in the forest,
    and the creak of the wind in the alder-
    tree."

"Benjamin Bailey, Benjamin Bailey, why
    do you stare so into the dark?"
"I saw white circles twining, floating,
    and in the centre a molten spark."

"Why are you restless, Benjamin Bailey?
    Why do you fling your arms so wide?"
"To keep the bat's wings from coming
    closer and push the grey rat from my
    side."

"What are you muttering, Benjamin
    Bailey? The room is quiet, the moon
    is clear."
"The trees of the forest are curling, sway-
    ing, writhing over the heart of my
    Dear."

"Lie down and cover you, Benjamin
    Bailey, you're raving, for never a wife
    or child
Has blessed your hearthstone; it is the
    fever, which startles your brain with
    dreams so wild."

"No wife indeed," said Benjamin Bailey,
    and his blue nails picked at the bed-
    quilt's edge.
"I gathered a rose in another man's gar-
    den and hid it from sight in a haw-
    thorn hedge.

I made her a chamber where green boughs
    rustled, and plaited river-grass for the
    floor,
And three times ten moonlight nights I

loved her, with my old hound stretch-
    ing before the door.

Then out of the North a knight came
    riding, with crested helm and pointed
    sword.
'Where is my wife?' said the knight to
    the people. 'My wife! My wife!' was
    his only word.

He tied his horse to the alder yonder, and
    stooped his crest to enter my door.
'My wife,' said the knight, and a steel-
    grey glitter flashed from his armour
    across the floor.

Then I lied to that white-faced knight,
    and told him the lady had never been
    seen by me;
And when he had loosed his horse from
    the alder, I bore him a mile of com-
    pany.

I turned him over the bridge to the val-
    ley, and waved him Godspeed in the
    twilight grey.
And I laughed all night as I toyed with
    his lady, clipping and kissing the hours
    away.

The sun was kind and the wind was
    gentle, and the green boughs over our
    chamber sang,
But on the Eastern breeze came a tinkle
    whenever the bells in the Abbey rang.

Dang! went the bell, and the lady heark-
    ened — once, twice, thrice — and her
    tears sprang forth.
"Twas three of the clock when I was
    wedded,' quoth she, 'in the castle to
    the North.

They praised us for a comely couple, in
truth my Lord was a joy to see;
I gave him my troth for a golden dowry,
and he gave me this ring on the stroke
of three.

Three years I lived with him fair and
stately, and then we quarrelled, as
lovers will.
He swore I wed for his golden dowry,
and I that he loved another still.

I knew right well that never another had
crossed the heart of my dearest Lord,
But still my rage waxed hot within me
until, one morning, I fled abroad.

All down the flickering isles of the forest
I rode till at twilight I sat me down,
And there a-weeping you found and took
me, as one lifts a leaf which the wind
has blown.

But to-night my ring burns hot on my
finger, and my Lord's face shines
through the curtained door.
And the bells beat heavy against my temples, two long strokes, and one stroke
more.

Loose me now, for your touch is terror,
my heart is a hollow, my arms are
wind;
I must go out once more and wander,
seeking the forest for what I shall find.'

Then I fell upon her and stifled her
speaking till the bells died away in the
rustling breeze,
And so I held her dumb until morning
with smothered lips, but I knew no
ease.

And every night that the bells came
clearly striking three strokes, like a
heavy stone
I would seal her lips, but even as I kissed
her, behind her clenched teeth I could
hear her moan.

The nights grew longer, I had the lady,
her pale blue veins and her skin of
milk,

But I might have been clasping a white
wax image straightly stretched on a
quilt of silk.

Then curdled anger foamed within me,
and I tore at her finger to take the
ring,
The red gold ring which burned her spirit
like some bewitched, unhallowed thing.

High in the boughs of our leafy chamber,
the lady's sorrowing died away.
All night I fought for the red gold circle,
all night, till the oak-trees reddened
to day.

For two nights more I strove to take it,
the red gold circlet, the ring of fear,
But on the third in a blood-red vision I
drew my sword and cut it clear.

Severed the ring and severed the finger,
and slew my Dear on the stroke of
three;
Then I dug a grave beneath the oak-trees,
and buried her there where none could
see.

I took the ring and the bleeding finger,
and sent a messenger swiftly forth,
An amazing gift to my Lord I sent them,
in his lonely castle to the North.

He died, they say, at sight of my present.
I laughed when I heard it — 'Hee!
Hee! Hee!'
But every night my veins run water and
my pores sweat blood at the stroke of
three."

"Benjamin Bailey, Benjamin Bailey, seek
repentance, your time is past."
"My Dearest Dear lies under the oak-
trees, pity indeed that the ring held
fast."

"Benjamin Bailey, Benjamin Bailey, sin-
ners repent when they come to die."
"Toll the bell in the Abbey tower, and
under the oak-trees let me lie."

GAVOTTE IN D MINOR

She wore purple, and when other people
    slept
She stept lightly — lightly — in her ruby
    powdered slippers
Along the flags of the East portico.
And the moon slowly rifting the heights
    of cloud
Touched her face so that she bowed
Her head, and held her hand to her eyes
To keep the white shining from her. And
    she was wise,
For gazing at the moon was like looking
    on her own dead face
Passing alone in a wide place,
Chill and uncosseted, always above
The hot protuberance of life. Love to her
Was morning and a great stir
Of trumpets and tire-women and sharp
    sun.
As she had begun, so she would end,
Walking alone to the last bend
Where the portico turned the wall.
And her slipper's sound
Was scarce as loud upon the ground
As her tear's fall.
Her long white fingers crisped and clung
Each to each, and her weary tongue
Rattled always the same cold speech:
    Gold was not made to lie in grass,
    Silver dints at the touch of brass,
    The days pass.

Lightly, softly, wearily,
The lady paces, drearily
Listening to the half-shrill croon
Leaves make on a moony Autumn night
When the windy light

Runs over the ivy eerily.
A branch at the corner cocks an obscene
    eye
As she passes — passes — by, and by —
A hand stretches out from a column's
    edge,
Faces float in a phosphorent wedge
Through the points of arches, and there
    is speech
In the carven roof-groins out of reach.
A love-word, a lust-word, shivers and
    mocks
The placid stroke of the village clocks.
Does the lady hear?
Is any one near?
She jeers at life, must she wed instead
The cold dead?
A marriage-bed of moist green mold,
With an over-head tester of beaten gold.
A splendid price for a splendid scorn,
A tombstone pedigree snarled with thorn
Clouding the letters and the fleur-de-lis,
She will have them in granite for her
    heart's chill ease.

I set the candle in a draught of air
And watched it swale to the last thin
    flair.
They laid her in a fair chamber hung
    with arras,
And they wept her virgin soul.
The arras was woven of the story of
    Minos and Dictynna.
But I grieved that I could no longer hear
    the shuffle of her feet along the portico,
And the ruffling of her train against the
    stones.

THE STATUE IN THE GARDEN

I

It was not a large garden, as gardens go,
But carefully patterned with row after
    row
Of flower-beds edged by low, clipped box
In the quaintly prim and orthodox
Manner of seventeen-eighty or there-
    abouts.

A couple of dolphins spurted out spouts
Of silver-blue water from a couple of
    fountains,
And the distant sky was suggestive of
    mountains.
I say suggestive, for it lay with the wind
If the sky were thicker or thinner skinned.
Even when the air was without a vapour
All one saw was a luminous blur

Which might have been a cloud of a trick
Of the eyes, smarting under the too sharp prick
Of the very clearness, till you looked again
And saw it still. It was never plain,
But hung like a whisper of something bright
In the large, slow blue, about half the height
From horizon to zenith. This dolomite
Which, for better disguise, I shall call Ghost Peak,
Was considered by Julius to be the unique
Cause of his coming, and presently buying,
The charming old house he was now occupying.
A writer may live where his fancies dictate
Provided his copy be kept up to date,
And Julius had certainly earned some repose
And might, if he wanted, play dominoes,
Or whist, or billiards, for the rest of his life,
Might even consider the taking a wife.
Not Julius, he sought only lapses of hours
Within reach of the sight and scent of flowers.
He loved the languor of faded chintz,
The strange nostalgia of coloured prints
To hang above Sheraton chairs, the sham
And exquisite classics of the brothers Adam.
His garden delighted him through and through,
With its peacocks and unicorns clipped in yew,
And the broad lines of the gravel walks,
Firm and flat between tall stalks
Of fox-glove, or monk's-hood, down which to betake
Himself to the edge of the long green lake
Which lay at the foot of the garden-close —
And over all the Ghost Peak rose.
On the days when it did; when it didn't, he fought
A weird depression which clenched his thought
And seemed to squeeze it between cold claws.

He harried his soul in a search for laws
Of the bonds of man with things, the caress
Of awe and horror in loveliness.
He burned his brain in a search to find
What the Ghostly Mountain meant to his mind,
What his chairs and tables held him by,
Whether or not he had heard a sly
Rustle, as he passed, from the peacock yews.
Once he thought that the cockatoos
On the chintz of his arm-chair flapped their wings.
These were most fearful and joyous things.
The mellow place had a sort of spell,
And it suited him thoroughly, blissfully well.
He was tired out with the old routine
Of man and man, now something between
Held him away and apart. Intense
Became his ultra-commonsense,
And he was happy and preened himself
On being an unusual sort of elf,
Not feeling the need of his fellows at all.
Julius was riding for a fall.

One day his luck, or his fate, or his fiend,
(Something sardonic, at least) intervened
Between him and the comfortable life he was leading,
And suggested a walk in the town. Too much reading
Had made his head buzz, so he put on his hat
And started out blithely, considering that
This bright afternoon was an excellent season
To visit a shop he had not, for some reason,
Yet entered. An antiquity dealer's, of course.
Such gentry, he mused, were the clear single source
Of his pleasures. How gaily he walked down the street!
I might almost say strutted, so very replete
Was he with good temper. The shop-door stood wide,
And Julius, poor devil, stepped squarely inside.

II

The place was dim, with shafts of dusty
light
Shocking the gloom to colour. On the
right,
A grim old cabinet whose worm-holed
wood
Was black as iron, reared its vastitude
Quite out of sight among the smoky
rafters.
Its front was carven with the grinning
laughters
Of broken-faced, libidinous dwarfs who
clung
Among the twistings of a snaky tongue
That proved itself a vine by flinging
clusters
Of grapes out here and there, which,
through the dust blurs,
Shimmered with subtle, polished, purple
lustres.
The thing was most intriguing, harsh, and
fine,
But, like a thunder-cloud which breaks
the line
Of open clearness in a Summer sky.
Worm-eaten oak could scarcely qualify
Among his painted satin-wood escritoires,
His Wedgwood vases and majolicas.
"The eighteenth century is my period,"
He told the shopman, who answered with
a nod,
And forthwith guided him among the
maze
Of torn brocaded chairs, the chipping
glaze
Of things which once were lacquer, and
the traps
Of sprawling andirons with trivets on
their laps,
Into a little yard behind the shop
All full of urns, and columns, and a crop
Of marble Mercuries, and Venuses, and
Floras,
Of cavaliers in *bautas* and black-silk-
masked signoras.
The shopman waved his hand and turned
away.

Well, Julius, take your stock of the array,
But never again can there be yesterday
As you will recollect, I dare to say,
Though sportsmen keep stiff upper lips
and pay.

The things were well enough at five yards
distance
But at a closer view did not entrance.
Julius, discouraged, was turning to go in
When some conceit of colour, vaguely
seen
Between two statues, struck his eager
sense
And set him threading through the very
dense
Concourse of mediocre marbles. Sud-
denly
She, charming feminine creature, held his
eye.
The seeing was a dazzle in his head,
But what he saw by every honest measure
Had not this shimmering denied him
leisure
To contemplate beyond his eager pleas-
ure,
Was just a garden figure made of lead.

A garden figure. Yes, but what a one!
Bright as a flower under a white sun,
Vigorous and frail, with tints as gay as
those
Which deck the saints in Fra Angelico's
Best adorations. Dressed in pink and
blue,
A rose-red bodice, whence a kerchief flew
Streaming behind her on a hidden wind,
Her azure skirt was gathered up and
pinned
A little to one side, her stockings shone
As though of very silk, and she had on
The blackest, shiniest pair of buckled
shoes
That ever bore a maiden through the dews
Of a Summer morning. Then there was
her hat
Of yellow straw, beribboned, wide, and
flat.
Her face and hands were all that hands
and face
Might be in hue and shapeliness, their
grace
A balance of perfections. At her belt,
In her up-curving arm, she held a nose-
gay
Of marigolds and phlox, the lively way
In which these flowers were modelled
made a play
Of movement seem among them, and the
scent

Just on the point of coming — yes, Julius
    smelt
Their pungent bitter sweetness as he bent
A little farther forward, then it went
Fading away, and Julius could have sworn
The lady smiled a little more. Was it
    scorn
Or only the shadow from the maple-tree?
What was it Julius saw or didn't see?
He scarcely stopped to wonder. Back he
    hurried
Into the shop, and though a trifle flur-
    ried
Achieved a tolerable bargain, for our
    hero
Was a shrewd business man, as you must
    know.
Well, that was done, the figure to be de-
    livered.
Did Julius hear a rusty sound which quiv-
    ered
Down the old cabinet, cracking in the
    heat?
Those grinning dwarfs pursued him to
    the street,
He felt their obscene jaws stretching and
    gobbling.
That cabinet was a disgusting thing,
A mouldering carcass which needed bury-
    ing.
And then he straight forgot it, thinking
    where,
Beside which tree and close to which
    parterre,
He should place his little leaden Jardin-
    ière.

III

That night the sun sank in a wheel of
    purple flame.
The Ghost Peak floated, an unapproach-
    able purity, in the opposite sky.
The lake was a violent splendour with no
    farther shore.
But Julius had chosen the place for his
    statue;
He was content to sit on a garden bench
    and smoke,
And watch the white lilies fuse into in-
    candescence under the fading of the
    sky.
At the end of a long vista,
Near, and not too near, a fountain,
Beneath an acacia whose drooping golden

chains of flowers brushed her hat and
    shoulder,
Stood the little garden maiden,
A gaiety of colour in a green and gold
    shade.
Her pinks, and blue, and yellows, were
    like the tinkling of glass bells to his
    senses.
A front foot lightly, firmly advanced,
A back foot just on its tiptoe,
She paused, waiting a farther reason for
    coming forward,
Abiding the final chord of a rhythm not
    yet completed.
A dancer without music,
A walker without a goal,
Seeking a purpose to fulfil a movement
Unwittingly begun.
Half bold, half shy, and wholly alluring,
Julius congratulated himself on having
    added to his garden
Just the touch it needed,
And more than ever, felt no concern to
    leave it.

Summer!
Summer!
Great gusts of surging Summer,
A breeze of perfume making its own
    wind!
Butterflies flickered among orange lilies,
Ruby-throated humming-birds drank
    from climbing nasturtiums
Hanging in a vanishing whirl of wings.
At night, the garden was a bowl of fire-
    flies,
And, when the moon rose, the Ghost
    Peak, suddenly, silently visible,
Bloomed in the half-height of the sky.
A fire-fly lit on the breast of the statue,
"As it might have been a diamond,"
    thought Julius,
"I had bought for her on Midsummer
    Day."
He was pleased with the fancy,
And slipped his ring on the finger of the
    statue
To see it gleam in the moonlight.
Pricks of sapphire, ripples of rose,
Basilisk eyes which open and close,
How the light of the moon ran across the
    diamond!
How it splashed deep down in the facets
    of the stone
And flung up sprays of iris and maroon.

Julius played the tale of lover to his dream
Until the moon set,
But when he tried to pull the ring off,
It held instead,
Caught in the crook of a knuckle of lead,
And the white stone was red — red —
And in its heart lay the bright, coiled
thread
Of a many-coloured snake with an eye in
its head.
And there were grimaces
Of misshapen faces
Peering out of a green snake-tree.
The diamond glittered horribly,
For the eye made a light
Which broke through the night
In a sort of bungling, dazzling flight
That splintered the garden's symmetry:
The trees were so tall
They had no tops at all,
And the lake stood straight like a painted
sea.
Then came the dark . . .
And the spark of the scratch
From a lighted match
As Julius sought to take the ring.
But he could not, it continued to cling.
Julius laughed.
"Good night, Madonna del Giardino,"
Said he,
"You may give the jewel back to me
To-morrow."
And he went in to bed.

But not to-morrow,
Or the morrow, or the next,
Could he take off the ring. Julius was
perplexed.
It was safe enough, for who would seek
gems
On a garden figure's finger, and as all his
stratagems
Had failed, why Julius left the matter
where it was.
In fact, he grew to think of it as
An added touch of coquetry
To the statue's charm, and let it be.

A week or two of amazing weather
He and the statue passed together.
Julius was never more enamoured
Of his quaint old house, but the garden
clamoured
With loud throat notes of yellow and red,
An orchestra in every bed,

The blaring brass of late Summer flowers.
In the early morning, the garden's blaze
Was softened by a half-Autumnal haze,
But by noon the colours were deafening.
I am not responsible for the sting
Of such a muddle of metaphors,
They were Julius's, and what was worse
He made many such as he sat by the
fountain,
Under the gleam of his Vision, the
Mountain,
Playing a game he delighted in:
That his garden lady was feminine
Flesh and blood to his masculine
Desire, a proper person before whom to
kneel.
The game as he played it became almost
real.
It was well no gardener was hovering
round
To overhear poor Julius expound
His love in his best poetic style.
I fear the man might have been tempted
to smile,
Or rather, more possibly, since persons so
menial
Find everything out of routine uncon-
genial,
He might even have taken his master for
mad;
A condition of things which, I hasten to
add,
Was not so. The truth is man is so multi-
plex
He confuses himself with his this and his
that,
And carries round constantly under his
hat
A thousand odd notions. Now 'twas
nothing but sex
Deprived its due reason, which set Julius
sighing
Before a lead statue instead of comply-
ing
With all mystic wisdom and seeking a
woman
Who, whatever she lacked, would be certainly human.

All the long Summer days, and soft Summer nights,
Julius sat by his statue, and sometimes
the flights
Of his fancy (or eyesight) made him
think he detected

A twitch or a shiver, he almost suspected
She might some day speak. So a month
    passed away,
Then a veer in the wind brought a cold
    rainy day.
No sitting and soaking for hours together,
And Julius was in for a real "spell of
    weather."
Like wires across the landscape fell the
    rain,
The lean, swift wind became a hurricane,
Leaves rocketed along the air, the lash-
    ing trees
Thundered as they drove their quivering
    knees
Deep in the muddy grass, some leapt and
    screamed
As a branch broke and left the trunk all
    seamed
With the running scar. The windows
    creaked like bones
As the old house raged and tore on its
    foundation stones.
Two days the fury lasted, then a smooth
And sudden calm fell with a change of
    wind,
But still the sky seemed a grey marble
    veined
With spots and drops of black. Like a
    broken tooth,
The ancient sycamore stood with its
    stumps
All hollow to the rainfall. Where were
    clumps
Of flowers was beaten offal; where were
    walks
Were spaces littered with the rotting
    stalks
Of headless plants. Beyond was only mist;
A hatching of water hid the sudden twist
Of the path to the Dolphin Fountain.
    How was she?
But Julius had no mind to go and see.
He wanted lights, and brick façades, and
    town,
Somewhere where no leaves were which
    could be blown,
A brief half-hour away these might be
    had,
And Julius sought them eagerly, most
    glad,
For once, to leave his consoles and
    clipped yews.
Blood ran again along his dusty thews.

IV

He could not grasp it,
Could not tear the shell
Off of his soul and see it as it was
Naked and green with life;
Nor could he see what tendrils from it
    held
Her tendrils. How his heart
Long since burst open with its fruit
    spilled out,
And so accustomed to a core of air,
Closed round her as a sheath
Fitted to its own kernel.
But these things were.
A month ago he was an amateur of taste,
To-day his footsteps rang like clanging
    bells,
The steps of self-sufficing, august man,
Beating a chime upon the universe.

A month he had been away, and when he
    came
Once more into his garden, late Septem-
    ber
Lay like a melted hoar-frost on the air.
The flowers were dahlias, marigolds, and
    phlox,
All spangled with the chilling of the haze.
Julius smiled at them as he recollected,
For were not phlox and marigolds the
    flowers
His garden lady carried for her nosegay.
He praised himself for buying the little
    figure,
Hildegarde would like it. Then he turned
The corner by the fountain and there she
    was,
A dazzling clarity of shape and colour,
For now and then the fountain tossed its
    spray
A little higher, and lightly spattered her
So that she shone. So did the diamond
Still on her finger.
But Julius was ashamed to see it there
And made a note to have it cut away
If nothing else would free it. He went on
Down to the lake and skipped a stone or
    two
Across its surface, noted how faint and
    edgeless
The Mountain was, then went indoors to
    work.
He worked all day, and in the evening
Sat down to write a line to Hildegarde.

What is that heavy, pungent smell?
Flowers, of course, but not in the room,
There are none in the room. He shut
The window long ago. Again
He smells it, tart and sweet.
"The phlox and marigolds are lovely
here,"
He writes, and stops astonished
For phlox and marigolds are what he
smells,
And all the windows tightly shut!
He dips his pen, but instantly the scent
Becomes submerging like a drug,
Becomes an ether clogged with dreams.
A step? Could there come a step
Fanning the floor as lightly as a leaf?
Julius startled looks, and all his muscles
Cease to cohere, they run apart like
sand.
He cannot move,
He must be drugged, for right before his
eyes
Are phlox and marigolds, and they are ar-
ranged
In the pattern of the garden lady's nose-
gay.
He makes himself look up, but it is tor-
ture
Even to turn his eyes, and there she is,
Holding out the flowers. "God in
Heaven's name!
What is this?" He speaks, but cannot
move an inch.
"I love you, Julius," and it is a voice
Brittle and sharp as glass, a crimson glass.
He hears and shudders.
"To whom are you writing, Julius?
Not to me, and you belong to me,
I have your ring, the ring of our be-
trothal."
Then Julius tears his muscles from the
coil
Of their inertia and leaps upon the statue,
Seizing her arm, her hand —
She folds upon him, smothering his face
with hers,
Her crimson voice enters his heavy ears.
His mouth is stopped . . .
Oh, God, how loud the ticking of the
clock!
How hard the sleep which will not let
him wake!
His eyelids are iron doors he cannot lift;
With all his strength he forces them to
open.

The clock says eight, and sunlight fills
the room.
There is no statue, so he must have
dreamed.
But the letter he was writing, Hildegarde's —
There is no letter!

Well, let us leave it there. This is the
first time,
And yesterday is a thing without a shape
Broken and scattered.
Can he build to-morrow and find his feet
a footing?
Such perchance may be, or otherwise —
A year has many days.

V

He might have thought the thing a dream
And steadied himself by that.
But when a wall dissolves between two
worlds
An honest man does not put himself off
With sophistries. Julius was honest.
He played no tricks of thinking,
And never got the chance. She saw to
that.
If he went down the garden to the lake,
She'd leave her pedestal and follow him
Pleading in her glassy, tinkling voice
That she was his.
He tried to work. What nonsense!
He could not see his paper, for her arm
Was always there holding out her flowers.
She ran the scale of coquetry, now cod-
dling him
With little Dresden china figure gestures,
Now raging in a heavy leaden fury.
Once she took up his manuscript
And threw it down and stamped upon it,
Then fell to weeping, bunched up on the
floor,
All crumpled to a sad humility.
She was very lovely, you remember,
So possibly, if Hildegarde —
And I'm not saying that there were no
moments
When he half wished to cross the line
Between the worlds.
It was not much to cross it,
Just leave his bedroom door unlocked at
night,
Or spend an Autumn evening by the
fountain.

Once done the other world was his,
But not the two.
No man can straddle both and be alive.
And yet he touched the edge, he knew it,
For the sycamore stumps were headless
snakes some evenings
Cut jaggedly across the middle section,
The top half gone.
They jerked half-circles, breaking in the
middle
Of a long whip-tail sweep. The move-
ment snapped directly on the edge
Which kept him in this world. If he
should cross
Then he would see the snakes' heads
fully winding.
He knew this. Luckily that moment did
not come,
At least, not then. Then he would face
about
And sternly order the figure to be gone.
When he was fierce like that, she went,
Drooping and tearful underneath the
trees,
And that night he was free of her. For
other nights
She passed beneath his window, wringing
her hands,
Those little hands which kept his dia-
mond,
Or else outside his door moaning and
moaning,
Pressing her mouth to the key-hole,
Squeezing herself full length against the
door,
Beating her hands upon it. It was anguish
To listen to her sobbing in the night,
And half betrayed himself, I must be-
lieve.
It was unbearable, he grew to loathe her,
And loathed her most when most near
being conquered,
For fact disports itself with paradox.
He knew her suffering, but hers was
single,
His double-darting. And then one after-
noon,
Worn out with sleeplessness and struggle,
he saw a way
To give her what she wanted and save
himself.
She was alone, the only figure
In all the silent garden. She should have
a mate,
He would seek her one; and instantly,

Next morning, he escaped, and went to
town,
Going directly to the shop
Where he had purchased her.

The bulging, broken faces
Fleered at him with crooked mouths,
With mouths like bloody gashes
Which made red stains on the oak wood,
The black oak wood of the cabinet.
Or was it the sun?
He heard them slobbering words,
He saw the words like smoke
Rising up and wreathing the rafters.
He saw the green snake-tree
Convulsed, contorted, and swaying.
He saw it was his sycamore
As he had never seen it.
The leaves were clapping and sighing.
The leaves and the faces together,
And the long snake boughs with heads
Which swept in terrible circles.
It was like a far-off screaming
Coming through time, not space,
Tenuously coming through time.
"Fool! Fool! Fool!" in a sort of smoky
echo,
Drawing from aeons of time,
Ending dark and still in the rafters.

And he saw a moon in the rafters
Shaped like the Ghost Peak Mountain,
A moon of copper and crystal,
In the midst of the flowing smoke.

Julius stood stock still, forcing his mind
To balance itself, to gain a solid kind
Of upright thinking. With his will drawn
tense
He held it sternly to obedience.
The swirl of smoke subsided, he ceased
to hear
The whispering, the faces frozen to mere
Grotesque immovable carvings on the
doors
Of an old oak cabinet, one among scores,
An excellent specimen. When Julius
Reached to that point and could quite
see it thus,
He had, he felt, attained a victory
Over himself, or over the incubi
Which always seemed about to haunt
him. So,
Relieved, he called out loudly, "Oh,
Hullo!

Is any one here?" At this, the proprietor
Appeared and inquired what Julius had
come for.
Easily explained, to find another
Lead statue to match and set off the
other.
Again they went into the little yard,
Past the forlorn Greek goddesses who
stared
At them with dull, nicked eyeballs grimed
with dust,
Gaunt in their marble robes beneath a
crust
Of mosses overscoring them like rust;
Past the poor chipped rococo cavaliers
Mincing their minuets, the gondoliers
Vigorously rowing on the cindered grass.
At length, beyond a crucifix of brass,
The proprietor stopped and pointed.
There it was,
The very thing, exactly the right size,
A little manikin in a gardener's guise,
With yellow breeches and a purple coat;
His loose white shirt was open at the
throat,
And he was idly leaning on a scythe.
A springy fellow, well set up and lithe,
Some rustic gallant decades and decades
dead
Achieved an immortality of lead.
The thing was done, the garden lady
mated,
The shopman more than amply compen-
sated.
And Julius, charmed with his expedient,
Passed through the shop, so happily in-
tent
Upon his ruse he did not look at all
At the old black cabinet against the wall.
Is it better to see, or not to see? A ques-
tion
Weighty as Hamlet's. This time no sug-
gestion
Of anything untoward struck his sense.
He preened himself upon his sapience.

Most appropriate and pleasing,
The little purple-coated gentleman
Stood between a clipped peacock and a
clipped unicorn,
An engaging bit of colour beside the
achromatic yews.
He leant on his scythe,
Agreeably regarding the little lady across
the path.

The Dolphin of the fountain appeared
unconcerned,
He spat out his jet of silver-blue water as
usual,
But then this was half-past four in the
afternoon,
And the sun was very bright in the sky,
The sun which lit this world and not the
other.
It was after it had set that things —
But Julius had installed his panacea,
And he went down to the lake to skip
stones.
Even when twilight came, he was un-
molested.
"So much for that," thought Julius.
But he went back to the house a round-
about way nevertheless.

VI

Tap! Tap! Tap! The sound of those
buckled shoes!
The little stealthy noise hurt his ears like
a bruise.
Three days she had not come, and he had
been so sure
The spell was broken, even had found
himself content
To relinquish the shadowy dawn of
something impermanent,
The vague and twilit edges which seemed
to circumfuse
The real, and sometimes almost suck it
or melt it away.
Had it been pleasure or pain? Julius
could not say.
He had taken his stand on the solid when
he bought the little man.
Tap! Tap! on the gravel, the footsteps
came — they came.
And each was like a crack in his smooth
and perfect plan.
Why did she come now, after three days
of waiting?
It was he who was eager to ask an ex-
planation.
She came in swiftly and knelt with her
marigolds and phlox
Held quivering out before her in a sort of
supplication.
"For you, dear Julius," she said. He
brushed by the evasion.
"Why?" he demanded, ironically conscious of the paradox,

The question sounded as if he had breath-
lessly watched the clocks
And counted the moments of absence.
    She took it so at once,
And with a certain majesty of loving
    stepped swiftly forward.
What was his response?

Julius, Julius, are you man or superman?
Can you pass the nether space
And keep a clue for returning?
As you stand in the flesh,
This woman, this leaden woman,
What is she that her wooing has at once
    the grace of flowers
And the horror of serpents?

Beware, Julius, and look
Through the window, someone is there,
And moonlight striking on the sharp
    hook
Of a scythe in the blue night air.
The face is sinister which you thought so
    debonair,
And the eyes are blood-grapes staring at
    the little Jardinière,
And at you also, Julius.
His leaden heart is green, green as an
    unripe pear,
For jealousy and hate is a choking thong
    in his throat —
Her beautiful, beautiful mouth, her suck-
    ing, intolerable mouth!
Julius feels his head throb, his stifled
    arteries bloat.
He is the tide of a sea, the thunder about
    to break,
With all his strength, he bursts himself
    awake
And flees up the stair.
The long, thin vapours of the nether
    space
Are closing down as he mounts the stair.
He feels a tenuous, flaccid air
Puffing against his upturned face.
The walls of the rooms are spinning and
    whirling,
The tables, with legs in the air, are curl-
    ing
Round and round like hoops on their
    polished edges.
Unfastened curtains are flaring and furl-
    ing
And racketing over the window-ledges.
A chiffonier glides across the floor

And catches at him with a golden claw.
Fire leaps from the seats of the chairs;
The flames break off and float like hairs.
The feathers of the red chintz cockatoos
Are burning convolvuli of reds and blues
Through the heat
Comes the awful beat
Of running — running leaden feet.
Panting and moaning, her little hands
Clutching and pulling at the air, the
    strands
Of her shredded petticoat dabbed with
    blood,
She follows Julius, the Gardener behind
Runs with a frothy, scarlet cud
Oozing out of his muoth. His hair is
    twined
With blotched and broken maple-leaves;
His arms below his rolled-up sleeves
Are hairy as apes; his scythe is a tongue
Whimpering for flesh. Julius has swung
Out of the window, he drops to the
    ground.
She, with the curve of a springing hound,
Is after; and the Gardener, flung on a
    bound
Like a bladder projected into light air,
Is next, and running with the others
    there.

Above in the gurgling tree-tops
Are whispering, misty mouths
Slobbering words like lava
Spilling them down the stems.
The mouths bleed words which drip
Into crawling slimy pools
And seep away like worms
Through the slit and cringing grass-blades.
Man-high is pausing stillness,
But the tree-leaves are whistling and cry-
    ing
With pallid childish voices.
A screaming comes out of the distance,
An old dead agony wailing.
The anguish of frozen planets
Engulfed in a timeless whirling.
No ear can catch it and hold it,
It hangs beyond hearing, a sense
Of sound aching into the flesh,
Never there; never quite silent.
The sycamore stumps are completed
Into white and hovering snakes
Which glitter and gloom like silver
And wave in a pattern of circles
Perpetually turning and coiling.

The peacocks and unicorns,
With the faces of men and women,
Dance with the blue-black dolphins
Or bathe themselves in the fountains.
They tear off their feathers and skin,
And stand up as golden figures
With red mouths, and red ears; their
  bellies
Are round and polished as brass,
In the centre of each is a diamond.
They sing, and gambol, and roll,
And pelt one another with flowers,
With marigolds and phlox,
And dash them into the fountain.
The Ghost Peak lies like a wound
In a puckered purple sky,
Sharp cut out of copper and crystal.
It throws a light on the garden
And streaks it with terrible shadows.
Through the shadows, in the glare of the
  copper light,
Goes Julius.
His breath scalds his lungs,
His feet stick and cling upon the gravel,
Behind him he hears the feet of the
  leaden figures
Nearer, louder, shattering his ears,
Confusing his steps with the rhythm of
  theirs.
His tongue is a red-hot ball in his mouth,
His lungs labour as though under sand.
The peacocks and unicorns skip round
  him,
They form a ring and dance before him,
Ogling him, thrusting upon him,
Strewing the ground with the diamonds
  plucked from their bellies.
Before him lies the lake,
Shuddering in sharp angles of copper and
  crystal.
He flogs his lungs, his feet,
He sees only the lake between the danc-
  ing unicorns and peacocks.
He hurls himself against the twined arms
And breaks through them.
He leaps, with a last pulse of effort,
Into the lake.
Water rises and blinds him,
Copper-flaming water like a great wall
  crushes upon him.
As he sinks — A clap! — loud and rever-
  berant as thunder.
Another clap! And a cleft wave rises to
  left and right,
Hangs a moment asunder,

And falls together with a noise of breaking crystals.
The Ghost Peak explodes
And tumbles in bloody atoms down the
  sky . . .

VII

Through quiet water, riffled by the
  moon,
Julius swims, toward the silent wharves
Of the little village. He hears the gentle
  grind
Of rowboats against the wharf-sides,
Reaches one and clambering into it feels
  for the gunwale
And then the bow and painter. He pulls
  the painter,
Hand over hand, until his fingers touch
The seamed wood of the wharf. Then,
  rising up,
He steps ashore as the boat rocks away.
A striking clock reminds him of the
  hour.
It is five o'clock. Already above the
  roofs
The sky is tinted, but there are still some
  stars
Like diamonds — Oh, damnable allusion!
Like diamonds! — A slightly twisted smile
Twitches his face. And now he sees but
  one,
Rayless and small, immensely bright to
  keep
Itself a sparkle in the coloured sky.
He sees it as the spectre of a death
Which might have been, eyeing the resur-
  rection
Which is. Thank God! Now he can
  watch it fade
Beneath the creeping daylight — just a
  star,
Going out in the morning. Stars are
  worlds;
But what has he to do with other worlds
Who knows so blunderingly of this? Well
  then
What's to do in this world? There's
  Hildegarde —
With which beginning he finds it is the
  end,
And other things superfluous. Why re-
  turn?
Why not start here directly where he
  stands?

He will go to town, and after Hildegarde
(He feels no qualm at seeing Hildegarde,
Some things are certain, Hildegarde is
    one),
Call at his agent's and give him strict
    instructions
To sell his house and all his furniture
At once. He has a written inventory.
It is correct except for two lead figures,
Small garden figurines of no great value,
Fallen into the lake by accident

And much too heavy to think of salvag-
    ing.
This plausible fiction happily invented,
The rising sun projected his sudden
    shadow
Before him on an earth of gold. Which
    noting,
He laughed and marched along the alley
    whistling
The broom song from the "Sorcerer's Ap-
    prentice."

DRIED MARJORAM

Over the moor the wind blew chill,
And cold it blew on the rounded hill
With a gibbet starting up from its crest,
The great arm pointing into the West
    Where something hung
    And clanked and swung.

Churchyard carrion, caged four-square
To every wind that furrows the air,
A poor unburied, unquiet thing,
The weighted end of a constant swing.
    It clanged and jangled
    But always dangled.

Lonely travellers riding by
Would check their horses suddenly
As out of the wind arose a cry
Hoarse as a horn in the weather-eye
    Of sleet at sea
    Blown desperately.

It would rise and fall, and the dissonance
As it struck the shrill of the wind would
    lance
The cold of ice-drops down the spine
And turn the blood to a clotted brine.
    Then only the hum
    Of the wind would come.

Never a sound but rasping heather
For minute after minute together.
Till once again a wail, long-drawn,
Would slice the night as though it were
    sawn,
    Cleaving through
    The mist and dew.

Such were the tales the riders told,
Sitting snugly out of the cold

In a wayside inn, with just a nip
Of cherry-brandy from which to sip,
    While rafters rattled
    And gossips prattled.

Rotted and blackened in its cage,
Anchored in permanent harborage,
Breeding its worms, with no decent clod
To weave it an apron of grassy sod.
    But this is no grief,
    The man was a thief.

He stole a sheep from a farmer's fold.
He was hungry, he said, and very cold.
His mother was ill and needed food.
The judge took snuff, his attitude
    Was gently resigned.
    He had not yet dined.

"To be hanged by the neck until you are
    dead."
That was the verdict, the judge had said.
A sheep had died so why not a man.
The sheep had an owner, but no one can
    Claim to own
    A man full-grown.

Nobody's property, no one to care,
But some one is sobbing over there.
"Most distressing, I declare,"
Says the judge, "take the woman out on
    the stair,
    And give her a crown
    To buy a new gown."

A gown for a son, such a simple ex-
    change!
But the clerk of the court finds it hard
    to arrange

This matter of sobbing, the fact is the sheep
Was stolen for her, and the woman will weep.
     It is most unreasonable.
     Indeed, well-nigh treasonable.

Slowly, slowly, his hands tied with rope,
The cart winds up the market slope.
Slowly, slowly, the knot is adjusted.
The tackle-pulleys whine, they are rusted,
     But free at a kick —
     Run — and hold with a click.

A mother's son, swung like a ham,
Bobbing over the heads of the jam.
A woman has fainted, give her air,
Drag her away for the people stare.
     The hanging is done.
     No more fun.

Nothing more but a jolting ride.
An ox-cart with a corpse inside,
Creaking through the shiny sheen
Of heather-stalks melted and bathed in green
     From a high-set moon.
     The heather-bells croon.

Heather below, and moon overhead,
And iron bars clasping a man who is dead.
Shadows of gorse-bushes under him bite
The shimmering moor like a spotted blight.
     The low wind chirrs
     Over the furze.

Slowly, slowly, panting and weak,
Some one wanders and seems to seek,
Bursting her eyes in the green, vague glare,
For an object she does not know quite where.
     Ah, what is that?
     A wild moor cat?

It scratches and cries above her head,
But here is no tree, and overspread
With clouds and moon the waste recedes,
And the heather flows like bent sea-weeds
     Pushed by an ebb
     To an arching web.

Black and uncertain, it rises before
Her dim old eyes, and the glossy floor
At its feet is undulant and specked
With a rhythmic wavering, and flecked
     By a reddish smudge
     Which does not budge.

Woman, that bundle is your son,
This is the goal your steps have won.
Over the length of the jewelled moor
You have travelled at last to the high-hung door
     Of his airy grave,
     Which does nothing but wave.

Dripping and dropping, his caged limbs drain,
And the spangled ground has a sticky stain.
She gave him this blood from her own dull veins,
And hers still runs, but her body's pains
     Turn back on her now,
     And each is a blow.

Iron-shrouded, flapping the air,
Sepulchred without a prayer,
Denied the comfort of bell and book.
Her tortured eyes do nothing but look.
     And from flower to flower
     The moon sinks lower.

Silver-grey, lavender, lilac-blue,
East of the moor the sun breaks through;
Cracking a bank of orange mist,
It shoulders up with a ruddy twist,
     And spears the spires
     Of heath with its fires.

Then a lark shoots up like a popgun ball
And turns to a spark and a song, and all
The thrushes and sparrows twitter and fly,
And the dew on the heather and gorse is dry.
     But brutal and clear
     The gibbet is here.

Slowly, slowly, worn and flagging,
With the grasshoppers jumping in front of her dragging
Feet, the old woman returns to the town.
But the seed of a thought has been deeply sown
     In her aching mind,
     Where she holds it enshrined.

Nights of moon and nights of dark,
Over the moor-path footsteps. Hark!
It is the old woman whose son is rotting
Above, on the gallows. That shadow
  blotting
    The Western sky
    Will be hers by-and-by.

Morning, and evening, and sun, and
  snow,
Months of weather come and go.
The flesh falls away from the withering
  bones,
The bones grow loose and scatter like
  stones.
    For the gallows-tree
    Shakes windily.

Every night along the path
Which her steps have beaten to a swath
Where heather and bracken dare not
  spring,
To the clack and grind of the gallows
  swing,
    The woman stumbles.
    The skeleton crumbles.

Bit by bit, on the ferns and furze,
Drop the bones which now are hers.
Bit by bit, she gathers them up
And carries them home in an old cracked
  cup.
    But the head remains
    Although its brains

Nourish the harebells and mullein-stalks.
Blow the wind high, the head still balks;
It rolls like an ivory billiard-ball,
But the bars are too close to let it fall.
    Still, God is just,
    And iron may rust.

November comes, this one after ten,
And the stiff bush-branches grate on the
  fen,
The gibbet jars to the sharp wind-strokes,
And the frazzled iron snarls and croaks.
    It blows a gale
    With snow and hail.

Two days, three nights, the storm goes
  on,
And the cage is tossed like a gonfalon
Above a castle, crumpled and slit,
And the frail joints are shattered apart
  and split.

The fissure gapes,
And the skull escapes.

An ostrich-egg on a bed of fern,
Restlessly rolled by the streams which
  churn
The leaves, thrust under and forced into
The roots and the mud which oozes
  through
    The empty pockets
    Of wide eye-sockets.

Two days, three nights, and the ferns are
  torn
And scattered in heaps, and the bushes
  shorn,
And the heather docked of its seeded
  bells.
But the glittering skull heaves high and
  swells
    Above the dank square
    Where the ferns once were.

Hers at last, all, all of hers,
And past her tears the red sun blurs,
Bursting out of the sleeve of the storm.
She brushes a busy, wriggling worm
    Away from the head
    Of her dearest dead.

The uprooted gibbet, all awry,
Crooks behind her against the sky.
Startled rabbits flee from her feet;
The stems of the bracken smell ripe and
  sweet.
    She pays no heed,
    But quickens her speed.

In the quiet evening, the church-bell tolls;
Fishermen wind up their fishing-poles;
Sheep-bells clink in farmstead closes;
A cat in a kitchen window dozes;
    And doors are white
    With candlelight.

In the old woman's house there is much
  to do.
Her windows are shuttered, no gleam
  comes through,
But inside, the lamp-shine strikes on a
  tub;
She washes, it seems, and her old hands
  rub
    And polish with care
    The thing that is there.

Gently, gently, sorting and sifting,
With a little psalm-tune shakily drifting
Across her lips, she works and watches,
Stealing moments in sundry snatches
    To note the tick-tock
    Of the hanging clock.

Decently, reverently, all displayed
Upon a cloth, the bones are laid.
Oh, the loving, lingering touch
Tenderly pausing on such and such!
    A cuckoo flings
    From the clock, and sings.

"Cuckoo! Cuckoo!" Eight times over.
Wrap them up in a linen cover.
Take the spade and snuff the lamp.
Put on a cloak for the night is damp.
    The door creaks wide,
    She steps outside.

All tottering, solemn, eager, slow,
She crawls along. The moon is low
And creeps beside her through the hedge,
Rising at last to peer over the edge
    Of the churchyard wall
    And brighten her shawl.

The flagstone path taps back to her tread.
She stops to listen, and whispers spread
All round her, hissing from trees and
    graves.
Before her is movement; something
    waves.
    But she passes on,
    The movement is gone.

Blind in the moon the windows shine,
Colourless, glinting, line and line,
The leaded panes are facets and squares
Of dazzle, arched in carven pairs.
    Ivy rustles.
    A yew-tree justles.

The corner last on the farthest side
Where the church, foreshortened, is
    heavy-eyed,
For only the chancel lancets pierce
The lichened mullions, designed in tierce,
    Whence the sun comes through
    Ruby and blue.

This corner is strangled in overgrowth;
Dock-leaves waver like elephants, loath
To move, but willing to flap their ears,

And huge stone blocks like unshaped
    biers
    Are sprawled among
    Clumps of adder's-tongue.

A bat swoops down and flitters away;
An owl whimpers like a child astray;
The slanting grave-stones, all askew,
Cock themselves obscenely, two and two.
    She stoops and pushes
    Between the bushes.

She lays her bundle on a stone.
Her bleeding hands are cut to the bone
And torn by the spines of thorn and brier.
Her shoulders ache. Her spade in the
    mire
    Sucks and slimes
    These many times.

Slowly she clears an open space,
Screened behind hollies, where wild vines
    lace
Their tendrils in angles and fractured
    turns.
But water is flooding the stems of the
    ferns.
    Alas for the dead
    Who lie in this bed!

But hanged men have no business where
The ground has been hallowed by chant
    and prayer.
Even to lie in the putrid seeping
Of consecrate mud is to be in God's keep-
    ing,
    And He will forget
    His judgment debt.

Poor lone soul, all palsied and dim,
As she lifts the bones, she quavers a
    hymn.
Then, as for years she laid him to sleep
In his crib, she sets the bundle deep
    In the watery hole,
    And prays for his soul.

"Rest, lad, now, surely God hears,
He has granted me this for my many
    tears.
Sleep, my Darling, for you are come
Home at last to stay at home."
    But the old voice stops,
    And something drops.

They found her dead on a sunny noon,
Clasping the ground, and overstrewn
With decent leaves which had dropped
    a shroud
All about her. The parson allowed
    Custom to waive
In making her grave.

Even the sexton said no word
When something under his shovel stirred,
And the parson read the burial prayer.
He seemed rather husky, but then the air
    Was bitter cold.
There was frost on the mold.

BEFORE THE STORM

THE LEGEND OF PETER RUGG

I

Over the hill snakes the dusty road, creeping up, and up, in a smother of sandy gravel, heaving the load of itself up against the horizon; a couple of yards of level, then a leap down between powdered barberry bushes; a narrow white line shot like a bolt between bushes and stone walls. It is appallingly still. Not a rustle of the white barberry-leaves, not a single moving stalk of Queen Anne's lace in the field over the wall. The sunshine lies like a flat, hot weight on the hill, a moment ago there were locusts grating in the branches, but not now. The ground is still, and hot to touch; the trees are still, with a hushing of innumerable leaves; the sky is still; but in the Southwest, great thunder-heads push up behind the mountain. A hushing of leaves, and a pushing of big, white clouds, up — up — puffing into wide silver balloons, gathering back into pigeon-grey pleats, up — up — into the hot yellow sky.

There is a shade over the sun, it is fading from yellow to white, from white to grey. Away down the hill is a tight, narrow wedge of wind, it cuts sharply over a field of barley; it is edged, and hard, and single. Another wind-wedge, with looser, vaguer edges. A mist swirls over the shoulder of Black Top, thickens, clouds the mountain.

A barberry-leaf jerks, and settles; two barberry-leaves quirk themselves upright, and fall back; from over the hill there is a quick skirling of crisp leaves — nearer. The trees begin to whisper, and the snaky road hurls its dust into the air and plunges down the hill into the blue-black

wind. All the leaves are blowing now, shivering, pulling, throwing themselves frantically hither and thither; they are not green any more, but blue and purple, and they play over the rolling thunder like flutes and mandolins over double basses.

Something races along the road. Sharp whip-cracks staccato upon the double basses and flutes. Who lashes a poor brute up a hill like that? On the two-yard level, something passes in a smear of yellow wheels and bright steel shoes. Who goes there? "Boston! Boston! . . ." But the stones of the down grade are already clattering and rolling as the horse goes over them. A spatter of rain slaps the barberry-leaves; patter — patter — rain, and a grieving, tearing wind. A flare of lightning! There is no one on the road. A long peal of thunder, and then beating rain.

II

"Lucindy-Ann, you run upstairs this minit and shut them guest-room winders, ther's a awful storm a-comin'."

Lucindy-Ann tears up the narrow stair, but pauses at the guest-room window to see the black water of the bay wrinkle and flow, and all the fishing-boats scud to their moorings. A flicker of lightning quicksilvers the window-panes. A crash of thunder sets them clapping in their frames.

"Somebody's caught," giggles Lucindy-Ann. "Well, ef that ain't a queer team!"

Along the shore road comes a high carriage with yellow wheels. It comes so fast it reels from side to side, swaying in a dreadful way. Standing up in it, lashing the white horse, is a man, in a long laced coat and cocked hat. "Did you ever see a figure of fun to beat that?" Lucindy-Ann leans from the window, and the lightning spots her out against the black room behind like a painted saint on a dark altar. Lucindy-Ann does not falter. There is a child beside the man, clinging and shaking. The horse is making for the house.

"You come right in," shouts Lucindy-Ann. "Drive around to the kitchen door," but before she can say more, the man has pulled his sweating horse up under the window.

"Which is the way to Boston?" he calls. And his voice quavers, and quivers, and falls. A clap of thunder, the child shrieks, the old apple-tree by the window creaks. The man looks up, and his clothes are torn — worn, draggled, caked with mud. His face is white, and his eyes a-stare, the lightning strikes him out to a glare: he, and the child, and the yellow-wheeled chaise, against a background of blue-black haze. The waves slap on the sandy shore, the apple-tree taps on the entry door. "Which way to Boston?" the cracked voice wails. "Boston — Boston . . ." the echo trails away through tossing trees. In the bay, the fishing-boats heel to the breeze.

A roll of thunder jags and cracks over the house roof. Rain-drops — clashing on a row of milk-pans set out to air.

"Boston, Sir, why you must be mad, you're twelve miles from Providence, and headed fair that way." A sharp whip cut, a snorting horse, a scrape and whir of the yellow wheels, round spins the chaise, and dashes for the gate.

"An' ef he ain't took the wrong turn agin!" gasps Lucindy-Ann, as she draws her head in. The milk-cans rattle, as the thunder bursts and tears out of the sky. Away down the road comes the clicking clatter of fast wheels, lessening the distance to Providence.

"I don't s'pose it matters," says Lucindy-Ann, but she scuttles down the stairway as fast as she can.

III

The sky is lowering and black, a strange blue-blackness, which makes red houses pink, and green leaves purple. Over the blowing purple trees, the sky is an iron-blue, split with forks of straw-yellow. The thunder breaks out of the sky with a crash, and rumbles away in a long, hoarse drag of sound. The river is the blue of Concord grapes, with steel points and oblongs, down the bridge; up stream, it is pale and even, a solid line of unpolished zinc.

Tlop — Tlop — Tlop — Tlop! Beyond the willows, the road bends; someone is coming down it at a tremendous speed. Indeed he is in a hurry, this someone. You can hear him lashing his horse. A flashing up of willows and road on a lightning jab. A high yellow-wheeled gig, or chair, fashion of a century ago. A man in a cocked hat, a child in a snood! What the devil gets into the blood when thunder is rumbling? Have a care, man, that horse is stumbling. Down on his knees, by Gravy! No, up again. Bear him on the rein. Hi! Do you hear? A queer swirling and sighing in the air. The crying of a desolate child. A quivering flare of lightning sparkling in the whirling spokes of turning wheels. Tlop! Tlop! on the wooden planks of the bridge. No thanks to you you're not over the edge. Lord, what a curve! He went round on one wheel. Do you hear anything? No, feel rather. Drifting over the grape-blue river, seeping through the willow-trees' quiver, is a faint, hoarse calling of "Boston — Boston — Will no one show me the way to Boston?" Poor Devil, he can't have left it above an hour. Listen to the bridge drumming to the shower. And the water all peppered with little white rounds, it's funny how a storm plays the mischief with sounds. Sights, too, sometimes. Cocked hat, indeed! I must have been dreaming.

IV

Guinea-gold, the State House dome, standing out against a wall of indigo cloud. Boldly thrust out in high relief, with its white façade, and its wide, terraced esplanade. It spurns the Common at its feet, treading on it as on a mat, cooling itself with the air from its fanning trees. Guinea-gold lightning glitters through the indigo-blue cloud, a loud muffled booming of thunder, then the rain, pin-pointing down on the stretched silk of umbrellas, clipping like hard white beans on glass awnings, double-streaming over the two edges of sidewalk clocks. Electric car gongs knock sharp warnings into the slipping crowd. A policeman humps himself into his rubber coat and springs to catch the head of a careering horse.

"Stop beatin' him, ye Fool. Didn't ye see me raised hand? Whoa! Stand still, ye beast. You advertisin' fellers think the least ye do is to own the city. I've a mind to run ye in. Fool-bumpin' along like that. What you pushin' anyway, breakfast food or automobiles? He was a clever guy rigged ye out, but I guess ye're about due for a new set of glad rags, judgin' by them ye got on. Here, Kiddie, don't cry, ye'll soon be home now, snug and dry. Listen to that thunder. Some storm! No wonder ye're scared; it's fierce. What's that? Mrs. Peter Rugg? Middle Street? See her, I ain't a direct'ry, ye'd better inquire at the post-office. Tell your breakfast food to put its name on ye next time."

There is a hissing of sparks as the steel shoes strike the wet asphalt. A clattering of iron tires on the metal roadway, drowned by a thunder peal. Wires and wires of linked rain, hatching over the disappearing yellow wheels.

The policeman rubs a wet, red ear. "That's a queer thing," he mutters, "very queer. I thought he asked me the way to Boston, just as he was drivin' off."

V

The yellow-wheeled chaise with the cocked-hatted man takes all of New England into its span. Logging-men, drifting down the Kennebec on floating rafts, see a moving speck of sulphur dust along the bank, an old-fashioned gig, drawn by a lank white horse, driving furiously before the storm. A moment later, a thunderbolt gashes across the sky, they can feel the raft jolt. Then the river swirls into lumpy waves and the logging men jump to their poles and staves.

An automobile, struggling up Jacob's Ladder on the way to Lenox in the teeth of a thunder-shower, sees glowering ahead on the down stretch, a wretched one-horse rig, which, in the uncertain light, seems as big as a locomotive. The driver switches on his klaxon and takes the down slope. But he might be a loping broncho, for all the gain he makes on the one-horse team. His klaxon screeches and echoes among the hills. Is it a dream that over its din, a thin voice reaches his ear? "Boston — Boston . . ." he seems to hear. "I left Menotomy a long time ago. Oh, when shall I get to Boston!"

Gloucester fishermen, moored to a wharf, hear a wheezy, coughing voice calling, pleading, in the middle of the night. It is a crazy wight, in a two-wheeled buggy of a pattern long gone by, driving a great white horse with a savage eye. The horse stamps on the thin boards of the wharf and champs his bit. There's a slip of a girl, too, who does nothing but cry. Rigging slaps and spars creak, for a gale is rising and the stars are hidden. The fishermen hear again the wail, "Tell me how to get to Boston." "Well, not that way, Idiot, you're going straight into the Atlantic Ocean." There is a terrible commotion on the wharf, the horse almost beats it through with his hoofs. Then, in the white gleam of a lightning spear, the chaise is seen rocking, shaking, making for the road above and turning toward Ipswich.

Through narrow wood-tracks where hermit-thrushes pair, staggers the yellow one-horse chair, just ahead of a lightning flare. Along elm-shaded streets of little towns, the high wheels roll, and leaves blow down on the man's cocked hat and the little girl's snood, and a moment later comes a flood of bright, white rain, and thunder so loud it stops the blood.

From Kittery Point down to Cape Cod, trundle the high, turning wheels;

they rattle at the Canadian line; they shine in the last saffron glitter of an extinguishing sun by the ferry over Lake Champlain; they are seen again as the moon dips into an inky cloud passing the Stadium in East Cambridge, the driver bowed over the dasher and plying his whip; they flash beside graveyards, and thunder lashes the graveyard trees. Always the chaise flees before the approaching storm. And always, down the breeze, blowing backwards through the bending trees, comes the despairing wail — "Boston! — For the love of God, put me on the road to Boston!" Then the gale grows louder, lightning spurts and dazzles, and steel-white rain falls heavily out of the sky. A great clap of thunder, and purple-black darkness blinding the earth.

FOUR SIDES TO A HOUSE

Peter, Peter, along the ground,
Is it wind I hear, or your shoes' sound?
Peter, Peter, across the air,
Do dead leaves fall, or is it your hair?
Peter, Peter, North and South,
They have stopped your mouth
With water, Peter.

The long road runs, and the long road
    runs,
    Who comes over the long road, Peter?
Who knocks at the door in the cold twi-
    light,
And begs a heap of straw for the night,
And a bit of a sup, and a bit of a bite —
    Do you know the face, Peter?

He lays him down on the floor and sleeps.
    Must you wind the clock, Peter?
It will strike and strike the dark night
    through.
He will sleep past one, he will sleep past
    two,
But when it strikes three what will he do?
He will rise and kill you, Peter.

He will open the door to one without.
    Do you hear that voice, Peter?
Two men prying and poking about,
Is it here, is it there, is it in, is it out?
Cover his staring eyes with a clout.
    But you're dead, dead, Peter.

They have ripped up the boards, they
    have pried up the stones,
    They have found your gold, dead
    Peter.
Ripe, red coins to itch a thief's hand,
But you drip ripe red on the floor's white
    sand,

You burn their eyes like a firebrand.
    They must quench you, Peter.

It is dark in the North, it is dark in the
    South,
    The wind blows your white hair, Peter.
One at your feet and one at your head.
A soft bed, a smooth bed,
Scarcely a splash, you sink like lead.
    Sweet water in your well, Peter.

Along the road and along the road,
    The next house, Peter.
Four-square to the bright and the shade
    of the moon.
The North winds shuffle, the South winds
    croon,
Water with white hair over-strewn.
    The door, the door, Peter!
Water seeps under the door.

They have risen up in the morning grey.
    What will they give to Peter?
The sorrel horse with the tail of gold,
Fastest pacer ever was foaled.
Shoot him, skin him, blanch his bones,
Nail up his skull with a silver nail
Over the door, it will not fail.
No ghostly thing can ever prevail
    Against a horse's skull, Peter.

Over the lilacs, gazing down,
    Is a window, Peter.
The North winds call, and the South
    winds cry.
Silver white hair in a bitter blowing,
Eel-green water washing by,
A red mouth floating and flowing.
    Do you come, Peter?

They rose as the last star sank and set.
 One more for Peter.
They slew the black mare at the flush of
   the sun,
And nailed her skull to the window-stone.
In the light of the moon how white it
   shone —
 And your breathing mouth, Peter!

Around the house, and around the house,
With a wind that is North, and a wind
   that is South,
 Peter, Peter.
Mud and ooze and a dead man's wrist
Wrenching the shutters apart, like mist
The mud and the ooze and the dead
   man twist.
 They are praying, Peter.

Three in stable a week ago.
 This is the last, Peter.
"My strawberry roan in the morning
   clear,

Lady heart and attentive ear,
Foot like a kitten, nose like a deer,
But the fear! The fear!"
 Three skulls, Peter.

The sun goes down, and the night draws
   in.
 Toward the hills, Peter.
What lies so stiff on the hill-room floor,
When the gusty wind claps to the door?
They have paid three horses and two
   men more.
 Gather your gold, Peter.

Softly, softly, along the ground
Lest your shoes sound.
Gently, gently, across the air
Lest it stream, your hair.
North and South
For your aching mouth.
But the moon is old, Peter,
And death is long, and the well is deep.
Can you sleep, sleep, Peter?

FIR-FLOWER TABLETS

PREFACE

LET ME STATE at the outset that I know no Chinese. My duty in Mrs. Ayscough's and my joint collaboration has been to turn her literal translations into poems as near to the spirit of the originals as it was in my power to do. It has been a long and arduous task, but one which has amply repaid every hour spent upon it. To be suddenly introduced to a new and magnificent literature, not through the medium of the usual more or less accurate translation, but directly, as one might burrow it out for one's self with the aid of a dictionary, is an exciting and inspiring thing. The method we adopted made this possible, as I shall attempt to show. The study of Chinese is so difficult that it is a life-work in itself; so is the study of poetry. A sinologue has no time to learn how to write poetry; a poet has no time to learn how to read Chinese. Since neither of us pretended to any knowledge of the other's craft, our association has been a continually augmenting pleasure.

I was lucky indeed to approach Chinese poetry through such a medium. The translations I had previously read had given me nothing. Mrs. Ayscough has been to me the pathway to a new world. No one could be a more sympathetic go-between for a poet and his translator, and Mrs. Ayscough was well-fitted for her task. She was born in Shanghai. Her father, who was engaged in business there, was a Canadian and her mother an American. She lived in China until she was eleven, when her parents returned to America in order that their children might finish their education in this country. It was then that I met her, so that our friendship is no new thing, but has persisted, in spite of distance, for more than thirty years, to ripen in the end into a partnership which is its culmination. Returning to China in her early twenties, she became engaged to an Englishman connected with a large British importing house in Shanghai, and on her marriage, which took place almost immediately, went back to China, where she has lived ever since. A diligent student of Chinese life and manners, she soon took up the difficult study of literary Chinese, and also accepted the position of honorary librarian of the library of the North China Branch of the Royal Asiatic Society. Of late years, she has delivered a number of lectures on Chinese subjects in China, Japan, America, and Canada, and has also found time to write various pamphlets on Chinese literature and customs.

In the Autumn of 1917, Mrs. Ayscough arrived in America on one of her periodic visits to this country. She brought with her a large collection of Chinese paintings for exhibition, and among these paintings were a number of examples of the "Written Pictures." Of these, she had made some rough translation which she intended to use to illustrate her lectures. She brought them to me with a request that I put them into poetic shape. I was fascinated by the poems, and, as we talked them over, we realized that here was a field in which we should like to work. When she returned to China, it was agreed that we should make a volume of translations from the classic Chinese writers. Such translations were in the line of her usual work, and I was anxious to read the Chinese poets as nearly in the original as it was possible for me to do. At first, we hardly considered publication. Mrs. Ayscough lives in Shanghai and I in Boston, and the war-time mails were anything but expeditious, but an enthusiastic publisher kept constantly before us our ultimate, if remote, goal. Four years have passed, and after many unavoidable delays the book is finished. We have not done it all by correspondence. Mrs. Ayscough has come back to America several times during its preparation; but, whether together or apart, the plan on which we have worked has always been the same.

Very early in our studies, we realized that the component parts of the Chinese written character counted for more in the composition of poetry than has generally been recognized; that the poet chose one character rather than another which meant practically the same thing, because of the descriptive allusion in the makeup of that particular character; that the poem was enriched precisely through this undercurrent of meaning in the structure of its characters. But not always — and here was the difficulty. Usually the character must be taken merely as the word it had been created to mean. It was a nice distinction, when to allow one's self the use of these character undercurrents, and when to leave them out of count entirely. But I would not have my readers suppose that I have changed or exaggerated the Chinese text. Such has not been the case. The analysis of characters has been employed very rarely, and only when the text seemed to lean on the allusion for an added vividness or zest. In only one case in the book have I permitted myself to use an adjective not inherent in the character with which I was dealing — and, in that case, the connotation was in the word itself, being descriptive of an architectural structure for which we have no equivalent — except in the "Written Pictures," where, as Mrs. Ayscough has stated in her Introduction, we allowed ourselves a somewhat freer treatment.

It has been necessary, of course, to acquire some knowledge of the laws of Chinese versification. But, equally of course, these rules could only serve to bring me into closer relations with the poems and the technical limits of the various forms. It was totally impossible to follow either the rhythms or the rhyme-schemes of the originals. All that could be done was to let the English words fall into their natural rhythm and not attempt to handicap the exact word by introducing rhyme at all. This is the method I followed in my translations of French poems in my book, "Six French Poets." I hold that it is more important to reproduce the perfume of a poem than its metrical form, and no translation can possibly reproduce both.

Our plan of procedure was as follows: Mrs. Ayscough would first write out the poem in Chinese. Not in the Chinese characters, of course, but in transliteration. Opposite every word she put the various meanings of it which accorded with its place in the text, since I could not use a Chinese dictionary. She also gave the analyses of whatever characters seemed to her to require it. The lines were carefully indicated, and to these lines I have, as a rule, strictly adhered; the lines of the translations usually corresponding, therefore, with the lines of the originals. In the few poems in which the ordering of the lines has been changed, this has been done solely in the interest of cadence.

I had, in fact, four different means of approach to a poem. The Chinese text, for rhyme-scheme and rhythm; the dictionary meanings of the words; the analyses of characters; and, for the fourth, a careful paraphrase by Mrs. Ayscough, to which she added copious notes to acquaint me with all the allusions, historical, mythological, geographical, and technical, that she deemed it necessary for me to know. Having done what I could with these materials, I sent the result to her, when she and her Chinese teacher carefully compared it with the original, and it was returned to me, either passed or commented upon, as the case might be. Some poems crossed continent and ocean many times in their course toward completion; others, more fortunate, satisfied at once. On Mrs. Ayscough's return to America this year, all the poems were submitted to a further meticulous scrutiny, and I can only say that they are as near the originals as we could make them, and I hope they may give one quarter of the pleasure to our readers that they have to us in preparing them.

INTRODUCTION

THERE HAS probably never been a people in whose life poetry has played such a large part as it has done, and does, among the Chinese. The unbroken continuity of their history, throughout the whole of which records have been carefully kept, has resulted in the accumulation of a vast amount of material; and this material, literary as well as historical, remains available to-day for any one who wishes to study that branch of art which is the most faithful index to the thoughts and feelings of the "black-haired race," which, besides, constitutes one of the finest literatures produced by any race the world has known.

To the confusion of the foreigner, however, Chinese poetry is so made up of suggestion and allusion that, without a knowledge of the backgrounds (I use the plural advisedly) from which it sprang, much of its meaning and not a little of its beauty is necessarily lost. Mr. Arthur Waley, in the preface to his "A Hundred and Seventy Chinese Poems," says: "Classical allusion, always the vice of Chinese poetry, finally destroyed it altogether." Granting the unhappy truth of this statement, the poetry of China is nevertheless so human and appealing as to speak with great force even to us who live under such totally different conditions; it seems worth while, therefore, to acquire a minimum of knowledge in regard to it and so increase the enjoyment to be derived from it. In the present collection, I have purposely included only those poems in which this national vice is less in evidence; and this was not a difficult task. There is such an enormous body of Chinese poetry that the difficulty has been, not what to take, but what to leave out. I have been guided somewhat by existing translations, not wishing to duplicate what has already been adequately done, when so much still remains untouched. Not that all these poems appear in English for the first time, but many of them do; and except for Mr. Waley's admirable work, English renderings have usually failed to convey the flavour of the originals.

Chinese scholars rank their principal poets in the following order: Tu Fu, Li T'ai-po, and Po Chü-i. Realizing that, naturally, in any literature, it is the great poets which another nation wishes to read, I have purposely kept chiefly to them, and among them to Li T'ai-po, since his poems are of a universal lyricism. Also, Mr. Waley has devoted his energies largely to Po Chü-i. Tu Fu is very difficult to translate, and probably for that reason his work is seldom given in English collections of Chinese poems. Some of his simpler poems are included here, however. A small section of the book is devoted to what the Chinese call "written-on-the-wall-pictures." I shall come back to these later.

The great stumbling-block which confronts the translator at the outset is that the words he would naturally use often bring before the mind of the Occidental reader an entirely different scene to that actually described by the Oriental poet. The topography, the architecture, the fauna and flora, to say nothing of the social customs, are all alien to such a reader's own surroundings and cannot easily be visualized by him. Let me illustrate with a modern poem, for it is a curious fact that there has lately sprung up in America and England a type of poetry which is so closely allied to the Chinese in method and intention as to be very striking. This is the more remarkable since, at the time of its first appearance, there were practically no translations of Chinese poems which gave, except in a remote degree, the feeling of the originals. So exact, in fact, is this attitude toward the art of poetry among the particular group of poets to whom I have reference and the Chinese masters, that I have an almost perfect illustration of the complications of rendering which a translator runs up against by imagining this little poem of Miss Lowell's being suddenly presented to a Chinese scholar in his grass hut among the Seven Peaks:

NOSTALGIA

By Amy Lowell

"Through pleasures and palaces" —
Through hotels, and Pullman cars, and steamships . . .

Pink and white camellias
    floating in a crystal bowl,
The sharp smell of firewood,
The scrape and rustle of a dog stretching himself
    on a hardwood floor,
And your voice, reading — reading —
    to the slow ticking of an old brass clock . . .

"Tickets, please!"
And I watch the man in front of me
Fumbling in fourteen pockets,
While the conductor balances his ticket-punch
Between his fingers.

As we read this poem, instantly pictures of American travel start before our eyes: rushing trains with plush-covered seats, Negro porters in dusty-grey suits, weary ticket-collectors; or marble-floored hotel entrances, clanging elevator doors, and hurrying bell-boys, also the vivid suggestion of a beautiful American house. But our scholar would see none of this. To him, a journey is undertaken, according to the part of the country in which he must travel, either in a boat, the types of which are infinitely varied, from the large, slow-going travelling barge capable of carrying many passengers, to the swifter, smaller craft which hold only two or three people; in one of the several kinds of carriages; in a wheelbarrow, a sedan chair, a mule litter, or on the back of an animal — horse, mule, or donkey, as the case may be. Again, there is no English-speaking person to whom "Home, Sweet Home" is not familiar; in a mental flash, we conclude the stanza suggested by the first line, and know, even without the title, that the subject of the poem is homesickness. Our scholar, naturally, knows nothing of the kind; the reference is no reference to him. He is completely at sea, with no clue as to the emotion the poem is intended to convey, and no understanding of the conditions it portrays. Poem after poem in Chinese is as full of the intimate detail of daily life, as dependent upon common literary ex-

perience, as this. There is an old Chinese song called "The Snapped Willow." It, too, refers to homesickness and allusions to it are very frequent, but how can an Occidental guess at their meaning unless he has been told? In this Introduction, therefore, I have endeavoured to give as much of the background of this Chinese poetry as seems to me important, and, since introductions are made to be skipped, it need detain no one to whom the facts are already known.

The vast country of China, extending from the plains of Mongolia on the North to the Gulf of Tonquin on the South, a distance of somewhat over eighteen hundred miles, and from the mountains of Tibet on the West to the Yellow Sea on the East, another stretch of about thirteen hundred miles, comprises within its "Eighteen Provinces" practically every climate and condition under which human beings can exist with comfort. A glance at the map will show the approximate positions of the ancient States which form the poetic background of China, and it will be noticed that, with the exception of Yüeh, they all abut either on the Huang Ho, better known as the Yellow River, or on the Yangtze Kiang. These two great rivers form the main arteries of China, and to them is largely due the character of the people and the type of their mythology.

The Yellow River, which in the old mythology was said to have its source in the Milky Way (in the native idiom, "Cloudy" or "Silver River"), really rises in the K'un Lun Mountains of Central Asia; from thence its course lies through the country supposed to have been the cradle of the Chinese race. It is constantly referred to in poetry, as is also its one considerable tributary, the Wei River, or "Wei Water," its literal name. The Yellow River is not navigable for important craft, and running as it does through sandy loess constantly changes its course with the most disastrous consequences.

The Yangtze Kiang, "Son of the Sea," often referred to as the "Great River," is very different in character. Its source lies among the mountains of the Tibetan border, where it is known as the "River of Golden Sand." After flowing due

South for several hundred miles, it turns abruptly to the North and East, and, forcing its way through the immense wall of mountain which confronts it, "rushes with incredible speed" to the far-off Eastern Sea, forming in its course the Yangtze Gorges, of which the most famous are the San Hsia, or "Three Chasms." To these, the poets never tire of alluding, for, to quote Li T'ai-po, the cliffs rise to such a height that they seem to "press Green Heaven." The water is low during the Winter months, leaving many treacherous rocks and shoals uncovered, but rises to a seething flood during the Summer, when the Tibetan snows are melting. The river is then doubly dangerous, as even great pinnacles of rock are concealed by the whirling rapids. Near this point, the Serpent River, so-called from its tortuous configuration, winds its way through deep ravines and joins the main stream. As may be imagined, navigation on these stretches of the river is extremely perilous, and an ascent of the Upper Yangtze takes several months to perform since the boats must be hauled over the numerous rapids by men, called professionally "trackers," whose work is so strenuous that they are bent nearly double as they crawl along the tow-paths made against the cliffs. In spite of the precipitous nature of the banks, many towns and villages are built upon them and rise tier on tier up the mountain sides. Having run about two-thirds of its course and reached the modern city of Hankow, the Great River changes its mood and continues on its way, immense and placid, forming the chief means of communication between the sea and Central China. The remarkably fertile country on either side is intersected by water-ways, natural and artificial, used instead of roads, which latter do not exist in the Yangtze Valley, their place being taken by paths, some of which are paved with stone and wide enough to accommodate two or three people abreast.

As travel has always been very popular, every conceivable form of water-borne craft has sprung up, and these the poets constantly used as they went from the capital to take up their official posts, or from the house of one patron to another, the ancient custom being for the rich to entertain and support men of letters with whom they "drank wine and recited verses," the pastime most dear to their hearts. The innumerable poems of farewell found among the works of all Chinese poets were usually written as parting gifts from the authors to their hosts.

As it nears the sea, the river makes a great sweep round Nanking and flows through what was once the State of Wu, now Kiangsu. This and the neighbouring States of Yüeh and Ch'u (the modern Chêkiang and parts of Hunan, Kweichow, and Kiangsi) is the country painted in such lovely, peaceful pictures by Li T'ai-po and his brother poets. The climate being mild, the willows which grow on the banks of the rivers and canals are seldom bare and begin to show the faint colour of Spring by the middle of January; and, before many days, the soft bud-sheaths, called by the Chinese "willow-snow," lie thick on the surface of the water. Plum-trees flower even while the rare snow-falls turn the ground white, and soon after the New Year, the moment when, according to the Chinese calendar, Spring "opens," the fields are pink with peach-bloom, and gold with rape-blossom, while the air is sweetly scented by the flowers of the beans sown the Autumn before. Walls and fences are unknown, only low ridges divide the various properties, and the little houses of the farmers are built closely together in groups, as a rule to the South of a bamboo copse which acts as a screen against the Northeast winds prevailing during the Winter; the aspect of the rich plain, which produces three crops a year, is therefore that of an immense garden, and the low, grey houses, with their heavy roofs, melt into the picture as do the blue-coated people who live in them. Life is very intimate and communistic, and the affairs of every one in the village are known to every one else. The silk industry being most important, mulberry-trees are grown in great numbers to provide the silk-worms with the leaves upon which they subsist, and are kept closely pollarded in order that they may produce as much foliage as possible.

This smiling country on the river-banks, and to the South, provides a striking contrast to those provinces lying farther North and West. Shantung, the birthplace of Confucius, is arid and filled with rocky, barren hills, and the provinces of Chili, Shansi, Shensi, and Kansu, which extend Westward, skirting the the Great Wall, are also sandy and often parched for lack of water, while Szechwan, lying on the Tibetan border, although rich and well irrigated, is barred from the rest of China by tremendous mountain ranges difficult to pass. One range, called the "Mountains of the Two-Edged Sword," was, and is, especially famous. It formed an almost impassable barrier, and the great Chu Ko-liang, therefore, ordered that a roadway, of the kind generally known in China as *chan tao* (a road made of logs laid on piers driven into the face of a cliff and kept secure by mortar) be built, so that travellers from Shensi might be able to cross into Szechwan. This road is described by Li T'ai-po in a very beautiful poem, "The Terraced Road of the Two-Edged Sword Mountains."

These varied scenes among which the poets lived differed again from those which flashed before their mental eyes when their thoughts followed the soldiers to the far Northwest, to the country where the Hsiung Nu and other Mongol tribes lived, those Barbarians, as the Chinese called them, who perpetually menaced China with invasion, who, in the picturesque phraseology of the time, desired that their horses should "drink of the streams of the South." These Mongol hordes harassed the Chinese State from its earliest days; it was as a defence against them that the "First Emperor" erected the Great Wall, with a length of "ten thousand *li*" as Chinese hyperbole unblushingly states — its real length is fifteen hundred miles. This defence could, however, merely mitigate, not avert, the evil; only constant effort, constant fighting, could prevent the Mongol hordes from overrunning the country.

Beyond the Jade Pass in Kansu, through which the soldiers marched, lay the desert and the steppes stretching to the very "Edge of Heaven," and on this "edge" stood the "Heaven-high Hills"; while, on the way, surrounded by miles of sand, lay the Ch'ing Hai Lake (Green, or Inland, Sea), a dreary region at best, and peopled by the ghosts of countless soldiers who had fallen in battle on the "Yellow Sand Fields."

In addition to these backgrounds of reality, that of the Fertile Empire and that of the Barren Waste, there was another — that of the "Western Paradise" inhabited by the *Hsi Wang Mu* (Western Empress Mother) and those countless beings who, after a life in this world, had attained Immortality and dwelt among the *Hsien*, supernatural creatures living in this region of perfect happiness supposed to lie among the K'un Lun Mountains in Central Asia. From the spontaneous manner in which they constantly refer to it, and from the vividness of the pictures suggested by their references to it, one can almost question whether this Fairy World, the World of Imagination, with its inhabitants, were not as real to the writers of the early days as was the World of Actuality. Thus the topography of Chinese poetry may be said to fall into three main divisions, and allusions are made to

1. The beautiful scenes in the Eighteen Provinces.
2. The desolate region beyond the Jade Pass.
3. The glorious "Western Paradise."

Ideals determine government, and government determines social life, and social life, with all that the term connotes, is the essence of every literature.

The theory upon which the Chinese State was established is exceedingly interesting, and although the ideal was seldom reached, the system proved enduring and brought happiness to the people who lived under it.

The Emperor was regarded as the Son of the Celestial Ruler, as Father of his people, and was supposed to direct his Empire as a father should direct his children, never by the strong arm of force, but by loving precept and example. In theory, he held office only so long as peace and prosperity lasted, this beneficent state of things being considered a proof that the ruler's actions were in accordance with the decree of Heaven. Rebellion and disorder were an equal proof that the Son of Heaven had failed in his great mission; and, if wide-spread discontent continued, it was his duty to abdicate. The "divine right of kings" has never existed in China; its place has been taken by the people's right to rebellion.

This system created a very real democracy, which so struck the Dutchman, Van Braam, when he conducted a commercial embassy to the Court of Ch'ien Lung in 1794, that he dedicated his account of the embassy to "His Excellency George Washington, President of the United States," in the following remarkable manner:

Sir,

Travels among the most ancient people which now inhabits this globe, and which owes its long existence to the system which makes its chief the Father of the National Family, cannot appear under better auspices than those of the Great Man who was elected, by the universal suffrage of a new nation, to preside at the conquest of liberty, and in the establishment of a government in which everything bespeaks the love of the First Magistrate for the people. Permit me thus to address the homage of my veneration to the virtues, which in your Excellency, afford so striking a resemblance between Asia, and America. I cannot shew myself more worthy of the title of Citizen of the United States, which is become my adopted country, than by paying a just tribute to the Chief, whose principles and sentiments, are calculated to procure them a duration equal to that of the Chinese Empire.

The semi-divine person of the Emperor was also regarded as the "Sun" of the Empire, whose light should shine on high and low alike. His intelligence was compared to the penetrating rays of the sun, while that of the Empress found its counterpart in the soft, suffusing brilliance of the moon. In reading Chinese poetry, it is important to keep these similes in mind, as the poets constantly employ them; evil counsellors, for instance, are often referred to as "clouds which obscure the sun."

The Son of Heaven was assisted in the government of the country by a large body of officials, drawn from all classes of the people. How these officials were chosen, and what were their functions, will be stated presently. At the moment, we must take a cursory glance at Chinese history, since it is an ever-present subject of allusion in poetry.

Two favourite, and probably mythical, heroes, the Emperors Yao and Shun, who are supposed to have lived in the semilegendary period two or three thousand years before the birth of Christ, have been held up ever since as shining examples of perfection. Shun chose as his successor a man who had shown such great engineering talent in draining the country, always in danger of floods from the swollen rivers, that the Chinese still say: "Without Yü, we should all have been fishes." Yü founded the first hereditary dynasty, called the Hsia Dynasty, and, since then, every time the family of the Emperor has changed, a new dynasty has been inaugurated, the name being chosen by its first Emperor. With Yü's accession to the throne in 2205 B.C., authentic Chinese history begins.

Several centuries later, when Yü's descendants had deteriorated and become effete, a virtuous noble named T'ang organized the first of those rebellions against bad government so characteristic of Chinese history. He was successful, and in his "Announcement to the Ten Thousand Districts," set forth what we should call his platform in these words: "The way of Heaven is to bless the good and punish the wicked. It sent down calamities upon the house of Hsia to make manifest its crimes. Therefore I, the little child, charged with the decree of Heaven and its bright terrors, did not dare forgive the criminal. . . It is given to me, the one man, to ensure harmony and tranquillity to your State and families; and now I know not whether I may not offend the Powers above and below. I am fearful and trembling lest I should fall into a deep abyss." The doctrine that Heaven sends calamity as a punishment for man's sin is referred to again and again in the ancient "Book of History" and "Book of Odes." It is a belief common to all primitive peoples, but in China it persisted until the present republic demolished the last of the long line of dynastic empires.

T'ang made a great and wise ruler. The Dynasty of Shang, which he founded, lasted until 1122 B.C., and was succeeded by that of Chou, the longest in the annals of Chinese history — so long, indeed, that historians divide it into three distinct periods. The first of these, "The Rise," ran from 1122 B.C. to 770 B.C.; the second, "The Age of Feudalism," endured until 500 B.C.; the third, "The Age of the Seven States," until 255 B.C. Starting under wise rulers, it gradually sank through others less competent until by 770 B.C. it was little more than a name. During the "Age of Feudalism," the numerous States were constantly at war, but eventually the strongest of them united in a group called the "Seven Masculine Powers" under the shadowy suzerainty of Chou. Although, from the political point of view, this period was full of unrest and gloom, from the intellectual it was exceedingly brilliant and is known as the "Age of Philosophers." The most famous names among the many teachers of the times are those of Lao Tzŭ, the founder of Taoism, and Confucius. To these men, China owes the two great schools of thought upon which her social system rests.

The "Age of the Seven States" (Masculine Powers) ended when Ch'in, one of their number, overcame and absorbed the rest. Its prince adopted the title of Shih Huang Ti, or "First Supreme Ruler," thus placing himself on an equality with Heaven. Is it to be wondered at that the scholars demurred? The literary class were in perpetual opposition to the Emperor, who finally lost patience with them altogether and decreed that all books relating to the past should be burnt, and that history should begin with him. This edict was executed with great severity, and many hundreds of the *literati* were buried alive. It is scarcely surprising, therefore, that the name of Shih Huang Ti is execrated, even to-day, by a nation whose love for the written word amounts to veneration.

Although he held learning of small account, this "First Emperor," to give him his bombastic title, was an enthusiastic promoter of public works, the most important of these being the Great Wall, which has served as an age-long bulwark against the nomadic tribes of Mongolia and Central Asia. These tribes were a terror to China for centuries. They were always raiding the border country, and threatening a descent on the fertile fields beyond the mountains. The history of China is one long struggle to keep from being overrun by these tribes. There is an exact analogy to this state of affairs in the case of Roman Britain, and the perpetual vigilance it was obliged to exercise to keep out the Picts.

Shih Huang Ti based his power on fear, and it is a curious commentary upon the fact that the Ch'in Dynasty came to an end in 206 B.C., shortly after his death, and only a scant half-century after he had founded it.

A few years of struggle, during which no Son of Heaven occupied the Dragon Throne, succeeded the fall of the Ch'in Dynasty; then a certain Liu Pang, an inconsiderable town officer, proved strong enough to seize what was no one's possession and made himself Emperor, thereby founding the Han Dynasty.

The Han is one of the most famous dynasties in Chinese history. An extraordinary revival of learning took place under the successive Emperors of Han. The greatest of them, Wu Ti (140–87 B.C.), is frequently mentioned by the poets. Learning always follows trade, as has often been demonstrated. During the Han Dynasty, which lasted until A.D. 221, intercourse with all the countries of the Near East became more general than ever before, and innumerable caravans wended their slow way across the trade routes of Central Asia. Expeditions against the harassing barbarians were undertaken, and for a time their power was scotched. It was under the Han that Buddhism was introduced from India, but deeply as this has influenced the life and thought of the

Middle Kingdom, I am inclined to think that the importance of this influence has been exaggerated.

This period, and those immediately preceding it, form the poetic background of China. The ancient States, constantly referred to in the poems, do not correspond to the modern provinces. As these States did not all exist at the same moment, it is impossible to define their exact boundaries, but how strongly they were impressed upon the popular mind can be seen by the fact that, although they were merged into the Chinese Empire during the reign of Shih Huang Ti, literature continued to speak of them by their old names and, even to-day, writers often refer to them as though they were still separate entities. The names of a few of the old cities are also given, as Chin Ling, the "Golden Mound" or "Sepulchre," and Ch'ang An, "Eternal Peace," for so many centuries the capital. Its present name is Hsi An-fu, and it was here that the Manchu Court took refuge during the Boxer madness of 1900.

Little more of Chinese history need be told. Following the Han, several dynasties held sway; there were divisions between the North and South and much shifting of power. At length, in A.D. 618, Li Shih-min established the T'ang Dynasty by placing his father on the throne, and the T'ang brought law and order to the suffering country.

This period is often called the Golden Age of Chinese Learning. The literary examinations introduced under the Han were perfected, poets and painters were encouraged, and strangers flocked to the Court at Ch'ang An. The reign of Ming Huang (A.D. 712–756), the "Brilliant Emperor," was the culmination of this remarkable era. China's three greatest poets, Li T'ai-po, Tu Fu, and Po Chü-i, all lived during his long reign of forty-five years. Auspiciously as this reign had begun, however, it ended sadly. The Emperor, more amiable than perspicacious, fell into the toils of his favourite concubine, the lovely Yang Kuei-fei, to whom he was slavishly devoted. The account of their love story — a theme celebrated by poets, painters, and play-wrights — will be found in the note to "Songs to the Peonies." A rebellion which broke out was crushed, but the soldiers refused to defend the cause of the Emperor until he had issued an order for the execution of Yang Kuei-fei, whom they believed to be responsible for the trouble. Broken-hearted, the Emperor complied, but from this date the glory of the dynasty was dimmed. Throughout its waning years, the shadow of the dreaded Tartars grew blacker and blacker, and finally, in A.D. 907, the T'ang Dynasty fell.

Later history need not concern us here, since most of the poems in this book were written during the T'ang period. Though these poems deal largely with what I have called the historical background, they deal more largely with the social background and it is, above all, this social background which must be understood.

If the Emperor were the "Son of Heaven," he administered his Empire with the help of very human persons, the various officials, and these officials owed their positions, great and small, partly to the Emperor's attitude, it is true, but in far greater degree to their prowess in the literary examinations. An official of the first rank might owe his preferment to the Emperor's beneficence; but to reach an altitude where this beneficence could operate, he had to climb through all the lower grades, and this could only be done by successfully passing all the examinations, one after the other. The curious thing is that these examinations were purely literary. They consisted not only in knowing thoroughly the classics of the past, but in being able to recite long passages from them by heart, and with this was included the ability to write one's self, not merely in prose, but in poetry. Every one in office had to be, perforce, a poet. No one could hope to be the mayor of a town or the governor of a province unless he had attained a high proficiency in the art of poetry. This is brought strikingly home to us by the fact that one of the chief pastimes of educated men was to meet together for the purpose of playing various games all of which turned on the writing of verse.

The examinations which brought about

this strange state of things were four. The first, which conferred the degree of *Hsiu Ts'ai*, "Flowering Talent," could be competed for only by those who had already passed two minor examinations, one in their district, and one in the department in which this district was situated. The *Hsiu Ts'ai* examinations were held twice every three years in the provincial capitals. There were various grades of the "Flowering Talent" degree, which is often translated as Bachelor of Arts, some of which could be bestowed through favour or acquired by purchase. The holders of it were entitled to wear a dress of blue silk, and in Chinese novels the hero is often spoken of as wearing this colour, by which readers are to understand that he is a clever young man already on the way to preferment.

The second degree, that of *Ch'ü Jên*, "Promoted Man," was obtained by passing the examinations which took place every third year in all the provincial capitals simultaneously. This degree enabled its recipients to hold office, but positions were not always to hand, and frequently "Promoted Men" had to wait long before being appointed to a post; also, the offices open to them were of the lesser grades, those who aspired to a higher rank had a farther road to travel. The dress which went with this degree was also of silk, but of a darker shade than that worn by "bachelors."

The third examination for the *Chin Shih*, or "Entered Scholar," degree was also held triennially, but at the national capital, and only those among the *Ch'ü Jên* who had not already taken office were eligible. The men so fortunate as to pass were allowed to place a tablet over the doors of their houses, and their particular dress was of violet silk.

The fourth, which really conferred an office rather than a degree, was bestowed on men who competed in a special examination held once in three years in the Emperor's Palace. Those who were successful in this last examination became automatically *Han Lin*, or members of the Imperial Academy, which, in the picturesque phraseology of China, was called the "Forest of Pencils." A member of the Academy held his position, a

salaried one, for life, and the highest officials of the Empire were chosen from these Academicians.

This elaboration of degrees was only arrived at gradually. During the T'ang Dynasty, all the examinations were held at Ch'ang An. These four degrees of learning have often been translated as Bachelor of Arts, Master of Arts, Doctor of Literature, and Academician. The analogy is so far from close, however, that most modern sinologues prefer to render them indiscriminately, according to context, as student, scholar, and official.

By means of this remarkable system, which threw open the road to advancement to every man in the country capable of availing himself of it, new blood was continually brought to the top, as all who passed the various degrees became officials, expectant or in being, and of higher or lower grade according to the Chinese measure of ability. Military degrees corresponding to the civil were given; but, as these called for merely physical display, they were not highly esteemed.

Since only a few of the candidates for office passed the examinations successfully, a small army of highly educated men was dispersed throughout the country every three years. In the towns and villages they were regarded with the reverence universally paid to learning by the Chinese, and many became teachers to the rising generation in whom they cultivated a great respect for literature in general and poetry in particular.

The holders of degrees, on the other hand, entered at once upon a career as administrators. Prevented by an inexorable law — a law designed to make nepotism impossible — from holding office in their own province, they were constantly shifted from one part of the country to another, and this is a chief reason for the many poems of farewell that were written. The great desire of all officials was to remain at, or near, the Court, where the most brilliant brains of the Empire were assembled. As may be easily imagined, the intrigues and machinations employed to attain this end were many, with the result that deserving men often found themselves banished to posts on the desolate outskirts of the country where, far from congenial intercourse, they suffered a mental exile of the most complete description. Innumerable poems dealing with this sad state are found in all Chinese anthologies.

There were nine ranks of nobility. The higher officials took the rank of their various and succeeding offices, others were ennobled for signal services performed. These titles were not hereditary in the ordinary sense, but backwards, if I can so express it. The dead ancestors of a nobleman were accorded his rank, whatever had been theirs in life, but his sons and their descendants had only such titles as they themselves might earn.

The desire to bask in the rays of the Imperial Sun was shared by ambitious fathers who longed to have their daughters appear before the Emperor, and possibly make the fortune of the family by captivating the Imperial glance. This led to the most beautiful and talented young girls being sent to the Palace, where they often lived and died without ever being summoned before the Son of Heaven. Although numberless tragic poems have been written by these unfortunate ladies, many charming romances did actually take place, made possible by the custom of periodically dispersing the superfluous Palace women and marrying them to suitable husbands.

In striking contrast to the unfortunates who dragged out a purposeless life of idleness, was the lot of the beauty who had the good fortune to capture the Imperial fancy, and who, through her influence over the Dragon Throne, virtually ruled the Middle Kingdom. No extravagancies were too great for these exquisite creatures, and many dynasties have fallen through popular revolt against the excesses of Imperial concubines.

It would be quite erroneous to suppose, however, that the Emperor's life was entirely given up to pleasure and gaiety, or that it was chiefly passed in the beautiful seclusion of the Imperial gardens. The poems, it is true, generally allude to these moments, but the cares of state were many, and every day, at sunrise, officials assembled in the Audience Hall to make their reports to the Emperor. Moreover, Court ceremonials were extremely solemn occasions, carried out with the utmost dignity.

As life at Court centred about the persons of the Emperor and Empress, so life in the homes of the people centred about the elders of the family. The men of wealthy families were usually of official rank, and led a life in touch with the outer world, a life of social intercourse with other men in which friendship played an all-engrossing part. This characteristic of Chinese life is one of the most striking features of the poetic background. Love poems from men to women are so rare as to be almost non-existent (striking exceptions do occur, however, several of which are translated here), but poems of grief written at parting from "the man one loves" are innumerable, and to sit with one's friends, drinking wine and reciting verses, making music or playing chess, were favourite amusements throughout the T'ang period.

Wine-drinking was general, no pleasure gathering being complete without it. The wine of China was usually made from fermented grains, but wines from grapes, plums, pears, and other fruits were also manufactured. It was carefully heated and served in tall flagons somewhat resembling our coffee-pots, and was drunk out of tiny little cups no bigger than liqueur glasses. These cups, which were never of glass, were made of various metals, of lacquered or carved wood, of semi-precious stones such as jade, or agate, or carnelian; porcelain, the usual material for wine-cups today, not having yet been invented. Custom demanded that each thimbleful be tossed off at a gulp, and many were consumed before a feeling of exhilaration could be experienced. That there was a good deal of real drunkenness, we cannot doubt, but not to the extent that is generally supposed. From the character of the men and the lives they led, it is fairly clear that most of the drinking kept within reasonable bounds. Unfortunately, in translation, the quantity imbibed at these wine-parties becomes greatly exaggerated. That wine was drunk, not merely for its taste but as a heightener of sensation, is evident; but the "three hundred cups" so often mentioned bear no such significance as might at first appear when the size of the cups is taken into account. Undoubtedly, also, we must regard this exact number as a genial hyperbole.

If husbands and sons could enjoy the excitement of travel, the spur of famous scenery, the gaieties of Court, and the pleasures of social intercourse, wives and daughters were obliged to find their occupations within the Kuei or "Women's Apartments," which included the gardens set apart for their use. The ruling spirit of the Kuei was the mother-in-law; and the wife of the master of the house, although she was the mother of his sons and the director of the daughters-in-law, did not reach the fulness of her power until her husband's mother had died.

The chief duty of a young wife was attendance upon her mother-in-law. With the first grey streak of daylight, she rose from her immense lacquer bed, so large as to be almost an anteroom, and, having dressed, took the old lady her tea. She then returned to her own apartment to breakfast with her husband and await the summons to attend her mother-in-law's toilet, a most solemn function, and the breakfast which followed. These duties accomplished, she was free to occupy herself as she pleased. Calligraphy, painting, writing poems and essays, were popular pursuits, and many hours were spent at the embroidery frame or in making music.

Chinese poetry is full of references to the toilet, to the intricate hair-dressing, the "moth-antennae eyebrows," the painting of faces, and all this was done in front of a mirror standing on a little rack placed on the toilet-table. A lady, writing to her absent husband, mourns that she has no heart to "make the cloud head-dress," or writes, "looking down upon my mirror in order to apply the powder and paint, I desire to keep back the tears. I fear that the people in the house will know my grief. I am ashamed."

In spite of the fact that they had never laid eyes on the men they were to marry before the wedding-day, these young women seem to have depended upon the companionship of their husbands to a most touching extent. The occupations of the day were carried on in the Kuei; but, when evening came, the husband and wife often read and studied the classics together. A line from a well-known poem says, "The red sleeve replenishes the incense, at night, studying books," and the picture it calls up is that of a young man and woman in the typical surroundings of a Chinese home of the educated class. Red was the colour worn by very young women, whether married or not; as the years advanced, this was changed for soft blues and mauves, and later still for blacks, greys, or dull greens. A line such as "tears soak my dress of coarse, red silk" instantly suggests a young woman in deep grief.

The children studied every day with teachers; the sons and daughters of old servants who had, according to custom, taken the family surname, receiving the same advantages as those of the master. These last were, in all respects, brought up as children of the house, the only distinction being that whereas the master's own children sat "above" the table, facing South, the children of the servants sat "below," facing North. A more forcible reminder of their real status appeared later in life, since they were debarred from competing in the official examinations unless they left the household in which they had grown up and relinquished the family surname taken by their fathers. A curious habit among families, which extended even to groups of friends, was the designation by numbers according to age, a man being familiarly known as Yung Seven or T'sui Fifteen. It will be noticed that such designations often occur in the poems.

Only four classes of persons were recognized as being of importance to society and these were rated in the following order: scholars, agriculturists, labourers, and traders — officials, of course, coming under the generic name of scholars. Soldiers, actors, barbers, etc., were considered a lower order of beings entirely and, as such, properly despised.

China, essentially an agricultural country, was economically self-sufficient, producing everything needed by her population. The agriculturalist was, therefore, the very backbone of the state.

In rendering Chinese poetry, the translator must constantly keep in mind the fact that the architectural background differs from that of every other country, and that our language does not possess terms which adequately describe it.

Apart from the humble cottages of the very poor, all dwelling-houses, or chia, are constructed on the same general plan. They consist of a series of one-story buildings divided by courtyards, which, in the houses of the well-to-do, are connected by covered passages running along the sides of each court. A house is cut up into chien, or divisions, the number, within limits, being determined by the wealth and position of the owners. The homes of the people, both rich and poor, are arranged in three or five chien; official residences are of seven chien; Imperial palaces of nine. Each of these chia consists of several buildings, the number of which vary considerably, more buildings being added as the family grows by the marriage of the sons who, with their wives and children, are supposed to live in patriarchal fashion in their father's house. If officials sometimes carried their families with them to the towns where they were stationed, there were other posts so distant or so desolate as to make it practically impossible to take women to them. In these cases, the families remained behind under the paternal roof.

How a house was arranged can be grasped from the following description. Doors lead to the garden from the study, the guest-room, and the Women's Apartments. These are made in an endless diversity of shapes and add greatly to the picturesqueness of house and grounds. Those through which a number of people are to pass to and fro are often large circles, while smaller and more intimate doors are cut to the outlines of fans, leaves, or flower vases. In addition to the doors, blank spaces of wall are often broken by openings at the height of a window, such openings being most fantastic and filled with intricately designed lattice-work.

I have already spoken of the Kuei, or Women's Apartments. In poetry, this part of the chia is alluded to in a highly figurative manner. The windows are "gold" or "jade" windows; the door by which it is approached is the Lan Kuei, or "Orchid Door." Indeed, the sweet-scented little epidendrum called by the Chinese, lan, is continually used to suggest the Kuei and its inmates.

Besides the house proper, there are numerous structures erected in gardens, for the Chinese spend much of their time in their gardens. No nation is more passionately fond of nature, whether in its grander aspects, or in the charming arrangements of potted flowers which take the place of our borders in their pleasure grounds. Among these outdoor buildings none is more difficult to describe than the lou, since we have nothing which exactly corresponds to it. Lous appear again and again in Chinese poetry, but just what to call them in English is a puzzle. They are neither summer-houses, nor pavilions, nor cupolas, but a little of all three. Always of more than one story, they are employed for differing purposes; for instance, the fo lou is an upper chamber where Buddhist images are kept. The lou generally referred to in poetry, however, is really a "pleasure-house-in-the-air," used as the Italians use their belvederes. Here the inmates of the house sit and look down upon the garden or over the surrounding country, or watch "the sun disappear in the long grass at the edge of the horizon" or "the moon rise like a golden hook."

Another erection foreign to Western architecture is the t'ai, or terrace. In early days, there were many kinds of t'ai, ranging from the small, square, uncovered stage still seen in private gardens and called yüeh t'ai, "moon terrace," to immense structures like high, long, open platforms, built by Emperors and officials for various reasons. Many of these last were famous; I have given the histories of several of them in the notes illustrating the poems, at the end of the book.

It will be observed that I have said

practically nothing about religion. The reason is partly that the three principal religions practised by the Chinese are either so well known, as Buddhism, for example, or so difficult to describe, as Taoism and the ancient religion of China now merged in the teachings of Confucius; partly that none of them could be profitably compressed into the scope of this Introduction; but chiefly because the subject of religion, in the poems here translated, is generally referred to in its superstitious aspects alone. The superstitions which have grown up about Taoism particularly are innumerable. I have dealt with a number of these in the notes to the poems in which they appear. Certain supernatural personages, without a knowledge of whom much of the poetry would be unintelligible, I have set down in the following list:

HSIEN

Immortals who live in the Taoist Paradises. Human beings may attain *"Hsienship,"* or Immortality, by living a life of contemplation in the hills. In translating the term, we have used the word "Immortals."

SHÊN

Beneficent beings who inhabit the higher regions. They are kept extremely busy attending to their duties as tutelary deities of the roads, hills, rivers, etc., and it is also their function to intervene and rescue deserving people from the attacks of their enemies.

KUEI

A proportion of the souls of the departed who inhabit the "World of Shades," a region resembling this world, which is the "World of Light," in every particular, with the important exception that it has no sunshine. Kindly *kuei* are known, but the influence generally suggested is an evil one. They may only return to the World of Light between sunset and sunrise, except upon the fifth day of the Fifth Month (June), when they are free

to come during the time known as the "hour of the horse," from eleven A.M. to one P.M.

YAO KUAI

A class of fierce demons who live in the wild regions of the Southwest and delight in eating the flesh of human beings.

There are also supernatural creatures whose names carry a symbolical meaning. A few of them are:

CH'I LIN

A composite animal, somewhat resembling the fabulous unicorn, whose arrival is a good omen. He appears when sages are born.

DRAGON

A symbol of the forces of Heaven, also the emblem of Imperial power. Continually referred to in poetry as the steed which transports a philosopher who has attained Immortality to his home in the Western Paradise.

FÊNG HUANG

A glorious bird, symbol of the Empress, therefore often associated with the dragon. The conception of this bird is probably based on the Argus pheasant. It is described as possessing every grace and beauty. A Chinese author, quoted by F. W. Williams in "The Middle Kingdom," writes: "It resembles a wild swan before and a unicorn behind; it has the throat of a swallow, the bill of a cock, the neck of a snake, the tail of a fish, the forehead of a crane, the crown of a mandarin drake, the stripes of a dragon, and the vaulted back of a tortoise. The feathers have five colours which are named after the five cardinal virtues, and it is five cubits in height; the tail is graduated like the pipes of a gourd-organ, and its song resembles the music of the instrument, having five modulations." Properly speaking, the female is *Huang,* the male *Fêng,* but the two words are usually given in combination to denote the species. Some one, probably in desperation, once translated the combined words as "phoenix," and this term has been employed ever since. It conveys, however, an entirely wrong impression of the creature. To Western readers, the word "phoenix" suggests a bird which, being consumed by fire, rises in a new birth from its own ashes. The *Fêng Huang* has no such power, it is no symbol of hope or resurrection, but suggests friendship and affection of all sorts. Miss Lowell and I have translated the name as "crested love-pheasant," which seems to us to convey a better idea of the beautiful Fêng Huang, the bird which brings happiness.

LUAN

A supernatural bird sometimes confused with the above. It is a sacred creature, connected with fire, and a symbol of love and passion, of the relation between men and women.

CHIEN

The "paired-wings bird," described in Chinese books as having one wing and one eye, for which reason two must unite for either of them to fly. It is often referred to as suggesting undying affection.

Real birds and animals also have symbolical attributes. I give only three:

CRANE

Represents longevity, and is employed, as is the dragon, to transport those who have attained to Immortality to the Heavens.

YUAN YANG

The exquisite little mandarin ducks, an unvarying symbol of conjugal fidelity. Li T'ai-po often alludes to them and declares that, rather than be separated, they would "prefer to die ten thousand deaths, and have their gauze-like wings torn to fragments."

WILD GEESE

Symbols of direct purpose, their flight being always in a straight line. As they follow the sun's course, allusions to their departure suggest Spring, to their arrival, Autumn.

A complete list of the trees and plants endowed with symbolical meanings would be almost endless. Those most commonly employed in poetry in a suggestive sense are:

CH'ANG P'U

A plant growing in the Taoist Paradise and much admired by the Immortals, who are the only beings able to see its purple blossoms. On earth, it is known as the sweet flag, and has the peculiarity of never blossoming. It is hung on the lintels of doors on the fifth day of the Fifth Month to ward off the evil influences which may be brought by the *kuei* on their return to this world during the "hour of the horse."

PEONY

Riches and prosperity.

LOTUS

Purity. Although it rises from the mud, it is bright and spotless.

PLUM-BLOSSOM

Literally "the first," it being the first of the "hundred flowers" to open. It suggests the beginnings of things, and is also one of the "three friends" who do not fear the Winter cold, the other two being the pine and the bamboo.

LAN

A small epidendrum, translated in this book as "spear-orchid." It is a symbol for noble men and beautiful, refined women. Confucius compared the *Chün Tzŭ*, Princely or Superior Man, to this little orchid with its delightful scent. In poetry, it is also used in reference to the Women's Apartments and everything connected with them, suggesting, as it does, the extreme of refinement.

CHRYSANTHEMUM

Fidelity and constancy. In spite of frost, its flowers continue to bloom.

LING CHIH

Longevity. This fungus, which grows at the roots of trees, is very durable when dried.

PINE

Longevity, immutability, steadfastness.

BAMBOO

This plant has as many virtues as it has uses; the principal ones are modesty, protection from defilement, unchangeableness.

WU-T'UNG

A tree whose botanical name is *sterculia platanifolia*. Its only English name seems to be "umbrella-tree," which has proved so unattractive in its context in the poems that we have left it untranslated. It is a symbol for integrity, high principles, great sensibility. When "Autumn stands," on August seventh, although it is still to all intents and purposes Summer, the wu-t'ung tree drops one leaf. Its wood, which is white, easy to cut, and very light, is the only kind suitable for making that intimate instrument which quickly betrays the least emotion of the person playing upon it — the *ch'in*, or table-lute.

WILLOW

A prostitute, or any very frivolous person. Concubines writing to their lords often refer to themselves under this figure, in the same spirit of self-depreciation which prompts them to employ the

euphemism, "Unworthy One," instead of the personal pronoun. Because of its lightness and pliability, it conveys also the idea of extreme vitality.

PEACH-BLOSSOM

Beautiful women and ill-success in life. The first suggestion, on account of the exquisite colour of the flower; the second, because of its perishability.

PEACH-TREE

Longevity. This fruit is supposed to ripen once every three thousand years on the trees of Paradise, and those who eat of this celestial species never die.

MULBERRY

Utility. Also suggests a peaceful hamlet. Its wood is used in the making of bows and the kind of temple-drums called *mo yü* — wooden fish. Its leaves feed the silkworms.

PLANTAIN

Sadness and grief. It is symbolical of a heart which is not "flat" or "level," as the Chinese say, not open or care-free, but of one which is "tightly rolled." The sound of rain on its leaves is very mournful, therefore an allusion to the plantain always means sorrow. Planted outside windows already glazed with silk, its heavy green leaves soften the glaring light of Summer, and it is often used for this purpose.

Nothing has been more of a stumbling-block to translators than the fact that the Chinese year — which is strictly lunar, with an intercalary month added at certain intervals — begins a month later than ours; or, to be more exact, it is calculated from the first new moon after the sun enters Aquarius, which brings the New Year at varying times from the end of January to the middle of February. For translation purposes, however, it is safe to count the Chinese months as always one later by our calendar than the number given would seem to imply. By this calculation the "First Month" is February, and so on throughout the year.

The day is divided into twelve periods of two hours each beginning at eleven P.M. and each of these periods is called by the name of an animal — horse, deer, snake, bat, etc. As these names are not duplicated, the use of them tells at once whether the hour is day or night. Ancient China's method of telling time was by means of slow and evenly burning sticks made of a composition of clay and sawdust, or by the clepsydra, or water-clock. Water-clocks are mentioned several times in these poems.

So much for what I have called the backgrounds of Chinese poetry. I must now speak of that poetry itself, and of Miss Lowell's and my method of translating it.

Chinese prosody is a very difficult thing for an Occidental to understand. Chinese is a monosyllabic language, and this reduces the word-sounds so considerably that speech would be almost impossible were it not for the invention of tones by which the same sound can be made to do the duty of four in the Mandarin dialect, five in the Nankingese, nine in the Cantonese, etc., a different tone inflection totally changing the meaning of a word. Only two chief tones are used in poetry, the "level" and the "oblique," but the oblique tone is subdivided into three, which makes four different inflections possible to every sound. Of course, like English and other languages, the same word may have several meanings, and in Chinese these meanings are bewilderingly many; the only possible way of determining which one is correct is by its context. These tones constitute, at the outset, the principal difference which divides the technique of Chinese poetry from our own. Another is to be found in the fact that nothing approaching our metrical foot is possible in a tongue which knows only single syllables. Rhyme does exist, but there are only a little over a hundred rhymes, as tone inflection does not change a word in that particular. Such a paucity of rhyme would seriously

affect the richness of any poetry, if again the Chinese had not overcome this lingual defect by the employment of a juxtaposing pattern made up of their four poetic tones. And these tones come to the rescue once more when we consider the question of rhythm. Monosyllables in themselves always produce a staccato effect, which tends to make all rhythm composed of them monotonous, if indeed, it does not destroy it altogether. The tones cause what I may call a psychological change in the time-length of these monosyllables, which change not only makes true rhythm possible, but allows marked varieties of the basic beat.

One of the chief differences between poetry and prose is that poetry must have a more evident pattern. The pattern of Chinese poetry is formed out of three elements: line, rhyme, and tone.

The Chinese attitude toward line is almost identical with that of the French. French prosody counts every syllable as a foot, and a line is made up of so many counted feet. If any of my readers has ever read French alexandrines aloud to a Frenchman, read them as we should read English poetry, seeking to bring out the musical stress, he will remember the look of sad surprise which crept over his hearer's face. Not so was this verse constructed; not so is it to be read. The number of syllables to a line is counted, that is the secret of French classic poetry; the number of syllables is counted in Chinese. But — and we come to a divergence — this method of counting does, in French practice, often do away with the rhythm so delightful to an English ear; in Chinese, no such violence occurs, as each syllable is a word and no collection of such words can fall into a metric pulse as French words can, and, in their *Chansons*, are permitted to do.

The Chinese line pattern is, then, one of counted words, and these counted words are never less than three, nor more than seven, in regular verse; irregular is a different matter, as I shall explain shortly. Five and seven word lines are cut by a caesura, which comes after the second word in a five-word line, and after the fourth in a seven-word line.

Rhyme is used exactly as we use it, at

the ends of lines. Internal rhyming is common, however, in a type of poem called a *fu*, which I shall deal with when I come to the particular kinds of verse.

Tone is everywhere, obviously, and is employed, not arbitrarily, but woven into a pattern of its own which again is in a more or less loose relation to rhyme. By itself, the tone-pattern alternates in a peculiar manner in each line, the last line of a stanza conforming to the order of tones in the first, the intervening lines varying methodically. I have before me a poem in which the tone-pattern is alike in lines one, four, and eight, of an eight-line stanza, as are lines two and six, and lines three and seven, while line five is the exact opposite of lines two and six. In the second stanza of the same poem, the pattern is kept, but adversely; the tones do not follow the same order, but conform in similarity of grouping. I use this example merely to show what is meant by tone-pattern. It will serve to illustrate how much diversity and richness this tone-chiming is capable of bringing to Chinese poetry.

Words which rhyme must be in the same tone in regular verse, and unrhymed lines must end on an oblique tone if the rhyme-tone is level, and *vice versa*. The level tone is preferred for rhyme.

In the early Chinese poetry, called *Ku-shih* (Old Poems), the tones were practically disregarded. But in the *Lü-shih* (Regulated Poems) the rules regarding them are very strict. The *lü-shih* are supposed to date from the beginning of the T'ang Dynasty. A *lü-shih* poem proper should be of eight lines, though this is often extended to sixteen, but it must be in either the five-word line, or the seven-word line, metre. The poets of the T'ang-Dynasty, however, were by no means the slaves of *lü-shih*; they went their own way, as good poets always do, conforming when it pleased them and disregarding when they chose. It depended on the character of the poet. Tu Fu was renowned for his careful versification; Li T'ai-po, on the other hand, not infrequently rebelled and made his own rules. In his "Drinking Song," which is in seven-word lines, he suddenly dashes in two three-word lines, a proceeding

which must have been greatly upsetting to the purists. It is amusing to note that his "Taking Leave of Tu Fu" is in the strictest possible form, which is at once a tribute and a poking of fun at his great friend and contemporary.

Regular poems of more than sixteen lines are called *p'ai lu*, and these may run to any length; Tu Fu carried them to forty, eighty, and even to two hundred lines. Another form, always translated as "short-stop," cuts the eight-line poem in two. In theory, the short-stop holds the same relation to the eight-line poem that the Japanese *hokku* does to the *tanka*, although of course it preceded the *hokku* by many centuries. It is supposed to suggest rather than to state, being considered as an eight-line poem with its end in the air. In suggestion, however, the later Japanese form far outdoes it.

So called "irregular verse" follows the writer's inclination within the natural limits of all Chinese prosody.

A *tzŭ* may be taken to mean a lyric, if we use that term, not in its dictionary sense, but as all modern poets employ it. It may vary its line length, but must keep the same variation in all the stanzas.

Perhaps the most interesting form to modern students is the *fu*, in which the construction is almost identical with that of "polyphonic prose." The lines are so irregular in length that the poem might be mistaken for prose, had we not a corresponding form to guide us. The rhymes appear when and where they will, in the middle of the lines or at the end, and sometimes there are two or more together. I have been told that Persia has, or had, an analogous form, and if so modern an invention as "polyphonic prose" derives, however unconsciously, from two such ancient countries as China and Persia, the fact is, at least, interesting.

The earliest examples of Chinese poetry which have come down to us are a collection of rhymed ballads in various metres, of which the most usual is four words to a line. They are simple, straightforward pieces, often of a strange poignance, and always reflecting the quiet, peaceful habits of a people engaged in agriculture. The oldest were probably composed about 2000 B.C. and the others at varying times from then until the Sixth Century B.C., when Confucius gathered them into the volume known as the "Book of Odes." Two of these odes are translated in this book. The next epoch in the advance of poetry-making was introduced by Ch'ü Yüan (312–295 B.C.), a famous statesman and poet, who wrote an excitable, irregular style in which the primitive technical rules were disregarded, their place being taken by exigencies of emotion and idea. We are wont to regard a poetical technique determined by feeling alone as a very modern innovation, and it is interesting to note that the method is, on the contrary, as old as the hills. These rhapsodical allegories culminated in a poem entitled "Li Sao," or "Falling into Trouble," which is one of the most famous of ancient Chinese poems. A further development took place under the Western Han (206 B.C.–A.D. 25), when Su Wu invented the five-character poem, *ku fêng*; these poems were in Old Style, but had five words to a line. It is during this same period that poems with seven words to a line appeared. Legend has it that they were first composed by the Emperor Wu of Han, and that he hit upon the form on an occasion when he and his Ministers were drinking wine and capping verses at a feast on the White Beam Terrace. Finally, under the Empress Wu Hou, early in the T'ang Dynasty, the *lü-shih*, or "poems according to law," became the standard. It will be seen that the *lü-shih* found the five and seven word lines already in being and had merely to standardize them. The important gift which the *lü-shih* brought to Chinese prosody was its insistence on tone.

The great period of Chinese poetry was during the T'ang Dynasty. Then lived the three famous poets, Li T'ai-po, Tu Fu, and Po Chü-i. Space forbids me to give the biographies of all the poets whose work is included in this volume, but as Li T'ai-po and Tu Fu, between them, take up more than half the book, a short account of the principal events of their lives seems necessary. I shall take them in the order of the number of their poems printed in this collection, which also, as a matter of fact, happens to be chronological.

I have already stated in the first part of this Introduction the reasons which determined me to give so large a space to Li T'ai-po. English writers on Chinese literature are fond of announcing that Li T'ai-po is China's greatest poet; the Chinese themselves, however, award this place to Tu Fu. We may put it that Li T'ai-po was the people's poet, and Tu Fu the poet of scholars. As Po Chü-i is represented here by only one poem, no account of his life has been given. A short biography of him may be found in Mr. Waley's "A Hundred and Seventy Chinese Poems."

It is permitted to very few to live in the hearts of their countrymen as Li T'ai-po has lived in the hearts of the Chinese. To-day, twelve hundred and twenty years after his birth, his memory and his fame are fresh, his poems are universally recited, his personality is familiar on the stage: in fact, to use the words of a Chinese scholar, "It may be said that there is no one in the People's Country who does not know the name of Li T'ai-po." Many legends are told of his birth, his life, his death, and he is now numbered among the *Hsien* (Immortals) who inhabit the Western Paradise.

Li T'ai-po was born A.D. 701, of well-to-do parents named Li, who lived in the Village of the Green Lotus in Szechwan. He is reported to have been far more brilliant than ordinary children. When he was only five years old, he read books that other boys read at ten; at ten, he could recite the "Classics" aloud and had read the "Book of the Hundred Sages." Doubtless this precocity was due to the fact that his birth was presided over by the "Metal Star," which we know as Venus. His mother dreamt that she had conceived him under the influence of this luminary, and called him T'ai-po, "Great Whiteness," a popular name for the planet.

In spite of his learning, he was no *Shu Tai Tzŭ* (Book Idiot) as the Chinese say, but, on the contrary, grew up a strong young fellow, impetuous to a fault, with a lively, enthusiastic nature. He was extremely fond of sword-play, and constantly made use of his skill in it to right the wrongs of his friends. However worthy his causes may have been, this propensity got him into a serious scrape. In the excitement of one of these encounters, he killed several people, and was forthwith obliged to fly from his native village. The situation was an awkward one, but the young man disguised himself as a servant and entered the employ of a minor official. This gentleman was possessed of literary ambitions and a somewhat halting talent; still we can hardly wonder that he was not pleased when his servant ended a poem in which he was hopelessly floundering with lines far better than he could make. After this, and one or two similar experiences, Li T'ai-po found it advisable to relinquish his job and depart from his master's house.

His next step was to join a scholar who disguised his real name under the pseudonym of "Stern Son of the East." The couple travelled together to the beautiful Min Mountains, where they lived in retirement for five years as teacher and pupil. This period, passed in reading, writing, discussing literature, and soaking in the really marvellous scenery, greatly influenced the poet's future life, and imbued him with that passionate love for nature so apparent in his work.

At the age of twenty-five, he separated from his teacher and left the mountains, going home to his native village for a time. But the love of travel was inherent in him, nowhere could hold him for long, and he soon started off on a sight-seeing trip to all those places in the Empire famous for their beauty. This time he travelled as the position of his parents warranted, and even a little beyond it. He had a retinue of servants, and spent money lavishly. This open-handedness is one of the fine traits of his character. Needy scholars and men of talent never appealed to him in vain; during a year at Yangchow, he is reported to have spent three hundred thousand ounces of silver in charity.

From Yangchow he journeyed to the province of Hupeh ("North of the Lake") where, in the district of the "Dreary Clouds," he stayed at the house of a family named Hsü, which visit resulted in his marriage with one of the daughters. Li T'ai-po lived in Hupeh for some years — he himself says three — then his hunger for travel reasserted itself and he was off again. After some years of wandering, while visiting a magistrate in Shantung, an incident occurred which had far-reaching consequences. A prisoner was about to be flogged. Li T'ai-po, who was passing, glanced at the man, and happening to be possessed of a shrewd insight into character, realized at once that here was an unusual person. He secured the man's release, and twenty-five years later this action bore fruit as the sequel will show. The freed prisoner was Kuo Tzŭ-i, who became one of China's most powerful generals and the saviour of the T'ang Dynasty.

It will be noticed that nothing has been said of the poet taking any examinations, and for the excellent reason that he never thought it worth while to present himself as a candidate. The simple fact appears to be that geniuses often do not seem to find necessary what other men consider of supreme importance. Presumably, also, he had no particular desire for an official life. The gifts of Heaven go by favour and the gifts of man are strangely apt to do the same thing, in spite of the excellent rules devised to order them. Li T'ai-po's career owed nothing to either the lack of official degrees or official interest. What he achieved, he owed to himself; what he failed in came from the same source.

About this time, the poet and a few congenial friends formed the coterie of "The Six Idlers of the Bamboo Brook." They retired to the Ch'u Lai Mountain and spent their time in drinking, reciting poems, writing beautiful characters, and playing on the table-lute. It must be admitted that Li T'ai-po was an inveterate and inordinate drinker, and far more often than was wise in the state called by his countrymen "great drunk." To this propensity he was indebted for all his ill fortune, as it was to his poetic genius that he owed all his good.

So the years passed until, when he was forty-two, he met the Taoist priest, Wu Yün. They immediately became intimate, and on Wu Yün's being called to the capital, Li T'ai-po accompanied him. Wu Yün took occasion to tell the Emperor of his friend's extraordinary talent. The Emperor was interested, the poet was sent for, and introduced by Ho Chih-chang, was received by the Son of Heaven in the Golden Bells Hall.

The native accounts of this meeting state that "in his discourses upon the affairs of the Empire, the words rushed from his mouth like a mountain torrent." Ming Huang, who was enchanted, ordered food to be brought and helped the poet himself.

So Li T'ai-po became attached to the Court and was made an honorary member of the "Forest of Pencils." He was practically the Emperor's secretary and wrote the Emperor's edicts, but this was by the way — his real duty was simply to write what he chose and when, and recite these poems at any moment that it pleased the Emperor to call upon him to do so.

Li T'ai-po, with his love of wine and good-fellowship, was well suited for the life of the gay and dissipated Court of Ming Huang, then completely under the influence of the beautiful concubine, Yang Kuei-fei. Conspicuous among the Emperor's entourage was Ho Chih-chang, a famous statesman, poet, and calligraphist, who, on reading Li T'ai-po's poetry, is said to have sighed deeply and exclaimed: "This is not the work of a human being, but of a *Tsê Hsien* (Banished Immortal)." To understand fully the significance of this epithet, it must be realized that mortals who have already attained Immortality, but who have committed some fault, may be banished from Paradise to expiate their sin on earth.

For about two years, Li T'ai-po led the life of supreme favourite in the most brilliant Court in the world. The fact that when sent for to compose or recite verses he was not unapt to be drunk was of no particular importance since, after being summarily revived with a dash of cold water, he could always write or chant with his accustomed verve and dexterity. His influence over the Emperor became so great that it roused the jealousy, and eventually the hatred, of Kao Li-shih, the Chief Eunuch, who, until then had virtually ruled his Imperial master. On one occasion, when Li T'ai-po was more than usually incapacitated, the Emperor ordered Kao to take off the poet's shoes. This was too much, and from that moment the eunuch's malignity became an active intriguing to bring about his rival's downfall. He found the opportunity he needed in the vanity of Yang Kuei-fei. Persuading this lady that Li T'ai-po's "Songs to the Peonies" contained a veiled insult directed at her, he enlisted her anger against the poet and so gained an important ally to his cause. On three separate occasions when Ming Huang wished to confer official rank upon the poet, Yang Kuei-fei interfered and persuaded the Emperor to forego his intention. Li T'ai-po was of too independent a character, and too little of a courtier, to lift a finger to placate his enemies. But the situation became so acute that at last he begged leave to retire from the Court altogether. His request granted, he immediately formed a new group of seven congenial souls and with them departed once more to the mountains. This new association called itself "The Eight Immortals of the Wine-cup."

Although Li T'ai-po had asked for his own dismissal, he had really been forced to ask it, and his banishment from the "Imperial Sun," with all that "Sun" implied, was a blow from which he never recovered. His later poems are full of more or less veiled allusions to his unhappy state.

The next ten years were spent in his favourite occupation of travelling, especially in the provinces of Szechwan, Hunan, and Hupeh.

Meanwhile, political conditions were growing steadily worse. Popular discontent at the excesses of Yang Kuei-fei and her satellite An Lu-shan were increasing, and finally, in A.D. 755, rebellion broke out. I have dealt with this rebellion earlier in this Introduction, and a more detailed account is given in the Notes; I shall, therefore, do no more than mention it here. Sometime during the preceding unrest, Li T'ai-po, weary of moving from place to place, had taken the position of adviser to Li Ling, Prince of Yung. In the wide-spread disorder caused by the rebellion, Li Ling conceived the bold idea of establishing himself South of the Yangtze as Emperor on his own account. Pursuing his purpose, he started at the head of his troops for Nanking. Li T'ai-po strongly disapproved of the Prince's course, a disapproval which affected that headstrong person not at all, and the poet was forced to accompany his master on the march to Nanking.

At Nanking, the Prince's army was defeated by the Imperial troops, and immediately after the disaster Li T'ai-po fled, but was caught, imprisoned, and condemned to death. Now came the sequel to the incident which had taken place long before at Shantung. The Commander of the Imperial forces was no other than Kuo Tzŭ-i, the former prisoner whose life Li T'ai-po had saved. On learning the sentence passed upon the poet, Kuo Tzŭ-i intervened and threatened to resign his command unless his benefactor were spared. Accordingly Li T'ai-po's sentence was changed to exile and he was released, charged to depart immediately for some great distance where he could do no harm. He set out for Yeh Lang, a desolate spot beyond the "Five Streams," in Kueichow. This was the country of the *yao kuai*, the man-eating demons; and whether he believed in them or not, the thought of existence in such a gloomy solitude must have filled him with desperation.

He had not gone far, luckily, when a general amnesty was declared, and he was permitted to return and live with his friend and disciple, Lu Yang-ping, in the Lu Mountains near Kiukiang, a place which he dearly loved. Here, in A.D. 762, at the age of sixty-one, he died, bequeathing all his manuscripts to Lu Yang-ping.

The tale of his drowning, repeated by Giles and others, is pure legend, as an authoritative statement of Lu Yang-ping proves. The manuscripts left to his care, and all others he could collect from friends, Lu Yang-ping published in an edition of ten volumes. This edition appeared in the year of the poet's death, and contained the following preface by Lu Yang-ping:

Since the three dynasties of antiquity
Since the style of the 'Kuo Fêng' and the 'Li Sao,'
During these thousand years and more, of those
*   who walked the "lonely path,"*
There has been only you, you are the Solitary Man,
*   you are without rival.*

Li T'ai-po's poetry is full of dash and surprise. At his best, there is an extraordinary exhilaration in his work; at his worst, he is merely repetitive. Chinese critics have complained that his subjects are all too apt to be trivial, and that his range is narrow. This is quite true; poems of farewell, deserted ladies sighing for their absent lords, officials consumed by homesickness, paeans of praise for wine — in the aggregate there are too many of these. But how fine they often are! "The Lonely Wife," "Poignant Grief During a Sunny Spring," "After being Separated for a Long Time," such poems are the truth of emotion. Take again his inimitable humour in the two "Drinking Alone in the Moonlight" poems, or "Statement of Resolutions after being Drunk on a Spring Day." Then there are the poems of hyperbolical description such as "The Perils of the Shu Road," "The Northern Flight," and "The Terraced Road of the Two-Edged Sword Mountains." Mountains seem to be in his very blood. Of the sea, on the other hand, he has no such intimate knowledge; he sees it afar, from some height, but always as a thing apart, a distant view. The sea he gazes at; the mountains he treads under foot, their creepers scratch his face, the jutting rocks beside the path bruise his hands. He knows the straight-up, cutting-into-the-sky look of mountain peaks just above him, and feels, almost bodily, the sheer drop into the angry river tearing its way through a narrow gully below, a river he can see only by leaning dangerously far over the cliff upon which he is standing. There is a curious sense of perpendicularity about these mountain rhapsodies. The vision is strained up for miles, and shot suddenly down for hundreds of feet. The tactile effect of them is astounding; they are not to be read, but experienced. And yet I am loth to say that Li T'ai-po is at his greatest in description, with poems so full of human passion and longing as "The Lonely Wife," and "Poignant Grief During a Sunny Spring," before me. There is no doubt at all that in Li T'ai-po we have one of the world's greatest lyrists.

Great though he was, it cannot be denied that he had serious weaknesses. One was his tendency to write when the mood was not there, and at these moments he was not ashamed to repeat a fancy conceived before on some other occasion. Much of his style he crystallized into a convention, and brought it out unblushingly whenever he was at a loss for something to say. Sustained effort evidently wearied him. He will begin a poem with the utmost spirit, but his energy is apt to flag and lead to a close so weak as to annoy the reader. His short poems are always admirably built, the endings complete and unexpected; the architec-tonics of his long poems leave much to be desired. He seems to be ridden by his own emotion, but without the power to draw it up and up to a climax; it bursts upon us in the first line, sustains itself at the same level for a series of lines, and then seems to faint exhausted, reducing the poet to the necessity of stopping as quickly as he can and with as little jar as possible. Illustrations of this tendency to a weak ending can be seen in "The Lonely Wife," "The Perils of the Shu Road," and "The Terraced Road of the Two-Edged Sword Mountains," but that he could keep his inspiration to the end on occasion, "The Northern Flight" proves.

Finally, there are his poems of battle: "Songs of the Marches, " "Battle to the South of the City," and "Fighting to the South of the City." Nothing can be said of these except that they are superb. If there is a hint of let-down in the concluding lines of "Fighting to the South of the City," it is due to the frantic Chinese desire to quote from older authors, and this is an excellent example of the chief vice of Chinese poetry, since these two lines are taken from the "Tao Tê Ching," the sacred book of Taoism; the others, even the long "Songs of the Marches," are admirably sustained.

In Mr. Waley's excellent monograph on Li T'ai-po, appears the following paragraph: "Wang An-shih (A.D. 1021–1086), the great reformer of the Eleventh Century, observes: 'Li Po's style is swift, yet never careless; lively, yet never informal. But his intellectual outlook was low and sordid. In nine poems out of ten he deals with nothing but wine and women.' " A somewhat splenetic criticism truly, but great reformers have seldom either the acumen or the sympathy necessary for the judgment of poetry. Women and wine there are in abundance, but how treated? In no mean or sordid manner certainly. Li T'ai-po was not a didactic poet, and we of the Twentieth Century may well thank fortune for that. Peradventure the Twenty-first will dote again upon the didactic, but we must follow our particular inclination which is, it must be admitted, quite counter to anything of the sort. No low or mean attitude indeed, but a rather restricted one we may, if we please, charge against Li T'ai-po. He was a sensuous realist, representing the world as he saw it, with beauty as his guiding star. Conditions to him were static; he wasted none of his force in speculating on what they should be. A scene or an emotion *was*, and it was his business to reproduce it, not to analyze how it had come about or what would best make its recurrence impossible. Here he is at sharp variance with Tu Fu, who probes to the roots of events even when he appears to be merely describing them. One has but to compare the "Songs of the Marches" and "Battle to the South of the City" with "The Recruiting Officers" and "Crossing the Frontier" to see the difference.

Tu Fu was born in Tu Ling, in the province of Shensi, in A.D. 713. His family was extremely poor, but his talent was so marked that at seven years old he had begun to write poetry; at nine, he could write large characters; and at fifteen, his essays and poems were the admiration of his small circle. When he was twenty-four, he went up to Ch'ang An, the capital, for his first examination — it will be remembered that, in the T'ang period, all the examinations took place at Ch'ang An. Tu Fu was perfectly qualified to pass, as every one was very well aware, but the opinions he expressed in his examination papers were so radical that the degree was withheld. There was nothing to be done, and Tu Fu took to wandering about the country, observing and writing, but with little hope of anything save poverty to come. On one of his journeys, he met Li T'ai-po on the "Lute Terrace" in Ching Hsien. The two poets, who sincerely admired each other, became the closest friends. Several poems in this collection are addressed by one to the other.

When Tu Fu was thirty-six, it happened that the Emperor sent out invitations to all the scholars in the Empire to come to the capital and compete in an examination. Tu Fu was, of course, known to the Emperor as a man who would have been promoted but for the opinions aired in his papers. Of his learning, there could be no shadow of doubt. So Tu Fu went to Ch'ang An and waited there as an "expectant official." He waited for four years, when it occurred to him to offer three *fu* to the Emperor. The event justified his temerity, and the poet was given a post as one of the officials in the Chih Hsien library. This post he held for four years, when he was appointed to a slightly better one at Fêng-hsien. But a year later, the An Lu-shan rebellion broke out, which put a summary end to Tu Fu's position, whereupon he left Fêng-hsien and went to live with a relative at the Village of White Waters. He was still living there when the Emperor Ming Huang abdicated in favour of his son, Su Tsung. If the old Emperor had given him an office, perhaps the new one would; at any rate it was worth an attempt, for Tu Fu was in dire poverty. Having no money to hire any kind of conveyance, he started to walk to his destination, but fell in with brigands who captured him. He stayed with these brigands for over a year, but finally escaped, and at length reached Fêng Chiang, where the Emperor was in residence.

His appearance on his arrival was miserable in the extreme. Haggard and thin, his shoulders sticking out of his coat, his rags literally tied together, he

was indeed a spectacle to inspire pity, and the Emperor at once appointed him to the post of Censor. But this did not last long. He had the imprudence to remonstrate with the Emperor anent the sentence of banishment passed upon the general Tan Kuan. Considering that this clever and extremely learned soldier had so far relaxed the discipline of his army during one of the Northern campaigns that, one night, when his troops were all peacefully sleeping in their chariots, the camp was surrounded and burnt and his forces utterly routed, the punishment seems deserved. But Tu Fu thought otherwise, and so unwisely urged his opinion that the Emperor lost patience and ordered an investigation of Tu Fu's conduct. His friends, however, rallied to his defence and the investigation was quashed, but he was deprived of the censorship and sent to a minor position in Shensi. This he chose to regard as a punishment, as indeed it was. He proceeded to Shensi, but, on arriving there, dramatically refused to assume his office; having performed which act of bravado, he joined his family in Kansu. He found them in the greatest distress from famine, and although he did his best to keep them alive by going to the hills and gathering fire-wood to sell, and by digging up roots and various growing things for them to eat, several of his children died of starvation.

Another six months of minor officialdom in Hua Chou, and he retired to Ch'êngtu in Szechwan, where he lived in a grass-roofed house, engaged in study and the endeavour to make the two ends of nothing meet. At length, a friend of his arrived in Szechwan as Governor-General, and this friend appointed him a State Counsellor. But the grass-house was more to his taste than state councils, and after a year and a half he returned to it, and the multifarious wanderings which always punctuated his life.

Five years later, when he was fifty-five, he set off on one of his journeys, but was caught by floods and obliged to take refuge in a ruined temple at Hu Kuang, where he nearly starved before help could reach him. After ten days, he was rescued through the efforts of the local magistrate, but eating again after so long a fast was fatal and he died within an hour.

Innumerable essays have been written comparing the styles of Li T'ai-po and Tu Fu. Yüan Chên, a poet of the T'ang period, says that Tu Fu's poems have perfect balance; that, if he wrote a thousand lines, the last would have as much vigour as the first and that no one can equal him in this, his poems make a "perfect circle." He goes on: "In my opinion, the great living wave of poetry and song in which Li T'ai-po excelled is surpassed in Tu Fu's work, he is shoulders higher than Li Po." Again: "The poems of Li T'ai-po are like Spring flowers, those of Tu Fu are like the pine-trees, they are eternal and fear neither snow nor cold."

Shên Ming-chên says: "Li Po is like the Spring grass, like Autumn waves, not a person but must love him. Tu Fu is like a great hill, a high peak, a long river, the broad sea, like fine grass and bright-coloured flowers, like a pine or an ancient fir, like moving wind and gentle waves, like heavy hoar-frost, like burning heat — not a quality is missing."

Hu Yu-ling uses a metaphor referring to casting dice and says that Li T'ai-po would owe Tu Fu "an ivory"; and Han Yü, speaking of both Li T'ai-po and Tu Fu, declares that "the flaming light of their essays would rise ten thousand feet."

Poetic as these criticisms are, it is their penetration which is so astonishing; but I think the most striking comparison made of Tu Fu's work is that by Tao Kai-yu: "Tu Fu's poems are like pictures, like the branches of trees reflected in water — the branches of still trees. Like a large group of houses seen through clouds or mist, they appear and disappear."

Sometime ago, in a review of a volume of translations of Chinese poetry in the London *Times*, I came across this remarkable statement: "The Chinese poet starts talking in the most ordinary language and voices the most ordinary things, and his poetry seems to happen suddenly out of the commonplace as if it were some beautiful action happening in the routine of actual life."

The critic could have had no knowledge of the Chinese language, as nothing can be farther from the truth than his observation. It is largely a fact that the Oriental poet finds his themes in the ordinary affairs of everyday life, but he describes them in a very special, carefully chosen, medium. The simplest child's primer is written in a language never used in speaking, while the most highly educated scholar would never dream of employing the same phrases in conversation which he would make use of were he writing an essay, a poem, or a state document. Each language — the spoken, the poetic, the literary, the documentary — has its own construction, its own class of characters, and its own symbolism. A translator must therefore make a special study of whichever he wishes to render.

Although several great sinologues have written on the subject of Chinese poetry, none, so far as I am aware, has devoted his exclusive attention to the poetic style, nor has any translator availed himself of the assistance, so essential to success, of a poet — that is, one trained in the art of seizing the poetic values in fine shades of meaning. Without this power, which amounts to an instinct, no one can hope to reproduce any poetry in another tongue, and how much truer this is of Chinese poetry can only be realized by those who have some knowledge of the language. Such poets, on the other hand, as have been moved to make beautiful renditions of Chinese originals have been hampered by inadequate translations. It is impossible to expect that even a scholar thoroughly versed in the philological aspects of Chinese literature can, at the same time, be endowed with enough of the poetic *flair* to convey, uninjured, the thoughts of one poet to another. A second personality obtrudes between poet and poet, and the contact, which must be established between the two minds if any adequate translation is to result, is broken. How Miss Lowell and I have endeavoured to obviate this rupture of the poetic current, I shall explain presently. But, to understand it, another factor in the case must first be understood.

It cannot be too firmly insisted upon that the Chinese character itself plays a considerable part in Chinese poetic composition. Calligraphy and poetry are mixed up together in the Chinese mind. How close this intermingling may be, will appear when we come to speak of the "Written Pictures," but even without following the interdependence of these arts to the point where they merge into one, it must not be forgotten that Chinese is an ideographic, or picture, language. These marvellous collections of brush-strokes which we call Chinese characters are really separate pictographic representations of complete thoughts. Complex characters are not spontaneously composed, but are built up of simple characters, each having its own peculiar meaning and usage; these, when used in combination, each play their part in modifying either the sense or the sound of the complex. Now it must not be thought that these separate entities make an over-loud noise in the harmony of the whole character. They are each subdued to the total result, the final meaning, but they do produce a qualifying effect upon the word itself. Since Chinese characters are complete ideas, it is convenient to be able to express the various degrees of these ideas by special characters which shall have those exact meanings; it is, therefore, clear that to grasp a poet's full intention in a poem there must be a knowledge of the analysis of characters.

This might seem bizarre, were it not for a striking proof to the contrary. It is a fact that many of the Chinese characters have become greatly altered during the centuries since they were invented. So long ago as A.D. 200, a scholar named Hsü Shih, realizing that this alteration was taking place, wrote the dictionary known as "Shuo Wên Chieh Tzŭ," or "Speech and Writing: Characters Untied," containing about ten thousand characters in their primitive and final forms. This work is on the desk of every scholar in the Far East and is studied with the greatest reverence. Many editions have appeared since it was written, and by its aid one can trace the genealogy of characters in the most complete manner. Other volumes of the same kind have followed in its wake, showing the importance of the subject in Chinese estimation. While translators are apt to ignore this matter of character genealogy, it is ever present to the mind of the Chinese poet or scholar who is familiar with the original forms; indeed, he may be said to find his overtones in the actual composition of the character he is using.

All words have their connotations, but this is connotation and more; it is a pictorial representation of something implied, and, lacking which, an effect would be lost. It may be objected that poems were heard as well as read, and that, when heard, the composition of the character must be lost. But I think this is to misunderstand the situation. Recollect, for a moment, the literary examinations, and consider that educated men had these characters literally ground into them. Merely to pronounce a word must be, in such a case, to see it and realize, half-unconsciously perhaps, its various parts. Even if half-unconscious, the *nuances* of meaning conveyed by them must have hung about the spoken word and given it a distinct flavour which, without them, would be absent. Now what is a translator to do? Shall he render the word in the flat, dictionary sense, or shall he permit himself to add to it what it conveys to an educated Chinese? Clearly neither the one nor the other in all cases; but one *or* the other, which the context must determine. In description, for instance, where it is evident that the Chinese poet used every means at his command to achieve a vivid representation, I believe the original poem is more nearly reproduced by availing one's self of a minimum of these "split-ups"; where, on the other hand, the original carefully confines itself to simple and direct expression, the word as it is, without overtones, must certainly be preferred. The "split-ups" in these translations are few, but could our readers compare the original Chinese with Miss Lowell's rendition of it, in these instances, I think they would feel with me that in no other way could the translation have been made really "literal," could the poem be "brought over" in its entirety. If a translation of a poem is not poetry in its new tongue, the original has been shorn of its chief reason for being. Something is always lost in a translation, but that something had better be the trappings than the essence.

I must, however, make it quite clear how seldom these "split-ups" occur in the principal parts of the book; in the "Written Pictures," where the poems were not, most of them, classics, we felt justified in making a fuller use of these analytical suggestions; but I believe I am correct in saying that no translations from the Chinese that I have read are so near to the originals as these. Bear in mind, then, that there are not, I suppose, more than a baker's dozen of these "split-ups" throughout the book, and the way they were managed can be seen by this literal translation of a line in "The Terraced Road of the Two-Edged Sword Mountains." The Chinese words are on the left, the English words on the right, the analyses of the characters enclosed in brackets:

Shang	Above
Tsê	Then
Sung	Pines
Fêng	Wind
Hsiao	Whistling wind (Grass — meaning the sound of wind through grass, to whistle; and in awe of, or to venerate.)
Sê	Gusts of wind (Wind; and to stand.)
Sê	A psaltery (Two strings of jade-stones which are sonorous.)
Yü	Wind in a gale (Wind; and to speak.)

Miss Lowell's rendering of the line was:

On their heights, the wind whistles awesomely in the pines; it booms in great, long gusts; it clashes like the strings of a jade-stone psaltery; it shouts on the clearness of a gale.

Can any one doubt that this was just the effect that the Chinese poet wished to achieve, and did achieve by means of the overtones given in his characters? Another, simpler, example is in a case where the Chinese poet speaks of a rising sun. There are many characters which denote sunrise, and each has some shade of difference from every other. In one, the analysis is the sunrise light seen from a boat through mist; in another, it is the sun just above the horizon; still another is made up of a period of time and a mortar, meaning that it is dawn, when people begin to work. But the poet chose none of these; instead, he chose a character which analyzes into the sun at the height of a helmeted man, and so Miss Lowell speaks of the sun as "head-high," and we have the very picture the poet wanted us to see.

Miss Lowell has told in the Preface the manner in which we worked. The papers sent to Miss Lowell were in exactly the form of the above, and with them I also sent a paraphrase, and notes such as those at the end of this book. Far from making the slightest attempt at literary form in these paraphrases, I deliberately made them as bald as possible, and strove to keep my personality from intruding between Miss Lowell and the Chinese poet with whose mood she must be in perfect sympathy. Her remarkable gift for entering into the feeling of the poet she is translating was first shown in "Six French Poets," but there she approached her authors at first hand. It was my object to enable her to approach these Chinese authors as nearly at first hand as I could. That my method has been justified by the event, the book shows; not merely are these translations extraordinarily exact, they are poetry, and would be so though no Chinese poet had conceived them fourteen hundred years ago. It is as if I had handed her the warp and the woof, the silver threads and the gold, and from these she has woven a brocade as nearly alike in pattern to that designed by the Chinese poet as the differences in the looms permit. I believe that this is the first time that English translations of Chinese poetry have been made by a student of Chinese and a poet working together. Our experience of the partnership has taught us both much; if we are pioneers in such a collaboration, we only hope that others will follow our lead.

The second section of the book,

"Written Pictures," consists of illustrations, or half illustrations, of an art which the Chinese consider the most perfect medium in which a man can express himself. These *Tzŭ Hua*, "Hanging-on-the-Wall Poems," are less known and understood than any other form of Oriental art. A beautiful thought perpetuated in beautiful handwriting and hung upon the wall to suggest a mental picture — that is what it amounts to.

In China, the arts of poetry and calligraphy are united in the ideographs which form the written language. There are several different styles in which these ideographs, or characters, may be written. The earliest are pictograms known as the "ancient pictorial script"; they were superseded in the Eighth Century B.C. by the "great seal" characters and later by the "lesser seal." These, which had been executed with the "knife pen," were practically given up when the invention of the writing-brush, which is usually translated as "pencil," revolutionized calligraphy (*circa* 215 B.C.). Their place was taken by a type of character known as *li* or "official script," a simplified form of the "seal," and this, being an improvement upon all previous styles, soon became popular. It created almost a new character in which the pictorial element had largely disappeared, and, with certain modifications, holds good to-day. The "model hand," the "running hand," and the famous "grass hand," so popular with poets and painters, are merely adaptations of the *li*; all three of these, together with the *li* itself, are used in the composition of written pictures.

The written pictures here translated were formerly in the possession of a Chinese gentleman of keenly aesthetic taste, and are excellent examples of the art. The names which follow the poems are not those of the authors, but of the calligraphists. In the case of two poems, the authors' names are also given. These written pictures had no titles, those given here were added simply for convenience; but the titles to the poems in the body of the book are those of the poets themselves, except in one or two instances where the Chinese title conveyed so little

to an Occidental mind that its meaning had to be paraphrased.

The Notes at the end of the book are intended for the general reader. For which reason, I have purposely excluded the type of note which consists in cataloguing literary cross-allusions. To know that certain lines in a poem are quoted from some earlier author, one of a class of facts which deeply interest scholars, but are of no importance whatever to the rest of the world.

A word as to the title of this book: There lived at Ch'êng-tu, the capital of Szechwan, early in the Ninth Century, a courtesan named Hsieh T'ao, who was famous for her wit and verse-writing. Hsieh T'ao made a paper of ten colours, which she dipped in a stream, and on it wrote her poems. Now, some years before, a woman had taken the stole of a Buddhist priest to this stream in order to wash it. No sooner had the stole touched the water than the stream became filled with flowers. In an old Chinese book, "The Treasury of Pleasant Records," it is told that, later in life, Hsieh T'ao gave up the "fir-flower tablets" and made paper of a smaller size. Presumably this fir-flower paper was the paper of ten colours. The mountain stream which ran near Hsieh T'ao's house is called the "Hundred Flower Stream."

I cannot close this Introduction without expressing my gratitude to my teacher, Mr. Nung Chu. It is his unflagging interest and never-failing patience that have kept me spurred on to my task. Speaking no word of English, Mr. Nung must often have found my explanations of what would, and what would not, be comprehensible to Occidental readers very difficult to understand, and my only regret is that he cannot read the book now that it is done.

FLORENCE AYSCOUGH

SONGS OF THE MARCHES
BY LI T'AI–PO

I

It is the Fifth Month,
But still the Heaven-high hills
Shine with snow.
There are no flowers

For the heart of the earth is yet too chilly.
From the centre of the camp
Comes the sound of a flute
Playing "The Snapped Willow."
No colour mists the trees,
Not yet have their leaves broken.
At dawn, there is the shock and shouting of battle,
Following the drums and the loud metal gongs.
At night, the soldiers sleep, clasping the pommels of their jade-ornamented saddles.
They sleep lightly,
With their two-edged swords girt below their loins,
So that they may be able in an instant to rush upon the Barbarians
And destroy them.

II

Horses!
Horses!
Swift as the three dogs' wind!
Whips stinging the clear air like the sharp calling of birds,
They ride across the camel-back bridge
Over the river Wei.
They bend the bows,
Curving them away from the moon which shines behind them
Over their own country of Han.
They fasten feathers on their arrows
To destroy the immense arrogance of the foe.
Now the regiments are divided
And scattered like the five-pointed stars,
Sea mist envelops the deserted camp,
The task is accomplished,
And the portrait of Ho P'iao Yao
Hangs magnificently in the Lin Pavilion.

III

When Autumn burns along the hills,
The Barbarian hordes mount their horses
And pour down from the North.
Then, in the country of Han,
The Heavenly soldiers arise
And depart from their homes.
The High General
Divides the tiger tally.
Fight, Soldiers!

Then lie down and rest
On the Dragon sand.
The frontier moon casts the shadows of bows upon the ground,
Swords brush the hoar-frost flowers of the Barbarians' country.
The Jade Pass has not yet been forced,
Our soldiers hold it strongly.
Therefore the young married women
May cease their lamentations.

IV

The Heavenly soldiers are returning
From the sterile plains of the North.
Because the Barbarians desired their horses
To drink of the streams of the South,
Therefore were our spears held level to the charge
In a hundred fights.
In straight battle our soldiers fought
To gain the supreme gratitude
Of the Most High Emperor.
They seized the snow of the Inland Sea
And devoured it in their terrible hunger.
They lay on the sand at the top of the Dragon Mound
And slept.
All this they bore that the Moon Clan
Might be destroyed.
Now indeed have they won the right
To the soft, high bed of Peace.
It is their just portion.

THE BATTLE TO THE SOUTH OF THE CITY

BY LI T'AI–PO

How dim the battle-field, as yellow dusk!
The fighting men are like a swarm of ants.
The air is thick, the sun a red wheel.
Blood dyes the wild chrysanthemums purple.
Vultures hold the flesh of men in their mouths,
They are heavy with food — they cannot rise to fly.
There were men yesterday on the city wall;
There are ghosts to-day below the city wall.
Colours of flags like a net of stars,
Rolling of horse-carried drums — not yet is the killing ended.

From the house of the Unworthy One
— a husband, sons,
All within earshot of the rolling horse-
drums.

THE PERILS OF THE SHU ROAD
BY LI T'AI–PO

Alas! Alas! The danger! The steepness!
O Affliction!
The Shu Road is as perilous and difficult
as the way to the Green Heavens.
No greater undertaking than this has
been since Ts'an Ts'ung and Yü Fu
ruled the land.
For forty-eight thousand years no man
had passed the boundary of Ch'in.
Westward, over the Great White Mountain, was a bird-track
By which one could cross to the peak of
Omei.
But the earth of the mountain fell and
overwhelmed the Heroes so that they
perished.
Afterwards, therefore, they made sky-
ladders and joined the cliffs with hanging pathways.
Above, the soaring tips of the high mountains hold back the six dragons of the sun;
Below, in the ravines, the flowing waters
break into whirlpools and swirl back
against the current.
Yellow geese flying toward the peaks
cannot pass over them;
The gibbons climb and climb, despairingly pulling themselves up higher and
higher, but even their endurance fails.
How the road coils and coils through the
Green Mud Pass!
With nine turns to a hundred steps, it
winds round the ledges of the mountain crests.
Clutching at Orion, passing the Well
Star, I look up and gasp.
I sit long with my hand pressed to my
heart and groan.
I ask my Lord how long this Westward
wandering will last, when we shall
return.
It is impossible to climb the terrible road
along the edges of the precipices.
Among the ancient trees, one sees only
cruel, mournful, black birds.
Male birds, followed by females, fly to
and fro through the woods.

Sometimes one hears a nightingale in
the melancholy moonlight of the lonely
mountain.
The Shu Road is as perilous and difficult
as the way to the Green Heavens.
The ruddy faces of those who hear the
story of it turn pale.
There is not a cubit's space between the
mountain tops and the sky.
Dead and uprooted pine-trees hang over
sheer cliffs.
Flying waterfalls and rolling torrents outdo one another in clamour and confusion;
They dash against the perpendicular
walls, whirl round ten thousand rocks,
and boom like thunder along the
ravines.
This is what the Two-Edged Sword
Mountains are like!
Alas! How endless a road for man to
undertake! How came he to attempt
it!
The Terraced Road of the Two-Edged
Sword twists between glittering and
rocky summits.
One man alone could hold it against a
thousand and mow them down like
grass.
If the guardian of the Pass were doubtful
whether those who came were enemies
of his kinsmen,
He could fall upon them as a ravening
wolf.
At dawn, one flees the fierce tigers;
In the evening, one flees the long
snakes
Who sharpen their fangs and suck blood,
Destroying men like hemp.
Even though the delights of the Em-
broidered City are as reported,
Nothing could equal the joy of going
home at once.
The Shu Road is as perilous and difficult
as the way to the Green Heavens.
I turn toward the West, and, gazing
long, I sigh.

LOOKING AT THE MOON
AFTER RAIN
BY LI T'AI–PO

The heavy clouds are broken and blowing,
And once more I can see the wide com-

mon stretching beyond the four sides of the city.
Open the door. Half of the moon-toad is already up,
The glimmer of it is like smooth hoar-frost spreading over ten thousand *li*.
The river is a flat, shining chain.
The moon, rising, is a white eye to the hills;
After it has risen, it is the bright heart of the sea.
Because I love it — so — round as a fan, I hum songs until the dawn.

THE LONELY WIFE
BY LI T'AI–PO

The mist is thick. On the wide river, the water-plants float smoothly.
No letters come; none go.
There is only the moon, shining through the clouds of a hard, jade-green sky,
Looking down at us so far divided, so anxiously apart.
All day, going about my affairs, I suffer and grieve, and press the thought of you closely to my heart.
My eyebrows are locked in sorrow, I cannot separate them.
Nightly, nightly, I keep ready half the quilt,
And wait for the return of that divine dream which is my Lord.

Beneath the quilt of the Fire-Bird, on the bed of the Silver-Crested Love-Pheasant,
Nightly, nightly, I drowse alone.
The red candles in the silver candlesticks melt, and the wax runs from them,
As the tears of your so Unworthy One escape and continue constantly to flow.
A flower face endures but a short season,
Yet still he drifts along the river Hsiao and the river Hsiang.
As I toss on my pillow, I hear the cold nostalgic sound of the water-clock:
Shêng! Shêng! it drips, cutting my heart in two.

I rise at dawn. In the Hall of Pictures
They come and tell me that the snow-flowers are falling.

The reed-blind is rolled high, and I gaze at the beautiful, glittering, primeval snow,
Whitening the distance, confusing the stone steps and the courtyard.
The air is filled with its shining, it blows far out like the smoke of a furnace.
The grass-blades are cold and white, like jade girdle pendants.
Surely the Immortals in Heaven must be crazy with wine to cause such disorder,
Seizing the white clouds, crumpling them up, destroying them.

THE PLEASURES WITHIN THE PALACE
BY LI T'AI–PO

From little, little girls, they have lived in the Golden House.
They are lovely, lovely, in the Purple Hall.
They dress their hair with hill flowers,
And rock-bamboos are embroidered on their dresses of open-work silk gauze.
When they go out from the retired Women's Apartments,
They often follow the Palace chairs.
Their only sorrow, that the songs and wu dances are over,
Changed into the five-coloured clouds and flown away.

THE YOUNG GIRLS OF YUEH
BY LI T'AI–PO
I

Young girls are gathering lotus-seeds on the pond of Ya.
Seeing a man on the bank, they turn and row away singing.
Laughing, they hide among the lotus-flowers,
And, in a pretence of bashfulness, will not come out.

II

Many of the young girls of Wu are white, dazzlingly white.
They like to amuse themselves by floating in little boats on the water.

Peeping out of the corners of their eyes,
    they spurn the Springtime heart.
Gathering flowers, they ridicule the
    passer-by.

WRITTEN IN THE CHARACTER OF A BEAUTIFUL WOMAN GRIEVING BEFORE HER MIRROR

BY LI T'AI-PO

I

Bright, bright, the gilded magpie mirror,
Absolutely perfect in front of me on the
    jade dressing-stand.
Wiped, rubbed, splendid as the Winter
    moon;
Its light and brilliance, how clear and
    round!
The rose-red face is older than it was
    yesterday,
The hair is whiter than it was last
    year.
The white-lead powder is neglected,
It is useless to look into the mirror. I
    am utterly miserable.

II

When my Lord went away, he gave
    me this precious mirror coiled with
    dragons
That I might gaze at my golden-threaded
    dress of silken gauze.
Again and again I take my red sleeve
    and polish the bright moon,
Because I love to see its splendour light-
    ing up everything.
In its centre is my reflection, and the
    golden magpie which does not fly
    away.
I sit at my dressing-stand, and I am like
    the green Fire-Bird who, thinking of
    its mate, died alone.
My husband is parted from me as an
    arrow from the bow-string.
I know the day he left; I do not know
    the year when he will return.
The cruel wind blows — truly the heart
    of the Unworthy One is cut to pieces.
My tears, like white jade chop-sticks, fall
    in a single piece before the water-
    chestnut mirror.

SONGS TO THE PEONIES SUNG TO THE AIR: "PEACEFUL BRIGHTNESS"

BY LI T'AI-PO

I

The many-coloured clouds make me
    think of her upper garments, of her
    lower garments;
Flowers make me think of her face.
The Spring wind brushes the blossoms
    against the balustrade,
In the heavy dew they are bright and
    tinted diversely.
If it were not on the Heaped Jade Moun-
    tain that I saw her,
I must have met her at the Green Jasper
    Terrace, or encountered her by acci-
    dent in the moon.

II

A branch of opulent, beautiful flowers,
    sweet-scented under frozen dew.
No love-night like that on the Sorceress
    Mountain for these; their bowels ache
    in vain.
Pray may I ask who, in the Palace of
    Han, is her equal?
Even the "Flying Swallow" is to be
    pitied, since she must rely upon ever
    new adornments.

III

The renowned flower, and she of a love-
    liness to overthrow Kingdoms — both
    give happiness.
Each receives a smile from the Prince
    when he looks at them.
The Spring wind alone can understand
    and explain the boundless jealousy of
    the flower,
Leaning over the railing of the balcony
    at the North side of the aloe-wood
    pavilion.

SPRING GRIEF AND RESENTMENT

BY LI T'AI-PO

There is a white horse with a gold bridle
    to the East of the Liao Sea.
Bed-curtains of open-work silk — em-

broidered quilt — I sleep with the Spring wind.

The setting moon drops level to the balcony, it spies upon me. The candle is burnt out.

A blown flower drifts in through the inner door — it mocks at the empty bed.

THE CAST–OFF PALACE WOMAN OF CH'IN AND THE DRAGON ROBES

BY LI T'AI–PO

At Wei Yang dwells the Son of Heaven.

The all Unworthy One attends beside The Dragon-broidered robes.

I ponder his regard, not mine the love Enjoyed by those within the Purple Palace.

And yet I have attained to brightening The bed of yellow gold.

If floods should come, I also would not leave.

A bear might come and still I could protect.

My inconsiderable body knows the honour Of serving Sun and Moon.

I flicker with a little glow of light, A firefly's. I beg my Lord to pluck The trifling mustard plant and melon-flower

And not reject them for their hidden roots.

THE POET IS DETAINED IN A NANKING WINE–SHOP ON THE EVE OF STARTING ON A JOURNEY

BY LI T'AI–PO

The wind blows. The inn is filled with the scent of willow-flowers.

In the wine-shops of Wu, women are pressing the wine. The sight invites customers to taste.

The young men and boys of Nanking have gathered to see me off;

I wish to start, but I do not, and we drink many, many horn cups to the bottom.

I beg them to look at the water flowing toward the East,

And when we separate to let their thoughts follow its example and run constantly in my direction.

FENG HUANG T'AI ASCENDING THE TERRACE OF THE SILVER–CRESTED LOVE–PHEASANTS AT THE CITY OF THE GOLDEN MOUND

BY LI T'AI–PO

The silver-crested love-pheasants strutted upon the Pheasant Terrace.

Now the pheasants are gone, the terrace is empty, and the river flows on its old, original way.

Gone are the blossoms of the Palace of Wu and overgrown the road to it.

Passed the generations of the Chin, with their robes and head-dresses; they lie beneath the ancient mounds.

The three hills are half fallen down from Green Heaven.

The White Heron Island cuts the river in two.

Here also, drifting clouds may blind the Sun,

One cannot see Ch'ang An, City of Eternal Peace.

Therefore am I sorrowful.

THE NORTHERN FLIGHT

BY LI T'AI–PO

What hardships are encountered in a Northern flight!

We fly Northward, ascending the T'ai Hang Mountains.

The mountain road winds round a cliff, and it is very steep and dangerous;

The precipice, sheer as though cut with a knife, rises to the great, wide blue of the sky.

The horses' feet slip on the slanting ledges;

The carriage-wheels are broken on the high ridges;

The sand, scuffed into dust, floats in a continuous line to Yo Chou.

The smoke of beacon fires connects us with the Country of the North.

The spirit of killing is in the spears, in
the cruel two-edged swords.
The savage wind rips open the upper gar-
ments, the lower garments.
The rushing whale squeezes the Yellow
River;
The man-eating beasts with long tusks
assemble at Lo Yang.

We press forward with no knowledge of
when we shall return;
We look back, thinking of our former
home;
Grieving and lamenting in the midst of
ice and snow;
Groaning aloud, with our bowels rent
asunder.
A foot of cloth does not cover the body,
Our skins are cracked as the bark of a
dead mulberry.
The deep gullies prevent us from getting
water from the mountain streams,
Far away are the slopes where we might
gather grass and twigs for our fires,
Then, too, the terrible tiger lashes his
tail,
And his polished teeth glitter like
Autumn frosts.
Grass and trees cannot be eaten.
We famish; we drink the drops of freez-
ing dew.
Alas! So we suffer, travelling Northward.
I stop my four-horse carriage, overcome
by misery.
When will our Emperor find a peaceful
road?
When, before our glad faces, shall we
see the Glory of Heaven?

FIGHTING TO THE SOUTH
OF THE CITY
BY LI T'AI–PO

Last year they fought at the source of the
Sang Ch'ien,
This year they fight on the road by the
Leek-green River.
The soldiers were drenched by the waters
of the Aral Sea,
The horses were turned loose to find grass
in the midst of the snows of the
Heaven High Hills.
Over ten thousand *li*, they attacked and
fought,

The three divisions are crumbled, de-
cayed, utterly worn and old
The Hsiung Nu use killing and slaughter
in the place of the business of plowing.
From ancient times, only dry, white
bones are seen on the yellow sand-
fields.
The House of Ch'in erected and pounded
firm the wall to make a barrier before
the dwelling-place of the Barbarians,
The House of Han still preserved the
beacon-stands where fires are lighted.
The lighting of beacon fires on the stands
never ceases,
The fighting and attacking are without a
time of ending.
In savage attack they die — fighting without arms.
The riderless horses scream with terror,
throwing their heads up to the sky.
Vultures and kites tear the bowels of
men with their beaks
And fly to hang them on the branches of
dead trees.
Officers and soldiers lying in mud, in
grass, in undergrowth.
Helpless, the General — Yes, incapable
before this!
We have learnt that soldiers are evil
tools,
But wise men have not accomplished the
ending of war, and still we employ
them.

THE CROSSWISE RIVER
BY LI T'AI–PO

I

There are people who say the Crosswise
River is good;
I say the Crosswise River is terrible.
The savage wind blows as if it would
overturn the Heaven's Gate Mountains.
The white waves are as high as the high
rooms in the Temple of Wa Kuan.

II

The sea tide flowing Southward passes
Hsün Yang.
From the beginning of things, the Ox
Ledge has been more dangerous than
the Standing Horse Hill.

Those who wish to cross the Crosswise
River
Find evil winds and waves.
The misery of that one stretch of water
draws out its length to ten thousand *li*.

III

When the Sea Demon passes by, a
vicious wind curves back.
The waves beat open the rock wall of
the Gate of Heaven.
Is the Eighth Month tide-bore of Chêkiang equal to this?
It seems as though the vast, booming
waves were part of the mountains —
they spurt out snow.

ON HEARING THE BUDDHIST
PRIEST OF SHU PLAY HIS
TABLE–LUTE

BY LI T'AI–PO

The Priest of the Province of Shu, carrying his table-lute in a cover of green,
shot silk,
Comes down the Western slope of the
peak of Mount Omei.
He moves his hands for me, striking the
lute.
It is like listening to the waters in ten
thousand ravines, and the wind in ten
thousand pine-trees.
The traveller's heart is washed clean as
in flowing water.
The echoes of the overtones join with the
evening bell.
I am not conscious of the sunset behind
the jade-grey hill,
Nor how many and dark are the Autumn
clouds.

CH'ANG KAN

BY LI T'AI–PO

When the hair of your Unworthy One
first began to cover her forehead,
She picked flowers and played in front
of the door.
Then you, my Lover, came riding a bamboo horse.
We ran round and round the bed, and
tossed about the sweetmeats of green
plums.

We both lived in the village of Ch'ang
Kan.
We were both very young, and knew
neither jealousy nor suspicion.
At fourteen, I became the wife of my
Lord.
I could not yet lay aside my face of
shame;
I hung my head, facing the dark wall;
You might call me a thousand times, not
once would I turn round.
At fifteen, I stopped frowning.
I wanted to be with you, as dust with its
ashes.
I often thought that you were the faith-
ful man who clung to the bridge-
post,
That I should never be obliged to ascend
to the Looking-for-Husband Ledge.
When I was sixteen, my Lord went far
away,
To the Ch'ü T'ang Chasm and the Whirl-
ing Water Rock of the Yü River
Which, during the Fifth Month, must
not be collided with;
Where the wailing of the gibbons seems
to come from the sky.
Your departing footprints are still before
the door where I bade you good-bye.
In each has sprung up green moss.
The moss is thick, it cannot be swept
away.
The leaves are falling, it is early for the
Autumn wind to blow.
It is the Eighth Month, the butterflies
are yellow,
Two are flying among the plants in the
West garden;
Seeing them, my heart is bitter with grief,
they wound the heart of the Unworthy
One.
The bloom of my face has faded, sitting
with my sorrow.
From early morning until late in the
evening, you descend the Three Ser-
pent River.
Prepare me first with a letter, bringing
me the news of when you will reach
home.
I will not go far on the road to meet
you.
I will go straight until I reach the Long
Wind Sands.

SORROW DURING A CLEAR AUTUMN

BY LI T'AI–PO

I climb the hills of Chiu I — Oh-h-h-h-h!
I look at the clear streams a long way off.
I see distinctly the three branches of the Hsiang River, I hear the sound of its swift current.
The water flows coldly; it is on its way to the lake.
The horizontal Autumn clouds hide the sky.
I go by the "Bird's Path." I calculate the distance to my old home. Oh-h-h-h-h!
I do not know how many thousand *li* it is from Ching to Wu.
It is the hour of the Western brightness, of the half-round sun.
The dazzle on the island is about to disappear;
The smooth lake is brilliantly white — from the moon?
Over the lake, the moon is rising.
I think of the moment of meeting — the long stretch of time before it.
I think of misty Yen and gaze at Yüeh.
The lotus-flowers have fallen — Oh-h-h-h-h! The river is the colour of Autumn.
The wind passes — passes. The night is endless — endless.
I would go to the end of the Dark Sea. How eagerly I desire this!
I think much of fishing for a leviathan from the Island of the Cold Sea.
There is no rod long enough to raise it.
I yield to the great waves, and my sorrow is increased.
I will return. I will go home. Oh-h-h-h-h!
Even for a little time, one cannot rely upon the World.
I long to pick the immortal herbs on the hill of P'êng.

POIGNANT GRIEF DURING A SUNNY SPRING

BY LI T'AI–PO

The East wind has come again.
I see the jade-green grass and realize that it is Spring.

Everywhere there is an immense confusion of ripples and agitations.
Why does the waving and fluttering of the weeping-willow make me sad?
The sky is so bright it shines; everything is lovely and at peace.
The breath of the sea is green, fresh, sweet-smelling;
The heaths are vari-coloured, blue — green — as a kingfisher feather. Oh-h-h-h — How far one can see!
Clouds whirl, fly, float, and cluster together, each one sharply defined;
Waves are smoothed into a wide continuous flowing.
I examine the young moss in the well, how it starts into life.
I see something dim — Oh-h-h-h-h — waving up and down like floss silk.
I see it floating — it is a cobweb, coiling like smoke.
Before all these things — Oh-h-h-h-h — my soul is severed from my body.
Confronted with the wind, the brilliance, I suffer.
I feel as one feels listening to the sound of the waters of the Dragon Mound in Ch'in,
The gibbons wailing by the Serpent River.
I feel as the "Shining One" felt when she passed the Jade Frontier,
As the exile of Ch'u in the Maple Forest.
I will try to climb a high hill and look far away into the distance.
Pain cuts me to the bone and wounds my heart.
My Spring heart is agitated as the surface of the sea,
My Spring grief is bewildered like a flurry of snow.
Ten thousand emotions are mingled — their sorrow and their joy.
Yet I know only that my heart is torn in this Spring season.
She of whom I am thinking — Oh-h-h-h-h — is at the shore of the Hsiang River,
Separated by the clouds and the rainbow — without these mists I could surely see.
I scatter my tears a foot's length upon the water's surface.
I entrust the Easterly flowing water with my passion for the Cherished One.

If I could command the shining of the Spring, could grasp it without putting it out — Oh-h-h-h —
I should wish to send it as a gift to that beautiful person at the border of Heaven.

TWO POEMS WRITTEN AS PARTING GIFTS TO TS'UI (THE OFFICIAL) OF CH'IU PU

BY LI T'AI–PO

I love Ts'ui of Ch'iu Pu.
He follows the ways of the Official T'ao.
At his gate, he has planted five willow-trees,
And on either side of the well, crowding it between them, stand two wu-t'ung trees.
Mountain birds fly down and listen while he transacts business;
From the eaves of his house, flowers drop into the midst of his wine.
Thinking of my Lord, I cannot bear to depart.
My thoughts are melancholy and endless.

II

My Lord is like T'ao of P'êng Tsê.
Often, during the day, he sleeps at the North window.
Again, in the moonlight, he bends over his table-lute and plays,
His hands follow his thoughts, for there are no strings.
When a guest comes, it is wine alone which he pours out.
He is the best of officials, since he does not care for gold.
He has planted many grains on the Eastern heights,
And he admonishes all the people to plow their fields early.

SENT AS A PARTING GIFT TO THE SECOND OFFICIAL OF CH'IU PU

BY LI T'AI–PO

In the old days, Ch'iu Pu was bare and desolate,
The serving-men in the Official Residence were few

Because you, my Lord, have planted peach-trees and plum-trees,
This place has suddenly become exuberantly fragrant.
As your writing-brush moves, making the characters so full of life, you gaze at the white clouds;
And, when the reed-blinds are rolled up, at the kingfisher-green of the fading hills;
And, when the time comes, for long at the mountain moon;
Still again, when you are exhilarated with wine, at the shadow of the moon in the wine-cup.
Great man and teacher, I love you.
I linger.
I cannot bear to leave.

THE SONG OF THE WHITE CLOUDS SAYING GOOD–BYE TO LIU SIXTEEN ON HIS RETURN TO THE HILLS

BY LI T'AI–PO

The hills of Ch'u,
The hills of Ch'in,
White clouds everywhere.
White clouds follow my Lord always,
From place to place. They always follow My Lord,
When my Lord arrives at the hills of Ch'u.
Clouds also follow my Lord when he floats
In a boat on the river Hsiang,
With the wild wistaria hanging above
The waters of the river Hsiang
My Lord will go back
To where he can sleep
Among the white clouds,
When the sun is as high
As the head of a helmeted man

WIND–BOUND AT THE NEW FOREST REACH.
A LETTER SENT TO A FRIEND

BY LI T'AI–PO

Tidal water is a determined thing, it can be depended on;
But it is impossible to make an appointment with the wind of Heaven.

In the clear dawn, it veers Northwest;
At the last moment of sunset, it blows
  Southeast.
It is therefore difficult to set our sail.
The thought of our happy meeting be-
  comes insistent.
The wide water reflects a moon no longer
  round, but broken.
Water grass springs green in the broad
  reach.
Yesterday, at the North Lake, there were
  plum-flowers;
They were just beginning to open, the
  branches were not covered.
To-day, at dawn, see the willows beyond
  the White Gate;
The road is squeezed between them, they
  drop down their bright green silk
  threads.
Everything stirs like this, with the year —
When will my coming be fixed?
Willow-blossoms lie thick as snow on
  the river,
I am worried, the heart of the traveller is
  sad.
"At daybreak I will leave the New Forest
  Reach" —
But what is the use of humming Hsieh
  T'iao's poem.

IN THE PROVINCE OF LU,
AT THE ANCESTRAL SHRINE
OF KING YAO.
SAYING FAREWELL TO WU FIVE
ON HIS DEPARTURE FOR
LANG YA

BY LI T'AI–PO

King Yao has been dead for three thou-
  sand years,
But the green pine, the ancient temple,
  remain.
As we are bidding you good-bye, we set
  out offerings of cassia wine;
We make obeisance, we bend our knees,
  and, rising, turn our faces to Heaven.
Our hearts and spirits are pure.
The colour of the sun urges our return.
Song follows song, we tip up the flagon
  of sweet-scented wine.
The horses whinny. We are all tipsy,
  yet we rise.
Our hands separate. What words are
  there still to say?

DRINKING ALONE IN THE
MOONLIGHT

BY LI T'AI–PO

I

A pot of wine among flowers.
I alone, drinking, without a companion.
I lift the cup and invite the bright moon.
My shadow opposite certainly makes us
  three.
But the moon cannot drink,
And my shadow follows the motions of
  my body in vain.
For the briefest time are the moon and
  my shadow my companions.
Oh, be joyful! One must make the most
  of Spring.
I sing — the moon walks forward rhyth-
  mically;
I dance, and my shadow shatters and be-
  comes confused.
In my waking moments, we are happily
  blended.
When I am drunk, we are divided from
  one another and scattered.
For a long time I shall be obliged to
  wander without intention;
But we will keep our appointment by the
  far-off Cloudy River.

DRINKING ALONE IN THE
MOONLIGHT

BY LI T'AI–PO

II

If Heaven did not love wine,
There would be no Wine Star in Heaven.
If Earth did not love wine,
There should be no Wine Springs on
  Earth.
Why then be ashamed before Heaven to
  love wine.
I have heard that clear wine is like the
  Sages;
Again it is said that thick wine is like
  the Virtuous Worthies.
Wherefore it appears that we have swal-
  lowed both Sages and Worthies.
Why should we strive to be Gods and
  Immortals?
Three cups, and one can perfectly under-
  stand the Great Tao;

A gallon, and one is in accord with all
nature.
Only those in the midst of it can fully
comprehend the joys of wine;
I do not proclaim them to the sober.

A STATEMENT OF RESOLUTIONS AFTER BEING DRUNK ON A SPRING DAY

BY LI T'AI–PO

This time of ours
Is like a great, confused dream.
Why should one spend one's life in toil?
Thinking this, I have been drunk all day.
I fell down and lay prone by the pillars
in front of the house;
When I woke up, I gazed for a long time
At the courtyard before me.
A bird sings among the flowers.
May I ask what season this is?
Spring wind,
The bright oriole of the water-flowing
flight calls.
My feelings make me want to sigh.
The wine is still here, I will throw back
my head and drink.

I sing splendidly,
I wait for the bright moon.
Already, by the end of the song, I have
forgotten my feelings.

RIVER CHANT

BY LI T'AI–PO

Fig-wood oars,
A boat of the wood of the sand-pear.
At either end,
Jade flageolets and pipes of gold.

Amidships,
Jars of delectable wine,
And ten thousand pints
Put by.

A boat-load of singing-girls
Following the water ripples —
Going,
Stopping,
Veering —

The Immortal waited,
Then mounted and rode the yellow crane.

But he who is the guest of the sea has no
such desire,
Rather would he be followed by the
white gulls.

The *tzu* and *fu* of Ch'u P'ing hang sus-
pended like the sun and moon.
The terraces and the pleasure-houses
Of the Kings of Ch'u
Are empty heaps of earth.

I am drunk with wine,
With the sweet taste of it;
I am overflowed with the joy of it.
When I take up my writing-brush,
I could move the Five Peaks.

When I have finished my poem,
I laugh aloud in my arrogance.
I rise to the country of the Immortals
which lies in the middle of the sea.
If fame followed the ways of the good
official,
If wealth and rank were long constant,
Then indeed might the water of the Han
River flow Northwest.

SEPARATED BY IMPERIAL SUMMONS FROM HER WHO LIVES WITHIN

BY LI T'AI–PO

I

The Emperor commands; three times the
summons. He who left has not yet
returned.
To-morrow, at sunrise, he will go out by
the Pass of Wu.
From the upper chamber of white jade,
I shall gaze far off; but I shall be able
to make out nothing.
Our thoughts will be with each other. I
must ascend the Looking-for-Husband
Hill.

II

As I left my door, my wife dragged my
clothes with all her strength.
She asked me in how many days I should
return from the West.
"When I return, supposing I wear at my
girdle the yellow gold seal,
You must not imitate Su Ch'in's wife
and not leave your loom."

III

The upper chamber of kingfisher jade,
the stairs of gold —
Who passes the night alone, leaning
against the door and sobbing?
She sits all night by the cold lamp until
the moon melts into the dawn.
Her streaming, streaming tears are exhausted — to the West of the Ch'u
Barrier.

A WOMAN SINGS TO THE AIR: "SITTING AT NIGHT"

BY LI T'AI–PO

A Winter night, a cold Winter night. To
me, the night is unending.
I chant heavily to myself a long time. I
sit, sit in the North Hall.
The water in the well is solid with ice.
The moon enters the Women's Apartments.
The flame of the gold lamp is very small,
the oil is frozen. It shines on the
misery of my weeping.

The gold lamp goes out,
But the weeping continues and increases.
The Unworthy One hides her tears in her
sleeve.
She hearkens to the song of her Lord, to
the sound of it.
The Unworthy One knows her passion.
The passion and the sound unite,
There is no discord between them.
If a single phrase were unsympathetic to
my thoughts,
Then, though my Lord sang ten thousand
verses which should cause even the dust
on the beams to fly, to me it would be
nothing.

THE PALACE WOMAN OF HAN TAN BECOMES THE WIFE OF THE SOLDIERS' COOK

BY LI T'AI–PO

Once the Unworthy One was a maiden
of the Ts'ung Terrace.
Joyfully lifting my moth-pencilled eye-
brows, I entered the carnation-coloured
Palace.
Relying on myself, my flower-like face,

How should I know that it would wither
and fade?
Banished below the jade steps,
Gone as the early morning clouds are
gone,
Whenever I think of Han Tan City
I dream of the Autumn moon from the
middle of the Palace.
I cannot see the Prince, my Lord.
Desolate, my longing — until daylight
comes.

THE SORREL HORSE

BY LI T'AI–PO

The sorrel horse with the black tail gal-
lops, gallops, and neighs,
Lifting, curving his grey-jade hoofs.
He shies from the flowing water, unwill-
ing to cross,
As though he feared the mud for his em-
broidered saddle-cloth.
The snow is white on the far frontier
hills,
The clouds are yellow over the misty
frontier sea.
I strike with my leather whip, there are
ten thousand *li* to go.
How can I accomplish it, thinking of
Spring in the Women's Apartments?

A POEM GIVEN TO A BEAUTIFUL WOMAN ENCOUNTERED ON A FIELD–PATH

BY LI T'AI–PO

The magnificent horse, galloping swiftly,
tramples the fallen flower.
Down comes the riding-whip, straight
down — it strikes the Five Cloud Cart.
The young person who lifts the pearl
door-screen is very beautiful. Moreover, she smiles.
She points to a Red Building in the distance — it is the home of the Flower
Maiden.

SAYING GOOD–BYE TO A FRIEND

BY LI T'AI–PO

Clear green hills at a right angle to the
North wall,
White water winding to the East of the
city.

Here is the place where we must part.
The lonely water-plants go ten thousand *li*;
The floating clouds wander everywhither
as does man.
Day is departing — it and my friend.
Our hands separate. Now he is going.
"Hsiao, hsiao," the horse neighs.
He neighs again, "Hsiao, hsiao."

DESCENDING THE EXTREME SOUTH MOUNTAIN; PASSING THE HOUSE OF HU SSU, LOVER OF HILLS; SPENDING THE NIGHT IN THE PREPARATION OF WINE

BY LI T'AI–PO

We come down the green-grey jade hill,
The mountain moon accompanies us
home.
We turn and look back up the path:
Green, green, the sky; the horizontal,
kingfisher-green line of the hills is fading.
Holding each other's hands, we reach the
house in the fields.
Little boys throw open the gate of thorn
branches,
The quiet path winds among dark bamboos,
Creepers, bright with new green, brush
our garments.
Our words are happy, rest is in them.
Of an excellent flavour, the wine! We
scatter the dregs of it contentedly.
We sing songs for a long time; we chant
them to the wind in the pine-trees.
By the time the songs are finished, the
stars in Heaven's River are few.
I am tipsy. My friend is continuously
merry.
In fact, we are so exhilarated that we both
forget this complicated machine, the
world.

THE TERRACED ROAD OF THE TWO–EDGED SWORD MOUNTAINS

BY LI T'AI–PO

Looking South and straight from Hsien
Yang for five thousand *li*,
One could see, among the full, blowing
clouds, the rocky sharpness of peaks,

Were it not for the horizontal line of
the Two-Edged Sword Mountains cutting across the view.
They are flat against the green sky, and
open in the middle to let the sky
through.
On their heights, the wind whistles awesomely in the pines; it booms in great,
long gusts; it clashes like the strings of
a jade-stone psaltery; it shouts on the
clearness of a gale.
In the Serpent River country, the gibbons — Oh-h-h-h-h — all the gibbons
together moan and grieve.
Beside the road, torrents flung from a
great height rush down the gully,
They toss stones and spray over the road,
they run rapidly, they whirl, they
startle with the noise of thunder.
I bid good-bye to my devoted friend —
Oh-h-h-h-h — now he leaves me.
When will he come again? Oh-h-h-h-h
— When will he return to me?
I hope for my dear friend the utmost
peace.
My voice is heavy, I sigh and draw my
breath haltingly.
I look at the green surface of the water
flowing to the East.
I grieve that the white sun hides in the
West.
The wild goose has taken the place
of the swallow — Oh-h-h-h-h — I hear
the pattering, falling noises of Autumn.
Dark are the rain clouds; the colour of
the town of Ch'in is dark.
When the moon glistens on the Road of
the Two-Edged Sword — Oh-h-h-h-h —
I and you, even though in different
provinces, may drink our wine opposite
each other,
And listen to the talking
Of our hearts.

HEARING A BAMBOO FLUTE ON A SPRING NIGHT IN THE CITY OF LO YANG

BY LI T'AI–PO

From whose house do the invisible notes
of a jade flute come flying?
The Spring wind scatters them. They
fill the City of Lo Yang.

To-night, as the phrases form, I hear
"The Snapped Willow."
To whom do they not bring back the
love of his old, early garden?

THE RETREAT OF HSIEH KUNG
BY LI T'AI–PO

The sun is setting — has set — on the
Spring-green Mountain.
Hsieh Kung's retreat is solitary and still.
No sound of man in the bamboo grove.
The white moon shines in the centre of
the unused garden pool.
All round the ruined Summer-house is
decaying grass,
Grey mosses choke the abandoned well.
There is only the free, clear wind
Again — again — passing over the stones
of the spring.

A TRAVELLER COMES TO THE OLD TERRACE OF SU
BY LI T'AI–PO

The old Imperial Park — the ruined
Terrace — the young willows.
The water-chestnut pickers are singing, a
simple song unaccompanied by instru-
ments — but joy is unbearable.
For now the moon over the Western
River is alone.
The time is past when she gazed upon
the concubines in the Palace of the
King of Wu.

THEME OF THE REST–HOUSE ON THE CLEAR WAN RIVER
BY LI T'AI–PO

I love the beauty of the Wan River.
One can see its clear heart shining a
hundred feet deep.
In what way does it not equal the river
Hsin An?
For a thousand times eight feet one can
see its bright bed,
The white sand keeps the colour of the
moon.
The dark green bamboos accentuate the
Autumn sounds.
Really one cannot help laughing to think
that, until now, the rapid current
celebrated by Yen
Has usurped all the fame.

DRINKING SONG
BY LI T'AI–PO

Do you not see the waters of the Yellow
River coming down from Heaven?
They rush with incredible speed to the
sea, and they never turn and come
back again.
Do you not see, in the clear mirror of
the Guest Hall, the miserable white
hair on my head?
At dawn it is like shining thread, but at
sunset it is snow.
In this life, to be perfectly happy, one
must drain one's pleasures;
The golden wine-cup must not stand
empty opposite the moon.
Heaven put us here, we must use what
we have.
Scatter a thousand ounces of silver and
you are but where you were.
Boil the sheep,
Kill the ox,
Be merry.
We should drink three hundred cups at
once.
Mr. Wise Gentleman Ts'en,
And you, Mr. Scholar Tan Ch'iu,
Drink, you must not stop.
I will sing one of my poems for you,
Please lean over and listen:
"Bells! Drums! Delicacies
Worth their weight in jade —
These things
Are of the slightest value.
I only want to be drunk
For ages and never wake.
The sages and worthies of old times
Have left not a sound,
Only those who drank
Have achieved lasting fame.
The King of Ch'ên, long ago, caroused
In the Hall of Peaceful Content.
They drank wine paid
At a full ten thousand a gallon;
They surpassed themselves in mirth,
And the telling of obscene stories.
How can a host say
He has very little money.
It is absolutely imperative
That he buy wine for his friends.
Horses of five colours, dappled flower
horses,
Fur coats costing
A thousand ounces of silver —

He sends his son to exchange
All these for delectable wine,
So that you and I together
May drown our ancient grief."

ANSWER TO AN AFFECTIONATE INVITATION FROM TS'UI FIFTEEN

BY LI T'AI–PO

You have the "bird's foot-print" characters.
You suggest that we drink together at the Lute Stream.
The characters you wrote are in the centre of a foot of pure white silk,
They are like exquisite clouds dropped from Heaven.
Having finished reading, I smile at the empty air,
I feel as though my friend were before me
Reciting verses for a long time.
The characters are not faded. I shall keep them in my sleeve, and they should last three years.

PARROT ISLAND

BY LI T'AI–PO

The parrots come, they cross the river waters of Wu.
The island in the river is called Parrot Island.
The parrots are flying West to the Dragon Mountain.
There are sweet grasses on the island, and how green, green, are its trees!

The mists part and one can see the leaves of the spear-orchid, and its scent is warm on the wind;
The water is embroidered and shot with the reflections of the peach-tree blossoms growing on both banks.
Now indeed does the departing official realize the full meaning of his banishment.
The long island — the solitary moon — facing each other in the brightness.

THE HONOURABLE LADY CHAO

BY LI T'AI–PO

Moon over the houses of Han, over the site of Ch'in.

It flows as water — its brightness shone on Ming Fei, the "Bright Concubine," Who took the road to the Jade Pass.
She went to the edge of Heaven, but she did not return;
She gave up the moon of Han, she departed from the Eastern Sea.
The "Bright Concubine" married in the West, and the day of her returning never came.
For her beautiful painted face, there was the long, cold snow instead of flowers.
She, with eyebrows like the antennae of moths, pined and withered.
Her grave is in the sand of the Barbarians' country.
Because, when alive, she did not pay out yellow gold,
The portrait painted of her was distorted.
Now she is dead no one can prevent the bright green grass from spreading over her grave,
And men weep because of it.

THINKING OF THE FRONTIER

BY LI T'AI–PO

At what season last year did my Lord leave his Unworthy One?
In the Southern garden, the butterflies were fluttering in the young green grass.
Now, this year, at what season does the Unworthy One cherish thoughts of her Lord?
There is white snow on the Western hills and the clouds of Ch'in are dark.
It is three thousand *li* from here to the Jade Barrier.
I desire to send the "harmonious writings," but how can they reach you?

A SONG OF RESENTMENT

BY LI T'AI–PO

At fifteen, she entered the Palace of Han,
Her flower-face was like a river in Spring.
The Prince chose her of the jade colour
To attend his rest within the embroidered screen.
As she presented the pillow, she was lovely as the evening moon.
He who wears the dragon robes de-

lighted in the sweetly scented wind of her garments.
How was it possible for the "Flying Swallow" to snatch the Emperor's love?
Jealousy unending! Profoundest grief which can so wound a person
And turn the black cloud head-dress to frosted thistledown!

If, for one day, our desires be not satisfied,
Verily the things of the world are nothing.
Change the duck-feather dress for sweet wine,
Cease to embroider dragons on the dresses for the wu dance.
She is chilly with bitterness,
Words cannot be endured.
For one's Lord one plays the table-lute of wu-t'ung wood with strings of silk,
But when one's bowels are torn with grief, the strings also break.
Grief in the heart at night is anguish and despair.

PICKING WILLOW
BY LI T'AI–PO

The drooping willow brushes the very clear water,
Beautifully it flickers in this East-wind time of the year.
Its flowers are bright as the snow of the Jade Pass,
Its leaves soft as smoke against the gold window.
She, the Lovely One, bound in her long thoughts;
Facing them, her heart is burnt with grief.
Pull down a branch,
Gather the Spring colour
And send it far,
Even to that place
Before the Dragon Gate.

AUTUMN RIVER SONG ON THE BROAD REACH
BY LI T'AI–PO

In the clear green water — the shimmering moon.
In the moonlight — white herons flying.

A young man hears a girl plucking water-chestnuts;
They paddle home together through the night, singing.

VISITING THE TAOIST PRIEST ON THE MOUNTAIN WHICH UPHOLDS HEAVEN. HE IS ABSENT
BY LI T'AI–PO

A dog,
A dog barking.
And the sound of rushing water.
How dark and rich the peach-flowers after the rain.
Every now and then, between the trees, I see deer.
Twelve o'clock, but I hear no bell in the ravine.
Wild bamboos slit the blue-green of a cloudy sky.
The waterfall hangs against the jade-green peak.
There is no one to tell me where he has gone.
I lean against the pine-trees grieving.

REPLY TO AN UNREFINED PERSON ENCOUNTERED IN THE HILLS
BY LI T'AI–PO

He asks why I perch in the green jade hills.
I smile and do not answer. My heart is comfortable and at peace.
Fallen peach-flowers spread out widely, widely, over the water.
It is another sky and earth, not the world of man.

RECITING VERSES BY MOON-LIGHT IN A WESTERN UPPER CHAMBER IN THE CITY OF THE GOLDEN MOUND
BY LI T'AI–PO

The night is still in Chin Ling, a cool wind blows.
I am alone in a high room, gazing over Wu and Yüeh.

White clouds shine on the water and blur the reflection of the still city.
The cold dew soaks my clothes, Autumn moonlight is damp.
In the moonlight, murmuring poems, one loses count of time.
From old days until now, people who can really see with their eyes are few,
Those who understand and speak of a clear river as being bright as silk.
I suggest that men meditate at length on Hsieh Hsüan Hui.

PASSING THE NIGHT AT THE WHITE HERON ISLAND

BY LI T'AI-PO

At dawn, I left the Red Bird Gate;
At sunset, I came to roost on the White Heron Island.
The image of the moon tumbles along the bright surface of the water.
The Tower above the City Gate is lost in the twinkling light of the stars.
I gaze far off, toward my beloved, the Official of Chin Ling,
And the longing in my heart is like that for the Green Jasper Tree.
It is useless to tell my soul to dream;
When it comes back, it will feel the night turned to Autumn.
The green water understands my thoughts,
For me it flows to the Northwest.
Because of this, the sounds of my jade table-lute
Will follow the flowing of its current and carry my grief to my friend.

ASCENDING THE THREE CHASMS

BY LI T'AI-PO

The Sorceress Mountain presses against Green Heaven.
The Serpent River runs terribly fast.
The Serpent River can be suddenly exhausted.
The time may never come when we shall arrive at the Green Heaven.
Three dawns shine upon the Yellow Ox.
Three sunsets — and we go so slowly.

Three dawns — again three sunsets —
And we do not notice that our hair is white as silk.

PARTING FROM YANG, A HILL MAN WHO IS RETURNING TO THE HIGH MOUNTAIN

BY LI T'AI-PO

There is one place which is an everlasting home to me:
The Jade Woman Peak on the High Southern Mountain.
Often, a wide, flat moonlight
Hangs upon the pines of the whirling Eastern stream.
You are going to pick the fairy grasses
And the shooting purple flower of the ch'ang p'u.

After a year, perhaps, you will come to see me
Riding down from the green-blue Heaven on a white dragon.

NIGHT THOUGHTS

BY LI T'AI-PO

In front of my bed the moonlight is very bright.
I wonder if that can be frost on the floor?
I lift up my head and look full at the full moon, the dazzling moon.
I drop my head, and think of the home of old days.

THE SERPENT MOUND SENT AS A PRESENT TO CHIA THE SECRETARY

BY LI T'AI-PO

Chia, the Scholar, gazes into the West, thinking of the splendour of the Capitol.
Although you have been transferred to the broad reaches of the river Hsiang, you must not sigh in resentment.
The mercy of the Sainted Lord is far greater than that of Han Wên Ti.
The Princely One had pity, and did not appoint you to the station of the Unending Sands.

ON THE SUBJECT OF OLD TAI'S WINE-SHOP

BY LI T'AI-PO

Old Tai is gone down to the Yellow Springs.
Yet he must still wish to make "Great Spring Wine."
There is no Li Po on the terrace of Eternal Darkness.
To whom, then, will he sell his wine?

DRINKING IN THE T'AO PAVILION

BY LI T'AI-PO

The house of the lonely scholar is in the winding lane.
The great scholar's gate is very high.
The garden pool lies and shines like the magic gall mirror;
Groves of trees throw up flowers with wide, open faces;
The leaf-coloured water draws the Spring sun.
Sitting in the green, covered passage-way, watching the strange, red clouds of evening,
Listening to the lovely music of flageolets and strings,
The Golden Valley is not much to boast of.

A SONG FOR THE HOUR WHEN THE CROWS ROOST

BY LI T'AI-PO

This is the hour when the crows come to roost on the Ku Su Terrace.
In his Palace, the King of Wu is drinking with Hsi Shih.
Songs of Wu — posturings of Ch'u dances — and yet the revels are not finished.
But already the bright hills hold half of the sun between their lips,
The silver-white arrow-tablet above the gold-coloured brass jar of the water-clock marks the dripping of much water,
And, rising, one can see the Autumn moon sliding beneath the ripples of the river,
While slowly the sun mounts in the East —
What hope for the revels now?

POEM SENT TO THE OFFICIAL WANG OF HAN YANG

BY LI T'AI-PO

The Autumn moon was white upon the Southern Lake.
That night the Official Wang sent me an invitation.
Behind the embroidered bed-curtain lay the Official Secretary — drunk.
The woven dresses of the beautiful girls who performed the wu dance took charming lines,
The shrill notes of the bamboo flute reached to Mien and O,
The phrases of the songs rose up to the silent clouds.
Now that we are parted, I grieve.
We think of each other a single piece of water distant.

DRINKING ALONE ON THE ROCK IN THE RIVER OF THE CLEAR STREAM

BY LI T'AI-PO

I have a flagon of wine in my hand.
I am alone on the Ancestor Rock in the river.
Since the time when Heaven and Earth were divided,
How many thousand feet has the rock grown?
I lift my cup to Heaven and smile.
Heaven turns round, the sun shines in the West.
I am willing to sit on this rock forever,
Perpetually casting my fish-line like Yen Ling.
Send and ask the man in the midst of the hills
Whether we are not in harmony, both pursuing the same thing.

A FAREWELL BANQUET TO MY FATHER'S YOUNGER BROTHER YUN, THE IMPERIAL LIBRARIAN

BY LI T'AI-PO

When I was young, I spent the white days lavishly.
I sang — I laughed — I boasted of my ruddy face.

I do not realize that now, suddenly, I am old.
With joy I see the Spring wind return.
It is a pity that we must part, but let us make the best of it and be happy.
We walk to and fro among the peach-trees and plum-trees.
We look at the flowers and drink excellent wine.
We listen to the birds and climb a little way up the bright hills.
Soon evening comes and the bamboo grove is silent.
There is no one — I shut my door.

IN THE PROVINCE OF LU, TO THE EAST OF THE STONE GATE MOUNTAIN, TAKING LEAVE OF TU FU

BY LI T'AI–PO

When drunk, we were divided; but we have been together again for several days.
We have climbed everywhere, to every pool and ledge.
When, on the Stone Gate Road,
Shall we pour from the golden flagon again?
The Autumn leaves drop into the Four Waters,
The Ch'u Mountain is brightly reflected in the colour of the lake.
We are flying like thistledown, each to a different distance;
Pending this, we drain the cups in our hands.

THE MOON OVER THE MOUNTAIN PASS

BY LI T'AI–PO

The bright moon rises behind the Heaven-high Mountain,
A sea of clouds blows along the pale, wide sky.
The far-off wind has come from nearly ten thousand *li*,
It has blown across the Jade Gate Pass.
Down the Po Têng Road went the people of Han
To waylay the men of Hu beside the Bright Green Bay.

From the beginning, of those who go into battle,
Not one man is seen returning.
The exiled Official gazes at the frontier town,
He thinks of his return home, and his face is very bitter.
Surely to-night, in the distant cupola,
He sighs, and draws heavy breaths. How then can rest be his?

THE TAKING–UP OF ARMS

BY LI T'AI–PO

A hundred battles, the sandy fields of battles, armour broken into fragments.
To the South of the city they are already shut in and surrounded by many layers of men.
They rush out from their cantonments.
They shoot and kill the General of the Barbarians.
A single officer leads the routed soldiers of the "Thousand Horsemen" returning whence they came.

A SONG OF THE REST–HOUSE OF DEEP TROUBLE

BY LI T'AI–PO

At Chin Ling, the tavern where travellers part is called the Rest-House of Deep Trouble.
The creeping grass spreads far, far, from the roadside where it started.
There is no end to the ancient sorrow, as water flows to the East.
Grief is in the wind of this place, burning grief in the white aspen.
Like K'ang Lo I climb on board the dull travelling boat.
I hum softly "On the Clear Streams Flies the Night Frost."
It is said that, long ago, on the Ox Island Hill, songs were sung which blended the five colours.
Now do I not equal Hsieh, and the youth of the House of Yüan?
The bitter bamboos make a cold sound, swaying in the Autumn moonlight.
I pass the night alone, desolate behind the reed-blinds, and dream of returning to my distant home.

THE "LOOKING–FOR–HUSBAND" ROCK

BY LI T'AI–PO

In the attitude, and with the manner,
of the woman of old,
Full of grief, she stands in the glorious
morning light.
The dew is like the tears of to-day;
The mosses like the garments of years
ago.
Her resentment is that of the Woman of
the Hsiang River;
Her silence that of the concubine of the
King of Ch'u.
Still and solitary in the sweet-scented
mist,
As if waiting for her husband's re-
turn.

AFTER BEING SEPARATED FOR A LONG TIME

BY LI T'AI–PO

How many Springs have we been apart?
You do not come home.
Five times have I seen the cherry-blos-
soms from the jade window,
Besides there are the "embroidered
character letters."
You must sigh as you break the seals.
When this happens, the agony of my
longing must stop your heart.
I have ceased to wear the cloud head-
dress. I have stopped combing and
dressing the green-black hair on my
temples.
My sorrow is like a whirling gale — like
a flurry of white snow.
Last year I sent a letter to the Hill of
the Bright Ledge telling you these
things;
The letter I send this year will again
implore you.

East wind — Oh-h-h-h!
East wind, blow for me.
Make the floating cloud come West-
ward.
I wait his coming, and he does not
come.
The fallen flower lies quietly, quietly,
thrown upon the green moss.

BITTER JEALOUSY IN THE PALACE OF THE HIGH GATE

BY LI T'AI–PO

I

The Heavens have revolved. The "Northern Measure" hangs above the Western
wing.
In the Gold House, there is no one;
fireflies flit to and fro.
Moonlight seeks to enter the Palace of
the High Gate,
To one in the centre of the Palace it
brings an added grief.

II

Unending grief in the Cassia Hall. Spring
is forgotten.
Autumn dust rises up on the four sides
of the Yellow Gold House.
At night, the bright mirror hangs against
a dark sky;
It shines upon the solitary one in the
Palace of the High Gate.

ETERNALLY THINKING OF EACH OTHER

BY LI T'AI–PO

(The Woman Speaks)

The colour of the day is over; flowers
hold the mist in their lips.
The bright moon is like glistening silk.
I cannot sleep for grief.
The tones of the Chao psaltery begin
and end on the bridge of the silver-
crested love-pheasant.
I wish I could play my Shu table-lute on
the mandarin duck strings.
The meaning of this music — there is
no one to receive it.
I desire my thoughts to follow the Spring
wind, even to the Swallow Mountains.
I think of my Lord far, far away, remote
as the Green Heaven.
In old days, my eyes were like horizontal
waves;
Now they flow, a spring of tears.
If you do not believe that the bowels of
your Unworthy One are torn and
severed,
Return and take up the bright mirror I
was wont to use.

(The Man Speaks)

We think of each other eternally.
My thoughts are at Ch'ang An.
The Autumn cricket chirps beside the
railing of the Golden Well;
The light frost is chilly, chilly; the colour
of the bamboo sleeping mat is cold.
The neglected lamp does not burn
brightly. My thoughts seem broken off.
I roll up the long curtain and look at the
moon — it is useless, I sigh continually.
The Beautiful, Flower-like One is as far
from me as the distance of the clouds.
Above is the brilliant darkness of a high
sky,
Below is the rippling surface of the clear
water.
Heaven is far and the road to it is long;
it is difficult for a man's soul to compass it in flight.
Even in a dream my spirit cannot cross
the grievous barrier of hills.
We think of each other eternally.
My heart and my liver are snapped in
two.

PASSIONATE GRIEF

BY LI T'AI–PO

Beautiful is this woman who rolls up the
pearl-reed blind.
She sits in an inner chamber,
And her eyebrows, delicate as a moth's
antennae,
Are drawn with grief.
One sees only the wet lines of tears.
For whom does she suffer this misery?
We do not know.

SUNG TO THE AIR:
"THE MANTZU LIKE AN IDOL"

BY LI T'AI–PO

The trees in the level forest stand in
rows and rows,
The mist weaves through them.
The jade-green of the cold hillside coun-
try hurts one's heart.
Night colour drifts into the high cupola.
In the cupola, a man grieves.

I stand — stand — on the jade steps,
doing nothing.
The birds are flying quickly to roost.

There is the road I should follow if I
were going home.
Instead, for me, the "long" rest-houses
alternate with the "short" rest-houses.

AT THE YELLOW CRANE
TOWER, TAKING LEAVE OF
MENG HAO JAN ON HIS
DEPARTURE TO KUANG LING

BY LI T'AI–PO

I take leave of my dear old friend at the
Yellow Crane Tower.
In the flower-smelling mist of the Third
Month he will arrive at Yang Chou.
The single sail is shining far off — it is
extinguished in the jade-coloured dis-
tance,
I see only the long river flowing to the
edge of Heaven.

IN DEEP THOUGHT, GAZING
AT THE MOON

BY LI T'AI–PO

The clear spring reflects the thin, wide-
spreading pine-tree —
And for how many thousand, thousand
years?
No one knows.
The late Autumn moon shivers along the
little water ripples,
The brilliance of it flows in through the
window.
Before I sit for a long time absent-
mindedly chanting,
Thinking of my friend —
What deep thoughts!
There is no way to see him. How then
can we speak together?
Joy is dead. Sorrow is the heart of man.

THOUGHTS FROM A
THOUSAND LI

BY LI T'AI–PO

Li Ling is buried in the sands of Hu.
Su Wu has returned to the homes of
Han.
Far, far, the Five Spring Pass,
Sorrowful to see the flower-like snow.
He is gone, separated, by a distant
country,
But his thoughts return,

Long sighing in grief.
Toward the Northwest
Wild geese are flying.
If I sent a letter — so — to the edge of
Heaven.

WORD–PATTERN

BY LI T'AI–PO

The Autumn wind is fresh and clear;
The Autumn moon is bright.
Fallen leaves whirl together and scatter.
The jackdaws, who have gone to roost,
are startled again.
We are thinking of each other, but when
shall we see each other?
Now, to-night, I suffer, because of my
passion.

THE HEAVEN'S GATE MOUNTAINS

BY LI T'AI–PO

In the far distance, the mountains seem
to rise out of the river;
Two peaks, standing opposite each other,
make a natural gateway,
The cold colour of the pines is reflected
between the river-banks,
Stones divide the current and shiver the
wave-flowers to fragments.
Far off, at the border of Heaven, is the
uneven line of mountain-pinnacles;
Beyond, the bright sky is a blur of rose-
tinted clouds.
The sun sets, and the boat goes on
and on —
As I turn my head, the mountains sink
down into the brilliance of the cloud-
covered sky.

POEM SENT ON HEARING THAT WANG CH'ANG–LING HAD BEEN EXILED TO LUNG PIAO

BY LI T'AI–PO

In Yang Chou, the blossoms are drop-
ping. The night-jar calls.
I hear it said that you are going to
Lung Piao — that you will cross the
Five Streams.
I fling the grief of my heart up to the
bright moon

That it may follow the wind and arrive,
straight as eyesight, to the West of
Yeh Lang.

A PARTING GIFT TO WANG LUN

BY LI T'AI–PO

Li Po gets into a small boat — he is on
the point of starting.
Suddenly he hears footsteps on the bank
and the sound of singing.
The Peach-Flower Pool is a thousand feet
deep,
Yet it is not greater than the emotion of
Wang Lun as he takes leave of me.

SAYING GOOD–BYE TO A FRIEND WHO IS GOING ON AN EXCURSION TO THE PLUM–FLOWER LAKE

BY LI T'AI–PO

I bid you good-bye, my friend, as you are
going on an excursion to the Plum-
Flower Lake.
You should see the plum-blossoms open;
It is understood that you hire a person to
bring me some.
You must not permit the rose-red fra-
grance to fade.
You will only be at the New Forest Reach
a little time,
Since we have agreed to drink at the City
of the Golden Mound at full moon.
Nevertheless you must not omit the wild-
goose letter,
Or else our knowledge of each other will
be as the dust of Hu to the dust of
Yüeh.

A POEM SENT TO TU FU FROM SHA CH'IU CH'ENG

BY LI T'AI–PO

After all, what have I come here to do?
To lie and meditate at Sha Ch'iu Ch'êng.
Near the city are ancient trees,
And day and night are continuous with
Autumn noises.
One cannot get drunk on Lu wine,
The songs of Ch'i have no power to
excite emotion.

I think of my friend, and my thoughts
are like the Wên River,
Mightily moving, directed toward the
South.

BIDDING GOOD–BYE TO YIN SHU

BY LI T'AI–PO

Before the White Heron Island — the
moon.
At dawn to-morrow I shall bid good-bye
to the returning traveller.
The sky is growing bright,
The sun is behind the Green Dragon
Hill;
Head high it pushes out of the sea clouds
and appears.
Flowing water runs without emotions,
The sail which will carry him away meets
the wind and fills.
We watch it together. We cannot bear
to be separated.
Again we pledge each other from the cups
we hold in our hands.

A DESULTORY VISIT TO THE FENG HSIEN TEMPLE AT THE DRAGON'S GATE

BY TU FU

I had already wandered away from the
People's Temple,
But I was obliged to sleep within the
temple precincts.
The dark ravine was full of the music of
silence,
The moon scattered bright shadows
through the forest.
The Great Gate against the sky seemed
to impinge upon the paths of the
planets.
Sleeping among the clouds, my upper gar-
ments, my lower garments, were cold.
Wishing to wake, I heard the sunrise bell
Commanding men to come forth and
examine themselves in meditation.

THE THATCHED HOUSE UNROOFED BY AN AUTUMN GALE

BY TU FU

It is the Eighth Month, the very height
of Autumn.
The wind rages and roars.

It tears off three layers of my grass-roof.
The thatch flies — it crosses the river —
it is scattered about in the open spaces
by the river.
High-flying, it hangs, tangled and floating,
from the tops of forest trees;
Low-flying, it whirls — turns — and sinks
into the hollows of the marsh.
The swarm of small boys from the South
Village laugh at me because I am old
and feeble.
How dare they act like thieves and rob-
bers before my face,
Openly seizing my thatch and running
into my bamboo grove?
My lips are scorched, my mouth dry, I
scream at them, but to no purpose.
I return, leaning on my staff. I sigh and
breathe heavily.

Presently, of a sudden, the wind ceases.
The clouds are the colour of ink.
The Autumn sky is endless — endless —
stretching toward dusk and night.
My old cotton quilt is as cold as iron;
My restless son sleeps a troubled sleep,
his moving foot tears the quilt.
Over the head of the bed is a leak. Not
a place is dry.
The rain streams and stands like hemp —
there is no break in its falling.
Since this misery and confusion, I have
scarcely slept or dozed.
All the long night, I am soaking wet.
When will the light begin to sift in?
If one could have a great house of one
thousand, ten thousand rooms —
A great shelter where all the Empire's
shivering scholars could have happy
faces —
Not moved by wind or rain, solid as a
mountain —
Alas! When shall I see that house
standing before my eyes?
Then, although my own hut were
destroyed, although I might freeze and
die, I should be satisfied.

THE RIVER VILLAGE

BY TU FU

The river makes a bend and encircles the
village with its current.
All the long Summer, the affairs and

occupations of the river village are quiet and simple.

The swallows who nest in the beams go and come as they please.

The gulls in the middle of the river enjoy one another, they crowd together and touch one another.

My old wife paints a chess-board on paper.

My little sons hammer needles to make fish-hooks.

I have many illnesses, therefore my only necessities are medicines;

Besides these, what more can so humble a man as I ask?

THE EXCURSION
A NUMBER OF YOUNG GENTLEMEN OF RANK, ACCOMPANIED BY SINGING–GIRLS, GO OUT TO ENJOY THE COOL OF EVENING. THEY ENCOUNTER A SHOWER OF RAIN

BY TU FU

I

How delightful, at sunset, to loosen the boat!

A light wind is slow to raise waves.

Deep in the bamboo grove, the guests linger;

The lotus-flowers are pure and bright in the cool evening air.

The young nobles stir the ice-water;

The Beautiful Ones wash the lotus-roots, whose fibres are like silk threads.

A layer of clouds above our heads is black.

It will certainly rain, which impels me to write this poem.

II

The rain comes, soaking the mats upon which we are sitting.

A hurrying wind strikes the bow of the boat.

The rose-red rouge of the ladies from Yüeh is wet;

The Yen beauties are anxious about their kingfisher-eyebrows.

We throw out a rope and draw in to the sloping bank. We tie the boat to the willow-trees.

We roll up the curtains and watch the floating wave-flowers.

Our return is different from our setting out. The wind whistles and blows in great gusts.

By the time we reach the shore, it seems as though the Fifth Month were Autumn.

THE RECRUITING OFFICERS AT THE VILLAGE OF THE STONE MOAT

BY TU FU

I sought a lodging for the night, at sunset, in the Stone Moat Village.

Recruiting Officers, who seize people by night, were there.

A venerable old man climbed over the wall and fled.

An old woman came out of the door and peered.

What rage in the shouts of the Recruiting Officers!

What bitterness in the weeping of the old woman!

I heard the words of the woman as she pled her cause before them:

"My three sons are with the frontier guard at Yeh Ch'êng.

From one son I have received a letter.

A little while ago, two sons died in battle.

He who remains has stolen a temporary lease of life;

The dead are finished forever.

In the house, there is still no grown man, Only my grandson at the breast.

The mother of my grandson has not gone,

Going out, coming in, she has not a single whole skirt.

I am an old, old woman, and my strength is failing,

But I beg to go with the Recruiting Officers when they return this night.

I will eagerly agree to act as a servant at Ho Yang;

I am still able to prepare the early morning meal."

The sound of words ceased in the long night,

It was as though I heard the darkness choke with tears.

At daybreak, I went on my way,

Only the venerable old man was left.

CROSSING THE FRONTIER

BY TU FU

I

When bows are bent, they should be bent strongly;
When arrows are used, they should be long.
The bow-men should first shoot the horses.
In taking the enemy prisoner, the Leader should first be taken;
There should be no limit to the killing of men.
In making a kingdom, there must naturally be a boundary.
If it were possible to regulate usurpation,
Would so many be killed and wounded?

II

At dawn, the conscripted soldiers enter the camp outside the Eastern Gate.
At sunset, they cross the bridge of Ho Yang.
The setting sun is reflected on the great flags.
Horses neigh.   The wind whines — whines —
Ten thousand tents are spread along the level sand.
Officers instruct their companies.
The bright moon hangs in the middle of the sky.
The written orders are strict that the night shall be still and empty.
Sadness everywhere. A few sounds from a Mongol flageolet jar the air.
The strong soldiers are no longer proud, they quiver with sadness.
May one ask who is their General?
Perhaps it is Ho P'iao Yao.

THE SORCERESS GORGE

BY TU FU

Jade dew lies upon the withered and wounded forest of maple-trees.
On the Sorceress Hill, over the Sorceress Gorge, the mist is desolate and dark.
The ripples of the river increase into waves and blur with the rapidly flowing sky.

The wind-clouds at the horizon become confused with the Earth. Darkness.
The myriad chrysanthemums have bloomed twice. Days to come — tears.
The solitary little boat is moored, but my heart is in the old-time garden.
Everywhere people are hastening to measure and cut out their Winter clothes.
At sunset, in the high City of the White Emperor, the hurried pounding of washed garments.

THINKING OF LI PO ON A SPRING DAY

BY TU FU

The poems of Po are unequalled.
His thoughts are never categorical, but fly high in the wind.
His poems are clear and fresh as those of Yü, the official;
They are fine and easy as those of Pao, the military counsellor.
I am North of the river Wei, looking at the Spring trees;
You are East of the river, watching the sunset clouds.
When shall we meet over a jug of wine?
When shall I have another precious discussion of literature with you?

AT THE EDGE OF HEAVEN. THINKING OF LI T'AI–PO

BY TU FU

A cold wind blows up from the edge of Heaven.
The state of mind of the superior man is what?
When does the wild goose arrive?
Autumn water flows high in the rivers and lakes.

They hated your essay — yet your fate was to succeed.
The demons where you are rejoice to see men go by.
You should hold speech with the soul of Yüan,
And toss a poem into the Mi Lo River as a gift to him.

SENT TO LI PO AS A GIFT

BY TU FU

Autumn comes,
We meet each other.
You still whirl about as a thistledown in
the wind.
Your Elixir of Immortality is not yet per-
fected
And, remembering Ko Hung, you are
ashamed.
You drink a great deal,
You sing wild songs,
Your days pass in emptiness.
Your nature is a spreading fire,
It is swift and strenuous.
But what does all this bravery amount to?

A TOAST FOR MENG YUN–CH'ING

BY TU FU

Illimitable happiness,
But grief for our white heads.
We love the long watches of the night,
the red candle.
It would be difficult to have too much of
meeting,
Let us not be in a hurry to talk of separa-
tion.
But because the Heaven River will sink,
We had better empty the wine-cups.
To-morrow, at bright dawn, the world's
business will entangle us.
We brush away our tears,
We go — East and West.

MOON NIGHT

BY TU FU

To-night — the moon at Fu Chou.
In the centre of the Women's Apart-
ments
There is only one to look at it.
I am far away, but I love my little son,
my daughter.
They cannot understand and think of
Ch'ang An.
The sweet-smelling mist makes the cloud
head-dress damp,
The jade arm must be chilly
In this clear, glorious shining.
When shall I lean on the lonely screen?
When shall we both be shone upon, and
the scars of tears be dry?

HEARING THE EARLY ORIOLE
(WRITTEN IN EXILE)

BY PO CHU–I

The sun rose while I slept. I had not
yet risen
When I heard an early oriole above the
the roof of my house.
Suddenly it was like the Royal Park at
dawn,
With birds calling from the branches of
the ten-thousand-year trees.
I thought of my time as a Court Official
When I was meticulous with my pencil
in the Audience Hall.
At the height of Spring, in occasional
moments of leisure,
I would look at the grass and growing
things,
And at dawn and at dusk I would hear
this sound.
Where do I hear it now?
In the lonely solitude of the City of
Hsün Yang.
The bird's song is certainly the same,
The change is in the emotions of the
man.
If I could only stop thinking that I am
at the ends of the earth,
I wonder, would it be so different from
the Palace after all?

THE CITY OF STONES.
(NANKING)

BY LIU YU–HSI

Hills surround the ancient kingdom; they
never change.
The tide beats against the empty city,
and silently, silently, returns.
To the East, over the Huai River — the
ancient moon.
Through the long, quiet night it moves,
crossing the battlemented wall.

SUNG TO THE TUNE OF "THE
UNRIPE HAWTHORN BERRY"

BY NIU HSI–CHI

Mist is trying to hide the Spring-coloured
hills,
The sky is pale, the stars are scattered
and few.

The moon is broken and fading, yet there is light on your face,
These are the tears of separation, for now it is bright dawn.

We have said many words,
But our passion is not assuaged.
Turn your head, I have still something to say:
Remember my skirt of green open-work silk,
The sweet-scented grasses everywhere will prevent your forgetting.

WRITTEN BY WANG WEI, IN THE MANNER OF CHIA, THE (PALACE) SECRETARY, AFTER AN IMPERIAL AUDIENCE AT DAWN IN THE "PALACE OF GREAT BRILLIANCE"

At the first light of the still-concealed sun, the Cock-man, in his dark-red cap, strikes the tally-sticks and proclaims aloud the hour.
At this exact moment, the Keeper of the Robes sends in the eider-duck skin dress, with its cloud-like curving feather-scales of kingfisher green.
In the Ninth Heaven, the Ch'ang Ho Gate opens; so do those of the Palaces, and the Halls of Ceremony in the Palaces.
The ten thousand kingdoms send their ambassadors in the dresses and caps of their ranks to do reverence before the pearl-stringed head-dress.
The immediately-arrived sun tips the "Immortal Palm"; it glitters.
Sweet-scented smoke rises and flows about the Emperor's ceremonial robes, making the dragons writhe.
The audience ended, I wish to cut the paper of five colours and write upon it the words of the Son of Heaven.
My jade girdle-ornaments clash sweetly as I return to sit beside the Pool of the Crested Love-Pheasant.

THE BLUE–GREEN STREAM
BY WANG WEI

Every time I have started for the Yellow Flower River,
I have gone down the Blue-Green Stream,

Following the hills, making ten thousand turnings.
We go along rapidly, but advance scarcely one hundred *li*.
We are in the midst of a noise of water,
Of the confused and mingled sounds of water broken by stones,
And in the deep darkness of pine-trees.
Rocked, rocked,
Moving on and on,
We float past water-chestnuts
Into a still clearness reflecting reeds and rushes.
My heart is clean and white as silk; it has already achieved Peace;
It is smooth as the placid river.
I long to stay here, curled up on the rocks,
Dropping my fish-line forever.

FARM HOUSE ON THE WEI STREAM
BY WANG WEI

The slanting sun shines on the cluster of small houses upon the heights.
Oxen and sheep are coming home along the distant lane.
An old countryman is thinking of the herd-boy,
He leans on his staff by the thorn-branch gate, watching.
Pheasants are calling, the wheat is coming into ear,
Silk-worms sleep, the mulberry-leaves are thin.
Labourers, with their hoes over their shoulders, arrive;
They speak pleasantly together, loth to part.
It is for this I long — unambitious peace!
Disappointed in my hopes, dissatisfied, I hum "Dwindled and Shrunken."

SEEKING FOR THE HERMIT OF THE WEST HILL; NOT MEETING HIM
BY CH'IU WEI

On the Nothing-Beyond Peak, a hut of red grass.
I mount straight up for thirty *li*.
I knock at the closed door — no serving boy.

I look into the room. There is only
the low table, and the stand for the
elbows.
If you are not sitting on the cloth seat of
your rough wood cart,
Then you must be fishing in the Autumn
water.
We have missed each other; we have not
seen each other;
My effort to do you homage has been in
vain.
The grass is the colour which rain
leaves.
From inside the window, I hear the
sound of pine-trees at dusk.
There is no greater solitude than to be
here.
My ears hear it; my heart spreads open to
it naturally.
Although I lack the entertainment of a
host,
I have received much — the whole doctrine of clear purity.
My joy exhausted, I descend the hill.
Why should I wait for the Man of Wisdom?

FLOATING ON THE POOL OF
JO YA. SPRING

BY CHI WU-CH'IEN

Solitary meditation is not suddenly
snapped off; it continues without interruption.
It flows — drifts this way, that way —
returns upon itself.
The boat moves before a twilight
wind.
We enter the mouth of the pool by the
flower path
At the moment when night enfolds the
Western Valley.
The serrated hills face the Southern Constellation,
Mist hangs over the deep river pools and
floats down gently, gently, with the
current.
Behind me, through the trees, the moon
is sinking.
The business of the world is a swiftly
moving space of water, a rushing,
spreading water.
I am content to be an old man holding
a bamboo fishing-rod.

SUNG TO THE AIR:
"THE WANDERER"
(COMPOSED BY SU WU IN THE
TIME OF THE EMPEROR
WU OF HAN)

BY MENG CHIAO

Thread from the hands of a doting
mother
Worked into the clothes of a far-off
journeying son.
Before his departure, were the close, fine
stitches set,
Lest haply his return be long delayed.
The heart — the inch-long grass —
Who will contend that either can repay
The gentle brightness of the Third
Month of Spring.

FAREWELL WORDS TO THE
DAUGHTER OF THE HOUSE
OF YANG

BY WEI YING-WU

Because of this, sad, sad has the whole
day been to me.
You must go forth and journey, far, very
far.
The time has come when you, the
maiden, must go.
The light boat ascends the great river.
Your particular bitterness is to have none
from whom you may claim support.
I have cherished you. I have pondered
over you. I have been increasingly
gentle and tender to you.
A child taken from those who have cared
for it —
On both sides separation brings the tears
which will not cease.
Facing, this, the very centre of the bowels
is knotted.
It is your duty, you must go. It is scarcely
possible to delay farther.
From early childhood, you have lacked a
mother's guidance,
How then will you know to serve your
husband's mother? I am anxious.
From this time, the support on which
you must rely is the home of your husband.
You will find kindness and sympathy,
therefore you must not grumble;
Modesty and thrift are indeed to be
esteemed.

Money and jewels, maid-servants and furnishings — are these necessary, a perfection to be waited for?
The way of a wife should be filial piety, respect and compliance;
Your manner, your conduct, should be in accord with this way.
To-day, at dawn, we part.
How many Autumns will pass before I see you?
Usually I endeavour to command my feelings,
But now, when my emotions come upon me suddenly, they are difficult to control.
Being returned home, I look at my own little girl.
My tears fall as rain. They trickle down the string of my cap and continue to flow.

SUNG TO THE AIR: "LOOKING SOUTH OVER THE RIVER AND DREAMING"

BY WEN T'ING–YUN

The hair is combed,
The face is washed,
All is done.

Alone, in the upper story of my Summer-house, I bend forward, looking at the river.
A thousand sails pass — but among all of them the one is not.
The slant sunlight will not speak,
It will not speak.
The long-stretched water scarcely moves.

My bowels are broken within me.
Oh! Island of the White Water Flowers!

TOGETHER WE KNOW HAPPINESS

WRITTEN BY A DESCENDANT OF THE FOUNDER OF THE SOUTHERN T'ANG DYNASTY

Silent and alone, I ascended the West Cupola.
The moon was like a golden hook.
In the quiet, empty, inner courtyard, the coolness of early Autumn enveloped the wu-t'ung tree.

Scissors cannot cut this thing;
Unravelled, it joins again and clings.
It is the sorrow of separation,
And none other tastes to the heart like this.

ONCE MORE FIELDS AND GARDENS

BY T'AI YUAN–MING

Even as a young man
I was out of tune with ordinary pleasures.
It was my nature to love the rooted hills,
The high hills which look upon the four edges of Heaven.
What folly to spend one's life like a dropped leaf
Snared under the dust of streets,
But for thirteen years it was so I lived.

The caged bird longs for the fluttering of high leaves.
The fish in the garden pool languishes for the whirled water
Of meeting streams.
So I desired to clear and seed a patch of the wild Southern moor.
And always a countryman at heart,
I have come back to the square enclosures of my fields
And to my walled garden with its quiet paths.

Mine is a little property of ten *mou* or so,
A thatched house of eight or nine rooms.
On the North side, the eaves are over-hung
With the thick leaves of elm-trees,
And willow-trees break the strong force of the wind.
On the South, in front of the great hall,
Peach-trees and plum-trees spread a net of branches
Before the distant view.

The village is hazy, hazy,
And mist sucks over the open moor.
A dog barks in the sunken lane which runs through the village.
A cock crows, perched on a clipped mul-berry.

There is no dust or clatter
In the courtyard before my house.

My private rooms are quiet,
And calm with the leisure of moonlight
through an open door.

For a long time I lived in a cage;
Now I have returned.
For one must return
To fulfil one's nature.

SONG OF THE SNAPPED WILLOW
WRITTEN DURING THE
LIANG DYNASTY

When he mounted his horse, he did not
take his leather riding-whip;
He pulled down and snapped off the
branch of a willow-tree.
When he dismounted, he blew into his
horizontal flute,
And it was as though the fierce grief of
his departure would destroy the
traveller.

THE CLOUDY RIVER
(FROM THE "BOOK OF ODES")

How the Cloudy River glitters —
Shining, revolving in the sky!
The King spoke:
"Alas! Alas!
What crime have the men of to-day com-
mitted
That Heaven sends down upon them
Confusion and death?
The grain does not sprout,
The green harvests wither,
Again and again this happens.
There is no spirit to whom I have not
rendered homage,
No sacrifice I have withheld for love.
My stone sceptres and round badges of
rank have come to an end.
Why have I not been heard?

Already the drought is terrible beyond
expression!
The heated air is overpowering; it is a
concentrated fierceness.
I have not ceased to offer the pure sacri-
fices,
I myself have gone from the border altars
to the ancestral temples.
To Heaven,
To Earth,
I have made the proper offerings,
I have buried them in the ground.

There is no spirit I have not honoured,
Hou Chi could do no more.
Shang Ti does not look favourably upon us.
This waste and ruin of the Earth —
If my body alone might endure it!

Already the drought is terrible beyond
expression!
I cannot evade the responsibility of it.
I am afraid — afraid; I feel in peril — I
feel in peril,
As when one hears the clap of thunder
and the roll of thunder.
Of the remnant of the black-haired
people of Chou
There will not be left so much as half
a man.
Ruler over the high, wide Heavens,
Even I shall not be spared.
Why should I not be terrified
Since the Ancestral sacrifices will be
ended?

Already the drought is terrible beyond
expression!
The consequences of it cannot be pre-
vented.
Scorching — scorching!
Blazing — blazing!
No living place is left to me.
The Great Decree of Fate is near its end.
There is none to look up to; none whose
counsel I might ask.
The many great officials, the upright
men of ancient days,
Cannot advise me in regard to these con-
sequences.
My father, my mother, my remote an-
cestors,
How can you endure this which has be-
fallen me?

Already the drought is terrible beyond
expression!
Parched and scoured the hills, the
streams.
Drought, the Demon of Drought, has
caused these ravages,
Like a burning fire which consumes everything.
My heart is shrivelled with the heat;
Sorrow rises from the heart as smoke
from fire.
The many great officials, the upright men
of ancient days,

Do not listen to me.
Ruler of the high, wide Heavens,
Permit that I retire to obscurity.

Already the drought is terrible beyond
expression!
I strive, and force myself in vain.
I dread that which will come.
How — why — should I bear this mad-
ness of drought?
I suffer not to know the reason for it.
I offered the yearly sacrifices for full
crops in good time.
I neglected not one of the Spirits of the
Four Quarters of the Earth.
The Ruler of the high, wide Heavens
Does not even consider me.
I have worshipped and reverenced the
bright gods,
They should not be dissatisfied or angry
with me.

Already the drought is terrible beyond
expression!
Everything is in confusion; all authority
is gone;
My officials are reduced to extremity.
My Chief Minister is afflicted with a
continuing illness.
My Master of the Horse, my Com-
mander of the Guards,
My Steward, my attendants of the Right
and of the Left,
Not one among them has failed to try
and help the people,
Not one has given up because powerless.
I raise my head and look at the Ruler
of the wide, bright Heavens.
I cry: 'Why must I suffer such grief!'

I look upwards. I gaze at the wide, bright
Heavens,
There are little stars twinkling, even those
stars.
My officers and the great men of my
country,
You have wrought sincerely and without
gain.
The Great Decree is near its end.
Do not abandon what you have partly
accomplished,
Your prayers are not for me alone,
But to guard the people and those who
watch over them from calamity.

I look upwards. I gaze at the wide,
bright Heavens.
When shall I receive the favour of rest?"

TO THE AIR: "THE FALLEN LEAVES AND THE PLAINTIVE CICADA"

BY THE EMPEROR WU OF HAN

There is no rustle of silken sleeves,
Dust gathers in the Jade Courtyard.
The empty houses are cold, still, with-
out sound.
The leaves fall and lie upon the bars of
doorway after doorway.
I long for the Most Beautiful One; how
can I attain my desire?
Pain bursts my heart. There is no peace.

WRITTEN IN EARLY AUTUMN AT THE POOL OF SPRINKLING WATER

BY CHAO TI OF HAN, THE "BRIGHT EMPEROR"

In Autumn, when the landscape is clear,
to float over the wide, water ripples,
To pick the water-chestnut and the lotus-
flower with a quick, light hand!
The fresh wind is cool, we start singing
to the movement of the oars.
The clouds are bright; they part before
the light of dawn; the moon has sunk
below the Silver River.
Enjoying such pleasure for ten thousand
years —
Could one consider it too much?

PROCLAIMING THE JOY OF CERTAIN HOURS BY THE EMPEROR LING OF (LATER) HAN

Cool wind rising. Sun sparkling on the
wide canal.
Pink lotuses, bent down by day, spread
open at night.
There is too much pleasure; a day cannot contain it.
Clear sounds of strings, smooth flowing
notes of flageolets — we sing the "Jade
Love-Bird" song.
A thousand years? Ten thousand? Nothing could exceed such delight.

A SONG OF GRIEF
BY PAN CHIEH–YU

Glazed silk, newly cut, smooth, glittering, white,
As white, as clear, even as frost and snow.
Perfectly fashioned into a fan,
Round, round, like the brilliant moon,
Treasured in my Lord's sleeve, taken out, put in —
Wave it, shake it, and a little wind flies from it.
How often I fear the Autumn Season's coming
And the fierce, cold wind which scatters the blazing heat.
Discarded, passed by, laid in a box alone;
Such a little time, and the thing of love cast off.

A LETTER OF THANKS FOR PRECIOUS PEARLS BESTOWED BY ONE ABOVE
BY CHIANG TS'AI–P'IN
(THE "PLUM–BLOSSOM" CONCUBINE OF THE EMPEROR MING HUANG)

It is long — long — since my two eyebrows were painted like cassia-leaves.
I have ended the adorning of myself. My tears soak my dress of coarse red silk.
All day I sit in the Palace of the High Gate. I do not wash; I do not comb my hair.
How can precious pearls soothe so desolate a grief.

DANCING
BY KANG KUEI–FEI
(THE "WHITE POPLAR" IMPERIAL CONCUBINE OF THE EMPEROR MING HUANG)

Wide sleeves sway.
Scents,
Sweet scents
Incessantly coming.

It is red lilies,
Lotus lilies,
Floating up,
And up,
Out of Autumn mist.

Thin clouds
Puffed,
Fluttered,
Blown on a rippling wind
Through a mountain pass.

Young willow shoots
Touching,
Brushing,
The water
Of the garden pool.

SONGS OF THE COURTESANS
(WRITTEN DURING THE LIANG DYNASTY)
ONE OF THE "SONGS OF THE TEN REQUESTS"
BY TING LIU NIANG

My skirt is cut out of peacock silk,
Red and green shine together, they are also opposed.
It dazzles like the gold-chequered skin of the scaly dragon.
Clearly so odd and lovely a thing must be admired.
My Lord himself knows well the size.
I beg thee, my Lover, give me a girdle.

AI AI THINKS OF THE MAN SHE LOVES

How often must I pass the moonlight nights alone?
I gaze far — far — for the Seven Scents Chariot.
My girdle drops because my waist is shrunken.
The golden hairpins of my disordered head-dress are all askew.

SENT TO HER LOVER YUAN AT HO NAN (SOUTH OF THE RIVER) BY CHANG PI LAN (JADE–GREEN ORCHID) FROM HU PEI (NORTH OF THE LAKE)

My Lover is like the tree-peony of Lo Yang.
I, unworthy, like the common willows of Wu Ch'ang.

Both places love the Spring wind.
When shall we hold each other's hands
again?

CH'IN, THE "FIRE–BIRD WITH PLUMAGE WHITE AS JADE," LONGS FOR HER LOVER

Incessant the buzzing of insects beyond
the orchid curtain.
The moon flings slanting shadows from
the pepper-trees across the courtyard.
Pity the girl of the flowery house,
Who is not equal to the blossoms
Of Lo Yang.

THE GREAT HO RIVER BY THE MOTHER OF THE LORD OF SUNG

(FROM "THE BOOK OF ODES")

Who says the Ho is wide?
Why one little reed can bridge it.

Who says that Sung is far?
I stand on tiptoe and see it.

Who says the Ho is wide?
Why the smallest boat cannot enter.

Who says that Sung is far?
It takes not a morning to reach it.

WRITTEN PICTURES

AN EVENING MEETING

The night is the colour of Spring mists.
The lamp-flower falls,
And the flame bursts out brightly.
In the midst of the disorder of the dress-
ing-table
Lies a black eye-stone.
As she dances,
A golden hairpin drops to the ground.
She peeps over her fan,
Arch, coquettish, welcoming his arrival.
Then suddenly striking the strings of her
table-lute,
She sings —
But what is the rain of the Sorceress
Gorge
Doing by the shore of the Western Sea?
LI HAI-KU, 19th Century

THE EMPEROR'S RETURN FROM A JOURNEY TO THE SOUTH

Like a saint, he comes,
The Most Noble.
In his lacquered state chariot
He awes the hundred living things.
He is clouded with the purple smoke of
incense,
A round umbrella
Protects the Son of Heaven.
Exquisite is the beauty
Of the two-edged swords,

Of the chariots,
Of the star-embroidered shoes of the
attendants.
The Sun and Moon fans are borne before
him,
And he is preceded by sharp spears
And the blowing brightness of innumer-
able flags.
The Spring wind proclaims the Em-
peror's return,
Binding the ten thousand districts to-
gether
In a chorded harmony of Peace and
Satisfaction,
So that the white-haired old men and
the multitudes rejoice,
And I wish to add my ode
In praise of perfect peace.
WEN CHENG-MING, 16th Century

ON SEEING THE PORTRAIT OF A BEAUTIFUL CONCUBINE

Fine rain,
Spring mud
Slippery as bean curds.
In a rose-red flash, she approaches —
Beautiful, sparkling like wine;
Tottering as though overcome with wine,
Her little feet slip on the sliding path;
Who will support her?
Clearly it is her picture

We see here,
In a rose-red silken dress,
Her hair plaited like the folds
Of a hundred clouds.
It is Manshu.
CH'EN HUNG-SHOU, 19th Century

CALLIGRAPHY

The writing of Li Po-hai
Is like the vermilion bird
And the blue-green dragon.
It drifts slowly as clouds drift;
It has the wide swiftness of wind.
Hidden within it lurk the dragon and
the tiger.

The writing of Chia, the official,
Is like the high hat of ceremonial.
It flashes like flowers in the hair,
And its music is the trailing of robes
And the sweet tinkling of jade girdle-
pendants.
Because of his distinguished position,
He never says anything not sanctioned by
precedent.
LIANG T'UNG-SHU, 18th Century

THE PALACE BLOSSOMS

When the rain ceases,
The white water flowers of Ch'ang Lo
stroll together at sunset
In the City by the River.
The young girls are no longer confined
In the gold pavilions,
But may gaze at the green water
Whirling under the bridge of many turn-
ings.
TAI TA-MIEN, 18th Century

ONE GOES A JOURNEY

He is going to the Tung T'ing Lake,
My friend whom I have loved so many
years.
The Spring wind startles the willows
And they break into pale leaf.
I go with my friend
As far as the river-bank.
He is gone —
And my mind is filled and overflowing
With the things I did not say.

Again the white water flower
Is ripe for plucking.

The green, pointed swords of the iris
Splinter the brown earth.
To the South of the river
Are many sweet-olive trees.
I gather branches of them to give to my
friend
On his return.
LIU SHIH-AN, 18th Century

FROM THE STRAW HUT AMONG THE SEVEN PEAKS

I

From the high pavilion of the great rock,
I look down at the green river.
There is the sail of a returning boat.
The birds are flying in pairs.
The faint snuff colour of trees
Closes the horizon.
All about me
Sharp peaks jag upward;
But through my window,
And beyond,
Is the smooth, broad brightness
Of the setting sun.

II

Clouds brush the rocky ledge.
In the dark green shadow left by the
sunken sun
A jade fountain flies,
And a little stream,
Thin as the fine thread spun by sad
women in prison chambers,
Slides through the grasses
And whirls suddenly upon itself
Avoiding the sharp edges of the iris-
leaves.
Few people pass here.
Only the hermits of the hills come in
companies
To gather the Imperial Fern.
LU KUN, 19th Century

ON THE CLASSIC OF THE HILLS AND SEA

In what place does the cinnabar-red tree
of the alchemists seed?
Upon the sun-slopes
Of Mount Mi
It pushes out its yellow flowers
And rounds its crimson fruit.
Eat it and you will live forever.

The frozen dew is like white jade;
It shimmers with the curious light of
gems.

Why do people regard these things?
Because the Yellow Emperor considers
them of importance.

Written by LI HAI-KU, 19th Century
Composed by T'AO CH'IEN

THE HERMIT

A cold rain blurs the edges of the river.
Night enters Wu.
In the level brightness of dawn
I saw my friend start alone for the Ch'u
Mountain.
He gave me this message for his friends
and relations at Lo Yang:
My heart is a piece of ice in a jade cup.

Written by LI HAI-KU, 19th Century
Composed by WANG CH'ANG-LING

AFTER HOW MANY YEARS

SPRING

The willows near the roadside rest-house
are soft with new-burst buds.
I saunter along the river path,
Listening to the occasional beating of
the ferry drum.
Clouds blow and separate,
And between them I see the watch towers
Of the distant city.
They come in official coats
To examine my books.
Months go by;
Years slide backwards and disappear.
Musing,
I shut my eyes
And think of the road I have come,
And of the Spring weeds
Choking the fields of my house.

SUMMER

The rain has stopped.
The clouds drive in a new direction.
The sand is so dry and hard that my
wooden shoes ring upon it
As I walk.
The flowers in the wind are very beauti-
ful.

A little stream quietly draws a line
Through the sand.
Every household is drunk with sacrificial
wine,
And every field is tall with millet
And pale young wheat.
I have not much business.
It is a good day.
I smile.
I will write a poem
On all this sudden brightness.

AUTUMN

Hoar-frost is falling,
And the water of the river runs clear.
The moon has not yet risen,
But there are many stars.
I hear the watch-dogs
In the near-by village.
On the opposite bank
Autumn lamps are burning in the win-
dows.
I am sick,
Sick with all the illnesses there are.
I can bear this cold no longer,
And a great pity for my whole past life
Fills my mind.
The boat has started at last.
O be careful not to run foul
Of the fishing-nets!

WINTER

I was lonely in the cold valleys
Where I was stationed.
But I am still lonely,
And when no one is near
I sigh.
My gluttonous wife rails at me
To guard her bamboo shoots.
My son is ill and neglects to water
The flowers.
Oh yes,
Old red rice can satisfy hunger,
And poor people can buy muddy, un-
strained wine
On credit.
But the pile of land-tax bills
Is growing;
I will go over and see my neighbour,
Leaning on my staff.

LI HAI-KU, 19th Century

THE INN AT THE MOUNTAIN PASS

I return to the inn at the foot of the
    Climbing Bean Pass.
The smooth skin of the water shines,
And the clouds slip over the sky.
This is the twilight of dawn and dusk.
On the top of Hsi Lêng
The hill priest sits in the evening
And meditates.
Two —
Two —
Those are the lights of fishing-boats
Arriving at the door.
          WANG CHING-TS'ENG, 19th Century

LI T'AI–PO MEDITATES

Li Po climbed the Flowery Mountain
As far as the Peak of the Fallen Precipice.
Gazing upward, he said:
"From this little space my breath can
    reach the God Star."
He sighed, regretting his irresolution, and
    thought:
"Hsieh T'iao alarms people with his
    poetry.
I can only scratch my head
And beseech the Green Heaven
To regard me."
          HO PING-SHOU, 19th Century

PAIR OF SCROLLS

Shoals of fish assemble and scatter,
Suddenly there is no trace of them.

The single butterfly comes —
Goes —
Comes —
Returning as though urged by love.
          HO SHAO-CHI, 19th Century

TWO PANELS

By the scent of the burning pine-cones,
I read the "Book of Changes."

Shaking the dew from the lotus-flowers,
I write T'ang poetry.
          LIANG T'UNG-SHU, 19th Century

THE RETURN

He is a solitary traveller
Returning to his home in the West.
Ah, but how difficult to find the way!
He has journeyed three thousand *li*.
He has attended an Imperial audience at
    the Twelve Towers.
He sees the slanting willows by the road
With their new leaves,
But when he left his house
His eyes were dazzled by the colours
Of Autumn.
What darkness fills them now!
He is far from the Autumn-bright hills
He remembers.
The spread of the river before him is
    empty,
It slides — slides.
          LI HAI-KU, 19th Century

EVENING CALM

The sun has set.
The sand sparkles.
The sky is bright with afterglow.
The small waves flicker,
And the swirling water rustles the stones.
In the white path of the moon,
A small boat drifts,
Seeking for the entrance
To the stream of many turnings.
Probably there is snow
On the shady slopes of the hills.
          KAO SHIH-CHI, 19th Century

FISHING PICTURE

The fishermen draw their nets
From the great pool of the T'an River.
They have hired a boat
And come here to fish by the reflected
    light
Of the sunken sun.
          TA CHUNG-KUANG, 19th Century

SPRING. SUMMER. AUTUMN

The stream at the foot of the mountain
Runs all day.
Even far back in the hills,
The grass is growing;
Spring is late there.
From all about comes the sound

Of dogs barking
And chickens cheeping.
They are stripping the mulberry-trees,
But who planted them?

What a wind!
We start in our boat
To gather the red water-chestnut.
Leaning on my staff,
I watch the sun sink
Behind the Western village.
I can see the apricot-trees
Set on their raised stone platform,
With an old fisherman standing
Beside them.
It makes me think
Of the Peach-Blossom Fountain,

And the houses
Clustered about it.

Let us meet beside the spring
And drink wine together.
I will bring my table-lute;
It is good
To lean against
The great pines.
In the gardens to the South,
The sun-flowers are wet with dew;
They will pick them at dawn.
And all night
In the Western villages
One hears the sound of yellow millet
being pounded.

LI HAI-KU, 19th Century

NOTES

SONGS OF THE MARCHES

NOTE 1

It is the Fifth Month,
But still the Heaven-high hills
Shine with snow.

The Fifth Month corresponds to June.
(See Introduction.) The Heaven-high
hills are the T'ien Shan Mountains,
which run across the Northern part of
Central Asia and in places attain a
height of 20,000 feet.

NOTE 2

Playing "The Snapped Willow."

The name of an old song suggesting
homesickness; it is translated in this
volume. It was written during the Liang
Dynasty (A.D. 502–557). References to
it are very common in Chinese poetry.

NOTE 3

So that they may be able in an instant to
rush upon the Barbarians.

The Chinese regarded the tribes of Central Asia, known by the generic name of
Hsiung Nu, as Barbarians, and often
spoke of them as such. It was during the
reign of Shih Huang Ti (221–206 B.C.)
that these tribes first seriously threatened
China, and it was to resist their incur-

sions that the Great Wall was built.
They were a nomadic people, moving
from place to place in search of fresh
pasture for their herds. They were
famous for their horsemanship and always fought on horseback.

NOTE 4

And the portrait of Ho P'iao Yao
Hangs magnificently in the Lin Pavilion.

Ho P'iao Yao was a famous leader whose
surname was Ho. He was given the
pseudonym of P'iao Yao, meaning "to
whirl with great speed to the extreme
limit," because of his energy in fighting.
His lust for war was so terrible that the
soldiers under him always expected to be
killed. After his death, the Emperor Wu
of Han erected a tomb in his honour. It
was covered with blocks of stone in order
that it might resemble the Ch'i Lien
Mountains, where Ho P'iao Yao's most
successful battles had been fought.
The Lin Pavilion was a Hall where the
portraits of distinguished men were hung.

NOTE 5

The Heavenly soldiers arise.

The Chinese soldiers were called the
"Heavenly Soldiers" because they fought

for the Emperor, who was the Son of Heaven.

NOTE 6

Divides the tiger tally.

A disk broken in half, worn as a proof of identity and authority. The General was given one half, the Emperor kept the other.

NOTE 7

The Jade Pass has not yet been forced.

In order to reach the Central Asian battle-fields, the soldiers were obliged to go out through the Jade Pass, or Barrier, which lay in the curious bottle-neck of land between the mountain ranges which occupy the centre of the continent.

NOTE 8

They seized the snow of the Inland Sea.

The Inland, or Green Sea, is the Chinese name for the Kokonor Lake lying West of the Kansu border.

NOTE 9

They lay on the sand at the top of the Dragon Mound.

The Dragon Mound is a high ridge of land on the Western border of Shensi, now comprising part of the Eastern boundary of Kansu. The native accounts say that the road encircles the mountains nine times, and that it takes seven days to make the ascent. "Its height is not known. From its summit, one can see five hundred *li*. To the East, lie the homes of men; to the West, wild wastes. The sound of a stone thrown over the precipice is heard for several *li*."

NOTE 10

All this they bore that the Moon Clan.

Name of one of the Hsiung Nu tribes. It was this tribe, known to Europeans under name of Huns, who overran Europe in the Fifth Century.

THE PERILS OF THE SHU ROAD

NOTE 11

During the reign of the T'ang Emperor, Hsüan Tsung (A.D. 712–756), better known as Ming Huang, a rebellion broke out under An Lu-shan, an official who had for many years enjoyed the Emperor's supreme favour. Opinions among the advisers to the throne differed as to whether or not the Emperor had better fly from his capital and take refuge in the province of Szechwan, the ancient Shu. Li T'ai-po strongly disapproved of the step, but as he was no longer in office could only express his opinion under the guise of a poem. This poem, which the Chinese read in a metaphorical sense, describes the actual perils of the road leading across the Mountains of the Two-Edged Sword, the only thoroughfare into Szechwan. Li T'ai-po's counsel did not prevail, however, and the Emperor did actually flee, but not until after the poem was written.

NOTE 12

No greater undertaking than this has been since Ts'an Ts'ung and Yü Fu ruled the land.

These were early Rulers. Ts'an Ts'ung was the first King of Shu, the modern Szechwan. He was supposed to be a descendant of the semi-legendary Yellow Emperor.

NOTE 13

But the earth of the mountain fell and overwhelmed the Heroes so that they perished.

An historical allusion to five strong men sent by the King of Shu to obtain the daughters of the King of Ch'in.

NOTE 14

Above, the soaring tips of the high mountains hold back the six dragons of the sun.

The sun is supposed to drive round the Heavens once every day in a chariot drawn by six dragons and driven by a charioteer named Hsi Ho.

NOTE 15

The gibbons climb and climb.

Gibbons, which are very common in this part of China, are a small species of tailless ape, thoroughly arboreal in their habits. They make the woods sound with unearthly cries at night, and are unsurpassed in agility and so swift in movement as to be able to catch flying birds with their paws.

NOTE 16

This is what the Two-Edged Sword Mountains are like!

In this range, the mountains are so high, the cliffs so precipitous, and the passes so few, that it was almost impossible to devise a means of crossing them. The Chinese, however, had invented an ingenious kind of pathway called a "terraced" or "flying" road. Holes are cut in the face of the cliffs, and wooden piles are mortised into them at an angle. Tree trunks are then laid across the space between the tops of the piles and the cliff wall, making a corduroy road, the whole being finally covered with earth. These roads are so solidly built that not only people, but horses and even small carts, can pass over them. As there are no railings, however, travel upon them is always fraught with more or less danger.

LOOKING AT THE MOON AFTER RAIN

NOTE 17

Half of the moon-toad is already up.

In Chinese mythology, the *ch'an*, a three-legged toad, lives in the moon and is supposed to swallow it during an eclipse. The toad is very long-lived and grows horns at the age of three thousand years. It was originally a woman named Ch'ang O, who stole the drug of Immortality and fled to the moon to escape her husband's wrath. The moon is often referred to as *ch'an*, as in the poem.

NOTE 18

The glimmer of it is like smooth hoar-frost spreading over ten thousand li.

A *li* is a Chinese land measurement, equal to about one third of a mile.

THE LONELY WIFE

NOTE 19

There is only the moon, shining through the clouds of a hard, jade-green sky.

The term "jade," in Chinese literature, includes both the jadeites and nephrites. These semi-transparent stones are found in a great variety of colours. There are black jades; pure white jades, described by the Chinese as "mutton fat"; jades with brown and red veins; yellow jades tinged with green; grey jades with white or brown lines running through them; and, most usual of all, green jades, of which there are an infinite number of shades.

These green jades vary from the dark, opaque moss-green, very much like the New Zealand "green-stone," to the jewel jade called by the Chinese *fei ts'ui*, or "kingfisher feather," which, in perfect examples, is the brilliant green of an emerald. As a result of this range of colouring, the Chinese use the term "jade" to describe the tints seen in Nature. The colours of the sky, the hills, the sea, can all be found in the jades, which are considered by the Chinese as the most desirable of precious stones. In addition to its employment in actual comparison, the word "jade" is very often used in a figurative sense to denote anything especially desirable.

NOTE 20

Beneath the quilt of the Fire-Bird, on the bed of the Silver-Crested Love-Pheasant.

The Fire-Bird is the *Luan*, and the Love-Pheasant the *Fêng Huang*; both are fully described in the table of mythical animals in the Introduction.

NOTE 21

As the tears of your so Unworthy One escape and continue constantly to flow.

The term "Unworthy One" is constantly used by wives and concubines in speaking of themselves to their husbands or to the men they love.

NOTE 22

As I toss on my pillow, I hear the cold, nostalgic sound of the water-clock.

The clepsydra, or water-clock, has been used by the Chinese for many centuries, one can still be seen in the North Worshipping Tower in Canton, and another in the "Forbidden" portion of the Peking Palace, where the dethroned Manchu Emperor lives. The following account of the one in Canton is taken from the "Chinese Repository," Volume XX, Page 430: "The clepsydra is called the 'copper-jar water-dropper.' There are four covered jars standing on a brickwork stairway, the top of each of which is level with the bottom of the one above it. The largest measures twenty-three inches high and broad and contains seventy catties or ninety-seven and a half pints of water; the second is twenty-two inches high and twenty-one inches broad; the third, twenty-one inches high and twenty broad; and the lowest, twenty-three inches high and nineteen inches broad. Each is connected with the other by an open trough along which the water trickles. The wooden index in the lowest jar is set every morning and afternoon at five o'clock, by placing the mark on it for these hours even with the cover through which it rises and indicates the time. The water is dipped out and poured back into the top jar when the index shows the completion of the half day, and the water is renewed every quarter."

THE PLEASURES WITHIN THE PALACE

NOTE 23

From little, little girls, they have lived in the Golden House.

The "Golden House" is an allusion to a remark made by the Emperor Wu of Han who, when still a boy, exclaimed that if he could marry his lovely cousin A-chiao he would build a golden house for her to live in.

Palaces were often given most picturesque names, and different parts of the precincts were described as being of "jade" or some other precious material, the use of the word "golden" is, of course, in this case, purely figurative.

The organization of the Imperial seraglio, which contained many thousands of women, was most complicated, and the ladies belonged to different classes or ranks.

There was only one Empress, whose title was *Hou*, and, if the wife of the preceding monarch were still alive, she was called *T'ai Hou*, or Greater Empress. These ladies had each their own palace. Next in rank came the principal Imperial concubines or secondary wives called *Fei*. As a rule, there were two of them, and they had each their palace and household. After them came the *P'in* described as "Imperial concubines of first rank," or maids of honour, who lived together in a large palace and who, once they had attained this rank, could never be dispersed. (See Note 69.) The ladies of the Court are often spoken of as *Fei-P'in*. Of lower rank than these were the innumerable Palace women called *Ch'ieh*, concubines or handmaids. The use of the word is not confined to the inmates of the Palace, as ordinary people may have *ch'ieh*. Little girls who were especially pretty, or who showed unusual promise, were often sent to the Palace when quite young, that they might become accustomed to the surroundings while still children. (See Introduction.)

NOTE 24

They are lovely, lovely, in the Purple Hall.

The Ruler of Heaven lives in a circumpolar constellation called the Tzŭ Wei, Purple Enclosure; therefore the Palace of his Son, the Ruler of Earth, is called "Purple."

NOTE 25

Their only sorrow, that the songs and wu dances are over.

The wu dance is a posturing dance for which special, very elaborately embroidered dresses with long streamers are worn. As the arms move, these scarves float rhythmically in the air.

NOTE 26

Changed into the five-coloured clouds and flown away.

The allusion to the five-coloured clouds is to the beautifully variegated clouds, bright with the five colours of happiness, upon which the Immortals ride.

WRITTEN IN THE CHARACTER OF A BEAUTIFUL WOMAN

NOTE 27

Bright, bright, the gilded magpie mirror.

Magpies are the birds of happiness. There is an old story of the Gold Magpie which tells that, ages ago, a husband and wife, at parting, divided a round mirror between them, each keeping a half as a guarantee of fidelity. Unhappily, the wife forgot her marriage vows, and to her horror the half circle she had kept turned into a magpie and flew away. Since then, magpies are often carved on mirror backs as reminders and warnings.

NOTE 28

I sit at my dressing-stand, and I am like the Green Fire-Bird who, thinking of its mate, died alone.

The Green Fire-Bird is a fabulous creature who is regarded as the embodiment of every grace and beauty. It is the essence of the Fire God, and reference to it in stories of love and marriage are frequent. One of the most popular of these tales is that of a King of India who caught a beautiful bird with green plumage of an extraordinary brilliance. He valued it greatly, and had an exquisite gold cage made for it. For three years it lived in captivity, and not a sound came from it in all that time. At last, the King, who was much puzzled at its silence, consulted his wife, saying: "Is the creature dumb?" She replied: "No, but every creature is the same, when it meets one of its own species it will speak." Not knowing how to obtain a mate for the Green Fire-Bird, the King placed a large mirror in its cage. The *Luan* danced with joy, uttered strange cries, and then, with all its strength, hurled itself against its own reflection and fell dead.

NOTE 29

My tears, like white jade chop-sticks, fall in a single piece.

It was said of the Empress Ch'ên of Wei (403-241 B.C.) that her tears fell so fast they formed connected lines like jade chop-sticks.

SONGS TO THE PEONIES

NOTE 30

The "Songs to the Peonies" were written on a Spring morning when Ming Huang, accompanied by Yang Kuei-fei, his favourite concubine, and his Court, had gone to see the blooms for which he had a passion. As he sat, admiring the flowers and listening to the singing of the Palace maidens, he suddenly exclaimed: "I am tired of these old songs, call Li Po." The poet was found, but unfortunately in a state best described by the Chinese expression of "great drunk." Supported by attendants on either side of him, he appeared at the pavilion, and while Yang Kuei-fei held his ink-slab, dashed off the "Songs." She then sang them to the air, "Peaceful Brightness," while the Emperor beat time.

The "Songs" compare Yang Kuei-fei to the Immortals and to Li Fu-jên, a famous beauty of whom it was said that "one glance would overthrow a city, a second would overthrow the State." But, unluckily, Li T'ai-po also brought in the name of the "Flying Swallow," a concubine of the Han Emperor Ch'êng, who caused the downfall of the noble Pan Chieh-yü (see Note 155) and is looked upon as a despicable character. Kao Li-shih, the Chief Eunuch of the Court, induced Yang Kuei-fei to take this mention as an insult, and it finally cost Li T'ai-po his place at Court.

In the third "Song," there is an allusion to the Emperor under the figure of the sun. When his presence is removed, the unhappy, jealous flowers feel as if they were growing on the North side of the pavilion.

Yang Kuei-fei, the most famous Imperial concubine in Chinese history, was a young girl of the Yang (White Poplar) family, named Yü Huan, or Jade Armlet; she is generally referred to as Yang Kuei-fei or simply Kuei-fei — Exalted Imperial Concubine.

The Chief Eunuch brought her before the T'ang Emperor, Ming Huang, at a time when the old man was inconsolable from the double deaths of his beloved Empress and his favourite mistress.

The story goes that the Emperor first

saw Yang Yü Huan, then fifteen years old, as she was bathing in the pool made of stone, white as jade, in the pleasure palace he had built on the slopes of the Li Mountains. As the young girl left the water, she wrapped herself in a cloak of open-work gauze through which her skin shone with a wonderful light. The Emperor immediately fell desperately in love with her, and she soon became chief of the Palace ladies wearing "half the garments of an Empress."

Yang Kuei-fei rose to such heights of power that her word was law; she had her own palace, her own dancing-girls, and was even allowed by the doting monarch to adopt the great An Lu-shan, for whom she had a passion, as her son. Her follies and extravagancies were innumerable, and her ill-fame spread about the country to such an extent that, when the rebellion broke out (see Note 37), the soldiers refused to fight until she had been given over to them for execution.

After her death, Ming Huang spent three inconsolable years as an exile in Szechwan, and his first act upon his return to the Empire, which he had ceded to his son, was to open her grave. It was empty. Even the gold hair-ornaments, and the half of a round gold box shared with the Emperor as an emblem of conjugal unity, had gone; the only trace of the dead beauty was the scent-bag in which she had kept these treasures. "Ah," cried the unhappy monarch, "may I not see even the bones of my beloved?" In despair, he sent for a Taoist magician and begged him to search the Worlds for Yang Kuei-fei. The Taoist burnt charms to enlist the help of the beneficent spirits, but these were unsuccessful in their search. He finally sat in contemplation until the "vital essence" issued from his body and descended to the World of Shades. Here the names of all the spirits who have passed from the World of Light are entered in classified books, but that of Yang Kuei-fei was not among them. The demon in charge insisted that if the name were not entered, the spirit had not arrived, and the Taoist left, sad and crest-fallen.

He then reflected that if she really were not at the Yellow Springs below,

she must be among the Immortals above. He therefore ascended to Paradise, and asked the first person he met, who happened to be the Weaving Maiden who lives in the sky, for news of the lost lady. The Weaving Maiden was most uncommunicative, and found much difficulty in believing that Ming Huang, who had consented to the execution of Yang Kuei-fei, really mourned her death, but finally admitted that she was living among the Immortals on the island of P'êng Lai in the Jade-grey Sea, and even assisted the Taoist to find her. She then told Yang Kuei-fei that, if she still loved the Emperor, the Moon Mother might be induced to allow a meeting at the full moon on the fifteenth day of the Eighth Month. Yang Kuei-fei eagerly assented, and giving the Taoist a gold hairpin and her half of the round box as a proof of her existence, begged that he hasten back to the World of Light and make all arrangements with her lover.

Accordingly, at the appointed time, the Taoist threw his fly-whip into the air, creating a bridge of light between this world and the moon, and over this Ming Huang passed. Yang Kuei-fei was waiting for him. She stood under the great cassia-tree which grows in the moon, and was surrounded by fairies.

The story, which is often sung to the air "Rainbow Skirts and Feather Collar," goes on to relate that the Weaving Maiden was moved to deep pity by their joy at meeting and arranged with the Jade Emperor, Chief Ruler of the Heavens, that the pair, immortalized by their great love, should live forever in the Tao Li Heaven.

THE PALACE WOMAN AND THE DRAGON ROBES

NOTE 31

I ponder his regard, not mine the love
Enjoyed by those within the Purple
  Palace.

The Palace woman of Ch'in was evidently one of the lower ranks of concubines who lived in the Women's Apartments and only appeared when sent for, not in one of the palaces given to ladies of higher rank.

NOTE 32

If floods should come, I also would not leave.
A bear might come and still I could protect.

Now that she is no longer needed, she reflects sadly on the stories of two heroines whose behaviour she would gladly have emulated. These are Fên Chieh-yü, a favourite of the Han Emperor, Yüan, who once protected her master with her own body from the attack of a bear which had broken out of its cage; and Liu Fu-jên, concubine of King Chao of Ch'u. It is told of Liu Fu-jên that one day she went with the King to the "Terrace by the Stream," where he told her to wait for him until he returned from the capital. While she waited, the river rose, but she refused to leave unless by Imperial command. By the time this arrived she was drowned.

NOTE 33

Of serving Sun and Moon.

The "Sun and Moon" are the Emperor and Empress.

THE NANKING WINE–SHOP

NOTE 34

In the wine-shops of Wu, women are pressing the wine.

Wine made from grain is fermented for several weeks in tubs and then strained or "pressed" through cloths. It is not red, like wine from grapes, but either a shade of yellow or pure white. Wines made from grapes, plums, apples, pears, lichis, and roses, are sometimes used, but are not nearly so strong as the decoctions from grains.

FENG HUANG T'AI

NOTE 35

The silver-crested love-pheasants strutted upon the Pheasant Terrace.

About A.D. 493, three strange and beautiful birds were noticed inside the city walls of Nanking, then called the "City of the Golden Mound." At first, the people did not suspect the identity of the birds, but when they saw that all the other birds assembled and appeared to be paying homage to the strangers, they realized that the visitors were the famous *Fêng Huang*. (See table of mythical birds in Introduction.) The terrace was built to commemorate the occasion.

NOTE 36

Here also, drifting clouds may blind the Sun.

The drifting clouds are supposed to be the evil courtiers who have poisoned the mind of the Emperor, i.e. the Sun, against Li T'ai-po.

THE NORTHERN FLIGHT

NOTE 37

The An Lu-shan rebellion, which broke out during the reign of the T'ang Emperor, Ming Huang, was very nearly successful, and, if the leader had not been assassinated in A.D. 757 by his son, might have caused the overthrow of the dynasty. As it was, the Emperor, having fled to Szechwan — a step strongly deprecated by Li T'ai-po in the poem, "The Perils of the Shu Road" (see Note 11) — abdicated in favour of *his* son, Su Tsung, who crushed the rebellion. The poem refers to the time when it was at its height, and the Emperor's forces were flying to the North.

NOTE 38

The rushing whale squeezes the Yellow River;
The man-eating beasts with long tusks assemble at Lo Yang.

During the rebellion, both sides of the Yellow River were lined with rebels, the population was obliged to fly, and the country was devastated as if a whale had rushed up the river and caused it to overflow its banks.
The "beasts" are fabulous creatures called *tso chih*, with tusks three feet long, who delight in eating the flesh of men. Li T'ai-po uses them meta-

phorically for the rebels who are threatening the capital.

NOTE 39

When, before our glad faces, shall we see
the Glory of Heaven?

The Emperor, under the usual figure of
the Sun.

THE CROSSWISE RIVER

NOTE 40

I say the Crosswise River is terrible.
The savage wind blows as if it would
overturn the Heaven's Gate Mountains.

The "Crosswise River" is that section of
the Yangtze which flows past steep cliffs
in Anhwei. The "Heaven's Gate Mountains" tower above, making a sharp defile.

NOTE 41

From the beginning of things, the Ox
Ledge has been more dangerous than
the Standing Horse Hill.

A very swift current runs past the Ox
Ledge, and boats are obliged to wait for
daylight before attempting to breast it.
The Standing Horse Hill, so called from
its resemblance to a standing horse, is
above a reach of the Yangtze where the
river is comparatively tranquil.

NOTE 42

Is the Eighth Month tide-bore of Chêkiang
equal to this?

The Ch'ien T'ang River in Chêkiang is
famous for its bore, or tidal wave. During the autumnal equinox, this bore sometimes attains a height of twenty feet and
more.

CH'ANG KAN

NOTE 43

I could not yet lay aside my face of
shame;
I hung my head, facing the dark wall.

In China, little girls are supposed to hide
their faces at the suggestion of marriage.

NOTE 44

I often thought that you were the faithful man who clung to the bridge-post.

A certain Wei Shêng had a great reputation for sincerity and reliability, which
was put to proof on an occasion when
he had an appointment with a lady to
meet on a bridge. The lady did not come.
But, in spite of the fact that the waters
rose to a flood, Wei Shêng would not
leave. Finally, as he stood there clinging
to the bridge-post to keep himself firm,
the waves engulfed him and he was never
seen again.

NOTE 45

That I should never be obliged to ascend
the Looking-for-Husband Ledge.

A hill on the banks of the Yangtze, so
called because of a legend that, many
centuries ago, a wife, whose husband
had been away for several years, went
daily to watch for his returning sail. In
the end, she was turned to stone on the
spot where she had kept her vigil.

NOTE 46

To the Ch'ü T'ang Chasm and the
Whirling Water Rock of the Yü River
Which, during the Fifth Month, must
not be collided with;
Where the wailing of the gibbons seems
to come from the sky.

The Ch'ü T'ang is the first of the three
noted chasms in the upper reaches of the
Yangtze. At the point where the River
Yü empties into the Yangtze, there is a
great rock which, when uncovered, is
more than two hundred feet high. In
the Fifth Month (June) the water from
the melting snows of the Tibetan mountains causes the river to rise to such an
extent that the rock is covered, which
makes it especially dangerous to navigation. The height of the cliffs on either
side of the gorge is so tremendous that
the wailing of the gibbons (see Note 15)
in the woods above sounds as though it
came from the sky.

NOTE 47

I will not go far on the road to meet you.
I will go straight until I reach the Long
Wind Sands.

The Long Wind Sands are many a day's
journey from the village of Ch'ang Kan,
which stands just outside the South Gate

of Nanking. What the lady implies is that she will go to "the ends of the earth" to meet her returning husband.

SORROW DURING A CLEAR AUTUMN

NOTE 48

I climb the hills of Chiu I.

The Chiu I, or "Nine Peaks," lie to the South of the Tung T'ing Lake into which the three divisions of the Hsiang River debouch after having united.

NOTE 49

I go by the "Bird's Path."

A term very often used for steep mountain paths.

NOTE 50

I think much of fishing for a leviathan from the Island of the Cold Sea.

The legend referred to at the end of the poem is as follows: A group of five islands in the Pi Hai, the Jade-grey Sea, were inhabited by the Immortals, who found themselves very uncomfortable as these islands, instead of standing firmly, rose and fell in the most disconcerting manner. The Immortals therefore applied to the Jade Emperor for assistance, and he commanded fifteen leviathans, three to each island, to raise their heads and support the islands, thus keeping them from rocking. All was well until a man from the Elder Dragon Country appeared and with one cast of his line caught six of the monsters, the result being that two of the islands toppled over and sank in the sea. The three which remain are known as the "Three Hills of the Immortals." This tale has become proverbial, and people who are disappointed in their ambition say "I have no rod with which to catch a leviathan."

POIGNANT GRIEF DURING A SUNNY SPRING

NOTE 51

I feel as one feels listening to the sound of the waters of the Dragon Mound in Ch'in.

(See Note 9.)

NOTE 52

The gibbons wailing by the Serpent River.

(See Note 15.)

NOTE 53

I feel as the "Shining One" felt when she passed the Jade Frontier, As the exile of Ch'u in the Maple Forest.

Two allusions which suggest homesickness. The "Shining One" is Chao Chün. (See Note 79.) The exile of Ch'u is Ch'ü Yüan, the famous statesman. (See Note 62.)

TWO POEMS WRITTEN TO TS'UI (THE OFFICIAL)

NOTE 54

In both these poems, Ts'ui is compared to T'ao Yüan-ming, author of "Once More Fields and Gardens," published in this volume. T'ao is the ideal of the educated scholar, who prefers a life in the fields to any official post. Many stories are told of him. He planted five willows in front of his house, and is therefore often spoken of as the "Teacher of the Five Willows." He was so fond of music that he declared he could imagine the sweet sounds of the *ch'in*, and often carried about a stringless instrument over which he moved his hands. The *ch'in*, or table-lute, is fully described in Note 114.

WIND–BOUND AT THE NEW FOREST REACH

NOTE 55

To-day, at dawn, see the willows beyond the White Gate.

The White Gate is the Western Gate. The points of the compass are governed by colours, elements, mythological beasts, and seasons, thus:

East: Green. Wood. The Blue-green Dragon. Spring. South: Red. Fire. The Vermilion Bird. Summer. West: White. Metal. The White Tiger. Autumn. North: Black. Water. The Black Warrior. Winter. Centre: Yellow. Earth.

DRINKING ALONE IN THE MOONLIGHT

NOTE 56

But we will keep our appointment by the far-off Cloudy River.

The Cloudy River is the Chinese name for the Milky Way.

NOTE 57

There would be no Wine Star in Heaven.

The Wine Star is a constellation composed of three stars, to the North of the Dipper.

NOTE 58

There should be no Wine Springs on Earth.

The Wine Springs lie, one in Kansu, and one in Shansi. The water of the one in Kansu is supposed to taste like wine, that of the one in Shansi is used in the making of wine.

RIVER CHANT

NOTE 59

Jade flageolets and pipes of gold.

The Chinese flageolet is a tube measuring a little more than a foot in length. It has five holes above, one below, and one at the end through which it is played. They are now made of bamboo, but formerly were made of copper, jadestone, or marble, as such materials were considered less liable to be affected by the weather.

NOTE 60

The Immortal waited,
Then mounted and rode the yellow crane.

Tou Tzŭ-an, who had attained Immortality by living a life of contemplation, was transported to the Taoist Paradise by a crane so old that it had turned yellow.

NOTE 61

Rather would he be followed by the white gulls.

This line refers to a story from a book treating of Taoist subjects long supposed to have been written by a philosopher called Lieh Tzŭ, but this is now known to have been a Second Century forgery. A translation of the story reads: "The man who lived by the sea loved the sea-gulls. Every day, as the sun rose above the horizon, the birds from the sea assembled in hundreds and flew about. His father said: 'I hear the sea-gulls follow you and fly round you. Catch some in your hands and bring them to me that I too may enjoy them.' The next day the birds from the sea all performed the posturing dance in the air, but did not descend."

NOTE 62

The *tzŭ* and *fu* of Ch'ü P'ing hang suspended like the sun and moon.

The *tzŭ* and *fu* are two irregular forms of verse, they are referred to in the Introduction in the part dealing with versification. Ch'ü P'ing is another name for Ch'ü Yüan, a famous poet and statesman who lived 332–295 B.C. (See Introduction.)

NOTE 63

I could move the Five Peaks.

The sacred mountains of the "four quarters" and the nadir (or the four points of the compass and the centre of the earth). They are the T'ai Shan in the East, the Hua Shan in the West, the Hêng Shan in the South, and the Sung Shan in the centre.

SEPARATED BY IMPERIAL SUMMONS

NOTE 64

The Emperor commands; three times the summons. He who left has not yet returned.

The official has not responded quickly to the summons from the capital, so the messenger has been obliged to come three times. Upon the third occasion, the official realizes that the matter is urgent and prepares to depart the next day at sunrise, before the messenger can have reached the Palace on his return journey.

NOTE 65

Our thoughts will be with each other. I must ascend the Looking-for-Husband Hill.

(See Note 45.)

NOTE 66

You must not imitate Su Ch'in's wife and not leave your loom.

Su Ch'in, who lived in the Fourth Century B.C., was away from home many years; when he returned, his wife took no notice whatever, and did not even leave the loom at which she sat weaving cloth.

A WOMAN SINGS TO THE AIR: "SITTING AT NIGHT"

NOTE 67

I sit, sit in the North Hall.

The "North Hall" is a term for the Women's Apartments, which always lie farthest from the Great Gate placed in the South wall of the house.

NOTE 68

Then, though my Lord sang ten thousand verses which should cause even the dust on the beams to fly, to me it would be nothing.

It is said that when Yü Kung, a man of the State of Lu who lived during the Han Dynasty, sang, the sounds were so exquisite that even the dust on the beams flew. "To cause the dust on the beams to fly" has therefore become a current saying.

THE PALACE WOMAN AND THE SOLDIERS' COOK

NOTE 69

Once the Unworthy One was a maiden of the Ts'ung Terrace.

The Ts'ung Terrace referred to by the sad lady who, in the dispersal of the Palace women (see Introduction), had fallen to such a low degree, stood in the Palace of King Chao, who lived at the time of the "Spring and Autumn Annals," many centuries before our era.

A BEAUTIFUL WOMAN ENCOUNTERED ON A FIELD–PATH

NOTE 70

Down comes the riding-whip, straight down — it strikes the Five Cloud Cart.

The Immortals used Five Coloured Clouds to ride upon, therefore the term, "Five Cloud Cart," has become a complimentary expression for a cart or carriage in which a beautiful young woman is travelling.

HEARING A BAMBOO FLUTE IN THE CITY OF LO YANG

NOTE 71

I hear "The Snapped Willow."

An allusion to the old song suggesting homesickness. (See Note 2.)

THE RETREAT OF HSIEH KUNG

NOTE 72

Hsieh Kung is the honorary title of the poet, Hsieh T'iao, who lived in the Fifth Century A.D. Li T'ai-po, who greatly admired him, constantly quoted his poems, and expressed a wish to be buried on the Spring-green Mountain where Hsieh Kung had lived. Some accounts say that he was first buried elsewhere, but that afterwards his body was removed and put where he desired.

A TRAVELLER COMES TO THE OLD TERRACE OF SU

NOTE 73

The old Imperial Park — the ruined Terrace — the young willows.

Early in the Fifth Century B.C., Fu Ch'ai, King of Wu, built the Ku Su Terrace to please Hsi Shih, one of the most famous beauties in history. It was nearly two miles long, and took three years to build. Its foundations can still be traced on the hills near Soochow, which was the capital of Wu.

THE REST–HOUSE ON THE CLEAR WAN RIVER

NOTE 74

I love the beauty of the Wan River.

A little river near Ning Kuo-fu in Anhwei.

NOTE 75

Really, one cannot help laughing to think that, until now, the rapid current celebrated by Yen
Has usurped all the fame.

The philosopher Yen Kuang (*circa* A.D. 25) is better known as Yen Tzŭ-ling. The river in which he loved to fish was the Hsin An.

ANSWER TO AN AFFECTIONATE INVITATION FROM TS'UI FIFTEEN

NOTE 76

A party of friends who are in the habit of meeting each other constantly are called by numbers according to age. The same custom is used to distinguish members of a family. (See Introduction.)

NOTE 77

You have the "bird's foot-print" characters.

Writing is supposed by the Chinese to have been invented by Ts'ang Chieh, a minister of the Yellow Emperor (2698–2598 B.C.) who, having "observed the shapes of things in the heavens and the forms of things on earth, also the footprints of birds and beasts on the sand and mud," suddenly conceived the idea of pictographic writing. It is highly complimentary to speak of a person's writing as being like the "bird's footprints."

NOTE 78

You suggest that we drink together at the Lute Stream.

The Ch'in Ch'i T'ai (Table-lute Stream Terrace) was a stone terrace where a famous player of the table-lute, who is said to have attained Immortality, lived. The legend is that he took a small dragon in the form of a carp from the Ch'in stream and kept it for a month, when it changed its shape into that of a dragon and ascended to Heaven.

THE HONOURABLE LADY CHAO

NOTE 79

Moon over the houses of Han, over the site of Ch'in.

Ch'in was the name of the State which overcame all the others and welded China into a homogeneous Empire instead of a loose federation. (See Introduction.) The lady Chao lived during the Han Dynasty.

Wang Ch'iang, known to posterity as Chao Chün, the "Brilliant-and-Perfect," lived in the First Century B.C. The daughter of educated parents, she was brought up in the strictest Confucian principles; in the words of the Chinese, she "did not speak loudly nor did she look beyond the doors, indeed, even within the house, she only walked the path which led to her mother's room. Her ears were closed to all distracting sounds, therefore her heart and mind were pure like those of the Immortals." Her father regarded her as a precious jewel, and although many suitors presented themselves, he refused to listen to their proposals, and finally, when she was seventeen, sent her to the capital as an offering to the Han Emperor Yüan.

Upon arriving at the Palace, the young girl was housed in the inner rooms, among the innumerable Palace women who lived there in constant hope of a summons to the Imperial presence. As the Son of Heaven never went into this part of his Palace, it was customary to catalogue the inmates and submit their portraits to him, a form of procedure which led to much bribery of the Court painters. The rigid principles of the daughter of the Wang clan forbade her to comply with this Palace custom, and the portrait which appeared in the catalogue was such a travesty of her exquisite features that it roused no desire in the Imperial breast.

Five or six dreary years passed, and the young girl remained secluded in the Women's Apartments. Shortly before this time, one of the Hsiung Nu tribes (see Note 3) had surrendered to the Chinese soldiers, and as a proof of good faith on both sides had received permission to serve as a frontier guard. Soon after, the head of the tribe sent to ask that one of Yüan Ti's ladies be sent him as Queen. The catalogue was consulted, and the decision fell upon the daughter of Wang as being the one among the Palace women who had the fewest charms. She was therefore told to prepare herself for a journey to the desert wastes where she would reign over a savage Central Asian tribe, a prospect terrifying to one brought up in strict seclusion among people of refinement.

Custom demanded that, on the point of departure, she should appear before the Son of Heaven in order to thank her Imperial Master for his kind thoughtfulness in thus providing for her future, and then be formally handed over to the envoys. The audience was held in one of the secondary halls, the Court was assembled, the envoys stood ready, and the lady entered. At the sight of her unusual beauty, every one was thunderstruck, even the Emperor could hardly refrain from springing off the Dragon Throne and speaking to her. But it was too late; there was nothing to be done. The most beautiful of all the Palace women was pledged to the Hsiung Nu Khan, the escort which was to convey her over the Jade Pass waited, and soon the broken-hearted girl set off.

Fury and consternation spread through the Palace; a camel laden with gold was sent in pursuit; the guilty painter, Mao Yen-shou, was executed and his immense fortune sent as a consolation to the Wang family; but all this could not save the young girl from her fate. The Hsiung Nu ambassador refused to ransom her, and she passed out through the Jade Barrier to the "Yellow Sand Fields" beyond.

The banished daughter of Han was true to the principles in which she had been schooled. Instead of committing suicide, as she longed to do, she submitted to the will of the Five Great Ones —Heaven, Earth, The Emperor, her Father, and her Mother — and performed her duties as a wife to the best of her ability in spite of the homesickness from which she suffered perpetually.

Upon the death of the Khan, she felt that her hour of deliverance had at last come and that she was at liberty to poison herself. This she did, and was buried in the desert, but the mound over her grave remained always green.

Because of her pseudonym "Brilliant-and-Perfect," she is often referred to as "Ming Fei," the "Bright Concubine." Allusions to her story always suggest homesickness.

THINKING OF THE FRONTIER

NOTE 80

I desire to send the "harmonious writings."

Letters from wives to husbands are often spoken of as though they carried sweet sounds.

NOTE 81

He who wears the dragon robes delighted in the sweetly-scented wind of her garments.

Appointments for the Emperor's use were all spoken of as "dragon" appointments, and the analysis of the character which means the Emperor's love, is a dragon under a roof. Ladies' clothes were, and are to-day, kept in cupboards in which scented woods were burned, therefore as the long sleeves of their dresses swayed back and forth a sweet perfume came from them.

NOTE 82

How was it possible for the "Flying Swallow" to snatch the Emperor's love?

The "Flying Swallow" was a famous concubine. (See Note 30.)

RECITING VERSES BY MOONLIGHT

NOTE 83

I suggest that men meditate at length on Hsieh Hsüan Hui.

A reference, under a pseudonym, to the poet Hsieh T'iao, whose work Li T'ai-po so much admired. (See Note 72.) "Hsüan" is applied to the names of gods to indicate that they deserve praise and worship, and "Hui" means bright, splendid, or a ray of the sun.

PASSING THE NIGHT AT THE WHITE HERON ISLAND

NOTE 84

At dawn, I left the Red Bird Gate.

An allusion to the bird which rules the South. (See Note 55.)

NOTE 85

At sunset, I came to roost on the White Heron Island.

According to the Chinese commentary, this island lies "in the heart's centre of the river, three *li* West of the district of the Golden Mound (Nanking), and many herons collect there."

NOTE 86

And the longing in my heart is like that for the Green Jasper Tree.

This tree grows in the Taoist Paradise, supposed to lie in the K'un Lun Mountains. Those who eat its blossoms become immortal.

ASCENDING THE THREE CHASMS

NOTE 87

These are the famous chasms of the Yangtze River, between Ichang and Chungking. Their names are: "The Terrifying Barrier," "The Sorceress Gorge," and "The Western Sepulchre." Joined together in one great line of precipitous cliffs, they are among the extraordinary natural objects of the world and are most awe-inspiring.

NOTE 88

The Serpent River runs terribly fast. The Serpent River can be suddenly exhausted.

A reference to the fact that, although the water of the river flows with terrible speed while the snow waters are coming down, during the Winter it is very low, and many parts are quite dry. (See Note 46.)

NOTE 89

Three dawns shine upon the Yellow Ox. Three sunsets — and we go so slowly.

A cliff beneath which are rapids so difficult and dangerous to pass that the utmost care must be taken in navigating them. Boats ascending this stretch of the river often take several days to pass a given point. (See Introduction for a description of the Yangtze River and travel upon it.)

PARTING FROM YANG, A HILL MAN

NOTE 90

You are going to pick the fairy grasses And the shooting purple flower of the *ch'ang p'u*.

"Hill men" is a term applied to those who desire to become worthy of joining the ranks of the Immortals, and for this reason lead a life of contemplation among the hills. The fairy grasses and the *ch'ang p'u* (see table of plants in Introduction) both grow in the Taoist Paradises.

NOTE 91

Riding down from the green-blue Heaven on a white dragon.

The dragon is one of the steeds of the Immortals.

THE SERPENT MOUND

NOTE 92

The mercy of the Sainted Lord is far greater than that of Han Wên Ti. The Princely One had pity, and did not appoint you to the station of the Unending Sands.

The allusion is to an incident which occurred in the Second Century B.C. when a famous scholar named Chia was sent to Ch'ang Sha, literally "Unending Sands," and died there of the damp vapours.

ON THE SUBJECT OF OLD TAI'S WINE–SHOP

NOTE 93

Old Tai is gone down to the yellow Springs.

The Yellow Springs lie in the nether world, where spirits go after death.

NOTE 94

There is no Li Po on the terrace of Eternal Darkness.

This world is known as the World of Light, and below it lies the World of Shades, where the sun never shines.

DRINKING IN THE T'AO PAVILION

NOTE 95

The garden pool lies and shines like the magic gall mirror.

The Magic Gall Mirror was a square of glittering, polished metal supposed to possess the miraculous power of betraying the thoughts of all who looked into it, by making the heart and "five viscera" visible. The ferocious First Emperor used it to examine his numerous Palace women, and those who, by a palpitating gall, showed lack of faith were put to death.

NOTE 96

The Golden Valley is not much to boast of.

A beautiful garden built by the rich and eccentric Shih Ch'ung (died A.D. 300) for his favourite concubine Lü Chu.

A SONG FOR THE HOUR WHEN THE CROWS ROOST

NOTE 97

This is the hour when the crows come to roost on the Ku Su Terrace.

(See Note 73.)

NOTE 98

The silver-white arrow-tablet above the gold-coloured brass jar of the water-clock marks the dripping of much water.

(See Note 22.)

POEM SENT TO THE OFFICIAL WANG OF HAN YANG

NOTE 99

The shrill notes of the bamboo flute reached to Mien and O.

Mien and O are the ancient names for Hankow and Wuchang.

DRINKING ALONE ON THE ROCK IN THE RIVER OF THE CLEAR STREAM

NOTE 100

Perpetually casting my fish-line like Yen Ling.

Yen Ling is one of the names of the philosopher Yen Kuang. (See Note 75.)

THE REST–HOUSE OF DEEP TROUBLE

NOTE 101

At Chin Ling, the tavern where travellers part is called the Rest-House of Deep Trouble.

An inn fifteen *li* South of the district in which Chin Ling (Nanking) stands.

NOTE 102

Like K'ang Lo I climb on board the dull travelling boat.

K'ang Lo is a pseudonym for the poet Hsieh Ling-yün, who lived in the Fifth Century A.D.

NOTE 103

I hum softly "On the Clear Streams Flies the Night Frost."

A line from one of Hsieh Ling-yün's poems.

NOTE 104

It is said that, long ago, on the Ox Island Hill, songs were sung which blended the five colours.

The "five colours" are blue-green, yellow, carnation, white, and black. Anything that is perfectly harmonious is spoken of figuratively as being blended like the five colours.

Rapids flow past the Ox Island Hill on the Yangtze, which is not to be confused with the Ox Hill at the Yangtze Gorges.

NOTE 105

Now do I not equal Hsieh, and the youth of the House of Yüan?

Yüan Hung lived in the time of the Chin Dynasty. His poems were both erudite and beautiful, but his extreme poverty forced him to take a position on a freight-boat plying up and down the Yangtze. One night, as the vessel lay below the dangerous Ox Rapids waiting for daylight, the official of the place, a learned man named Hsieh Shang, heard Yüan Hung's exquisite songs and was so delighted that he insisted upon the singer's accompanying him to the Official Residence. Here the days and nights were passed in conversation, and upon Yüan Hung's departure, Hsieh gave him much silver and gold, and eventually used his influence to enable the young man to become an official. Since then all men have heard of Yüan Hung. Li T'ai-po compares his lonely lot to that of the youth who possessed a faithful friend.

NOTE 106

The bitter bamboos make a cold sound, swaying in the Autumn moonlight.

The ancient Chinese divided bamboos into two classes: the bitter and the tasteless.

THE "LOOKING–FOR–HUSBAND" ROCK

NOTE 107

In the attitude, and with the manner, of the woman of old.

A reference to a legend of a woman who was turned to stone. (See Note 45.)

NOTE 108

Her resentment is that of the Woman of the Hsiang River.

O Huang and her sister Nü Ying were the wives of Shun, the "Perfect Emperor" (2317–2208 B.C.). When he died, and was buried near the Hsiang River,

they wept so copiously over his grave that their tears burned spots on the bamboos growing there, and thus was the variety known as the "spotted bamboo" created. Eventually the despairing ladies committed suicide by throwing themselves into the river.

NOTE 109

Her silence that of the concubine of the King of Ch'u.

Ts'u Fei, concubine of the King of Ch'u, was much distressed because her lord was of a very wild disposition, and only took pleasure in hunting and such pursuits. She constantly expostulated with him on his mode of life, but at last, finding that all her entreaties were in vain, she ceased her remonstrances and sank into a silence from which she could not be roused.

AFTER BEING SEPARATED FOR A LONG TIME

NOTE 110

Besides there are the "embroidered character letters."

In the Fourth Century A.D., a lady, whose maiden name was Su, embroidered a long lament of eight hundred and forty characters in the form of a poetical palindrome and sent it to her husband who was exiled in Tartary.

BITTER JEALOUSY IN THE PALACE OF THE HIGH GATE

NOTE 111

The Heavens have revolved. The "Northern Measure" hangs above the Western wing.

The "Northern Measure" is the Chinese name for the "Dipper," and on the fifteenth day of the Eighth Month, when it can be seen sinking in the West before bed-time, a festival is held. This is essentially a festival for women, who object to being parted from their husbands at that time. Incense is burned to the full moon, and many fruits and seeds, all of a symbolical nature denoting the desire for posterity, are set out for the moon goddess.

NOTE 112

In the Gold House, there is no one.
(See Note 23.)

ETERNALLY THINKING OF EACH OTHER

NOTE 113

The tones of the Chao psaltery begin and end on the bridge of the silver-crested love-pheasant.

"The *sê*, or psaltery, is made on the principle of the *ch'in*, and like that instrument has been made the subject of numerous allegorical comparisons. The number of strings has varied . . . but the *sê* now in use has twenty-five strings. Each string is elevated on a movable bridge. These bridges represent the five colours: the first five are blue, the next red, the five in the middle are yellow, then come five white, and lastly five black." ("Chinese Music," by J. A. Van Aalst.) The most desirable specimens came from Chao, a place in Shensi. The allusion to the love-pheasants is, of course, symbolical. By it, the lady says that this instrument is only properly used for love-songs, with the implication that it is therefore impossible for her to play it now.

NOTE 114

I wish I could play my Shu table-lute on the mandarin duck strings.

The *ch'in*, or table-lute, lies on a table like a zither, and is played with the fingers. It is "one of the most ancient instruments, and certainly the most poetical of all. . . The dimensions, the number of strings, the form, and whatever is connected with this instrument had their principles in Nature. Thus the *ch'in* measured 3.66 feet, because the year contains a maximum of 366 days; the number of strings was five, to agree with the five elements; the upper part was made round, to represent the firmament; the bottom was flat, to represent the ground; and the thirteen studs stood for the twelve moons and the intercalary moon. The strings were also subjected to certain laws. The thickest string was composed of two hundred and forty threads and represented the Sovereign."

("Chinese Music," by J. A. Van Aalst.) The "Shu table-lute" is an allusion to Ssŭ Ma Hsiang-ju, a great poet and musician, who was a native of Shu. The mandarin ducks are emblems of conjugal love, and in speaking of them the wife expresses the wish that her husband were present to listen.

NOTE 115

I wish my thoughts to follow the Spring wind, even to the Swallow Mountains.

The Yen Jan, or "Swallow Mountains," lie several thousand miles to the West of Ch'ang An, in Central Asia.

NOTE 116

The neglected lamp does not burn brightly.

The lamps were little vessels filled with natural oil, upon which floated a vegetable wick. Unless constantly attended to, and this was the duty of the woman, the flame was small and insignificant.

SUNG TO THE AIR: "THE MANTZŬ LIKE AN IDOL"

NOTE 117

The Mantzŭ are an aboriginal tribe still living in the far Southwest of China. It was here that Li T'ai-po was to have been exiled had not the sentence been commuted. (See Introduction.)

NOTE 118

Instead, for me, the "long" rest-houses alternate with the "short" rest-houses.

On the "great roads," which we should speak of as paths, rest-houses for the convenience of travellers are erected every five *li* (a *li* is one-third of a mile). These are called "short road rest-houses" and are simply shelters. There are also "long road rest-houses" every ten *li*, where the care-takers serve travellers with tea and food, and which are equipped with altars and idols for the convenience of the pious.

AT THE YELLOW CRANE TOWER, TAKING LEAVE OF MENG HAO JAN

NOTE 119

I take leave of my dear old friend at the Yellow Crane Tower.

Mêng Hao Jan (A.D. 689–740) was a very famous poet, one of whose idiosyncrasies was riding a donkey through the snow in a search for inspiration.

The Yellow Crane Tower is still standing at Wuchang. (see Note 60.)

THOUGHTS FROM A THOUSAND LI

NOTE 120

Li Ling is buried in the sands of Hu.

Li Ling lived during the reign of the Emperor Wu of Han (140–87 B.C.) at a time when the Hsiung Nu tribes were very troublesome. He penetrated far into the Hsiung Nu country, with a force of only five thousand infantry, and was there surrounded by thirty thousand of the enemy. After his men had exhausted their arrows, he was forced to surrender, and spent the rest of his life as a captive in Central Asia.

NOTE 121

Su Wu has returned to the homes of Han.

Su Wu lived during the same period as did Li Ling, and was sent by the Emperor Wu upon a mission of peace to the Hsiung Nu. By the time he reached the Court of the Khan, however, relations between the Chinese and the Barbarians were again strained, and he was taken prisoner. Various attempts were made to induce him to renounce his allegiance to China; he was thrown into prison and subsisted for days on the moisture which he sucked from his clothes, but all efforts to undermine his loyalty failed, and eventually he was sent to tend sheep on the grazing fields of the steppes. Years passed, Wu Ti, the "Military Emperor," died, and his successor Chao Ti made peace with the Central Asian tribes and sent envoys to ask for the return of the faithful Su Wu. The Khan replied that he was dead, but the envoy was able to answer that such could not be the case, as, not long before, the Emperor himself while hunting in his park had shot a wild goose, and had found a letter from Su Wu tied to its leg. The loyal official was therefore sent back to China. He had gone off in the prime of life; when

he returned, in 86 B.C., he was a broken-down, white-haired old man.

NOTE 122

Wild geese are flying.
If I sent a letter — so — to the edge of Heaven.

An allusion to the story of Su Wu. Letters anxiously awaited are often spoken of as "wild-goose" letters.

SAYING GOOD–BYE TO A FRIEND WHO IS GOING TO THE PLUM–FLOWER LAKE

NOTE 123

I bid you good-bye, my friend, as you are going on an excursion to the Plum-Flower Lake.

This lake lies about seven miles Southwest of Nanking. The legend is that, many years ago, a raft loaded with flowering plum-trees sank in it, and ever since, during the plum-blossom season, the lake is covered with plum-trees in bloom.

NOTE 124

Nevertheless you must not omit the wild-goose letter.

(See Notes 121 and 122.)

NOTE 125

Or else our knowledge of each other will be as the dust of Hu to the dust of Yüeh.

Hu is the Mongols' country to the North and West of the Great Wall, and Yüeh is the province of Chêkiang in the Southeast of China.

A DESULTORY VISIT TO THE FENG HSIEN TEMPLE AT THE DRAGON'S GATE

NOTE 126

I had already wandered away from the People's Temple.

The Fêng Hsien is one of the so-called Chao Ti temples. These temples are erected by the people, not by Imperial command, which fact is proclaimed on an inscription written on a horizontal board placed over the main doorway. The Fêng Hsien temple stands in the Lung Mên, or Dragon Gate, a defile cut in the mountains of Honan by the great Yü when he drained the Empire about two thousand B.C. (See Introduction.) He is supposed to have been helped by a dragon who, with one sweep of its tail, cleft the mountain range in two, thus forcing the river I, a confluent of the Lo which is one of the tributaries of the Yellow River, to confine itself within the defile through which it runs in a series of rapids.

CROSSING THE FRONTIER — II

NOTE 127

Sadness everywhere. A few sounds from a Mongol flageolet jar the air.

The Hsiung Nu soldiers, against whom the Chinese are fighting, are so near that the sounds of their flageolets can be plainly heard.

NOTE 128

Perhaps it is Ho P'iao Yao.

(See Note 4.)

AT THE EDGE OF HEAVEN. THINKING OF LI T'AI–PO

NOTE 129

The demons where you are rejoice to see men go by.

The demons are of the man-eating variety, the *yao kuai*. (See table of supernatural beings in Introduction.)

NOTE 130

You should hold speech with the soul of Yüan.

Ch'ü Yüan (see Note 62) drowned himself in the Mi Lo River.

SENT TO LI PO AS A GIFT

NOTE 131

And remembering Ko Hung, you are ashamed.

Ko Hung, author of "Biographies of the Gods," lived in the Fourth Century A.D.

Although very poor, he pursued his studies with such zeal that he became an official. Having heard that the cinnabar, from which the Elixir of Immortality is distilled, came from Cochin China, he begged to be appointed to a magistracy in the South in order that he might obtain a supply for experimental purposes on the spot. Arrived in Kwangtung, he spent his time on Mount Lo Fo attempting to compound this elixir, and so, working at his experiments, passed into a tranquil sleep. When his friends went to wake him, they found his clothes empty. Ko Hung had ascended to the Taoist Paradise to live forever among the Immortals.

HEARING THE EARLY ORIOLE

NOTE 132

The sun rose while I slept. I had not yet risen.

The poem alludes to the curious Chinese custom of holding Imperial audiences at dawn. This custom was persisted in until the fall of the Manchu Dynasty in 1912. One of the most noticeable peculiarities of Peking in Imperial days was the noise during the night, which never seemed to stop. Officials came to the Palace in their carts, while it was still dark, in order to be ready for the audience at dawn. It is clear from Po Chü-i's poem that he is no longer in office, since, although the sun has risen, he himself is still in bed.

AN IMPERIAL AUDIENCE AT DAWN

NOTE 133

At the first light of the still-concealed sun, the Cock-man, in his dark-red cap, strikes the tally-sticks and proclaims aloud the hour.

The Cock-men, whose badge of office was a red cloth, were in charge of the water-clock, and their business was to announce the time of day. Near the water-clock were kept bamboo tallies, one for each division of the twenty-four hours. (See Introduction.) When the arrow of the water-clock registered the moment of the change from one division into another, the Cock-man on duty struck the appropriate tally-stick on a stone set for that purpose beside the door of the Palace. At sunrise, which took place during the hour of the monkey (three to five A.M.) or during the hour of the cock (five to seven A.M.), according to the season, he gave a loud, peculiar cry to warn the inmates of the Palace that day had come.

NOTE 134

At this exact moment, the Keeper of the Robes sends in the eider-duck skin dress, with its cloud-like curving feather-scales of kingfisher green.

The "Keeper of the Robes" was one of the six offices instituted by the Ch'in Dynasty (255–209 B.C.), the other five were those of the "Imperial Head-dresses," "Food-stuffs," "Washing Utensils," "Sitting Mats," and "Writing Materials." Robes were, and are, made from the skins of the various eider-ducks found in Northern Asia. The king eider's head is blue; the Pacific eider's black and green; while the spectacled eider has a white line round the eye, which accounts for its name. The feathers are so close and soft that garments made of them feel exactly like fine fur.

NOTE 135

In the Ninth Heaven, the Ch'ang Ho Gate opens.

The Ninth Heaven is the centre from which the points of the compass radiate, and it is there that the first of all the entrances to Heaven, the Ch'ang Ho Gate, stands.

NOTE 136

The immediately-arrived sun tips the "Immortal Palm."

The "Immortal Palm" was a very tall bronze pillar which the Emperor Wu of Han erected in the grounds of the Variegated Colours Palace. On the top was a colossal hand, with the fingers curled up so that the falling dew might be caught in the palm, for, of course, the ancient Chinese firmly believed that dew fell. As dew was the drinking-water of the Immortals, to drink it was to advance a step on the road to Immortality. The hand was brightly polished, and was one of the first objects about the Palace to glitter when the sun rose.

SEEKING FOR THE HERMIT OF THE WEST HILL

NOTE 137

On the Nothing-Beyond Peak, a hut of red grass.

Huts were built of a certain hill grass, now very rare. It turns red in the Autumn, and is fine and strong like wire.

NOTE 138

I look into the room. There is only the low table and the stand for the elbows.

Much of the furniture in the T'ang period was like that used now by the Japanese. It was customary to sit on the floor and write at a low table, and the use of the elbow-stand was general.

NOTE 139

I have received much — the whole doctrine of clear purity.

The principles of Taoism are called literally "the clear pure doctrines."

NOTE 140

Why should I wait for the Man of Wisdom?

An allusion to the eccentric Wang Hui-chih (A.D. 388), who made a long journey through the snow to see a friend, but missed him.

FAREWELL WORDS TO THE DAUGHTER OF THE HOUSE OF YANG

NOTE 141

The sacredness with which the Chinese regard their family ties is well known, but it is perhaps not realized that the Chinese conception of the duties owed to friendship entails very great responsibilities. If a friend dies, it is a man's duty to see that his family do not suffer in any way. Wei Ying-wu is probably addressing the daughter of some dead friend whom he has brought up in his own family, or she may be a poor relation on his mother's side, but that she is not his own daughter is clear from the fact that her clan name differs from his, which is Wei.

ONCE MORE FIELDS AND GARDENS

NOTE 142

But for thirteen years it was so I lived.

The text reads "three ten," which is the way the Chinese say "thirty," but native commentaries state that it should read "ten three," or thirteen. This is far more in accordance with the facts of T'ao's life. He lived A.D. 365–427, and although he became an official, he soon resigned his post, saying that he "could not crook the hinges of his back for five pecks of rice a day." (See Note 54.)

NOTE 143

Mine is a little property of ten *mou* or so.

A *mou* is a Chinese land measurement which is equal to about one-sixth of an acre.

SONG OF THE SNAPPED WILLOW

NOTE 144

A very famous song written during the Liang Dynasty (A.D. 502–557). Allusions to it always suggest homesickness.

THE CLOUDY RIVER

NOTE 145

There seems to be no doubt that although King Hsüan of Chou (876–781 B.C.) is not mentioned by name in the poem, which appears in the "Decade of Tang" division of the "Book of Odes," he is the King referred to. All the old Chinese commentators agree in ascribing the authorship to a certain Jêng Shu, an officer of the Court during the reign of that monarch, who is known to have had a profound admiration for the King. Opinions differ as to the exact date of

the great drought, but the standard chronology places it in the sixth year of King Hsüan's reign, 812 B.C. This ode illustrates the Chinese conception of kingship described in the Introduction.

NOTE 146

How the Cloudy River glitters.

The Chinese call the Milky Way the "Cloudy" or "Silver River." Stars are peculiarly bright and glittering during a drought.

NOTE 147

My stone sceptres and round badges of rank.

The badges of office were made of nephrite. There are references in both the "Book of History" and the "Book of Odes" to the fact that, after certain sacrifices, they were buried in the ground. In this case, the sacrifices had been performed so often that the supply of these tokens was exhausted.

NOTE 148

I myself have gone from the border altars to the ancestral temples.

According to Confucius, the sacrifices to Heaven and Earth were performed at the border altars, and those to the ancestors took place at the temples especially provided for the purpose.

NOTE 149

Hou Chi could do no more.

Hou Chi is the deity of grain, and from him King Hsüan was supposed to be descended.

NOTE 150

Shang Ti does not look favourably upon us.

Shang Ti, literally the "Above Emperor," is the supreme ruler of the universe. Earthly Emperors receive the decree which empowers them to rule from him.

NOTE 151

Why should I not be terrified
Since all the ancestral sacrifices will be ended?

To the Chinese, this is the greatest calamity that can be conceived, since without these sacrifices the ancestral spirits would suffer greatly, and might visit their wrath upon their descendants.

NOTE 152

Drought, the Demon of Drought, has caused these ravages.

The "Book of Spirits and Prodigies" states that in the Southern regions there is a hairy man, two or three cubits in height, with eyes in the top of his head and the upper part of his body bare. His name is Po. He runs with the speed of the wind, and in whatever part of the country he appears a great drought ensues.

NOTE 153

I offered the yearly sacrifices for full crops in good time.

It was the custom for the King to pray and make offerings to Shang Ti during the first Spring month (February), in order to propitiate this chief of the Chinese pantheon and ensure good harvests from the grain then being sown. During the first Winter month (November), other prayers and sacrifices were offered to the "Honoured Ones of Heaven" (the sun, moon, and stars) for a blessing on the year to follow.

NOTE 154

I neglected not one of the Spirits of the Four Quarters of the Earth.

Sacrifices of thanksgiving to the "Spirits of the Four Earth Quarters" were offered at the end of the harvest season.

SONG OF GRIEF

NOTE 155

Pan Chieh-yü, the talented and upright concubine of the Han Emperor, Ch'êng, is one of the ladies most often referred to in literature. She was supplanted by the beautiful, but unscrupulous, "Flying Swallow," who accused her to the Emperor of denouncing him to the *kuei* and the *shên*. (See table of supernatural beings in Introduction.) The Emperor, therefore, sent for Pan Chieh-yü who, kneeling before him, answered him as follows: "The Unworthy One of the

Emperor has heard that he who cultivates virtue still has not attained happiness or favour. If this be so, for him who does evil what hope is there? Supposing that the demons and spirits are aware of this world's affairs, they could not endure that one who was not faithful to the Emperor should utter the secret thoughts hidden in the darkness of his heart. If they are not conscious of this world's affairs, of what use would the uttering of those secret thoughts be?" Then, rising, she left the Imperial presence, and immediately obtained permission to withdraw from the Palace. Not long after, she sent the Emperor "A Song of Grief," and ever since then the term, "Autumn Fan," has been used to suggest a deserted wife.

LETTER OF THANKS FOR PRECIOUS PEARLS

NOTE 156

One of the ladies swept aside by Yang Kuei-fei (see Note 30) was the lovely Chiang Ts'ai-p'in, known as the "Plumblossom" concubine. As she liked to differ from other people, she painted her eye-brows in the shape of wide cassialeaves instead of the thin-lined willowleaf, or "moth-antennae," the form so much used. Soon after her departure from the Palace, some pearls were received as tribute, and the Emperor, who still had a lingering regard for "Plumblossom," sent them to her in secret. She refused the pearls, and returned them to the Emperor with this poem.

SONGS OF THE COURTESANS

NOTE 157

I gaze far — far — for the Seven Scents Chariot.

The "Seven Scents Chariot" was a kind of carriage used in old days by officials, and only those above the sixth rank might hang curtains upon it. It was open on four sides, but covered with a roof. The hubs of the wheels were carved. Ai Ai implies that the person she is waiting for is very grand indeed.

THE GREAT HO RIVER

NOTE 158

This song, which was probably written about 600 B.C., has been elucidated by succeeding generations of Chinese commentators in the following tale.

The lady was a daughter of the Lord of Wei, and the divorced wife of the Lord of Sung. On the death of her husband, her son succeeded to his father's position as feudal chief of Sung. Because of her divorce, the unhappy woman, who was deeply attached to her son, was forbidden to enter Sung, where he lived.

AN EVENING MEETING

NOTE 159

The lamp-flower falls.

An old-fashioned Chinese lamp was simply a vessel in which a vegetable wick floated in oil. If the oil were very pure, the wick burned evenly, leaving no charred end; but if the oil were impure, the wick turned red-hot and formed a glowing tip called the "lamp-flower." Its appearance was looked upon as the happy omen which foretold a lover's speedy return.

NOTE 160

But what is the rain of the Sorceress Gorge.

The Sorceress Gorge (see Note 87) is often referred to in a figurative sense, as it is in this poem. The allusion is to the story of a certain prince who dreamed that a fairy, calling herself the Lady of the Sorceress Mountain, came and passed the night with him. On leaving in the morning, she told him that it was she who ruled over the clouds and rain, which would ever after be symbols of their love. Since then, the expression "clouds and rain" has become a euphemism for the relation of the sexes.

CALLIGRAPHY

NOTE 161

The writing of Li Po-hai.

Li Yung (A.D. 678–747) is often called "Po Hai" in reference to a place where he held office. He was a person who displayed astounding knowledge at a very early age, and rose to be very powerful. When he was nearly seventy, he was overthrown by the machinations of his enemies and put to death. He wrote many inscriptions and was noted for his beautiful, spirited calligraphy.

NOTE 162

The writing of Chia, the official.

Chia K'uei (A.D. 30–101) was known as the "Universal Scholar." He was an eminent teacher, and many of his pupils came from great distances. As the payment he received was in grain, he was said to "till with his tongue," which phrase has now become a current expression for earning one's living as a teacher. Toward the end of his life, he was appointed Imperial historiographer. He was also a noted calligraphist. (See Note 77.)

ONE GOES A JOURNEY

NOTE 163

Are many sweet-olive trees.

The *olea fragrans*, or sweet-olive, is employed in a metaphorical sense to denote literary honours. Scholars who have successfully passed their examinations are said to have gathered its branches.

ON THE CLASSIC OF THE HILLS AND SEA

NOTE 164

Because the Yellow Emperor considers them of importance.

The Yellow Emperor is one of the five mythical sovereigns who ruled *circa* 2697 B.C. and is supposed to have reigned a hundred years.

THE SOLITARY TRAVELLER

NOTE 165

He has attended an Imperial audience at the Twelve Towers.

The "Twelve Towers" was a palace built by Ming Huang (see Note 30) for the use of his ladies. It was an attempted imitation of a building supposed to have been erected by the Yellow Emperor (see Note 164) for the use of the Immortals. By his reference to it, one knows that the traveller has been to Court and is returning disappointed.

SPRING. AUTUMN. WINTER

NOTE 166

It makes me think
Of the Peach-Blossom Fountain

An Allusion to a well-known allegory, "The Peach-Blossom Fountain," by T'ao Yüan-ming. (See Note 142.) It tells how a fisherman, who was lost, found himself in a beautiful country where the people all wore strange clothes of very old-fashioned cut. On coming home, he told many stories about this enchanting land, but it could never be found again. The gods had permitted the fisherman to return for a short time to the "peach-blossom" days of his youth, although he could never remember the road he had taken, nor even point out the direction in which it lay.

A CRITICAL FABLE

A CRITICAL FABLE

There are few things so futile, and few so
amusing,
As a peaceful and purposeless sort of per-
using
Of old random jottings set down in a
blank-book
You've unearthed from a drawer as you
looked for your bank-book,
Or a knife, or a paper of pins, or some
string.
The truth is, of course, you'd forgotten
the thing,
And all those most vitally important
matters
You'd preserved in its pages, just so many
spatters
The wheel of your life kicked up in its
going
Now hard as caked clay which nothing
can grow in.
You raved over Browning, you discovered
Euripides,
You devoured all volumes from which
you could snip idees
(No one need be surprised if I use the
vernacular
Whenever it fits with my text. It's spec-
tacular.
And what smacks of the soil is always
tentacular.) —
Astronomy, botany, palaeontology —
At least you acquired their strange
phraseology
And sprinkled it over your pages in
splendid
Profusion because that was what learned
men did.
Having one day observed daffodils in a
breeze,
You remarked as a brand new impression
that these
Were beautiful objects; you filled quite
two pages
With extracts from all those esteemed
personages
Whose sayings are found to their last
adumbrations

In any respectable book of quotations.
You heard "Pelléas" and returned in a
stutter
Of rainbows, and bomb-shells, and thin
bread and butter;
And once every twenty odd entries or so
You recorded a fact it was worth while
to know.
At least that was my blank-book, but one
of the "odds"
Gave my memory two or three violent
prods.
All it said was, "A gentleman taking a
walk
Joined me, and we had a most interest-
ing talk."
We certainly did, that day is as clear
As though the whole circumstance hap-
pened this year.
But when it did happen I really can't say,
The note is undated, except it says
"May."
Put it, then, when you please, whether
last year or next
Doesn't matter a rap, and I shall not be
vext
If you think I just dreamt it, it swings
in my mind
Without root or grapple, a silvery kind
Of antique recollection, that's all I can
say.
The sun shone — I remember the scat-
tering way
It shot over the water. I stood by the
river.
The plane-trees were just leaving out,
and a shiver
Of sunshine and shadow twitched over
the grass.
I was poking at something which glit-
tered like glass
With my stick when he joined me and
stopped, and his stick
Helped mine to dig up a long bottle-
neck, thick,
Brown, and unctuous with memories of
cool yellow wine
From some pre-bellum vineyard on the
banks of the Rhine:

"Berncastler Doctor," perhaps, or "Rüde-
sheimer,"
"Liebfraumilch" — could nomenclature
e'er be sublimer?
Our dear cousins German are so deftly
romantic!
Where else in the world could you meet
such an antic
Idea, such a sentiment oily to dripping?
The pot-bellied humbugs deserved a good
whipping,
With their hands dropping blood and
their noses a-sniffle
At some beautiful thought which burns
down to mere piffle.
As I rubbed off the dirt (with my hand-
kerchief mainly)
I may have said this, for he answered
profanely,
"But their wine was damned good!" I
dispensed from replying,
His remark held a truth I was far from
denying.
The gentleman seemed not to notice my
silence.
"Could you tell me," said he, "if that
place a short mile hence
Is really Mt. Auburn?" I said that it was,
And went on to observe I had never had
cause
To enter its precincts. "Why should
you?" he said.
"The living have nothing to say to the
dead.
The fact is entirely the other way round,
The dead do the speaking, the living are
wound
In the coil of their words." Here I
greatly demurred.
His expression provoked me to utter
absurd
Refutations. "In America," I began,
with bombast —
"Tut! Tut!" the old gentleman smiled,
"not so fast.
Fold your wings, young spread-eagle, I
merely have stated
That the worth of the living is much
over-rated.
I was young once myself some few decades ago,
And I lived hereabouts, so I really should
know.
This parkway, for instance, is simply
man's cheating

Himself to believe he is once more re-
peating
A loveliness ruthlessly uptorn and lost.
Those motor-horns, now, do you really
dare boast
That they please you as marsh-larks' and
bobolinks' songs would?
That shaven grass shore, is it really so
good
As the meadows which used to be here,
and these plane-trees,
Are they half as delightful as those
weather-vane trees,
The poplars? I grant you they're quaint,
and can please
Like an old gouache picture of some
Genevese
Lake-bordering highway; but it is just
these
Trans-Atlantic urbanities which crowd
out the flavour,
The old native lushness and running-wild
savour,
Of mulleins, and choke-cherries in a con-
fusion
So dire that only small boys dared in-
trusion;
Beyond, where there certainly wasn't a
shore,
Just tufted marsh grass for an acre or
more
Treading shiftily into the river and
drowned
When the high Spring tides turned in-
conveniently round,
And on the tall grass-sprays, as likely as
not,
Red-winged blackbirds, a score of them,
all in one spot.
This place had the taste which a boy
feels who grapples
With the season's first puckery, bitter-
green apples.
Regardless of consequence, he devours
and crams on
Does maturity get the same joy from a
damson?
But we, with our marshes, were more
certainly urban
Than you with your brummagem, gilded
suburban,
Which you wear like a hired theatrical
turban.
You move and you act like folk in a play
All carefully drilled to walk the same way.

Just look at this bottle, we were free in
    my time,
But I think you are free of nothing but
    rhyme."
Now here was a thing which was not to
    be stood,
Poking fun at a soul just escaped from
    the wood
Like a leaf freshly burst from the bark of
    its twig.
"At least," I said hotly, "we are not a
    mere sprig
From an overseas' bush, and we don't
    care a fig
For a dozen dead worthies of classic
    humdrum,
And each one no bigger than Hop-o'-my-
    thumb
To our eyes. Why, the curse of their
    damned rhetoric
Hangs over our writers like a school-
    master's stick."
Here I caught a few words like "the dead
    and the quick."
I admit I was stung by his imperturba-
    bility
And the hint in his eyes of suppressed
    risibility.
"We are breaking away . . . " Here he
    tossed up the bottle,
Or the poor jagged neck which was left
    of the hot Hell
Container, as I think Mr. Volstead might
    say.
How thankful I am I preceded his day
And remember the lovely, suave lines of
    these flasks.
To piece them together will be one of
    the tasks
Of thirty-third century museum curators,
Subsidized and applauded by keen legis-
    lators.
It flashed in the sun for an instant or
    two,
And we watched it in silence as men al-
    ways do
Things that soar, then it turned and fell
    in chaotic
Uprisings of spray from a sudden aquatic
Suppression beneath the waves of the
    Charles.
"Yet that, like so much, is but one of the
    snarls,"
He dusted his fingers. "And if a man
    flings

His tangles in air, there are so many
    strings
To a single cat's-cradle of impulse, who
    knows
When you pull at one end where the
    other end goes.
We were worthy, respectable, humdrum,
    quite so,
An admirable portrait of one Edgar Poe."
"Oh, Poe was a bird of a different
    feather,
We always rank him and Walt Whitman
    together."
"You do?" The old gentleman tugged at
    his whisker.
"I could scarcely myself have imagined
    a brisker
Sarcasm than that to set down in my
    'Fable.'
I did what I could, but I scarcely was
    able
To throw leaves of grass to Poe's raven
    as sops
For his Cerberus master, who would be
    mad as hops
At a hint of your excellent juxtaposition,
Since that book was not yet in its first
    slim edition.
You remember I said that Poe was three
    parts genius.
As to Whitman, can you think of an ac-
    tion more heinous
Than to write the same book every two
    or three years?
It's enough to reduce any author to tears
At the thought of this crime to the writ-
    ing fraternity.
A monstrous, continual, delaying pater-
    nity.
But I wax somewhat hot, let's have done
    with the fellows.
Your strange estimation has made me
    quite jealous
For those of my time whose secure repu-
    tations
Gave us no concern. These are trifling
    vexations,
But they itch my esteem. Is there really
    not one
You sincerely admire?" "Yes, Miss Dick-
    inson,"
I hastily answered. At this he stopped
    dead
In his walk and his eyes seemed to pop
    from his head.

"What," he thundered, "that prim and
perverse little person
Without an idea you could hang up a
verse on!
Wentworth Higginson did what he could,
his tuition
Was ardent, unwearied, but bore no
fruition.
You amaze me, young man, where are
Longfellow, Lowell,
With Whittier, Bryant, and Holmes? Do
you know well
The works of these men? What of
Washington Irving,
And Emerson and Hawthorne, are they
not deserving
A tithe of your upstart, unfledged admir-
ation?
In the name of the Furies, what's come
to the nation!"
Here I thought it was prudent to say, as
to prose
I was perfectly willing to hand him the
rose.
But I could not admit that our poets
were so backward.
I thought, if he knew them, he'd see
they'd a knack would
Command his respect. For the matter of
liking,
The men he had mentioned might be
each a Viking,
While we, very probably, were merely the
skippers
Of some rather lively and smartish tea-
clippers;
Or, to put it in terms somewhat more
up to date,
Our steamers and aeroplanes might be
first-rate
As carriers for a particular freight.
Each time for its heroes, and he must
excuse
The terms I employed, I'd not meant to
abuse
Our forerunners, but only to speak of a
preference —
Anno Domini merely. So classic a reference
Should cool him, I thought. Here I went
on to better a
Most happy allusion, and continued —
et caetera.
I will not repeat all the soothing remarks

With which I endeavoured to smother
the sparks
Of his anger. Suffice it to say I succeeded
In clouding the issue of what had preceded.
I enjoyed it myself and I almost think he
did.
I admit there was something a trifle
pragmatical
In my method, but who wants the truth
mathematical?
It sours good talk as thunder does cream.
I ignore, for the nonce, a disquieting
gleam
In his eye. "But your critics," he an-
swered demurely,
"For your poets, by-and-by; with your
critics you surely
Surpass what we did. I was not fond of
critics;
If I rightly remember, I gave them some
sly ticks.
I called them, I think, poor broken-
kneed hacks."
"We've advanced," I replied, "to the
office boot-blacks.
We are quite democratic, and the news-
papers think
One man is as good as another in ink.
The fluid that's paid for at so much a
sprinkling
Is a guaranteed product, quite free of all
inkling
That standardized morals, and standard-
ized criticisms,
And a standardized series of cut-and-
dried witticisms,
Are poor stuff to purvey as a full reading
ration,
Though they suit to a T the views of a
nation
Which fears nothing so much as a per-
sonal equation.
Subscribers demand that their thoughts
be retailed to them
So often and plenteously that they be-
come nailed to them
And when travelling are lost if their
journal's not mailed to them.
By this safe and sane rule our newspapers
get on
Without any gambling, since there's
nothing to bet on.
Of course I refer to things of import

Such as stock-exchange news, murders, fashions, and sport,
With a smattering of politics, garbled to fit
Editorial policy; if they admit
Puerilities like music and art, these are extras
Put in to augment, by means of a dexterous
Metropolitan appearance, their own circulation,
For a paper's first duty is self-preservation.
If they will run book columns, why some one must feed them,
And, after all, few take the trouble to read them.
With a pastepot and scissors to cut up his betters
And any young numskull is equal to letters.
He scans what the publisher says on the jacket,
Then the first paragraph and the last, and the packet
Goes off to the second-hand book-shop, the bunch
Polished off in the minutes he's waiting for lunch.
I believe there's no record of any one feeling
As he pockets his pay that he may have been stealing.
The thing would be murder, but that time has gone by
When an author can be made or marred by such fry.
Some good paper is spoiled, that's the long and the short of it."
Here I watched the old gentleman to see what he thought of it.
"There reviews which you speak of have one great advantage,"
He remarked, "they are brief. In our less petulant age
They had not that merit. But I see we agree
On essentials. Yet we had a very few men
Who wielded a passably powerful pen."
"And one woman," I slyly put in. He grimaced.
"That's the second you've dug up and greatly displaced.
Since you criticize thus, do I err if I doubt

Whether you are the boot-black on his afternoon out?"
Fairly touched and I owned it, and let Margaret Fuller
Slide softly to limbo. 'Twas unmanly to rule her
Out of count in this way, but the fish I must fry
Required considerable diplomacy
To keep in the pan and not drop in the fire.
'Twas an expert affair, and might shortly require
I knew not what effort to induce him to grant
That whatever we are is worth more than we aren't.
So I instantly seized on his "very few men"
And assured him that we also, now and again,
Found a youth who was willing to write good reviews
While learning to tickle the publishers' views
And make them believe he was worth while to back.
"The thing after all is a question of knack,
Ten to one if you have it you turn out a quack;
If you don't, and win through, you've arrived without doubt,
But the luck's on your side if you're not quite worn out."
"Good old world," he remarked, as he prodded the ground
With the point of his cane, "I observe it goes round
In the same soothing, punctual way. This pastiche
Of the quite unfamiliar is merely a bleach,
A veneer, acid-bitten, on a colour we knew.
By the way, when it's finished, who reads your review?"
"The fellow who wrote it, on all those occasions
When his fine self-esteem has received some abrasions.
Then the fellow who's written about cons the thing
Over several times in a day till the sting
Of its strictures becomes just the usual pedantic

Outpouring, and its granules of praise
grow gigantic.
Once acquire this excellent trick for
benumbing
What you don't want to hear by an extra
loud strumming
On the things which you do and you
fast are becoming
A real going author. Then there are the
gentry
Who must read reviews to fill out an
entry
In next week's advertisement; and others
peruse
The paper with care to note down its
abuse
Of their dear brother writer, and suck up
each injurious
Phrase to retail with a finely luxurious
Hypocritical pretense of its being unsuitable,
While all the time showing it quite
irrefutable.
Then there are the sisters, and cousins,
and aunts
Of the writer and wrote about; some
sycophants
Who pry into favour by announcing
they've read it,
And praise or deride to heighten their
credit
With the interested person. There are
others who edit
Gossip columns, and who must go
through at a dead-heat
The news of the day for the spicy tid-
bits
And who greatly prefer the more virulent
hits.
By the time we are through, a fairly
large public
Has skimmed through the paper." He
gave a quick flick
To a stone which arose with a circular
twist
And plopped into the river. "But if I
insist
On your people of parts?" "Oh, they
do not exist,"
I assured him, "or only as sparsely as
daisies
In city back-yards. And if one of them
raises
His voice it is drowned in the whirligig
hazes

Of mob murmurings. If these men hold
the key
To the spacious demesne known as pos-
terity
The gate must have shrunk to a postern,
I think.
Every one worth his salt glues his eye to
the chink
'Twixt the frame and the door, but it's
long to keep looking
With never a chance to get even a hook
in
And pull open a door where it's 'Skele-
tons Only.'
A notice designed to make any one lonely.
It stares over the gate in huge letters of
red:
'No person admitted until he is dead.'
Small wonder if some of them cannot
hold out.
As they dwindle away, the watchers, no
doubt,
Feel a sort of cold envy creep through
their contempt.
Then perhaps the door opens and one
is exempt,
Gone over to dust and to fame. As it
slams,
The requiem fraternal, a chorus of
'Damns!'
Cracks the silence a moment. More still
break away,
But the shrivelled remainder waits each
one his day.
It takes marvellous force and persistence
to tarry on
When your own special corpse may be
counted as carrion
And left where it lies to await decom-
posing
While that devilish door shows no sign
of unclosing.
These custodians of keys are ill to rely on
As the last Day of Judgment to the fol-
lowers of Zion.
There are folk who dress up in the very
same guise
And boast of a power that's nothing but
lies.
They shout from their chosen, particular
steeple
Of some weekly review: 'We are surely
the people!
We know what posterity wants, for we
know

What other posterities have wanted, and
so
We affirm confidently the true cut and
fashion
Which the future will certainly dote on
with passion.
There is no need at all of making a fuss
For all generations are exactly like us.
We represent that which is known as the
Vox
Populi, species *Intelligentsia*, or Cocks
Of the Walk on the Dunghill of High
Erudition,
Referred to more elegantly as Fields
Elysian.'
The matter of clocks may be readily
dropped,
Every Ph.D. knows that they long ago
stopped.
What are colleges for with their dignified
massiveness
But just to reduce all time-pieces to
passiveness."
"The picture you draw does not greatly
attract
One who seeks for the absolute even in
fact.
That fanciful bit you put in about clocks
Borders rather too smartly upon paradox.
We had a few poets, and we had a few
colleges,
And something like half of your bundle
of knowledges.
We delivered our lectures and wrote our
lampoons,
And I venture to say that the fire-balloons
Of our verse made as lively a sputter as
yours.
If things are so changed, what, pray, is
the cause?"
I groaned. Poor old gentleman, should I
be tempted
To tell him the fault was that he had
preëmpted,
He and the others, the country's small
stock
Of imagination? The real stumbling-block
Was the way they stood up like Blake's
angels, a chorus
Of geniuses over our heads, no more
porous
Than so much stretched silk; rain, sun,
and the stellar
Effulgences balked by our national um-
brella

Of perished celebrities. To mention a
trifling
Fact, underneath them the air's somewhat
stifling.
Youthful lungs need ozone and, con-
sidering the tent,
No man can be blamed if he punches a
rent
With his fist in the stiff, silken web if he
can.
A feat, I assured him, more horrible than
Cataclysmic tide-waters or Vesuvian
Explosions to all those quaint, straightly-
laced folk
Who allow a man only the freedom to
choke.
"We may buckle the winds and rip open
the sea,
But we mayn't poke a finger at authority."
"A nursery game," the old man spoke
benignly,
"To all school-boys, convention's a matter
divinely
Ordained, and the youngster who feels
himself bold enough
To step out of the ring will soon find
himself cold enough.
To be chips from a hardened old tree
may be crippling,
But it's nothing compared to the lot of
the stripling.
For the sake of the argument, let us
agree
That we were the last surge of life which
the tree
Could produce, that our heart-wood was
long ago rotted,
Our sap-wood decaying, and all our roots
spotted
With fungus; the Spring of our flourishing over,
The first Winter storm would most likely
have rove a
Great cleft through the trunk, and the
next year's out-leaving
Would unbalance the whole without
hope of retrieving.
The gentlest of breezes would then send
it crashing.
Good luck to the striplings if they escape
smashing.
When an oak, having lasted its time, is
once thrown,
What is left are the acorns it cast, and
these grown

Are the forest of saplings in which it lies
prone.
But 'twould be a dull acorn who should
dare to declare
It was sprung only from earth's connec-
tion with air,
The miraculous birth of a marvellous rut.
Such an acorn indeed would be a poor
nut."
He quickened his steps and I followed
along,
Listening partly to him, and partly to the
song
Of the little light leaves in the plane-
trees. Said he,
Stopping short quite abruptly, "I think
it should be
Somewhere about here that a house I
once knew
Used to stand. It was not much to look
at, 'tis true,
But its elms were superb and it had a
fine view
Of the river. A friend of mine owned it,
indeed
He was born here and loved every tree,
every weed.
Circumstance loosed his moorings, but
he came back to die,
To envisage the past with a chill, older
eye,
And dwelt a few years with the bitter-
sweet ghosts
Of his earlier dreams, with the shadowless
hosts
Of the things he had never brought
farther than planning.
How often he wished there were some
way of spanning
The past and the present, to go back
again
And drink to the dregs the austere cup of
pain.
Instead, he allowed the nepenthe of
change
To smother that loneliness by which the
range
Of his soul might have reached to some
highest achievement
Through the vision won out of a grievous
bereavement.
He'd a wit and a fancy, a hint of some
deepness,
An excellent humour quite unmarred by
cheapness,

But somehow his work never got beyond
soundings.
I wonder sometimes if it was his sur-
roundings
Or the fact that he fled them. With a
grim taciturnity,
He admitted no masterpiece owed its
paternity
To him. Now they've pulled down his
house, I suppose.
Thistles spring up and die, and the thistle-
down goes
Anywhere the wind blows it." "Wait,"
I said, "if you mean
James Lowell's house, 'Elmwood,' you
can see it between
That brick porch and that window, and
those are its chimneys.
The grounds are cut up and built over,
their trimness
Is due to that cluster of very new
houses.
In its rather bedraggled condition, it
rouses
My ire each time I come anywhere near
it.
It deserved better treatment." "I fear it!
I fear it!"
He murmured. "Was it lack of success,
or those years
I spent in escaping the tonic arrears
Of a grief not lived through. I cannot
bear more."
He turned and walked rapidly down to
the shore
Of the river and seated himself on the
bank.
Many minutes went by, then he asked
me point-blank
Who were the young poets of the day.
"Since my mood
Will admit no more sorrowful past, be
so good
As to marshal your forces, I shall find it
quite pleasant
To stroll for a little with you in the
present.
So bring them out, lock, stock, and barrel,
the whole of them,
I'm really most anxious to get a good toll
of them.
Recount me their merits, their foibles
and absurdities,
Such a tale is too saccharine without
some acerbities."

His gesture of challenge was so debon-
naire
I could only accept with as devil-may-care
A grace as I could. But our Ostrogothic
Modern manners, I fear, made me seem
sans-culottic,
I know that I felt supremely idiotic.
Still "out of the mouths of the babes and
the sucklings,"
And I was prepared with some brave
ugly ducklings
I was willing to swear would prove to be
swans,
Or, to tone up the metaphor, Bellero-
phons.
At least they'd no fear of a chase round
the paddock
After Pegasus, who "might be lamed by
a bad hock
And so easily mounted" — I can hear
the malicious
Sneers of the critics when one dare be
ambitious
And attempt a bold thing, yet it's hard
to decry a
Flight its existence when above you the
flyer
Is gyrating and plunging on his way to
the zenith,
And he grins the best who at the last
grinneth.
But my unknown old friend seemed to
need no acquainting
With this style of horseflesh, he would
notice my painting,
No chance then at all to confuse him by
feinting.
I must prove that my horse had his quota
of wings,
Was sound wind and limb, that his sidles
and swings
Were no circus parade, that the man who
would stride him
Knew perfectly well why he wanted to
ride him.
That 'twas bareback or die, that the
fellow was game
For whichever result was the end of his
aim.
As I pondered, I harboured no little
aversion
At having embarked on so great an excursion,
Nothing less, be it said, than his total
conversion.

"Come, come," he urged quickly, "you're
taking some time
To trot out your up-to-date dabblers in
rhyme."
I pouted, I think. "Ha! Ha! you're
offended!
Because I said 'dabblers' or because I
pretended
Not to know that rhyme's lost its erst-
while predominance?"
I assured him at once that we gave no
prominence
To rhyme or the lack of it. To which
he said "Good!
We've got somewhere at last; now let's
have the whole brood
In their rareness and rawness. I am
surely no prude,
I shall not be satisfied if you exclude
Any atom of character, any least mood.
Give your men as you see them from
their toes to their chin.
Only, for God's sake, my dear fellow,
begin."
Since he and I wanted the same thing
exactly,
I started to put it quite matter-of-factly.
He had spoken of acorns, so poets in a
nutshell
Should please him, I thought, and they're
none of them but shell.
To hesitate longer would smack of the
boyish,
And a prophet's ill served by an attitude
coyish,
Like a diffident girl asked to play the
piano.
I detest all such feminine ruses, and
so
I hitched up my mind as sailors and
whalers
Are reported to do with their trousers
(why tailors
Should so fashion these garments that
this act must precede
Every truly stupendous and heroic deed
I am quite at a loss to surmise). To
continue,
I exerted each muscle and braced every
sinew
For the duty in hand. In a fiery burst
Which I hoped might be eloquence, I
took up the first
Poet I happened to think of, explaining
quite clearly

That my order of precedence meant nothing really.
Number ten might be easily rated as equal
To one or fifteen, if we lived for the sequel.
Here I saw with concern he had fixed both his eyes on
That soothing Nirvana we call the horizon.
There was danger of slumber I felt, so embarking
On my story with gusto, I began by remarking
(And here I must add for my just self-esteem
That the minute I spoke he awoke from his dream
And never thereafter did so much as blink,
Though I thought, once or twice, I detected a wink.)
But I'm straying again. I remarked then succinctly,
Without farther preamble:

   "To name them distinctly,
There's Frost with his blueberry pastures and hills
All peopled by folk who have so many ills
'Tis a business to count 'em, their subtle insanities.
One half are sheer mad, and the others inanities.
He'll paint you a phobia quick as a wink
Stuffed into a hay-mow or tied to a sink.
And then he'll deny, with a certain rich rapture,
The very perversion he's set out to capture.
Were it not for his flowers, and orchards, and skies,
One would think the poor fellow was blind of both eyes
Or had never read Freud, but it's only his joke.
If we're looking for cheer, he's a pig in a poke.
But he's such a good chap, he is welcome to say
Tweedledum's Tweedledee if he's feeling that way.
When he calls a thing yellow and you know it is pink,

Why, you've purchased his book and you're welcome to think.
He's a foggy benignity wandering in space
With a stray wisp of moonlight just touching his face,
Descending to earth when a certain condition
Reminds him that even a poet needs nutrition,
Departing thereafter to rarefied distances
Quite unapproachable to those persistencies,
The lovers of Lions, who shout at his tail —
At least so he says — when he comes within hail.
Majestic, remote, a quite beautiful pose,
(Or escape, or indulgence, or all three, who knows?)
Set solidly up in a niche like an oracle
Dispensing replies which he thinks categorical.
No wonder he cleaves to his leafy seclusion,
Barricading his door to unlawful intrusion,
The goal of the fledgling, a god in a thicket,
To be viewed only Tuesdays and Fridays by ticket.
Yet note, if you please, this is but one degree
Of Frost, there are more as you'll presently see,
And some of them are so vexatiously teasing
All this stored heat is needed to keep him from freezing.
Life is dreadfully hard on a man who can see
A rainbow-clad prophet a-top of each tree;
To whom every grass-blade's a telephone wire
With Heaven as central and electrifier.
He has only to ring up the switch-board and hear
A poem lightly pattering into his ear,
But he must be in tune or the thing takes a kink,
An imminent lunch-bell puts it all on the blink.
Some one to be seen in the late afternoon
Throws all his poetical thoughts in a swoon.

He can't walk with one foot on Parnassus, and stutter
Along with the other foot deep in the gutter,
As many poets do, all those who have tamely
Submitted to life as men live it, and lamely
Continue to limp, half man-in-the-street,
Half poet-in-the-air. How often we meet
Such fellows, they throng the bohemian centres,
The 'Blue Cats' and 'Pink Moons' those artistic frequenters
Who eat at the house's expense for the fame
Their presence ensures have conceived as a name
Full of rich innuendo. Though why a strange hue
Connected with something — moons pink or cats blue —
Should make it so vicious, I can't see, can you?
These double-paced bardlings are marvels at talking,
But their writing seems curiously given to balking,
A result, like as not, of their manner of walking.
Not so Frost, he divides his life into two pieces,
Keeping one for himself while the other he leases
To various colleges. He's eclectic in choice
And at least half-a-dozen have cause to rejoice
That he's sojourned among them; for his unique duty,
What they pay him to do and regard as their booty,
Is the odd one of being on hand, nothing more.
He's an unexplored mine you know contains ore;
Or rather, he acts as a landscape may do
Which says one thing to me and another to you,
But which all agree is a very fine view.
Such a sight is experience, a wonderful thing
To have looked at and felt. This establishing

Of a poet in a college like a bird in a cage
Is a happy endowment for art which our age
Is the first to have thought of and made quite the rage.
That the poet cannot function while kept as a zoo,
Does not matter at all to the wiseacres who
Invented the scheme. They secure for the year
That desideratum, a high atmosphere.
If the poet who provides it be drained to the pith,
That is nothing to leaving their college a myth,
A tradition, to hand down to all future classes.
A thing and its shadow are one to the masses.
The man's written his poems, now he can recite them;
As for new ones, he is a great fool to invite them,
Notoriety offers a constant repose,
Like a time-honoured rose-bush which now bears no rose.
Instead of one poet, we've a score of poetasters.
Are we wise in our method or ignorant wasters?
Frost suffers himself to be bled for the small fry
While Pegasus, never a quiescent palfrey,
Stamps at the hitching-post. Still, I'm not saying
There is really much harm in this lengthy delaying.
There's the other half-year and his telegraph grasses
And no college thrives on a diet of asses;
A man must be sacrificed now and again
To provide for the next generation of men.
So if, once in a while, a real poet is captured
And bled for the future, we should all be enraptured.
The violence done to his own special nature
Is a thing of no moment if he add to the stature
Of a handful of students, and business is booming

For the troubadour poets in the town
he's illuming.
They come, called in shoals by the in-
terest he rouses,
And talk of themselves to preposterous
houses.
But who, in the end, has the best of the
luck,
The migrating birds or the poor decoy
duck?
Small surprise, when Commencement
has ended the year,
If our poet's first free action is to dis-
appear.
Chained up on a campus creating diurnal
Poetic fine weather must be an eter-
nal
Annoyance, a horror, growing always more
biting.
How pleasant his mountains must look,
how exciting
The long leisured moments to think, with
no gaping
Importunate youths whose lives he is
shaping
Forever observing his least little move-
ment.
Why, a bleak desert island would be an
improvement
On such an existence. Though we should
be proud
That there is such a man to let loose on
a crowd
Of young bears, any one of whom may
become President,
We should be even prouder to know
him a resident
Of our woods and our hills, a neighbour
of neighbours,
A singer of country-sides and country
labours,
Like a hermit thrush deep in a wood
whose fresh fire
Of song burns the whole air to music,
and higher
Up-soars till it seems not one voice but
a choir —
The choir of his people whose hearths
are the altars
Of that deep race-religion which in him
never falters,
His life is its worship, his songs are its
psalters.
Prophet, seer, psalmist, is the world so
importunate

As to leave you no peace even here?
You are fortunate
At least to abide, remote as the fables,
In a place much neglected by railroad
time-tables.
I promise, for one, when I turn from the
wicket,
That the name of your town will not be
on my ticket.
You have as much right to protect your
seclusion
As any old monk of the order Carthusian,
Though solitude really is but an illusion
As most men find out to their utter con-
fusion.

To speak of seclusion is to think of a
man
Who is built on a totally otherwise plan.
I mean, and I rather imagine you know
it,
Edwin Arlington Robinson, excellent poet,
And excellent person, but vague as a wood
Gazed into at dusk. His preponderant
mood
Is withdrawal, and why? For a man of
his stamp,
So conscious of people, it seems odd to
scamp
Experience and contact, to live in a
hollow
Between the four winds and perpetually
swallow
The back draughts of air from a swift
forward motion.
It takes a huge strength to withstand
all emotion,
But Robinson stays with his feet planted
square
In the middle of nothing, the vacuum
where
The world's swinging starts and whirls
out, where is left
The dead root of movement, an emptiness cleft
In the heart of an aim, of all aims, peering
out
At the dust and the grass-blades that
swirl all about.
He notes who is here, who is coming
along,
Who has passed by alone, who is one
of a throng.
He peers with intentness bent all into
seeing,

A critical eye finely pointed on being.
He is cruel with dispassion, as though
    he most dreaded
Some shiver of feeling might yet be
    imbedded
Within him. And if this occurrence
    should happen,
He would probably see himself with a
    fool's cap on
And feel himself sinking to shipwreck at
    once;
Of the two, much preferring disaster to
    dunce.
For the dunce is contingent on a sort of
    a curse
He thinks he is doomed with. A curious,
    perverse
Undercutting of Fate which decrees him
    observer
And hoods him in ice from all possible
    fervour.
The slightest conceivable hint of a thaw
Wounds his conscience as though he had
    broken a law
He had sworn to uphold. Are there
    demons in hiding
Within his ice-mail? Can he feel them
    abiding
A time to break loose and disrupt into
    tatters
The scheme of existence he has taught
    himself matters,
A barrier raised betwixt him and his
    satyrs?
For he has them; his quaint, artificial
    control
Is a bandage drawn tightly to hold down
    his soul.
Should a nail or a thorn tear the least
    little mesh, it
Would let all his nature go leaping in
    freshet
Overflowing his banks and engulfing his
    dams
In a flurry of life. But the desolate calms
He has cherished so long would be lost
    in the slams,
The torrential vortices of a swift current
Exploding in motion. Some uncouth,
    deterrent
Complex in his make-up enforces recoil
Before the fatigue and the wrench of
    turmoil.
He compounds with inertia by calling
    it Fate,

Deeply dreading the rush of emotion in
    spate,
Distrusting his power to outwit disaster
In the realization that with him fast
    means faster,
And refusing to see that a turbulent strife
Is the valuable paradox given to life
Which only the few may possess. With
    the prize
In his hand, he turns sadly away, crucifies
His manhood each day with the old
    dog's-eared lies,
The heritage, left by those Puritan heirs.
His bogies and satyrs are grandsons of
    theirs.
Could he see them as fruit-trees distorted
    by mist,
He might unknot himself from the terrible
    twist
He has suffered through fear of them.
    Now, with vicarious
Experience in verse, he cheats all the
    various
Impulses within him which make him a
    poet;
But, try as he will, his poems all show
    it.
His tight little verses an inch in diameter,
His quatrains and whole-book-long tales
    in pentameter,
With never a hint of what he'd call a
    sham metre —
Though some people style his kind *ad
    nauseam* metre —
With gimlets for eyes and a sensitive
    heart,
All battened down tight in the box of
    his art,
And we have his rare merits and his
    strange deficiencies
Which mix to a porridge of peculiar
    efficiencies.
Admired by every one dowered with wit,
He has scarcely the qualifications to hit
The unlettered public, but the fact that
    his name
Is already spotted with the lichens of
    fame
Opens up a most fecund and pertinent
    query
And is one of the pedestals on which my
    theory
Is based: whether now we have not
    reached the stage
Of a perfectly genuine coming-of-age.

I am willing to swear that when he has
    retired
His books will be listed as 'reading re-
    quired,'
And poor sweltering youths taking exam-
    inations
Will crown him with the bays of their
    wild lamentations.
Our beautiful system is to make every
    course able
To render delight quite sterile through
    forcible
Insistence upon it. But these are the
    laurels
With which no man who's not insane
    ever quarrels.
Perhaps it's as well not to look at the
    guerdon
Too closely or no one would shoulder
    the burden
Of being a poet.

           The next I shall take up
Is a fellow as utterly different in make-up
As you're likely to see if you scour the land
With field-glasses and microscopes. This
    is Carl Sand-
burg, a strange, gifted creature, as slow
    as a fog
Just lifting to sunshine, a roughly hewn
    Gog,
Shorn of his twin Magog, set over the
    portal
Through which brawls the stream of
    everything mortal.
Day and night he observes it, this river
    of men,
With a weary-sweet, unflagging interest,
    and ten
Times in a day he seeks to detach
Himself from the plinth where he's
    destined to watch,
And mingle as one of them, mistaking
    his stature
To be but that generally ordained by
    nature
For the run of humanity. His miscal-
    culations
Of the possible height to which civiliza-
    tions
May rightly aspire are constantly leading
Him into positions whence there's no
    proceeding.
Because he can easily reach to the stars,
He cannot believe that a short arm debars

Any others from doing the same, and
    declares
His qualifications assuredly theirs.
Endowing each man whom he meets with
    his own
Stretch and feeling, he takes for the
    foundation stone
Of his creed the ability to walk cheek by
    jowl
With the sun, at the same time not losing
    control
Of feet always set on the earth. It is
    droll
To hear him announce neither giants nor
    pigmies
Exist, that there's only one knowable
    size,
Which by implication's as tall as the
    skies.
What he feels about souls, he has brought
    into speech,
But since perfect English is a hard thing
    to teach
To those brought up without it, he
    changes his tactics
And declares correct use the hypochon-
    driactics
Of language too timid for red-blooded
    slang.
This theory of his is a swift boomerang
Overturning his balance and flooring him
    pell-mell, he
Presents the strange sight of a man on
    his belly
Proclaiming that all men walk that way
    from preference
And the manner, though new, must be
    treated with deference.
Since his own natural speech is correct
    to a dot,
His theory, to use the red-blooded, is
    'rot,'
And as man does not wiggle along like
    a jelly
When he walks, to affect that laid flat
    on the belly
Is the easiest position to attain locomo-
    tion
Must surely be called a preposterous
    notion.
But what's the poor fellow to do? It
    is plain
He overtops folk if he stands; once again
It's the hill and Mohammed, since he
    can't raise the others

He must lie if he'd be the same height
as his brothers.
It may weary his readers to see a true
poet
Who apparently has not the instinct to
know it,
And so burdens his beauty with wild
propaganda
That much of his work is a hideous
slander
Against his remarkable genius, but scratch
it
With a prudent pen-knife and there's
nothing to match it
Going on in the whole world to-day. He
has sight
Of a loveliness no man has seen, and a
might,
A great flowing power of words to express
Its hugeness and littleness. All the excess
Of his passion for living leaps out from
his pen
In a gush of fresh imminence; again and
again
We read him to fill our soul's withering
lungs
With the wind-over-water sweep which
is his tongue's
Particular gift — though I should have
said 'prairies,'
Not 'water,' he is no result of the seas,
But in every whiff of him, flat and ex-
tended,
A man of the plains, whose horizons are
ended
By the upreach of earth to that sky which
he touches
And carries off great fragments of in his
clutches.
Wood-smoke, and water-smoke rising from
runnels
At sunrise, long lines of black smoke from
the funnels
Of engines and factories, steel of man's
forging
And steel he's forged into; the slow,
passive gorging
Of earth with mankind, blood of souls,
blood of hearts,
Swallowed into the fields where the
sprouting grain parts
A right rail from a left rail, and always
asunder
Go marching the fields cleft in two by
the wonder

Of man gauging distance as magic and
burning it
Under boot-heels or car-wheels and all
the time earning it
For the silt of his mind from which a
new soil
Is gradually risen. This turgescent coil
Is the crawling of glaciers, the upheave
of hills,
The process of making and change, the
huge spills
Of watersheds seeking their oceans, the
miracle
Of creeping continuance. This is the
lyrical
Stuff Sandburg works into something as
lazy
And deep as geology planting its clays, he
Makes keenly, unhastingly, as evolution,
And yet, poor blind eagle, he dreams
revolution.
With the centuries his if he could but
decide
To pocket his picayune, popular pride,
Give up his day-dreams and his tin-penny
logic,
Be Gog as God made him and not dema-
gogic,
Sit solidly down with his eyes and his
heart,
And a file and a chisel, to fashion great
art —
If he would, but will he? It really is
vexing
To see such a fellow perpetually flexing
His knees to false idols, a mere artizan
When he might be an artist. Some his-
torian
Of the future will round him up in an
abstract
By denouncing the times as too matter-
of-fact,
Not observing what might well be seen
for the looking
That it's simply a case of not quite
enough cooking.
An accredited hero or a dream-blinded
sloven
Is entirely a matter of stoking the oven.
The material's certainly A number one,
It will be his own fault if he dies under-
done.

The man whom I next shall bring to the
fore

Is becoming, I fear, an impossible bore.
Some few years ago, Minerva mislaid
Her glasses, and unable to see in the shade,
Feeling also, quite naturally, rather afraid
To proclaim that she wore them, like any old maid
Teaching school — for a Goddess is loath to parade
Her antiquity, even as others — she said
No word of the matter at home on Olympus.
A pity, because a very bad *impasse*
Might have so been averted. The hand-maids and lackeys,
Who are always possessed of both front door and back keys,
Would have hunted the palace from cellar to roof
And most probably found them not very aloof
From the spot where poor Vulcan, in playing Tartuffe,
Had received a convincing and permanent proof
That the lady was chaste. Indeed, how-ever frigid,
No woman of spirit admits to the rigid
Mathematical count of the years after forty,
And even immortals, though reputed quite 'sporty,'
And figuring time by the so many cen-turies,
Still scarcely desire to add up the entries
And publish the total. Minerva, then, hid
The fact that she could not quite see what she did,
And since it would give things away to inquire, 'Oh
She could not do that!' And after a *giro*
Which blindly confused every main street and by-row,
In the end she conferred a great book on a tyro.
The author in question, though an excel-lent notary,
Could scarcely be classed at that time as a votary
Worth Minerva's attention. But, however unsuitable,
The deed, once accomplished, became quite immutable.

No matter how foolish she felt, the poor Goddess
Must carry it through in a pitiless prog-ress.
For be sure, when her family learnt of her blunder,
Which they very soon did, she'd have welcomed Jove's thunder
To be quit of his really abominable quiz-zing.
His jokes were caught up by Neptune and sent whizzing
For Vulcan to cap them, and as he was still smarting
Beneath the rebuke she'd not spared him at parting,
He gave her good measure now he'd got the upper
Hand. Then the women joined in; what at supper
Was observed was rehashed for break-fast and dinner,
Even Venus said 'Minnie, you *have* picked a winner!
From all that I hear, your man is verbose.
He'll print in ten volumes, a very large dose
For you to inspire.' 'Oh, Minnie is game,'
Cried Mercury, kind-hearted boy. 'All the same,'
Growled Vulcan, 'if Min can hold out, 'twould be speedier
To imbue him at once with an ency-clopedia.'
Here Minerva, in tears which begemmed her found glasses,
Declared her relations were all of them asses,
That she cared not a fig for their tup-penny threats
Having settled the book to be done in vignettes.
The Gods broke out laughing. 'Give Minnie the handle
And not one of you is worth even her sandal,'
Shouted Jove, 'she's arranged for a *suc-cès de scandal.*'
Which she had, and her poet, never doubting the giver,
Wrote steadily on without the least quiver,
And at last, in due course, was pub-lished 'Spoon River.'

Now having explained the volume's true
genesis,
Let me say it is not for a party where
tennis is
In order, or bridge. If you like porcu-
pining
Your soul with your conscience, here's
a chance for refining
On misery, and since Minerva'd a hand
in it
No person need doubt that there's plenty
of sand in it.
Of course the thing's genius no matter
how squint-eyed,
And the reader who never once weeps
must be flint-eyed.
But hey, Mr. Masters, how weary and
dreary
You make all your folk! How impossibly
smeary
And sticky they are with old amorous
contacts,
A series of ticketed, sexual facts
Tucked away, all unwashed, in the
ground. Who once told you
The great, biological truths with a few
Dirty smudges you've never forgotten, like
plasters
Thumbed tight to your mind? They're
the trade-mark of 'Masters.'
Whatever he's writing — Minerva inspired
As this book, 'Spoon River'; or, nervous
and tired,
Worrying his public as a dog does a bone
As in 'Domesday Book,' done, you'll
agree, quite alone —
They all have the stamp of back-alley
lust
Which you stand as you can, for stand
it you must
If you'd read him at all. I've no wish
to cloud over
The fame of a book which, from cover
to cover,
Shows the trace of Minerva's most help-
ful collusion.
The hall-marks of genius are here in pro-
fusion.
People swarm through its pages like ants
in a hill,
No one's like the others, a personal will
Makes each man what he is and his life
what it was.
The modern Balzac? Not at all — the
new 'Boz!'

Where the Frenchman employed an
urbane moderation,
The Englishman gloried in exaggeration.
But, in spite of his gargoyles, his fine
gift of humour
Kept even his quaintness from the taint
of ill-rumour.
In a grin of delight, he played tricks
with his drawing,
And no matter how far from the real he
was yawing
His object were merely a louder guffaw-
ing.
He never believed his grotesques were
true pictures
Of life, he knew perfectly well men are
mixtures
Of rather more this or a little less that;
No man is pure angel and none is sheer
brat.
Where he painted them so, it was done
to enhance
Some meaning he wished to make clear;
circumstance
Induced him to stress both the gall and
the honey,
And no one knew better just when to be
funny.
Mr. Masters, quite otherwise, thinks his
creations
Reveal abstract truth in their vilest rela-
tions.
He sees every one as the suffering
prey
Of some low, hidden instinct, his business
to flay
The decency off them and show them all
naked,
A few of them zanies, the rest downright
wicked.
In all his vast gallery there's but one
exception,
And that, I hold, is to have wrought
with deception.
If some excellent sense of the really
amusing
Had led him to practise a little more
fusing
Of the good and the bad, his book had
succeeded
In being the great masterpiece we have
needed
Ever since the beginning. As it is, his
caprice
Has given us only a great Masters' piece.

How Minerva deserted him all through
the sequel,
We can easily see if we hunt for an equal
Success in the list of his subsequent works.
Each hitches along in a series of jerks.
He tries lyrics, and ballads, and novels
in verse,
But lacks always the wit to return to the
terse.
In the last, 'Domesday Book,' he relied
upon Browning
To replace Minerva and keep him from
drowning.
Shallow hope! He achieved a self-hitting
satire,
Mr. Masters looked so odd in Browning's
attire.
The huge bulk of his book brought to
mind the old fable
Of the bull-frog who, seeing an ox in
the stable,
Puffed up till he burst in a vain-glorious
trying
To attain the same size. But no magni-
fying
Can make of unripeness a thing brought
to a finish,
For blowing it up only makes it look
thinnish.
If asked my opinion, I think that Minerva
Was cruel to abandon the rôle of pre-
server.
To lift a man suddenly out of obscurity
And leave him quite solus in his pre-
maturity
Was not, I think, cricket. (I like to
imply an
Acquaintance with idioms as remote as
the Chian,
They read like a dash of the pepper called
Cayenne.)
To conclude, I believe, when the Gods
have done chaffing,
Minerva will one morning catch herself
laughing,
And, as laughing's a good-natured act to
fall into,
I should not be surprised if she found
she had been too
High-handed and harsh in her speedy
desertion
Of an author who might have become
her diversion
Had her relatives not been so prompt
with their jeers.

Then, totalling up the count of the years
And the works she'd permitted her erst-
while protégé
To publish without her assistance, 'Hey-
day!'
I can hear her exclaiming. 'This will
scarcely redound
To my credit, and since the world knows
that I found
Him and helped him, I really think it
would be better
If I helped him again to become the
begetter
Of another 'Spoon River,' or at least
some quite fine thing
Which folk will acknowledge to be a
divine thing.'
I should not be astonished if, touched to
the marrow,
Minerva set out in her largest Pierce
Arrow,
Or else (since I would not pretend to a
choice)
Departed in her most expensive Rolls-
Royce,
With a dozen or two extremely sharp
axes,
Three or four different saws, and various
waxes,
A hammer and nails, also scissors and
strings,
The whole bundle of tools which a good
workman brings
To a job who's no wish to go back for
his 'things.'
Arriving *chez* Masters, there'll be a short
parley,
And I conjure the world not to miss the
finale."

At this point in my tale, there suddenly
grew
On my ear a low sound like wind sweeping through
Many acres of pine-trees; but, even as I
listened,
It changed into bird-calls which merrily
glistened
Like sun-spattered feathers of tone
through the glancing
Of leaves over water where shadows are
dancing.
Once again was a change, and I heard
the low roar
Of surf beating up against a rock shore;

This gave place to the clanging of bells over valleys
And the long monotone of horns blown from Swiss chalêts.
I'd scarcely determined that fact when again
It transmuted itself into pattering rain,
Which fused in its turn to harsh drums and to blares
Of tin trumpets, the kind that you meet with at fairs.
But before I'd accustomed myself to the noise,
It rose quiet, single, enduring in poise,
Held high to a balance above growling thunder
As though I were harkening to the world's wonder,
The organ at Harlem, while the "Mourning of Rachel"
Was played — and I knew I was listening to Vachel.
"Who else has, or ever has had, such a voice
As is his, Vachel Lindsay's? Whether his choice,
Be it singing, exhorting, making fun, prophesying,
It is equally lovely and soul-satisfying.
He's a composite choir, whether shouting or chanting,
Whoever's heard once must admit to a haunting
Nostalgia to hear him again. It's enchanting.
A Sunday-school orator, plus inspiration,
The first ballad-singer, bar none, of the Nation.
When he is performing, I acknowledge to being
More delighted with hearing than I am with seeing.
Perhaps I'm self-conscious, but his postures and poses
Do not strike me as happily chosen for Moses
Bearing down from the mountain his Tables of Stone,
Otherwise the part fits him as though 'twere his own.
When he starts in proclaiming his credo of new laws,
They appear to be vaudeville stunts dashed with blue laws.

He's so desperately earnest there's no modifying him,
And that wonderful voice is forever enskying him.
There's a sober old owl and a bright dragon-fly in him,
But clearly there's nothing at all of the dry in him.
An odd, antic fellow, but if you insist
On the unvarnished truth, a sublime egotist
Delighting to cover his titles and fly-leaves
With the personal notes his omnipresent 'I' leaves.
This trait should endear him to every collector
Long after his ego's become a mere spectre.
If his writing's so *chic* that you can't read a particle,
Why, all the more grist for a bibliophile's article.
He's a sort of mad xylophone, twinkling his bells
Before all the doors of the thirty-six Hells.
No whirligig dervish gyrating his piety
Can ever be less moved than he with anxiety
Lest his furious rhythms may show impropriety
And injure his creed in the eyes of society.
He knows his own heart and its innate sobriety
And cares nothing for fools who may note with dubiety
A worship which ranges through so much variety.
A mighty jazz dancer before the Lord! —
I can think of no happier term to record
His effect when reciting. He's astoundingly mystic
Even when he purports to be most naturalistic,
A queer ancient trait we may call Judaistic,
Engraft on a style which is pure Methodistic.
He is always attempting to fathom his soul,
But he cannot get hold of a long enough pole.
As he uses an ancient one which he inherited,
Perhaps, after all, his failure is merited.

It's a battered old thing might be John
   Wesley's staff,
Good enough in its day, but too short by
   half
To reach to his bottom. Still there's
   something so stable
In his love for the heirloom, it might
   pass for a label.
The fellow has scarce an iota of logic
Though he leans rather strongly toward
   the pedagogic.
These two traits make his teaching less
   vivid than taking,
He appears as the herald of some proud
   awaking,
But what it's to be, I dare swear he's no
   whit
More enlightened than we are, not one
   little bit.
I like his conceit of the amaranth apples,
(The word is so charming, the look of it
   dapples
His page with sunshine) and his modern
   Valkyri,
A cross between Joan of Arc and a
   fairy —
I, too, should have relished some good
   latakia
At a table for two behind clumps of
   spirea
At the top of his Truth Tower cafeteria
With this twenty-first century wise young
   Medea.
Who wouldn't, indeed! But the sweep-
   ings and shavings
I gather up after her talk seem mere
   ravings,
The opaline fancies of moonlight and
   youth.
Among them I scarcely can plot out one
   truth
Plain enough to be platformed by some
   voting sleuth
And paraded before the precinct polling-
   booth.
What's the difference, say I, since the
   book is as airy
As the dew-dripping song of a young wild
   canary.
Who dotes on perusing economists'
   tracts?
There are millions of volumes which deal
   with mere facts.
I prefer this spiced basket of rose and
   camelia,

And a populace dancing a gay seguidilla
Under Tajes Mahal, with the star-chimes
   all ringing.
(That term, by the way, simply does its
   own singing.)
'Amaranth apple-trees, sandal-wood thick-
   ets!'
Bless the man who has shown us the way
   through the wickets
Which lead to this pleasance, and haply
   the leaven
Works none the less well because he calls
   it Heaven.
The book is the whole of him, minus his
   rhythm.
But the others — how often I pass a day
   with them,
Boomlaying and shouting, 'creeping
   through the black,'
With a whole troop of nigger-gods yell-
   ing at my back,
And the motors whizzing with their
   'crack-crack-crack,'
Till at last I strike the wheat-ridge track
And up along a mulberry lane
I listen to the song of the Rachel-Jane.
And as I listen, perhaps it is absurd,
The singer changes to a small grey bird,
And then I see the purple quiver
Of a rainbow junk on a silver river.
I know that 'Spring comes on forever.'
I know it by heart, I have heard the tale
From Lindsay's jade-grey nightingale.
I shall never forget it, because I know it
By heart. This tribute? Do I not owe
   it!
Forgive me then, most fanciful poet,
If I find in you rarest, gravest delight
When you would have brought me to
   Heaven's height.
I am very well off where I am, I think,
Still you certainly write with a golden ink,
But I wish you would give us more of
   the Chink."

At which juncture, I paused to see if my
   friend,
Who had not said a word, might have
   ceased to attend.
Far from it, his eyes were fixed on my
   face
With an eager insistence as if he would
   trace
My meaning beyond the mere words.
   "What you say,"

He broke silence at last in his impassive way,
"Proves your poets to be certainly not of my day.
You put the fact gently, but we are passé.
At least that I presume's what you wish to convey."
With a horrified gesture I started to say —
But what? Thank the Lord I had no time to get in
The something I should have wrapt up my regret in,
Like a pill in a sugar-plum, since he went on:
"I should not be surprised, as your judgment anon,
If I heard you correctly, was for Miss Dickinson,
With Whitman and Poe. To throw off constraint,
I will say I consider your pronouncement quaint.
But I'm not so at sea to account for the cause
As before your narration I certainly was.
For the men, I'll admit there is room for dispute;
But the choice of Miss Dickinson I must refute."
Then seeing me shrug, he observed, "I am human,
And hardly can bear to allow that a woman
Is ever quite equal to man in the arts;
The two sexes cannot be ranked counterparts."
"My dear Sir," I exclaimed, "if you'd not been afraid
Of Margaret Fuller's success, you'd have stayed
Your hand in her case and more justly have rated her."
Here he murmured morosely, "My God, how I hated her!
But have you no women whom you must hate too?
I shall think all the better of you if you do,
And of them, I may add." I assured him, "A few.
But I scarcely think man feels the same contradictory

Desire to love them and shear them of victory?"
"You think wrong, my young friend," he declared with a frown,
"Man will always love woman and always pull down
What she does." "Well, of course, if you will hug the cynical,
It is quite your affair, but there is the pinnacle.
She's welcome to climb with man if she wishes."
"And fall with a crash like a trayful of dishes,"
He answered at once, "but if there's no gainsaying her,
There's certainly not the least use in delaying her."
"Very well," I assured him, and quite without mockery,
"But I know several women not yet broken crockery.
Amy Lowell, for instance," I spoke a bit clammily.
"Good Heavens!" he shouted, "not one of the family!
I remember they used to be counted by dozens,
But I never was interested in immature cousins."
"They grow, I believe." The retort was so pat
There was nothing to say, and he pulled down his hat.
I continued: "But since this is not genealogy,
You'll permit me to waive any sort of analogy
Between her and your friend. No one likes to be bound
In a sort of perpetual family pound
Tied by esprit de corps to the wheels of the dead.
A poet above all people must have his head.
Indeed it's been whispered the lady sees red
When the subject is broached, she will find her own latitude."
"My friend, were he here, would extol such an attitude,"
He said very gravely. "But proceed, Sir, I pray."
I hastened as fast as I could to obey:
"Conceive, if you can, an electrical storm

Of a swiftness and fury surpassing the
norm;
Conceive that this cyclone has caught up
the rainbow
And dashed dizzily on with it streaming
in tow.
Imagine a sky all split open and scis-
sored
By lightnings, and then you can picture
this blizzard.
That is, if you'll also imagine the clashes
Of tropical thunder, the incessant
crashes
Which shiver the hearing and leave it in
ashes.
Remember, meanwhile, that the sky is
prismatic
And outrageous with colour. The effect
is erratic
And jarring to some, but to others
ecstatic,
Depending, of course, on the idiosyncratic
Response of beholders. When you come
to think of it,
A good deal is demanded by those on
the brink of it.
To be caught in the skirts of a whirling
afflatus
One must not suppose is experienced
gratis.
Broncho-busting with rainbows is scarcely
a game
For middle-aged persons inclined to the
tame.
Likewise, who'd enjoy a sunrise from the
Matter-
horn — something all travellers agree is
the attar
Of distilled perfection — must be ready
to reap
The mid-afternoon pangs of too little
sleep.
I might go on forever commingling my
metaphors,
And verse by this means does undoubtedly get a force,
But persons who so air their fancy are
bores,
A thing every bone in my body abhors,
And you'll guess by this time, without
farther allusion,
That the lady's unique and surprising profusion
Creates in some minds an unhappy confusion.

No one's to be blamed who's not something and twenty,
But it's lucky for her that young folks are
so plenty.
The future's her goose and I dare say
she'll wing it,
Though the triumph will need her own
power to sing it.
Although I'm no prophet, I'll hazard a
guess
She'll be rated by time as more rather
than less.
Once accustom yourself to her strange
elocution,
And milder verse seems by contrast mere
dilution.
Then again (for I've kept back a very
great part),
Despite her traducers, there's always a
heart
Hid away in her poems for the seeking;
impassioned,
Beneath silver surfaces cunningly fash-
ioned
To baffle coarse pryings, it waits for the
touch
Of a man who takes surfaces only as such.
Her work's not, if you will, for the glib
amateur,
But I wonder, would it be improved if it
were?
Must subtlety always be counted a flaw
And poetry not poetry which puzzles the
raw?
Let me turn for an instant to note the
reverse
Of my poet, who employs many manners
of verse
And when not hurricaning's astoundingly
terse;
Yet here the poor creature but makes
matters worse.
There are plenty of critics who say they
can't hear
When she sings *sotto voce*, the sensa-
tion's queer
And inspires a species of horrible fear.
To be told there's a sound and catch
nothing at all,
Is a circumstance fairly designed to appal
Most casual people, for here is the hitch:
The admission that one's own ears can't
grasp a pitch
Clear and lovely to others. Whereupon a
bow-wow

Which swells to a perfectly hideous row.
They've accused her of every description
    of quackery,
Of only concerning herself with knick-
    knackery,
It has all been enough to set any one's
    back awry.
She's a fool to resent it, a man would
    have grinned?
Quite so, but then poets are created thin-
    skinned,
And when one is more than a little
    volcanic,
With a very strong dash of the ultra-
    tyrannic,
The retort contentious will be simply
    Titanic.
Behold, then, our poet, by the lash of
    atrociousness
Goaded into an attitude much like
    ferociousness.
Every book that she writes has a preface
    to guard it
Which spits fire and cannon-balls, mak-
    ing each hard hit
Tell, and mow down its swathe of ob-
    jectors.
But critics have ever been good resur-
    rectors.
Since she keeps the fight going, they rise
    to do battle,
When the whole mess is only so much
    tittle-tattle.
So it goes back and forth with the cries
    and the cheering,
And there's no sign at all of the atmos-
    phere clearing.
Her books follow each other despite all
    the riot,
For, oddly enough, there's a queer,
    crumpled quiet
Perpetually round her, a crazy-quilt tent
Dividing her happily from the event.
Armed to the teeth like an old Samurai,
Juggling with jewels like the ancient
    genii,
Hung all over with mouse-traps of metres,
    and cages
Of bright-plumaged rhythms, with pages
    and pages
Of colours slit up into streaming confetti
Which give the appearance of something
    sunsetty,
And gorgeous, and flowing — a curious
    sight

She makes in her progress, a modern
    White Knight,
Forever explaining her latest inventions
And assuring herself of all wandering at-
    tentions
By pausing at times to sing, in a duly
Appreciative manner, an aria from Lully.
The horse which she rides will suit any
    part
Either Peg (with the 'asus,') or 'Peg o'
    my heart.'
To avoid making blunders, he's usually
    known
Without any suffix as 'Peg' all alone.
This style of address has become a tradi-
    tion
Most offendingly silly, since no erudition
Unaided can ever produce a magician.
For the magic she has, I see nothing
    demonic
In the use of free verse (the 'free' is quite
    comic!)
Or even that mule of the arts, polyphonic.
No matter what pedants may find that's
    awry in him,
There's plenty of kick and plenty of fly
    in him.
Taking this thing and that, and con-
    sidering on it,
I believe there are more guesses under
    her bonnet
Than in any two hats you are likely to
    meet
(Straw or felt, take your choice, so the
    shape be discreet,
Not too flap-brimmed and weird, nor too
    jaunty and neat)
In any particular city or street
You may happen to pick. Note, I only
    say questions,
Which leaves the mind open to many
    suggestions,
Up or down, there's the rub. (The mere
    matter of hats
Is too nice, by the way, to be dealt with
    as 'Rats!'
There's a temperature here which the
    best thermostats
Could not regulate better. We're all
    diplomats
Now the 'Arrys have ousted the aris-
    tocrats.)"

I looked at my friend, his face was
    averted.

"You make it quite clear why we are
    deserted,
Old men are tough customers. Now, as a
    foil,
Give me something as smooth and slow-
    running as oil,
Something clear, uncontentious, it even
    may be
A bit chilly in beauty perhaps." "There's
    'H. D.,'"
I was tempted to shout, she fitted so
    rightly
His immediate preference: frost falling
    lightly
In delicate patterns on thin blades of
    grass.
(Since oil does not fit, I let that figure
    pass,
Though it did well enough up above
    where it was.)
"This author's become a species of
    fable
For she masks her identity under a label.
If others have ancestors, she would for-
    get hers
And appear the spontaneous child of two
    letters,
The printing of which is the ban of type-
    setters.
They have called her a dryad just stepped
    from a bosk,
But I see an ice maiden within an ice
    kiosk,
With icicle stalactites hanging around
    her,
And the violets frozen with which they
    have crowned her —
The man who would filch them would be
    an icebounder,
Which I surely am not. If each lovely,
    veined petal
Becomes by the contact a trifle too brittle
And cold to give out its usual warm scent,
They make it up amply by such dazzle-
    ment
Of sun-shot-through-ice that the shine of
    her shrine
Seems the sky-piercing glitter of some
    Apennine.
I have told you before that my mind
    teems with similes.
It's a shocking bad habit persists in some
    families,
I've an uncle — but there, I spread out
    like a runnel,

When I should flow as straight as though
    poured through a funnel.
So take this digression in the light of an
    interlude
Leading up to a change which I wish to
    obtrude
On the form of my speech, for I find I
    am freezing
Before the remarkably chilly, though
    pleasing,
Ice image I've painted, and soon shall be
    sneezing.
My Muse must immediately seek out a
    clime
Where her trippings and flittings are not
    above rime,
Or dew that is duly congealed, or hoar-
    frost.
I'm indifferent to science, so the mean-
    ing be tossed
Into some sort of shape which fits well
    with my pattern,
For, whatever the faults of said Muse,
    she's no slattern.
My verse, I'll allow, is the species fan-
    tastic,
I've been *épris* for years of the style
    Hudibrastic,
But my rhyming morale is, I trust, in-
    elastic.
Which preamble means I have searched
    for a week
To rouse neither my Muse's nor heroine's
    pique
In the matter of climate. I've found it
    in Greek.
'H. D.' (for it's time we got back to the
    girl)
Might be some ancient mirror, with
    mother-of-pearl
Let into its metal, a thing which a nation
Deems well worth the cost of its own
    exhumation,
A prize to count up to the whole excava-
    tion.
This mirror, which carries the breath of
    the past
On its scarcely stained surface, is no
    scholiast,
But a living replica of what once was
    living
At the touch of a rare adoration reviv-
    ing.
Here youths in scant armour, on the way
    to the galleys,

Woo maidens in dark ilex-groves; in the valleys,
Anemone-sprinkled, young shepherds guard flocks
Clad in ram's fleeces only; above the sharp rocks
Jutting into the purple Ionian sea
Are the white, fluted columns of —
Fiddle-de-dee!
Such lyrical bursts in a mere *jeu d'esprit*
Are like brandy poured into a cup of bohea,
A transaction called 'lacing' in old days, *on dit*.
I can't say for myself, being no devotee
Of either diluted or straight *eau-de-vie*,
And the eighteenth amendment is nothing to me.
Still, I don't like a law couched in hyperbole,
It gets any one's goat. To return to 'H. D.,'
Whom I've really kept waiting most outrageously,
She's the thing as it was, not the thing we have made it
And with insolent ornament quite overlaid it.
She descends to no commonplace, flock-guarding shepherds.
No pompous Victorian gush ever jeopards
Her reticent, finely-drawn line. No Greek marble
Has less of the puerile and less of the garble.
Her sea is the sea of a child or a Neriad,
And yet no false word lifts it out of its period.
Her flowers of shore and of cliff those we seek
On our cliffs and our shores, but hers somehow are Greek.
Her poems are excitement and rest, and the glory
Of living a life and not reading a story.
Archaeology? Yes, in the very same way
That geology's the mountain we climb every day.
The armour she welds, the dyed cloth she weaves,
Are so perfect in artistry, every word cleaves
To the substance as though that would crackle without it

And split. Read her books (there are two) if you doubt it.
Perhaps, after all, this quintessence of Greece
Is the wool on a century-garlanded fleece;
Underneath is, and was, a tough fibre of leather.
Is the Greece she has given us Greece altogether?
As well might one ask if the youth of Praxiteles
Is an everyday chap or a scheme to belittle ease
By exalting the sharp line of young masculinity.
In her method and his is there not some affinity?
Each sheers to the soul, to the base of a nemesis,
And the hard, glancing residue is the ultimate genesis.
For out of the past is the future; a truism,
You must pardon, since man has invented no new 'ism'
Since the days of the cavemen. I wish merely to prove
That this most modern poet runs along an old groove,
That the erudite novelties filling her pages
Are as old as this morning and as new as the ages."

Here a voice interrupted my long peroration,
Speaking, I detected, in some irritation.
"I think," it announced, "though I may be mistaken,
There's a poet whom you've not mentioned yet, Conrad Aiken."
Such an ill-governed mind as I've got, and the porter
Never keeps out intruders who call, as he ought to.
(That rhyme will be cursed as "a regular snorter"
By every stand-pat, Tennysonian supporter.
I am sorry myself to be forced to distort a
Fine line unduly, and if I or my thought err
I am willing to own it without the least *hauteur*.
I rhyme as I can, and am never a courter

For all suffrages.) The doorman, I said,
Who, between you and me, is a crass
dunderhead,
Had let this extremely irascible gentle-
man
Pass through the door, and of course he
began
At once to upbraid me. It's the method
he uses
To force himself into the sight of the
Muses.
"Young man," I replied with some heat,
"you mistake
My preoccupation. If you wish to make
Your entrance at once with the ladies, I'll
see to it,
But I should have supposed you'd im-
mediately veto it."
This was rather a staggerer, to be grouped
with the women
Would tax the endurance of any male
human;
Yet to wait any longer, when I might be
weary
Before his turn came, did not strike him
as cheery.
He puffed and he fumed, with pride pull-
ing both ways;
It was pitiable to see the poor fellow's
malaise.
But finally, with a great bluffing of
chivalry,
He declared he had no sort of feeling of
rivalry
Against the fair sex who adorned his profession.
A very neat way, this, to blur a confes-
sion,
For the long and the short of it was he'd
go on
The carpet at once, if I pleased. There-
upon
I hastily made my excuses to one
Or two ladies I'd meant to have been
next presented.
Being sensible persons, they seemed quite
contented.
Perhaps 'twas as well, for I'd rather a
hunch
The irascible poet might make good with
his "Punch"
And land me that terrible "one on the
jaw,"
When I'm sure I should "measure my
length" in the straw.

It will clearly be seen that my anxious
perusal
Of a recent combat has done much to
bamboozle
The erstwhile classic grace of my natural
diction.
You see I obeyed a strong predilection
In Carpentier's favour to the tune of a
tenner
And, with other good sportsmen, I found
my Gehenna.
"Mr. Aiken's a poet so cram full of
knowledge
He knows all about poetry that's taught
in a college.
His versification's as neat as a pin,
His metre so fine it becomes finikin.
I say nothing of rhythm, for he's some-
thing fanatical
Anent the advantage of the beat mathe-
matical.
Within his set limits, the pulse of his
verse
Is often most subtle, and even his worse
Attempts are by no means either jejune
or lacking
In form, one can hardly imagine him
slacking
In pains or desire. He's all that a poet
Can make of himself when he sets out
to do it
With his heart, and his soul, and his
strength, and his mind.
For years now, he's had a most horrible
grind
With his work, with the public, but what
stands in his way
Is the awkward necessity of something to
say.
A man of sensations, of difficult cheerful-
ness
Which the fog in his brain has tor-
mented to fearfulness,
Possessed of much music and little
idea,
Always steeping his soul in the strange
undersphere
Of the brain. Since all thought in him
tends to grow hazy
When his sentiment's roused, he is lost
in a mazy
Vortex where he swings like some pale
asteroid.
Seeking orientation, he's stumbled on
Freud.

With the Austrian's assistance, he's become neurological,
A terrible fate to befall the illogical.
Being born with an ultra-sensitive cuticle,
We must realize his verse in a sense therapeutical.
If he doesn't quite state any fact, his oblique
Side-glances at subjects are just hide-and-seek
He's playing with all his frustrated ambitions
And gaining, thereby, some vicarious fruitions.
He's so young as to think that he proves his maturity
By boldly colliding with all sorts of impurity.
His ladies are, most of them, a little bit dusty,
But we're learning to think any other kind musty.
The true modern artist would face destitution
Were it not for that universe-wide institution
Plain people frown down on and call prostitution.
No matter how shopworn the plots he has made,
They'll always pass muster if he mentions a spade.
At least this is true with that type of Bohemia
Which is not yet aware that such art spells anaemia.
Not so Aiken — his brothels, streetwalkers, dope-eaters
Are merely the web he weaves over with metres.
He uses them chiefly because they are easy
And sure to produce an effect on the queasy.
For more than all else he dreads falling flat;
The fear of it teases his brain like a gnat.
He would rather be called wicked, incomprehensible,
Anything, so long as the world's not insensible.
In his anxious desire to escape being tepid,
He makes too great a show of the overintrepid,

But his real interest lies in quite other directions:
In noting the faintest of fleeting reflections
In tone or in colour; in catching the magic
Of words against words; and it simply is tragic
How few apprehend his remarkable quality.
But was ever a public more lost in frivolity
Than ours? It cannot tell feathers from lead
Till you hit it a crack with the last on the head.
His volumes are filled with a sea-green miasma
Shot and sprinkled throughout with the grotesque phantasma
Of an egoist's brain, or a man's when he's sleepy.
They revolve unrelated and sink into creepy
Sight and sound mutterings, yet sometimes so vivid
They are that they seem to stand out in a livid
And flaming protrusion. Take, for instance, the scene
Of his satyrs and maenads, which is white striped on green,
With red, sudden explosions. Sometimes, more surprising,
The fog lifts a moment before a sun rising
As clear and as thin as though painted on china
By some eighteenth century Dresden designer.
His sordid back rooms disappear and the groans
Of dying dope-fiends, and we hear 'three clear tones,'
The tones of his bird in the china-berry tree.
What a mercy that such a tree happened to be!
Otherwise, I believe, he must have invented it.
Never mind, here it is, and he's simply cemented it
On the botany of poetry for ever and every.
I say that superbly, without the least quiver.

If the rest of his work's neither Saint
    Paul's nor Kremlin,
He's built a basilica surely in 'Senlin.'
At least in that 'Morning Song,' which,
    until lately,
Was the sole, single fragment he'd done
    adequately.
Till 'Punch,' ah! with 'Punch' now, he
    should achieve fame,
But there's nothing so dogging as a once-
    come-by name.
If this were his first, he'd be up like a
    rocket,
Now I think he'll burn steadily on in his
    socket
Making beautiful poems though the
    public won't stand 'em
Because he can't drive style and tale in a
    tandem.
Since the books as they are stick so hard
    in the gizzard,
The sensible thing is to have each one
    scissored.
Cut out from each volume the one or
    two scraps
You might like on a third or fourth read-
    ing perhaps;
Paste them into a scrap-book, and some
    rainy day
Just glance over the lot and I think you
    will say:
'By Jove! What a fellow he is in his
    way!'
And I'll thank you for that as a true leaf
    of bay.
If he, the arch-sceptic, finds other folk
    doubting,
He makes a mistake to be seen always
    pouting.
He has not his deserts, yet to publish the
    fact
Is a childish and most unintelligent act,
But every one knows he's deficient in
    tact.
A man who can work with such utter
    devotion
Can afford to wait patiently for his pro-
    motion,
And that it will come, I've a very strong
    notion.
One thing we can say, he will certainly
    wait
And either get in or turn dust at the gate.
Since Fame is a very good hand at the
    shears,

I shall not be surprised if he gets his
    arrears,
For quality counts in the long run of
    years."
I turned to the shade in my mind, but
    unused
To listening with patience, the thing had
    vamoosed.

Not so my old friend, he was listening
    intensely,
And as I stopped speaking, he said, "I'm
    immensely
Intrigued by that man, he's a curious
    fellow.
Too bad he's permitted himself to see
    yellow.
A jaundiced perspective's a great handi-
    cap.
Well, what other poets have you got in
    your lap?
I commend you, young man, as an excel-
    lent etcher."
"The next I shall notice will be John
    Gould Fletcher,"
I answered, "but before I begin my nar-
    ration
Don't *think*; if you can, *see* an irradia-
    tion
Spreading out over roofs, over trees, over
    sky,
The gold screen of a moment, on which
    you descry
Such oddments as heaps of 'vermilion
    pavilions'
And Gabriel's angels all riding on pil-
    lions
On the backs of cloud horses, blowing
    trumpets of thunder,
Above forests of elephant trees standing
    under
The precipitous cone of some steep after-
    noon.
The whirling wind 'screams,' the stars
    'shrill,' the streets 'croon.'
A cataract of music swirls out of the
    throats
Of the long scarlet trumpets, the pris-
    matic notes
Sweep over the city like sun-spray and
    laughter,
Embroidered with all colours . . . Then
    what comes after?
More colours, a rain of them, hanging,
    delaying,

To sprinkle cool 'jade balustrades' with
their staying.
Golden flakes, silver filaments, what
pandemonium!
The rainbow joined in wedlock to a bursting harmonium.
Elephantine surrenders, prodigious re-
lapses,
Speech turned to a fire-ball which soars
and collapses
And spills down its words like the whole
spectrum falling
In a broken excitement. My eye, it's ap-
palling!
Such a chaotic shooting and drifting of
particles,
Mere loveliness solus, not stuck tight to
articles,
For what it all means does not matter a
jot;
You are filled with delight at it, or you
are not.
But suppose that you weary of the poly-
chromatic —
Some natures, I realize, are far too
lymphatic
To derive any pleasure from what is not
static —
There are corners to rest in with foun-
tains, and grass
Streaming up in long slopes, and if you
should pass
Just over the hill, there's a house where
each column
Is wreathed and entangled with the half-
gay, half-solemn
Recollections of childhood. There you
can eat luncheon,
And drink slow well-water from some old
grey puncheon,
And listen to tale of hobgoblins and
genie
Till I venture to say you'll be a bit
spleeny
And welcome the rising of white-faced
Selene.
(Rather pretty, that last, such touches do
garnish
One's writing, I think, and I'm not above
varnish.
I like a bright lustre in poems or medal-
lions,
The polish one sees in the later Italians.
Here a friend who's dropped in says I've
mixed my mythology.

Such a slip, if I've made it, deserves an
apology:
Selene, Cybele, Diana — I care
Not at all for mere names. You may take
Lemprière
And choose any Goddess you think op-
portune
So you quite understand I refer to the
moon.)
As you sit in the moonlight, the gist of
your summary
Will be: Here at last, is a poet without
flummery.
A score or two words are his total of
plunder,
But the whole is a boyhood imprisoned in
wonder.
A boy, and the things all about him —
plain stuff,
And not even new, but the measure's
enough.
Not the kind which they want for a
penny-a-liner;
It's too sharp, and too sheer, but for
that all the finer.
Have you ever gone into a dim, disused
attic
And poked about there among the
erratic
Remains of worn toys, legless soldiers,
chipped blocks,
And suddenly come on an old music-
box?
As you twist round the handle, the notes
seem to squeeze
Through the dust, some are lost and the
rest choke and wheeze,
But you make out a tune, and the mere
broken hint of it
Is the agonized joy of remembrance, by
dint of it
You suffer and love with an ache you'd
forgotten.
It were wiser, perhaps, were your ears
stuffed with cotton.
So Fletcher's not only the rainbow in
spate,
He's the soul of a music-box which can
create
All our childhood again. If the tune's a
bit scrappy,
What's the odds, just so long as the
sound makes us happy?
So far, Mr. Fletcher, for that's only a
mood,

We'll not whistle until we are out of the
wood.
Were your publishers mad, or why bind
together
Your 'Old House' and 'Symphonies'? One
wonders whether
You were bent on emptying out your
portfolio.
You created, at any rate, quite an im-
broglio.
This break-up of feeling with one or two
vile hacks
Of discord is as jarring as gumdrops and
smilax
Giving suddenly place to red-peppers and
asters.
The symphonies, come on this way, call
for plasters.
This arrangement, indeed, was the worst
of disasters.
Up bright in the morning, shoes tied and
hair brushed,
On a Sunday, maybe, when you're not
too much rushed,
You can seek ancient China in Symphony
Blue;
Or, if you prefer, you may take a stroll
through
Any Spring, in the Green; you may sail
over oceans
With the Red glare of stoke-holes to
thrill your emotions;
You may fight in the Scarlet, and laugh
in the Yellow,
You may do what you please in the Gold.
A fine fellow
Whose palette is full if a little bit messy.
But you have a good deal of the world
here in *esse.*
At least, you would have, were it not for
a doubt
About what any symphony's really about.
He writes, it appears, in a prismatic
spasm;
This phase of his work is complete proto-
plasm.
He is whirling his atoms before quite
cohering them,
But there's no doubt at all that he soon
will be steering them.
Yet, hold on a bit, my dear chap, do you
think
You can set all America down in cold ink?
Here you are, aeroplaning from Boston
to Texas,

And taking snapshots as you fly to per-
plex us.
If you see a sky-scraper, down it goes, and
the next
Shot's a square of Chicago — fit it into
the text.
Joggle niggers and Mexicans, some of
them dead 'uns,
And for spirit, bring in a few battles
where reddens
The smoke of proud guns, for your richest
of gravies
Is the sauce of Bull Run and the bier of
Jeff Davis.
You've done it, my cock, as well as a
man
Who is chiefly the slave of his sensa-
tions can;
For somehow your genius has a habit of
shying
Whenever your heart is involved. It's
most trying.
You can work yourself up to a towering
passion
Over landscapes and peoples, but when
you would fashion
A love lyric — Puff! and the substance
dissolves
And melts out of your fingers. A thou-
sand resolves
To break through with yourself, to have
done with objectives,
Leave you still where you were, explor-
ing perspectives.
I declare I could weep, did I not know
that life
Is only achieved through a vast deal of
strife.
You stand in the midst of a cosmic
heterogeny,
But I do not despair of your rearing a
progeny.
If chaos at last jelled into a man,
What a big chaos did, your small chaos
can.
You were built, you perceive, as the first
of your clan.
And, whatever you want, you've got what
no other
Poet ever has had. So a truce to the
pother!
Bless the man, you've done something as
new as tomorrow,
And I cannot consider your case with
much sorrow.

Just wait" . . . But, most gently, my old
    friend interrupted,
"Don't go on, Sir, I beg, I am being cor-
    rupted.
Your poets are so diverse. One thing I
    can say,
Good or bad, they're more various than
    poets were in my day.
If you've more in your bag, produce
    them, I pray."

Thus adjured, I remembered the one or
    two ladies
I'd deserted, and mentally crying "Oh,
    Hades!
Will they be mad as hops or affect a
    quite staid ease?
Whichever it is, I shall get a good wig-
    ging,
To be kept waiting's always a bit *infra*
    digging.
I must cudgel my brain for a really apt
    whopper,
Women don't pardon blunders when
    their *amour propre*
Is in question." But all of the chickens
    I'd counted,
When I'd tallied them up to a total,
    amounted
To just nothing at all, for your modern
    Egeria
Is far too advanced to give way to
    hysteria.
Approaching the first, I said no woman
    like her
Had yet been considered. She replied
    "Oh, you piker!
A poet learns to see, and you need not
    dissemble.
We will go up at once. Grace, here is
    your thimble."
Then jumping up quickly from where she
    was sitting
She quite overturned a little girl's knit-
    ting
Who was there by some chance, I'll come
    back to that later.
Said I to myself, no man living can hate
    her,
She is what I should call a born fas-
    cinator.
Upon reaching my friend — and let me
    explain
That these scenes in the scene all take
    place in my brain —

I began with a few neatly turned words
    on love
As the poet's own bourne, and declared
    that no glove
Ever fitted a hand with less wrinkling and
    snugger
Than this theme this poet. Here I
    noticed her shrug her
Shoulders a little, which was rather up-
    setting.
However, it may have been only coquet-
    ting.
Still I thought it was wise to get on with
    my tale:
"Our love-poet, *par excellence,* Sara
    Teasdale,"
I said with a flourish. Now that was a
    whale
Of a compliment, such things deserve an
    entail,
'Twas so brilliantly super even if it were
    true,
And I knew very well 'twas but one of a
    cue.
"This poet," I went on, "is a great niece
    of Sapho,
I know not how many 'greats' laid in a
    row
There should be, but her pedigree's per-
    fectly clear;
You can read it in 'Magazine Verse' for
    the year.
She is also a cousin, a few times re-
    moved,
Of dear Mrs. Browning, that last can be
    proved.
The elder poet hid in a shrouding man-
    tilla
Which she called Portuguese. Was ever
    trick sillier?
Our Sara is bolder, and feels quite at ease
As herself; in her mind there is nothing
    to tease.
Dale and valley, the country is hers she
    traverses,
She has mapped it all out in a bushel of
    verses.
Sara Teasdale she is — was — for our
    minnesinger,
Behind her front door, is now Mrs.
    Filsinger.
A hard question this, for a hand-maid of
    Muses,
When she's once made a name in cold
    print which she loses

On taking a husband, the law's masculinity
Would seem to demand a perpetual vir-
ginity
For all married poets of the down-trodden
sex.
To forfeit the sale of a new volume
checks
Even marital ardour, to say nothing of
cheques.
It's just this sort of thing which so frequently wrecks
The artistic composure, and must surely
perplex
Any husband who's not in the class of
henpecks.
Still I think the poor man should find
some consolation
In two or three volumes of sheer adoration.
It's the price he receives for never im-
posing
Himself on his wife when the lady's composing.
Under whatever name, the world grows
awarer
Every year of the prize we have got here
in Sara.
She has no colours, no trumpets, no plat-
forms, no scepticisms,
She has no taste for experiments, and
joins in no schisms;
She just sings like a bird, and I think
you'll agree
This is clearly the place for the china-
berry tree —
With a difference, the bird in that pleas-
ant, arboreal
Importation had three tones, while her
repertorial
Range is compassed in one, the reflex
amatorial.
She loves in a charming, perpetual way,
As though it just came when she was
distrait,
Or quite occupied in affairs of the day.
Or else, and I think the remark's more
acute,
She lives as the flower above a deep root.
Like a dedicate nun, she tells bead after
bead
At Matins, Tierce, Vespers. You'd think
she'd be treed
Just once in a while to find something to
say.

Not at all, she's a vast *catalogue raison-
née*
Of the subject. No one's so completely
au fait.
Her poetry succeeds, in spite of fragility,
Because of her very remarkable agility.
There is no single stunt in the style
amatory
Which is not included in her category,
We may as well take that at once *a
priori.*
So easy to her seems the work of creation
She might be just jotting down lines
from dictation.
There is nothing green here, each poem's
of the ripest.
The income tax lists her as Cupid's own
typist.
Of course, it is true that she's not intel-
lectual,
But those poets who are, are so apt to
subject you all
To theories and treatises, the whole gal-
vanometry
Of the bardling who thinks verse a sort
of geometry.
Now Sara's as easy to read as a slip
On a piece of banana, and there's no
need to skip,
For each poem's so peculiarly like every
other
You may as well stay where you are and
not bother.
She's that very rare compost, the dainty
erotic;
Such a mixture can't fail to produce a
hypnotic
Effect on the reader, whose keenest sen-
sation
Will consist in a perfect identification
Of himself with the poet, and her sorrows
and joys
Become his, while he swings to the deli-
cate poise
Of a primitive passion so nicely refined
It could not bring a blush to the most
squeamish mind.
Though the poems, I may add, are all
interlined
For the ready perusal of those not too
blind.
For Sara, if singer, is also a woman,
I know of no creature more thoroughly
human.
If woman, she's also a lady who realizes

That a hidden surprise is the best of surprises.
She seems a white statue awaiting unveiling,
But raised on a platform behind a stout railing
Whence she lures and retires, provoking a nearer
Contact which is promised to be even dearer
If we find we have courage enough not to fear her."
I looked at my subject to find she'd departed,
It's a habit of hers when a party's once started
To vanish unnoticed. My poetess had flown.
Seeing which, I remarked that I'd better postpone
The rest of my discourse. "I think you have shown
The outlines at least, my young cicerone,"
Said my friend. "Have you others? I see the sun's setting.
If you have many more, why we must be getting
On faster." I promised to use all despatch
Which I saw was most needed when I took out my watch.

"There's a child here I've not yet had leisure to mention,
Both she and her mother are worth your attention.
And one or two more I can think of, but most of them
Will not take up much time. After that, there's a host of them
We'll consider, if you are agreeable, *en masse.*"
"You spoke of a child, a child in this class!"
He asked me astonished. "I suppose that betrays me
A fogey indeed, but the thing does amaze me."
"No wonder," I answered, "America's youth
Symbolized with a vengeance as plainest of truth.
The poets I've presented may none of them be
Among the top boughs of that flourishing tree,

The *Genus Poeticus, Anglice-folia,*
Whose flowers have rivalled the greater magnolia,
But no shoot we know of has blossomed so early
As ours, and that makes a distinction clearly.
A ten-year-old child, half elf and half sage,
Where else can you find a poet of her age?
This is no little girl, though the critics preëmpt her
As the essence of childhood, but, *caveat emptor;*
It is easy to say, which is all that they care about,
For where is the critic one can see is aware about
Any essence whatever. This child's no more childhood
Than the wolf was the grandmother for donning her mild hood.
Hilda Conkling (I see I've forgotten to name her)
Is a greater phenomenon than they would proclaim her.
She is poetry itself, for her slight little soul
Is not yet of a size to encompass the whole
She gives out. Without knowing who really is speaking,
She speaks, and her words fall without the least seeking.
There's no need for allowances, the poems that she writes
May be certainly reckoned among the high lights
Of their *genre,* and although I'm no hyperbolist
I say flatly this child is the first Imagist.
But you will remember that Jove sometimes naps,
And the baby in Hilda not seldom entraps
The genius. But what of that! Such handicaps
May be reckoned as *nil* in the total, perhaps.
If she sometimes descends from Parnassus crescendo
To play with her dolls, why, the greatest of men do

The same in their fashion, and no innuendo
Need follow so natural a way of proceeding.
It is merely the little girl in her stamped-
ing.
Since she's neither a freak, nor a ghoul,
nor a Houyhnhnm,
We may thank the good fate which has
left her a minim
Of usual childhood — but, bless my soul,
what
Has become of her now, she was here,
was she not?"
"Oh," her mother joined in, "she ran
off to catch
A white kitten she saw. There's no fear
of a scratch,
She understands kittens." "Did she hear
what I'm saying?"
I asked. "I am really afraid she was paying
But little attention, her fingers were
drumming
In time to some sort of a tune she was
humming.
Now she and the kitten are disposed to
agree,
We have lost her, I fear, so you'll have
to take me."

Now what can a gallant gentleman do
On receiving a challenge so couched?
"*Entre nous,*
I think you're delightful," I said in aside,
"Your verses have made many poets
emerald-eyed.
What you seem to do without turning a
hair
Is just the one trick makes the less gifted
swear.
Who would copy you, digs for himself
a fine snare."
But when a man whispers inside of his
mind
He can scarcely expect an onlooker to
find
His abstraction amusing. My friend woke
me smartly
From my silent flirtation by announcing,
quite tartly,
"The child, as you've proved, is a *lusus
naturae,*
A verdict I'm sure any qualified jury

Would agree to at once were her case
up for trial.
Why even our feminophobe on the 'Dial'
Never dared to bring forward young ladies
of ten
As serious rivals to middle-aged men.
Poor Margaret Fuller, how she would
have doted on
Your remarkable age, and how happily
floated on
Its dawn-coloured currents and all its
forensical
Preoccupations! We were so common-
sensical.
Perhaps we were tainted with some senti-
mentalism,
But your *beau ideal* seems to be ele-
mentalism.
I can cap you, however, by mentioning one
Poet who never grew up, your friend,
Miss Dickinson."
"The comparison's just," I declared. "As
to Hilda,
Your juxtaposition need never bewilder
The admirers of either. One you failed
quite to scotch;
The other, I think, you should certainly
watch."
"Well, well," he said hastily, "but I
protest
At sitting all night with you and your
quest.
Who's the next, and be quick." As if
riding a race
I dashed at my subject: "Let me intro-
duce Grace
Conkling, no one is so handy at brooks.
They chatter and spatter through all of
her books.
And her fish — every angler is on tenter-
hooks
Lest they should escape him. The same
with her birds.
My land, what a fluttering they make!
Quite two thirds
Of her work is concerned with them, so
that her pages
Present the appearance of so many cages.
Then mountains — yes, mountains —
she crams them in too.
The little nearby ones all green, and all
blue
The more distant peaks. She is great on
perspective.

And whatever her theme, she is always
selective.
Take her love-poems, for instance, she
serves, piping hot,
A lyric of passion, and chooses the spot
For its setting somewhere where you go
in a yacht:
South America, Mexico, wherever not,
So there is a garden with grapefruit,
kumquat,
A score or two peach-trees and some
apricot.
For her flowers, one should be an en-
cyclopedia.
No less an abundance of knowledge the
medea
Could possibly be to surmount and re-
count 'em.
(Here I've got in a mess. There's no
rhyme except 'fount.' Hem!
Take no notice I beg of the exceedingly
thin ice
I'm skating on; if you find my heroine
nice,
Which she certainly must be to all
masculine eyes,
I care not a whit with what names I am
twitted.
On account of my subject, the claim's
manumitted.)
Now turn back six lines, so you capture
the gist
Of my tale where I left it — I will jot
down a list
Of a few of her flowers which must not
be missed.
There's magnolia first, of the kind grand-
iflora,
With its moons of blooms scenting the
air where Señora
Jimenez, Alcaro — take your pick, I
would banish
Such names if I could, but the Señora's
Spanish —
Walks under daturas whose cups of per-
fume
Hang above her, with jasmine so thick
there's scant room
To pass down the path to the beds where
the lilies
Are standing together in a stately and
still ease.
The dates are in blossom, or is it in
fruit? —

One should not make a list unless able
to do't,
And this Mexican flora trips any one's
foot —
Never mind, it's enough that the lady's
en route
To a clandestine tryst, when a tingling
sol fa
Shakes the garden to life, for he's
brought his guitar.
I acknowledge I've taken a few auto-
cratic
Liberties with my author, who's never
dramatic,
But the garden alone seemed to me
miasmatic,
With its scents and its sounds, but for
the rest solus.
If we must not embroider, why she must
parole us.
Since I've given no promise, and the
scene, without doubt,
Should have been there although the
poet left it out,
It shall stand in my version — and there's
a night-piece.
But what of the mornings, as soft as
crêpe-lisse
Till the mists burn away with the sun
and leave staring
A peacock-hued dome, with gilt cornices,
flaring
Above an old market-place crowded with
fig-trees
And the flame-coloured awnings of
booths where the big trees
Make a thunder-cloud shade, and
Giuseppe, Felice,
(These Mexican names make our own
sound so screechy!)
Are vociferously selling figs, melons, and
grapes?
It's the rainbow gone mad in all colours
and shapes.
There are smoky blue plums and raw-
striped cucumbers,
Red slits of pomegranates, gold loquats,
the umbers
Of nuts and the green of almonds not yet
husked;
Huge elephant baskets of flowers all be-
tusked
With long sprays of yucca — the poet
has attacked us

With all of her armoury at once — spears of cactus
Shoot out between passion-vines spreading their discus-
Like blooms just above a bouquet of hibiscus.
The trees, I observe, are all festooned with monkeys,
Long necklaces of them, and the square's choked with donkeys.
The bell in the peacock dome clatters and clangs,
Parakeets flash through leaves like so many whiz-bangs
On the fourth of July, there are orchids exploding
New flowers each minute over hand-carts unloading
Bread-fruit and bananas, and the hot, dry sirocco
Tips it all to a sparkle so bright and rococo
The book should be bound in a purple morocco
If the contents and cover were made to agree,
This dismal sage-green is a catastrophe;
But what publisher thinks of aught else but his fee.
I have written my best, but it's so multiplex I can
Never compete with her when she's on Mexican
Horticulture, zoölogy, and I don't know what all,
Unless I've Gray's 'Botany' handy, and Nuttall,
With Wilson and Chapman close by on the table;
And as to the speech, it is just so much Babel
To me if each word is not tagged with a label
In good easy English. Well, no matter for that,
I've told you she's got every atmosphere pat.
She's as happy with pine-trees and an orchard of apples
And the clouds which a 'slender sky' scatters and dapples
Over grass-and-stone hillsides, as with lotus-brimmed fountains,
And I'll swear that no poet has done better with mountains.

Her flickers, and veeries, and finches, and thrushes
Are as good as her nightingale hid in a bush is,
And when she would sing of the Old Mohawk Trail
I toss up my hat with a shout of 'All hail!
Troubador of New England, who knows that white pine is
Her very soul's self,' and I write in gold, 'Finis!' "

"Dear me," said my friend, "so you think she's a laureate
Of poor old New England." "If there's any one bore I hate
More than another," I answered, "it's the man
Who pretends to see farther than any one can.
Considering   we've   Robinson,   Miss Lowell, and Frost
Such a statement were rash. I'm afraid you have lost
Just the shade I intended; there's a difference, be sure,
Between a poet laureate and a troubador."
"The point is well taken," he admitted at once.
"Was I laureate or troubador? The distinction confronts
Me now rather unpleasantly. For, was I able
To go her one better in my famous 'Fable'?
That I loved my New Egland you'll find by the space
I devoted to her in that book. Face to face
With her new poets, I'm wondering who'll win in the race.
Am I in the lead since they've quickened the pace?
I'm beginning to doubt it as far as mere praise
Counts at least, I was Frost and she mixed, hence my bays,
If I really deserved any. But with this poetess
I find myself back on old ground, none the less
Delightful, be sure, and there is a slight change

In her manner, I do detect that, but her range
Does not carry me out of the depth of my sympathy."
"The next fellow will," was my succinct reply.
"Alfred Kreymborg, deft master of the oddest machine
Made of strings and of gut which I ever have seen.
A hybrid of sorts yclept mandolute.
Queer instrument? Very. His voice is the flute
Playing over the strings, and his songs epigrams
Tinkled up into rhythm. Oh, yes, they're called shams
By the public at large, but who wants a large public?
Kreymborg's manner to his is a kiss and a kick.
He's the monkey of poetry who climbs on a stick,
But that's only his way to conceal by a trick
The real truth he has. Oh, he's impolitic
To a fault, but the fellow is no lunatic,
Nor mountebank either, though some people think
He has squeezed not two drops of his blood in his ink
And regard him as jester with more than suspicion.
The fact is he's an untaught, but natural musician.
His poems and his tunes come straight out of his pestle
And fall as they will. Unbaked clay's not a vessel,
However, and though I believe he has made
Some excellent poems, that's not really his trade,
Which I grieve to admit consists largely of bluffing.
The gems in his books are half smothered in stuffing.
He's an ironist pure, but I can't call him simple;
More than one of his efforts may be classed as a pimple
On the fair face of poetry, but others delight us
As much for their beauty as the first kind affright us

By their horrible ugliness, wry-formed and waxy.
He's a man flinging queer little toys from a taxi.
If you scrabble round fast enough you may pick a good one,
But the chances are ten to one you'll get a wooden
Contraption of rude, creaky springs, badly gilt,
Just words nailed together haphazard, no lilt,
And no sense you can find. It's a real 'hunt the slipper'
To read what he writes, and you may come a tripper
Or you may win a prize, that's the whole proposition.
How does it affect his poetic position?
I tell you quite frankly I feel at a loss
For an answer to give you, we might try a toss
Or leave it in peace on the lap of the Gods.
To put it quite plainly, dear Sir, what's the odds?
When we come to his singing, it's another concern.
However on earth did the chap come to learn
Of those strange sweeping chords and that odd whispered singing
Which cleaves to the heart and sets the nerves stinging,
And where did he find his sawed-off mandolin
Or guitar, or banjo? Good Lord, it's a sin
When there is such an instrument no one else knows it,
But the luckier for him, I say, and therefore — *prosit!*
The poems he writes down never end, scarce begin,
If the truth must be told; in the music, a thin
Silver chord holds a something, a glitter of fable,
And the tale and its moral lie strung on a cable,
Half-music, half-thought, but what we have heard
Is more echo than music, more music than word.
He's a poet in the core of him, a bit of a clown,

And two-thirds of a vagabond drifting
round town,
Seeing whimsical nothings at every street
corner.
A lover possessed, an inveterate scorner,
Engaged in a pulling of plums like Jack
Horner —
There's the man, Alfred Kreymborg."
"We had no counterpart
To your monkey-musician. Do you call
the thing art
You've been talking about?" The old
gentleman's tone
Betrayed just a trace of annoyance. "I've
shown
You a figure, make of him whatever you
can,
To tag him as this or that's not in my
plan.
You asked me to give you each phase of
the time."
"And I could not stand Whitman be-
cause he'd no rhyme!"
He gasped. "You may banish all verse
that's harmonious,
But it's not so far short of being felo-
nious
When you ask us to substitute for it the
simious.
You will find what that means in the
pages of Linnaeus.
We raised roses, but you seem to culti-
vate zinnias,
Not to call your verse anything more
ignominious."
"You forget," I reminded him, "his
mandolute;
To judge him without it is hardly acute."
The old gentleman suddenly turned and
snapped "Nonsense!"
"On the contrary, Sir, it's the *sine quâ
non* sense.
We have Lindsay, a voice; and Kreym-
borg, an instrument."
"Is your poetry a junk-shop? I am now
quite convinced you meant
All this as hoaxing." I tried to protest.
He went on in a stream like a person
possessed:
"A junk-shop indeed! There is Frost, a
dim Buddha
Set high on a shelf; there is Sandburg, a
cruder
Carved god of some sort, neither English
nor Gothic —

Assyrian, Egyptian, perhaps — a huge
Thothic
Sacerdotal presentment placed over the
door;
There are two Chinese vases, a spy-glass,
three score
Or so dog's-eared books, flower-pots, and
a spinet,
This odd jumble's Miss Lowell; there's a
little green linnet
Hung up in a cage, Sara Teasdale, I
think;
And a battered old desk all bespattered
with ink,
That's Masters; and just up above is a
palette
Smudged over with paint, that is
Fletcher; a mallet
Thrown down on a heap of new books
which it crushes
Is Aiken; and there is a bundle of rushes
Just picked and brought in to the shop to
set off
A stone-lantern — 'H.D.'; just behind is
a trough
To water poor readers, it's not overflow-
ing
But full to the brim and seems always
just going
To spill, but that never quite happens,
you guess
At once this is Robinson; in a recess
Just under the counter are two or three
chromos
Of tropical scenes, Mrs. Conkling is
those;
And the blocks which you see have just
come from the gilder
I need hardly tell you are your precious
Hilda,
They are specially made to build Castles
in Spain.
There's your junk-shop of poets, and I
tell you again
I don't like to be quizzed." Poor old
soul, he was furious,
But when once convinced his suspicions
were spurious
He was eager as ever. "For," said I,
"there's no quarrel.
The shop sign's a wreath and it's pos-
sibly laurel."
"Perhaps I have half a suspicion of that
Myself," he smiled broadly, "now give tit
for tat,

And confound all my quondam ridiculous
    ires
With something so pleasant and . . . "

                    "The Untermeyers!"
The shout which I gave cut his sentence
    in two,
And we lost the last part in the hullabaloo
I made as I served up my marital dish.
"Two poets, and between them whatever
    you wish.
If they haven't the depth, they've more
    range than the Brownings,
It runs all the way from complexes to
    clownings,
With love-songs so frank they pursue
    more than follow man
Being made on the pattern approved by
    King Soloman.
(My so spelling that name is nothing to
    look solemn on,
I've a black-letter precedent one might
    write a column on.
Orthographical pedantry was not in King
    Solomon.)
At least hers are, a perfectly natural law
Vide Freud, D. H. Lawrence, and George
    Bernard Shaw.
For woman possesses, it seems, an atomic
Attraction for man, and his serio-comic
Pretence of pursuit is a masculine blind
To keep up his prestige within his own
    mind.
If the lady appears to be fleeing, the
    stroke
Is a masterly one and just her little joke.
But when this same woman, in some
    bright confection
Of boudoir attire, gives herself to reflec-
    tion
And writes down her heart in a freak of
    exposure,
The result will most certainly jar the
    composure
Of elderly persons brought up more
    demurely,
While youth will retire, with doors locked
    securely,
And read what to them is a gorgeous dis-
    play
Of Paradise opened on visiting day.
The best gifts of our time are these
    pure revelations
Of facts as they are in all human rela-
    tions

With no understatements or exaggera-
    tions.
And the West is the East, with the puri-
    tan night
Swallowed up in a gush of approaching
    daylight —
At least, so our cherished delusion mis-
    takes it,
And since everything is as man's attitude
    makes it,
What the Orient knew we are learning
    again
For the next generation to laud with
    'Amen!'
In this wise are the poems of Jean Unter-
    meyer,
Though the whole of her output takes
    less than a quire
Of paper to hold it. Not at all so with
    Louis,
He's as rich and eclectic as a bowl of
    chop-suey.
If his wife plays a timbrel, he plays a
    ram's horn,
His ardour for worship is never outworn,
One of Joshua's soldiers, protecting his
    candle
With the pitcher he eagerly holds by
    the handle,
Tramping his turn at a long sentry-go
Round and round the high walls of our
    new Jericho;
Or, again, on a harp which, if slightly
    archaic,
Has lost nothing in tone or in timbre
    since Hebraic
Psalmists once plucked it in stern exhor-
    tations
Before kneeling hosts of then wandering
    nations.
Through the streets of to-day, with his
    shoulders set square,
He walks, full of business, and yet one's
    aware
Of a something he sees which surrounds
    and encloses
His vision, he might be just gazing on
    Moses
Descending the mountain, but his tables
    of stone
Have Marx written on them and Debs,
    while his own
Name has no place at all, and that's
    characteristic;
His ego's too eager to be egotistic.

When everything beckons, why sit at
home brooding
On the opposite wall; he's no taste for
secluding
Himself or his interests, and they're only
controlled
By the small slice of time which he hap-
pens to hold.
Punctiliously present in this exact mo-
ment,
His dates began when he learnt what
'proximo' meant.
No glance of his, scanning the past, finds
it prizable,
The only real worth is in the realizable;
Neither history nor legend induce him
to vary
His perfect allegiance to the mere tem-
porary.
When he takes on himself the rôle of
appraiser,
His words spout and gush like a Yellow-
stone geyser,
At least for the poet whose political ways
err
From those of society, an apt paraphraser
Of the poems of such men, he becomes
a sharp razor
To others, no hint of the sham senti-
mental
Escapes his smooth blade, and he is not
gentle
With the scenes or the poses in which
'temperamental'
Poets indulge, and he's scarcely parental
To persons with leanings toward the
transcendental.
His dictums, it's true, are less poignant
than plenty,
And do not rank too high among
cognoscenti,
Who are usually college boys not quite
turned twenty.
He has a blind spot; he cannot keep his
eye on
A world without man. Why, a fresh
dandelion
Is nothing to him without someone to
pick it,
Observe it alone and he hands you the
ticket
For exit at once, and it's not a return
check.
He hopes in this way to act as a stern
check

On all those untoward imaginative flights
In which he is sure he descries signal-
lights
Of a shower of earth-wrecking meteor-
ites.
Now why should a man who is so pyro-
technical
Find a mere meteoric display apoplectical,
While many consider it a beautiful
spectacle?
That's a matter for wonder; but, speak-
ing of rockets,
He carries them round like small change
in his pockets.
A touch and they're off, and the whiz
and the flare
And the burst of bright balls are quite
his affair.
What a crackle of rhymes! They go off
like red crackers
Beneath a tin pan. And there are some
whackers
Exploding at intervals when you least
expect them,
And long trailing assonances set to con-
nect them.
His wit is a pin-wheel which at first jerks
and spits
Then whirls suddenly round as though
ten thousand fits
Were in it, and all is one sparkling gyra-
tion
In every known manner of versification.
But the best of his fire-works comprise
his set-pieces
Which are really so many bright-coloured
esquisses.
(Please pardon a liberty in pronunciation.
Le mot juste, I believe, needs no justifi-
cation,
Even when it involves a slight deviation
From the speech of a friendly but jaw-
breaking nation,
Who, I trust, will regard this brief ex-
planation
In the light of a willing, though painful,
libation.)
But how I run on! To return to my
symbol:
A bare two or three poets have ever been
nimble
Enough to depict their confrères and
show them
Drawn to scale in each feature as all
their friends know them.

Just glance at them now, each hung on a
    hook
Awaiting the match — Ftt! Presto! Now,
    look —
How they flicker and burn, each one to
    his trick:
There are Robinson's quatrains, Frost's
    long, pliant stick
Of blank-verse which he carries when
    taking his walks,
And Sandburg with his suit-case all
    crammed full of talks
With murderers and hobos and such
    worth while gentry;
Here is Lindsay retreating at speed to the
    entry
To stand on the stair and harangue new
    arrivals
With the very same stunts they employ
    at revivals,
While Amy Lowell, close by the library
    door,
Announces her theories and tries hard
    to score
More disciples than Lindsay; though,
    with his and her medium,
It's a matter of choice which produces
    least tedium.
Whoever the poet and whatever his
    foibles,
Even dull ones like — well, I won't
    say — are enjoyables
When he touches them up to a glare
    with his slow-match.
At this sort of thing every one else is no
    match
For him, and the best simply rank as
    '— and Other Poets.'
A terrible fellow with his black line to
    smother poets,
And that line is become the poetical
    plank
From which he dives into posterity's tank.
It's a curious conceit, and his one bit of
    swank,
To flaunt himself under a long line of
    blank.
But what poet, quick or dead, would dare
    to decline
An immortal existence conferred by one
    line.
Take it then, Untermeyer, irrepressible
    Louis,
And observe, as you touch it, that the
    leaves are still dewy.

That dew is the proof that it's not
    bombazine,
One has to be careful with a housewife
    like Jean.
The lady, you know, is a trifle impulsive,
And I should not like my gift to receive
    a propulsive
Reception. For fame's rather like mil-
    linery,
To-day it's a blossom, to-morrow a cherry,
The day after, glass flowers in some
    cemetery.
But who, even in fame, would remain
    stationary?
Not you certainly, Louis, your deepest
    devotion
Is involved in this question, but you
    have no notion
How nearly you come to perpetual mo-
    tion."
Here I ended abruptly. When he's car-
    ried a man
To the centre of movement, the historian
Does well to leave off. I left off there-
    fore.
My old friend somewhat wearily asked,
    "Is there more?"
"A few odds and ends, but not much
    you need heed,"
I replied. "Very well, run them over at
    speed,"
He commanded.

Now if he had wielded a bludgeon
I could not have more quickly obeyed,
    no curmudgeon
Could have forced my direction more
    surely than he did.
His imperious courtesy was all that I
    needed
To start off again with my tale: "The
    expatriates
Come next," I began, "but the man who
    expatiates
Upon them must go all yclad in cold
    steel
Since these young men are both of them
    most *difficile*,
And each is possessed of a gift for satire.
Their forked barbs would pierce any usual
    attire.
In order of merit, if not of publicity,
I will take Eliot first, though it smacks
    of duplicity
To award Ezra Pound the inferior place

As he simply won't run if not first in a race.

Years ago, 'twould have been the other way round,

With Eliot a rather bad second to Pound.

But Pound has been woefully free with the mustard

And so occupied has quite ruined his custard.

No poems from his pen, just spleen on the loose,

And a man who goes on in that way cooks his goose.

T. S. Eliot's a very unlike proposition,

He has simply won through by process of attrition.

Where Pound played the fool, Eliot acted the wiseacre;

Eliot works in his garden, Pound stultifies his acre.

Eliot's always engaged digging fruit out of dust;

Pound was born in an orchard, but his trees have the rust.

Eliot's mind is perpetually fixed and alert;

Pound goes off anywhere, anyhow, like a squirt.

Pound believes he's a thinker, but he's far too romantic;

Eliot's sure he's a poet when he's only pedantic.

But Eliot has raised pedantry to a pitch,

While Pound has upset romance into a ditch.

Eliot fears to abandon an old masquerade;

Pound's one perfect happiness is to parade.

Eliot's learning was won at a very great price;

What Pound calls his learning he got in a trice.

Eliot knows what he knows, though he cannot digest it;

Pound knows nothing at all, but has frequently guessed it.

Eliot builds up his essays by a process of massing;

Pound's are mostly hot air, what the vulgar call 'gassing.'

Eliot lives like a snail in his shell, pen protruding;

Pound struts like a cock, self-adored, self-deluding.

Pound's darling desire is his ego's projection;

Eliot tortures his soul with a dream of perfection.

Pound's an ardent believer in the value of noise;

Eliot strains every nerve to attain a just poise.

Each despises his fellows, for varying reasons;

Each one is a traitor, but with different treasons.

Each has left his own country, but Pound is quite sick of it,

While for Eliot's sojourn, he is just in the nick of it.

Pound went gunning for trouble, and got it, for cause;

Eliot, far more astute, has deserved his applause.

Each has more brain than heart, but while one man's a critic

The other is more than two-thirds tympanitic.

Both of them are book-men, but where Eliot has found

A horizon in letters, Pound has only found Pound.

Each man feels himself so little complete

That he dreads the least commerce with the man in the street;

Each imagines the world to be leagued in a dim pact

To destroy his immaculate taste by its impact.

To conceive such a notion, one might point out slyly,

Would scarcely occur to an author more highly

Original; such men seldom bother their wits

With outsiders at all, whether fits or misfits.

Where they are, whom they see, is a matter of sheer

Indifference to a poet with his own atmosphere

To exist in, and such have no need to be preachy

Anent commonplaceness since they can't write a *cliché* —

In toto, at least, and it's *toto* that grounds

All meticulous poets like the Eliots and Pounds.

Taking up Eliot's poetry, it's a blend of intensive

And elegant satire with a would-be of-
fensive
Kind of virulent diatribe, and neither
sort's lacking
In the high type of polish we demand of
shoe-blacking.
Watteau if you like, arm in arm with
Laforgue,
And both of these worthies laid out in
a morgue.
The poems are expert even up to a vice,
But they're chilly and dead like corpses
on ice.
Now a man who's reluctant to heat his
work through,
I submit, is afraid of what that work will
do
On its own, with its muscles and sinews
unfrozen.
Something, I must think, which he would
not have chosen.
Is there barely a clue here that the action
of heat
Might reveal him akin to the man in the
street?
For his brain — there's no doubt that
is up on a steeple,
But his heart might betray him as one
of the people.
A fearful dilemma! We can hardly abuse
him
For hiding the damaging fact and excuse
him
If it really be so, and we've more than
a hint of it,
Although I, for one, like him better by
dint of it.
Since the poet's not the half of him, we
must include
The critical anchorite of his 'Sacred
Wood.'
'This slim duodecimo you must have
your eye on
If you'd be up to date,' say his friends.
He's a sly one
To have chosen this format — the book's
heavy as iron.
I'm acutely aware that its grave erudi-
tion
Is quite in the line of a certain tradi-
tion,
That one which is commonly known as
tuition.
To read it is much like a lengthy so-
journing

In at least two or three institutions of
learning.
But, being no schoolboy, I find I'm not
burning
For this sort of instruction, and vote for
adjourning.
What the fellow's contrived to stuff into
his skull
May be certainly classed as a pure miracle.
But the way he imparts it is terribly dull.
This may not be fair, for I've only begun
it,
And one should not pronounce on a book
till one's done it,
But I've started so often, in so many
places,
I think, had there been any livelier spaces
I must have encountered at least one of
those
Before falling, I say it with shame, in a
doze.
We must take Ezra Pound from a dif-
ferent angle:
He's a belfry of excellent chimes run to
jangle
By being too often and hurriedly tugged
at,
And even, when more noise was wanted,
just slugged at
And hammered with anything there was
lying round.
Such delicate bells could not stand so
much Pound.
Few men have to their credit more
excellent verses
Than he used to write, and even his
worse is
Much better than most people's good.
He'd a flair
For just the one word indispensably there,
But which few could have hit on. An-
other distinction
Was the way he preserved fledgeling poets
from extinction.
Had he never consented to write when
the urge
To produce was not on him, he'd have
been on the verge
Of a great reputation by now, but his
shoulder
Had always its chip, and Ezra's a scolder.
Off he flew, giving nerves and brain up
to the business
In a crowing excitement not unmixed
with dizziness,

Whenever he could get any sort of news-
paper
To lend him a column and just let him
vapour.
But while he was worrying his gift of
invention
For adequate means to ensure the pre-
vention
Of any one's getting what he had not
got,
His uncherished talent succumbed to dry
rot.
When, after the battle, he would have
employed her,
He learnt, to his cost, that he had de-
stroyed her.
Now he does with her ghost, and the
ghosts of the hosts
Of troubadors, minstrels, and kings, for
he boasts
An acquaintance with persons of whose
very names
I am totally ignorant, likewise their
fames.
The foremost, of course, is Bertrand de
Born,
He's a sort of pervasively huge leprecawn
Popping out from Pound's lines where
you never expect him.
He is our poet's chief lar, so we must not
neglect him.
There is Pierre de Maensac, and Pierre
won the singing —
Where or how I can't guess, but Pound
sets his fame ringing
Because he was *dreitz hom* (whatever
that is)
And had De Tierci's wife; what happened
to his
We don't know, in fact we know nothing
quite clearly,
For Pound always treats his ghosts cava-
lierly.
There is John Borgia's bath, and be sure
that he needed it;
Aurunculeia's shoe, but no one much
heeded it.
There's a chap named Navighero and
another Barabello,
Who prods a Pope's elephant; and one
Mozarello;
Savairic Mauleon — Good Lord, what a
dance
Of impossible names! First I think we're
in France,

Then he slides in Odysseus, and Eros,
and Atthis —
But I'm not to be fooled in my Greek,
that's what that is.
Yet, look, there's Italian sticking out in
italics
And French in plain type, the foreign
vocalics
Do give one the feeling of infinite back-
ground,
When it's all just a trick of that con-
summate quack, Pound,
To cheat us to thinking there's some-
thing behind it.
But, when nothing's to find, it's a hard
job to find it.
The tragedy lies in the fact that the man
Had a potentiality such as few can
Look back or forward to; had he but
kept it,
There's no bar in all poetry but he
might have leapt it.
Even now, I believe, if he'd let himself
grow,
He might start again. . ." "We will have
no 'although'
In your gamut of poets. Your man is a
victim
Of expatriation, and, as usual, it's licked
him.
It has happened more times than I care
to reflect,
And the general toll is two countries'
neglect."
The old gentleman sighed. "I presume
that you've finished,"
He went on at last. "The ranks are
diminished,"
I answered, "but still there remain one
or two
Whose names, at the least, I must pass
in review.

There's William Rose Benét, his poems
have no beaters
In their own special *genre*; he's a wonder
with metres,
A sleight of hand artist, and one of his
mysteries
Is his cabinet trick with all the world's
histories.
There's Bodenheim, trowel in hand, bent
on laying
A tessellate floor with the words he is
saying.

Squares of marble, moss-agate, and jade,
and carnelian,
Byzantium *in pleno*, never Delphic nor
Delion.
A perfect example of contemporaneity,
But with too little force and too much
femineity.
The man's a cascade of verbose spon-
taneity.
Except when he's giving Advice, there he
shines
And La Fontaine plays hide and seek in
his lines.
As a maker of Fables, no one ever quar-
rels
With his style, and old Aesop must look
to his laurels.
There's another young man who strums
a clavier
And prints a new poem every third or
fourth year.
Looking back, I don't know that anything
since
Has delighted me more than his 'Peter
Quince.'
He has published no book and adopts this
as pose,
But it's rather more likely, I think, to
suppose
The particular gift he's received from the
Muses
Is a tufted green field under whose grass
there oozes
A seeping of poetry, like wind through a
cloister;
On occasion it rises, and then the field's
moister
And he has a poem if he'll trouble to
bale it,
Address it to 'Poetry,' and afterwards mail
it.
His name, though the odds overbalance
the evens
Of those who don't know it as yet's
Wallace Stevens,
But it might be John Doe for all he
seems to care —
A little fine work scattered into the
air
By the wind, it appears, and he quite
unaware
Of the fact, since his motto's a cool
'laisser-faire.'
There's Edna Millay with her 'Aria da
Cap-

O'h, she dealt all society a pretty sharp
rap
With that bauble of hers, be it drama or
fable,
Which I certainly trust won't be laid
on the table
In my time. Her 'Bean-Stalk' is a nice
bit of greenery,
For one of her charms is her most
charming scenery,
Few can handle more deftly this sort of
machinery.
But I must call a halt, or your brain will
be flooded
With big poets, and little poets, and
poets not yet budded."
"Have you really so many?" my old
friend desired
To know. "If you count all the ones
who've aspired,
I could go on all night. You see we have
got
A Renaissance on." "Dear me, I forgot,"
He remarked somewhat dryly. "We were
not renaissant,
But also I note we were far less com-
placent
Than you seem to be, and this beggar-
my-neighbour
Game you all indulge in was no part of
our labour."
"No," I told him, "you played on a pipe
and a tabour;
We go girt with a shield and drawing a
sabre.
And yet you, with Miranda. . ." I
talked to the swell
Of the wide-running river, to a clock-
striking bell.
There was no one beside me. A wave
caught the sedge
Of the bank and went ruffling along its
soft edge.
Behind me a motor honked twice, and
the bridges
Glared suddenly out of the dusk, twinkling ridges
Notched into the dim river-line. Wind
was whirling
The plane-trees about, it sent the waves
curling
Across one another in a chuckle of
laughter —
And I recollect nothing that happened
thereafter.

Who my gentleman was, if you hazard
a guess,
I will tell you I know nothing more,
nothing less,
Than I here have set forth. For I never
have met him
From that day to this, or I should have
beset him
With questions, I think. My unique
perseverance
Kept me haunting the river for his re-
appearance,
Armed with two or three books which
might serve as a primer
To point my remarks, for I am no skim-
mer,
When I push at a wheel it must go or
I'll break it,
Once embarked on a mission I never
forsake it.
Did he guess my intention and think
he'd enough
Of me and my poets, a sufficient rebuff;
But I've never believed he went off in a
huff.
Did I dream him perhaps? Was he only
a bluff
Of the past making sport with my brain?
But that's stuff!
Take it what way you like, if he were a
spectre
Then the ghosts of old poets have re-
ceived a correcter
Account than they had of us, and may
elect a

Prize winner and vote over post-prandial
nectar.
Suppose that, before awarding the prize,
The poets had determined to sift truth
from lies
And had sent an ambassador down to
enquire
Whose flames were cut tinsel and whose
were real fire.
Selecting a man once employed in the
trade,
They had only to wait the report that he
made
And discuss it at *al fresco* lunch in the
shade
Of some cloudy and laurel-embowered
arcade.
Supposing it happened that their emis-
sary
Determined to take me as a tutelary
Genius to guide him, and after he'd
pumped me
Of all that I knew, quite naturally
dumped me
And returned whence he came. You call
this bizarre?
But then, after all, so many things
are!
If it were so, at least the conclave knows
who's who,
And will see there's no reason at all to
pooh-pooh.
I, for one, am most eager to know what
they'll do.
Aren't you?

WHAT'S O'CLOCK

EAST, WEST, NORTH, AND SOUTH OF A MAN

I

He rides a white horse,
  Mary Madonna,
Dappled as clouds are dappled,
  O Mary, Mary,
And the leather of his harness is the colour of the sky.

On his head is a casque with an azure plume
Which none may observe with unswerving eyes.
  A proud gentleman, Mary Madonna.
A knight to fill the forest, riding it cross-wise,
  O Mary, Mary.
His hoof-prints dint the beech-mast,
His plume brushes the golden leaves.

No flute man this, to sigh at a lady's elbow.
This is a trumpet fellow, proper for jousting or battle,
  Mary Madonna,
To hack an enemy to pieces, and scale his castle wall.
  O Mary, Mary,
A point for piercing, an edge for shearing, a weight for pounding, a voice for thundering,
And a fan-gleam light to shine down little alleys
Where twisted houses make a jest of day.

There are dead men in his hand,
  Mary Madonna,
And sighing women out beyond his thinking.
  O Mary, Mary,
He will not linger here or anywhere.
He will go about his business with an ineradicable complaisance,
Leaving his dead to rot, his women to weep and regret, his sons to wax into his likeness,
Never dreaming that the absurd lie he believes in
Is a gesture of Fate forcing him to the assumption of a vast importance
Quite other than the blazoning of ceremonial banners to wave above a tomb.

II

Hot with oranges and purples,
In a flowing robe of a marigold colour,
He sweeps over September spaces.
  Scheherezade, do you hear him,
  And the clang of his scimitar knocking on the gates?
The tawny glitter of his turban,
Is it not dazzling —
With the saffron jewel set like a sun-flower in the midst?
The brown of his face!
Aye, the brown like the heart of a sun-flower.
Who are you to aspire beyond the petals,
To touch the golden burning beneath the marigold robe?
His sash is magnificence clasped by an emerald;
His scimitar is the young moon hanging before a sun-set;
His voice is the sun in mid-heaven
Pouring on whirled ochre dahlias;
His fingers, the flight of Autumn wasps through a honey-coloured afternoon.
So, Scheherezade, he has passed the dragon fountains
And is walking up the marble stairway, stopping to caress the peacocks.
He will lean above you, Scheherezade, like September above an orchard of apples.
He will fill you with the sweetness of spice-fed flames.
Will you burn, Scheherezade, as flowers burn in September sunlight?
Hush, then, for flame is silence,
And silent is the penetrating of the sun.

The dragon fountains splash in the court-yards,
And the peacocks spread their tails.

There are eyes in the tails of the peacocks,
But the palace windows are shuttered and
barred.

III

Pipkins, pans, and pannikins,
China teapots, tin and pewter,
Baskets woven of green rushes.
Maudlin, Jennifer, and Prue,
What is lacking in your kitchens?
Are you needing skewers or thimbles,
Spools of cotton, knots of ribbon,
Or a picture for your pantry,
Or a rag-rug for the bed-side?
Plodding, plodding, through the dusty
Lanes between the hawthorn hedges,
My green wheels all white and dusty,
I as dusty as a miller,
White as any clown among them
Dancing on the London stages.
Here I have Grimaldi's latest,
Songs and ballads, sheets of posies
For your feet to ring-a-rosy.
Songs to make you sigh and shudder,
Songs to win you bright eye-glances,
Choruses, and glees, and catches.
Do your cupboards need refilling?
Take a peep into these hampers.
I have goods to loose your purse-strings:
Smocks, and shifts, and fine clocked
stockings
Aprons of a dozen sizes,
Muslin dresses sprigged and patterned.
Can you look and not be buying?
Maudlin, Jennifer, and Prue,
Here are dainties for sweetheartings,
Tinsel crackers plumped with mottoes,
Twisted barley sticks and pear-drops.
Here are ear-rings, chains, and brooches,
Choose what gift you'll have him give
you.
If the sweetheart days are over,
I have silver forks and bodkins,
Leather breeches, flannel bed-gowns,
Spectacles for eyes grown feeble,
Books to read with them and candles
To light up the page of evenings.
Toys, too, to delight the children,
Rocking-horses, tops, and marbles,
Dolls with jointed arms, and flying
Kites, and hoops, and even the Royal
Game of Goose the world is playing.
When I camp out on a common,

Underneath an oak or linden,
And my horse crops at his supper,
Finding it along the hedge-rows,
Then I play at Goose with one hand
Taking sides against the other.
First my right hand holds the dice-cup,
Then my left, each has its counter.
'Tis a pastime never tires.
Coppers, coppers, for the pedlar.
Maudlin, Jennifer, and Prue,
Fare you well, I must be jogging.
Horse-bells tinkle at the lane-sides,
Green wheels growing whiter, whiter,
Lurching van of whims and whimsies
Vanishing into the distance.

IV

Who would read on a ladder?
But who can read without a ladder?
Cheerful paradox to be resolved never.
Book by book, he steps up and off to all
the four quarters
Of all the possible distances.
Minerva have a care of him,
For surely he has none for himself.
His eyes are dim with the plague of print,
But he believes them eagle-seeing.
His spectacles have grown to his nose,
But he is unaware of the fact since he
never takes them off.
A little black cap on his head;
A rusty dressing-gown, with the quilts
run together,
To keep out the cold;
A window out of which he never looks;
A chair from which he never rises.
But do you not know a wharf-side when
you see it,
And are you not moved at watching the
putting off of the caravels of dream?
Food gets into his mouth by accident
As though fish swam the seas to come
there,
And cattle crowded the thoroughfares to
reach his lips.
If there are intermediaries, he is un-
conscious of them,
As he is of everything but his cat,
Who shares his vigils
And has discovered the art of projecting
herself into his visions.
He loves a thousand ladies, and fore-
gathers with a thousand caravans.
To-day is as remote as yesterday,

And he is avid of either with the intensity of a partaker of each;
He could hobnob as blithely with Julius Caesar as with King George or Samuel Gompers,
And his opinions on affairs of the moment are those of an eye-witness
Although he never sets foot out-of-doors.
Indeed, Minerva, you should watch the step of this gentleman,
For he runs so swiftly past events and monuments it seems incredible he should not trip.
The walls of forbidden cities fall before him;
He has but to tap a sheepskin to experience kingdoms,
And circumstance drips from his fingers like dust.
An habituated eye sees much through a pin-prick,
And are not his observations folio wide?
He eats the centuries
And lives a new life every twenty-four hours,
So lengthening his own to an incalculable figure.
If you think you see only an old man mouldering between four walls,
You are greatly mistaken.
Minerva over the door could tell you better
If her stone face would speak.
Talk to him and he will not hear you;
Write a book and he knows you better than you know yourself.
Draw the curtains, then, and bring in tea, with plenty of buttered scones.
Since neither the old gentleman nor Minerva will speak to us,
I think we had best ignore them and go on as we are.

EVELYN RAY

No decent man will cross a field
Laid down to hay, until its yield

Is cut and cocked, yet there was the track
Going in from the lane and none coming back.

But that was afterwards; before,
The field was smooth as a sea off shore

On a shimmering afternoon, waist-high
With bent, and red top, and timothy,

Lush with oat grass and tall fescue,
And the purple green of Kentucky blue;

A noble meadow, so broad each way
It took three good scythes to mow in a day.

Just where the field broke into a wood
A knotted old catalpa stood,

And in the old catalpa-tree
A cat-bird sang immoderately.

The sky above him was round and big
And its centre seemed just over his twig.

The earth below him was fresh and fair,
With the sun's long fingers everywhere.

The cat-bird perched where a great leaf hung,
And the great leaf tilted, and flickered, and swung.

The cat-bird sang with a piercing glee
Up in the sun-specked catalpa-tree.

He sang so loud and he sang so long
That his ears were drowned in his own sweet song.

But the little peering leaves of grass
Shook and sundered to let them pass,

To let them pass, the men who heard
Nothing the grass said, nothing the bird.

Each man was still as a shining stone,
Each man's head was a buzzing bone

Wherein two words screeched in and out
Like a grinding saw with its turn about:

"Evelyn Ray," each stone man said,
And the words cut back and forth through his head,
And each of them wondered if he were dead.

The cat-bird sang with his head cocked up
Gazing into the sky's blue cup.

The grasses waved back into place,
The sun's long fingers stroked each face,

Each grim, cold face that saw no sun.
And the feet led the faces on and on.

They stopped beside the catalpa-tree,
Said one stone face to the other: "See!"

The other face had nothing to say,
Its lips were frozen on "Evelyn Ray."

They laid their hats in the tall green
grass
Where the crickets and grasshoppers pass
and pass.

They hung their coats in the crotch of a
pine
And paced five feet in an even line.

They measured five paces either way,
And the saws in their heads screeched
"Evelyn Ray."

The cat-bird sang so loud and clear
He heard nothing at all, there was nothing
to hear.

Even the swish of long legs pushing
Through grass had ceased, there was only
the hushing

Of a windless wind in the daisy tops,
And the jar stalks make when a grasshopper hops.

Every now and then a bee boomed over
The black-eyed Susans in search of clover,

And crickets shrilled as crickets do:
One — two. One — two.

The cat-bird sang with his head in the
air,
And the sun's bright fingers poked here
and there,

Past leaf, and branch, and needle, and
cone.
But the stone men stood like men of
stone.

Each man lifted a dull stone hand
And his fingers felt like weaving sand,

And his feet seemed standing on a ball
Which tossed and turned in a waterfall.

Each man heard a shot somewhere
Dropping out of the distant air.

But the screaming saws no longer said
"Evelyn Ray," for the men were dead.

· · · · ·

I often think of Evelyn Ray.
What did she do, what did she say?
Did she ever chance to pass that way?

I remember it as a lovely spot
Where a cat-bird sang. When he heard
the shot,
Did he fly away? I have quite forgot.

When I went there last, he was singing
again
Through a little fleeting, misty rain,
And pine-cones lay where they had lain.

This is the tale as I heard it when
I was young from a man who was three-
score and ten.
A lady of clay and two stone men.

A pretty problem is here, no doubt,
If you have a fancy to work it out:
What happens to stone when clay is
about?

Muse upon it as long as you will,
I think myself it will baffle your skill,
And your answer will be what mine is —
nil.

But every sunny Summer's day
I am teased with the thought of Evelyn
Ray,
Poor little image of painted clay.
And Heigh-o! I say.
What if there be a judgment-day?

What if all religions be true,
And Gabriel's trumpet blow for you
And blow for them — what will you do?

Evelyn Ray, will you rise alone?
Or will your lovers of dull grey stone
Pace beside you through the wan

Twilight of that bitter day
To be judged as stone and judged as
clay,
And no one to say the judgment nay?

Better be nothing, Evelyn Ray,
A handful of buttercups that sway
In the wind for a children's holiday.

For earth to earth is the best we know,
Where the good blind worms push to
and fro
Turning us into the seeds which grow,

And lovers and ladies are dead indeed,
Lost in the sap of a flower seed.
Is this, think you, a sorry creed?

Well, be it so, for the world is wide
And opinions jostle on every side.
What has always hidden will always hide.

And every year when the fields are high
With oat grass, and red top, and timothy,
I know that a creed is the shell of a lie.

Peace be with you, Evelyn Ray,
And to your lovers, if so it may,
For earth made stone and earth made
clay.

THE SWANS

The swans float and float
Along the moat
Around the Bishop's garden,
And the white clouds push
Across a blue sky
With edges that seem to draw in and
harden.

Two slim men of white bronze
Beat each with a hammer on the end of
a rod
The hours of God.
Striking a bell,
They do it well.
And the echoes jump, and tinkle, and
swell
In the Cathedral's carved stone polygons.

The swans float
About the moat,
And another swan sits still in the air
Above the old inn.

He gazes into the street
And swims the cold and the heat,
He has always been there,
At least so say the cobbles in the square.
They listen to the beat
Of the hammered bell,
And think of the feet
Which beat upon their tops;
But what they think they do not tell.

And the swans who float
Up and down the moat
Gobble the bread the Bishop feeds them.
The slim bronze men beat the hour again,
But only the gargoyles up in the hard
blue air heed them.

When the Bishop says a prayer,
And the choir sing "Amen,"
The hammers break in on them there:
Clang! Clang! Beware! Beware!
The carved swan looks down at the
passing men,
And the cobbles wink: "An hour has
gone again."
But the people kneeling before the
Bishop's chair
Forget the passing over the cobbles in
the square.

An hour of day and an hour of night,
And the clouds float away in a red-
splashed light.
The sun, quotha? or white, white
Smoke with fire all alight.

An old roof crashing on a Bishop's tomb,
Swarms of men with a thirst for room,
And the footsteps blur to a shower,
shower, shower,
Of men passing — passing — every hour,
With arms of power, and legs of power,
And power in their strong, hard minds.
No need then
For the slim bronze men
Who beat God's hours: Prime, Tierce,
None.
Who wants to hear? No one.
We will melt them, and mold them,
And make them a stem
For a banner gorged with blood,
For a blue-mouthed torch.
So let the men rush like clouds,
They strike their iron edges on the
Bishop's chair

And fling down the lanterns by the tower
stair.
They rip the Bishop out of his tomb
And break the mitre off of his head.
"See," say they, "the man is dead;
He cannot shiver or sing.
We'll toss for his ring."

The cobbles see this all along the street
Coming — coming — on countless feet.
And the clockmen mark the hours as they
go.
But slow — slow —
The swans float
In the Bishop's moat.
And the inn swan
Sits on and on,
Staring before him with cold glass eyes.
Only the Bishop walks serene,
Pleased with his church, pleased with his
house,
Pleased with the sound of the hammered
bell,
Beating his doom.
Saying "Boom! Boom! Room! Room!"
He is old, and kind, and deaf, and blind,
And very, very pleased with his charming
moat
And the swans which float.

ONCE JERICHO

Walking in the woods one day,
I came across a great river of rye
Sweeping up between tall pine-trees.
The grey-green heads of the rye
Jostled and flaunted
And filled all the passage with a tossing
Of bright-bearded ears,
It was very fine,
Marching and bending
Under the smooth, wide undulation of
the upper branches of pines.

"Yi! Yi!" cried the little yellow cinque-
foil.
"What is this bearded army which
marches upon us?"
And the loosestrife called out that some-
body was treading on its toes.
But the rye never heeded.
"Bread! Bread!" it shouted, and wagged
its golden beards.
"Bread conquering the forest."
I stood with the little cinquefoil

Crushed back against a bush of sheep's
laurel.
"I am sorry if I crowd you," said I.
"But the rye is marching
And the green and yellow banners blind
me,
Also the clamour of the great trumpets
Is confusing."
"But you are trampling me down,"
wailed the loosestrife.
"Alas! Even so.
Yet do not blame me,
For I too have scarcely room to stand."

Then a gust of wind ran upon the tall
rye,
And it flung up its glittering helmets and
shouted "Bread!" again and again,
And the hubbub of it rolled superbly
under the balancing pines.

"Three times the trumpets," thought I,
And I picked the cinquefoil.
"Why not on my writing-table," I said,
caressing its petals with my finger.
And that, I take it, is the end of the
story.

MERELY STATEMENT

You sent me a sprig of mignonette,
Cool-coloured, quiet, and it was wet
With green sea-spray, and the salt and
the sweet
Mingled to a fragrance weary and dis-
creet
As a harp played softly in a great room
at sunset.

You said: "My sober mignonette
Will brighten your room and you will
not forget."

But I have pressed your flower and laid
it away
In a letter, tied with a ribbon knot.
I have not forgot.
But there is a passion-flower in my vase
Standing above a close-cleared space
In the midst of a jumble of papers and
books.
The passion-flower holds my eyes,
And the light-under-light of its blue and
purple dyes
Is a hot surprise.

How then can I keep my looks
From the passion-flower leaning sharply
    over the books?
When one has seen
The difficult magnificence of a queen
On one's table,
Is one able
To observe any colour in a mignonette?
I will not think of sunset, I crave the
    dawn,
With its rose-red light on the wings of a
    swan,
And a queen pacing slowly through the
    Parthenon,
Her dress a stare of purple between pillars
    of stone.

FOOTING UP A TOTAL

I moved to the sound of gold, and brass,
    and heavily-clashed silver.
From the towers, the watchers see the
    flags of my coming:
Tall magenta flags
Stinging against a pattern of light blue.
Trumpets and tubas
Exult for me before the walls of cities,
And I pass the gates entangled in a dance
    of lifted tambourines.

But you — you come only as a harebell
    comes;
One day there is nothing, and the next
    your steepled bells are all,
The rest is background.
You are neither blue, nor violet, nor red,
But all these colours blent and faded to
    a charming weariness of tone.
I glare; you blossom.
Yes, alas! and when they have clanged
    me to my grave
Wrapped gaudily in pale blue and
    magenta;
When muted bugles and slacked drums
Have brayed a last quietus;
What then, my friend?

Why, someone coming from the funeral
Will see you standing, nodding under-
    neath a hedge
(Picking or not is nothing).
Will that person remember bones and
    shouting do you think?
I fancy he will listen to the music

Shaken so lightly from your whispering
    bells
And think how very excellent a thing
A flower growing in a hedge most surely
    is.
And so, a fig for rotting carcasses!

Waiter, bring me a bottle of Lachryma
    Christi,
And mind you don't break the seal.
Your health, my highly unsuccessful con-
    frère,
Rocking your seed-bells while I drift to
    ashes.
The future is the future, therefore —
Damn you!

TWENTY–FOUR HOKKU ON A MODERN THEME

I

Again the larkspur,
Heavenly blue in my garden.
They, at least, unchanged.

II

How have I hurt you?
You look at me with pale eyes,
But these are my tears.

III

Morning and evening —
Yet for us once long ago
Was no division.

IV

I hear many words.
Set an hour when I may come
Or remain silent.

V

In the ghostly dawn
I write new words for your ears —
Even now you sleep.

VI

This then is morning.
Have you no comfort for me
Cold-coloured flowers?

VII

My eyes are weary
Following you everywhere.
Short, oh short, the days!

VIII

When the flower falls
The leaf is no more cherished.
Every day I fear.

IX

Even when you smile
Sorrow is behind your eyes.
Pity me, therefore.

X

Laugh — it is nothing.
To others you may seem gay,
I watch with grieved eyes.

XI

Take it, this white rose.
Stems of roses do not bleed;
Your fingers are safe.

XII

As a river-wind
Hurling clouds at a bright moon,
So am I to you.

XIII

Watching the iris,
The faint and fragile petals —
How am I worthy?

XIV

Down a red river
I drift in a broken skiff.
Are you then so brave?

XV

Night lies beside me
Chaste and cold as a sharp sword.
It and I alone.

XVI

Last night it rained.
Now, in the desolate dawn,
Crying of blue jays.

XVII

Foolish so to grieve,
Autumn has its coloured leaves —
But before they turn?

XVIII

Afterwards I think:
Poppies bloom when it thunders.
Is this not enough?

XIX

Love is a game — yes?
I think it is a drowning:
Black willows and stars.

XX

When the aster fades
The creeper flaunts in crimson.
Always another!

XXI

Turning from the page,
Blind with a night of labour,
I hear morning crows.

XXII

A cloud of lilies,
Or else you walk before me.
Who could see clearly?

XXIII

Sweet smell of wet flowers
Over an evening garden.
Your portrait, perhaps?

XXIV

Staying in my room,
I thought of the new Spring leaves.
That day was happy.

THE ANNIVERSARY

Ten years is nothing,
Yet I do not remember
What happened before.

Morning flings shadows,
But midday is shadowless.
So I have found it.

I have no flowers,
Yet I give you these roses.
Humour my pretence.

Have I satisfied?
Who can be sure of himself.
Touch me with your love.

Knowing my weakness,
Spread your hands above my head.
See only your hands.

Watching you daily,
I dare not think what I see.
It is better so.

Since I am only
What you may consider me,
Have merciful thoughts.

Shield me from myself.
At times I have wounded you.
I do not forget.

Take what I give you.
Foolishness is in my words,
But not in my heart.

Cease urging your ears,
My speech has little for them.
Hearken otherwise.

You wrong me, saying:
One death will not kill us both.
Your veins hold my sap.

Keep in remembrance:
Peonies do not blossom
Till Spring is over.

You prefer Spring? Why?
A season's length of hours —
Incalculable.

Days and days — what then?
Is not recurrence a smile
On the face of age?

Now, in the pale dawn,
How strange to consider time.
What is it to us?

Grains of rice counted —
Can any one so spend life?
Be spacious and wise.

The bowl is still full.
We will not be niggardly.
Plunge in both your hands.

I have known terror.
I swear to know it no more,
Each day a new dawn.

Youth is incautious.
Wisdom learns to tread softly,
Valuing moments.

Cherishing what is,
The wise man sees it depart
Without emotion.

Time is rhetoric,
A mad logician's plaything.
O pitiful world!

Listen to the wind;
Man has not learnt to measure
The wind of his thought.

Blowing asunder,
Yet we shall be as the air
Still undivided.

Sleep until day-spring.
With morning we start again,
Another ten years.

SONG FOR A VIOLA D'AMORE

The lady of my choice is bright
As a clematis at the touch of night,
As a white clematis with a purple heart
When twilight cuts earth and sun apart.
Through the dusking garden I hear her
   voice
As a smooth, sweet, wandering, windy
   noise,
And I see her stand as a ghost may do

In answer to a rendez-vous
Long sought with agony and prayer.
So watching her, I see her there.

I sit beneath a quiet tree
And watch her everlastingly.
The garden may or may not be
Before my eyes, I cannot see.
But darkness drifting up and down
Divides to let her silken gown
Gleam there beside the clematis.
How marvellously white it is!
Five white blossoms and she are there
Like candles in a fluttering air
Escaping from a tower stair.

Be still you cursed, rattling leaf,
This is no time to think of grief.

The night is soft, and fire-flies
Are very casual, gay, and wise,
And they have made a tiny glee
Just where the clematis and she
Are standing. Since the sky is clear,
Do they suppose that, once a year,
The moon and five white stars appear
Walking the earth; that, so attended,
Diana came and condescended
To hold speech with Endymion
Before she came at last alone.

The lady of my choice is bright
As a clematis at the fall of night.
Her voice is honeysuckle sweet,
Her presence spreads an April heat
Before the going of her feet.
She is of perfectness complete.
The lady whom my heart perceives
As a clematis above its leaves,
As a purple-hearted clematis.
And what is lovelier than that is?

PRIME

Your voice is like bells over roofs at dawn
When a bird flies
And the sky changes to a fresher colour.

Speak, speak, Beloved.
Say little things
For my ears to catch
And run with them to my **heart.**

VESPERS

Last night, at sunset,
The foxgloves were like tall **altar** candles.

Could I have lifted you to the roof of
the greenhouse, my Dear,
I should have understood their burning.

IN EXCELSIS

You — you —
Your shadow is sunlight on a plate of
silver;
Your footsteps, the seeding-place of lilies;
Your hands moving, a chime of bells
across a windless air.

The movement of your hands is the long,
golden running of light from a rising
sun;
It is the hopping of birds upon a garden-
path.

As the perfume of jonquils, you come
forth in the morning.
Young horses are not more sudden than
your thoughts,
Your words are bees about a pear-tree,
Your fancies are the gold-and-black striped
wasps buzzing among red apples.
I drink your lips,
I eat the whiteness of your hands and
feet.
My mouth is open,
As a new jar I am empty and open.
Like white water are you who fill the
cup of my mouth,
Like a brook of water thronged with
lilies.

You are frozen as the clouds,
You are far and sweet as the high clouds.
I dare reach to you,
I dare touch the rim of your brightness.
I leap beyond the winds,
I cry and shout,
For my throat is keen as a sword
Sharpened on a hone of ivory.
My throat sings the joy of my eyes,
The rushing gladness of my love.

How has the rainbow fallen upon **my**
heart?
How have I snared the seas to lie in **my**
fingers
And caught the sky to be a cover for **my**
head?
How have you come to dwell with me,

Compassing me with the four circles of
your mystic lightness,
So that I say "Glory! Glory!" and bow
before you
As to a shrine?

Do I tease myself that morning is morning
and a day after?
Do I think the air a condescension,
The earth a politeness,
Heaven a boon deserving thanks?
So you — air — earth — heaven —
I do not thank you,
I take you,
I live.
And those things which I say in conse-
quence
Are rubies mortised in a gate of stone.

WHITE CURRANTS

Shall I give you white currants?
I do not know why, but I have a sudden
fancy for this fruit.
At the moment, the idea of them
cherishes my senses,
And they seem more desirable than flaw-
less emeralds.
Since I am, in fact, empty-handed,
I might have chosen gems out of India,
But I choose white currants.
Is it because the raucous wind is hurtling
round the house-corners?
I see it with curled lips and stripped
fangs, gaunt with a hunting
energy,
Come to snout, and nibble, and kill the
little crocus roots.
Shall we call it white currants?
You may consider it as a symbol if you
please.
You may find them tart, or sweet, or
merely agreeable in colour,
So long as you accept them,
And me.

EXERCISE IN LOGIC

I gave you a picture once,
A great crimson sun floating beside a
gnarled bamboo.
The sun has faded;
For which reason, I think nothing of the
painter,

Until I reflect that many pigments cannot bear the dazzle of excessive light.
For, my Dear, have you not sat opposite
it daily?
I ask you, is there truth in this?

OVERCAST SUNRISE

The sky is spattered with clouds,
Pink clouds,
And behind them is the reluctant blue
of dawn.
The hemlock-trees move to a weary wind,
And the clouds lose their brightness,
Gathering to a dull day.

Morning, you observe —
But the night was more shining in my
thoughts.
O realistic generation,
Who do not get abroad while still the
clouds are pink
And the sky concerned only with how
much colour it will choose to wear!

AFTERGLOW

Peonies
The strange pink colour of Chinese porce-
lains;
Wonderful — the glow of them.
But, my Dear, it is the pale blue lark-
spur
Which swings windily against my heart.
Other Summers —
And a cricket chirping in the grass.

A DIMENSION

To-night I stood among roses
Watching the slow studding of the sky
with stars.
The cat fawned upon me to play with
him.
Poor little cat, you have only me,
Unless we add that delightful feather on
the end of a whip.
I have flowers and the high green love-
liness of an evening sky,
And I find them not worth your feather,
Since the earth happens to be round as
an orange
And I am not possessed of seven league
boots.

MACKEREL SKY

I ride, ride,
Through the spotted sunlight of an April
    forest
Down a pathway bewildered with crocus
    cups,
The wind dallies with the plume of my
    helmet.
I ride, ride,
Seeking those adventures to which I am
    dedicate,
Determined, but without alertness,
Ungraciously ignoring the salutations of
    the young, jocund leaves.

Lady,
Far as you are from me in distance of
    place,
I know you yet farther off in good will
    of heart.
Wherefore,
Although I make a brave show in armour
    of green and carnation
Riveted with the flowers which are
    called "you-love-me-not" of white and
    yellow,
And on my shield a waning moon in a
    field of azure,
I am gayer in my colours than in my
    heart.

THE ON-LOOKER

Suppose I plant you
Like wide-eyed Helen
On the battlements
Of weary Troy,
Clutching the parapet with desperate
    hands.
She, too, gazes at a battle-field
Where bright vermilion plumes and
    metal whiteness
Shock and sparkle and go down with
    groans.
Her glances strike the rocking battle,
Again — again —
Recoiling from it
Like baffled spear-heads fallen from a
    brazen shield.
The ancients at her elbow counsel pa-
    tience and contingencies;
Such to a woman stretched upon a bed
    of battle,

Who bargained for this only in the
    whispering arras
Enclosed about a midnight of enchant-
    ment.

LILACS

Lilacs,
False blue,
White,
Purple,
Colour of lilac,
Your great puffs of flowers
Are everywhere in this my New England.
Among your heart-shaped leaves
Orange orioles hop like music-box birds
    and sing
Their little weak soft songs;
In the crooks of your branches
The bright eyes of song sparrows sitting
    on spotted eggs
Peer restlessly through the light and
    shadow
Of all Springs.
Lilacs in dooryards
Holding quiet conversations with an
    early moon;
Lilacs watching a deserted house
Settling sideways into the grass of an
    old road;
Lilacs, wind-beaten, staggering under a
    lopsided shock of bloom
Above a cellar dug into a hill.
You are everywhere.
You were everywhere.
You tapped the window when the preacher
    preached his sermon,
And ran along the road beside the boy
    going to school.
You stood by pasture-bars to give the
    cows good milking,
You persuaded the housewife that her
    dish pan was of silver.
And her husband an image of pure gold.
You flaunted the fragrance of your blos-
    soms
Through the wide doors of Custom
    Houses —
You, and sandal-wood, and tea,
Charging the noses of quill-driving clerks
When a ship was in from China.
You called to them: "Goose-quill men,
    goose-quill men,
May is a month for flitting."
Until they writhed on their high stools

And wrote poetry on their letter-sheets
   behind the propped-up ledgers.
Paradoxical New England clerks,
Writing inventories in ledgers, reading
   the "Song of Solomon" at night,
So many verses before bed-time,
Because it was the Bible.
The dead fed you
Amid the slant stones of graveyards.
Pale ghosts who planted you
Came in the night-time
And let their thin hair blow through your
   clustered stems.
You are of the green sea,
And of the stone hills which reach a long
   distance.
You are of elm-shaded streets with little
   shops where they sell kites and marbles,
You are of great parks where everyone
   walks and nobody is at home.
You cover the blind sides of greenhouses
And lean over the top to say a hurry-
   word through the glass
To your friends, the grapes, inside.

Lilacs,
False blue,
White,
Purple,
Colour of lilac,
You have forgotten your Eastern origin,
The veiled women with eyes like pan-
   thers,
The swollen, aggressive turbans of jewelled
   Pashas.
Now you are a very decent flower,
A reticent flower,
A curiously clear-cut, candid flower,
Standing beside clean doorways,
Friendly to a house-cat and a pair of
   spectacles,
Making poetry out of a bit of moonlight
And a hundred or two sharp blossoms.

Maine knows you,
Has for years and years;
New Hampshire knows you,
And Massachusetts
And Vermont.
Cape Cod starts you along the beaches
   to Rhode Island;
Connecticut takes you from a river to
   the sea.
You are brighter than apples,
Sweeter than tulips,

You are the great flood of our souls
Bursting above the leaf-shapes of our
   hearts,
You are the smell of all Summers,
The love of wives and children,
The recollection of the gardens of little
   children,
You are State Houses and Charters
And the familiar treading of the foot to
   and fro on a road it knows.
May is lilac here in New England,
May is a thrush singing "Sun up!" on a
   tip-top ash-tree,
May is white clouds behind pine-trees
Puffed out and marching upon a blue
   sky.
May is a green as no other,
May is much sun through small leaves,
May is soft earth,
And apple-blossoms,
And windows open to a South wind.
May is full light wind of lilac
From Canada to Narragansett Bay.

Lilacs,
False blue,
White,
Purple,
Colour of lilac.
Heart-leaves of lilac all over New Eng-
   land,
Roots of lilac under all the soil of New
   England,
Lilac in me because I am New England,
Because my roots are in it,
Because my leaves are of it,
Because my flowers are for it,
Because it is my country
And I speak to it of itself
And sing of it with my own voice
Since certainly it is mine.

PURPLE GRACKLES

The grackles have come.
The smoothness of the morning is
   puckered with their incessant chatter.
A sociable lot, these purple grackles,
Thousands of them strung across a long
   run of wind,
Thousands of them beating the air-ways
   with quick wing-jerks,
Spinning down the currents of the South.
Every year they come,

My garden is a place of solace and rec-
      reation evidently,
For they always pass a day with me.
With high good nature they tell me what
      I do not want to hear.
The grackles have come.

I am persuaded that grackles are birds;
But when they are settled in the trees,
I am inclined to declare them fruits
And the trees turned hybrid blackberry
      vines.
Blackness shining and bulging under
      leaves,
Does not that mean blackberries, I ask
      you?
Nonsense! The grackles have come.

Nonchalant highwaymen, pickpockets, sec-
      ond-story burglars,
Stealing away my little hope of Summer.
There is no stealthy robbing in this.
Who ever heard such a gabble of thieves'
      talk!
It seems they delight in unmasking my
      poor pretence.
Yes, now I see that the hydrangea
      blooms are rusty;
That the hearts of the golden glow are
      ripening to lustreless seeds;
That the garden is dahlia-coloured,
Flaming with its last over-hot hues;
That the sun is pale as a lemon too small
      to fill the picking-ring.
I did not see this yesterday,
But to-day the grackles have come.

They drop out of the trees
And strut in companies over the lawn,
Tired of flying, no doubt;
A grand parade to limber legs and give
      wings a rest.
I should build a great fish-pond for them,
Since it is evident that a bird-bath, meant
      to accommodate two goldfinches at
      most,
Is slight hospitality for these hordes.
Scarcely one can get in,
They all peck and scrabble so,
Crowding, pushing, chasing one another
      up the bank with spread wings.
"Are we ducks, you, owner of such
      inadequate comforts,
That you offer us lily-tanks where one
      must swim or drown,

Not stand and splash like a gentleman?"
I feel the reproach keenly, seeing them
      perch on the edges of the tanks, trying
      the depth with a chary foot,
And hardly able to get their wings under
      water in the bird-bath.
But there are resources I had not con-
      sidered,
If I am bravely ruled out of count.
What is that thudding against the eaves
      just beyond my window?
What is that spray of water blowing past
      my face?
Two — three — grackles bathing in the
      gutter,
The gutter providentially choked with
      leaves.
I pray they think I put the leaves there
      on purpose;
I would be supposed thoughtful and
      welcoming
To all guests, even thieves.
But considering that they are going South
      and I am not,
I wish they would bathe more quietly,
It is unmannerly to flaunt one's good
      fortune.

They rate me of no consequence,
But they might reflect that it is my gutter.
I know their opinion of me,
Because one is drying himself on the
      window-sill
Not two feet from my hand.
His purple neck is sleek with water,
And the fellow preens his feathers for all
      the world as if I were a fountain
      statue.
If it were not for the window,
I am convinced he would light on my
      head.
Tyrian-feathered freebooter,
Appropriating my delightful gutter with
      so extravagant an ease,
You are as cool a pirate as ever scuttled
      a ship,
And are you not scuttling my Summer
      with every peck of your sharp bill?

But there is a cloud over the beech-tree,
A quenching cloud for lemon-livered suns.
The grackles are all swinging in the tree-
      tops,
And the wind is coming up, mind you.
That boom and reach is no Summer gale,

I know that wind,
It blows the Equinox over seeds and
scatters them,
It rips petals from petals, and tears off
half-turned leaves.
There is rain on the back of that wind.
Now I would keep the grackles,
I would plead with them not to leave me.
I grant their coming, but I would not
have them go.
It is a milestone, this passing of grackles.
A day of them, and it is a year gone by.
There is magic in this and terror,
But I only stare stupidly out of the
window.
The grackles have come.

Come! Yes, they surely came.
But they have gone.
A moment ago the oak was full of them,
They are not there now.
Not a speck of a black wing,
Not an eye-peep of a purple head.
The grackles have gone,
And I watch an Autumn storm
Stripping the garden,
Shouting black rain challenges
To an old, limp Summer
Laid down to die in the flower-beds.

MEETING–HOUSE HILL

I must be mad, or very tired,
When the curve of a blue bay beyond a
railroad track
Is shrill and sweet to me like the sudden
springing of a tune,
And the sight of a white church above
thin trees in a city square
Amazes my eyes as though it were the
Parthenon.
Clear, reticent, superbly final,
With the pillars of its portico refined to
a cautious elegance,
It dominates the weak trees,
And the shot of its spire
Is cool, and candid,
Rising into an unresisting sky.
Strange meeting-house
Pausing a moment upon a squalid hill-
top.
I watch the spire sweeping the sky,
I am dizzy with the movement of the
sky,
I might be watching a mast

With its royals set full
Straining before a two-reef breeze.
I might be sighting a tea-clipper,
Tacking into the blue bay,
Just back from Canton
With her hold full of green and blue
porcelain,
And a Chinese coolie leaning over the
rail
Gazing at the white spire
With dull, sea-spent eyes.

TEXAS

I went a-riding, a-riding,
Over a great long plain.
And the plain went a-sliding, a-sliding
Away from my bridle-rein.

Fields of cotton, and fields of wheat,
Thunder-blue gentians by a wire fence,
Standing cypress, red and tense,
Holding its flower rigid like a gun,
Dressed for parade by the running wheat,
By the little bouncing cotton. Terribly
sweet
The cardinals sing in the live-oak trees,
And the long plain breeze,
The prairie breeze,
Blows across from swell to swell
With a ginger smell.
Just ahead, where the road curves round,
A long-eared rabbit makes a bound
Into a wheat-field, into a cotton-field,
His track glitters after him and goes still
again
Over to the left of my bridle-rein.

But over to the right is a glare — glare —
glare —
Of sharp glass windows.
A narrow square of brick jerks thickly up
above the cotton plants,
A raucous mercantile thing flaring the
sun from thirty-six windows,
Brazenly declaring itself to the lovely
fields.
Tram-cars run like worms about the feet
of this thing,
The coffins of cotton-bales feed it,
The threshed wheat is its golden blood.
But here it has no feet,
It has only the steep ironic grin of its
thirty-six windows,

Only its basilisk eyes counting the fields,
Doing sums of how many buildings to a
city, all day and all night.

Once they went a-riding, a-riding,
Over the great long plain.
Cowboys singing to their dogey steers,
Cowboys perched on forty-dollar saddles,
Riding to the North, six months to get
there,
Six months to reach Wyoming.
"Hold up, paint horse, herd the little
dogies,
Over the lone prairie."
Bones of dead steers,
Bones of cowboys,
Under the wheat, maybe.

The sky-scraper sings another way,
A tune of steel, of wheels, of gold.
And the ginger breeze blows, blows all
day
Tangled with flowers and mold.
And the Texas sky whirls down, whirls
down,
Taking long looks at the fussy town.
An old sky and a long plain
Beyond, beyond, my bridle-rein.

CHARLESTON, SOUTH CAROLINA

Fifteen years is not a long time,
But long enough to build a city over and
destroy it.
Long enough to clean a forty-year growth
of grass from between cobblestones,
And run street-car lines straight across
the heart of romance.
Commerce, are you worth this?
I should like to bring a case to trial:
Prosperity versus Beauty,
Cash registers teetering in a balance
against the comfort of the soul.
Then, to-night, I stood looking through a
grilled gate
At an old, dark garden.
Live-oak trees dripped branchfuls of
leaves over the wall,
Acacias waved dimly beyond the gate,
and the smell of their blossoms
Puffed intermittently through the wrought-
iron scroll-work.
Challenge and solution —

O loveliness of old, decaying, haunted
things!
Little streets untouched, shamefully paved,
Full of mist and fragrance on this rainy
evening.
"You should come at dawn," said my
friend,
"And see the orioles, and thrushes, and
mocking-birds
In the garden."
"Yes," I said absent-mindedly,
And remarked the sharp touch of ivy
upon my hand which rested against
the wall.
But I thought to myself,
There is no dawn here, only sunset,
And an evening rain scented with flowers.

THE MIDDLETON PLACE
CHARLESTON, S.C.

What would Francis Jammes, lover of
dear, dead elegancies,
Say to this place?
France, stately, formal, stepping in red-
heeled shoes
Along a river shore.
France walking a minuet between live-
oaks waving ghostly fans of Spanish
moss.
La Caroline, indeed, my dear Jammes,
With Monsieur Michaux engaged to
teach her deportment.
Faint as a whiff of flutes and hautbois,
The great circle of the approach lies be-
neath the sweeping grasses.
Step lightly down these terraces, they are
records of a dream.

Magnolias, pyrus japonicas, azaleas,
Flaunting their scattered blooms with the
same bravura
That lords and ladies used in the prison
of the Conciergerie.
You were meant to be so gay, so sophis-
ticated, and you are so sad,
Sad as the tomb crouched amid your
tangled growth,
Sad as the pale plumes of the Spanish
moss
Slowly strangling the live-oak trees.

Sunset wanes along the quiet river.
The afterglow is haunted and nostalgic,

Over the yellow woodland it hangs like
   the dying chord of a funeral chant;
And evenly, satirically, the mosses move
   to its ineffable rhythm,
Like the ostrich fans of palsied dowagers
Telling one another contentedly of the
   deaths they have lived to see.

THE VOW

Tread softly, softly,
Scuffle no dust.
No common thoughts shall thrust
Upon this peaceful decay,
This mold and rust of yesterday.
This is an altar with its incense blown
   away
By the indifferent wind of a long, sad
   night;
These are the precincts of the dead who
   die
Unconquered. Haply
You who haunt this place
May deign some gesture of forgiveness
To those of our sundered race
Who come in all humility
Asking an alms of pardon.
Suffer us to feel an ease,
A benefice of love poured down on us
   from these magnolia-trees.
That, when we leave you, we shall know
   the bitter wound
Of our long mutual scourging healed at
   last and sound.

Through an iron gate, fantastically
   scrolled and garlanded,
Along a path, green with moss, between
   two rows of high magnolia-trees —
How lightly the wind drips through
   the magnolias.
How slightly the magnolia bend to the
   wind.

It stands, pushed back into a corner of
   the piazza,
A jouncing-board, with its paint scaled
   off,
A jouncing-board which creaks when you
   sit upon it.
The wind rattles the stiff leaves of the
   magnolias:
So may tinkling banjos drown the
   weeping of women.

When the Yankees came like a tide of
   locusts,
When blue uniforms blocked the ends of
   streets
And foolish, arrogant swords struck
   through the paintings of a hundred
   years.
From gold and ivory coasts come the
   winds that jingle in the tree-tops;
But the sigh of the wind in the un-
   shaven grass, from whence is that?

Proud hearts who could not endure dese-
   cration,
Who almost loathed the sky because it
   was blue;
Vengeful spirits, locked in young, arro-
   gant bodies,
You cursed yourselves with a vow;
Never would you set foot again in
   Charleston streets,
Never leave your piazza till Carolina was
   rid of Yankees.
O smooth wind sliding in from the sea,
It is a matter of no moment to you
   what flag you are flapping.

Ocean tides, morning and evening, slipping past the sea-islands;
Tides slipping in through the harbour,
   shaking the palmetto posts,
Slipping out through the harbour;
Pendulum tides, counting themselves
   upon the sea-islands.

So they jounced, for health's sake,
To be well and able to rejoice when once
   again the city was free,
And the lost cause won, and the stars
   and bars afloat over Sumter.
The days which had roared to them
   called more softly,
The days whispered, the days were silent,
   they moved as imperceptibly as mist.

And the proud hearts went with the days,
   into the dusk of age, the darkness
   of death.
Slowly they were borne away through a
   Charleston they scarcely remembered.
The jouncing-board was pushed into a
   corner,
Only the magolia-trees tossed a petal to
   it, now and again, if there hap-

pened to be a strong wind when the blooms were dropping.

Hush, go gently,
Do not move a pebble with your foot.
This is a moment of pause,
A moment to recollect the futility of cause.
A moment to bow the head
And greet the unconcerned dead,
Denying nothing of their indifference,
And then go hence
And forget them again,
Since lives are lived with living men.

THE CONGRESSIONAL LIBRARY

The earth is a coloured thing.
See the red clays, and the umbers and salt greys of the mountains;
See the clustered and wandering greens of plains and hillsides,
The leaf-greens, bush-greens, water-plant and snow-greens
Of gardens and forests.
See the reds of flowers — hibiscus, poppy, geranium;
The rose-red of little flowers — may-flowers, primroses;
The harlequin shades of sweet-peas, orchids, pansies;
The madders, saffrons, chromes, of still waters,
The silver and star-blues, the wine-blues of seas and oceans.
Observe the stars at night time, name the colour of them;
Count and recount the hues of clouds at sunset and at dawn.
And the colours of the races of men —
What are they?
And what are we?
We, the people without a race,
Without a language;
Of all races, and of none;
Of all tongues, and one imposed;
Of all traditions and all pasts,
With no tradition and no past.
A patchwork and an altar-piece,
Vague as sea-mist,
Myriad as forest-trees,
Living into a present,
Building a future.
Our colour is the vari-coloured world.
No colours clash,

All clash and change,
And, in changing, new colours come and go and dominate and remain,
And no one shall say which remain,
Since those that have vanished return,
And those no man has seen take the light and are.

Where else in all America are we so symbolized
As in this hall?
White columns polished like glass,
A dome and a dome,
A balcony and a balcony,
Stairs and the balustrades to them,
Yellow marble and red slabs of it,
All mounting, spearing, flying into colour.
Colour round the dome and up to it,
Colour curving, kite-flying, to the second dome,
Light, dropping, pitching down upon the colour,
Arrow-falling upon the glass-bright pillars,
Mingled colours spinning into a shape of white pillars,
Fusing, cooling, into balanced shafts of shrill and interthronging light.
This is America,
This vast, confused beauty,
This staring, restless speed of loveliness,
Mighty, overwhelming, crude, of all forms,
Making grandeur out of profusion,
Afraid of no incongruities,
Sublime in its audacity,
Bizarre breaker of moulds,
Laughing with strength,
Charging down on the past,
Glorious and conquering,
Destroyer, builder,
Invincible pith and marrow of the world,
An old world remaking,
Whirling into the no-world of all-coloured light.

But behind the vari-coloured hall?
The entrails, the belly,
The blood-run veins, the heart and viscera,
What of these?
Only at night do they speak,
Only at night do the voices rouse themselves and speak.
There are words in the veins of this creature.

There are still notes singing in its breast:
Silent voices, whispering what it shall
speak,
Frozen music beating upon its pulses.
These are the voices of the furious dead
who never die,
Furious with love and life, unquenchable,
Dictating their creeds across the vapours
of time.
This is the music of the Trumpeters of
the Almighty
Weeping for a lost estate,
Sounding to a new birth which is to-
morrow.
Hark! This hurricane of music has no
end,
The speech of these voices has neither
end nor beginning;
They are inter-riven as the colours of the
sky
Over the graveyards of ten thousand gen-
erations.

When we are as Nineveh, our white col-
umns thrown and scattered,
Our dome of colours striped with the
crawling of insects,
Spotted with the thrust of damp clay —
Our words, our music, who will build a
dome to hive them?
In whose belly shall we come to life?
A new life,
Beyond submergence and destruction,
The implacable life of silent words,
Of tumultuous stillness of never-ceasing
music,
Lost to being that so it may triumph
And become the blood and heat and urge
Of that hidden distance which forever
whips and harries the static present
Of mankind.

WHICH, BEING INTERPRETED, IS AS MAY BE, OR OTHERWISE

Underneath the dim, criss-crossing beams
Grown edgeless with the litter of decay,
Where spiders hung their everlasting
webs
To wave, tier upon tier, across the gloom
Whenever any little cranny wind
Whined in on them and tumbled up the
dust
Upon the flaking beams and on the floor

Startling the nosing rats to sudden cold,
Old Neron sat, cuddling his withered
bones.
Above his head, the great Cathedral bells
Scattered their hallelujahs round the sky
On Sundays, holy days, and festivals;
But Neron took no note of them, his ears
Were inadvertent to such happenings
As cry themselves with bells. He sat un-
moved,
Scuffing his naked feet in the thick dust
Poured from the mouldering beams by
the bells' jar,
Sorting his pleasure from old heaps of
thoughts.
Below his garret, stairs and stairs below,
Men skinned their fingers tugging at the
ropes
That swung the clappers of the chiming
bells.
No kith nor kin to Neron, these; his
bones
Were liker to the shafts and traceries
And gargoyled gutters shining on the
town
In twitched and twisted angles. Neron
paid
No least attention to them, nor the
church
Which harboured him; and yet it was a
jewel,
A very rose of Gothic merriment,
Blooming symbolic beasts on every arch
And sprouting columns like a Summer
wood.
All up and down were flights of spiral
stairs,
Contrived within the hollow core of
walls,
Leading to chambers of hewn stone, and
lofts
Where slits for windows pierced the
granite blocks
More than an arm's length to reach open
air,
And distant so far down that sums of
steps
Ran into figures to affright the mind,
God lived upon an altar bright with
lights
Where snivelling priests might wish him
well-a-day.
Now Neron was a man preoccupied
With the huge spectacle of impotence
Swarming upon an ether-floating planet

Which only people called astronomers
Paused to take any heed of. Other men
Hurried and worried over this and that,
And passed from birth to death in one
    short eye-wink
Of aching agitation. Fools, parlous fools,
To aged Neron, but a stupendous jest
Fit for the crumpling of old bones in
    laughter.
Sneering was a capable sort of sport
If one had learnt the trick of balancing
On an impalpable circumference
To whirl a quite detached and sharpened
    vision
Over inanities a decent planet
Might be ashamed to carry. Neron took
His younger self as motto; every phase
Which others linger in had once been
    his,
But in the end he had flung clear of
    all.
They served him in the way of illustra-
    tion.
He built them up like blocks to knock
    them down
And chuckle at the noise they made in
    falling.
These visions of himself were warlock
    dreams
Conjured up with a wand-stroke from the
    air
And swept away as easily upon
The imperious order of another gesture.
This pastime lifted Neron to a god,
Or something similar, if only language
Had found a word for it. But superstition
Held words too rigid in a certain groove
For any purpose Neron had for them;
Giving a thing no name exacts obedience
To any chasing colour or humour one
May need to clap to it, and he, at least,
Swam high above convention in his
    thoughts.
Under the criss-cross beams and chiming
    bells
Old Neron sat, cheating himself with
    dreams,
Spreading them out before him, one by
    one,
As dowagers tap down their playing cards
With claw-like hands in games of soli-
    taire.
His frozen eyes gleamed at them as they
    came
Out of the darkness from an eldritch past

Which seemed no longer his, yet tasted
    sweet
In far-off recollection. Childhood first —
But what was childhood? A small, fragile
    thing
Of gay mishaps, and silly, bootless joys,
An eagerness of folly over tops,
Or kites which tugged and sharply broke
    their strings
Leaving a heartache Neron chirped to
    think
No greatest misery could give him now.
Youth bettered this. His jellied blood
    became
Less solid pondering upon the heat
Which burns youth into powder; his old
    bones
Were brittle, maybe, but not to that fire,
And yet its simulacrum was most fit
To muse upon and glow vicariously,
Warming safe fingers at a painted flame.
And Neron felt a queasy sort of pride
In mocking his old wounds with jibes
    that pricked
To a delicious flood of memory.
The hurt outgrown was tonic to his years.
He plied his ridicule so lustily
His body shook and rattled where he sat.
But manhood, flattering itself with windy
    praise,
Hugging the spiky guerdon of a name
With letters to it, gratified beyond
Desire by the cheap grace of epithet —
What monument of satire was this!
What exquisite lampooning! — O, the
    mirth
Of stars and ribbons viewed from the
    vast height
Of Neron's imperturbability!
To chip a quondam purpose to a grin
Was sport to make him hug his pointed
    knees
And rock for very glee, until his thighs
Were bruised with teetering upon the
    floor
Whose only cushion was the heaped-up
    dust.
How good to lick the sauce from all those
    years
And leave them icy bare and shivering,
With no illusion for their nakedness,
Turned playthings for a man of doting
    age
Who had no other joy but these, and
    sleep.

A little sift of daylight wandered in
Where one of the roof-tiles had blown
    away
And rain and sun had rotted through the
    wood.
This wisp of light was company to Neron.
He watched the floor-boards change from
    dark to glare,
Saw the glow creep upon a cock of dust
And leave it flat in shadow, traced its
    course
To where the hole's edge snapped it
    swiftly off,
Striking him blind to the accustomed
    dusk.
Now Neron had a friend he never met,
A verger who winked at his being there
In the sky-loft where no one ever came,
And left him scraps of broken meat and
    bread
Upon a step of the third stairway down.
The light was Neron's clock; it lit a crack
Jagged and strange, not like another
    crack,
So Neron knew the time. With many a
    curse
And groan he twitched his shaking bones
    upright
And tottered down the stair to get his
    meat,
For he must eat to live and dream his
    dreams.
He hated it, the aching journey down
And up again, he hated even his bones
Whose insolence in so demanding food
Sent him to get it whatever cost
To old, unable feet and quaking knees;
He loathed the verger's charitable dole,
The need of it became an injury.
But Neron still must eat, and so he went
Wearily down the stair to get his food.
It was not easy eating with the rats
Swarming upon him, but Neron long
    ago
Had crawled about his loft and gathered
    in
Such bits of bars, and bolts, and wooden
    blocks
As workmen leave, and sitting there he
    shied
These craftily into the horde of rats
And kept them from him while he eat his
    meat.
And afterwards, filled for more cursing,
    he

Would fumble round and pick his
    weapons up,
Treasuring them with canny, careful
    count
Lest one among the number might be
    missed,
To serve him for another meal to-mor-
    row.
So the days went, one pea-like to another,
The seasons unremarked, the years a loss.
No Monday, Tuesday, Wednesday were,
    for Neron,
Just when the light was there and when
    'twas not,
With dreams and slumber as each chose
    to come —
This, he would think, was sure philos-
    ophy,
Proper to please the minds of dry old
    men
Outgrown of creeds and fallals, seeing far
Beyond the hazards itching younger folk
With livelier arteries, whose dumb-bell
    heads
Were crowned with donkey's ears. Old
    bones are wise
And undisturbed by any hum of flesh;
He knew this with a wizened irony.
Weighing the world and life against his
    bones,
He tipped the scales down heavily, he
    thought,
And so was satisfied. His cackling laugh
Piped to the rats and hanging spiders'
    webs
And smothered in the muffle of decay.
The wine of his conceit was very old
And heady; like a drug, it ran beneath
His skin and flushed his veins so that
    they stood
Out on him like blue worms. A queer
    old man,
Building content with each new creaking
    thought
That jarred across his draughty, shrivelled
    brain.

One day as he was groping in the dusk,
The dusty dusk through which the light-
    streak clove
And showed it such for some few broom-
    stick lengths,
His startled fingers closed about a foot,
Two feet, in fact, a pair of human feet,
Palpable to his touch, but cold as snow.

Old Neron cringed from them and hid
  his eyes.
For might he not be going mad? Yes,
  mad!
That last cold horror haunting vacant
  age?
His toothless jaws chattered and slab-
  bered now
For one pale moment, then he looked
  and saw
Two wooden statues in the golden dusk:
A king with orb and sceptre, and a beard
As black as ink, beside him was his
  queen,
And both were crowned. The beard held
  Neron's eyes.
Waist-long and vast, its heaviness of hair
Stamped the king's sullen masculinity
With something of grave terror. Neron
  felt
An instant loathing, tingled with shrewd
  fear;
And yet, although he shuddered, a sly
  spark
Of admiration twinged him like a pain.
This was a terrible and virile king.
But for the queen — old Neron gasped
  before
Her sudden loveliness. A slender plant
Swung in a wind, crowned by a pyramid
Of fragile, jostling bells, was not more
  like
Itself than she to it. Her eyes were kind,
But wise withal, and hooded with fatigue.
She drooped in standing, yet remained
  upright
Wistfully conscious of an effort so.
Her pleated robe of green, or blue, or
  green,
Pushed out or hollowed as her body
  pressed
Upon it or withdrew within its folds;
She stood as naked to old Neron's eyes
As though no robe were there. Her small
  white hands
Held a red fox-glove, charming in its
  poise;
Her feet, which caught the sliding spray
  of light,
Appeared to tread on gold. Neron beheld
Them, bitter bearded king, mighty in
  power,
And gentle queen all weariful repose.
The light moved on and Neron saw no
  more.

Who were they? Neron plagued his
  memory
For some stray fact he might have heard
  of them.
But nothing came. He probed a curious
  mind
Into the reason for their banishment
To this lost corner whence no one had
  climbed
For desert lengths of years; he did not
  know
How long he had himself been there,
  death-long
He thought, and tallied up his distant
  dreams
As glittering from the other side of life.
Day after day he pondered why so late
He had encountered them. His wisp of
  light
Fell always to a line; but this was fact
Which baffled speculation. His own
  dreams
Fogged to a hueless essence, here was
  more
To work upon; with such a king and
  queen
Things had moved gaudily — if that were
  all.
He guessed the word ill-chosen, half a
  truth,
And seeking the other half, he wrought
  them both
Into a tale of tragic circumstance,
Of bargained marriage hurried on
  through lust,
Of desolate surrender where no hope
Of moving iron wills could have a place,
Of girlhood torn upon the state of queen.
With scraps of ancient myths, and fairy-
  tales,
And half-remembered tags of history,
Neron made up a story his old dreams
Could nowise counter with. He let them
  be,
Forsaking his life to consider theirs:
The terrible and unrelenting king,
The queen with a red fox-glove in her
  hands.
So Neron changed the order of his
  dreams
And irony became magnificence.
The queen, composed and cool, bent to
  his will,
Moving with stately graciousness within
The frame of his imaginings. She fringed

His dream with filigrees of excellence,
A lace of buds and scarcely opened
    flowers
Just touched with morning hoar-frost.
    But the king
Had his own dreams and would not enter
    Neron's,
Black dreams peculiar to a bearded king.
They injured Neron in his own esteem,
Chafing him to achieve a greater thing
Than he had yet conceived. His ardour
    grew
To match himself against the king, and
    crack
The shell of high omnipotence in two
And gloat upon the scattered empty
    halves
Lolling lopsided on the dusty floor.
So gradually he wrought a miracle,
Merging himself into the royal dream —
But not as ancient Neron, that old man
Had plumped himself with visions of the
    queen
Into a proper youth whose sap ran hot
Over his gusty body, ripe for love,
Fresh with the bursting agony of love,
And she a very distant, youthful queen.
As long as he could see them, Neron sat
Before the statues, while the light-streak
    crawled
From king to queen and left them in the
    dark.
Bit after bit he added to his dream.
He found the castle where they lived,
    above
A meadow of fair trees, whose flickering
    leaves
Chequered the placid water of a moat,
Weed-spotted, sound asleep, beneath the
    walls,
Except when the portcullis, clanging
    down,
Shattered its sky and trees to sliding
    planes
Of colour tipping with the tilt of waves.
Above the angry walls was gleam of grass
Shuttled with gold and white, for on a
    terrace
A peacock strutted between carven
    shields
Flanking the angles of a balustrade.
Sometimes, at night, Neron would climb
    the hill,
And crouching down beside the brooding
    moat

Gaze at the silent glisten of the roof
And ivy-twinkling walls, and speculate
Which hollow window opened on the
    room
Where the queen slept, and curse the
    bearded king
With full-mouthed curses.   Then, as
    dreaming grew,
He saw the queen at work within her
    bower
Surrounded by her ladies, stitching on
A blue-green tapestry where hunters ran,
And spotted dogs plunged into a blue
    stream
After an otter. Neron boldly stepped
Into the bower and nodded to the ladies
Who crept away and left him with the
    queen.
But nothing happened, for that night
    the king came,
Though Neron luckily escaped before.
He wrenched his wits to find some casual
    way
When he might urge himself upon her
    thought
Whose numb inconsequence was salt and
    flame
Set to the green wound of his smarting
    flesh.
But the dream halted at this very spot,
He could not push it to a consumma-
    tion.
He heaved upon it with his new-found
    strength,
Fully persuaded that he served her cause
By this he had in mind. The dream gave
    way,
The queen surrendered on the very terrace
Where the white peacock strutted. She
    whispered Neron
Where she would be at sunset, gave him
    the key
Of a small turret-chamber. He found her
    there,
Her slender shadow stretching to the door
To welcome him; and she, beyond her
    shadow,
Stood waiting in the crimson sunset light,
A slender silver fox-glove flushed with
    rose.
There was no sound except the golden
    boom
Of bees among the honeysuckle flowers
Stirring against the wall. For neither
    spoke,

Being removed past any reach of speech
Into that silent space of holiness
Where flesh creates the everlasting world.
But there the bearded king broke in upon
    them,
The king whose dream would never enter
    Neron's.
When Neron saw that thorny face, he
    leapt
To hide it from the queen. Calling his
    dream,
He strode upon the king, and the dream
    followed
Inch by inch after him, close as a shadow.
But Neron's dream was mighty with ful-
    filment,
It strove with the king's dream, and he
    and Neron
Stood each beside his dream and urged
    it forward
With shouts and cries. The battle
    roared between them.
The king's dream crowded down on
    Neron's dream
To smother it. But Neron's dream arose,
Flinging the king's dream off, and towered
    up
Tremendous in its brilliance. Then the
    king,
To save his dream, threw his black beard
    upon it,
The heaviness of hair shut out the bril-
    liance,
At which his dream, revived to fearful
    fury,
Came on at Neron's dream, and the two
    clashed
With a great noise together, and their
    bodies
Rang each on each like cymbals in the
    gloom
Sprung suddenly about them. With the
    dark,
The king's dream waxed monstrous in
    shape and stature,
Behemoth treading on a puny earth.
So did it stand and move, a ponderous
    bulk,
The nimbleness of Neron's dream was
    nothing.
The king's dream lifted like a rock and
    drove
The air snarling before it to a height
Past vision, thence it fell on Neron's
    dream,

Splitting its back from end to end, and
    Neron
Waggled his palsied hands about and
    wept.

The verger, coming up with Neron's food,
Found what was left the day before un-
    touched.
But being somewhat slow of wit, indeed
A person of marked unagility
Where thinking was concerned, what
    speculations
Another might have had, he was without.
So laying the second dole beside the first
He stumped downstairs to dust the chan-
    cel rail.
But when, next day, two baskets greeted
    him,
Both full, he felt enough perplexity
To risk a whistle on it; and the third
Encounter with the baskets, all of them,
Induced such lively wonder that he
    climbed
The three long flights of curling stairs
    to see
What ailed old Neron. Scratching match
    on match
He came at last upon him, crushed be-
    neath
A fallen wooden statue, dead as nails.
"The poor old beggar was dead as last
    year's fly,"
He told his mates, and later told the
    Dean,
And also mentioned something of a
    figure
Of painted wood. And there were two
    of them,
A king and queen, so wondrously pre-
    served
They looked quite new, although the
    architect
Pronounced them very early specimens
Of thirteenth century work, at which the
    Dean
And Chapter all said "Ah!" and spent
    a week
Searching old records for a hint of them.
The local antiquaries blew the dust
From ancient chronicles and seared their
    eyes
With cryptic script to learn what history
Made mention of an inky-bearded king
Whose iron mien portended fearful
    things,

And who the queen, so obviously mis-
mated?
But not a dusty chronicle gave tongue.
Baffled, they placed them in the town
museum
Cautiously labelled, "Ancient King and
Queen,
Fine specimens of Thirteenth Century
Carving."
And what of Neron? Neron was a pauper,
They buried him, of course, in Potter's
Field,
Where you can see him turned to purple
thistles
Purveying exquisite delight to donkeys
On Sundays, holidays, and festivals,
When the white sky is filled with
hallelujahs
Profusely scattered by Cathedral bells.

THE SISTERS

Taking us by and large, we're a queer lot
We women who write poetry. And when
you think
How few of us there've been, it's queerer
still.
I wonder what it is that makes us do it,
Singles us out to scribble down, man-wise,
The fragments of ourselves. Why are we
Already mother-creatures, double-bearing,
With matrices in body and in brain?
I rather think that there is just the reason
We are so sparse a kind of human being;
The strength of forty thousand Atlases
Is needed for our every-day concerns.
There's Sapho, now I wonder what was
Sapho.
I know a single slender thing about her:
That, loving, she was like a burning birch-
tree
All tall and glittering fire, and that she
wrote
Like the same fire caught up to Heaven
and held there,
A frozen blaze before it broke and fell.
Ah, me! I wish I could have talked to
Sapho,
Surprised her reticences by flinging mine
Into the wind. This tossing off of gar-
ments
Which cloud the soul is none too easy
doing
With us to-day. But still I think with
Sapho

One might accomplish it, were she in
the mood
To bare her loveliness of words and tell
The reasons, as she possibly conceived
them,
Of why they are so lovely. Just to know
How she came at them, just to watch
The crisp sea sunshine playing on her
hair,
And listen, thinking all the while 'twas
she
Who spoke and that we two were sisters
Of a strange, isolated little family.
And she is Sapho — Sapho — not Miss
or Mrs.,
A leaping fire we call so for convenience;
But Mrs. Browning — who would ever
think
Of such presumption as to call her "Ba."
Which draws the perfect line between
sea-cliffs
And a close-shuttered room in Wimpole
Street.
Sapho could fly her impulses like bright
Balloons tip-tilting to a morning air
And write about it. Mrs. Browning's
heart
Was squeezed in stiff conventions. So
she lay
Stretched out upon a sofa, reading Greek
And speculating, as I must suppose,
In just this way on Sapho; all the need,
The huge, imperious need of loving,
crushed
Within the body she believed so sick.
And it was sick, poor lady, because words
Are merely simulacra after deeds
Have wrought a pattern; when they take
the place
Of actions they breed a poisonous miasma
Which, though it leave the brain, eats
up the body.
So Mrs. Browning, aloof and delicate,
Lay still upon her sofa, all her strength
Going to uphold her over-topping brain.
It seems miraculous, but she escaped
To freedom and another motherhood
Than that of poems. She was a very
woman
And needed both.

        If I had gone to call,
Would Wimpole Street have been the
kindlier place,
Or Casa Guidi, in which to have met her?
I am a little doubtful of that meeting.

For Queen Victoria was very young and strong
And all-pervading in her apogee
At just that time. If we had stuck to poetry,
Sternly refusing to be drawn off by mesmerism
Or Roman revolutions, it might have done.
For, after all, she is another sister,
But always, I rather think, an older sister
And not herself so curious a technician
As to admit newfangled modes of writing —
"Except, of course, in Robert, and that is neither
Here nor there for Robert is a genius."
I do not like the turn this dream is taking,
Since I am very fond of Mrs. Browning
And very much indeed should like to hear her
Graciously asking me to call her "Ba."
But then the Devil of Verisimilitude
Creeps in and forces me to know she wouldn't.
Convention again, and how it chafes my nerves,
For we are such a little family
Of singing sisters, and as if I didn't know
What those years felt like tied down to the sofa.
Confounded Victoria, and the slimy inhibitions
She loosed on all us Anglo-Saxon creatures!
Suppose there hadn't been a Robert Browning,
No "Sonnets from the Portuguese" would have been written.
They are the first of all her poems to be,
One might say, fertilized. For, after all,
A poet is flesh and blood as well as brain
And Mrs. Browning, as I said before,
Was very, very woman. Well, there are two
Of us, and vastly unlike that's for certain.
Unlike at least until we tear the veils
Away which commonly gird souls. I scarcely think
Mrs. Browning would have approved the process
In spite of what had surely been relief;

For speaking souls must always want to speak
Even when bat-eyed, narrow-minded Queens
Set prudishness to keep the keys of impulse.
Then do the frowning Gods invent new banes
And make the need of sofas. But Sapho was dead
And I, and others, not yet peeped above
The edge of possibility. So that's an end
To speculating over tea-time talks
Beyond the movement of pentameters
With Mrs. Browning.
                    But I go dreaming on,
In love with these my spiritual relations.
I rather think I see myself walk up
A flight of wooden steps and ring a bell
And send a card in to Miss Dickinson.
Yet that's a very silly way to do.
I should have taken the dream twist-ends about
And climbed over the fence and found her deep
Engrossed in the doing of a humming-bird
Among nasturtiums. Not having expected strangers,
She might forget to think me one, and holding up
A finger say quite casually: "Take care.
Don't frighten him, he's only just begun."
"Now this," I well believe I should have thought,
"Is even better than Sapho. With Emily
You're really here, or never anywhere at all
In range of mind." Wherefore, having begun
In the strict centre, we could slowly progress
To various circumferences, as we pleased.
We could, but should we? That would quite depend
On Emily. I think she'd be exacting,
Without intention possibly, and ask
A thousand tight-rope tricks of understanding.
But, bless you, I would somersault all day
If by so doing I might stay with her.
I hardly think that we should mention souls
Although they might just round the corner from us

In some half-quizzical, half-wistful
metaphor.
I'm very sure that I should never seek
To turn her parables to stated fact.
Sapho would speak, I think, quite openly,
And Mrs. Browning guard a careful
silence,
But Emily would set doors ajar and slam
them
And love you for your speed of observa-
tion.

Strange trio of my sisters, most diverse,
And how extraordinarily unlike
Each is to me, and which way shall I
go?
Sapho spent and gained; and Mrs. Brown-
ing,
After a miser girlhood, cut the strings
Which tied her money-bags and let them
run;
But Emily hoarded — hoarded — only
giving
Herself to cold, white paper. Starved
and tortured,
She cheated her despair with games of
patience
And fooled herself by winning. Frail
little elf,
The lonely brain-child of a gaunt
maturity,
She hung her womanhood upon a bough
And played ball with the stars — too long
— too long —
The garment of herself hung on a tree
Until at last she lost even the desire
To take it down. Whose fault? Why
let us say,
To be consistent, Queen Victoria's.
But really, not to over-rate the queen,
I feel obliged to mention Martin Luther,
And behind him the long line of Church
Fathers
Who draped their prurience like a dirty
cloth
About the naked majesty of God.
Good-bye, my sisters, all of you are great,
And all of you are marvellously strange,
And none of you has any word for me.
I cannot write like you, I cannot think
In terms of Pagan or of Christian now.
I only hope that possibly some day
Some other woman with an itch for
writing
May turn to me as I have turned to you

And chat with me a brief few minutes.
How
We lie, we poets! It is three good hours
I have been dreaming. Has it seemed so
long
To you? And yet I thank you for the
time
Although you leave me sad and self-dis-
trustful,
For older sisters are very sobering things.
Put on your cloaks, my dears, the motor's
waiting.
No, you have not seemed strange to me,
but near,
Frightfully near, and rather terrifying.
I understand you all, for in myself —
Is that presumption? Yet indeed it's
true —
We are one family. And still my answer
Will not be any one of yours, I see.
Well, never mind that now. Good night!
Good night!

VIEW OF TEIGNMOUTH
IN DEVONSHIRE

*"Atkins the coachman, Bartlett the
surgeon, and the Girls over at the Bonnet-
shop, say we shall now have a month of
seasonable weather — warm, witty, and
full of invention."*
Letter from Keats to Reynolds.
March 14, 1818

It's a soppy, splashy, muddy country
And he is dead sick of stair and entry,
Of four walls cuddling round his chair,
And breathing full as much water as air.
London is so far away
It dreams, like Latmos. He has sat all
day
Copying that cursed Fourth Book and
he's struck
A snag, and his drying sand won't suck.
His mind's like a seed gone to rot with
rain,
And — Damn it, there's poor Tom
coughing again!

Mr. John Keats crams his hat well on
Over his ears and walks up and down
The soggy streets of Teignmouth town.
Mr. John Keats walks along the streets
Of Teignmouth and asks every soul he
meets

If the sun ever shines in Devonshire,
Whether the weather they live with here
Is sometimes what one might really call
    fair,
With the sun in the sky and a brisk to
    the air?
The hat of Mr. John Keats is wet,
But his eyes are sharp and ferret-set,
He is seeking the sun with a quicksilver-
    rod,
Noting the veer in a neighbour's nod,
Gauging the drift of a neighbour's words
As they might be a flock of South-come
    birds.

Atkins, the coachman, sets his mug
Down on the counter and gives a shrug,
"Lor' love you, Sir, if I was to tell
The way I know, you might call it smell.
I smell it right across the rain,
Dry and gentle; it's plain as plain
To-day, I give it a week to run,
This rain, and then we'll have the sun,
As skittish as a piebald colt
And sudden as a thunderbolt.
All full o' notions, that's the way
Of the sun down here on a Summer's
    day.
Just take my word, before you've said
'Jack Robinson,' you'll be hugging the
    shade
Of every wall, and sweatin' in
A steam like my team when I bring 'em
    in.
Well, thank ye, Sir, I don't mind if I do,
Brandy neat is my usual brew."

Smell it, could he? The man's insane.
Smell the sun through a week of rain!
Yet the thought has a kind of glamour
    to it,
A relish of wit, however you view it,
A rainbow quip for a rainy day.
Mr. Keats, plodding through wet clay,
Is aware of a certain direct effect
Of joy in his heart. He stands erect.
Surely the mist is silvering
His footsteps sound with a livelier ring.
If anything glitters in Teignmouth streets
This afternoon, it is John Keats.

Mr. Bartlett is hurrying by
At a speed which announces that minutes
    fly,
But he pauses briefly just to say

"Ah, Mr. Keats, how are you to-day?
The sun? Oh, very shortly now.
We shall be scorched before we know.
Didn't you hear the crows this morning?
They always give one plenty of warning.
And Mrs. Bartlett talks of house-cleaning,
Every married man can read the meaning
Of that. When the women begin to
    clack
It's a surer sign than the almanac.
The barometer's risen a point or two
Since yesterday, and this mist is blue,
Not grey. I am sorry I cannot stop,
But a surgeon is always on the hop,
If it's not for one thing, it's another.
Of course you're anxious because of your
    brother.
Tell him he'll soon have all the basking
In sunlight he wants, and just for the
    asking.
But I must go, Mrs. Green's brought to
    bed —
Oh, tell him to keep it off of his head."

Smash! Bang! Mr. Keats. Another chain
Is snapped, and there's a gold tint to the
    rain.

Simmons the barber's as shrunk as a
    pippin
Hung on a beam which you might nick a
    chip in,
But never could suck for its juice is all
    dried.
This afternoon he is standing inside
His doorway, just behind his pole,
With the mien of a migratory soul
Perching an instant before departing
Otherwise, he seems always just starting
To leave, a whirling weather-cock
On the edge of flight, but tied to a block.
"Good afternoon, Mr. Keats," says he,
"Brushing up a bit for good weather, I
    see.
That's the way, young men can tell
A season's turn uncommonly well.
I've had a full day, the whole town at
    once.
But when I learnt my trade every dunce
Who could snap a scissors did not dare
    hoist a pole.
I remember one day when they called out
    the roll
In the old sixty-third, every man of the
    lot

Was new shaved and powdered and
wound, and my pot
And razors all cleaned and I with the
rest of them
As spick and as span I could match with
the best of them.
To cut a round head requires some skill,
But nothing to binding a cue, there's a
thrill
In a nicely tied cue, I can't see how the
girls
Can put up with a man who wears his
own curls.
But fashion is fashion, the hussy, and I've
Been her very devoted since I've been
alive.
And, thank God, she has not yet set her
approval
On beards except in the way of removal.
I wish you could feel the delight I re-
ceive
When my razor slides over your skin, I'd
as leave
Shave a man in his twenties as go to a
play,
There's romance in it, Sir, when you see
the soap spray
Into bubbles and lather, and your blade
cuts a line
And lets through the smooth face like a
moon, it's so fine
That I dream it sometimes. I've a soul
for such fancies,
Old barbers like shaving as young girls
like dances.
And one makes the other. Who would
dance a quadrille
With a rough, stubble chin? That
fellow who will
Is a hater of women, a thief in the
egg,
He's just ripe for a ball attached to his
leg.
Why look, Sir, and tell me if fully two-
thirds
Of the unshaven men do not end as jail-
birds.
Our prisons are full of them, I dare to
swear
No convict's without a two-days' growth
of hair.
I don't hold with this personal shaving,
it's sordid.
A man should spend well on himself, I
wish more did.

But no man can cut his own hair, that's
a fact,
And a hair-cut requires a vast deal of tact.
A doctor wants his to look sober and
grave,
Tradesmen are addicted to a float and
a wave,
And again, one must know the sort of
commodity
Your client purveys or there's danger of
oddity.
A butcher cut like a silk-mercer won't do.
And a military man must carry a clue
To his martial exploits in the style of his
head,
While a poet — you're a poet, Sir, I
think I've heard said —
Oh, no, Sir, indeed, not a bit more con-
fined,
A poet's hair should seem the least trifle
inclined
To a graceful disorder, it should look
well when tossed;
If you cut it too short this effect is quite
lost.
Oh, I beg, Mr. Keats, not another least
snip.
Oh, dear, I do really regret that last clip.
I am glad you are pleased, but I don't
think a poet
Should order his hair so that no one can
know it.
Still, you look very well, though I should
have preferred
More dash and confusion for you. I have
heard
That Lord Byron measures his hair with
a rule
Before it is cut, and the least thimbleful
Too much taken off sets him all in a
taking.
I've been told of men who couldn't cut
him for shaking.
The weather will change in less than a
week,
I have felt it these last few days on my
cheek,
My skin always answers to the slightest
degree
Of more or less moisture. You'll hardly
agree
That it's dryer and warmer, but my touch
is so fine
I can tell a South wind when it's over
the line.

Of course they'll say different, these poor
rustic churls,
But you be all ready for sparking the girls
By Tuesday. I'll tip you the wink. We
old men
Remember our own young days, now and
again."

Mr. John Keats has a jaunty swing
In his gait, as he leaves the chattering
Old barber, bowing beside his door.
Of course he feels the sort of core
Of golden sun the mist falls through.
What is a day, what is two?
The sun is coming up from the line
Like a fifty-four with its sails ashine.
He feels the flower-scented South
Like a taste of apricot in his mouth.
He thinks of primroses under the hedge
Where the pathway runs by the sheer
cliff edge;
Of the downs above where sheep have
trod
Crooked grey patterns across the sod,
And the shadows of turf-walls, cool and
still,
Mark who owns where all down the
hill;
Of a long slow ocean, so dazzling bright
Its blue is smothered in spangled white.
He thinks of queer sea-paths cross-run-
ning,
Smooth on ripple, of the quiet sunning
Of rocks and meadows, of violets
Creeping through grass, of drying nets,
Of poetry read with the sun on his book
And the freckling of leaves for an over-
look.
Somebody laughs, somebody calls,
"Good-day, Mr. Keats." It drops from
the walls,
A perfume of laughter which flutters and
falls.
Lime-tree blossoms by turret stairs,
Laughter of flowers no more than theirs,
Sunny golden acacia blooms
Peeping into maidens' rooms,
Snap a spray and throw it over
The window-ledge to a waiting lover.
Mr. Keats comes to a stop
For the girls are over the Bonnet-shop
Leaning out like waving roses
Over a gate, most lovely of poses.
"Stay where you are, Girls," says Mr.
Keats,

"You pose as the dryads of Teignmouth
streets.
If Haydon were here he would jot you
down
In a jiffy, with your hair wet and blown
And your little laughing faces like pansies."
"La! Mr. Keats, you do have such
fancies."
"Fancies or no, I believe it clears.
Don't you feel the sun on your cheeks,
my Dears?
Or smell it perhaps? What do you think?
There's a hocus-pocus to-day in my
ink
Which would not let me write a line,
And I itch for the sight of a columbine.
Tell me, have you noticed anything
Which points to a near-by Summering?"
"Oh yes," said little Number One,
"All day I have felt the sun,
I saw it on a wheat-straw bonnet
I was making, the sun lay upon it,
And I thought the muslin blue-bells were
sweet."
"That," said Mr. Keats, "is proof com-
plete."
Said Number Two, "I pricked my thumb
Three times running, and fair days come
After three pricks, it is always so.
Grandmother taught me long ago."
"I dreamt last night," said Number
Three,
"Of a great thick-leaved fuchsia-tree
Full of blossoms, purple and red,
And the blossoms played music over my
head
Like bells of glass and copper bells
And wind in the trees when the ocean
swells
Flood tide over the beach, and shells
Glisten like rubies with the water sheen
And the sky at the back of the town is
green."
"You prophesy in a parable,"
Said Mr. Keats. "Oh, April-fool!"
Cried the girls who were over the Bonnet-
shop.
And their laughter was sweet as a lolli-
pop
To an urchin's palate in his ears.
With a gesture, he brushed aside their
jeers.
"But will it clear?" "Of course it will,"
Said the three, "If you patiently wait
until

It does." And they laughed in a rain-
bow chord,
High, and low, and middleward.
And Mr. Keats laughed too, though he
knew
That they had not said one word in two
Of what he'd imagined they might have
said.
But who cares a button who bakes the
bread
So the bread is baked? And a Bonnet-
shop
May be what you please, even Latmos
top.
So Mr. Keats went blithely on,
Quite as if the round sun shone,
Back to his copying his Fourth Book.
And the girls watched him until a crook
In the street, when he turned it, hid him
from sight.
Then they noticed that it was growing
night.
So they put their bonnets away, and the
three
Lit the lamp and sat down to tea,
Immortal for always, because John Keats
Had taken a walk through Teignmouth
streets,
And stopped when one of them said
"Good-day."
Clio is odd in her ways, they say.
The coachman, the surgeon, the barber,
the girls —
Islands raised out of darkening swirls.
Who else was in Teignmouth that after-
noon?
Vainly may we importune
The shadows, only these have come down
A century from Teignmouth town.
These only from the dark are won
Because John Keats had a hunger for
sun.

FOOL O' THE MOON

The silver-slippered moon treads the blue
tiles of the sky,
And I
See her dressed in golden roses,
With a single breast uncovered,
The carnation tip of it
Urgent for a lover's lip.
So she dances to a stately
Beat, with poses most sedately
Taken, yet there lies

Something wanton in her gestures,
And there is surprise of coquetry
In the falling of her vestures.
Why?

Out of old mythology,
With a pulse of gourds and sheep-skins,
Banging bronze and metal thunders,
There is she,
Wonderfullest of earth's wonders.
As for me,
Head thrown back and arms spread wide
Like a zany crucified,
I stand watching, waiting, gazing,
All of me spent in amazing,
Longing for her wheat-white thighs,
Thirsting for her emerald fire,
My desire
Pounding dully from my eyes.
And my hands
Clutch and cuddle the vast air
Seeking her where she's most fair.

There,
On the cool blue tiles of heaven,
She is dancing coolly, coldly,
Footsteps trace a braid of seven,
And her gauzy garments fleet
Round her like a glittering sleet.
Suddenly she flings them boldly
In a streaming bannerall
Out behind,
And I see all.
God! I'm blind!

And a goodly company
Of men are we,
Lovers she has chosen,
Laughing-stocks and finger-posts
To the wise, a troupe of ghosts
Swelled by every century.
Mad, and blind, and burnt, and frozen,
Standing on a hilly slope
At bright midnight,
And our hope
Is in vain, or is it not?
Legend knows the very spot
Where the moon once made her bed.
But the pathway as it led
Over rock-brows to that valley
Is an alley choked and dead.
One by one our fates deceive us,
One of hundreds will be shown
Ferny uplands whose great bosses
Of tall granite hide the mosses

Where our Lady's lying prone,
All her stars withdrawn, alone.
So she chooses to receive us,
Out of hundreds, only one.

Such a vale of moss and heather
Spreads about us, hither — thither.
Hush!
Shall I tell what befell
Once behind that bush.
When the rattling pods at noon
Made a music in September.
Shall I say what I remember —
While the long, sea-grasses croon,
And the sea-spray on the sand
Chips the silence from the land?
Hush, then, let me say it soon.
I have lain with Mistress Moon.

TOMB VALLEY

Down a cliff-side where rock-roses,
Shallow-rooted, scantly bloom,
And the mountain goats in passing
Barely find a foothold's room,
While the boulders of the summit
Cast an everlasting gloom.

Leaps a torrent from behind
The jutted angle of a wall
In a long, unbroken sliding,
For it touches not at all
Any rock, or stone, or pebble
For a thousand feet of fall.

For a thousand feet it rushes
Like a heavy, laden air,
Playing over some tremendous
Sound which surely must be there,
For you hear it, lose it, hear it.
Does it come from anywhere?

Seething, bubbling, churning, groaning,
Has the water in its flight
Shattered on the stony bottom
Of the valley, while its height
Drawing upward like a ribbon
Palely grows upon the sight?

But the sound is chiller, deeper,
Long and dreary like a moan
Caught forever on an echo
'Twixt two balanced shafts of stone,
Whence it surges and resurges
In protracted monotone.

Far below, within the valley,
Runs a river, cold and sleek,
Never oar has cut its smoothness,
It has shattered on no beak
Of shallop or of galley,
Its tide is slow and meek.

And the trees within that valley,
Of every broad-leaved kind,
Wave to and fro compactly,
For there's never any wind.
Ten thousand branches blowing
All one way is hard to find.

And the shadows which their movement
Casts upon the sandy ground
Are like footsteps weaving dances
To that ghastly, haunting sound
Ringing round the chilly valley,
Round and round and round and round.

Where the river curves about it,
And the water lilies strew
Silver petals on the pebbles
Mingling with dropped cones of yew,
Stands a sepulchre of granite
Striped with bars of green and blue.

Green and blue bars painted crosswise
From its bottom to its crown,
At its apex is a statue,
Coldly, boldly, gazing down,
Gazing fiercely, gazing wildly,
In an everlasting frown.

And upon its knees a woman
Kneels and clasps the granite thighs,
And clings upon the roughened stone
While tears drop from her eyes.
The surly yews wave back and forth
Beneath a red moonrise.

And a hollow, draughty moaning
Fills the valley like a gong.
Women's voices weeping, wailing,
All the waving trees among,
Where no shapes or shadows flicker
But the low moon, broad and long.

Slowly rising from the cliff-tops,
Like a gnawed and crumbled cone,
It appears in perfect semblance
To a sepulchre of stone,
And the bars are striped upon it
Like cross-sticks of blackened bone.

In a bitter orange moonlight
Lies the woman on the knees
Of that austere thing of granite,
All surrounded by the trees,
And the curling, sneering river,
And nothing else but these.

On a sudden, she has risen,
And with clenched fists beats the face
Of that frozen granite horror,
And her blows in that drear place
Are as thunder-claps resounding
Upon vastnesses of space.

For an instant still she batters
At that changeless, mocking frown,
Then flings her bleeding hands
Above her head and plunges down
To the smooth and careful river
With sere rushes overgrown.

But no ripple marks her entrance
To that water, bright as flame,
And no pucker stirs the granite face
To tell she ever came.
The trees blow and the moaning
Continues just the same.

But every moonlight night, they say,
She drowns herself once more,
And by the queasy daylight
You can see her from the shore
Lying like a lily petal
On the river's glassy floor.

So they say, but no one proves it.
No one ever ventures in
To that valley. Only passers-by
Above can hear a thin
Weary wailing, if they note it
Through the torrent's distant din.

As they wander on the cliff-edge
Where the scant rock-roses blow,
And the mountain goats go shrewdly
In the footways that they know,
While the crash of tumbling water
Sounds a thousand feet below.

THE GREEN PARRAKEET

"Three doors up from the end of
    the street
Hung a golden cage with a green
    parrakeet."

His feet shambled in the dust of the road,
    and the little barberry bushes
    hung out red tongues and leered
    at him.
He shuffled on, down the road, bent as
    though it might be a load he was
    carrying, while tiers and tiers of
    poplars, birches, hemlocks, pines,
    peered to see who it might be
    who stumbled and flung the dust
    about,
And the grey grape-vines, in and out
    between the bushes, ran beside
    him and looked in his face.
But his pace never changed a whit for
    all their staring. He shuffled on
    at his long way-faring.

    "Morning and night, to the green
        parrakeet
    She sang, and Oh, her singing was
        sweet!"
The road dipped down to a marsh, and
    the meadow-larks sang as he
    passed them, but his ears rang
    with another singing so that he
    heard nothing.
"By the North Wind's whistle, he is
    blind!" said a mouse-wood to an
    elder-bush.
"Hush," cried the grape-vines, "you do
    not catch his dust. It is the dust
    of something a long way off."

    "Her kisses were a flower red;
    I saw them on the bird's green head.
    Her breasts were white as almond
        bean
    And the parrakeet nestled in be-
        tween."
"Oh, gently, gently," sighed the senti-
    mental vines, but the long lines
    of trees behind them objected
    that he took a great while to go
    by.
"We are better employed," they de-
    clared, "contemplating the sky."

    Then I knocked at the door and
        entered in
    Like the orange flame of a hidden
        sin.
    I stood before her and there were
        three —
    The parrakeet and I and she.

I tossed her arms apart and pressed
Myself upon her, breast to breast,
And the parrakeet was my bidden
    guest.
I forced her lips till they caught on
    mine,
And poured myself down her throat
    like wine.
I mingled with her, part for part,
But the parrakeet lay next her heart.
Oh, sweeter than her lips were sweet
Was my utter hate for that par-
    rakeet.
She fell from me like the withered
    shell
Of a cranberry, and it was well;
I stood on the other side of Hell.
Slowly, slowly, she raised her head,
But the parrakeet fell down like lead
Upon the matting, still and dead.
Softly, softly, she gazed at me,
And I saw a thing which I dared not
    see.
"My love!" she said, and the tones
    were sweet
As ever she used to the parrakeet.
But I had made my flaming breast
A weapon to kill a bird on its nest —
A single flame for the bird and me,
And I was as smothered as he could
    be.
I stared at her from the farther side
Of Hell, no space is great beside
This space. I could not see her face
Across such vastitude of space,
And over it drowsed a darkened
    thing:
A monster parrakeet's green wing.
The air was starred with parrakeets.
I turned and rushed into the streets.
For days and days I wandered there,
For Oh! My love was very fair!
Each night I watched her lean and
    stand,
With empty heart and empty hand,
While every passer-by she scanned.
But I beheld what was not meet
For all to see — a parrakeet
Of gauzy substance which could cast
No slightest shadow where it passed,
Fluttering with indecent glee
Between my hungering love and me.
Ten months went by, and then one
    day
It struck my face and flew away.

Some odd obedience in my feet
Compelled me after, street by street,
And then along a country lane.
I had no power to turn again.
Next morning took me farther still,
My feet usurped the place of will.
And now I walk a weary road,
Bent double underneath the load
Of memory and second sight.
That bird is always on my right
And just ahead, I follow where
His body flickers through the air.
Sometimes it is as plain as print,
Sometimes no better than a hint
Of colour where no leaves are green
But I can see what I have seen.
How many years is that ago?
I notice night and morning flow
Each into each, the seasons run
Against the turning of the sun,
But more or fewer — 'tis all one.
She may be dead, and I may be
A ghost myself, eternally
Dreaming the short, ironic bliss
Of one long, unrepeated kiss.

The man scuffed across a bridge and up
    a steep hill. "Quietly, quietly,"
    whispered the barberry-bushes,
    and hid their scarlet tongues
    under the leaves. "Weep, Tree-
    Brothers," said the grape-vines.
    But the long lines of trees only
    rustled and played hide and seek
    with the peeping moon. They
    were too tall to pay much heed to
    anything so small as an old man
    limping up a hill.

TIME'S ACRE

Beat, beat, with your soft grey feet,
Tear at the cold, rough stone.
His grave is here, but it's many a year
Since the grass on it was mown.

His ears are crumbled to bitter dust,
His eyes are a hollow bone.
Your twisting hair is bright and fair,
But he is under a stone.

Go back again to your own wide tomb,
Leave him in peace within
His grave that is narrow and shallow and
    small,

There is no room for two between either
    wall,
And the walls are caving in.

There are nests of worms in the under-
    ground,
And the grass-roots wind across,
Like a counterpane to keep out the rain
Is the green-eyed, clutching moss.

Go back to your tomb a mile away,
Go back through the still bronze door.
The arms which are carven upon its front
Are there as they were before.

No trace of escutcheon is on this stone,
And burdocks have pushed it awry,
And the flowers on tiptoe out of his
    mouth
Are staring into the sky.

Over his grave is a moan of wind,
And hemlock-trees bow down,
And a hemlock cone lies on the stone
Stained with smoke from the town.

What have you to do in this dismal place
By a dingy, broken stone?
He has no hands and he has no face,
And bone cannot wed with bone.

You took his flesh and you took his
    heart,
But his bones are his own to keep.
Knuckle and straight, he has them all
Down in the gravel deep.

Perhaps he laughs with his hard grey
    mouth,
Perhaps he shouts with glee,
And cuddles his bones up one by one,
And wishes that you could see.

Perhaps he plays jackstones with his
    bones,
And bets how long you will stay,
He knows all about those bright bronze
   doors
Waiting a mile away.

For you in the flesh teased him in the
    flesh
And would not let him be,
Till you teased him out of his flesh for
    good
And into Eternity.

But what is fire to a living man
Is nothing at all to a bone.
He lies at ease in the cold and the mold,
And he lies at ease alone.

He will be part of the earth in time,
You will be only dust,
And your carven door will be nothing
    more
Than a heap of eating rust.

So much for your azure fleur-de-lis,
And your cross in a chevron d'or.
He will be lilies in a morning breeze
At the foot of a sycamore.

The world goes round, and the world goes
    round,
And who knows what may come out of
    the ground
When a man is planted under a mound.

SULTRY

To those who can see them, there are
    eyes,
Leopard eyes of marigolds crouching above
    red earth,
Bulging eyes of fruits and rubies in the
    heavily-hanging trees,
Broken eyes of queasy cupids staring from
    the gloom of myrtles.
I came here for solitude
And I am plucked at by a host of eyes.

A peacock spreads his tail on the balus-
    trade
And every eye is a mood of green malice,
A challenge and a fear.
A hornet flashes above geraniums,
Spying upon me in a trick of cunning.
And Hermes,
Hermes the implacable,
Points at me with a fractured arm.

Vengeful god of smooth, imperishable
    loveliness,
You are more savage than the goat-legged
    Pan,
Than the crocodile of carven yew-wood.
Fisherman of men's eyes,
You catch them on a three-pronged spear:
Your youth, your manhood,
The reticence of your everlasting revela-
    tion.

I too am become a cunning eye
Seeking you past your time-gnawed surface,
Seeking you back to hyacinths upon a dropping hill,
Where legend drowses in a glaze of sea.

Yours are the eyes of a bull and a panther,
For all that they are chiselled out and the sockets empty.
You — perfectly imperfect,
Clothed in a garden,
In innumerable gardens,
Borrowing the eyes of fruits and flowers —
And mine also, cold, impossible god,
So that I stare back at myself
And see myself with loathing.

A quince-tree flings a crooked shadow —
My shadow, tortured out of semblance,
Bewildered in quince boughs.
His shadow is clear as a scissored silhouette.
Heat twinkles and the eyes glare.
And I, of the mingled shadow,
I glare
And see nothing.

THE ENCHANTED CASTLE

To Edgar Allan Poe

Old crumbling stones set long ago upon
The naked headland of a suave green shore.
Old stones all riven into cracks and glands
By moss and ivy. Up above, a peak
Of narrow, iron windows, a hooded tower
With frozen windows looking to the West.
When the sun sets, a winking, fiery light
Riffles the window-panes above the gloom
Of purple waters heaving evenly,
Waters moving about the naked headland
In sombre slowness, with no dash of spray
To strike the stagnant pools and flash the weeds.
A rack of shifting clouds
Darkens the waters' margin. On the shore
Are clusters of great trees whose brittle leaves
Crackle together as the mournful wind

Takes them and shakes them. But the tower windows
Fling bloody streams of light across the dusk,
Planges of bloody light which the upper sky
Has hurled at them and now is drawing back.
Behind the tower, where no windows are,
A little wisp of moon catches the stones
So that they glitter palely from the shore,
The suave green shore with all its leaden trees.

AUTUMN AND DEATH

They are coy, these sisters, Autumn and Death,
And they both have learnt what it is to wait.
Not a leaf is jarred by their cautious breath,
The little feather-weight
Petals of climbing convolvulus
Are scarcely even tremulous.

Who hears Autumn moving down
The garden-paths? Who marks her head
Above the oat-sheaves? A leaf gone brown
On the ash, and a maple-leaf turned red —
Yet a rose that's freshly blown
Seals your eyes to the change in these,
For it's mostly green about the trees.

And Death with her silver-slippered feet,
Do you hear her walk by your garden-chair?
The cool of her hand makes a tempered heat,
That's all, and the shadow of her hair
Is curiously sweet.
Does she speak? If so, you have not heard;
The whisper of Death is without a word.

The sisters, Autumn and Death, with strange
Long silences, they bide their time,
Nor ever step beyond the range
Allotted to a pantomime.
But the soundless hours chime,
One after one, and their faces grow
To an altered likeness, slow — slow.

Grim is the face which Autumn turns
To a sky all bare of obscuring leaves,
And her hair is red as a torch where it
　burns
In the dry hearts of the oaten sheaves.
But Death has a face which yearns
With a gaunt desire upon its prey,
And Death's dark face hides yesterday.

Then Autumn holds her hands to touch
Death's hands, and the two kiss, cheek
　by cheek,
And one smiles to the other, and the
　smiles say much,
And neither one has need to speak.
Two gray old sisters, such
Are Autumn and Death when their tasks
　are done,
And their world is a world where a
　blackened sun
Shines like ebony over the floes
Of a shadeless ice, and no wind blows.

FOLIE DE MINUIT

No word, no word, O Lord God!
Hanging above the shivering pillars
Like thunder over a brazen city.

Pity, Is there pity?
Does pity pour from the multiform
　points
Of snow crystals?
If the throats of the organ pipes
Are numb with cold,
Can the boldest bellows' blast
Melt their now dumb hosannas?

No word, august and brooding God!
No shrivelled spectre of an aching tone
Can pierce those banners
Which hide your face, your hands,
Your feet at whose slight tread
Frore water curds to freckled sands
Seaweed encrusted.
The organ loft is draughty with faint
　voices
Weeping,
Which are not mine, nor would be.
I purposed anthems, copper-red and
　golden,
Thrusting to the hearts of Babylonian
　Kings,
Bowed down before Judea and its Highest,

That God of Hosts who screens himself
　with banners.
My finger-tips are cast in a shard of
　silence;
The wormy lips of these great, narrow
　tunnels, the pipes,
Are choked with silence;
The banners, the banners, are brittle with
　decay
And rusted out of colour.

The candles gutter in their sconces,
Curling long welts of evil-smelling smoke
　about my head.
The organ's voice is dead,
Or is it mine?
The banners flap
Like palls upon a bier
On windy midnight burials
Where torches flare a glittering imposture
About the loneliness of violated sod
Gashed open for a grave.

Pity me, then,
Who cry with wingless psalms,
Spellbound in midnight and chill organ
　pipes.
Above my eyes the banners bleed
Their dripping dust-specks,
Proclaiming the gaunt glories of success-
　ful battles.
It would enchant me to see you afloat
　behind them,
Blown for a moment to an eye-catch.
But who are you to come for frozen
　hallelujahs!

And yet I go on silently playing.

THE SLIPPERS OF THE
GODDESS OF BEAUTY

*"It is easy, like Momus, to find fault
with the clattering of the slipper worn
by the Goddess of beauty; but 'the serious
Gods' found better employment in admiration of her unapproachable loveliness."*

They clatter, clatter, clatter on the floor,
Her slippers clack upon the marble
　slabs,
And every time her heels clap, I count
　one,

And go on counting till my nerves are
sick
With one and one and one told out in
claps.

He shot a hand out, clutching at my arm
With bony fingers. "Young man," said
he, "look up.
Is that a starry face, or am I blind?
Do stars beset her like a crown of pearls?
Does sunset tinge and tangle in her hair,
And moonlight rush in silver from her
breasts?
Look well, young man, for maybe I am
blind."

I looked, and agony assailed my brain.
He chirruped at me. "So — so! Ancient
eyes
Know better than to keep upon the floor.
What dazzles you is kindly sight to me,
One gets accustomed. But I interrupt
Your count. What figure had you
reached?" I shook
Him off and staggered to my room,
bright pain
Stabbing my head.
                    I've never found that count,
Nor started on another. Every day
I look a little longer when she comes,
And see a little more, and bear to see.
But that queer man I've never met again,
Nor very much desired to, perhaps.
Gratitude is an irksome thing to youth,
And I, thank Hermes, am still reckoned
young,
Though old enough to look above the
floor,
Which is a certain age, I must admit.
But I'll endure that, seeing what it brings.

THE WATERSHED

You say you are my friends,
Coming mistily to greet me in your
streets and places,
Handing me roses which are not tinsel
surely,
That much is no gainsaying, but there it
ends.
For you, the friendly people, are a vision
of massed faces,
A large wavering smile of something I
shrink to call derision.
And yet I take your roses demurely

And express my obligation with a nice
precision.
Why should I quarrel with what Fate
sends?

Poppycock! For indeed I am not a fool.
Next year, perhaps, I shall be no more
to you than a sick mountebank.
Therefore, while I thank you for your
roses,
I hold apart and I too smile,
Bitterly, if you will have it so; but while
I wonder you should laud me for a minute,
I wonder more by what strange finger-
rule
You find your praise so easy to be spilt —
The brimful ease of it your chief of poses.
Am I the creature you have swiftly built
Since yesterday, who, formerly, for all you
thought,
Printed too light a circle even to round
a naught?
Or am I what you'll have me by to-
morrow?
There's worry to keep me busy dabbling
in it,
And pricks enough to start a pretty sor-
row.

Don't think, you polype blur of friendli-
ness,
That any attitude you choose to take
Affects me otherwise than so much less
Than atom's atom. Scarcely for your
sake
Would I consent even to notice where
You seem most thickly to invest the air,
Making a coloured rose-bud of the sun.
Your sneers, I think, would leave me well
aware
Of something I might boast a bit of
having;
Your smooth and pitiless content with
what I do
Shows up each whorl and roughness in
the grain
Of that harsh article I call my brain,
Of that queer heart all twisted like a
shaving
I seldom fret about. So after being
Encumbered for a brief space by your
roses
I think to find your subsequent composure
As apt and cheerful as a new disclosure
Broke suddenly across a weary seeing.

Your waning praise will mark a time of
day,
And afternoon approaching finds my way
So far advanced, that's all. You are a
stage
We reach at ten o'clock and twelve is
age.
If I'm an episode, why so are you.
We'll make a kindliness of that — what
else is there to do?

LA RONDE DU DIABLE

"Here we go round the ivy-bush,"
And that's a tune we all dance to.
Little poet people snatching ivy,
Trying to prevent one another from
snatching ivy.
If you get a leaf, there's another for me;
Look at the bush.
But I want your leaf, Brother, and you
mine,
Therefore, of course, we push.

"Here we go round the laurel-tree."
Do we want laurels for ourselves most,
Or most that no one else shall have any?
We cannot stop to discuss the question.
We cannot stop to plait them into
crowns
Or notice whether they become us.
We scarcely see the laurel-tree,
The crowd about us is all we see,
And there's no room in it for you and
me.
Therefore, Sisters, it's my belief
We've none of us very much chance at
a leaf.

"Here we go round the barberry-bush."
It's a bitter, blood-red fruit at best,
Which puckers the mouth and burns the
heart.
To tell the truth, only one or two
Want the berries enough to strive
For more than he has, more than she.
An acid berry for you and me.
Abundance of berries for all who will eat,
But an aching meat.
That's poetry.
And who wants to swallow a mouthful
of sorrow?
The world is old and our century
Must be well along, and we've no time
to waste.

Make haste, Brothers and Sisters, push
With might and main round the ivy-
bush,
Struggle and pull at the laurel-tree,
And leave the barberries be
For poor lost lunatics like me,
Who set them so high
They overtop the sun in the sky.
Does it matter at all that we don't know
why?

MORNING SONG, WITH DRUMS

The pheasants cry in the dawn,
Mocking the glitter of the nearby city
Struck upon the sky.

Ivy in a wind,
Smooth grass,
Old cedar-trees.

Change is a bitter thing to contemplate
Across a grey dawn.
Puff-ball world, forsooth,
A kick and it is broken into smoke.

The pheasant's cry is raucous in the
dawn.

A GRAVE SONG

I've a pocketful of emptiness for you, my
Dear.
I've a heart like a loaf was baked yes-
teryear,
I've a mind like ashes spilt a week
ago,
I've a hand like a rusty, cracked cork-
screw.

Can you flourish on nothing and find it
good?
Can you make petrification do for food?
Can you warm yourself at ashes on a
stone?
Can you give my hand the cunning which
has gone?

If you can, I will go and lay me
down
And kiss the edge of your purple gown.
I will rise and walk with the sun on my
head.
Will you walk with me, will you follow
the dead?

A RHYME OUT OF MOTLEY

"I grasped a thread of silver; it cut me
    to the bone —
I reached for an apple; it was bleak as
    a stone —
I reached for a heart, and touched a raw
    blade —
And this was the bargain God had made
For a little gift of speech
Set a cubit higher than the common
    reach,
A debt running on until the fool is dead."

Carve a Pater Noster to put at his head
As a curse or a prayer,
And leave him there.

THE RED KNIGHT

I saw him,
Standing in red armour before an altar
Under the fish-scale roof of a church
In a river valley in mid-France.
The organ was crying an anthem along
    the great nave
And the eddy of it tickled the noses of
    the impish stone manikins with foxes'
    tails curled beneath the architraves.
When the organ ceased crying, he lifted
    his head
And gazed through the clear-story win-
    dows at the white-blue of an after-
    rain sky.
Suddenly a thin scatter of sunlight smote
    upon his armour
And it flamed like a bonfire, and he in
    the midst, unnoticing.

White wood of poplar beneath green bark,
A man, the height and spread of a tall
    man,
Beneath a burning armour.
I would have flung my kerchief to him
    to bind upon his helmet,
But kerchiefs fall obliquely through back-
    ward centuries,
And already the light was growing too
    dim to see a silken nothing upon a
    shadowed floor.
Steel footsteps on stone make a strange
    sound;
I never heard the like before, and I think
    I never shall again.
For which unreasonable reason
I am determined to remain a virgin.

NUIT BLANCHE

I want no horns to rouse me up to-night,
And trumpets make too clamorous a ring
To fit my mood, it is so weary white
I have no wish for doing any thing.

A music coaxed from humming strings
    would please;
Not plucked, but drawn in creeping
    cadences
Across a sunset wall where some Marquise
Picks a pale rose amid strange silences.

Ghostly and vaporous her gown sweeps by
The twilight dusking wall, I hear her feet
Delaying on the gravel, and a sigh,
Briefly permitted, touches the air like sleet.

And it is dark, I hear her feet no more.
A red moon leers beyond the lily-tank.
A drunken moon ogling a sycamore,
Running long fingers down its shining
    flank.

A lurching moon, as nimble as a clown,
Cuddling the flowers and trees which
    burn like glass.
Red, kissing lips, I feel you on my gown —
Kiss me, red lips, and then pass — pass.

Music, you are pitiless to-night.
And I so old, so cold, so languorously
    white.

ORIENTATION

When the young ladies of the boarding-
    school take the air,
They walk in pairs, each holding a blush-
    red parasol against the sun.
From my window they look like an
    ambulating parterre
Of roses, I cannot tell one from one.

There is a certain young person I dream
    of by night,
And paint by day on little two-by-three
    inch squares
Of ivory. Which is she? Which of all
    the parasols in sight
Covers the blithe, mocking face which
    stares
At me from twenty miniatures, con-
    fusing the singleness of my delight?

You know my window well enough —
the fourth from the corner. Oh, you
know.
Slant your parasol a bit this way, if you
please,
And take for yourself the very correct bow
I make toward the line of demure young
ladies
Perambulating the street in a neat row.
It is true I have never seen beneath your
parasol,
Therefore my miniatures resemble one
another not at all.

You must pick yourself like a button-hole
bouquet,
And lift the parasol to my face one day,
And let me see you laughing at the
sun —
Or at me. Then I will choose the one
Of my twenty miniatures most like you
And destroy the others, with which I shall
have nothing more to do.

PANTOMIME IN ONE ACT

Certainly the furniture was of satin-wood,
Painted with a lovely design of strawberry flowers and heliotrope,
And the carpet was Aubusson, all pinks
and golds.
On it stood frail chairs, their seats
covered with green and yellow silk,
A striped pattern, continued and broken
in the folds
Of the window-curtains. The clock on
the mantel-piece
Was a gay conceit of porcelain flowers
springing from fantastic sprigs of ormolu,
And in the book-cases that lined the walls,
three book-cases with glass doors and
gilded locks, were volumes bound in
blue.
The smell of clipped box floated in from
the garden outside, and the sound of
a rake
On gravel stirred the silence with an
impression of placid order
Peacefully repeated through a season and
seasons perhaps, but the odour of the
box was an ache
After the same perfection which existed
inevitably in every parterre and border.
Mirrors of a yellow-silver shining topped
the consoles at either end,

Behind twin alabaster vases, and in
tarnished and golden duplicate, a blend
Of fact and potent possibility, the room
stretched dreamily through
Walls that were solid or not as one beheld them, depending on the point of
view.
Sunlight fell on the satin-wood escritoire between the windows,
And on a single Malmaison rose
And the green Ming vase which held it,
Also on a letter, I suppose.
White paper with ink upon it may be
taken for such, I opine.
But the letter, being without superscrip-
tion, could hardly be considered mine.
On the whole, I preferred to leave it
untouched and preserve the nicety of
my honour.
(Positively I thought I heard a giggle
from the lips of the Botticelli Ma-
donna
On the chimney-breast; but that was solely
her affair.)
I was a poltroon maybe, or wise with a
wisdom which haunted the air,
Coquettish reserve, that was it, but brazen
armour could have stayed me less.
Ah, Madame, did I obey your desire, or
possibly disobey it ruthlessly? I confess
I never became aware of your attitude, for
I tiptoed to the door,
And left the room which had caught
your trick of smiling,
Exactly as it was before: a beautiful
entourage, bien entendu,
But to me nothing more.

IN A POWDER CLOSET

Early Eighteenth Century

My very excellent young person,
Since Fate has destined you to play the
rôle of coiffeur,
You will permit that I admire your quite
unsurpassed skill,
Together with your polished, if a trifle
over-pronounced, manners,
Without by an inch lessening the distance
Which the hazard of birth and the arti-
fice of custom
Have placed between us.
My mirror tells me that you are a per-
sonable man;

But, indeed, it is my own image in this
  same mirror
Which most occupies my attention.
That such a subject as I offer
Engages you to put forth your best efforts
Is only natural;
That I should remain indifferent is equally
  so.
Be satisfied that the exigencies of your
  profession
Admit you to privileges from which a
  more exalted station would exclude
  you.
My maid will, I am sure, be most happy
  to accommodate herself to your wishes,
She is a worthy girl and entertains a not
  unjustifiable belief in my continued
  recognition of her services.
The spray of heliotrope is well placed.
Do you think a patch just here — at the
  corner of the eye?
Ah, yes. It adds perceptibly.
You are, Sir, a consummate artist.
To-morrow at four I shall expect you.

ATTITUDE UNDER AN
ELM TREE

Seeing that you pass your life playing
  upon the virginals
In an upper chamber with only a slit of
  a window in it,
I wonder why I,
Roaming the hills on a charger red as
  maple-leaves,
Should find the thought of you attrac-
  tive.
You were veiled at the jousting, you re-
  member,
Which enables me to imagine you with-
  out let or hindrance from the rigidness
  of fact;
A condition not unproductive of charm
  if viewed philosophically.
Besides, your window gives upon a walled
  garden,
Which I can by no means enter without
  dismounting from my maple-red charger,
And this I will not do,
Particularly as the garden belongs in-
  dubitably to your ancestors.
But I thank you for the spray of myrtle
  I have wound about my sleeve.
As it over-topped the wall,
My plucking it was without malice.

ON READING A LINE
UNDERSCORED BY
KEATS

In a Copy of "Palmerin of England"

You marked it with light pencil upon a
  printed page,
And, as though your finger pointed along
  a sunny path for my eyes' better
  direction,
I see "a knight mounted on a mulberry
  courser and attired in green armour."
I think the sky is faintly blue, but with a
  Spring shining about it,
And the new grass scarcely fetlock high
  in the meads.
He rides, I believe, alongside an overflown river,
By a path soft and easy to his charger's
  feet.
My vision confuses you with the green-
  armoured knight:
So dight and caparisoned might you be in
  a land of Faery.
Thus, with denoting finger, you make of
  yourself an escutcheon to guide me to
  that in you which is its essence.
But for the rest,
The part which most persists and is re-
  membered,
I only know I compass it in loving and
  neither have, nor need, a symbol.

THE HUMMING–BIRDS

Up — up — water shooting,
Jet of water, white and silver,
Tinkling with the morning sun-bells.
Red as sun-blood, whizz of fire,
Shock of fire-spray and water.
It is the humming-birds flying against the
  stream of the fountain.
The trumpet-vine bursts into a scatter of
  humming-birds,
The scarlet-throated trumpet flowers ex-
  plode with humming-birds.
The fountain waits to toss them dia-
  monds.
I clasp my hands over my heart
Which will not let loose its humming-
  birds,
Which will not break to green and ruby,
Which will not let its wings touch air.
Pound and hammer me with irons,

Crack me so that flame can enter,
Pull me open, loose the thunder
Of wings within me.
Leave me wrecked and consoled,
A maker of humming-birds
Who dare bathe in a leaping water.

SUMMER NIGHT PIECE

The garden is steeped in moonlight,
Full to its high edges with brimming
silver,
And the fish-ponds brim and darken
And run in little serpent lights soon
extinguished.
Lily-pads lie upon the surface, beautiful
as the tarnishings on frail old silver,
And the Harvest moon droops heavily
out of the sky,
A ripe, white melon, intensely, magnifi-
cently, shining.
Your window is orange in the moonlight,
It glows like a lamp behind the branches
of the old wistaria,
It burns like a lamp before a shrine,
The small, intimate, familiar shrine
Placed reverently among the bricks
Of a much-loved garden wall.

WIND AND SILVER

Greatly shining,
The Autumn moon floats in the thin sky;
And the fish-ponds shake their backs and
flash their dragon scales
As she passes over them

NIGHT CLOUDS

The white mares of the moon rush along
the sky
Beating their golden hoofs upon the glass
Heavens;
The white mares of the moon are all
standing on their hind legs
Pawing at the green porcelain doors of
the remote Heavens.
Fly, Mares!
Strain your utmost,
Scatter the milky dust of stars,
Or the tiger sun will leap upon you and
destroy you
With one lick of his vermilion tongue.

FUGITIVE

Sunlight,
Three marigolds,

And a dusky purple poppy-pod —
Out of these I made a beautiful world.
Will you have them —
Brightness,
Gold,
And a sleep with dreams?
They are brittle pleasures certainly,
But where can you find better?
Roses are not noted for endurance,
And only thirty days are June.

THE SAND ALTAR

With a red grain and a blue grain, placed
in precisely the proper positions, I
made a beautiful god, with plumes of
yard-long feathers and a swivel eye.

And with a red grain and a blue grain,
placed in precisely the proper positions, I made a dragon, with scaly
wings and a curling, iniquitous tail.

Then I reflected:
If, with the same materials, I can make
both god and dragon, of what use is
the higher mathematics?

Having said this, I went outdoors and
stood under a tree and listened to the
frogs singing their evening songs in
the green darkness.

TIME–WEB

The day is sharp and hurried
As wind upon a dahlia stem;
It is harsh and abrupt with me
As a North-east breeze
Striking a bed of sunflowers.
Why should I break at the root
And cast all my fragile flowers in the
dust —
I who am no taller than a creeping pansy?
I should be sturdy and definite,
Yet am I tossed, and agitated, and prag-
matically bending.

PREFACE TO AN OCCASION

How witless to assail the carven halls
Of memory! To climb the high stone
steps,
Picking a foothold through the crisp, dry
leaves

Whirled in the corners, crunching under foot
Those scattered in the centre, to clap at doors
With battered hauberk, till some seneschal,
Drowsy with age and oversleeping, creaks
Them open an inhospitable inch,
And, grumbling, lets himself be pushed aside
By a determined entrance! Where's the sense
Of striding by tarnished furniture from one
Mournful deserted chamber to another,
Seeking for roses in a vase of dust,
For tapestries where rusty armour hangs,
For blithe allurement under spider-spun
Ceilings corroded to a dripping ash?
What can you find here? A little powdered dust
To pinch up with your finger and your thumb
And fasten in a knotted handkerchief!
Look from the window, Friend, the sky is blue,
The leafless trees blow to a merry wind,
Your horse is tethered at the stairway's foot,
He twitches at the skipping of the leaves.
Pocket your handkerchief and ride away.
Was the trip worth while? I'll wager guinea gold
Within a week you'll wish you had not come,
And send your handkerchief knotted to the wash.
Life's the great cynic, and there's an end of that.

PRIMAVERA

Spring has arrived.
It is no use your telling me to look at the calendar,
And saying that it is five good days to the twenty-first of March.
Is the year bound to obey the almanac-makers?
O model of all egregious pedants!
Would you shackle Spring to times and seasons,
And catch her back by her long green skirt
Till the moment you have planned for her?

She has stolen a march this year, for certain.
To-day, at sunrise, I saw a white-breasted nut-hatch
Running up the branch of the oak-tree
That was so broken by the ice-storm last December,
And in the garden a pheasant was picking grains
Out of the manure covering the garden-beds.
There is a snowdrop up by the porch,
Shot clean through the tulip-straw;
And the crows are all agog over my neighbour's pine-trees.
It is a game of catch-who-catch-can with that green skirt then.
Even though, in your passion for order, you bring about a snow storm to-morrow,
It will not matter to me.
This morning, beyond the shadow of a doubt, I saw the Spring.

KATYDIDS

SHORE OF LAKE MICHIGAN

Katydids scraped in the dim trees,
And I thought they were little white skeletons
Playing the fiddle with a pair of finger-bones.

How long is it since Indians walked here,
Stealing along the sands with smooth feet?
How long is it since Indians died here
And the creeping sands scraped them bone from bone?
Dead Indians under the sands, playing their bones against strings of wampum.
The roots of new, young trees have torn their graves asunder,
But in the branches sit little white skeletons
Rasping a bitter death-dirge through the August night.

TO CARL SANDBURG

I think I am cousin-german to Endymion,
Certainly I have loved the moon a long time.

I have seen her, a faint conceit of silver,
Shooting little silver arrows into a marsh
  pool at twilight.
I have seen her, high, round, majestic,
Making herself a jewel of fire out of a
  sea bay.
I have seen the morning moon, grievously
  battered,
Limping down a coloured sky.
To-night I saw an evening moon
Dodging between tree-branches
Through a singing silence of crickets,
And a man was singing songs to a black-
  backed guitar.

To-day I saw a country I knew well but
  had never seen.
A country where corn runs a mile or
  more to a tree-line,
A country where a river, brown as bronze,
  streaked green with the flowing heads
  of water-plants,
Slips between a field of apples and a
  field of wheat.
A country where the eye seeks a long
  way
And comes back on the curve of a round
  sky,
Satisfied with greens and blues, tired
  with the stretch and exhilarated by it.

The moon stops a moment in a hole
  between leaves
And tells me a new story,
The story of a man who lives in a house
  with a pear-tree before the door,
A story of little green pears changing and
  ripening,
Of long catalpa pods turning yellow
  through September days.
There is a woman in the house, and
  children,
And, out beyond, the corn-fields are
  sleeping and the trees are whispering to
  the fire-flies.
So I have seen the man's country, and
  heard his songs before there are
  words to them.
And the moon said to me: "This now I
  give you," and went on, stepping
  through the leaves.
And the man went on singing, picking
  out his accompaniment softly on the
  black-backed guitar.

IF I WERE
FRANCESCO GUARDI

I

I think you are a white clematis
Climbing the wall of a seaside garden,
When there is a green haze on the water
And a boy is eating a melon in a boat
  with a brown sail.

II

I think you are the silver heart of a great
  square,
Holding little people like glass beads,
Watching them parade — parade — and
  gather,
When the sun slips to an opposite angle,
And a thunder of church bells lies like
  a bronze roof beneath the sky.

ELEONORA DUSE

I

Seeing's believing, so the ancient word
Chills buds to shrivelled powder flecks,
  turns flax
To smoky heaps of straw whose small
  flames wax
Only to gasp and die. The thing's absurd!
Have blind men ever seen or deaf men
  heard?
What one beholds but measures what
  one lacks.
Where is the prism to draw gold from
  blacks,
Or flash the iris colours of a bird?
Not in the eye, be sure, nor in the ear,
Nor in an instrument of twisted glass,
Yet there are sights I see and sounds I
  hear
Which ripple me like water as they pass.
This that I give you for a dear love's sake
Is curling noise of waves marching along
  a lake.

II

A letter or a poem — the words are set
To either tune. Be careful how you slice
The flap which is held down by this
  device
Impressed upon it. In one moment met
A cameo, intaglio, a fret

Of workmanship, and I. Like melted ice
I took the form and froze so, turned
  precise
And brittle seal, a creed in silhouette.
Seeing's believing? What then would you
  see?
A chamfered dragon? Three spear-heads
  of steel?
A motto done in flowered charactry?
The thin outline of Mercury's winged
  heel?
Look closer, do you see a name, a face,
Or just a cloud dropped down before a
  holy place?

III

Lady, to whose enchantment I took shape
So long ago, though carven to your grace,
Bearing, like quickened wood, your sweet
  sad face
Cut in my flesh, yet may I not escape
My limitations: words that jibe and gape
After your loveliness and make grimace
And travesty where they should interlace
The weave of sun-spun ocean round a
  cape.
Pictures then must contain you, this and
  more,
The sigh of wind floating on ripe June
  hay,
The desolate pulse of snow beyond a
  door,
The grief of mornings seen as yesterday.
All that you are mingles as one sole cry
To point a world aright which is so
  much awry.

IV

If Beauty set her image on a stage
And bid it mirror moments so intense
With passion and swift largess of the
  sense
To a divine exactness, stamp a page
With mottoes of hot blood, and dis-
  engage
No atom of mankind's experience,
But lay the soul's complete incontinence
Bare while it tills grief's gusty acreage.
Doing this, you, spon-image to her needs,
She picked to pierce, reveal, and soothe
  again,
Shattering by means of you the tinsel
  creeds

Offered as meat to the pinched hearts of
  men.
So, sacrificing you, she fed those others
Who bless you in their prayers even
  before their mothers.

V

Life seized you with her iron hands and
  shook
The fire of your boundless burning out
To fall on us, poor little ragged rout
Of common men, till like a flaming
  book
We, letters of a message, flashed and
  took
The fiery flare of prophecy, devout
Torches to bear your oil, a dazzling
  shout,
The liquid golden running of a brook.
Who, being upborne on racing streams of
  light,
Seeing new heavens sprung from dusty
  hells,
Considered you, and what might be your
  plight,
Robbed, plundered — since Life's cruel
  plan compels
The perfect sacrifice of one great soul
To make a myriad others even a whit
  more whole.

VI

Seeing you stand once more before my
  eyes
In your pale dignity and tenderness,
Wearing your frailty like a misty dress
Draped over the great glamour which
  denies
To years their domination, all disguise
Time can achieve is but to add a
  stress,
A finer fineness, as though some caress
Touched you a moment to a strange sur-
  prise.
Seeing you after these long lengths of
  years,
I only know the glory come again,
A majesty bewildered by my tears,
A golden sun spangling slant shafts of
  rain,
Moonlight delaying by a sick man's bed,
A rush of daffodils where wastes of dried
  leaves spread.

EAST WIND

THE DOLL

You know, my Dear, I have a way, each
   Summer
When leaves have changed from ecstasies
   in green
To something like a crowd with raised
   umbrellas
Pushing for places at a theatre door,
Whenever there's a reasonable wind —
And when there isn't, why I think it's
   worse,
They droop so underneath the copper
   sun
Sitting upon them like a metal cover;
I think the trees look positively tired
Holding the mass of them up all the
   time.
Well, as I say, when every breeze is
   smothered
By heavy, lagging leaves on dusty trees,
And all I smell is asphalt and hot tar,
And motor horns destroy the moonlight
   nights,
I pack myself, and some stray sheets of
   music,
Into a train and hie me to South Norton.
I came from there, and little drowsy town
Although it is, I still go back (or used to)
And find it with a narrow odd content-
   ment
As grey and glistening as it always was,
Some of it painted, some a silver shim-
   mer
Of weathered clapboards melting to decay.
There always is a blaze of Summer flowers
Cramming the dooryards — stocks and
   portulaca,
And golden glow above the first floor
   windows,
And China asters mixed with marigolds.
White paint looks very well indeed be-
   hind them
And green blinds, always down, you
   understand,
South Norton people will not risk the
   daylight
Upon their best room furniture, and
   really

When you possess an inlaid teak-wood
   table,
With mother-of-pearl and ebony in squares,
And on it, set precisely in their order,
Stand ivory chess-men, red and white,
   the queens
A pair of ancient Maharanies copied
To every quaintness of their grand attire
And not a button or embroidery
Skimped by the Hindu carver; when your
   chairs
Are waxed as never chair is waxed to-day,
And there are corners lit by golden silks,
And mandarin fruit-dishes in high glass
   cupboards,
Perhaps you may at least be half forgiven
For only opening the room for weddings
Or when some guest from Boston comes
   to call.
I have called often in such drawing-
   rooms,
Confused at first by coming from the
   dazzle
Of a white August sea, and almost
   groping
To find my hostess in the green-blind
   dusk,
While all the time my nose was being
   grateful
For the great puffs of pot-pourri and
   cloves,
The gusts of myrrh, and sandalwood,
   and ginger
Invisibly progressing up and down.
These scented rooms are just a paraphrase
Of something penetrant, but never clear,
Never completely taken nor rejected,
Unrealized flotsam of the tides of trade;
And these frail, ancient ladies are like
   tea-dust
Left in the bottom of a painted chest,
Poor fluttering souls, surrounded by their
   "things,"
Oblivious of the sea which brought them
   here.
My Dear, I prose, you really must not
   let me,
For after all I have something to say.
I never make these duty calls until

My music lessons are a week away
And each day's mail is stuffed with
  pupils' letters
Asking for dates and prices, then I go
The rounds and drink a dish of tea with
  each
Old fragile chrysalis and so come home.
For many years I've always ended up
With the two Misses Perkins. They were
  a whiff
Of eighteen-forty, and I rather liked
To talk to them and then come back and
  play
Debussy, and thank God I had read
  Freud;
The contrast was as genial as curry.
I only wish that I could make you see
  them,
Their garden path with spice-bushes and
  lilacs,
The scraper by the door, the polished
  knocker,
And then the hall with the model of a
  clipper
Upon a table in a square glass case.
She is a replica of the "Flying Dolphin"
And Captain Perkins made her on a
  voyage
Of eighteen months to China and Ceylon,
Miss Julia just remembers when he
  brought
The model home and put it where it
  stands.
I always laid my gloves upon the table
Just by the clipper's stern, and stood my
  sunshade
Against the corner, and tiptoed up the
  stairs.
Miss Perkins was an invalid, for years
She had not left her bed, so I was sum-
  moned
Up slippery stairs and over cool, long
  matting
Into her room, and there in a great four-
  poster
The little lady would greet me with
  effusion.
"Clara, Dear, how good of you to come,
Julia and I were wondering if you would.
You'll have a cake and a small glass of
  sherry.
Hannah will bring them in directly. Now
How is the music getting on? To think
You play at concerts! Julia and I read
About your triumphs in the newspapers."

And all the time, behind the house, the
  sea
Was moving — moving — with a long,
  slow sound.
I could not hear it, but I clung to it,
For naturally this room looked on the
  street.
It was a pretty room with bright glazed
  chintz,
And Naples bay in staring blue gouache,
Flanked by Vesuvius at night, both pic-
  tures framed
In peeling gold. Upon the mantelpiece
Were silhouettes: the Captain and his
  wife,
Miss Perkins and Miss Julia in pantalettes,
A China bear for matches, and a clock
Suspended between alabaster pillars.
But what I never could keep long from
  seeing
Was a large wax doll, dressed in the Paris
  fashion
Of sixty years ago, with a lace tippet
And much-flounced skirt over a crinoline,
Upright in a winged arm-chair by the bed.
She sat and gazed with an uncanny ardour
Straight at the andiron, her hands palms
  upward,
Her feet in heelless slippers wide apart.
She fascinated me. Those blue glass eyes
Had an unearthly meaning, staring straight
Before her in her faded finery.
I had to draw a chair up from the wall,
For never did Miss Perkins or Miss Julia
Suggest that I should sit in the winged
  chair.
I found my mind all drawn upon a focus,
I thought wax doll and very nearly said
  so,
And I am very much afraid I missed the
  point
Of one or two quite artless little sallies.
They never said a word, and I with rigour
Suppressed my curiosity and merely lis-
  tened
With sometimes half a mind and some-
  times none.
I drank the sherry and I eat the cake,
I kissed Miss Perkins when I came to go,
Bending over the bed, my skirt just
  touching
The doll, I think, and then the call was
  over.
Of course at first the thing made no
  impression.

I thought they had been clearing out the attic
And come upon the doll; but when each year
She was still sitting there, I grew to dread
Encountering her, she seemed so full of tales,
Tell-tales of maiden ladies left alone
With still things on the walls and mantle-pieces
And nothing moving round them but the sea
Kept out of reach beyond the matted entry.
One year, in early April, coming in
All flushed with having played Mous-sorgski's "Pictures"
To an enthusiastic audience,
I found a black-edged letter on my table,
Miss Julia writing that "Dear Sister Jane
Had passed away, she wanted me to know."
The words were quaintly quiet and re-signed,
The slim and pointed writing very calm,
But still there seemed a wistful hint of dread.
I knew, in fact, Miss Julia was alone.
I wrote — oh, what one always writes, the things
One does not think, and does not want to think.
I sent the letter, and the answer came
As slim, and pointed, and reticent as ever.
And that was all until I reached South Norton.
Of course I went at once to see Miss Julia.
She greeted me beside the clipper-ship,
And there was something grim about that vessel
Placidly sailing on its painted waves
With coffins passing through the door beside it,
From time to time, while nothing ever came.
I wondered what would be its fate, some junk-shop
Probably, when Miss Julia too had gone.
Poor soul, she seemed to flicker with excitement
And sorrow all in one. The great im-portance

Of doing something which was not com-manded
Appeared in vague authoritative gestures
Which seemed but half controlled and faded off
Into a quiver of movement so pathetic
It made me want to cry. She begged me
To go upstairs. "I cannot bear to be
In any other room but Jane's," she told me.
"I've sat there so much with her, quite ten years
It was she did not leave it." So we mounted
The broad old stairs, and softly trod the matting,
Walking gently as in a house of mourning.
I was resentful, it was four full months
Since I had got that lonely little letter.
Was this a mausoleum? Was Miss Julia
To find her only company with ghosts?
The gaudy paper of the narrow hallway,
Flashing its minarets to a sapphire Heaven
Seemed to be mocking us with Eastern splendour,
With Eastern customs and an Eastern languor.
The conch shells roared a siren song of oceans,
Flanking the newel posts, as we passed by them.
Miss Jane's room was a lovely blaze of sunlight,
The empty bed was orderly and sane,
The Bay of Naples gladdened without hurting.
I shook myself free of the swarming still-ness
And saw with satisfaction that the chair,
The doll chair, had been moved, it stood beside
The window with its back toward the room.
Why did I walk up to it? I don't know.
Some feeling that the usualness of streets
Comes kindly over a long spent emotion
Perhaps. At any rate, I did so, saying
How bright and gay the portulacas were,
Or something of the sort. And then I started
To sit down in the chair and saw the doll
With palms stretched out and little slip-pered feet

Pointing before her. There she sat, her
    eyes
Fixed glassily upon the window-pane.
I may have jumped, at any rate Miss
    Julia
Flushing a painful pink said steadily:
"It was so dull for her after Jane died,
I moved her here where she could see the
    street.
It's very comforting to watch the passing,
I think. I always find it so." That's all,
I don't know how the visit went, nor
    what
I said, nor where I sat. I only know
I took the train that evening back to
    town
And stayed up half the night playing
    Stravinsky.
I dreamt wax doll for three weeks after-
    wards,
And I shall go to London this vacation.

THE HOUSE IN MAIN STREET

You want I should tell yer 'bout old
    James Boott, do yer, boys?
Well, 'tain't much of a story, I guess,
But I ain't never fergot it.
Hitch yer cheer up t' th' stove, Sam.
And, 'Lige, you fetch that cracker-box out
    o' th' corner,
Two o' you can set on that.
Now jest wait a mite till I git my pipe
    a-drawin'—
Ther'!
Well, you know I warn't raised here,
My father didn't hold with farmin'.
He was a carpenter over to Pelham,
An' I was a real town boy all my growin'
    up.
Only Pelham warn't near th' city 'tis now.
It set in th' middle o' a great space o'
    fields
An' I couldn't never ha' done with run-
    nin' over 'em.
I'd hire out with th' farmers fer Satur-
    day afternoons,
An' I never was so happy as when I was
    hoein' beans,
Or pitchin' hay,
Or beatin' a tin pan when a beehive
    swarmed.
I can see th' critters now,
Black, an' gold, an' buzzin'.
They was like sparks from a pin-wheel,

All scatterin' up in th' sunlight,
An' th' great trees bendin' over 'em like
    butterfly nets.
No, I couldn't relish carpenterin',
An' when th' time come fer me to fix
    on a trade
I went to farmin';
An' I been at it fifty year now,
Fifty year o' freeze, an' thaw, an' drought.
Well! Well! 'Tain't no bed o' eider-
    down, farmin' ain't,
An' that's th' Lord's truth.
Now don't you worrit me, Sam,
I'll git to James Boott presently.
When we old fellers once starts in re-
    memberin',
Ther' ain't no beginnin' nor end, I guess.

James Boott was a fine man to look at,
Bearin' his years right smart,
Only fer a stoop he had,
An' a lameness th' rheumatiz settled on
    him.
But he was queer as Dick's hat-band.
He come by it straight 'nough;
One o' his brothers shot himself,
An' t' other died in th' 'sylum,
But old James warn't really mad,
He was jest diff'rent.
He had a mint o' money,
All his own an' what his brothers lef'
    him,
But for all that he boarded in a couple
    o' rooms to Parson Tole's.
He could ha' bought half th' town
Ef he'd been so minded,
As 'twas he owned a house,
An' I do think 'twas th' prettiest house I
    ever see.
It stood right up in th' main street,
With th' Common jest acrost th' road;
Th' Court House cornered it one end,
An' Parson Tole's church, with th' new
    spire peekin' over th' barberry hedge,
Was on th' South side.
'Twas a mighty fine house,
An' tidy warn't th' word fer th' way
    James Boott kep' it.
He had th' box borders either side th'
    stone path to th' front door
As flat an' square as a plate.
An' my, but th' hollyhocks he had under
    th' winders!
They was as big an' bright es ef they was
    stamped chintz

An' not jest wood an' sap.
Nobody ever see 'em fade.
One day they was ther'
An' th' next day they warn't,
An' that was all ther' was to it.
'Twas th' same way with all th' flowers,
Pansies, an' gillyflowers, an' snapdragons,
Nobody ever could pint out a faded
flower
In James Boott's yard.
It costs a sight o' money
To keep things redded up that way,
But James had th' money,
An' his yard showed it.
Why, even th' laylocks warn't let ripen;
I never see nothin' like it.
Seemed es ef th' place was painted on
cardboard
An' held to th' drawin'.
He was pertic'lar 'bout th' house-paintin'
too,
He couldn't never abide no blisters
An' 'twas all burnt down to th' bare
wood
Every time it needed a new coat.
That paintin' brought it out elegant;
Ther' was th' pilasters, an' th' twisted
tops o' th' pillars,
As spick an' span as washed ivory.
But th' blinds was al'ays shut,
An' that made th' house seem kind o'
lonesome
Spite o' th' grand bloomin' o' th' flowers.
I guess 'twas a little mite sad fer him
too.
Folks said he'd bought it to marry
on,
An' then he never did marry.
But ther' set th' house,
Starin' at him with its white paint
An' sort o' pintin' back'ards.
I guess when he bought it, it told him
"Bimeby, Bimeby," all th' time,
But afterwards it fairly hollered, "Too
late!"
It stood like a lady all 'dizened up fer
a party
An' carryin' a bouquet,
But when you come to look at her, she
was blind.
I mind I used to think 'twas awful creepy
When th' moon dazzled it of a June
evenin'.
An' th' flowers was noddin', and' jostlin',
An' whisperin'.

I used to commence runnin' at th' Court
House
An' keep on clear past th' church
When I had to pass it.
An' that was queer too,
Fer Joseph Peters, th' hired man,
Lived in th' back part,
An' I'd go in once in a while with young
Joe
An' git a ginger-cookie.
Mrs. Peters liked us to come in.
Maybe she felt lonesome with that great,
empty, echoin' house
Behind her.
Yer see, boys,
The kitchen part give on a lane
So we didn't have to go through the yard
at all.
Even Joe didn't care about th' front after
sunset.
'Twas like two houses,
One livin' an' one dead,
An' th' dead house meant th' most, I
guess.

I was goin' on fer twelve year old
When a new doctor come to Pelham.
He'd had hospital trainin' down to Boston,
An' only fer his havin' a weak heart
He'd never ha' left th' city.
'Twas a fine thing fer Pelham to git him.
He was full o' notions 'bout sprains an'
fevers,
An' one o' them was that th' old doc-
tor's house was a pesky little place
Fer th' likes o' him,
He must have somethin' better.
Well, boys, you know how 'tis,
Most o' th' houses was lived in a'ready,
So Doctor Busby he peered roun' and
roun'
But couldn't hit on a place to suit him
'Ceptin' James Boott's house,
An' that he fixed his mind to
Till ther' warn't no movin' him.
Folks told him 'twouldn't do,
That James wouldn't sell,
But he only said, "Tut! Tut! We'll see,"
And walked off down th' street, steppin'
out real jaunty
In a way he had.

One day I was shootin' marbles all alone,
Playin' one hand ag'in t'other,
In th' drive by th' Court House,

When I seed 'em comin'.
Doctor Busby was hustlin' 'long with his
    big stride,
An' James Boott was creepin' toward him
Tappin' th' flags with his malaccer stick.
I guess 'twas th' tappin' o' th' stick
Made me look up.
They stopped jest opposite th' white
    house
An' I thought it 'peared brighter'n usual
With th' big, shiny clouds blowin' over
    th' chimblies.
"Good-mornin', Mr. Boott," says Doctor
    Busby.
"Good-mornin', Doctor," says James.
An' 'twas jest like a little fife
Answerin' a big bass drum.
Well, th' doctor started right in sayin'
    he wanted to buy th' house.
And James listened to him,
Leanin' on his stick, an' sort o' quiverin'.
Leastways I thought he quivered,
But maybe 'twas only th' shadows o' th'
    leaves from th' great elm-tree
Dancin' on his shoulders.
"Th' house ain't fer sale," says James,
Short and quick.
"But you don't live in it," persisted th'
    doctor.
"My hired man does," snapped James,
An' jerked up as though fer walkin' on.
"But, my dear sir," the doctor was al'ays
    polite
Even when he was drawin' a tooth,
"Surely you ain't a-goin' to keep a val-
    uable house empty
Jest fer th' sake o' your servant?"
Now that's what all Pelham had been
    saying fer years
But nobody hadn't never durst say it to
    James afore.
"That, Doctor Busby, is my affair," the
    old man lashed out,
An' I declare he was stan'in' up as straight
    as a new willer shoot,
An' gimletin' his eyes right into th' doc-
    tor.
I cal'late Doctor Busby thought he'd gone
    too fer,
Fer he started praisin' th' hollyhocks an'
    dahlias,
An' after a while he got round to th' way
    th' house was built,
An' kep' a-speakin' o' Doric columns, an'
    th' fan-light over th' door,

An' a heap o' things I couldn't under-
    stan'.
I could see th' old gentleman was pleased,
But when th' doctor come to money
He shied like a colt
An' turned off on to somethin' else quick
    as a flash.
I declare I felt es ef I was to a badger-
    baitin'.
The doctor he up an' at it ag'in and ag'in,
But James give him the slip every time.
An' all th' while th' little shadows kep'
    bobbin' over 'em,
An' th' great clouds breezin' above.
I call to mind I watched 'em
An' tried to figger out how many men
    like them two
Could stand on one of 'em.
Boys do have queer fancies sometimes.
Well, th' long an' th' short o' it was
That th' doctor didn't git ahead a mite.
It made me chuckle
To think o' that old man, teeterin' on
    his cane
An' not able to take a step without it,
Jest blockin' th' way fer that great big
    doctor.
In th' end he give over an' 'lowed he
    was beaten.
"I see you won't sell," says he,
"But maybe at least you'll let me see th'
    inside o' that beautiful house, Mr.
    Boott."
I 'most squealed at that;
I'd 'bout come to believin' ther' warn't
    no inside.
Old James he stroked his chin.
"It's a handsome house,
A handsome house, doctor,
But I ain't kep' it up inside," he says.
That fair riled me,
Not kep' up th' inside,
With all th' outside fixed like a parlour!
But th' doctor didn't seem to care,
He said the woodwork would be ther'
An' th' chimbley-pieces.
'Twarn't woodwork an' chimbley-pieces
    I was set on,
But my ears was fit to bust listenin', jest
    th' same.
I wondered would James hit him with
    his cane,
Or would he take him into th' Court
    House
An' have th' law on him fer trespassin'.

But he didn't do neither.
He jest turned a sort o' dark pink
All over his wrinkled face,
An' then he said, hollow-like,
"Very well, Doctor Busby,
I will take you into th' house.
Would four o'clock on Thursday after-
    noon suit you?"
The doctor said 'twould,
An' then they parted.
I heer'd th' tappin' o' that malaccer cane
Fer three good minutes after th' doctor's
    steps
Had stopped soundin' in th' other direc-
    tion.

I guess Thursday was awful long a-comin'
    ter me,
Fer, you understan', I'd made my mind
    up
To see th' house too.
So I sized up that yard
Same as though I was huntin' fer a jack-
    knife I'd lost.
I squatted behind th' flower beds
An' squeezed under th' bushes,
An' when four o'clock Thursday come
I was ther';
But I guess 'twould ha' taken more'n old
    James Boott's eyes ter see me
Even with his spectacles on.
I can't tell you how I felt when I heer'd
    th' key
Strikin' on th' lock.
I couldn't see nothin' where I was hidin',
But I'd heer'd th' malaccer cane a-comin'
Way down th' road,
An' I was ready.
I declare I git gooseflesh now,
Jes rememberin' th' awful moan th' door
    give
When James pushed it open.
'Twas like a livin' thing cryin' out,
An' somethin' come rushin' out o' that
    door too,
Damp an' musty,
An' ther' warn't nothin' at all.
'Twas mortal hard fer me to git up and
    go in,
But I did.
They was ahead o' me,
I could hear 'em talkin' in one o' th'
    rooms.
Oh, Lor! How queer that house was!
'Twas August,

But that hall was so cold my teeth chat-
    tered,
An' th' floor felt funny.
'Twas like walkin' on velvet,
An' th' softness give me a dret'ful start.
You see I was barefoot,
An' th' dust was so thick
It oozed up between my toes
An' sucked me down,
The way snow does.
'Twas dark too,
'Count o' th' shut blinds,
Didn't seem like th' same world was out-
    side.
I looked out o' th' door,
An' th' glassy green o' th' box hedges,
An' th' swingin' chains o' th' Common
    fence beyond,
Helped me some,
They looked so nat'ral.
Bimeby I got used to it bein' so dim in
    ther'
An' I could see th' steps they'd made in
    th' dust,
An' th' little round plop where th'
    malaccer cane had set.
So I follered,
Makin' no noise
'Cause o' my bare feet.

Oh, it was a house!
Ther' was carvin's everywher',
Flowers an' vines all runnin' an' blowin',
Ther' was a whole orchard over th'
    chimblies,
But th' paint was all peelin' off
An' th' dust choked th' ribs o' th' pillars
    till they was pretty near smooth.
Ther' was a great glass chandelier in
    every room
Hangin' so still.
They didn't shine much,
But they did a little,
An' that shinin' was so empty an' cold,
I had to go under 'em without lookin'.
'Twas es ef they hadn't had nothin' to
    reflect
Fer so many years
They was makin' up time by reflectin' me
    double.
Not that I seed anythin',
I jest sensed it.
Halfway up th' stairs was a great standin'
    glass,
A mirror, I think they call it.

It didn't show what was in front of it
Bein' all run as 'twere,
An' yet I seemed to see things movin'
    through it.
When I looked, they wern't ther',
An' when I didn't look, they war.
It kep' me on th' stairs a terr'ble time,
An' I had to rec'lect George Washington
    real hard
To git by at all.
When I got up to th' first floor,
I heer'd James Boott an' th' doctor
In a room over th' front porch,
So I crep' over an' peeked thru' th' crack
    o' th' door.
I don't know what I seed,
Nothin' at first, I guess,
Fer th' blue light from th' blinds didn't
    make fer seein',
But, Gosh! What I smelled!
Apples, boys!
Apples!
They was so sweet an' strong
I thought I'd ha' dropped with th' sur-
    prise o' it.
They did make my mouth water.
Then I heer'd th' doctor say:
"Why, Mr. Boott, what are you doing
    with all these apples on th' mantel-
    piece?"
An' old Boott's voice, like a cracked
    fiddle, answerin':
"I find this an excellent place to ripen
    apples, Dr. Busby."
"Do you mean to tell me you keep this
    house to ripen a few dozen apples
    in?"
That voice did me good,
An' I braced up an' stared into th' blue
    room
An' there was old James fingerin' his
    apples
With a queer, scared look on his face.
He was pattin' 'em,
An' cossetin' 'em,
I don't know why, but it made me shiver
    to see him.
He picked up a red Bald'in
An' sniffed it,
An' his eyes looked narrer an' greedy.
"I like apples," he said.
Then I give a awful jump
For th' malaccer cane fell down on th'
    floor with a clatter.
I guess I pushed th' door some, too,

'Cause I seem to remember standin' up
    ther' in th' doorway
Lookin' straight at 'em.
But they didn't see me.
The doctor started forward an' grabbed
    th' old man's arm.
"You poor soul!" he said.
That was all,
An' it didn't seem much,
But James Boott jest crumpled up
An' would ha' fell only fer th' doctor's
    holdin' him.
Somethin' seemed to claw out o' his
    throat.
I suppose 'twas a sob,
But it sounded like some critter inside
    fightin' loose.
It echoed an' echoed 'bout that room
An' set th' chandelier jiggin';
It seemed everywher',
Back an' front,
An' when I turned roun',
Ther' was somethin' wigglin' in th' big
    mirror, fer sartin.
I guess now 'twas th' reflection
O' th' movin' chandelier,
But I didn't think so then.
Anyhow, I jumped down them stairs
Quicker'n winkin',
An' I out into th' yard
An' run till I was in bed in my own room.
My mother thought I had a chill
But I knowed diff'rent.
I knowed a lot,
But I never found out what 'twas I really
    knowed.
Fer nothin' happened.
James Boott lived a couple o' years after
    that
An' when he died Doctor Busby bought
    th' house,
An' his daughter was livin' in it when I
    was last to Pelham.
'Twarn't much, was it?
An' yet I don't know —
I ain't never forgot it.

ONE WINTER NIGHT

"Have another cruller, Mis' Sanders.
You ain't eat nothin'."

"They're proper good, Mis' Bixby,
But Em'ly comin' down sick all of a sud-
    din like that

Has took all th' relish out o' me.
I can't git a morsel down my throat.
My own brother's child, you know.
It ain't in th' fam'ly, Mis' Bixby.
We never had no spasms on our side.
'Course I ain't so sure 'bout her mother's
   people,
But I never heer'd o' nothin'.
I wish th' doctor'd come.
Waitin's awful tryin'."

"Guess he'll be right along now.
Len took his sorrel mare,
An' th' roads is beat down fine fer
   sleighin'."

"Do you think she really saw anythin',
   Mis' Bixby?"

"Laws, no! Ther' wa'n't nothin' to see."

"I dunno, o' course. I was up to my
   room,
Spickin' up my new bunnit fer meetin'
   termorrer,
When I heerd her scream.
I'm all shook up with th' sound of it;
I can't git it out o' my head.
Jest what was it happened, Mis' Bixby?
You was here, wasn't you?"

"Yes, I was here; but I wa'n't ther' —
   down cellar, I mean.
I heerd th' scream, too,
But 'fore I could git out o' th' rocker
She come stumblin' up th' cellar stairs
White as a dish-cloth.
'He's ther'!' she says,
'He popped right out o' a apple-barrel
An' made faces at me.'
Then down she goes on th' floor in a
   faint."

"Maybe 'twas one o' th' neighbors playin'
   tricks."

" 'Deed no, Mis' Sanders.
Nobody'd durst play any such a trick on
   Em'ly.
Why't be murder.
She's most died o' these takin's a couple
   o' times."

"Th' poor child! She never give so much
   as a hint in her letters.
An' me her father's own sister,

An' th' only blood relation she has in
   th' world, too.
I do wish that doctor'd come."

"Now don't you fret.
He'll be right along.
An' Susan Ellen understands her real
   well.
But as to anythin' she might ha' seed,
She couldn't.
Why them barrels is chock full to th'
   brim,
An' shove so close ther' ain't 'nough room
   between 'em for a rat to pass 'thout
   gnawin'.
It's jest took her ag'in, that's all.
I'm afeer'd they'll have to put her away
One o' these days."

"Has she been took often?"

"Five or six times, I guess.
Le' me see:
Ther' was th' Post Office.
She 'lowed she'd seed Si throw up a
   winder over th' shop.
She said he leaned out so fer he'd ha' fell
Only fer th' sill ketchin' him at th' waist
An' keepin' him danglin'.
'Twas 'nough to scare th' life out o' ye
T' hear her tell th' way he looked.
Mr. Jones was real kind.
He searched th' whole house himself.
But ther' wa'n't nobody ther'
'Cept Mrs. Jones and th' hired girl.
Then once when she was over to Stone-
   ham,
Buyin' some 'lastic,
She went right over in a faint on th'
   counter,
An' when she come to,
She said 'twas Si was sellin' it to her.
'Course it wa'n't.
Why th' young man that 'tended her
   was right ther',
An' he didn't look no more like Si
Than I look like Drake's red bull.
He was ten years younger, fer one thing.
That's twice't I remember.
Then ther' was th' time in th' clo'es-yard,
And another in th' cars comin' from
   Boston.
Ther's been a good many,
First an' last."

"Was she an' Si happy?"

"Happy as cranberries, I should say.
'Course Si was a kind o' quiet feller,
An' Em'ly's al'ays been smart and lively.
But they hit it off nicely
'Spite o' th' diff'rence in disposition."

"I s'pose ther' ain't no doubt he's dead?"

"Doubt! 'Course ther' ain't no doubt.
Why th' man was drowned.
Len was with him when't happened."

"You don't say!"

"Oh, yes! Len was ther'.
Not that he seen it happen 'xactly.
'Twas this way.
They was cuttin' ice up to Breed's pond
That Winter.
All th' boys was at it,
But that night they'd all gone home
'Cept Len an' Si.
Them two was ambitious,
An' they was sort o' racin' each other
    with th' cuttin',
So they kep' on by lantern light
After th' others left.
Well, bimeby it got near supper time,
An' Len figgered he'd better be gettin'
    home.
So he hollered to Si,
An' started loadin' his things into th'
    sleigh.
Si didn't answer,
An' he hollered ag'in.
Then he started out over th' ice
Lookin' fer him.
Ther' was a patch o' open water
Where they'd cut th' ice clear away,
An' after Len'd been all over th' hard
    part
He got ther'.
Well, that water give him a turn.
'Twas jest skimmin' over ag'in
All 'cept one place,
An' he could see that wa'n't froze
'Cause th' wind ruffed it up
Jest as he got to it,
An' th' lantern light was all broke to bits
By th' waves.
Well, when Len seed that,
He give over huntin'.
He jest run fer th' sleigh

An' drove back home with his horse on
    th' gallop
An' scared up th' folks.
Th' whole town went out with tools an'
    grapples,
But 'twas all thick ice when they got to
    th' pond.
They couldn't find nothin'.
They searched th' woods,
But 'twan't no use.
Mr. Marvin, th' coroner
Said as how th' body would come up
When th' ice melted.
But it didn't.
Then he said it must ha' been Si's axe
    got caught
In th' weeds somehow an' held him
    down.
I forgot to tell you th' axe was gone."

"Didn't they drag the pond?"

"They tried to,
But it's awful deep.
Anyhow they never found th' body.
But ther' ain't a mite o' doubt it's ther'."

"How long after was it Len married
    Em'ly?"

"Oh, goin' on a year and half, I guess.
Len felt dreadful 'bout th' whole
    thing.
He's one o' th' sens'tive sort,
An' he kep' blamin' himself
He hadn't kep' a watch on what Si was
    doin'.
He felt he wanted to make it up to
    Em'ly some way.
So he used to go up ther' twice a day,
An' saw her firewood,
An' redd up her horses,
An' 'tend to things generally.
It made a lot o' trampin'
An' I 'spec they thought 'twould be
    easier if he jest stayed for keeps,
So they got married."

"He took a good deal on himself, didn't
    he?"

"Well, I dunno.
Em'ly hadn't had no spells then.
Ther' didn't seem no risk."

"Good Land! Mis' Bixby.
What could ha' brought 'em on!
Our folks ain't never been subject to
fits.''

"No, 'deed, Mis' Sanders,
Nor Em'ly neither, fer as th' neighbors
knew.
They come on all to onc't,
After she and Len'd been married a year
or more."

"It's awful strange 'bout th' body not
floatin'."

"Mr. Marvin said 'twas th' axe."

"But you'd ha' s'posed he'd ha' let go
o' th' axe
When he felt th' water sousin' over him."

"I never thought o' that.
P'raps 'twas tied onto him somehow."

"What would he want to tie his axe on
fer?
Would he ha' drove home that way?"

"Laws Sakes! I dunno.
But if 'twa'n't fastened on him,
Why didn't he float clear?"

"That was what I was thinkin'."

"Good Land o' God, Mis' Sanders!
You don't mean —"

"I don't mean nothin', Mis' Bixby.
I was jest thinkin' —
More hot water, Susan Ellen?
'Course, we'll have it in a jiffy."

THE DAY THAT WAS THAT DAY

The wind rose, and the wind fell,
And the day that was that day
Floated under a high Heaven.

"Home! Home! Home!"
Sang a robin in a spice-bush.
"Sun on a roof-tree! Sun on a roof-tree!"
Rang thin clouds
In a chord of silver across a placid sky.

Rachel Gibbs stepped up the path
To pass the time of day

With Haywood Green's Minnie.
My, ef she ain't shut th' door!
An' all th' breeze this side th' house too.
She must like to stew.
"Minnie,
Minnie,
You ain't gone out have yer?
I'll skin my knuckles ef I knock agin.
I wonder did she lock th' door —
Well, I never!
Have you gone hard o' hearin'?
Have you —
Minnie, child, what's th' matter?
Why do you look like that?
What you doin'?
Speak I tell yer,
What you hidin' that cup fer?
God A'mighty, gal, what you doin' with
    wood-alcohol
In a drinkin'-cup?
Here, give it ter me,
An' I'll set it on th' table.
Set down Minnie dear,
Set right here in th' rocker
An' tell me
What ails yer to be wantin'
To drink stuff like that?
There, there, you poor lamb,
Don't look so scared.
Jest tell me all about it,
An' ease your heart.
Minnie, I'll have to shake yer
Ef you don't stop starin'
In that dretful way.
Poor Dear,
You just lay your head up agin me
An' let me soothe yer.
Poor little thing.
Poor little thing."

"Don't, don't, Rachel,
I can't bear it.
I'm a wicked woman,
But I jest couldn't stand no more."

"No more o' what?
Ain't yer Pa good to yer?
What's come over yer, Minnie?
My! I'm jest as sorry as I can be."

"Oh, it ain't nothin' like that.
An' don't be so good to me,
You'll make me want to cry agin,
An' I can't cry.
I'm all dried up.

An' it's like squeezin' my heart sick
To want to cry, an' can't."

"But what is it?
Ain't yer never goin' ter tell me?"

"Why ther' ain't nothin' to tell
'Cept that I'm tired."

"Now, look-a-here, Minnie,
No one don't drink poison jest 'cause
    they're tired."

"I didn't drink it, as it happens."

"No, you didn't, 'cause I come in an'
    stopped yer.
But I'm mighty afeered you would have.
Lord, it makes me shudder!"

"I guess yer right,
I would have.
An' I wish you'd ha' let me be.
Now it's all to do over agin,
An' I don't know as I'll git th' courage
A second time.
I guess you ain't never been right down
    tired, Rachel."

"Well, never to th' poison point, no, I
    haven't
But what's gone wrong to wear yer out
    so?"

"The cat's sick."

"Minnie Green, was you takin' poison
'Cause you got a sick cat?
That's down-right foolishness."

"Yes, it does sound so.
But I couldn't face nussin' her.
Look here, Rachel,
I may be foolish, or mad, or jest plain
    bad,
But I couldn't stan' another thing.
I'm all fretted now
An' more's one too many.
I can't go on!
Oh, God! I can't go on!
I ain't got no more'n most women,
I know that,
But I fuss a lot more.
There's al'ays th' same things

Goin' roun' like th' spokes to a cart-
    wheel,
Ef one ain't a-top it's another,
An' th' next comin' up all th' time.
It's breakfast, an' dinner, an' supper,
Every day.
An' th' same dishes to wash.
I hate them dishes.
I smashed a plate yesterday
'Cause I couldn't bear to see it
Settin' on th' sink waitin' fer me.
An' when I go up to make Father's bed
I git seasick
Thinkin' I'll have to see that old check
    spread agin.
I've settled it,
An' twitched it this way an' that,
For thirty year,
An' I hate th' sight o' th' thing.
Sometimes I've set an hour on th' stair
Ruther'n go in an' touch it.
Oh my God! Why couldn't yer let me
    be?
Why'd you have to come interferin'?
Why?
Why?"

"Thank th' Everlastin' Mercy I did!
But, Minnie, how long's this been goin'
    on?
I never had no idea anythin' was wrong."

"I don't know.
For ever an' ever, I guess.
Rachel, you can't think how hard it is
    fer me
To set one foot after th' other sometimes.
I hate lookin' out th' winder,
I'm so tired o' seein' th' path to th' barn.
An' I can't hardly bear
To hear father talkin' to th' horses.
He loves 'em.
But I don't love nothin'
'Cept th' cat,
An' cats is cold things to cling to,
An' now mine's sick!"

"Don't take on so, Minnie.
She'll git well.
There, you rest awhile
You can tell me afterwards."

A wind rose, and a wind fell,
And the day that was that day
Hung against a turning sun.

The robin sang "Home! Home! Home!"
In an up-and-down scale of small, bright
*   notes.*
The clouds rang silver arpeggios
Stretched across a pleasant sky.

"I wish I loved somethin', Rachel."

"Bless your heart, Child, don't you love
    yer Father?"

"I suppose so. But he don't mean nothin'
    ter me.
He don't say nothin' I want ter hear.
My ears is achin' to hear words,
Words like what's written in books,
Words that would make me all bright
    like a Spring day.
I lay awake nights
Thinkin' o' hearin' things,
An' seein' things.
I'm awful tired o' these hills,
They crowd in so.
Seems sometimes ef I could see th' ocean,
Or a real big city,
'Twould help.
Kind o' lay my eyes out straight fer a
    while,
Everythin's so short here
My eyes feels pushed in,
An' it hurts 'em.
I love laylocks,
But I git so tired o' watchin'
Th' leaves come an' th' flowers
Every year th' same,
I'd like to root 'em up.
I've set an' set in th' kitchen evenin's
Awful late,
Fer not bein' able to git up an' light th'
    lamp
To go ter bed.
I'm all lead somehow.
I guess ef anybody did say anythin'
I'd be deaf
Jest with listenin' so long.
I'm plumb tired out."

"Look-a-here, Minnie,
Why don't you go away
Fer a spell?"

"Me go away!
Oh, no, I couldn't never do that.
I couldn't go no place.
I can't hardly git over to Dicksville

Fer my week with Aunt Abby now.
I'm all wrong away from home.
I can't do nothin'!
Nothin' at all.
I'm so awful tired."

"Minnie, did you ever love anybody?
Any man, I mean?"

"No, Rachel, I never did.
I know that sounds queer, but it's a fact
I've tried to think I did,
But 'twarn't true.
I hadn't hardly no time fer men-folks,
Mother was sick so long,
An' then ther' was Father.
I never was much account with 'em any-
    way,
But I s'pose I might ha' had one
Ef I'd fixed my mind so.
But I al'ays waited.
An' now I'm through waitin',
I'm through waitin' fer anythin', Rachel.
It's jest go, go, go,
With never no end,
And nothin' done that ain't to do over
    agin.
Ther' now it's six o'clock,
An' I must be gittin' supper.
You needn't move that cup, Rachel.
I ain't a-goin' to touch it.
I'll jest keep on now till th' Lord takes
    me
An' I only hope he'll do it soon."

The robin flew down from the spice-bush
And pecked about for worms.
The clouds were brazen trumpets
Tumbled along the edge of an apple-
*   coloured sky.*
The shadow of the house
Fell across the path to the barn
Confusing it with the grass and the
*   daisies.*

A wind rose, and a wind fell,
And the day that was that day
Vanished in the darkness.

A DRACULA OF THE HILLS

Yes, I can understan' ther's a sort o'
    pleasure collectin' old customs
An' linin' 'em up like a card o' butterflies.
Some on 'em's real quaint, I dessay,

But lookin's one thing an' livin's another.
Folks don't figger on th' quaintness o' th'
   things they're doin',
Ther' ain't no knick-knack about it then,
   I guess.
Times is changed since my young days,
Don't seem like th' same world I used
   to live in.
What with th' telephones an' th' auto-
   mobiles,
An' city folks rampin' all over th' place
   Summers,
Lots o' things has kind o' faded out.
But I remember some queer goin's
   on;
They seem queer 'nough to me now,
   lookin' back.
We had good times a-plenty, nat'rally,
But they're all jumbled up together when
   I think on 'em,
I can't git aholt o' one more'n another,
While ther's some fearful strange things
   I can't ever lose a mite of,
No matter how I try.
I'd like to forget 'bout Florella Perry,
But I ain't never be'n able to.
I don't know as you'd call it a custom,
'Twarn't th' first time th' like had hap-
   pened, I know,
But ther' ain't never no such doin's now-
   adays.
Do the Lord's ways change, I wonder?
Superstition, you call it — but I don't
   know.
Seein's believin' all th' world over,
An' 'twas my own father seed
An' others besides him.
I didn't, 'cause I was a young girl an'
   not let,
But I watched th' beginnin's;
An' what my eyes didn't see, my ears
   heerd,
An' that afore other folks' seein' was
   cold, as you might say.
'Twas all of forty year ago;
I was jest a slip of a girl drawin' toward
   th' beau stage but not yit ther'.
One day I'd be thinkin' o' nothin' but
   ribbons,
An' th' next I'd go coastin' bellybumps
   all afternoon with th' boys.
Florella made me a woman for fair;
P'raps that was a good thing, 'twas time
   for it,
But I be'n a woman long 'nough now

An' I kind o' like to look back to what
   went afore.
I warn't livin' here then;
My husband was a Rockridge man
An' I come here when I married.
I was raised t'other side o' Bear Moun-
   tain to Penowasset.
Father kep' th' store ther'.
They thought a heap o' him in th' town
An' I had a happy childhood.
We didn't live over th' shop,
But quite along by th' end o' th' village
In a house my mother got from her
   father.
We had a couple o' fields an' a wood lot
An' kep' a hired man.
Father used to drive back an' forth in a
   buggy mornin's an' evenin's,
But Mother an' me didn't miss for neigh-
   bors.
Jared Pierce owned a fine big farm just
   beyond us,
An' Joe Perry's was t'other side th' road.
Florella was Joe's wife,
An' a real pretty creatur she was,
Fragile as a chiney plate
An' bright an' tidy as a June pink in sun-
   shine.
She loved flowers;
Her door-yard was like a nosegay from
   May till October.
I never seen sich flowers as hers;
Nobody else couldn't make 'em bloom
   so,
Even when she give 'em th' seeds.
Her snowdrops was al'ays first up in th'
   Spring,
An' it took more'n a couple o' frosts to
   kill her late asters.
Th' way we knew she was ill was when
   th' garden begun to git weedy.
She an' Joe'd be'n married 'bout seven
   year then,
An' My! but they'd be'n happy!
Exceptin' for not havin' a child, I don't
   think ther' was a thing they wanted.
An' then Florella took sick.
It come with a cough one Winter,
An' she couldn't seem to git back her
   stren'th.
Come plantin' time, she couldn't do it.
Joe done his best, but that year th'
   garden warn't nothin' perticlar.
Florella used to set in her rocker on th'
   piazza lookin' at it an' cryin'.

Many's th' time I've slipped over an'
done a little rakin' for her.
At first she liked me to do it,
But after a while she said to let it alone;
Ef it warn't her garden, she said, she
didn't care nothin' 'bout it.
She spoke almost fierce, I thought, an' I
didn't go over agin for quite a spell.
When I did, Florella had took to her
bed.
She was a queer kind of invalid. You
couldn't seem to help her any.
She'd let you do things an' thank you,
But she al'ays seemed angry that you had
to come.
One day I was dustin' her room, an' she
said to me:
"Becky, I ain't a-goin' to die."
" 'Course you ain't, Florella," says I,
"Whatever put that into your head?"
She flared up at that.
" 'Tain't no use lyin' to me, Becky Wales,
I know I'm dyin'.
But I won't die. You'll see.
I'll find some way o' livin'.
Even ef they bury me, I'll live.
You can't kill me, I ain't th' kind to kill.
I'll live! I'll live, I tell you,
Ef there's a Devil to help me do it!"
She screamed this out at me, settin' up
in bed
An' p'intin' with her finger.
I was so scared I had to grab a chair to
keep from fallin',
An' Joe come runnin' in from th' barn.
He took her in his arms an' soothed her,
An' she bust out cryin' an' sunk into a
little heap in th' big bed
So's you couldn't hardly see her, she was
so thin.
Joe sent me home. He said not to mind
Florella,
That she was flighty an' didn't know
what she was sayin'.
Well, after that things got worse.
Florella had spell after spell;
You could hear her cryin' an' hollerin'
way down th' road.
It was al'ays th' same thing: she wouldn't
die,
Nobody could make her die.
'Twas awful pitiful to hear her takin' on.
Sometimes she'd moan an' moan,
An' then she'd break out crazy mad an'
angry, screamin' for life.

Joe was at his wits' end.
Dr. Smilie said ther' warn't nothin' to
do for her
'Cept give her quietin' draughts.
But Florella wouldn't take 'em;
She said they was a little death,
An' she'd throw down th' cup every time
they give it to her.
Then she took a notion to see Anabel
Flesche.
She was a queer sort of woman, was
Anabel,
She lived in a little shed of a place over
Chester way.
Some said she had Indian blood in her,
Anyway she was learn'd in herbs an'
semples;
She claimed to know jest when to pick
'em,
An' she talked a lot o' foolishness about
th' full o' th' moon,
An' three hours before dawn, an' th' dew
o' th' second Friday,
An' things like that.
Well, Florella had her in,
An' she made her camomile teas an'
lotions, out o' leaves an' plants she'd
gathered,
An' fussed around with bits o' wax an'
string,
But Florella didn't change none.
She kep' sinkin' an' sinkin',
An' th' cryin' spells got to comin' oftener.
She cried most o' th' time then.
I used to set in th' stair winder
When I'd oughter be'n in bed, listenin'.
It made my flesh creep to hear her poor
cracked voice declarin' she wouldn't
die,
An' all th' time she was dyin' plain as
pikestaff.
I never see nobody so hungry for life;
She was jest starvin' for it.
Why, even when ther' warn't nothin' lef'
of her but eyes an' bones,
She'd talk an' talk 'bout th' life she'd a
right to, an' she was goin' to have,
come what or nothin'!
It was kind o' lonesome out our way then;
Most o' th' passin' got to go by th' Brook
Road.
'Twarn't so handy by a good two mile,
But nobody couldn't a-bear to hear
Florella
Callin' an' wailin'.

You couldn't count ten th' times she was
    still.
'Twas a awful witchin' sound, comin'
    through th' night th' way it did;
I know I got all frazzled out losin' my
    sleep for hearin' it.
Mother an' Mis' Pierce used to take it in
    turns to watch her,
An' 'twas a real kindness to do it,
It wore th' nerves so.
One Saturday afternoon Mis' Pierce was
    with her,
When all of a suddint she jumped out
    o' bed,
Cryin' she was goin' int' th' garden,
That she was well now an' wouldn't be
    kep' back no more.
Mis' Pierce caught her just as she was
    goin' through th' door
An' ther' was a struggle, I guess.
Joe heerd where he was out in th' yard
    hoein' beans.
He was scared to death, an' jest heaved
    his hoe up onto his shoulder
An' run in as he was.
Florella seed him comin' with th' hoe up
    on his shoulder,
An' she screamed a fearful wild scream:
"You too, Joe!" she said,
"You want to kill me same as th' others?
But you shan't do it.
I'll live to spite you,
I'll live because o' you."
She was mockin', an' grinnin', an'
    coughin',
An' menacin' him with her finger,
An' her head joggin' back an' forth from
    shoulder to shoulder like a rag-doll's.
Mis' Pierce run'd over an' tell'd Mother
    soon's she could git a minit,
An' them was her very words.
Now Florella loved Joe as only a rare
    few women do love;
But she was jest plumb crazy by this
    time,
Worryin' 'bout th' life was leavin' her,
    an' all eat up with consumption.
But it didn't make no diff'rence to Joe,
He loved her al'ays.
He jest picked her up an' laid her back
    in bed,
An' she went off unconscious an' never
    come to.
She died that night.

I mind it well, 'cause th' whippoorwills'd
    be'n so loud th' night before;
When I'd heerd 'em I'd thought Flor-
    ella's time was come.
I've al'ays hated funerals,
I can't a-bear to look on a corpse
An' Florella's was dretful.
Not that she warn't pretty;
She was. Even her sickness hadn't sp'iled
    her beauty.
She was like herself in a glass, somehow,
An old glass where you don't see real
    clear.
'Twas like music to look at her,
Only for her mouth.
Ther' was a queer, awful smile 'bout her
    mouth.
It made her look jeery, not a bit th' way
    Florella used to look.
Ef I shut my eyes I can see that face
    now,
Blue, an' thin an' th' lips all twisted up
    an' froze so.
I guess I've seen that face in my mind
    every day for forty year, more or less.
Well, they buried her, an' we girls set
    pansies an' lobelia all about her grave
An' took turns tendin' 'em, week by week.
I'd loved Florella,
An', when she was dead, I rec'llected her
    as she was 'fore her sickness come
An' forgot th' rest.
Two years is a long time to watch a
    person die,
An' Joe'd done more nussin' than most
    husbands.
He kind o' pined when 'twas all finished,
But th' neighbors kep' a-droppin' in to
    see him,
An' Mother an' Mis' Pierce did him up
    every so often,
An' bimeby he got aholt of himself,
An' seemed to be gittin' on nicely.
He was a proper good farmer
An' things was goin' well with him,
All 'ceptin' his sorrow, which nothin'
    couldn't lift, nat'rally,
When th' next Winter he caught a bad
    cold.
I guess he let it go too far afore he saw
    th' doctor;
Anyhow it got a good settle on him an'
    he couldn't shake it off.
Nobody'd have thought much of it, I

guess, but for Florella beginnin' th'
same way.
Joe warn't concerned, he said he'd be all
right come Spring,
But he warn't. He'd try to do his work
as usual,
But soon he'd give over an' set down.
He was real patient, but he didn't git no
better.
Dr Smilie begun to look grave.
One day I went over with a bowl o' soup
from Mother.
Joe was settin' in th' garden, by a bed
o' portulaca;
They's cruel bright flowers, an' Joe looked
so grey beside 'em
I got a start to see him.
"Becky," says he, "I know you loved
Florella,
An' I should like you to have her
flowers," says he.
"I've willed th' farm to my brother over
to Hillsborough,
But you can dig up th' flowers afore he
takes possession."
"Joe," I said, "Joe — " an' I couldn't git
out another word for th' life o' me.
"Yes," he went on, "o' course I'm goin'.
I've give her all I could, but it can't
last.
Anabel Flesche was here yesterday, an'
she told me.
I'm glad to ease her any, you know that,
But it can't last."
Glad to ease Anabel Flesche — I
thought,
But I know'd he didn't mean that.
I run right home an' told Mother, an'
she told Father,
An' that evenin' they druv down to Dr.
Smilie's.
The doctor 'lowed 'twas consumption,
but he was angry enough 'bout Anabel
Flesche.
"I'll see that hussy stops her trapesin',"
he said,
"Rilin' up a sick man with her witch
stories," he said.
"I'll witch her, I'll run her out o' town
if she comes agin."
Anabel didn't come agin, but I guess she
done it th' first time,
For Joe didn't seem to take much int'rest
in gittin' well.

When a man don't want to live, he don't
live, an' that's gospel.
Joe went down hill so fast that by Mid-
summer ther' warn't no hope.
I used to set with him a good deal,
An' 'twas queer how diff'rent he was to
Florella.
I think he was th' quietest man I ever see.
He didn't seem to have no pleasure 'cept
in speakin' 'bout Florella.
By times he told me everythin':
How he courted her, an' what she said,
an' th' way she looked when he
brought her home.
I got awful near life for a young girl
with th' things he told me.
I've be'n married an' widowed since, but
I don't know as I ever got nearer to
things than Joe's talk brought me.
Men ain't alike, an' women ain't alike,
an' marriages is th' most unlike of all.
My marriage, when it come, was no more
like Joe's an' Florella's
Than a piney's like a cabbage.
But this ain't my story.
"Florella had a strong will," says Joe to
me one afternoon.
Autumn had come by then, an' some o'
th' leaves had fell,
An' those that hung on were so bright
they seemed to fairly smarten up th'
sun.
Joe was layin' in his bed with a patch-
work quilt over him,
A lovely one 'twas, the State House Steps
pattern;
Florella'd made it, she was wonderful
clever with her needle.
Th' whole room was a blaze o' sunshine.
Right on th' chimbley hung a picture o'
Florella
Some travellin' artist had painted th' year
she was married.
I don't suppose city folk would have
made much of it,
But I thought 'twas a sweet pretty thing,
an' th' spon-image o' Florella.
"Florella had a mighty strong will," says
Joe agin.
"She owned me body an' soul, an' that
was a rare pride to me."
I couldn't figger what to answer, so I
didn't.
"I guess she owns me still," he says, an'

I don't know ef he was really talkin'
to me.
"I'm glad she does. It's got to be both
o' us, all or neither, together."
He smiled at that, very slow an' tired, al-
most as though it hurt his lips to do it.
"Perhaps you don't understand, little
Becky," said he.
I don't know whether I did or not, an' I
didn't have a chance to say,
For all of a sudden crash down come
Florella's picture on th' floor with th'
cord broke.
I jumped nearly out o' my skin, I expect
I screamed too,
But Joe didn't so much as shiver.
"Yes," he said, lookin' at me with his
steady smile,
"This proves it. You mark my words.
It can't go on much longer. Poor
Florella!"
He sighed then an' layed down, an' I
thought he went to sleep.
I picked up th' picture, but th' glass had
cut it badly,
All about th' mouth too.
It make it look th' way Florella's corpse
did an' give me a turn.
I was afeerd Joe'd see it when he waked
up,
So I set it with its face aginst th' wall.
But I needn't have bothered, for Joe
never waked up.
When Mother come, she didn't think he
looked right,
An' she sent for Dr. Smilie.
He warn't dead when th' doctor got ther',
But he was unconscious an' hardly
breathin';
He stayed like that for a day an' a night
An' then 'twas all over.
All over for Joe, yes,
But not for us.
About a week after th' funeral, Father
met Anabel Flesche.
"So Joe Perry's dead," whined Anabel,
an' Father was sure th' old hag looked
pleased.
He only said, "Yes, he's dead," an' was
pushin' on when Anabel stopped him.
"Florella's a determined woman," she
cackled, "ain't you afeerd she'll try
somebody else?"
"What th' Hell do you mean?" cried out
Father.

"She loved life," said Anabel, in a queer,
sly way,
"Joe's gone, but ther's others."
Father was so angry he couldn't trust
himself to speak,
He jest touched up his horse an' druv on.
But what Anabel said rankled.
He an' Mother talked it over that night.
I warn't supposed to hear, but I did.
I was all shook up with th' things had
happened
An' I daresn't stay in bed alone with no-
body near,
So I used to creep out an' set on th' stairs
Till Father an' Mother come up.
It comforted me to know they was in
th' next room,
An' I could sleep then.
Mother was real strict, an' I was al'ays
sent to bed at nine;
They'd come up 'bout ten, an' I'd set
that hour on th' stairs
Where I could look int' th' kitchen an'
see 'em.
That's how I come to hear.
Afterwards I 'lowed I knew, an' they told
me everythin'.
Well, to make a long story short,
Father an' Jared Pierce went straight to
th' Selectmen,
An' told 'em what Anabel was hintin'.
Then some old people rec'llected things
which had happened years ago,
An', puttin' two an' two together, they
decided to see for themselves.
The Selectmen was all ther', an' Father,
an' Jared Pierce;
They did it at night so's not to scare
folks.
I warn't ther', but Father told it so I
think I seen it:
Th' leaves blowin' an' sidlin' down,
Th' lantern light jerkin' 'long th' ground,
Th' noise o' th' pickaxes an' spades.
They got up th' coffin an' opened it.
Florella's body was all gone to dust,
Though 'twarn't much more'n a year
she'd be'n buried,
But her heart was as fresh as a livin'
person's,
Father said it glittered like a garnet when
they took th' lid off th' coffin.
It was so 'live, it seemed to beat almost.
Father said a light come from it so
strong it made shadows

Much heavier than th' lantern shadows
an' runnin' in a diff'rent direction.
Oh, they burnt it; they al'ays do in such
cases,
Nobody's safe till it's burnt.
Now, sir, will you tell me how such
things used to be?
They don't happen now, seemingly, but
this happened.
You can see Joe's grave over to Peno-
wasset buryin'-ground
Ef you go that way.
The church-members wouldn't let Flor-
ella's ashes be put back in hers,
So you won't find that.
Only an open space with a maple in th'
middle of it;
They planted th' tree so's no one
wouldn't ever be buried in that spot
agin.

THE NOTE–BOOK IN THE GATE–LEGGED TABLE

Richardson, Erik Follows, Reed and I
Were all comparing notes on our vaca-
tions
One evening after dinner. Richardson
Had been to Labrador on a coasting
steamer
And run across a half a dozen whales
In the mating season. He has an eye for
colour
And picturesque detail, his flashing ocean
And his superb, preoccupied great whales
Love-hunted into fighting, was a thing
I might not have forgotten, but — you'll
see,
We'd something bigger even than his
whales
To occupy us later on. Tom Reed
Had climbed Mount Everest and broken
his leg,
And crawled and starved for near a week
before
A searching party found him. I had been
Playing the miner for socialistic reasons,
And I thought I had a pretty tale to
tell
Until I heard the others. I began,
A bit puffed up to start with, then came
Reed,
Then Richardson, the last was Erik
Follows.
I rather think he'd needed his vacation

More than the rest of us; he worked so
hard.
A doctor can work himself down to bare
nerves
If he's in love with his profession, and
Follows
Cared more for his than any man I know.
An alienist has many leads to follow,
But Erik's leads all seemed to follow
him;
They ran him down a dozen times a
day
And even tracked him into his vacations.
That's why we'd left his tale until the
last,
For he was sure to have encountered
something.
He had; he showed it to us. A gate-
legged table
Of old mahogany, as soft as skin,
The colour of maple-syrup, with slender
legs,
And just a touch of brass to liven it —
The round-ringed handle of its one small
drawer.
And out of this drawer it came, the amaz-
ing thing.
A little, pigskin-bound, octavo booklet,
Ruled for accounts, but kept for notes,
it seemed.
Half of the pages were blank, the rest
were scrawled
With a large, oafish sort of pencil-writing,
So blurred and rubbed, it hardly could be
read.
But Follows had read it; you see it was
a lead.
"Well?" — we all said, for we could
see at once
That Follows had a clue which stretched
away
From just this note-book. "Well" — he
said at last,
"I took a little trip into the Berkshires
Last Autumn in my car. One afternoon
I chanced to pass a farm-house where an
auction
Was being held, and went in just for fun.
It was a pretty place. A little brook
Nuzzled its way along a boggy meadow
Behind a barn with a ship weather-vane,
Which should have struck me, but some-
how it didn't,
And, just beyond, one of those odd-
shaped hills

You see in Hiroshige's prints ran up,
A slope of hemlocks, right into the sky.
The house was low and wide, with both its porches
So thickly covered with Virginia creeper
The lattice laths might have been creeper-stems.
The crimson of the leaves in the Autumn sunlight
Against the old white paint was strangely cheerful.
I liked the place at once; it seemed a shame
To scatter all the queer, comfortable old things
Had been there for so long. I stopped to look
A moment at the crowd, trampling the garden
And shuffling through the house, then I went in
And bought that table in a sort of pity
That all these things spread round were up for sale.
The old stock ended — it was the usual story —
Gone West, or dead, no one to keep the farm.
I bought the table, ordered it expressed,
Pondered the natural queries which an auction
Always arouses for a day or so,
And finished out my trip without adventure.
Without adventure, yes, that was to come.
It must have been at least two weeks before
I found a moment to unbox my table.
I set it up, dusted it, opened the leaves,
And in the drawer I found this diary;
For that is what it is, a diary.
There is no date, but I can tell you now
The notes were made in eighteen eighty-nine.
But I don't know who wrote them. There's no name;
And that, I think, I never shall discover.
The diary begins — I'll read it to you,
Just a few pages, and then tell the rest."
He picked the book up from the table and read
Slowly and quietly, yet it rang my nerves
It was so still and horrible.

"My God!
Why have they sent me up here to the grass?
Sent me to live among the hateful grass!
The terrible, creeping, creeping, pitiless grass!
What is this thing, this gorging, endless thing,
Moving so slowly that it baffles sight,
But never stopping either night or day?
We mow it down, and in a week again
It covers all the place we have laid bare.
Man builds his roads through grass. With breaking toil,
With sweat and muscle-ache he forces his way
Across the earth. He shears the grasses down
And keeps them there with infinite stress of wheels,
But if he pauses in his travelling,
If for a space he rests, worn with fatigue,
The ravening grass has run across his paths
And choked them utterly away. Oh, God!
The chatter, chatter, chatter, of the grass!
I hear it in the night crying for men
To feed its vitals with their own. I see
It crawling toward this thin, unstable house,
Thrusting its clutching fingers through the boards,
Swallowing the poor weak flowers in their beds.
What is this house? A flimsy, man-made thing
Besieged on all sides by the gluttonous grass.
They speak of spears of grass, but I see bellies
Bellies which feed on man-blood; feet which suck
Entrails of human beings. I am mad,
Tortured to see this island of a house
Waiting to be engulfed. And they have sent
Me here for rest! Oh, Fools! Fools! I, alone —
The myriads of grass are more than I.
I cannot eat, for I will feed no grass.
I cannot sleep for listening to it drink
And fortify its waiting strength with dew.
They tell me to go sit upon the hill

Under the hemlocks where no grass can
　　grow.
But do not trees themselves flourish on
　　graves?
They laugh, the farmer and his sons, they
　　do not think
Of the fat, waving grass that I have seen
In the churchyard. I often go to watch
How green, how wicked green, it grows
　　just there.

.　　.　　.　　.　　.

Last night I heard a little quiet noise,
A wood-pecker noise, but very, very soft,
And it was in the middle of the night.
I listened for hours till the grey light
　　came,
And then it stopped, and then at last I
　　slept."

.　　.　　.　　.　　.

The doctor paused, but not one of us
　　spoke.
He turned some pages over and went on:
"I hear it now on almost every night
And all day long my head aches. Lack of
　　sleep,
I know. And that is very bad, for when
I do not sleep, my hearing is so sharp
I very nearly catch the words they say,
The grasses. Only not quite, not quite;
　　and this
Hearing and not is piercing my head
　　through,
Burning it up with irons, hot and cold,
So that I break out in a chilly sweat.
The farmer's wife tells me I'm looking
　　badly,
Should go out more. But that I will not
　　do.
I never go out now. The grass is there.
I have no money; the town doctors saw
To that. 'No care at all,' they said, 'just
　　grow
As the grass grows.' I laughed, oh, I did
　　laugh!
And still they sent me here to rest. My
　　ears!
My ears! They hurt with all the noise.
　　The tapping
Is louder every night. It seems as though
It tried to drown the whimper of the
　　grass,
But nothing can do that. And I can't go
Away, I have no money, not a cent.

I cannot walk, for I must walk through
　　grass.
I've whittled bits of wood to stop my
　　ears,
But, with them in, I think I hear the
　　leaves
Of some dead tree stuttering out my
　　name
In a ghoulish whisper. So I take them
　　out.
The tapping is better, even the stealthy,
　　licking
Murmur which comes from all that tide
　　of grass.

.　　.　　.　　.　　.

I've found it out at last. I made them
　　tell me.
I threatened them one evening with a
　　knife,
And said I'd go to bed like a good boy
When once they'd told. It seems that,
　　years ago,
Fifty years or a hundred, I don't remem-
　　ber,
An old sea-captain came up here to live.
He'd left the sea, and as his daughter was
　　married
To the man who owned this place, they
　　took him home
To die, whenever that might happen.
　　But he
Was marvellously afraid of just this dy-
　　ing,
Because he felt like me about the grass.
He used to swear that it should never get
　　him,
And begged his daughter to cast him in
　　the sea.
But she, a decent, quiet woman, was
　　shocked,
And he could never make her give her
　　promise.
At length he hit upon a compromise
And made the two of them agree to
　　it.
His coffin was to be slung from a high
　　beam
Beneath the roof-peak of the barn, and
　　left
To rot and crumble. When they'd given
　　their words,
He had that vane I've often wondered at
Set up there on the barn, he liked to
　　watch

The wind-flaws veer it round and round,
he said,
And they were satisfied and never
thought
Beyond his reason. But I know more
than they.
I know he set it for a sign, a symbol,
A monument. He died at last quite happy
Believing he had overcome the grass.
Way up under the roof-peak swung the
coffin,
And mostly folk forgot that it was there.
It gathered dust and cobwebs and grew
dim,
You couldn't rightly see it when you
looked,
For all the chaff and hayseed floating
round
Made a kind of blur to any one below.
But, one day, many years after that time,
The farmer's son, going to feed the
horses,
Heard a loud, intermittent sort of bang-
ing
Under the roof, and when he took the
ladder
And climbed up there to see, he found a
strap
Had given way, and the coffin hung head
down
Suspended by the other, and there it
teetered
To and fro with every gust of wind
When the barn-door was open. So he
said
He'd fix it in the morning. But that night
He woke to hear a rap-tap-tapping, so
like
A hammer — but that was a foolish
thought,
He knew directly what the thing must be,
Some stanchion broken loose in the high
wind.
It was a stormy night, so he decided
He'd leave the shutter, or whatever it
was,
Until next day, and fell asleep again.
But in the morning, when he went to
see
About the coffin, it was all nailed up
As firm as could be with a harness-strap.
They thought that very odd, they little
knew
What men can do who have the fear of
grass,

What fear can make men do although
they're dead.
But I have found a hero I can worship.
Napoleon, Julius Caesar, what are these?
They never ruled the grass, it sucked
them up
And drank their brains, and overscored
their towns.
O rare and mighty Captain, here's my
hand.
Mightier than all men have been before!
Dominant Master, even over grass!
Not by the accident of death at sea,
But by compelling force in your own soul
To be forever above these miles of grass,
As no one ever in the world has been.
I feel a leaping fervour to join my hand
With yours, to grasp your bony, brittle
fingers
Unstained by grass-roots. To-morrow I
will go
And offer sacrifices to your manes.
How soaring my thoughts are released at
last
From all the demon grasses that have
gnawed
At them these months past! Now I go to
bed,
And I shall sleep to-night.

.   .   .   .   .

Oh, merciless God! The coffin is not
there!
They tell me it crumbled many years ago,
And where the bones are no one knows.
A jelly-fish
With oozing, pulpy brain, a worthless
polype
Tossed in the air by a Devil-God for fun,
That's what I am, and have been, ever
to think
One could cheat grass! The squirming,
oily grass!
It waited, lapping round and round the
walls
Of the old barn to catch him as he fell.
The terrible, blind grass, feeling its way
With little patting hands. Feeling its
way
Slowly, horribly, over all mankind.
There is no safety anywhere at all
For any people. The clapboards of this
house
Will peel off one by one, the floor will
crack

And through the cracks will come the grinning grass.
My legs will find it stifling them in nets,
My open hands be shut with thongs of grass,
My mouth will hold its roots, my nose its heads,
And in my ears the clatter of its laughter
Will burst my brain and cleave my senseless skull.
I cannot wait and watch, the strain is fire
Stretching and shrivelling me till my bones twist
And drive their needle ends out through my flesh,
And all I see is blood struck through with green,
The bloated green of over-nourished grass.
You dastard God, who set this hideous thing
Upon us! Curse you! Curse you! And all this
Foul, beastly, eating Earth. You shall not have me,
I'll die before I'm eaten. I'll squeeze my hands
About my neck until my eyes spit out
And after them the blood which is my life.
I cannot do it, my fingers are too thin.
But I will find a way to strengthen them,
I'll think of nothing but how to find a way,
I'll kill myself with thinking — "
                    Follows stopped,
And closed the book. "That entry is the last,"
He said, quite simply, "but there's more to tell.
For I went back to Oakfield — that was the nearest
Village to the farm — and found a man
Who'd known the Crawfords in the eighteen eighties.
And when I asked him if they'd had a boarder,
He said, 'Oh, yes, a poor demented fellow,
Sent up there for the quiet of the country.'
He'd been there just about three months, he told me,
And then, one day when no one was about,

He'd hanged himself by an old harness-strap
To one of the barn beams. He said no more.
Perhaps he did not know about the coffin,
And clearly he knew nothing of the man.
I think I've learned a salutary lesson.
I might myself have been one of those doctors
Prescribing easily 'Rest in the country.'
But, all the same, I wish I'd had a chance
To try my hand. And even as I say it,
I realize what harpies science makes us.
I pity him profoundly — yet a case
Like his to perish on a harness-strap!
Good Lord, what brutes we are! And now let's talk
Of something cheerful. Richardson, your whales — "

THE ROSEBUD WALL–PAPER

So you been peekin' int' th' winders o' th' old porch house to th' Four Corners,
Have ye?
Wall, I dunno as anybody wouldn't be puzzled
Not knowin' nothin' 'bout it, an' seein' it th' way 'tis.
I bet you had a time pushin' through them cat-briers
That's growed up all about it.
Terrible stiff bushes they be, an' th' scratchiest things goin'.
Oh, you needn't tell me!
Many's th' first-class tear I've got from 'em in my time.
Not those pertic'ler ones, I ain't no call to go shovin' through them,
An' what on earth you wanted to tackle 'em for beats me.
But, since you been ther',
It's just nater you should want to know.
A house all sagged down an' rotted, an' th' chimbley fell,
An' every room spick an' span with new wall-paper!
Sort o' creepy, was it?
I guess th' creeps is ther' all right,
But we figgered we'd smothered 'em with that rosebud paper.
Mrs. Pearson, th' doctor's wife, had th' choosin' of it.

She went to Boston a-purpose when th'
town decided to put it on.
I al'ays thought 'twas kind o' gay for
what they wanted it for,
But Mrs. Pearson said it had ought to
be gay
An' she's a real tasty woman;
Nobody darsn't go agin her judgment in
this town,
Least of all th' selectmen with th' doctor
chairman o' th' board.
Well, Mr. Day, ther's a good long story
to that wall-paper.
Th' beginnin's way back, all of thirty
year, I guess.
Ther' was a storekeeper here at that time,
name o' Amos Sears.
He warn't a native o' th' place,
I've heerd he come from somewheres
down Cape Cod way,
He just sort o' drifted here an' stuck.
His wife was dead, an' he had a son,
young Amos,
Who used to play around with us boys.
You know what boys be, al'ays in an'
out o' one another's pockets.
Young Amos was a fine, upstandin' chap.
We all favoured him, but he an' Luke
Bartlett was like a plum an' its skin,
You couldn't peel 'em apart.
They beat th' band for mischief an' high
jinks,
Th' rest of us just follered along an'
caught th' lickin's.
'Bout th' time we was gittin' through
school, old Amos died.
We thought, o' course, young Amos'd
settle right down to th' shop,
But he wouldn't hear to it, said he
couldn't rest quiet without he'd done
a bit o' trapesin'
Afore he took root for keeps;
An' first thing we knew, he'd hired Tom
Wetherbee to look after th' business
An' was off.
He wanted Luke should go with him,
But Luke was a real steady youngster,
he'd 'prenticed himself to a stone-
mason
An' wouldn't budge.
I guess now he wishes some he'd gone,
But I dunno, 'tain't easy seein' into other
folks' minds.
I went studyin' surveyin' to Barre
An' warn't here when Amos left.

Luke heerd from him two or three times,
But pretty soon th' letters stopped.
Tom Wetherbee went on 'tendin' to th'
shop
An' payin' his own wages out o' th' earn-
in's.
What he didn't need for repairin' an' to
keep th' stock up, he put in th' bank
for Amos,
But Amos never drawed any of it,
So it just piled up.
What Amos lived on, I dunno, he never
told nobody to my knowledge.
But he lived somehow, an' after ten years
He come back with a wife.
Mrs. Amos was a fine figger of a woman,
With eyes like steel traps, an' a tongue
like a mowin' machine.
She al'ays reminded me of a sumach
when it's turned in th' Autumn,
Sort o' harsh an' bright. You couldn't
see nothin' else
When she was around, but she warn't th'
easy kind,
Her nerves was like a bundle o' fire-
crackers,
An' it didn't take no slow-match to light
'em.
She could do anythin' she set her hand
to,
But she made such a touse doin' it
You'd full as lives not have it done.
Amos found quite a bit o' money wait-
in' for him in th' Wiltshire bank,
An' he found th' store in extra good
shape,
So th' first thing he done was to buy a
house.
Not th' one you see, that didn't come
till later,
Th' third house from th' post-office was
his.
Then he took Tom Wetherbee into partnership
An' moved into his new house, an' things
begun.
They begun with a vengeance, but we
didn't know nothin' for some time.
Th' house, maybe you noticed, stands
quite a piece above th' road.
Did you see anythin' queer 'bout th'
grass either side th' steps?
Well, that was 'cause Amos an' Mrs.
couldn't come to no agreement 'bout
fixin' up th' lawn.

He set by a straight slope an' she wanted
    terraces,
So they had a straight slope to one side
    an' terraces to th' other.
Amos made a joke of it, but Mrs. Amos
    she made a grievance;
She made most everythin' a grievance.
She was al'ays runnin' roun' an' tattlin'
    aginst Amos.
I expect she had one o' them tongues
    they say's hung in th' middle;
If one end got tired, all she had to do
    was let it be an' go right along with
    th' other.
When she warn't scoldin' Amos, she was
    scoldin' 'bout him.
But in th' end 'twarn't him as give, t'was
    her.
She up an' runned away, boarded th'
    afternoon train to Boston
One day while he was mindin' th' shop.
When Amos found out she'd gone
He got Bill Rivers (Rivers kep' th' livery
    stable then) to hitch up his Morgan
    mare in a couple o' shakes
An' drive him over to th' junction, lickety
    split, to ketch th' night train from
    Fitchburg.
He ketched it all right, but 'twas nip
    an' tuck,
Th' conductor was hollerin' "All aboard!"
    when they come in sight o' th' depot.
I mind Rivers was some put out 'cause
    Amos didn't say a single word
All th' way over,
Didn't even think to thank him when
    he got him ther'.
Amos was back in a little over a week,
But he didn't bring Mrs. Amos with him.
Luke went up to see him right away,
An' he told Luke Mrs. Amos had gone
    for a stewardess on a Halifax steam-
    boat.
She had th' sea in her blood, he said,
An' he guessed she couldn't be happy
    livin' so far from it.
It seems she was a New Bedford woman,
An' all her folks had been whalers.
Everybody supposed as how Amos would
    sell his house an' shop
An' go an' settle somewheres his wife
    would like.
But he didn't do no such thing.
He just hung on, lookin' as gloomy as a
    rainy Fourth o' July;

An' he kep' a-hangin', neither here nor
    ther' exactly,
He didn't seem fixed to stay, an' he
    didn't go.
Things went on like that for more'n a
    year,
An' then Amos bought that parcel o'
    land to th' Four Corners, an' put up
    th' house you see.
When 'twas finished, he sold th' old
    house an' moved in.
He druv into town every day to th'
    store,
But folks didn't go out to see him.
He'd turned terr'ble glum an' pernickety
An' Luke was th' only man on real terms
    with him.
You couldn't git anythin' out o' Luke,
He was mum as a fish,
That's how we didn't come to hear 'bout
    Mrs. Richards bein' with Amos
Till she'd been ther' quite a spell.
I dunno's we'd ever have heerd but for
    Bill Rivers drivin' some Summer
    boarders
Up Hog Back one August afternoon.
One o' th' ladies had a faintin' fit or
    somethin',
An' Rivers stopped to Amos's to ask if
    she couldn't rest ther' while th' others
    went on.
He was took all aback when Mrs. Rich-
    ards come out.
Rivers was a awful talker,
He'd twist a bit o' news under his tongue
    same as if 'twas a chaw o' tobaccer
An' I never see a man take such relish in
    spreadin' it.
So th' whole town knowed 'bout Mrs.
    Richards 'fore he'd been back an
    hour.
You know how folks be, once git a story
    started
An' it's off rampagin' like a forest fire,
Somebody said Luke'd know, an' two or
    three went up to Luke's
An' asked him.
But Luke just said "Why not? Amos
    had to have some one to do for him,
An' Mrs. Richards was a respectable
    widow from Millbridge."
Ther' warn't no gainsayin' that, when
    Luke pointed it out,
But what folks don't say ain't al'ays a
    handle to what they thinks.

Luke was a real smart man, an' he
wouldn't listen to a word aginst her
an' Amos,
An' nobody darsn't say a thing to Amos
himself nat'rally.
So it went on. Amos had a hired house-
keeper, said Luke;
Amos had somethin' he shouldn't have
had, said others.
But that was only hearsay, an' Mrs.
Richards' husband had been th' post-
master to Millbridge for years
Until he'd been took off by th' pneumony
three years before,
An' left nothin'.
"So his widow had to work," said Luke's
friends.
Amos's friends didn't say nothin' seein'
he didn't rightly have any,
Barrin' Luke, but that was enough.
Luke was a powerful perseverin' man, an'
wouldn't stand no nonsense.
But, spite o' Luke, ther' was talk, heaps
of it.
You can't keep women from enjoyin' a
story like that,
Nor men neither, I guess.
A good few o' th' boys went out to
Amos's
An' they telled how cozy 'twas out ther',
With white curtings to th' winders
An' th' chiny on th' dresser all set out
elegant,
Nothin' out o' place an' a sort o' cheery
look to everythin'.
Amos had planted apple-trees an' they
was just come to bear.
Early sugar apples they was, you know
th' kind,
Yaller streaked with red an' sweet as
honey.
To hear th' talk you'd think no one else
in th' town
Had apples. Boys will be boys, even
when they ain't,
An' ther' was somethin' 'bout Mrs.
Richards menfolk couldn't have
enough of.
But Amos didn't turn a hair, he know'd
his woman.
'Twas al'ays th' same — apples, an'
cookies, an' blackberry jam, an' a welcome.
Amos warn't like th' same man he was
to th' store,

He'd laugh an' joke, for all th' world like
he used to do in th' old days,
'Twas good to hear him.
Th' women didn't go, though I guess
they was itchin' to,
But none on 'em darst begin.
Women is sticklers for custom,
An' all that whisperin' made a sort o'
fence
They couldn't break through.
I've sometimes wondered if that ain't th'
real use o' women,
To keep things goin' on even an' straight,
with no bumps an' jumps to onsettle ye.
O' course ther's th' other kind o' women,
th' Mrs. Amos kind,
But, praise th' Lord, I ain't had much
to do with them.
But, however stiddy they be, women is
terr'ble cur'ous critters,
They can't git along without a deal o'
worritin' 'bout th' neighbours' con-
cerns.
An' I do believe our Parson's wife was
th' most cur'ous woman ever was.
She was at th' Parson from mornin' till
night to go out to Amos's.
You see she wanted to know how things
was at first hand,
But she know'd better'n to say so.
What she said was that his duty called
him to go an' see if Amos was a errin'
man;
If he kep' a scarlet woman to th' Corners,
th' Parson ought to try an' git him
away from her
An' save his soul.
'Twas a bitter strong argiment to use to
a Parson,
An' she used it every day an' all day.
'Twas clear he wouldn't git no peace till
he went,
An' Parson Eldridge loved peace.
He was a meek little man
An' didn't hold with pokin' in wher'
'twarn't agreeable,
But he had to go, an' he did.
Mrs. Eldridge must have been mortal dis-
appointed,
For all he said when he come back was
That Amos didn't appear to be livin' in
sin.
He didn't say he warn't, mind you,
But he 'lowed to his wife he couldn't see
no openin' to start savin' his soul.

"Th' Almighty works in his own ways,"
he said,
"An' Amos has had a heavy cross to
bear."
He didn't name no names, but it set us
all to thinkin' o' Mrs. Amos
An' what a dance she'd led Amos.
It made us feel sorry for him,
An' after that we kind o' sidelooked his
failin'
If so be as 'twas one,
An' th' tittle tattle an' speculatin' died
down.
Also we was gittin' used to things, I
guess.
Well, they kep' that way for a good fif-
teen year
An' then one night Amos called th' doc-
tor on th' telephone.
His voice was gritty an' shakin', so th'
doctor said afterwards,
An' he know'd at once somethin' had
happened.
Mrs. Richards was real bad, Amos said,
Could th' doctor come right away.
So Dr. Pearson got out his flivver an'
started for th' Corners.
'Twas just commencin' to snow, but
'twarn't so deep th' car couldn't run,
Nor it warn't so light it didn't matter.
'Twas one o' them stingin' snow-storms,
With th' flakes so little you can't hardly
see 'em
But drivin' with a awful force.
That kind o' snow don't seem to lay none
at first,
But ther' ain't no melt to it, an' it goes
on an' on,
Comin' every way to oncet, an' blowin'
up into drifts which you can't make
out wher' they be or ain't till you're
on 'em.
One side th' road'll be swep' clear,
An' th' other all piled up with snow
higher'n your head,
An' all th' time you're as good as blind
'Count o' th' flakes bein' so sharp an'
sheddin' down so almighty fast.
Some men wouldn't have gone out,
Dr. Blake to Millbridge wouldn't, I
know,
But Dr. Pearson went wher' he was
needed;
Battle an' murder an' suddin death
couldn't stop him if any one was sick.

It took him all of an hour to git to th'
Corners,
An' he know'd when he got ther' he
couldn't git back.
Amos met him at th' door,
"I mistake but you're too late, Doctor,"
says he.
And so 'twas. Mrs. Richards was dead.
She'd had a heart attack, and died while
th' doctor was on his way.
Th' doctor done what he could just to
comfort Amos by doin' somethin',
But in th' end he had to tell him 'twas
all over.
Then th' doctor was scared, Amos acted
so queer.
He turned as white as marble, an' as
stiff.
He stood ther', lookin' down at th'
bed,
Lookin' with his eyes like stones o' fire,
Froze an' burnin' at th' same time.
He never moved 'em from th' dead face,
Just stared still as ice, as if he was all
shelled in it,
But somethin' hot an' hard was scaldin'
him inside.
Th' doctor tried to rouse him, but he
didn't seem to hear.
Then th' doctor took his hand an' raised
it up,
But when he let it go, it fell down by his
side agin,
An' Amos didn't seem to notice that he'd
took it an' dropped it.
Dr. Pearson couldn't leave him ther'
alone,
An' he couldn't go anyway 'cause o' th'
storm.
Th' snow kep' risin' higher an' higher on
th' winders.
Th' door was clean blocked, an' when
mornin' come
Th' doctor couldn't see his car, 'twas all
buried in.
All night long Amos had stood just th'
same way
Starin' at th' dead woman.
He might have been dead himself, or a
moniment.
He didn't give a sign he was livin',
Only ther' was mist on a hand-glass th'
doctor held to his mouth.
Th' doctor tried to force some coffee
down his throat,

But his jaw was clinched an' he couldn't
prize it open.
He tried to throw him over so's he could
git him layin' down,
But he couldn't budge him no more'n if
he'd been a granite boulder.
Seem's he had th' stren'th o' ten men
Just to keep standin' ther' lookin' at that
dead body.
'Twas a Sunday night Amos called th'
doctor,
An' 'twas Wednesday mornin' afore th'
storm broke.
An' all that time Amos had stood ther'
without movin' a muscle,
Only he'd sort o' shrunk together; not
stoopin', I don't mean,
But collapsin' in sideways.
Th' doctor put it he looked brittle
Like you might snap him in two but
couldn't overset him nohow.
Maybe 'twas th' sunlight done it. The
sun shone straight in his eyes,
But he never even winked 'em, just kep'
on lookin' an' lookin'.
'Bout 'leven o'clock a sleigh come for
th' doctor.
They'd been tryin' to git to him for two
days
But couldn't, th' drifts was so high,
They'd had to shovel most o' th' way as
'twas.
When th' doctor let 'em in ('twas th'
two Fowler boys an' Sam Gould)
Th' first thing he told 'em was to come
upstairs an' help him with Amos.
But they hadn't hardly set foot in th'
room
When Amos tumbled over on th' floor
— same as a tree, they said,
Stiff from head to foot, not limp like a
man in a faint.
Th' boys picked him up an' laid him on
th' bed in th' next room,
An' th' doctor worked over him; but
'twas hours 'fore he give a sign o'
life,
An' when he did, he went right out of
his head with fever.
He warn't sensible for some days, an' by
that time th' funeral was over an' done
with.
They telled him how 'twas when they
thought he could stand it,
But he didn't seem to care,

I guess he'd buried her in his mind long
before,
Durin' th' storm.
Folks was awful sorry for Amos,
But he didn't act to take much stock in
that neither.
He got up an' went about,
But he didn't go to th' store no more,
An' he didn't take no steps to git a new
housekeeper.
Mrs. Eldridge had a string o' middle-aged
women to suggest for th' place,
But th' Parson kep' her off him some-
how.
I al'ays had a likin' for th' Parson after
that;
Maybe he'd sensed more'n we thought,
all along.
He was a good man, too good to go in-
terferin' with th' Almighty's doin's,
An' that's what you can't say o' most
parsons.
Come Spring, one afternoon when Luke
Bartlett was workin' in his yard,
Tinkerin' at a funeral urn for Elder
Townsend's moniment,
Who should come creepin' in but Amos
Sears.
Luke was all took aback seein' him
comin' in so quiet,
Almost stealin' in, you might say,
'Cause Amos had shown him pretty plain
that he didn't set nothin' by seein'
him.
Luke was a sensitive man, an' Amos
turnin' from him had hurt him dretful.
Amos crep' up to him, peerin' as if he
couldn't see very well,
An' hangin' onto his stick like 'twas a
third leg he couldn't do without.
"Luke," says he, "Luke, we been old
friends, you an' me."
"We have, Amos," says Luke.
"Luke," says Amos agin, "I've had a
sight to bear in my life."
"You have, Amos," says Luke.
"'Tis you, Luke, an' you only can ease
me now, if you will," says Amos, an'
ther' was tears in his eyes.
Luke seen 'em an' they made him feel
sick all over,
Amos warn't one to cry.
Now what do you s'pose it was he wanted
Luke should do?
Why, make a gravestone for Mrs.

Richards, an' that was all ther' was
to it.
Everythin' went slick as paint till they
come to th' inscription;
Amos had that all writ out nice on a
piece of paper
An' he read it to Luke.
"Here lies th' body o' Mary Richards,
Beloved friend an' onlawful wife o' Amos
Sears,
For seventeen years his sole comfort by
th' grace o' God.
Blessed be th' name of th' Lord whose
ways are inscrutable.
Erected by her bereaved husband in th'
sight o' Heaven wher' ther's no mar-
riage nor givin' in marriage,
But joyful meetin' without end for ever
an' ever. Amen."
Luke took th' paper when Amos handed
it to him,
But he couldn't git aholt o' no words
quick enough to speak 'em.
Maybe he'd know'd al'ays, same as
Parson Eldridge,
Maybe he'd thought what he said he
did.
But anyways you look at it that inscrip-
tion was a baffler.
Here was Amos givin' himself away to
th' whole town.
He put it to him so, but Amos said he
wouldn't keep it hid no more,
That 'twas like th' burnin' bush to him,
Th' love they'd bore each other.
Then Luke argid 'twas sacrilege to ask
th' blessin' o' th' Lord for a onsanc-
tified union.
"Who says 'twarn't sanctified," shouted
Amos,
"She was th' Lord's givin' to lighten th'
sorrow He'd set so heavy on me.
God's just, as I've heerd from the pulpit
many a time,
An' I don't cal'ate you're denyin' it,
An' He done th' square thing by me.
I'd be a limpin' coward if I didn't pro-
claim it to all an' sundry,
Witness as I be to His mercy an' com-
prehendin' kindness."
That was too much for Luke He was a
Godfearin' man,
An' he thought Amos had gone blas-
phemin' crazy.
But Amos hadn't, not then.

They went at it, hammer an' tongs,
Each talkin' nineteen to th' dozen.
Then th' pity of it come over Luke,
An' he said he'd try to see it Amos's
way
An' tell him in a month th' stone'd be
near done.
An' Amos had to do with that for th'
time bein'.
Luke made th' gravestone just as Amos
said,
Of good black slate, with th' top poked
up in a little round just big enough for
a angel's head.
An' th' wings reachin' out right an' left
underneath —
Luke had a won'erful knack with angels,
he put on most all his stones —
But when it come to th' inscription, he
couldn't stomach it.
So he just put "Here lies Mary Richards.
God's will be done."
He'd worked it out that them words'd
fit anythin' an' they wouldn't shock
nobody.
If Amos was right 'bout th' Almighty's
designin's, they'd mean that,
An' if he warn't, they'd mean otherwise.
They'd come in handy either way.
Then he went an' set it up himself,
I guess he was kind o' afeared Amos might
break it or somethin'.
Well, th' month was up by then, an' he
had to give his answer to Amos.
I dessay he didn't look forward to it any,
But Luke warn't th' man to shirk a duty,
An' that very evenin', soon's supper was
over, he started for th' Corners.
Luke never telled what happened that
night, but I know for a fact that him
an' Amos never spoke agin.
Ther' warn't much time for speakin', as
a matter o' fact,
For 'twas th' next Tuesday I went up
to th' graveyard.
I don't mind now why, I hadn't buried
none o' my folks for years,
Butt I did go up, an' wandered round
for a spell,
An' all of a suddin I come on Mrs.
Richards' grave.
I didn't know nothin' bout th' inscrip-
tion,
Luke didn't say anythin' 'bout it till 'twas
all over,

So 'twarn't that made me look at th'
  stone.
Then I couldn't scarcely b'lieve my eyes,
Th' stone was all writ over with red
  letters.
First I thought they was blood,
But then I see they was red chalk runnin'
  straight between th' lines Luke had cut.
Yes, Sir, you've guessed it. 'Twas Amos's
  inscription,
Fixed so's to read right along with Luke's;
An' Luke's letters was chalked too, it
  looked all of a piece a little ways off.
Thinks I, th' man who could do that must
  be goin' through blazes,
His grievin' must have plumb crazed him,
I guess 'twould be a Christian act to go
  an' see how he be.
I warn't anxious for goin', but I didn't
  see how any decent man
Could leave them letters an' just go off
  home.
I'll never forgit that drive to th' Corners,
  never.
Every tree I passed looked so's I'd never
  seen it till that minit,
They stuck out at me an' made me
  notice 'em,
I can almost tell you how many leaves
  ther' was to every branch.
An' ther' was th' Ford chuggin' away,
An' th' thrushes singin' their sunset songs,
An' th' sun goin' down behind Hog Back.
My! How black th' mountain was with
  th' sky turnin' all kinds o' colours be-
  hind it,
An' th' air comin' cool an' damp when
  we struck th' shadow o' th' mountain!
'Twas all shadow to Amos's, but back
  yonder t'other side o' th' valley was
  full o' sun,
It holds a good hour longer down ther'.
I jumped out o' th' car an' knocked on
  th' door,
But nobody answered.
Then I done th' same as you did, I peeked
  int' th' winders.
But I couldn't see if Amos was inside
  or not.
In th' end I just made bold an' opened
  th' door.
Red chalk, did I say?
Red, an' white, an' green, an' blue, an'
  purple chalk!
'Twas chalk, chalk, all roun' th' room!

An' 'twas ships done with chalk!
Ther' was a steamboat fightin' waves as
  tall as th' funnels,
Roarin' over her they was, with a noise
  like artil'ry,
I swear I heerd 'em, an' I sensed she'd
  be swamped in a minit.
'Twas a rackin' thing to watch her strug-
  glin' to keep up
With no more chance than a fly under
  a pump-spout.
An' another steamboat (they was all
  steamboats) runnin' on rocks, black
  rocks, with red an' green waves dashin'
  th' ship onto 'em.
Th' next was th' ship goin' to pieces,
An' th' waves was all full o' people clingin'
  to bits o' wood.
Some was hangin' on a little longer,
  some was drownin' as you looked.
I can't describe how awful 'twas.
One ship was afire, with great tongues
  o' yaller flame bustin' through black
  smoke.
Not another vessel was near, just th'
  heavin' sea wallowin' in th' glitter o'
  th' flames.
Ther' was a steamer struck by a bolt o'
  lightnin',
Riv' clear down th' middle, an' th' crew
  was takin' to th' life-boats,
An' th' life-boats was over-loaded an'
  sinkin' as fast as they was launched.
I was cold all over with lookin' 'fore I
  come to th' last,
An' that was th' worst of all.
'Twas a dismasted hulk driftin' with th'
  run o' th' waves,
Only ther' warn't no waves, th' ocean was
  calm,
So calm it made you want to scream.
Dawn was comin', an' th' light was just
  showin' that ther' was a ocean at all,
But 'twarn't no good to see it for ther'
  warn't nothin' to see but it.
'Twas done pretty big, an' you could
  make out ther' was somebody on th'
  ship,
An' that 'twas a woman.
Somehow you know'd she was all th'
  folks ther' was,
An' th' hulk had drifted out o' th' way
  o' other ships,
An' that 'twas just goin' to float along
  like that with th' woman on it

Till th' food give out an' she died o'
starvation.
By that time I was in a sweat all over.
There was a lonesomeness an' a down-
right nastiness 'bout them picters
I can't describe to ye,
But you'd have felt it too, if you'd seen
'em.
I'm glad you didn't, I wouldn't wish any
one to be haunted by 'em same as I
been.
I'd just finished an' was startin' all over
agin 'cause I couldn't keep from it,
When Amos come in.
"You didn't know I could do nothin'
like that, did you?" says Amos,
Beginnin' in th' middle, with not so much
as a "How d'you do" to set things
goin'.
"No," says I, "I didn't. Be these your
doin'?"
"They be," says he. "I'm pretty smart
at drawin' now.
I guess there's more in a man than he
knows till he tries."
I didn't answer, not findin' what to say,
But he didn't notice that.
"I been at it all Winter," he says,
"Quick as I worked out a new way for
th' sea to kill
I slapped it down on th' wall yonder.
I guess I ain't left out a single one; if I
learn I have, I'll put it on th' ceilin'.
Curse that woman! One on 'em must
strike!
Th' sea's so notional at killin' 'twon't
leave her be much longer,
Stan's to reason she's nearin' her term.
Eighteen year she's been at it, temptin'
it an' floutin' it
Same's she's flouted me.
Th' sea won't desert me th' way Luke
done,
Th' sea'll be my friend.
Ain't I prayed to it every night an' mornin'
To git her quick.
I shall go mad 'fore long if somethin'
don't happen.
Joshua"— an' he grabbed my arm —"you
think it'll git her pretty soon, don't
ye?"
I was scared, Mr. Day, scared to hear him
sayin' such things.
He was tremblin' from head to foot, an'
his eyes had a mean, dry look in 'em

I'd never see in nobody's.
"Amos," I says, "be you speakin' o' your
wife?"
"You tarnation fool!" says he, droppin'
my arm an' ragin' off roun' th' room,
"Of course I be. If I warn't a God damn
coward, I'd kill her with my own hands.
But th' sea's my depity; I've appointed
it in my place, an' I'm just waitin' for
news.
An' I'll wait till Hog Back's a valley, an'
don't you go doubtin' it."
I didn't doubt, I was beginnin' to know
Amos,
But what he said riled me so, I couldn't
keep from hollerin' out:
"God in Heaven, man, don't you know
she was drownded in a wreck two year
ago!"
'Twarn't right to tell him like that, an'
I was ashamed to th' marrer at what
I'd done th' minit after,
For Amos went down as if he'd been
shot.
You see, Mr. Day, he couldn't git a
divorce
'Count o' havin' signed a paper agreein'
to a separation when his wife left him,
An' that queered his case accordin' to
law.
An' here he might ha' been married to
Mrs. Richards for two years anyway,
If he'd ha' know'd.
I can't think how he didn't, 'cept that
'twas in a Portland paper I read it
One time when I was down that way.
'Twas enough to upset any man comin'
on him suddin like that,
But I warn't prepared for his way o'
takin' it.
I hadn't had time to think o' th' half
o' what I'm tellin' you
When he was up an' runnin' at me with
a chair.
"Get out!" he screamed, "you get out or
I'll smash you into hell."
Chair for chair, I was no match for him,
It was just dodge an' run for me.
When I got to the door I made a dash
for it,
An' I'd just got my car goin' when he
reached me,
But a motor on high ain't a thing to fool
with
An' I got away.

I druv for all th' car was worth to Parson
    Eldridge's
An' telled him th' whole story.
He got a posse o' men together an' off
    we all went back to Amos's.
But we couldn't find him anywheres
    about th' place.
Parties searched th' woods, and th' ponds
    was dragged,
But we never come on a thing, not till
    this day.
Nobody knows if he's dead or livin'.
All th' towns for miles was notified,
But he warn't never found,
No one ain't ever see hair or hide of him
    since that day.
That was six Summers come next,
An' anybody you don't know's dead ain't
    lawfully such for I don't know how
    many years,
So nothin' couldn't be done with his
    effects.
Ther' stood th' house an' them fearsome
    picters
Any one could see 'em through th' winders
    if they was lookin' for 'em,
An' they was scary as I can't tell ye.
It got to be a dare with th' little fellers
    to go out an' peek,
An' some o' th' boys couldn't sleep nights
    for 'em.
After John Baxter's youngest screamed
    himself into fits,
Th' selectmen took it on themselves to
    order th' walls papered.
'Twouldn't injure his property none to
    put it on, they 'lowed,
He could rip it off when he come back,
    if he'd a mind to.
Th' house must ha' been jerrybuilt to
    have fell away so in th' time,
But that was kind o' like Amos's life,
    warn't it?
'Twas jerrybuilt clear through, I guess.
But you just thank your stars for them
    rosebuds, that's all.

THE CONVERSION OF A SAINT

"Why, Sallie Williams,
I'm proper glad to see ye.
Go straight in t' th' clock-room,
I blazed a fire in ther' this afternoon to
    take th' chill off
An' it's nice an' warm.

Now you set right down in th' red plush
    rocker
An' git your breath,
You look all beat out.
Just you set still an' rest
And I'll run out t' th' kitchen
And git ye a good strong cup o' tea an'
    some cookies.
I won't be a minute."

"You're real good, Lidy,
But I don't hold with snacks between
    meals,
Never did, an' I don't dar'st begin now.
Th' tea'll be enough an' plenty.
I been a long walk
An' I do feel a mite tired."

"I'll leave th' door open
So's we can talk through.
It's been some consid'able time since you
    was here,
All of two months, I do b'lieve.
I was goin' to git Oren to drive me into
    town
For a visit with you one o' these days.
However did you happen out here?
On foot too.
We ain't so young as we was, you an'
    me."

"We ain't, Lidy, that's a fact,
Though I keep pretty spry, consid'rin'."

"It's awful ugly footin' this time o' year,
Th' roads ain't dry yet.
A couple more weeks should harden 'em.
Now you just drink that,
I made it fire-strong a-purpose,
As Father used to say."

"It's real revivin',
I feel better a'ready."

"To think o' your trapesin' way out here,
An' in your best magenta silk too.
I must say I take it very kind.
But 'pears like we be gittin' strangers
When you have to dress up for me."

"To tell th' truth, Lidy,
You ain't just th' reason I put on this
    dress.
I had another,
But I'm most afraid to tell it."

"Don't you be silly, an' le' me take your
cup.
This ain't no time o' day to be keepin'
things from me.
Wa'n't you th' first I told
When I brought my mind to marry Oren,
An' ain't I been sharin' my troubles with
ye ever since!
You got somethin' on your mind, Sallie,
I thought as much when you first come
in.
Now you tell me right out what 'tis.
We're old to be hangin' back with one
another
An' I'm bound to git it sooner or later.
If you didn't come out a-purpose to see
me
What did you come for?
Ther' ain't nobody else to visit out this
way
As I'm aware."

"Ther's a lot o' folks, Lidy,
Only they're dead.
You're forgittin' th' buryin'-ground."

"Sakes alive! What be you a-doin' to th'
buryin'-ground?
I didn't know you ever went near it
'Cep' on Decoration Day."

" I never did before.
I wanted to see Miss Ziba's grave."

"Miss Ziba's grave!
Well, you do take me all aback.
I al'ays thought you hated her."

"Hate ain't no word for th' way I felt
'bout that woman.
That's why I wanted to see her grave."

"I don't sense your meanin', Sallie.
You'd best begin right at th' beginnin'
An' tell me straight through."

"I guess I'll have to.
It's preyin' on me somethin' awful.
What's done's done, an' I'm glad,
But I'm kind o' scared too.
Lidy, you promise you won't tell a soul,
Not even Oren."

"I won't if it'll ease you. Ther'!
Now you git it right out, dear,
I'm listenin'."

"You mind th' trouble, Lidy?"

"Don't I? Why even us girls was all
sides 'bout it.
I've never had nothin' to do with Hannah
Williams
Nor Addie Belle Dyer since."

"Well, that trouble sp'iled my life.
I never telled you how it laid on me.
I couldn't bring myself to speak on't even
to you.
But it's been a dwellin' horror all my life,
Like a ghost-story,
Only 'twas I was ha'nted, not a house.
It begun when I was goin' on ten year
old.
Miss Ziba'd al'ays been friendly with my
folks,
I used to call her Aunt Ziba.
She made lovely paper-dolls;
Many's th' Sat'day afternoon I spent over
to her house
Playin' with 'em,
An' an old doll's-house she had when she
was a little girl.
Then all at once it come, th' quarrel.
Mother telled me I wa'n't never to go to
Miss Ziba's agin.
I mind how she looked when she said
it,
Not like Mother at all, but a stranger.
That look chilled me clear to th' marrer,
I git th' shivers now, thinkin' of it.
'Twas as if Mother was hid away an'
someone else'd took her place,
I ain't never had a shock to beat that,
So lonely as 'twas, an' never been nothin'
else since, not once.
I ran away up garret an' cried all after-
noon.
I don't run now,
Habit keeps folks quieter if that's all it
does.
One day I met Miss Ziba out walkin'
An' she stared right through me as if I
wa'n't ther'.
That made me feel creepy
As though I wa'n't ther' myself.
O' course in a village like ours
You can't help meetin's,
But I never got used to Miss Ziba actin's
though she could put her foot right
down on me
An' feel th' boards under, just th' same.

I used to look in t' th' windows o' Mr.
    Gale's shop
To see if I could see myself in 'em
After she'd gone by.
Then th' girls begun.
Addie Belle took a notion to stick her
    tongue out at me
Whenever Miss Price's back was turned.
She'd do it a dozen times a forenoon.
An' then she an' Hannah Williams'd
    h'ist up their desk tops, an' whisper
    an' giggle behind 'em
Till Miss Price ketched 'em at it.
Tricky wa'n't th' word for them two.
Hannah'd say she wanted a drink an' ast
    to go out to th' well;
She had to pass me to git to th' door,
An' goin' an' comin' she'd give me a
    nasty pinch.
I'd ha' complained to Miss Price, only
    I darsn't,
Knowin' ther' was somethin' 'bout me,
Somethin' terrible, an' 'couldn't guess
    what.
If it hadn't ha' been for you an' one or
    two o' th' others
I think I'd ha' died for shame."

"Why, Sallie dear, you're tremblin'.
I hadn't no knowledge you took it so
    hard.
We wouldn't let Addie Belle or Hannah
See our poppy-shows, I remember.
You said they shouldn't see yours for a
    whole packet o' pins.
I've laughed over it lots o' times since."

"I expect you thought my dander was
    up, Lidy,
An' it ought to ha' been.
But th' peth was all gone out o' me,
I wanted to cry all th' time,
An' I wouldn't ha' gone to school
Only Mother made me."

"What was it all about anyway?
I don't b'lieve I ever heerd."

"That's th' awful part.
I don't know no more'n th' dead.
I ast Mother once, but she wouldn't say
    a word,
An' th' look she give me settled me not
    to ast agin,
'Twas like th' first time only worse.

Mother an' me wa'n't never th' same
    after.
I couldn't feel to love her like I should
With that secret in between."

"Sallie! You don't say!
An' you an' your Mother livin' alone
    together twenty year;
It must ha' been all o' that."

"It was, twenty-three.
We lived together, but we didn't speak,
Not really speak, I mean.
I used myself for her hard as I could,
But that was all ther' was to it.
I've al'ays been good at flourishin' flowers
An' Mother liked a posy by her bed,
But them flowers was th' nearest we come
    to speakin'.
I wa'n't no lonelier after she died
Than I was with her livin'.
Did I hate Miss Ziba, Lidy?
'Tis past expressin', I tell ye.
Wa'n't it her took my Mother away
    from me,
An' all th' youth an' splendour I'd a
    right to?
Girls needs cossetin' all through th'
    growin' years
But I didn't never have any,
An' I just lost heart for gay times an'
    junketin's.
I was a sort o' Ishmael to my own seemin'.
I read his story every night 'fore I went
    to bed one Winter,
He got to be a kind o' blood cousin,
An' th' thought of ther' bein' another
    of us comforted me some.
If it hadn't ha' been for you, Lidy —
But ther', if it hadn't been so between
    us
I wouldn't be here now, tellin' ye.
Don't mind me, dear, tears is a help
    sometimes,
An' I feel dretful low-sperited."

"But what about th' buryin'-ground,
    Sallie?"

"Yes, th' buryin'-ground. I'm comin' to
    that.
When I heerd last Tuesday Miss Ziba
    was dyin'
It acted like a crust broke up in me
    somewheres,

I was so rej'iced 'twas like a jubilee.
I tried to pray aginst it,
But 'twa'n't no use.
I was as happy as though I'd heerd
    trumpetin' angels
Callin' me to dance before th' ark,
Th' way they done in th' Bible.
I couldn't go to th' buryin', nat'rally,
But I watched it from th' garret window
Windin' up along,
An' when I couldn't see it no more
I went an' got out this dress
An' pressed it nice an' tidy, an' put new
    lace to th' neck an' sleeves.
Ther' was somethin' I had to do, Lidy.
You needn't feel obleeged to remark it
    none,
'Cause I had to do it.
I'd got to feelin' old scores must be paid,
An' I was goin' to pay 'em for keeps.
I waited a couple o' days
Till I 'lowed all th' tendin' an' visitin'd
    be done
An' nothin' left to fix but th' stone,
An' you couldn't expect that for some
    weeks;
Asa Frye makes real pleasin' stones, but
    he's slow.
When I got up this mornin' an' see
    what a day 'twas,
With th' wind Southerly an' th' snow-
    drops up an' noddin',
I know'd 'twas just time.
So I dressed me all up,
Same's I planned,
An' come right along up here to th'
    buryin'-ground.
I can't go on, Lidy.
It's too dretful now.
Don't, don't let me go on.
Lidy, you mustn't let me go on,
I can't do it."

"There now, dearie, don't you fret.
You better tell it all out,
It's th' holdin' in's hurtin' ye.
What'd you do, Sallie?
I want to know complete."

"It's awful, Lidy,
A great deal more awful'n you'd think
    'twould be.
I walked right up to Miss Ziba's grave
    an'— kicked it.
Th' earth was all soft, o' course,

An' mounded up th' way they al'ays
    leaves 'em.
I kicked that soft loam hard's ever I
    could,
An' I kep' kickin' till I made a big hole.
When I got through I felt as light as
    air,
All my hate was gone.
I was all full up with lovin' kindness.
Then I went to work an' filled up that
    hole with my bare hands
An' come right over to you.
Oh, Lidy, don't look at me like that!
I had to do it, an' I feel so happy,
So diff'rent from common,
Like ther' was was wings on my feet
An' my eyes peerin' to a sunrise."

"But 'twas wicked, Sallie,
A wicked, wicked thing.
I don't see how you, a church member,
Could bring yourself to do such a thing."

"Neither do I.
Half of me's just as shocked as you
    be,
But th' other half's so glad I could clap
    my hands."

"Don't, Sallie.
It ain't like you.
'Tis a very wrong thing to meddle with
    a grave.
Oh, whatever shall you do now
With such a mem'ry?
Poor little Sallie!
Poor child! I can't see my way at all."

"Now don't you go on like that, Lidy.
Half of me's happy an' I ain't wishful to
    lose it.
You were plumb right,
Tellin' you's done me a heap o' good.
Th' happy half's drownin' out th' other
    quicker every minute.
What am I goin' to do?
I settled that when I was pressin' out
    my dress.
I'm goin' to take in boarders.
I do enjoy havin' company around.
I sent a couple o' notices to the Boston
    papers yesterday.
I'll bring th' answers right along to you
Soon's I git any.
P'raps I can git a real nice young man,

An' maybe a mother an' daughter.
I should love to have a romance goin'
on
Right under my own roof.
That house has had nothin' but gloomy
things happen in it
Long's I can remember.
Now I'm goin' to give it smilin' things
if I can git to do it."

"But, Sallie, what will th' minister say?
You can't go on goin' to meetin'
With this on your mind.
You'll have to tell him."

"I shan't do no such a thing.
I guess I'll give up goin' to meetin' for a
spell.
I been steady at it all my life,
But I can't see's any good come from
it.
I'm goin' to be a errin' sperit for th'
rest o' my days,
Hell can't be no worse nor what I've had;
Anyhow, I'm goin' to resk it.
If th' boardin' works, maybe I'll take a
house down to Boston
An' keep at it Winters.
Oh, we're goin' to have a beautiful time,
Lidy!
An' I'll git my folks to hire Oren's auto-
mobile for picnics an' things.
My! If ther' ain't Oren now, drivin' in
t' th' barn.
I must be goin' on along home.
Don't you tell him, Lidy.
If I'm goin' to live with a sin on my
conscience
Th' fewer knows it th' better.
An' don't you worrit 'bout me a mite,
Like's not I'll be sorry as can be one o'
these days,
But I can't see my way to it now.
I'll be up agin soon's th' answers come.
Ain't th' snow-drops lovely with th' moon
on 'em?
I don't know as I rec'lect a forwarder
Spring,
Ther'll be cherry-blows in next to no
time.
No, I won't stay, dear.
I'll just git me a bit o' supper,
An' set that new knittin' stitch on a
needle 'fore I go to bed.
I'm so glad I come in."

THE GRAVESTONE

"That was a funny thing. I guess you
were startled
Finding it that way underneath the stairs."

"Startled I was, and something a good
deal more.
For I was thinking of nothing but my
ball
And how I couldn't say that I had lost
it
Not being allowed to play with it in-
doors.
I didn't want a licking or a lecture,
But mightily I wanted back my ball,
And fumbling round there in the dark
I touched
Stone, shivering stone, a cold long stretch
of slate,
Waist-tall, about, going clear down to the
floor.
I hardly dared to trust the feel of it,
So I struck a match and there it was,
a head-stone
With writing on it, good, square, march-
ing letters;
I saw that much before the match went
out.
The dark was rather awful afterwards.
Being twelve years old by our Bible, and
a healthy chap,
I didn't really suppose that any one
Was buried there under Grandfather's
staircase,
But I couldn't help thinking a little it
might be so.
It might — and then I went and got a
candle.
Of course there wasn't any grave; the
stone
Just stood there, leaning up against the
stair-back,
Dusty the way old furniture is dusty,
House-dust, you know, not weather-dust,
no rain
Had run its mark upon it, top to bottom;
There were no bird-stains, nor snail trails,
nor anything
Like creeper smears, it might have been
a table
Without its legs, shoved out of the way
in there,
But for the letters. They were plain
enough,

And so I read them: 'Here lies the mortal
body
Of Joseph Crocker, entered into rest . . . '
After that came a gap with nothing on it,
Where the surface was all neatly scraped
and chiselled
So that the date was gone, but down
below
I read again: 'Beloved Son of Joel
And Maryum Crocker,' and then there
came some poetry,
A hymn, I think, but I don't remember
that;
My mind was taken up with Joseph
Crocker
Whose tombstone stood here like a
table-top
Gathering household dust under the stairs.
I crept out, sober enough, as you may
think,
And left the ball behind me with the
stone.
A stone without a grave didn't seem
religious;
It shocked me, and I couldn't figure why.
I didn't like the fact of its being there,
With all the family going up and down
Over the legend of a 'mortal body,'
Which wasn't there as it should have
been, and shouldn't;
That would be worse, of course, and yet
more fitting.
It was rather a nasty riddle for a boy
Of twelve, set down so in the family
Bible,
And as the sixth James Crocker. But that
was why
I knew immediately I couldn't take it
As an omen or anything like that. I
couldn't
Recollect a single Joseph. We had Johns,
And Amoses and Joels, and lots of others,
But not a Joseph could I bring to mind.
Yet it would seem that once there must
have been one,
For people don't keep gravestones as
ornaments
With fancy names on them, at least, not
now,
Perhaps they used to, that I didn't know.
I didn't like it anyway, and after a time
I liked it so little I screwed my courage
up
To speak to Grandfather. How well I
see

The old book-room, with the October
sun
Shining on gold and leather up and down
The walls, and getting a sort of extra
spryness
From the crimson maple-leaves outside
the window.
The fire, a sunny fire, crackled and tried
To burn with solar brilliance, and impress
As white a star in the balls of the brass
andirons.
Grandfather was smoking and reading as
he always did
Just before sunset until supper time.
I sidled in and wandered round the room
Staring at the book-backs I knew by
heart,
And fingering the pistols Great Uncle
John
Had used in Egypt on his famous tour,
And pretty soon Grandfather saw me
there.
'Well, Jim,' said he, taking his spectacles
off,
'What do you want here at this time of
day?'
That was a good beginning, I knew the
signs,
Twelve years might say a word to seventy
When seventy laid its spectacles aside.
I ventured round the table and sat down
Gingerly in the writing-table chair,
And perching on its edge I said my word,
Somewhat in haste as doing a fearful
thing,
And one not altogether warranted,
But which admitted of a subtle doubt
As to its perfect impropriety.
Armed with this doubt to cover my in-
trusion,
If such it were, on ground where tres-
passers
Would not be welcomed, I advanced my
query.
'Grandfather,' said I, for I was in it then,
Committed to the hazard of even chances,
'Why do you keep a gravestone under
the stairs?'
My ears sang in the silence that came
after.
The ticking of the banjo clock on the
chimney
Was brass and fury banging on chill
doom.
The fire roared like a great conflagration.

But Grandfather put his finger-tips to-
gether
And carefully tapped them one upon
another.
Then he looked up and smiled, and with
a sigh
I settled my unbroken back against the
chair-back,
Wondering a little, but vastly comforted,
And found the fire good, and the sun
most pleasant,
And thought how pretty all the gold and
calf-skin
Book-backs were looking, and the maple-
tree
Crimson-red, standing outside the win-
dow.
'So you've found the tombstone,' Grand-
father was saying,
When I got back enough to listen to him
After considering the beauty of the world
And all its special attributes just there
And then, where I was at the moment
sitting.
'It's a curious tale, my boy, but you shall
have it,
It will tell you something of your family.
You know, of course, we're comfortably
off,
Very well off indeed. Well, we owe that
To thrifty forebears. Prudence was their
motto.
They saved their pennies, perhaps a bit
too much
For modern notions. My great-grand-
father
Was a certain Joel Crocker, a driving
man
Who farmed this place and pulled good
crops by force
Of will out of the rocks, and made them
yield
More profit by double than his neigh-
bours' land,
Or they themselves, could ever learn the
trick of.
He worked the farm alone with his two
sons.
James, a steady lad, was like his father,
But Joseph favoured his mother's people
more.
He wasn't wild or bad, but he hated
farming,
And used to steal what time he could
to read

Geography, always geography, he was
daft about it,
Could name the cities of China like a
teacher,
And tick off rivers as fast as you could
count,
While as to exports and imports, you
couldn't stump him
Jumping all round the map. He used to
draw
India and Asia from memory, and all the
Islands
That men then knew of in the Pacific
Ocean,
And give them to his mother, and she
would frame them
With bits of silk and ribbon from her
piece-bag
And hang them in her bedroom. It didn't
please Joel
To have him do it, but after all 'twas
better
Than hanging round the store where they
kept a bowl
Of rum punch on the counter all the
time.
So Joel said nothing, and Joseph made
his maps.
One Winter, James came down with a
sudden fever.
Three days sufficed, poor chap, for him
to turn
His toes up, and there was an end of
James,
The very darling of his father's heart.
Old Joel was staggered, James was more
than the apple
Of his eye, more like the eye itself he
was,
The ripe, sweet kernel of his father's soul.
As I have said, Joel was a thrifty man,
And hated like blazes to part with hard-
earned money;
But James, the rapture of his life, was
dead.
He had not given much to James when
living,
It had not been his way, but now he
grieved
At things he did not speak of, only he
went
A whole day's journey down to Nashua
To Jacob Crufts, the mason, and ordered
a stone
Of fine blue slate to put at James's grave.

Well, by and by, the stone came home,
but somehow
Jacob had blundered at the name and
carved
"Joseph" where he should have chiselled
"James."
Old Joel was just beside himself to see it.
The whole stone spoilt and the money
gone for nothing.
He loaded that stone into a cart at once,
Although the sun had just that moment
gone
Down behind Greyback. He wouldn't
wait for supper
He was so angry, but took it in a pail,
And jogged the night long down to
Nashua,
And there he got at dawn, fussed as a
rooster
All spurred and spanked up for a cocking
bout.
Crufts was in bed, but Joel had him
out
In no time, and standing with him in the
street,
He damned and tongue-lashed very hand-
somely,
Not caring a brass farthing who might
hear.
He told Crufts he had ordered plainly
"James,"
But Crufts said "No, 'twas Joseph was
the name."
Joel said that couldn't be, he never
thought
Of Joseph, never, and he always thought
of James,
And more than usual now that he was
dead.
Crufts didn't know anything about that,
of course,
And said so with an acid sullenness,
Business was business, and his was making
gravestones.
Joel, being a father, knew which son was
dead
As he insisted. Crufts, a dogged man,
Replied that might be so or not, he
couldn't say,
But Joseph was the name was given him.
"Joseph's alive," roared Joel. "That's a
pity,"
Admitted Crufts, "for it's a handsome
stone."
Joel said he wouldn't pay a cent for it,

Crufts might have it back, but Crufts
declared
It was no use to him, which fact indeed
Was evident. Finally when they'd been
at it
Hot and heavy for an hour or more,
Crufts was visited by inspiration.
"But you have a son named Joseph," he
shouted out,
"And he'll die some day, keep the stone
for him."
Joel, indignant, pointed to the date,
"He'll die some time," he said, "but not
that time.
That's passed." A quivering argument to
plant
In the other's bosom. Poor Crufts
scratched his head.
Then suddenly he swore, "By Gum! I
have it!
The date's done shaller, I can cut it
out.
You take the stone at half price, and set
it by
Till such time as it's needed. And I'll
make another
And put 'James' on it right as a trivet
this time."
So the bargain was struck with no great
satisfaction
On either side, but the best that could be
done.
The stone with "James" was set up in
the graveyard,
And the "Joseph" stone put by for later
use.
Now whether it was the presence of his
gravestone
Here in the house, or the lonesomeness
now James
Was gone, or what it was, Joseph grew
moody.
He couldn't stand the farm, he almost
sickened
At staying on it, and one fine Summer
morning
He ran away to Portsmouth and went to
sea.
He came back three years later for a
week,
But after that he never came again,
And they heard at last that his ship and
every soul
On board of her was lost. Joel was sorry,
Of course, but no one ever rightly knew

Which he was sorrier for, the loss of
Joseph
Or the fact that now he couldn't use the
tombstone.
However, after his first grief was over,
He used to say, "There'll be another
Joseph
Some day, and they'll be glad to have
this gravestone
Handy, so they won't have to buy an-
other."
But he was wrong, there's been no other
Joseph,
It seems like flying in the face of Fate
To give a boy a name that's on a tomb-
stone,
As if you put him like money in a bank
Waiting until it's called for. No Crocker
woman
Would name a son of hers Joseph. No,
Jim,
There never will be another Joseph
Crocker.'
Then I, with all the bravery of twelve,
Rose from my chair and solemnly averred
That I would name my first son Joseph.
But
I have not kept that vow, though I've
five sons.
Do you think my wife would ever agree
to Joseph?
A bachelor is prodigal with vows,
Wait till you're married, my friend, and
you will see."

THE REAL ESTATE AGENT'S TALE

The furniture goes with the house. Oh,
yes.
There ain't no silver, but silver's never
let,
At least I never heard of that being
done.
There's lots of dishes though, and only
a few
Are cracked or chipped, the owner was
very careful.
She washed her plates as though they
were her babies,
And everything's spick and span, just as
she left it.
Maybe you'll want a little bit more comfort
In your chairs. But you can send up one
or two

If these don't suit, and probably a spring
sofa
For the sitting-room, the one there's hard
as nails
And I don't fancy you'll like its horse-
hair cover,
Folks don't to-day. My wife couldn't
abide ours,
We broke it up for fire-wood long ago.
It's a pretty place, the more you look it
over,
And the rent is very reasonable indeed.
Now just you let me make a note or two:
You'll take it as it stands without the
sofa,
And you don't want the bed in the East
Chamber,
Nor the kitchen things, and you do want
an ice-chest.
Nothing more? Well, now, there's just
one thing
Which may surprise you, but I wouldn't
keep
That clock if I was you. Oh, it goes all
right.
It hasn't missed its strike in fifty years.
I've come here every Sunday and wound
it up,
Sam Gould, Miss Bartlett's nephew, told
me to.
He's all that's left of the family, he and
the clock,
But I don't notice he's sent for it to
Boston.
It's a very handsome thing, the sort that
dealers
Hunting old furniture can't get enough
of —
We have a good few of the tribe up here,
Nosing about whenever there's an auc-
tion —
But for all that I wouldn't want it round.
I guess I'm mighty poor at real estating
To say a thing like that, but still I
wouldn't,
Not if 'twas me. You needn't laugh, Mr.
Brooks,
I've got a funny feeling about that clock.
I want to let it stop, and tie a rope
Around it good and tight just where the
wood
Juts out to hold the face, and then I want
To hang it up in the old apple-tree
Outside my office and let it swing and
rot

With snow, and rain, and sun, until it
drops.
You think I'm mad, I guess. Well, Sir,
I'm not.
But I've got my own ideas about that
clock.
It's a whole hour to train time, if you
care
To hear why I feel so, I'll tell you why.
That clock's been in the Bartlett family
Time out of mind, ever since Simon
Bartlett
Brought it from England on one of his
long voyages,
The longest voyage he ever took and the
last.
He was captain of a ship trading the
Indies,
Not the West Indies, of course you un-
derstand,
But the other Indies, off around Cape
Horn.
This time he'd been away above two
years
And back he came, slapping along as fast
As winds would blow him, expecting to
be married
Soon as his ship had got her anchor down.
The war of eighteen-twelve was on and
booming,
But Cap'n Si didn't know a thing about
it,
Until a British ship fired plunk at him.
He made what fight he could with only
muskets,
But the British ship had a bellyful of
cannon,
And pretty soon 'twas strike or go down
flyin',
So Cap'n Si, being prudent, hauled his
flag.
They put a prize crew on him just for
luck,
And off he went under the Union Jack,
And found himself clapped into Dart-
moor jail,
With no way of sending word back to his
Sweetheart
That he wasn't hobnobbing down with
Davy Jones.
They let him out after the war was over.
He'd made some money carving little
toys,
For sailors in those days knew how to
whittle

And visitors were always keen on buying,
And I guess he had some more sewed in
his clothes
The warden had overlooked. But all his
keepsakes
Were gone, the presents he was bringing
home
To give his bride. He wouldn't come
empty-handed,
He bought this clock, now he had time
again,
It seemed to him time had been all
choked up,
Clogged somehow, like the wheels of a
dirty watch,
While he had been in prison. He might
have thought
Amanda would have married, but he
didn't,
And she hadn't. So that at least was
right as rain,
And they set up housekeeping with the
clock.
You bet he wound it every week, he
wouldn't
Have let it stop for a hundred thousand
dollars.
He'd got time back, and he meant to hold
on to it.
He did, being over a hundred when he
died.
And I don't suppose the jail seemed more
than five minutes
When he looked back. He'd given up
sea-fearing
And moved quite a ways inland, to
Nashua,
And then on here to Franklin. Here he
stuck,
And here his folks have been sticking ever
since,
Till Sam Gould went away and Miss
Bartlett died.
The Bartlett family just lived by that
clock.
You never caught one of them being late
For meals, or getting up, or going to bed.
The clock was in at all the goings on.
No Bartlett woman was married from a
church,
They used to stand the minister in front
Of the clock to marry them, and all the
guests
Looked right into that clock face all the
time

The wedding was going on, and ten to
one
The clock would strike and you couldn't
hear a thing
Was said. It was the same with christen-
ings.
Every Bartlett baby was baptized
In front of the clock, and every Bartlett
corpse
Got prayed off into Heaven with that
clock
Tick-tocking up above, and striking too,
Funerals weren't more serious to Bart-
letts
Than the clock's striking. I've heard my
mother say
They purposely arranged to have it so.
It really was uncanny how their lives
Moved and circled about that grim old
clock.
Bartletts were born, and Bartletts died,
but the clock
Was always the same, it never changed
a bit.
When I was a boy I used to come with
Sam
And stand for hours watching those
rocking ships
Up there. But when Sam's father died
and I
Saw those ships rocking up above his
coffin
They turned me sort of sick, I wanted to
smash them.
That clock was treated as if it was alive,
And there it stood, grinning with all its
ships,
Not caring a brass farthing what occurred
To any one. I got a hunch that day
That the clock had a nasty soul, that it
liked to watch
The family like puppets in a show
And that some day it would get bored
and do
Some horrid thing. It was a curious fancy,
Wasn't it? But maybe I was righter
Than I could ever dare believe I was.
The Bartletts owned a lot of land round
here,
Old Si had spread himself when it came
to land.
Some of it was farm, some woodland,
some was nothing,
And kept as such for a full century.
I guess the Captain started the first store

They had here. He did a thriving trade
In groceries, and calicoes, and hardware,
But somehow the family drifted out of
business
And long before my day they'd sold the
store
And only kept the farm. But the new
West
Cut farming into bits all through this
country.
Only some folks don't know when they've
had enough
And the Bartlett family hated change like
poison.
George Bartlett, having only girls, the
neighbours
Used to wonder what would happen when
he died.
At first, of course, they thought the girls
would marry,
And Jane, the youngest, did — but not
a farmer,
Her husband was the doctor here, and a
good one,
But country practice ain't a roarin' gold
mine.
Still it kept them, and Jerusha found a
man
To rent the farm, and things went on like
that
For a good many years. Then the doctor
died
And left his wife and Sam without a cent.
Jerusha took them in, but the farm rent
Didn't go far with three of them, so
Jerusha
Sold off her wood; not the land, you
understand,
But the trees on it. The Diamond Match
people
Sent saw-mills in and cut down every-
thing.
There were miles and miles looked like
the Day of Judgment,
Stumps, and dead twigs, and rotting
chips, and cinders.
The city folks were mad as hops about it,
But if Jerusha cared she didn't say so.
I went to Hanover about that time,
And then to Law School. How they got
the money
To send Sam down to study pharmacy,
I've only just found out. They borrowed
it,
And at enormous interest. By that time

Sam's mother had died, and there was
just those two,
Sam and Miss Bartlett, with the measly
farm rent
To carry them. Miss Bartlett made it do,
Pinching along on next to nothing here
Till Sam got his diploma. Just a year
After he'd started working in a drug-
store,
The man who rented the farm got sick
and died.
And there was poor Miss Bartlett with no
money,
Not a single dollar bill that she could
count on,
And owning acres and acres of useless
land!
If dirt was only dollars now — but it
isn't.
Land-poor she was, and a very bad case
of it.
Of course she meant to let the farm again,
But no one wanted it, and her wood land
Was nothing but a six years' growth of
saplings.
One afternoon Miss Bartlett sent me word
She wanted to see me. So I went right
down
And had a talk with her. She told me
everything
And asked me whether I could sell her
land.
I didn't think I could, and said so frankly.
"Martin," says she, "I'll give you just
six months,
If it ain't sold then, I know what I will
do."
Now she might have meant she'd join
Sam in the city,
Or take in washing, or go out for a house-
keeper.
But she didn't mean any of those things,
She meant she'd kill herself. I don't
know how
I got that, but I did. She might sell land,
The same as you might have your teeth
pulled out,
But she couldn't leave that house. It
seemed to me
As though she and the clock were wound
together
And the house was the shell of both. The
clock was ticking
In the silence that followed after she had
spoken.

It ticked so loud I heard it in the parlour
Where we were sitting. It seemed as
though her heart
Was ticking with it somehow, or that
what
I listened to was not the clock at all
But her heart beating, pounding on the
silence
To break it down. 'Twas fearfully un-
canny,
And when I left her and went into the
entry
There were those everlasting ships rock-
ing and rocking,
And telling me something plainly all the
time.
I couldn't pass them, and I got the no-
tion
That they were shouting at me I could
sell
The old land if I dared — just if I dared.
I hauled my feet away at last, and when
I got outside I called myself some names
I wouldn't like another man to call me.
I thought I knew the clock was only
fancy,
But I couldn't shake the idea of Miss
Bartlett.
I knew I'd got that right, it was suicide
She had in mind. You bet I didn't leave
A stone unturned about selling that land.
I advertised it out of my own pocket.
Five months went by and I was almost
crazy,
And then one morning I landed a cus-
tomer.
He was rich as mud and mad as a March
Hare,
He wanted rural solitude, he said.
I told him he would find it at the farm
And he agreed he should. But, mad as
he was,
I couldn't plant on him a single acre
Of that poor spindly, second-growth wood
land.
What ever had been the farm he wanted
badly,
But he wouldn't touch a yard of anything
else.
I didn't blame him, the wood lots were
a sight,
And 'twas luck you couldn't see them
from the farmhouse.
For Miss Jerusha couldn't touch the
farm trees

They being rented at the time, you re-
member.
I tell you, Sir, I simply soaked that fellow,
I made him pay twice what the farm
was worth.
And he stood for it, he liked the place
so much.
Well, that was that, and he had signed
the deed
A good two weeks before the month was
up.
It was a Saturday I took it over
To get Miss Bartlett's signature. I can't
forget
How quiet and genteel the old house
looked,
With the lilacs by the door all in full
bloom
And the window-beds with their red-and-
yellow tulips
The way they'd always been. When I
was a boy
I never could pass that yard without
looking in
To see Miss Bartlett's flowers and sniff
the scent of them.
I used to smell it for hours afterwards.
I felt as though I'd gained a lot of time
That day and I didn't hurry to ring the
bell.
But when I did, and Miss Bartlett opened
the door,
The entry seemed as black as pitch to
me
Coming in from the sunlight, and the
tick
Of that infernal clock seemed to break
the air
The same as you break water skipping
pebbles,
I could scarcely hear Miss Bartlett greet-
ing me,
And when I looked at her I half expected
To see the ships rocking upon her fore-
head.
I got myself together in a minute
And gave her the papers and showed her
where to sign them.
It took an age, I thought, and then I
found
That I was breathing in time to the
ticking clock
And counting — counting. I'd got to
eighteen hundred
Before she finished. Then I tried to say

Something appropriate, but nothing came.
Miss Bartlett was like an image run in-
side
By clockwork. Her face was wax — wax-
white,
And wax-still too, she thanked me like a
doll
Who speaks because you press it.
I'd saved her life, perhaps, and yet I
seemed
To be pressing it out at the very instant.
At any rate, there was nothing more to
do
And I got up. Miss Bartlett got up with
me
And walked to the door, and for some
sudden reason
Turned round and went directly to the
clock.
She had the papers still, and she held
them up
Before the clock-face with a curious ges-
ture,
Defiance it might have been, or supplica-
tion.
It had a nasty look to me, the way
She braced herself and cringed at the
same time,
Like I was watching some beastly cere-
mony,
With torture in it and things one
wouldn't think of.
I might be seeing a heathen devotee
Making oblation to a heathen god,
A wood and metal thing without a
soul
But furious with abominable intention.
Ten breaths I counted before the clock
fell over.
It started to strike, then with a hideous
screech
Of grating wheels and rapping bells, it
tottered,
Poised on its edge and suddenly came
down
And crashed Miss Bartlett with it to the
floor.
I got it off her somehow, she was breath-
ing
And muttering something. When I
stooped to hear,
She whispered, "Go and put the clock
up, Martin.
Put it up before you touch me." And I
did.

And you would have done the same, Sir.
    All she wanted
Was to see that clock in place before she
    died.
She saw it so, but when I went to lift her
I did not lift Miss Bartlett, but a corpse
With hands and feet already growing
    cold.
But nothing ailed the clock. I looked at
    it,
Its ships were rocking, cool as cucumbers,
Over and back, over and back. I carried
Miss Bartlett into the parlour and laid
    her down
On the sofa, and I could hardly pass the
    clock
For loathing, and a sort of fear, I guess.
I passed it twice, and it was ticking softly
And purring too, it might have been a
    cat,
When I went out to call the doctor.
    They tell me
It was the wires jarring, but I know better.
Well, now you know the story, you can
    choose
Whether you want the clock or not. I
    thought so.
You'll never make me think it didn't
    kill her,
If there are homicidal clocks or no.
It may be foolishness, but I believe it,
Believe that clock has got a sort of mania.
If it were mine, I'd smash the case to
    pieces
And bury the works out under those rank
    saplings,
But Sam will have a word to say to that.
And now, Sir, we'll be starting for the
    train.

THE LANDLADY OF THE
WHINTON INN TELLS A STORY

Yes, indeed, Sir,
'Tis pretty up here this time o' year,
With th' sumachs an' th' maples fer red,
An' th' birches an' th' oaks fer yaller,
Sometimes you'd think th' sun was shinin'
When 'tain't nothin' but leaves.
Ef you was to go up Tollman's hill,
You'd see th' country layin' out in front
    o' yer
Jest like a big flower garden.
I don't wonder city folks is so partial to
    th' mountains in th' Fall.

But they don't all care enough fer it
To come a-ridin' shanks's mare
The way you're doin'.
What was it you wanted I should tell yer?
Oh, yes, 'bout th' brick house over on
    th' Danbridge road.
I know well th' one you mean.
Sort o' tumble down, ain't it?
Run to seed?
That's th' one.
Th' old Steele farm, we call it.
It's in a dretful state.
Th' last folks had it was a pack o' Finns,
An' I never see such a shiftless set as they
    be.
Don't seem to have no idea o' nothin'.
But th' way they can grub a livin' outer
    stones
Do beat all.
Ther's a whole lot on 'em settled around
    here,
But I guess they wouldn't ha' got aholt
    o' th' Steele place
Only fer it havin' a kind o' bad name.
Sort o' got set in a streak o' cross luck,
    somehow.
You hitch your chair up clost t' th' fire,
And I'll tell yer 'bout it.
It's a funny story;
An' it ain't so funny neither,
Come to think of it.
I remember Tim'thy Adams well
When I was a girl.
He was innercent an' feeble enough by
    then.
My father's told me th' story often,
But it all happened long 'fore my day.
It must ha' been nigh on to eighty year
    ago.
Ther' was two brothers livin' over to
    Danbridge at that time,
Name of Steele.
George an' Clif Steele.
Between 'em, they owned that farm you
    seen,
An' a hardware store to Main Street.
My father used ter say
Nobody hereabouts thought they could
    cut a rakeful o' hay
Or split a log,
Onless they'd bought th' scythe, or th'
    saw, or th' sickle,
To Steele's.
Funny name for a hardware store, warn't
    it,

But them things do happen.
Well, as I said,
They owned th' store an' th' farm, 'tween
    'em,
Old Steele left it that way.
But 'twas real onhandy,
An' nat'rally, they kep' a-treadin' on
    each other's toes.
So 'bout th' time I'm speakin' of,
They made up their minds to do th'
    splittin' themselves,
An' they'd fixed it up that George was
    to have th' store
An' Clif was to take th' farm.
Clif warn't more'n five an' twenty, then,
An' he warn't married,
An' he seen, well as another,
That a farm without a wife's a mighty
    ticklish thing.
So he told his brother
He'd look around a bit,
And when he found a likely woman,
He'd marry her,
An' settle right away.
I guess he warn't quite square 'bout th'
    lookin' around,
'Cause everyone knowed he'd be'n keep-
    in' comp'ny
Fer some time.
Mirandy Eccles, 'twas;
And Father al'ays said she was a fine,
    sensible girl,
And a credit to th' man that chose her.
Clif used ter take her buggy-ridin'
With a fast sorrel mare he had,
Done two thirty or somethin'
Over to th' County Fair.
Clif was proud as punch of her, an' of
    th' girl too.
Father said th' whole street 'ud set up to
    look
When they two druv along it
Like a streak o' lightnin'.
Clif thought his courtin' was goin' ele-
    gant,
An' I guess 'twas,
When all of a suddint,
He was drawed for jury duty.
That put a stop to th' junketin's,
An' Clif was like a bear with a sore head.
'Twas a kind of a queer case.
A man called Tim'thy Adams was bein'
    tried
Fer 'saulting his employer an' stealin'
    four dimonds.

I don't rec'lect th' name o' th' man whose
    store 'twas,
But he was a jeweler an' watch-maker,
Th' only one ther' was to Danbridge.
One mornin' they found him most beat
    to a jelly,
An' bound an' gagged,
An' four big dimonds was missin' outer
    th' stock.
Ther' was a candle in th' store
Guttered to nothin',
An' Mrs.—— th' storekeeper's wife —
Said when she last seed it,
Jest as she was goin' to bed,
It was good an' long,
An' would ha' burned a couple o' hours,
    anyway.
Tim'thy used to come mornin's an' open
    up th' store.
He had a key,
An' that was th' only other ther' was,
So suspicion fastened on him, good an'
    tight.
He said he hadn't be'n ther' at all
Sence closin' time.
That he'd be'n fer a walk up th' moun-
    tain.
But he hadn't be'n gunnin',
'Cause he didn't take no gun;
An' he hadn't be'n fishin',
'Cause he didn't take no pole;
An' nobody b'lieved a man 'ud go walkin'
    up th' mountain
Jest fer th' pleasure o' gittin' ther',
So it looked bad fer Tim'thy.
Clif set in that Court Room,
An' twiddled his fingers,
An' thought o' Mirandy,
An' never heerd so much as a haystraw
    o' th' evidence,
An' when lockin'-up time come,
He didn't know no more about th' case
Than th' town pump.
In them days,
Juries was locked up fer fair.
They didn't 'low 'em home nights,
An' they sent their meals in,
'Stead o' marchin' 'em out to a hotel.
Clif had got awful sick o' bein' ther'.
He'd cut his name on th' table in th'
    jury room
Till 'twas all pickled over with it,
(I've seed th' table, with th' name on,
    myself),
An' th' night after th' ev'dence was in,

Ther' was a dance to th' Town Hall,
An' Clif wanted like pisen to be ther'.
He set in that jury room,
Hackin' at th' table,
Till he couldn't stand it another minit,
Then he jumped outer th' winder,
An' shinned down a big elm-tree was
  outside,
An' went to th' party,
An' th' first person he run acrost when
  he got inter th' room
Was th' Judge!
That was a awful fix fer Clif,
But th' Judge had be'n young once,
An' he jest turned his back, an' never
  seed a thing.
Clif didn't waste no time.
He went straight up to Mirandy an' asked
  her to marry him,
An' she'd missed him so,
She said "yes" right out,
An' Clif went back, an' shinned up th'
  elm agin,
An' ther' he was, spick an' span,
When th' door was unlocked next
  mornin'!
But he hadn't voted on th' case,
An' th' foreman jest whispered to him,
  would he agree,
As they went inter Court.
Clif was in such good sperrits,
He'd ha' agreed to anythin',
So he jest nodded,
An' poor Tim'thy Adams was convicted
  o' 'sault an' batt'ray,
With stealin',
An' sent to State's Prison for twenty
  year.
I told you 'twas a queer story,
But it's a heap queerer than you've heerd
  yit.

Clif married Mirandy,
An' they went to live to th' farm.
They was a well-matched pair,
An' everythin' went as fine as roses in
  July,
'Cept they didn't have no children.
But after it had all be'n goin' on like
  that fer most fifteen year,
Somethin' turned Clif's mind back to that
  old jury case.
Bits o' things he'd heerd in th' Court
  Room
Kep' a-risin' up in his mind.

They must ha' be'n ther' all th' time,
But he'd never sensed 'em.
An' now they up an' slapped him in th'
  face.
Th' more he thought, th' more he felt
That Tim'thy couldn't ha' done it.
He was a bit of a dreamer himself,
An' he knowed a man could go up a
  mountain,
'Ithout hankerin' to shoot or fish.
He thought an' thought, Clif did,
Till he was so nervous an' jumpy,
He was all of a twitch from head to foot.
Then one day he druv over to Danbridge
To see Judge Proctor.
Th' Judge was a old man, an' retired,
But Clif thought it 'ud ease him some
To see him.
He told th' Judge all about it,
But th' Judge said 'twas past an' gone,
An' he'd better lay some of his fields
  down to red rye,
An' try replantin' his wood-lot.
But Clif didn't buy no red rye seed that
  day;
He went straight to th' lib'ry
An' read a lot o' old newspapers.
Then he ferreted out th' Court clerk,
An' fussed an' fussed,
Till he let him see th' records.
He druv back an' forth to Danbridge fer
  weeks,
Readin' all th' papers 'bout that trial.
An' th' more he read 'em, th' more he
  knowed
Tim'thy hadn't had no head nor hand
  to do with it.
Clif was most beside himself with worry,
An' no wonder,
He felt he'd sent a feller critter to State's
  Prison
Who didn't b'long ther' no more'n he
  did himself.
He act'ally got to feelin' he was th' one
  b'longed,
He'd committed a wicked crime,
An' he'd got t' expiate it.
I guess he was most mad;
Father often said so.
He was thin as a rail,
An' he couldn't eat nor sleep,
An' th' farm all went to smithereens
'Cause he hadn't no time to work it,
Fer readin' ev'dence.
He didn't know much law,

An' it 'curred to him,
That ef he got all th' jury that done th'
    convictin'
To change their minds,
That would stop th' sentence right where
    'twas,
An' Tim'thy could walk out o' jail.
So th' poor lunatic started to git aholt
    o' th' jury.
'Twarn't no easy matter to do,
Fer some was moved away, an' some was
    dead;
But he wrote, an' he travelled,
An' he run here an' ther' like a hen with-
    out its head,
An', in th' end, he got all th' livin mem-
    bers o' that jury
To sign papers reversin' their decision.
Is that very remarkable, Sir?
P'r'aps you're right.
Anyhow, he done it.
When he'd got all th' papers,
He went back to Judge Proctor,
An' asked him, would he please arrange
    things
So Tim'thy'd be free.
O' course, th' Judge told him 'twarn't no
    manner o' use.
That all th' papers in th' world wouldn't
    git Tim'thy out,
Onless ther' was new ev'dence,
Which, don't you see, ther' warn't,
Not a scrap.
So Clif went home, all broke to bits,
An' put his papers in th' chimbly cup-
    board,
An' Mirandy had all she could do
To git a little bacon an' coffee down him.
It's al'ays th' women gits it in th' end,
    you know, Sir?

Well, bimeby it come time fer Tim'thy
    to be let out o' jail.
He'd served his term, barrin' what was
    took off fer good conduct.
Th' very day he stepped out o' prison,
Standin' directly in front o' th' gate
Wher' he couldn't miss him,
Was Clif Steele.
Tim'thy was took all aback
An' made to git out o' th' way,
But Clif up an' hitched his arm inter his
An' marched him off, real brotherly.
"Tim'thy Adams," says Clif,
"I done yer a great wrong.

I know you never 'saulted nobody
An' never took no dimonds,
An' I come here to-day to make it up to
    yer best I can," he says.
"Come to yer senses, have yer?" says
    Tim'thy.
"Yes, I have," says Clif.
"An' I'm goin' to take yer right along
    home with me."
Mebbe Tim'thy wouldn't ha' gone,
Only his sperrits was all squeezed to
    nothin'
By bein' so long in jail.
Anyhow, Cliff wouldn't hear no.
An' them two went home together
Like a pair o' old shoes.
Folks wondered, would Mirandy like
    it?
All I c'n say is, ef she didn't, she darsn't
    say so.
I guess she was some feared 'bout Clif's
    stayin' in his right mind.
Whatever was th' reason, she acted
    pleased as pie.
So th' three on 'em lived in th' brick
    house,
An' after a little, nobody heeded 'em no
    more.
But Clif was all played out;
Th' worry'd done fer him,
An' two year come th' next Winter
He died o' pneumonia.

Tim'thy an' th' widder
Stuck it out fer a bit as they was.
But tongues got to waggin'
An' they must ha' heerd 'em,
Anyways, one fine day they up an' got
    married,
An' that settled th' talk fer keeps.
Then th' good times seemed come fer
    Tim'thy an' Mirandy.
They warn't young no more, but they
    was real well suited.
Folks kind o' fergot 'bout th' jail,
An' Mirandy took a new lease o' life.
Why, th' kitchen winders was all jammed
    full o' flower-pots!
You never seed sich rose-geraniums,
Everybody wanted slips from 'em.
I don't know jest how it come 'bout,
But one way or 'tother, Tim'thy took to
    tinkerin' clocks agin.
He had a wonderful knack at makin' 'em
    go.

Not th' batteredest old clock as ever was,
beat him.
He'd set ther' in that kitchin,
Snuffin' up th' smell o' them geraniums
An' foolin' with little wheels an' wires,
An' all of a suddint he'd have th' clock
as good as new.
Most everybody has a broken clock;
Well, they brought 'em all to Tim'thy.
Th' house was full on 'em.
Now comes th' queer part,
An' ther' ain't no explainin' it, no how.
Many's th' time I've heerd my Father tell
it,
But I never give over startin' when I
think of it.
One day, Tim'thy was overhaulin' a fine
wall clock,
Th' kind with big weights hangin' down
under it,
When he give a cry,
So loud Mirandy heerd it out in th' clo'es-
yard.
She come runnin' in
With her heart in her mouth,
An' ther' was Tim'thy,
Starin' as though he seed a ghost,
An' holdin' four big dimonds in his hand.
They was sparklin' like icicles on a South
winder,
All green, an' blue, an' red.
Father seed 'em,
An' he said they was so bright
You could most see to read by th' flashin'
they made.
"Wher'd you git them things, Tim'thy
Adams?" Mirandy hollered out.
She was struck all of a heap
An' couldn't scarcely fetch her breath fer
wonder.
"Out o' th' clock," says Tim'thy, quick,
as ef a bee stung him.
"Who put 'em in?" asked Mirandy, kind
o' snappin' out th' words.
"I ain't no notion,' says Tim'thy.
Now ther' was a fine fix, an' dimonds
agin!
Mirandy leaned up agin th' door-jamb to
save herself from fallin' —
"Whose clock is it?" says she.
'Twas old man Smart's clock, an' Tim'thy
telled her so.
Well, not to keep a-talkin' all day, they
sent fer old man Smart,
An' showed him th' dimonds.

But he said they warn't none o' his.
Tim'thy acted as ef he was afeared on 'em.
He'd put 'em on th' chimbly,
An' he wouldn't tech 'em agin, nohow.
Mirandy said she couldn't sleep with 'em
in th' house,
An' ther' was a fine hurrah-boys.
Th' neighbours got wind on it somehow,
An' they all come flockin' to ask fool
questions
An' git a sight o' th' dimonds.
Tim'thy seemed kind o' crazed, all to
oncet.
He jest set ther', an' whispered: "In th'
clock! In th' clock!"
Nobody couldn't git another thing out
o' him.
Mirandy'd got to cryin' by then,
An' all th' women was soothin' her,
An' burnin' feathers under her nose.
'Twas th' awfullest mess ever was,
An' all along o' them pesky dimonds.
Somebody called in Lawyer Cary to Dan-
bridge,
An' he took charge o' th' dimonds,
An' they got th' house cleared somehow.
But nothin' ever warn't th' same after.
Mirandy went inter a sort o' decline,
An' died 'fore Thanksgivin'.
Tim'thy didn't die, but he didn't git well
neither.
He wouldn't tech a clock agin fer love
nor money.
If anyone said: "Clock," he'd commence
shiv'rin'
As though he had th' ague.
Then a nasty whisper got about,
You know how folks talk,
Well, 'twas said th' dimonds warn't really
in th' clock at all.
That Tim'thy had 'em all these years,
An' that he only pretended to find 'em
So's he could sell 'em at last.
Some said 'twas a trade 'twixt him an'
Clif.
Clif had kep' 'em fer him while he was
to State's Prison.
I guess that was all foolishness,
But what made 'em think so
Was that old man Smart 'lowed he'd
bought th' clock
To a auction;
An' it turned out 'twas th' auction o'
that jewel'ry store
Where Tim'thy worked.

Th' man that owned it had sold out an'
gone away.
Lawyer Cary tried to trace him,
But 'twarn't a mite o' use.
He'd gone to Boston, an' they couldn't
find out another thing.
But ther' was th' dimonds, an' ther' was
poor old Tim'thy,
Half cracked with findin' 'em.
Property like that's a terrible nuisance.
Old man Smart wouldn't look at th'
things,
An' he told how he'd burnt th' clock,
Considerin' it a sort o' party.
They warn't Tim'thy's, that was sure,
An' Lawyer Cary said he wouldn't keep
'em after New Year's.
So th' Selectmen voted to sell 'em,
An' buy books for th' lib'ry with th'
money.
You c'n see 'em now, with a card in 'em:
"Bought with th' proceeds o' th' sale o'
four dimonds."
I must ha' be'n 'bout ten when Tim'thy
died,
I mind it well, 'cause Father told th'
story at supper
Th' day they buried him,
An' I ain't never fergot it.
Ther' was some trouble 'bout th' house
too.
George Steele had moved to Boston years
afore
An' his daughter (he didn't have no son)
had married,
An' they had a time findin' her under
her new name.
Anyhow, she didn't want th' farm, an'
'twas sold.
It's be'n goin' down hill ever sence.
Lor's Mercy! Ain't this world a queer
place!
Ther' was three lives all gone to smash
Over them dimonds,
An' nothin' to show fer it but a ram-
shackle house,
An' a passel o' books in th' lib'ry!
Well, that's th' story,
An' I must be seein' to your supper.
It's gittin' late.

"AND PITY 'TIS, 'TIS TRUE"

"Will they do anythin' to her, do you
think, Mirandy?"

"Do you mean prison?
No, I guess not.
That doctor from Boston said she wa'n't
no ways responsible."

"She's over to th' 'sylum, ain't she?"

"Yes, but th' doctor said she'd be right
as a trivet
In a month or two."

"I never seed th' child but once,
But now I mind, it 'peared awful big
fer five weeks, ter me."

"You may say so, 'Melia.
Ef you was a married woman
You'd ha' sensed right off
Somethin' was wrong.
Why 'twas all of a year an' more.
I guess that was th' reason she let you
see it.
You not bein' knowin' in such things.
I ast her ter le' me look at it a hunder'd
times
But she al'ays put me off
One way or another.
Bless you! She was as nervous as a witch
Fear o' bein' found out."

"Old man Drew wouldn't think nothin'
o' course."

"That's why she come here.
She was safe with only her Grandsir in
th' house.
He's in a terrible tew now, they say.
Eighty year old and al'ays respectable.
It do seem hard."

"How does 'Lisha take it?
He's one o' them husbands as sets a store
by their wives.
I remember his courtin',
He'd ha' pulled th' stars out o' th' sky
To lay a path so's Claribel could step
easy."

"He won't hear a word agin her now.
Says 'twas his fault fer bein' 'way when
'twas born.
Eben said he jest bust out cryin'
When they tell'd him th' baby wa'n't
his."

"Travels, don't he?"

"Yes, stoves.
Doin' elegant.
Only, o' course it takes him 'way most o' th' time."

"She should ha' come home fer her layin' in,
Then nothin' wouldn't ha' happened."

"I dunno.
'Tain't in nater to leave yer own home
When a baby's comin'.'"

"But she did leave her home, didn't she?
Went to a hospital or somethin'."

"Well, she had ter do that
Jest at th' last.
'Lisha was off West, you see,
An' somebody had to 'tend her."

"My! Ain't it a shame!
Poor little thing!
Ef she'd ha' sent fer me
I'd gone right down to Boston next train."

"Anybody would.
But she was al'ays proud as Lucifer,
Was Claribel.
An' that baby comin' made her prouder'n ever.
Why th' letters she writ 'bout it!
I declare they sounded like th' Bible.
She was all keyed up,
Seemed she wa'n't steppin' on no common earth,
An' she most sewed her eyes out
Makin' th' clo'es.
She didn't need nobody
But jest her thoughts.
She'd kep' that baby on her mind so long
It went all to shivers when ther' wa'n't none."

"The Almighty's ways do be past understandin'.
Why couldn't her baby ha' lived, I wonder?
Most on 'em does."

"Seems she slipped on th' ice or somethin'.

Anyway th' baby was born dead.
They do say she took on 'bout it somethin' awful,
An' she wouldn't let nobody write to 'Lisha.
That doctor said they oughtn't never to ha' let her out o' th' hospital alone.
But they did,
An' she was walkin' home
When she seed a baby-carriage settin' outside a drug-store
With th' baby in it.
Th' mother'd gone inside fer a minit,
An' 'fore she knowed what she was doin'
She had th' baby in her arms an' was cuddlin' it.
She's a born mother, is Claribel,
An' her milk wa'n't dry,
An' I guess she jest couldn't put it down.
It's wicked to think o' what she must ha' suffered
To do such a thing;
But she took that baby off home with her,
An' she 'lowed to 'Lisha 'twas her own
She'd brought from th' hospital.
'Lisha was new to babies,
An' he didn't think nothin' 'bout its size."

"I wonder why she come up here?"

"To git farther away, I guess.
'Twas all right an' proper
To bring th' baby home to visit with her Grandsir fer a spell.
An' she never figured as they could trace her up here.
When anybody wanted to see th' baby
She'd say she didn't want it should be waked up.
It might ha' gone on till th' Day o' Judgment
Ef th' Sheriff hadn't been a fam'ly man."

"You don't say!"

"Yes. You see th' other mother was right down sick with fussin',
Nat'rally.
An' she an' her husband got th' perlice on it.
An' they sent all over th' state,
An' to New York.
I guess they spent a mint o' money

Ef you was to count it.
Sheriff, he read th' papers,
An' one day he seed Claribel
In th' village
Wheelin' th' baby.
It looked awful large ter him,
An' he stopped an' ast a heap o' ques-
tions.
Claribel was at her wits' ends,
An' bimeby she muddled herself 'bout
somethin',
An' he took her right into Cole's store
An' had a good look at th' baby.
That settled it.
They do say that Claribel most killed th'
Sheriff
With a pitchfork was standin' ther'
'Fore they got th' baby from her.
I dunno's I blame her
She's got mother in her blood."

"Blame her! Mirandy, you'd do th' same.
So would I ef th' Lord had seed fit ter
gi' me a child."

"Ther's th' other woman, 'Melia."

"Yes, that's so.
My! But th' ways of th' Almighty do
beat all,
An' I al'ays says so.
Why, it's only a week ago I says to
Parson Davis,
'Parson,' says I, 'ther' ain't no manner
o' use
You expounding Scripture th' way you
do,
Day in an' day out.
We'll never understan',' I says,
'Not till Gabriel's trump starts us all
puttin' on our bunnits fer th' Resur-
rection.'
Mirandy, d'you s'pose Claribal'd care fer
one o' my spice cakes,
She used to be real partial to 'em?
Jason could drive over to th' 'sylum with
one most any day,
Now th' apples is picked."

"So do, so do, 'Melia.
An' I'll jest slip some o' them new jars
o' quince conserve into a basket
An' send 'em along too.
I got a plenty."

THE HOUSE WITH THE MARBLE STEPS

He built the house to show his neigh-
bours
That decent thrift could lead to this,
A giddy reason for his labours,
A bright brick apotheosis.

He was not one to be bulldozed
By sentiment, and he had planned
Past whispered sneers when he fore-
closed
The mortgage on this very land.

He'd forced his way with prudent greed
While they at best remained the same.
He gauged the folly of a creed
Which keeps a lame purse always lame.

Well, here it was, and in the road
He stood and tallied beam and rafter.
The cost would be a heavy load
He'd tell you, twisting into laughter.

The window-edges were of stone,
A soapy limestone smooth and fair.
The floors were all hard wood and none
Tailed off to pine beneath a stair.

If he were old and quite infirm,
His house was very fresh and young,
And envy is a winding worm —
These thoughts were pepper to his
tongue.

And so he watched it grow and grow,
And jotted down the things he heard,
Scheming to balance by the blow
His house should deal as final word.

To crown the whole and go beyond
Whatever yet had been attempted
In his small town, he signed a bond
Which would most certainly have emp-
tied

The pockets of quite half his friends.
Even to him it was a point,
But when a man aims at such ends
He must keep stiff in every joint.

He bought a quarry's good half year
Of first-class, fine-grained marble output,

He paid a mason very near
As much again to have it cut.

The sharp white polished steps were grand
Descending from the stucco porch.
They glittered like a marching band,
They mounted upward like a torch.

But he had taken to his bed
Before the last was set in place,
And one week later he was dead
With a slow smile upon his face.

The marble flashed beneath the fall
Of undertakers' feet who carried
His coffin to the funeral
Within the house. And there he tarried

For fifteen minutes more or less,
And "dust to dust" they read above him.
Now who had gained in bitterness —
For not one soul was there to love him?

They gaped upon the shining floors,
Their eyes scanned ceiling heights and blocked them.
When all was done, they shut the doors
And shrugged their shoulders as they locked them.

The house is charming now with weeds
Sprung all about, the steps are mellow
With little grass and flower-seeds
Drifting across their sun-stained yellow.

Empty it stands and so has stood
More years than the town clerk can tell.
No legend has it he was good,
No tale reports that he did well.

They've tried to sell it, off and on,
But not a person wants to buy,
Though visitors who've come and gone
Remember it against the sky
In shrewd and sweet proportions glowing
Above a flight of marble steps where grass is growing.

BALLADS FOR SALE

BALLADS FOR SALE

Fresh, New Ballads, with the Ink Scarce
Dried upon Them

Have a ballad, good people
A sheet of song-words just pulled from
    the press.
A new song all a-flutter in the wind.
Did you hear the drums and fife,
And the boys and girls calling down the
    side streets?
Throw up your windows,
You, who live in the Square,
For I am passing by your doors
With sheets and sheets of songs,
To tickle your tears and your laughter
And set your feet a-jigging.

Will you have a penny posy of daisies and
    dandelions,
    and true love under a hedge?
For another penny, I can give you
    roses,
Fountains, fish-ponds,
    and a dim old palace streaked with
    moonlight.
If the sea is your choice,
You must give me silver.
The sea is a hard thing to get into a
    song.
Martial ballads bring silver too.
They are a bit out of style,
But I have two or three,
    with guns popping like the Fourth of
    July,
Printed in red ink,
    with a skull and cross-bones at the
    corners.
Then there is a merry song of a moor and
    and a cocoanut,
    and a clown who went to Heaven in a
    fire-balloon.
Ha! Ha! You will hold your sides,
    and all for a bit of white silver.
But it is yellow gold I must have for love
    songs,
A drop of blood for a drop of gold,
    and fourteen lines is a guinea.

See the wind flutter my songs,
They almost sing themselves out here in
    the sunshine.
Step up, good people,
And buy a fine ballad crisp from the
    press,
    with the ink scarce dried upon it.

TO A GENTLEMAN WHO
WANTED TO SEE THE FIRST
DRAFTS OF MY POEMS IN THE
INTERESTS OF PSYCHOLOGICAL
RESEARCH INTO THE WORKINGS
OF THE CREATIVE MIND

So you want to see my papers, look what
    I have written down
'Twixt an ecstasy and heartbreak, con
    them over with a frown.
You would watch my thought's green
    sprouting ere a single blossom's blown.

Would you, friend? And what should I
    be doing, have you thought of that?
Is it pleasant, think you, being gazed
    upon from feet to hat,
Microscopically viewed by eyes com-
    missioned just for that?

Don't assure me that your interest does
    not lie with me at all.
I'm a poet to be dissected for the good
    of science. Call
It by any name, I feel like some old root
    where fungi sprawl.

Think you, I could make you see it, all
    the little diverse strands
Locked in one short poem? By no means
    do I find your prying hands
Pleasure bearing and delightful straying
    round my lotus lands.

Not a word but joins itself with some
 adventure I alone
Could attach consideration to. You'd
 wrench me flesh from bone,
Find the heart and count its tappings. At
 your touch, 'twould turn to stone.

What is I, and what that other? That's
 your quest. I'll have you know
Telling it would break it from me, it
 would melt like travelled snow.
I will be no weary pathway for another's
 feet to go.

Seize the butterfly and wing it, thus you
 learn of butterflies.
But you do not ask permission of the
 creature, which is wise.
If I did consent, to please you, I should
 tell you packs of lies.

To one only will I tell it, do I tell it all
 day long.
Only one can see the patches I work
 into quilts of song.
Crazy quilts, I'm sure you'd deem them,
 quite unworthy of your prong.

One must go half-way with poets, feel the
 thing you're out to find,
Wonder even while you name it, keep it
 somehow still enshrined,
Still encased within its leafage like an
 arbour honey-vined.

Lacking just this touch and tremour, how
 can I but shrink and clutch
What I have to closer keeping. Little
 limping phantoms, such
Are my poems before I've taught them
 how to walk without a crutch.

You mean well, I do not doubt it, but
 you're blind as any mule.
Would you question a mad lover, set his
 love-making to rule?
With your pulse upon his finger, watch
 him play the sighing fool?

Would he win the lady, tell me, with
 you by? Your calculations
Might frustrate a future teeming with
 immeasurable equations.
Which will prove the most important,
 your research or his relations?

Take my answer then, for, flatly, I will
 not be vivisected.
Life is more to me than learning. If you
 clumsily deflected
My contact with what I know not, could
 it surely be connected?

Scarcely could you, knowing nothing,
 swear to me it would be so.
Therefore unequivocally, brazenly, I tell
 you "No!"
To the fame of an avowal, I prefer my
 domino.

Still I have a word, one moment, stop,
 before you leave this room.
Though I shudder thinking of you wan-
 dring through my beds of bloom,
You may come with spade and shovel
 when I'm safely in the tomb.

ON LOOKING AT A COPY OF ALICE MEYNELL'S POEMS, GIVEN ME, YEARS AGO, BY A FRIEND

Upon this greying page you wrote
A whispered greeting, long ago.
Faint pencil-marks run to and fro
Scoring the lines I loved to quote.

A sea-shore of white, shoaling sand,
Blue creeks zigzagging through marsh-
 grasses,
Sand pipers, and a wind which passes
Cloudily silent up the land.

Upon the high edge of the sea
A great four-master sleeps; three hours
Her bowsprit has not cleared those
 flowers.
I read and look alternately.

It all comes back again, but dim
As pictures on a winking wall
Hidden save when the dark clouds fall
Or crack to show the moon's bright rim.

I well remember what I was,
And what I wanted. You, unwise
With sore unwisdom, had no eyes
For what was patently the cause.

So are we sport of others' blindness,
We who could see right well alone.

What were you made of — wood or
stone?
Yet I remember you with kindness.

You gave this book to me to ease
The smart in me you could not heal.
Your gift a mirror — woe or weal.
We sat beneath the apple-trees.

And I remember how they rang,
These words, like bronze cathedral bells
Down ancient lawns, or citadels
Thundering with gongs where choirs
sang.

Silent the sea, the earth, the sky,
And in my heart a silent weeping.
Who has not sown can know no reaping!
Bitter conclusion and no lie.

O heart that sorrows, heart that bleeds,
Heart that was never mine, your words
Were like the pecking Autumn birds
Stealing away my garnered seeds.

No future where there is no past!
O cherishing grief which laid me bare,
I wrapped you like a wintry air
About me. Poor enthusiast!

How strange that tumult, looking back.
The ink is pale, the letters fade.
The verses seem to be well made,
But I have lived the almanac.

And you are dead these drifted years,
How many I forget. And she
Who wrote the book, her tragedy
Long since dried up its scalding tears.

I read of her death yesterday,
Frail lady whom I never knew
And knew so well. Would I could strew
Her grave with pansies, blue and grey.

Would I could stand a little space
Under a blowing, brightening sky,
And watch the sad leaves fall and lie
Gently upon that lonely place.

So cried her heart, a feverish thing.
But clay is still, and clay is cold,
And I was young, and I am old,
And in December what birds sing!

Go, wistful book, go back again
Upon your shelf and gather dust.
I've seen the glitter through the rust
Of old, long years, I've known the pain.

I've recollected both of you,
But I shall recollect no more.
Between us I must shut the door.
The living have so much to do.

WHO HAS NOT, CANNOT HAVE

Lances slanted against a froward sky,
So do the days of my life appear before
me,
O verily Beloved.
Tempt me not, therefore, that I linger
With my long, pointed, red morocco
shoes
Scuffing the fallen vine-leaves
A-skip upon the lozenged marbles of
your floor.
I am not a man for chess and blue
cushions,
For sheep's-eyeing across lute-strings
Of a dapper afternoon.
What were you among the cooks and
water-boys,
Camping on a wind-vexed plain at night-
fall
Amid the chattering stalks of last year's
grasses,
While I, in some lost distance, wage a war
Against the goblins of a mouldering gen-
eration?
Would you follow my torn banners where
they flicker
In and out of the cloven bellies of moun-
tains,
And the hail-stones gash like javelins,
And the sun dries up the roots of hair
Till my horse is naked as a woman
Bartered for an arid territory?
There are such, my lady,
And I have lands and lances to compel
them,
And owe them nothing but a five-petalled
kiss
Blooming between a brace of bloody
battles.

MID–ADVENTURE

Mist, vapour,
A little whiff of wind,
Noticed as nothing and as soon forgotten,

Such was my purpose.
It would have held, too,
No doubt of that,
And you and I no other than we were.
You would not have it so.
Your call cloaked me in the seeming of
reality,
I entered, bidden, to your consciousness.
And here I stand,
Waiting, for so you will for me,
Waiting.
For what?
Would you have me like a caryatid,
Holding above your head some shelter-
ing sky
Of softened, tempered sunlight?
Would you keep me as a gathered curio
To say: "See, this I found, and kept for
luck"?
Or do you guess at possibilities,
A warmth to draw from me when nights
grow cold
And gales whine bitterly in window
cracks?
For myself,
I have lost recollection how I came.
Returning shows a dim, uneasy way
My feet refuse to follow.
Yet suppose,
Suppose the very custom of my long
Vacant delaying just inside the door
Blurs me to an impassive bibelot,
A bit of furniture which, neither used
Nor looked at, is most likely to be left
Totally unregarded and ignored —
My summons nothing,
A caprice outworn —
Standing forsaken in an empty room.
How the wind howls!
The fire is a red recumbent ash.
The future, strange chameleon to the
drift of time,
Turns round on me a grinning paste-
board face
Dropped from a masker at a carnival.
Hola! then. I'll be harlequin and dance
In checkers of blood-red and black hearse
plumes,
Capering, dead drunk, upon a coffin lid.

CORRESPONDENCE

I wrote her a letter, she wrote me three,
And the cadence was that of a leafing
tree.

I wrote her four letters, she wrote me
none,
And the scuffled leaves lay dim and dun.

I broke my pen and wrote no more,
Lacking the postman's knock at the door.

I scored that year with a mark of chalk:
Second-hand compliments, windy talk,

Pleasant platitudes hung on a nail
Useful to plump an uneven sale.

It will all come out in the wash, they say,
And to-morrow but duplicates yesterday.

Even great Pharaoh takes no more room
Than his huddled bones, though the
spacious gloom

Containing them goes by his stately
name.
Dead leaves, dead kings, it is much the
same.

Cocks crow daily on hills of dung,
And no song is the first, nor the last,
that's sung.

TO A LADY OF UNDENIABLE
BEAUTY AND PRACTISED CHARM

No peacock strutting on a balustrade
Could air his feathers with a cooler grace,
Assume a finer insolence of pace,
Or make his sole advance a cavalcade
Of sudden shifts of colour, slants of
shade,
Than you, the cold indifference of your
face
Sharpening the cunning lure of velvets,
lace,
Greens, blues, and golds, seduction on
parade.
You take the accolade of staring eyes
As something due your elegance of pose,
Feeding your vanity on pecks of dust,
The weary iteration which supplies
No zest. I see you as a cankered rose
Its silver petals curled and cracked with
rust.

AND SO, I THINK, DIOGENES

I told them to look at an apple-tree
In a gust of blossom. They could not see.

I told them to notice people's faces
In quiet, unexpected places;

To catch the flying speech of eyes,
And stumble on some young surprise

Of joy as sharp as any dawn
Or afternoon across a lawn.

I told them to look at a thin, white
   steeple
Soaring above a throng of people,

And listen to the people's cheers
When some one spoke. They had no ears.

Instead, they led me to a hill
Above a bay. The noon was still.

The water in the bay was cold;
The hanging air was slack with mould.

Gravestones were scattered through the
   grass
So close there was no room to pass

For any save the narrow dead
Who need no paths on which to tread.

Each scraggy gravestone bore a name
And some brief episode of fame,

Some pious irony of grief,
Draped in the tatters of belief.

Misshapen flowers stood awry,
Too weak to face the staring sky.

The wind upon that barren hill
Was strangely sleek and strangely still.

A dreary shadow crept and crept
Across the gaunt graves where they slept

Who died so many years ago
And lay here softly, row on row,
With nowhere else at all to go.

. . . .

They led me up and down the hill.
They said no word. The dusk was chill.

They left me at the edge of town;
They gazed at me and up and down.

Their eyes were ghastly white and cool
Like fishes in a frozen pool.

They left me where I stood, and bent
With feverish ague, turned and went

Back to the hill. "But they are dead,
They do but wander home," I said.

MESDAMES ATROPOS AND CLIO ENGAGE IN A GAME OF SLAP–STICK

*"And better there for her than at that
inn he left her at to pine and watch the
Royal Sovereign come swing come smirk
in sailor blue and star and meet the rain."*
   "THE AMAZING MARRIAGE"

Come swing, come smirk, in sailor blue
   and star,
And I, poor lad, dead as Balaam's donkey,
Nothing left but a coat and star
And anyone's face clapped on top of 'em.
I was a round chuck-penny for fortune.
   I was,
A fellow to straddle a quarter deck, step
   up step down,
Guns, and runs, and the wind's eye wink-
   ing.
So I stood it, swallowing the harbour
   jauntings
Like so many puffs of cream,
And off to windward, clip at a black
   squall
With a snap of my fingers.
Now I'm the laughing-stock of a cat's-
   paw;
Come swing, come smirk, to every little
   sniff of air,
Sailor blue and star, up and down,
With my hinges squealing like a cracked
   serpent,
And every window behind mocking the
   sight of me
And my silly star, gone no one knows
   whither.
I was a man to stand the slash of hurri-
   canes,
With a bowsprit of good metal spitting
   mouthfuls of water and liking it.
Come swing, come smirk now,
With the black rain snivelling down my
   front,
And the apple-faced sun wizening me to
   a cranberry.

Come swing, come smirk, all day long,
Watching a boy jabbing a goose-quill into
  paper,
By candle-light, when the moon fails,
And Zip! they go out of window like so
  many fire-balloons,
And some take the trees, and some foul
  the mud,
And some give me a pinch in passing.
Once I had a belly-ful of good sea-salt
  in me,
And a cocked hat of brine to brisk me up,
Me and my star;
Now I eat that fellow's ripped-up papers,
Whenever there's a breeze.
And the sight of him, red-haired ninny,
Sitting there with his head like a bon-
  fire,
And his heart too, I daresay,
Is a bitterer thing to spy at than the
  march of a China Seas typhoon.
Come swing, come smirk, in sailor blue
  and star,
To catch the rain, and catch his papers,
Hot to blister the paint off me,
And the white rain spoiling 'em,
And the blue, morning rain sticking 'em
  together,
And I in the drift creaking my rust at
  the flight they make.

Faugh! I say,
This is a pretty heaven, this is!
Dead and gone and should be let lie,
Not swinging and smirking after other
  men's scribblings.
Sailor blue and star,
To tell the world here's an inn to stop at,
And a young fellow blazing his eyes blind
  in a worm-hole
After something he can't see.
Pretty world he's made for me to swing
  in,
Smirking at him with my star that's only
  paint
When the bells toll of a Sunday,
And a grinning churchyard underneath
Rots the man I was.
Can he cheat it when his time's come,
Or will he, too, be strung up on a pair
  of whining hinges,
Sailor blue and star, or something like it?
Ding-dong bell on a sign-board,
And the old goose gobbled full of papers
Waddling down to the ditch.

That's a song for a Sunday morning,
Come swing, come smirk, till your boards
  give way,
And you go to grind shoe-leather,
And the wind can't peck you from the
  dust.
Grand world, come swing, come smirk,
Baby Bunting world of painted nonsense,
Up and down to a scrape of rusty bear-
  ings
Like a man with a cold at the back of
  his nose;
Holy-ghost world with a star on it like
  a cold pancake,
And the devil's beer brewed of sick brains
Which should be let lie and aren't,
And go for the choking of geese
Laid out stark in a green ditch
Of a Sunday morning for the church-folk
  to see.

A COMMUNICATION

You deceived me handsomely
With your inconsolable grief at parting.
I really believed in your crocodile tears
And suffered at the exhibition of your
  suffering;
A little for myself also at the breaking of
  an old tie,
A habit grown as comfortably pleasant
As the wearing of a friendly dressing-
  gown.
For we had passed the stage of exhilara-
  tion
And reached the solace of a quiet domes-
  ticity.
I was prepared to linger over it in retro-
  spect,
Not too unhappily, for had we not agreed
  a thousand times
That this sundering was merely geograph-
  ical.
And now a month has passed and not a
  word have I had from you,
Not so much as a scrawl to say you could
  not write!
Fate lays innumerable springes for per-
  sons of imagination.
Because I wished to believe,
I saw in your Byronic gesture of woe,
Not what it purported to be, certainly,
But something not too different.
You cast a larger shadow than yourself,
  that I realized.

But even I, who should have known
  better,
Believed it was your shadow.
I crave your pardon for my blunder.
The mask was well assumed,
I should have been critical enough to
  understand it was an artistic produc-
  tion.
I congratulate you on the verisimilitude
  of it,
But I shall not be fooled again, be sure
  of that.
In future I shall see you as you are:
A plaster figure of a man that's grown a
  little dusty.
We all have knick-knacks round which
  once meant something.
It is rather a wrench to take them from
  their niches,
But life goes on, imperious, and bric-à-
  brac accumulates.
Still, because I cherished you once, I will
  not throw you away just yet.
I will put you on an upper shelf in the
  pantry of my mind,
Among old flower-vases I no longer use,
  being of a bygone fashion.
It may interest you to know that the
  place you occupied
Looks a little strange to me without you,
But that, of course, will pass.

THE IMMORTALS

I have read you, and read you, my
  Betters,
Piling high on the clear brown shelves,
Mountain high, your very selves
Disguised in a garb of letters.

I have poked and pried beyond,
Seeking past words for how you did it,
While my mind was one tormented
  fidget
Like a stone-struck, shallow pond.

I have ravelled your patterns out,
And matched them piece by piece as
  they were,
Till your hearts flashed again from the
  erstwhile blur.
Did I know then the rule from the rout?

Do I know how a flower comes —
A spurt of blue or a shoot of rose?

Plant a seed and watch while it grows.
Chrysanthemums — geraniums —
Let the scientists crack their craniums!

I know what paper is,
And I've handled pencils, and pens, and
  ink.
Does grammar teach us the way men
  think?
Can you narrow a man to a synthesis?

Build him from his parts if you can.
Shade him to colour and cut him to
  shape,
Docket his method, something will
  escape,
And, presto! Where is the man?

Two and two make four.
If your two and two will amalgamate,
But who knows the way to add moon-
  shine to paint.
And there we touch the core.

I read you as I look at the sky,
Gratefully wondering at its fresh-flowing
  blue.
If I'm not, why I'm not, so why this
  to-do —
Must I disqualify?

Well, I won't, my Masters, so reckon
On the valiant rivalry of a flea.
I should lie to you if I never said "We."
You great gods, why do you beckon?

Clearly the fault is yours,
Flaunting a challenge I can't resist.
I declare my back has a permanent twist,
And my boot-straps are counted by scores.

Out of your anguish we see,
Out of your mighty rejoicing we are.
Your burning has seared us with a bleed-
  ing scar,
We strive in irony.

You most Serene and Dead
In your bright gardens! Our Gethsemane
Is planted with your immortality.
We walk with feet of lead.

With leaden feet we move,
And still with heads flung up and bared.
Fools, in that seeing, yet we dared
To follow you and prove.

Prove whether stars or ashes.
That's the touchstone, is it not?
Graven tablets or dry-rot.
Well, the mist has sunny flashes.

APOTHEOSIS

The mountains were both far and high,
Their jagged peaks along the sky
Broke it like splintered porphyry.

I stood beneath a cherry-tree
Whose thick leaves fluttered ceaselessly,
And there were cherry clusters — three.

Prone at my feet was one who slept;
At my right hand, a maid who wept;
And at my left, a youth who kept

Vigil before a naked sword
Which gleamed and sparkled on the sward
As though it were a holy word.

An eery moonlight lit the place,
Just bright enough to show each face
And each lithe body's proper grace.

The weeping maiden raised her head:
"I die for want of food," she said,
And in her famished gaze I read

The wasting of her life in tears.
Her face was shattered as though years
Had nicked it with an iron shears.

"Peace, Mournful Lady," I replied,
"Within these leaves dark cherries hide."
I raised my hand, but in a stride,

Catching his sword up, so he came,
The youth. His helmet burst to flame,
And on it shone a fearful name.

The maiden moaned and sank beneath
The tree's foot, like a fallen wreath
Of myrtle-buds, stripped of their sheath.

Once more we were as we had been:
One wept, one slept, one watched his keen
Sword lying in the grasses green.

Then she who slumbered stirred and woke,
And throwing back her ample cloak
She lifted heavy eyes and spoke:

"I faint for hunger," whispered she,
"And though above me I can see
Cherries, I am spent utterly.

Reach me the fruit for kindness, so
My blood may once more course and flow
As it was used, oh, long ago."

The words were faint as is the jar
Of air behind a falling star
Felt in a forest where ghosts are.

"Be still," I answered, "if I fail
To succour you, no burning mail
Will be the force to which I quail."

Brave words to whip my spirit on.
Under the leaves the cherries shone.
A moment and I should have done.

But, as the thought came, so did he,
And stood beside the cherry-tree,
And struck his sword upon her knee.

Even while she fell, he went his way,
And laid his sword as erst it lay,
And mournfully awaited day.

Then, drearily, above the rim
Of mountains, rose a sun so dim
I only knew day watching him.

For, as the morning slowly grew,
He took another ghastly hue,
And what was pale had turned to blue.

His corselet was corroded rust,
Between his greaves a briar thrust
Its long head up, his eyes were dust.

His sword still lay upon the ground,
But all at once it moved and wound
Among the grass-blades to a mound

Of heaped-up earth, and entered in,
Inch after inch, for what had been
A sword was now become a thin

Long line of ants, who crawled and went
With the strange, multiple consent
Of myriads working one intent.

Sick and distraught, I turned to where
The weeping maid had been, and there
Was nothing but a gusty air

Which blew upon a ruined town.
Tall girders, stripped of stone, looked
down
On crumbled streets where weeds had
grown.

A doorway opened a gaunt eye
Upon the rats which scurried by.
A roofless window watched the sky.

And all the frayed and brittle soil
Of that dead city seemed to boil
With insects laden down with spoil.

Again I turned and sought the spot
Where one had slumbered, and my hot
Eyes rested on a graveyard plot.

A devastating plague of sand
Had swept it, piled on either hand
Were broken headstones, and a band

Of plundering ants crept in and out
Among the graves and round about.
The very air smarted with drought.

The valley burned without a sun,
Gasping beneath a twilight, dun
And twitched with heat, through which
gnats spun.

And, sweeping it, my eyes could see
No semblance of a cherry-tree,
The plain was flat as plain could be.

But where that long night I had stood
Lay a sarcophagus of wood
Covered with ants as red as blood.

Then suddenly a frozen cry
Tingled along the brazen sky,
And he who uttered it was I.

Tangled in scorching sand I fled.
The mountains closed about my head.
The stifled air proclaimed me dead.

I woke — for I had slept, it seemed.
My head ached and I must have dreamed.
Above me, cherry blossoms gleamed

A slant of whiteness to a sky
So blue it glared bewilderingly.
I crushed an ant and wondered why.

BEHIND TIME

On days when the sky is grey, not blue,
My mind strays back for an age or two,
And amuses itself in a little place
I have made to provide a breathing space
Whenever our twentieth-century air
Heats to a temperature so rare
It stifles fancy, and our thundering cities,
Weighted down by cares and pities,
Load my soul with a heap of dust
Through which no least conceit may
thrust
A single stalk or a single bloom
In a free-flung way. Keats made a room
To house him on afternoons like this;
Poe followed him, and created a bliss
Of black and silver furniture;
And Samain, obedient to the lure
Of both these chambers, builded his
Like as a pea, a sort of *bis*
To the others. But Browning broke new
ground
In Italy, and what he found
Was "a gash in a wind-grieved Apennine"
With a castle a-top. Now this of mine
Is no rock-perched castle, not even a pink
House of scaling stucco just at the brink
Of a blue Neapolitan bay. Browning's
love
Outsoars mine as he soars above
Whatever little there is in me,
I am more modest, as you will see.
My dream is a cottage, trim and neat
As paint can make it, the village street
Runs past, beyond a grove of trees,
But only my gable-ends show through
these
To any one walking up and down
The sleepy street of that sea-side town
Where even the fishermen merely fish
When someone's table's in need of a dish
Of oysters, or eels, or cod. My eaves
Peep archly over the bustling leaves
Of Virginia creeper, and down below
The wall-beds glitter with golden glow,
And asters, and black-eyed sun-flowers,
And a strawberry-bush with its dun
flowers
That smell of allspice stands at each
end
Just where the lawn takes a sudden bend
And turns the corner. A foot or two
From the creaking piazza, a naval review
Of seventy-eights and ninety-fours

Whirls round on a wheel without a
    pause:
Four-masted schooners luff and jibe,
Fill again with wind, and circumscribe
The limit of their revolution,
And in the centre, the "Constitution"
Points always at the very eye
Of whatever wind is blowing by.
Beyond the lawn, a little cliff
Drops to the shore, held firm and stiff
By rooted broom. The chuckling lap
Of waves on shingle, the sudden flap
Of a fisherman's sail as he hoists it up,
A grumbling rowlock — you may sup
On a sunset silence such as this
Each afternoon. The clematis
Drops a petal on the old sea wall
As purple as the lights which crawl
And melt and flow across the bay.
Whipped green and silver with streaks of
    grey
Differently mingled every day.
Along the tall horizon slips
A dim procession of sailing ships
So slowly that they scarcely change
Positions from morning till night. The
    range
Of the telescope planted on the green
Brings illusions of sound where no sound
    has been,
The bustle of shipboard suddenly grown
Near and clear through the glass half-
    crown
Of the eye-piece, but take away your eye,
The ships are still as tapestry.
Here is a foot-path, let us go
And see the place where my flowers grow.
Sunken a foot or two below
The bowling-green, my garden lies,
Flanked by hemlocks of every size
Clipped into peacocks and unicorns,
And monstrous dragons for the scorns
Of noble St. Georges. A hedge of thorns
Protects the tiger-lilies set
In rigid rows. The mignonette
Smells sweet, I see a bunch of it
Plucked by a hand which wears a mit,
Just as I see the pansy faces
Peeking from kerchiefs of Mechlin laces,
And not the trace of rowelled spurs
In the monk's-hood bed where a late bee
    stirs.
Here is a maid and a manikin
Of painted bisque, half-hidden in
An old laburnum's dropping shade.

The little man rests on his spade
And ogles the maiden's broad-brimmed
    hat
Since he can see nothing of her but that.
Paul and Virginia, he and she,
Mincingly fashioned in pottery.
Now up three steps where the sunlight
    sifts
Through a thick pleached alley, when
    one lifts
The latch of the gate, the click as it
    closes
Is like the snap of buds into roses.
See the little apples are taking shape
And colour above our heads, they gape
And gossip between the latticed leaves.
Look down at your feet where the sun-
    light weaves
Quaint patterns of stems and fruit and
    we
Walk round in them deliciously.
Now let us go through my open door
And tread the black-and-white-squared
    floor
And hang our hats on the horns of a deer
I've put in the corner over here.
Four rooms as uneven as carpenter's rule
Ever dared to leave. The first is full
From floor to ceiling of maps and books;
Poetry mostly, by the looks.
Thick little duodecimos,
Slender cloth-covered octavos,
Musty, and fusty, and fingered all,
Make a faded rainbow of each wall.
Within them, faint as a scent of musk
Are words which glimmer through the
    dusk
Of that vanished world which lies just
    over
The hither side of each marbled cover.
The fireplace is low and wide
With a rusty crane against the side
And an oven behind, where I keep my
    cherry
Brandy. Mahogany, pale as sherry,
My writing-table is; the locks
Are brass in the form of crested cocks.
Here are chairs of red and brown
Crumbling leather, pliant as down;
On the arms is manifest
The very spot where my elbows rest
When I balance my mighty folios
And read of men with timber-toes
Who discovered archipelagoes
Or rotted for weeks in a bear-skin tent

With moss for their sole nourishment
Beneath Auroran boreal
Nights for phantasmagorial
Possession of a goodish slice
Of that part of the earth which is noth-
ing but ice.
Now cross the hall and I'll introduce
You to something else; a ship's caboose
Saved from the wreck of the Minnie B.
Gone on the sands in seventy-three.
Here is a lantern which used to scan
The foaming wake of an Indiaman;
These chessmen were scrimshawed out of
the teeth
Of a whale; that knife in its lacquer
sheath
Was filched from the deck of a Chinese
junk
A half-an-hour before she sunk
With her pirate crew; this necklace of
shells
Was strung for the Indian Jezebels
Of Pitcairn Island, who smiled long years
Ago at the "Bounty" mutineers.
The floor of this room seems to careen
Beneath one's feet, and walls of green
Sea-water to dash against the slim
Matched boards of the sides. I hear the
swim
Of a deck-wash sliding from scupper to
scupper,
And down through the flanges of the
upper
Air, faintly flying above the swell,
The everlasting cry: "All's well!"
Or "There she blows!" or "Breakers
ahead!"
I wonder if anything's really dead.
Well, well, there's enough of that. In
here
Is a totally different atmosphere.
A pretty shape, this room, the leather
Hangings keep out all notion of weather,
They are Spanish, embossed in gold and
blue.
That little picture is a view
Of Venice by Guardi, the Piazzetta
In Carnival, a floweret, a
Shimmer, a perfume, an age in petto
Eighteenth century allegretto.
Considerably unlike it hangs
A Turner, where a mountain's fangs
Close over the plunge of a waterfall
With a slant of sunlight striking it all
To the doom of a planet's evenfall.

Jagged, haggard, splintered steep,
Swept with gold above the deep
Abysmal hollow curving under
The bow of the torrent, grim rotunda
Tawny lit and shocked with thunder.
Here's a picture of nothing but the tops
of trees,
Wind-blown, cloud overlooked. If you
please
'Tis the life-like portrait of a breeze,
No more, no less, what Constable saw
On Hampstead Heath when a brisk cat's-
paw
Flurried out of the West-North-West the
prize
Of an Autumn morning. I see your eyes
Stray to the corner where stands my
spinet.
Suppose we consider it a minute,
Salvator Rosa painted the case
Of satin-wood. Is it out of place
To put a drawing by William Blake
Just above? Does it seem to shake
A symmetry? Perhaps, but it's done.
Observe the rolling, crimson sun
Glitter along the huge outline
Of that weary form, relaxed, supine,
A man on the edge of a rocky world
Balanced above an ocean curled
And frozen. All Eternity
Shouts in that over-borne man for me.
Let us sit awhile and hark to the speech
Of a century beyond our reach,
Colossal, fastidious, witty, brave,
Importuning us from the grave.
Shift on your spindle-legged gold-white
chair,
You will not find the answer where
You seek it. Science cannot raise the flap
Between us and these, nor know what gap
Divides Reynolds's, Romney's, Gains-
borough's
Population from men like us.
There seems the fragilest sort of parti-
tion
Between then and now. But what condi-
tion
Do we subscribe to a cruel decree
That what is, for us, is but what we see?
The world shrinks daily; must we confine
Ourselves to a geographer's line,
Choosing our friends by accident
Of almanac? What impertinent
Design is this, which would control
Free intercourse of soul with soul,

Because, forsooth, an airy thing
Brushes us with its bat-like wing.
A thing we cannot see or touch!
Shall such a nothing dare a clutch
At us in passing? So I sit
Considering time and hating it,
Until I glance at that strange clock
Upon the mantel. With a shock,
I see the face is changed, the numbers
Are there no more, something else en-
cumbers
The dial, a half-moon something, writ
About the upper edge of it.
I notice that the iron hands
Point to this crescent, and each stands
Stock still; then I behold the words,
Contrived grotesquely of crossing swords,
And what I read in crimson ink
Is, "It is later than you think!"
I rise and take my latch-key down
And through the peaceful, sleeping town
I walk back to my century,
The dun, dumb years reserved for me
To wander in and call them mine
And be called theirs in every line
Historians may choose to write
Upon my night, my night, my night.

GOUACHE PICTURES OF ITALY
PALAZZO CONTARINI

Beside the high window, but partly withdrawn
And concealed by the fold of a gold-
lacquered screen,
This admirable day-bed discovers the
sheen
Of its hooped salmon satin and yellowing lawn.

On spindle legs, thin as a spider's, it
stands.
The gilding has scaled to a faint silver
tone.
A lavender dust, as of hours outgrown,
Drifts past on a quaver of old sarabands.

Bewilderingly fragile, it baffles decay
With the porcelain pinks on the ormolu
spray
Twined about the Saxe clock. Hark! the
weary sweet chime

Of the hour it strikes. At precisely this
minute

The Duke would declare he was wasting
his time
And the lady half-languidly rise from her
spinet.

Poor flesh and blood lovers long dead,
the fine bloom
Of your coquetry crumbles and smiles in
this room.

THE LIME AVENUE

With a crunching of gravel and flapping
upon it
Of scarlet soutanes, down an alley of
limes,
Where the tree-boles, as evenly distanced
as rhymes,
Cut their long promenade into bars like
a sonnet,

Two cardinals whispering under the trees,
Discussing the doctor's last news of the
Pope,
And artfully hiding an indiscreet hope
With a long pinch of snuff and its con-
sequent sneeze.

Lowsy eyes, pendant jowls, immense
purple-sashed waist,
Soft labial words dripping out on the
taste
Of a greedy ambition. The other —
succinct,

Lips of wire, and face all one cold,
chiselled piece,
Pronouncing his bribe with each word
quite distinct:
"To your connoisseur's palate I offer my
niece."

Pope's arms in a moss-confused lozenge,
an ache
Of slow wind, and the whine of a
gardener's rake.

THE WATER STAIR

Under cypresses, ilexes, myrtles, within
Granite edges, or slipped over broad-
ended stairs,
Is a moving of water, and large tranquil
squares
Stain its umber and gold with a green
lily skin.

No splash, just a ripple which jars the
smooth air
Into damp undulations. Remote and
suspended
Winds pause in the trees, and the shadows are blended
With gleams as of moonlight entangling
drowned hair.

Steps — steps — phantom footsteps.
They shuffle and blur
And crowd the wide stairs with an odd,
timid stir
Thinly teasing the sense where there's
nothing to hear.

Crimson heels, silver clocks, the shock of
them whines
With the shrillness of flutes in the thick
atmosphere.
Purple flutes fading silver and rose
through the pines.

Liquid lap of old water, and I am confused
With the scent of crushed violets my feet
have bruised.

THE STABLE

Two rows of stiff poplars, wind-bitten
and grey,
Flank the high-cobbled courtyard in long,
serried lines;
And between them the old stable-clock
dimly shines
With its cracked yellow dial defying
decay.

It was here that six lumbering, thick-
barreled mares
Were wont to be harnessed to my Lord's
glass coach
When he drove out to call on his neighbours and broach
Some scheme of importance to landed
affairs.

Now the leaves of the poplars may settle
and fall
And drift where they will in the juts of
the wall,
While the grass has half-buried the sharp-
pointed stones.

A ripple of pigeons waves over the yard,
And a toothless old bitch, who is nothing but bones,
Growls drowsily at them to prove she's
on guard.

With a wheeze, and a whirr, and a horrible catch,
The clock strikes eighteen; it is two by
my watch.

FETE AT CASERTA
THE QUEEN OF NAPLES RECEIVES

But tickets, of course, at the door of
the theatre
Scrutinized by a Lord of the Court.
What a blaze
Of wax candles reflected in gilding, a
haze
Of cross-lights like a halo! Is this not
Caserta?

The pit is a ball-room, the stage a bright
stair
Of musicians in livery; the dazzle becomes
An effulgent wax sun where the great
kettle-drums
Crown the apex. Can eyesight endure
such a glare?

The Queen! Hist! The Queen! Though
she's wearing a mask,
No one can mistake her. She approaches
to ask
If the strangers liked France, if they'd
met the Dauphine?

At midnight exactly, proclaimed by six
flutes,
Enter soldiers with plates and a great
galantine
Of hot macaroni, with cream and iced
fruits.

But the Queen sups on two dishes only,
and these
Are prepared by her own special cooks —
Viennese.

SANTA SETTIMANA

On a carpeted bench, thirteen well-
chosen priests,
All tutored and drilled in an excellent
miming.

The Last Supper staged to the sonorous chiming
Of the Pope's special choir in silks and batistes.

His Holiness, bibbed with an apron of lace,
Arises sedately from his great purple chair
And draws off thirteen socks leaving thirteen feet bare,
Washes each in a basin of gold, and with grace

Presents thirteen bouquets, and a paper of coins,
Returns to his carved purple chair, bows, and joins
His well-mannered hands in a semblance of prayer.

Thirteen silver plates laid on exquisite lawn,
Thirteen eager priests' noses snuffing the fare:
Herring salad, broccoli in oil. And each pawn

Gulps the wine the Pope pours. While behind the Pope's guards,
In a stiff inattention, plan their next game of cards.

THE AMBASSADOR

Coat of purple stamped with velvet, satin breeches to match
Of the same sober, elegant hue, white silk stockings
Of a texture so fine that their silver-thread clockings
Seem embroidered on nothing. A great gold-sealed watch.

The slightly bull neck is concealed by the fall
Of a cascade of point-lace imported from Brussels,
And ruffles of lace at the sleeve-ends hide muscles
Too thick for a man who would shine at a ball.

Monsieur l'Ambassadeur aims at all things, it seems:
Wit, duellist, banker, his lottery schemes
Are the whisper of Paris. He glitters to-day

Sardinia's envoy to France, whose finesse
Has taught him the power there is in display;
Note the painstaking fanfaronade of his dress.

The coat was embroidered in China! His air
Is a trifle bombastic as he walks up the stair.

FROM NICE TO ONEGLIA

An astonishing view, she regards it with eyes
All astare at its glitter and space. Where the sea,
Creeping up to the cliffs, leaves a foot or two free,
Runs the path she is following with such gay surprise.

A lady, a Countess, whose long flowing habit
Proclaims her as English by every known rule,
Perched up on a deft little mouse-coloured mule
Stepping daintily, softly, as any jack-rabbit.

What a heavenly journey, this coming by land
From Nice to Oneglia, outriding her train!
She is vastly amused — why, even the sand . . .

The mule shies, she pulls him up sharply and sees,
Just over the edge of her tightly held rein,
A skull, water-washed, grimly bright in the breeze.

The guide, coming up, shrugs his shoulders with shady
Indifference, "It's only the pirates, my Lady."

VILLA CAPOUANA

In the grounds of the Villa Capouana where now,
By municipal order, is a vast cemetery,

The noble and good rest in row after row,
But a single great grave, far more spacious
     and airy,

Is allotted to those so unwise as to die
Or be killed out of spite in the late revo-
     lution.
Here they lie in a heap underneath the
     blue sky,
A heap of white bones in a mixed dis-
     tribution.

What excellent playthings! Giannina has
     wound
A thigh-bone in bright purple rags.
     "This," says she,
"Is Brighella.' And Tito, having pulled
     from the mound

A great hollow skull, gathers violets and
     yew
To put round its head. "See, a King,
     now he's crowned,
And the King asks Brighella to a monster
     review."

So the children set arms, fingers, jaws,
     in platoon,
And play soldiers and kings all the long
     afternoon.

THE CHURCH OF SANTA CHIARA, NAPLES

The day has arrived when the marvellous
     earth
Beneath Santa Chiara has leave to exhibit
The dead it preserves in the stature and
     girth
They displayed when alive, which most
     earths prohibit.

Since even such dead cannot stand, they
     are held
By a rope round the waist concealed by
     their dress.
To be sure they loll oddly, as though they
     rebelled
At this forced resurrection in its full
     loathliness.

But the populace, come by the dozens
     to see
Its neighbours and friends, comments in
     high glee:

"Look at Niccolò Baldi, how rakish he
     looks.

That's because Margherita hangs her
     head right beside him.
She is teasing him still, though they're
     nothing but spooks."
"She's a fright now, at least. I could
     never abide him."

"Nor he you, I believe." They titter and
     leer.
Too bad such a show comes but one day
     a year.

IN THE CAMPAGNA

With his wide crimson cloak and his
     cardinal's hat,
Like an emphasized flower, amazing the
     grass
Of the Autumn Campagna, he stands
     with his fat
Fingers quick on the lock of his gun and
     the glass

Which is tied to an owl on a perch glints
     and glitters
Attracting the larks and the finches that
     fly
In a dazzling confusion of wings and
     sharp twitters.
The cloud of them hides several yards of
     blue sky.

Behind him, two liveried grooms load
     fresh guns
And watch larks and goldfinches fall in
     dozens, quenched suns
Attesting his skill, for the Cardinal's
     game

Is how many small song-birds he can take
     as his booty
Without shooting the owl who is flus-
     tered though tame.
A rare sportsman this Cardinal in his
     moments off duty!

To-night at the Contessa's supper he'll
     boast
That she owes to his prowess the larks
     served on toast.

PORTRAITS, PLACES, AND PEOPLE

TO ELEONORA DUSE

IN ANSWER TO A LETTER

"Regrets and memories these short
    December days."
How the words cut and scar themselves
Across my heart!
Dear lady of the great compassion,
All tenderness enmeshed in withes of
    truth,
Experience harboured for its seeking
    flame,
Clean burning flame of knowledge be-
    yond thought,
Sword-blade of sheerest beauty,
As the sun sinks wanly,
Branch by branch,
Through the shaking, leafless trees,
How cruelly the twilight comes —
I watch it here,
At this long distance from you,
And rage at impotence
Which can give you no brighter present
Than the flicker of a small red candle
Lit by you long ago.
You wrong yourself dwelling upon the
    past;
I have it from your lips:
"The past is dead. The future alone has
    life."
The past is dead, save in the continuity
Of your most inaccessible loveliness.
Where touch is healing should be no
    regret
At that which makes it so.
You walked, and walk, incarnate soul
Of human needs and meetings.
This sight of you is the clarity of courage;
Your movements, insistent, compelling,
    muted trumpets in a still air;
Your voice, ah, dear, that voice, as April
    rain
Dropping at evening on beds of unsprung
    tulips.
Where has there ever been a flesh
So rightly framing such a spirit? Tell me.
You cannot.
Words are pebbles,
A gravel-path for you to tread and spurn.
Music is liker to encase your essence,
Yet you escape, for what you really are
Hangs to no swiftest flash of evocation,

But floats in rondure of its perfectness
Out of our sight as possible, impossible,
Peak of a human capability,
Infinite spirit with the lightest shadowing
Of merciful and finite flesh.
Has any one ever so held the cords of
    life,
Of all our lives, as you?
You dare not say there has and gaze
    truth in the eye.
Look back, then, if you must,
But see plain fact,
Yourself the soul's wine of a generation,
The whispered bourne of blessings to a
    world.

TO ELEONORA DUSE

1923

If you believed my words,
O tragic, incommunicable lady,
Would they lure you for an instant
From your long, rapt contemplation
Of the sunset-tinted clouds
Lowering in grim and huddled spendour
Over the broken turrets of your ruined
    sorrows?
Dead to the sting of anguish,
The misery that you ache no more
Is aching so preponderant and huge
You walk within it as an atmosphere
And breathe its bitterness like some
    gaunt poison
Easing you into numbness
Even of its slow insidious advance.
Where grief has watched
Sits now the ghost of grief.
Where tenderness once held out arms to
    gather
A universe's loneliness,
Reigns now a weariness of feeling,
A kindliness too spent to give itself,
To smile less calmly than a sculptured
    saint
Enduring anthems in an incensed niche.
The small dried cones of my fardel of
    years
Make a poor faggot to light before you,
And yet if you believed them wood not
    wax
Might not the little raw flame of them
Warm you to a single throb of your lost
    life?
I see you there before me,

Distant as the shattered past, the shape-
less future.
The sprig of your sowing withers in my
hands,
Your remoteness is too vast to cherish it.
See, I please it where your somnambulis-
tic feet
May tread upon it
Crushing its fragrance to play round
your dreams
I could give much,
Give back what you will not believe your
own,
Give laughter, tears.
I am not poor in such,
Richer than you are now, perhaps.
You put me by
Gently, as something in your path
Which, scarcely seeing, yet you brush
aside.
You hurt less in the days of your revolt
Than in this quietude of charity.
The sight of you is piercing as a cry,
Your loveliness betrays my eyes to tears,
They smart in falling.
I am no hero-worshipper,
Yet for your sake I long to babble prayers
And overdo myself in services.
Is this not love, then?
My I not write myself disciple, follower?
Unworthy, doubtless, but authentic grain
Sprung from your scattered seed?
Yet you smile and say:
"Of course, it is not true."
If this be not truth,
Then truth and I have never made a
company.
You want no service, no compassion, no
refreshment.
Tranquillity you think you have, or call
it so,
I call it poison dripped from traitorous
urns.
You pass me like a legend sprayed with
flowers,
The legend of my youth, and now hence-
forward
Of my age.
Pass, lady,
To whom I can give nothing, nothing.
Yet here again I say it,
With the doggedness of custom grown
inveterate:
What you gave I give back again and
shall,

Along the smooth years where you wan-
der now,
Perfectly heedless of your heedlessness.
Truth is a brazen thing, and I,
Banging against the brass of utter fact,
Do make perhaps a horrid din
To your peace-longing ears.
So be it, I am silent,
But still here, believed or not,
A chance creation not at all desired,
Yet so existing while our double names
Shall carry any meaning to men's minds.

THE MADONNA OF CARTHAGENA

Where a chain of sandy beaches
Cuts across an open sea,
Blue as asters, pink as peaches
Out beyond the farthest reaches
For a distant eye to see,
Every colour that one wishes
May be witnessed hereabout
From the sand-dunes to the ocean.
If the tide is going out,
There are sea-gulls in commotion
Flying over where a fish is;
In a pool as green as grass
Crimson shatterings may pass
Or a blackness blowing over
Quench the colour like a cover;
And the fronds of water-weeds,
Thick as leather, wave and feather,
Tossing stems blown out with beads
As wave after wave recedes.
If the tide is coming in,
What a thunder! What a din!
With the slappings and the swishes,
Creeping slowly and a thin
Line of little forward breakers
Licking onward up the sand
Like the fingers of a hand
Tapping where they'll soon be takers
For the sea has grabbed the land.
Up beyond the sand and eel-grass
Is a sunny little town
Built of palm-tree and palmetto.
It's a city here in petto,
With its huts all golden brown,
And above, upon the thatches
Of its roofs are purple patches
Where the bougainvillaea's sown
Light-heeled seeds to wax and bloom
there,
Always finding ample room there
For the forest's fleecy down.

Here were Indians long ago
In the days before a prow,
Topped by carven saint or sinner,
Sailed across the Spanish Main.
When the caravels and galleons
Of an overweening Spain
Had not found the precious metals
Of the Incas, or in vain
Wasted men and blood and treasure
Forcing Indians from their leisure
Just to glut the greed of gain.
When the opal orchid petals
Were no scientific find,
But a shimmer in the wind.
Ere the feet of dappled stallions
Set the print of iron shoe
On a sandy sunken shore,
But the dappled stallions waited
All in vain, for they were fated
To recross the sea no more.
And their masters often died
Waiting with them, side by side,
An emaciated crew.
All that happened long ago.
Now the vessels, to and fro,
Come as punctually as clock-work
Or at least they mean to do.
And they carry under hatches
All things needed by the cities
They have planted on the sands.
And the monasteried monks,
Hearing tales in quiet cells,
Whispered low in broken snatches
To an undertone of bells
From some wanderer overseas,
Find their hearts moved by strange pities
At the listening to these,
And they volunteer in bands
To convert the simple dwellers
Of these unimagined lands,
Worshipping as they should not.
Manner bringers, pardon sellers,
Vessels carry them in hordes
With a zeal that's piping hot.
Bishops lay aside their croziers,
Hew palmettos into boards,
Build them churches as a duty,
Fill them with whatever booty
They can find of silk or wax,
Woolen fabric, cloth of flax,
Goods of tailors, mercers, hosiers,
In the bottoms that come in,
And for payment wink at sin.
So the church grows, hung with feathers
Woven by the tired Indians,

Lined with these and Spanish leathers,
For at bargains none are keener
Than the potentates of churches.
So it was with Carthagena.
On a hill that rises straightly
From the town, it stands in stately
Isolation, gazing far
All across the stretching ocean.
Privateers and men of war,
Lost in reckoning, see its spire
Burning like a sacred fire
From the broad-leaved palms which rise
Just to where the windowed eyes
Stare forever out to sea.
And the captain calls his people,
Points to where that far-off shining
Glitters like a distant star,
Tells them, not without emotion,
That he knows now where they are,
They may cease their long repining
For that shimmering has been a
Joy to many, 'tis the steeple
Of the Church of Carthagena.
Sailors call the sunny flame
By another, fragrant name:
When the sparkle in the sky
First appears, they raise a cry
"Look! It is our Lady's eye!"
"The Madonna of the Ships" —
So she is to sailors' lips.
And indeed she is a sweetly
Lovely image, most discreetly
Veiled in gauzy stars and roses
With an iridescent cloak,
Made, at least so one supposes,
Noticing its changing sheen —
Ruby sometimes, sometimes green —
Of the wings of humming-birds.
From the hem of it, there poke
Little shoes of gold and blue,
Sewn with gems, not one or two,
But a toe-full flashing through
The beholder's head as though
He were watching the rainbow.
On her head a crown is set
Where great moons of carven jet
Are in fact no jet at all,
But black opals; and the fall
Of her wimple wrought of lace
Half obscures her wondrous face.
Only half, for there's her mouth,
And her nose, an awkward feature
For so heavenly a creature:
There's a sauciness of shape,
And the tip points upward slyly,

But her mouth is most demurely
Small and wistful, yet to see it
Is to know a sudden drouth.
But the priest, who's old and wily,
If you question him says, "Surely
God has ordered, and so be it!"
Glorious, excellent Madonna,
She of ships, and furious oceans,
Here at the Antipodes,
How should she resemble these
Dim Cathedral Virgins, hearing
Ancient fly-blown sins forever,
Snivelled into their dull ears
For eternities of years.
Sins here have a different flavour.
We must cast our hide-bound notions
Of her manner of appearing.
Here she is in perfect semblance
Of what she should be, her lips
Frame her name, or its resemblance:
"The Madonna of the Ships."

But there is a curious story
You may hear about the streets.
Though they tell it to her glory,
Every second man one meets
Winks his eye when you address him
Speaking of her brave attire,
And if you go on and press him,
He will cross himself and say
'Tis no wonder, for the day
That the pirate ship caught fire
At the entrance of the bay
Was when last the priests arrayed her
Newly for a festival
Offered for the town's escape
From a sacking; they displayed her
In the morning. All agape,
Lacking reason's wherwithal
To digest this information,
You may beg for farther light
On so dim a revelation.
But your man is nothing loth,
For his city's praise and pride,
To detail upon his oath
What no citizen will hide:
The possession of a Blessing
Such as nowhere else can be,
Not in any place soever
All along that spacious sea,
At no river-mouth or harbour
Of that many-harboured sea.
So you learn that that same night
For a space of several hours
The high altar was deserted,

Not a trace of waxen image,
Only dropped and withered flowers
Shaken from her feather cape.
Then the church's doors were closed,
But a panic was averted
For the priests gave out she dozed
Being weary. All that night
The priests knelt and said their masses,
Swung their censers left and right,
Moved before the empty altar
With their passes and repasses,
And their sacred psalms and droning.
A great wind outside was moaning.
And the whirled palmettos scratching
On the walls, their great leaves catching
In the flimsy window shutters.
Streams of rain poured from the gutters.
One young priest began to falter
Fearing doom or miracle,
Or a Demon out of Hell.
But his fellows chanted on
Orison for orison.
Suddenly a fearful gale
Shook the church, and furious hail
Rattled on the wooden roof,
Like a squad of eager devils
Spitting flame from horn to hoof
Showering down a thousand evils.
And a window burst asunder.
There was heard a peal of thunder,
A distracting, dooming thunder,
Bearing omen in its rolling,
Tolling dolefully and slowly,
While the church stood slightly under
This reverberate and wholly
Overhanging dome of thunder.
Every joist and rafter quivered,
And the leather hangings shivered.
So protracted was the thunder,
Such an everlasting thunder,
That the priests both old and young
Were quite paralyzed of tongue,
And they ceased their weary singing,
Saying nothing after that.
Truth to tell, they fell down flat.
Each one wanted to be hid,
None saw what the others did.
Each priest's eyes were shut, each prayed.
But the storm seemed to be laid.
For a perfect calm was there,
Not a flutter nicked the air
Which appeared to hold its breath
Folding round them like a wreath
From the open window where
The palmetto leaf hung in

Still as stone, but dripping wet.
And the dripping made a noise
Like a nail which strikes on tin
Or a tinkling little bell
Palpitating for a spell
From some lonely hermitage
At the bottom of a dell.
And the pause endured an age,
Till each priest was moved to see,
Dared once more to look and see,
What that tinkling noise might be.
And they saw the altar set
For high mass and on it standing
Their dear Lady, and her poise
Was that of a flying gull
Just an instant after landing.
The priests gasped: "A Miracle!"
Sobbing, kneeling down before
Their Madonna, on the floor.
But the image made no sign,
Only her far-looking eyes
Gazed upon them with benign
Pleasantness, as one who sighs
And, in sighing, smiles again,
Pitiful to mortal men.
But they might not long indulge
Their great wonder and alarm,
Which no telling may divulge,
Seeing her escaped from harm.
For the old priest bade them haste
To relieve their Lady's plight
From the ravage of the night.
She was mud from foot to waist,
In her crown long weeds were tangled,
One of her bejewelled shoes
Was not there, and sea-shells jangled
Caught upon her feathered dress.
No time this to stare and pray,
Even though the wits confuse,
She must be well comforted,
Cherished, cosseted, and tended
Now her voyaging is ended,
Bathed, and combed, and clothed, and
    fed
With the sacred wine and bread.
Awed before her holiness,
Frightened priests ran to obey,
Getting in each other's way
In their eagerness to serve her,
Be the one most to deserve her.
In the end the task was done;
And the instant that the sun,
Calculated to exalt her,
Shone upon the wooden altar,
There they placed her reverently,

Crossing breast and bowing knee
To their "Lady of the Sea"
Blazoned in new finery.
When the clock that hung inside
The tall steeple stood at ten,
The church door was opened wide,
Everyone could enter then,
And the priests were told the news:
How the pirates nearly came
To the city, when a flame
Burst up from the nearing ship;
How they let the cable slip
Trying to put the fire out;
How the ship went on the shore
Lacking room to put about;
That the drowned were a full score,
And the others clapped in jail.
So the populace filed slowly
Past the altar, meek and lowly,
Saying "Mary, Mary, Hail!"
And the young priest, cold and pale,
Whispered the thing that befell,
How it was a miracle!
But the old priest said, " 'Tis well,"
Joining ancient finger-tips,
"Bless our Lady of the Ships!"

TUNE

There's a lilt abroad in my head to-night
Like a nodding columbine,
It joins to no words, it draws no breath
From any idea of mine.
Yet it crosses and recrosses through my
    brain
With a sweetness of mulberry wine.

There are tapping red heels in the heart
    of this tune,
And the flirt of flickered fans,
There are meadows a-spray with a but-
    tercup June
And halted caravans,
Where a gipsy fiddle cries "down the
    middle"
To a light that is Aldebaran's.

'Tis a tune to wake mummied kings and
    make
Fra Angelico's angels by scores
Cease their harping and hymns and in-
    dulge in the whims
Of a *bal masqué*, Louis Quatorze,
Where the little devils of rhythm perch
On the shoes of ambassadors.

Pavans? No! No! Nor sarabands,
Nor minuets for me.
But capriccioso, a stamping bolero
With a crowd come in to see,
And the moon winking over a curtain's
edge
Like a peeping Tom Mercury.

Not a thought, no words, not anything
But a lilt in my head to-night.
Inconsequent as a butterfly's wing
Or the skim of a meteorite.
Put me down as the slave of a toss and
a tune
A humble neophyte
With the trees and the breeze, as
Terpsichore's
Dedicate eremite.

But, listen, the gusty wind is hushed,
The corn is stiff and still,
The moon like a beetle upside down
Sheds no more light on the hill,
And a little goblin spirited thought
Steals in against my will
Arousing me to the sight of inimical day.
Give the goblin creature its breakfast then,
I say,
And loaded with morning I crawl upon
my way
To the world where men ravel and rave
but none of them dares to play.

GRIEVANCE

All these years I have remembered a night
When islands ran black into a sea of silk,
A bay and an open roadstead set to a
shimmer like cool, white silk
Under an August moon.
Trees lifted themselves softly into the
moonlight,
A vine on the balcony glittered with a
scattered brilliance,
The roofs of distant houses shone solidly
like ice.
Wind passed,
It touched me.
The touch of the wind was cool, im-
personal;
The fingers of the wind brushed my face
and left me.
I remember that I shivered,
And that the long, continuous sound of
the sea beneath the cliff

Seemed the endless breathing of the days
I must live through alone.
I grieve for that night as for something
wasted.
You are with me now, but that was
twenty years ago,
And the future is shortened by many days.
I no longer fear the length of them,
I dread the swiftness of their departure.
But they go — go —
With the thunderous rapidity of a water-
fall,
And scarcely can we find a slow, cool
night
To consider ourselves,
And the peaceful shining of the moon
Along a silken sea.

PARADOX

You are an amethyst to me,
Beating dark slabs of purple
Against quiet smoothnesses of heliotrope,
Sending the wine-colour of torches
Rattling up against an avalanche of pale
windy leaves.

You enter my heart as twilight
Seeping softly among the ghosts of beeches
In a glade where the last light cleaves for
an instant upon the swung lash of a
waterfall.
You oversweep me with the splendid
flashing of your darkness,
And my flowers are tinted with the light
of your thin grey moon.

An amethyst garden you are to me,
And in your sands I write my poems,
And plant my heart for you in deathless
yew trees
That their leaves may shield you from
the falling snow.

Open your purple palaces for my enter-
tainment,
Welcome my feet upon your polished
floors,
And keep in your brazier always
One red hot coal;
For I come at the times which suit me,
Morning or evening,
And I am cold when I come down the
long alleys to you.

Clang the doors against the multitude
who would follow me.
Is not this my chamber where I would
sleep?

HIPPOCRENE

With you,
    I sup on singing birds
And drink hot sunlight cooled with clouds.

With you,
    I ride the slanting winds,
Toss coloured balls back and forth over
    the moon,
Swing up through trees,
And slide down swiftly upon beds of
    irises.

When you are here,
    we stack words at the end of a
    rainbow
And bowl at them with swans' eggs.

We run races through grass
    to old bronze temples,
And sitting under marble porches,
Count daisy petals
    to the tapping of a bell.

We leap from steeples,
And land in flowered palaces.

In cedar-scented parlours you tell me
    tales,
Long, slow tales,
    strummed lightly on a lute;
And I lie on blue cushions and watch the
    sea
    and hear your voice.

With you,
    I do all these things —
How therefore should I care
    to gabble with the donkey-men,
To gossip with the old women
    who sell turkeys,
To watch my next-door neighbour plait
    her hair
    and lament the untoward price of
    butter.

Until you come I will sit here
    alone, by a quiet window,
And, with a fine brush,
    trace little pictures
To show when you return.

THORN PIECE

Cliffs,
Cliffs,
And a twisted sea
Beating under a freezing moon.
Why should I,
Sitting peaceful and warm,
Cut my heart on so sharp a tune?

Liquid lapping of seething fire
Eating the heart of an old beech-tree.
Crack of icicles under the eaves,
Dog-wind whining eerily.

The oaks are red, and the asters flame,
And the sun is warm on bark and stones.
There's a Hunter's Moon abroad to-
    night —
The twigs are snapping like brittle bones.

You carry a lantern of rose-green glass,
Your dress is red as a Cardinal's cloak.
I kneel at the trace of your feet on the
    grass,
But when I would sing you a song, I
    choke.

Choke for the fragile careless years
We have scattered so easily from our
    hands.
They flutter like leaves through an
    Autumn sun,
One by one, one by one.

I have lived in a place,
I shall die in a place,
I have no craving for distant lands.
But a place is nothing, not even space,
Unless at its heart a figure stands

Swinging a rose-green lantern for me.
I fear the fall of a rose-green gate,
And the cry of a cliff-driven, haunted sea,
And the crackle of ice while I wait —
    wait!

Your face is flowers and singing sun,
Your hands are the cool of waters falling.
If the rose-green bars should drop be-
    tween
Would you know that I was calling?

For the stars I see in that sky are black.
The kind earth holds me and laughs in
    my ear.

I have nothing to do with the planet's
  track,
I only want you, my Dear.

Beyond is a glaze, but here is fire,
And love to comfort, and speech to bind,
And the common things of morning and
  evening,
And the light of your lantern I always
  find.

One or the other — then let it be me,
For I fear the whirl of the cliff-wrung sea,
And the biting night. You smile at my
  fears,
But the years — years —
Like leaves falling.

ON CHRISTMAS EVE

What is the thing I would say to you
Ere the time when we can say nothing at
  all,
Neither you to me nor I to you,
And between us is sprung a smoky wall?
If I am left, I shall push the mist
And crack my eyes to a gimlet point
Striving to pierce its every twist
And bore a hole through some weakened
  joint.
But I know very well it will disappoint
My keenest urge, and I shall be left
Baffled, forsaken, and blind to boot,
But with still the feeling that in some
  cleft
You linger and watch and maybe hear
The dim and feeble substitute
For speech which may travel from sphere
  to sphere
And hold itself perpetual
Merging the there and here.

I am counted one who is good at words,
And yet, in placing my thought of you
Where I can see it, hard and clear,
This, that, and the other, in review,
I think that only the songs of birds
Are adequate for the task which I
Can never even make the attempt
To come at ever so haltingly.
I earn my own contempt
That I should presume to try.

You have lifted my eyes, and made me
  whole,
And given me purpose, and held me faced

Toward the horizon you once had placed
As my aim's grand measure. Your starry
  truth
Has shown me the worm-holes in Earth's
  apple,
You have soothed me when I dared not
  look,
And forced me on to seek and grapple
With the nightmare doubts which block
  the ways
Of a matrix-breaking, visioning soul
When, lacking the arrogance of youth,
I started to carve the granite days
Into tablets of a book.

The hundred kindly daily things,
I have numbered them all though I may
  not speak them.
Sitting here on this Christmas Eve,
I think of you asleep above,
And the house has a gentleness which
  clings,
And a wide content of love.
What you have said and what you have
  done,
I should not have known enough to seek
  them,
But now the very rooms you leave
Have a peace which hangs like a hyacinth
  scent
All about them.
Your ways, your thoughts,
I would surely rather lose the sun
Than be without them.
So absolutely is it I am bent
To know how you are excellent.

Dearest, I have written it down
For your Christmas Day, but not half is
  said.
I might write so long it would span the
  town
And yet scarce mention more than a
  shred
Of you and you, and you and me;
And of all that I know so well to be,
How wretchedly I have scratched the
  stone!
You must know the end instead.

A NEW YEAR'S CARD

Everyone has his fancies, I suppose,
And to-night I should like to walk round
  a towered city

Blowing a blue silver trumpet.
Then, when all the people had run out
To see me circling the walls
Playing on a blue trumpet,
I would stop and sing them a song all
   about your loveliness.
I would make it of the flicker of the air
   and the sweep of the sun,
And when I had finished, they would see
   you sitting on a cloud
And know how far you surpassed others
   in everything.
But there is no towered city,
And I have no blue trumpet,
And those who meet you seem to feel
   about you much as I do without the
   aid of these accessories,
Which proves how very useless a thing
   a poet is, after all.

FACT

Sea-roses blowing on a high, white cliff
Rayed out above their leaves, bent by a
   whiff
Of salty wind. White snowdrops over
   snow.
The colour of a field where violets grow.
The tingling rings of honeysuckle bines.
Cloud shadows drawing over Apennines.
Young paper birches, with their lustred
   stems
Brightening old woods . . . . But similes
   like these
Are stock in trade with all poets. If you
   please,
Therefore, we'll put aside such brum-
   magems
And merely state a proven certainty,
Which is that you are fine exceedingly
And all that matters in Heaven or Earth
   to me.

HERALDIC

I have often a vision of your face,
Seen through the crossing branches of
   young trees.
Your face, as a white, flowing water,
At a little distance, beyond the reeds of
   a shallow shore.
Ironical, my lady, that Spring, the barb
   and whet-stone of my love,
Should net you from me in leaves and
   whisperings!

Yet I would not lose even this,
Although the sight and leashing tease
   me to madness.

QUINCUNX

A lady was given a shell which kept in
   its convolutions
The dash and sucking of waves.
At first the lady played with it,
Putting it to her ear.
But soon tiring of this,
She gave it into the hands of a skilful
   carver
Who fashioned out of it an intaglio of
   great beauty;
This the lady set in a band of gold
And placed in a cabinet for all to admire.
Now people praise the delicate gem and
   pass on,
And it lies on its velvet,
Flat, and cold, and admirable;
But the fresh sound of waves
Is no longer about it.

CARREFOUR

O you,
Who came upon me once
Stretched under apple-trees just after
   bathing,
Why did you not strangle me before
   speaking
Rather than fill me with the wild white
   honey of your words
And then leave me to the mercy
Of the forest bees?

GRANADILLA

I cut myself upon the thought of you
And yet I come back to it again and
   again.
A kind of fury makes me want to draw
   you out
From the dimness of the present
And set you sharply above me in a wheel
   of roses.
Then, going obviously to inhale their
   fragrance,
I touch the blade of you and cling upon
   it,
And only when the blood runs out across
   my fingers
Am I at all satisfied.

CAUSTIC

Certainly you gave me your heart,
I don't in the least deny it.
And a splendid heart it was,
Of white sea jade strewn over with ochre
shadings and polished to the tip touch
of brilliance.
I strung it on my watch-chain.
But then, I seldom wear a watch nowa-
days;
I do not need it to tell that the black
sun
Is sinking into a sea of garnet flame.

ONE! TWO! THREE!

Poems,
Poems,
What are poems but words
Set edgewise up like children's blocks
To build a structure no one can inhabit.

I fling you words,
Raw and bleeding
Out of my desolation.
Tock! Tock! The clock is no more mo-
notonous than I,
Beating your name to every new vibra-
tion,
Aching upon remembrance with a dura-
bility
Which wears a knife-edge all along each
shouting nerve.

Day and night wind round upon my lone-
liness
Coiling me in a serpent strangle of time.
One morning opens like another:
Sun on each wet bush and tree;
They laugh and rustle,
But I shut my eyes.
How wide the sky is!
And all that way the sun must go
Before another day will have been ended.

Lamps, work, and sunrise,
And again — again —
Always again, and each day tastes like
powder
Brittle and salt.
And each night goes like water
Weeping along a heavy wall of stone.

And nothing comes.
It cannot come,

Since you are all that ever could have
come.
I count them — one, two, three, and
ten's a bundle;
A tally of burnt sticks
A heap of twigs,
With not one little bell-flower nodding
up between them.

So then I take my blocks
And neatly place them
One balancing another.
I mock that ghastly clock and make a
cupola of windows
And out of each I gaze awhile
Looking down long roads for you.
Then I put in a paved forecourt-yard,
And lay my smoothest squares,
And plant wide borders of campanulas.
But what I plant is nothing;
What comes up
Is fire-weed.
How often have I seen it
Glaring above the silver-grey of rotted
boards
Where a deserted farmhouse
Was falling gently,
Each year a little more of it would settle.

Tush! This is fooling.
Words,
Words,
I think I hate them.
You cannot live in them,
And so they are no more to me
Than spiders' webs:
Tall, floating, ghostly webs.
Hanging above the candles of a church
When someone's to be buried.

Therefore I will put my words away,
And count the ticking of the clock
As men count pins in solitary cells.
To-morrow it may rain
And then, at least,
I shall not have to watch the terribly
slow spanning
Of the sun
Across that reach of sky.

ALTERNATIVES

You mistake me, Madame, I ask for
nothing.
I give arrogantly and with indifference.

These are no wall-fruits, soft and sugary,
    I offer you,
But dragon-berries,
Burnt black with their own fire,
Grown on brambles in the Courts of
    Destiny.
You may refuse them if you please,
Since choice is not denied you.
Then you will be lone as a rattling leaf
On an upland oak-tree,
Flinging its single shadow
Across a treeless snow.

THRENODY

On an evening of black snow
I walked along the causeway,
Wishing that I too might melt
Between the agitated fingers
Of a stuttering, intolerable sea.

TANKA

Roses and larkspur
And slender, serried lilies;
I wonder whether
These are worth your attention.
Consider it, and if not —

REFLECTION

Why does my clock persist in marking
    the hour after that which it is?
Scornful clock!
Do you wish to remind me that there is
    never any present,
Only a future and a long, long past?

PASTIME

*"Whose pretty pawn is this
And what shall be done to redeem it?"*
                CHILDREN'S GAME

I am immoderately fond of this place.
My thoughts run under it like the roots
    of trees and grasses,
They spread above it like fluttering, in-
    consequential leaves.
Spring comes to me with the blossoming
    of the snow-drop under the arbor-vitae.
So all Springs come, and ever must do.
Spring ripens with the crocus cups on
    the South lawn,
Blue and white crocuses, remains of an
    ancient garden,
By the side of an ancient house —
So they told me, so I believed.

That shadowy structure holds a distant
    charm,
I see its walls printed upon the air, in
    certain moods,
And build it back into solidity with awed
    enjoyment.
But that is fairy-tale or history,
And I am more concerned with recollection.

How perpetually the seasons mark them-
    selves!
Tulips for April,
Peonies for May.
The pillar-rose has not lacked its robin's
    nest since I remember,
Nor the pink horse-chestnut its mob of
    honey-bees:
The boom of them is essence of sleep
    and flowers,
Of Summer sleep and poetry mixed to-
    gether.
Yet there are differences even in the
    repeated lilt of time.
I seem to think the humming-birds are
    fewer,
And I have not seen a luna-moth for
    years.

Now, suddenly, here is a grosbeak
Perched in the double-cherry near the
    door.
He suggests that I look him over,
His striped black and white,
His rose-red triangle of waistcoat.
He is clearly on view for commendation,
Displaying himself as though I were his
    wife or his tailor
Observing to pronounce a verdict.
I had contemplated second childhood,
But scarcely believed it imminent,
And here I am plunged in it.
A rose-breasted grosbeak indeed,
And the last I saw was in that long, first
    childhood.
Senility may have its compensations,
I shall hunt up my old butterfly-net
And prowl about to-night seeking luna-
    moths.

AFTER AN ILLNESS

TO A CAT FROM WHOM ONE HAS BEEN
    SEPARATED FOR A LONG TIME

I have come back, Winky.
After a long time — yes.

There was a heavy sodden sea,
And I in the midst of it.
Before me, white snakes swam in a slime
of seaweed.
They drew their bodies through the sea-
weed with a dreadful rustle
Like dead leaves on sand,
And left long open lanes behind them
Which glowed a clotted purple
Under the rays of a bursting, half-sunk
sun.
Somewhere, on the right, were shores
With high glass cliffs.
The cliffs were hot and leapt up and
down unceasingly,
And the heat from them blistered my
body
Even under the water as I swam.
A wind rose
And drove the weeds faster upon me,
And I struggled in fear of the snakes who
came swiftly — swiftly —
Then I sank down somewhere out of the
sea
Into a place of mist.
I was blind,
But my ears were shrunken points of
awareness,
I was anguished by the keenness of my
ears,
For all round were loud voices
Shouting harsh, unintelligible things
Which I strove to understand, but could
not.
I trod upon the voices,
But they shifted like pebbles beneath my
feet.
I fought with them,
Flinging them from me,
Pushing them down with my hands.
At last I had them under me and I was
rising —
I saw nothing, but I was rising —
Then my mouth choked with salt,
And the salt entered my eyes and unsealed
them.
Light was an explosion in my brain,
And I floated again in the seaweed
sea
Under the bloody cliffs which leapt like
flame.

Now I am sitting in a room again,
With fire-light fluttering on the walls
And you in my lap — purring.

Little cat, are you as glad to have me to
lie upon
As I am to feel your fur under my hand?
Your purr sounds like the blowing of
feathers in a wind;
It is a strangely comfortable sound,
And there is no other,
For the night smiles and says nothing.

"RODE THE SIX HUNDRED"

A June-bug has just flown in through my
window,
And to-day I sat among narcissus and
grape-hyacinths
Drinking the sudden sun.
The terrible Winter has passed
Flinging my garden full of flowers
But for me I think it will not be long,
Not long,
Before it is the end.

Ah, my flowers!

THE SILENT HUSBAND

The gifts of Heaven to you and me have
not been equal.
You play your table-lute even when it is
stringless,
With the movement of your hands draw-
ing forth the five-coloured sounds which
delight you.
Your Unworthy One is dull,
She hears only what is.
I beg you, therefore, my Lord,
Speak the words which I am fain to
believe abide in your heart.

THE "PLUM–BLOSSOM"
CONCUBINE WRITES TO THE
EMPERER MING HUANG

I have painted my eyebrows like willow-
leaves to delight you.
I have painted them like cassia-leaves to
attract your fancy.

Now the leaves of all the trees have
fallen,
And snow hisses from the sky.

My Lord,
Could you look in this mirror,
You would see

My face, white as heaped snow,
My lips, red as sunset
Between peaks of ice.

OLD EXAMINATION HALL

CHINA

Thickly green is the moss on the corroded
    roof-tiles of this hall,
Loud, loud, the cry of the wind striking
    and moving the hinges of the old doors,
Silver as evening mist the spiders' webs
    spun about the corners.

They broke their hearts here, bending
    over the pen-brushes,
They tore their hearts upon the glittering
    words of the T'ang poets,
They went mad, babbling Confucius and
    Mencius to the cold clouds passing
    above an open window.

All this they did to wear a violet coat
    and a belt-clasp of agate stones set in
    rubies.
Now through the windy hall sucks a ca-
    dence of falling seas,
Seas withdrawn along an ancient shore,
Backward seas
Turned,
Running in great strides upon a bold and
    distant continent.

PILLAR PRINTS

THE CUT SHADOW

Who sees the metal of the Temple mirrors
Across the blowing lustre of reflected
    trees?
So those who look into my heart
See only the faint, surging vision of your
    face.

LUSTRE

Your face to me is like the slope of a
    snow-mountain
In moonlight.
You, too, I cannot look at steadily.

ACCOLADE

"The garden was admirable," she said,
    nine hundred years ago,
And in saying so, made it immortal.

GREEN SHADOWS

The moon on the very white sand of the
    garden
Is more pleasing to my eyes
Than the silver embroidered dress of the
    Lady Yasurahi,
Since she permits the Lieutenant-General
    of the Right Bodyguard
To row her in his boat.

DEBIT

Passing my nights with books,
The morning moon brings a sad greeting.

PAYMENT

After a night of labour
Better a misty sky than a white sunrise.

THE AUTUMN HEART

Faint and far the cry of the migrating
    geese,
Neither do they come near my house.

TO TWO UNKNOWN LADIES

Ladies, I do not know you, and I think
I do not want to. And a strange begin-
    ning
I make with that. Admitted; there's the
    odds.
You live between the covers of a book,
At least for me, but then I've known a
    crowd
Of other people who do that. My mind
Is stuffed with phantoms out of poets'
    brains.
But you are out of nothing but the air,
Or were, rather, for one of you is dead.
Dead or alive, it is the same to me,
Since all our contact lies in printer's ink.

But even this, peculiar as it is,
Is but a thread of singularity.
Here is another, that I see you double,
Each one beheld in profile, as it were.
And yet the full-face view is not com-
    posite,
But shows two totally specific halves
Which do not blend and still are not
    distinct.
And again why should I perplex my eyes
With trying so hard to draw you both
    together

As though you were a lighted candle, split
Upon an oculist's dissecting spectacles?

You see the thing is really not so simple
As A.B.C., or Keats, or "Christabel,"
And that is where the plague comes in for me.
For here, sitting quite calmly in my chair,
Settled down comfortably to an evening's reading,
I open up the queerest possibility,
Namely: the visitation of a ghost.
Suppose I throw you down the glove at once
And say I'm haunted, does that bring the answer?
If so, it blurs beyond what I can grasp
And foggy answers leave us where we were.

If either of you much attracted me
We could fall back upon phenomena
And make a pretty story out of psychic
Balances, but not to be too broad
In my discourtesy, nor prudish neither
(Since, really, I can hardly quite suppose
With all your ghostliness you follow me),
I feel no such attraction. Or if one
Bows to my sympathy for the briefest space,
Snap — it is gone! And, worst of all to tell,
What broke it is not in the least dislike
But utter boredom.

Now I acknowledge you are sensible,
And so I put it squarely; is there not
A strange absurdity in being haunted
By ghosts who crack one's jaws upon a yawn?
If that were all of it! But nothing's all.
For just as I am oozing into sleep,
See-sawing gently out of consciousness,
A phrase of yours will laugh out loud and clang
Me broad awake. And still there's more to come:
Sometimes I catch the faintest whiff of flutes.
And that I hold to be a paradox.

Did ever ladies lead so dull a life
As you? At least according to my taste
(I'll be polite enough to put it so).

You wrote, but, Great Saint Peter, tell me how!
With half a destiny. Now we, poor devils,
Fill our ink-wells with entrails, pour our veins
To wet a pencil point, and end at last
As shrivelled as a pod of money-wort,
And (let me say this in a neat aside)
We hope as shining. So do artists live,
And skulls are best when turned to flower-pots.

Now your way: Half a year, or more, or less;
A book tossed off between two sets of tennis,
Or jotted down some morning of hard frost
When the hounds could not run. Pale Jesus Christ,
Is this an effort worthy to be classed
Beyond the writing of cake recipes?
One of you painted. Well, you have no shame
To call such trash a picture. Years and years
You studied with the patient, stupid zeal
Of every amateur, and to this day
You never guess how badly you have done.

You speak of music, and my nerve-ends sting
Thinking of Chopin sentimentalized
By innocent young ladyhood; of Liszt
Doted upon, his tinsel rhodomontade
Held for high romance. And the ghastly nights
On cracked hotel pianos! It would be
Experience to read of washier stuff.
And yet — and yet — this clearly is not all.
Or why should I go back to you again,
Evening and evening, in a kind of thirst,
Surprising my tongue upon an almond taste.

A puzzling business. Everything comes back
And hooks upon a question. I suspect
Myself of cheating, stacking a full pack
With diamond Jacks extraordinary and Queens
Of Spades enough to make a declaration
Of quite superb inviolability.

But if the pack were dealt again, what then?
So what's the truth behind my set of it,
If I can keep my eyes clear long enough
To get a squint thereat? Almonds, I said,
Smooth, white, and bitter, wonderfully almonds.

Your fingers were unequal to the task
Of fashioning pictures, they were not enough.
For pictures take the whole and whip it round
To something out of you; and this you could
Contrive, but not as artists, since this thing
Was not your making. You were pigment, line.
I will not split you up to parts and parts,
Suffice it that the pictures here are you.
Double and single, like chrysanthemums,
Each of one family, but with just differences
Of colour and habit and the arch of stem.

Two halves, I said, and here I patterned rightly.
A frail half and a virile, but both shoots
Of one straight mother tree. It is your nobleness
That shocks a fire across these photographs
And makes them a contentment for strained eyes
Hurt by the ugliness of crowds in streets,
Stumbling short-sighted in a group of gargoyles.
You might have posed for caryatides,
With wind-drawn garments sucking round your limbs,
Your beauty blushing through their flattened gauze,
Before a temple, on a sunny day.

I wonder I am Greek enough to feel
Such solace in mere outline. But again,
As always where I find you are concerned,
This does not finish your effect. For when
I write down Greek, it is inadequate.
Marble you are, but there's that jet of fire
Like a red sunset on a fall of snow.
I feel a wind blowing off heather hills,

Am vaguely conscious of the moan of waves,
And seaweed fronds pulsating in a pool.
Now this, of course, is anything but Greek.

Horses and dogs! You say yourself that they
Are stuck with limpet-closeness to your life.
And there, I think, is more than parallel.
For dogs and horses have a wistfulness,
A pathos, in their bursts of gaiety
Which tears the heart, even when crinkytail
Sets dogs in bundles racing round a lawn,
Or snaps a horse's feet to jigging springs
Cat-dancing with a sudden twitch of ears.
And you are both like that, for your jokes bob
Under taut flags across a bay of tears.

That figure is so old, I feel a twinge
Of hot compunction at using it again.
But even artists stub their toes sometimes
Upon the fallen centuries, and Helen
Was much considered by the youth of Troy.
I think perhaps your prototypes in Sparta
Called forth that metaphor. But let it pass.
It is a fact that my eyes itch and burn
At this of you on horseback. Foolish! Oh,
Shall you call it folly at this time of day,
You, who tell tales of banshees in a park!

Again a facet. Like a lapidary
I cut and cut in microscopic flakes,
But never get the gem for all these sides.
There's more to you than single flesh and blood
Though these be fine and clear as new-stripped almonds.
And more than tears; but what it is drifts out
Beyond the surf-line of my consciousness
And blurs in dazzle so I lose its edge.
The puzzle grows as I unravel it,
For all these feelings come out of a book
And you, who cannot write, have written it.

There's food for many solitary munchings,
And sticks to beat an artist's soul withal.

You cannot write, and look what you
    have written:
Two lives which stare and twinkle on the
    page
So that I blind in looking. That's a glare
To put out farthing candles of profes-
    sionals.
Had I not seen your drawings, I might
    almost
Have been bewitched by that hotel piano
And guessed you better understood your
    Chopin.
Now I am all at sea again and clinging
To horses and a cat-leap at a fence.

Well, there it stands, and what I get is
    life,
And love held back and breaking up and
    out.
Your heart is never on your sleeve, you
    say;
But try your hardest, it is in your pen,
And death is nothing to vitality
Swinging across a second heart. At best
One sees a breeding like those draperies
Which cool my naked caryatides.
Why, I'm not dead, but merely gone in
    space
And that you slap away with easy hand
Drawing me closer much than you intend.

Perhaps the very queerest of these facts
Is that I feel apologies are due
For just this thing which wakes my ad-
    miration.
You do not want me crowding in behind
That carefully embroidered sleeve, and yet
What I behold mounts to a blazing altar,
And both are there before it, worship-
    ping.
Will you forgive this little pinch of in-
    cense,
For one of you is dead and she will know,
Perhaps, at least, what magic brought
    me here.
And I will never seek to meet the other,
I only write to exorcise a ghost.

WRITTEN ON THE REVERSE

He told me, one night, when we were off
    duty,
And with a pride which might have been
    Lord Nelson's
Detailing Emma to a fellow Admiral —

Only that's one thing Nelson never did —
And Lady Hamilton was gold and rubies
While this girl was a circus-rider's spangles,
As real as they, at least not one whit
    more so,
And he, poor boy, as far from Nelson's
    honour.
Well, there you have it, tucked up in our
    tent,
Propping our spurs against an iron stove-
    pipe
And talking as I'm wishing now we
    hadn't.
But he was at it, and I couldn't stop him.
I swear the fellow's talk became quite
    lyric,
A sort of chucking stars, and into saw-
    dust —
It seemed to me the lady was no better;
She scuffled underneath a press of foot-
    steps,
His among others. I had liked him hugely.
A great, big, honest, rather clumsy chap,
Just off of middle-age, and such a baby,
Playing the soldier in a uniform,
And playing it damned well, you under-
    stand;
We had no better in the regiment.
I used to chuckle just to see him acting
His own ideal. But somehow as I lis-
    tened
The folly in him rasped upon my nerves.
What right had he to be so innocent
To whip a tawdry intrigue up to poetry
And set me shivering who had not got it.
He painted her exactly. I could see
Not only what he said, but what he didn't.
I guessed the sort of talcum-powder
Kind of woman who had picked him up.
Cheap smartness, one who pats her hair
    in order
Before shop-windows, and pays for what
    she buys
With crumpled bills fished from a small
    mesh purse
Whose gold is gilding and wearing off at
    that;
Add, too, a passion for gold-tipped cig-
    arettes
And blue-sashed bon-bon boxes. But she
    was shrewd,
I knew as much because he was so
    pleased —
With her, of course, and also with himself.
He saw her Cleopatra on high Nile

Floating between blue lupins, graciously
According to him, Anthony, her heart.
And that was just the way he wasn't
    Nelson,
Who saw her Emma — and nothing else
    at all.
The thing stopped there, it seemed, for
    he was married
And decent enough before she came, I
    know.
He filled the ache in him with high-
    falutin,
I wondered how long that would satisfy
And felt his charmer would draw him
    farther in
To cheques of somewhat high denomina-
    tion
Paid, naturally, upon receipt of value.
Well, when he took to glowing like the
    sun
Upon a hayrick on a Summer morning
I thought the lady had achieved her
    figure.
But what I didn't reckon was just the
    man.
The thing was epic to him now, I saw.
War and his love — a fearful combina-
    tion
To snarl the simple structure of his life.
He twisted to it and turned upon himself
With such a marvellous gyration, that
    in some way
He pulled it up to grandeur, and he a-top
Mystically bright and crowned with bitter
    laurel.
And all the time, behind, there was his
    wife.
He got her so at last, fuddled his wits
To it, that she became the smirch upon
His unique glory. I used to marvel at
    the paradox
He'd hung cocooning round him, but so
    it was.
The fellow grew to something greatly
    larger
Than I could have believed. I never said
This was a moral tale, you understand,
It's simply true.
        Well, we went over, both
In the same company, I Captain to his
    Lieutenant,
And, in due course, were sent on to the
    front.
A month went by, and then a bit of
    shell

Took him between the shoulder-blades
    and gouged
Into a lung and stayed there. We were
    caught,
A handful of us, right between barrages.
I'd got a leg, or rather hadn't one,
So there we sat, and cursed, and bled,
    and died.
I didn't, you observe. Worse luck, per-
    haps.
I'll never get the joy that fellow had
Coughing, and spitting, and whimpering
    her name.
He met that shell toting a wounded ser-
    geant
Through our barrage, and, coming back,
    it hit.
Tough luck? Oh, I don't know. He had
    his time.
When the delirium struck him, I covered
    my ears,
Hearing a man like that is too close
    cornered,
Like something naked hurting you with
    beauty.
It ended then for him, but I came home.
His wife was cool and stately as a widow.
The talcum-powder lady changed her
    man.
And yet I think the person was an artist
To carve a hero out of what he was
When she first ran across him. I wonder
    sometimes
What she can think about it. As for me,
I always give it up at just this point.
Poor dear old chap, God bless his silly
    soul.

SILHOUETTE WITH SEPIA BACKGROUND

He moved in, with two thousand books,
    and a bed, and an armchair,
Into a little room under the roof of the
    great building with the pointed, carved
    stone doorway.
At eleven o'clock precisely, he would
    come out of the pointed stone doorway
And cross the street to the Common to
    feed the squirrels,
Then he would wander on to the Public
    Garden to gaze at the geometrical
    flower-beds.
He did this every day, and the orange-
    vendor at the corner told the time by

him; it saved crossing Tremont Street to look up at the clock on Park Street Church.

One morning he did not come, and the traffic policeman missed him.

So did the park policeman, and they talked about it together when they should have been minding their business.

On the second day, they spoke to the orange-vendor, but he knew nothing;

It would have been wiser to ask the pigeons who fly everywhere, but they never thought of that.

On the third day, they consulted the janitor, and, come to think of it, the janitor had not seen him either.

Then the janitor and the park policeman (for the traffic policeman dared not leave his post)

Went upstairs together ever so high, a flight higher than the elevator ran.

They had to break in the door, but that was no great thing,

It was an old door, and rickety.

They found him sitting quietly in his chair, with the book he had been reading fallen on the floor beside him.

He had been dead three days, but only the pigeons knew that.

AQUATINT FRAMED IN GOLD

Six flights up in an out-of-date apartment house

Where all the door-jambs and wainscots are of black walnut

And the last tenant died at the ripe age of eighty.

Tick-tock, the grandfather's clock,
Crowded into a corner against the black walnut wainscot.

Surrounded by the household gods of her family for three generations:

Teak-wood cabinets, rice-paper picture books, slim, comfortless chairs of spotted bamboo.

Too many house gods for the space allotted them, exuding an old and corroding beauty, a beauty faded and smelling of the past.

Tick-tock, the grandfather's clock,
Accurately telling the time, but forgetting whether it is to-day or yesterday.

Sleeping every night in a walnut bedstead
With a headboard like the end of a family pew;

Waking every morning to the photographs of dead relations,

Dead relations sifted all over the house,
Accumulated in drifts like dust or snow.

Tick-tock, the grandfather's clock,
Indifferently keeping up an old tradition,

Unconcernedly registering the anniversaries of illnesses and deaths,

But omitting the births, they were so long ago.

The lady is neither young nor old,
She walks like a wax-work among her crumbling possessions,

She is automatic and ageless like the clock,
And she, too, is of a bygone pattern.

She sits at her frugal dinner,
Careful of its ancient etiquette,
Opposite the portrait of a great-aunt
Done by a forgotten painter.

The portrait lived once, it would seem,
To judge by the coquetry of its attire;
But the lady has always been a wax-work,
Of no age in particular,
But of an unquestioned ancestry.

Tick-tock, the grandfather's clock,
Ironically recording an hour of no importance.

MINIATURE

Because the little gentleman made nautical instruments

And lived in a street which ran down to the sea,

The neighbours called him "Salt Charlie."

I wonder what they would have said if they had known

That he stole out every evening to a sweet-shop

And bought sticks of red-and-white sugar candy.

It was a pleasant thing to see him,
Standing meekly before the custom-house,
Sucking a sugar-stick,
And gazing at the dead funnels of anchored steamers

Against a star-sprung sky.

I thought of him in an oval gilt frame
Against sprigged wall-paper,

Done in Fra Angelico pinks and blues
Of a clear and sprightly elegance.
Wherefore, being convinced of his value
    as ornament,
I have set him on paper for the delecta-
    tion
Of sundry scattered persons
Who consider such things important.

EASEL PICTURE

DECORATION DAY

She is a washerwoman most of the time,
But to-day she is a widow.
Important distinction which warrants a
    plaintive manner
And her best black bombazine.
To be sure, she is only a plain widow,
And her husband was a drunkard who
    ill-treated her,
But she never forgets that it is owing to
    him that she ranks third in the cemetery,
Next to the war-widows and gold-starred
    mothers.
She regrets that he did not enlist
Instead of lying about his age and dying
    coldly of pneumonia,
Until she reflects that he might have re-
    turned from overseas and beaten her
    according to custom.
The thought purges her of envy, and she
    sprinkles woe-begone, contented tears
On the bell-glass of artificial flowers she
    lays on his grave;
It is a beautiful offering and has been
    much admired.
With a blissful sense of bereavement, she
    bows her head over the bell-glass,
Then rises to totter to the gate on the
    arm of a friend who has offered to give
    her a lift home.
In her attic room, she carefully folds the
    bombazine,
Whispering to herself: "It was a beautiful
Decoration Day."

THE IRONY OF DEATH

A FUNERAL

You were always so vigorous,
And your mind was as full of movement
    as your body.
When you sprang over rocks and boulders,
Or pushed waist-high through the fern,
I used to envy your strength,
And your buoyant lightness.
You were a true pagan
And Nature was your God.
You had no use for other gods,
And said so.
The day before you died you said so,
And you died bravely as you had lived,
With the farewell of a staunch comrade
    upon your lips.

I went to the funeral which they gave
    you.
No other of your real friends was there,
This was not the manner in which they
    were used to meet you.
The room was crowded with your hus-
    band's colleagues and their wives,
And people who had come for the sake
    of appearances.
We were shut in the stifling room,
With the scent of the flowers on your
    coffin.
A clergyman read the funeral service
Which you despised,
And the flowers wilted in the hot air.
Then I knew that you were dead
And I was glad,
For you would have wept to see how your
    foolish husband exposed his soul
In his endeavour to give you a proper
    funeral.

THE GRAVE

I left the horse outside,
For there were no roads in the little
    graveyard,
No paths,
Only a disorder of gravestones,
And moss, and ragged grass,
And broken twigs fallen from the trees
    overhead.
The ground was hummocked and hol-
    lowed
Between the gravestones,
And I stumbled among them
Reading the inscriptions
To guide me.
Your monument was to be designed by
    a great architect
They had told me,
But not yet, although you had been dead
    four months.
Such things require consideration.

So I went from stone to stone,
Seeking the child's grave
Near which they had laid you.
Suddenly I tripped,
And jerking forward to save myself
On the uneven ground,
I saw in front of me two fruit jars
Leaning crookedly against each other,
And half-full of water foul to the colour
of tobacco juice.
They were smeared with the splashings of
rain,
And the rims of the covers were red with
rust;
In one a leaf was still clinging to a dying
stalk,
In the other the stalk was quite dead.
Above them a tablet to a dead child
Was let into a rock.

THE MIRROR

Opaque because of the run mercury at its
back,
White with a breath of yellow, like tarnished silver,
The old mirror hangs over the chimney-
piece
Incased in its carved frame, and reflects
the room beneath.
It is warped and bulging, because of the
great fires
Of other years; and dim with the sun
shining in it every Spring.
Old men and children move before it,
and it reflects them all,
Pulling them this way and that in its
uneven surface.
The pictures pass over it like mist over
a morning window,
And it hangs in its carved frame, tarnished and beautiful,
And reflects everything.

PORTRAIT OF AN
ORCHESTRA LEADER

A young man on a platform?
A white flame upreared in a silver dish,
Swaying to the wind of horns and oboes,
Bending to the undulate waves of violins.
Do you think you see a young man in a
swallow-tailed coat leading an orchestra?
I tell you it is a white, pointed flame in
a silver dish.

PORTRAIT
(E.R.B.)

This lady is like a grass-blade sheathed in
ice,
Like hoar-frost running along the borders
of a formal garden.
She is like violets under the misted glass
of a cold frame
On an Autumn morning with the sun
scarcely above the trees.

The air has a smart twinge to it, I think,
And the asters are black and broken;
But what can equal the glitter of the
frosty grass-blades,
Held to a rigid radiance,
Bent and motionless,
Answering nothing to the wind?
No, do not lift the frames.
The violets are a lovely touch of colour,
And I would rather forego the scent of
them
Than run the risk of their freezing.

MAGNOLIA GARDENS
CHARLESTON, S. C.

It was a disappointment,
For I do not like magenta,
And the garden was a fire of magenta
Exploding like a bomb into the light-
coloured peace of a Spring afternoon.
Not wistaria dropping through Spanish
moss,
Not cherokees sprinkling the tops of trees
with moon-shaped stars,
Not the little pricked-out blooms of
banksia roses,
Could quench the flare of raw magenta.
Rubens women shaking the fatness of
their bodies
In an opulent egotism
Till the curves and colours of flesh
Are nauseous to the sight,
So this magenta.
Hateful,
Reeking with sensuality,
Bestial, obscene —
I remember you as something to be for-
gotten.
But I cherish the smooth sweep of the
colourless river,
And the thin, clear song of the red-
winged blackbirds
In the marsh-grasses on the opposite bank.

A SOUTH CAROLINA FOREST

Hush, hush, these woods are thick with
shapes and voices,
They crowd behind, in front,
Scarcely can one's wheels break through
them.
For God's sake, drive quickly!
There are butchered victims behind those
trees,
And what you say is moss I know is the
dead hair of hanged men.
Drive faster, faster.
The hair will catch in our wheels and
clog them;
We are thrown from side to side by the
dead bodies in the road,
Do you not smell the reek of them,
And see the jaundiced film that hides
the stars?
Stand on the accelerator. I would rather
be bumped to a jelly
Than caught by clutching hands I can-
not see,
Than be stifled by the press of mouths
I cannot feel.
Not in the light glare, you fool, but on
either side of it.
Curse these swift, running trees,
Hurl them aside, leap them, crush them
down,
Say prayers if you like,
Do anything to drown the screaming
silence of this forest,
To hide the spinning shapes that jam the
trees.
What mystic adventure is this
In which you have engulfed me?
What no-world have you shot us into?
What Dante dream without a farther
edge?
Fright kills, they say, and I believe it.
If you would not have murder on your
conscience,
For Heaven's sake, get on!

CIRCUS TENTS BY LAKE MICHIGAN

I looked from my window at the great
lake,
And Shakespeare, and Keats, and Whitman stood beside my chair
And pointed out to me things I might not
have seen.

They bade me observe the feather lights
lying upon the lake surface,
The blue enlarging upon a greater blue
of the flat, approaching water,
The crispness of its line against the shore.
But the trains ran beneath my window,
puffing and grinding,
And from the circus tents beyond the
railroad tracks
Came the incessant, teasing bleat of the
heard notes of a brass band.
"Mr. Shakespeare," I urged, "be so kind
as to repeat what you just said,
I did not quite hear it.
And, Mr. Keats, say that once again, if
you please, I wish to lose nothing."
Only Walt Whitman kept on speaking,
Rolling out words which swept through
the noise like a heavy moon through
clouds,
And his stretched arm pointed to the
lake, cutting the tent in two, blotting
out the middle flag.

So it went on all day,
And the poets withdrew, baffled,
And the circus tent swelled to a prodigious
size and hung before me as all America.
And the sorrow of jungle animals wasting
themselves upon sawdust entered my
heart,
And the glory and grief of the trapeze
artists and their useless perfection
Rasped my nerves with the prick of hail.
So it was all day.
And all day I watched and saw my country
swallowed up by the huge tent,
Far from trees, sweltering in a hot dust,
Crying its delight cheaply and violently
through the voices of peanut-men and
clowns.

Night came, and the band droned on and
bright lights glared in the tents.
I had ceased to think. I stared out of
the window and beat time to the band
on the arm of my chair.
Beyond the tent, the great lake crouched
in darkness, waiting.
I thought it waited to say a word to the
caged, jungle animals,
To the trapeze artists who had cheated
death another day.
I too waited until the tent lights went
out,

And the lighthouses shone, red and white,
in even pulsations,
Half-way up my black window.
And Shakespeare, and Keats, and Whitman came back and watched the turning lights with me,
Silently we watched them half-way up the window.
Then an elephant trumpeted, dreaming of water and lush trees,
And a jackal, forgetting his cage, howled to the smell of the creeping water,
And I wrote a poem for the trapeze artists which they will never read,
And showed it to my companions, who only nodded,
For they were watching the turning lighthouse lanterns, revolving red and white — red and white — slowly, evenly, half-way up the window.

ST. LOUIS

JUNE

Flat,
Flat,
Long as sight
Either way.
An immense country,
With a great river
Steaming it full of moist, unbearable heat.
The orchards are little quincunxes of Noah's Ark trees,
The plows and horses are children's toys tracing amusingly shallow lines upon an illimitable surface.
Great chunks of life to match the country,
Great lungs to breathe this hot, wet air.

But it is not mine.
Mine is a land of hills
Lying couchant in the angles of heraldic beasts
About white villages.
A land of singing elms and pine-trees.
A restless up and down land
Always mounting, dipping, slipping into a different contour,
Where the roads turn every hundred yards or so,
Where brooks rattle forgotten Indian names to tired farm-houses,
And faint spires of old meeting-houses
Flaunt their golden weather-cocks in a brave show of challenge at a sunset sky.

Here the heat stuffs down with the thickness of boiled feathers,
The river runs in steam.
There, lilacs are in bloom,
Cool blue-purples, wine-reds, whites,
Flying colour to quiet dooryards.
Grown year on year to a suddenness of old perfection,
Saying "Before! Before!" to each new Spring.
Here is "Now,"
But "Before" is mine with the lilacs,
With the white sea of everywhither,
With the heraldic, story-telling hills.

THE REVENGE

All night I read a little book,
A very little book it was.
It had a pretty, shimmering look
Like silver threaded into gauze.

I read it till the windows turned
Into blue ghosts which stared at me.
The fire twittered as it burned.
A dwarfish sneer perched on my knee.

Who was it put the poison there?
Who has conceived this hellish thing —
To lay a sightless, soundless snare
Amid its lovely whispering?

So gently came the rush of rhymes,
So lightly breathed the poison in —
Who thinks of cinquecento crimes
White hellebore on jessamine?

I took that little shy, sleek book
And set a crimson match to it.
It crinkled like a freshet brook,
And flaked and vanished, bit by bit.

There was no book my hands could hold,
No book my eyes could ever see,
But round my head it ran, a bold
Ironical phylactery.

I cannot read the book again,
But there's no need, it scalds my head,
A strip of livid, living pain
I shall not lose till I am dead.

For hate is old as eagle peaks,
And hate is new as sunrise gulls,
And hate is ravening vulture beaks
Descending on a place of skulls.

Hate is a torch, hate is a spur,
Hate will accomplish my design:
The author's first biographer!
I pray, O Hate, that task be mine.

I shall not need to criticize
Nor look the subject up at all,
But simply turn round both my eyes
And gaze at my brain's inner wall.

There I shall see a fresco wreath
Of letters moulded of dried tears,
And annotated underneath
The things I've thought and thought for
    years.

'Twill be a pleasant job, I think,
To crumble up those dusty tears,
And stir them thickly in my ink;
Hate paid at last his long arrears.

My foot-notes will enrich the brew
With colours I've brought back from Hell.
I'll write down all I every knew.
By Satan's ears, I'll write it well!

By Satan's tongue! I'll tell the truth,
And not one word will add to it,
From his egregious, twisted youth
To his last frozen torture fit.

I'll write down his biography
So that the world will die of laughter.
I'll pin him like a squirming fly,
A comic spasm of hereafter.

I'll make his sins a jig of mirth,
His loves so many masterpieces
Of high derision. I will dig
Bare the cold roots of his caprices.

I'll sling about him every soul
He squeezed and drained to give him
    drink.
His wife gone mad — I'll make it droll.
Bless the Hell colours in my ink!

I'll leave him not a decent rag
Of tragedy to wrap about him.
I'll hang him up as a red flag
Till every street boy learns to shout him.

I've taken up a pretty whim,
But tit for tat, he had his chance.

And I may end by blessing him,
My partner in this ghoulish dance.

He slew me for a time, admitted;
But I shall slay him for all time.
Poor shrivelled clown whom I've out-
    witted,
I pardon you your poisoned rhyme.

Go peacefully, for I have done
With you and your false book is dead.
There's sorrow, too, in having won.
Go softly then, and go well sped.

CHILL

I thought of myself as a walnut
Hung above fallen leaves,
Desperately clinging and jerking
At the edge of a hollow wind.

I counted the leaves below me,
Scuffling and grating together.
I feared lest my withered stem
Should drop me too soon upon them.

The hollow wind played music,
Running over the branches.
The sapless chords of the branches
Whined a shrunken, glimmering tune.

The moon with a hump-backed shoulder
Shook a cloud off as though it were water,
And her light dripped down like water
Over the crackling leaves.

And shadows rose from the tree-trunks,
Cocking their legs and their ankles,
Dancing a dance of snapped elbows,
Distorting the beds of the leaves.

The owls flew shrieking above them,
Field-mice, their long tails twisted,
Ran like an army of ants
Gnawing and nudging each other.

And the wind played cymbals and tubas
To the beat of a tarantella,
Rocking in broken circles,
Chaining the tops of the tree.

And I was the kettle-drum tapping,
Tap-tapping my shell on the branch,
Terribly pulled and contorted,
Fearing the dance of the shadows.

Then there came to me the vision of a
hepatica
Standing thinly out of a mould of Winter
leaves,
Star-white, calling Good-morning to a
soft sky.
Gently swayed the white hepatica,
Drinking the wet mould.
I felt the roots streaming through it,
I felt the moisture rising into the white
petals.
I saw the sun reach down and answer
the bright hepatica.

I loosened my stem and fell — fell —
Into blackness,
For the cloud had re-captured the moon.

SNOW

It snowed yesterday,
And to-day I have been choked with the
pale falling of snow.
It drops steadily,
Slowly,
Sliding in slant lines of white
Against green trees.
The trees burn through it
Like slabs of green water
Beneath the foam of a waterfall.
The trees are permanent and still,
The snow is permanent also,
Light as dust,
Grim as the heave of massed water,
Continuous as the beat of death.
A snow-flake on a path,
A foot treads upon it and it is gone.
Millions by millions of snow-flakes
And a hundred thousand people
Struggle under a smooth, smothering
desolation.
In a bitter white twilight
The snow creeps upon the city,
Coming gently,
Little crystals of no account
Dropping down between solid houses,
The warm streets melt it,
But soon their power fails,
The roadways disappear,
The sidewalks sink and fade,
From doorway to opposite doorway
Lies a prairie of sudden snow.
My rhododendron bushes
Are single leaves gasping for air.
My windows are dull eyes

Gazing at a crushed heaven.
The wind flings rattles of sneering
laughter
Down the chimneys.
Once there was a sun;
I saw it weeks ago
Commanding a blue sky,
Driving the hours before it in a coloured,
satisfactory procession.
Now there is no sky,
Merely a descending of grey particles,
Ordered, open,
A sequence of irony
Deftly possessing itself of the world.
Long ago,
On nights like this,
Wolves howled among these trees;
Now there is silence,
And the sibilant sifting murmur of the
snow.
But I expect to hear the wolves,
I expect the house-roof to crumble
And leave me pushing against white
drifts,
Chattering nonsense with a parched
tongue,
Gone mad with whiteness,
Drowned under the feathers of the snow.
There used to be sleigh-bells,
Little shaken sprays of music,
To make the snow human.
Strong, friendly horses
Trampling the storm with living sinews.
Now —
It slips,
Slips,
Cool,
Still,
Fragile and irrefragable,
And I see it falling on a dead continent
Where there is no more life,
No more desire,
Only the windless cold of an old planet
Voyaging a perpetuity of stars.

OLD SNOW

The earth is iron,
The winds are bands of steel,
The snow is a pock-marked beggar·
woman
Crouching at a street corner
Whining an old misery over and over.
They say she was white once, and a
virgin.

But who remembers it —
Seeing her lie indecently huddled upon
    an iron earth,
Cringing under the strokes of the steel-
    band wind?

NEW HEAVENS FOR OLD

I am useless.
What I do is nothing,
What I think has no savour.
There is an almanac between the win-
    dows:
It is of the year when I was born.

My fellows call to me to join them,
They shout for me,
Passing the house in a great wind of
    vermilion banners.
They are fresh and fulminant,
They are indecent and strut with the
    thought of it,
They laugh, and curse, and brawl,
And cheer a holocaust of "Who comes
    firsts!" at the iron fronts of the houses
    at the two edges of the street.
Young men with naked hearts jeering be-
    tween iron house-fronts,
Young men with naked bodies beneath
    their clothes
Passionately conscious of them,
Ready to strip off their clothes,
Ready to strip off their customs, their
    usual routine,
Clamouring for the rawness of life,
In love with appetite,
Proclaiming it as a creed,
Worshipping youth,
Worshipping themselves.
They call for women and the women
    come,
They bare the whiteness of their lusts
    to the dead gaze of the old house-
    fronts,
They roar down the street like flame,
They explode upon the dead houses like
    new, sharp fire.

But I —
I arrange three roses in a Chinese vase:
A pink one,
A red one,
A yellow one.
I fuss over their arrangement.
Then I sit in a South window

And sip pale wine with a touch of hem-
    lock in it,
And think of Winter nights,
And field-mice crossing and re-crossing
The spot which will be my grave.

THE SIBYL

She was an aggressively unattractive old
    woman,
Sitting there behind the table in the hotel
    corridor.
Nothing could make her interesting or
    pathetic,
Although to be on duty at midnight
Proved her lot unfortunate.
From her topknot of grey, escaping,
    withered hair
To her fat, delaying hands,
She precluded pathos;
Even her melancholy attempt at finery,
A faded imitation coral necklace,
Seemed only dirty and dull.
Hers was a hard lot indeed,
Yet I could not pity her.
I asked for a pencil.
She gave me one, and grudged the doing
    it heartily.
When I reached my room, I found that
    the pencil had a rubber on the end.
Cursed old sibyl!
What do you mean by uttering proph-
    ecies
At midnight,
In a hotel corridor!

THE MADMAN

My house burnt down, I saw the stars
Where a dull ceiling once had been.
The smoky rafters stood like bars
With glittering planets in between.

My neighbours came and saved the shell
Of my burnt house. I took no heed.
They called to me that all was well.
I strid a rafter like a steed.

My neighbours stamped the flower beds,
Imploring me to clamber down.
And all the time above their heads
The steady stars were like a crown.

I chirruped to my rafter horse
That he might flee across the sky,

Galloping in a planet's course
As I directed. Who was I?

I heard the shouts shot up at me,
I heard the cry: "The man's a fool!"
The rafter leapt amazingly
Among the stars. The air was cool.

The stars ran swiftly past my ear.
Chirping and chuckling, so they came.
They whispered to me not to fear.
I did not fear, the stars were tame.

They fawned and licked my hands and
      feet,
I rode enwound in fondling stars.
They grouped themselves to make a
      street,
And Venus flew with me, and Mars.

Jupiter strode along ahead
To push the crowding stars aside,
And Mercury, with fluttering tread,
Held back the rear that I might ride.

Now who would own a house of wood,
Of clay, or even morticed stone?
A hundred years I might have stood
Under the ceilings hanging prone.

"Blest fire!" I thought, and dug my heels
Into the rafter. On it slid.
The stars were road-dust blown from
      wheels
Behind my flight. I reached the lid.

There was the cover of the sky.
I cried out to my rafter, "Stop!"
It heeded not at all, and I
Came bump against the awful top.

The shock deprived me of my breath
And shuttlecocking down I went.
A palsied thought that this was death
Scattered my senses and I bent.

All huddled up upon my steed
I clung, but with a swoop the rafter
Dropped through my legs which could
      not speed
So fast. I fell alone thereafter.

I fell and fell again. I fell
For years and years. It was so dark

I only knew the door of Hell
Because it glowed with a red spark.

The stars had gone, the years had gone,
A memory was all I had.
I sat in a burnt dusk alone
And heard a voice say, "He is mad!"

Perhaps, thought I, it may be so,
But it's a poor man who'll not pay
For pleasures had when pleasures go.
Thank Fortune, I'm not made that way.

They brought a wife and child to me
And called them mine. The silly dolts!
I turned my back upon their plea.
They put me behind bars and bolts.

I did not care a tinker's damn
For this or that. For I am he
Who rode with stars, that's what I am,
And will be to Eternity.

I've sold my life for one short night
And it was worth the payment due.
A man has certainly a right
To do as he desires to do.

They tell me 'twas my wife and child
Who owned my life. But these are
      names
I've never heard before. Who build
Such flimsy lies can make no claims.

Fiddlesticks! fellows. Leave me be;
Here or elsewhere, it matters not.
Blinded by stars, I cannot see.
A memory is all I've got.

Leave me alone to dree my weird.
It always comes, the paying day.
And I remember I once steered
A rafter through a milky way.

DIRGE

I left her there in the rushes by the river,
Where the aspen leaves make a quiver —
      quiver — quiver —
And the breeze through the trees casts a
      silver shiver,
   I left her floating there.
She swore to die and I left her dead
For what I answered to what she said.

Was there anything I could have done
      instead?
Oh, the bitter, bitter beauty of her
      hair!

For days I had heard the call of the
      town.
But there was no need for her to drown.
Oh, the bubbles that came up as she
      went down,
And the creak of the displaced reeds!
Snakes of hair-strands mounting through
      the green,
Nosing past the reed-stems, catching in
      between,
And a pallid shadow like a sunken tam-
      bourine.
Was it she I saw in the weeds?

My boat drew out and drifted away,
What was the need for me to stay?
A drowned body is but water-logged clay.
I must pull for the night comes on.
But the water spurns the oars off as
      though it were ice,
The boat is held as if wedged in a vice.
A gull cries once, a gull cries twice,
And a fog conceals the sun.

Red water-snakes with glimmering eyes
And bells on their tails, I see them rise
Here, there, everywhere. A swart crow
      flies
Croaking toward the shore
And fastened to the snakes are pale
      strange things
With waving, weaving tentacles like
      arms, and rings
Clinging tight and tidily to misty pen-
      cillings.
I have seen those rings before.

Not one face, alone, nor two, nor three,
But faces as many as the shells in the sea,
Their lank jaws trailing beside them
      crookedly.
The river sighs and moans.
The tossing snakes are the hideous hair
Sprung from these heads. And the white
      eyes glare
At my boat stuck still in a musty air
Jolted by the clatter of bones.

It's a lie! A lie! She wished to die,
Could any one have stopped her? There
      was no time to try.

But the whimpering air seems to jellify.
My heart-beats slow and fail.
The bells on the snakes shrill an angelus.
The oily sky drips its yellow pus
Through the twilight — and I? You see
      me thus.
A murderer locked in jail.

But all of every night and all of every day
I see her body with the rushes sway,
And the needles of the sun in the dis-
      array
Of her glorious, undulant hair.
Her face smiles at me through the cool,
      calm green
Of the water pool like a Florentine
Image set in lilies, but the lilies intervene.
I cannot reach her there.

Farewell, loveliest, azure-lidded, parted
By your misunderstanding and my wrath.
      Ah, eager-hearted,
Prone to take offence at jests scarcely
      even started,
      There you lie with hope.
Both lost together at a single turn.
Water soaks your eyes and brain, mine
      only burn.
Jailer put the clock on, upset the urn,
      Be pitiful and hurry with the rope.

ANECDOTE

First Soliloquy

Her breasts were small, upright, virginal;
Even through her clothes I could feel the
      nipples pointing upward when   I
      touched her inadvertently.
The chastity of her garments was pro-
      nounced,
But no disposal of material could keep
      the shape of her breasts unseen.

And you would walk as a Spring wind,
You would order your demeanour as
      though there were still frost in the air,
You would keep me to my distance by
      the cool agreeableness of your speech.
You are foolish, Madam, or deceived.
Is it possible you underrate my sensibility
And do not realize that I hold your
      breasts
In the hollow of my hand?

SECOND SOLILOQUY

His voice was a dagger tipped with honey,
His touch a scimitar dripping myrrh and
gall.
He parted me from myself
And I stood alone in sunshine and
trembled.
I caught my garments about me,
But they withered one by one as leaves
wither, and fell.
I was alone in the wide sunlight;
His eyes were winds which would not
leave me.
I would have sought a tree,
But the place where I was was bare and
light.
Merciless light he shed upon me,
And I stretched my arms in shame and
rejoicing.
Why do you stand there watching me?
Are you blind to what is really happen-
ing
That you talk so lightly of trifles?
Stop talking, you suffocate me.
Does any one notice?
Why do you strip me before all these
people —
You, who care nothing for my naked-
ness?
Unbearable the anguish of my body,
The ache of my breasts,
The strain of covering myself is choking
me.
Why do you do nothing but talk?
Have you no hands, no heart,
Or are you so cynical that you expose me
for a whim?
Oh, I am well-trained, be sure of that,
But can you not see through my pretense?
It is agony to hold myself away from
you,
Yet you are as impassive as a stone
Hermes before whom Venus herself
would need no cloak.
Now that you are gone, what have you
left me?
No privacy at all, I think.
You have stolen my secrecy, and flung
it back as something not worth tak-
ing.
I have only the harsh memory of your
eyes,
Your dull, stone eyes which haunt me in
the dark.

EPITHALAMIUM IN THE MODERN MANNER

The round, red moon ran a level eye
along the hayfield,
Appraising conditions with a view to
possibilities.
It was the moon's business to see that the
shadows of the cocks were of
sufficient size,
As a preliminary to the seasonable arrival
of the next generation.

"To one enamoured of dragonflies,
What is a chip hat with a ribbon
round it?
To one engrossed in a game of crib-
bage,
What is the importance of the
Treaty of Ghent?"
Which shows that Archibald was in a
naughty humour,
And Joanna more than usually occupied
with the counting of grass-blades.
The moon caught them in her long
orange arms
And jostled them together with so
thorough a completeness
That they fell, giggling, into a haycock
shadow,
As perfect a pair of young animals as
need be
For the maintenance of the species man
on an ant-corroded planet.

POINTS OF VIEW

Youth cocks his hat and rides up the
street.
Age cocks his eye only to see it.

Youth puts his horse at a five-barred
gate.
Age chuckles grimly and sits down to
wait.

Youth limps by with a broken-kneed
horse.
Age, through the shutters, mutters "Of
course!"

Youth curses Fate for his splitting
head.
Age lights the candle and hobbles to
bed.

SHOOTING THE SUN

Four horizons cozen me
To distances I dimly see.
Four paths beckon me to stray,
Each a bold and separate way.
Monday morning shows the East
Satisfying as a feast.
Tuesday I will none of it,
West alone holds benefit.
Later in the week 'tis due
North that I would hurry to.
While on other days I find
To the South content of mind.
So I start, but never rest
North or South or East or West.
Each horizon has its claim
Solace to a different aim.
Four-soul'd like the wind am I,
Voyaging an endless sky,
Undergoing destiny.

THE CUSTOMER

She came into my shop to-day,
The old maid from across the way,
With her pursed-up lips and disdainful
  mien
And her walk, each step with another be-
  tween.

Her mouth drew up above her nose,
No wrinkles ever so sniffed as those.
Her dress was too long, too short, too
  square,
Each inch measured out with what
  should be there.

Her hair, a twisted wad of grey,
Tipped her hat in the strangest way
So that every angle hurt like a noise,
There was discord in its very poise.

Her eyeglass crystals made her eyes
Puff out to a prodigious size:
The opaque white of eggs much cooked
Shone dully everywhere she looked.

She minced up to the counter, said:
"I want three yards of ribbon — red."
Sat down upon a stool and waited.
The tranquil atmosphere vibrated.

I bowed and brought a brilliant red,
Flaming and smooth as though each
  thread

Were new-run blood or molten glass.
She gave one look and let it pass.

I brought her scarlet, a poppy shade
Hot as a subaltern's cockade,
It darted out between my hands
Like a spurted flame of many strands.

She shook her head and murmured,
  "Crude."
I brought her a damask whose lassitude
Was of pale boudoirs and midday wak-
  ings;
It slid from the roll in languid snakings.

Annoyed, she pushed it to one side.
A clear carnation next I tried,
Fresh as Spring wind. "Oh, no," said
  she,
And tapped her foot impatiently.

I urged a cardinal crimson — she pouted.
Magenta, vermilion — both were flouted.
Carbuncle, ruby, cinnabar,
The counter looked like a mad bazaar.

One was too dull, the next too gay,
The next she fingered and turned away.
I tried thin ribbons of madder and lake,
Or wide russet sashes I hoped she would
  take.

I offered maroon with intriguing bright-
  nesses,
I tendered a cherry streaked with white-
  nesses.
I gave her the claret of evening skies,
The silver-salmon of faint sunrise.

I brought down carmine doubled with
  gold.
I found pale buffs under which rolled
A faint suggestion of watchet or blue.
Nothing I showed her seemed to do.

I gave her plaid ribbons, chequered, shot.
Always she asked what more I had got.
I proffered striped satins, or grosgrain
  plain.
Whatever it was, I must try again.

The uncoiled ribbons grew and grew
Until I only saw her through

A hole in the pile. But her voice came clear:
"Have you no more, there is nothing here."

I climbed down ladders with boxes balanced
In either hand. Under the valanced
Counters I dove for still more bolts.
She pronounced all ribbon designers dolts.

Neither colour, nor texture, nor price would suit,
She must see more. So to the root
Of my stock I went, unwinding, displaying —
Her chilly voice simply went on saying

That all was wrong, one way or another.
I began to wonder if I should smother
Under those rubicund twining strips,
When wanly fell from the pursed-up lips:

"You have so little to choose from here,
And what you have so excessively dear,
I will take two packets of pins. Nothing more."
And paying me she tripped through the door.

The sun was setting, the ribbons looked dull,
The heap had assumed the form of a skull.
The hollow eyes winked, the loose jaw made
A grimace at the fool who sold beauty in trade.

The wind whispered under the shop-door sill,
"Loveliness! Loveliness! Where you will.
Make it, give it, but put it on sale,
A bale of goods is only a bale."

The primrose moon through the window-pane
Misted the skull with saffron rain.
Gold as a guinea it lured and shone
At the tradesman standing there alone.
From the old clock tower of carven stone
The hour chimed in a hollow tone,
Three peals of bells for a quarter past one.

THE SEWING-BOOK

I've been reading a book about sewing,
And I look at my useless hands,
They know nothing at all of a needle's going
Over and under through linen strands.

My hands are a foolish sort of toys,
They can hold a pencil, that is all they know.
Now, reading, they would aspire to the joys
Of setting a thousand little stitches in a row.

A row of neat little stitches in some particularly fine cloth.
Cloth is perhaps sweeter than its grand-child — paper.
But these clumsy hands of mine are worth
Whatever value there is in a sky-scraper
Hewn of cold clouds, airily morticed with grey vapour.

Nainsooks, linen-lawns and cambrics,
Even mercerized cotton has an agreeable style
In reading. My hands build towers of flame-bricks,
But I burn in their fire all the while.

Imbroidering monograms is a cool pursuit, and stitching
A monotonous thing like a hem means rest
I can quite believe, rest uninterrupted by the itching
Torment to mold a weather-cock of fire into a crest.

Is a needle sharper than a pencil? That
Hinges of course on this matter of hands.
A cardinal may be weighed down by his hat,
And a pencil weary for the smooth, white bands
Of a linen cuff, perchance. There it stands.

Two or three spools of coloured thread,
And whatever flower comes into your head
Blooms on the muslin tranquilly,

Evenly patterned as a tree.
I consume with a pencil's lead,
Making a thought, a grief, a laughter.
You will last while fibres hold fibres. I, dead,
Tempt a future of nothing and nothing.
No dafter
Aim in the world than that what I have said
May be seeded, harvested, ground into bread
And so on hereafter, and that to be
Till the hungry find nothing to eat in me,
And no fit dwelling in my smouldering towers
Only the crumbling of mouldy hours.
Oh, the peace, the peace of your silken flowers!
The smooth, white dust of your exquisite, faded flowers!

STILL LIFE

Moonlight Striking Upon a Chess–Board

I am so aching to write
That I could make a song out of a chess-board
And rhyme the intrigues of knights and bishops
And the hollow fate of a checkmated king.
I might have been a queen, but I lack the proper century;
I might have been a poet, but where is the adventure to explode me into flame.
Cousin Moon, our kinship is curiously demonstrated,
For I, too, am a bright, cold corpse
Perpetually circling above a living world.

BALLAD OF GRINNING DEATH

Upon a decent truckle-bed
A woman lay, and she was dead.
A curtain flapped before a pane
Of glass made sharp and thick by rain.
A mouse ran softly on the floor.
Beyond the rattling attic door,
A wind was moaning more and more,
It wailed as waves against a shore.

A candle with a drowning wick
Swaled in an old tin candlestick.

A haggard man was writing there,
Composing words with dreadful care.
He ran his fingers through his hair,
And sang a song which cut a glare
Like purple lightning through the gloom
Of that wind-muffled, quiet room.

He sang: "Come, comrades, drink it up,
The bubbling, beading, blazing cup,
The licking, glittering serpent wine,
Drink, Bully Boys, the candles shine,
Women, and lights — " The strained voice cracked
Upon a chilly sob which hacked
The melody to bits, and left
Only a poor old man bereft.

He rose and wavered through the room,
His fingers struck upon the doom
Of Death and rang a hollow sound
As pulses beating round and round,
All round and round, but in that place
Where lay her tired, peaceful face,
He knelt as in a neutral space.

He kissed the glassy hands, a moan
Wrenched from him by their feel of stone;
He passed his arms about the thin
Old shrunken form and held it in
His shivering grasp, and called her name,
And told her it was he who came;
He babbled love words, beating them
Harshly against Death's frozen phlegm.

The rain struck loud upon the sash.
Over the roof, the rain-drops' dash
Drew thickly to a single fall
Of water leaping down a wall.
He must not pause, he could not wait,
The hour was growing very late.
The money for the funeral.
He crept back to his blotted scrawl.

And there all night he wept and tore
Out of his bleeding mind a score
Of rousing drinking-songs, that rang
In obscene choruses, a clang
Of goblets clattered through the staves,
And on he wrote as one who raves:
"Drink, Men, for wine is crowning sweet" —
He dropped his head upon the sheet,
He clutched his hands until the bones
Stood out upon the skin like stones,

And cursed God as a frantic child
Screams at a dream. Then, weak and
mild,
He pleaded: "Do not leave me, Dear.
Oh, Mary, Mary, can you hear?"
The silence hissed upon his ear.

Then he would jerk upright and sing:
"A ring-a-ding, a ring-a-ding.
For brandy is a handsome thing.
Ale is for topers who have to be careful,
Claret for gentlemen grown somewhat
fearful.
Sherry for men with a long roll of
yellows,
But brandy and rum for the best of good
fellows.
Ho! Boys! Drinking boys,
Clap your glasses and make a noise,
Shouting brandy and rum, Ho! Ho! Ho!
Calling for whiskey and gin." Below
He heard the choking gutters spill,
The wind beyond the door was shrill,
The corpse beneath its sheet lay still.

To him this was not something dead,
He did not know her so. Instead
What lay there was his sleeping wife,
The hair-spring of his dredged-out life,
The reason why his dreams were good,
The springing freshness of his blood.
The edges of his life drew in
And hung about him, curled and thin,
He felt himself an empty shell
Swirled by a wind across a fell,
And Heaven was just a sneer of Hell.

A near-by steeple rang a chime,
For time is time, and passing time,
And wearily he found a rhyme
And nailed it to a loud-laughed jest.
He cursed the man at whose request
The drinking-songs were ordered. Then
He rose and came to her again,
And stood and stifled in his pain.

The near-by steeple chimed and tolled
That life was old and songs were gold,
And drinking-songs were red and sweet,
And morning crawling down the street.
He smoothed her quiet, quiet hair,
He pulled the curtain so no glare
Should be upon her anywhere,
Then took his songs and left her there.

Outside the wind blew sharp and strong.
A dwindled sunlight fled along
The endless streets. He ached for sleep,
His eyes were eyes which may not weep.
He had no thought about it all
But money for a funeral.
His brains were leaping in a fire
To gratify her last desire.
A hearse, a coffin, and a pall
To give her decent burial.
And then the snow began to fall.

POETIC JUSTICE

Double-flowering trees bear no fruit, they
say,
And I have many blossoms,
With petals shrewdly whirled about an
empty centre,
White as paper, falling at a whiff of wind.
But when they are gone
There are only green leaves to catch at
the sunlight,
Green monotonous leaves
Which hide nothing.

TO FRANCESCA BRAGGIOTTI

After Seeing Her Dance:
"Fragrance"

White —
As the dawn on white roses,
Bright —
As sunlight on your rope of roses;
As a feather tossed in the quick of the
wind,
As a crystal figure swept by a rainbow
rain.
Dancer of silver shadows,
You are all youth and freshness,
Like a sharp spear against ivy,
Like a bow pulled to quivering,
Like an arrow rushed from a shaking bow.
Your arms are gestures of a morning
earth,
The arc of your leaping legs a shout of
loveliness,
Your movements the shining silence of
the on-coming sun.
You dance in the dawn,
You dance over green lawns in a leaf-
rhythm,
Weaving patterns with your rope of
roses,

Printing a white, fleeting pattern of
yourself,
Of your bright body against sudden,
startled green.

DANCE FIGURE

I would pray for thunder
Clanging across a copper sky.
For the scissors of the lightning
Rending green clouds.

As a tempest in the tree-tops,
I scream into the fiery wind;
As rain, wing-footed,
I fleet over dim valleys.

I am the silver of storm,
The gold of shuddering mist-tissues
Clouded about the head of that God
Whose name is fury to the world.

Speak, joints,
Wrists, ankles, knee-sockets!
Shout — arms, legs,
Shoulder-reaches and finger-tips!
Cry the song of an iron chariot
Rolling wheel and wheel
Along the wind tracks.

I leap in an angle of lightning.
I bend, spring, glitter,
Ripping the cloud-veils.
Who has seen the passion of my heart?
Are there eyes which can bear the sight
of me
Approaching in the darkness?

The black horses snort at my coming,
The trees fling the roses of their leaves
before me.
Sing —
While the leaves tear from the trees.
I leap from the heavens —
Shall you not behold me?

Daughter of thunder and the flake of it,
The deep pools wait for me.
I am the flash of a single body
Shivering to a million reflections.

As the thunder walks upon the sky
With steps of brass and ochre,
So I walk,
Upon a tower where no light is,

Slightly gauzed,
A moon whose clouds escape her.

You who desire me,
Where are you that I may reach you?
For whom am I come
If not for you?

Thunder of midnight,
Thunder of the morning,
I have made my waist supple for you.
I have taught my hands an unknown
cunning.
My legs are the pillars of a flowing sky.

Dance then,
You who are curved to receive me.
Fling a new shadow from my brightness.
I am as you would have me,
The breaker of moulds and medallions,
Fashioning all things to a heaviness of
thunder,
To a glory of unquenchable lightnings,
Whose image shall endure
To everlasting time.

Torch of thunder,
You burn upon the mountains,
And the lesser peaks
Fly up with flame.
Dazzling torch of aconite and silver,
Blaze — flare —
Penetrate the chasms of the great rocks,
The clefts in the mountain sides.
O radiant valleys,
Catch fire and sing with it in your
mouths!
Light is forever,
For the fire of the sky has no end.

. . . . .

Thunder-dancer,
I am tranquil,
Tranquil.
Slow drops drip from the trees,
Unevenly falling.
Slowly, with the slow rain-drops,
Dance,
And sleep.

JAZZ DANCE

How-do! How-do!
Pigeon-wing and toe.
Click your heels together

And away we go.
Snappin' our fingers
And slitherin' our feet,
Beatin' out a sugar tune
Sticky and sweet.
Grab your lovely lady
And whirl her off the floor,
Slip and slide her down the room,
Steer her up once more.
Hear the drums a-beatin',
But they're goin' awful slow.
Hit her up, you jazz-men,
We're sleepin' in this row.
What's the bones a-doin'
Blowin' on his thumbs?
Sets my ribs a-jiggin'
To hear them drums.
How-do! How-do!
Out there in the night
All the birds am listenin'
And quiverin' with fright.
I reckon they 'low it's Judgment come
Them rattles is makin' such a terrible
    hum.
Don't you hear the sizzlin' out in the
    grass?
It's snakes, Honey, snakes, all a-hustlin'
    to pass.
They thinks we's devils, with the bawlin'
    and yellin',
An' they've only got a minute to run
    away from Hell in.
Watch me playin' possum,
Slinkin' through the crowd.
Peek past the folks, Lamb,
Ain't yo' proud
When I leap up sudden
On a great round swing
With the flicker-flap-flash
Of a woodpecker's wing?
'Pears like you
Is a honeysuckle flower
Smellin' like a bunch of 'em
After a shower.
'Pears like you
Is a great gold queen
Settin' on a high throne
All red an' green.
These here niggers
Am just yo' people,
But I am yo' fancy-man
Tall as a steeple,
With my head in the clouds
Bobbin' roun' an' roun',
An' my feet rejoicin'

At the boom-boom sound.
Step along with me, Honey,
What's the music for?
Your little fire-feet am cracklin',
Snappin' on the floor.
They'm scorchin' my toes
An' burnin' my eyes
An' shootin' an' scootin'
Like they was fire-flies
All a-razzle an' a-dazzle
An' a whirligiggin' wonder,
Mockin' the old jazz drums
Poundin' there like thunder.
Don't you keep me waitin',
Ain't I achin' to begin,
Itchin' for it, Lady Bird,
Like it was a sin.
Your wild-cat eyes is callin' me
They'm clawin' at my face,
I can't stand still no longer,
Jump in an' take your place.
Tickle up your shins, Girl,
Look mighty smart.
Grab me round the waist and — Whoo!
There we start.
How-do! How-do!
Throw your little heels so,
Same as colts do, that's the style.
Double shuffle for a mile.
Swing your hips and bend your head.
Say, the music's all gone dead.
Beat your drums up, player-men,
Do that cake-walk reel again.
Shake the tambourines a bit,
Bang the cymbals till they split,
Throw your drum-sticks up and catch
    'em.
We can bunny-jump to match 'em.
Whirl your rattles to a spin,
Prod the fiddler with a pin,
That ole nigger's pow'ful lazy,
Makes us all go just plumb crazy.
Do you hear that shudderin' whine?
There's an owl in the old pine.
Guess he's lonesome all out there
Nothin' roun' but just cold air.
My! it's hot in here an' steamy.
Makes my head go kind of creamy
Seein' that great big flat moon
Gallivantin' roun' in tune
Every time we pass the door.
Shoot away now down the floor,
Dizzy, whizzy, loo-for-Lizzie,
Buckle-rappin', tap-tap-tappin'.
Guess my bones am gwine to loosen,

Guess I can't no more be choosin',
Guess I'll dance till Kingdom come,
Guess I need a drop of rum.
Holy Moses! hold me tighter,
'Pears the moon am growin' whiter.
Drum, you niggers, skin yo' wrists,
Ain't we done a heap o' twists!
How-do! How-do!
Heel and toe,
Forty couples in a glow,
Eight rose-bud hearts a-quakin'.
Looks it might be dawn a-breakin'!
How-do! How-do!
Pigeon-heel and rabbit-toe,
Till the candles all burn low
And the drums am tellin' sleepy
Tappin' ghosty-short an' creepy,
An' a bluejay up an' screeches
Outside in his purple beeches.
Kiss me, Honey, that's all right.
Maybe I'll be round to-night.

PROPER INVECTIVE

Followed by an Aria of Ironic Consequence

Rust, moth, fungus, canker-worm,
Hemlock, nightshade, Upas tree,
All the horrors that there be
Loose upon this pachyderm.

Gods of grottoes, caves, and mountains,
Oracles and visions dire,
Spirits of the air and fire.
Dryads, naiads, nymphs of fountains.

Leave your eagle crags and eyries,
Fly your apple-leaved seclusions,
Bring your dreadfullest confusions,
Mumbled magic misereres.

Spell, and curse, and incantation
Heap upon this froward man,
Every charm and patteran
Use to his complete damnation.

Call in wizards, witches, seers,
With their lore of plant and planet,
Bid them forge a charm of granite
Lasting for a thousand years.

Bid them pick the square-stemmed briars
Out of swamps where vapours ooze,
Watch the faggots that they choose,
Proper for their magic fires.

Watch them come by one and one,
With the fog-web in their hair,
And their yellow eyes astare,
Bearing treasures hardly won.

Slowly tramping round about
The red cauldron, in they drop
Mince and morsel, sip and sop,
Rabbit's paw or weasel's snout,

Snakeskin sloughed at middle moon,
Hair of brindled, five-toed cat,
Spotted burdock which a rat
Gnawed where frosty gibbets croon.

Tail of skunk and owlet's ear,
Earthworms digged from a Jew's grave,
Splinter of a coffin stave
Nicked from off a miser's bier.

Roots of adder's tongue, and yew
Stripped at dawn on Easter even.
"Seven, seven, seven, seven,
Seven stars which buzzed and flew.

Seven devils, flying, dipping,
Diving round the weather-cock
Of the church, while tolls the clock
Seven long strokes without skipping."

Infant's finger singed and brittle
Stuck upon a dragon's fang,
And, to give the brew a tang,
Seven drops of blindman's spittle.

Rumble, rumble, stir the stew
Round and round in widdershins,
Faster, faster, till it spins.
But there's more I'd have you do.

Summon Gods of Ind and Indies:
Thoth, Sesostris, Voodoo, Bel,
With their sorceries from Hell
And their weird outlandish shindies.

Sibyls, with your erudition,
Read him all the sooth and sin
Under his name written in
Your long records of perdition.

Ancient oracles declaim
Fates concealed in dream and trance,
Tragic jests of circumstance.
Speak them smoothly like a flame.

Every rune and every rite
Shower on him, spare not one,
Till from sun to rising sun
Never lived a sadder wight.

Let the spinning shapes of mist
Lure him to high rocky edges
Over surfy seas, let sedges
Hide the river's sudden twist.

Urge him with the voice of lovers
Into fenny bogs and quakes
Where the tufted marsh-mud shakes
And a green light swoops and hovers.

Elves and pixies, pique him, prick him,
Knot the grass to trip his feet.
Goblin, djinn, and black afreet
Pommel, pound, confuse, and kick him.

Star his darkness thick with faces,
Mewing, mouthing, white as yeast;
Bloody lips on which ghouls feast
Leer at him with foul grimaces.

Beetles, bugs, and dragon-flies,
Sting him with your poisoned stings,
Crawling fogs fold your cold wings
Round about his arms and thighs.

Itching fevers, let him be
Your most constant bourn, attend him
With such pangs that they may send him
Forthright to Eternity.
. . . . .

So far done! O Warlocks, Witches,
Thanks. And Gods of cloud and mountain,
And ye nymphs of tree and fountain,
Upland wold and leafy ditches,

I am gratitude unending.
Flit back to your woods and caverns,
Your high palaces, and taverns
Under junipers down bending.

I will lay you jars of wine
At the entrance to your grottoes,
I will carve the trees with mottoes:
Aspen, birch, and scowling pine.

Not a wind shall blow between them
But my words will show the brighter,

Cut through bark to wood that's whiter.
Everyone will soon have seen them.

Everyone will pilgrimage
To your mountains and your rills,
Trampling down the daffodils,
Hauling marble for a stage.

Column, court, and colonnade
Will appear by due degrees,
Overhung with locust-trees
Casting purple pools of shade.

Medals, coins, and carven gems
Will be dropped into your shallows,
Chequered by the brooding sallows
With their pink and silver stems.

Youths and maidens wreathed in crocus
Will parade your solemn larches,
Pruned and fashioned into arches
With the temple as their focus.

All because, you Ancient Spirits,
Sibyls, Oreads, and Elves,
Hoary Gods, you gave yourselves,
Each with his peculiar merits,

To avenge a mortal who
Had received a grievous slight
From a witty, witless wight.
Tell no one what I tell you.

Priests and Vestals shall not know
Why this temple stands to prove
My high gratitude and love.
Why I have proclaimed you so.

Listen then, to solemn truth,
In the arrogance of youth,
What that fellow dared to do:
Write a long, adverse review!

See now, in my rage and rancour,
Goaded by tormenting canker,
What I've done. It might be worse.
Founding creeds upon a curse
Is no new thing, you'll admit.
Take what is and build on it,
Be obliged with what you find,
Wisdom does not pry behind
Any curtain hung between
What is now with what has been.
If you do not wish to see
Your fine temple utterly

Doomed and ruined, never tell.
Gods and oracles, farewell.

DISSONANCE

From my window I can see the moon-
   light stroking the smooth surface of
   the river.
The trees are silent, there is no wind.
Admirable pre-Raphaelite landscape,
Lightly touched with ebony and silver.
I alone am out of keeping:
An angry red gash
Proclaiming the restlessness
Of an incongruous century.

THE BOOK OF STONES
AND LILIES

I read a book
With a golden name,
Written in blood
On a leaf of flame.

And the words of the book
Were clothed in white,
With tiger colours
Making them bright.

The sweet words sang
Like an angel choir,
And their purple wings
Beat the air to fire.

Then I rose on my bed,
And attended my ear,
And the words sang carefully
So I could hear.

The dark night opened
Like a silver bell,
And I heard what it was
The words must tell:
"Heaven is good.
Evil is Hell."

The night shut up
Like a silver bell.
But the words still sang,
And I listened well.

I heard the tree-winds
Crouch and roar,
I saw green waves
On a stony shore.

I saw blue wings
In a beat of fire.
My hands clutched the feathers
Of all desire.

I cried for hammers,
For a hand of brass,
But my soul was hot
As melted glass.

Then the bright, bright words,
All clothed in white,
Stood in the circle of the silver night,
And sang:
"Energy is Eternal Delight.
Energy is the only life."

And my sinews were like bands of brass,
And the glass of my soul hardened and
   shone
With all fires, and I sought the ripeness
   of sacrifice
Across the dew and the gold of a young
   day.

STALACTITE

I am a dead thing,
A brittle mummy swathed in canvas,
Gazing with cracked, painted eyes
At a high dome above a still hall.
There is thunder,
And I hear it;
There is lightning,
And I see the tongues of it;
There are many bodies beside mine,
And I see them too.
I died a thousand years ago,
And yet I remember long since,
Drifts of ages since,
Watching,
With other eyes than these,
Diana gathering white poppies upon a
   seaside hill.

THE SPLENDOUR FALLS FROM
CASTLE WALLS

(Adapted from Tennyson)

The windows of the gallery
Are tall, with rounded tops, so high
They cramp the ceiling. Through their
   panes,
Fogged and streaked with dust and rains,

An August sunshine slants and veers
Over the walls and the chandeliers
Of faceted crystal, but scarce a gleam
Can these give back, the ancient dream
Of dust is on them. The sunlight floats
On a stream of dust, the dropping motes
Sift like mist through the empty room
Filling it with a golden bloom.
The moth-eaten velvet of the chairs
Placed along the walls in pairs
Is pitilessly obvious,
The gilded arms and legs are worse,
Scaled to the wood. All is hushed and
      bright,
An ancient splendour crushed with light,
An aristocratic refinement, lying
Bare to the eyes in the act of dying.
Not a sound from the courtyard, not a
      bang
From a distant door. The pictures hang
Undisturbed, the scenes they show
All occurred so long ago
They are nothing to nothing.
But how fresh the paint
Upon armoured hero and martyred saint.
How steadily the pennants curl
From the masts of battleships! How they
      whirl,
The javelins on that brazen gate!
Here is passion coagulate,
Stiffened at its highest flux,
An agony not worth the chucks
Of a copper-coin, or the bandolier
Of a sixteenth century cavalier.
What knots of roses these battles were
To the painter commissioned to disinter
A thousand graves and decorate
One general at his moment of spate.
How gaily and safely they plied their
      trade,
Turning a fight to a harlequinade,
A holocaust to a pirouet.
What of the blood, the groans, the sweat,
The squeal of wounded horses, the
      cries
Of disembowelled companies —
What, think you, becomes of these
On his commissioned canvases?
Blow the trumpet! Bang the drum!
Tootle the fife! The armies come
Home from the wars, and what did they
Do there, painter, can you say?
Of course he can, he's the man to tell
What he's never seen, he imagines so
      well.

In his pictures, cavalry advance
To the jaws of cannon, so sprightly a
      prance
Shows the rose-wreath courage of horses
      and men.
One cannon ball has just slain ten,
Another is bursting like a rocket
An inch beyond the embroidered pocket
Of a gold-laced gentleman, unconcerned
By the fact that his uniform may be
      burned.
His noble horse, on hind legs only,
Dashes ahead of the troop in lonely
Magnificence. Earthworks bar the way,
But what of that? This is Malplaquet
With Marlborough rampant. Hooray!
      Hooray!
I am almost inclined to toss my hat
Up on a chandelier for that.
Such a roseate riot of marshal exploit!
A leader so bold, well-dressed, and adroit
At high-school horsemanship, one of the
      true bits
Of earth's tempered metal; why even his
      cubits
Outspan those of any behind him that
      drew bits
And gave him his distance to open the
      breach
In fiery solitude. What do they teach?
"Marlbrouck s'en va-t-en guerre!" Such
      is speech;
Even I am ignited.
                    A curious sound,
Something between a step and a pound,
Startles my trance. A man comes in,
A pallid person, and so thin
His bones crook the angles of his dress.
He limps, poor soul, and his breathless-
      ness
Is pitiable, after his climb
Up the slippery stairs. It is closing time
He tells me dully. But I beg
Him to sit and rest. His wooden leg
Is a heavy burden, I suppose.
He shakes his head and slowly goes
On his round of closing the high win-
      dows.
"It's nothing, Sir, I've got the use
Of this timber now. They cooked my
      goose
When they conscripted me. If I'd known
In time I'd have broke my leg with a
      stone
Rather than this. I've a churlish bed

To lie on, but what's done is done," he
    said.
A miserable philosophy
To catch a man so young as he.
I risked a question gingerly.
"Yes, Sir, a wife and youngster, so
I got this job. It's all I can do.
Damn beastly business, war!" He spat
A curse or two, and after that
He moved to show me out, but when
I asked his age, he spat again
Another curse: "That's it, Sir, see,
I'm only just gone twenty-three."
I gave him silver. His stump came fainter
Round the corner of the kitchen wing.
Coincidence is an eery thing —
As I walked away, I damned that painter.

SONGS OF THE PUEBLO INDIANS

I

WOMEN'S HARVEST SONG

I am waving a ripe sunflower,
I am scattering sunflower pollen to the
    four world-quarters.
I am joyful because of my melons,
I am joyful because of my beans,
I am joyful because of my squashes.

The sunflower waves.
So did the corn wave
When the wind blew against it,
So did my white corn bend
When the red lightning descended upon
    it,
It trembled as the sunflower
When the rain beat down its leaves.

Great is a ripe sunflower,
And great was the sun above my corn-
    fields.
His fingers lifted up the corn-ears,
His hands fashioned my melons,
And set my beans full in the pods.
Therefore my heart is happy
And I will lay many blue prayer-sticks at
    the shrine of Ta-wa.

I will give corn to Ta-wa,
Yellow corn, blue corn, black corn.
I wave the sunflower,
The sunflower heavy with pollen.
I wave it,
I turn it,

I sing,
Because I am happy.

II

BASKET DANCE

Dance!
Dance!
The priest is yellow with sunflower meal,
He is yellow with corn-meal,
He is yellow as the sun.
Dance!
Dance!
His little bells are ringing,
The bells tinkle like sunlight,
The sun is rising.
Dance!
Dance!
Perhaps I will throw you a basket,
Perhaps I will throw you my heart.

Lift the baskets, dancing,
Lower the baskets, dancing,
We have raised fruits,
Now we dance.
Our shadows are long,
The sunlight is bright between our
    shadows.
Do you want my basket?
Catch it!
Catch it!
But you cannot catch me,
I am more difficult.

III

WOMEN'S SONG OF THE CORN

How beautiful are the corn rows,
Stretching to the morning sun,
Stretching to the evening sun.
Very beautiful, the long rows of corn.

How beautiful is the white corn,
I husk it,
I grind it,
Very beautiful, my white corn.

How beautiful is the red corn,
I gather it and make fine meal,
I am glad doing this.
Very beautiful, my red corn.

How beautiful is the black corn,
I give it to my father,
To my mother,

I give it to my child.
Very beautiful, the black corn.

How beautiful is the mottled corn,
Like the sky with little clouds,
I eat it looking at the sky.
Very beautiful, my mottled corn.

IV

PRAYER FOR A PROFUSION OF SUNFLOWERS

Send sunflowers!
With my turkey-bone whistle
I am calling the birds
To sing upon the sunflowers.
For when the clouds hear them singing
They will come quickly,
And rain will fall upon our fields.
Send sunflowers!

V

PRAYER FOR LIGHTNING

My corn is green with red tassels,
I am praying to the lightning to ripen
my corn,
I am praying to the thunder which car-
ries the lightning.
Corn is sweet where lightning has fallen.
I pray to the six-coloured clouds.

VI

FLUTE-PRIEST SONG FOR RAIN
Ceremonial at the Sun Spring

Whistle under the water,
Make the water bubble to the tones of
the flute.
I call the bluebird's song into the water:
Wee-kee! Wee-kee-kee!
Dawn is coming,
The morning star shines upon us.
Bluebird singing to the West clouds,
Bring the humming rain.

Water-rattles shake,
Flute whistles,
Star in Heaven shines.
I blow the oriole's song,
The yellow song of the North.
I call rain clouds with my rattles:
Wee-kee-kee, oriole.
Pattering rain.

To the South I blow my whistle,
To the red parrot of the South I call.
Send red lightning,
Under your wings
The forked lightning.
Thunder-rattles whirl
To the sky waters.
Fill the springs.
The water is moving.
Wait —

Whistle to the East
With a magpie voice:
Wee-kee! Wee-kee-kee!
Call the storm-clouds
That they come rushing.
Call the loud rain.

Why does it not come?
Who is bad?
Whose heart is evil?
Who has done wickedness?
I weep,
I rend my garments,
I grieve for the sin which is in this place.
My flute sobs with the voice of all birds
in the water.
Even to the six directions I weep and
despair.
Come, O winds, from the sides of the
sky,
Open your bird-beaks that rain may fall
down.
Drench our fields, our houses,
Fill the land
With tumult of rain.

UNCOLLECTED POEMS

ON "THE CUTTING OF AN AGATE" (BY W. B. YEATS)

Reading this book, I see an attic room
  Brimful of heaps of dimly-shining
    stuff,
  Tumbled upon the floor. Here is
    enough
To fashion wingèd Caps till day of doom.
This yarn is shimmering with a frosty
    bloom
  Of colours overlaid as with a rough
Patina of snow crystals. See! A puff
Of wind blows jewelled chaff to spark the
    gloom.
  It seems the storehouse of raw poesy,
Where unspun dreams are waiting to be
    bought,
And where unwoven tapestries of thought
  Lie ripe for the large looms of
    prophecy.
A little handful of this harvesting
Would make most poets an ample cover-
    ing.

A RAINY NIGHT

Shadows,
And white, moving light,
And the snap and sparkle of rain on the
  window,
An electric lamp in the street
Is swinging, tossing,
Making the rain-runnelled window-glass
Glitter and palpitate.
In its silver lustre
I can see the old four-post bed,
With the fringes and balls of its canopy.
You are lying beside me, waiting,
But I do not turn,
I am counting the folds of the canopy.
You are lying beside me, waiting,
But I do not turn.
In the silver light you would be too
  beautiful,
And there are ten pleats on this side of
  the bed canopy,
And ten on the other.

A COMPARISON

This man is like a mechanical toy
Which runs, and streaks, and veers over
  the carpet,
With a noise of thin edges of tin
Whirring upon one another
In spirals of shrillness.
Even when you pick it up,
The wheels of the toy continue to whirl,
Grating incessantly.
They beat, and wobble, and whiz,
Inconceivably rapid rings of blurred
  spokes,
And the shrill scraping pierces one's ear-
  drums
Like an auger.

MAY EVENING IN CENTRAL PARK

Lines of lamp-light
Splinter the black water,
And all through
The dim park
Are lamps
Hanging among the trees.
But they are only like fire-flies
Pricking the darkness,
And I lean my body against it
And spread out my fingers
To let it drift through them.
I am a swimmer
In the damp night,
Or a bird
Floating over the sucking grasses.
I am a lover
Tracking the silver foot-prints
Of the moon.
I am a young man,
In Central Park,
With Spring
Bursting over me.

The trees push out their young leaves,
Although this is not the country;
And I whisper beautiful, hot words,
Although I am alone,
And a few more steps

Will bring me
The glare and suffocation
Of bright streets.

THE ROAD TO THE MOUNTAIN

He rode along the turnpike way,
    With yellow daffodils a-springing,
A poet on a flea-bitten gray.
    The birds were singing.

Out from behind an oak-tree came
    An ancient man, all bent and
        tangled;
Like unwound wire, he was lame,
    And his body jangled.

"So up the mountain is your speed!"
    He shook his stick and coughed and
        cackled.
"Up the great mountain, riding a steed
    That's spavined and hackled.

Each hock is apple-puffed, his knees
    Are broken, and he's badly
        winded." —
The rusty voice stopped on a sneeze,
    For no one minded.

The poet rode on through spotted shade,
    His harness buckles ting-a-linging,
When down a forest-path skipped a
        maid,
    With wide skirts swinging.

She stopped a moment to gape and gaze,
    And the budding elm-trees sprigged
        her over
With sliding meshes of crown-green haze,
    A butterfly cover.

"Your horse is very small," said she.
    "If those four feet cannot trot faster,
You might as well stay where you be.
    Think of it, Master.

An hour hence and scarce a mile
    Will you be from where you now are
        faring.
Why not dismount and stay a while,
    For the sun is flaring."

Pit-pat, pit-pat, the beating hoofs
    Scatters of pebbles and dust are
        flinging,

Under the weaving, waving roofs,
    Like birds a-winging.

Through the cobbled street of a little
        town,
    Round a corner, and past a turning,
The poet and his flea-bitten gray are
        blown,
    Like leaf-smoke burning.

A puff of gray, a darting feather;
    Gravel pecking a window-pane;
A spark underfoot, a creak of leather;
    They are up the lane.

Up the lane to the leaves again,
    And trees and trees in endless string-
        ing.
A flat, green square like a counterpane
    And churchbells ringing.

Kettledrum strokes on an organ's drone,
    The flea-bitten gray past the church
        door canters,
Thudding drum echoes out of the stone,
    Confusing the chanters.

Round hoofs pick, and nick, and fly.
    A shadow close to white dust cling-
        ing,
Shot at a line of purple sky,
    And a hill wind stinging.

Waves awash and a ferry stalled.
    Thunder-darkened, rain-ringed river.
Frantic cries of boat-men appalled.
    A splash, a quiver.

Snorting rise on the further bank,
    A flat-bellied gallop far on again,
Between thick bushes, steaming and dank,
    Till sun dries rain.

He rides along the turnpike way,
    With blue hills over green hills
        springing.
A poet on a flea-bitten gray,
    And the poet is singing.

ELEONORA DUSE

The talk is hushed,
In the domed theatre's self the lights go
        out
While other lights flash on the eyes,

As the concealing curtain slowly lifts
Upon a mimic world, or grave or gay,
As artist's hand hath wrought.

The silent throng
Is bound together by one common aim,
One animating thought has brought
them there
In rows that curve expectant towards the
stage,
For they have come to see the self-same
play.
But this the only bond that makes them
one,
For each is here upon a different quest,
A difference rooted deep as are their
lives;
For they have minds as various
As are the shells the ebbtide leaves upon
The shingle of some island beach.

For some are here on pure amusement
bent,
Others come lured by the far fame of her
Who tonight will image forth the tragic
fate
Of one who lived and died long since,
Or else imbue the shadowy figment of
A poet's dream with palpitating life.
Others there are in search of sparks to
kindle
The slow fire of their torpid brains.
Others have wandered in they scarce
know how;
As sand that sifts all imperceptibly
Into some ancient temple's columned
hall,
The desert wind that urged it is so far
It hardly seems impelled by any law
But drifting aimlessly has drifted here.

Yet all have come to see the self-same
play.
But what they take away is not the same,
For none can go beyond what he has
known
And none can feel what was not felt
before;
No wandering half-forgotten moment
passed,
No volume read, no music heard, but
now
Bears fruit in deeper comprehension.

For she whom we have come to see to-
night
Is more to be divined and felt than seen,
And when she comes one yields one's
heart perforce,
As one might yield some noble instru-
ment
For her to draw its latent music forth.

For she herself vibrates to every thought,
And shades of feeling cross her face like
clouds
That trail their shadows over distant
hills.
Her being is like an aeolian harp
Clasped in a casement on some summer
night
Whence every breeze that passes draws a
sound,
Now harsh and wild, now sweet, now
quaintly gay,
But always musical, and always true.

Her voice is vibrant with a thousand
things;
Is sharp with pain, or choked with tears,
Or rich with love and longing.
Her little inarticulate sounds are sprung
From depths of inner meaning which
embrace
A life's chaotic, vast experience.

As if a little, sudden gust of wind
Should blow aside the branches of a tree,
Revealing for an instant to our eyes
The deep night sky all twinkling full of
stars,
And then the branch sweep back and
shut it out
And leave us wondering, 'neath the rus-
tling leaves.

And as the evening lengthens, bit by bit,
Little by little, we discern the real.
'Tis that which holds us spellbound far,
far more
Than even her most consummate art can
do,
Through all the passion of a simulated
grief
And through the studied anguish learnt
by rote
We feel the throbbing of a human soul,
A woman's heart that cries to God and
fears!

INDEX OF FIRST LINES OF POEMS

A bird chirped at my window this morning, 213
A black cat among roses, 212
A bullet through his heart at dawn, 103
A cold rain blurs the edges of the river, 363
A cold wind blows up from the edge of Heaven, 353
Across the newly-plastered wall, 206
A dog, 344
A drifting, April, twilight sky, 27
A face seen passing in a crowded street, 16
A flickering glimmer through a window-pane, 14
After all, what have I come here to do, 350
Again the larkspur, 441
A great tall column spearing at the sky, 124
A hundred battles, the sandy fields of battles, armour broken into fragments, 347
A June-bug has just flown in through my window, 561
A ladder sticking up at the open window, 223
A lady was given a shell which kept in its convolutions, 558
Alas! Alas! The danger! The steepness! O Affliction, 330
A little brown room in a sea of fields, 220
A little garden on a bleak hillside, 15
A little old man, 238
All day I have watched the purple vine leaves, 204
All day long I have been working, 210
All night I read a little book, 571
All night I wrestled with a memory, 19
All night our room was outer-walled with rain, 213
All the afternoon there has been a chirping of birds, 219
All these years I have remembered a night, 555
Alone, I whet my soul against the keen, 226
Although so many years, 207
Always we are following a light, 16
A man made a symphony, 230
A minstrel stands on a marble stair, 11
A music-stand of crimson lacquer, long since brought, 142
Anaemic women, stupidly dressed and shod, 230
An arid daylight shines along the beach, 37
An astonishing view, she regards it with eyes, 548
A near horizon whose sharp jags, 12
A pot of wine among flowers, 338
April had covered the hills, 2
A scholar, 205
As for a moment he stands, in hardy masculine beauty, 9
As I crossed over the bridge of Ariwarano Narikira, 203
As I sit here in the quiet Summer night, 217
As I wandered through the eight hundred and eight streets of the city, 203
As I would free the white almond from the green husk, 73
As one who sails upon a wide, blue sea, 3
At Chin Ling, the tavern where travellers part is called the Rest-House of Deep Trouble, 347
At dawn, I left the Red Bird Gate, 345
At dawn, the conscripted soldiers enter the camp outside the Eastern Gate, 353

At fifteen, she entered the Palace of Han, 343
At first a mere thread of a footpath half blotted out by the grasses, 9
A thousand years went to her making, 236
At Matsue, 205
At the first light of the still-concealed sun, the Cock-man, in his dark-red cap, strikes the tally-sticks and proclaims aloud the hour, 355
At Wei Yang dwells the Son of Heaven, 333
At what season last year did my Lord leave his Unworthy One, 343
Autumn comes, 354
A Winter night, a cold Winter night. To me, the night is unending, 340
A wise man, 205
A yellow band of light upon the street, 44
A young man on a platform, 569
Bang, 116
Beat, beat, with your soft, grey feet, 468
Beautiful is this woman who rolls up the pearl-reed blind, 349
Because of this, sad, sad has the whole day been to me, 356
Because the little gentleman made nautical instruments, 567
Because the moonlight deceives, 207
Because there was no wind, 207
Before me, 225
Before me lies a mass of shapeless days, 36
Before the Altar, bowed, he stands, 1
Before the White Heron Island — the moon, 351
Being thirsty, 204
Beneath this sod lie the remains, 43
"Benjamin Bailey, Benjamin Bailey, why do you wake at the stroke of three," 278
Be not angry with me that I bear, 36
Be patient with you, 35
Beside the high window, but partly withdrawn, 546
Between us leapt a gold and scarlet flame, 43
Beyond the porcelain fence of the pleasure garden, 204
Birds are calling through the rain, 241
Black clouds slowly swaying, 224
Blow softly, 207
Blue and pink sashes, 104
Blue as the tip of a salvia blossom, 153
Blue through the window burns the twilight, 14
Bright, bright, the gilded magpie mirror, 332
Brighter than fireflies upon the Uji River, 204
Bring pencils, fine pointed, 222
But tickets, of course, at the door of the theatre, 547
But why did I kill him? Why? Why, 56
By day you cannot see the sky, 25
By the scent of the burning pine-cones, 364
Cat, 232
Certainly the furniture was of satin-wood, 475
Certainly you gave me your heart, 559
Chia, the Scholar, gazes into the West, thinking of the splendour of the Capitol, 345

Clear green hills at a right angle to the North wall, 340
Cliffs, 556
Cloud-topped and splendid, dominating all, 15
Coat of purple stamped velvet, satin breeches to match, 548
Cold, wet leaves, 204
Come swing, come smirk, in sailor blue and star, 539
Coming to you along the Nihon Embankment, 206
Coming up from my boat, 205
Cool wind rising. Sun sparkling on the wide canal, 359
Cross-hatchings of rain against grey walls, 150
Cross-ribboned shoes; a muslin gown, 111
Crows are cawing over pine-trees, 221

Dance, 588
Dear Bessie, would my tired rhyme, 13
Dearest, forgive that with my clumsy touch, 37
Dearest, we are like two flowers, 218
Dear Virgin Mary, far away, 55
Diagonally between the cryptomerias, 206
Did the door move, or was it always ajar, 215
Double-flowering trees bear no fruit, they say, 581
Down a cliff-side where rock-roses, 466
Do you not see the waters of the Yellow River coming down from Heaven, 342
Draw your hoods tightly, 207
Due East, far West, 162

Earth, Air, Water, and Fire, 177
Even as a young man, 357
Even the iris bends, 205
Everyone has his fancies, I suppose, 557
Every time I have started for the Yellow Flower River, 355

Fifteen years is not a long time, 450
Fig-wood oars, 339
Fine rain, 361
Fireflies flicker in the tops of trees, 211
Flat, 571
Forever the impenetrable wall, 20
Four horizons cozen me, 578
Frau Concert-Meister Altgelt shut the door, 88
From little, little girls, they have lived in the Golden House, 331
From my window I can see the moonlight stroking the smooth surface of the river, 586
From out the dragging vastness of the sea, 35
From the high pavilion of the great rock, 362
From whose house do the invisible notes of a jade flute come flying, 341

Give me sunlight, cupped in a paint brush, 222
Glazed silk, newly cut, smooth, glittering, white, 360
Glinting golden through the trees, 2
Goaded and harassed in the factory, 15
Golden peacocks, 203
Good ev'nin', Mis' Priest, 131
Grass-blades push up between the cobblestones, 227
Greatly shining, 477
Great master! Boyish, sympathetic man, 21
Guarded within the old red wall's embrace, 74

Gushing from the mouths of stone men, 73

Hanging from the ceiling by threads, 219
Happiness, to some, elation, 37
"Have another cruller, Mis' Sanders, 488
Have at you, you Devils, 40
He asks why I perch in the green jade hills, 344
He built the house to show his neighbours, 532
Hedges of England, peppered with sloes, 173
He died of "Stranger's Fever" when his youth, 20
He earned his bread by making wooden soldiers, 237
He is a solitary traveller, 364
He is dead, 273
He is going to the Tung T'ing Lake, 362
He moved in, with two thousand books, and a bed, and an armchair, 566
He perches in the slime, inert, 35
Her breasts were small, upright, virginal, 576
"Here we go round the ivy-bush," 473
He rides a white horse, 435
He rode along the turnpike way, 592
He said he saw the spangled wings of angels, 230
He shouts in the sails of the ships at sea, 25
He told me, one night, when we were off duty, 565
He was a landscape architect, 238
He wore a coat, 206
Hey! Crackerjack — jump, 224
Hey! My daffodil-crowned, 73
High up above the open, welcoming door, 3
High up in the apple tree climbing I go, 24
Hills surround the ancient kingdom; they never change, 354
Hold your apron wide, 42
Hold your soul open for my welcoming, 43
Holy Mother of God, Merciful Mary, 71
How beautiful are the corn rows, 588
How delightful, at sunset, to loosen the boat, 352
How dim the battle-field, as yellow dusk, 329
How-do! How-do!, 582
How empty seems the town now you are gone, 19
How fresh the Dartle's little waves that day, 76
How is it that, being gone, you fill my days, 18
How long shall I tarnish the mirror of life, 37
How many Springs have we been apart? You do not come home, 348
How should I sing when buffeting salt waves, 35
How still it is! Sunshine itself here falls, 10
How the Cloudy River glitters, 358
How the slates of the roof sparkle in the sun, 113
How witless to assail the carven halls, 477
"Hullo, Alice," 134
Hush, hush, these woods are thick with shapes and voices, 570

I am a dead thing, 586
I am a woman, sick for passion, 233
I am immoderately fond of this place, 560
I am so aching to write, 580
I am so tired, 239
I am useless, 574
I am waving a ripe sunflower, 588
I ask but one thing of you, only one, 18
I beg you, 212
I bid you good-bye, my friend, as you are going on an excursion to the Plum-Flower Lake, 350
I build my poems with little strokes of ink, 229

I came from the country, 227
I cannot see your face, 216
I climb the hill of Chiu I — Oh-h-h-h-h! I look at the clear streams a long way off, 336
I cut myself upon the thought of you, 558
I do not care to talk to you although, 18
If Heaven did not love wine, 338
If I could catch the green lantern of the firefly, 204
If you believed my words, 550
I gave you a picture once, 445
"I grasped a thread of silver; it cut me to the bone, 474
I had already wandered away from the People's Temple, 351
I have a flagon of wine in my hand, 346
I have been temperate always, 42
I have come back, Winky, 560
I have drunk your health, 206
I have often a vision of your face, 558
I have painted a picture of a ghost, 205
I have painted my eyebrows like willow-leaves to delight you, 561
I have read you, and read you, my Betters, 541
I have whetted my brain until it is like a Damascus blade, 42
I know a country laced with roads, 10
I lay them before you, 213
I learnt to write to you in happier days, 19
I left her there in the rushes by the river, 575
I left the horse outside, 568
Illimitable happiness, 354
I looked from my window at the great lake, 570
I love the beauty of the Wan River, 342
I love Ts'ui of Ch'iu Pu, 337
I made a song one morning, 227
I moved to the sound of gold, and brass, and heavily-clashed silver, 441
I must be mad, or very tired, 449
In Autumn, when the landscape is clear, to float over the wide, water ripples, 359
In front of my bed the moonlight is very bright, 345
In the attitude, and with the manner, of the woman of old, 348
In the brown water, 72
In the clear green water — the shimmering moon, 344
In the cloud-grey mornings, 208
In the far distance, the mountains seem to rise out of the river, 350
In the grounds of the Villa Capouana where now, 548
In the old days, Ch'iu Pu was bare and desolate, 337
In the sky there is a moon and stars, 207
Into the brazen, burnished sky, the cry hurls itself, 125
In what place does the cinnabar-red tree of the alchemists seed, 362
In Yang Chou, the blossoms are dropping. The night-jar calls, 350
I own a solace shut within my heart, 4
I pray to be the tool which to your hand, 36
I put your leaves aside, 211
I read a book, 586
I return to the inn at the foot of the Climbing Bean Pass, 364

I ride, ride, 446
I saw him, 474
I should tremble at the falling showers of ashes, 206
Is it a dragonfly or a maple leaf, 205
Is it the tinkling of mandolins which disturbs you, 236
I sought a lodging for the night, at sunset, in the Stone Moat Village, 352
I stood in my window, 221
I take leave of my dear old friend at the Yellow Crane Tower, 349
It had been a trim garden, 235
I think I am cousin-german to Endymion, 478
I think you are a white clematis, 479
I thought, 204
I thought of myself as a walnut, 572
It is late, 215
It is long — long — since my two eyebrows were painted like cassia-leaves, 360
It is not the bright light in your window, 207
It is only a little twig, 227
It is the Eighth Month, the very height of Autumn, 351
It is the Fifth Month, 328
I told them to look at an apple-tree, 538
It's a soppy, splashy, muddy country, 461
It snowed yesterday, 573
It was a disappointment, 569
It was a gusty night, 139
It was not a large garden, as gardens go, 280
It winds along the face of a cliff, 5
I've a pocketful of emptiness for you, my Dear, 473
I've been reading a book about sewing, 579
I walk down the garden paths, 75
I walked along a street at dawn in cold, grey light, 213
I wandered through a house of many rooms, 237
I want no horns to rouse me up to-night, 474
I want to be a carpenter, 228
I went a-riding, a-riding, 449
I will mix me a drink of stars, 42
I would pray for thunder, 582
I wrote her a letter, she wrote me three, 538

Jade dew lies upon the withered and wounded forest of maple-trees, 353
Jangle of cow-bells through pine-trees, 224
Jolt of market-carts, 214

Katydids scraped in the dim trees, 478
King Yao has been dead for three thousand years, 338

Ladies, I do not know you, and I think, 562
Lances slanted against a froward sky, 537
Last night, at sunset, 444
Last year they fought at the source of the Sang Ch'ien, 334
Leisure, thou goddess of a bygone age, 15
Life! Austere arbiter of each man's fate, 17
Life is a stream, 2
Like a saint, he comes, 361
Like black ice, 226
Like Don Quixote, I tilted at a windmill, 228
Lilacs, 446

Li Ling is buried in the sands of Hu, 349
Lines of lamp-light, 591
Li Po climbed the Flowery Mountain, 364
Li Po gets into a small boat — he is on the point of starting, 350
Little cramped words scrawling all over the paper, 209
Little hot apples of fire, 226
Look, Dear, how bright the moonlight is to-night, 9
Looking at myself in my metal mirror, 206
Looking South and straight from Hsien Yang for five thousand li, 341

Mist is trying to hide the Spring-coloured hills, 354
Mist, vapour, 537
Moon over the houses of Han, over the site of Ch'in, 343
Must all of worth be travailled for, and those, 17
My corn is green with red tassels, 589
My cup is empty to-night, 41
My Grandpapa lives in a wonderful house, 24
My heart is like a cleft pomegranate, 42
My heart is tuned to sorrow, and the strings, 19
My house burnt down, I saw the stars, 574
My skirt is cut out of peacock silk, 360
My thoughts, 212
My very excellent young person, 475

Naughty little speckled trout, 25
Near where I live there is a lake, 23
No decent man will cross a field, 437
No peacock strutting on a balustrade, 538
No word, no word, O Lord God, 471
Now what in the name of the sun and the stars, 129

Oblong, its jutted ends rounding into circles, 234
Oh! To be a flower, 5
Old China sits and broods behind her ten-thousand-miles-great wall, 251
Old crumbling stones set long ago upon, 470
Old Tai is gone down to the Yellow Springs, 346
On a carpeted bench, thirteen well-chosen priests, 547
On an evening of black snow, 560
Once, in the sultry heats of Midsummer, 204
Once the Unworthy One was a maiden of the Ts'ung Terrace, 340
On days when the sky is grey, not blue, 543
One night, 203
On the floor of the empty palanquin, 206
On the Nothing-Beyond Peak, a hut of red grass, 355
On winter nights beside the nursery fire, 12
Opaque because of the run mercury at its back, 569
Our meeting was like the upward swish of a rocket, 230
Outside the long window, 41
Over the hill snakes the dusty road, 295
Over the housetops, 31
Over the moor the wind blew chill, 291
Over the shop where silk is sold, 206
Over the yawning chimney hangs the fog, 60
O You, 558

Pale, with the blue of high zeniths, shimmered over with silver, brocaded, 72
Panels of claret and blue which shine, 65
Paul Jannes was working very late, 66
Peonies, 445
Perched upon the muzzle of a cannon, 205
Peter, Peter, along the ground, 298
Pierrot had grown old, 231
Poems, 559
Poor foolish monarch, vacillating, vain, 21

Reading this book, I see an attic room, 591
Red foxgloves against a yellow wall streaked with plum-coloured shadows, 211
Red slippers in a shop-window, 149
"Regrets and memories these short December days," 550
Richardson, Erik Follows, Reed and I, 499
Roses and larkspur, 560
Rust, moth, fungus, canker-worm, 584

Sea-roses blowing on a high, white cliff, 558
Sea Shell, Sea Shell, 23
See! He trails his toes, 216
See! I give myself to you, Beloved, 41
Seeing's believing, so the ancient word, 479
Seeing that you pass your life playing upon the virginals, 476
Send sunflowers, 589
Shadows, 591
Shall I give you white currants, 445
She came into my shop to-day, 578
She is a washerwoman most of the time, 568
She sat in a Chinese wicker chair, 235
She was an aggressively unattractive old woman, 574
She wore purple, and when other people slept, 280
Shoals of fish assemble and scatter, 364
Silent and alone, I ascended the West Cupola, 357
Silver-green lanterns tossing among windy branches, 204
Since an empty kago can be carried upon the back of one man, 207
Six flights up in an out-of-date apartment house, 567
Slipping softly through the sky, 24
Slowly, without force, the rain drops into the city, 125
Smoke-colour, rose, saffron, 223
Snow is still on the ground, 220
Softly the water ripples, 7
Solitary meditation is not suddenly snapped off; it continues without interruption, 356
So, Master, the wine gave you something, 209
Some men there are who find in nature all, 8
"So . . ." they said, 147
So you been peekin' int' th' winders o' th' old porch house to th' Four Corners, 503
So you want to see my papers, look what I have written down, 535
Spread on the roadway, 33
Spring has arrived, 478
"Stop! What are you doing," 235
Streaks of green and yellow iridescence, 151
Stupefy my heart to every day's monotony, 3
Sunlight, 477
Sunshine, 216

Suppose I plant you, 446
Swept, clean, and still, across the polished floor, 15
Swift like the tongues of lilies, 224

Taking us by and large, we're a queer lot, 459
Tang of fruitage in the air, 72
Tell me, 210
Ten years is nothing, 443
That sputter of rain, flipping the hedge-rows, 212
"That was a funny thing. I guess you were startled, 516
The anchorite, Kisen, 207
The Autumn moon was white upon the Southern Lake, 346
The Autumn wind is fresh and clear, 350
The Bell in the convent tower swung, 61
The birds sing to-day, 207
The branches of the trees lie in layers, 221
The bright moon rises behind the Heaven-high Mountain, 347
The cat and I, 233
The chatter of little people, 226
The chirping of crickets in the night, 206
The clear spring reflects the thin, wide-spreading pine-tree, 349
The colour of the day is over; flowers hold the mist in their lips, 348
The day has arrived when the marvellous earth, 549
The day is fresh-washed and fair, 145
The day is sharp and hurried, 477
The disappearing guns, 239
The drooping willow brushes the very clear water, 344
The earth is a coloured thing, 452
The earth is iron, 573
The East wind has come again, 336
The Emperor commands; three times the summons. He who left has not yet returned, 339
The fishermen draw their nets, 364
The Fool Errant sat by the highway of life, 5
The fountain bent and straightened itself, 57
The furniture goes with the house. Oh, yes, 520
The garden is steeped in moonlight, 477
The gifts of Heaven to you and me have not been equal, 561
The grackles have come, 447
The great painter, Hokusai, 204
The hair is combed, 357
The Heavens have revolved. The "Northern Measure" hangs above the Western wing, 348
The heavy clouds are broken and blowing, 330
The hills of Ch'u, 337
The house of the lonely scholar is in the winding lane, 346
The inkstand is full of ink, 58
The lady of my choice is bright, 443
The lake is steel-coloured and umber, 215
The lawyer, are you, 136
The little boy pressed his face against the window pane, 141
The magnificent horse, galloping swiftly, tramples the fallen flower, 340
The many-coloured clouds make me think of her upper garments, of her lower garments, 332
The mist is thick. On the wide river, the water-plants float smoothly, 331

The moon is cold over the sand-dunes, 214
The mountains were both far and high, 542
The neighbor sits in his window and plays the flute, 73
The night is still in Chin Ling, a cool wind blows, 344
The night is the colour of Spring mists, 361
The noise of the city sounds below me, 215
The nursery fire burns brightly, 126
The old Imperial Park — the ruined Terrace — the young willows, 342
The paper carp, 205
The parrots come, they cross the river waters of Wu, 343
The path runs straight between the flowering rows, 18
The pheasants cry in the dawn, 473
The poems of Po are unequalled, 353
The Poet took his walking-stick, 34
The pool is edged with the blade-like leaves of irises, 203
The Priest of the Province of Shu, carrying his table-lute in a cover of green, shot silk, 335
The rain gullies the garden paths, 42
The rain is dark against the white sky, 203
There are few things so futile, and few so amusing, 389
There are people who say the Crosswise River is good, 334
There is a white horse with a gold bridle to the East of the Liao Sea, 332
There is no moon in the sky, 207
There is no rustle of silken sleeves, 359
There is one place which is an everlasting home to me, 345
There once was a man whom the gods didn't love, 38
There's a lilt abroad in my head to-night, 554
There was a man, 128
The river makes a bend and encircles the village with its current, 351
The round, red moon ran a level eye along the hayfield, 577
The scent of hyacinths, like a pale mist, lies between me and my book, 209
The silver-crested love-pheasants strutted upon the Pheasant Terrace, 333
The silver-slippered moon treads the blue tiles of the sky, 465
The sky is spattered with clouds, 445
The slanting sun shines on the cluster of small houses upon the heights, 355
The snow whispers about me, 208
The Sorceress Mountain presses against Green Heaven, 345
The sorrel horse with the black tail gallops, gallops, and neighs, 340
The South wind blows open the folds of my dress, 208
The stars hang thick in the apple tree, 7
The stream at the foot of the mountain, 364
The sudden April heat, 221
The sun has set, 364
The sun is setting — has set — on the Spring-green Mountain, 342
The sun rose while I slept. I had not yet risen, 354

The swans float and float, 439
The talk is hushed, 592
The tall yellow hollyhocks stand, 32
The throats of the little red trumpet-flowers are wide open, 109
The trees in the level forest stand in rows and rows, 349
The Turkey-buzzard was chatting with the Condor, 245
The vine leaves against the brick walls of my house, 217
The white mares of the moon rush along the sky, 477
The white snows of Winter, 205
The willows near the roadside rest-house are soft with new-burst buds, 363
The wind blows. The inn is filled with the scent of willow-flowers, 333
The wind has blown a corner of your shawl, 210
The wind is singing through the trees to-night, 17
The windows of the gallery, 586
The wind rose, and the wind fell, 491
The writing of Li Po-hai, 362
They are coy, these sisters, Autumn and Death, 470
They brought me a quilled, yellow dahlia, 215
They clatter, clatter, clatter on the floor, 471
They have watered the street, 33
The young gentleman from the foreign nation, 229
They say there is a fairy in every streak'd tulip, 221
Thick dappled by circles of sunshine and fluttering shade, 223
Thickly green is the moss on the corroded roof-tiles of this hall, 562
Thimble-rig on a village green, 231
Thin-voiced, nasal pipes, 148
This afternoon was the colour of water falling through sunlight, 241
This is the hour when the crows come to roost on the Ku Su Terrace, 346
This lady is like a grass-blade sheathed in ice, 569
This little bowl is like a mossy pool, 7
This man is like a mechanical toy, 591
This time of ours, 339
Thou dear and well-loved haunt of happy hours, 21
Thou father of the children of my brain, 13
Thou yellow trumpeter of laggard Spring, 16
Thread from the hands of a doting mother, 356
"Three doors up from the end of the street, 467
Throughout the echoing chambers of my brain, 20
"Through pleasures and palaces," 217
Through the Spring-thickened branches, 219
Throw the blue ball above the little twigs of the tree-tops, 228
Tidal water is a determined thing, it can be depended on, 337
Tinkling of ankle bracelets, 221
'T is you that are the music, not your song, 16
To-day I went into a shop where they sell spectacles, 217
To-night I stood among roses, 445
To-night — the moon at Fu Chou, 354
To those who can see them, there are eyes, 469
Tread softly, softly, 451
Two rows of stiff poplars, wind-bitten and grey, 547

Under cypresses, ilexes, myrtles, within, 546
Underneath the dim, criss-crossing beams, 453
Under red umbrellas with cream-white centres, 206
Under the broken clouds of dawn, 208
Under the plum-blossoms are nightingales, 203
Upon a decent truckle-bed, 580
Upon the maple leaves, 203
Upon this greying page you wrote, 536
Uprightness, 240
Up — up — water shooting, 476

Walking beside the tree-peonies, 204
Walking in the woods one day, 440
Wax-white, 149
Wax-white lilies, 220
We come down the green-grey jade hill, 341
Well, John Keats, 242
What charm is yours, you faded old-world tapestries, 33
What fell upon my open umbrella, 207
What hardships are encountered in a Northern flight, 333
What instinct forces man to journey on, 17
What is a rainbow, 206
What is poetry? Is it a mosaic, 7
What is the thing I would say to you, 557
What torture lurks within a single thought, 18
What would Francis Jammes, lover of dear, dead elegancies, 450
When a hero fails of his purpose, 207
When bows are bent, they should be bent strongly, 353
When drunk, we were divided; but we have been together again for several days, 347
When he mounted his horse, he did not take his leather riding-whip, 358
When I am alone, 204
When I go away from you, 43
When I have baked white cakes, 212
When I hear your runners shouting, 206
When I looked into your eyes, 208
When I stand under the willow-tree, 203
When I think of you, Beloved, 210
When I was young, I spent the white days lavishly, 346
When night drifts along the streets of the city, 218
When the Goose Moon rose and, 261
When the hair of your Unworthy One first began to cover her forehead, 335
When the leaves of the cassia-tree, 206
When the rain ceases, 362
When the young ladies of the boarding-school take the air, 474
When you came, you were like red wine and honey, 217
When you, my Dear, are away, away, 4
Where a chain of sandy beaches, 551
Whistle under the water, 589
White, 581
White, glittering sunlight fills the market square, 20
White phlox and white hydrangeas, 215
Who says Ho is wide, 361
Who sees the metal of the Temple mirrors, 562
Who shall declare the joy of the running, 4

Why does my clock persist in marking the hour after that which it is, 560
Why does the clanking of a tip-cart, 216
Why do the lilies goggle their tongues at me, 216
Why do you not sleep, Beloved, 214
Why do you subdue yourself in golds and purples, 211
"Why, Sallie Williams, 512
Wide sleeves sway, 360
Wild little bird, who chose thee for a sign, 1
William Blake and Catherine Bourchier, 230
"Will they do anythin' to her, do you think, Mirandy," 530
"Witch, 276
With a crunching of gravel and flapping upon it, 546
With a red grain and a blue grain, placed in precisely, 477
With his wide crimson cloak and his cardinal's hat, 549
Within the gold square of the proscenium arch, 150
With you, 556

Yellow-green, yellow-green, yellow-green and silver, 224
Yes, I can understan' ther's a sort o' pleasure collectin' old customs, 493
Yes, indeed, Sir, 525
You are an amethyst to me, 555
You are beautiful and faded, 73
You are ice and fire, 214

You are like the stem, 229
You ask me for a sonnet. Ah, my Dear, 43
You came to me bearing bright roses, 13
You came to me in the pale starting of Spring, 214
You deceived me handsomely, 540
You glow in my heart, 41
You hate me and I hate you, 228
You have taken our love and turned it into coins of silver, 208
You have the "bird's foot-print" characters, 343
You know, my Dear, I have a way, each Summer, 481
You marked it with light pencil upon a printed page, 476
You mistake me, Madame, I ask for nothing, 559
Young girls are gathering lotus-seeds on the pond of Ya, 331
Your footfalls on the drum bridge beside my house, 206
Your voice is like bells over roofs at dawn, 444
You say you are my friends, 472
You sent me a sprig of mignonette, 440
You stand between the cedars and the green spruces, 211
Youth cocks his hat and rides up the street, 577
You walk under the ice trees, 213
You want I should tell yer 'bout old James Boott, do yer, boys, 484
You want to know what's the matter with me, do yer, 130
You were always so vigorous, 568
You — you, 444

GENERAL INDEX OF TITLES

(The titles of major works and general divisions are set in SMALL CAPITALS*)*

Absence, 41
After an Illness, 560
After an Imperial Audience, 355
After a Storm, 213
After Being Separated for a Long Time, 348
Afterglow, 445
After Hearing a Waltz by Bartók, 56
After How Many Years, 363
Aftermath, 19
Afternoon Rain in State Street, 150
After Writing "The Bronze Horses," 239
Again the New Year Festival, 206
Aliens, 226
Allies, The, 125
Alternatives, 559
Ambassador, The, 548
"And Pity 'Tis, 'Tis True," 530
And So, I Think, Diogenes, 538
Anecdote, 576
Angles, 203
Anniversary, The, 443
Answer to an Affectionate Invitation, 343
Anticipation, 42
Apology, 36
Apotheosis, 542
Apples of Hesperides, 2
Appuldurcombe Park, 233
April, 213
Aquarium, An, 151
Aquatint Framed in Gold, 567
Artist, An, 207
Artist, The, 211
Ascending the Three Chasms, 345
Astigmatism, 34
As Toward Immortality, 242
As Toward One's Self, 225
As Toward War, 237
At Night, 17
At the Ancestral Shrine of King Yao, 338
At the Bookseller's, 219
At the Edge of Heaven, 353
At the Yellow Crane Tower, 349
Attitude Under an Elm Tree, 476
Aubade, 73
August, 223
Autumn, 204
Autumn, 215
Autumnal Equinox, 214
Autumn and Death, 470
Autumn Haze, 205
Autumn River Song, 344
Azure and Gold, 2

Back Bay Fens, The, 219
Ballad of Footmen, A, 129
Ballad of Grinning Death, 580
Ballads for Sale, 535
Balls, 228
Basket, The, 58
Basket Dance, 588
Bather, A, 223

Battle to the South of the City, The, 329
Beautiful Woman Encountered on a Field-Path, A, 340
Beech, Pine, and Sunlight, 221
Before Dawn, 17
Before the Altar, 1
Before the Storm, 295
Behind a Wall, 4
Behind Time, 543
Bidding Good-Bye to Yin Shu, 351
Bitter Jealousy in the Palace of the High Gate, 348
Blockhead, A, 36
Blue-Green Stream, The, 355
Blue Scarf, The, 72
Bombardment, The, 125
Book of Hours of Sister Clotilde, The, 61
Book of Stones and Lilies, The, 586
Bookshop, The, 231
Boston Athenaeum, The, 21
Bright Sunlight, 210
Broken Fountain, The, 234
Bronze Horses, The, 177
Bronze Tablets, 111
Bullion, 212
Bungler, The, 41
Burnt Offering, A, 207
By Messenger, 203

Calligraphy, 362
Camellia Tree of Matsue, The, 205
Camouflaged Troop-Ship, 240
Can Grande's Castle, 153
Captured Goddess, The, 31
Carrefour, 558
Castles in Spain, 229
Caustic, 559
Ch'ang Kan, 335
Charleston, South Carolina, 450
Charm, The, 213
Chill, 572
Chinoiseries, 208
Chopin, 233
Church of Santa Chiara, Naples, The, 549
Circumstance, 203
Circus Tents by Lake Michigan, 570
City of Stones, The, 354
Clear, with Light Variable Winds, 57
Climbing, 24
Clocks Tick a Century, 139
Cloudy River, The, 358
Coal Picker, The, 35
Coloured Print by Shokei, A, 5
Communication, A, 540
Comparison, A, 591
Congressional Library, The, 452
Constancy, 207
Convalescence, 35
Conversation of a Saint, The, 512
Coq d'Or, 213
Corner of Night and Morning, The, 221

Correspondence, 538
Country House, The, 215
Cremona Violin, The, 88
Crépuscule du Matin, 19
Crescent Moon, The, 24
CRITICAL FABLE, A, 389
Crossing the Frontier. I, 353
Crossing the Frontier. II, 353
Cross-Roads, The, 103
Crosswise River, The, 334
Crowned, 13
Customer, The, 578
Cyclists, The, 33

Daimio's Oiran, A, 206
Dance Figure, 582
Dancing, 360
Dawn Adventure, 221
Daybreak. Yoshiwara, 207
Day That Was That Day, The, 491
Decade, A, 217
ΔIΨA, 9
Descending the Extreme South Mountain, 341
Desolation, 203
Dimension, A, 445
Dinner-Party, The, 147
Dirge, 575
Disillusion, 205
Dissonance, 586
Document, 204
Dog-Days, 223
Doll, The, 481
Dolphins in Blue Water, 224
DOME OF MANY-COLOURED GLASS, A, 1
Dracula of the Hills, A, 493
Dreams, 18
Dreams in War Time, 237
Dried Marjoram, 291
Drinking Alone in the Moonlight. I, 338
Drinking Alone in the Moonlight. II, 338
Drinking Alone on the Rock in the River, 346
Drinking in the T'ao Pavilion, 346
Drinking Song, 342
Dusty Hour-Glass, The, 235

Early Autumn at the Pool of Sprinkling Water, 359
Easel Picture, 568
East, West, North, and South of a Man, 435
EAST WIND, 481
Eleonora Duse, 479
Eleonora Duse, 592
Ely Cathedral, 230
Emperor's Garden, The, 204
Emperor's Return, The, 361
Enchanted Castle, The, 470
End, The, 20
Entente Cordiale, 229
Ephemera, 204
Epithalamium in the Modern Manner, 577
Epitaph in a Church-Yard in Charleston, South Carolina, 20
Epitaph of a Young Poet, 43
Eternally Thinking of Each Other, 348
Eucharis Amazonica, 220
Evelyn Ray, 437
Evening Calm, 364

Evening Meeting, An, 361
Excursion, The, 352
Exercise in Logic, 445
Exeter Road, The, 65
Exiled Emperor, The, 207
EYES, AND EARS, AND WALKING, 218

Fact, 558
Fairy Tale, A, 12
Falling Snow, 208
Fanatic, The, 228
Farewell Banquet, A, 346
Farewell Words to the Daughter of Yang, 356
Farm House on the Wei Stream, 355
Fatigue, 3
Fêng Huang T'ai, 333
Fête at Caserta. The Queen of Naples Receives, 547
Fighting to the South of the City, 334
FIGURINES IN OLD SAXE, 75
Fireworks, 228
FIR-FLOWER TABLETS, 301
Fisherman's Wife, The, 204
Fishing Picture, 364
Fixed Idea, A, 18
Flame Apples, 226
Floating on the Pool of Jo Ya, 356
Flotsam, 235
Flute, The, 235
Flute-Priest Song for Rain, 589
Folie de Minuit, 471
Fool Errant, The, 5
Fool o' the Moon, 465
Fool's Money Bags, 41
Footing up a Total, 441
Foreigner, The, 40
Forsaken, The, 71
Fort, The, 239
Four Sides to a House, 298
Fragment, 7
Francis II, King of Naples, 21
Frankincense and Myrrh, 19
Free Fantasia on Japanese Themes, 219
Frimaire, 218
Fringed Gentians, 23
From a Window, 206
From China, 204
From Nice to Oneglia, 548
From One Who Stays, 19
From the Straw Hut Among the Seven Peaks, 362
Frosty Evening, 207
Fruit Garden Path, The, 18
Fruit Shop, The, 111
Fugitive, 477
Funeral Song for the Indian Chief Blackbird, 273

Garden by Moonlight, The, 212
Gargoyles, 231
Gavotte in D Minor, 280
Generations, 229
Gift, A, 41
Giver of Stars, The, 43
Gold-Leaf Screen, 208
Good Gracious! 221
GOUACHE PICTURES OF ITALY, 546
Granadilla, 558
Grave, The, 568

Grave Song, A, 473
Gravestone, The, 516
Great Adventure of Max Breuck, The, 44
Great Ho River, The, 361
Green Bowl, The, 7
Green Parrakeet, The, 467
Grievance, 555
Grocery, The, 134
Grotesque, 216
Guns as Keys: and the Great Gate Swings, 162

Hammers, The, 116
Happiness, 37
Haunted, 216
Hearing a Bamboo Flute in the City of Lo Yang, 341
Hearing the Early Oriole, 354
Heaven's Gate Mountains, The, 350
Hedge Island, 173
Heraldic, 558
Hermit, The, 363
Hero-Worship, 16
Hilly Country, 224
Hippocrene, 556
Hoar-Frost, 208
Honourable Lady Chao, The, 343
Hora Stellatrix, 7
House in Main Street, The, 484
House with the Marble Steps, The, 532
Humming-Birds, The, 476

If I Were Francesco Guardi, 479
Illusion, 204
Immortals, The, 541
Impressionist Picture of a Garden, 222
In a Castle, 60
In a Garden, 73
In Answer to a Request, 43
In a Powder Closet, 475
In a Time of Dearth, 225
Incident, An, 230
In Darkness, 17
In Deep Thought, Gazing at the Moon, 349
In Excelsis, 444
Inn at the Mountain Pass, The, 364
Interlude, 212
In the Campagna, 549
In the Stadium, 238
In Time of War, 206
Irony, 37
Irony of Death, The, 568

J-K. Huysmans, 14
Japanese Wood-Carving, A, 3
Jazz Dance, 582
July Midnight, 211

Kagoes of a Returning Traveller, The, 206
Katydids, 478

LACQUER PRINTS, 203
Lady, A, 73
Lady to Her Lover, A, 205
Lamp of Life, The, 16
Landlady of the Whinton Inn Tells a Story, The, 525
La Ronde du Diable, 473

Last Quarter of the Moon, The, 37
Late September, 72
La Vie de Bohême, 226
Lead Soldiers, 126
Left Behind, 215
Legend, 206
Legend of Porcelain, A, 251
LEGENDS, 245
Leisure, 15
Letter, The, 209
Letter of Thanks for Precious Pearls, A, 360
Letter Written from Prison by Two Political Offenders, 207
Lilacs, 446
Lime Avenue, The, 546
Listening, 16
Li T'ai Po, 209
Li T'ai Po Meditates, 364
Little Garden, The, 15
Little Ivory Figures Pulled with a String, 236
Little Song, A, 4
London Thoroughfare. A. 2 A.M., 33
Lonely Wife, The, 331
Looking at the Moon after Rain, 330
"Looking-For-Husband" Rock, The, 348
Loon Point, 7
Lover, A, 204
LYRICAL POEMS, 1

Mackerel Sky, 446
Madman, The, 574
Madonna of Carthagena, The, 551
Madonna of the Evening Flowers, 210
Magnolia Gardens, 569
Maladie de l'Après-Midi, 216
Malmaison, 113
Many Swans, 261
March Evening, 14
Market Day, 20
Matrix, The, 15
May Evening in Central Park, 591
Meditation, 205
Meeting-House Hill, 449
Memorandum Confided by a Yucca to a Passion-Vine, 245
MEN, WOMEN AND GHOSTS, 75
Merchandise, 227
Merely Statement, 440
Mesdames Atropos and Clio Engage in a Game of Slap-Stick, 539
Mid-Adventure, 537
Middle Age, 226
Middleton Place, The, 450
Miniature, 567
Mirage, 18
Mirror, The, 569
Miscast I, 42
Miscast II, 42
Mise en Scène, 210
Misericordia, 237
Monadnock in Early Spring, 15
Moon Haze, 207
Moon Night, 354
Moon Over the Mountain Pass, The, 347
Morning Song, with Drums, 473
Motor Lights on a Hill Road, 224
Music. 73

Nanking Wine-Shop, The, 333
Near Kioto, 203
Nerves, 215
New Heavens for Old, 574
New Year's Card, A, 557
New York at Night, 12
Night Before the Parade, The, 241
Night Clouds, 477
Nightmare: A Tale for an Autumn Evening, 139
Night Thoughts, 345
Northern Flight, The, 333
Nostalgia, 217
Note-Book in the Gate-Legged Table, The, 499
November, 217
Nuance, 205
Nuit Blanche, 206
Nuit Blanche, 474
Number 3 on the Docket, 136

Obligation, 42
Off the Turnpike, 131
Old Examination Hall — China, 562
Old Snow, 573
Old Tai's Wine-Shop, 346
Ombre Chinoise, 211
On a Certain Critic, 242
On Carpaccio's Picture, 15
On Christmas Eve, 557
Once Jericho, 440
Once More Fields and Gardens, 357
One Goes a Journey, 362
One of the "Hundred Views of Fuji" by Hokusai, 204
One! Two! Three! 559
One Winter Night, 488
On Hearing that Wang Ch'ang-ling Had Been Exiled, 350
On Hearing the Buddhist Priest Play His Lute, 335
On-Looker, The, 446
On Looking at a Copy of Alice Meynell's Poems Given Me, Years Ago, by a Friend, 536
On Reading a Line Underscored by Keats in a Copy of "Palmerin of England," 476
On the Classic of the Hills and Sea, 362
On "The Cutting of an Agate" (By W. B. Yeats), 591
On the Mantelpiece, 236
Opal, 214
Opera House, An, 150
Orange of Midsummer, 214
Orientation, 474
Outside a Gate, 206
Overcast Sunrise, 445
OVERGROWN PASTURE, THE, 130
Ox Street, Takanawa, 206

Painted Ceiling, The, 24
Painter on Silk, The, 128
Pair of Scrolls, 364
Palace Blossoms, The, 362
Palace Woman and the Dragon Robes, The, 333
Palace Woman and the Soldiers' Cook, The, 340
Palazzo Contarini, 546
Pantomime in One Act, 475
Paper Fishes, 205
Paper Windmill, The, 141

Paradox, 555
Parrot Island, 343
Parting from Yang, a Hill Man, 345
Parting Gift to Wang Lun, A, 350
Passing the Bamboo Fence, 207
Passing the Night at the White Heron Island, 345
Passionate Grief, 349
Pastime, 560
Patience, 35
Patterns, 75
Peace, 205
Peach-Colour to a Soap-Bubble, 230
Peddler of Flowers, The, 227
Penumbra, 217
Perils of the Shu Road, The, 330
Petals, 2
Petition, A, 36
Picking Willow, 344
Pickthorn Manor, 76
PICTURES OF THE FLOATING WORLD, 203
Pike, The, 72
Pilgrims Ascending Fuji-yama, 206
Pillar Prints, 562
PLANES OF PERSONALITY, 209
Planning the Garden, 222
Pleasures Within the Palace, The, 331
Pleiades, The, 25
"Plum-Blossom" Concubine Writes to the Emperor Ming Huang, The, 561
PLUMMETS TO CIRCUMSTANCE, 230
Poem, The, 227
Poem Sent to the Official Wang, 346
Poem Sent to Tu Fu, A, 350
Poet, The, 17
Poetic Justice, 581
Poetry, 206
Poet's Wife, A, 208
Poignant Grief During a Sunny Spring, 336
Points of View, 577
Pond, The, 204
POPPY SEED, 44
Portrait, 569
Portrait of a Beautiful Concubine, 361
Portrait of an Orchestra Leader, 569
PORTRAITS, PLACES, AND PEOPLE, 550
Prayer for a Profusion of Sunflowers, 589
Prayer for Lightning, 589
Precinct, The. Rochester, 32
Preface to an Occasion, 477
Preparation, 217
Primavera, 478
Prime, 444
Proclaiming the Joy of Certain Hours, 359
Promise of the Morning Star, The, 13
Proper Invective, 584
Proportion, 207
Purple Grackles, 447
Pyrotechnics, 230

Quincunx, 558

Rainy Night, A, 591
Real Estate Agent's Tale, The, 520
Reaping, 130
Reciting Verses by Moonlight, 344
Recruiting Officers, The, 352
Red Knight, The, 474

Red Lacquer Music-Stand, The, 142
Red Slippers, 149
Reflection, 560
Reflections, 208
Reply to an Unrefined Person, 344
Rest-House on the Clear Wan River, The, 342
Retreat of Hsieh Kung, The, 342
Return, The, 205
Return, The, 364
Revenge, The, 571
Rhyme out of Motley, A, 474
Ring and the Castle, The, 278
River Chant, 339
River Village, The, 351
Roads, 10
Road to Avignon, The, 11
Road to the Mountain, The, 592
Road to the Yoshiwara, 206
"Rode the Six Hundred," 561
Rosebud Wall-Paper, The, 503
Roxbury Garden, A, 104

St. Louis.   June, 571
Sancta Maria, Succure Miseris, 55
Sand Altar, The, 477
Santa Settimana, 547
Saying Good-Bye to a Friend, 340
Saying Good-Bye to a Friend Going to the Plum-
    Flower Lake, 350
Sea-Blue and Blood-Red, 153
Sea Coal, 224
Sea Shell, 23
Seeking for the Hermit of the West Hill, 355
Sent as a Parting Gift to the Second Official, 337
Sent to Li Po as a Gift, 354
Separated by Imperial Summons, 339
September.   1918, 241
Serpent Mount, The, 345
1777, 109
Sewing-Book, The, 579
Shadow, The, 66
Shooting the Sun, 578
Shore Grass, 214
Shower, A, 212
Sibyl, The, 574
Silent Husband, The, 561
Silhouette with Sepia Background, 566
Sisters, The, 459
Sixteenth Floor, The, 215
Slippers of the Goddess of Beauty, The, 471
Snow, 573
Snow in April, 216
Solitaire, 218
Song, 5
Song for a Viola d'Amore, 443
Song for the Hour When the Crows Roost, A, 346
Song of Grief, A, 360
Song of Resentment, A, 343
Song of the Rest-House of Deep Trouble, A, 347
Song of the Snapped Willow, 358
Song of the White Clouds, The, 337
Songs of the Courtesans, 360
Songs of the Marches, 328
SONGS OF THE PUEBLO INDIANS, 588
Songs to the Peonies, 332
SONNETS, 15
Sorceress Gorge, The, 353

Sorrel Horse, The, 340
Sorrow During a Clear Autumn, 336
South Carolina Forest, A, 570
Spectacles, 238
Splendour Falls from Castle Walls, The, 586
Sprig of Rosemary, A, 216
Spring Dawn, 206
Spring Day, 145
Spring Grief and Resentment, 332
Spring Longing, 208
Spring.   Summer.   Autumn, 364
Stable, The, 547
Stalactite, 586
Starling, The, 20
Statement of Resolutions After Being Drunk, A,
    339
Statue in the Garden, The, 280
Still Life, 580
Storm by the Seashore, 207
Storm-Racked, 35
Strain, 215
Stravinsky's Three Pieces "Grotesques," for
    String Quartet, 148
Street, A, 206
Streets, 203
Stupidity, 37
Suggested by the Cover of a Volume of Keats's
    Poems, 1
Sultry, 469
Summer, 8
Summer Night Piece, 477
Summer Rain, 213
Sung to the Air: "Looking South," 357
Sung to the Air: "The Mantzŭ like an Idol," 349
Sung to the Air: "The Wanderer," 356
Sung to the Tune of "The Unripe Hawthorn
    Berry," 354
Sunshine, 203
Sunshine through a Cobwebbed Window, 33
Superstition, 205
Swans, The, 439
SWORD BLADES, 31
SWORD BLADES AND POPPY SEED, 27
Sword Blades and Poppy Seed, 27

Taking Leave of Tu Fu, 347
Taking-Up of Arms, The, 347
Tale of Starvation, A, 38
Tanka, 560
Taxi, The, 43
Teatro Bambino, 10
Temple, The, 43
Temple Ceremony, 207
Terraced Road, The, 341
Texas, 449
Thatched House Unroofed by an Autumn Gale,
    The, 351
Thinking of Li Po on a Spring Day, 353
Thinking of the Frontier, 343
Thompson's Lunch Room — Grand Central Sta-
    tion, 149
Thorn Piece, 556
Thoughts from a Thousand Li, 349
Threnody, 560
Time, 206
Time-Web, 477
Time's Acre, 468

To a Friend, 18
To a Gentleman Who Wanted to See the First Drafts of My Poems in the Interests of Psychological Research into the Workings of the Creative Mind, 535
To a Husband, 204
To a Lady of Undeniable Beauty and Practised Charm, 538
To an Early Daffodil, 16
Toast for Mêng Yün-Ch'ing, A, 354
To Carl Sandburg, 478
To Eleonora Duse. In Answer to a Letter, 550
To Eleonora Duse. *1923*, 550
To Elizabeth Ward Perkins, 13
To Francesca Braggiotti, 581
Together We Know Happiness, 357
To John Keats, 21
Tomb Valley, 466
"To-morrow to Fresh Woods and Pastures New," 9
To the Air: "The Fallen Leaves," 359
To Two Unknown Ladies, 562
To Winky, 232
TOWNS IN COLOUR, 149
Trades, 228
Traveller Comes to the Old Terrace of Su, A, 342
Travelling Bear, The, 227
Tree of Scarlet Berries, The, 42
Trees, 221
Trees in Winter, 224
Trout, The, 25
Tulip Garden, A, 74
Tune, 554
Twenty-Four Hokku on a Modern Theme, 441
Two Panels, 364
Two Poems Written to Ts'ui, 337
Two Porters Returning along a Country Road, 207
Two Rains, The, 221
TWO SPEAK TOGETHER, 209
Two Travellers in the Place Vendôme, 124

UNCOLLECTED POEMS, 591

Venetian Glass, 3

Venus Transiens, 210
Vernal Equinox, 209
Vespers, 444
Vicarious, 203
View of Teignmouth in Devonshire, 461
Villa Capouana, 548
Vintage, 42
Violin Sonata by Vincent d'Indy, 220
Visiting the Taoist Priest, 344
Visit to the Fêng Hsien Temple, A, 351
Vow, The, 451

Wakefulness, 214
WAR PICTURES, 125
Watershed, The, 472
Water Stair, The, 546
Way, The, 9
Weather-Cock Points South, The, 211
WHAT'S O'CLOCK, 435
Wheat-in-the-Ear, 211
Wheel of the Sun, The, 212
Which, Being Interpreted, Is as May Be, or Otherwise, 453
White and Green, 73
White Currants, 445
Who Has Not, Cannot Have, 537
William Blake, 230
Wind, 25
Wind and Silver, 477
Wind-Bound at the New Forest Reach, 337
Winter Ride, A, 4
Winter's Turning, 220
Witch-Woman, 276
Woman Sings, A, 340
Women's Harvest Song, 588
Women's Song of the Corn, 588
Word-Pattern, 350
Written in the Character of a Beautiful Woman, 332
Written on the Reverse, 565
WRITTEN PICTURES, 361

Year Passes, A, 204
Yoshiwara Lament, 203
Young Girls of Yüeh, The, 331